Lecture Notes in Computer Science　　　9431

Commenced Publication in 1973
Founding and Former Series Editors:
Gerhard Goos, Juris Hartmanis, and Jan van Leeuwen

More information about this series at http://www.springer.com/series/7412

Thomas Bräunl · Brendan McCane
Mariano Rivera · Xinguo Yu (Eds.)

Image and Video Technology

7th Pacific-Rim Symposium, PSIVT 2015
Auckland, New Zealand, November 25–27, 2015
Revised Selected Papers

Springer

Editors
Thomas Bräunl
The University of Western Australia
Crawley, Perth, WA
Australia

Brendan McCane
University of Otago
Dunedin
New Zealand

Mariano Rivera
Centro de Investigación en Matematicas A.C.
Guanajuato
Mexico

Xinguo Yu
Central China Normal University
Wuhan, Hubei
China

Cover illustration: Photo by Dongwei Liu, Auckland, New Zealand

ISSN 0302-9743   ISSN 1611-3349   (electronic)
Lecture Notes in Computer Science
ISBN 978-3-319-29450-6   ISBN 978-3-319-29451-3   (eBook)
DOI 10.1007/978-3-319-29451-3

Library of Congress Control Number: 2015961033

LNCS Sublibrary: SL6 – Image Processing, Computer Vision, Pattern Recognition, and Graphics

Printed on acid-free paper

This Springer imprint is published by SpringerNature
The registered company is Springer International Publishing AG Switzerland

Preface

The Pacific-Rim Symposium on Image and Video Technology (PSIVT) 2015 took place in beautiful Auckland, New Zealand. Nicknamed the "City of Sails," Auckland welcomed us with warm spring weather and lots of boats sailing across the bay.

Previous PSIVT symposiums were held in Taiwan, Chile, Japan, Singapore, South Korea, and Mexico; all host countries sharing a coastline with the Pacific Ocean.

PSIVT 2015 attracted 133 submissions to the main conference of which 61 were accepted (overall acceptance rate of 46 %). Of these, 26 papers were delivered as oral presentations and 35 papers as posters.

Submissions came from all over the world, with major contributing countries Japan (19 papers) and Germany (seven papers). Each paper was reviewed in full by at least two (and up to four) reviewers, followed by a brief rebuttal, before the area chairs made their recommendations. None of the four program co-chairs was allowed to be a co-author on any paper submission for PSIVT 2015.

For the 2015 issue of PSIVT, we invited three keynote speakers:

- Victor Erukhimov from Itseez3D, Moscow, presented a talk on "Embedded Real-Time Computer Vision." Victor is CEO of Itseez3D, the company behind the open source library OpenCV and a driving force of the new OpenVX working group. The talk highlighted image processing standards and hardware acceleration for embedded vision systems.
- Joe Wünsche from UBM München talked about "Perception for Off-Road Driving." Joe presented UBM's history of vision-based autonomous driving and demonstrated his group's latest ELROB-winning driverless vehicles for off-road terrain.
- Richard Green from the University of Canterbury, New Zealand, gave an overview on "Computer Vision for Precision Agriculture." In his talk, Richard highlighted projects such as robotic vine pruning and potential agricultural applications for intelligent drones.

As program co-chairs, we selected three outstanding papers this year for awards:

- The IAPR Best Paper at PSIVT 2015 was awarded to Zexuan Ji, Jinyao Liu, Hengdong Yuan, Yubo Huang, and Quansen Sun for their paper "A Spatially Constrained Asymmetric Gaussian Mixture Model for Image Segmentation."
- The IAPR Best Application Paper at PSIVT 2015 was awarded to Vijay John, Zheng Liu, Chunzhao Guo, Seiichi Mita, and Kiyosumi Kidono for their article "Real-Time Lane Estimation Using Convolutional Neural Networks and Extra Trees Regression."
- The IAPR Best Paper Presentation at PSIVT 2015 was awarded to Domingo Mery, Erick Svec, and Marco Arias for their contribution "Object Recognition in Baggage Inspection Using Adaptive Sparse Representations of X-ray Images."

The social program of PSIVT 2015 included a welcome reception, a bus excursion to Muriwai, a banquet at a fantastic countryside restaurant, and a "survivors' party." These social events certainly also contributed to the success of the conference.

We thank our PSIVT 2015 sponsors Auckland University of Technology (AUT), IMIT Chiba University, Nagoya Institute of Technology, KAIST Korea, and IEEE New Zealand North Section, all reviewers and area chairs, the local Organizing Committee (especially Amy Claughton and Tessa Lloyd-Hagemann of UoA), the University of Auckland (UoA) for providing the venue, Linda Barbour (UWA) for remote conference–office support, and of course, last but not least, our general co-chairs, Reinhard Klette (AUT) and In So Kweon (KAIST).

We also thank IAPR, the International Association for Pattern Recognition, for endorsing PSIVT 2015, and Springer's *Lecture Notes in Computer Science* team, especially Alfred Hofmann and Anna Kramer, for the efficient communication when submitting and finalizing this volume.

We look forward to seeing you all again at PSIVT 2017 in Wuhan, China, nicknamed the "Chicago of Asia."

December 2015

Thomas Bräunl
Brendan McCane
Mariano Rivera
Xinguo Yu

Organization

PSIVT 2015 Organizing Committee

Program Co-chairs

Thomas Bräunl	The University of Western Australia, Australia
Brendan McCane	Otago University, New Zealand
Mariano Rivera	Central Institute for Mathematics and Applications (CIMAT), Mexico
Xinguo Yu	Central China Normal University, China

Area Chairs

Phil Bones	University of Canterbury, New Zealand
Li Chen	University of the District of Columbia, USA
Jian Cheng	Chinese Academy of Sciences, China
Uwe Franke	Daimler AG, Germany
Hanseok Ko	Korea University, Korea
Chilwoo Lee	Chonnam National University, Korea
Wen-Nung Lie	National Chung Cheng University, Taiwan
Chia-Yen Chen	National University of Kaohsiung, Taiwan
Rick Millane	University of Canterbury, New Zealand
Takeshi Oishi	Tokyo University, Japan
Lei Qin	Chinese Academy of Sciences, China
Shin'ichi Satoh	NII Tokyo, Japan
Terence Sim	National University of Singapore, Singapore
Zhixun Su	Dalian University of Technology, China
Yue Wang	Institute for Infocomm Research, Singapore

General Co-chairs

Reinhard Klette	Auckland University of Technology, New Zealand
In So Kweon	KAIST, Korea

Workshop Co-chairs

Fay Huang	National Ilan University, Taiwan
Akihiro Sugimoto	National Institute of Informatics, Japan

Demo Co-chairs

Michael Cree   The University of Waikato, New Zealand
Nicolai Petkov   Groningen University, The Netherlands

Tutorial Co-chairs

Domingo Mery   Universidad Católica de Chile, Chile
Huang Qing Ming   University of Chinese Academy of Sciences, China

Submission Site and Author Instructions

Jean-Bernard Hayet   CIMAT, Mexico

Web Developers

Davis Dimalen   The University of Auckland, New Zealand
Alexandr Shirokov   The University of Auckland, New Zealand

Program Committee

Akihiko Torii	Ichiro Ide	Rudolf Mester
Andrew Lambert	Itaru Kitahara	Rui Huang
Andrew Martin	Jian Sun	Ryo Furukawa
Antonio M.López	Jimmy Lee	Ryusuke Sagawa
Arun Ross	Jing-Ming Guo	Shih-Hsuan Yang
Beng Hai Lee	Jinqiao Wang	Shohei Nobuhara
Bingpeng Ma	Jiunn-Lin Wu	Shuhui Wang
Bo Zheng	Jong Chul Ye	Shyi-Chyi Cheng
Chao-Ho Chen	Julian Maclaren	Stefan Gehrig
Chia-Hung Yeh	Jun Li	Takahiro Okabe
Chih-Yang Lin	Junbin Gao	Tariq Khan
Ching-Chun Huang	Kar-Ann Toh	Ting-Lan Lin
Chunhong Yoon	Karthik Nandakumar	Tingting Jiang
Chunjie Zhang	Keita Takahashi	Tomokazu Sato
Daniel Kondermann	Li-Wei Kang	Wangmeng Zuo
Darin O'Keeffe	Mahdi Rezaei	Wankou Yang
David Wojtas	Manuel Guizar-Sicairos	Wei-Ta Chu
Deng-Yuan Huang	Ming-Chih Chen	Wei-Yang Lin
Duane Loh	Norihiko Kawai	Wei-Yun Yau
Fridtjof Stein	Norimichi Ukita	Wengang Zhang
Guo-Shiang Lin	Peter Doerschuk	Wu-Chih Hu
Hajime Nagahara	Reinhard Koch	Xiangyu Chen
Hideaki Uchiyama	Richang Hong	Xiaoshuai Sun
Hiroshi Kawasaki	Rongrong Ji	Xiaoyi Jiang

Contents

Color and Motion

Image/Video Coding and Transmission

Computational Photography and Arts

Computer Vision and Applications

Image Segmentation and Classification

Video Surveillance

Biomedical Image Processing and Analysis

Object and Pattern Recognition

Computer Vision and Pattern Recognition

Image/Video Processing and Analysis

Pattern Recognition

Color and Motion

Color Conversion for Color Blindness Employing Multilayer Neural Network with Perceptual Model

Hideaki Orii[1]([✉]), Hideaki Kawano[2], Noriaki Suetake[3], and Hiroshi Maeda[2]

[1] Fukuoka University, 8-19-1 Nanakuma, Jonan-ku, Fukuoka 814-0180, Japan
oriih@fukuoka-u.ac.jp
[2] Kyushu Institute of Technology, 1-1 Sensui-cho, Tobata-ku,
Kitakyushu-shi, Fukuoka 804-8550, Japan
[3] Yamaguchi University, 1677-1 Yoshida, Yamaguchi-shi, Yamaguchi 753-8511, Japan

Abstract. In this paper, we propose a novel digital image color conversion algorithm for color blindness using a multilayer neural network. The symptoms of "color blindness" are due to an innate lack or deficit of cone cells that recognize colors, and people with color blindness have difficulty discriminating combinations of specific colors. Those people require color conversion for the presented image such that the image can be a perceptible color representation. In the proposed method, we design a multilayer neural network composed of three building blocks: layers for image color conversion, layers for perceptual model of color blindness, and layers for color discrimination. In proposed framework, a neural network is learning about a relationship of an image data and a discrimination performance of colors in an image, and a color conversion rule is trained as a part of a neural network. To validate the effectiveness of proposed method, it is applied to several images that have various color combinations.

Keywords: Color conversion · Neural network · Color blindness

1 Introduction

Human eyes perceive colors via a group of cells known as cone cells. The three types of cone cells are L, M, and S, which react to red, green, and blue, respectively. The magnitudes of these reactions determine the color that is perceived. When all three types of cone cells are present, this state is referred to as trichromatic. If there is a decrease or complete deficiency in either the L or M cone cells, these conditions are known as protanopia and deuteranopia, respectively. A deficiency of S cone cells is known as tritanopia by only 5 % and 0.2 % of Japanese males and females have this condition, respectively.

Expressing information using colors has important roles in modern society. For example, newspapers, books, and cell phones all use colors to express information. Some information represented by colors gives users directions, such as route maps and road signs. From a Color Universal Design perspective, these

© Springer International Publishing Switzerland 2016
T. Bräunl et al. (Eds.): PSIVT 2015, LNCS 9431, pp. 3–14, 2016.
DOI: 10.1007/978-3-319-29451-3_1

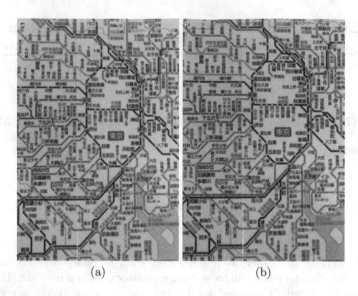

(a)   (b)

Fig. 1. Example of visibility with respect to vision type. (a) general color vision, (b) protanopia color vision.

maps and roads signs are designed to be easily understood. Cases where colors are used to make information easy to understand have increased over the last few decades. Many methods have also been developed, such as using shapes and color names with colors, or using colors that are easily distinguishable.

However, some route maps and road signs are still not understandable by people with color blindness. For example, train route maps are discretized by color to avoid confusing complex routes. People with color blindness cannot distinguish the different routes, which make the maps difficult to use (Fig. 1).

People with color blindness cannot differentiate between a specific set of colors. Colors that are hard to discretize by people with colorblindness are known as indiscriminable colors. Recently, to help people with colorblindness, some technologies have been developed that alters the colors in images so the contrast of indiscriminable colors is improved. K. Rasche et al. [1,2], J. B. Huang et al. [3] and G. Tanaka et al. [4] treat the color conversion as the optimization problem relates to the combination of colors in the image, and convert the color by solving the problem. While the legibility of colors in the resultant image is enhanced by these methods, the problem that undermines the impression of color to have of the original image is a color that was significantly different from the original color could occur.

M. Ichikawa et al. [5,6] and M. Meguro et al. [7] proposed the color conversion methods based on color clustering. In these methods, the color conversion rule is determined based on a relationship of centroids of color obtained by clustering. However, there are the some procedures to be performed by the hand of man, and the processes of these algorithms are complicated when many colors are in an image.

In this paper, we propose a novel digital image color conversion algorithm for color blindness employing a multilayer neural network. We focused that a discrimination performance of colors in an image is depend on a color difference of the colors on the boundary of regions. In proposed framework, a neural network is learning about a relationship of an image data and a discrimination performance of colors in an image, and a color conversion rule is trained as a part of a neural network. By perceptual model of color blindness is also embed for the layers of the neural network, a color conversion rule for keeping a color differences in images in presence of lack of a color information could be obtained.

2 Proposed Method

In the proposed method, we design a multilayer neural network composed of three building blocks: layers for image color conversion, layers for perceptual model of color blindness, and layers for color discrimination as shown in Fig. 2. In learning, the neural network train a relationship of pixel values, i.e. color map, and a discrimination performance of colors, i.e. color edge map, in an image. The 2nd block and the 3rd block are predesigned based on perceptual model of color blindness and color discrimination, and these models are fixed while the neural network is learning overall. Therefore, a color conversion rule for keeping a color differences in images in presence of lack of color information can be obtained as the 1st block of the trained neural network.

The overview of neural networks and color model for colorblindness are described in Sects. 2.1 and 2.2. The detail of the neural network model for color blindness and color edge is described in Sect. 2.3. The entire algorithm of proposed method is described in Sect. 2.4.

2.1 Neural Networks

Neural network models are essentially simple mathematical models defining a function $g : X \rightarrow Y$. In a neural network, the j-th neuron in a layer calculates and output a value y_j as follows:

$$y_j = f(\Sigma_i x_i \cdot w_{ij} + b_j). \tag{1}$$

Here, x_i is a i-th input value for a layer. w_{ij} is a weighted value of the j-th neuron for a i-th input value. b_j is a bias value of the j-th neuron. $f(\cdot)$ is a transfer function of the j-th neuron. Therefore, when a number of neurons of a layer is M, an output vector $y = [y_1, y_2, \ldots, y_M]^T$ of this layer with respect to an input vector $x = [x_1, x_2, \ldots, x_N]^T$ can be obtained as follows:

$$y = f\left(\begin{bmatrix} w_{11} & w_{12} & \cdots & w_{1N} \\ w_{21} & w_{22} & \cdots & w_{2N} \\ \vdots & \vdots & \ddots & \vdots \\ w_{M1} & w_{M2} & \cdots & w_{MN} \end{bmatrix} \begin{bmatrix} x_1 \\ x_2 \\ \vdots \\ x_N \end{bmatrix} + \begin{bmatrix} b_1 \\ b_2 \\ \vdots \\ b_M \end{bmatrix}\right) \tag{2}$$

$$= f(Wx + b). \tag{3}$$

Figure 3 shows this process schematically.

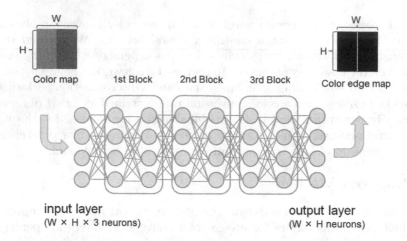

Fig. 2. Overview of our multilayer neural network framework. The neural network composed of three building blocks: layers for image color conversion, layers for perceptual model of color blindness, and layers for color discrimination.

As mentioned above, a relationship of an input vector and an output vector in a layer is defined by weighted value matrix W, bias vector b, and transfer function $f(\cdot)$. In multilayer neural network, neurons in each layer calculate output vector based on previous layer output and send the vector as next layer input. Therefore, an input vector of multilayer neural network is mapped a number of times from input layer to output layer. The training of neural network is supervised generally, training data set, i.e. many pairs of an input vector and its desirable output vector of neural network. The weighted value matrix W and bias vector b of each layer are updated based on error of output vector. This called backpropagation algorithm. To use backpropagation algorithm, transfer functions of each layer must be differentiable. Figure 4 shows popular transfer functions for neural networks.

2.2 Color Model for Colorblindness

To simulate the vision of colorblindness for an input image, we convert color space of the input image. The CIE XYZ color space is defined by quantitative relationship between physical pure colors, i.e. wavelengths, in the electromagnetic visible spectrum, and physiological perceived colors in human color vision. The simulated image for colorblindness can be obtained using, "RGB to XYZ" and "XYZ to RGB".

For efficient color conversion, our proposed method linearly converts the RGB values to the XYZ color system. The conversion from RGB to XYZ is calculated using the following equation.

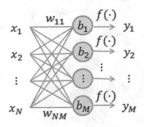

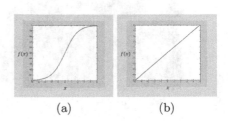

input values   output values   (a)   (b)

Fig. 3. Relationship of an input vector and an output vector in a layer on
neural network.

Fig. 4. Examples of a transfer function.
(a) sigmoid function, (b) pure linear
function.

$$\begin{bmatrix} X \\ Y \\ Z \end{bmatrix} = \begin{bmatrix} 0.4124 & 0.3756 & 0.1805 \\ 0.2126 & 0.7152 & 0.0722 \\ 0.0193 & 0.1192 & 0.9505 \end{bmatrix} \begin{bmatrix} R \\ G \\ B \end{bmatrix} = A_{RGB2XYZ} \begin{bmatrix} R \\ G \\ B \end{bmatrix} \tag{4}$$

Then, the conversion from XYZ to RGB is calculated using the following equation.

$$\begin{bmatrix} R \\ G \\ B \end{bmatrix} = \begin{bmatrix} 0.4124 & 0.3756 & 0.1805 \\ 0.2126 & 0.7152 & 0.0722 \\ 0.0193 & 0.1192 & 0.9505 \end{bmatrix}^{-1} \begin{bmatrix} X \\ Y \\ Z \end{bmatrix} = A_{XYZ2RGB} \begin{bmatrix} X \\ Y \\ Z \end{bmatrix} \tag{5}$$

Human perceive color by the ratio of the reaction value of each L, M, S cone
to light. In other words, it is possible to simulate the color model of color vision
defective by adjusting the reaction value of LMS cone. Relationship between
XYZ and spectral sensitivity value of LMS cone is given as follows [8]:

$$\begin{bmatrix} L \\ M \\ S \end{bmatrix} = \begin{bmatrix} 0.1551 & 0.5431 & -0.03286 \\ -0.1551 & 0.4568 & 0.03286 \\ 0.0 & 0.0 & 0.01608 \end{bmatrix} \begin{bmatrix} X \\ Y \\ Z \end{bmatrix} \tag{6}$$

In LMS cone, the response of the P-type color vision (L_p, M_p, S_p), i.e. protanopia,
and the D-type color vision (L_D, M_D, S_D), i.e. deuteranopia, are calculated as
follows [9,10]:

$$\begin{bmatrix} L_p \\ M_p \\ S_p \end{bmatrix} = \begin{bmatrix} 0.0 & 2.02 & -2.52 \\ 0.0 & 1.0 & 0.0 \\ 0.0 & 0.0 & 1.0 \end{bmatrix} \begin{bmatrix} L \\ M \\ S \end{bmatrix} \tag{7}$$

$$\begin{bmatrix} L_d \\ M_d \\ S_d \end{bmatrix} = \begin{bmatrix} 1.0 & 0.0 & 0.0 \\ 0.49 & 0.0 & 1.25 \\ 0.0 & 0.0 & 1.0 \end{bmatrix} \begin{bmatrix} L \\ M \\ S \end{bmatrix} \tag{8}$$

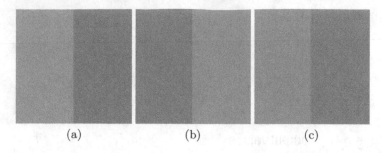

(a)   (b)   (c)

Fig. 5. Example of a simulation image of color vision for colorblindness. (a) an image, (b) simulated protanopia color vision of (a), (c) simulated deuteranopia color vision of (a).

The legibility of an image for the P-type color vision or the D-type color vision can be estimated using these equations. From the Eqs. 6 and 7, XYZ value of P-type color vision $(X_p, Y_p, Z_p)^T$ is obtained as following equation:

$$\begin{bmatrix} X_p \\ Y_p \\ Z_p \end{bmatrix} = \begin{bmatrix} -0.3813 & 1.1228 & 0.1730 \\ -0.4691 & 1.3813 & 0.0587 \\ 0.0 & 0.0 & 1.0 \end{bmatrix} \begin{bmatrix} X \\ Y \\ Z \end{bmatrix} = A_{XYZ2XYZp} \begin{bmatrix} X \\ Y \\ Z \end{bmatrix} \tag{9}$$

Then, XYZ value of D-type color vision $(X_d, Y_d, Z_d)^T$ is obtained as follows:

$$\begin{bmatrix} X_d \\ Y_d \\ Z_d \end{bmatrix} = \begin{bmatrix} 0.1884 & 0.6597 & 0.1016 \\ 0.2318 & 0.8116 & -0.0290 \\ 0.0 & 0.0 & 1.0 \end{bmatrix} \begin{bmatrix} X \\ Y \\ Z \end{bmatrix} = A_{XYZ2XYZd} \begin{bmatrix} X \\ Y \\ Z \end{bmatrix} \tag{10}$$

Therefore, RGB value of P-type color vision $(R_p, G_p, B_p)^T$ can be calculated from RGB value (R, G, B) as follows:

$$\begin{bmatrix} R_p \\ G_p \\ B_p \end{bmatrix} = A_{XYZ2RGB} A_{XYZ2XYZp} A_{RGB2XYZ} \begin{bmatrix} R \\ G \\ B \end{bmatrix} \tag{11}$$

Using color conversion matrix as mentioned above, we can simulate P-type or D-type color vision of a image. Figure 5 shows a example of a simulation image of color vision for colorblindness using this color model.

2.3 Neural Network Model for Simulating Colorblindness and Extraction of Color Edge

As mentioned in Sect. 2.1, input-output relationship of a layer of a neural network can be described as a matrix operation. At the same time, a color simulation of colorblindness can be also described as a matrix operation as mentioned Sect. 2.2. Therefore, we can define a neural network model for simulating colorblindness

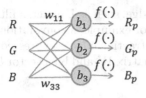

Color value   Color value
of P-type color vision

(a)   (b)

Fig. 6. A neural network model for simulating colorblindness. Here, the weighted value matrix W and bias vector b of this model is defined as Eq. (13), and transfer function $f(\cdot)$ is pure linear function (Fig. 4(b)).

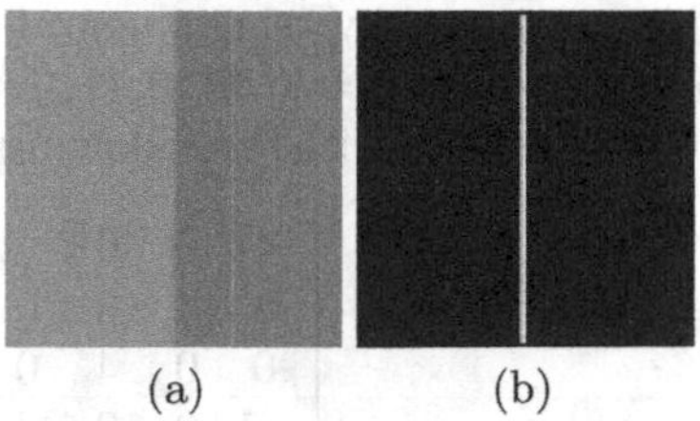

Fig. 7. An input image and an output image of this two-layered neural network (Eqs. (15) and (16)). (a) input image, (b) output image.

by using the color conversion matrix as the weighted value matrix of a layer of a neural network.

Figure 6 shows a neural network model of simulating colorblindness for RGB value of a pixel. Here, the weighted value matrix W and bias vector b of this model is defined as the following equations, and transfer function $f(\cdot)$ is pure linear function (Fig. 4(b)).

$$W = \begin{bmatrix} w_{11} & w_{12} & w_{13} \\ w_{21} & w_{22} & w_{23} \\ w_{31} & w_{32} & w_{33} \end{bmatrix} = A_{XYZ2RGB} A_{XYZ2XYZp} A_{RGB2XYZ} \quad (12)$$

$$b = \begin{bmatrix} 0 \\ 0 \\ 0 \end{bmatrix} \quad (13)$$

To input the entire image for a neural network, the weighted value matrix W should be extended as the following equation:

$$W = \begin{bmatrix} w_{11} & w_{12} & w_{13} & 0 & 0 & 0 & \cdots & 0 \\ w_{21} & w_{22} & w_{23} & 0 & 0 & 0 & \cdots & 0 \\ w_{31} & w_{32} & w_{33} & 0 & 0 & 0 & \cdots & 0 \\ 0 & 0 & 0 & w_{11} & w_{12} & w_{13} & \cdots & 0 \\ 0 & 0 & 0 & w_{21} & w_{22} & w_{23} & \cdots & 0 \\ 0 & 0 & 0 & w_{31} & w_{32} & w_{33} & \cdots & 0 \\ 0 & 0 & 0 & 0 & 0 & 0 & \ddots & \vdots \\ 0 & \cdots & \cdots & \cdots & \cdots & \cdots & \cdots & w_{33} \end{bmatrix} \quad (14)$$

Here, W a square matrix of size n (= the height of input image × the width of input image × 3). The input vector of this neural network should compose of RGB values of an image.

In a similar way, an image filter for extraction of edge, such as Laplacian filter, can be expressed by using a neural network model. For example, a convolution of laplacian kernel k (= $[0, -1, 0; -1, 4, -1; 0, -1, 0]$) for extraction edge is expressed as a neural network with the following weighted value matrix W and bias vector b:

$$
W = \begin{bmatrix}
4 & 0 & 0 & -1 & 0 & 0 & \cdots & 0 \\
0 & 4 & 0 & 0 & -1 & 0 & \cdots & 0 \\
0 & 0 & 4 & 0 & 0 & -1 & \cdots & 0 \\
-1 & 0 & 0 & 4 & 0 & 0 & \cdots & 0 \\
0 & -1 & 0 & 0 & 4 & 0 & \cdots & 0 \\
0 & 0 & -1 & 0 & 0 & 4 & \cdots & 0 \\
0 & 0 & 0 & -1 & 0 & 0 & \ddots & \vdots \\
0 & \cdots & & & & & \cdots & 4
\end{bmatrix}, \quad b = \begin{bmatrix} 0 \\ 0 \\ 0 \end{bmatrix} \quad (15)
$$

Here, an input vector of this neural network should be RGB values of an image, the order of components of the vector is $[R_1, G_1, B_1, R_2, G_2, \ldots, G_{(H \times W)}, B_{(H \times W)}]^T$. (R_i, G_i, B_i) is RGB value of the i-th pixel. W a square matrix of size n (= the height of input image × the width of input image × 3). The output vector this layer of neural network express an edge image of each color plane (R, G, B) of an input image. Next, to obtain a color edge image, the output vector input to the layer defined as the following equation:

$$
W = \begin{bmatrix}
0.333 & 0.333 & 0.333 & 0 & 0 & 0 & \cdots & 0 \\
0 & 0 & 0 & 0.333 & 0.333 & 0.333 & \cdots & 0 \\
0 & 0 & 0 & 0 & 0 & 0 & \cdots & 0 \\
\vdots & \cdots & \cdots & \cdots & \cdots & \cdots & \ddots & \vdots \\
0 & \cdots & \cdots & \cdots & \cdots & \cdots & \cdots & 0.333
\end{bmatrix}, \quad b = \begin{bmatrix} 0 \\ 0 \\ 0 \end{bmatrix} \quad (16)
$$

W is a matrix of size n (= the height of input image × the width of input image) × m (= the height of input image × the width of input image × 3), and the output vector of this layer express a mean of edge image of each color plane (R, G, B) of an input image. Figure 7 shows an input image and an output image of this two-layered neural network. This network can extract a map of the discrimination performance of colors.

2.4   Algorithm of Proposed Method

In the proposed method, we design a multilayer neural network composed of three building blocks as shown in Fig. 2. The 1st block assumes a function of color conversion for an input image. The 2nd block simulates a perceptual model of colorblindness using a layer model (Eq. (14)) as mentioned Sect. 2.3. The 3rd block extract color edge for a simulated image of colorblindness using layers model of neural network (Eqs. (15) and (16)). In the training, this neural network is learned about a relationship of pixel values, i.e. color map, and a discrimination performance of colors, i.e. color edge map, in an image (as shown in Fig. 7), and the models of 2nd block and the 3rd block, i.e. weighted value matrix W and bias vectors b, are fixed while the neural network is learning overall. Thus, a color conversion rule for colorblindness is trained as a part of a neural network (1st Block). Because of perceptual model of color blindness is embed for the layers of the neural network, a color conversion rule for keeping a color differences in images in presence of lack of a color information can be obtained.

The learning of color conversion in proposed method is performed as following procedure:

(1) generate training dataset from some images
(2) construct a multilayer neural network composed of three building blocks
(3) train the neural network with the models of the 2nd block and the 3rd block are fixed
(4) a color conversion rule for colorblindness can be obtained as the 1st block of the trained neural network

Here, a training dataset is pairs of input vector and desirable output vector of the neural network. In this study, RGB values of pixel of an image is used an input vector, and its color edge values of pixel of same image is used an output vector.

The 1st block of a neural network of our framework should have N (= the height of input image × the width of input image × 3) neurons as an input layer, and M (= the height of input image × the width of input image × 3) neurons as an output layer. The output vector of this block as RGB values of a image send to the 2nd block. The weighted values and biases of neurons of the 1st block are updated based on back propagation algorithm in the training.

3   Experimental Results and Discussions

In this section, we apply the proposed method to the images have various colors, to verify its effectiveness.

Figure 8 shows experimental results of our color conversion method. In this experiment, the images of Fig. 8(a) are used as training images for our multilayer neural network in advance, and the images of Fig. 8(c) are obtained as the output vectors of the 1st block of our neural network. As can be seen from the images of Fig. 8(b) and (d), the color conversion is functioning effectively.

Figure 9 shows experimental results of the color conversion using the pre-trained neural network. In this experiment, we apply the pre-trained color conversion neural network to other images. The images of Fig. 9(c) are obtained from the same neural network as above experiment. As can be seen from the images of Fig. 9(b) and (d), the color conversion is effectively although the images of Fig. 9(a) are not the training images.

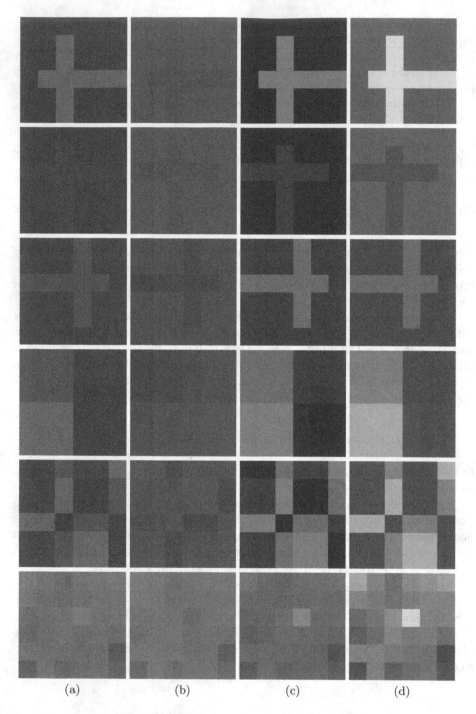

Fig. 8. Experimental results 1. (a) input images, (b) simulated protanopia color vision of (a), (c) color conversion images by proposed method, (d) protanopia color vision of (c).

Fig. 9. Experimental results 2. (a) input images, (b) simulated protanopia color vision of (a), (c) color conversion images by proposed method, (d) protanopia color vision of (c).

4 Conclusions

We proposed a novel digital image color conversion algorithm for color blindness employing a multilayer neural network. We focused that a discrimination performance of colors in an image is depend on a color difference of the colors on the boundary of regions. In the proposed method, we design a multilayer neural network composed of three building blocks: layers for image color conversion, layers for perceptual model of color blindness, and layers for color discrimination. The 2nd block and the 3rd block are predesigned based on perceptual model of color blindness and color discrimination, and these models are fixed while the neural network is learning overall, and a color conversion rule for colorblindness is trained as a part of a neural network (1st Block). In the experiment, we apply the proposed method to the test image have various colors. The results show the effectiveness of proposed method.

Acknowledgments. This work was supported in part by funds (No. 157202) and (No. 155006) from the Central Research Institute of Fukuoka University.

References

1. Rasche, K., Geist, R., Westall, J.: Detail preserving reproduction of color images for monochromats and dichromats. IEEE Comput. Graph. Appl. **25**(3), 22–30 (2005)
2. Rasche, K., Geist, R., Westall, J.: Re-coloring images for gamuts of lower dimension. Comput. Graph. Forum **24**(3), 423–432 (2005)
3. Huang, J.B., Tseng, Y.C., Wu, S.I., Wang, S.J.: Information preserving color transformation for protanopia and deuteranopia. IEEE Signal Process. Lett. **14**(10), 711–714 (2007)
4. Tanaka, G., Suetake, N., Uchino, E.: Lightness modification of color image for protanopia and deuteranopia. Opt. Rev. **17**(1), 14–23 (2010)
5. Ichikawa, M., Tanaka, K., Kondo, S., Hiroshima, K., Ichikawa, K., Tanabe, S., Fukami, K.: Web-page color modification for barrier-free color vision with genetic algorithm. In: Cantú-Paz, E. (ed.) GECCO 2003. LNCS, vol. 2724, pp. 2134–2146. Springer, Heidelberg (2003)
6. Ichikawa, M., Tanaka, K., Kondo, S., Hiroshima, K., Ichikawa, K., Tanabe S., Fukami K.: Preliminary study on color modification for still images to realize barrier-free color vision. In: Proceedings of IEEE International Conference on Systems, Man, and Cybernetics, vol. 1, pp. 36–41 (2004)
7. Meguro, M., Takahashi, C., Koga, T.: Simple color conversion method to perceptible images for color vision deficiencies. In: Proceedings of SPIE, vol. 6057, pp. 1–11 (2006)
8. Smith, V.C., Pokorny, J.: Spectral sensitivity of the foveal cone photopigments between 400 and 500 nm. Vis. Res. **15**(2), 161–171 (1975)
9. Viénot, F., Brettel, H., Mollon, J.D.: Digital video colourmaps for checking the legibility of displays by dichromats. Color Res. Appl. **24**(4), 243–252 (1999)
10. Suetake, N., Tanaka, G.: Color transformation techniques for gamuts of lower dimension -color transformation for monochrome display / print and dichromacy-. IEICE Fundam. Rev. **6**(2), 102–113 (2012)

Synthesis of Oil-Style Paintings

Fay Huang$^{(\boxtimes)}$, Bo-Hui Wu, and Bo-Ru Huang

Department of Computer Science and Information Engineering,
National Ilan University, Yi-lan, Taiwan, ROC
fay@niu.edu.tw

Abstract. Non-photorealistic rendering is an important research topic in computer graphics, where painterly (or stroke-based) rendering has received intensive attention from researchers in recent years. The goal of this paper is to design a fully automatic algorithm, which is able to turn a photograph into an oil-style painting. Different from the existing approaches that use real brush stroke images as templates, our brush strokes were created in random manner according to the characteristics of the local image region. For determining the direction of a brush stroke, we also proposed a new method based on template-matching to evaluate the major orientation of edge features within a local image window. Moreover, a novel method of deciding stroke locations was proposed, which is simple yet effective. All these features together significantly reduce the undesirable systematic impression, which appears to be a common artifact of painterly rendering.

Keywords: Non-photorealistic rendering · Painterly rendering · Stroke-based painting · Texture synthesis

1 Introduction

Non-photorealistic rendering (NPR) is an active research topic in computer graphics. One of the interesting applications of NPR technique is to simulate different types of art mediums and different styles of paintings/drawings. The task is to turn a photo into a specific type of painting or drawings by a computer algorithm. Many digital image acquisition devices nowadays include built-in software, which allow users to change the style of photos. Various commercial image editing software provide filters which are able to simulate different styles of artistic impressions. However, none of those is able to deliver quality oil-style painting synthesis automatically. Either manual assistance or the knowledge of specific combination of different filtering functions is required.

There are many artistic-style simulation algorithms for some specific type of art medium, such as pencil, crayon, link, watercolor, and etc., as well as a well-known artist's style. Among these researches, two major approaches are,

F. Huang—This research project is funded by Ministry of Science and Technology, Taiwan (MOST 104-2221-E-197 -020 -MY2).

© Springer International Publishing Switzerland 2016
T. Bräunl et al. (Eds.): PSIVT 2015, LNCS 9431, pp. 15–26, 2016.
DOI: 10.1007/978-3-319-29451-3_2

first, considering the simulation task as texture synthesis, and second, imitating the way an artist paints a picture. In the first approaches, an example painting, which is sometimes referred to as a sample image, is required. The essential pre-processing step of approaches in this category is performing texture analysis to the patches of the sample image. The algorithms then transform a photo into an artistic style picture following the painting style of the given example by various texture synthesis techniques [1,6,10].

In the second approaches, the major concerns are the design of the brush strokes and the method of applying them (e.g., orientation and order). The painting synthesis results are generated by stacking various sizes and orientations of strokes. Since brush stroke templates are the principal elements for methods belonging to this category, the approaches are often referred to as painterly rendering [2,3,8,9] or stroke-based rendering [4,5,7].

Meier [8] at Walt Disney first introduced the concept of painterly-style rendering for animation and Hertzmann [3] proposed the modelling of curved brush strokes. Both papers received great attention in the early development of NPR technology. Brush strokes in [3] are represented by anti-aliased thick cubic B-splines. The termination of each stroke and the painting order are two important subjects discussed in Hertzmann's paper. Lee et al. [5] refined Hertzmann's approach by proposing a new painting order which reduced the undesirable color scattering artifacts at the objects boundaries. A 3D curved brush stroke model was introduced by modifying the actual brushstroke samples provided by an artist. Gooch et al. [2] proposed a new method of constructing brush strokes based on the medial axes of the segmented regions. Shiraishi and Yamaguchi [9] defined a set of brush stroke attributes such as color, location, orientation, and size. Stroke distribution was determined according to the stroke area image. Stroke size was specified by user. Kang et al. [4] presented a unified scheme for automatically generating various types of artistic illustrations from photographs. A set of eleven parameters were used to classify different styles of illustrations. However, Kang's approach required manual assistance to calculate the importance map, which served as a reference for direction map generation. The goal of this paper is to design a fully automatic painterly rendering algorithm, which is able to turn a photograph into an oil-style painting.

2   Program Framework

Paintbrushes come in various shapes and sizes, each with a different purpose. One most intuitive way of selecting different sizes of paintbrushes is according to the area of the specific color to be painted on the canvas. Usually, one would use large paintbrushes to paint the large color-homogeneous region, and use smaller paintbrushes for the detailed areas. Therefore, the proposed synthesis algorithm first analyzes the color complexity of the different portions of the input photograph. A complexity map will be established and is used as a reference to select the size of a paintbrush for later painting process. The framework of the proposed synthesis algorithm is depicted in Fig. 1. In this figure, the outlined

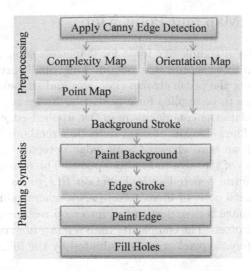

Fig. 1. The flowchart of the proposed approach. The outlined rectangles indicate the tasks to be performed, and the un-outlined rectangles denote the items to be created.

rectangles indicate the tasks to be performed, and the un-outlined rectangles denote the items to be created.

Once the brush size is determined, the next things to decide are where to apply a stroke and in which direction the brush should be moved. The directions of the brush strokes are essential, especially for creating an oil painting effect. In the preprocessing stage of the framework, a point map and an orientation map are constructed based on the complexity map and the edge features of the input image, respectively. The point map indicates the locations where the brushes are to be applied. The orientation map stores the suggested orientations of the strokes. A novel edge orientation determination algorithm is proposed, which is robust to noise and thus the common preprocessing such as noise removal can be waived. The definition and generations of complexity, point, and orientation maps are elaborated in Sects. 3 and 4.

Artists usually use relatively large brushes to paint the background or large color-homogeneous regions first, and use smaller brushes to add complex details to the foreground objects last. To imitate this behavior, the developed painting algorithm also performs background painting first, and then paints the edge regions on top of the resultant image. In the painting synthesis stage of the framework, the paintbrush generation is divided into two categories: one is background stroke and the other is edge stroke. The size of the background strokes depends on their associated values in the obtained complexity map. Edge strokes are designed to be thin and longish to emphasize their orientations. The detailed stroke generation methods will be explained in Sect. 5.

Finally, after the painting process, if there are still small unpainted regions, then the hole filling will take place to complete the oil-style painting synthesis. The unpainted regions can be filled by colors obtained from the input photograph.

3   Complexity Map and Point Map

In this paper, the term complexity for a local image region is defined by the color or intensity variation within that region. The complexity map serves as a reference for designing the brush strokes (i.e., size and shape) and determining the amount of strokes to be applied for a particular image region.

In order to calculate the complexity map, we applied edge detection to the input photograph. The selection of edge detection methods is not critical in our application and we have chosen Canny edge detector and modified it to increase the thickness of the edge to be three pixels. The resulting edge image is stored in binarized form, denoted as B. Function $B(x, y)$ returns the binarized intensity value, either 0 or 1, of image pixel (x, y), where value 1 indicates the edge location. The image is then partitioned into $i \times j$ rectangular regions. Each region is of size $m \times n$ pixels. The complexity map is a $i \times j$ matrix. The complexity value $C(i, j)$ of a reference pixel (x, y) is evaluated by the following equation.

$$C(i, j) = \frac{1}{mn} \sum_{h=0}^{m-1} \sum_{l=0}^{n-1} B(x + h, y + l)$$

where $x = jn + 1$ and $y = im + 1$. Based on the experience from the experiments, according to the size of input image, we would recommend partitioning the image into 120 to 200 rectangular regions. For instance, a 400×600 pixels image would be partitioned into 10×15 regions, and in this case, values m and n are both equal to 40, $i = 15$, and $j = 10$. Figure 2 illustrates an example of the aforementioned preprocesses, where (a) shows the result after increasing the thickness of Canny edges of the image in Fig. 7. The image partitions are depicted by grids and the associated complexity values of four selected regions are shown in Fig. 2(b).

Next, a point map is generated according to the complexity map. The point map indicates the locations where the brush strokes are to be applied. The task is to assign an amount of random dots within each of the specified rectangular image regions of Fig. 2(b). The total amount of stroke to be applied (i.e., the total number of dots) for the whole image, is defined to be $\frac{1}{k}$ of the total number of edge pixels within the image. The default value of k is 10. This parameter k can be altered by user to control the abstractness of the painting style. (Note: to increase the abstraction level, the value of k should be increased within the range between 10 to 20, and the source image should be blurred accordingly to be used in the hole filling process.) Based on the complexity value for each region and the total number of strokes, the program assigns dots in random manner to every image region. The number of dots within each region is proportional to the associated complexity value. Figure 2(c) illustrates an example of the point map.

4   Orientation Map

An orientation map is created to guide the painting direction of each stroke. We proposed a new method to obtain the major orientation of edges within a local

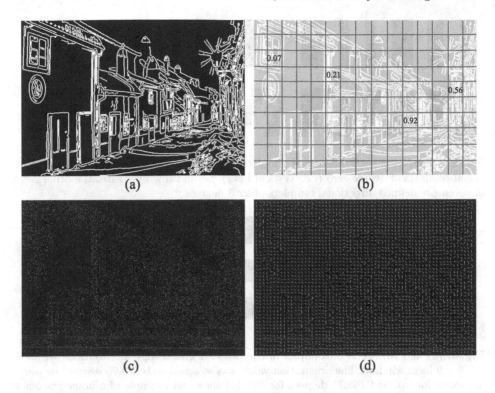

Fig. 2. (a) the result after applying a modified Canny edge detection to photo in Fig. 7. Examples of a 10×15 complexity map (b), a point map (c), and a orientation map (d). Numbers in the complexity map illustrate examples of the complexity values of that particular regions.

window. This method is very useful especially when multiple edges are clustered within a small region. The artist often paints a stroke along the major orientation of structures within the neighborhood, especially in the abstract-style painting. In the case when there is no edge within a local window, the orientation value of a homogenous region is obtained by considering the orientation values of the closest edge pixels in top, down, left, and right directions.

A set of 56 directional templets were designed and used to determine the major orientation of edges within a 9×9 local window region. We defined seven varieties of templets for each of the eight directions, namely 0, 22.5, 45,..., 157.5 degrees. In particular, zero degree corresponds to vertical edges and 90 degrees to horizontal edges, respectively. Figure 3 shows the zero and 22.5 degrees examples of the directional templets. Let T_{dn} denote the nth templet of degree d, and function $T_{dn}(u,v)$ returns the intensity value of the (u,v) pixel, which is either 0 (black) or 1 (white). For each reference pixel (x,y) in the binarized image B, if $B(x,y) = 1$, we calculate the following:

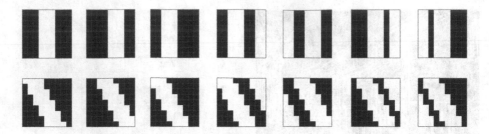

Fig. 3. Examples of 9 × 9 directional templates. First row shows seven pre-defined directional templets of degree zero (i.e., vertical lines). Second row illustrates the other set of seven pre-defined directional templets of 22.5 degrees.

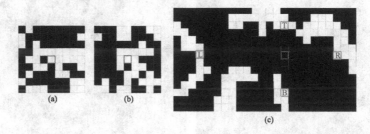

Fig. 4. (a) and (b) are two examples of complicated image edge distributions within the 9 × 9 local window. The orientation value was assigned to be 78.75 degrees by our approach for (a), and 168.75 degrees for (b). (c) shows an example of a homogeneous region, and the orientation value for this reference pixel (outlined square) is obtained by linear combinations of orientation values of pixels L, T, R, and B.

$$Similarity(T_{dn}) = \sum_{u=-4}^{4} \sum_{v=-4}^{4} NOT(XOR(T_{dn}(u+5, v+5), B(x+u, y+v)))$$

for all d and n. Then all the similarity values are sorted in descending order. The greater the similarity value indicates the more closely the template matches the local edge distribution. The finial orientation value for the edge pixel (x, y) is set to the average degrees associated with the highest two similarity values. By this way, our approach is able to identify 16 different orientations. Consequently, more variety of strokes can be created. Figure 4(a) and (b) show two examples of complicated distributions of image edges within the 9 × 9 local window. It is not trivial to determine the gradient values for the respective reference pixels (outlined square) using the standard gradient formula. After applying our orientation estimation, Fig. 4(a) obtained an orientation value of 78.75 degrees, and 168.75 degrees for Fig. 4(b).

Figure 4(c) gives an example of the possible homogeneous region. In order to obtain an orientation value for its reference pixel (outlined square), our approach searches for the existing orientation values associated to the nearest neighbors in four directions, namely top, down, left and right. The distances between the reference pixel and those neighborhood pixels were used to decide a set of weighting coefficients. The final orientation value is set to equal to the sum of weighted orientation values of those neighborhood pixels. For the photograph shown in Fig. 7, the corresponding orientation map is illustrated by a needle map displaying only every tenth pixel in Fig. 2(d).

5   Stroke Design and Painting

The design of painting strokes is the most essential task in a painting simulating process. Some researchers [5] and commercial products used real brush strokes as templates to paint the entire picture. Only the size and the orientation of the stroke template was varied accordingly during the painting process. In their approaches a pre-established database of real brush strokes is required. Moreover, if painting a picture using only a few types of strokes, then it would create an undesirable systematic impression to the final artwork. Therefore, we proposed a method to design our own brush strokes instead of using a real brush stroke database. In our approach, parameters are the keys to change the appearance of a stroke. The parameter values are determined according to the characteristic of the local edge features, and each stroke is created by random manner. The parameters include the color, the width and height, the density, the orientation, and the thickness of the stroke.

5.1   Background Region

Background in this paper is defined to be the non-edge region of the binarized image B. It corresponds to the locally color-homogeneous region in the input image. First of all, the size (i.e., width and height) of a background stroke is decided based on the complexity value associated with this stroke location on the image. The smaller the complexity value indicates the higher possibility that this location lies within a larger color-homogeneous region. Therefore, the size of the stroke to be applied at this location should likely to be greater in comparison to the other strokes. A maximum stroke length L is evaluated by $L = k * max(W, H) * (1 - C(i, j))/100$, where W and H are the width and height of the input image, $C(i, j)$ is the corresponding complexity value, and k defines the abstractness level as described earlier. The width w and height h of the stroke is obtained independently by w or $h = ceil(rand * L) + 5$, where $ceil$ and $rand$ are the ceiling and the random functions provided in Matlab. The number 5 in the formula is to ensure the size of a background stroke to be at the least five.

Next, the pattern of the stroke is mainly affected by the density value. Here, the density of a stroke can be analogous to the density of the paint (or pigment) on the brush. In general, the overall usage of paints (or pigments) on brushes to create the entire piece of artwork is somehow consistent. Therefore, a single average density value is assigned for each artwork, which influences the style

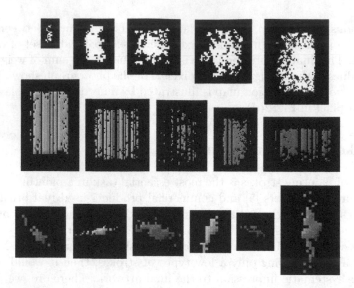

Fig. 5. Top row shows some examples of stroke masks of various intensity values. Middle row illustrates few examples of simulated background strokes. Bottom row shows some examples of generated edge strokes of different orientations.

of the painting. The default value is 0.5. The way to create a stroke mask is by adding random dots within a predefined rectangular region of size $w \times h$. The number of dots is equal to $wh * (randn * 0.1 + 0.5)$, where $randn$ is a normally distributed random function provided in Matlab. After this, more dots are randomly added towards the center region to simulate the appearance of an actual brush stroke. Some examples are illustrated in the top row of Fig. 5.

In order to create more realistic brush textures, the stroke mask is then subtracted from another mask containing randomly placed vertical lines. This gives a good simulation of oil paint texture. Before applying the stroke mask, it would be rotated according to the direction specified in the orientation map. Finally, certain thickness is added to the stroke by applying a proper shading. The middle row of Fig. 5 demonstrates few examples of simulated background strokes without performing the rotation step.

The program generates a new background stroke for each point, say (x, y), in the point map which lies in the background region, and applies (or paints) this stroke to the corresponding location (x, y) on the resulting image. The color of a stroke is assigned to be the same as the pixel (x, y) in the original input image. By this way, an image pixel is possible to be painted multiple times. When it occurs, the colors of overlapping strokes are averaged. The effect of averaging colors proposed in our approach appears to be somehow similar to the real world situation when mixed colors are used. But, averaging too many difference colors might eventually turn to gray. Therefore, our program accepts at most four colors to be applies on each pixel. The effect of overlapping strokes is shown in Fig. 6.

Fig. 6. Enlarged portions of the resulting simulation to demonstrate the strokes textures.

5.2 Edge Region

The role of the edge strokes is to enhance the outlines of the objects or to add details to the complex image regions. Orientation characteristic is essential for the edge strokes. Artists usually apply brush strokes according to the main direction of surrounding structures. In order to serve those purposes, our program generates thin strokes for edges and rotates it to meet the majority of the local edges directions. The generation procedure for an edge stroke is the same as that for background strokes. The only differences are the values for size and density parameters. The program specifies the aspect ratio of edge stroke to be about 5 : 1, and the length of the stroke is determined by $k*min(W, H)*(1-C(i,j))/200$. The average density for edge stroke is set to 0.7. Bottom row of Fig. 5 shows examples of generated edge strokes. For each point in the point map which lies in the edge region of B, an edge stroke is created and applied to the resulting image on top of the already painted background region. The edge stroke color will directly overlay the existing background color. Only colors of overlapping edge strokes will be averaged.

6 Experiment Results

The implemented oil-style painting synthesis program has been applied to a diverse set of photos, including sceneries, indoor views, animal photos, and portraits etc. The input photograph that was used to illustrate the concepts of our approach is shown in Fig. 7(a) and the final synthesis result is shown in (b). Figure 7(c) and (d) show the results of increasing levels of abstraction, where the value of k was set to 15 and 20 respectively.

Fig. 7. (a) the original input photo. (b) the final synthesis result. (c) and (d) are results of increasing levels of abstraction to $k = 15$ and $k = 20$ respectively.

The proposed method was also compared with existing approaches based on the availability of the original input images. In the first column of Fig. 8, our synthesis result was compared to Hertzmann [3] and Lee et al.'s [5] approaches. Our method demonstrates a good simulation of oil-painting strokes at enhancing the shading of the fruits. In the middle column of Fig. 8, Shiraishi and Yamaguchi's [9] approach creates a slightly blurring effect to the resulting image. Our method remains the sharpness of the contents and at the same time provides good abstraction of the details, for instance, see the head of the dog. In the right column of Fig. 8, our result was compared to Litwinowicz's [7] approach. It shows that even in the large color-homogeneous regions, our method is able to simulate the paintbrush effects without the noticeable repetition of brushes. In general, the painting simulation results of our approach contain less systematic impression normally caused by similar shapes of strokes. Our program creates individual unique stroke based on the characteristics of the local image region. For a 600×400 pixel image as shown in Fig. 7, the processing time of the developed MATLAB code is 109 s running on an Intel Core i7 computer with 16 GB of RAM. The code has not yet been optimized to increase its efficiency.

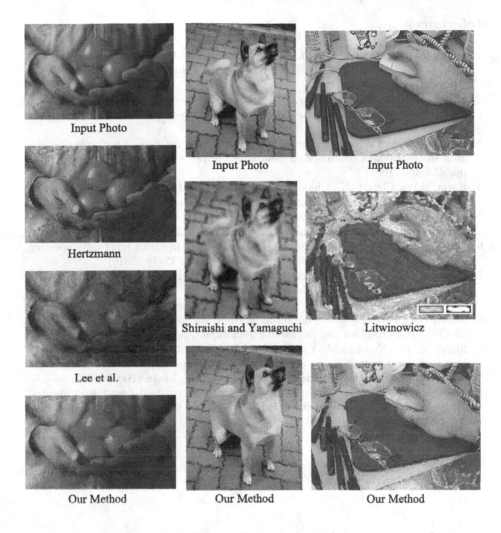

Fig. 8. The comparison of our synthesis results to the exiting approaches.

7   Conclusion

A stroke-based oil-painting simulation algorithm has been proposed. The main contributions of the proposed approach different from the existing works include: First, the newly introduced concepts of a complexity map and a point map, both serve as important components in the entire simulation process. Second, the novel method for calculating the main edge direction within a local window, by which an orientation map can be achieved. The proposed method is able to distinguish 16 different orientations. Third, a newly developed stroke generation procedure, by which each stroke can be uniquely created based on the edge distribution within the local image region. Finally, the proposed synthesis approach is also able to simulate different level of abstractions by varying the value of a parameter.

References

1. Chang, W.-H., Cheng, M.-C., Kuo, C.-M., Huang, G.-D.: Feature-oriented artistic styles transfer based on effective texture synthesis. J. Inf. Hiding Multimedia Signal Process. **6**(1), 29–46 (2015)
2. Gooch, B., Coombe, G., Shirley, P.: Artistic vision: painterly rendering using computer vision techniques. In: 2nd International Symposium on Non-photorealistic Animation and Rendering, pp. 83–90 (2002)
3. Hertzmann, A.: Painterly rendering with curved brush strokes of multiple sizes. In: 25th International Conference on Computer Graphics and Interactive Techniques, pp. 453–460 (1998)
4. Kang, H.W., Chui, C.K., Chakraborty, U.K.: A unied scheme for adaptive stroke-based rendering. Vis. Comput. **22**(9), 814–824 (2006)
5. Lee, K.J., Kim, D.H., Yun, I.D., Lee, S.U.: Three-dimensional oil painting reconstruction with stroke-based rendering. Vis. Comput. **23**(9), 873–880 (2007)
6. Lee, H., Seo, S., Ryoo, S., Yoon, K.: Directional texture transfer. In: Symposium on Non-Photorealistic Animation and Rendering, pp. 43–48 (2010)
7. Litwinowicz, P.: Processing images and video for an impressionist effect. In: 24th International Conference on Computer Graphics and Interactive Techniques, pp. 407–414 (1997)
8. Meier, B.J.: Painterly rendering for animation. In: 23rd International Conference on Computer Graphics and Interactive Techniques, pp. 477–484 (1996)
9. Shiraishi, M., Yamaguchi, Y.: An algorithm for automatic painterly rendering based on local source image approximation. In: First International Symposium on Non-Photorealistic Animation and Rendering, pp. 53–58 (2000)
10. Wang, B., Wang, W., Yang, H., Sun, J.: Efficient example-based painting and synthesis of 2D directional texture. IEEE Trans. Vis. Comput. Graph. **10**(3), 266–277 (2004)

Multi-frame Feature Integration
for Multi-camera Visual Odometry

Hsiang-Jen Chien[1]($^{\boxtimes}$), Haokun Geng[2], Chia-Yen Chen[3],
and Reinhard Klette[1]

[1] School of Engineering, Auckland University of Technology,
Auckland, New Zealand
jchien@aut.ac.nz

[2] Department of Computer Science, University of Auckland,
Auckland, New Zealand

[3] Department of Computer Science and Information Engineering,
National University of Kaohsiung, Kaohsiung, Taiwan

Abstract. State-of-the-art ego-motion estimation approaches in the context of visual odometry (VO) rely either on Kalman filters or bundle adjustment. Recently proposed multi-frame feature integration (MFI [1]) techniques aim at finding a compromise between accuracy and computation efficiency. In this paper we generalise an MFI algorithm towards the full use of multi-camera-based visual odometry for achieving more consistent ego-motion estimation in a parallel scalable manner. A series of experiments indicated that the generalised integration technique contributes to an improvement of above 70 % over our direct VO implementation, and further improved the monocular MFI technique by more than 20 %.

Keywords: Visual odometry · Ego-motion estimation · Feature tracking

1 Introduction

The development of visual odometry contributed not only to robotics, it is also of growing importance for self-driving vehicles. The recovery of camera motion and 3D structures from video sequences has been studied since the early 80s [15]. The vision-guided rovers on Mars defined one of the early milestones. They operate by applying the framework of structure from motion (SfM). Since then, an extensive amount of work has been added to theories and practice for solving the ego-motion estimation problem in fields of visual odometry (VO) and simultaneous localisation and mapping (SLAM).

Existing visual odometry algorithms include patch-based and feature-based methods, depending on how inter-frame pixel correspondences are established. Patch-based methods, e.g. by following common optical flow, deploy search windows to track each pixel, while feature-based approaches perform a matching in feature spaces where each feature vector encodes the regional characteristics centering at the tracked pixel [6]. Feature-based approaches dominated the development of visual odometry in the last decade [7].

© Springer International Publishing Switzerland 2016
T. Bräunl et al. (Eds.): PSIVT 2015, LNCS 9431, pp. 27–37, 2016.
DOI: 10.1007/978-3-319-29451-3_3

Although the tracking of features has been a well-studied topic in the field of computer vision, for the use in visual odometry more strict conditions apply, and hence a generic feature tracker can often fail. Some filtering mechanisms and temporal constraints need to be considered in order to remove incorrect inter- frame feature matches which could hazard the ego-motion estimation process [12].

The drift caused by the accumulation of ego-motion estimation is yet another major concern [11]. Bundle adjustment (BA) is considered to be the "golden standard" to solve this issue [5]. BA reduces the accumulated error by a global optimisation process designed to converge to the maximum-likelihood estimate that optimally fits the observed feature locations and their 3D coordinates. However, many BA approaches are implemented only in a local scale since it requires a huge amount of computation involving the solution of large linear systems.

Multi-frame feature integration (MFI), proposed in [1], provides a cost-effective yet comparable solution for drift suppression as well as for improving the tracking process. By integrating multiple measurements of the same feature at different times, the 3D measurement noise is canceled under certain conditions. The integration of feature also implicitly introduces a dependency of the ego-motion estimation between each frame. Such dependency is helpful in the reduction of drift. Figure 1 shows an example of the growth of accumulated drift and the suppression of the drift.

However, we noticed that the original MFI algorithm uses the right camera of a stereo-vision system only for 3D calculation, while the feature detection and tracking is done in a monocular manner. In this work we propose a generalisation of a similar idea, which uses multi-camera data to enhance the robustness of feature tracking, and to further reduce the drift.

The paper is organised as follows. In Sect. 2 we formulate the VO problem. In Sect. 3 the MFI algorithm is described. In Sect. 4 we generalise the MFI algorithm to make a full use of a multi-camera system. Experimental results are discussed in Sect. 5 to study the improvement of the proposed method, while Sect. 6 concludes this paper.

2   Feature-Based Visual Odometry

The pipeline of binocular visual odometry, as shown in Fig. 2, involves several domains in computer vision. The input of the pipeline is a pair of images captured time-synchronised by a left and right camera. It produces the estimated 3D structure of tracked scene points and motion of the vision system relative to the pose where the previous input images were taken. In this work we follow a feature-based framework which derives the motion of the cameras by tracking sparse features instead of coping with dense image patches. The advantage of a binocular framework over a monocular one is that the 3D information can be acquired using stereo matching and triangulation, hence it is preferable in high-precision applications.

Motion estimation can be achieved in either Euclidean space, projective space, or by means of both spaces. Solving the motion in Euclidean space is less

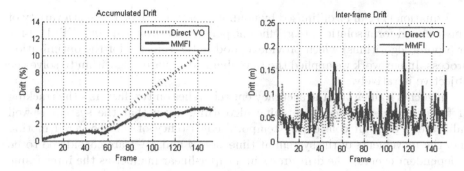

Fig. 1. The accumulation of inter-frame estimation error grows in a super-linear manner when a direct VO method is applied, as can be seen on the left plot, which also shows that the drift is effectively suppressed when the proposed multi-camera multi-frame feature integration (MMFI) method is used. By the introduction of inter-frame dependency the drift slightly increases in a local scale as can be observed on the right.

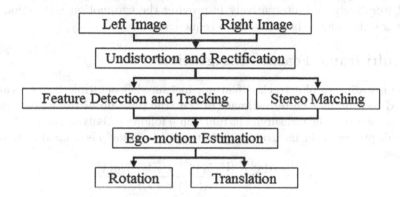

Fig. 2. Pipeline of a stereo visual odometry system using 3D-to-2D correspondences

favourable due to the highly anisotropic error covariances in the case where the 3D structure is measured using a stereo-based disparity value. On the other hand, the projective approach does not provide reliable metric information, hence the 3D-to-2D correspondences are considered as being a better choice for ego-motion estimation [15].

Optimised motion is found by a minimisation of the re-projection error. Given two sets of features F and F', and a mapping $M \subseteq F \times F'$. We also assume defined 3D and 2D measurement functions g and ρ that transform a feature into the Euclidean coordinates in $\mathbb{R}^3$ or into the image coordinates in $\mathbb{R}^2$, respectively. Furthermore, consider the perspective projection function $\pi : \mathbb{R}^3 \to \mathbb{R}^2$. Optimal motion is defined by the rotation matrix $\mathbf{R}$ and translation vector $\mathbf{t}$ which minimise the sum of squares of the re-projection error, formally given by

$$\phi(\mathbf{R}, \mathbf{t}) = \sum_{\forall(\chi, \chi') \in M} \left\| \pi\left(\mathbf{R} g\left(\chi\right) + \mathbf{t}\right) - \rho\left(\chi'\right) \right\|^2 \tag{1}$$

Equation (1) can be optimised by nonlinear optimisation. There is a variety of linear closed-form solutions (e.g. efficient perspective-from-n-point (EPnP [14]), or 5-point algorithms) which provide a good initial solution for the optimisation process. In our work we applied the Levenberg-Marquardt algorithm to solve the objective iteratively.

In such a framework, the accuracy entirely relies on two factors - the tracking of features and the stereo matching algorithm, given that the system is well calibrated. Without considering temporal consistency of the recovered motion (i.e. the movements of the system at time slots j and $j + 1$ are considered to be independent events), the drift grows in a super-linear manner as the inter-frame ego-motion estimations are chained to derive the global trajectory of the system. A state-of-the-art solution to suppress the drift is to use either Kalman filters or a sliding-window bundle adjustment [16].

Recently, the multi-frame integration (MFI) technique has been proposed to achieve drift suppression by introducing a dependency between the recovered ego-motion at j, and feature tracking between frame j and $j + 1$, based on the idea of iteratively and alternatively improving the ego-motion estimation and feature tracking along the given video sequence.

3   Multi-frame Feature Integration

The 3D coordinates of a tracked feature, measured in multiple frames, can be averaged to acquire a better estimate of the true position of the feature in the Euclidean space, if the measurement function g follows a Gaussian error. According to this property, the integrated measurement function $\bar{g}$ is defined recursively as follows:

$$\bar{g}(\chi_i^j) = \frac{\alpha(\chi_i^j) \cdot [\mathbf{R}_j \bar{g}(\chi_i^{j-1}) + \mathbf{t}_j] + g(\chi_i^j)}{\alpha(\chi_i^j) + 1} \tag{2}$$

where $(\mathbf{R}_j, \mathbf{t}_j)$ defines the rigid transformation from frame $j - 1$ to j, and $\alpha(\chi_i^j)$ denotes the accumulated number of measurements of feature χ_i at moment j. If the feature χ_i is first discovered in frame j_0, it is defined that $\bar{g}(\chi_i^j) = \mathbf{0}^\top$ and $\alpha(\chi_i^j) = 0$ for all $j < j_0$.

Before the states of features are updated by Eq. (2), the optimal ego-motion $(\mathbf{R}_j, \mathbf{t}_j)$ is estimated first by minimising

$$\phi_j(\mathbf{R}, \mathbf{t}) = \sum_{i=1}^{n} \eta \cdot \varepsilon(\chi_i^j, g; \mathbf{R}, \mathbf{t}) + (1 - \eta) \cdot \alpha(\chi_i^j) \cdot \varepsilon(\chi_i^j, \bar{g}; \mathbf{R}, \mathbf{t}) \tag{3}$$

where $\eta = [0, 1]$ controls the significance of the feature integration and ε measures the deviation of the projection of feature χ_i in frame t versus its tracked position:

$$\varepsilon(\chi_i^j, g; \mathbf{R}, \mathbf{t}) = \omega(\chi_i^j) \cdot \left\| \pi \left(\mathbf{R} g(\chi_i^{j-1}) + \mathbf{t} \right) - \rho \left(\chi_i^j \right) \right\|^2 \tag{4}$$

By ω we denote the weighting term of feature χ_i at moment j. If feature χ_i is not discovered at that moment, we have $\omega(\chi_i^j) = 0$ so that the feature is not taken into account for the estimation of $\mathbf{R}_j$ and $\mathbf{t}_j$.

The estimated motion can also be used to improve the tracking of features. The prediction of a feature's location in the current frame is calculated by projecting its previously integrated 3D coordinates into the current frame. The projection is then compared to the image coordinates obtained by feature matching. The deviation between both is then used to denote the reliability of the measurement, and taken into account to adjust the weighting term ω accordingly. The MFI algorithm keeps tracking the mean of such deviations, every time a feature's state is updated. When the cost of an update is higher than a predefined threshold, then the tracking process for a feature is marked "lost", and hence terminated.

Instead of terminating the tracking immediately, an attempt to re-discover the missing feature can be optionally carried out. The feature vector of the pixel, at the projection of the integrated feature, is extracted and compared with the feature being tracked. If a significantly high similarity is found, then the tracking process is resumed.

4   Multi-camera Multi-frame Feature Integration

To maximise the robustness of the feature tracking mechanism, the MFI [1] is extended in our work to use images taken by all cameras at moments j and $j+1$. The four steps of the proposed algorithm, to be walked through in the rest of this section, are as follows:

1. *Feature detection and cross matching.* Image features are detected, extracted and then matched for all camera combinations in consecutive frames.
2. *Ego-motion estimation.* The optimal rotation and translation of the inter-frame motion is calculated by minimising re-projection error *subject to all cameras.*
3. *Update of the integrated features.* The states of all the actively tracked features are updated to take into account the new observations based on the solved ego-motion. Features having significantly different prediction and observation locations are marked as lost. Attempts will be carried out to resume the tracking of these features at a later stage.
4. *Lost feature recovery.* For those features, failed to update their states due to missed matches, a prediction-and-check strategy is performed to re-discover their corresponding image features.

4.1   Spatial-Temporal Feature Matching

Considering an m-camera visual odometry system, image features are initially detected and extracted from images I_k^j and I_k^{j+1} for each camera $k = 1, 2, .., m$. Let F_k^j and F_k^{j+1} denote these features, respectively. The cross matching is initiated in feature space for each pair of feature sets $(F_k^j, F_{k'}^{j+1})$, where $1 \leq k, k' \leq m$.

The mutual Euclidean distances between feature vectors are calculated, and similar features are associated. For each feature $\chi \in F_k^j$, we have the distances

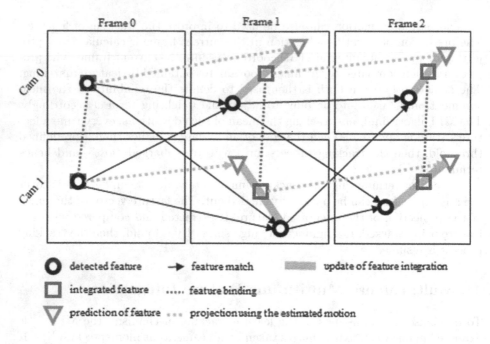

Fig. 3. Illustration of the generalised multi-frame feature integration and ego-motion estimation process

to its best match $\chi_1' \in F_{k'}^{j+1}$ and its second best match $\chi_2' \in F_{k'}^{j+1}$. A differential ratio is calculated as

$$\delta(\chi, \chi_1', \chi_2') = \frac{\|\nu(\chi) - \nu(\chi_1')\|}{\|\nu(\chi) - \nu(\chi_2')\|} \tag{5}$$

where ν transforms a feature to its vector representation in feature space. If the ratio is lower than a defined threshold, say 0.8, then such matching is considered ambiguous, hence rejected at this stage.

The initial matches are then verified in projective space for outlier rejection. The fundamental matrix-based RANSAC strategy is typically carried out at this stage to reject geometrically inconsistent correspondences [9]. In this work, we instead use an LMeD estimator which is considered to be a more strict and stable model for outlier identification [4]. The mislabeled inliers at this stage will still have a chance to be amended later in the lost feature recovery stage. The detected features and the matched correspondences are depicted in Fig. 3 as black circles and black solid lines, respectively.

It is worth a mention that, despite being developed independently, the described cross matching mechanism shares a similar idea of the spatial-temporal network implemented in the open source library LIBVISO2 [2]. In particular, for each frame j the implementation maps features from F_1^j to F_1^{j+1}. For those mapped features $\chi \in F_1^{j+1}$ the matching is performed again, but this time from

F_1^{j+1} to F_2^{j+1} (i.e. doing a left-right feature matching in j-th frame.) After repeating such process through $F_2^{j+1} \rightarrow F_2^j \rightarrow F_1^j$, in the way that χ finally travels back to F_1^j, it checks if χ is mapped to itself in the end. Feature matches failed to fulfill such circular consistency are rejected by LIBVISO2 to prevent outliers being used in the ego-motion stage.

4.2   Ego-Motion Estimation

The direct 3D measurement function g is extended for also using the mean of the measurements from all k cameras:

$$g(\chi_i^j) = \sum_{1 \le k \le m} \frac{1}{m} \cdot g_k(\chi_i^j) \tag{6}$$

Here, each component $g_k(\chi_i^j)$ denotes a 3D measurement made by the k-th camera. The definition allows us to develop a generalised multi-camera version of Eq. (3) such that, once minimised, a system-wide consistent solution is found.

4.3   Feature Integration and State Update

Initially as $j = 0$ only the direct measurement $g(\chi_i^0)$ is used in Eq. (3) to find $(\mathbf{R}_1, \mathbf{t}_1)$. After the first ego-motion estimation, $(\mathbf{R}_1, \mathbf{t}_1)$ is taken into account to compute the integration of feature χ_i at moment $j = 1$, which yields

$$\bar{g}(\chi_i^1) = \frac{[\mathbf{R}_1 g(\chi_i^0) + \mathbf{t}_1] + g(\chi_i^1)}{2} \tag{7}$$

according to Eq. (2). Such an update is performed for each tracked feature every time when the ego-motion is solved between frames j and $j + 1$.

The magnitude of the update in Eq. (7) indicates the accuracy of the recovered ego-motion as well as the reliability of the direct measurement, and can be useful to take out unreliable 3D data in further ego-motion estimation. To this purpose we also update the running covariance by

$$\sigma^2(\chi_i^j) = \frac{\alpha(\chi_i^j) \cdot \sigma^2(\chi_i^{j-1}) + [\bar{g}(\chi_i^j) - g(\chi_i^j)]^\top [\bar{g}(\chi_i^j) - g(\chi_i^j)]}{\alpha(\chi_i^j) + 1} \tag{8}$$

and use it to adjust $\omega(\chi_i^j)$ accordingly to decrease the significance of features as more unreliable measurements are integrated.

Projecting the integrated $\bar{g}(\chi_i^j)$ to frame $j+1$ yields prediction of a previously tracked feature χ_i; (depicted as blue triangles in Fig. 3.) The prediction is also helpful to indicate problematic feature tracking. Let $\pi_k(\cdot)$ be the projection function of camera k and $\rho_k(\chi_i^j)$ the observation of feature χ_i by camera k in frame j. The prediction is defined as

$$\bar{\rho}_k(\chi_i^j) = \pi_k \left(\mathbf{R}_{j+1} \bar{g}(\chi_i^j) + \mathbf{t}_{j+1} \right) \tag{9}$$

The deviation $\|\bar{\rho}_k(\chi_i^j) - \rho_k(\chi_i^j)\|$ is checked before the update of an integrated feature is actually performed. If the projection error (depicted as green thick line in Fig. 3) is greater than a predefined threshold, then the feature is marked as lost and the update of $\bar{g}(\chi_i^j)$ will be set on hold for further investigation.

4.4 Lost Feature Recovery

A feature $\chi_i^j \in F_k^j$ is lost in frame $j+1$ between camera k and k' if either there exists no matched feature $\chi' \in F_{k'}^j$, or the difference between its prediction and the observation $\rho_{k'}(\chi')$ is not acceptable.

To resume the tracking of a lost feature, the feature vector is extracted from the predicted location $\bar{\rho}(\chi_i^j)$. Then the Euclidean distance between the extracted descriptor and $\nu_k(\chi_i^j)$ is checked against the statistics of successfully tracked features. If the distance is within 1-σ then the feature is considered recovered.

Figure 4 shows some examples of re-discovery of lost features in the image taken by another camera from frame j and $j+1$. Please note the matched patches are not found by any means of explicit feature matching. Only the solved ego-motion and integrated feature states are used to establish the correspondences in sub-pixel accuracy.

5 Experimental Results

The proposed method is compared with direct VO and MFI approaches. We use the KITTI dataset [8], with the stereo monochrome images as input data,

Fig. 4. Four lost features (always in the *left* image) recovered in another frame taken by another camera (see the *right* image of each pair) using the multi-camera multi-frame integration technique. The image patches are enlarged 5 times to illustrate the sub-pixel accuracy of the feature recovery algorithm

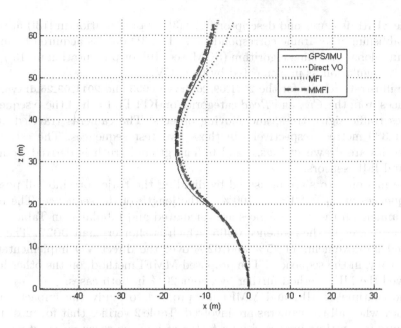

Fig. 5. Visual odometry of KITTI sequence 0005

Table 1. Ego-motion estimation errors and improvements

Sequence	Component	Unit	Direct	MFI	MMFI
0005	Rotation	deg/m	0.22	0.07 (68 %)	0.06 (72 %)
	Translation	%	9.42	6.10 (35 %)	4.49 (52 %)
0027	Rotation	deg/m	0.06	0.02 (67 %)	0.01 (83 %)
	Translation	%	13.2	5.79 (59 %)	2.74 (79 %)

and the GPS/IMU data as ground truth. The direct VO implementation uses only inter-frame feature matching of the left camera to solve ego-motion. The MFI method uses the same camera while the tracked features are integrated over time. The MMFI makes a full use of images taken from both cameras.

Table 2. Averaged time profile per frame

	MFI	MMFI
Feature matching	8.04 ms	38.61 ms
Feature integration	3.70 ms	11.49 ms
Ego-motion estimation	28.12 ms	26.34 ms
Lost feature recovery	5.83 ms	41.52 ms

The SURF features and descriptors (see [3], or presentation in [13]) are used for establishing inter-frame correspondences. The 3D data is acquired by means of a semi-global matching algorithm (SGM, see [10], or presentation in [13]), and stereo triangulation as implemented by OpenCV.

We illustrate results for the 2011_09_26_drive_0005 and 2011_09_26_drive_0027 sequences from the *City* and *Road* categories on KITTI. Each of these sequences includes traffic signs, trees, and moving objects. The cameras traveled about 70 and 380 metres, respectively, in those two test sequences. The estimated trajectories are drawn in Figs. 5 and 6. The ground truth is derived from the GPS and IMU sensors.

The motion errors are measured by dividing the trajectory into all possible subsequences of 10 %, 20 %, .., 100 % of the length of the sequence. The mean errors among all the subsequences are calculated and tabulated in Table 1. The errors are lower in the sequence **0005**, which is shorter than **0027**. The MFI achieved improvements of 45 % and 62 % over the direct VO implementation, respectively, in the sequences. The proposed MMFI method, on the other hand, improved the MFI method further by about 20 % in both cases.

The runtime of MFI and MMFI are profiled to study the impact on the efficiency when all the cameras are involved. Table 2 verifies that for most tasks the computation time increased by a factor of four, as three more inter- frame feature integrations are introduced by the MMFI. However, the computation time of the nonlinear optimisation for ego-motion estimation remains at the same level. This is a desired property as the stages of the original MFI, generalised in our work, can be easily parallelised for optimising the procedure. It is therefore possible to further improve the efficiency of MMFI by parallel implementation to match the original MFI method.

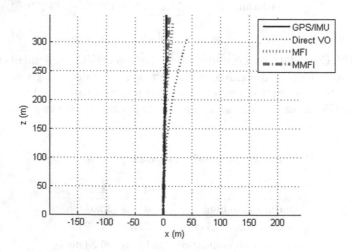

Fig. 6. Visual odometry of KITTI sequence 0027

6   Conclusions

In this paper we generalised the recently proposed multi-frame integration technique to make a full use of a multi-camera visual odometry system. The proposed approach enhances the robustness of the feature integration algorithm and achieves a better ego-motion estimation by taking into account multiple observations.

References

1. Badino, H., Yamamoto, A., Kanade, T.: Visual odometry by multi-frame feature integration. In: International Workshop on Computer Vision Autonomous Driving (ICCV) (2013)
2. Geiger, A., Ziegler, J., Stiller, C.: StereoScan: dense 3D reconstruction in real-time. In: Intelligent Vehicles Symposium (IV) (2011)
3. Bay, H., Van Gool, L., Tuytelaars, T.: SURF: speeded up robust features. In: Leonardis, A., Bischof, H., Pinz, A. (eds.) ECCV 2006, Part I. LNCS, vol. 3951, pp. 404–417. Springer, Heidelberg (2006)
4. Choi, S., Kim, T., Yu W.: Performance evaluation of RANSAC family. In: Proceedings of the British Machine Vision Conference (2009)
5. Engels, C., Stewenius, H., Nister, D.: Bundle adjustment rules. In: Proceedings of Photogrammetric Computer Vision (2006)
6. Forster, C., Pizzoli, M., Scaramuzza, D.: SVO: Fast semi-direct monocular visual odometry. In: Proceedings of the IEEE International Conference on Robotics Automation, pp. 15–22 (2014)
7. Fraundorfer, F., Scaramuzza, D.: Visual odometry: part II - matching, robustness, and applications. IEEE Robot. Autom. Mag. **19**, 78–90 (2012)
8. Geiger A., Lenz, P., Urtasun, R.: Are we ready for autonomous driving? The KITTI vision benchmark suite. In: Proceedings of the Conference on Computer Vision Pattern Recognition (2012)
9. Hartley, R.I., Zisserman, A.: Multiple View Geometry in Computer Vision, 2nd edn. Cambridge University Press, Cambridge (2004)
10. Hirschmüller, H.: Accurate and efficient stereo processing by semi-global matching and mutual information. In: Proceedings of the Conference Computer Vision Pattern Recognition, vol. 2, pp. 807–814 (2005)
11. Jiang, R., Wang, S., Klette, R.: Statistical modeling of long-range drift in visual odometry. In: Koch, R., Huang, F. (eds.) ACCV 2010 Workshops, Part II. LNCS, vol. 6469, pp. 214–224. Springer, Heidelberg (2011)
12. Kitt, B., Geiger, A., Lategahn, H.: Visual odometry based on stereo image sequences with RANSAC-based outlier rejection scheme. In: Proceedings of the IEEE Intelligent Vehicles Symposium, pp. 486–492 (2010)
13. Klette, R.: Concise Computer Vision. Springer, London (2014)
14. Lepetit, V., Moreno-Noguer, F., Fua, P.: EPnP: an accurate O(n) solution to the PnP problem. Int. J. Comput. Vis. **81**, 155–166 (2009)
15. Scaramuzza, D., Fraundorfer, F.: Visual odometry: part I - the first 30 years and fundamentals. IEEE Robot. Autom. Mag. **18**, 80–92 (2011)
16. Zhang, Z., Shan Y.: Incremental motion estimation through local bundle adjustment. Technical report MSR-TR-01-54, Microsoft (2001)

A Robust Identification Scheme for JPEG XR Images with Various Compression Ratios

Hiroyuki Kobayashi[1]([✉]), Shoko Imaizumi[2], and Hitoshi Kiya[3]

[1] Tokyo Metropolitan College of Industrial Technology, Shinagawa,
Tokyo 140-0011, Japan
hkob@metro-cit.ac.jp
[2] Chiba University, Chiba 263-8522, Japan
shoko@chiba-u.jp
[3] Tokyo Metropolitan University, Hino, Tokyo 191-0065, Japan
kiya@sd.tmu.ac.jp

Abstract. A robust scheme for identifying JPEG XR coded images is proposed in this paper. The aim is to identify the images that are generated from the same original image under various compression ratios. The proposed scheme is robust against a difference in compression ratios, and does not produce false negative matches in any compression ratio. A new property of the positive and negative signs of lapped biorthogonal transform coefficients is considered to robustly identify the images. The experimental results show the proposed scheme is effective for not only still images, but also video sequences in terms of the querying such as false positive, false negative and true positive matches.

Keywords: Image identification · JPEG XR · Robustness

1 Introduction

The use of digital images and video sequences has greatly increased recently because of the rapid growth of the Internet and multimedia systems. It is often necessary to identify a certain image in a database that has a large number of images in various types of the applications of digital images/videos, such as security and evaluation of image validity. The image database generally consists of images in a compressed form to reduce the amount of data. Several international standards for searching for images/videos have been developed [1–4] in connection to this. "Identification" in this work is defined as the operation of finding an image that is identical to a given original image from an image database. In this paper, a robust scheme for identifying JPEG XR coded images is proposed.

JPEG XR is an image coding standard from the JPEG committee [5,6]. It allows lossy and lossless coding for still images and videos. It supports not only images with 8 bits but also images with over 8 bits and floating point representation. Thus, it can support various kinds of images including high dynamic range(HDR) images [7–9] for a new generation of digital cameras. Therefore the proposed scheme is widely available for identifying many kinds of images.

© Springer International Publishing Switzerland 2016
T. Bräunl et al. (Eds.): PSIVT 2015, LNCS 9431, pp. 38–50, 2016.
DOI: 10.1007/978-3-319-29451-3_4

Fig. 1. Process of image identification

So far, several schemes have been developed for identifying compressed images [10–19]. The schemes described in [13–17] are for the JPEG standard, and the schemes in [17–19] are for the JPEG 2000 standard, where some properties of transform coefficients i.e. DCT(Discrete Cosine Transform) and DWT(Discrete Wavelet Transform) coefficients, play an important role for image identification. In addition, they have been extended to image identification schemes in the encrypted domain securely to operate images/videos [20,21]. However, there is still none for the JPEG XR standard. Moreover the previous schemes are not available for JPEG XR images, because JPEG XR is the only image coding standard that uses a lapped biorthogonal transform(LBT), which is different from DCT and DWT [22].

Because of this situation, a scheme for identifying JPEG XR coded images is considered in this paper. The aim of the proposed scheme is to identify JPEG XR images that are generated from the same original image under various compression ratios. The proposed scheme does not produce false negative matches in any compression ratio. A new property of the positive and negative signs of LBT coefficients is utilized to identify the images. The experimental results shows the proposed scheme is effective for not only still images, but also video sequences in terms of the retrieval performance such as false positive, false negative and true positive matches.

2 Background

2.1 Image Identification Model

Let us consider that there are two or more compressed images, which have different or the same compression ratios. Those images are originated from the same image and compressed by the same compression method. In this paper, the identification of those images is referred to as image identification. In other words, if the images do not originate from the same image, or are not compressed by the same compression method, they are unidentifiable from each other.

A simplified model of the image identification system is shown in Fig. 1. The system consists of three components: namely, a client (user), an image identifier, and a database. The database may contain various types of data, such as compressed images, parameter (feature) of the images, and image information (metadata). An identification is initialized by the user, by sending a query, which can be any kind of the data mentioned above to the image identifier. Then the image identifier checks the availability of the query in the database. Afterwards, if the query information is available, it can be directly sent or confirmed to the user. This paper focuses on querying some properties of JPEG XR images.

2.2 Applications

There are numerous applications for the previously mentioned identification model. Some examples are described in the following.

a. Security

In a compressed image environment, it is important to identify any alterations in image caused by disturbances or alterations other than the compression itself. For instance, identifying the presence of malicious attacks, such as intentional cropping, or the addition or removal of objects.

b. Detection of Errors in Images

In image and video communications, a slight quality degradation due to compression noise is commonly accepted. However, the image quality degradation due to other causes, such as transmission and decoding errors, are usually unacceptable. A method to identify those errors in a fast and automatic way is required in such applications.

c. Evaluation of Image Validity

Let us consider two images of the same scene, for example: chest X-ray images of two patients. Those images may have been labelled by name, date, or content description. However, this approach is very sensitive to human error, such as mislabelling. The mislabelled images can cause a misdiagnosis, which in turn could threaten a patient's life. Therefore, a more efficient and save method to guarantee the image validity is required.

d. Image Information Retrieval

In addition to image querying to obtain identical image, image querying to obtain image information (metadata) is comparably important. For the images, the metadata may include: photographer's name, image format, and date and time. The digital library is one area where metadata identification is important.

2.3 JPEG XR

JPEG XR is an image coding standard from the JPEG committee. It allows lossy and lossless coding for still images and videos. It supports not only fixed point representation but also floating point representation. Thus, it can support various kinds of images including HDR images for a new generation of digital cameras.

The block diagram of JPEG XR encoding is illustrated in Fig. 2. JPEG XR is based on a block transform design, and it uses some of the same high level building blocks as in most image compression schemes, such as color conversion, spatial transformation, scalar quantization, coefficient scanning, and entropy coding. The encoding consists of the following basic steps:

(1) Performing a color conversion.
(2) Dividing an image into non-overlapped consecutive 16×16 blocks, called macro block, and then each macro block into consecutive 4×4 blocks, called block (see Fig. 3(a)).

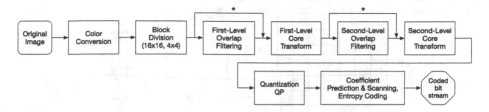

Fig. 2. Basic block diagram of JPEG XR encoding (* There are three modes)

(3) Applying two basic operators i.e. core transform and optional overlap filtering to the blocks, where the operators are hierarchically executed twice shown in Fig. 3(b).
(4) Applying a coefficient quantization approach controlled by quantization parameters (QPs).
(5) Executing adaptive coefficient scanning to convert the two-dimensional array transform coefficients within a block into a one-dimensional vector to be encoded. Finally, the coefficients are entropy encoded.

In step (3), one temporally DC coefficient and 15 HP coefficients are obtained for each block by the 1st-level core transform, and 16 temporally DC coefficients are gathered from each macro block as shown in Fig. 3(b). The 2nd-level core transform is then applied to them. As a result, one DC coefficient, 15 LP coefficients and 15×16 HP coefficients are calculated for each macro block, where core transform, referred to as lapped biorthogonal transform (LBT), is common between two levels. Therefore, the transform coefficients are often called LBT coefficients, which consist of DC, LP and HP ones.

The overlap filtering may be used to reduce blocking artifacts. JPEG XR has three overlapping-modes. When mode 0 is chosen, no overlap filtering is performed. Otherwise, only the 1st-level overlap filtering is performed for mode 1, and both filtering operations are done for mode 2.

3 Proposed Identification Scheme

The aim of the proposed scheme is to identify JPEG XR images that are generated from the same original image under various compression ratios. The proposed scheme does not produce false negative matches in any compression ratio. A new property of the positive and negative signs of LBT coefficients is utilized to identify the images.

3.1 Notation and Terminologies

Several notations and terminologies used in the following sections are listed here.

- x represents an image. x can be "Q" for image Q, "D" for image D and "O" for the original image, where all images have the same size.
- B represents the number of blocks in an image.

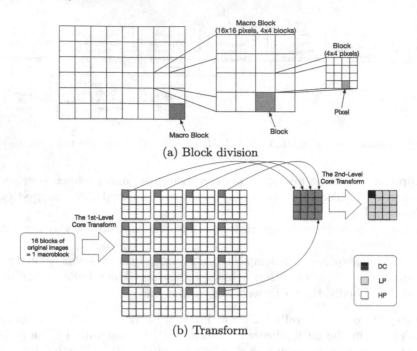

(a) Block division

(b) Transform

Fig. 3. Lapped biorthogonal transform used in JPEG XR

- M represents the number of macroblocks in an image.
- N represents the number of coefficients in a 4×4 core transform, and the number of blocks in a macroblock, where $N = 16$.
- $DC_x(m)$ represents the DC coefficient of the mth macroblock in image x, where $0 \leq m < M$.
- $LP_x(m, n)$ represents the nth LP coefficient of the mth macroblock in image x, where $0 \leq m < M, 1 \leq n < N$.
- $HP_x(b, n)$ represents the nth HP coefficient of the bth block in image x, where $0 \leq b < B, 1 \leq n < N$.
- P represents the number of all coefficients in an image, where $P = MN + B(N-1)$.
- $\text{sgn}(c)$ represents the sign of a real value c as

$$\text{sgn}(c) = \begin{cases} -1, & c < 0, \\ 0, & c = 0, \\ 1, & c > 0. \end{cases} \tag{1}$$

- $C_x(k)$ represents LBT coefficients sequence given by

$$C_x(k) = \begin{cases} DC_x(k), & 0 \leq k < M, \\ LP_x(m, n), & M \leq k < MN, \\ \quad m = \text{mod}(k, M), n = \lfloor (k-M)/M \rfloor, \\ HP_x(b, n), & MN \leq k < P, \\ \quad b = \text{mod}(k - MN, B), n = \lfloor (k - MN)/B \rfloor + 1. \end{cases} \tag{2}$$

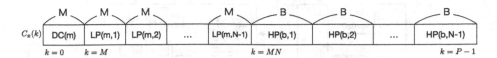

Fig. 4. LBT coefficients sequence $C_x(k)$

where $\mathrm{mod}(x, d)$ denotes the remainder when x is divided by d, and $\lfloor x \rfloor$ denotes the integer part of x. The length of $C_x(k)$ is $P = MN + B(N-1)$, (see Fig. 4).

3.2   Identification Scheme

The proposed scheme focuses on the positive and negative signs of LBT coefficients, which can be obtained by entropy-decoding from JPEG XR bit streams. It is verified that quantized LBT coefficients have the following property.

- When images Q and D_i are generated from the same original image O, the positive and negative signs of LBT coefficients of the two images are equivalent in the corresponding location, even though quantization parameters (QPs) are different. Namely, the relation is given as

$$\mathrm{sgn}(C_Q(k)) = \mathrm{sgn}(C_{D_i}(k)), (0 \le k < P) , \tag{3}$$

where this property does not apply in zero-value coefficients.

The above property, which can be theoretically explained, is illustrated in Fig. 5. Figure 5(a) and (b) are examples of quantized LBT coefficients of images Q and D_1 that are generated from the same original image O. It is confirmed that the positive and negative signs of LBT coefficients of the two images are equivalent in the corresponding location, except for the case in zero-value coefficients. On the other hand, image D_2 in Fig. 5(c) that is generated from the other original image, does not have the same signs as those in Fig. 5(a). In this manner, there is no guarantee that two images generated from different original images have the same signs. Note that the number of zero-value coefficients depend on quantization parameters (QPs).

-349	0	4	-1
4	2	-6	7
-1	-3	-3	-4
0	3	3	-1

-116	0	1	0
1	1	-2	2
0	-1	-1	-1
0	1	1	0

-29	-15	7	-8
1	1	7	-25
-8	10	-2	-2
-24	7	6	-1

(a) Image Q ($QP = 10$) (b) Image D_1 ($QP = 30$) (c) Image D_2 ($QP = 10$)

Fig. 5. Examples of LBT (DC and LP) coefficients. Image D_1 has the same signs as image Q except for zero-value coefficients

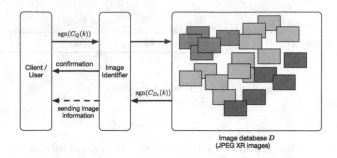

Fig. 6. Image identification for JPEG XR images

Let us define image Q as a JPEG XR coded image that is given by user (a query image) and image D_i is a JPEG XR image that is given from a database $\boldsymbol{D}$, where $D_i \in \boldsymbol{D}$ (see Fig. 6). The positive and negative signs of the quantized LBT coefficients of the images Q and D_i in the corresponding locations are compared, and the results are used to decide whether the images are compressed from the same original image.

When compressed image Q and image D_i ($i = 1, 2, \cdots$) are compared, the identification algorithm is accomplished according to the following steps.

(a) Set the value of L, where L is the number of LBT coefficients used for identification ($1 \leq L \leq P$).
(b) Set $k := 0$.
(c) For the kth coefficients A, extract the positive and negative signs. If $\text{sgn}(C_A(k)) = 0$, proceed to step (e).
(d) If $\text{sgn}(C_Q(k)) \neq \text{sgn}(C_{D_i}(k))$, the algorithm decides that image Q and D_i were not compressed from the same original image, and the process is halted. Otherwise, proceed to step (e)
(e) Set $k := k + 1$.
(f) If $k = L$, it is decided that image Q has the same original image as image D_i. Otherwise, continue to step (c).

When $L = M$ is chosen, only DC coefficients are used for identification. Otherwise, DC and LP coefficients are used for $L = MN$, and all LBT coefficients are done for $L = P$, respectively.

4   Simulation

To evaluate the performance of the proposed scheme, several simulations are conducted.

4.1   Simulation Conditions

The simulation conditions are presented in Table 1. Two still images with 8×3 bpp(bit per pixel), two still HDR images with the OpenEXR format

Table 1. Simulation conditions

Image 1	Lena still image (color 512×512, 8×3 bpp)
Image 2	Mandrill still image (color 512×512, 8×3 bpp)
Image 3 (OpenEXR format)	Spirals still image (color 1040×1040, 16×4 bpp)
Image 4 (OpenEXR format)	Blobbies still image (color 1040×1040, 16×4 bpp)
Video 1	Mobile video sequence (color 352×288, 8×3 bpp, 100frames)
Video 2	Flower video sequence (color 352×288, 8×3 bpp, 100frames)
Video 3	Deadline video sequence (color 352×288, 8×3 bpp, 100frames)
OM(Overlapping mode)	0(non overlapping), 1(HP only), 2(LP &HP)
QP	10, 20, 30, 40, 50, 60, 70, 80, 90
The number of LBP coefficients	$L = M$(DC only), MN(DC and LP), P(all)

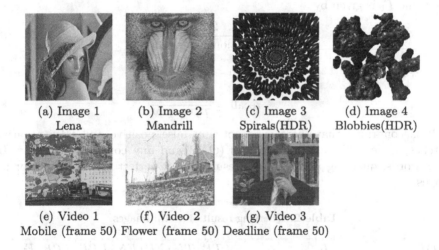

(a) Image 1 Lena   (b) Image 2 Mandrill   (c) Image 3 Spirals(HDR)   (d) Image 4 Blobbies(HDR)

(e) Video 1 Mobile (frame 50)   (f) Video 2 Flower (frame 50)   (g) Video 3 Deadline (frame 50)

Fig. 7. Images and videos used in simulation

(16×4 bpp) [23] and three video sequences, i.e. "Mobile", "Flower" and "Deadline" were used in the simulation (Fig. 7). "Mobile" and "Flower" are in a class of images with large object movements between subsequent frames. "Deadline" is vice versa. All images were compressed with 9 different quantization parameters (QP). In the following section, for example, "Mobile" frame No.5 with $QP = 10$ will be referred to as "Mobile5-10". The JPEG XR reference software 1.8 [24] was used in the simulation. The simulation was run on a PC, with a 2.7 GHz processor and a main memory of 16 Gbytes.

4.2 Evaluation for Still Images

Four still images including HDR ones were compressed with nine different quantization parameters (QPs) shown in Table 1 to generate 36 compressed images, of which four images with $QP = 50$ were in the database $\boldsymbol{D}$, and $4 \times 9 = 36$ compressed images were used as a query image. The original uncompressed versions were not included in the simulation. Identification was accomplished by querying a compressed image.

Querying results for still images are shown in Table 2. Table 2 summarizes the number of true-positive (TP), true-negative (TN), false-positive (FP) and false-negative (FN) matches. Besides, the table shows the false-positive-rate (FPR) and true-positive-rate (TPR) [25], defined by

$$FPR = FP/(FP + TN) \,, \tag{4}$$
$$TPR = TP/(TP + FN) \,. \tag{5}$$

Moreover, the F_1-score (F_1) [25] is known to be one measure used in the field of information retrieval for measuring the performance of search, document classication, and query classification. A higher F_1-score means better performance. The value F_1 is given by

$$F_1 = \frac{2}{1/\text{precision} + 1/\text{recall}} \,, \tag{6}$$
$$\text{precision} = \frac{TP}{TP + FP} \,, \tag{7}$$
$$\text{recall} = \frac{TP}{TP + FN} \,. \tag{8}$$

It is confirmed that there were not any false positive and false negative matches, under all overlapping modes (OM) and any compression ratios. In other words, querying with all QPs resulted in a perfect identification for all images.

Table 2. Querying results for still images

OM	L	TP	TN	FP	FN	FPR (%)	TPR (%)	F_1 score
0 (non overlapping)	M (DC only)	36	108	0	0	100	0	1.0
	MN (DC and LP)	36	108	0	0	100	0	1.0
	P (all)	36	108	0	0	100	0	1.0
1 (HP only)	M (DC only)	36	108	0	0	100	0	1.0
	(DC and LP)	36	108	0	0	100	0	1.0
	P (all)	36	108	0	0	100	0	1.0
2 (LP and HP)	M (DC only)	36	108	0	0	100	0	1.0
	MN (DC and LP)	36	108	0	0	100	0	1.0
	P (all)	36	108	0	0	100	0	1.0

4.3   Evaluation for Videos

The three video sequences shown in Table 1 were used to confirm the effectiveness of the proposed scheme. Originally, there were 100 uncompressed frames for each video sequence. All video frames were compressed with three different quantization parameters i.e. $QP = 10, 50$ and 90. As a result, 300 compressed frames were generated from each sequence, and 900 compressed frames were used in total in the simulation. Three video sequences with $QP = 50$ i.e. 300 frames in total were in the database D, and all compressed frames i.e. 900 frames were used as a query image. The original uncompressed versions were not included in the simulation. Therefore, 900×300 combinations were carried out to evaluate the proposed scheme.

Querying results for videos are shown in Table 3. From the results, it is confirmed that a larger L proves higher recognition accuracy and a smaller QP also gives higher one, because these conditions enable to supply a large number of the positive and negative signs of LBT coefficients to image identifier. In particular, for $L = P$, querying with all QPs resulted in a perfect identification for all video sequences. The performance trends can be reconfirmed via F_1-scores as shown in Fig. 8. Besides, compared to "Mobile" and "Flower", F_1-scores decrease

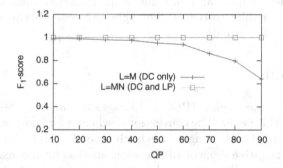

Fig. 8. F_1-scores for experimental results (Flower)

| (a) mobile50-10 | (b)mobile50-90 | (c) mobile49-90 |
| PSNR 44.37[dB] | PSNR: 20.14[dB] | PSNR: 17.49[dB] |

Fig. 9. Compressed frames with different QPs (Mobile frame 50 and 49)

Table 3. Querying results for video images (Overlapping mode = 1)

Video	QP	L = M(DC only)						L = MN(DC & LP)					
		TP	TN	FP	FN	FPR (%)	F_1	TP	TN	FP	FN	FPR (%)	F_1
Mobile	10	100	29898	2	0	0.01	0.990	100	29900	0	0	0.00	1.000
	50	100	29898	2	0	0.01	0.990	100	29900	0	0	0.00	1.000
	90	100	29896	4	0	0.01	0.980	100	29900	0	0	0.00	1.000
Flower	10	100	29895	5	0	0.02	0.976	100	29900	0	0	0.00	1.000
	50	100	29890	10	0	0.03	0.952	100	29900	0	0	0.00	1.000
	90	100	29788	112	0	0.37	0.641	100	29900	0	0	0.00	1.000
Deadline	10	100	29888	12	0	0.04	0.943	100	29900	0	0	0.00	1.000
	50	100	29874	26	0	0.09	0.885	100	29900	0	0	0.00	1.000
	90	100	29763	137	0	0.46	0.593	100	29893	7	0	0.02	0.966

for "Deadline", since it does not include large objective movements between subsequent frames. For all conditions, it is worth noting that there were no false negatives.

Figure 9 shows examples of compressed frames with different QPs, where PSNR(Peak Signal to Noise Ratio) is a measure of image quality. From these examples, it is shown that the successive frames are very similar and moreover compressed frames include large amount of quantization noise in general. The proposed scheme enables to detect the slight difference between frames, even though there is such a situation.

5   Conclusion

A novel scheme for identifying JPEG XR images in the compressed domain has been proposed in this paper. The conventional schemes for compressed images are not available for JPEG XR images, due to the use of a LBT. A new property of the positive and negative signs of LBT coefficients has been considered robustly to identify the images. The proposed scheme does not produce false negative matches in any compression ratio. The experimental results have showed the proposed scheme is effective for not only still images, but also video sequences in terms of the retrieval performance such as false positive, false negative and true positive matches. In particular, in the case of using DC and LP coefficients, i.e. $L = MN$, querying with all QPs resulted in a near-perfect identification for all images and videos. The proposed scheme will be extended to a identification scheme in the encrypted domain as a future work.

References

1. Information technology - JPSearch - Part 1: System framework and components. International Standard ISO/IEC TR-24800-1 (2007)
2. Compact descriptors for visual search: Applications and use scenarios. ISO/IEC JTC1/ SC29/WG11/N11529 (2010)

3. Compact descriptors for visual search: Context and objectives. ISO/IEC JTC1/SC29/WG11/N11530 (2010)
4. Compact descriptors for visual search: Requirements. ISO/IEC JTC1/SC29/WG11/N11531 (2010)
5. Rec, ITU.-T., T.832: Information technology - JPEG XR image coding system - Image coding specification. http://www.itu.int/rec/T-REC-T.832
6. Dufaux, F., Sullivan, G., Ebrahimi, T.: The JPEG XR image coding standard [Standards in a Nutshell]. IEEE Signal Process. Mag. **26**(6), 195–204 (2009)
7. Dobashi, T., Tashiro, A., Iwahashi, M., Kiya, H.: A fixed-point implementation of tone mapping operation for HDR images expressed in floating-point format. APSIPA Trans. Signal Inf. Process. **3**(e11), 1–11 (2014)
8. Iwahashi, M., Kiya, H.: Two layer lossless coding of HDR images. In: Proceedings of the IEEE International Conference on Acoustics, Speech and Signal Processing, pp. 1340–1344 (2013)
9. Reinhard, E., Ward, G., Pattanaik, S., Debcvec, P., Heidrich, W., Myszkowski, K.: High Dynamic Range Imaging - Acquisition, Display and Image Based Lighting. Morgan Kaufmann, Burlington (2010)
10. Mandal, M.K., Liu, C.: Efficient image indexing techniques in the JPEG2000 domain. J. Electron. Imaging **13**(1), 182–187 (2004)
11. Uchida, Y., Sakazawa, S.: D-12-93 near-duplicate video detection considering temporal burstiness of local features. In: Proceedings of the IEICE General Conference 2011 (2011)
12. McIntyre, A.R., Heywood, M.I.: Exploring content-based image indexing techniques in compressed domain. In: Proceedings of the IEEE Canadian Conference on Electrical & Computer Engineering, vol. 2, pp. 957–962 (2002)
13. Arnia, F., Iizuka, I., Fujiyoshi, M., Kiya, H.: Fast and robust identification methods for JPEG images with various compression ratios. In: Proceedings of the IEEE International Conference on Acoustics Speech and Signal Processing, vol. II, no. IMDSP-P4.6 (2006)
14. Arnia, F., Iizuka, I., Fujiyoshi, M., Kiya, H.: "Fast Method for Joint Retrieval and Identification of JPEG Coded Images Based on DCT Sign," Proc. IEEE International Conference on Image Processing, vol. II, no.MP-P1.10, pp. 229–232 (2007)
15. Jiang, J., Armstrong, A., Feng, G.C.: Web-based image indexing and retrieval in JPEG compressed domain. Multimedia Syst. **9**, 424–432 (2004)
16. Shneier, M., Abdel-Mottaleb, M.: Exploiting the JPEG compression scheme for image retrieval. IEEE Trans. Pattern Anal. Mach. Intell. **18**(8), 849–853 (1996)
17. Cheng, K.O., Law, N.F., Siu, W.C.: A fast approach for identifying similar features in retrieval of JPEG and JPEG 2000 images. In: Proceedings of APSIPA ASC 2009 (2009)
18. Watanabe, O., Iida, T., Fukuhara, T., Kiya, H.: Identification of JPEG 2000 Images in encrypted domain for digital cinema. In: Proceedings of the IEEE International Conference on Image Processing, no. MA.PJ.PJ8, pp. 2065–2068 (2009)
19. Watanabe, O., Fukuhara, T., Kiya, H.: Fast identification of JPEG 2000 images for digital cinema profiles. In: Proceedings of the IEEE International Conference on Acoustics, Speech and Signal Processing, no. IVMSP-L4.6, pp. 881–884 (2011)
20. Dobashi, T., Watanabe, O., Fukuhara, T., Kiya, H.: Hash-Based Identification of JPEG 2000 images in encrypted domain. In: Proceedings of the IEEE International Symposium on Intelligent Signal Processing and Communication Systems, no. D2.4, pp. 469–472. (2012)

21. Watanabe, O., Fukuhara, T., Kiya, H.: Codestream-based identification of JPEG 2000 images with different coding parameters. IEICE Trans. Inf. Sys. **E95–D**(4), 1120–1129 (2012)
22. Taubman, D.: High performance scalable image compression with EBCOT. IEEE Trans. Image Process. **9**(7), 1158–1170 (2000)
23. Bogart, R., Kainz, F., Hess, D.: The OpenEXR image file format. In: Proceedings of the ACM SIGGRAPH Technical Sketches, San Diego, CA, USA (2003)
24. ITU-T Rec. T.835: Information technology - JPEG XR image coding system - Reference software. http://www.itu.int/rec/T-REC-T.835
25. Fawcett, T.: An introduction to ROC analysis. Pattern Recogn. Lett. **27**(8), 861–874 (2006)

Challenge to Scalability of Face Recognition Using Universal Eigenface

Hisayoshi Chugan$^{(\boxtimes)}$, Tsuyoshi Fukuda, and Takeshi Shakunaga

Department of Computer Science, Okayama University,
Okayama-shi, Okayama 700-8530, Japan
{chugan,fukuda,shaku}@chino.cs.okayama-u.ac.jp

Abstract. This paper approaches to the scalability problem of face recognition using the weight equations in a universal eigenface. Since the weight equations are linear equations, the optimal solution can be generated even when the number of registered faces exceeds the dimensionality of universal eigenface. Based on the characteristics of the underdetermined linear systems, this paper shows that effective preliminary elimination is possible with little loss by the parallel underdetermined systems. Finally, this paper proposes a preliminary elimination followed by a small-scale face recognition for a scalable face recognition.

Keywords: Face recognition · Eigenface · Weight equations · Underdetermined systems · Orthogonal partitions · Scalability

1 Introduction

Eigenspaces have been widely utilized in computer vision for various applications, including object recognition [6,8]. Eigenspaces constructed from face images are often called eigenfaces [11] and widely used in face recognition [1,7], tracking [2] , and so on. On the other hand, face recognition has still been a hot topic in computer vision and discussed from various view points [10,12], since this problem is a big problem for computer vision applications. Among them, Oka and Shakunaga [9] proposed an efficient method for real-time face tracking and recognition to cover pose and photometric changes. In their method, linear equations, called the weight equations, are used for both the face recognition (person identification) and the shape inference. Although the number of faces was at most 25 in their implementation, and the scalability seemed severe in this approach, Chugan et al. [3] showed that the weight equations also work in underdetermined systems, and they are effective for 100-face tracking and recognition when 140d eigenface is used.

This paper will show how much more faces can be recognized using the underdetermined systems. For the purpose, a framework of face recognition by weight equations is shown in Sect. 2. Section 3 discusses details of the parallel underdetermined approach. Section 4 shows final challenge to 2197-face recognition using 169d eigenface.

© Springer International Publishing Switzerland 2016
T. Bräunl et al. (Eds.): PSIVT 2015, LNCS 9431, pp. 51–62, 2016.
DOI: 10.1007/978-3-319-29451-3_5

2   Framework of Face Recognition by Weight Equations

2.1   Universal and Individual Eigenfaces

Let $\mathbf{V}_{kl}$ denote an n-d intensity vector of k-th person under l-th lighting condition. K and L indicate the number of persons, and the number of lighting conditions, respectively. The universal and individual eigenfaces are constructed and used as follows:

(1) Construction of universal eigenface. When a set of intensity vectors, $\{\mathbf{v}_{kl}\}$ are calculated by $\mathbf{v}_{kl} = \mathbf{V}_{kl}/\mathbf{1}^\top\mathbf{V}_{kl}$, the universal eigenface is constructed by average vector $\overline{\mathbf{v}}$ and m-principal eigenvectors $\mathbf{\Phi}_m$. Let it described as $\langle\overline{\mathbf{v}}, \mathbf{\Phi}_m\rangle$.

(2) Projection to universal eigenface. Let $\mathbf{PV}$ denote a part of image, where $\mathbf{P}$ is an $n \times n$ diagonal matrix, of which each diagonal element is 1 or 0. The projection $\mathbf{s}$ of $\mathbf{PV}$ is calculated by

$$\widetilde{\mathbf{s}} = (\mathbf{P}\widetilde{\mathbf{\Phi}}_m)^+(\mathbf{PV}) \tag{1}$$

when $\widetilde{\mathbf{\Phi}}_m = [\mathbf{\Phi}_m \ \overline{\mathbf{v}}]$ and $\widetilde{\mathbf{s}} = [\alpha\mathbf{s}^\top \ \alpha]^\top$, and $(\mathbf{P}\widetilde{\mathbf{\Phi}}_m)^+$ denotes (Moore-Penrose) pseudo inverse of $\mathbf{P}\widetilde{\mathbf{\Phi}}_m$. Once $\widetilde{\mathbf{s}}$ is calculated from a given part of image $\mathbf{PV}$, the normalized projection of $\widetilde{\mathbf{s}}$ is given by $\widehat{\mathbf{s}} = [\mathbf{s}^\top \ 1]^\top$.

(3) Construction of individual eigenfaces. In the learning stage, an individual eigenface is constructed in the universal eigenface, from a set of face images. When a set of $\mathbf{s}$-representations, $S_k = \{\mathbf{s}_{kl} \mid l = 1,\cdots,L\}$, are calculated for person k by projection of a set of intensity vectors $\{\mathbf{V}_{kl} \mid l = 1,\cdots,L\}$ to the universal eigenface, the k-th individual eigenface $\langle\overline{\mathbf{s}}_k, \eta_k\rangle$ is constructed from S_k in $\mathbf{s}$-domain, where $\overline{\mathbf{s}}_k$ and η_k denote the average and k-th individual eigenspace.

2.2   Face Recognition by Weight Equations

In Oka and Shakunaga [9], linear equations, called the weight equations, are proposed for both the face recognition (person identification) and the shape inference. The weight equations are used for face recognition in this paper, as follows:

(1) Projection to universal eigenface. When an unknown image vector $\mathbf{V}$ is given, the projection $\mathbf{s}$ of $\mathbf{PV}$ to the universal eigenface is calculated using Eq. (1) where $\mathbf{P}$ is an appropriate part indicator matrix. We can set $\mathbf{P} = \mathbf{I}$, when a full projection is necessary. If a set of parts are required, a set of partial projections might be used. (Refer to Oka and Shakunaga [9].)

(2) Photometric adjustment. In $\mathbf{s}$-domain, for each k, a projection of $\mathbf{s}$ to the k-th individual eigenface is calculated by

$$\mathbf{s}_k = \eta_k{\eta_k}^\top(\mathbf{s} - \overline{\mathbf{s}}_k) + \overline{\mathbf{s}}_k. \tag{2}$$

(3) Fundamental weight equations. After all $\mathbf{s}_k$ are calculated from $\mathbf{s}$, the following linear equations are given, named the fundamental weight equations

$$\widehat{\mathbf{S}}_K \mathbf{w} = \widehat{\mathbf{s}} \tag{3}$$

where $\widehat{\mathbf{S}}_K = [\widehat{\mathbf{s}}_1 \cdots \widehat{\mathbf{s}}_K]$ and $\mathbf{w} = [w_1 \cdots w_K]^\top$. The optimal solution of Eq. (3) is given by

$$\mathbf{w} = \widehat{\mathbf{S}}_K^+ \widehat{\mathbf{s}} \tag{4}$$

and the optimal solution indicates the weights of individual persons.

(4) Face recognition. Face recognition is accomplished by selecting

$$k_{max} = \operatorname{argmax} w_k. \tag{5}$$

2.3 Scalability Problem with Face Recognition

In the face recognition scheme mentioned above, the weight equations serve an essential role. Let K and M denote the number of persons and $m + 1$, where m is the dimensionality of the universal eigenface. Then, the computational cost for solving the weight equations is $O(MK^2)(O(KM^2))$ in the overdetermined(underdetermined) system. In the overdetermined system, K should be sufficiently less than M for reliable solutions. On the other hand, M could not be so large because the dimensionality of the universal eigenface cannot be too big. To solve the dimensionality problem, Chugan et al. [3] has shown a solution in the underdetermined system. In [3], the case of $M = 141$ and $K = 249$ was solved by parallel underdetermined approach. This paper discusses, from now on, the parallel underdetermined approach for $K >> M$, and how and why the approach is possible.

3 Parallel Underdetermined Approach

3.1 Solution of Underdetermined Weight Equations

Let us summarize characteristics and properties of the parallel underdetermined approach according to Chugan et al. [3]. When the fundamental weight equations are underdetermined, Eq. (4) provides $\mathbf{w}$ so as to minimize $\mathbf{w}^\top \mathbf{w}$ in the solution space of Eq. (3).

When $\mathbf{B}$ is a $K \times K$ diagonal matrix defined by

$$\mathbf{B} = diag\left(d^{-1}(\mathbf{s}, \mathbf{s}_1) \cdots d^{-1}(\mathbf{s}, \mathbf{s}_K)\right) \tag{6}$$

$$\text{where} \quad d(\mathbf{s}, \mathbf{s}_k) = \sqrt{(\mathbf{s} - \mathbf{s}_k)^\top (\mathbf{s} - \mathbf{s}_k)}, \tag{7}$$

diagonal terms of $\mathbf{B}$ indicate inverse distances from $\mathbf{s}$ to each $\mathbf{s}_k$. When $\mathbf{s}_k = \mathbf{s}$, a large number should be used for the k-th diagonal term instead of ∞.

By substituting $\mathbf{w} = \mathbf{B}\mathbf{w}'$ to Eq. (3), the biased weight equations are provided in

$$\widehat{\mathbf{S}}_K \mathbf{B}\mathbf{w}' = \widehat{\mathbf{s}}. \tag{8}$$

From the optimal solution of Eq. (8), the weight vector is estimated in

$$\mathbf{w} = \mathbf{B}[\widehat{\mathbf{S}}_K \mathbf{B}]^+ \widehat{\mathbf{s}}. \tag{9}$$

Equation (9) still provides a solution of the fundamental weight equations, Eq. (3). Since $\mathbf{w}'^{\top}\mathbf{w}'$ is minimized in the biased weight equations, $\mathbf{w}$ is optimized with considering distances between $\mathbf{s}$ and each $\mathbf{s}_k$.

As shown in [3], there is a simple relation between the biased weight equations and nearest neighbor criterion. When the weight equations are specified in 0d space, Eq. (9) becomes

$$\mathbf{w} = \mathbf{B}[\mathbf{1}^{\top}\mathbf{B}]^+ = \frac{1}{\sum d^{-2}(\mathbf{s}, \mathbf{s}_k)} \begin{bmatrix} d^{-2}(\mathbf{s}, \mathbf{s}_1) \\ \vdots \\ d^{-2}(\mathbf{s}, \mathbf{s}_K) \end{bmatrix}. \tag{10}$$

Therefore, the heaviest person indicated by Eq. (5) becomes equivalent to the nearest person.

3.2   Parallel Underdetermined Systems

A simple parallelism is implemented by partitioning the universal eigenface into subspaces. When m' denotes the dimensionality of each subspace in m-d eigenspace, and $m = Jm'$ holds, J-parallel underdetermined systems are implemented.

In the parallel implementation, the j-th fundamental weight equations are represented as

$$\begin{bmatrix} \mathbf{S}_K^{(j)} \\ \mathbf{1} \end{bmatrix} \mathbf{w}^{(j)} = \begin{bmatrix} \mathbf{s}^{(j)} \\ 1 \end{bmatrix}, \tag{11}$$

$$\text{where } \mathbf{w}^{(j)} = [w_1^{(j)} \cdots w_K^{(j)}]^{\top}, \tag{12}$$

$$\mathbf{S}_K = \left[\mathbf{S}_K^{(1)\top} \cdots \mathbf{S}_K^{(J)\top} \right]^{\top}, \tag{13}$$

$$\text{and } \mathbf{s} = \left[\mathbf{s}^{(1)\top} \cdots \mathbf{s}^{(J)\top} \right]^{\top}. \tag{14}$$

After solving all the equations, average over all the solutions

$$\mathbf{w} = \frac{1}{J} \sum_{j=1}^{J} \mathbf{w}^{(j)} \tag{15}$$

provides a final weight vector. In the parallel implementation, each underdetermined system could be transformed to the biased weight equations with using the same distances measured in the universal eigenface.

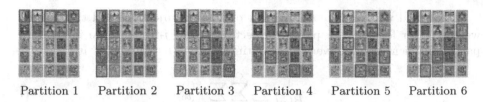

Partition 1   Partition 2   Partition 3   Partition 4   Partition 5   Partition 6

Fig. 1. Example of orthogonal subspace partitions

(1) Concurrency by orthogonal subspace partitions. In the parallel under-determined approach, the entire eigenfaces should be decomposed into exclusive subspaces. Let us call the decomposition *a subspace partition*. This paper proposes a parallel implementation of the underdetermined weight equations using a set of subspace partitions to improve recognition performance.

In the parallel implementation, a set of subspace partitions should satisfy the following requirement: Between a subspace in a partition and a subspace in another partition, intersection of them is at most 1d subspace.

When a set of subspace partitions satisfy it, let these partitions called *orthogonal subspace partitions*. An example of orthogonal subspace partitions is as shown in Fig. 1 when 25 eigenbases are arranged in a 5×5 matrix. In each partition, 5 colors indicate 5d subspaces, respectively. Since any two partitions in the figure satisfy the above requirement, they are orthogonal subspace partitions. For example, Partitions 1 and 2 are row-wise and column-wise partitions and they obviously satisfy the requirement. Since the other partitions are complete Latin squares [5], they are mutually orthogonal and orthogonal to Partitions 1 and 2, too. Note that when K is a prime number, there are exactly $K + 1$ orthogonal subspace partitions for K^2-d eigenface, since $K - 1$ complete Latin squares and row-wise and column-wise partitions are orthogonal to each other.

(2) Face recognition by orthogonal partitions. Let C and $\mathbf{w}_{(c)}^{(j)}$ denote the number of orthogonal subspace partitions and the optimal weight vector of the j-th subspace of the c-th partition. Then, average over all the optimal vectors is represented in

$$\mathbf{w} = \frac{1}{CJ} \sum_{c=1}^{C} \sum_{j=1}^{J} \mathbf{w}_{(c)}^{(j)}, \tag{16}$$

and used for face recognition.

(3) Utilization of parallel partial projections. It is widely known that parallel partial projections are also useful for robust face recognition [9]. When partial projections are combined with weight equations, partial sub images are more precisely approximated by weighted averages of dictionary images. In the cases, weights are calculated in each sub image in each underdetermined system. In this paper, face recognition is performed by combining the orthogonal subspace partitions and the parallel partial projections.

Let B and $\mathbf{w}_{(bc)}^{(j)}$ denote the number of partial projections and the optimal weight vector for the b-th partial projection of the j-th subspace in the c-th partition. Then, average over all the optimal vectors is represented in

$$\mathbf{w} = \frac{1}{BCJ} \sum_{b=1}^{B} \sum_{c=1}^{C} \sum_{j=1}^{J} \mathbf{w}_{(bc)}^{(j)}, \tag{17}$$

3.3 Preliminary Elimination by Parallel Underdetermined System

In conventional pattern recognition, supervised learning is performed before recognition. When a big number of classes should be learned, however, clustering is widely used for efficient selection of candidate classes from all classes. In these approaches, if clustering (or unsupervised learning) is accomplished for all the classes a priori, a smaller number of clusters are considered in the first stage of recognition. However, the clustering problems often suffer from computational cost and quality of clustering result. These problems are often serious for scalability of recognition algorithm.

In unsupervised learning, all the classes should be considered between each other without knowing what input is provided. Although the rough optimization seems valid for a wide variety of unknown inputs, only a small part of the rough optimization works for each particular input in the recognition stage.

In the parallel underdetermined approach, the number of classes has no limit in principle, and no clustering is necessary before the recognition stage. However, an average of a set of the weight equations can provide a weight ranking list of all the classes for each particular input. The result is regarded as a local but precise clustering result just around the particular input.

4 Experimental Challenge to Scalability

4.1 Construction of Scalable Database

In this paper, a subset of CMU Multi-PIE [4] is used for construction of the universal eigenface. The subset is composed of 141 faces (included in 249 neutral faces in session 1) of CMU Multi-PIE. The subset, called Data-1, is composed of 141 faces taken under 20 lighting conditions. The other 108 faces are excluded from the subset because they include glasses, mustache or teeth in his/her images.

Face shapes are different from person to person. The fact means that a geometric normalization is required for making a meaningful eigenface used in recognition of faces in monocular images. For this purpose, three points, which are located in centers of right and left eyes, and a center of lips on each face surface, are transposed to standard positions by affine transform in this paper, as shown in Fig. 2. After the geometric normalization, a normalized face image is made up by cropping a face region. In the current implementation, the face region is fixed as shown in Fig. 2(b).

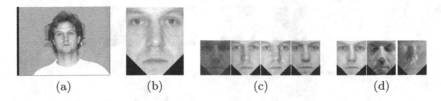

(a)   (b)   (c)   (d)

Fig. 2. Example of geometric normalization: (a) and (b) show a face image before/after geometric normalization. (c) and (d) show 4 images for an individual person and constructed individual eigenface, respectively.

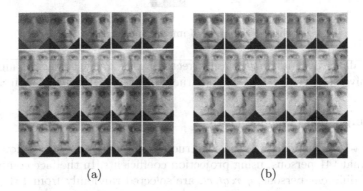

(a)   (b)

Fig. 3. Example of 20 images for an individual; (a) and (b) show a face image before/after image correction.

4.2 Refinement of Universal Eigenface

After the geometric normalization, 169d universal eigenface, called EF-1, was constructed by PCA on all (141x20) images in Data-1. In this process, universal eigenface was refined by the method described as follows:

Since the original image set includes a lot of kinds of noise including reflections and shadows, the universal eigenface is affected by these noise factors if the original images are directly used for the eigenface construction.

In order to suppress these noise factors in the original images, the following image correction is applied to the original images. Then, the universal eigenface is reconstructed from the corrected images.

For the image correction, 2d individual eigenface, as shown in Fig. 2(d), is constructed from 4 images (No. 0, 6, 8, 16) of 20 original images, as shown in Fig. 2(c).

Then, each original image is projected to the 2d individual eigenface, denoted by $\widetilde{\mathbf{\Psi}}$, and the following equation corrects each original image, $\mathbf{V}$, to

$$\mathbf{V'} = \widetilde{\mathbf{\Psi}} \widetilde{\mathbf{\Psi}}^{+} \mathbf{V}. \tag{18}$$

Figure 3 (a) shows an example of 20 original images, and (b) shows images after the image correction.

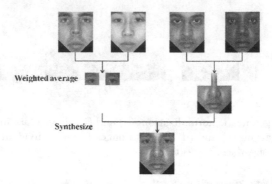

Weighted average

Synthesize

Fig. 4. Example of image composition.

When all the original images are corrected by the image correction algorithm, refined universal eigenface can be constructed by the method shown in Sect. 2.1.

4.3 Composition of Face Data

From Data-1, Extended-Data-1 is constructed by repetitive composition of faces from original 141 persons, using projection coefficients. In the face composition, at first, 4 different persons, $q, r, q\prime, r\prime$, are selected randomly from 141 persons. Then, the whole face image is composed of a weighted average of q and r, and the eye-part image is composed of a weighted average of $p\prime$ and $r\prime$. In these compositions, 2 parameters, β_1 and β_2, randomly selected between 0 and 1, are also used for weight control between two persons. The following equations show how to compose the whole and eye images, when $\mathbf{P}_e$ denotes a part indicator matrix for eyes region.

$$\mathbf{v}_{kl} = (\mathbf{I} - \mathbf{P_e})\mathbf{v}'_{kl} + \frac{\mathbf{1}^\top \mathbf{P_e} \mathbf{v}'_{kl}}{\mathbf{1}^\top \mathbf{P_e} \mathbf{v}''_{kl}} \mathbf{P_e} \mathbf{v}''_{kl} \qquad (19)$$

$$\text{where} \quad \mathbf{v}'_{kl} = \beta_1 \mathbf{v}_{ql} + (1 - \beta_1)\mathbf{v}_{rl}, \qquad (20)$$

$$\text{and} \quad \mathbf{v}''_{kl} = \beta_2 \mathbf{v}_{q'l} + (1 - \beta_2)\mathbf{v}_{r'l}. \qquad (21)$$

Figure 4 shows how a virtual image is composed from four faces according to Eq. (19).

We can make an arbitrary number of virtual faces by Eq. (19). For any virtual face, 20 virtual images are synthesized that were taken under 20 lighting conditions.

4.4 Specifications of Face Recognition Experiments

On Extended-Data-1, 4 of 20 images (No. 1, 13, 14, 18 of 20 images) were used for training data, to construct 2d individual eigenface in EF-1. The other 16 images were used for test. The training data and the test data are exclusive to each other.

(a)   (b)

Fig. 5. Example of noise suppression for training data: (a) and (b) show a face image before/after noise suppression.

In the learning stage, an input image often includes some reflections and shadows. These noise factors directly affect the face model synthesis. In order to suppress these noise factors in the input image, another image correction algorithm is used. In the image correction, the universal eigenface $\mathbf{\Phi}_m$ is used. The image correction algorithm is specified using a residue r_i that is calculated for the i-th pixel of $\mathbf{v}$ by

$$r_i = \mathbf{e}_i^T(\mathbf{v} - \tilde{\mathbf{\Phi}}_m\hat{\mathbf{s}}), \tag{22}$$

where $\mathbf{e}_i$ is a unit vector which has 1 in the i-th element and 0 s in the others. When $|r_i|$ is more than 3σ, where σ is a standard deviation of the absolute residuals over the input image, the i-th pixel of $\mathbf{v}$ should be replaced by $\mathbf{e}_i^T(\tilde{\mathbf{\Phi}}_m\hat{\mathbf{s}})$. The image correction makes an intensity value to be consistent with the projection. For example, shadows and reflection regions are corrected. It is noted that the normality of the image doesn't hold after the correction. Therefore, the corrected image should be re-normalized when all the pixels are checked and corrected (Fig. 5).

4.5 Fundamental Experiments of Face Recognition

As fundamental experiments of face recognition, face recognition rates were compared between the nearest neighbor (NN) method and the parallel underdetermined systems (PUS). In both methods, full projection (FP) and parallel partial projections (PPP) were also compared. In the experiments, the nearest neighbor method was implemented by Eq. (10) since it provides equivalent results.

When K^2 or K^3 persons were registered, the recognition rates were shown in Table 1, for $K = 7, 11, 13$. In the experiment, K^2-d universal eigenface was used for each K, and in the PUS approach K-d subspace was used in each PUS.

For the full projection, a subspace partition, which consists of K subspaces, was used when concurrency $= K$. When concurrency $= 4K$, 4 orthogonal subspace partitions were used. When concurrency $= (K + 1)K$, $K + 1$ orthogonal subspace partitions were used. Note that when K is a prime number, there are exactly $K + 1$ orthogonal subspace partitions. For the parallel partial projections, 6 partial projections were used along with a full projection. Therefore, concurrency is magnified 7 times by the parallel partial projections.

Table 1 shows that the PUS method provided much better results than the NN method in both the full and parallel partial projections. In the PUS method, recognition rates were improved when the concurrency increases. The table also shows that results of full projection were worse than those of the parallel partial

Table 1. Face-recognition rates (%) for K^2 and K^3 registrations

method	concurrency	K^2 registration			K^3 registration		
		K=7	K=11	K=13	K=7	K=11	K=13
NN(FP)	1	72.45	78.46	79.07	62.92	64.74	64.96
PUS(FP)	K	92.86	98.50	99.11	84.49	95.46	95.24
	4K	90.94	98.30	99.37	83.71	95.49	96.57
	(K+1)K	90.69	98.45	99.52	83.33	95.59	96.67
NN(PPP)	7	91.07	92.30	90.01	89.50	87.04	84.22
PUS(PPP)	7*K	99.49	99.95	99.96	98.92	99.77	99.73
	7*4K	99.62	100	100	99.22	99.79	99.78
	7*(K+1)K	99.62	100	100	99.23	99.81	99.80

projections for both the NN and PUS methods. In K^3 registration, combination of PUS and parallel partial projections gave the best recognition rate for each K, but a perfect recognition could not be obtained even when the concurrency was $7(K+1)K$. However, it is noted that recognition rates reached 99.8 % for $K = 11, 13$ at the maximum concurrency. The PUS method could accomplish almost perfect recognition for 1331 and 2197 faces. In K^2 registration, the PUS method accomplished a perfect recognition for 121 and 169 faces.

Because the dimensionality of the universal eigenface was set to K^2, recognition rate got worse in NN(FP), PUS(FP) and PUS(PPP), while K decreased. However, in NN(PPP), recognition rates of two partial projections lowered as K increased, and affected the final recognition rates.

4.6 Fundamental Experiments of Preliminary Elimination

As fundamental experiments of preliminary elimination, face selection rates were compared between the nearest neighbor (NN) method and the parallel underdetermined system (PUS). In both methods, only the parallel partial projections (PPP) was used because of the face recognition results in Sect. 4.5.

Table 2 shows K- and K^2-face selection rates for K^3 faces. The result shows that PUS method could perfectly select K candidates from K^3 candidates for $K = 11, 13$ with any concurrency, and K^2 candidates for $K = 7$. Therefore, the PUS method is effective for preliminary selection of K^2 candidates from K^3 faces.

The table also shows that rank-K^2 selection rates of the NN method could not reach 100 %, and the simple NN method was less scalable to the number of registered faces than the PUS method.

4.7 Challenge to Scalability of Face Recognition

From experimental results shown above, the parallel underdetermined systems could effectively work for preliminary elimination. Table 2 shows that

Table 2. Rank-K and K^2 selection rates (%) from K^3 persons

method	concurrency	Rank-K			Rank-K^2		
		K=7	K=11	K=13	K=7	K=11	K=13
NN(PPP)	7	96.47	94.89	93.26	99.03	98.50	98.02
PUS(PPP)	7*K	99.98	100	100	100	100	100
	7*4K	99.98	100	100	100	100	100
	7*(K+1)K	99.98	100	100	100	100	100

Table 3. Final recognition rate and rank-13 selection rates(%) for 2,197 faces

Preliminary	Final	Recognition	Rank-13
-	PUS(7*13)	99.73	100
-	PUS(7*14*13)	99.80	100
PUS(7*13)	PUS(7*13)	99.85	100
PUS(7*13)	PUS(7*14*13)	99.87	99.997

169-candidate selection was perfectly done from 2,197 faces using 169d universal eigenface. Furthermore, Table 1 shows that face recognition from 169 was also perfectly done using the same eigenface. Therefore, if 169 candidates selected by the preliminary elimination has similar properties to the 169 faces used in Table 1, combination of the two methods can accomplish a scalable face recognition. Otherwise, the two methods may be inconsistent.

In order to confirm if the combination works or not, the following experiment was tried for 2,197 faces. In the experiment, PUS was used for final recognition, and the final recognition rate and rank-13 selection rates were compared between the cases with/without preliminary elimination.

Experimental result as shown in Table 3 indicates that the combination of preliminary elimination and final recognition works well. The final recognition rates of 99.85 % and 99.87 % were better than those of the cases without using the preliminary elimination. In our current implementation, the processing time of the combination of preliminary elimination and final recognition using PUS (PPP, $2, 197$ persons, concurrency $= 7 * 14 * 13$) was about 0.8 seconds/image on Intel Corei7-5820K 3.30 GHz without any GPU.

5   Conclusions

This paper reported a challenge to scalability of face recognition using the universal eigenface and the parallel underdetermined systems of linear equations. Based on the characteristics of the underdetermined linear systems, this paper indicated that effective preliminary elimination is possible with little loss by the parallel underdetermined systems. From these experimental results, this paper proposed a preliminary elimination followed by a small-scale face recognition.

In order to confirm the effectiveness of the method, a scalable database was constructed by an extension database of CMU Multi-PIE. Our final experiments show that the proposed method worked well on 2,197 faces with 99.87 % correct face recognition. Comparison of the proposed method and the state-of-the-art methods is in future work. We hope the proposed method will effectively work in wide variety of computer vision and pattern recognition problems.

References

1. Belhumeur, P., Hespanha, J., Kriegman, D.: Eigenfaces vs. fisherfaces: Recognition using class specific linear projection. IEEE Trans. Pattern Anal. Mach. Intell. **19**(7), 711–720 (1997)
2. Black, M., Jepson, A.: Eigentracking: Robust matching and tracking of articulated objects using a view-based representation. Int. J. Comput. Vis. **26**(1), 63–84 (1998)
3. Chugan, H., Oka, Y., Shakunaga, T.: Underdetermined approach to real-time face tracking and recognition. In: Proceedings of IAPR Conference on Machine Vision and Applications, pp. 242–246 (2013)
4. Gross, R., Matthews, I., Cohn, J., Kanade, T., Baker, S.: Multi-pie. In: Proceedings of IEEE Conference on Automatic Face and Gesture Recognition, pp. 1–8 (2008)
5. Laywine, C.F., Mullen, C.M.: Discrete Mathematics using Latin Squares. Wiley Interscience, New York (1998)
6. Leonardis, A., Bischof, H.: Robust recognition using eigenimages. Comput. Vis. Image Underst. **78**, 99–118 (2000)
7. Moghaddam, B., Pentland, A.: Probabilistic visual learning for object representation. IEEE Trans. Pattern Anal. Mach. Intell. **19**(7), 696–710 (1997)
8. Murase, H., Nayar, S.: Visual learning and recognition of 3-d objects from appearance. Int. J. Comput. Vis. **14**, 5–24 (1995)
9. Oka, Y., Shakunaga, T.: Real-time face tracking and recognition by sparse eigentracker augmented by associative mapping to 3d shape. Image Vis. Comput. J. **30**(3), 147–158 (2012)
10. Tan, X., Triggs, B.: Enhanced local texture feature sets for face recognition under difficult lighting conditions. IEEE Trans. Image Process. **19**(6), 1635–1650 (2010)
11. Turk, M., Pentland, A.: Eigenfaces for recognition. J. Cogn. Neurosci. **3**(1), 71–86 (1991)
12. Wagner, A., Wright, J., Ganesh, A., Zhou, Z., Mobahi, H., Ma, Y.: Toward a practical face recognition system: Robust alignment and illumination by sparse representation. IEEE Trans. Pattern Anal. Mach. Intell. **34**(2), 372–386 (2012)

From Optimised Inpainting with Linear PDEs Towards Competitive Image Compression Codecs

Pascal Peter[1]([✉]), Sebastian Hoffmann[1], Frank Nedwed[1], Laurent Hoeltgen[2],
and Joachim Weickert[1]

[1] Mathematical Image Analysis Group, Faculty of Mathematics
and Computer Science, Campus E1.7, Saarland University,
66041 Saarbrücken, Germany
{peter,hoffmann,nedwed,weickert}@mia.uni-saarland.de
[2] Applied Mathematics and Computer Vision Group, Brandenburg University
of Technology, Platz der Deutschen Einheit 1, 03046 Cottbus, Germany
hoeltgen@b-tu.de

Abstract. For inpainting with linear partial differential equations (PDEs) such as homogeneous or biharmonic diffusion, sophisticated data optimisation strategies have been found recently. These allow high-quality reconstructions from sparse known data. While they have been explicitly developed with compression in mind, they have not entered actual codecs so far: Storing these optimised data efficiently is a non-trivial task. Since this step is essential for any competetive codec, we propose two new compression frameworks for linear PDEs: Efficient storage of pixel locations obtained from an optimal control approach, and a stochastic strategy for a locally adaptive, tree-based grid. Suprisingly, our experiments show that homogeneous diffusion inpainting can surpass its often favoured biharmonic counterpart in compression. Last but not least, we demonstrate that our linear approach is able to beat both JPEG2000 and the nonlinear state-of-the-art in PDE-based image compression.

Keywords: Linear diffusion inpainting · Homogeneous · Biharmonic · Image compression · Probabilistic tree-densification

1 Introduction

For a given image, the core task of image compression is to store a small amount of data from which the original can be reconstructed with high accuracy. Homogeneous and biharmonic partial differential equations (PDEs) can restore images with a high quality from a small fraction of prescribed image points, if their position and value are carefully optimised [1,2,6,15]. This suggests the viability of linear, parameter-free PDEs for image compression. Unfortunately, all these data optimisation efforts are in vain, as long as one cannot store the data efficiently.

© Springer International Publishing Switzerland 2016
T. Bräunl et al. (Eds.): PSIVT 2015, LNCS 9431, pp. 63–74, 2016.
DOI: 10.1007/978-3-319-29451-3_6

Currently, PDE-based compression is dominated by nonlinear models that require parameter optimisation, e.g. edge-enhancing anisotropic diffusion (EED) [25]. In particular, the general purpose codec R-EED by Schmaltz et al. [23] can beat popular transform-based coders like JPEG [18] and JPEG2000 [24]. In contrast, homogeneous diffusion has only been applied for specialised applications (e.g. cartoon compression in [16]) which do not employ the sophisticated data optimisation methods mentioned above. Moreover, there is no compression codec based on biharmonic inpainting at all. This shows the lack of general purpose codecs with linear inpainting PDEs.

Our Contribution. To fill this gap, we investigate how to embed powerful data optimisation strategies for harmonic and biharmonic inpainting into two codecs: (1) A compression scheme that combines free choice of known pixels by optimal control [2,6] with tailor-made entropy coding. (2) A stochastic method that restricts pixel selection to a locally adaptive grid, but allows to store these positions efficiently as a binary tree. We evaluate how individual restrictions and lossy compression steps of both frameworks affect the performance of harmonic and biharmonic inpainting. In addition, we compare our best methods against the state-of-the-art in PDE-based compression and the quasi-standards in transform-based compression.

Related Work. Homogeneous diffusion has been applied for the compression of specific classes of images. In particular, Mainberger et al. [14] have proposed a highly efficient codec for cartoon images, and there are several successful coders for depth maps [5,7,12]. However, unlike our approach, these methods rely primarily on semantical image features such as edges. This choice is motivated by the theoretical results of Belhachmi et al. [1] which suggest to choose known data at locations with large Laplacian magnitude. Köstler et al. [11] apply homogeneous diffusion for real-time video playback on a Playstation 3.

General purpose codecs with PDEs are mainly based on edge-enhancing anisotropic diffusion (EED) [25] and efficient representations of data locations by binary trees. Initially, this class of methods was proposed by Galić et al. [4], while the current state-of-the-art is the R-EED codec by Schmaltz et al. [23]. Modifications and extensions of R-EED include colour codecs [19], 3-D data compression [23], and progressive modes [22].

In addition, there are several works that are closely related to compression, but do not consider actual encoding [1,2,6,15]. Instead, they deal with optimal reconstruction from small fractions of given data. We directly use results from the optimal control scheme for harmonic PDEs by Hoeltgen et al. [6] and its biharmonic extension. Our densification approach on restricted point sets is inspired by the approach of Mainberger et al. [15]. They consider a stochastic sparsification on unrestricted point sets.

Organisation of the Paper. We begin with a short introduction to PDE-based inpainting and the optimisation of spatial and tonal data in Sect. 2. Section 3 proposes solutions to general challenges of PDE-based compression algorithms. These form the foundation for our codecs. In Sect. 4 we describe a new general compression approach for exact masks, and we apply it to the optimal control method of Hoeltgen et al. [6]. Section 5 introduces a stochastic, tree-based method that imposes restrictions on the location of known data. We evaluate both compression frameworks in Sect. 6. Section 7 concludes our paper with a summary and outlook on future work.

2   PDE-Based Inpainting

Image Reconstruction. In PDE-based image compression, we want to store only a small fraction of the original image data and reconstruct the missing image parts. To this end, consider the original image $f : \Omega \to \mathbb{R}$. It maps each point from the rectangular image domain Ω to its grey value. Let us assume that the set of known locations $K \subset \Omega$, the *inpainting mask*, is already given and we want to reconstruct the missing data in the *inpainting domain* $\Omega \setminus K$.

For a suitable differential operator L, we obtain the missing image parts u as the steady state for $t \to \infty$ of the evolution that is described by the PDE

$$\partial_t u = Lu \quad \text{on } \Omega \setminus K. \tag{1}$$

Here, we impose reflecting boundary conditions at the image boundary $\partial\Omega$. In addition, the known data is fixed on K, thus creating Dirichlet boundary conditions $u = f$. In our work, we consider two different parameter-free choices for the differential operator L. In the simplest case, we apply *homogeneous diffusion* [9]: $Lu = \Delta u = \text{div}(\nabla u)$. Since experiments suggest that the *biharmonic operator* $Lu = -\Delta^2 u$ may give better reconstructions [2,4,23], it is also considered.

Both operators propagate known information equally in all directions and behave consistently throughout the whole image evolution. In contrast, more complex models in compression are nonlinear and anisotropic: edge-enhancing diffusion (EED) [25] inhibits diffusion across image edges. In principle, this allows EED to obtain more accurate reconstructions from the same amount of known data [4,23]. However, the price for this increase in quality are algorithms with higher computational complexity and the need for parameter optimisation. Note that the compression frameworks that we propose in the following Sections work in a discrete setting. To this end we consider the finite difference approximations of the inpainting equation in the same way as in [15].

3   From Inpainting to Compression

Spatial and Tonal Optimisation. For a pure inpainting problem, predetermined missing image regions are reconstructed from known data. This is fundamentally different in compression, where the whole image is known and the encoder actively chooses known pixels. Many research results have confirmed that the choice of known data influences the reconstruction significantly [1,2,6,15]. At the same mask density, i.e. the same amount of known data, choosing optimal positions and pixel values is vital for a good reconstruction. In our

---

Input: Original image f, admissible set of quantised grey values $Q := \{q_1, ..., q_n\}$,
   inpainting mask c.
Initialisation: $u := r(c, f)$ and $g := f$.
Compute:
   For all $i \in K$:
   Compute the inpainting echo b_i.

   Do
      For all $i \in K$:
      1. Compute the correction term $\alpha := \frac{b_i^\top (f - u)}{|b_i|^2}$.
      2. Set $u^{\mathrm{old}} := u$.
      3. Update the grey value $g_i := g_i + \alpha$.
      4. Apply coarse quantisation: $g_i' := \mathrm{argmin}_{q \in Q} |g_i - q|$
      5. Update reconstruction $u := u + \alpha' \cdot b_i$ with $\alpha' = g_i' - u_i$.
   while $|\mathrm{MSE}(u, f) - \mathrm{MSE}(u^{\mathrm{old}}, f)| > \varepsilon$.
Output: Optimised quantised grey values g.

Algorithm 1: Quantisation-aware grey value optimisation.

paper we consider a separate optimisation process of both types of data. First we optimise the locations of data and then perform a grey value optimisation (GVO) step.

Efficient Storage. In PDE-based image compression, the reconstruction capability of the inpainting operator is only one of two important factors for the success of a codec. The other key element is the efficient storage of known data. There is a straightforward trade-off between a desired sparsity of stored points and reconstruction quality. In addition, a codec can influence the final file size by combining multiple other lossless and lossy compression steps. In the following, we discuss different possibilities for such compression steps and how they can be combined with the aforementioned spatial and tonal optimisation.

Entropy Coding is an essential concept of compression that is employed in most successful codecs. It aims at removing redundancy from data and thereby stores it losslessly, but with a reduced file size. Huffman coding [8], adaptive arithmetic coding [21] and PAQ [13] have been successfully used in PDE-based compression [23]. In our setting there are always two different kinds of known data that must be stored: grey values and locations on the pixel grid. In addition, some header information like file sizes or parameters need to be stored. Therefore, we choose to use PAQ for our codecs, since it is a context mixing scheme that can locally adapt to different types of data. PAQ combines models that predict the next bit in a file from a history of already compressed bits. With neural networks, it adapts the weighting of these models to changing content types throughout a single file. Thus, it can be directly applied as an efficient container format for both positional and brightness data.

Quantisation. For brightness data, the performance of the aforementioned entropy coders can be improved by a coarser quantisation. Instead of storing grey values with float precision, we only consider a finite number $q \leq 256$ of different discrete brightness values. Since this introduces an error to the known data, it is a lossy preprocessing step to the lossless entropy coding. In a PDE-based setting, the benefits of grey value optimisation (GVO) can be diminished if such a quantisation is applied afterwards. Therefore, grey values should be optimised under the constraint of the coarse quantisation (see [23]).

To this end, we propose *quantisation-aware GVO* in Algorithm 1. Since both PDEs we consider are linear, we can use so-called inpainting echos [15] to speed up the optimisation. For a given mask c and corresponding grey values g, let $r(c, g)$ denote the inpainting result according to Sect. 2. Then, an echo is computed as $r(c, e(i))$ where in the image $e(i)$ the ith known pixel is set to 1 and all other known data is set to zero. Thereby, each echo represents the influence of a single known data point. As long as the mask c is constant, we can compute the reconstruction for arbitrary grey values in g as $r(c, g) = \sum_{i \in K} g(x) r(c, e(i))$. Note that the echoes only need to be computed once.

During optimisation, a Gauss-Seidel scheme successively updates the grey values at mask positions one by one. The crucial difference to [15] is that we directly quantise the grey values after every update. In our experiments, we observe that this algorithm already converges after only a few iterations over all mask points. Since the inpainting mask remains constant, the echoes can be reused for arbitrary quantisation parameters q. Thus, in contrast to the non-linear inpainting case in R-EED [23], we are able to optimise q thoroughly and efficiently with the help of a simple grid search.

The number q of quantised grey values also influences the overall file size, since the entropy coding of the grey values becomes more efficient for smaller numbers of different grey values. Therefore, for smaller q, also the file size becomes smaller in general. Simultaneously, the error increases, since the constraints to the GVO become more strict. For a given mask, the best trade-off between file size and reconstruction quality must be found, i.e. the inpainting error and the file size have to be minimised simultaneously. For a given quantisation q, let $s : \{0, ..., 255\} \rightarrow \mathbb{N}$ be the file size in byte and $e : \{0, ..., 255\} \rightarrow \mathbb{R}$ the corresponding mean square error. By normalising both quantities to the range [0,1] and combining them additively, we define the *trade-off coefficient* μ:

$$\mu := \frac{s(q)}{s(255)} + \frac{e(q)}{e(255)}.$$

The smaller this coefficient, the better the trade-off for a given q. Our goal is to find the best q for a given mask. In our algorithms, we minimise μ with respect to q in combination with quantisation-aware GVO.

Efficient Representations of Positional Data. In the previous paragraphs we have covered how compression steps influence tonal optimisation. In the following sections we propose two different approaches to perform the spatial optimisation: in Sect. 4, we allow free choice of point positions on the pixel grid and in Sect. 5 we restrict ourselves to a coarser, locally adaptive mesh. For both cases we discuss efficient storage. Note that for both codecs, decompression follows the same pattern: first we extract the entropy-coded mask data, then we apply inpainting to reconstruct the image.

Input: Original image f, fraction α of tree nodes used as candidates for densification, fraction β of candidate nodes that are added in each iteration, desired final mask density d.

Initialisation: Splitting tree T containing only the root node t_0. Initial leaf node set $L := \{t_1, t_2\}$ containing child nodes of t_0.

Compute:
  Do
  1. Compute reconstruction u from mask $C(T)$ and image data f.
  2. Choose randomly a candidate set $A \subset L$ containing $\alpha \cdot |L|$ nodes.
  3. For all $t_i \in A$ compute the subimage error $e(t_i)$.
  4. Add a subset of $\beta \cdot |A|$ candidate nodes t_i with the largest errors $e(t_i)$ to the tree T.
  5. Update L to contain all children of single split nodes from T.
  while $|C(T)| < d \cdot |\Omega|$.

Output: Tree T with corresponding mask $C(T)$ of density d.

Algorithm 2: Stochastic tree densification.

4   Encoding with Exact Masks

Finding optimal positions on the pixel grid for a fixed amount of mask points is nontrivial. Besides the greedy approaches in [15], the algorithms in [2,6] find masks by formulating an optimisation problem. As proposed in these papers, a primal-dual scheme can be employed for finding a solution. While [6] focuses on homogeneous diffusion, biharmonic inpainting is considered in [2]. Thus, we use both PDEs to find optimised masks for our compression scheme. Note that we use the variants of both methods that produce binary masks.

An inpainting mask acquired from the aforementioned algorithms is essentially a binary image of the same size as the original image. This suggests to use compression schemes like JBIG [10] to store the mask, in particular since it has been successfully applied in edge-based compression [16]. However, JBIG is optimised for binary images that obey a connectivity, since its primary intention was the use in fax machines. This is not the case for sparse inpainting masks which makes them hard to compress for JBIG.

Therefore, we have also evaluated other compression methods for binary image data. While block coding schemes [3,17,26,27] and coordinate coding [17] are not competitive to JBIG on their own, they can act as a preprocessing step for entropy coders such as Huffman Coding [8], arithmetic coding [21] and PAQ [13]. We experimentally found that a simple block coding scheme [27] in combination with PAQ is a good choice. It reduces the file size by up to 10 % in comparison to JBIG. Together with the grey value and quantisation optimisation from Sect. 3, we obtain the following three-step compression for exact masks:

1. Select p % of total pixels with the optimal control approach [6].
2. Perform GVO with quantisation optimisation (Algorithm 1).
3. Optimise block size for optimal compression with PAQ.

Input: Original image f, binary tree T, parameters $n < m$.
Compute: Repeat
    1. Create a backup copy T_{old} of the splitting tree T.
    2. Compute reconstruction u_{old} from mask $C(T_{\text{old}})$ and image data f.
    3. Remove the children of n randomly chosen single split nodes from T.
    4. Randomly select a set A containing m leaf nodes from T.
    5. For all $t_i \in A$ compute the subimage error $e(t_i)$.
    6. Add the children of the n nodes with the largest error $e(t_i)$ to T.
    7. Compute reconstruction u from mask $C(T)$ and image data f.
    8. If $\text{MSE}(u, f) > \text{MSE}(u_{\text{old}}, f)$
        Reset changes, i.e. $T = T_{\text{old}}$.
  until number of maximum iterations is reached.
Output: Optimised tree T.

Algorithm 3: Nonlocal node exchange.

5 Encoding with Stochastic Tree-Building

In this section, we pursue an approach that imposes restrictions to spatial optimisation. To define an adaptive regular grid, we start by storing a fixed point pattern for a given image: its four corner points and its midpoint. We can refine this grid by splitting the image in half in its largest dimension and add the same point pattern to its two subimages. Each split in this partitions the original image into smaller subimages and thereby refines the grid locally.

Compared to the free choice of the previous sections, this restriction reduces the size of the search space for optimal known data at the potential cost of reconstruction quality. In addition, it offers a lower coding cost for the locations by using *binary tree representations*. We represent each subimage of a given partition as a leaf node of the tree. For a tree T consisting of nodes $t_0, \ldots, t_n$, the root node t_0 stands for the original image and the root's children for the halves of the original. By adding more nodes to the tree, the image corresponding to their parent node is split further. We can consider *leaf nodes* as indicators for termination, i.e. the subimage corresponding to a leaf node is not split further. This allows us to represent the tree as a bit sequence (0 for leaf nodes, 1 for other nodes). In [23], such an efficient representation of the point positions is obtained with a heuristic method. We propose to use a more powerful stochastic mask selection approach inspired by Mainberger et al. [15] instead.

The original idea in [15] for unrestricted point sets is to start with a full mask that contains all image points. From this mask, we remove a fixed percentage α of known data. After inpainting with the smaller mask, we add a fraction β of the removed pixels with the highest reconstruction error back to the mask. This sparsification algorithm iterates the aforementioned steps until the target mask density is reached.

If we transfer this concept to a binary tree representation, there are some key differences: We have experimentally determined that densification is more efficient for tree structures than sparsification. Therefore, we start with a small amount of data and iteratively add more points at locations with large error until the target density is reached. In addition, we consider to add nodes to the tree instead of dealing with mask points directly. The tree structure dictates that only subimages corresponding to leaf nodes may be split. Such a split is equivalent to adding two child nodes to the former leaf node, each corresponding to one new subimage. Note that several mask points might be added by a single subdivision and that these mask points can also be contained in several of the neighbouring subimages. For our probabilistic method, we also need an appropriate error computation. In order to avoid a distortion of the influence of each node, we do not consider the mean square error in each subimage, but the sum $e(t_k)$ of unnormalised squared differences

$$e(t_k) = \sum_{(i,j) \in \Omega_k} (f_{i,j} - u_{i,j})^2 \tag{2}$$

where Ω_k denotes the image domain of the subimage corresponding to the tree node t_k. Without this unnormalised error measure, the same per-pixel-error in small subimages would be weighted higher than in large subimages. Taking all of these differences into account, we define *stochastic tree densification* in Algorithm 2. For a target density d, it produces an optimised tree T with a corresponding pixel mask $C(T) \subset \Omega$.

Just as the original sparsification algorithm, there is a risk that Algorithm 2 is caught in a local minimum. To avoid this problem, we propose an adapted version of the nonlocal pixel exchange from [15] in Algorithm 3. The method from [15] first generates a candidate set containing m non-mask pixels. Afterwards, the n pixels with the largest reconstruction error are exchanged with n randomly chosen mask pixels. If the new mask yields a better reconstruction it is kept, otherwise the change is reverted.

In our case, we have to adapt the node selection to respect the tree structure in order to define a nonlocal node exchange. In particular, the candidate set that is removed from the tree can only consist of nodes that are only split once. This is the case if and only if both children are leaf nodes. We call these nodes *single split node* and the reversion of their associated split comes down to removing their children which converts the single split node to a leaf node. These modifications lead to Algorithm 3.

The binary trees obtained from the densification and nonlocal node exchange can finally be stored as a sequence of bits. As in [23], we store a maximum and minimum tree depth and only save the node-structure explicitly inbetween. As header data, only the image size and the number of quantised grey values have to be stored. In total, this leads to the following encoding procedure:

1. Select a fraction p of total pixels with tree densification (Algorithm 2).
2. Optimise the splitting tree with nonlocal node exchange (Algorithm 3).
3. Perform GVO with quantisation optimisation (Algorithm 1).
4. Concatenate header, positional, and grey value data and apply PAQ.

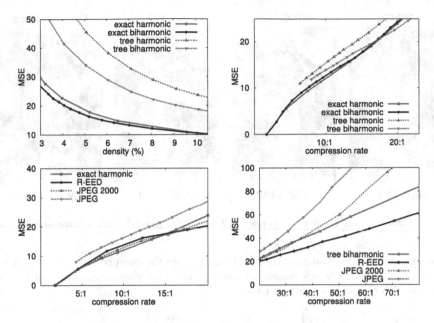

Fig. 1. Comparisons for the test image 256 × 256 image *peppers*. The top row compares harmonic and biharmonic versions of our codecs, the bottom row compares our best methods to transform coders and R-EED. **(a) Top Left:** Comparison at same mask density. **(b) Top Right:** Comparison at same compression ratio. **(c) Bottom Left:** Low to medium compression ratios. **(d) Bottom Right:** High compression ratios.

6   Experiments

In the following we evaluate the capabilities of harmonic and biharmonic inpainting for the two compression methods from the previous sections. Our experiments rely on a set of widely-used test images. We start with a pure comparison of the inpainting operators on the test image *peppers*: We optimise exact and restricted masks with different densities, perform GVO and compare the mean square error (MSE) at the same mask density. The results in Fig. 1 (a) show that, in general, biharmonic performs better than harmonic inpainting given the same amount of known data. This is consistent with previous results [2]. The restriction of the mask to an adaptive grid has a significant negative impact on the quality. This affects harmonic inpainting more than its biharmonic counterpart.

Interestingly, an evaluation of the actual compression performance with the codecs from Sects. 4 and 5 in Fig. 1(b) shows a significantly different ranking than in the density comparison. For exact masks, harmonic inpainting can even surpass its biharmonic counterpart. The coding cost for the known data is similar in both cases, but since harmonic inpainting is less sensitive to a coarse quantisation of the grey values, it performs overall better than biharmonic inpainting. The drawbacks of the restrictions in the tree-based approach are attenuated by the reduced positional coding cost. After a break-even point around ratio 20:1, the biharmonic tree-based method outperforms both exact approaches.

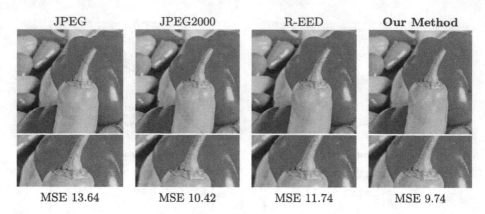

Fig. 2. Compression results for *peppers* (256 × 256 pixels) with compression ratio ≈ 8:1.

Table 1. MSE comparison on several test images. For the compression rate of 15:1 we use exact masks with homogeneous inpainting. The high compression rate of 60:1 is obtained with the biharmonic tree codec.

Ratio	≈ 15 : 1				≈ 60 : 1			
Image	elaine	lena	trui	walter	elaine	lena	trui	walter
JPEG	34.69	20.06	16.24	6.73	77.39	97.37	116.98	69.40
JPEG2000	31.23	14.73	12.27	5.70	54.18	60.48	88.96	47.09
R-EED	35.48	16.56	11.27	5.48	49.87	56.96	44.38	24.05
Our method	31.38	17.00	14.85	6.94	55.96	62.01	60.92	34.95

In relation to transform-based coders, the tree-based method performs consistently better than JPEG and in many cases also outperforms JPEG2000 for compression rates larger than 35:1. Nevertheless, R-EED copes better with the restriction to the adaptive grid and remains the preferable choice at high compression ratios. In comparison to other PDE-based methods, linear diffusion performs best in the area of low to medium compression rates (up to 15:1). Figs. 1, 2 and Table 1 show that, it can beat R-EED, mostly outperforms JPEG, and comes close to the quality of JPEG2000. Only on images that contain partially smooth data with high-contrast edges, R-EED is significantly better (e.g. on *trui* and *walter*). This demonstrates how powerful simple PDEs can be.

7   Conclusion

We have shown that codecs with parameter-free linear inpainting PDEs can beat both the quasi standard JPEG2000 of transform-based compression and the state-of-the-art in PDE-based compression. Comparing the different inpainting operators yields a valuable general insight: *The performance of PDEs for compression can only be evaluated in the context of actual codecs.* Comparisons that do not consider all compression steps can lead to false rankings of inpainting operators that do not reflect their real compression capabilities. In particular, the sensitivity of the biharmonic operator to coarsely quantised known data makes the simpler harmonic diffusion the preferable choice for compression.

Currently, the algorithms for mask selections are not competitive to JPEG2000 in regard to runtime. In our ongoing research, we focus on speeding up our algorithms for mask selection, such that PDE-based codecs are not only fast for decompression [11], but also for compression. Moreover, we will consider combinations of linear PDEs with patch-based inpainting for highly textured images, since this concept is already successful for nonlinear PDEs [20].

References

1. Belhachmi, Z., Bucur, D., Burgeth, B., Weickert, J.: How to choose interpolation data in images. SIAM J. Appl. Math. **70**(1), 333–352 (2009)
2. Chen, Y., Ranftl, R., Pock, T.: A bi-level view of inpainting-based image compression. In: Proceedings of the 19th Computer Vision Winter Workshop, Křtiny, Czech Republic, pp. 19–26, February 2014
3. Fränti, P., Nevalainen, O.: Compression of binary images by composite methods based on block coding. J. Vis. Commun. Image Represent. **6**(4), 366–377 (1995)
4. Galić, I., Weickert, J., Welk, M., Bruhn, A., Belyaev, A., Seidel, H.-P.: Towards PDE-based image compression. In: Paragios, N., Faugeras, O., Chan, T., Schnörr, C. (eds.) VLSM 2005. LNCS, vol. 3752, pp. 37–48. Springer, Heidelberg (2005)
5. Gautier, J., Meur, O.L., Guillemot, C.: Efficient depth map compression based on lossless edge coding and diffusion. In: Proceedings of the 29th Picture Coding Symposium, Krakow, Poland, pp. 81–84, May 2012
6. Hoeltgen, L., Setzer, S., Weickert, J.: An optimal control approach to find sparse data for Laplace interpolation. In: Heyden, A., Kahl, F., Olsson, C., Oskarsson, M., Tai, X.-C. (eds.) EMMCVPR 2013. LNCS, vol. 8081, pp. 151–164. Springer, Heidelberg (2013)
7. Hoffmann, S., Mainberger, M., Weickert, J., Puhl, M.: Compression of depth maps with segment-based homogeneous diffusion. In: Pack, T. (ed.) SSVM 2013. LNCS, vol. 7893, pp. 319–330. Springer, Heidelberg (2013)
8. Huffman, D.A.: A method for the construction of minimum redundancy codes. In: Proceedings of the IRE, vol. 40, pp. 1098–1101 (1952)
9. Iijima, T.: Basic theory on normalization of pattern (in case of typical one-dimensional pattern). Bull. Electrotechnical Lab. **26**, 368–388 (1962). in Japanese
10. Joint Bi-level Image Experts Group: Information technology progressive lossy/lossless coding of bi-level images. Standard, International Organization for Standardization (1993)
11. Köstler, H., Stürmer, M., Freundl, C., Rüde, U.: PDE based video compression in real time. Technical report 07–11, Lehrstuhl für Informatik 10, University Erlangen-Nürnberg, Germany (2007)
12. Li, Y., Sjostrom, M., Jennehag, U., Olsson, R.: A scalable coding approach for high quality depth image compression. 3DTV-Conference: The True Vision - Capture. Transmission and Display of 3D Video, Zurich, Switzerland, pp. 1–4, October 2012
13. Mahoney, M.: Adaptive weighing of context models for lossless data compression. Technical report CS-2005-16, Florida Institute of Technology, Melbourne, Florida, December 2005

14. Mainberger, M., Bruhn, A., Weickert, J., Forchhammer, S.: Edge-based compression of cartoon-like images with homogeneous diffusion. Pattern Recogn. **44**(9), 1859–1873 (2011)
15. Mainberger, M., Hoffmann, S., Weickert, J., Tang, C.H., Johannsen, D., Neumann, F., Doerr, B.: Optimising spatial and tonal data for homogeneous diffusion inpainting. In: Bruckstein, A.M., ter Haar Romeny, B.M., Bronstein, A.M., Bronstein, M.M. (eds.) SSVM 2011. LNCS, vol. 6667, pp. 26–37. Springer, Heidelberg (2012)
16. Mainberger, M., Weickert, J.: Edge-based image compression with homogeneous diffusion. In: Jiang, X., Petkov, N. (eds.) CAIP 2009. LNCS, vol. 5702, pp. 476–483. Springer, Heidelberg (2009)
17. Mohamed, S.A., Fahmy, M.: Binary image compression using efficient partitioning into rectangular regions. IEEE Trans. Commun. **43**(5), 1888–1893 (1995)
18. Pennebaker, W.B., Mitchell, J.L.: JPEG: Still Image Data Compression Standard. Springer, New York (1992)
19. Peter, P., Weickert, J.: Colour image compression with anisotropic diffusion. In: Proceedings of the 21st IEEE International Conference on Image Processing, Paris, France, pp. 4822–4862, October 2014
20. Peter, P., Weickert, J.: Compressing images with diffusion- and exemplar-based inpainting. In: Aujol, J.-F., Nikolova, M., Papadakis, N. (eds.) SSVM 2015. LNCS, vol. 9087, pp. 154–165. Springer, Heidelberg (2015)
21. Rissanen, J.J.: Generalized Kraft inequality and arithmetic coding. IBM J. Res. Dev. **20**(3), 198–203 (1976)
22. Schmaltz, C., Mach, N., Mainberger, M., Weickert, J.: Progressive modes in PDE-based image compression. In: Proceedings of the 30th Picture Coding Symposium, San Jose, CA, pp. 233–236, December 2013
23. Schmaltz, C., Peter, P., Mainberger, M., Ebel, F., Weickert, J., Bruhn, A.: Understanding, optimising, and extending data compression with anisotropic diffusion. Int. J. Comput. Vis. **108**(3), 222–240 (2014)
24. Taubman, D.S., Marcellin, M.W. (eds.): JPEG 2000: Image Compression Fundamentals, Standards and Practice. Kluwer, Boston (2002)
25. Weickert, J.: Theoretical foundations of anisotropic diffusion in image processing. Comput. Suppl. **11**, 221–236 (1996)
26. Zahir, S., Naqvi, M.: A near minimum sparse pattern coding based scheme for binary image compression. In: Proceedings of the 2005 IEEE International Conference on Image Processing, vol. 2, Genova, Italy, pp. II-289, September 2005
27. Zeng, G., Ahmed, N.: A block coding technique for encoding sparse binary patterns. IEEE Trans. Acoust. Speech Signal Process. **37**(5), 778–780 (1989)

A Study on Size Optimization of Scanned Textual Documents

Nidhi Saraswat$^{(\boxtimes)}$ and Hiranmay Ghosh

TCS Research, New Delhi, India
{nidhi.saraswat,hiranmay.ghosh}@tcs.com

Abstract. This paper reports a study on compression achieved on document images with different image formats, including PNG, GIF, PBM (zipped), JBIG and JBIG2. It also examines the issue of perceptual quality of the bi-level document images in these formats. It analyzes the impact of a common pre-processing step, namely the adaptive thresholding, on compression ratio and perceptual image quality in different image formats. We conclude that adaptive thresholding improves the compression ratio for common image formats, like the PNG and GIF, and make them comparable to JBIG/JBIG2 encoding; they result in significant improvement in perceptual image quality also. We also observe that the simple pre-processing step prevents perceptual information-loss in JBIG/JBIG2 encoding in certain situations.

Keywords: Image compression · Adaptive thresholding · Utilization of Image formats · Scanned document size optimization

1 Introduction

Digitization of paper documents is necessary for several reasons, such as for supporting computerized work-flow and long-term convenient archival. Many business processes and archival systems need to handle very large number, often in the order of millions, of documents. Optimization of document image size, maintaining readability, is important in these systems to reduce storage as well as handling time while transporting them over networks. In particular, big file-sizes are a major hindrance for consumption of documents over mobile networks. While several compression techniques have been proposed and several image representation formats have evolved to optimize document image sizes, their blind use often results in loss of readability. While confronted with such a situation, we experimented with several image compression schemes and some pre-processing algorithms. We present our key findings in this paper.

Generally, the commercial scanners produces color or gray-level document images that are stored in jpeg (or, pdf-encapsulated jpeg) formats. In many documents, the content is solely characterized by the text and graphics therein and color or texture do not contribute to its information value. Examples of such documents include business mails, doctors' prescriptions, various forms and

© Springer International Publishing Switzerland 2016
T. Bräunl et al. (Eds.): PSIVT 2015, LNCS 9431, pp. 75–86, 2016.
DOI: 10.1007/978-3-319-29451-3_7

answer-books from examinations. Use of bi-level images drastically reduces the numbers of bits per pixels and is a pragmatic option for such documents. Various lossy and lossless techniques available for image compression are described in [3]. The image formats using these compression techniques is explained in details in [2,4]. Different scenarios where certain image formats are more useful as compared to others are described as well. We also aim to experiment the proposed approach with JBIG [6,7] and JBIG2 [8–10] standards designed and developed specially for bi-level images.

While JBIG / JBIG2 provides excellent compression on document images, degradation in perceptual quality of text and graphics are often observed in such encoding, especially when an image segment consists both. Our experimentation shows that some pre-processing steps like use of adaptive threshold for binarization helps in retaining the quality. We also show that such simple pre-processing technique can significantly reduce the file-size in other common document formats, such as PNG and GIF, and make their sizes almost comparable to those of JBIG/JBIG2 formats. Moreover, such pre-processing step often results in significant improvement in perceptual quality of the document.

The rest of the paper is organized as follows: Sect. 2 gives an overview of factors contributing to the large size of scanned documents, various compression techniques and the utilization of these compression techniques in image formats is summarized in Sect. 3, the proposed approach and the experimental results with discussion are elaborated in Sects. 4 and 5 respectively. Section 6 concludes the paper with the findings and recommendations from proposed approach.

2   Contributing Factors to Large Scanned Document Size

The possible reasons for large size of scanned documents are:

- **High Resolution while scanning:** Resolution selected at the time of document scan can add to the size of scanned document. A document scanned at 300 dpi resolution is sufficient for printing, while a document scanned at 150–200 dpi is good enough for screen reading.
- **Scan Mode:** On one hand, Black and White Text pages can be scanned at Line Art Scan Mode while, Black and White Photos can be scanned at Gray Tones. In Line art scan of a given document the aliasing are very pronounced at the edges which can be smoothend by increasing the resolution at the time of scan. But,the main benefit of small size of line art scan of documents is lost by increasing resolution(in order to get smooth-edged scan of documents). The gray-scale scan of documents has larger files size as compared to Line Art Scan of Documents.
- **Physical dimension of scanned document:** A legal-size scan will be larger than a letter-size scan, with all other factors being equal.
- **Compression Techniques:** The compression technique followed to compress the scanned document greatly defines the file size.
- **Scanning Noise:** The principle source of noise in digital images arise during image acquisition. The performance of imaging sensors is affected by a variety of factors such as environmental conditions during image acquisition, and by the quality of sensing elements themselves.

We aim to reduce the size of scanned documents while enhancing the image clarity to simplify the process of upload/download of these documents.

3   Compression and Image Formats

The image format used for saving the scanned images can be interpreted as the compression technique used for scanned documents. The following sub-sections give a brief description of the broad categorization of compression techniques along with some commonly used image formats and the compression techniques used by them.

3.1   Compression Techniques

1. *Lossy Compression:* Lossy compression is the class of data encoding methods that uses inexact approximations (or partial data discarding) for representing the content that has been encoded. Lossy compression algorithms preserve a representation of the original uncompressed image that may appear to be a perfect copy, but it is not a perfect copy. Often lossy compression is able to achieve smaller file sizes than lossless compression.
   - **DCT (Discrete Cosine Transform):** The discrete cosine transform (DCT) helps separate the image into parts (or spectral sub-bands) of differing importance (with respect to the image's visual quality). The DCT is similar to the discrete Fourier transform: it transforms a signal or image from the spatial domain to the frequency domain.
   - **Vector Quantization:** Vector quantization (VQ) is a classical quantization technique from signal processing which allows the modeling of probability density functions by the distribution of prototype vectors. It works by dividing a large set of points (vectors) into groups having approximately the same number of points closest to them. Each group is represented by its centroid point, as in k-means and some other clustering algorithms.
2. *Lossless Compression:* Lossless data compression is a class of data compression algorithms that allows the original data to be perfectly reconstructed from the compressed data.
   - **Run Length Encoding:** Run-length encoding (RLE) is a very simple form of data compression in which runs of data (that is, sequences in which the same data value occurs in many consecutive data elements) are stored as a single data value and count, rather than as the original run. There are a number of variants of run-length encoding. Image data is normally run-length encoded in a sequential process that treats the image data as a 1D stream, rather than as a 2D map of data.
   - **LZW:** The LZW Compression Algorithm can summarized as a technique that encodes sequences of 8-bit data as fixed-length 12-bit codes. The codes from 0 to 255 represent 1-character sequences consisting of the corresponding 8-bit character, and the codes 256 through 4095 are created in a dictionary for sequences encountered in the data as it is encoded. At each stage in compression, input bytes are gathered into a sequence until the

next character would make a sequence for which there is no code yet in the dictionary. The code for the sequence (without that character) is added to the output, and a new code (for the sequence with that character) is added to the dictionary.
- **Zlib:** zlib is a software library used for data compression. Zlib is an abstraction of the DEFLATE compression algorithm used in their gzip file compression program. Deflate is a data compression algorithm that uses a combination of the LZ77 algorithm and Huffman coding.
- **Huffman Coding:** Huffman coding is based on the frequency of occurrence of a data item (pixel in images). The principle is to use a lower number of bits to encode the data that occurs more frequently. Codes are stored in a Code Book which may be constructed for each image or a set of images. In all cases the code book plus encoded data must be transmitted to enable decoding.

3.2 Image Formats

There are a number of image formats available that use either a lossless, or lossy form of compression (or their variation). Given below are a few image formats that use either of the forms of compression.

PNM: A Netpbm format is any graphics format used and defined by the Netpbm project. The portable pixmap format(PPM), the portable graymap format (PGM) and the portable bitmap format (PBM) are image file formats designed to be easily exchanged between platforms. They are also sometimes referred to collectively as the portable anymap format (PNM). The ASCII formats allow for human readability and easy transfer to other platforms (so long as those platforms understand ASCII), while the binary formats are more efficient both in file size and in ease of parsing, due to the absence of white spaces. In the binary formats, PBM uses 1 bit per pixel, PGM uses 8 bits per pixel, and PPM uses 24 bits per pixel: 8 for red, 8 for green, 8 for blue. PNM in itself does not provide any compression to encoded data, but a PNM format file when combined with some other compression techniques (e.g. .gz) can greatly reduce the size of given files.

JPEG: Jpeg support up to 16.7 million colors, which makes them the right choice for complex images and photographs. But for normal documents which does not include any complex drawings or images, but only line drawings (text), jpeg is not a suitable choice. JPEG supports lossy format that uses DCT to compress given files. JPEG images are full-color images that dedicate at least 24 bits of memory to each pixel, resulting in images that can incorporate 16.8 million colors. Hence the image takes up more bits/pixel to store image information resulting in larger file size. [12] explains in detail about JPEG Still picture Compression Standard.

PNG: Portable Network Graphics (PNG) is a raster graphics file format that supports lossless data compression [11]. PNG supports palette-based images (with palettes of 24-bit RGB or 32-bit RGBA colors), gray-scale images (with or without alpha channel), and full-color non-palette-based RGB[A] images (with or without alpha channel). PNG uses a 2-stage compression process: (1) pre-compression: filtering (prediction), (2) compression: DEFLATE. PNG uses a non-patented lossless data compression method known as DEFLATE, which is the same algorithm used in the zlib compression library. When storing images that contain text, line art, or graphics – images with sharp transitions and large areas of solid color – the PNG format can compress image data more than JPEG can.

GIF: The Graphics Interchange Format is a bitmap format. The format supports up to 8 bits per pixel for each image, allowing a single image to reference its own palette of up to 256 different colors chosen from the 24-bit RGB color space. GIF images are compressed using the Lempel-Ziv-Welch (LZW) lossless data compression technique (LZW compression technique is more efficient than run length encoding) to reduce the file size without degrading the visual quality. PNG files can be much larger than GIF files in situations where a GIF and a PNG file were created from the same high-quality image source, as PNG is capable of storing more color depth and transparency information than GIF. GIF is a good choice for storing line drawings, text, and iconic graphics at a small file size.

JBIG: JBIG is a lossless image compression standard from the Joint Bi-level Image Experts Group, standardized as ISO/IEC standard 11544 and as ITU-T recommendation T.82 [6,7]. JBIG is based on a form of arithmetic coding patented by IBM, known as the Q-coder, but using a minor tweak patented by Mitsubishi, resulting in what became known as the QM-coder. It bases the probabilities of each bit on the previous bits and the previous lines of the picture. In order to allow compressing and decompressing images in scanning order, it does not reference future bits. JBIG also supports progressive transmission with small (around 5) overheads.

JBIG2: JBIG2 is an International Telecommunication Union format that represents a revolutionary breakthrough in captured document technology [8–10]. Using JBIG2 encoding, a scanned image can be compressed up to 10 times smaller than with TIFF G4. This facilitates creating, for the very first time, scanned image documents whose file size is the same as OCR-converted text files. The power behind JBIG2 technology is its ability to support both lossless and perceptually lossless black and white image compression.

The scanned textual documents cannot rely much on lossy compression as it may lead to loss of information. On the other hand, various lossless compression techniques can be useful for compression of scanned textual documents. The study of few commonly used image formats leads to the conclusion of experimenting the proposed approach with formats like .png/ .gif/ .pbm/ .jbg/ .jb2. JPEG is a lossy image format that is more suitable for complex pictures as it removes high frequency values. PNG and GIF formats can be more efficient and useful for saving line arts, texts and graphics, while PBM in itself is a binary format but gives large file size when used individually. The application of gzip compression on pbm files gives high compression. JBIG and JBIG2, the comparatively new standards, are specially suited for bi-level images. So we propose to experiment the proposed approach with these formats to achieve files of reduced size.

4   Approach

On the basis of study of the factors contributing to the large file size of scanned documents in Sect. 2, it is understood that one cannot have control over the Scanning noise and physical dimension of document being scanned. A minimal resolution required for clear reading of documents without any aliasing is dependent on resolution at the time of scan and scan mode, hence limiting the control on these factors. On the other hand, acquisition of textual documents' images through scanning is accompanied by inclusion of irrelevant data points due to environmental factors, that acts as scanning noise. So, we precisely try to reduce scanning noise to achieve greater compression. Therefore, our approach towards size optimization of scanned documents is directed towards binarization of scanned documents which not only reduces file size, but also increases legibility of the documents. For any scanned textual document, the color may not be of great importance, hence it is significant to convert it into a binary image. Noise, one of the factors contributing to large size of scanned documents,is also removed by the process of binarization. The output images with adaptive thresholding are anti-aliased bi-level images that are saved in different image formats to utilize the compression techniques supported by them. The resultant images, hence are clear to read with optimal file size.

The novelty in this paper lies in the use of adaptive thresholding to binarize a given image that not only reduces the size of scanned textual docu-

Fig. 1. Overview of proposed Algorithm

ments but also enhances document clarity. Figure 1 shows an overview of proposed approach. Considering the input to be a gray-scale scan of documents, the approach to reduce the size of scanned text documents is explained as follows:

- **Binarization and Cleaning:** The less colors that are in input image, smaller the file size will be. So for any given document, we can easily convert value of each pixel to either 0 or 1, i.e., black or white, hence reducing the number of colors in given image to only two. The input image is applied with adaptive thresholding to convert it into a bi-level image.
  Unlike simple (global) binary thresholding, where a fixed threshold is used for all the pixels in the image, adaptive thresholding uses a local threshold for every pixel in an image. The threshold value is calculated based on the intensities of the neighbouring pixels. Adaptive thresholding has an edge over global thresholding in the scenarios where there is large variation in background intensity, which is true for scanned document images (because of noise).

Adaptive thresholding typically takes a gray-scale or color image as input and, in the simplest implementation, outputs a binary image representing the segmentation. For each pixel in the image, a threshold has to be calculated. If the pixel value is below the threshold it is set to the background value, otherwise it assumes the foreground value. It calculates thresholds in regions of size block-size surrounding each pixel (i.e. local neighborhoods). Each threshold value is the weighted sum of the local neighborhood minus an offset value [1]. While we have used an open-source implementation of standard adaptive thresholding algorithm, our contribution lies in deciding an optimal neighbourhood size and an optimal offset value that determines the performance of adaptive thresholding. These parameters are decided based on extensive experimentation over a large set of documents[1].

The conversion of scanned grayscale documents to binary cleans the image, making it more legible. The adaptive thresholding acts as an agent to cleaning the given image since any such pixel value which is below the calculated threshold is set to white.

– **Compression Technique:** The image is saved in an appropriate image format (see Sect. 2) to get suitable level of compression on scanned document along with maintenance of image quality.

The reason behind binarising the input image is not only to convert the image to bi-level but also to remove noise. Noise, being the unwanted data in input image, is removed by the process of adaptive thresholding leading to file size reduction. The binarization of image along with noise removal greatly optimizes on the size of input image saved in .png/ .gif/ .pbm (zipped)/ .jbg/ .jb2 formats due their suitability on type of content and bi-level nature.

Binarization of image is followed by saving it in an appropriate format to get desired compression. The image formats use different algorithms to encode the given image. Therefore, the judgment of image format is based on type of image and its content type. Every image format have their own pros and cons. They were created for specific, yet different purposes. Section 3 gives a deep insight into various image formats, compression technique used and their utility in various scenarios.

5 Results and Discussions

We experimented the proposed algorithm on 8 data sets containing in total of about 224 gray-scale scanned images. The images were scanned at 150–200 ppi with resolution in between 1240×1753 to 2136×1700. The images in data set mostly had handwritten text with graphs and figures. The compression percentage varied from 52 % to 87 % for various image formats used to save the processed images. The compression achieved is not only dependent on encoding format but is also driven by encoder used. The experiments for the proposed approach are

---

[1] The block size and offset for adaptive thresholding are selected on the basis of experimental evaluation of images.

performed using OpenCV library and ImageMagick tool. The source of encoder used for saving as JBIG2 file is [5].

Table 1 summarizes the compression achieved with the state of the art methods and implementation of proposed approach. Various formats used to save the binarized images may have their utility in various areas of application. The Compression % defined in Table 1 can be defined as: If a given image has originally scanned size of 'x' and the size of this image changes to 'y' after the application of proposed methodology, then the "Compression %" is defined as:

$$Compression\% = (x - y)/x * 100$$

The grayscale scanned document images form the set of input images. There are two classes of image formats: (1) the JPEG family: designed for optimizing natural images, and (2) PNG, GIF, JBIG family, etc., which are more generic and work better for bi-level document images. Based on the nature of the set of input images, we experimented with the latter set of image formats to get compression. Hence, the set of scanned input images are encoded in .png/ .gif/ .pbm (zipped)/ .jbig/ .jbig2 formats for experimentation purpose. We have compared our results with publicly available encoders for these formats, besides an publicly available encoder for a standard lossless compression technique .gz. The results in Table 1 are shown in 2 parts , the upper rows indicating the compression achieved by state of the art methods, and the lower rows indicating the compression achieved with proposed approach. We observed that we get much better compression with the pre-processed images than when the encoding methods are directly applied for all except for .jbig2 format. For .jbig2, we find a little degradation in compression performance with pre-processing step. In all the image formats (including .jbig2), the perceptible quality of the document images are much better when pre-processed than when directly encoded. This is illustrated in Fig. 2.

The scanned input images encoded directly as .png/ .gif formats seemingly do not suit the compression needs of the documents. On the other hand, the images processed with adaptive thresholding when encoded as .png/ .gif format give a significant compression in the file size of scanned textual documents. The compression achieved in latter is due to the type of content in the scanned documents that fits in well with lossless compression techniques followed by these formats.

The pbm files generated by any of the two methods have large size, but the use of gzip format (lossless compression format) on the pbm encoded images gives a significant compression in the file size of scanned images. The input images encoded in raw .pbm files followed by the use of .gz compression, without the use of pre-processing step of Adaptive Thresholding, gives reasonable compression in scanned files' size. Although the important aspect in this regard is that the pbm file format is a binary format. Hence grayscale images when encoded directly as .pbm files can potentially hamper the image completely. Therefore, in order to encode a scanned file as .pbm directly (Without Adaptive Thresholding), a thresholding is required. Such a thresholding, known as

Table 1. Results achieved for proposed approach on 8 data sets with 224 images in total (All sizes in KB and compression in percentage).

Images (state of the art Methods)

	Source (jpeg) Size	.png Size	.png Compression%	.gif Size	.gif Compression%	.pbm-gz Size	.pbm-gz Compression%	.jbg Size	.jbg Compression%	.jb2 Size	.jb2 Compression%
DS1	5632	24268.8	-330.91	30105.6	-434.55	1638.4	70.91	1433.6	74.55	461.7	91.8
DS2	3584	28057.6	-682.86	33484.8	-834.29	946.9	73.58	1536	57.14	298.3	91.68
DS3	3788.8	36454.4	-862.16	35737.6	-843.24	2150.4	43.24	2355.2	37.84	491.9	87.02
DS4	3584	27238.4	-660	31846.4	-788.57	1843.2	48.57	2252.8	37.14	474.1	86.77
DS5	5529.6	19968	-261.11	24576	-344.44	1024	81.48	1126.4	79.63	368	93.34
DS6	3788.8	11980.8	-216.22	13107.2	-245.95	1024	72.97	785.6	79.27	402.6	89.37
DS7	3276.8	10240	-212.5	11059.2	-237.5	894	72.72	691.6	78.89	365.7	88.84
DS8	11366.4	45875.2	-303.6	59904	-427.03	1843.2	83.78	1638.4	85.59	322.1	97.17
Total	40550.4	204083.2	-403.28	239820.8	-491.41	11364.1	71.98	11819.6	70.85	3184.4	92.15

Processed Images (With Adaptive Thresholding)

	.png Size	.png Compression%	.gif Size	.gif Compression%	.pbm-gz Size	.pbm-gz Compression%	.jbg Size	.jbg Compression%	.jb2 Size	.jb2 Compression%
DS1	2457.6	56.36	1843.2	67.27	1331.2	76.36	809.1	85.63	760.9	86.49
DS2	1843.2	48.57	1433.6	60	1024	71.43	531.7	85.16	521.4	85.45
DS3	4710.4	-24.32	3481.6	8.11	1740.8	54.05	766.5	79.77	740.5	80.46
DS4	2764.8	22.86	2048	42.86	1433.6	60	786.3	78.06	754.4	78.95
DS5	1433.6	74.07	1126.4	79.63	936.5	83.06	530.1	90.41	529.8	90.42
DS6	2048	45.95	1536	59.46	1126.4	70.27	630.3	83.36	577.1	84.77
DS7	1740.8	46.88	1331.2	59.38	1024	68.75	573	82.51	539.3	83.54
DS8	2252.8	80.18	1638.4	85.59	1536	86.49	820.2	92.78	761.6	93.3
Total	19251.2	52.53	14438.4	64.39	10152.5	74.96	5447.2	86.57	5185	87.21

global thresholding, might not be feasible for all the scenarios. For calculating the impact of state of the art method in this case, we experimented with the input images by applying a global threshold(220), to get result images. On the other hand, use of Adaptive thresholding on input images binarizes the images. The resultant binarised images can be directly encoded as .pbm format followed by .gzip to get compressed images. Hence, the compression achieved by the use of pbm(zipped) in the latter case is comparatively better than former with the additional benefit of adaptive and feasible nature of adaptive thresholding in all scenarios.

JBIG and JBIG2 give a good compression percentage with both state of the art method and proposed approach. The approach of separating textual, halftones and generic regions from given image to apply different encoding techniques results in higher compression in JBIG2 as compared to JBIG. The proposed approach of using adaptive thresholding followed by JBIG encoding gives higher compression than state of art method. On the other hand, the experimental results show that the compression achieved through direct JBIG2 format encoding of input image is higher than the other case.

Apart from the compression achieved in file size of scanned document images, another crucial aspect that cannot be neglected is legibility of images after compression. A group of people were shown images from both state of the art method and proposed approach, for each of the image format considered in experimental setup, to rate on the quality of images. The assessment of perceptual quality of images was done by taking into consideration collective feedback. The adaptive thresholding on scanned input images along with binarization also leads to image cleaning, hence, improving the quality of images. The png and gif encoded input images hold perceptually similar quality of images for both the cases. The images produced by the state of art method and proposed approach (for pbm zipped) have gap in legibility. The pbm files generated after adaptive thresholding are smudge free and more clear to read. Thus,the scanned documents binarized through adaptive threshold, followed by pbm(zipped) encoding Fig. (2(d)) not only makes the approach a lot more reliable and robust but also gives higher legibility as compared to state of the art method Fig. (2(a)).

JBIG and JBIG2 give a good compression percentage with both state of the art method and proposed approach. JBIG and JBIG2 standards are mainly developed for bi-level images but can be used on other types of images as well. Figure 2(b) and (c) shows input image encoded directly in JBIG and JBIG2 format while Fig. 2(e) and (f) shows input image applied with Adaptive thresholding followed by JBIG and JBIG2 format encoding. The perceptual quality of image encoded with JBIG after adaptive thresholding format is better than directly encoded JBIG images.

It can be seen that the images directly encoded as JBIG in Fig. 2(b) have faded horizontal rulers as compared to Fig. 2(e). Also, the higher compression achieved by JBIG2 encoding, without the pre-processing step, comes at a cost of perceptual degradation of image quality. Figure 2(c) also shows that the horizontal lines in the text are lost (which are still there in JBIG2 files after adaptive thresholding in Fig. 2(f)) which points towards the fact that a grayscale/colored image input

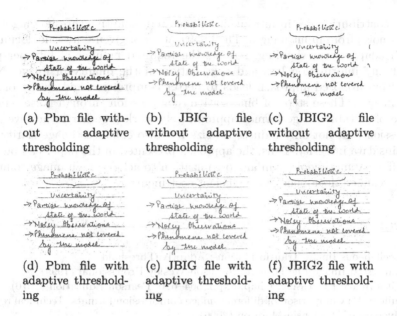

(a) Pbm file without adaptive thresholding

(b) JBIG file without adaptive thresholding

(c) JBIG2 file without adaptive thresholding

(d) Pbm file with adaptive thresholding

(e) JBIG file with adaptive thresholding

(f) JBIG2 file with adaptive thresholding

Fig. 2. Comparison of image formats with and without adaptive thresholding

encoded directly may lead to loss of legibility in a few cases. JBIG2 when used in lossy mode, can potentially alter text in a way that's not discernible as corruption. This is in contrast to some other algorithms, which simply degrade into a blur, making the compression artifacts obvious. Since JBIG2 tries to match up similar-looking symbols, the numbers '6' and '8' may get replaced for example.

The PBM, JBIG, and JBIG2 are bi-level formats. Though they themselves are sufficient in binarising given images when a given image is saved in these formats, but the quality of saved images need not necessarily be satisfactory for all the cases. Hence, the adaptive thresholding of grayscale images in accordance to the proposed approach not only binarizes the image at good quality without any perceptual degradation but also helps in optimizing the compression achieved by various image formats. Different image formats used to save the binarized files may have different system/software requirements at the time of their use. For example JBIG2 format, despite giving the highest compression after proposed algorithm, is a fairly new format to save files, hence there are not many image viewers that incorporate the decoder for the image format. The inference, hence, drawn from given results and discussions is that the file size can be greatly reduced by using the suitable file format on noise free bi-level images.

6   Conclusion

In this paper, we have presented a simple, but reliable and efficient approach to reduce the size of scanned textual documents. The varied results achieved by different methods can be opted on the basis of requirements of operational units.

Our contribution lies in introducing the step of adaptive thresholding which removes noise from input images. The binarization of given grayscale document, through adaptive thresholding, reduces the required number of bits per pixel without any information loss and degradation of the quality of image. Noise removal by proposed approach leads to better compression and clarity of document images. These steps of binarization, compression through noise removal and use of suitable image format appropriately work together to achieve good compression that not only reduces file size but also enhances image clarity and maintains data integrity. Thus, the approach presented in the paper can be used as an effective methodology in any organization to achieve high image compression for scanned documents with efficient cost incurred.

References

1. Miscellaneous Image Transformations: AdaptiveThreshold
2. Compressed Image File Formats. Addison-Wesley Professional (1999)
3. Digital Image Processing, Chap. 8, pp. 564–626. Pearson Education (2010)
4. Aguilera, P.: Comparison of different image compression formats. Technical report, University of Wisconsin-Madison (2006)
5. Github. jbig2enc. Technical report, GitHub
6. Gutierre. Jbig compression
7. Kyrki, V.: Jbig image compression standard
8. Joint Bi level Image Experts Group. Jbig2.com: An introduction to jbig2. Technical report
9. Ono, F., Rucklidge, W., Arps, R.: Jbig2-the ultimate bi-level image coding standard. In: 2000 International Conference on Image Processing, Proceedings, vol. 1 (2011)
10. Howard, P.G., Kossentini, F., Martins, B., Ren Forchhammer, S., Rucklidge, W.J., Ono, F.: The emerging jbig2 standard. In: IEEE Transactions on Circuits and Systems for Video Technology
11. Roelofs, G.: History of the portable network graphics (png) format. In Linux Gazette
12. Wallace, G.K.: The jpeg still picture compression standard. In: IEEE Transactions on Consumer Electronics

Combination of Mean Shift of Colour Signature and Optical Flow for Tracking During Foreground and Background Occlusion

M. Hedayati, M.J. Cree$^{(\boxtimes)}$, and J. Scott

School of Engineering, University of Waikato, Hamilton 3240, New Zealand
mh267@student.waikato.ac.nz, {cree,scottj}@waikato.ac.nz

Abstract. This paper proposes a multiple hypothesis tracking for multiple object tracking with moving camera. The proposed model makes use of the stability of sparse optical flow along with the invariant colour property under size and pose variation, by merging the colour property of objects into optical flow tracking. To evaluate the algorithm five different videos are selected from broadcast horse races where each video represents different challenges that present in object tracking literature. A comparison study of the proposed method, with a colour based mean shift tracking proves the significant improvement in accuracy and stability of object tracking.

Keywords: Object tracking · MeanShift · Optical flow · LK · Occlusion

1 Introduction

Object tracking is a common computer vision task and it is the backbone of many applications like video surveillance, robotics, human computer interaction (HCI) and video analysis. The primary task of video tracking is to localize the object of interest in frame $t + 1$ by having its location at time t.

Although for the past decades enormous study was dedicated to object tracking, due to various problems encountered in this area, object tracking still is a challenging topic in computer vision. These challenges are mainly caused by change in size or pose of the object, noise produced at the image acquisition level, variation of light, and partial or full occlusion of the object with the background or foreground [1]. Depending on the characteristics of the scene these challenges need to be considered in building any tracking system.

Colour-based models [2–6] have achieved considerable success in video tracking applications. This success is due to the invariant property of colour under size and pose changes. However using the colour property has two main drawbacks, first the colour is sensitive to illumination changes [7], and second the occlusion of objects with similar colour may lead to incorrect tracking [8]. These shortcomings can be compensated by merging extra information such as edge features [9,10] or spatiotemporal motion [11,13–16] of the object with the colour property.

© Springer International Publishing Switzerland 2016
T. Bräunl et al. (Eds.): PSIVT 2015, LNCS 9431, pp. 87–98, 2016.
DOI: 10.1007/978-3-319-29451-3_8

This paper introduces a model for long-term object tracking by building a probability distribution from corners, motion and colour. The proposed model uses stability of corner features in light variation to extract spatio-temporal motion of the object and stability of colour under pose and size changes to handle various challenges like light variation, occlusion and object pose changes. To have fair evaluation under a highly dynamic environment, the five different videos are selected from broadcast horse races. The selected videos cover almost all the challenges in the object tracking literatures.

The rest of this article is organized as follows: Sect. 2 is a review of significant literature on object tracking; Sect. 3 describes our approaches for multiple object tracking; Sect. 4 compares Meanshift tracking with our proposed model and discusses the final result; and, finally, Sect. 5 concludes and provides recommendations for further work.

2   Literature Study

Among various tracking systems, Meanshift [2,3,7,10] and optical–flow based [11,12,14–17,19] tracking are two well-known tracking systems that have proven their reliability. The mean shift [18] is a statical method to find local maxima of any kind of probability distribution. The mean shift algorithm was not originally intended for tracking purposes. It was first applied to object tracking by Bradski et al. [2]. Their model calculates the centroid of the 2D colour probability distribution within its 2D window, then moves the window centre to the centroid of distribution. Thus it is called Continuously Adaptive Mean Shift (CAMSHIFT).

Over time various adaptations have been made on CAMSHIFT to improve its accuracy. Comaniciu et al. [6] used the weighted probability distribution in order to assign higher weighting to pixels nearer to the centre of window, based on the assumption that the foreground pixel is more likely selected near to the centre of the tracking window rather than its border. Allen et al. [19] introduced a background–weighted histogram by assigning lower weight to colour features that belong to the background. The background weighted–histogram weights the probability distribution by considering the distribution ratio between background colour (pixels outside tracking window) and the foreground colour (pixels inside tracking window). To handle occlusion Kai She et al. [9] build statistical models based on a hue–saturation–value (HSV) colour map and Haar–like features [20] and apply the Meanshift algorithm on each of these features to localize the object.

Optical flow basically refers to the displacement of intensity patterns and is widely used in computer vision from medical image registration to automated video surveillance [21]. The fundamental optical flow equation is based on the assumption that the pixel intensity does not change due to a small displacement, and is given by,

$$f(x + \triangle x; y + \triangle y; t + \triangle t) \approx f(x; y; t), \tag{1}$$

where $f(x; y; t)$ is the intensity of the image at position (x, y) at time t, $(\triangle x, \triangle y)$ is the change in position, and $\triangle t$ is the change in time.

The optical flow itself can be divided into a dense and a sparse model. In the dense model the optical field is built based on the motion of all pixels in the image. Horn and Schunk's model [13] is classic dense optical flow which estimate the motion by imposing additional constraints, such as smoothness, to the system. The smoothness constraint is an assumption that the optical flow field should vary smoothly and have few discontinuities. The dense optical flow algorithm has difficulty in calculating flow in homogeneous regions or in edges where only orthogonal displacement can be found. Sparse optical flow solves these issues by only considering points that have strong gradients in both x and y direction. In the literature these points are called *corners*.

The corner detection methods themselves are a broad topic but useful reviews are given by Tuytelaars et al. [22] and Kerr et al. [23].

The Lucas-Kanade (LK) technique [11] is a well-known sparse optical flow method due to it reliable and robust performance. This method solved the optical flow Eq. (1) by assuming that pixels in the small neighbourhood (patch) have the same displacement. The flow vector at pixel (x,y) is approximated by

$$E_v = \sum_{P \in N} W^2(p)[\nabla I(p)[u.v] + I_t(p)], \tag{2}$$

where $\nabla I(p)$ and $I_t(p)$ represent the spatial and temporal gradient at neighbouring pixels, N is the number of pixels inside the patch, u and v are x and y displacement respectively, and $W(p)$ is the weight parameter associate with neighbouring pixels. If in Eq. (2) N is bigger than two then u and v can be approximated by least squares solution as:

$$A^T W^2 A V = A^T W^2 b \Rightarrow V = (A^T W^2 A)^{-1} A^T W^2 b, \tag{3}$$

where $A = [\nabla I(p_1), ...]^T, V = [u, v]^T, b = -[I_t(p_1), ...]^T$ and W is the weight matrix.

LK optical flow is widely used in tracking applications. Yin et al. [15] used the LK model to suppress the object tracking problem under camouflage by modelling the motion pattern of the object and the background then object detection is achieved by cluster motion pattern using flow magnitude.

MedainFlow [14] tracking is another LK–based tracker. This model starts by initialising a set of points in the rectangular grid within the object bounding box. These points are then tracked by Lucas-Kanade tracker and the quality of the points is estimated by forward-backward error. The object displacement is approximated by calculating median displacement over remaining points. The forward-backward error first finds the forward trajectory of the object from the first to the last frame, then the backward trajectory is obtained by backward tracking from the last frame to the first one. Finally the two trajectories are compared and if they differ significantly, the forward trajectory is considered incorrect.

The tracking system proposed by Oshima et al. [17] is the closest approach to our proposed model. They designed a model to track a single object with a static near-infrared camera. They build three different histograms, based on flow magnitude, flow direction and colour. Values of magnitude and direction of each flow vector are estimated on based dense optical flow [13] and then fitted into two separate histograms. Final object localization is achieved by applying Meanshift on a combination of magnitude, flow and colour histograms.

3 The Proposed Model

This paper proposes a multiple hypothesis model for multiple object tracking in video captured with a single moving camera. The proposed model takes advantage of the invariance of object colour under size and pose changes as well as the stability of sparse optical flow to build the probability distribution of the object. As this model used corner, motion, and colour features to build an object model, the proposed model name is CMC tracker.

CMC tracker can be separated into four blocks, namely, pre-localization, filtering, weighing and updating, (See Fig. 1).

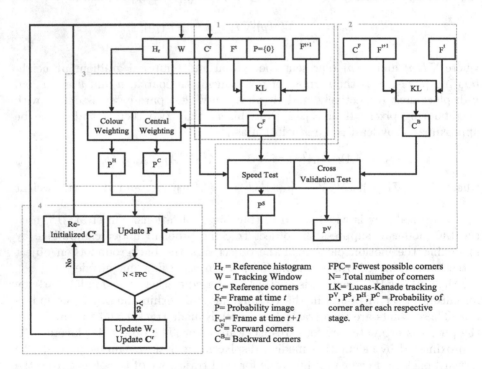

Fig. 1. Flow diagram of proposed model. The blocks are identified with numbered grey boxes.

The pre-localization, block 1, roughly estimates the location of the object in the next frame by applying the LK tracker [11] using the set of corner points.

The filtering, block 2, deals with removing the corner points that do not satisfy two constraints. The first constraint is based on the assumption that the speed of corner points are almost constant therefore the corners should not accelerate much. Any corner violating this constraint is removed. The second constraint is based on the forward-backward error [14]. Forward-backward error is used to remove the corner if its forward trajectory significantly differs from its backward trajectory.

The weighting, block 3, adjusts the significance of corners based on colour similarity with the reference object colour and by their distance from the centre of the tracking window. The corners tracked by the LK tracker are not necessarily reliable because they only consider motion of the object, hence these corners can not handle occlusion when two or more objects are moving in the same direction and with similar speed. To handle this situation the colour property of the object merges into the tracked corners, therefore the colour similarity of corners with the reference target colour is measured, and then they are given weights according to their distance to the centre of the tracking window.

The Updating, block 4, applies Meanshift on the probability distribution of image to find the new location of the object and finally update related parameters. The probability distribution image here refers to the corners which passed filtering block and weighted in weighting block. The effect of each of these blocks can be seen in Fig. 2.

To initialize the tracking at the start frame, the rectangular box is placed manually around each object (jockey's upper body). Three sets of features are extracted from these reference targets, as follows:

I. The first feature is the coordinate of the reference target, window (W), in the 2D image plane.
II. The second feature is the colour distribution of the reference targets or reference histogram. A reference histogram is calculated from the colour distributions of objects in the hue and saturation channel in an HSV colour map and it is represented by $H_r = \{h_n^r\}_{(n=1...b)}$ where b is the number of bins.
III. The LK gives better tracking performance if it operates on stable points like corners, therefore as last feature the well-known Shi and Tomasi [16] method is used to extract corner points from reference target. These points called reference corners are represented by $C^r = \{c_n^r\}_{(n=1...N)}$ where N is total number of reference corners.

In brief, the CMC tracker aims to utilize the above information and build a probability image P to feed to the Meanshift tracking. The probability image is a 2D matrix with the same size as the input frame with all of its elements set to zero at the beginning of tracking. The rest of this section gives further detail on each block.

3.1 Pre-localization

The pre-localization block roughly estimates the location of the object in the next frame by applying the LK tracker [12] on the set of corners points. LK estimates the locations of reference corners in the consecutive frame by calculating their sparse motion field. In the literature these tracked points are called forward corners (C^F). The forward corners alone are not reliable in a highly dynamic environment with various occlusion and pixel intensity changes, therefore a series of assumptions are exploited in the filtering and weighting stage to refine these points as much as possible.

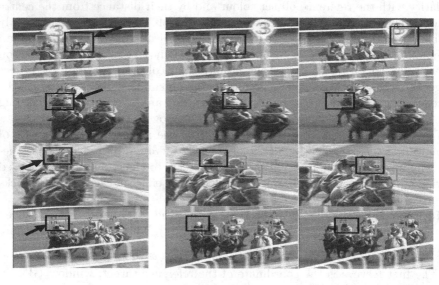

Fig. 2. The effect of filtering and weighting. The arrows in the first column show the notable contenders, the sample result using the proposed model for the subsequent frame is shown in the second column, and third column shows how tracking is lost without the speed test, the cross validation test, and the central and colour weighting from top to bottom.

3.2   Filtering

The filtering block deals with removing the corner points that do not satisfy two assumptions. These two assumptions are called "speed filtering" and "cross validation" testing.

Speed Filtering: After tracking reference corners using the LK model the speed of the object can be estimated by taking the median value from the displacement vector. The displacement vector itself is a vector that represents the distance value between each pairs of points (4).

$$S^t = \{\| c_n^F - c_n^r \|\}_{(n=1...N)} \tag{4}$$

where S^t is the displacement vector at time t, and c_n^F and c_n^r are forward and reference corners respectively.

Having estimated the speed of the object at time $t - 1$ and displacement vector at time t the speed errors E^s can be calculated by

$$E^s = \{\| S_n^t - \text{Md}(S^{t-1}) \|\}_{(n=1...N)}, \tag{5}$$

and a the new probability is assigned to each corner by

$$P^S(C^F) = \begin{cases} 0 \text{ for } E_n^s > \text{Md}(E^s) + \alpha \\ 1 \text{ for } E_n^s \leq \text{Md}(E^s) + \alpha \end{cases} \tag{6}$$

where $P^S(C^F)$ indicates the speed filtering weight function, α is the margin of error and $\text{Md}(E^s)$ is the median function.

Cross Validation Testing: To increase the accuracy of optical flow tracking the forward-backward error [14] is calculated for two consecutive frames. In this process, reference corners are tracked from frame at time t to frame at $t + 1$ (forward test). Next the tracked corners are tracked backward to the frame at time t (backward test). Then a distance error E^V can be calculated for each reference corner using

$$E^V = \{\| c_n^r - c_n^B \|\}_{(n=1...N)}, \tag{7}$$

where E^V is forward-backward error vector. Eventually the forward corners are given the weights by

$$P^V(C^F) = \begin{cases} 0 \text{ for } E_n^V > \epsilon \\ 1 \text{ for } E_n^V \leq \epsilon, \end{cases} \tag{8}$$

where $P^V(C^F)$ is cross validation testing function and ϵ is the maximum distance error.

3.3 Weighting

The cross validation and speed filtering simply eliminate the points that are likely to be in error considering some margin of error. Typically these corners do not handle occlusion well when two or more objects are moving in the same direction and with similar speed. These corners are weighted by the distance of the corners to the centre of the tracking window (central weighting), and by the colour similarity between surrounding patch around each corner and the reference histogram (colour weighting).

Central Weighting: Normally the foreground region is more likely to be at the centre of the window, therefore the corner point near the window's centre should be weighted by a higher value. The distance r of the forward corner from the window centre,

$$r = \{\| W_{center} - c_n^F \|\}_{(n=1...N)} \tag{9}$$

is calculated and the corner is given the central weight,

$$P^C(C^F) = \begin{cases} 0 \text{ for } r_n > W_{radius} \\ \frac{1}{r_n} \text{ for } r_n \leq W_{radius}. \end{cases} \tag{10}$$

Colour Weighting: The final step to build the probability distribution of the object is the colour similarity estimation. This process differs from the traditional histogram matching, which compares the entire tracked window with the reference histogram. The histograms of 7 by 7 patches around forward corners are calculated and compared with the reference histogram using the Bhattacharyya distance [24].

Lower values of Bhattacharyya distance indicate higher similarity, a perfect match is indicated by zero and a total mismatch by one. Thus the inverse value of Bhattacharyya distance is used to weight the corners (11)

$$P^H(C^F) = 1 - \sqrt{1 - \sum_i \frac{\sqrt{H(c_n^F)(i).H_r(i)}}{\sqrt{\sum_i H(c_n^F)(i).H_r(i)}}} \tag{11}$$

where P^H indicate the probability of forward corners after colour matching, $H(c_n^F)$ is the histogram of patches around each corners and i is the bin number.

3.4 Updating

In the updating block all weighted corners are merged together to form a probability image by (12)

$$P = \begin{cases} 0 & \text{if} \quad P_n^{FB} = 0 \vee P_n^S = 0 \vee P_n^C = 0 \vee P_n^H = 0 \\ P_n^{FB} \times P_n^S \times P_n^C \times P_n^H & Otherwise, \end{cases}$$

$$\tag{12}$$

and the reference corners are updated by

$$C^r = \{C_n^F \mid P_n > 0, 0 < n < N\}. \tag{13}$$

Eventually, to locate the new position of window the probability image (P) is fed to a Meanshift. Note if the total number of reference corners is below some pre-defined number, the forward corners can not represent the object well and can result in mistracking. If the model reaches this critical point, the reference corners (C^r) are reinitialized and the process is repeated from the filtering stage. This number is called the fewest possible corners(FPC).

4   Evaluation Methodology

The tracking algorithm was implemented using a C++-based computer vision library (OPENCV) on an Intel (R) core (TM) i7- 4770 @ 3.4 GHz CPU with 16 GB RAM.

In order to detail assessment of the proposed model five challenging videos of horse races are selected and the tracking results are compared with the Meanshift model proposed by Allen et al. [19]. Each video highlights different challenges that are faced in object tracking literature. These challenges can be identified

Table 1. Property of sample videos

Video ID	Duration (Secound)	Frame Size(Pixel)	Frame Rate(fps)	Challenges	Sample Frame
V1	8s	800 × 450	28	C1, C3	
V2	10s	800 × 450	28	C1, C3	
V3	13s	800 × 450	28	C1, C2 C3, C6	
V4	31s	800 × 450	28	C1, C3 C6, C7	
V5	50s	640 × 480	25	C1, C2, C3 C4, C5, C6 C7	

Table 2. The parameter used for the implementation

No.Hue Bin	No.Sturation Bin	Patch Size	ϵ	α	W	FPC
128	128	7 × 7	5	5	40 × 40	15

as light variation (C1), partial occlusion with the background (C2) or the foreground (C3), full occlusion with the background (C4) or the foreground (C5), camera zoom in/zoom out (C6) and angle changes of camera (C7). The properties of the test videos are listed in Table 1. The parameters used in the proposed model are tabulated in Table 2.

To estimate the accuracy of the tracking model, the contenders (i.e. jockeys) at the first quarter (T1), half way (T2), third-quarter (T3) and at the end (T4) of each video were manually selected as ground truth. The contender tracking is considered successful if the centre of the tracking window lays inside the ground truth window. The performance of a tracking algorithm is then measured by

Table 3. Number of total contenders actually present in the frame at the test point.

Video ID	T1	T2	T3	T4
V1	12	12	12	9
V2	12	12	12	12
V3	12	12	12	5
V4	12	12	10	9
V5	9	9	9	9

calculating ratio of successful tracked contenders to the total number of contenders, and is called the percentage of correct tracking (PCT). The number of total contenders actually present in the frame at the test point for five samples shows in Table 3.

5   Result and Discussion

Figure 3 shows the mean PCT for five sample videos and Table 4 tabulates the tracking accuracy based on PCT at the test points. The overall PCT (Fig. 3) clearly indicate that the proposed model improves the tracking accuracy compared to the colour-based Meanshift tracker.

By observing the PCT at each interval (Table 4) it can be observed that Meanshift accuracy significantly drops with respect to time. One main reason behind this drop is change in illumination which cause a shift in significant colours of the object.

The light variation is unpredictable, therefore under light changes the behaviour of Meanshift tracking is also unpredictable. This instability can be clearly seen in V1 and V2 where both cases suffer from same challenges but one result (V2) is comparable to CMC tracker while the other one (V1) is notably lower than CMC.

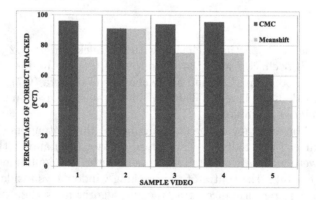

Fig. 3. Mean percentage correct tracking of contenders in the horse races for five sample videos

The partial occlusion is one common problem in all of the video samples. Meanshift tracking has difficulty in handling partial occlusion especially where occlusion happens between two objects with similar colour. The CMC is more robust to occlusion because, first, CMC only uses the colour property around stable corners for the colour matching, therefore it makes objects more recognisable under foreground occlusion, and second CMC estimates the object speed using optical flow, hence it can overcome background occlusion by estimating relative speed of the object with respect to its background (sample V3).

As it can be observed from sample V5 (Table 4) the PCTs of the proposed model is better than Meanshift at the first three intervals, however the Meanshift gives better tracking at the last interval. The reason behind this problem lays in the characteristic of CMC and the challenges in video V5.

Video V5 suffers from one main problem which is full occlusion with other contenders, therefore as contenders fully cover one another, all reference corners are swept from the target and stick to the obstacle. As a result the reference corners are no longer there to represent the desired target and cause false tracking.

Table 4. Results of percentage of correct tracking for both Meanshift and CMC at the test points.

Video ID	T1		T2		T3		T4	
	CMC	Mean shift	CMC	Mean shift	CMC	Mean shift	CMC	Mean shift
V1	100	91	91	75	91	66	100	55
V2	91	91	91	91	91	91	91	91
V3	100	83	91	91	83	66	100	60
V4	100	91	100	81	90	70	88	55
V4	77	55	77	44	55	33	33	44

6 Conclusion

This paper proposed a novel model for multiple object tracking under highly dynamic environment. The tracking accuracy of the model is evaluated by five broadcast videos in four different intervals. The statistical result shows this model improves the accuracy of tracking under occlusion, light variation, size and pose changes by overall PCT average of 27 % respect to colour based Meanshift tracking.

References

1. Maggio, E., Cavallaro, A.: Video Tracking: Theory and Practice. Wiley Publishing, Chichester (2011)
2. Bradski, G.R.: Real time face and object tracking as a component of a perceptual user interface. In: 4th IEEE Workshop on Applications of Computer Vision, pp. 214–219. IEEE Computer Society, Washington (1998)
3. Pérez, P., Vermaak, J., Gangnet, M., Hue, C.: Color-based probabilistic tracking. In: Heyden, A., Sparr, G., Nielsen, M., Johansen, P. (eds.) ECCV 2002, Part I. LNCS, vol. 2350, pp. 661–675. Springer, Heidelberg (2002)
4. Van Gool, L., Nummiaro, K., Koller-Meier, E.: Object tracking with an adaptive color-based particle filter. In: Van Gool, L. (ed.) DAGM 2002. LNCS, vol. 2449, pp. 353–360. Springer, Heidelberg (2002)
5. Isard, M., Blake, A.: Condensationconditional density propagation for visual tracking. Int. J. Comput. Vis. **29**(1), 528 (1998)

6. Comaniciu, D., Visvanathan, R., Meer, P.: Kernel-based object tracking. IEEE Trans. Pattern Anal. Mach. Intell. **25**(5), 564–577 (2003)
7. Hayashi, Y., Fujiyoshi, H.: Mean-shift-based color tracking in illuminance change. In: Visser, U., Ribeiro, F., Ohashi, T., Dellaert, F. (eds.) RoboCup 2007: Robot Soccer World Cup XI. LNCS (LNAI), vol. 5001, pp. 302–311. Springer, Heidelberg (2008)
8. Chandel, H., Vatta, S.: Occlusion detection and handling: a review. Int. J. Comput. Appl. **120**(10), 33–38 (2015)
9. She, K., Bebis, G., Gu, H., Miller, R.: Vehicle tracking using on-line fusion of color and shape features. In: 7th International Conference on Intelligent Transportation Systems, pp. 731–736. IEEE (2004)
10. Zhou, H., Yuan, Y., Shi, C.: Object tracking using SIFT features and mean shift. Comput. Vis. Image Underst. **113**(3), 345–352 (2009)
11. Lucas, B.D., Kanade, T.: An iterative image registration technique with an application to stereo vision. In: 7th International Joint Conference on Artificial Intelligence, pp. 674–679. Vancouver (1981)
12. Bouguet, J.Y.: Pyramidal implementation of the affine lucas kanade feature tracker description of the algorithm. Intel Corporation **5**, 1–10 (2001)
13. Horn, B., Schunck, B.: Determining optical flow. Artif. Intell. **17**, 185203 (1981)
14. Kalal, Z., Mikolajczyk, K., Jiri Matas, J.: Forward-backward error: automatic detection of tracking failures. In: 20th International Conference on Pattern Recognition, pp. 2756–2759. IEEE Computer Society, Washington (2010)
15. Hou, J.Y.Y.H.W., Li, J.: Detection of the mobile object with camouflage color under dynamic background based on optical flow. Procedia Eng. **15**, 2201–2205 (2011)
16. Shi, J., Tomasi, C.: Good Features to Track. Technical Report. Cornell University, Ithaca (1993)
17. Oshima, N., Saitoh, T., Konishi, R.: Real time mean shift tracking using optical flow distribution. In: Joint Conference on SICE-ICASE, pp. 4316–4320. IEEE (2006)
18. Cheng, Y.: Mean shift, mode seeking, and clustering. IEEE Trans. Pattern Anal. Mach. Intell. **17**(8), 790–799 (1995)
19. Allen, J.G., Xu, R.Y., Jin, J.S.: Object tracking using camshift algorithm and multiple quantized feature spaces. In: Proceedings of the Pan-Sydney Area Workshop on Visual Information Processing, pp. 3–7. Australian Computer Society Inc, Darlinghurst (2004)
20. Viola, P., Jones, M.: Robust real-time object detection. Int. J. Comput. Vis. **4**, 51–52 (2001)
21. Fortun, D., Bouthemy, P., Kervrann, C.: Optical flow modeling and computation: a survey. Comput. Vis. Image Underst. **134**, 1–21 (2015)
22. Tuytelaars, T., Mikolajczyk, K.: Local invariant feature detectors: a survey. Found. Trends Comput. Graph. Vis. **3**(3), 177–280 (2008)
23. Kerr, D., Coleman, S., Scotney, B.: Comparing cornerness measures for interest point detection. In: 8th Machine International Confrence on Vision and Image Processing, pp. 105–110. IEEE, Portrush (2008)
24. Kailath, T.: The divergence and bhattacharyya distance measures in signal selection. IEEE Trans. Comm. Technol. **15**, 52–60 (1967)

Rendered Benchmark Data Set for Evaluation of Occlusion-Handling Strategies of a Parts-Based Car Detector

Marvin Struwe[1]([⊠]), Stephan Hasler[2], and Ute Bauer-Wersing[1]

[1] Frankfurt University of Applied Sciences, Frankfurt, Germany
{mstruwe,ubauer}@fb2.fra-uas.de
[2] Honda Research Institute Europe GmbH, Offenbach, Germany
stephan.hasler@honda-ri.de

Abstract. Despite extensive efforts, state-of-the-art detection appro-aches show a strong degradation of performance with increasing level of occlusion. A fundamental problem for the development and analy-sis of occlusion-handling strategies is that occlusion information can not be labeled accurately enough in real world video streams. In this paper we present a rendered car detection benchmark with controlled levels of occlusion and use it to extensively evaluate a visibility-based exist-ing occlusion-handling strategy for a parts-based detection approach. Thereby we determine the limitations and the optimal parameter settings of this framework. Based on these findings we later propose an improved strategy which is especially helpful for strongly occluded views.

Keywords: Object detection · Benchmark data set · Occlusion-handling

1 Introduction

Perception of traffic participants is a fundamental component in driver assistant systems. Despite extensive research visual detection of objects in natural scenes is still not robustly solved. The reason for this is the large appearance variation in which objects or classes occur. A very challenging variation is occlusion which is caused by the constellation of objects in a scene. Occlusion reduces the num-ber of visible features of an object but also causes accidental features. Current object representations show acceptable results during a low to medium level of occlusion but fail for stronger occlusions. Methods like [1,11] train a holistic object template in a discriminative manner and focus resources on differences between classes. This strong specialization on the training problem results in a stronger decrease of performance for occluded objects when trained on unoc-cluded views. In contrast to this parts-based methods like [7,8] accumulate local features in a voting manner. Also when trained with unoccluded views, these methods can handle arbitrary occlusion patterns, but require that sufficiently many features can still be detected. However, in general the voting methods

© Springer International Publishing Switzerland 2016
T. Bräunl et al. (Eds.): PSIVT 2015, LNCS 9431, pp. 99–110, 2016.
DOI: 10.1007/978-3-319-29451-3_9

perform worse than the discriminative ones, whenever test and training set do not show such systematic differences, as discussed in [15] and confirmed by the detection results in [2]. In this paper we want to extensively evaluate visibility-based occlusion-handling strategies for a parts-based detection approach using a rendered benchmark data set.

Some methods make use of context to explicitly deal with occlusion information, i.e. to exploit knowledge about the possible constellation of objects. The two approaches in [4,14] use Markov-Random-Fields to infer if neighboring features are consistent with a single detected instance of an object or have to be assigned to different ones. This allows both approaches to reason about relative depth of objects and to produce a coarse segmentation. However, the process over the whole input image leads to a time consuming iteration. Besides instance-instance relations, also knowledge about general occlusion patterns can be used. In [13] the authors handle vertical occlusion generated by the image border, which means that they have some knowledge about the occlusion constellation. This idea can be extended to the whole image if information about the occluding object is provided.

Occlusion is related to the 3D relation of objects. A general cue of 3D information is depth which can be used to check the physical plausibility of an object's position and size [6] or to segment and put attention to individual scene elements [12]. In [12] temporal differences between RGB-D(epth) views are used to discover movable parts for action representation.

Other strategies make use of 3D annotated data of car views. A common strategy for occlusion-handling is the use of the deformable part model (DPM) [3]. In [10] the 3D annotated data of the KITTI data set [5] is used to generate bounding boxes of the occluder, the occluding object, and their union and for each of the three types a separate DPM is trained. In [16] the authors used hand-annotated 3D CAD models and generated part models additionally to the full car view. A single component DPM detector is trained for each part configuration. To handle occlusion 288 occluder masks are generated for the training data. The approach works not in real time and can handle only occlusion cases which match somehow with the generated occlusion masks.

A parts-based detection approach with explicit occlusion-handling is shown in [9]. For the occlusion-handling depth information is used to determine the visibility of a car hypothesis. This information is used for a re-weighting of the score.

In general most approaches with explicit occlusion-handling make use of information of the occluding object delivered from different methods or sensors. We also want to integrate mask information of the occluding object to reason about visibility of features and to re-weight the activation score of a possible car hypothesis. The occluding mask can be provided in a real system by 3D or depth information. We want to show the limitations and the optimal parameter setting for parts-based detection approaches which provides a mask of the occluding object.

In Sect. 2 we describe how we generated a rendered benchmark data set. Section 3 outlines the used parts-based detection framework. Finally, in Sect. 4

we extensively evaluate a visibility-based occlusion-handling strategy for a parts-based detection approach, before we propose an improved strategy. Finally we are drawing the conclusions and further work in Sect. 5.

2   Rendered Benchmark Data Set

Benchmark data sets like KITTI show precise bounding boxes for objects but do not provide pixel-level information of the constellation of the occlusion, which is quite important to evaluate different occlusion strategies. To get more accurate labeling and a better control of the scene conditions we used a render framework to generate a data set. With the render framework we can define the position of the car, the position of the light source, the intensity of the light, and the angle of rotation of the car. Additionally we can estimate which pixels of the rendered image belongs to which object and can store this information in a mask which is more precise than a bounding box. After rendering we pasted the car models in the center of a car free street scene to get realistic clutter in the background. For our data set we defined the ranges of variation for the parameters for the scene conditions. At the rendering randomly values for the different parameters are used inside the defined ranges. An overview of the different car models with the changing scene conditions can be seen in Fig. 1.

The size of each rendered segment is set to 175×70 which correlates to the optimal size for our car models plus a border. We normalized the size of each car model in a way that the side view covers a given width of the segment. In general parts-based detection approaches are trained to a limited view of rotation of an object. For full rotation several detectors have to be trained. Since we want to concentrate on the evaluation of occlusion-handling strategies we only used side views of cars in a range of 30 degrees of variation at a total side view and omit the rotation handling. We randomly shifted the center position of the car for a better generalization after training. Because we want to evaluate occlusion strategies we use a fixed size for each car. In the upper line of Fig. 2 some segments with cluttered background for the training can be seen. In the bottom line the corresponding masks are shown.

For our data set we used for each car model 400 views. Segments of 44 car models each with 400 views are used for the training set while the other 44 car models each with 400 views are used for the test set. The training set includes non-occluded car views with a segment size of 175×70 pixels.

We generated different test sets with different rates of occlusion. The set with 0 percent of occlusion only shows a car object in the center of a car free street scene. These images were then used with an occluding object to generate test sets with 20, 40, 60, and 80 percent of occlusion. To get a car like shape for the occluding object we used an ellipse shaped patch. Instead a black colored occluding object which is unnatural since it includes no features we cropped patches out of car free street scenes. Figure 3 shows an example for a generated test image and the corresponding masks. For a consistence evaluation of the investigated occlusion-handling approach we also generated occluding constellations without any car. For the training set we generated in total 17600 segments

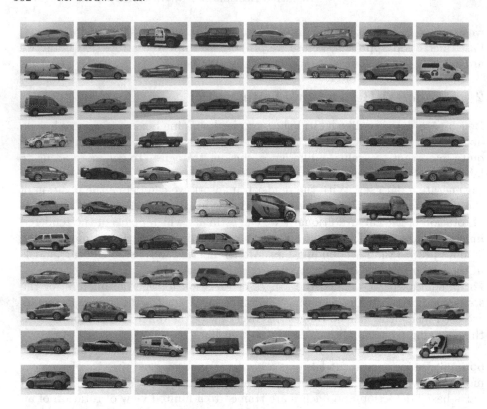

Fig. 1. Data set with different scene conditions: A data set with randomly chosen conditions for light position, light intensity, and angle of rotation is generated.

of un-occluded car views and for the test set 105600 images with different rates of occlusion.

In the next section we will use this data set to train and test our parts-based car detector.

3   Parts-Based Car Detector

Parts-based approaches detect the occurrence of part features over the image where each feature can vote casts for the object center. At the end a confidence map determines plausible detections. In this section we describe which descriptors are used for the features. We also show how the visual feature codebook is build and later used for detection.

3.1   Extraction of Texture Descriptors

Voting methods like [7] use a key point detector to localize interest points in the input image. At these points some texture descriptors are used, e.g. SIFT [8].

Fig. 2. Segments used for training: The upper line shows car segments with a cluttered background while the bottom line shows the corresponding masks.

Fig. 3. Example of the test set: At the left a test image with an occluding ellipse is shown. The two other images show the mask for the background object without any occlusion and the mask of the occluding object, respectively.

We noticed that these points often result only at high textured areas. To handle this drawback we decided to use a dense grid over the image for the extraction of texture descriptors. We tested several distances for the gap between grid points. A gap of 5 pixels shows the best compromise between the number of keypoints and the computing time. After some evaluation we decided to use SIFT descriptor without scaling what means that the receptive field size of 16 pixels correlates with the size of the patches used in the segment. To avoid the extraction of untextured descriptors we use an edge detector with the same size of the receptive field as the descriptor on each grid point. Only patches with corners or edges provide enough texture information to get specific features. We simply check if the resulting patch of the edge detector shows a minimum percentage of marked pixels. Patches that do not achieve this criterion are unselected. With those we can see a threefold reduction of the numbers of features (Fig. 4).

3.2 Learning of Parts-Based Object Representation

The object representation of a parts-based detector is stored in a visual codebook. The codebook includes the features and the relative position to the object's center. One method to build the codebook is to use a clustering method. The resulting clusters are the features of the codebook. Approaches that are trained on natural data use the whole training segment which leads to extraction of descriptors also at the background. These accidental non-car features have to be filtered out which is a challenging task by itself. By using our rendered data we can use the mask information of the object to limit the extraction on the object that should be learned. For training we used the training segments without occlusion. To build the codebook a MiniBatchKMeans clustering is performed.

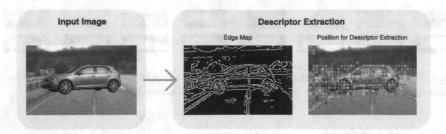

Fig. 4. Extraction of Texture Descriptors: The extraction layer shows the edge map and the resulting position for the descriptor extraction.

In contrast to the normal KMeans this clustering method splits the data into chunks to save memory and computing time.

Figure 5 shows two features of the visual codebook. On the left the so called feature maps are shown which describe the distribution of the occurrence of each stimuli of the codebook cluster. The sum of each feature map is normalized to one. On the right some corresponding stimuli of the descriptor clusters are shown. A well-balanced amount of clusters have to be used to get feature maps that are not too specific but also not too general. Too specific maps show only activations at small compact areas and represent non-generalized training results. Too general maps show a broad distribution of the stimuli and a non-specific training result. In our case 220 clusters provided a good compromise between both criteria. In the next section we show how the codebook is used for detection.

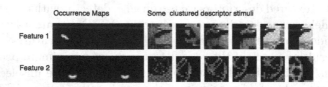

Fig. 5. Example of codebook features: On the left the so called occurrence maps are shown which describe the distribution of the occurrence of each stimuli of the codebook cluster. On the right some corresponding stimuli of the descriptor cluster are shown.

3.3 Parts-Based Detection Framework

In this section we will show a parts-based framework for car detection. First we extract descriptors for the full test image like described in Sect. 3.1. For each descriptor we determine the best matching feature. This feature votes with its occurrence map for the objects' center. An accumulation of all votes of all features at the test image is used to build the activation map. We refer to the accumulated score at each single position with γ (Fig. 6).

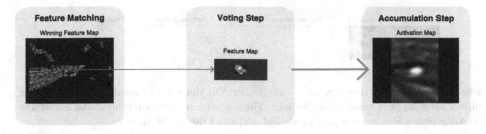

Fig. 6. Detection framework: The winning feature map shows the best matching feature for each pixel. Each feature votes with its occurrence map for the objects' center. An accumulation of all features is used to build the activation map.

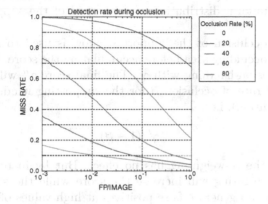

Fig. 7. Detection Performance: The ROC plot shows the detection result of our visibility-based parts-based car detector for five rates of occlusion.

Figure 7 shows the detection performance of this parts-based car detector for 0, 20, 40, 60, and 80 percent of occlusion. A loss in detection performance with an increase of occlusion rate can be seen. Car hypothesis that shows a minimal overlap of 80 percent in the height and 60 percent in the width of the ground truth are marked as detected car.

4 Occlusion-Handling of the Parts-Based Car Detector

As described in Sect. 1 parts-based methods like [9] use an explicit occlusion-handling to re-weight the accumulated score by making use of the predicted visibility of the car hypothesis. Motivated by this we will show a visibility-based occlusion-handling strategy for our parts-based detection framework. Like described before the parts-based approaches use an accumulative step to calculate the score for the car hypothesis. Occlusion will reduce this score. A visibility-based occlusion-handling strategy is to predict the occlusion of an object by

Fig. 8. Uniform contribution for β calculation: On the left the mask of the occluding object for a support window can be seen. The feature contribution map shows a uniform contribution which results in a predicted occlusion rate of 20 percent.

using the mask of an occluding object and to re-weight the score γ by taking the predicted occlusion β into account. For this we use a so called support window. The support window covers the field of the features that potentially contribute to the hypothesis. The support window has the same size like our feature maps. To calculate β a uniform distribution of each pixel of the support window is supposed (Fig. 8).

The predicted occlusion of the support window is used to reject detected features inside the occluding area before accumulating the score. We refer to the score without occlusion-handling with γ'. The final score γ'' will be calculated with the predicted rate of occlusion β for the supporting window (Fig. 9 with (A) for the re-weighting), i.e.

$$\gamma'' = \gamma'/(1 - \beta) \tag{1}$$

If β is 0 than the re-weighting has no effect. But by increasing β at the evaluation the re-weighting will increase the score while the support of γ' is getting lower. This can generate false positives at high values of β. Our goal is to find the maximum value for β that improves the detection performance. So we need a limitation of β up to a defined maximum occlusion rate for the use of the occlusion-handling. To find the optimal value for this limit β_{max} we evaluate the detection performance of our car detector by using values from 0.1 to 0.9 in steps of 0.1 for β_{max}. To see also effect of β_{max} at different rates of occlusion we use occlusion rates of 20, 40, 60, and 80 percent at the evaluation. The detection results can be seen in Fig. 10. For 20 percent occlusion a β_{max} of 0.2 shows the best results while for 80 percent occlusion a β_{max} of 0.5 yields the best results. In general the best detection performance can be seen if β_{max} is equal or in most cases lower than the predicted occlusion rate.

However, the results show that for each occlusion rate another β_{max} has to be used. For a detection system only a fixed β_{max} can be used. So we need an optimal β_{max} for all occlusion rates. To find such a value we plotted the result for the full data set including all occlusion rates for each β_{max} of an occlusion rate. Figure 11(left) shows the best improvements at all occlusion rates by using a β_{max} of 0.2. Figure 11(right) shows an improved detection performance for all occlusion rates by using the determined optimal value of 0.2 for β_{max}. The most gain can be seen at 40 and 60 percent of occlusion.

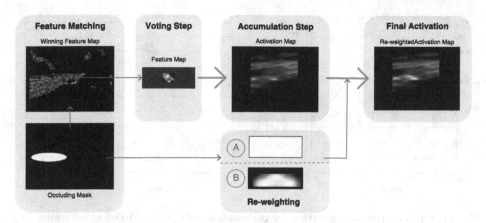

Fig. 9. Detection framework with occlusion-handling strategy: The mask of the occluding object is used to calculate the activation score by deselect the winning features at the occluding area. For the uniform occlusion-handling the re-weighting (A) is used to generate the final score. For the contribution-aware occlusion-handling the re-weighting (B) is used and will be explained in Sect. 4.1.

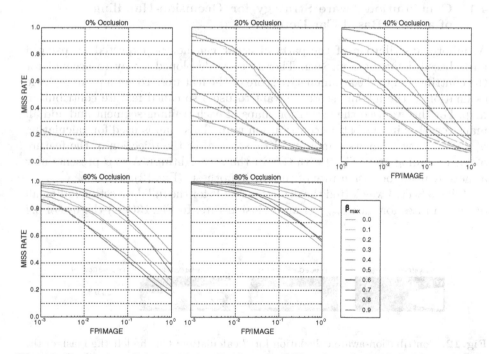

Fig. 10. Evaluation of the Detection Performance: The plots show the detection result for 0, 20, 40, 60, and 80 percent of occlusion separately.

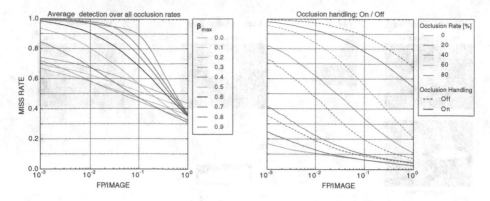

Fig. 11. Optimal parameter setting for occlusion-handling: (Left) Detection result for the full data set including all occlusion rates for each β_{max}. (Right) shows the detection performance for different occlusion rates by using the determined optimal value of 0.2 for β_{max}. The dotted lines show the detection result by using the parts-based car detector without occlusion-handling while the solid lines belong to the detector with uniform occlusion-handling.

4.1 Contribution-Aware Strategy for Occlusion-Handling of a Parts-Based Car Detector

A uniform distribution of the parts of a car can not be expected by using a parts-based detection approach. Therefore we developed a way to account for the contribution to the accumulative score of the features. To get a more realistic estimation of the missing score we want to use a so called feature contribution map. For this we used the activation maps of each training segment and add all maps together in the feature contribution map. This map is used for calculating γ' and β. Now γ' shows a more realistic score after the rejection of the feature of the occluding area (Fig. 9 with (B) for the re-weighting). Also β presents now a more realistic occlusion rate of the car hypothesis (Fig. 12).

Like in Sect. 4 we plotted the detection result for the full data set including all occlusion rates for each β_{max} of an occlusion rate. In Fig. 13(left) the use of 0.4

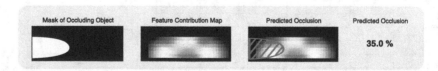

Fig. 12. Contribution-aware calculation for β calculation: On the left the mask of the occluding object for a support window can be seen. The feature contribution map shows a realistic contribution what result in a predicted occlusion rate of 35 percent by covering 20 percent of the area of the supporting window.

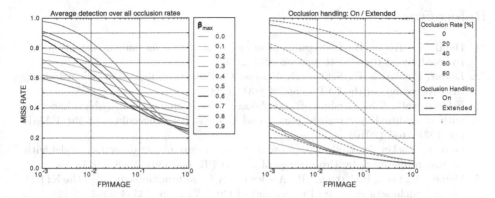

Fig. 13. Optimal parameter setting for contribution-aware occlusion-handling: (Left) Detection result for the full data set including all occlusion rates for each β_{max}. (Right) shows the detection results by using the determined optimal value of 0.4 for β_{max}. The dotted lines show the detection performance using the uniform occlusion-handling while the solid lines results from the contribution-aware occlusion-handling.

for β_{max} shows the best result. We used this β_{max} of 0.4 for the car detector with the contribution-aware occlusion-handling and show the detection performance in Fig. 13(right). The plot shows an improved detection performance at occlusion rates of 40, 60, and 80 percent while a small lost can be seen for 20 percent of occlusion.

5   Conclusion and Further Work

In this paper we introduced a rendered benchmark data set with controlled levels of occlusion and scene conditions. We determined the limitations and the optimal parameter settings of a parts-based car detector by extensively evaluating a visibility-based occlusion-handling strategy. The result of this evaluation is used to configure the car detector, which shows an improved detection performance at all occlusion rates. We also showed an improved strategy for occlusion-handling which boosts the detection performance specially for higher occlusion rates. The proposed occlusion-handling strategies are applicable to other detection approaches that include an accumulation step, like e.g. [3,10]. The results in Fig. 13 show that the detection performance can not be improved for 80 percent of occlusion as much as for 40 and 60 rates of occlusion. A very challenging effect is the number of false positives that are generated at very high levels of occlusion if too strong re-weighting is applied. This limitation of the system can not be solved by the used input information. More scene understanding and information is necessary to have a kind of possibility check to reduce the number of said false positives and to boost the detection performance.

References

1. Dalal, N., Triggs, B.: Histograms of oriented gradients for human detection. In: Proceedings of the CVPR, pp. 886–893 (2005)
2. Dollar, P., Wojek, C., Schiele, B., Perona, P.: Pedestrian detection: a benchmark. In: Proceedings of the CVPR, pp. 304–311 (2009)
3. Felzenszwalb, P.F., Girshick, R., McAllester, D., Ramanan, D.: Object detection with discriminatively trained part based models. In: Proceedings of the PAMI, pp. 1627–1645 (2010)
4. Gao, T., Packer, B., Koller, D.: A segmentation-aware object detection model with occlusion handling. In: Proceedings of the CVPR, pp. 1361–1368 (2011)
5. Geiger, A., Lenz, P., Urtasun, R.: Are we ready for autonomous driving? the KITTI vision benchmark suite. In: Proceedings of the CVPR, pp. 3354–3361 (2012)
6. Gould, S., Baumstarck, P., Quigley, M., Ng, A.Y., Koller, D.: Integrating visual and range data for robotic object detection. In: ECCV Workshop M2SFA2 (2008)
7. Leibe, B., Schiele, B.: Interleaved object categorization and segmentation. In: Proceedings of the BMVC, pp. 759–768 (2003)
8. Lowe, D.G.: Distinctive image features from scale-invariant keypoints. IJCV **60**(2), 91–110 (2004)
9. Makris, A., Perrollaz, M., Laugier, C.: Probabilistic integration of intensity and depth information for part-based vehicle detection. IEEE Trans. Intell. Transp. Syst. **14**, 1896–1906 (2013)
10. Pepik, B., Stark, M., Gehler, P., Schiele, B.: Occlusion patterns for object class detection. In: Proceedings of the CVPR, pp. 3286–3293 (2013)
11. Struwe, M., Hasler, S., Bauer-Wersing, U.: Using the analytic feature framework for the detection of occluded objects. In: Mladenov, V., Koprinkova-Hristova, P., Palm, G., Villa, A.E.P., Appollini, B., Kasabov, N. (eds.) ICANN 2013. LNCS, vol. 8131, pp. 603–610. Springer, Heidelberg (2013)
12. Stückler, J., Behnke, S.: Hierarchical object discovery and dense modelling from motion cues in RGB-D video. In: Proceedings of the IJCAI, pp. 2502–2509 (2013)
13. Vedaldi, A., Zisserman, A.: Structured output regression for detection with partial truncation. In: Proceedings of the NIPS, pp. 1928–1936 (2009)
14. Winn, J., Shotton, J.D.J.: The layout consistent random field for recognizing and segmenting partially occluded objects. In: Proceedings of the CVPR, pp. 37–44 (2006)
15. Yi-Hsin, L., Tz-Huan, H., Tsai, A., Wen-Kai, L., Jui-Yang, T., Yung-Yu, C.: Pedestrian detection in images by integrating heterogeneous detectors. In: IEEE Computer Symposium (ICS), pp. 252–257 (2010)
16. Zia, M.Z., Stark, M., Schindler, K.: Explicit occlusion modeling for 3D object class representations. In: Proceedings of the CVPR, pp. 3326–3333 (2013)

Moving Object Detection Using Energy Model and Particle Filter for Dynamic Scene

Wooyeol Jun(✉), Jeongmok Ha, and Hong Jeong

Department of Electrical Engineering,
Pohang University of Science and Technology (POSTECH),
Cheongam-ro 77, Pohang, South Korea
{wyjun,jmokha,hjeong}@postech.ac.kr

Abstract. We proposed an algorithm that uses an energy model with smoothness assumption to identify a moving object by using optical flow, and uses a particle filter with a proposed observation and dynamic model to track the object. The algorithm is based on the assumption that the dominant motion is background flow and that foreground flow is separated from the background flow. The energy model provides the initial label foreground object well, and minimizes the number of noise pixels that are included in the bounding box. The tracking part uses HOG-3 as an observation model, and optical flow as the dynamic model. This combination of models improves the accuracy of tracking results. In experiments on challenging data set that have no initial labels, the algorithm achieved meaningful accuracy compared to a state-of-the-art technique that needs initial labels.

Keywords: Moving Object Detection · Object tracking · Initial label estimation · Particle filter · Optical flow

1 Introduction

Use of computers to recognize moving objects in a dynamic scene video image is a challenging problem in computer vision. Moving Object Detection (MOD) in dynamic scene is a requirement before deployment of smart cars is feasible. The smart car industry demands accurate MOD in dynamic scene algorithms to detect objects that may pose a danger to a driver or vehicle. However many MOD algorithms cannot satisfy these demands.

The main objective of MOD is to find a moving an object in a video. Several approaches to solve this problem have been suggested: to use a detection algorithm in every video frame; or uses geometry or image feature to cluster background pixels and foreground pixels; or to track an object after it has been detected.

Part-based models assume that an object is a combination of its parts and generate a part model for detection [5]. Detection schemes based on neural networks train their own network to identify features that can be used to detect

© Springer International Publishing Switzerland 2016
T. Bräunl et al. (Eds.): PSIVT 2015, LNCS 9431, pp. 111–122, 2016.
DOI: 10.1007/978-3-319-29451-3_10

a target object [11,18]. However these models consider every object, including immobile ones, and can find only predefined objects such as humans or vehicles.

Some algorithms use homography, or a combination of homography and parallax to find foreground objects [19]. However if a foreground object is relatively large, the background flow is distorted. These algorithms have the serious deficit that they lose detected objects if they stop moving. Some methods try to estimate the feature of a moving object such as motion estimation and appearance model by using information from several image frames [1,3,9,17]. This online background subtraction needs long-term trajectories, and therefore is unsuitable in rapidly-changing conditions. Another method is try to represent background in combinations of image column called low rank representation [2]. This approaches fails when background moves fast or camera moves fast.

Tracking scheme can be divided into pixelwise tracking and objectwise tracking. Pixelwise tracking label every pixel as foreground or background in every frame. Objectwise tracking follow the foreground object as area like bounding box.

Pixelwise tracking schemes combined models of the foreground and of the background. Generalized background subtraction uses motion segmentation to find an initial label and to form foreground and background models for superpixels [4,12,13]. Each model classifies each pixel as foreground or background by matching each pixel to models. However if the initial label contains background pixels, the foreground label spreads out over time. Furthermore if the foreground objects has similar color to backgrounds, the foreground label also spreads out over time. Pixelwise tracking-based algorithms use an initial label assumption to find an object to track. Motion segmentation uses point trajectories for long term observation, and segmentation to detect moving objects [15,16]. These approaches can assign a good initial label but include some background pixels. Detection algorithms use the learned image features to find target object, and the result of detection contains many background pixels.

Objectwise tracking uses dynamic model and observation model to estimate objects position. Estimated objects is compared with the object in previous frame. A particle filter uses samples to track objects [7,8]. The filter assembles samples based on their dynamic models and uses the observation model to find the best matching sample. However if the dynamic model cannot follow an object's motion, tracking fails or if the observation model is ambiguous to given foreground object and background, tracking also fails.

We propose an algorithm that can detect a moving object and track it with low computation cost. Given frames and pixelwise optical flow, we use a smoothing assumption and the distance between foreground and background flow to form an energy function to decouple the moving object label from image. The decoupled initial labels are grouped, and each label is marked with a bounding box.

We used Histogram Of Gradients-3 (HOG-3) which is robust to gradient [10] as a particle filter's observation model to track each bounding box respectively with optical flow dynamic model. Because of it the proposed algorithm can find a stopped object that was previously moving. The main contribution and characteristics of the proposed algorithm are described below.

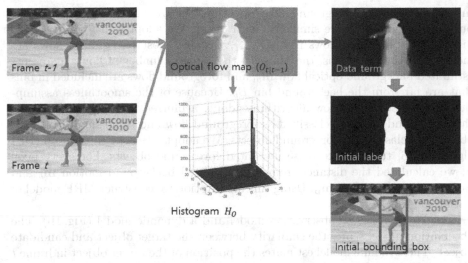

(a) The flow of initial label estimation procedure

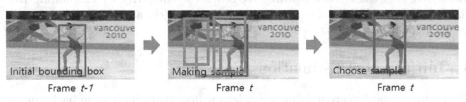

(b) The flow of tracking procedure

Fig. 1. The flow of the proposed algorithm, optical flow map shows the movement vector of pixel in frame $t - 1$. (a) The red box represents estimated initial bounding box. (b) The red box represents tracked bounding box and the blue box represents samples expected to include target object (Color figure online).

1. We used a well-defined energy model to find the initial label of a moving object and to avoid motion smoothing that can cause the initial label to spread out.
2. We used HOG-3 in the particle filter's observation model; use of HOG-3 improves the tracking quality by ensuring that observations are accurate.
3. We apply an optical flow model to a particle filter's dynamic model to estimate the foreground's motion.

2   Overview

The proposed algorithm consists of initial label estimation and tracking (Fig. 1). To estimate the initial label, which we assume to be foreground, we used an optical flow map (Fig. 1a). At time t, optical flow map $\mathbf{O}_{t|t-1}$ for frame $t - 1$ to t is calculated [14]. $\mathbf{O}_{t|t-1}$ consists of background flows and foreground flows.

In our assumption, foreground flows are different from the background flow, but background flows are similar to each other. We adopt a histogram H_O to distinguish foreground flows from $O_{t|t-1}$. Because most background flows are included in the same bins, the bin with the largest number of flows represents estimated background optical flow m_b, and foreground flows are included in bins that are far from the background bin B_b. Because of the smoothness assumption that most optical flow algorithms adopt, a blurred background flow near the foreground object is classified as foreground flow and some small irrelevant objects are classified as foreground objects. We adopt a Belief Propagation (BP) algorithm [6] to eliminate these unwanted foreground objects. For every pixel $\mathbf{p}$, we calculated the distance from the estimated background motion m_b and each pixel's optical flow $m_\mathbf{p}$. Using this assumption we construct MRF model of initial label.

Tracking applies an observation model and a dynamic model (Fig. 1b). The observation model scores the similarity between the target object and candidate object. The dynamic model estimates the position of the target object in frame t using optical flow $O_{t|t-1}$ and target position in frame $t-1$. The observation model calculated uses the HOG-3 feature. We score the similarity by calculating the distance between HOG-3 descriptor for the target object and HOG-3 descriptors for each candidate objects.

3   Initial Label Estimation

We assumed that foreground flow has relevant flow that differs from background flow. We used this assumption to guide construction of a foreground probability map. First, optical flow map $O_{t|t-1}$ for frame $t-1$ to t is calculated. Each pixel $\mathbf{p}$ has its own optical flow $m_\mathbf{p} = O(\mathbf{p})$. Denote background pixel as $\mathbf{p}_b$ and foreground pixel as $\mathbf{p}_f$, then all $m_{\mathbf{p}_b}$ are similar to each other and differ from $m_{\mathbf{p}_f}$.

Second, we construct a histogram of optical flow H_O that has 50×50 bins. Most background optical flows $m_{\mathbf{p}_b}$ are included in one bin B_b and foreground optical flows $m_{\mathbf{p}_f}$ are included in bin that is far from the background flow. A background bin can be estimated as

$$B_b = \Gamma(\arg\max_{\mathbf{m}} H_O(\mathbf{m})), \tag{1}$$

where $\Gamma(\cdot)$ is a function for input $\mathbf{m}$ to output bin that includes $\mathbf{m}$. Estimated background flow is calculated by

$$\overline{m}_b = \Theta(B_b), \tag{2}$$

where $\Theta(\cdot)$ is a function for input bin to output bin's representative value.

Third, use the background flow $\overline{m}_b$ and flow map $O_{t|t-1}$ to we construct a label distribution. By the Bayesian Rule,

$$P(\mathbf{l}|\mathbf{o}) = \prod_{\mathbf{p}} P(o|l)P(l), \tag{3}$$

where o means observation image at pixel $\mathbf{p}$ and l means label at pixel $\mathbf{p}$. We assumed that $p(o|l)$ has a Gaussian distribution

$$P(o|l) = \exp(\frac{-||\mathbf{m_p} - \overline{\mathbf{m}}_b||^2}{2\sigma^2}), \tag{4}$$

where σ means variance. However due to the smoothness assumption, $\mathbf{m}_{\mathbf{p}_b}$ near $\mathbf{p}_f$ is blurred by the foreground flow that is misclassified as $\mathbf{p}_f$. Furthermore, the label for foreground can have hole or disconnection for one object. We used prior information $P(l)$ to prevent these problem. l is assumed to be smooth, big enough and follow image data as

$$P(l) = \exp((1 - 2\eta)(l - l') + \eta), \tag{5}$$

where l' denotes label at neighbor pixel $\mathbf{p}$ and η is a balance constant. Finally, an energy model of initial label problem is defined by

$$\begin{aligned} E &= E_d + E_s \\ &= D^d(\mathbf{m_p}, \overline{\mathbf{m}}_b) + D^s(l, l'), \end{aligned} \tag{6}$$

where $D^d(\mathbf{m_p}, \mathbf{m}_b)$ from Eq. (4) and $D^s(l, l')$ from Eq. (5). To solve this equation, we adopt the BP algorithm and constant message weight. BP refines the smooth area of a foreground label and connects the label for each object. Then we count disconnected labels and surround each label by a bounding box.

4 Tracking

The initial calculated labels contain several background pixels. Other tracking algorithms [4, 12, 13] spread the foreground when the initial label is inaccurate. Our idea follows the particle filter sequence, in which the computation cost is small and a relatively inaccurate initial label is acceptable.

We adopt optical flow to reinforce the sample prior, and the HOG-3 feature to complement the observation model. The particle filter uses weighted samples to estimate the posterior probability $P(x_t|z_{1:t})$ in a sequential Bayesian filtering manner, where x means state and z means observation. By sequential Bayesian filtering,

$$P(x_t|z_{1:t}) = P(z_t|x_t) \int P(x_t|x_{t-1})P(x_{t-1}|z_{1:t-1})dx_{t-1}, \tag{7}$$

where $P(z_t|x_t)$ is the observation model and $\int P(x_t|x_{t-1})P(x_{t-1}|z_{1:t-1})dx_{t-1}$ is the dynamic model. In a tracking manner, we must find the maximum posterior bounding box; i.e., the box in which x is the vector of the top-left pixel and the bottom-right pixel. Therefore every sample represents a bounding box, and a box's posterior means the probability that the box is suitable.

The dynamic model represents their assumed position. For this purpose we used optical flow with a Gaussian assumption. We assumed that most pixels in a bounding box are foreground, and that the average optical flow of a bounding box is foreground optical flow $\mathbf{O}_f$. $\mathbf{O}_f$ is used in the sample prior,

$$P(x_t|x_{t-1}) = \mathcal{N}(\mathbf{O}_f, \Sigma), \tag{8}$$

where $\mathcal{N}(\cdot, \cdot)$ means Gaussian distribution and Σ means variance. When choosing the best sample in the Maximum a Posterior (MAP) rule, we eliminate other samples. Therefore we make samples based on one x_{t-1} sample with that bounding box's optical flow.

A particle filter can use any reasonable observation technique. We adopted HOG-3 feature which generates a histogram of zero-gradients, first-gradients, and second-gradients. The observation model $P(z_t|x)$ can be substituted to

$$P(z_t|x_t^i) = \frac{1}{D(\mathcal{H}(z_{t-1}, \overline{x}_{t-1}), \mathcal{H}(z_t, x_t^i))}, \tag{9}$$

where $D(\cdot, \cdot)$ means distance between the input descriptor, $\mathcal{H}(a, b)$ calculates HOG-3 descriptor of input a cropped by left top of b and right bottom of b, i means index of candidate object, and $\overline{x}_{t-1}$ means the chosen sample in frame $t - 1$. Finally, we choose MAP sample x_t at frame t, remove other samples, and used it as x_{t-1} for the next frame.

5   Experiment

The proposed method was tested in many challenging videos that include fast background motion and complex foreground. We analyze our algorithm quantitatively by comparison to a simple particle filter, and qualitatively compare our algorithm to the state-of-the-art algorithm.

5.1   Experimental Environment

We performed our experiment on a quad core i7-3770CPU @3.40 GHz with 8 GB DDR3 RAM. The algorithms were tested in MATLAB 2015a. To compute dense optical flow maps, we used SIFT flow, which is a state-of-the-art optical flow algorithm [14]. The optical flow map is smooth at the boundary of the foreground and its result can affect the result of our algorithm. We can use any optical flow algorithm but we do not consider this option in our experiment.

The experiment was processed in two environment. The first experiment quantified the tracking accuracy of the proposed algorithm and the particle filter algorithm with changing parameters. The second experiment compared the tracking accuracy of the proposed algorithm qualitatively with that of Generalized background subtraction using superpixels with label integrated motion estimation (GBS-SP) and Generalized background subtraction based on hybrid inference by belief propagation and bayesian filtering (GBS-BP), and showed the characteristics of our algorithm. The proposed algorithm, GBS-SP and GBS-BP

Table 1. Comparison of the proposed algorithm and particle filter. PF represents the particle filter and Ours represents the proposed algorithm. All IOUs are determined by averaging the IOU of the whole frames.

Scenarios	The number of particles n									
	20		50		80		110		140	
	PF	Ours	PF	Ours	PF	Ours	PF	Ours	PF	Ours
skating	0.44	**0.68**	0.50	**0.72**	0.64	**0.74**	0.72	**0.76**	0.74	**0.75**
car1	0.87	**0.88**	0.88	**0.89**	0.88	**0.89**	0.89	**0.90**	0.89	**0.91**
car2	**0.93**	0.84	**0.94**	0.84	0.93	**0.94**	0.86	**0.95**	0.88	**0.96**
people1	0.82	**0.91**	0.87	**0.91**	0.80	**0.88**	0.88	**0.90**	0.88	**0.90**
people2	**0.56**	0.55	0.53	**0.56**	0.59	**0.61**	0.61	**0.62**	0.47	**0.64**
PV person	0.68	**0.69**	**0.66**	0.61	0.67	**0.69**	0.70	0.70	0.69	**0.70**

involve several free parameters. We fixed them for each algorithm in the first experiment, then used the best parameters in the second experiment. In the second experiment, because GBS-SP and GBS-BP does not inform the motion segmentation for the initial label in the paper, we used the ground truth initial label, as in their experiment environment. We also used our initial label for GBS-SP and GBS-BP, which works poorly and compared all of this in qualitative manner. To evaluate the proposed algorithm, we used the proposed video set in GBS-SP and GBS-BP which includes a variety of foreground objects and situations, and real car-embedded camera videos.

5.2 Performance Evaluation for Tracking

We compared our algorithm and particle filters. To evaluate the tracking accuracy we use Intersection of Union (IOU) for frame t as

$$I_t = \frac{area(E \cap G)}{area(E \cup G)} \tag{10}$$

where, E is the estimated bounding box and G is the ground truth bounding box. We calculate IOU of the proposed algorithm and particle filter with a range of sample number n. All IOUs were determined by averaging the IOU of the whole frame. To consider the effect of the proposed observation model and dynamic model, we tested them on a dynamic scene (Table 1). In all of the dataset, the proposed algorithm achieved better IOU than did the particle filter. In skating video that camera and foreground movement was fast, IOU of the proposed algorithm was much larger than that of particle filter. This is because as the scene continues, the particle filter missed the target object (Fig. 2). This result means that the proposed algorithm works well in dynamic scenes and that the model is better than the regular particle filter.

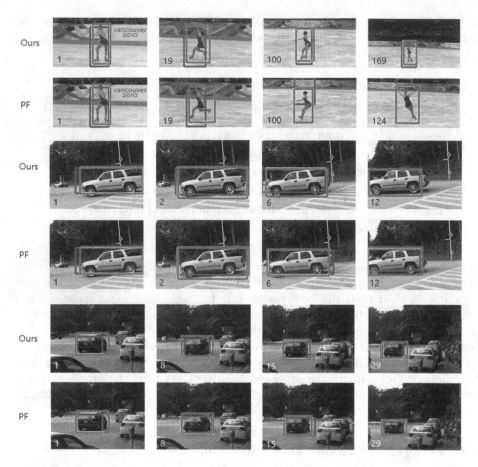

Fig. 2. Comparison with the proposed algorithm and particle filter for *skating*, *car1* and *car2* video. The images in each column represents the tracking result of each algorithm. The blue box represents the ground truth bounding box and the red box represents the tracked bounding box. Notice that the particle filter can not follow the foreground object in *skating* video (Color figure online).

5.3   Performance of Challenging Environment

We compared our algorithm, GBS-SP, and GBS-BP. The proposed algorithm track foreground in a bounding box, whereas GBS-SP and GBS-BP use pixelwise tracking, so quantitative comparison of the two algorithms is impossible. Instead we tested in variety of videos and showed characteristics of the proposed method with regard to GBS-SP and GBS-BP. Because GBS-SP and GBS-BP need a fine initial label, which is hard to pick out in real world scenes, the foreground area is spread out with a smoothed initial label. Furthermore, in a driving environment, the optical flow spreads out from the vanishing point, so the background optical flow will be ambiguous and the color of driving environment similar to foreground object that the foreground area is spread out.

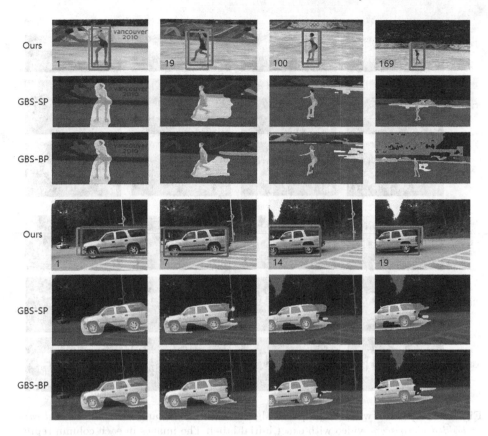

Fig. 3. Comparison with the proposed algorithm, GBS-SP, and GBS-BP for *skating* video with inexact initial label. The images in each column represents the tracking result of each algorithm. The blue box represents the ground truth bounding box and the red box represents the tracked bounding box. Notice that the foreground label of GBS-SP and GBS-BP are spread out over time (Color figure online).

We tested two environments: one with a smoothed initial label and one for a real car-embedded video scene in which the car moves and the foreground is relatively ambiguous. In the smoothed initial label experiment, we used the proposed initial label algorithm and compared the proposed algorithm, GBS-SP and GBS-BP. To compare in the car-embedded camera video data, we used the initial ground truth label to compare each algorithm.

The proposed algorithm followed the object well when the initial label was relatively smooth, whereas GBS-SP and GBS-BP spread the foreground label (Fig. 3). In the car-embedded video scene, our algorithm followed the target well, but GBS-SP and GBS-BP spread out the given ground truth foreground label (Fig. 4). These results mean that in a real car-embedded video scene the proposed method works better than GBS-SP and GBS-BP.

Fig. 4. Comparison with the proposed algorithm, GBS-SP, and GBS-BP for *real car-embedded video scene* video with exact initial label. The images in each column represents the tracking result of each algorithm. The red box represents the tracked bounding box of our algorithm and white area represent the tracked foreground label of GBS-SP and GBS-BP. Notice that the foreground label of GBS-SP and GBS-BP are spread out over time and the proposed method can follow the foreground object well (Color figure online).

6   Conclusions

For MOD, we showed a solution that uses a proposed initial label estimation method and an improved particle filter. The proposed method to estimate initial labels is based on the assumption that the foreground's optical flow differs from the background optical flow. Using this assumption, we proposed a data term for the initial label, and a new energy model for it. The estimated initial label is tracked by the particle filter using the proposed observation model and dynamic model. The proposed method was evaluated on a video set in GBS-SP, GBS-BP, and a challenging car-embedded camera video data. The proposed algorithm achieved higher IOU than the particle filter and in challenging video tracked objects more accurately than did GBS-SP and GBS-BP. When a smoothed initial label is given, the proposed algorithm can track the foreground. The proposed algorithm can used in the challenging problem in smart car industry that need fast and accurate MOD algorithm.

Acknowledgments. This work was supported by the Human Resource Training Program for Regional Innovation and Creativity through the Ministry of Education and National Research Foundation of Korea (NRF-2014H1C1A1066380).

References

1. Brox, T., Malik, J.: Object segmentation by long term analysis of point trajectories. In: Daniilidis, K., Maragos, P., Paragios, N. (eds.) ECCV 2010, Part V. LNCS, vol. 6315, pp. 282–295. Springer, Heidelberg (2010)
2. Cui, X., Huang, J., Zhang, S., Metaxas, D.N.: Background subtraction using low rank and group sparsity constraints. In: Fitzgibbon, A., Lazebnik, S., Perona, P., Sato, Y., Schmid, C. (eds.) ECCV 2012, Part I. LNCS, vol. 7572, pp. 612–625. Springer, Heidelberg (2012)
3. Elqursh, A., Elgammal, A.: Online moving camera background subtraction. In: Fitzgibbon, A., Lazebnik, S., Perona, P., Sato, Y., Schmid, C. (eds.) ECCV 2012, Part VI. LNCS, vol. 7577, pp. 228–241. Springer, Heidelberg (2012)
4. Ess, A., Leibe, B., Gool, L.V.: Depth and appearance for mobile scene analysis. In: IEEE 11th International Conference on Computer Vision, 2007. ICCV 2007, pp. 1–8. IEEE (2007)
5. Felzenszwalb, P.F., Girshick, R.B., McAllester, D., Ramanan, D.: Object detection with discriminatively trained part-based models. IEEE Tran. Pattern Anal. Mach. Intell. **32**, 1627–1645 (2010)
6. Felzenszwalb, P.F., Huttenlocher, D.P.: Efficient belief propagation for early vision. Int. J. Comput. Vis. **70**, 41–54 (2006)
7. Gordon, N., Ristic, B., Arulampalam, S.: Beyond the Kalman Filter: Particle Filters for Tracking Applications. Artech House, London (2004)
8. Haug, A.: A Tutorial on Bayesian Estimation and Tracking Techniques Applicable to Nonlinear And Non-gaussian Processes. MITRE Corporation, McLean (2005)
9. Hayman, E., Eklundh, J.O.: Statistical background subtraction for a mobile observer. In: Ninth IEEE International Conference on Computer Vision, 2003. Proceedings, pp. 67–74. IEEE (2003)
10. Jiang, Y., Ma, J.: Combination features and models for human detection. In: Proceedings of the IEEE Conference on Computer Vision and Pattern Recognition, pp. 240–248 (2015)
11. Krizhevsky, A., Sutskever, I., Hinton, G.E.: Imagenet classification with deep convolutional neural networks. In: Advances in Neural Information Processing Systems, pp. 1097–1105 (2012)
12. Kwak, S., Lim, T., Nam, W., Han, B., Han, J.H.: Generalized background subtraction based on hybrid inference by belief propagation and bayesian filtering. In: 2011 IEEE International Conference on Computer Vision (ICCV), pp. 2174–2181. IEEE (2011)
13. Lim, J., Han, B.: Generalized background subtraction using superpixels with label integrated motion estimation. In: Fleet, D., Pajdla, T., Schiele, B., Tuytelaars, T. (eds.) ECCV 2014, Part V. LNCS, vol. 8693, pp. 173–187. Springer, Heidelberg (2014)

14. Liu, C., Yuen, J., Torralba, A., Sivic, J., Freeman, W.T.: SIFT flow: dense correspondence across different scenes. In: Forsyth, D., Torr, P., Zisserman, A. (eds.) ECCV 2008, Part III. LNCS, vol. 5304, pp. 28–42. Springer, Heidelberg (2008)
15. Mittal, A., Huttenlocher, D.: Scene modeling for wide area surveillance and image synthesis. In: Proceedings of the IEEE Conference on Computer Vision and Pattern Recognition, 2000, vol. 2, pp. 160–167. IEEE (2000)
16. Ochs, P., Malik, J., Brox, T.: Segmentation of moving objects by long term video analysis. IEEE Trans. Pattern Anal. Mach. Intell. **36**, 1187–1200 (2014)
17. Sheikh, Y., Javed, O., Kanade, T.: Background subtraction for freely moving cameras. In: 2009 IEEE 12th International Conference on Computer Vision, pp. 1219–1225. IEEE (2009)
18. Szarvas, M., Yoshizawa, A., Yamamoto, M., Ogata, J.: Pedestrian detection with convolutional neural networks. In: Proceedings of the IEEE, Intelligent Vehicles Symposium, 2005, pp. 224–229. IEEE (2005)
19. Yuan, C., Medioni, G., Kang, J., Cohen, I.: Detecting motion regions in the presence of a strong parallax from a moving camera by multiview geometric constraints. IEEE Trans. Pattern Anal. Mach. Intell. **29**, 1627–1641 (2007)

Logarithmically Improved Property Regression for Crowd Counting

Usman Khan[1]([✉]) and Reinhard Klette[2]

[1] Centre for Advanced Studies in Engineering, Islamabad, Pakistan
usmankhanakbar@gmail.com
[2] Auckland University of Technology, Auckland, New Zealand

Abstract. Crowd counting based on video camera recordings faces two major problems, namely inter-occlusion among the people, and perspective scaling. Though the former issue has been adequately addressed using different regression- and model-based schemes, a solution to the later problem remains an open problem so far. This paper proposes a novel scene-independent solution to perspective scaling. We show that it supports promising results. A property matrix, combining both a grey-level co-occurrence matrix and segmentation properties, is first obtained which is subsequently weighted using logarithmic relationships between pixel distances and foreground regions. We apply a Gaussian process regression, using a compounded kernel, to acquire an estimate for the crowd count. We show that results are comparable to those obtained when using more complex and costly techniques.

Keywords: Crowd counting · Perspective scaling · Grey-level co-occurrence matrix · Gaussian process

1 Introduction

Crowd density estimation of moving humans gains increasing attention in the field of video surveillance due to its importance for crowd statistics, monitoring, crowd control, and security-related observations.

Crowd counts are directly dependent upon pixel regions occupied by the crowd itself [8]; therefore, one commonly used step is *foreground extraction* using segmentation. This process is supported by having stationary cameras. A segmentation step is followed by relevant property or feature extraction tools. (A *property* is a measured value; a *feature* is defined by a location in an image and a property vector [16].) Subsequently, property regression is then used to map extracted properties into a crowd count.

Another technique used for crowd counting is a model-based template matching method [3] in which a template of a human head and shoulder moves across the scene. Most probable matches in the scene are declared as being humans. Both these methods (i.e. property regression and model-based crowd counting) are mainly focused on blob refinement and measurement.

© Springer International Publishing Switzerland 2016
T. Bräunl et al. (Eds.): PSIVT 2015, LNCS 9431, pp. 123–135, 2016.
DOI: 10.1007/978-3-319-29451-3_11

In the property-regression technique, perspective distortion is catered for by using two basic methods. The first method is scene-specific perspective correction based on a linear perspective-map formulation, whereas in the second method low-level features have been used. In both cases, the feature set or the property vector expand at a level where the complexity of property regression escalates exorbitantly, resulting in over-fitting. On the other hand, template scaling for the head-shoulder template-matching scheme is also confined to a specific scenario, and needs to be redefined for different scenes. Consequently, researchers have been adopting more complex methods to achieve better estimates.

The paper is structured as follows: Sect. 2 provides a brief review of related work. Section 3 outlines the proposed approach. Section 3.1 elaborates the usefulness of the selected textural feature set based on a *grey-level co-occurrence matrix* GLCM. In Sect. 3.2, techniques defined elsewhere used for segmenting extracted features, including the ViBe algorithm and the optical flow method, are briefly introduced. Section 3.3 proposes our novel approach adopted in this work for the correction of perspective distortion. Gaussian process regression, using a compounded kernel, is detailed in Sect. 4. Section 5 provides an experimental evaluation of the proposed approach, including a comparison of our algorithm with some benchmark techniques. Section 6 concludes.

2   Literature Review

The crowd estimation problem is mainly handled as a classification problem where crowd density is categorised as being low, medium, or high. A well-known example of crowd-density estimation [18] is by applying improved local binary patterns for obtaining a histogram of the considered crowd, for comparing it against model histograms by calculating their inter-distance. This supports categorising the crowd as being of very low, low, medium, high, or very high density. Crowd-count estimation, on the other hand, is a tedious problem which focuses mainly on accurately counting the number of people making up the given crowd. This problem is mainly tackled in one of the following three ways:

1. *Counting by detection* uses a visual object detector which segments individual objects of interest. Reference [11] shows a unique crowd-segmentation method which uses Fourier descriptors for shape indexing of crowd blobs while [22] uses a generic head detector to segment and count the number of people making up the crowd.
2. *Counting-by-regression* methods do not consider solving the task by a detection of individual objects. In these methods, the number of object counts is learnt mainly through a supervised learning methodology [21]. The main interest of this technique lies in the number of people determined by foreground pixels. Regression-based techniques involve background segmentation followed by foreground-property measurements (e.g. the area of regions, or texture characteristics) and then using linear, Bayesian, support vector machine (SVM), or neural-network regression techniques to learn the human

count. An example of regression counting is reference [6] where neural-network regression is applied.

Another distinguished technique is Chan's method; for example, see [18]. Here, the problem of counting people in a moving crowd is addressed by using a Poisson regression in a Bayesian framework over low-level features extracted from the images. A crowd count is taken as an outcome of a linear function by presenting a prior distribution on the weights of selected low-level features.

In [12], the perspective distortion problem has been addressed by assigning linear weights to the *scale-invariant feature transform* (SIFT) based on interest points at different locations in the image. These weights are assigned with respect to the ratio between height of a reference individual at two different locations in the video. Subsequently, Gaussian process regression is used to map interest points into a people count.

3. A *hybrid method* uses both detection and regression techniques. For example, [20] focuses on the fact that each blob in a crowd at a different perspective should be dealt with separately. Weights are assigned to each pixel based on a perspective plot. Multiple feature extraction is the second step after which each feature is assigned a different weight based on least-square regression. An *artificial neural network* (ANN) is used to obtain a number-of-people count in each blob based on distinct features and corresponding weights assigned.

3 Proposed Approach

Our approach focuses on crowd counting by regression. It presents a novel and natural solution to the problem of perspective distortion, thereby improving results by keeping time complexity of the regression algorithm at a low level.

For counting moving people, a set of textural and geometric segment features is extracted from each frame of a video sequence. Foreground segmentation of moving people is obtained using optical flow (for an original paper, see [15], or for a recent text on optic flow, see [16]) and a variant of the ViBe algorithm [2,5]. This allowed us to improve the handling of illumination invariance, "foreground erosion", and "stationary object blindness", all known as being issues in this area. Segmentation is further improved by using morphological dilation and erosion. A fundamental segmentation feature, which is directly proportional to the crowd count, is the foreground area. Logarithmic perspective correction is applied to the foreground blob area-property with respect to its centroid location in the image. Thereafter, this property set is mapped to the crowd count using a Gaussian process regression.

The proposed method outperforms methods presented in [1,9,10,12,20] in terms of simplicity of selected features, clustering method, perspective correction, and, altogether, better results.

3.1 Textural Feature Selection

Textural content descriptors provide useful information about distinguishing characteristics of an image such as coarseness, homogeneity, or smoothness.

Gonzalez [14] categorises approaches of textural analysis or synthesis into three main classes, called structural, spectral, or statistical. [23] added a model-based class to the three classes mentioned by Gonzalez. We decided for a statistical approach, and the textural features, chosen to obtain accurate estimates of crowd counts, are derived from a *grey-level co-occurrence matrix* (GLCM). A GLCM elaborates the frequency and combination of pixels with different brightness values (e.g., see the text [16]). Common GLCM features are defined with respect to contrast, homogeneity, energy, or correlation.

3.2   Geometric Feature Extraction for Segments

Foreground segmentation of the images is carried out by using two different sets of algorithms, including background subtraction and image foreground clustering algorithms. ViBe and optical flow are the two background subtraction algorithms, whereas *Gaussian mixture model* (GMM), k-means clustering, adaptive GMM, and *hidden Markov model and expectation maximisation* (HMM-EM) frameworks have been used to classify the foreground into distinct clusters. Experimentally it was observed that the background subtraction algorithms provided faster segmentation owing to lesser complexity and comparatively better results.

GMM Segmentation. GMM-based segmentation [17] distributes the image into a set of different classes, assuming that each class can be modelled as a normal distribution with a separate mean and variance. This assumption, though not accurate, provides a fairly reasonable segmented image as shown in Fig. 1, using an image from the PETs 2009 dataset [13].

Fig. 1. Foreground segmentation using GMM for a sample from PETS 2009

Optimum result obtained for this sample of the PETs 2009 dataset is by using four classes. The algorithm does not need to be trained using background images. Segmentation results are obtained directly without the need of background subtraction. However, some of the background is still being classified as human blobs. Another problem with the algorithm is that for each new scene, a number of classes is required to be set separately, and processing time increases with an increase in the number of classes.

ViBe Segmentation. A ViBe algorithm does not rely on one particular pixel distribution assumption such as for the GMM. It results in faster processing, provides illumination invariance by uniformly updating a background model, and has reduced mathematical complexity. Classification of a pixel as foreground or background in ViBe is based on the simple criteria of considering a disk of specified radius around the current pixel and determining the cardinality of the set of pixel values arising from intersecting the disk in the image with the disk at the same location in the background model.

Fig. 2. Foreground segmentation using a ViBe algorithm. *Left*: Input sample from PETS 2009. *Right*: Segmentation result using a ViBe algorithm

To ensure intensity invariance and ghost suppression, a background pixel model is updated randomly using a uniform distribution. The erosion of the foreground is suppressed by disallowing an already declared foreground pixel in the current frame to become a part of the background in the next frame. Finally, morphological operations [14], including opening, closing and hole filling, are used to ensure the desired level of foreground segmentation. See Fig. 2 for an example.

HMM-EM Algorithm Based on GMM and k-Means Clustering. Taking its lead from segmentation of human brain images, the HMM-EM framework proposed in [25] is an edge-prior preserving segmentation algorithm which was also used for obtaining accurate segmentation labels for the PETS-2009 dataset. In this algorithm, an initial segmented image is obtained using k-means clustering or GMM with estimated parameters including mean and variance. Subsequently, these estimates are then refined using the HMM-EM framework.

The algorithm was tested for a number of classes starting from 2 to 8. See Fig. 3 for an example.

Optical Flow Segmentation. For segmentation using optical flow, we apply the original Horn-Schunck algorithm [15]. Optic flow is the relative motion of

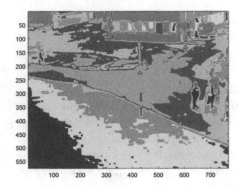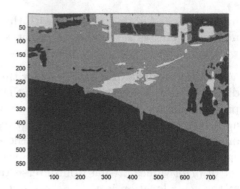

Fig. 3. Image segmentation using the HMM-EM framework. *Left*: Initial segmentation obtained using k-means clustering. *Right*: Initial segmentation obtained using GMM clustering

visible texture w.r.t. an observer in time and space. For calculating optic flow, the Horn-Schunck algorithm uses the *intensity constancy assumption* (ICA, see [16]) that reflectance is directly proportional to surface brightness, and also that surface brightness varies continuously with time. It is known that these assumptions are limiting the accuracy of calculated optic flow, especially the ICA is harmful. However, the Horn-Schunck algorithm is time-efficient and proved to be sufficient for our purpose.

Fig. 4. Foreground segmentation using optical flow. *Left*: Input sample from the PEDS dataset. *Right*: Segmented foreground

In our experiments with data of the PEDS database [24], foreground segmentation was obtained by applying a threshold to the minimum optical flow magnitudes at a pixel in both directions. We decided for a value of 3 as a threshold for flow velocities u and v in both x and y directions (i.e. $u > 3$ and $v > 3$); this produced the desired results. For an example, see Fig. 4.

Neither ViBe nor optical flow-based segmentation provide accurate segments of visible persons. However, this is also not required for the considered application as we will verify below.

3.3 Perspective Correction

Properties of fundamental importance, drawn from the segmented foreground, are blob area and perimeter. Due to the camera pose, an individual blob entering from one side of the image and traveling to the other side, suffers from shortening of both height and width which is a result of perspective distortion. This problem has been treated as a linear problem in previous work such as in [7,8,12,20] by taking into account height-to-distance ratios to cater for perspective distortion. However, a perspective linearization approach is not scene-independent, which means that for each new scenario, camera calibration is required again. Moreover, the formulation of an inherently nonlinear problem as a linear problem is an inappropriate simplification which causes errors in the final result.

Another method, which can be used to correct perspective distortion in images, is camera calibration [4]. This method involves a conversion from the 2D camera plane into the 3D real world. The complexity of the approach requires extra processing power despite followed optimisation efforts, thus making it unsuitable for real-time applications. This method has basically not been adopted into crowd-counting algorithms.

The *inverse square law* explains the relationship between the intensity of light and the distance of a point-light source from an object which is being illuminated by this light source. The *Weber-Fechner law* (identified as being a psycho-physical law) is another important relationship between human eye intensity response and contrast sensitivity. These two laws have been tested to automate perspective correction. Experiments have shown that a Weber-Fechner law implementation provides far better results compared to the inverse square law. The perspective scaling problem has been modelled in terms of logarithmic ratios as follows:

$$R_D = \sqrt{R_{IO}^2 + R_{IA}^2} \tag{1}$$

$$A_{corr} = \frac{A_{blob}}{\log C_{blob}} \log R_D \tag{2}$$

$$P_{corr} = \frac{P_{blob}}{\log C_{blob}} \log R_D \tag{3}$$

where, R_{IO} is the reference image ordinate, R_{IA} the reference image abscissa, R_D the reference distance, A_{blob} and P_{blob} are the blob area and perimeter. C_{blob} is the distance of the blob centroid from the reference point. Obtained corrected area and perimeter variables are A_{corr} and P_{corr}, respectively.

First a reference blob is selected. The distance from a specified reference point in the image, preferably from a corner point to the reference blob's centroid, is then used as the *reference distance*. In the second step, distances are calculated from the selected reference point to centroids of the remaining blobs in the scene, and we call those *blob-centroid distances*. A logarithmic ratio between the reference distance and a blob-centroid distance provides a weighted factor which can scale blob area or perimeter, basically normalising a blob's size to the selected reference blob's centroid location. This is equivalent to shifting foreground blobs to the same location, thereby, removing perspective distortion (Fig. 5).

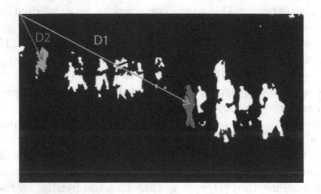

Fig. 5. D_1: Distance of the reference blob from the reference point, selected to be the image origin. D_2: Distance of another blob to the reference point selected to be the image origin. *Perspective correction:* The logarithmic ratio between D_1 and D_2 provides the required factor which is used for perimeter and area correction of the segmented blobs, i.e. virtually shifting blobs to the reference point.

4   Gaussian Process Regression with Compounded Kernel

After a representing property set is obtained for a given image I_i, it is mapped into a $D \times 1$ input vector $\mathbf{x}_i$, where D is the dimension of the collected property set. The goal is to design a function f which, if applied to the input property vector, provides the desired crowd count y_i for the given image [19]:

$$y_i = f(\mathbf{x}_i) + \varepsilon \tag{4}$$

with some error tolerance ε.

In generalisation, a set of vectors $\mathbf{x}_i$, obtained for a sequence $I_1, \ldots, I_n$ of n images, is collected into a matrix $\mathbf{X}$ of dimension $D \times n$, and we want to estimate

$$\mathbf{y} = [y_1, \ldots, y_n]^\top = f(\mathbf{X}) + \varepsilon \tag{5}$$

In case of linear regression, the function f can be expressed in terms of a weight vector as follows:

$$f(\mathbf{x}_i) = \mathbf{x}_i^\top \mathbf{w} \tag{6}$$

A Bayesian treatment of the above mentioned regression problem, applying a Gaussian distribution, assumes that noise is independent and identically distributed (i.e. Gaussian noise with zero mean and variance σ_n^2).

The likelihood of an observation is mutually independent, i.e. we have that

$$p(\mathbf{y}|\mathbf{X}, \mathbf{w}) = \prod_{i=1}^{n} p(y_i|\mathbf{x}_i, \mathbf{w}) \tag{7}$$

The weight vector has zero mean with a covariance matrix $\mathbf{Q}$.

With these assumptions the posterior distribution of the weight vector $\mathbf{w}$ is as follows:

$$p(\mathbf{w}|\mathbf{y}, \mathbf{X}) = \frac{p(\mathbf{y}|\mathbf{X}, \mathbf{w})p(\mathbf{w})}{p(\mathbf{y}|\mathbf{X})} \tag{8}$$

$$p(\mathbf{w}|\mathbf{y}, \mathbf{X}) = N(\mathbf{w} = \frac{1}{\sigma_n^2}\mathbf{A}^{-1}\mathbf{X}\mathbf{y}, \mathbf{A}^{-1}) \tag{9}$$

$$\mathbf{A} = \sigma_n^2 \mathbf{X}\mathbf{X}^\top + \mathbf{Q} \tag{10}$$

Therefore, a predictive distribution of values of f, for a set of property vectors $\mathbf{x}$, can be written as follows:

$$p(f|\mathbf{x}, \mathbf{X}, \mathbf{y}) = N(\frac{1}{\sigma_n^2}\mathbf{x}^\top \mathbf{A}^{-1}\mathbf{X}\mathbf{y}, \mathbf{x}^\top \mathbf{A}^{-1}\mathbf{x}) \tag{11}$$

The defined property-vector matrix $\mathbf{X}$ needs to be projected to a higher-dimensional property space using an unknown basis function $\phi_{\mathbf{x}}$ which converts a D-dimensional property vector into an N-dimensional array. Therefore, the model for f can be expressed in terms of $\phi_{\mathbf{x}}$ as follows:

$$p(f|\mathbf{x}, \mathbf{X}, \mathbf{y}) = N(\frac{1}{\sigma_n^2}\phi_{\mathbf{x}}^\top \mathbf{A}^{-1}\phi_{\mathbf{X}}\,\mathbf{y}, \phi_{\mathbf{x}}^\top \mathbf{A}^{-1}\phi_{\mathbf{x}}) \tag{12}$$

The basis function is unknown; however, fortunately there is no need to find the exact basis function. Instead the kernel trick is used to obtain the best possible approximation of a predictive distribution f. We suppose that $\mathbf{K}$ is the kernel matrix on the unknown basis function matrix $\phi_{\mathbf{X}}$. For the property vector basis function $\phi_{\mathbf{x}}$ it is represented as $\mathbf{k}$. With the help of kernel trick, instead of utilizing the property vector for functional prediction, approximation of the kernel is used instead. After a few mathematical manipulations of Eq. (12), $\mathbf{K}$ is represented as

$$\mathbf{K} = \phi_{\mathbf{X}}\,\mathbf{Q}\,\phi_{\mathbf{X}}^\top \tag{13}$$

$$\mathbf{k} = \phi_{\mathbf{x}}\,\mathbf{Q}\,\phi_{\mathbf{x}}^\top \tag{14}$$

Let $\mathbf{X}^*$ be the test set property matrix for the training set matrix $\mathbf{X}$, and let $\mathbf{I}$ be the identity matrix. The training and test set property matrices contain property vectors for each image arranged in columns. For the property matrices, the predictive distribution of the output vector $\mathbf{f}$, containing the desired crowd count, can be represented as follows:

$$\begin{aligned}
p(\mathbf{f}|\mathbf{x}, \mathbf{X}, \mathbf{y}) = N\big[&\mathbf{K}(\mathbf{X}^*, \mathbf{X})[\mathbf{K}(\mathbf{X}, \mathbf{X}) \\
&+ \sigma_n^2 \mathbf{I}]^{-1}\mathbf{y}, \mathbf{K}(\mathbf{X}^*, \mathbf{X}^*) \\
&- \mathbf{K}(\mathbf{X}^*, \mathbf{X})[\mathbf{K}(\mathbf{X}, \mathbf{X}) \\
&+ \sigma_n^2 \mathbf{I}]^{-1}\mathbf{K}(\mathbf{X}, \mathbf{X}^*)\big]
\end{aligned} \tag{15}$$

The kernel function can be a single covariance function, or a combination of covariance functions. In this work, a compounded kernel function has been used. To cater for local and global nonlinear trends, a sum of constant, linear and exponential covariance functions has been used to formulate a compounded kernel:

$$k(x, x^*) = \sigma_0{}^2 + \sum_{i=1}^{D} \sigma_i^2 x_i x_i^* \exp \frac{-||x_i - x_i^*||}{2l^2} \tag{16}$$

In order to estimate the best possible hyper-parameters σ_0^2, σ_i^2, and $\bar{x}$, and the characteristic length scale l, maximum likelihood estimation is used by maximising the logarithmic function

$$\begin{aligned}
\log p(\mathbf{f}|\mathbf{X}) = &-\frac{1}{2}\mathbf{y}^\top (\mathbf{K} + \sigma_n^2 \mathbf{I})^{-1}\mathbf{y} \\
&- \frac{1}{2}\log |\mathbf{K} + \sigma_n^2 \mathbf{I}| - \frac{n}{2}\log 2\pi
\end{aligned} \tag{17}$$

Maximum likelihood estimation provides the best possible estimate for the unknown hyper parameters. For relevant details, see [19].

5   Experiments and Results

In order to evaluate the algorithm, experiments were conducted on two different datasets, the PETS 2009 dataset and the Peds-1 dataset, with an intention to establish scene-independence for the algorithm.

For both datasets, half of the frames have been used for training purpose whereas the other half has been used for testing. The training set of images has been annotated by manual counting. The testing part remained fully automated with no requirement of manual interaction for specifying a *region of interest* (ROI), to segment a scene into different regions, or any linear interpolation for scene-specific perspective corrections or separate identifications of pedestrians walking towards or away from the camera. This, altogether, characterises our algorithm as being automated in distinction to benchmark techniques published in [7–9,12].

Figure 6, left, reports about a comparison between estimated crowd count and ground truth using the Peds-1 dataset. The ground truth or actual crowd count is indicated by green markers whereas the estimated count is shown by red dots. For obtaining a better idea about acquired result validity, mean square

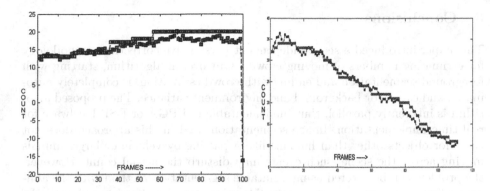

Fig. 6. Comparisons between ground truth and estimated counts (green dots represent ground truth, red dots represent estimated results). *Left:* PEDS dataset results. *Right:* PETS 2009 dataset results (Color figure online)

error, mean relative error, and mean absolute errors have been calculated using the proposed algorithm. The results are comparable to [7] but better than those reported in [12].

By using the logarithmic perspective scaling, *Gaussian process regression* (GPR) based crowd estimation results have improved compared to [7]. The minimum MSE obtained for the *scene motion class* in [7] is 3.654 using GPR, whereas by using the proposed algorithm, the MSE has been reduced to 3.093 which is comparable to 2.910, the result obtained when using a more complex *Bayesian Poisson regression* (BPR) method and a *digital terrain model* (DTM) segmentation in [7].

PET-2009 dataset results (i.e. manually annotated ground truth versus estimated count) are shown in Fig. 6, right. The red dots show estimated counts whereas the green dots represent the ground truth which has been manually annotated. The performance for the PETS-2009 dataset was also evaluated using mean-square error, mean absolute error, and mean relative error. See Table 1, which also summarises comparisons against benchmark methods.

Table 1. Examples of results

Error type	Mathematical notation	PETS 2009	Hajer Fradi	PEDS-1 (GPR)	*Chan's* (BPR)
MSE	$\frac{1}{N}\sum_{i=1}^{N}(EC_i - GT_i)^2$	1.422	-	3.093	2.910
MRE	$\frac{1}{N}\sum_{i=1}^{N}\frac{(EC_i - GT_i)^2}{GT_i}$	0.046	0.071	0.079	-
MAE	$A\frac{1}{N}\sum_{i=1}^{N}\frac{|EC_i - GT_i|}{GT_i}$	0.951	1.38	1.458	1.308

6   Conclusions

This paper introduced a scene-independent perspective correction methodology for estimating numbers of moving crowds. Our overall algorithm, starting with foreground segmentation and ending with crowd estimation, is completely automated and caters for background and environment variance. The proposed algorithm is inherently parallel, thus implementable in FPGA or DSP hardware for real-time implementation. Image segmentation used in this approach does not cater for objects other than humans like a passing-by vehicle or large animals moving across the scene; such events may disturb the actual count. However, the problem can be catered using a suitable segmentation method with the ability to filter out unnecessary objects. The algorithm has been tested with the reported results on pedestrians moving on a road with negligible traffic, and can be recommended for comparable scenarios.

References

1. Albiol, A., Silla, M.J., Albiol, A., Mossi, V.: Video analysis using corner motion statistics. In: Proceedings of IEEE International Workshop PETS, pp. 31–37 (2009)
2. Barnich, O., Droogenbroeck, M.: ViBe: A universal background subtraction algorithm for video sequences. IEEE Trans. Image Process. **20**, 1709–1724 (2011)
3. Fu, H., Ma, H., Xiao, H.: Real-time accurate crowd counting based on RGB-d information. In: Proceedings of ICIP, pp. 2685–2688 (2012)
4. Beardsley, P., Murray, D.: Camera calibration using vanishing points. Int. J. Comput. Vis. **4**, 127–139 (1992)
5. Barnich, O., Droogenbroeck, M.M.V., Paquot, O.: Background subtraction: experiments and improvements for ViBe. In: Proceedings of CVPR Workshop Change Detection, pp. 32–37 (2012)
6. Garcia-Bunster, G., Torres-Torriti, M., Oberli, C.: Crowded pedestrian counting at bus stops from perspective transformations of foreground areas. Comput. Vis. IET **6**, 296–305 (2012)
7. Chan, A., Vasconcelos, N.: Counting people with low-level features and Bayesian regression. IEEE Trans. Image Process. **21**, 2160–2177 (2012)
8. Chan, A.B., Liang, Z.S.J., Vasconcelos, N.: Privacy preserving crowd monitoring: counting people without people models or tracking. In: Proceedings Computer Vision Pattern Recognition, pp. 1–7 (2008)
9. Chan, A.B., Morrow, M., Vasconcelos, N.: Analysis of crowded scenes using holistic properties. In: IEEE International Workshop Performance Evaluation Tracking Surveillance (2009)
10. Conte, D., Foggia, P., Percannella, G., Tufano, F., Vento, M.: A method for counting people in crowded scenes. In: Proceedings of IEEE International Conference Advanced Video Signal Based Surveillance, pp. 225–232 (2010)
11. Dong, L., Parameswaran, V., Ramesh, V., Zoghlami, I.: Fast crowd segmentation using shape indexing. In: Proceedings International Conference Computer Vision, pp. 1–8 (2007)
12. Fradi, H., Dugelay, J.L.: People counting system in crowded scenes based on feature regression. In: Proceedings of European Signal Processing Conference, pp. 27–31 (2012)

13. Fraile, R.: IEEE International Workshop Performance Evaluation Tracking Surveillance (PETS 2009) (2009). www.cvg.reading.ac.uk/PETS2009/
14. Gonzales, R.C., Wintz, P.: Digital Image Processing, 3rd edn. Prentice Hall, Upper Saddle River (2009)
15. Horn, B.K.P., Schunck, B.G.: Determining optical flow. Artif. Intell. **17**, 185–203 (1981)
16. Klette, R.: Concise Computer Vision. Springer, London (2014)
17. Lalit, G., Thotsapon, S.: A Gaussian-mixture-based image segmentation algorithm. Pattern Recogn. **31**(3), 315–325 (1998)
18. Mousavi, S.M., Shahdi, S.O., Abu-Bakar, S.A.R.: Crowd estimation using histogram model classification based on improved uniform local binary pattern. Int. J. Comput. Electr. Eng. **4**, 256–259 (2012)
19. Rasmussen, C.E., Williams, C.K.I.: Gaussian Processes for Machine Learning. MIT Press, Cambridge (2006)
20. Ryan, D., Denman, S., Fookes, C.: Crowed counting using multiple local features. In: Proceedings of Digital Image Computing: Techniques Applications, pp. 81–88 (2009)
21. Shimosaka, M., Masuda, S., Fukui, R., Mori, T., Sato, T.: Counting pedestrians in crowded scenes with efficient sparse learning. In: Proceedings of Asian Conference Pattern Recognition, pp. 27–31 (2011)
22. Subburaman, V.B., Descamps, A., Carincotte, C.: Counting people in the crowd using a generic head detector. In: Proceedings of IEEE International Conference Advanced Video Signal-Based Surveillance, pp. 470–475 (2012)
23. Tuceryan, M., Jain, A.K.: Texture analysis. In: The Handbook of Pattern Recognition and Computer Vision, pp. 207–248 (1998)
24. UCSD: UCSD Anomaly Detection Dataset (2013). http://www.svcl.ucsd.edu/projects/anomaly/dataset.htm
25. Wang, Q.: HMRF-EM-image: implementation of the hidden Markov random field model and its expectation-maximization algorithm, arXiv: 1207.3510 [cs.CV] (2012)

Lesioned-Part Identification by Classifying Entire-Body Gait Motions

Tsuyoshi Higashiguchi, Toma Shimoyama, Norimichi Ukita$^{(\boxtimes)}$,
Masayuki Kanbara, and Norihiro Hagita

Nara Institute of Science and Technology, Ikoma, Japan
ukita@is.naist.jp

Abstract. This paper proposes a physical motion evaluation system based on human pose sequences estimated by a depth sensor. While most similar systems measure and evaluate the motion of only a part of interest (e.g., knee), the proposed system comprehensively evaluates the motion of the entire body. The proposed system is designed for observing a human motion in daily life in order to find the sign of aging and physical disability. For daily use, in this paper, we focus on walking motions. Walking motions with a variety of physical disabilities are recorded and modeled for classification purpose. This classification is achieved with a set of pose features extracted from walking motion sequences. In experiments, the proposed features extracted from the entire body allowed us to identify where a subject was injured with 81.1 % accuracy. The superiority of the entire-body features was also validated in estimating the degree of lesion in contrast to local features extracted from only a body part of interest (77.1 % vs 65 %).

Keywords: Gait motion · Entire-body motion · Lesioned part · Depth sensor · 3D human pose

1 Introduction

The number of people suffering from chronic diseases is constantly rising. Today, more than three quarters of the elderly population are suffering from chronic diseases, independent of the economic, social, and cultural background [21]. Such diseases can be possibly avoided or decreased if people often undergo a medical examination and find the early symptoms of these diseases [3]. It is, however, difficult for most people to frequently have supports by experts such as medical doctors and therapists. While complete diagnosis systems must be able to find a variety of diseases, we focus on the physical fitness of a lower body, in particular, a gait motion, which is crucial to maintain the quality of life.

As people get older, most of them may have the symptoms of lesions and/or aging on the lower body more or less. For example, a prevalence of knee osteoarthritis ranges from 19 % in women aged 50–59 to 56 % in men in the 70–90 year-old age group [6]. Such symptoms transfer in various ways such as

© Springer International Publishing Switzerland 2016
T. Bräunl et al. (Eds.): PSIVT 2015, LNCS 9431, pp. 136–147, 2016.
DOI: 10.1007/978-3-319-29451-3_12

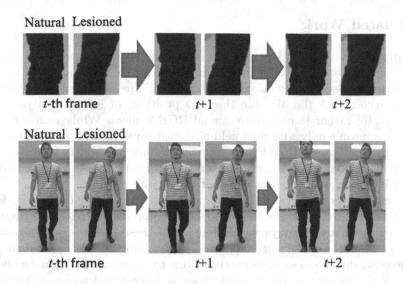

Fig. 1. Lesioned-part identification using a local appearance (upper row) versus an entire-body appearance (lower row). In examples shown in this figure, the right knee of a subject was tightly bandaged. At each frame, gait-phase-synchronized bodies in a natural motion (left side at each frame) and a motion with a lesioned right knee (right side at each frame) are shown. While differences between these two motions at each frame are not significant, the pose of the entire body with the lesioned right knee differs from the one in the natural motion.

insensitive sensation, and motor malfunction [10,23]. In terms of the motor malfunction, people may have muscle weakness [12] and/or knee osteoarthritis [1]. These symptoms cause a change in the patterns of a gait motion [5]. The change in the gait motion increases the risk of slipping and falling [2].

The goal of this work is to develop easy-to-use diagnosis systems that support the evaluation of physical patterns in the gait motion. For this evaluation, this paper proposes a method for classifying several symptoms of lesions on the lower body (e.g., knees and ankles), which are observed in the gait motion.

For precisely evaluating symptoms observed in gait motions, our contribution is to employ appearance information extracted from the entire body rather than local body parts such as knees and ankles. Figure 1 allows us to intuitively understand the effectiveness of the entire body appearance. In the upper row, the local appearance of a lesioned right knee is shown. This local appearance reveals less difference between a natural motion (shown in the left-hand side at each frame) and a motion with a lesioned right knee (shown in the right-hand side at each frame). On the other hand, we can easily see differences between these two motions in the appearance of the entire body shown in the lower row; for example, the upper body with the lesioned right knee is inclined backward and to the left for balancing. In this paper, a set of gait features is employed and appropriately pruned for robust lesioned-part identification.

2 Related Work

The proposed system employs a depth sensor for the evaluation of a 3D gait motion, which is expected to be more informative for lesioned-part identification than silhoette-based gait motions (e.g., [24,25]). The depth sensor is able to robustly reconstruct the 3D pose (i.e., 3D positions of joints) of a person of interest [7,13] rather than a conventional RGB camera. While such a camera can observe people only within its field of view, people are not required to carry any wearable sensors [17] and their motions are not affected by these sensors. In addition, for our goal (i.e., finding the symptoms in a gait motion), 24-hour observation using wearable sensors is not necessarily required.

A temporal sequence of a 3D body pose is defined as a gait motion. From the gait motion, we can extract several features representing physical symptoms caused by aging and/or physical disability. For these features, walking speed, stride, pace, etc. are useful [8]. For example, walking speed, stride, and pace become slow, short, and slow, respectively, due to the motor function decline [2]. As well as the walking speed, its acceleration is different between healthy people and elderly and/or disabled people [4,16]. It is also known that the anteversion of pelvis becomes smaller and left-right asymmetric due to the hemiplegia arthrosis [9].

The aforementioned features are well known in the literature in physiotherapy and biomechanics. However, these features are extracted from only target body parts/joints in previous work mentioned above. However, we know intuitively that not only the motion of lesioned part(s) but also the one of the entire body is affected as the symptom of aging and/or physical disability. This paper proposes a system that identifies lesioned part(s) based on gait motion features extracted from the entire body. While the closest work to our system is presented in [11], this method [11] analyzes the motion variation of the entire body under an assumption that a lesioned body part is known. For the purpose of finding such lesioned part(s), this is a kind of chicken-and-egg problem. On the other hand, our proposed system finds lesioned part(s) and estimated their symptoms (i.e., how severe the symptom is) from gait features extracted from a temporal sequence of a 3D body pose.

3 Overview of the System

The overview of the proposed system is illustrated in Fig. 2.

In its learning step (bottom row in Fig. 2), a number of gait patterns including the symptoms of lesions on various body parts are observed by a depth sensor. Each observed depth sequence is used to estimate the sequence of 3D body poses (i.e., skeletons) by using a pose estimation model [7,13], as shown in "Gait measurement" in Fig. 2. From the sequence of estimated 3D skeletons, a set of gait features are extracted. Since each set of gait features is labeled with the lesioned body part, a classifier ("Classification model" in Fig. 2) can be trained.

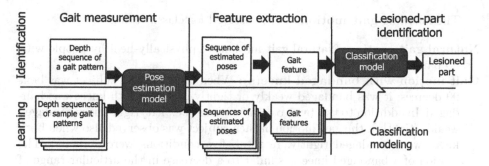

Fig. 2. Overview of the proposed system. The learning and identification steps are shown in lower and upper rows, respectively. Data are enclosed by rectangles and their flows are visualized by arrows in the figure.

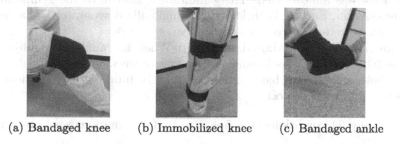

(a) Bandaged knee   (b) Immobilized knee   (c) Bandaged ankle

Fig. 3. Spurious lesions given for our experiments.

When the depth sequence of a gait motion is observed for lesioned-part identification, its gait features are extracted as in the learning step. Then the set of the gait features is classified in order to identify the lesioned part.

4   Gait Features for Lesioned-Part Identification

4.1   Dataset Collection for Lesioned-Part Identification

For realistic data and applications, it's better to collect and use the data of people who are actually lesioned. It is, however, difficult to collect a number of such data[1]. Instead of the real data, in this paper, spurious lesions were given to several body parts by bandaging or immobilizing them as shown in Fig. 3. Then gait motions with these spurious lesions were collected and used for classification. The spurious lesions, which were determined under the direction of a physiotherapist for our experiments, emulate the functional decline of joints caused by aging; for example, bending and stretching the knee [15] and the plantar flexion and dorsiflexion of the ankle [14].

---

[1] The authors have just collecting a dataset of gait motions of elderly people. So far, the motions of around 200 elderly people have been collected. After this dataset is ready to use, it will be used for further investigation.

The following **gait motions** were observed for classification:

Natural gait motion: Natural gait motions of physically-healthy people with no bandage.

Gait motion with bandaged knee(s): When the knee of a subject was bent 90 degrees, it was bandaged weakly or tightly. Each of both knees was bandaged. In addition to two by two combinations (i.e., left/right knees bandaged weakly/tightly), the gait motion of each subject was observed also when both knees were bandaged tightly. In total, five conditions were observed. The motion of a bandaged knee is similar to a decrease in the articular range of motion due to aging.

Gait motion with immobilized knee(s): When the knee of a subject was straight, it was immobilized with a splint. In this immobilization condition, the knee was almost fixed. This condition is similar to the symptom of a muscle strain. Each of both knees was immobilized separately. That is, two conditions were observed for each subject.

Gait motion with bandaged ankle(s): When the ankle of a subject was bent 90 degrees, it was bandaged. For experiments, left ankle, right ankle, and both ankles were bandaged separately. In total, three conditions were observed for each subject.

Eventually, 11 conditions $(1 + 5 + 2 + 3)$ of gait motions were observed for each subject.

4.2   Gait Features Representing the Motion of the Entire Body

As described in Sect. 3, the temporal sequence of a 3D skeleton is obtained by a depth sensor. In our experiments, a Kinect V2 sensor and its SDK were used together for 3D skeleton estimation.

A set of gait features are detected from the 3D skeletons of one gait cycle. This gait cycle is extracted from the observed sequence of the 3D skeleton so that each cycle begins and ends when the left knee is in front of and furthermost from the pelvis. All gait cycles are temporally normalized so that all of them consist of the same number of frames. In the normalized gait cycle, the 3D skeleton of each frame (denoted by $\boldsymbol{P}_i$ for i-th frame) is synthesized from observed skeletons with linear interpolation:

$$\boldsymbol{P}_i = \left(\frac{d_{i(+)}}{d_{i(-)} + d_{i(+)}} \hat{\boldsymbol{P}}_{i(-)} \right) + \left(\frac{d_{i(-)}}{d_{i(-)} + d_{i(+)}} \hat{\boldsymbol{P}}_{i(+)} \right)$$

where $\hat{\boldsymbol{P}}_{i(-)}$ and $\hat{\boldsymbol{P}}_{i(+)}$ denote the observed skeletons whose observed times are closest to the time of i-th frame. $\hat{\boldsymbol{P}}_{i(-)}$ and $\hat{\boldsymbol{P}}_{i(+)}$ are observed prior to and later than $\boldsymbol{P}_i$, respectively. $d_{i(-)}$ and $d_{i(+)}$ denote respectively the time differences from the time of i-th frame to the observed times of $\hat{\boldsymbol{P}}_{i(-)}$ and $\hat{\boldsymbol{P}}_{i(+)}$.

From each frame in the normalized temporal sequence, the following **gait features** are computed in our proposed system:

1. Relative x, y, z positions between the mid-spine and each joint/endpoint
2. Relative x, y, z velocities between the mid-spine and each joint/endpoint
3. Relative x, y, z accelerations between the mid-spine and each joint/endpoint
4. Angle of each joint
5. Angular velocity of each joint
6. Walking velocity along a moving direction
7. x, y, z positions of a body centroid
8. x, y, z velocities of a body centroid

From a 3D skeleton reconstructed using a Kinect V2, relative positions, velocities, and accelerations from the mid-spine to the head, neck, pelvis, both shoulders, both elbows, both wrists, both groins, both knees, both ankles, and both feet (in total, 17 points) are computed for the aforementioned features 1, 2, and 3, respectively. Joint angles and angular velocities are computed in the spine, neck, both shoulder blades, both shoulders, both elbows, both groins, both knees, and both ankles (in total, 14 points) for the features 4 and 5, respectively. The joint angle (radian) of joint j is represented by the 3D position of j and those of j's parent and child joints. A body centroid is determined based on a weight distribution in a human body; according to a report from a physiotherapy, the weights of the head, neck, both arms, torso, and both legs are 4 %, 3 %, 10 %, 48 %, and 35 %, respectively.

In addition to eight features listed above, each of them is subtracted from the mean of natural gait motions in training data. These features are called **mean-normalized features**. In total, $8 + 8 = 16$ features are extracted from each frame. All of these features extracted from all frames are concatenated to compose a **gait feature vector**.

The dimension of the above mentioned gait feature vector is huge. Specifically speaking, the concatenation of 16 gait features is a 376-dimensional vector: $((17 \times 3) + (17 \times 3) + (17 \times 3) + 14 + 14 + 1 + 3 + 3) \times 2 = 376$. For improving the discriminativity of the gait feature vector, its dimension is reduced by two schemes, namely backward search (a.k.a. backward feature elimination) and linear discriminant analysis (LDA), as follows:

Step 1: Assume the current dimension of a gait feature is N; initially, $N = 376$. For backward search, a LDA is trained with N components of all training samples. In the same way, N LDAs are trained with $(N - 1)$ components of all training samples so that one of N components in the gait feature vector is not used for each of N LDAs.

Step 2: All of these $(N + 1)$ LDAs are tested with validation data; a cross validation scheme is performed.

Step 3: If one of LDAs with $(N - 1)$ components (which is trained without k-th component) gets the best score in this validation, k-th component is removed from the gait feature vector. Then, go back to Step 1. Otherwise, namely if the LDA with N components is the best, the backward search ends. This LDA is used for lesioned-part identification.

With training data stored in the selected LDA space, k-Nearest Neighbor is employed for lesioned-part identification.

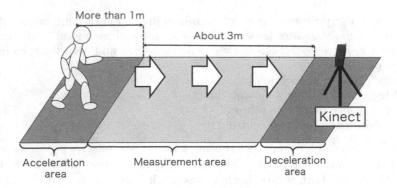

Fig. 4. Environment for capturing our gait dataset. A subject begins to walk in the acceleration area. While the subject walk through the measurement area, the temporal sequence of gait features are extracted.

5   Experiments

For experiments, the gait motions of 10 subjects were observed in a laboratory setup (Fig. 4). All of them were adult males, whose height and weight was 170 cm and 63 kg on average. Each of 11 gait motions was captured 10 times for each subject. From each gait sequence, one gait cycle was extracted. In total, 110 gait cycles were captured for each subject. In all experiments shown below, leave-one-out cross validation was used.

The effect of dimensionality reduction was investigated with each individual data (i.e., all data observed from each subject). As the result of backward search, gait features (1), (5), (8), (1′), (6′), (7′), and (8′), which are described in Sect. 4.2, were selected[2]. (l′) denotes the mean-normalized feature of feature (l). Comparison between results using all features and the selected features is shown in Table 1. This table shows the percentage of correctly-identified lesions. The performance was increased by around 10 % on average.

With the selected features, a confusion matrix is computed. Each value in the confusion matrix is the mean of results for all subjects. Table 2 shows the results of lesioned-part identification when all 11 kinds of gait motions were classified. This result is equivalent to the one shown in Table 1; the mean of diagonal values in Table 2 is 81.1, which is also shown as the mean in Table 1. As expected, it can be seen that it was difficult to discriminate between weakly- and tightly-bandaged knees.

To improve the discriminativity between different symptoms (e.g., weak and tight bandages) in the same body part, a two-step identification scheme was tested. In this scheme, only the position of lesion is identified initially. In our experiments, motions of tightly- and weakly- bandaged joints as well as

---

[2] For efficiency, backward search was executed so that (1) one gait feature is selected from 16 gait features and (2) all components in the selected gait feature were not used at each search step rather than each component of a gait feature vector.

Table 1. Effect of dimensionality reduction using backward search for lesioned-part identification. The mean of all gait motions is shown in each subject. For identification in i-th subject, training data of only i-th subject was used to train the LDA.

Subjects	All features (%)	Selected features (%)
A	62.7	73.6
B	60.5	66.8
C	67.7	80.5
D	76.8	87.2
E	61.8	75.9
F	67.3	80.5
G	86.8	91.4
H	86.3	91.4
I	71.8	83.6
J	73.6	79.6
Mean	71.6	81.1

Table 2. Confusion matrix of lesioned-part identification for 11 gait motions. All results were obtained with the selected features. Values above 10 % are highlighted in read cells.

Condition		Natural	Right knee			Left knee			Both knees	Right ankle	Left ankle	Both ankles
			Weak	Tight	Fixed	Weak	Tight	Fixed				
Natural		91.5	1.5	0.5	0.0	3.0	0.5	0.0	1.0	1.5	0.0	0.5
Right knee	Weak	0.0	84.0	12.0	0.0	1.5	0.0	0.0	1.5	1.0	0.0	0.0
	Tight	2.0	16.0	74.5	0.0	2.5	1.5	0.0	2.0	1.0	0.0	0.5
	Fixed	0.0	1.0	1.5	95.5	0.0	0.0	0.5	1.5	0.0	0.0	0.0
Left knee	Weak	3.0	1.5	1.0	0.0	69.0	18.0	0.0	3.0	1.0	3.0	0.5
	Tight	2.0	0.5	2.5	0.0	24.0	57.5	0.0	4.5	1.0	6.5	1.5
	Fixed	0.0	0.0	0.0	0.0	2.0	0.0	98.0	0.0	0.0	0.0	0.0
Both knees		0.0	2.5	3.5	0.5	1.5	2.5	0.5	88.0	0.5	0.5	0.0
Right ankle		0.5	1.0	3.0	0.0	2.5	1.0	0.0	1.5	81.5	1.0	8.0
Left ankle		1.5	0.0	0.0	0.0	6.0	3.5	0.0	0.5	4.0	74.5	10.0
Both ankles		0.0	0.0	1.0	0.0	2.0	0.5	1.0	0.0	8.5	9.5	77.5

immobilized joints were merged in each of right and left knees. If such a part is considered to be lesioned by the initial identification, the degree of the lesion is determined by a classification model that is trained by only the samples of lesions in this part; for example, the motions of weakly- and tightly-bandaged knees and immobilized knees are used for training for each of right and left knees. The results of initial classification (i.e., classification among 7 gait motions) are shown in Table 3. Table 4 shows the results of the second step where the motions of weakly- and tightly-bandaged knees and immobilized knees are classified after

Table 3. Confusion matrix of lesioned-part identification for 9 gait motions. Both for right and left knees, tightly- and weakly- bandaged motions were merged. All results were obtained with the selected features.

Condition	Natural	Right knee	Left knee	Both knees	Right ankle	Left ankle	Both ankles
Natural	90.0	5.0	2.0	1.0	0.5	1.0	0.5
Right knee	0.3	93.8	2.7	1.8	0.7	0.0	0.7
Left knee	1.3	2.7	91.7	1.3	0.7	2.0	0.3
Both knees	0.0	8.5	5.0	85.5	0.5	0.5	0.0
Right ankle	0.5	5.5	4.0	0.5	79.0	2.0	8.5
Left ankle	0.5	0.0	6.5	0.0	4.0	79.0	10.0
Both ankles	0.0	1.0	1.0	0.5	7.0	10.0	80.5

Table 4. 3-class classification accuracy. This classification identifies the symptom on a lesioned part, after the initial classification, whose results are shown in Table 3, determines the lesioned part (right or left knees in examples shown in this table). The mean of classification accuracy is 77.1 %.

	Right knee (%)	Left knee (%)
Weakly-bandaged	85.0	87.0
Tightly-bandaged	82.5	87.0
Immobilized	99.1	98.5

Table 5. Results of 3-class classification using local features. While this classification employs only several features extracted around a target part (i.e., right or left knee), the results shown in Table 4 were obtained with the features of the entire body. The mean of classification accuracy is 65.0 %.

Local features	Right knee (%)	Left knee (%)
Weakly-bandaged	58.0	69.5
Tightly-bandaged	44.0	50.0
Immobilized	85.5	83.0

the initial classification. The final mean score of this two-step identification is 83.1 %[3], which is 2 % above the result shown in Tables 1 and 2.

Next, the effect of gait features extracted from the entire body is validated. This effect is validated by comparing the results obtained with the entire-body gait features with those with local parts. Results obtained with only local features are shown in Table 5. Specifically, the local features consist of gait features

---

[3] This accuracy is computed from the diagonal values of the confusion matrix in Table 3 and the results of 3-class classification in Table 4 as follows: $(90.0 + 3 \times (93.8 \times \frac{85.0+82.5+99.1}{3}) + 3 \times (91.7 \times \frac{87.0+87.0+98.5}{3}) + 85.5 + 79.0 + 79.0 + 80.5)/11 = 83.1$.

Table 6. Confusion matrix of lesioned-part identification using gait features extracted from only the lower body.

Condition		Natural	Right knee			Left knee			Both knees	Right ankle	Left ankle	Both ankles
			Weak	Tight	Fixed	Weak	Tight	Fixed				
Natural		83.5	2.5	2.5	0.0	4.0	0.5	0.0	0.5	2.5	3.0	1.0
Right knee	Weak	0.0	64.5	27.0	0.5	2.0	0.5	0.0	4.0	0.0	0.5	1.0
	Tight	1.5	33.0	55.0	0.5	3.5	1.0	0.0	4.0	1.5	0.0	0.0
	Fixed	0.0	1.5	2.0	95.0	0.5	0.0	0.0	0.5	0.0	0.0	0.5
Left knee	Weak	3.5	1.0	1.5	0.0	57.0	21.5	1.5	4.0	1.5	5.0	3.5
	Tight	1.0	1.5	0.5	0.0	33.5	55.0	0.5	3.5	1.0	2.5	1.0
	Fixed	0.0	0.0	0.0	0.0	1.0	0.5	98.5	0.0	0.0	0.0	0.0
Both knees		1.0	2.5	2.5	0.5	4.5	3.5	1.0	83.5	0.0	0.5	0.5
Right ankle		2.5	1.5	3.0	0.0	2.0	0.5	0.0	0.0	78.5	2.0	10.0
Left ankle		1.5	0.0	1.0	0.0	4.5	2.0	0.0	0.5	4.5	74.0	12.0
Both ankles		0.0	0.0	0.0	0.0	3.0	1.5	0.0	0.0	11.5	14.0	70.0

Table 7. Confusion matrix of lesioned-part identification using gait features extracted from only the upper body.

Condition		Natural	Right knee			Left knee			Both knees	Right ankle	Left ankle	Both ankles
			Weak	Tight	Fixed	Weak	Tight	Fixed				
Natural		86.5	5.5	1.5	0.5	1.5	1.0	0.0	1.5	0.5	1.0	0.5
Right knee	Weak	3.5	68.5	14.5	1.0	4.5	0.0	0.5	3.0	3.0	0.5	1.0
	Tight	0.5	13.5	50.0	3.0	7.5	7.5	0.5	6.5	2.5	7.0	1.5
	Fixed	1.0	2.0	4.5	85.5	0.0	1.0	0.5	2.5	2.0	0.5	0.5
Left knee	Weak	0.5	6.0	3.0	0.0	41.5	19.0	1.5	6.0	6.0	9.5	7.0
	Tight	2.5	2.0	4.0	0.0	23.0	43.0	1.0	6.5	2.0	6.0	10.0
	Fixed	0.0	1.0	0.5	0.5	2.0	1.5	87.0	1.5	1.0	2.5	2.5
Both knees		1.5	3.5	10.5	1.0	5.5	6.5	1.5	61.0	4.0	3.5	1.5
Right ankle		0.5	2.5	4.0	0.0	7.0	4.0	0.5	3.0	53.0	12.5	13.0
Left ankle		0.5	1.5	2.5	0.5	8.5	6.0	0.5	1.0	12.0	53.5	13.5
Both ankles		0.5	2.5	2.0	0.5	8.0	4.0	0.5	2.5	7.5	15.5	56.5

(1), (2), (3), (4), (5), (1′), (2′), (3′), (4′), and (5′) where (l′) denotes the mean-normalized feature of feature (l), all of which are described in Sect. 4.2. Comparison between Tables 4 and 5 reveals the preponderance of the entire-body features over the local features.

For further analysis between entire-body and local features, confusion matrices obtained with gait features of lower- and upper-body parts are shown in Tables 6 and 7, respectively. The mean values of the percentages of correctly-identified lesions in Tables 6 and 7 are 74.1 % and 62.4 %, respectively, while the one of the entire-body features is 81.1 %. From these results, it has been demonstrated that the entire-body features are useful for lesioned-part identification.

In all experiments shown above, a training data for each subject consists of only this subject's data; a classification model was trained individually. For universal models that can be used by anybody, a classification model must be trained by training data of all subjects and applied to anybody. To examine the effectiveness of the proposed system for such universal models, the percentage of correctly-identified lesions was computed with a leave-one-out cross validation procedure. The mean percentage among all subjects and all gait motions was 66%, which is much lower than the one computed with individual models (i.e., 81.1%). This is a natural consequence because people have their own gait patterns, which are utilized for gait recognition [22].

Improving the performance of lesioned-part identification using a universal model is one of important future issues. To this end, gait features robust to individual variation should be explored.

6   Concluding Remarks

This paper proposed a system using a depth sensor for finding the symptoms of lesions on the lower body. For finding the lesioned part and its degree of lesion, the proposed system employs a set of gait features representing the motion of the entire body rather than local features around each body part. Compared with the local features, the effectiveness of the entire-body gait features was demonstrated in experiments; 11-class classification rates were improved: for example, 74.1% by the features of the lower body vs 81.1% by the features of the entire body.

Future work includes experiments with a large number of elderly people rather than people with spurious lesions. As discussed at the end of Sect. 5, it is important to improve lesioned-part identification using universal models for more general use. For basic techniques for estimating more accurate 3D pose sequences, a human motion prior [18–20] is useful.

References

1. Blagojevic, M., Jinks, C., Jeffery, A., Jordan, K.: Risk factors for onset of osteoarthritis of the knee in older adults: a systematic review and meta-analysis. Osteoarthritis Cartilage 18(1), 24–33 (2010)
2. Salzman, B.M.: Gait and balance disorders in older adults. Am. Fam. Physician 82(1), 61–68 (2010)
3. Cadore, E.L., Rodrguez-Maas, L., Sinclair, A., Izquierdo, M.: Effects of different exercise interventions on risk of falls, gait ability, and balance in physically frail older adults: a systematic review. Rejuvenation Res. 16(2), 105–114 (2013)
4. Derawi, M.O., Bours, P., Holien, K.: Improved cycle detection for accelerometer based gait authentication. In: Sixth International Conference on Intelligent Information Hiding and Multimedia Signal Processing (2010)
5. Duffell, L.D., Southgate, D.F., Gulati, V., McGregor, A.H.: Balance and gait adaptations in patients with early knee osteoarthritis. Gait Posture 39(4), 1057–1061 (2014)

6. Englund, M., Guermazi, A., Gale, D., Hunter, D.J., Aliabadi, P., Clancy, M., Felson, D.T.: Incidental meniscal findings on knee mri in middle-aged and elderly persons. N. Engl. J. Med. **359**(11), 1108–1115 (2008)
7. Girshick, R.B., Shotton, J., Kohli, P., Criminisi, A., Fitzgibbon, A.W.: Efficient regression of general-activity human poses from depth images. In: ICCV (2011)
8. de-la Herran, A.M., Garcia-Zapirain, B., Mendez-Zorrilla, A.: Gait analysis methods: an overview of wearable and non-wearable systems, highlighting clinical applications. Sensors **14**(2), 3362–3394 (2014)
9. Manca, M., Ferraresi, G., Cosma, M., Cavazzuti, L., Morelli, M., Benedetti, M.G.: Gait patterns in hemiplegic patients with equinus foot deformity. BioMed Res. Int. **2014** (2014)
10. Megumi, K., Stryker, M.P.: Sensory experience during locomotion promotes recovery of function in adult visual cortex. eLife **3**(3) (2014)
11. Ogawa, T., Yamazoe, H., Mitsugami, I., Yagi, Y.: The effect of the knee braces on gait – toward leg disorder estimation from images. In: Proceedings of the 2nd Joint World Congress of ISPGR and Gait and Mental Function, Akita, Japan, June 2013
12. Peterson, M., Rhea, M., Sen, A., Gordon, P.: Resistance exercise for muscular strength in older adults: a meta-analysis. Ageing Res Rev. **9**(3), 226–237 (2010)
13. Shotton, J., Fitzgibbon, A.W., Cook, M., Sharp, T., Finocchio, M., Moore, R., Kipman, A., Blake, A.: Real-time human pose recognition in parts from single depth images. In: CVPR (2011)
14. Simoneau, E., Martin, A., Hoecke, J.V.: Muscular performances at the ankle joint in young and elderly men. J. Gerontol. A Biol. Sci. Med. Sci. **60**(4), 439–447 (2005)
15. Sugiura, H., Demura, S.: The effects of knee joint pain and disorders on knee extension strength and walking ability in the female elderly. Adv. Phys. Educ. **2**(4), 139–143 (2012)
16. Tao, W., Liu, T., Zheng, R., Feng, H.: Gait analysis using wearable sensors. Sensors **12**, 2255–2283 (2012)
17. Taylor, P.E., Almeida, G.J.M., Kanade, T., Hodgins, J.K.: Classifying human motion quality for knee osteoarthritis using accelerometers. In: IEEE EMBS, pp. 339–343 (2010)
18. Ukita, N.: Simultaneous particle tracking in multi-action motion models with synthesized paths. Image Vision Comput. **31**(6–7), 448–459 (2013)
19. Ukita, N., Hirai, M., Kidode, M.: Complex volume and pose tracking with probabilistic dynamical models and visual hull constraints. In: ICCV (2009)
20. Ukita, N., Kanade, T.: Gaussian process motion graph models for smooth transitions among multiple actions. Comput. Vis. Image Underst. **116**(4), 500–509 (2012)
21. Vergados, D.J., Alevizos, A., Mariolis, A., Caragiozidis, M.: Intelligent services for assisting independent living of elderly people at home. In: PETRA (2008)
22. Wang, J., She, M.F., Nahavandi, S., Kouzani, A.Z.: A review of vision-based gait recognition methods for human identification. In: DICTA (2010)
23. Weinberger, B., Herndler-Brandstetter, D., Schwanninger, A., Weiskopf, D., Grubeck-Loebenstein, B.: Biology of immune responses to vaccines in elderly persons. Clin. Infect. Dis. **46**(7), 1078–1084 (2013)
24. Zhou, C., Mitsugami, I., Yagi, Y.: An attempt to detect impairment by silhouette-based gait feature. In: Annual Meeting of the European Society for Movement Analysis in Adults and Children, Glasgow, Scotland, September 2013
25. Zhou, C., Mitsugami, I., Yagi, Y.: Which gait feature is effective for impairment estimation? In: Korea-Japan Joint Workshop on Frontiers of Computer Vision (FCV 2014) (2014)

Variable-Length Segment Copy for Compressing Index Map of Palette Coding in Screen Content Coding

Yao-Jen Chang[1], Ching-Chieh Lin[1], Chao-Hsiung Hung[1],
Jih-Sheng Tu[1], Chun-Lung Lin[1(✉)], and Pei-Hsuan Tsai[2]

[1] Industrial Technology Research Institute, Hsinchu, Taiwan
{britpablo, JackLin, chhung, sunriseJSTu,
Chunlung}@itri.org.tw
[2] Institute of Manufacturing Information and Systems,
National Cheng Kung University, Tainan, Taiwan
peihsuan.tsai@gmail.com

Abstract. With the emerging applications, such as screen mirroring, and remote play, screen contents coding (SCC) plays important role in video coding recently. Since the characteristics of screen contents are different from nature contents, palette coding is adopted in the current draft standard of HEVC-SCC. The basic idea of the palette coding is to represent the colors of a coding unit (CU) by the indices of selected representative colors. This paper presents that the produced index maps exhibit considerably high spatial correlation. To utilize the spatial correlation among indices, a general 2-D search method is proposed firstly for index map compression. To reduce the memory access and implementation complexity, three simplified search schemes are proposed to balance the coding performance and complexity. The experimental results show that the three simplified methods can achieve 0.6 %, 0.5 % and 0.9 % BD-rate saving respectively, as compared to HM-13.0 + RExt-6.0 test model.

Keywords: Segment matching mode · Line-based · Palette · Screen content coding

1 Introduction

With rapid development of technologies and increased internet bandwidth, such as GPON, 3G and 4G etc., people are no longer satisfied with only communicating with each other via text or speech. More and More applications have started to provide services with many still images or videos to attract more users. These multimedia signals not only improve working efficiency but also enrich our daily life. In recent years, wireless displaying, cloud computing and gaming, screen sharing and collaboration, remote desktop, etc. are booming and have attracted a lot of attention. These emerging use cases can obliviously re-use the existing video compression technologies such as the state-of-the-art AVC [1] or HEVC [2] to fulfill purposes.

However, screen contents are fully or partial generated by computers. Console desktop, spreadsheet, slides and web browsers are typical examples for the screen

© Springer International Publishing Switzerland 2016
T. Bräunl et al. (Eds.): PSIVT 2015, LNCS 9431, pp. 148–159, 2016.
DOI: 10.1007/978-3-319-29451-3_13

contents with mixing lots of text, graphics, nature still images and nature video sequences. In addition, the screen contents usually contain sharp edges of the objects, background with simple colors and many thin lines. On the other hand, nature contents captured by video camcorders generally have rich colors, complex texture/shape and smooth-edged objects. Therefore, HEVC provides up to 35 spatial directions to code the nature contents. [2].

Since the state-of-the-art AVC and HEVC standards are mainly developed for the nature contents, the coding efficiency may not be adequate for the screen contents which have dissimilar characteristics from the nature contents. Therefore, ISO/IEC Moving Picture Experts Group (MPEG) and ITU-T Video Coding Experts Group (VCEG) issued a joint Call for proposal (CfP) for screen content coding (SCC) [3] in January 2014. Several responses were proposed and evaluated by the Joint Collaborative Team on Video Coding (JCT-VC) group in April 2014.

These responses all proposed two major coding tools for SCC: Intra Block Copy (IBC) [4] and Palette mode [5, 6]. IBC mode uses an estimated block vector to locate a similar block for the current partition in the current frame. The IBC mode is similar to the Inter Motion Estimation; however, the IBC mode only uses the current frame as a reference frame. The palette coding conceptually uses palette tables and index maps to represent the current CU. Overall, the palette coding has two major processing steps: palette table generation and index map compression. A palette table is generated by classifying the colors in the current CU and then reordering them according to the frequency of occurrence. After that, an index map is created by converting each sample to indices via the established palette table. Both palette tables and index maps need to be transmitted to the decoder.

Palette mode was proposed by Microsoft and Qualcomm in the 16th JCT-VC meeting [7, 8]. They are named PM and PQ respectively in this paper. In order to code the index map efficiently, we introduce advance segment matching mode on top of PM which is a line-based palette coding. Since many blocks or lines repeatedly appear in one frame for screen contents, similar or identical blocks/lines have high opportunities to be found from the previous decoded indices in the current coding CU for the palette coding. Splitting a line into several segments with various lengths plus 2-D searching is proposed first in this paper. However, using 2-D searching with various length segments not only requires a huge amount of data access but also increases the difficulties of the hardware implementation. Therefore, this paper further presents three simplified methods to reduce the complexity. The maximum BD-rate saving can achieve 0.6 %, 0.5 % and 0.9 % for "YUV, text & graphics with motion, 1080p" class for All Intra test condition.

The rest of this paper is organized as follows. Section 2 gives the overview of the palette coding and its related works. The proposed advanced segment matching tool and the three simplified methods are presented in Sect. 3. The performance evaluations are carried out and discussed in Sect. 4. The concluding remarks and possible future works are drawn in Sect. 5.

2 Overview

Palette coding has been studied in JCT-VC for many meeting cycles. It analyzes the colors in the current CU at first to generate the palette table and transmit the converted color indices to the decoder. Since neighboring samples in the screen contents generally have high contrasts such as sharp edges, conventional spatial coding tools may not be able to compress the screen contents efficiently. In addition, the screen contents contain limited colors. Therefore, the palette mode does not need to maintain a huge palette table for a color-index mapping process. Meanwhile, less numbers of the colors in the palette table reduce the coded bits to represent the palette indices. It improves the index map coding performance.

During the investigation of the palette mode, there were two main solutions with different implementations. The first one was a run-based palette coding PQ [8]. Compared with the conventional HEVC coding tools, the PQ packs the three components, e.g. YCbCr or GBR, for the palette table generation. The encoder first generates a color histogram according to the frequency of the color appearance and then groups similar colors together as major colors via an error allowance threshold value. Since the palette table needs to be transmitted to the decoder, the last decoded palette table is used as a palette table predictor in order to avoid resending the identical major colors. This is done by simply signaling reuse flags to indicate which colors in the last decoded palette table are reused in the current coding CU. Then, un-predicted major colors need to be signaled directly to the decoder. After applying the color to index mapping, the encoder can use two copy-run methods to compress the index map. When the current and the following color indices are the same with the above indices, Copy Above Run mode (CAR) is valid. If the current coding color index and the followed indices are the same, the Copy Left Run mode (CLR) is available. The number of the identical indices is defined as run value. In addition, CLR is also used for coding index when the run value equals one. Both the mode flag for the two modes and their run value are signaled. For the decoding process, the decoder parses the reuse flags and the signaled major colors to regenerate the palette table for the current decoding CU at first. After that, the index map is reconstructed by inversing the indices encoding process. The last step is to convert the decoded indices to color samples.

The line-based palette coding PM basically shares the same ideas for palette table generation and index map compression. Instead of packing all the three components together for selecting the major colors, PM generates triple palette tables for each component. In order to signal the major colors more efficiently, PM also uses the last decoded palette tables as predictors. After converting the color samples in the current coding CU by referencing the palette tables individually, triple index maps are created. For index maps compression, PM provides three copy modes: Vertical, Horizontal and Normal modes. The Vertical mode is similar to CAR in PQ. The main difference is that Vertical mode is valid if the current line is the same as the above line. The Horizontal mode is available when the whole color indices of the current line are all the same. For Normal mode, there are three sub-modes inside. They are Above, Left and No Prediction modes. When Normal mode is applied, each color indices will be coded in a pixel-by-pixel manner. Above mode and Left mode use the above and the left neighboring index of the current coding index as the predictor respectively. No prediction handles unpredictable indices. On the decoder side, the decoder regenerates the three palette tables and the procedure is similar to PQ. Then, the triple index maps are reconstructed by parsing the three modes. Lastly, the decoder converts the index map to color samples by looking up the palette tables.

3 Proposed Algoriths

In the current PM design, Vertical mode is only allowed to use the above one neighboring row to perform matching process. In addition, it also requires that every index in the above row should be identical to the current line. Owing to the special characteristics of screen contents such as repeatedly occurred objects/lines and simple background, the decoded indices excluding the above row may have useful information that can improve the coding efficiency. In the following sections, we first report the analysis about the correlations between the current line and the previous decoded lines in the current CU. After that, we present four novel methods for index map compression.

3.1 Previous Line Matching Analysis and General 2-D Index-Segment Copy Scheme

Our analyzing result is illustrated in Table 1. In this table, "occur once" means that only one matched line is found. "Occur twice" and "occur repeatedly" represent two and more than two matched lines, respectively.

As an obvious consequence, once the Vertical mode has been selected, it is highly possible to find an exactly matched line in the same CU (more than 90 % in Table 1). Hence, we can make a hypothesis based on the results in Table 1. If the current line differs from its above one, it still may find a matched line in the current CU. We can further extend this hypothesis by supposing that partial concatenation indices called a "segment" in the current line may find a matched segment in the already decoded part of the current CU. According to this hypothesis, a palette coding improvement algorithm is proposed. This algorithm includes two parts:

Extremely Search. For a current line, it can be considered as a combination result of segments. And there may be many possible combination results for the current line. For the segments in one combination result, the encoder could find their matched segments in the previous lines. If a matched segment is found, a shift vector and a segment length need to be recorded. The vector and the length are used to indicate where and how long do the start position of a segment can copy the indices from the reconstructed frame. If the current start position can't find any matched index, then it is coded as Normal mode.

Calculate the Cost of the Coded-Bins. If several search results are found in the search stage, the encoder would calculate the cost of the coded-bins of each pair's vector and length.

Table 1. The analysis result of Vertical mode

Category	Test Sequence	QP	Occur once (%)	Occur twice (%)	Occur repeatedly (%)
RGB, text & graphics with motion, 1080p	Flyinggraphicstext	27	4.80	4.65	90.54
		37	4.33	4.16	91.51
	Desktop	27	5.27	5.10	89.63
		37	4.50	4.50	91.00
	Console	27	3.87	3.87	92.26
		37	3.49	3.44	93.07
RGB, text & graphics with motion,720p	WebBrowsing	27	4.34	4.34	91.32
		37	3.27	3.27	93.45
	Map	27	15.48	12.50	71.43
		37	5.63	4.93	89.44
	Programming	27	7.33	7.33	85.34
		37	6.47	6.47	87.06
	SlideShow	27	10.00	10.00	83.33
		37	5.45	5.45	90.91
RGB, mixed content, 1440p	BasketballScreen	27	5.97	5.60	88.43
		37	4.92	4.92	90.15
	MissionControlClip2	27	6.94	6.36	86.71
		37	4.04	4.04	91.93
YUV, text & graphics with motion, 1080p	Flyinggraphicstext	27	4.82	4.65	90.53
		37	3.86	3.86	92.27
	Desktop	27	4.41	4.35	91.19
		37	3.89	3.89	92.22
	Console	27	3.14	3.14	93.68
		37	2.97	2.97	94.06
YUV, text & graphics with motion,720p	WebBrowsing	27	4.44	4.44	91.24
		37	2.50	2.50	95.01
	Map	27	9.33	8.00	81.33
		37	4.49	4.49	89.89
	Programming	27	7.82	7.41	84.77
		37	7.04	7.04	85.92
	SlideShow	27	8.57	8.57	85.71
		37	2.78	2.78	93.06
YUV, mixed content, 1440p	BasketballScreen	27	5.73	5.73	88.89
		37	4.65	4.65	90.70
	MissionControlClip2	27	4.48	4.48	91.42
		37	4.59	4.59	89.91

The pairs of the vector and the length with the minimum cost for the current line would be the final search result. Figure 1 illustrates an example of this search method.

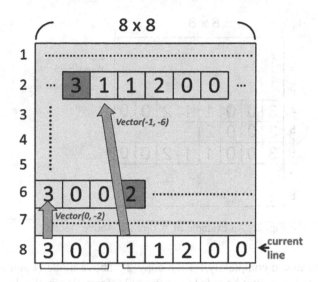

Fig. 1. An example of "segment search" result.

In Fig. 1, it is an 8 × 8 block and the 8th line is the current line. The current line is separated into two segments after the search stage. For these two segments, the matched segments locate in the 6th and the 2nd line. The shift vector and length of the first segment are (0, −2) and 3. Those of second segment are (−1, −6) and 5. These information all need to be coded.

However, there is no doubt that the high complexity of the aforementioned algorithm would lead to a huge overhead in computing time or memory usage. Therefore, we provide three simplified designs for the proposed algorithm. In the next sections, we will introduce these methods in detail.

3.2 1st Simplified Mode: Copy 2nd Above Mode

As the analysis shown in Sect. 3.1, the encoder and the decoder may find an identical line in the decoded indices for the current line easily. It is straightforward to force the encoder and the decoder to search one more line instead of only using the above line. Compared with the original three mode in PM for index map compression, we introduce an additional mode: copy 2nd above mode. When the current line and the above line are different, the encoder will bypass the Vertical mode and use the second line above the current line as a reference in our proposed mode. If the second line above the current line is identical to the current line, the proposed mode is valid. The decoder can parse the mode flag and copy the second line above the current line to the current line.

Figure 2 is an example for the first simplified mode. For the original Vertical mode, the 5th and the 6th lines are different. Therefore, the Vertical mode is unavailable. Meanwhile, in our proposed copy 2nd above mode, the 4th line is the same as the current 6th line. In this case, our proposed mode can be used here to improve the coding efficiency.

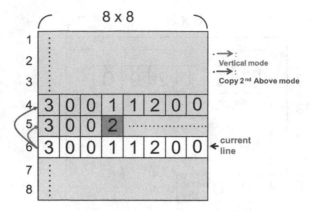

Fig. 2. An example of "Copy 2nd Above" mode.

The extra hardware complexity for the copy 2nd above mode is almost negligible. However, this mode may not be able to use the full information in the decoded indices. To approach the general 2-D searching, we propose the following two simplified designs.

3.3   2nd Simplified Mode: Sliding Half Line Mode

Our previous analysis shows a line has matched one in above processed region with high probability. Thus we partition a Normal-processed line into small segments and find matched ones. We provide two more simplified modes based on this idea.

Figure 3(a) shows an example of sliding half line mode based on this idea. The half-length segment *L1* is located arbitrarily within the current line. This simplified mode is also called match mode. This is a new model and proposed to replace original Normal mode.

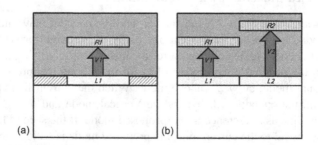

Fig. 3.   (a) Sliding half line mode (b) splitting half line mode.

Figure 4 illustrates the operation of the match mode. In the match mode, each current segment *L1* has many reference segments *R1* ~ *Ri* above in Fig. 4(a). In Fig. 4 (b), the match mode will evaluate whether the current segment *L1* matches one of the

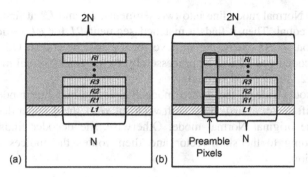

Fig. 4. Match mode. (a) Reference segments *Ri* above current segment *L1*. (b) Operation of match mode.

above reference segments. In order to simplify and accelerate the matching process, we take previous two indices before each segment for pre-matching process. This group of indices is preamble indices in Fig. 4(b). The preamble indices and the reference segments $R1 \sim Ri$ are already decoded while the current segment *L1* is going to be coded now.

If the current line is processed by the match mode, there are four steps to code *L1* in Fig. 4(b).

Step 1: For the preamble indices before *L1*, it finds the matched preamble indices of *Ri* above. If the preamble indices have no matched ones, the first index of *L1* will be processed by three sub-modes in original Normal mode. Then it goes to next index and re-starts the step 1.

Step 2: If the matched preamble indices of *Ri* exist, it then checks the corresponding *Ri* and *L1*.

Step 3: If no *Ri* matches *L1*, it transmits a flag "0" and codes the first index of *L1* by three sub-modes in original Normal mode. Then it goes to the next index and re-starts the step 1.

Step 4: If at least one *Ri* match *L1*, it labels these reference segments by matching indices starting from 0. It then transmits the flag "1" and the corresponding matching index. Then it goes to the index next to the end of *L1* and re-starts the step 1.

For the decoding process, the decoder has to parse the specific flag and the corresponding matching index at first. With the inversed encoding steps, the decoder then can use the matching index to find the preamble. After that, the decoder can copy the half line width indices after the preamble to the current decoding position.

3.4 3rd Simplified Mode: Splitting Half Line Mode

Previous simplified mode requires the additional pre-matching process which may complicate the hardware implementation. In consequence, we propose another simplified mode, splitting half mode in Fig. 3(b). This simplification is a modified Normal mode.

It splits the Normal mode line into two segments, *L1* and *L2* at first. The width of *L1* and *L2* are equal. Then it finds a matched segment *R1* for *L1* vertically in above processed region. If *R1* exists, the shift vector *V1* will be coded. Otherwise, a zero vector will be coded and *L1* will be processed by the original Normal mode. The other half segment *L2* is processed similarly.

On the decoder side, if the parsed mode flag is the half line mode, the decoder decodes the shift vector at first. If the shift vector is zero, the decoder decodes this half segment by the original Normal mode. Otherwise, the decoder finds the identical segment according to the shift vector and then copies the indices to the current decoding position.

4 Experimental Results

We integrated the line-based palette coding PM [2] into MPEG reference software HM-13.0+RExt-6.0. We then compare the coding performance of integrated software (PM+HM-13.0+RExt-6.0) and the reference software (HM-13.0+RExt-6.0). The experimental conditions are subject to the test conditions issued by JCT-VC in the 16th meeting [9]. Each test sequences must be tested under All Intra, Random Access, and Low-delay B conditions.

Since the palette coding is one of the intra-prediction coding tools, we are more interested in evaluating the All Intra experimental results. Our proposed methods are tested only under All Intra test conditions. The integrated software and the four simplified methods run on the different simulation platform. Encoding time and decoding time may not be reliable. Therefore, the comparisons of the averaged encoding and decoding time are not reported in our experimental results.

The improvement of the integrated software is investigated at first. Table 2 gives the All Intra results in BD-rate. The more negative value means better coding performance. Table 2 shows that the palette coding improves the coding performance, especially for the screen content test sequences.

Table 2. All Intra experimental results. The test algorithm and the anchor are the integrated software and the reference software respectively.

	AllIntra		
	Y	U	V
RGB, text & graphics with motion, 1080p	-8.3%	-8.0%	-8.4%
RGB, text & graphics with motion, 720p	-3.8%	-3.5%	-3.7%
RGB, mixed content, 1440p	-1.0%	-0.8%	-1.0%
RGB, mixed content, 1080p	-1.3%	-1.1%	-1.2%
RGB, Animation, 720p	0.1%	-0.1%	0.0%
YUV, text & graphics with motion, 1080p	-8.7%	-6.7%	-7.4%
YUV, text & graphics with motion, 720p	-3.0%	-2.8%	-4.0%
YUV, mixed content, 1440p	-1.2%	-1.4%	-1.4%
YUV, mixed content, 1080p	-1.1%	-0.9%	-0.9%
YUV, Animation, 720p	0.1%	0.0%	0.0%

The integrated software is the platform for implementation of our proposed modes. Tables 3, 4 and 5 give the All Intra experimental results. The anchors are the integrated software. It shows that the proposed simplified modes improve the palette coding performance.

Table 3. All Intra experimental results. The test algorithm and the anchor are the copy 2nd above mode and the integrated software respectively.

	All Intra		
	Y	U	V
RGB, text & graphics with motion, 1080p	-0.5%	-0.5%	-0.5%
RGB, text & graphics with motion, 720p	0.0%	0.0%	-0.1%
RGB, mixed content, 1440p	0.0%	0.0%	0.0%
RGB, mixed content, 1080p	0.0%	0.0%	0.0%
RGB, Animation, 720p	0.0%	0.0%	0.0%
YUV, text & graphics with motion, 1080p	-0.6%	-0.3%	-0.4%
YUV, text & graphics with motion, 720p	0.0%	0.0%	0.0%
YUV, mixed content, 1440p	0.0%	0.0%	0.0%
YUV, mixed content, 1080p	0.0%	0.0%	0.0%
YUV, Animation, 720p	0.0%	0.0%	0.0%

Our proposed copy 2nd above mode achieves 0.5 % and 0.6 % BD-rate saving in "RGB, text & graphics with motion, 1080p" and "YUV, text & graphics with motion, 1080p" classes with minor change. However, there is no coding gain in the rest of the testing classes. The reason may be caused by not using the full information provided by the decoded indices in the current CU.

Meanwhile, the sliding half mode provides much adaption of the current segment location with maximum 0.5 % coding gain as shown is Table 4. Comparing to the splitting half mode, the slightly worse coding performance may be caused by the pre-matching process. The size of the preamble indices is two in our current design to reduce the computations and accelerate the matching process. However, the preamble indices, which can be considered as predictors, cannot perfectly reflect the matching process. It is a tradeoff between coding performance and complexity.

Table 4. All Intra experimental results. The test algorithm and the anchor are the sliding half line mode and the integrated software respectively.

	AllIntra		
	Y	U	V
RGB, text & graphics with motion, 1080p	-0.5%	-0.5%	-0.5%
RGB, text & graphics with motion, 720p	-0.2%	-0.2%	-0.2%
RGB, mixed content, 1440p	-0.1%	0.0%	-0.1%
RGB, mixed content, 1080p	-0.1%	-0.1%	-0.1%
RGB, Animation, 720p	0.0%	0.0%	0.0%
YUV, text & graphics with motion, 1080p	-0.5%	-0.3%	-0.3%
YUV, text & graphics with motion, 720p	-0.2%	-0.3%	-0.2%
YUV, mixed content, 1440p	-0.1%	-0.1%	-0.1%
YUV, mixed content, 1080p	-0.1%	-0.1%	-0.1%
YUV, Animation, 720p	0.0%	0.0%	0.0%

Table 5. All Intra experimental results. The test algorithm and the anchor are the splitting half line mode and the integrated software respectively.

	All Intra		
	Y	U	V
RGB, text & graphics with motion, 1080p	-0.8%	-0.8%	-0.8%
RGB, text & graphics with motion,720p	-0.3%	-0.3%	-0.3%
RGB, mixed content, 1440p	-0.1%	-0.1%	-0.1%
RGB, mixed content, 1080p	-0.1%	-0.1%	-0.1%
RGB, Animation, 720p	0.0%	0.0%	0.0%
YUV, text & graphics with motion, 1080p	-0.9%	-0.5%	-0.6%
YUV, text & graphics with motion,720p	-0.3%	-0.2%	-0.3%
YUV, mixed content, 1440p	-0.1%	-0.2%	-0.2%
YUV, mixed content, 1080p	-0.1%	-0.1%	-0.1%
YUV, Animation, 720p	0.0%	0.1%	0.0%

The final proposed mode, the splitting half mode, provides better coding performance with the simple and clear design. It handles each line with the simple process and consumes less computing resources. In Table 5, the splitting half mode can achieve 0.8 % and 0.9 % BD-rate saving in " RGB, text & graphics with motion, 1080p" and " YUV, text & graphics with motion, 1080p" classes. For all the three proposed methods, there is no improvement for the animation classes. It may be caused by too many rich colors and complicated textures in the class.

5 Conclusions

In this paper, we have analyzed the probability of finding above matched lines for current processing line at first. The analysis shows that there exists a high correlation between the current line and the previous lines. Then, we have proposed a general 2-D palette indices search method and three simplified methods from Sects. 3.2 to 3.4. The first simplification use an additional mode to check the second line above the current line. Coding improvement is only shown in the "text & graphics with motion, 1080p" classes. The second simplified method uses our observed feature to provide obvious coding benefit. Then, the third simplified method further reduces the syntax overhead in coded-bins to achieve better coding gain. All of our proposed methods improve the coding efficiency significantly on top of the line-based palette coding. As the simulation results show, the third proposed simplified method gets 0.8 % to 0.9 % coding gain at the "RGB, text & graphics with motion, 1080p" and the "YUV, text & graphics with motion, 1080p" test sequence categories individually. Since the run-based and the line-based palette coding share the similar ideas for compression, integrating our proposed methods on top of the run-based palette coding will be our next step.

References

1. Wiegand, T., Sullivan, G.J., Bjontegaard, G., Luthra, A.: Overview of the H.264/AVC video coding standard. IEEE Trans. Circuits Syst. Video Technol. **13**(7), 560–576 (2003)
2. Sullivan, G.J., Ohm, J., Han, W.-J., Wiegand, T.: Overview of the high efficiency video coding (HEVC) standard. IEEE Trans. Circuits Syst. Video Technol. **22**(12), 1649–1668 (2012)
3. Joint call for proposals for coding of screen content, ISO/IEC JTC1/SC29/WG11 MPEG, MPEG N14715 (2014)
4. Chang, T.-S., Liao, R.-L., Chen, C.-C., Peng, W.-H., Hang, H.-M., Lin, C.-L., Jou, F.-D.: RCE3: results of subtest B.1 on Nx2N/2NxN intra block copy. Document JCTVC-P0176 (2014)
5. Guo, L., Karczewicz, M., Sole, J.: RCE3: results of Test 3.1 on palette mode for screen content coding. Document JCTVC-N0247 (2013)
6. Zhu, W., Xu, J., Ding, W.: RCE3 Test 2: multi-stage base color and index map. Document JCTVC-N0287 (2013)
7. Guo, X., Lu, Y., Li, S.: RCE4: Test 1. Major-color-based screen content coding. Document JCTVC-P0108 (2014)
8. Guo, L., Pu, W., Karczewicz, M., Sole, J., Joshi, R., Zou, F.: RCE4: results of Test 2 on palette mode for screen content coding. Document JCTVC-P0198 (2014)
9. Rosewarne, C., Sharman, K., Flynn, D.: Common test conditions and software reference configurations for HEVC range extensions. Document JCTVC-P1005 (2014)

Automatic Construction of Action Datasets Using Web Videos with Density-Based Cluster Analysis and Outlier Detection

Nga Hang Do$^{(\boxtimes)}$ and Keiji Yanai

The University of Electro-Communications, Chofugaoka 1-5-1,
Chofu, Tokyo 185-8585, Japan
dohang@mm.cs.uec.ac.jp

Abstract. In this paper, we introduce a fully automatic approach to construct action datasets from noisy Web video search results. The idea is based on combining cluster structure analysis and density-based outlier detection. For a specific action concept, first, we download its Web top search videos and segment them into video shots. We then organize these shots into subsets using density-based hierarchy clustering. For each set, we rank its shots by their outlier degrees which are determined as their isolatedness with respect to their surroundings. Finally, we collect upper ranked shots as training data for the action concept. We demonstrate that with action models trained by our data, we can obtain promising precision rates in the task of action classification while offering the advantage of a fully automatic, scalable learning. Experiment results on UCF11, a challenging action dataset, show the effectiveness of our method.

Keywords: Automatic construction · Action datasets · Web videos · Density-based clustering · Outlier detection

1 Introduction

High quality datasets play important roles in computer vision and pattern recognition tasks. With sufficient and high quality training data, most pattern recognition methods have achieved promising results. As data sources, most recently released datasets exploit Web data which are extremely numerous and easy to obtain. However, since Web data are generated and uploaded by general users, data corresponding to the concept of interest account for only a small proportion among retrieved results. Therefore, constructing high quality datasets with Web data requires extensive human effort of manual annotation. In case of constructing action datasets, in general, we need annotators to localize relevant video parts (shots) of the pre-defined actions in video sources by watching the whole of them carefully. Since the task is too exhausted, even largest action datasets cover not more than 101 concepts with only several thousands of video shots. This situation has given rise to the need for constructing action datasets with less human effort.

© Springer International Publishing Switzerland 2016
T. Bräunl et al. (Eds.): PSIVT 2015, LNCS 9431, pp. 160–172, 2016.
DOI: 10.1007/978-3-319-29451-3_14

Previous work which aim to automatically obtain action shots of specific action concepts from noisy data [1–3] generally require textual information provided together with videos such as movie script [1] or metadata (tags) [2,3]. Laptev et al. [1,4,5] proposed methods to automatically associate movie scripts with actions and obtain video shots in movie representing particular classes of human actions. Their methods actually can help reduce human effort on construction of realistic action database. However, targeted videos are only the movies with available scripts and trainable actions are limited to only actions appeared in movies. On the other hand, our proposed system can be applied to extract data for various types of actions which are distributed over much more immense video source.

As an approach which also targets on more various actions and use broader data sources, Nga et al. [2,6,7] proposed to collect video shots corresponding to any kind of action concept using Web videos. They conducted experiments for more than 100 action concepts and obtained promising results. Their work is the most related work to ours and treated as our baseline in this paper. According to their methods, before video downloading, videos are ranked based on usage frequencies of tags. Videos which have tags with high co-occurrence frequencies are considered as relevant videos. Therefore, their approach cannot make use of videos without associated tags. In this work, we propose an approach which also exploits videos without tags. As visual features, we extract temporal features using a ConvNet trained on UCF-101 dataset [8] following a recent state-of-the-art approach for action recognition [9].

In action recognition, in almost cases, a primary action is considered as a target in both training videos and test videos. Even with only one action, the task is still challenging due to variability of human actions. The actions can look different when they are seen from different views or operated by different people. They even can be manipulated in many disparate ways. Thus, to obtain good recognition performance, training data should capture actions in many different conditions. In other words, a high quality action database should reflect as much as possible the diversity of the concept. However, previous approaches for automatic construction of action database do not cope with concept diversity. Especially, our baseline [6] applies VisualRank [10] which is originally an image ranking method with a visual feature based similarity matrix to rank shots. Shots sharing the most visual characteristics with others are ranked to the top and selected as relevant shots. Therefore, this method tends to obtain only visually similar shots. In this paper, we propose to group related shots into clusters before shot ranking by a hierarchy clustering method [11]. Different clusters while sharing some appearance characteristics still hold unique aspects of the concept. Consequently, our obtained shots are much more diverse than shots obtained by the baseline [6]. According to our experiment results, the more diverse the training data are, the better recognition performance we can achieve.

After obtaining clusters, we rank instances in each cluster by outlier factor [12]. Outliers are instances deviating from the major distribution of the data. In other words, outliers belong to sparse regions while relevant instances lie in dense regions. The most densely linked instances from each cluster are ranked to the top and then used as training data for the concept. As action concepts, we experiment on those used in YouTube (also called as UCF11) dataset [13]. Furthermore, we train action models with our automatically collected data and test them on the test data of these datasets. We performed action classification by a popular supervised framework with the intention of comparing classification performance using manually constructed dataset and the dataset collected automatically by our proposed approach. Experiment results show that even though our data are not qualified as "clean" data as standard training data (manually collected data), classification rates are promising and show potential for development of approaches for automatic construction of action databases. Our work is inspired by [14] which uses density analysis of Web images for automatic image dataset construction.

Our contributions can be summarized as follows: (1) We propose a simple yet effective and feasible approach for fully automatic construction of action datasets; (2) We address intra-class variations within a concept resulting in multiple groups of shots; (3) We validate our automatically constructed datasets on standard datasets to show the potential of automatic construction for action datasets. To the best of our knowledge, we are the first to do that.

Remainder of this paper is constructed as follows. We first introduce some more related work for dataset construction and action recognition in Sect. 2. In Sect. 3 we describe our proposed approach. We then report the results of our experiments in Sect. 4 and finally, conclude this work in Sect. 5.

2   Related Work

We discuss here several related work on two topics: dataset construction and action recognition.

Dataset Construction: Many recent work have tackled the problem of building qualified training datasets automatically from data retrieved by Web search engines but most of them have been applied only on images [14–17]. Collins et al. [15] presented a framework for incrementally learning object categories from Web image search results. Given a set of seed images a non-parametric latent topic model is applied to categorize collected Web image. Schoroff et al. [16] proposed to first filter out the abstract images (e.g., drawings, cartoons) and then use text and metadata surrounding the images to re-rank the images searched in Google. Chen et al. [14] proposed NEIL (Never Ending Image Learner) which is a program using a semi-supervised learning algorithm that jointly discovers common sense relationships and labels instances of the given visual categories. NEIL learns multiple sub-model automatically for each concept. As an approach which also alleviates the multi-modal problem of concepts, [17] divides seed images into multiple groups and trains classifiers on each group separately. Images obtained from different groups usually capture some different looks of the concept.

As for automatic construction of action datasets using unconstrained videos, there are very few approaches as we introduced in the previous section. Moreover, these approaches require textual information associated with videos [1,2]. Adrian et al. [3] proposed a method to learn automatically concept detectors from YouTube videos for any kind of concepts including objects, actions and events. Their method also requires textual description of the target concept provided by YouTube users. Furthermore, each concept must be manually assigned a canonical YouTube category and low-quality videos are eliminated to improve the quality of downloaded material. In this work, we propose a fully automatic approach for action dataset building which exploits only visual features of raw videos retrieved from video sharing sites. Our approach neither needs additional information nor manual annotation.

Action Recognition: Most action recognition methods followed the standard framework of pattern recognition. First, a sufficiently large corpus of training data is collected, in which the concept labels are generally obtained through expensive human annotation. Next, concept classifiers are learned from the training data. Finally, the classifiers are used to detect the presence of the actions in the test data. We also adopt this standard framework in action recognition task, except that instead of using provided training data, we use our automatically collected data to train concept classifiers.

As popular video presentation, successful hand-crafted features such as HOG, HOF or MBH extracted along dense trajectories [18] have been adopted and developed in many work recently [19,20]. These features are generally encoded by Bag-of-Visual-Words or Fisher Vectors. In very recent years, followed by their success in image recognition field, deep learning Convolutional Neural Networks (CNNs) have received great attention and obtained promising results in action recognition [9,21,22]. Following this trend, we also train a temporal CNN using a method proposed in [9] and use this model to extract features from video shots.

3   Approach

In this work, we present an approach which autonomously extracts from noisy Web videos relevant video shots for given action concepts. Our approach consists of three steps: shot collection, shot clustering and shot selection. See Fig. 1 for the illustration of our proposed framework. In shot collection, we download videos of the concepts and segment them to shots. These shots are then organized into subsets by hierarchical clustering [11]. Finally, relevant shots are ranked by outlier factors [12] and selected from each of all clusters using a simple selection strategy. In the followings, we explain in detail each step.

3.1   Shot Collection

We first prepare keywords for given action concepts. The concepts can be defined in any form: either "verb" (such as "dive") or "verb+non-verb" (such as "throw+hammer", "cut+in+kitchen") or "non-verb" (such as "pole vault"). In case verb included in the keyword, we search for its videos in both forms: "verb" and "verb-ing" (such as "diving", "throwing+hammer"). We filter out videos

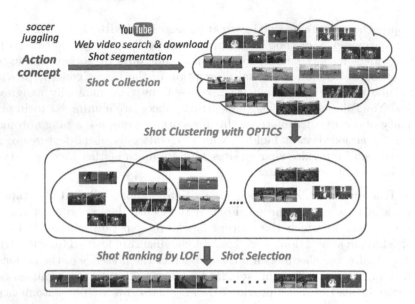

Fig. 1. Framework of our approach for automatic construction of action shot datasets which consists of three steps: shot collection, shot clustering and shot ranking.

belonging to "entertainment", "music", "movies", "film" and "games" categories during searching since these categories generally contain extremely long videos. Top search results are downloaded and segmented into video shots using color histogram. RGB histograms of every frame are computed and then segmentation points are put between frames whose histogram intersection is larger than a predefined constant. Each shot represents one single scene. For each concept, we download around 100–200 videos and obtain around 700–2000 shots.

3.2 Shot Clustering

With shots obtained after above step, we group related shots into clusters before shot ranking and selection. This step helps deal with concept diversity. With web data retrieved for a given concept, there will also be common characteristics shared among subsets of data. Therefore, rather than hard clustering data into a specific number of subsets as some approaches which also aim to deal with intra-class variations in concepts [17,23], we use hierarchy clustering which allows different clusters to share the same instances. We adopt OPTICS ("Ordering Points To Identify the Clustering Structure") [11] to find clusters. Rather than the popular Mean Shift, OPTICS is prefer due to its computational efficiency. The hierarchical structure of the clusters can be obtained based on the density of the data distributed around their points. Follows are our brief introduction of this clustering algorithm. For the detail, please refer to [11].

The basic idea of a density-based clustering algorithm is that for each object of a cluster the neighborhood of a given radius has to contain at least a given

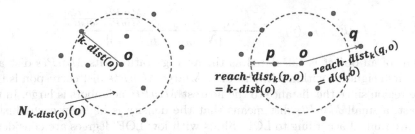

Fig. 2. k-distance and reachability distance (k = 4)

minimum number of objects ($MinPts$). Clusters are formally defined as maximal sets of density-connected objects. We introduce here some important definitions while briefly reviewing OPTICS algorithm.

Let p be an object from a dataset D, k be a positive integer and d be a distance metric, then (Fig. 2):

Definition 1: $k - \text{dist}(p)$, the k-distance of p, is defined as the distance $d(p, o)$ between p and object $o \in D$ satisfying: 1. at least k objects $q \in D$ having $d(p, q) \leq d(p, o)$, and 2. at most $(k\text{-}1)$ objects $q \in D$ having $d(p, q) < d(p, o)$.

Definition 2: $N_{k-\text{dist}(p)}(p) = \{q | q \in D, d(p, q) \leq k - \text{dist}(p)\}$ denotes the k-distance neighborhood of p.

Definition 3: $reach - \text{dist}_k(p, o) = max(k - \text{dist}(o), d(p, o))$ represents reachability distance of an object p with respect to object o.

The OPTICS-algorithm computes a "walk" through the data, and calculates for each object the smallest reachability-distance with respect to an object considered before it in the walk. A low reachability-distance indicates an object with a cluster, and a high reachability-distance indicates a noise object or a jump from one cluster to another cluster. Each cluster should hold different characteristics of the concept. The differences are caused by variations of conditions which videos taken under (viewpoints, scenes, illumination and so on) or diversity in meaning of the concept itself.

3.3   Shot Selection

For each obtained cluster, we assign outlier factor for each shot based on outlying property relative to its surrounding space. Differently from shot clustering step, in this step surrounding space of a shot is limited within in its own cluster. We use calculation method of LOF (Local Outlier Factor) proposed in [12]. There are numerous methods of outlier detection which have been proposed so far in the literature [24]. Among those, LOF is one of the most efficient and easy-to-implement. Especially, it makes use of computation during clustering ($k - \text{dist}, N_{k-\text{dist}}$). Therefore, we chose it to simplify the calculation process. Actually, the combination of OPTICS and LOF is quite natural and has been employed in some previous work [25]. LOF of a point p is formally defined as follows.

$$LOF_{MinPts}(p) = \frac{\sum_{o \in N_{MinPts-dist(p)}(p)} \frac{MinPts-dist(p)}{MinPts-dist(o)}}{|N_{MinPts-dist(p)}(p)|} \qquad (1)$$

LOF of an object is calculated as the average ratio of its $MinPts$-dist and that of its neighbors within $MinPts$-dist. A large $MinPts$-dist corresponds to a sparse region since the distance to the nearest $MinPts$ neighbors is large. In the contrast, a small $MinPts$-dist means that the density is high. In each cluster, shots are ranked according to LOF. Shots with low LOF degrees are considered as relevant shots and brought to the top of the cluster. $MinPts$ is the most important parameter for finding clusters and calculating LOF. Larger $MinPts$ means more clusters. Optimized value of $MinPts$ varies on the concept. In our experiments, we try several values and report the one with the best performance on average.

Algorithm 1. Shot selection

$N_t \leftarrow 0$
$N_m \leftarrow N_s/N_c$
for $c = 1$ to N_c **do**
   $C(c).is \leftarrow 1$
   $C(c).av \leftarrow 1$
end for

while $N_t < N_s \& \exists c : C(c).av = 1$ **do**
   for $c = 1$ to N_c **do**
     if $C(c).av = 1$ **then**
       if $C(c).ts > 2 * N_m$ **then**
         $C(c).ns \leftarrow N_m$
       else
         $C(c).ns \leftarrow C(c).ts/2$
         $C(c).av \leftarrow 0$
       end if
     end if
   end for
   for $c = 1$ to N_c **do**
     for $i = C(c).is$ to $C(c).ns$ **do**
       if $C(c).S[i] \notin \mathbb{S}$ **then**
         $push(C(c).S[i], \mathbb{S})$
         $N_t \leftarrow N_t + 1$
       end if
     end for
   end for
   for $c = 1$ to N_c **do**
     $C(c).is \leftarrow C(c).is + C(c).ns$
   end for
   $N_m \leftarrow N_m + (N_s - N_t)/N_c$
end while

We propose a simple shot selection strategy which can guarantee that shots are selected from all clusters. Let N_s be number of shots we want to collect for a concept and N_c be number of clusters we obtained. Since some shots are shared among some clusters, simply selecting top N_s/N_c shots from each cluster obtains less than N_s shots. Our selection strategy tries to keep selecting shots from clusters which are still available until number of selected shots reaches N_s or no available clusters left. An "available cluster" must have more shots than twice of its maximal number of shots to be selected. This definition of available cluster is inspired by experimental results in the baseline [6] which show that only shots ranked among top-half should be considered as relevant shots. Selection order for clusters is determined by the mean LOF of their shots. Our selection strategy is summarized in Algorithm 1.

In Algorithm 1, N_t and N_m represent the total number of selected shots and the maximal number of shots can be selected from each cluster, respectively. $\mathbb{C} = \{C(c)|c = 1 : N_c\}$ is the group of obtained clusters. Each cluster $C(c)$ has following fields: $C(c).is$ means index of start-to-select shot, $C(c).ns$ means the number of shots to select from $C(c)$, $C(c).ts$ is the total number of shots in $C(c)$ and $C(c).av$ represent the availability of $C(c)$. If $C(c)$ is available, $C(c).av = 1$, otherwise $C(c).av = 0$. Collection of shots in $C(c)$ is denoted as $C(c).S$. Since shots are ranked as mentioned above, $C(c).S[1]$ is supposed to be the most relevant shot and $C(c).S[C(c).ts]$ should be the least relevant one in cluster $C(c)$. $\mathbb{S}$ is the collection of selected shots.

4   Experiments and Results

4.1   Experimental Setup

We conduct two experiments: dataset construction and action recognition to validate the efficiency of our method. For dataset construction, we use 11 actions defined in UCF YouTube Action (UCF11) dataset [13]: "basketball shooting", "biking/cycling", "diving", "golf swinging", "horse riding", "soccer juggling", "swinging", "tennis swinging", "trampoline jumping", "volleyball spiking", and "walking with a dog". Note that in this experiment, we do not use videos of that dataset. Our videos are automatically collected from Web source (YouTube) as described in Sect. 3.2. As for action recognition experiment, we use videos of that dataset which contains a total of 1168 videos. The dataset is challenging due to large variations in camera motion, object appearance and pose, object scale, viewpoint, cluttered background and illumination conditions. We train three SVM multi-class classifiers: one based on our collected data, one based on data retrieved by the baseline [2] and one based on standard training data. Finally, we use these classifiers to perform action recognition on the standard test data.

Our baseline is our most related work [2]. According to this method, first videos are ranked based on usage frequencies of tags. Shots are collected from videos which have tags with high co-occurrence frequencies. Next shots are ranked using VisualRank [10] which is a ranking method with a visual feature

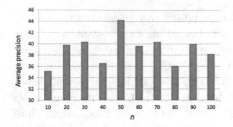
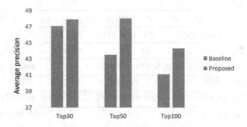

Fig. 3. Average precisions by the proposed method in different cases of n when $N = 100$.

Fig. 4. Average precisions by the proposed approach and the baseline in different cases of N.

Table 1. Precision rates of 11 action keywords with $N = 100$.

Action	Proposed	Baseline
basketball	**50**	35
biking	**23**	17
diving	**35**	28
golf_swing	52	**54**
horse_riding	**50**	42
soccer_juggling	**68**	63
swing	**36**	31
tennis_swing	47	**51**
trampoline_jumping	**54**	**54**
volleyball_spiking	58	**69**
walking	**14**	9
Average	44.3	41.1

based similarity matrix. Since it became hard to obtain tag information, we could not perform tag co-occurrence based video ranking step as proposed in the baseline. Here we use our method of shot collection and apply their idea of using VisualRank to shot ranking to compare with our proposed method of shot selection which composed of diversity based shot clustering and LOF based shot ranking. We show that our method can obtain higher precision rate for most of experimented actions and importantly, our results look more diverse than those by the baseline in all cases.

As distance metric, we use Rank-order distance [26] which has been demonstrated as a better density measurement than commonly used Euclidean distance [17]. We train a temporal ConvNet using UCF101 dataset [13] (split 1) following the approach proposed in [9] except that we insert a normalization layer between pool2 layer and conv3 layer. Using this modified network architecture, we obtained slightly better performance than the original one: 82.1 % versus 81.2 % [9] on UCF101 (split 1). We use 2048 dimensional full7 features

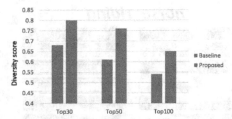

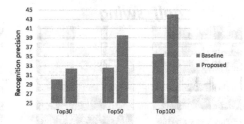

Fig. 5. Results of diversity evaluation. As opposed to the baseline, our approach retrieved more diverse shots from various videos. This explains for significant improvements in recognition performance (Fig. 6).

Fig. 6. Results of action recognition with automatically obtained training data. As shown in this figure, action model trained with shots obtained by the proposed method achieved better recognition rates in all cases of N.

extracted using the trained temporal ConvNet. $MinPts$ is set as T/n where T is total number of shots for a concept obtained after shot collection step (Sect. 3.1) and n is a constant. Ten values of n are experimented: 10, 20,..., 100.

4.2 Dataset Construction

In this experiment, we want to validate the quality of automatically constructed dataset regarding precision and diversity. Precision rate is calculated as percentage of relevant shots among top N shots following our baseline [2]. Three values of N are taken into consideration: 30, 50, 100. We evaluate relevance of upper ranked shots manually.

First we examine the effect of parameter settings on the performance of our proposed approach. Figure 3 shows average precision rates in different cases of n with $N = 100$. According to our empirical results, $n = 50$ obtained best performance. All results related to our proposed method that we report from here on refer to the case of $n = 50$. Figure 4 compares average precision rates in different cases of N between the proposed approach and the baseline. As shown in this figure, the proposed approach outperformed the baseline in all cases of N, especially when $N \geq 50$. In all of our results, "Proposed" means our approach and "Baseline" corresponds to VisualRank based shot ranking with our shot collection. Precision for all actions when $N = 100$ are shown in Table 1.

As shown in Table 1, for most of the actions, more relevant shots could be ranked to the top using our method. In many cases, top ranked shots by the baseline are although relevant to the concept but actually look similar to each other (See Fig. 7 for some example results). Even though average precision is not significantly improved, shots retrieved by our proposed method look much more diverse as shown in the followings.

Regarding evaluation for diversity of ranking results, we use evaluation method as described in [7]. Diversity score of a ranking result is defined as the ratio of the number of identical videos in its top ranked N video shots to N. This definition is based on the fact that shots from the same video tend to

golf_swing   **horse_riding**

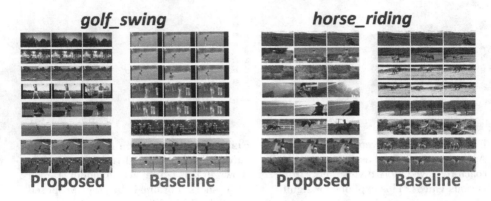

Proposed   Baseline   Proposed   Baseline

Fig. 7. Relevant shots among top 15 shots retrieved by our proposed method and the baseline for "golf_swing" and "horse_riding". As seen here, shots by the baseline tend to look similar while shots by our method are taken from various view points against different background.

look similar. The results of diversity evaluation are summarized in Fig. 5. As shown in Fig. 5, overall, the diversity score was significantly enhanced by using the proposed method. Figure 7 shows some examples of relevant shots among top 15 shots obtained by our method and the baseline.

4.3   Action Recognition

In this experiment, we validate performance of our automatically collected training data for the task of recognition on standard test data. To evaluate recognition performance, we follow the original setup [13] using leave one out cross validation for a pre-defined set of 25 folds. Average accuracy over all classes is reported as performance measure. We use top ranked N shots to train action classifiers. Similar to the previous experiment, three values of N are taken into consideration: 30, 50 and 100.

Figure 6 shows recognition accuracy rates by the proposed approach and the baseline in all cases of N. As shown in this figure, we obtained significant precision gain compared to the baseline. The recognition precision was boosted from approximately 35 % to 44 % in case of $N = 100$. This can be explained mostly by the improvements regarding diversity in the results (Sect. 4.2). Since many shots obtained by the baseline look similar, the information we can gain from them is much less than that from shots retrieved by our proposed approach. These results verified the fact that a high quality action database should reflect as well as possible the diversity of the concepts. The precision rate is further improved as more top-ranked shots are used to train.

In case of using standard training data, the average recognition rate was 81.5 %. This result is comparable to other approaches on the same dataset [18,27]. [27] with probabilistic fusion of multiple motion descriptors and scene context descriptors achieved 73.2 %. Especially, the state-of-the-art motion hand-crafted features (dense trajectory based MBH) [18] achieved 80.6 %. To the best

of our knowledge, there are no reports with CNN features on this dataset for us
to compare.

5 Conclusions

In this paper, we proposed a fully automatic approach for action dataset construction with noisy Web videos. Our approach aims to solve the problem of
limitation in quantity of training data for the task of action recognition. In our
experiments, we first constructed a database for 11 actions in UCF11 dataset
using YouTube videos with our proposed approach. We then employed this database to train action classifiers and applied them to classify standard test data of
UCF11. Even though collected training data by it is still far from "clean data"
as standard training data, it offers the advantage of a fully automatic, scalable
learning and shows the potential for development of approaches for automatic
construction of action databases.

References

1. Laptev, I., Marszalek, M., Schmid, C., Rozenfeld, B.: Learning realistic human
   actions from movies. In: Proceedings of IEEE Computer Vision and Pattern Recognition (2008)
2. Do, H.N., Yanai, K.: Automatic extraction of relevant video shots of specific actions
   exploiting Web data. Comput. Vis. Image Underst. **118**, 2–15 (2014)
3. Adrian, U., Christian, S., Markus, K., Thomas, M.B.: Learning automatic concept
   detectors from online video. Comput. Vis. Image Underst. **114**, 429–438 (2010)
4. Marszalek, M., Laptev, I., Schmid, C.: Actions in context. In: Proceedings of IEEE
   International Conference on Computer Vision (2009)
5. Duchenne, O., Laptev, I., Sivic, J., Bach, F., Ponce, J.: Automatic annotation of
   human actions in video. In: Proceedings of IEEE Computer Vision and Pattern
   Recognition, pp. 1491–1498 (2009)
6. Do, H.N., Yanai, K.: Automatic construction of an action video shot database
   using web videos. In: Proceedings of IEEE International Conference on Computer
   Vision, pp. 527–534 (2011)
7. Do, H.N., Yanai, K.: VisualTextualRank: an extension of visualrank to large-scale
   video shot extraction exploiting tag co-occurrence. IEICE Trans. Inf. Syst. **e98–D**,
   166–172 (2015)
8. Khurram, S., Amir, R.Z., Mubarak, S.: UCF101: A Dataset of 101 Human Actions
   Classes from Videos in the Wild. CoRR abs/1212.0402 (2012)
9. Simonyan, K., Zisserman, A.: Two-stream convolutional networks for action recognition in videos. In: Proceedings of Advances in Neural Information Processing
   Systems, pp. 568–576 (2014)
10. Jing, Y., Baluja, S.: VisualRank: applying pagerank to large-scale image search.
    IEEE Trans. Pattern Anal. Mach. Intell. **30**, 1870–1890 (2008)
11. Mihael, A., Markus, M.B., Hans-Peter, K., Jorg, S.: OPTICS: ordering points to
    identify the clustering structure. In: Proceedings of the ACM SIGMOD Interna-
    tional Conference on Management of Data, pp. 49–60 (1999)
12. Chiu, A.L.M., Fu, A.C.: Enhancements on local outlier detection. In: Proceedings
    of IEEE Database Engineering and Applications Symposium, pp. 298–307 (2003)

13. Jingen, L., Jiebo, L., Shah, M.: Recognizing realistic actions from videos. In: Proceedings of IEEE Computer Vision and Pattern Recognition, pp. 1996–2003 (2009)
14. Chen, X., Abhinav, S., Abhinav, G.: Neil: extracting visual knowledge from web data. In: Proceedings of IEEE International Conference on Computer Vision (2013)
15. Collins, B., Deng, J., Li, K., Fei-Fei, L.: Towards scalable dataset construction: an active learning approach. In: Forsyth, D., Torr, P., Zisserman, A. (eds.) ECCV 2008, Part I. LNCS, vol. 5302, pp. 86–98. Springer, Heidelberg (2008)
16. Schroff, F., Criminisi, A., Zisserman, A.: Harvesting image databases from the web. IEEE Trans. Pattern Anal. Mach. Intell. **33**, 754–766 (2011)
17. Xia, Y., Cao, X., Wen, F., Sun, J.: Well begun is half done: generating high-quality seeds for automatic image dataset construction from web. In: Fleet, D., Pajdla, T., Schiele, B., Tuytelaars, T. (eds.) ECCV 2014, Part IV. LNCS, vol. 8692, pp. 387–400. Springer, Heidelberg (2014)
18. Wang, H., Schmid, C.: Action recognition with improved trajectories. In: Proceedings of IEEE International Conference on Computer Vision, pp. 3551–3558 (2013)
19. Oneata, D., Verbeek, J., Schmid, C.: Action and event recognition with fisher vectors on a compact feature set. In: Proceedings of IEEE International Conference on Computer Vision, pp. 1817–1824 (2013)
20. Peng, X., Zou, C., Qiao, Y., Peng, Q.: Action recognition with stacked fisher vectors. In: Fleet, D., Pajdla, T., Schiele, B., Tuytelaars, T. (eds.) ECCV 2014, Part V. LNCS, vol. 8693, pp. 581–595. Springer, Heidelberg (2014)
21. Jeff, D., Lisa, A.H., Sergio, G., Marcus, R., Subhashini, V., Kate, S., Trevor, D.: Long-term Recurrent Convolutional Networks for Visual Recognition and Description. CoRR abs/1411.4389 (2014)
22. Joe, Y.H.N., Matthew, J.H., Sudheendra, V., Oriol, V., Rajat, M., George, T.: Beyond Short Snippets: Deep Networks for Video Classification. CoRR abs/1503.08909 (2015)
23. Golge, E., Duygulu, P.: ConceptMap: mining noisy web data for concept learning. In: Fleet, D., Pajdla, T., Schiele, B., Tuytelaars, T. (eds.) ECCV 2014, Part VII. LNCS, vol. 8695, pp. 439–455. Springer, Heidelberg (2014)
24. Chandola, V., Banerjee, A., Kumar, V.: Anomaly detection: a survey. Proc. ACM Comput. Surv. **41**, 15:1–15:58 (2009)
25. Breunig, M.M., Kriegel, H.-P., Sander, J., Ng, R.T.: OPTICS-OF: identifying local outliers. In: Żytkow, J.M., Rauch, J. (eds.) PKDD 1999. LNCS (LNAI), vol. 1704, pp. 262–270. Springer, Heidelberg (1999)
26. Chunhui, Z., Fang, W., Jian, S.: A rank-order distance based clustering algorithm for face tagging. In: Proceedings of IEEE Computer Vision and Pattern Recognition, pp. 481–488 (2011)
27. Reddy, K., Shah, M.: Recognizing 50 human action categories of web videos. Mach. Vis. Appl. **24**, 971–981 (2013)

Image/Video Coding and Transmission

Fast Coding Strategy for HEVC by Motion Features and Saliency Applied on Difference Between Successive Image Blocks

Pallab Kanti Podder[1]([✉]), Manoranjan Paul[1], and Manzur Murshed[2]

[1] School of Computing & Mathematics, Charles Sturt University,
Bathurst, NSW 2795, Australia
{ppodder,mpaul}@csu.edu.au
[2] School of Information Technology, Federation University,
Churchill, VIC 3842, Australia
manzur.murshed@federation.edu.au

Abstract. Introducing a number of innovative and powerful coding tools, the High Efficiency Video Coding (HEVC) standard promises double compression efficiency, compared to its predecessor H.264, with similar perceptual quality. The increased computational time complexity is an important issue for the video coding research community as well. An attempt to reduce this complexity of HEVC is adopted in this paper, by efficient selection of appropriate block-partitioning modes based on motion features and the saliency applied to the difference between successive image blocks. As this difference gives us the explicit visible motion and salient information, we develop a cost function by combining the motion features and image difference salient feature. The combined features are then converted into area of interest (AOI) based binary pattern for the current block. This pattern is then compared with a previously defined codebook of binary pattern templates for a subset of mode selection. Motion estimation (ME) and motion compensation (MC) are performed only on the selected subset of modes, without exhaustive exploration of all modes available in HEVC. The experimental results reveal a reduction of 42 % encoding time complexity of HEVC encoder with similar subjective and objective image quality.

Keywords: HEVC · Motion features · Saliency feature · Area of Interest (AOI) · Intermode selection

1 Introduction

The prime goal of the latest HEVC [1] standard is to provide the same perceptual quality compared to its antecedent H.264 [2], at approximately 50 % bitrate reduction for efficient transmission and storage of high volume video data [3]. HEVC introduces inventive approaches, including the coding unit (CU) size extension from 16×16 up to 64×64-pixels, variable size transform unit (TU), and symmetric/asymmetric block partitioning phenomenon that have achieved

© Springer International Publishing Switzerland 2016
T. Bräunl et al. (Eds.): PSIVT 2015, LNCS 9431, pp. 175–186, 2016.
DOI: 10.1007/978-3-319-29451-3_15

on improved performance gain, but at a cost of more than 4 times algorithmic complexity for a particular implementation [4,5]. For this reason, any electronic devices with limited processing capacity could not fully exploit HEVC encoding and decoding features. This motivated us to reduce the computational time of HEVC encoder by appropriate selection of inter-prediction modes. For this to happen, only the AOI in a video is taken into account that comprise with phase correlation based motion features and the saliency feature after applying it on the difference between successive image blocks. Unlike *HEVC test model* (HM12.1) [6], the selected CUs with, and without, AOI are motion estimated and motion compensated with modes in the higher and lower depth levels, respectively. Thus, exhaustive exploration of all modes in each coding depth level can be avoided (level 64×64, 32×32, 16×16 and 8×8 are denoted as depth level 0, 1, 2, 3 respectively) by proposed method. This results in computational time reduction. To select a particular motion prediction mode, HM exhaustively checks the *Lagrangian cost function* (LCF) [7]using all modes in each coding depth level. The LCF, $\Theta(k_n)$ for mode selection (kn is the nth mode) is defined by:

$$\Theta(k_n) = D(k_n) + \lambda \times R(k_n) \tag{1}$$

where λ is the Lagrangian multiplier, $D(k_n)$ is the distortion, and $R(k_n)$ is the resultant bit, which are determined by modes for each CU. In order to select the best partitioning mode in a coding depth level, HM checks at least 8, and at most 24, inter-prediction modes with lowest LCF. This process is time consuming due to the exploration of all modes in one or more coding depth levels. Moreover, only the LCF-based mode decision could not always provide the best *rate distortion*(RD) performance in different operational coding points due to advanced parameter settings in HEVC. Therefore, instead of merely depending on LCF, some consecutive pre-processing stages are executed by the proposed technique that makes mode decision process more appropriate and less time consuming (shown in Fig. 1).

In literature, some researchers have contributed to reduce time complexity [8,9]. In order to terminate the exploring modes in lower level, Hou *et al.* [10] recommend a RD cost based threshold to explore modes only in the higher level that results in 30 % time savings with 0.5 % quality loss. Vanne *et al.* [11] propose an efficient inter-mode decision scheme by finding the candidate PU modes of symmetric and asymmetric motion partition. The tested results reveal the reduction of HEVC encoder complexity by 31 %–51 % at the cost of 0.2 %–1.3 % bit-rate increment. Pan *et al.* [12] introduce an early MERGE mode decision algorithm to reduce computational complexity of HEVC encoder. They achieve 35 % time savings with the bit-rate increment of 0.32 %, and quality loss of 0.11 dB peak signal to noise ratio (PSNR).

The *energy concentration ratio* (ECR) from phase correlation was extracted and employed for mode selection in HEVC by Podder *et al.* [13](used in [14] for H.264 standard). They save computational time by sacrificing 0.24 dB PSNR on average compared to the full search approach of HM. As ECR stipulates only the residual error between current block and motion-compensated reference block, it would not provide expected compression results. For more accurate decision on ME and MC modes, in this paper, we extract three motion features from phase correlation. Other than motion, visual attentive areas are also extracted by exploiting the saliency feature. Compared to the current image, as the difference between two successive images provides the actual displacement and salient information, we apply the saliency feature on image difference to capture motion and saliency dominated precise areas perceived by human visual system. Moreover, as there is no difference of color or contrast in static areas, the image difference produced motion and salient information would be the premier option to determine visual observant areas. The features are incorporated by developing a weighted cost function to actuate AOI-based binary pattern for the current block to select a subset of inter-modes. From the selected subset, the final mode is determined based on their lowest LCF. The proposed method not only reduces the computational time by appropriate selection of AOI based ME and MC modes but also demonstrates similar subjective and objective image quality.

The remainder of this paper is structured as follows: Sect. 2 describes all the key steps of the proposed method; experimental results and discussions are detailed in Sect. 3, while Sect. 4 is the conclusion of the paper.

2   Proposed Mode Selection Technique

The phase-correlation renders relative displacement information between current block and the reference block by Fast Fourier Transformation (FFT). We first extract phase-correlation related three motion features including (i) ECR (α), (ii) predicted motion vector (dx, dy) and (iii) phase correlation peak (β) and combine them with saliency feature (γ) that is applied on the difference between successive image blocks. We evolve a unified AOI based cost function using the normalized motion features and weighted average of the saliency values to determine a unified AOI feature for the current block. The binary AOI pattern from the unified AOI features is then configured by applying threshold and to select a sub-set of inter-prediction modes. The final mode from the selected subset is determined by their lowest LCF. The whole process is shown as a block diagram in Fig. 1.

2.1   Motion Features Extraction

The phase correlation is calculated by applying the FFT and then *inverse* FFT (IFFT) of the current and reference blocks and finally applying the FFTSHIFT function as follows:

$$\Omega = fftshift \left| ifft \left(e^{j(\angle F_r - \angle F_c)} \right) \right| \tag{2}$$

where Fc and Fr are the Fast Fourier transformed blocks of the current C and reference R blocks respectively and $\angle$ is the phase of the corresponding transformed block. Note that Ω is a two dimensional matrix. We evaluate the

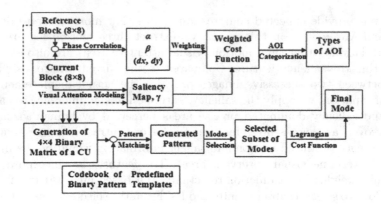

Fig. 1. Block diagram of the proposed mode selection process.

phase correlation peak (β) from the position of $(dx + blocksize/2 + 1, dy + blocksize/2 + 1)$ as follows:

$$\beta = \Omega\left(dx + blocksize/2 + 1, dy + blocksize/2 + 1\right) \tag{3}$$

where the blocksize is 8 if 8×8-pixel block is used for phase correlation. Then we compute the predicted motion vector (dx, dy) by subtracting blocksize-1 from the (x, y) position of Ω where we find the maximum value of Ω. We use the phase of the current block and magnitude of the motion-compensated block in the reference frame and finally calculate the matched reference block (Ψ) for the current block by:

$$\Psi = \left| ifft\left(|F_r|\, e^{j(\angle F_c)}\right) \right| \tag{4}$$

Now the displacement error (§) is enumerated by: §=C-Ψ. We then apply the *discrete cosine transform* (DCT) to error §and calculate the ECR (i.e., α) as the ratio of low frequency component and the total energy of the error block by:

$$\alpha = \left(D_{error\_low}/D_{error\_total}\right) \tag{5}$$

where D_{error_low} and D_{error_total} represent the top-left triangle energy and the whole area energy of a particular block.

2.2   Saliency Feature Extraction

The saliency map is operated as a tool (based on [15,16]) and incorporated into our coding architecture. The exploited graph-based visual saliency (GBVS) technique gives us the variance map of AOI based human visual features for an 8×8-pixel block consisting of the values ranging from 0 to 1. We extract the saliency feature, γ, by averaging all values of a given 8×8 block. Our focus is to encode the AOI based salient portions with more bits to achieve better compression and improve coding performance.

2.3 Cost Function Based AOI Categorization

After evaluating the phase correlation extracted motion features (i.e., α, β and (dx, dy) and saliency extracted variance map (i.e., γ), we finally determine a cost function $\eta(i, j)$ from these four features for (i, j)th block by-

$$\eta(i,j) = \omega_1\alpha(i,j) + \omega_2(1 - \beta) + \omega_3((\frac{|dx|}{\delta}) + (\frac{|dy|}{\delta})) + \omega_4(\gamma) \qquad (6)$$

where δ is the maximum block size, and $\omega 1$ to $\omega 4$ are the weights with $\sum_{i=1}^{4} \omega_i = 1$. We innovatively derive weights for each feature and only consider 0.50, 0.25, 0.125, and 0.125 weights based on the relative texture deviation of the current block against that of the whole frame. First we sort four features based on their values and if the value of the *Standard Deviation*(STD) of the block is smaller than the value of the current frame then the highest weight (i.e., 0.50) is applied to the feature 1 (i.e., sorted) and the lowest weight (i.e., 0.125) is applied to the feature 4 (according to sorted list); otherwise, inverse weighted order is applied. If the resultant value of the cost function (i.e., η) is greater than a predefined threshold the block is tagged by '1' otherwise tagged by '0' where binary '1' and '0' corresponds to AOI and non-AOI respectively. The rationality of the proposed weight selection strategy is that if the current block has higher texture variation compared to the current frame, the current block should be encoded with more bits compared to the rest of the blocks to achieve similar/improved RD performance. The relationship of the quantitative motion and salience features with the human visual features are depicted in Fig. 2. Figure 2 (b-d) shows the categories of motion-peak (β) and their corresponding values provided by ECR (Fig. 2 (e)) and saliency feature (Fig. 2 (f)) for *Tennis* video. Figure 3 illustrates

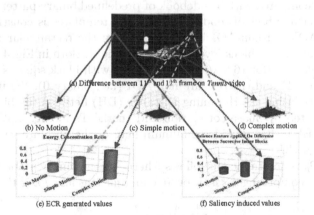

Fig. 2. Illustration of motion features and saliency feature generated at different CUs of 12th frame on Tennis video; (b-d) are the phase shifted plots for no motion (0.4), simple motion (0.7) and complex motion (0.8); (e-f) corresponds to the respective values generated by ECR and saliency map for CUs at positions (3, 1), (3, 10) and (5, 7) respectively. For clear visualization we use 32×32 block size.

the impact of saliency map and from Fig. 3 (a), we clearly depict the ellipse like red marked area as the table tennis court edge (obviously a visually attentive area) that is precisely identified by the saliency feature (red marked ellipse like area in Fig. 3 (c)) although three motion features of phase correlation could not grasp the court edge as it does not have any motion (white marked ellipse like area in Fig. 3 (b)). Thus, the proposed combined strategy improves the RD performance by recognizing not only the AOI-based motion features of phase correlation but also the AOI-based visually attentive areas inside the videos.

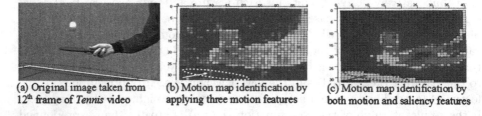

(a) Original image taken from 12th frame of *Tennis* video

(b) Motion map identification by applying three motion features

(c) Motion map identification by both motion and saliency features

Fig. 3. Identification of motion and salient areas with and without saliency feature based cost function (Color figure online).

2.4   Intermode Selection

For the generation of binary matrix, we exploit each of the 8×8 pixel blocks from the 32×32 pixel blocks (i.e., CU) and produce a matrix of 4×4 binary values for each CU (applying threshold). The cost function generated 4×4 binary matrix is then compared with a codebook of predefined binary pattern templates (BPT) to select a subset of modes. Each of the templates is constructed with a pattern of AOI and non-AOI block focusing on the rectangular and regular object shapes at 32×32 block level as shown in Fig. 4. Both in Fig. 4 (for 32×32 level) and Table 1(b) (for 16×16 level), the cells with black squares present the AOI (i.e., binary 1) and the rest are non-AOI (i.e., binary 0). We use a simple similarity metric using the Hamming Distance (DH) between the binary matrix of a CU generated by phase correlation and the BPTs in Fig. 4. We select the best-matched BPT that provides minimum sum of the absolute values of their differences for a CU.

The DH, D_h is determined as follows where S is the binary motion prediction matrix of a CU comprising 4×4 '1' or '0' combinations and Tk is the k-th BPT:

$$D_h(x,y) = \sum_{x=0}^{4} \sum_{y=0}^{4} |S(x,y) - T_k(x,y)| \tag{7}$$

The best-matched j-th BPT is selected from all BPTs as follows:

$$B_j = arg_{T_k \forall BPT} \min(D_h) \tag{8}$$

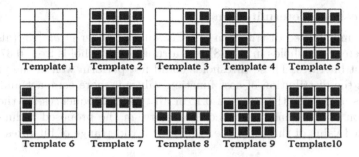

Fig. 4. Codebook of the proposed binary pattern templates for subset of inter-mode selection where template cells with black squares present AOI (i.e., binary 1) and the rest are non-AOI (i.e., binary 0).

The mode selection process from the BPTs at 32×32 and 16×16 coding depth levels is illustrated in Table 1 (a) and (b) respectively. Once a particular template selects a subset of candidate modes at 32×32 level, the final mode is decided by their lowest Lagrangian cost function. Again, at 32×32 level, if any of the 16×16 coding depth level modes is selected, we further explore smaller modes at 16×16 level using the AOI pattern (i.e., presence or absence of binary 1 and 0 as shown in Table 1 (b)).

Table 1. Selection technique of inter-modes at 32×32 and 16×16 coding depth levels.

Templates Based on AOI at 32×32 Block Level	Selection of Modes at 32×32 Block Level
Template 1	Skip or 32×32
Template 2	Intra 16×16 or Inter 16×16
Template 3 & 4	32×16 or Inter 16×16
Template 5	32×8 or Inter 16×16
Template 6	32×24 or Inter 16×16
Template 7 & 8	16×32 or Inter 16×16
Template 9	8×32 or Inter 16×16
Template 10	24×32 or Inter 16×16

(a) Mode selection at 32×32 block level based on predefined binary pattern templates

Pattern of AOI at 16×16 Block Level	Selected Subset of Inter-modes
	16×8, 8×16 or 8×8
	16×8 and 8×16
	16×12, 16×4, 12×16 or 4×16

(b) Subset of mode selection at 16×16 block level based on AOI pattern

Then the equation for the final mode (ξ) selection is given by:

$$\xi = arg_{\forall k_n} \min(\Theta(k_n)) \tag{9}$$

where $\Theta(k_n)$ is the Lagrangian cost function for mode selection.

2.5   Threshold Determination

Due to the imbalanced distribution of ECR values Podder *et al.* [13] (also mentioned different thresholds in [17,18]) use a range of thresholds from 0.37 to 0.52 for different bit-rates. Those thresholds could not perform well in the proposed method as the distribution of cost function values is more compact and almost in all cases it exceeds the value of 0.15 in all types of sequences for the blocks with motion and dominant salience. Therefore, in the proposed technique, we use the fixed value of threshold (i.e., 0.15) for a wide range of bit-rates.

3   Experimental Results and Analysis

To verify the performance of the proposed algorithm, experimental results are presented with six *standard definition* (SD) videos- *Tennis, Tempete, Waterfall, Silent, Paris, Bridgeclose,* four *high definition* (HD) videos- *Pedestrian, Bluesky, Rushhour, Parkrun* and two *multiview* (MV) videos- *Exit and Ballroom.* Each of the video sequences are encoded with 25 frame rate and search length ±64. We compare the proposed method results with HM of HEVC standard as HM outperforms the existing mode selection techniques in the literature. We use IPPP format with Group of picture (GOP) 32 for both techniques and two reference frames.

Table 2. Average time savings (%) by the proposed method (against HM) in terms of mode selection for each type of sequences-a theoretical analysis.

Sequence types	Average no. of inter-modes selected per CU by HM	Average no. of inter-modes selected per CU by proposed method	Average time savings (%) in terms of mode selection
SD	16.89	7.24	57.14
HD	18.92	9.63	49.11
MV	19.58	11.16	43.01
Average percentage (%) of time savings			49.75

3.1   Experimental Setup

In this paper, the experiments are conducted by a dedicated desktop machine (with Intel core i7 3770 CPU @ 3.4 GHz, 16 GB RAM and 1TB HDD) running 64 bit Windows operating system. The proposed scheme and HEVC with exhaustive mode selection scheme are developed based on the reference software HM (version 12.1) [6]. RD performance of both schemes are compared considering the maximum CU size of 32×32 by enabling both symmetric and asymmetric partitioning block size of 32×32 to 8×8 depth levels for a wide range of bit-rates (using QP=20, 24, 28, 32 and 36). The calculations of BD-PSNR and BD-Bit Rate were performed according to the procedures described in [19].

3.2   Results and Discussions

For the theoretical justification of computational time of all type of sequences, we first compare the average number of modes selected in each CU by HM12.1 and the proposed method. The results in Table 2 shows that HM checks more options in all cases and normally requires more computational time. From Table 2, the overall average percentage of encoding time savings by the proposed method is 49.75 and the reason of this acquisition is the efficient subset of intermode selection with simple criteria. However, we cannot ignore the pre-processing stages of the proposed method, and by calculation we notice that over twelve sequences on average 6.71 % extra encoding time is required to execute phase correlation and saliency related pre-processing overheads (see Fig. 1). Thus, theoretically we anticipate to acquire 43.04 % computational time savings on average. The experimental evaluation reveals that over twelve different sequences, and for a wide range of bit-rates, the proposed method reduces on average 42 % (range: 37 %–45 %) computational time as shown in Fig. 5 (a). The equation for the time savings (TS) is defined as:

$$TS = \frac{(T_o - T_p)}{T_o} \times 100\% \tag{10}$$

where T_0 and T_p denote the total encoding time consumed by HM and the proposed method respectively. For comprehensive performance test, we execute the computational time analysis of both techniques based on video categories and find that the proposed method achieves on average 41 % encoding time savings compared to HM12.1 as shown in Fig. 5 (b). The figure also reveals that the proposed technique saves more computational time for SD video type (48 %).

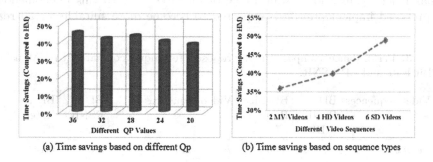

(a) Time savings based on different Qp   (b) Time savings based on sequence types

Fig. 5. Illustration of time savings by the proposed method against HM.

To test the performance of the proposed method objectively, we first compare the RD performance against HM using three different sequence types (one SD, HD and MV) for a wide range of bit-rates as demonstrated in Fig. 6. The figure shows that the proposed method achieves similar RD performance with HM12.1 especially caring about the AOI based CUs and partitioning them by efficient

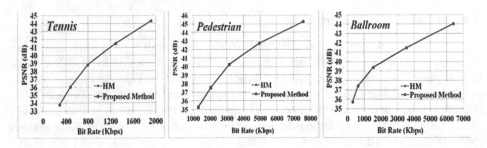

Fig. 6. Comparative study on RD performance by HM12.1 and the proposed method for a wide range of bit-rates.

selection of appropriate block partitioning modes. Table 3 represents the performance comparison of the proposed method for twelve divergent video sequences. The results reveal that compared to the mode selection approach in HM, the proposed technique achieves an almost similar RD performance (small average reduction of 0.021 dB PSNR) with a negligible bit-rate increment of 0.14 %.

Figure 7(a) shows the original image of *Tennis* video taken for subjective quality test and Fig. 7(b) and Fig. 7(c) illustrate the reproduced images by HM and the proposed method respectively. To present the comparison in image quality let us concentrate on the cuff and sleeve sections of the shirt in the three images which are marked by the red, yellow, and white ellipses respectively. It can be perceived that the three ellipse marked sections have almost similar image quality. It was presented earlier in this manuscript that the proposed method requires less encoding time. Hence it can be concluded that the proposed technique shows significant computational time savings compared to HM12.1 with similar image quality for a wide range of bit-rates. Due to this phenomenon, the proposed implementation is expected to become more suitable for all real

Table 3. Performance comparison of proposed technique compared to HM using BD-Bit Rate and BD-PSNR.

Video sequences	BD-PSNR (dB)	BD-Bit Rate (%)	Video sequences	BD-PSNR (dB)	BD-Bit Rate (%)
Tennis	−0.010	0.06	*Pedestrian*	−0.025	0.14
Tempete	−0.021	0.14	*Bluesky*	−0.039	0.22
Waterfall	−0.018	0.11	*Rushhour*	−0.031	0.18
Silent	−0.024	0.16	*Parkrun*	−0.023	0.15
Paris	−0.013	0.10	*Ballroom*	−0.026	0.20
Bridgeclose	−0.012	0.13	*Exit*	−0.013	0.19
Average BD-PSNR and BD-Bit Rate over twelve sequences				−0.021	0.14

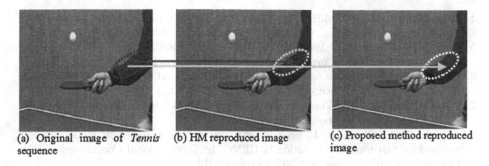

(a) Original image of *Tennis* sequence   (b) HM reproduced image   (c) Proposed method reproduced image

Fig. 7. Subjective quality assessment for HM12.1 and the proposed method for *Tennis* video sequence. The figures are achieved from the 20*th* frame of the *Tennis* video at the same bit-rate (Color figure online).

time video coding applications especially for a number of electronic devices with limited processing power and battery capacity.

4 Conclusion

In this work, a novel coding framework for HM performance improvement is presented. This is implemented by exploiting the AOI based mode selection technique comprising three different motion features of phase correlation and saliency features of human visual attention. The motion features focus on three different aspects of motions in each CU and the saliency feature captures the visual attentive areas. An adaptive cost function is formulated to determine a subset of inter-modes using predefined AOI based binary pattern templates. The Lagrangian optimization criterion is employed in the selected subset of modes to fix the final mode. Compared to HM with exhaustive mode selection strategy, the proposed scheme reduces on average 42 % computational time (range: 37 %–45 %) while providing similar image quality for a wide range of bit-rates.

Acknowledgement. This work was supported in part by the Australian Research Council under Discovery Projects Grant DP130103670.

References

1. High Efficiency Video Coding, document ITU-T Rec. H.265 and ISO/IEC 23008-2 (HEVC), ITU-T and ISO/IEC, April 2013
2. Wiegand, T., Sullivan, G.J., Bjontegaard, G., Luthra, A.: Overview of the H.264/AVC video coding standard. IEEE Trans. Circ. Syst. Video Technol. **13**(7), 560–576 (2003)
3. Bross, B., Han, W.J., Ohm, J.R., Sullivan, G.J., Wiegand, T.: High efficiency video coding text specification draft 8. JTCVC- J1003, Sweden (2012)

4. Bossen, F., Bross, B., Suhring, K., Flynn, D.: HEVC complexity and implementation analysis. IEEE Trans. Circ. Syst. Video Technol. **22**(12), 1684–1695 (2012)
5. Lu, Y.: Real-Time CPU Based H.265/HEVC Encoding Solution with Intel Platform Technology. Intel Corporation, Shanghai, PRC (2013)
6. Joint Collaborative Team on Video Coding (JCT-VC), HM Software Manual, CVS server (2013) (http://hevc.kw.bbc.co.uk/svn/jctvc-hm/)
7. Paul, M., Murshed, M.: Video coding focusing on block partitioning and occlusions. IEEE Trans. Image Process. **19**(3), 691–701 (2010)
8. Lee, A., Jun, D.S., Kim, J., Seok, J.: An efficient interprediction mode decision method for fast motion estimation in HEVC. In: International Conference on ICT Convergence (ICTC), pp. 502–505, October 2013
9. Tan, H.L., Liu, F., Tan, Y.H., Yeo, C.: On fast coding tree block and mode decision for high efficiency video coding. In: International Conference on Acoustic and Speech Signal Processing (ICASSP), pp. 825–828, March 2012
10. Hou, X., Xue, Y.: Fast coding unit partitioning algorithm for HEVC. In: IEEE International Conference on Consumer Electronics (ICCE), pp. 7–10 (2014)
11. Vanne, J., Viitanen, M., Hamalainen, T.: Efficient mode decision schemes for HEVC inter prediction. IEEE Trans. Circ. Syst. Video Technol. **24**(9), 1579–1593 (2014)
12. Pan, Z., Kwong, S., Sun, M.T., Lei, J.: Early MERGE mode decision based on motion estimation and hierarchical depth correlation for HEVC. IEEE Trans. Broadcast. **60**(2), 405–412 (2014)
13. Podder, P., Paul, M., Murshed, M., Chakrabarty, S.: Fast intermode selection for HEVC video coding using phase correlation. In: IEEE International Conference on Digital Image Computing: Techniques and Applications (DICTA), pp. 1–8 (2014)
14. Paul, M., Lin, W., Lau, C.T., Lee, B.S.: Direct inter-mode selection for H.264 video coding using phase correlation. IEEE Trans. Image Process. **20**(2), 461–473 (2011)
15. Harel, J., Koch, C., Perona, P.: Graph-Based Visual Saliency. California Institute of Technology, Pasadena, (2006)
16. January 2015. http://www.vision.caltech.edu/~harel/share/gbvs.php and http://libra.msra.cn/Publication/4113493/graph-based-visual-saliency
17. Paul, M., Frater, M., Arnold, J.: An efficient mode selection prior to the actual encoding for H.264/AVC encoder. IEEE Trans. Multimedia **11**(4), 581–588 (2009)
18. Podder, P., Paul, M., Murshed, M.: A novel motion classification based intermode selection strategy for HEVC performance improvement. Elsevier J. Neurocomputing **173**(3), 1211–1220 (2016). doi:10.1016/j.neucom.2015.08.079
19. Bjontegaard, G.: Calculation of average PSNR differences between RD curves. ITU-T SC16/Q6, VCEG-M33, Austin, USA (2001)

Neighboring Sample Prediction Coding
for HEVC Screen Content Coding

Yao-Jen Chang[1], Ching-Chieh Lin[1], Jih-Sheng Tu[1],
Chun-Lung Lin[1(✉)], Chao-Hsiung Hung[1], and Pei-Hsuan Tsai[2]

[1] Industrial Technology Research Institute, Hsinchu, Taiwan
{britpablo, JackLin, sunriseJSTu,
Chunlung, chhung}@itri.org.tw
[2] Institute of Manufacturing Information and Systems,
National Cheng Kung University, Tainan, Taiwan
peihsuan.tsai@gmail.com

Abstract. High Efficiency Video Coding (HEVC) Screen Content Coding (SCC) is under standardizing for the screen-captured contents. Because many areas are composed of the texts and lines featuring non-smooth textures, the traditional intra prediction is not suitable for those areas. Therefore, this paper proposes a neighboring sample prediction coding (NSPC) for HEVC SCC, which represents the samples of the coding unit (CU) by the indexes of samples selected from the neighboring CUs. A unified sample selection scheme (USSS) based on a neighboring sample list is also proposed to determine the priority ordering of the selected neighboring samples. The index coding with a single sample index skipping method is also designed for coding the converted indexes. Different NSPC signaling methods are evaluated under the common test condition for HEVC SCC, and the results show that the NSPC improves the Bjontegaard-Delta bitrate saving of Screen Content Coding Test Model 2.0 up to 1.0 %.

Keywords: Screen content coding · High efficiency video coding · Intra prediction · Palette coding

1 Introduction

In recent years, screen-content applications, such as wireless screen mirroring, remote desktop, remote play and cloud gaming, have attracted attention in the video standard community. In 2014, Joint Collaborative Team on Video Coding (JCT-VC), established by Moving Picture Experts Group (MPEG) and Video Coding Experts Group (VCEG), held a joint call-for-proposals[1] to extend High Efficiency Video Coding (HEVC) standard [2] to screen content coding (SCC). Now the HEVC SCC [3] is being standardized under the HEVC coding platform with newly additional tools specializing in coding screen contents.

Screen contents generally include a random mixture of text and computer-generated graphic. This emerging screen-captured video contents exhibit very different characteristics from camera-captured video. Since the objects, such as texts and lines with

© Springer International Publishing Switzerland 2016
T. Bräunl et al. (Eds.): PSIVT 2015, LNCS 9431, pp. 187–198, 2016.
DOI: 10.1007/978-3-319-29451-3_16

sharp edges, mainly feature non-smooth textures with irregular directions, the traditional intra prediction which predicts the samples of a coding unit (CU) by the intra samples with a regular direction is not suitable for these objects. To address the feature of screen contents, major-color-based coding tools, called palette mode (PM) [4–6], are proposed and comprehensively evaluated using the test sequences released by JCT-VC. The basic idea of the PM is to select a number of major colors which are the most representative pixel samples for the CU. Then each pixel in the CU is converted to an index corresponding to the nearest one of the major colors.

Usually, there is high correlation of pixel samples between the CU and the neighboring CUs. Therefore, this paper proposes a neighboring sample prediction coding (NSPC) to represent the pixel samples of the current CU by the indexes of the samples selected out of the neighboring CUs. A unified sample selection scheme (USSS) based on a neighboring sample list is also proposed to determine the priority ordering of the selected neighboring samples. The index coding with a single sample index skipping method is also designed for coding the converted indexes. For comparing the performance, we propose two versions of NSPC for implementation on the reference software Screen Content Coding Test Model 2.0 (SCM2.0) [7]: one views it as an additional tool which is independent of the other ones, and the other incorporates it into the existing PM, where the signaling are within the signaling of the PM. Due to the information on the neighboring CUs available for the decoder, there is no need to signal the neighboring samples and thus no burden on the bitstream. Both versions of NSPC are evaluated under the common test condition (CTC) [8] for HEVC SCC, and the evaluation results show that the NSPC can improve the Bjontegaard-Delta bitrate (BD-rate) [9] saving up to 1.0 % as compared to SCM 2.0

The rest of this paper is organized as follows. Section 2 introduces the palette mode in HEVC SCC. Section 3 presents the proposed NSPC. Section 4 shows the analyses of the NSPC. Section 5 presents two versions of NSPC to be evaluated in Sect. 6. Section 7 concludes this paper.

2   Palette Mode in HEVC SCC

The PM tool [4–6] is one of new coding tools adopted in the HEVC SCC. The concept of the PM is to analyze the pixel samples in the CU first, select several major colors out of the pixel samples to represent the CU, and convert each pixel in the CU to the index which corresponds to the major color nearest to the pixel sample.

The encoder first selects the most representative major colors by considering the combined pixel samples of the three components (Y/G, U/B and V/R) in the CU, and then establishes a look-up table of major colors, called major color table. Each major color would be given an index. A group of pixels gathering around a major color are represented by this major color and converted to the index corresponding to the major color. In the SCM2.0, the maximum amount of major colors is set to thirty-one.

Another important stage in the encoder is to code and transmit the major color table and the converted indexes. The major colors listed in the major color table must be coded by using a lossless coding because the decoder will need the major color table to reconvert the indexes to the major colors. Subsequently, the converted indexes are

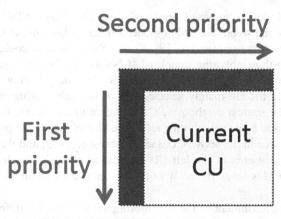

Fig. 1. The fixed order for selecting the neighboring samples of N_2, N_3, ..., N_{10} in the proposed USSS

coded based on two copy run modes: one is copy above run mode, and the other is copy left run mode. A flag is first signaled to indicate which copy run mode is selected. The copy above run mode is activated if the current and following color indexes are identical to the indices of the above pixel line. The copy left run mode is used when there are identical color indexes followed by the color index of the current coding pixel. For the copy left run mode, the color index is signaled to decoder to indicate the value of the index. For two copy run modes, a run value is further signaled to indicate the amount of pixels that copied from the above pixel line or the left pixel.

On the decoder side, it first decodes the major colors to reconstruct the major color table of the CU. Meanwhile, the indexes are also decodes to represent each pixel of the CU. By looking up the major color table, each index is reconverted to one of the major colors. Finally, the reconstructed samples of the CU are those colors reconverted from indexes.

3 Proposed Neighboring Sample Prediction Coding

The pixels in the CU are able to be predicted by the samples out of the neighboring blocks. The traditional intra prediction coding in the HEVC is the prediction method employing neighboring samples under the assumption of the CU with a regular texture or the smooth area. However, many areas of the screen captured content are composed of texts and lines located in the software such as websites and word-editing, which features a non-smooth texture with irregular directions. Therefore, the original intra prediction coding is no longer suitable for those areas. In this section, the NSPC is proposed to represent each pixel sample of the CU by the nearest one of the neighboring samples, which are selected from the nearest neighboring CUs and the previously encoded palette CU. Differing from the traditional intra prediction coding, the NSPC does not follow the rules of the texture direction or smoothing, and thus is suitable for the screen captured content.

The NSPC includes a number of neighboring sample (NS) modes, which are 1-NS mode, 2-NS mode, and so on. For M-NS mode, a neighboring sample list is established based on M neighboring samples, i.e., $\{S_1, S_2, ..., S_M\}$, where M could be 1, 2, and so on, and S_m is the m-th neighboring sample of M-NS mode. Then each sample in the CU is predicted by one of M neighboring samples. The neighboring samples in the neighboring sample list are mainly selected out of the neighboring reference blocks, which are inside the nearest neighboring CUs relative to the current CU. As shown in Fig. 1, the grey region is the neighboring reference blocks, where the parameter H is the height of the grey area in the above CU and the above-left CU, and the parameter W is the width of the grey area in the left CU and the above-left CU. In this paper, the maximum value of M is set as 10 and W and H are set as 2 based on the performance on BD-rate.

To unify the establishment of the neighboring sample lists for different NS modes, the USSS is proposed to select the neighboring samples following a certain ordering. Because there are ten neighboring samples at most for the NS modes in the proposed NSPC, the USSS orderly selects ten neighboring samples and denotes the ordering samples as the list $\{N_1, N_2, ..., N_{10}\}$, where N_i is defined as the i-th neighboring sample. The first sample N_1 is the most frequently occurring sample out of the neighboring reference blocks, and then the rest of samples $N_2, N_3, ..., N_{10}$ are filled with the neighboring samples from the neighboring reference blocks in a fixed order as shown in Fig. 1, where the first priority is the top sample to the bottom sample in the left neighboring reference block, and the second priority is the sample of the above-left CU, the left sample to the right sample of the above neighboring reference block. Note that a neighboring sample will not be filled with the list if its value is identical to the value of the previously derived sample N_i. If empty entry exists in the list followed by the filling process, the color samples from the major color table of the previously coded CU are employed to fill in those empty entries. After setting up the ordering sample list $\{N_1, N_2, ..., N_{10}\}$, the neighboring sample lists for ten different NS modes can be easily established as follows:

1-NS mode: $\{N_1\}$,
2-NS mode: $\{N_1, N_2\}$,
3-NS mode: $\{N_1, N_2, N_3\}$,

and so on. The last NS mode is 10-NS mode, whose neighboring sample list is $\{N_1, N_2, ..., N_{10}\}$.

After the USSS establishes the neighboring sample lists, each NS mode will convert each pixel of the CU to the index corresponding to the nearest neighboring sample out of its own neighboring sample list. The converting process for the M-NS mode can be illustrated as follows:

Step 1: The pixel $p(x,y)$ is predicted by the nearest neighboring sample $n(x,y)$, where (x,y) is the coordinate in the CU:

$n(x, y) = \arg \min_N abs(N_i - p(x, y))$.

Step 2: The prediction sample $n(x,y)$ is converted to the corresponding index $r(x,y)$ based on the look up table as shown in Table 1. The indexes $r(x,y)$ for all (x,y) in the CU are the results of the converting process.

During the signaling process at the encoder, a CU-level enabling flag is signaled to indicate whether to enable the proposed NSPC. If the NSPC tool is enabled, a flag is further signaled to indicate which NS mode is selected. Note that the best mode out of different NS modes will be selected based on the rate distortion (RD) optimization. The indexes $r(x,y)$ for all (x,y) in the CU are also required to be coded. The copy left run mode and copy above run mode proposed in the PM are applied to the index coding for different NS modes. However, for the 1-NS mode, a single sample index skipping method is designed to skip the signaling of the copy left run mode and copy above run mode. Because the indexes $r(x,y)$ for 1-NS mode must be a constant value '0', the decoder can readily parse the indexes $r(x,y)$ to be zeros without any further singling of copy run modes after it knows the mode is 1-NS mode.

Table 1. The look up table of the index corresponding to each neighboring samples in the M-NS mode $\{N_1, N_2, ..., N_M\}$

The neighboring sample	The sample index
N_1	0
N_2	1
$\vdots$	$\vdots$
N_M	M-1

Compared to the traditional intra prediction coding, the assignment of the prediction sample $n(x,y)$ of the pixel $p(x,y)$ for the NSPC is not based on a regular texture direction. Therefore, the NSPC is suitable for the texts and lines with irregular texture direction, which is often appeared in the screen-captured contents. The PM selects a number of prediction samples, i.e., the major colors, out of the current CU to represent each pixel samples in the CU. However, the PM requires to transmit the prediction samples to the decoder by a lossless coding, and thus the syntax of the PM would code a huge amount of bits to carry the information on the prediction samples. Differing from the PM, the NSPC uses the neighboring samples to predict the pixels of the CU. Because the neighboring samples from the neighboring blocks are available for the decoder, the syntax of the NSPC does not carry the information on the prediction samples, and thus NSPC results in a shorter syntax than PM.

4   Analysis for Neighboring Sample Prediction Coding

The number of neighboring samples for NSPC is chosen between one and ten as mentioned above. The number of major color samples for the PM, however, is set by the value between one and thirty-one. A large number of samples for each tool would be required when the CU is composed of much more colors, but a small number of samples would be preferable as the CU only covers a few colors. To understand the percentage of the number of samples for the NSPC-based the PM-based CUs, we analyze both tools under the sequence category of "text & graphic with motion", which

Table 2. Percentages of the number of the major color samples employed for the PM-based CU for different screen-content sequences

Sequences	The number of samples			
	1	2	3	4 ~ 31
YUV, FlyingGraphics, 1080p	0.54 %	15.27 %	21.02 %	63.17 %
YUV, Desktop, 1080p	0.06 %	30.33 %	6.00 %	63.61 %
YUV, Console, 1080p	0.13 %	48.36 %	12.60 %	38.91 %
YUV, web_browsing, 720p	0.00 %	2.23 %	4.56 %	93.21 %
YUV, Map, 720p	0.37 %	4.88 %	6.47 %	88.28 %
YUV, Programming, 720p	0.71 %	38.01 %	5.10 %	56.18 %
YUV, SlideShow, 720p	0.87 %	46.14 %	13.71 %	39.28 %
RGB, FlyingGraphics, 1080p	0.64 %	13.07 %	19.57 %	66.72 %
RGB, Desktop, 1080p	0.03 %	22.62 %	6.94 %	70.41 %
RGB, Console, 1080p	0.20 %	43.91 %	15.16 %	40.73 %
RGB, web_browsing, 720p	0.05 %	2.63 %	4.72 %	92.60 %
RGB, Map, 720p	0.19 %	2.43 %	3.86 %	93.52 %
RGB, Programming, 720p	0.84 %	30.58 %	3.62 %	64.96 %
RGB, SlideShow, 720p	0.64 %	26.32 %	14.10 %	58.94 %

Table 3. Percentages of the number of the neighboring samples employed for the NSPC-based CU for different screen-content sequences

Sequences	The number of sample			
	1	2	3	4 ~ 10
YUV, FlyingGraphics, 1080p	85.71 %	1.41 %	1.70 %	11.18 %
YUV, Desktop, 1080p	44.12 %	37.07 %	14.01 %	4.8 %
YUV, Console, 1080p	6.63 %	63.40 %	20.86 %	9.11 %
YUV, web_browsing, 720p	96.89 %	0.21 %	0.38 %	2.52 %
YUV, Map, 720p	69.12 %	7.72 %	7.25 %	15.91 %
YUV, Programming, 720p	89.89 %	0.58 %	1.39 %	8.14 %
YUV, SlideShow, 720p	95.52 %	1.28 %	0.50 %	2.7 %
RGB, FlyingGraphics, 1080p	80.00 %	0.24 %	1.74 %	18.02 %
RGB, Desktop, 1080p	37.45 %	43.63 %	14.64 %	4.28 %
RGB, Console, 1080p	7.58 %	63.92 %	19.87 %	8.63 %
RGB, web_browsing, 720p	97.74 %	0.22 %	0.28 %	1.76 %
RGB, Map, 720p	76.41 %	1.66 %	3.43 %	18.50 %
RGB, Programming, 720p	93.47 %	0.63 %	0.67 %	5.23 %
RGB, SlideShow, 720p	95.81 %	1.32 %	0.56 %	2.31 %

comprises 14 screen-content video sequences for the SCC CTC issued by JCT-VC [8]. All-intra configuration and quantization parameter 22 are specified for simulations.

The percentage results for the PM-based CU and the NSPC-based CU are listed in Tables 2 and 3, respectively. In Table 2, there are around 60 ~ 90 % CUs in a frame to use 4 or above color samples for the PM, but less than 1 % CUs are represented by

1 color sample. The results suggest that the PM could efficiently address the CU composed of many diverse colors. However, Table 3 shows a converse results, where there are around 70 ∼ 95 % CUs in a frame to use 1 or 2 neighboring samples for the NSPC, but around 2 ∼ 15 % CUs are represented by 4 or above neighboring samples. The results in Table 3 infer that the NSPC would be more effective for the CU with few colors. This is attributes to the high possibility of the neighboring samples hitting the pixel samples in the current CU as the number of the pixel samples is rather less. According to the percentages of one sample in both tables, it suggests that the CU with one or few colors can be more efficiently predicted by the NSPC than the PM which requires a huge number of bits to signal the major colors to the decoder. The analyses show the importance of the single sample index skipping method for the NSPC mentioned in Sect. 3. Because of forcing to signal the major colors for the PM, the results in Table 2 and the bitrate will remain unchanged even if the single sample index skipping method is applied to the PM.

5 Signaling of Neighboring Sample Prediction Coding for HEVC SCC

The proposed NSPC is integrated into the reference software SCM2.0 [7] for evaluation in HEVC SCC. This section contributes to studying the syntax integration between the NSPC and the existing PM tool in HEVC SCC. We propose two implementation methods for the integration: one is to view the NSPC as an independent mode, and the other is to incorporate the NSPC into the existing PM. The former transmits the NSPC signals independently, and the latter inserts the signaling of the NSPC within the signaling of the PM.

The signaling [7] of the PM in the HEVC SCC can be shown in Fig. 2. A CU-level PM flag is signaled to indicate whether to enable the PM tool. If the PM tool is enabled, the major colors in the established major color table and the indexes of the pixels in the CU are coded and transmitted. The first implementation method is as shown in Fig. 3, which puts the signaling of the NSPC on the same level of the signaling of the PM. A CU-level NSPC flag is signaled to indicate whether to enable the independent NSPC tool. Suppose that the independent NSPC tool is enabled and the M-NS mode is selected. Then the number of M and the indexes of the pixels in the CU are coded and transmitted. The second implementation method is as shown in Fig. 4, which puts the signaling of the NSPC within the signaling of the PM. In this method, the NSPC signaling is incorporated into the PM signaling. Based on the CU-level NSPC flag, the PM tool can decide how to predict the pixel samples of the CU. If the CU-level NSPC flag is enabled, the PM selects the neighboring samples from the neighboring reference blocks to represent the pixel samples of the CU. Otherwise, the PM selects some of the pixel samples from the current CU to represent the whole pixel samples of the CU. This paper will take advantage of the both implementation methods of the NSPC for performance evaluation. The evaluation results will be discussed in Sect. 6, which shows that there is no conflicts between the NSPC and the PM even when the NSPC is implemented within the PM.

```
A coding unit (CU) {
  ...
  Signaling CU-level_PM_flag
  If (CU_level_PM_flag) {
    Signaling the major colors
      Signaling the indexes of the pixels in CU
  }
  ...
}
```

Fig. 2. The signaling of the PM in HEVC SCC

```
Suppose that M-NS mode is selected:
A coding unit (CU) {
  ...
  Signaling CU_level_NSPC_flag
  If(CU_level_NSPC_flag) {
    Signaling the selected value of M
    Signaling the indexes of the pixels in CU
  }
  else {
    ...
    Signaling CU-level_PM_flag
    If (CU_level_PM_flag) {
      Signaling the major colors
        Signaling the indexes of the pixels in CU
    }
    ...
  }
}
```

Fig. 3. The signaling integration of the NSPC and the PM by viewing the NSPC as an independent tool

6   Simulation Results

The proposed NSPC is evaluated based on the CTC [8] for SCC reference software version SCM2.0 [7] with the following configurations:

1. All-intra (AI) configuration is used.
2. The intra block copy (IBC) tool is enabled with search range up to full frame.
3. Four quantization values are evaluated: 22, 27, 32 and 37.
4. There are totally 26 test sequences [8], which are classified into ten categories according to the video content, video size, and color format. Among 26 sequences, those in class "text & graphic with motion" are the standard screen-content videos, and those in class "mixed content" are the videos composed of screen content and natural content.

BD-rate measure [9] is used to evaluate objective coding efficiency. A negative BD-rate number means that the tool has coding gains.

Table 4. BD-rate results of NSPC-I versus anchor SCM2.0 under AI-lossy coding

	All Intra		
	G/Y	B/U	R/V
RGB, text & graphics with motion, 1080p	−1.0 %	−0.9 %	−1.0 %
RGB, text & graphics with motion,720p	−1.0 %	−1.0 %	−1.0 %
RGB, mixed content, 1440p	−0.4 %	−0.3 %	−0.4 %
RGB, mixed content, 1080p	−0.4 %	−0.3 %	−0.3 %
RGB, Animation, 720p	0.0 %	0.0 %	0.0 %
RGB, camera captured, 1080p	−0.1 %	0.0 %	0.0 %
YUV, text & graphics with motion, 1080p	−0.7 %	−0.6 %	−0.6 %
YUV, text & graphics with motion,720p	−0.8 %	−0.8 %	−0.8 %
YUV, mixed content, 1440p	−0.5 %	−0.5 %	−0.6 %
YUV, mixed content, 1080p	−0.5 %	−0.4 %	−0.4 %
YUV, Animation, 720p	0.0 %	−0.2 %	−0.2 %
YUV, camera captured, 1080p	−0.1 %	−0.1 %	−0.1 %
Enc Time[%]	103 %		
Dec Time[%]	96 %		

```
Suppose that M-NS mode is selected:
A coding unit (CU) {
    ...
    Signaling CU-level_PM_flag
    If (CU_level_PM_flag) {
        Signaling CU_level_NSPC_flag
        If (CU_level_NSPC_flag) {
            Signaling the selected value of M
        }
        else {
        Signaling the major colors
        }
        Signaling the indexes of the pixels in CU
    }
    ...
}
```

Fig. 4. The signaling integration of the NSPC and the PM by inserting the NSPC signaling underneath the PM signaling

For comparisons, both versions of the NSPC discussed in Sect. 5 are evaluated in this section. The two versions are, respectively, denoted as NSPC-I and NSPC-II. The NSPC-I is the first implementation version which puts the NSPC signaling onto an identical level to the PM signaling. The NSPC-II is the second implementation version which puts NSPC underneath the PM signaling. The BD-rate results for NSPC-I and NSPC-II are, respectively, summarized in Tables 4 and 5. It is seen that the BD-rate saving for the NSPC-I and the NSPC-II can both achieve up to 1.0 % coding gain for "text & graphic with motion". The results in Table 5 show that the NSPC-II is no conflict with the PM when the NSPC is viewed as a special mode of the PM. It means that the NSPC without any signaling of the major colors can be beneficial to improve the coding performance of the PM which requires to signal a huge number of the major colors. Comparing the two implementation methods with each other, the results show that the NSPC-I as an independent mode is still superior to the NSPC-II in terms of the BD-rates.

Table 5. BD-rate results of NSPC-II versus anchor SCM2.0 under AI-lossy coding

	All Intra		
	G/Y	B/U	R/V
RGB, text & graphics with motion, 1080p	−0.9 %	−0.8 %	−0.8 %
RGB, text & graphics with motion,720p	−1.0 %	−0.9 %	−0.9 %
RGB, mixed content, 1440p	−0.4 %	−0.3 %	−0.4 %
RGB, mixed content, 1080p	−0.4 %	−0.3 %	−0.3 %
RGB, Animation, 720p	0.0 %	0.0 %	0.0 %
RGB, camera captured, 1080p	0.0 %	0.0 %	0.0 %
YUV, text & graphics with motion, 1080p	−0.6 %	−0.4 %	−0.5 %
YUV, text & graphics with motion,720p	−0.6 %	−0.7 %	−0.5 %
YUV, mixed content, 1440p	−0.4 %	−0.4 %	−0.4 %
YUV, mixed content, 1080p	−0.4 %	−0.3 %	−0.3 %
YUV, Animation, 720p	0.0 %	−0.2 %	−0.2 %
YUV, camera captured, 1080p	−0.1 %	−0.1 %	−0.1 %
Enc Time[%]	102 %		
Dec Time[%]	97 %		

Table 6. BD-rate results of the modified PM versus anchor SCM2.0 under AI-lossy coding

	All Intra		
	G/Y	B/U	R/V
RGB, text & graphics with motion, 1080p	−0.2 %	−0.2 %	−0.2 %
RGB, text & graphics with motion,720p	−0.2 %	−0.2 %	−0.1 %
RGB, mixed content, 1440p	−0.1 %	−0.2 %	−0.2 %
RGB, mixed content, 1080p	−0.2 %	−0.3 %	−0.2 %
RGB, Animation, 720p	0.0 %	−0.1 %	−0.1 %
RGB, camera captured, 1080p	0.0 %	0.0 %	0.0 %
YUV, text & graphics with motion, 1080p	−0.2 %	−0.4 %	−0.4 %
YUV, text & graphics with motion,720p	−0.1 %	−0.3 %	−0.6 %
YUV, mixed content, 1440p	−0.1 %	−0.4 %	−0.4 %
YUV, mixed content, 1080p	−0.1 %	−0.1 %	−0.3 %
YUV, Animation, 720p	0.0 %	−0.3 %	−0.2 %
YUV, camera captured, 1080p	0.0 %	0.0 %	0.0 %
Enc Time[%]	104 %		
Dec Time[%]	100 %		

The NSPC uses the proposed USSS to establish a sample list $\{N_1, N_2, ..., N_{10}\}$, whose samples are composed of the neighboring samples out of the neighboring CUs. There are ten NS modes based the sample list to run the RD costs as described in Sect. 3. Then the best NS mode with the lowest RD cost will be selected. To verify the effectiveness of the NSPC being along with the USSS, we propose to modify the encoder of the PM in the original reference software SCM2.0 by adding a sample list $\{C_1, C_2, ..., C_{10}\}$, whose samples are the major colors in the original major color table. Similarly, there are ten additional PM modes: $\{C_1\}$, $\{C_1, C_2\}$, ..., $\{C_1, C_2, ..., C_{10}\}$. Each PM mode has different size of major color table. Then the best PM mode with the lowest RD cost will be selected. Note that it is a non-normative modification of the PM in HEVC SCC. The results of the modified PM are summarized in Table 6. It shows that the modified PM can achieve up to 0.2 % BD-rate saving for the screen-captured video categories "text & graphic with motion". However, there is 0.8 % BD-rate loss for the modified PM compared with the both versions of the NSPC. It verifies that encoder-only modification of the PM can achieve a minor gain, but cannot hit a higher gain achieved by the NSPC.

7 Conclusion

The proposed NSPC for HEVC SCC has been presented in this paper. The NSPC represents the samples of the CU by the indexes of samples selected from the neighboring CUs, such as the nearest CUs and previously encoded palette CU. The USSS based on a neighboring sample list is also proposed for determining the priority ordering of the selected neighboring samples. Two signaling methods of the NSPC are evaluated under the CTC for HEVC SCC, where the former is to view the NSPC as an independent mode, and the latter is to incorporate the NSPC into the existing PM mode. The experimental results show that both signaling methods of NSPC can improve the BD-rate saving of SCM2.0 up to 1.0 %, and the NSPC without any signaling of the major colors can be beneficial to improve the coding performance of the PM which requires to signal a huge number of the major colors. The analyses are also given in this paper to understand the statistical distribution of the number of the neighboring samples, and the results indicate that the NSPC is more effective than the PM for coding the CU with a small number of pixel samples. It verifies that there is no conflict between the NSPC and the PM on the BD-rate performance.

References

1. Joshi, R., Cohen, R., Yu, H.: BoG report on summary of objective performance and tools for SCC CfP responses. Document JCTVC-Q0239 (2014)
2. Boyce, J., Chen, J., Chen, Y., Flynn, D., Hannuksela, M.M., Naccari, M., Rosewarne, C., Sharman, K., Sole, J., Sullivan, G.J., Suzuki, T., Tech, G., Wang, Y.-K., Wegner, K., Ye Y.: Edition 2 Draft Text of High Efficiency Video Coding (HEVC), Including Format Range (RExt), Scalability (SHVC), and Multi-View (MV-HEVC) Extensions. Document JCTVC-R1013 (2014)

3. Joshi, R., Xu, J.: HEVC Screen Content Coding Draft Text 1. Document JCTVC-R1005 (2014)
4. Guo, X., Lu, Y., Li, S.: RCE4: Test1. Major-color-based screen content coding. Document JCTVC-P0108 (2014)
5. Pu, W., Guo, X., Onno, P., Lai, P., Xu, J.: AHG10: Suggested software for palette coding based on RExt6.0. Document JCTVC-Q0094 (2014)
6. Onno, P., Xiu, X., Huang, Y.-W., Joshi, R.: Suggested combined software and text for run-based palette mode. Document JCTVC-R0348 (2014)
7. Joshi, R., Xu, J., Cohen, R., Liu, S., Ma, Z., Ye, Y.: Screen content coding test model 2 encoder description (SCM2). Document JCTVC-R1014 (2014)
8. Yu, H., Cohen, R., Rapaka, K., Xu, J.: Common test conditions for screen content coding. Document JCTVC-R1015 (2014)
9. Bjøntegaard, G.: Calculation of average PSNR differences between RD curves. Document VCEG-M33 (2001)

Computational Photography and Arts

Aesthetic Interactive Hue Manipulation
for Natural Scene Images

Jinze Yu[1]([✉]), Martin Constable[2], Junyan Wang[3], Kap Luk Chan[4],
and Michael S. Brown[5]

[1] Institute of Industrial Science, The University of Tokyo, Tokyo, Japan
jzyu@iis.u-tokyo.ac.jp
[2] School of Art, Design and Media, Nanyang Technological University,
Singapore, Singapore
mconstable@ntu.edu.sg
[3] Doheny Eye Institute/Jules Stein Eye Institute, University of California,
Los Angeles, USA
[4] School of Electrical and Electronic Engineering, Nanyang Technological University,
Singapore, Singapore
[5] School of Computing, National University of Singapore, Singapore, Singapore
brown@comp.nus.edu.sg

Abstract. One of the most common ways to adjust the aesthetic quality of a natural scene image is by editing its color. However, while lightness and saturation manipulation is well understood in computational terms, hue manipulation is poorly understood and non-trivial to affect. As a result, modifications made to hue with existing photo-editing tools often impart an unnatural look to the image. In this paper, we discuss a framework for hue manipulation and its contribution to the aesthetics of an image inspired by the use of hue in the visual arts. Our framework is designed to work with a segmentation approach based on superpixels that can segment the image into regions of similar color at varying scales. This allows the user the ability to quickly select semantically similar regions. These local regions also provide the basic region of operation for three proposed hue operations: (1) hue spread; (2) hue compression; and (3) hue shift. We show that when combined with superpixel segmentation these operations are capable of increasing, decreasing and changing regions of local hue contrast in a manner that produces natural or artistic looking images. We demonstrate our framework on a variety of input images and discuss its evaluation from the feedback of several expert users.

Keywords: Hue manipulation · Color transfer · Hue contrast · Superpixels segmentation

1 Introduction and Motivation

The ability to aesthetically improve a photograph has long been a popular subject. Software tools such as Photoshop[1] and GIMP[2] provide users a wide range

---

[1] http://www.adobe.com/ru/products/photoshop.html.
[2] http://www.gimp.org/.

© Springer International Publishing Switzerland 2016
T. Bräunl et al. (Eds.): PSIVT 2015, LNCS 9431, pp. 201–214, 2016.
DOI: 10.1007/978-3-319-29451-3_17

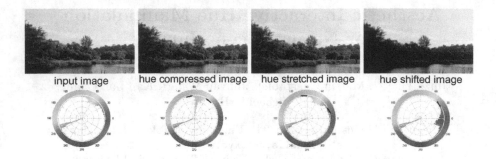

Fig. 1. Results of the three defined hue operations. Top row shows the original image, hue compressed image, hue stretched image and hue shifted image. Bottom row shows the corresponding hue histograms (Color figure online).

of image editing functions to manipulate the appearance of an image. Most popular adjustments are those made to lightness and saturation values in order to modify the global or local contrast and vividness of the image respectively. The modification of hue, however, is more challenging and less understood.

To better understand hue, we turn our attention to methods traditional painters use to organize the formal attributes of their paintings in such a way as to maintain a particular aesthetic quality. This is done to gain insight into how such organization can be applied in a computational manner. Similar approaches have been taken when examining lightness and saturation contrast. For example, Zhang et al. [16] compared the difference of lightness and saturation contrast within the artistic concept of the four depth regions. Using paintings as reference they developed a computational method to enhance the lightness and saturation contrast of photographs.

While lightness contrast and saturation contrast are fairly well understood as computational problems [6], hue is unique for the close relationship it has to the meaning of an object [10]. For example, foliage needs to be green, tomatoes needs to be red. Edits to hue risks damaging this relationship. Another problem is that there is little discussion or agreement as to what constitutes hue contrast.

Johhanes Itten was a Swiss artist and theorist whose work is well recognized in the art community. He identified a set of seven color contrasts [5] by which the colors of an artwork may be evaluated. Of these seven contrasts, three are hue specific. Two refer to the property of hue values on opposite sides of the hue wheel: the contrast of temperature and the contrast of complimentaries. The third, described as contrast of hue, refers simply to the property of there being many colors in an image or a region of an image.

Painters habitually variegate local regions of contiguous color so that they extend to include neighboring hue values. Hence the green of a tree would be painted so that it also encompasses yellow and blue, which border green on either side of the color spectrum. By either reducing or increasing this contrast the aesthetic properties of an image may be acted upon. Supporting this the art theorist Rudolph Arnheim wrote that: *configuration of colors will strive either*

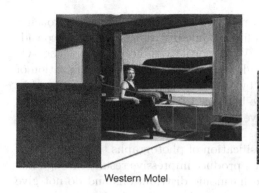

Western Motel   Orchard at La Louvière

Fig. 2. Edward Hopper, 'Western Motel', 1957 and Alfred William Finch, 'Orchard at La Louvière', 1890. Note the contiguous color of detail with subtle hue contrast in the first painting and variegated green with additional blue and yellows to give notable hue contrast in the second (Color figure online).

toward contrast or toward assimilation [2]. Figure 2 shows a detail of a painting by the painter William Finch (1854 – 1930) that shows a region of green grass being extended to cover the yellow and blue values. This effect may be understood as being an increase of Itten's hue contrast. Conversely, a region of naturally variegated hue may be decreased and rendered as a single coherent hue. An example of such is shown in Fig. 2 in the painting 'Western Motel' by Edward Hopper.

Contribution. Inspired by Itten's description of hue contrast, we propose an interactive image editing framework that allows the user to perform three operations for aesthetic hue manipulation. These are hue compression, stretching, and shifting (see Fig. 1), the first two being broadly analogues to an increase and decrease respectively of Itten's contrast of hue. As discussed above, hue manipulation is more appropriately defined for local image regions and therefore needs to be coupled with image segmentation. To this end, we incorporate a superpixel-based interactive segmentation method that allows the user to easily select image regions at different superpixel scales (see Fig. 6). These segmented regions not only give users a way to select objects in the image content, but also provide the basic local region for hue manipulation as shown in Fig. 8.

The remainder of this paper is organized as follows: Sect. 2 describes work related to our framework. Section 3 describes our overall framework. Section 4 shows several results generated with our framework as well as comparisons with results from existing image-editing software. Section 5.2 provides feedback from several expert users in image-editing and color manipulation who have used our system. Section 6 concludes this paper with a short summary.

2   Related Work

2.1   Hue Manipulation

Although the manipulation of hue is well known and well adopted by artists, it has seen relatively little focus in image editing. Probably the best known hue manipulation is the creation of color harmony within an image. These approaches manipulate input hue such that values fit to a hue distribution that are considered to comprise of harmonic color sets. Well known examples include, Cohen-Or et al. [3]'s method that uses a template-driven approach to the harmonization of images derived from models developed by Matsuda [7] and Tokumaru et al. [14]. Wang et al. [15] proposed a knowledge-based system which adopts established color design rules into a comprehensive interactive framework to aid users in the selection of colors for scene objects. Nishiyama et al. [9] used a similar color harmony idea for aesthetic quality classification of photographs to obtain better aesthetic results. While these approaches produce impressive results through hue manipulation, they rely on established harmonic distributions and do not give as much flexibility to hue manipulation as our proposed method.

The most similar approach to our work is that by Constable et al. [4]. In this work, the authors mapped the hue histogram of their images onto a color wheel. If mapped in this manner the combined angle of spread reflected the total amount of perceived hue variety. This was used as an indicator of hue contrast: a large hue spread angle indicating high hue contrast and a small one indicating low. The advantage of defining hue contrast in this way is that it is made computationally available and that it can therefore be quantified and changed to the aesthetic benefit of the image.

2.2   Image Editing Software

There is a number of image editing software solutions that allow hue manipulation. For example, Adobe Photoshop and GIMP give the function to change the hue of an image through hue shifting. These are generally very hard to control and can easily impart an unnatural look to an image. More specific software solutions exist. HueShifter[3] is a tool created specifically to change the hue of a region of an image in a manner that does not affect its perceptual lightness. Other kinds of software solutions, such as Color Schemer[4] and Color Wheel Expert[5], although not able to process an image directly, nonetheless provide a tool by which a harmonious color set could be designed that has been based on traditional color theory. Compared to such prior work, our framework is unique in its coupling of segmentation and the three hue manipulations: compression, stretching, and shifting using a single unified interface.

3   Hue Manipulation Framework

In this section we present the core concepts of our approach.

3.1   System Overview

Saturation and lightness values can be defined as pixel-wise variations of 'amount'. Manipulation of these values act upon this amount. Hue can be

---

[3] http://www.bergdesign.com/hueshifter/.

[4] http://www.colorschemer.com/.

[5] http://www.abitom.com/.

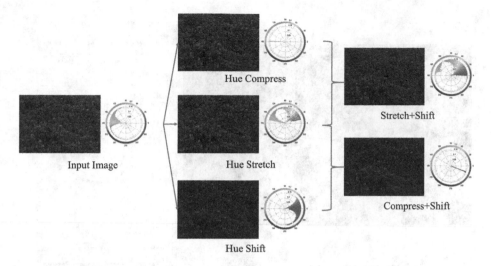

Fig. 3. Possible operations of our hue transfer system (Color figure online).

measured as an amount if regarded as range of increasing wavelength along a short sequence of the electro magnetic spectrum. However, a more conventional and perceptually correct way of presenting hue is one where the two ends of this sequence are bent round to join each other forming the color wheel [8]. This arrangement reflects the non-hierarchical nature of hue, with no single hue term being greater than another. Therefore, hue can not be operated upon in the same manner as lightness and saturation. A novel approach is therefore needed.

Our framework combines two main operations: image segmentation and hue adjustment. Figure 4 shows a screenshot of our software framework. As discussed earlier, our method provides three operations for hue: hue compression, hue stretch and hue shift. These three operations do not need to be used independently. As can be seen in Fig. 3, they can be combined to produce rich aesthetic results. As will be shown in Sect. 4, combining hue compression or stretching with hue shifting on different regions can significantly change the aesthetic appearance of an image. We chose to perform our color operations in the HSI color space. This color space presents hue as a separate channel in a manner that has its historic roots in the Munsell color system, wherein color is separated into its perceptually relevant components. HSI was derived from RGB color space in the following manner:

$$\alpha = \frac{1}{2}(2R - G - B), \quad \beta = \frac{\sqrt{3}}{2}(G - B), \quad H = atan2(\beta, \alpha),$$

$$m = min(R, G, B), \quad I = \frac{1}{3}(R + G + B), \quad S = \begin{cases} 0 & if\ I = 0, \\ 1 - \frac{m}{I} & otherwise \end{cases}, \quad (3.1)$$

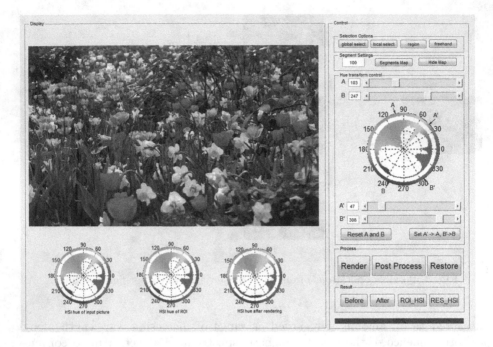

Fig. 4. The user interface developed for the hue transfer.

where R, G, B are red, green and blue values in the RGB space and H, S, I are the hue, saturation and brightness values in the HSI space, respectively. Note that is possible to use other color spaces that present hue as a unique channel, such as HSV and HSL.

We note that the hue value becomes more ambiguous as the saturation and brightness decreases. For brightness and saturation values equal to zero, the value of hue may not be meaningful. As such, we only process the pixels with saturation (S) and brightness (I) larger than a certain threshold. Here we define the threshold to be $t_s = 0.10$ and $t_i = 0.15$ (assuming that S and I are within the range $[0, 1]$), respectively.

We discuss each component of our framework in detail in the following sections.

3.2   Image Segmentation

As discussed in Sect. 1, hue manipulation is best defined in a local region of an image. This means that it will be necessary for the user to segment the image for hue processing. To this end, we use a segmentation strategy based on super-pixels. In particular, we use the SLIC method [1] for superpixel segmentation that is spaced using color information. As a result, each superpixel semantically contains the pixels that are clustered together by their similarity of color and location. This is in agreement with human perception, since the items that we

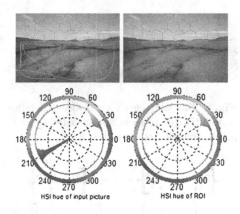

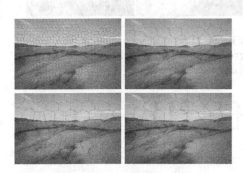

Fig. 5. Top: segmentations of size 30 and 100 (regularizor is 1). Bottom: segmentations with regulators 0.1 and 0.8 (size 100), respectively.

Fig. 6. Top: shows the process of super-pixel selection (selected super pixels are highlight in green on the right column). Bottom: shows the hue histogram of the whole image and the selected region (Color figure online).

Fig. 7. Global hue transfer result. From left: input, hue compress, hue spread. In the bottom row are the corresponding hue histograms.

are considering are regions defined by likeness of hue and location, and not individual pixels. The user can select regions by simply drawing a scribble through the super pixels they want to select. Moreover, our system allows the user to control the size of the superpixels through a simple parameter selection. Larger superpixels increase the speed in which objects can be selected, whilst smaller superpixels provide access to finer grain regions. Examples of different superpixel segmentation are shown in Fig. 5.

The final superpixel segmentation will provide the basic unit of hue manipulation. That is, hue manipulation is applied to each superpixel independently.

Fig. 8. Sky and earth are processed independently due to local hue transfer. (superpixels are selected as in Fig. 6).

Fig. 9. Hue shift can change the background of the image without affecting the foreground.

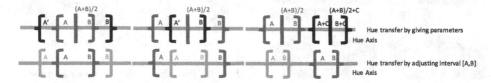

Fig. 10. Hue transfer by setting scale parameters and adjusting interval. The first, second and third columns are hue compression, stretching and shifting, respectively.

3.3 Hue Histogram Selection

As with existing image editing software such as Photoshop or GIMP, our tool allows users to manipulate a range of hue in a selected region. To isolate the hue range, the user can select a pixel in the image the hue value of which will be shown on the color wheel. A default interval centred at that hue value will be selected for the next step of hue transfer (we set 15° distance from both sides of the indicated hue value by default), since our hue transfer operations are processed for a range of hues. The user can also manually adjust the two sides of the interval being processed by adjusting the position of the starting hue, denoted as A and ending hue, denoted as B on the hue wheel. A simple global hue transfer result (by the algorithms in Sect. 3.4) is shown in Fig. 7. Our system will automatically calculate the hue histogram of the selected region and denote it in the hue ramp using the markers A and B, which facilitates the next step of hue transfer. A local hue transfer result can be seen in Figs. 7 and 8 (by the algorithms in Sect. 3.4). Following the automatic selection of A and B, users can adjust markers to obtain accurately the part of the histogram they want to process. This can also be used to filter the part of the histogram they want to keep untouched. With the idea of superpixels, we can locally deal with hue in a meaningful way and process different parts of an image independently.

3.4 Hue Transfer Operators

After selecting a region of interest (or the whole image in the case of global transfer), users can decide to process one of the three designed operators: hue compress, hue stretch or hue shift. We provide two categories of operations: hue transfer by setting scale parameters and by adjusting interval (see Fig. 10).

As indicated in previous steps in Sect. 3.3, markers A and B denote the two sides of the region that will be processed. Resulting interval is denoted by

Fig. 11. Left: an image of a flower bed before treatment. Middle: after hue compression, note the lessening of the variety of greens. Right: after hue stretch. Note the increase of the variety of greens that spreads into yellow (Color figure online).

markers A' and B'. Without losing generality, we consider that the hue axis is infinitely long with periodicity of $360°$, and $A < B$, $A' < B'$ on the hue axis (e.g. Fig. 10). These 3 hue operators work by referring to the center of interval which is $\frac{A+B}{2}$.

In the case of hue transfer by setting scale parameters, for hue compress and hue stretch users can input a scale t that reflects the degree that the selected part of the hue histogram is compressed or stretched. The resulting $[A', B']$ is calculated as $A' = \frac{A+B}{2} - t\frac{B-A}{2}$ and $B' = \frac{A+B}{2} + t\frac{B-A}{2}$. Moreover, to make the two operations meaningful, t needs to be non-zero for hue compress and to be smaller that certain value so that $B' - A'$ will not be larger than $360°$ for hue stretch. For hue shift users can input a shift amount C reflecting the color that they want to shift the selected region to. The resulting $[A', B']$ becomes $[A + C, B + C]$.

For hue transfer by adjusting interval $[A, B]$, users give directly the positions of A' and B' on the hue wheel. A 1-D Example for the 3 operators can be seen in Fig. 10. Performing hue transfer by setting scale parameters gives users the roughly quantitative control on the hue histogram, whereas performing hue transfer by adjusting interval gives users the possibility to fine tune the hue.

Given the hue values $H(x, y)$ of pixel (x, y) defined in the region of interest whose histogram is bounded by A and B, hue transfer aims to transform the current histogram of the hue function $H(x, y)$ within $[A, B]$ to a new histogram of interval $[A', B']$. We update the hue values $H'(x, y)$ using the following rule:

$$H' = \frac{B' - A'}{B - A}(H - A) + A'. \tag{3.2}$$

The *modulo* operation is needed to make sure that the final hue value H' is located within the meaningful range $[0, 360]$.

4 Results

The following shows several results from our software. In Sect. 5.2 we provide feedback from expert users on their experience with hue operations and their opinions of our software.

Input images   Results of hue transfer

Fig. 12. Examples of compound hue transfer operations.

4.1 Hue Shift, Compress and Stretch

Hue shift can be used to change the emotional ambience of a photograph. For example, a warm color is often used in the foreground against a cool background to give a harmonious result. Alternately, the local contrast between two or more different semantic parts of a photograph may be increased to improve its quality. An example of a hue shift result can be seen in Fig. 9.

Hue compression has the aesthetic effect of lessening the differences in hue within local regions (middle image of Fig. 11). This was very different from what could be achieved with the tool in stretch mode (bottom image of Fig. 11). Using a hue compression, the naturally variegated appearance of a tropical jungle can be compressed so that it more closely resembles the more monolithic hue of a European forest (Fig. 1).

The ideal image for the hue stretching and compression is one where there is an existing hue variety within the target region. This is in line with expectations, hue stretching and compression being conceptually impossible within regions of hue homogeneity. Hue stretch and compress produced some noticeable results when it was applied to such images (in Figs. 1, 7 and 11). Scenes featuring foliage, rocks, soil and other natural phenomenon are excellent examples of scenes with strong hue variation that can be amplified through hue stretching. Most man-made materials, being generally homogeneous in their hue values, do not make good subjects for our approach. However, those that displayed a degree of hue variation produced some interesting though unnatural results.

Generally good hue stretch results were possible if the target hue range did not span more than one hue term and if the degree of stretch did not also span

Fig. 13. Examples of hue transfer compared to Photoshop. Row 1 shows the results after hue stretch. Row 2 shows the results after hue compression. Row 3 shows the result after hue shift.

more than one hue term on either side of the hue spectrum for one object or one group of similar objects. This is again in line with expectations regarding the importance of hue terms to the semantic reading of an image.

4.2 Combining the Three Operations

In Fig. 3 we can see that by a combination of hue stretch and hue shift a variety of color effects can be derived which together makes the scene look like summer or autumn.

Our image processing method by hue can be decomposed to a series of hue transfer operations. To each operation can be attached semantic significance since color has a close relation with human experience. In Fig. 12 we show other examples of combining the three operations.

5   Discussion

5.1 Comparison with Other Software

Some of the existing image editing software, though to some extent allow hue to be adjusted separately to saturation and lightness, but none of them offer the regional and contextual control over hue spread that our approach offers.

Almost all of the state-of-the art of color manipulation methods are example-based (e.g. [11–13,16]), which means a reference image is needed. Different from them, our method requires user interaction. Here we compare our method with the existing commercial bitmap editor Photoshop CS6. Other software, such as GIMP can perform similar tasks with slightly different operations. Here we specifically compare their hue processing functions.

To test our result we invited some professional Photoshop artists to attempt to match our results using Photoshop. For the example of hue stretch, they were able to do reasonable job, however their results did not match ours in the subtlety and richness of the hue variegation across the tonal range. Importantly, their results required a complex multilayered approach. For one good achieved result shown in Fig. 14, in all, the artist used 4 layers and 2 masks and the whole operation required 9 separate steps. To control the effect spilling over into the sky region, it was necessary to mask out the effect. Note that our result is produced by the global hue transfer, without selecting out some specific region by superpixels to further carry out processing.

Three more comparison examples regard to hue compress, stretch and shift are shown in Fig. 13 in such order. The results compared to were done by some artists using the hue functions provided by Photoshop. Here the 3 hue transfers were done globally. We can see that our results are more natural and give more harmonic effects than those achieved with Photoshop when both of the two method only processes the hue.

Some commercial software, such as Lightroom[6], provide individual sections of the hue range manipulation where user can shift hue within some defined operations. However, such kind of hue operations are still limited and different from our idea of manipulating the hue histogram and hue contrast.

Fig. 14. Comparison of our result and one of Photoshop with complicate operation. The Photoshop result required 4 layers and 9 separate operations to achieve. Ours were done globally and required only one operation after well selecting interested region $[A, B]$ and transferred region $[A', B']$.

5.2 User Feedback

Additional feedback was gathered from a group of ten professionals in the film-making postproduction industry. These professionals were used to using a wide

---

[6] http://www.adobe.com/ru/products/photoshop-lightroom.html.

range of professional software, much of it developed in-house. Amongst this group was one who supervised an Oscar award winning visual effects team and another whose work was recognised with a prestigious Annie award. They therefore constitute a very capable group of users who operate at the very highest level of professional practice. The principles behind the tool were described to them and a sample of results was shown. They were asked if they thought the tool would be useful and if they could reproduce the same effects using existing tools. All of them were convinced of the usefulness of our tool and that its function was not naturally served by any existing solutions. Results achieved using such methods usually require masking before they are usable. Additionally, hue expansion is more achievable than hue compression. Others thought that in the right circumstances a hue replace would suffice if moderated with a mask. If a slight hue spread or compression was needed, then it could sometimes produce good results. Neither of the suggested approaches were as intuitive to manage as ours and both of them would be difficult to effect in Photoshop (RGB to HSI conversation is not naturally supported, though optional plugins are available).

6 Conclusion

We have presented an image editing framework to adjust the aesthetic quality of an image by manipulating its hue. Modifications made to hue with existing photo-editing tools can easily impart an unnatural look to the image. Considering that hue is poorly understood and non-trivial to affect, we propose three hue transfer operations for color manipulation. To realize our idea, we developed a user interaction tool that incorporates image segmentation to provide the user the possibility to deal with hue in a flexible and powerful way. The before and after values of the hue adjustment are presented in an intuitive and easy-to-understand manner. We demonstrate the effectiveness of our methods by comparing the results with those produced using Photoshop.

References

1. Achanta, R., Shaji, A., Smith, K., Lucchi, A., Fua, P., Süsstrunk, S.: SLIC superpixels compared to state-of-the-art superpixel methods. IEEE Trans. Pattern Anal. Mach. Intell. **34**(11), 2274–2282 (2012)
2. Arnheim, R.: Art and Visual Perception. University of California Press, Berkeley (1977)
3. Cohen-Or, D., Sorkine, O., Gal, R., Leyvand, T., Xu, Y.-Q.: Color harmonization. In: ACM SIGGRAPH, pp. 624–630 (2006)
4. Constable, M., Zhang, X.: Depth-based analyses of landscape paintings and photographs according to Itten's contrasts. In: Fourth Pacific-Rim Symposium on Image and Video Technology (2010)
5. Itten, J.: The Art of Color: The Subjective Experience and Objective Rationale of Color. Wiley, New York (1974)
6. Majumder, A., Stevens, R.: Perception-based contrast enhancement of images. ACM Trans. Graph. (TOG) **24**(1), 118–139 (2007)

7. Matsuda, Y.: Color Design. Asakura Shoten, Tokyo (1995)
8. Newton, I.: Newton, Isaac. 1730. Opticks, 1730. (Repr. New York: Dover, 1979.)
9. Nishiyama, M., Okabe, T., Sato, I., Sato, Y.: Aesthetic quality classification of photographs based on color harmony. In: Proceedings of IEEE Computer Society Conference on Computer Vision and Pattern Recognition, June 2011
10. Ostergaard, A.L.: Some effects of color on naming and recognition of objects. J. Exp. Psychol.: Learn. Mem. Cogn. **11**(3), 579–587 (1985)
11. Pitie, F., Kokaram, A.C., Dahyot, R.: N-dimensional probability density function transfer and its application to color transfer. In: IEEE International Conference on Computer Vision (2005)
12. Reinhard, E., Adhikhmin, M., Gooch, B., Shirley, P.: Color transfer between images. IEEE Comput. Graph. Appl. **21**(5), 34–41 (2001)
13. Tai, Y.-W., Jia, J., Tang, C.-K.: Soft color segmentation and its applications. IEEE Trans. Pattern Anal. Mach. Intell. **29**(9), 1520–1537 (2007)
14. Tokumaru, M., Muranaka, N., Imanishi, S.: Color design support system considering color harmony. In: Proceedings of IEEE International Conference on Fuzzy Systems (2002)
15. Wang, L., Giesen, J., McDonnell, K.T., Zolliker, P., Mueller, K.: Color design for illustrative visualization. IEEE Trans. Visual. Comput. Graphics **14**(6), 1739–1754 (2008)
16. Zhang, X., Chan, K.L., Constable, M.: Atmospheric perspective effect enhancement of landscape photographs through depth-aware contrast manipulation. IEEE Trans. Multimedia **16**(3), 653–667 (2014)

Cross-View Action Recognition
by Projection-Based Augmentation

Chien-Quang Le[1]([✉]), Thanh Duc Ngo[2], Duy-Dinh Le[3],
Shin'ichi Satoh[3], and Duc Anh Duong[2]

[1] The Graduate University for Advanced Studies (SOKENDAI), Hayama, Japan
{lqchien,ledduy,satoh}@nii.ac.jp
[2] University of Information Technology, Ho Chi Minh City, Vietnam
{thanhnd,ducda}@uit.edu.vn
[3] National Institute of Informatics, Tokyo, Japan

Abstract. Challenging issue in cross-view action recognition is the difference between training viewpoint and testing viewpoint. Existing research deals with this problem by transferring knowledge, i.e., finding a viewpoint independent latent space in which action descriptors from different viewpoints are directly comparable. In this paper, we propose a novel approach to tackle the problem based on exploiting the discrimination in action execution through various viewpoints. We take the advantages of depth data to augment viewpoints from an initial camera viewpoint. In our framework, the local motion features and dedicated classifiers are built from the augmented viewpoints. We conduct experiments on the benchmark dataset, the Northwestern-UCLA Multiview Action 3D (N-UCLA3D) dataset. The experimental results indicated that our proposed method leads to outperform the state-of-the-art on the benchmark. In addition, we show the important role of viewpoints to improve the performance of action recognition.

Keywords: Cross-view · Action recognition · Projection · Augmentation

1 Introduction

Human action recognition is one of the important research tasks of various fields, such as, patient care, human-computer interaction, and smart surveillance [9,10]. In this task, cross-view action recognition has been becoming a key problem due to the unpredictable recognition performance when we need recognize actions from unseen viewpoints. According to [2,3] actions are best defined as patterns in four-dimensional space. However, in practice, video recordings of actions can be similarly defined as patterns in three-dimensional space of image-space and time. This issue causes cross-view action recognition to become more challenging.

In order to deal with this challenging issue, the majority of recent research is based on the idea of knowledge transfer and achieves good results [8,13–19]. The aim of knowledge transfer is to find a view independent latent space in which

© Springer International Publishing Switzerland 2016
T. Bräunl et al. (Eds.): PSIVT 2015, LNCS 9431, pp. 215–227, 2016.
DOI: 10.1007/978-3-319-29451-3_18

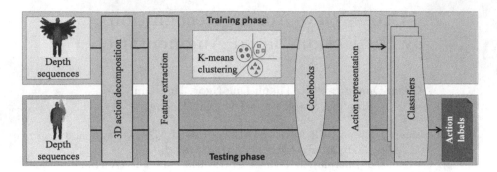

Fig. 1. Illustration of our multi-projection-based framework for human action recognition.

action representations mapped from different viewpoints are directly comparable. Therefore, the performance of this approach largely depends on the discrimination power of the local features in practice.

In this study, we approach the cross-view action recognition from another interesting perspective: augmenting a sufficiently large number of viewpoints from a single viewpoint in which actions are performed. To address that, we leverage the advantages of depth data in comparison with intensity data, i.e., less sensitive to variations in illumination, appearance and texture. First we obtain 3D actions from depth sequences which are shot by depth cameras, e.g., Kinect camera. We then decompose each 3D action into a set of 2D actions corresponding to augmented viewpoints in 3D space. The decomposed actions, afterwards, are used to build dedicated features and classifiers. With this approach, we do not completely rely on the discrimination power of local features. In addition, we can exploit the state-of-the-art 2D techniques (e.g., spatio-temporal interest points [6], motion patterns [4,5]) to effectively recognize 3D actions across different viewpoints.

Figure 1 illustrates our multi-projection-based framework. In the training phase, we extract local motion features from augmented viewpoints. Inspired by the success of the bag-of-words (BoW) model, we build a codebook corresponding to an augmented viewpoint by clustering dense trajectory motion features with K-means. We then describe an action sample in the augmented viewpoint by a histogram of codewords and build classifiers corresponding to the augmented viewpoint. In the testing phase, processes, such as, 3D action decomposition and feature extraction, are similar to the processes in the training phase. We use the built codebooks to generate action representations corresponding to the augmented viewpoints. And, classifiers built in the training phase are used to predict action labels.

We evaluate the proposed framework on the benchmark dataset, the N-UCLA3D dataset. Experimental results show two key points:

1. Augmented viewpoints provide more useful information to improve the performance of action recognition.

2. The discrimination performance of our method outperforms the state-of-the-art methods at cross-view action recognition with depth sequences.

The outline of this paper is as follows. We first provide a brief review of the related work in Sect. 2. We then describe our multi-projection-based framework in Sect. 3. Finally, experimental results, evaluation and conclusion are presented in Sect. 4 and in Sect. 5.

2 Related Work

Based on the data type, the literature on action recognition can be divided into two categories including 2D video-based and 3D video-based methods. In 2D videos, the majority of existing work focuses on single view action recognition, where actions in training and testing datasets are captured from the same view. In order to deal with viewpoint changes, one possible approach is to transfer knowledge. This approach builds an intermediate domain in which features extracted from different viewpoints are directly comparable. Works [13,14] treat each viewpoint as a language and build corresponding vocabularies. Actions in different viewpoints are modeled by the corresponding vocabularies. Then the modeled actions are translated into an "action view interlingua". Another method is to learn a transferable dictionary pair which includes a source dictionary and a target dictionary using shared action videos across the source and target views [15,16]. Unlike the previous works, [17,18] seek a set of linear transformations connecting source and target views, called "virtual views". In a similar manner, [19] learns a non-linear knowledge transfer model that transfers knowledge from multiple views to a canonical view. However, such methods, in general, are either not adaptable or not enough effective when target actions are from unseen viewpoints.

To overcome this problem, [20] relies on unlabeled 3D human motion examples to learn a probabilistic model for feature transformations due to viewpoint changes. Although this method can be applied to action recognition from unseen viewpoints, data source, captured from motion capture systems, is so ideal that is applicable for realistic applications.

In 3D videos, more recently, [11] proposed a hierarchical compositional model to effectively express the geometry, appearance and motion variations across multiple view points. However, requirement related to 3D skeleton data for training is not always available. Another method [12] extended spatio-temporal interest point-based approach for 3D video. They proposed a Histogram of Oriented Principal Components descriptor that is well integrated with their spatio-temporal keypoint detection algorithm. However, interest point-based methods are often sensitive to changes in the surroundings. Therefore, the method effectiveness is directly affected since depth data is always unstable. In this paper, our proposed method uses the trajectory-based feature extracted from some selected viewpoints to generate dedicated representations and classifiers for action recognition.

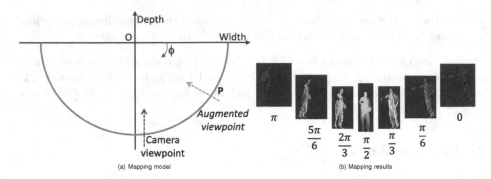

(a) Mapping model   (b) Mapping results

Fig. 2. Illustration of the geometric mapping. (a) describes the mapping model with a mapping angle ϕ. (b) results the mappings of human pose corresponding to augmented viewpoints.

(a) $\phi = 0$ (b) $\phi = \pi/6$ (c) $\phi = \pi/3$ (d) $\phi = \pi/2$

Fig. 3. Visualization for dense trajectories with action *Stand up*. This action is shot by camera 2. Examples correspond to 4 different viewpoints.

In comparison with the literature, this paper makes the following contributions:

- We give a novel view for human action recognition based on augmenting data from 3D actions to enrich information for training and testing phrases.
- In addition, we can apply the success of the state-of-the-art 2D techniques into 3D data and achieve good results.
- The experimental results are outstanding, and they are applicable to real-world applications.

3   Multi-projection-Based Framework

In this section, we describe our framework in detail. We first present the mapping procedure to decompose each 3D action to a set of 2D actions. Secondly, we give a review of the dense trajectory feature extraction. We then present action representation in each augmented viewpoint with the BoW model. Finally we provide an effective evaluation procedure to accurately predict action labels.

3.1 3D Action Decomposition

Recognizing arbitrary human action is a challenging task as it has to take into account the variations in executing the same action across different viewpoints. We have used the 2D motion pattern-based features directly with data classifiers such as Support Vector Machines (SVM) to recognize actions from different viewpoints. The complementary property of the 2D motion pattern-based features, suggests that the recognition of 3D actions can be achieved by recognizing a subset of 2D actions. In this section, we propose a method for decomposing arbitrary input 3D action as a subset of 2D actions. With this method, we can leverage the effectiveness of the state-of-the-art techniques in 2D action recognition for cross-view action recognition with 3D videos.

Given a camera viewpoint, we generate a mapping model defined by only one parameter, the azimuthal angle ϕ. Figure 2 presents the mapping model and specific results in mapping. In this model, we define $\phi = \pi/2$ as the camera viewpoint. We only consider viewpoints in $[0 \ \pi]$. After decomposing a 3D action, we adapt a trajectory-based feature extraction method to the 2D actions.

3.2 Feature Extraction

Dense trajectories [21] have indicated to be effective for action recognition. Our motivation for using dense trajectories is to capture discriminative motion patterns from 2D actions decomposed from 3D actions. To extract trajectories from videos, Wang et al. [21] proposed sampling on a dense grid. The sampling is performed at multiple scales. And tracking the dense points uses displacement information from a dense optical flow field. The tracking is implemented by using:

$$P_{t+1} = P_t + (\mathcal{M} * \omega)|_{(\bar{x}_t, \bar{y}_t)}, \tag{1}$$

where:

- P_{t+1}: is the point tracked from the point P_t.
- $\mathcal{M}$: is the kernel of median filtering.
- ω: denotes the dense optical flow field.
- $(\bar{x}_t, \bar{y}_t)$: is the rounded position of P_t.

Figure 3 visualizes dense trajectories of action *Stand up* from specific viewpoints. Once the trajectories have been extracted, two kinds of descriptor, i.e., a trajectory shape descriptor and a trajectory-aligned descriptor can be used. In our experiments, we only used the Motion Boundary Histogram (MBH), an trajectory-aligned descriptor, due to its effectiveness [21].

3.3 Decomposed Action Representation

So far we have augmented M viewpoints $\mathcal{V}_j$. From each viewpoint $\mathcal{V}_j$, we have corresponding decomposed actions. We represent the actions by using the BoW model. We first extract dense trajectory-based features (i.e., MBH descriptors)

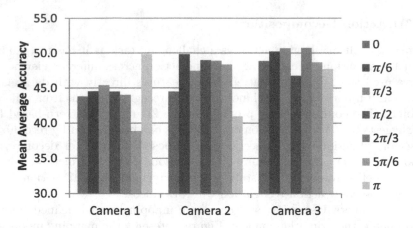

Fig. 4. The performance of each augmented viewpoint in the action recognition from the seen viewpoint.

[21] from the actions. Then, we build a codebook $\mathcal{CB}_j$ corresponding to viewpoint $\mathcal{V}_j$. We only use the development data to build the codebook $\mathcal{CB}_j$. Building the codebook $\mathcal{CB}_j$ is performed by using K-means method to cluster over all action descriptors. Each cluster is considered as a codeword that represents a specific motion pattern shared by the MBH descriptors in that cluster. We represent an action descriptor by the histogram encoding method [1]. The method means that one codeword is assigned to each MBH descriptor based on the minimum Euclidean distance. For classification, corresponding to each viewpoint $\mathcal{V}_j$, we train N binary classifiers, Support Vector Machines (SVM), to perform multi-class classification to N action classes.

4   Experiments

4.1   Prediction Procedure

For a given testing sample (i.e. samples from target view), we obtain its BoW representations corresponding to pairs of training and testing viewpoints $\mathcal{X} = \{x^{(k,l)}\}$, $k = 1..M_{tr}$, $l = 1..M_{ts}$, where M_{tr} and M_{ts} are respectively number of augmented viewpoints from the training and testing data. Through the trained classifiers, each $x^{(k,l)}$ have a corresponding score vector $y(x^{(k,l)})$ as follows:

$$y(x^{(k,l)}) = [s_1^{(k,l)}, s_2^{(k,l)}, ..., s_N^{(k,l)}], \quad k = 1..M_{tr}, \ l = 1..M_{ts}, \tag{2}$$

where:

- $s_{j(k,l)}$: is a response score from the jth classifier at the kth training viewpoint and the lth testing viewpoint.
- N: is a number of action classes.

Table 1. Comparison for six combinations of training and testing cameras

Training camera	Cam 1		Cam 2		Cam 3		Average accuracy
Testing camera	Cam 2	Cam 3	Cam 1	Cam 3	Cam 1	Cam 2	
The 1st setting	47.2	54.6	57.3	75.4	41.2	40.3	52.6
The 2nd setting	53.8	58.7	59.8	77.1	30.9	46.6	54.5
The 3rd setting	64.2	64.5	66.0	75.2	34.6	45.2	58.3
The 4th setting	62.3	67.7	67.5	77.7	29.4	36.0	56.8

Viewpoint 1   Viewpoint 2   Viewpoint 3

Fig. 5. The viewpoint variation in action "Pick Up With One Hand" from 3 different views.

Finally, we get the max-max score to find its label using (3).

$$j^* = \arg\max_{j} s_j^*, \quad j = 1..N, \tag{3}$$

where $s_j^* = \max(s_j^{(k,l)})$, $k = 1..M_{tr}$, $l = 1..M_{ts}$: is the maximal response score from the jth classifier of each pair of training and testing viewpoints.

Our proposed method was evaluated on the benchmark N-UCLA3D dataset [11]. We compare our method to the state-of-the-art cross-view action recognition methods including Domain Adaptation [8], Discriminative Virtual Views [17], And-Or Graph [11], and Histogram of Oriented Principal Components [12].

4.2 Implementation Details

Viewpoint Augmentation. The first step is to sample viewpoints which are used to decompose a 3D action. We empirically sample viewpoints with a step of $\pi/6$. In total, we obtain a few number ($n = 7$) of viewpoints (azimuthal angle $\phi \in \Phi = \{0, \pi/6, \pi/3, \pi/2, 2\pi/3, 5\pi/6, \pi\}$). We define $\phi = \pi/2$ as the camera viewpoint.

Dense Trajectory Extraction. We take the trajectory length of 15 frames and a dense sampling step size of 5 pixels. The sampling is performed at multiple scales with a factor of $1/\sqrt{2}$. In our experiments, we only used the trajectory-aligned

Table 2. Comparison to the state-of-the-art methods

Method	Average accuracy
Domain adaptation [8]	29.4
Discriminative virtual views [17]	32.3
And-Or graph [11]	32.1
Histogram of oriented principal components [12]	56.4
Ours *(the 1st setting)*	52.6
Ours *(the 2nd setting)*	54.5
Ours *(the 3rd setting)*	**58.3**
Ours *(the 4th setting)*	**56.8**

Pick up with one hand	Pick up with two hand	Drop trash	Walk around	Sit down
Stand up	Donning	Doffing	Throw	Carry

Fig. 6. Action samples are shot by camera 2 in the N-UCLA Multiview Action 3D dataset. The action samples are presented with depth data.

descriptor MBH [7]. The descriptor is computed within a 32×32 space-time volume around the trajectory. We then adapt the BoW model to represent actions. At each viewpoint, we cluster the corresponding dense trajectory descriptors into $k = 2000$ clusters using k-means to make viewpoint-specific codebooks.

4.3 Northwestern-UCLA Multiview Action 3D Dataset [11]

The N-UCLA3D dataset contains data categories: RGB, depth, and skeleton information captured simultaneously by three Kinect cameras (see Fig. 5). This dataset consists of 10 action classes: *pick up with one hand, pick up with two hand, drop trash, walk around, sit down, stand up, donning, doffing, throw, and carry*, see action samples in Fig. 6. Each action is performed by 10 persons. We only use depth data for our experiments. In order to evaluate our proposed framework, we make two evaluation settings:

- Action recognition from the seen viewpoint
- Action recognition across different viewpoints

4.4 Action Recognition from the Seen Viewpoint

In this setting, we employ the cross-validation method for each camera. Steps
are conducted as follows:

Step 1: Generate subsets

For a given video dataset $\mathcal{D}$, we first divide it into K parts:

$$\mathcal{D} = \bigcup_{i=1}^{K} D_i, \tag{4}$$

where D_i is the ith subset and $\bigcap_{i-1}^{K} D_i = \varnothing$. We obtain D_i across subjects. It
means that if a subject S_k belongs to D_i then D_j does not contain $S_k, \forall i \neq j$.

Step 2: Create development and validation data

We define $\mathcal{P}$ as a set of pairs of development and validation data:

$$\mathcal{P} = \{\mathcal{P}_i\} = \{(\mathsf{Dev}_i, \mathsf{Val}_i)\} \qquad , i = 1..K, \tag{5}$$

where:

- $\mathsf{Val}_i = \{D_i\}$: corresponds to the validation data.
- $\mathsf{Dev}_i = \mathcal{D}\backslash \mathsf{Val}_i$: represents the development data.

With such development and validation data, our framework is evaluated in the
cross-subject setting.

Step 3: Compute average accuracy for each augmented viewpoint

Given M augmented viewpoints, we calculate average accuracy $\overline{A}_j$ with classifiers trained from the jth augmented viewpoint and test samples from M viewpoints. Since we have K combinations $\mathcal{P}_i$, we evaluate the role of jth viewpoint
relied on mean average accuracy $\mathcal{A}_j$, as follows:

$$\mathcal{A}_j = \frac{1}{K} \sum_{i=1}^{K} \overline{A}_j^{(i)}, \tag{6}$$

Figure 4 shows the role of viewpoints to action recognition. The experimental
results indicate that the original camera viewpoints are not the best for action
recognition. We achieve the best results at 49.8 %, 49.8 % and 50.7 % respectively
corresponding to $\phi = \pi$, $\phi = \pi/6$ and $\phi = 2\pi/3$ from data on camera 1, camera
2, and camera 3. The results provide the benefit of selecting camera location to
mount in several realistic surveillance systems. We also take the advantages to
apply for action recognition across different viewpoints.

Table 3. Comparison for six combinations of training and testing cameras

Training camera	Cam 2	Cam 3	Cam 1	Cam 3	Cam 1	Cam 2	Average accuracy
Testing camera	Cam 1		Cam 2		Cam 3		
The 1st setting	46.8		47.3		70.9		55.0
The 2nd setting	42.2		57.8		75.6		58.5
The 3rd setting	46.0		58.2		77.9		60.7
The 4th setting	47.2		55.4		81.4		61.3

4.5   Action Recognition Across Different Viewpoints

In this section, we evaluate our framework at action recognition in the cross-view setting. As described in [12], we use samples from one camera for training phase, and samples from the two remaining cameras for testing phase. Table 1 shows the recognition accuracy of our method for six possible combinations of training and testing cameras. We report the recognition accuracy in four following settings:

– *The first setting*: We use all M viewpoints for both training and testing phases.
– *The second setting*: We use K best viewpoints which we obtained in Sect. 4.4 in the training phase, and predict action labels over all M viewpoints.
– *The third setting*: We use the K best viewpoints for both training and testing phases.
– *The fourth setting*: We follow the 3rd setting but perform recognition from the same viewpoints seen in the training data.

The experimental results in Table 1 show that our framework not only improves the computational cost (i.e., we used a smaller number of viewpoints in the 2nd, 3rd and 4th settings) but also achieves the better performance. We achieve the best result at the 3rd setting. Since the final prediction depends on the maximal response from pairs of training and testing viewpoints, using only the same viewpoints as described in the 4th settings restrict the recognition performance. In contrast, the 2nd setting is a mixture of the 1st and 3rd settings. It guarantees the reasonably computational cost in training phase, but easily cause confusions in testing phase.

Table 2 presents the performance of our method in comparison with the state-of-the-art methods. The results show that our method outperforms the other methods. The recognition accuracy of our method is significantly higher than the methods [8,11,17]. Unlike [12], our method does not depend on human body segmentation which is not a trivial task. Our method has proved the effectiveness for cross-view action recognition in much noise environments.

In addition, we also conduct the evaluation on another training/testing setting. In this setting, we use samples from two cameras for training and samples from the remaining one for testing. The experimental results, as shown in Table 3, indicate that providing more information from other viewpoints can lead to an improvement in recognition.

Table 4. Confusion matrix of our method on the N-UCLA3D dataset in the *fourth* setting.

(a) Training on camera 2 and testing on camera 3

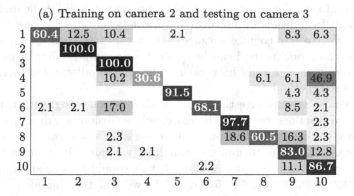

(b) Training on camera 1, 2 and testing on camera 3

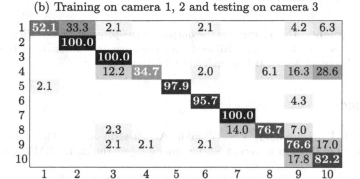

In Table 4, we show confusion matrices of our method on the N-UCLA3D dataset in the 4th setting. Table 4a shows the confusion matrix when using training samples from camera 2 and testing samples from camera 3. Action (4) *walk around* and action (10) *carry* have maximum confusion with each other because the majority of movement within action *carry* is walking. Action pairs, such as (6,3) and (8,7) (i.e., (*throw, drop trash*) and (*doffing, donning*)) have some confusion due to some similarity in motion and appearance. Table 4b shows the improvement to the confusion of the action pairs mentioned in advance. With more information provided from camera 1, we return the better results. We can easily realize the effectiveness when evaluate the recognition performance on action (6) *stand up*. In this case, we achieve the significant improvement from 68.1 % to 95.7 %.

5   Conclusion

This paper presents a study on human action recognition with depth sequences. In this paper, we discuss about the role of viewpoints to action recognition.

We evaluate their role through our multi-projection-based framework. Our method exploits the diversity in action execution to enrich useful information. It takes advantages of state-of-the-art 2D techniques to build dedicated features and classifiers. In addition, evaluating the information from some best viewpoints enables to effectively recognize actions that can be from unseen camera viewpoints. Therefore, our method can be applied for several realistic camera-based system. Experimental results have clearly shown the outstanding performance of our proposed method.

In this study, we only investigated cross-view action recognition using depth data obtained from one camera. Therefore, self-occlusion is still a problem that can influence the discrimination power. One possible way forward is to use multiple cameras [22,23]. With multiple cameras, we can collect much more discriminative motion information. As a result this should lead to an improvement in recognition accuracy. In the future work, we will try this idea within our viewpoint augmentation-based framework.

Acknowledgment. This research is the output of the project *"Action Recognition on 3D Video"* under grant number D2015-04 which belongs to University of Information Technology-Vietnam National University HoChiMinh City.

References

1. Chatfield, K., Lempitsky, V.S., Vedaldi, A., Zisserman, A.: The devil is in the details: an evaluation of recent feature encoding methods. In: BMVC, vol. 2, no. 4, p. 8 (2011)
2. Neumann, J., Fermller, C., Aloimonos, Y.: Animated heads: From 3d motion fields to action descriptions. In: Magnenat-Thalmann, N., Thalmann, D. (eds.) Deformable Avatars, pp. 1–11. Springer, USA (2001)
3. Weinland, D., Ronfard, R., Boyer, E.: Free viewpoint action recognition using motion history volumes. Comput. Vis. Image Underst. **104**(2), 249–257 (2006)
4. Matikainen, P., Hebert, M., Sukthankar, R.: Trajectons: action recognition through the motion analysis of tracked features. In: 2009 IEEE 12th International Conference on Computer Vision Workshops (ICCV Workshops), pp. 514–521. IEEE (2009)
5. Messing, R., Pal, C., Kautz, H.: Activity recognition using the velocity histories of tracked keypoints. In: 2009 IEEE 12th International Conference on Computer Vision, pp. 104–111. IEEE (2009)
6. Laptev, I.: On space-time interest points. Int. J. Comput. Vis. **64**(2–3), 107–123 (2005)
7. Dalal, N., Triggs, B., Schmid, C.: Human detection using oriented histograms of flow and appearance. In: Leonardis, A., Bischof, H., Pinz, A. (eds.) ECCV 2006. LNCS, vol. 3952, pp. 428–441. Springer, Heidelberg (2006)
8. Gopalan, R., Li, R., Chellappa, R.: Domain adaptation for object recognition: an unsupervised approach. In: 2011 IEEE International Conference on Computer Vision (ICCV), pp. 999–1006. IEEE (2011)
9. Aggarwal, J.K., Ryoo, M.S.: Human activity analysis: a review. ACM Comput. Surv. (CSUR) **43**(3), 16 (2011)

10. Weinland, D., Ronfard, R., Boyer, E.: A survey of vision-based methods for action representation, segmentation and recognition. Comput. Vis. Image Underst. **115**(2), 224–241 (2011)
11. Wang, J., Nie, X., Xia, Y., Wu, Y., Zhu, S.-C.: Cross-view action modeling, learning, and recognition. In: 2014 IEEE Conference on Computer Vision and Pattern Recognition (CVPR), pp. 2649–2656. IEEE (2014)
12. Rahmani, H., Mahmood, A., Huynh, D., Mian, A.: Histogram of Oriented Principal Components for Cross-View Action Recognition (2014). (arXiv preprint) arXiv:1409.6813
13. Li, B., Camps, O., Sznaier, M.: Cross-view activity recognition using hankelets. In: 2012 IEEE Conference on Computer Vision and Pattern Recognition (CVPR), pp. 1362–1369. IEEE (2012)
14. Liu, J., Shah, M., Kuipers, B., Savarese, S.: Cross-view action recognition via view knowledge transfer. In: 2011 IEEE Conference on Computer Vision and Pattern Recognition (CVPR), pp. 3209–3216. IEEE (2011)
15. Zheng, J., Jiang, Z., Jonathon Phillips, P., Chellappa, R.: Cross-view action recognition via a transferable dictionary pair. In: BMVC, vol. 1, no. 2, p. 7 (2012)
16. Zheng, J., Jiang, Z.: Learning view-invariant sparse representations for cross-view action recognition. In: 2013 IEEE International Conference on Computer Vision (ICCV), pp. 3176–3183. IEEE (2013)
17. Li, R., Zickler, T.: Discriminative virtual views for cross-view action recognition. In: 2012 IEEE Conference on Computer Vision and Pattern Recognition (CVPR), pp. 2855–2862. IEEE (2012)
18. Zhang, Z., Wang, C., Xiao, B., Zhou, W., Liu, S., Shi, C.: Cross-view action recognition via a continuous virtual path. In: 2013 IEEE Conference on Computer Vision and Pattern Recognition (CVPR), pp. 2690–2697. IEEE (2013)
19. Rahmani, H., Mian, A.: Learning a non-linear knowledge transfer model for cross-view action recognition. In: Proceedings of the IEEE Conference on Computer Vision and Pattern Recognition, pp. 2458–2466 (2015)
20. Gupta, A., Shafaei, A., Little, J.J., Woodham, R.J.: Unlabelled 3D motion examples improve cross-view action recognition. In: Proceedings of the British Machine Vision Conference. BMVA Press (2014)
21. Wang, H., Kläser, A., Schmid, C., Liu, C.-L.: Dense trajectories and motion boundary descriptors for action recognition. Int. J. Comput. Vis. **103**(1), 60–79 (2013)
22. Nakajima, H., Mitsugami, I., Yagi, Y.: Depth-based gait feature representation. Inf. Media Technol. **8**(4), 1085–1089 (2013)
23. Sivapalan, S., Chen, D., Denman, S., Sridharan, S., Fookes, C.: The backfilled GEI-a cross-capture modality gait feature for frontal and side-view gait recognition. In: 2012 International Conference on Digital Image Computing Techniques and Applications (DICTA), pp. 1–8. IEEE (2012)

Star-Effect Simulation for Photography Using Self-calibrated Stereo Vision

Dongwei Liu[1]([✉]), Haokun Geng[1], and Reinhard Klette[2]

[1] Department of Computer Science, The University of Auckland,
Auckland, New Zealand
dliu697@aucklanduni.ac.nz
[2] School of Engineering, Auckland University of Technology, Auckland, New Zealand

Abstract. Star effects are an important design factor for night photos. Progress in imaging technologies made it possible that night photos can be taken free-hand. For such camera settings, star effects are not achievable. We present a star-effect simulation method based on self-calibrated stereo vision. Given an uncalibrated stereo pair (i.e. a base image and a match image), which can be just two photos taken with a mobile phone with about the same pose, we follow a standard routine: Extract a family of feature-point pairs, calibrate the stereo pair by using the feature-point pairs, and obtain depth information by stereo matching. We detect highlight regions in the base image, estimate the luminance according to available depth information, and, finally, render star patterns with an input texture. Experiments show that our results are similar to real-world star effect photos, and that they are more natural than results of existing commercial applications. The paper reports for the first time research on automatically simulating photo-realistic star effects.

Keywords: Star effect · Computational photography · Stereo vision · Self-calibration

1 Introduction

Night photos with compelling lighting show sometimes star patterns around highlights, known as *star effect* in photography. Such star patterns are often essential for defining the aesthetic meaning of night photographs.

Recently, an increasing number of photos are taken with compact cameras or mobile phones. The technological progress (e.g. large aperture lenses or high-sensitivity image sensors) made it possible to shoot night photos free-hand.

Normally, to obtain a star effect, a photo has to be shot with a small aperture (e.g., f22). Such an aperture setting is unfit for free-hand shooting because it requires several seconds of exposure time; the photo would be largely blurred by hand shake. Alternatively, star effects can be achieved with a *star filter* in front of the lens. This is also not really appropriate for casual shooting with compact cameras or mobile phones because special equipment is needed. See Sect. 2.1 for

© Springer International Publishing Switzerland 2016
T. Bräunl et al. (Eds.): PSIVT 2015, LNCS 9431, pp. 228–240, 2016.
DOI: 10.1007/978-3-319-29451-3_19

details about generating star effects in photography. The question arises: How to obtain a star effect in case of casual hand-held photography?

Generating star effects by post-processing is a possible way, for example by adding star effects manually using available photo-editing applications. This might be a time consuming process for a complex scene because the size and color of each star should be carefully set, one by one. Professional skills are also needed. Dedicated applications such as *Topaz Star Effects plugins*, or instructions given in some online tutorial videos [7,17], draw uniform-sized star patterns to all the overexposed regions of a photo. Though it may also look beautiful, such effects typically look unnatural and different to the star effect generated by a small aperture. It is desirable to have an automatic star-effect generator which corresponds to the actual content of a photo.

Research on computational photography [16] explores the simulation of various photo effects such as fog [12], bokeh [13], or high dynamic range photos [23]. With this paper we present first time research on automatically simulating photo-realistic star effects.

This paper presents an automatic method for adding star effects to a photo using self-calibrated stereo vision. Given an uncalibrated stereo pair (e.g. two pictures of the same scene taken with a mobile phone at about "near-parallel" poses), we first detect a family of feature point-pairs and do a self-calibration. By stereo matching we estimate depth information of the scene. Next, "star-capable" highlights are detected, and luminance and color information (clipped by over-exposure) is recovered according to the available depth information. Finally, we render star patterns considering the luminance and color of the highlights using an input templet.

The rest of the paper is structured as follows. Section 2 briefly recalls theories and techniques related to our work. In Sect. 3 we provide details for our self-calibrated depth-estimation method. Section 4 discusses our method for the detection of highlights and the estimation of luminance and color of highlights. Then, Sect. 5 discusses our star effect rendering method. Experimental results are shown in Sect. 6. Section 7 concludes.

2   Basic and Notation

This section lists notation and techniques used. RGB color images I are defined on a rectangular set Ω of pixel locations, with $I(p) = (R(p), G(p), B(p))$ for $p \in \Omega$ and $0 \leq R(p), G(p), B(p) \leq G_{\max}$. Let N_{cols} and N_{rows} be width and height of Ω, respectively. Position O be the center of Ω (as an approximation of the principle point). We suppose lens distortion has been corrected in cameras, otherwise we can correct it by using the lens profile provided by the manufacturer. Altogether, we consider input image I as being generated by undistorted central projection. In the following, a *star-effect photo* refers to a photo taken of a night scene with a very small aperture, in which star patterns appear around highlights.

2.1   Star Effects in Photography

A star effect is normally caused by *Fraunhofer diffraction* [2]. Such a phenomenon is most visible when bright light from a "nearly infinite" distance passes through a narrow slit, causing the light to spread perpendicular to the slit. This spreads a point-like beam of light into a pair of streaks. Suppose a rectangular aperture A with width w_1 and height w_2, located in an x_1x_2 plane having its origin at the centroid of A; axes x_1 and x_2 are parallel to the edges with width w_1 and w_2, respectively. Suppose an axis y perpendicular to the x_1x_2 plane. When A is illuminated by a monochromatic plane wave of wavelength λ, the intensity $I(\theta_1, \theta_2)$ of the light through A forms a pattern that is described by

$$I(\theta_1, \theta_2) \propto \mathrm{sinc}^2 \left(\frac{\pi w_1 \sin \theta_1}{\lambda} \right) \mathrm{sinc}^2 \left(\frac{\pi w_2 \sin \theta_2}{\lambda} \right) \quad (1)$$

with $\tan \theta_1 = x_1/y$ and $\tan \theta_2 = x_2/y$. Similarly, for a parallelepiped aperture with edge lengths w_1, w_1, and w_1, we have a pattern defined by

$$I(\theta_1, \theta_2, \theta_3) \propto \mathrm{sinc}^2 \left(\frac{\pi w_1 \sin \theta_1}{\lambda} \right) \mathrm{sinc}^2 \left(\frac{\pi w_2 \sin \theta_2}{\lambda} \right) \mathrm{sinc}^2 \left(\frac{\pi w_3 \sin \theta_3}{\lambda} \right) \quad (2)$$

Fig. 1. Relationship between aperture shape and star effect. From left to right: Five straight blades aperture, eight straight blades aperture, eight curved blades aperture, nine curved blades aperture, and a circular aperture with a star filter

Figure 1 shows some real-world star patterns shot with different aperture shapes. It can be seen that each blade of the aperture contributes a pair of streaks to the star pattern. Due to overlapping, in case of a lens with an even number a of blades, generated star patterns have the same number a of streaks.

In fact, every beam of light that goes to the image sensor through a small aperture, spreads a star pattern to its neighboring region due to diffraction. In normal-contrast regions of an image, the star pattern is very slight and not visible (it only causes a reduction of local sharpness). Only in very high-contrast cases, such as highlights in a night photo, the star pattern is noticeable.

As described above, the shape of the star pattern depends on the shape of the aperture, which is not a user-controllable parameter. A modern-designed lens normally uses a near-circular aperture (in order to obtain good *bokeh* quality [13]), which generates only weak and scattered streaks. Our method provides controllable star pattern styles, which is convenient for photo-art creation.

A *star filter* can be used to simulate a star effect as introduced by small aperture. Such filter embeds a very fine diffraction grating or some prisms. A star effect can be obtained even at large aperture when using such a filter in front of the lens. The star pattern generated by a star filter is visually a little different from that one generated by a small aperture. Our method can simulate both styles by introducing different templates.

2.2 Stereo Vision

For stereo vision, we take a *stereo pair* (i.e. a *base image* I_b and a *match image* I_m) as input, and estimate depth information for a scene by searching for corresponding pixels in the stereo pair [10]. For reducing the complexity, the given stereo pair is normally geometrically rectified into *canonical stereo geometry* [10], in which I_b and I_m are as taken by identical cameras, only differing by translation distance b along the *base line* on the X-axis of the camera coordinate system of I_b. Rectification transform matrices $\mathbf{R}_b$ and $\mathbf{R}_m$ can be calculated in a stereo calibration process. Our proposed method is not very sensitive to accuracy of available depth values. For convenience, we use a self-calibration method with only a few assumed camera parameters. After rectification, a stereo matching method such as belief-propagation [3], or semi-global matching [5,6], can be used for calculating a disparity map. Depth information is then obtained by using standard *triangulation*.

Self-calibrated stereo vision is a convenient and easy to achieve setting for obtaining depth information of a scene (i.e. an image), compared to other depth sensors such as *structured lighting* as used in the *Kinect* [8], *depth from defocus (DFD)* [20], a *light-field camera* [18], or 3D laser imaging systems [1].

3 Depth Estimation

Given an uncalibrated stereo pair I_b and I_m, we do self-calibration by detecting a family of feature pairs, then we rectify the given stereo pair and obtain a disparity map through stereo matching. The disparity map is warped into the coordinates of the unrectified image I_b for avoiding any composition damage.

Feature detection and matching is the key step of the self-calibration method. A number of mainstream feature detectors are evaluated by [21], which suggests that the *oriented BRIEF* (ORB) (see [19] for an implementation) detector appears to be reasonably rotation invariant and noise resistant by also ensuring time efficiency.

First of all, two families of features $\mathcal{F}_b$ and $\mathcal{F}_m$ are collected from I_b and I_m using ORB. An ideal case would be that all the features are uniformly distributed in all the interesting regions of the input images.

The k-nearest neighbors (kNN) method is then used to detect best matches $\mathcal{F}_{\text{pairs}}$ between the two families of features. The feature pairs are filtered by a distance ratio test [15] and a cross-symmetry test:

$$\forall [p_b^{(i)}, p_m^{(i)}] \big(\; [p_b^{(i)}, p_m^{(i)}] \in \mathcal{F}_{\text{filtered}} \leftrightarrow [p_b^{(i)}, p_m^{(i)}] \in \mathcal{F}_{\text{pairs}}$$
$$\wedge \; \delta_1(p_b^{(i)}) < T_{\text{distance}} \cdot \delta_2(p_b^{(i)})$$
$$\wedge \; \|x_b^{(i)} - x_m^{(i)}\|_2 < T_{\text{cross,x}} \wedge \|y_b^{(i)} - y_m^{(i)}\|_2 < T_{\text{cross,y}} \big) \qquad (3)$$

where $\delta_1(p_b^{(i)})$ is the similarity distance to the closest neighbor of $p_b^{(i)}$ in kNN matching, and $\delta_2(p_b^{(i)})$ is the similarity distance to the second-closest neighbor. We use a ratio $T_{\text{distance}} = 0.8$. According to the statistics in [15], such a threshold eliminates 90 % of the false matches while discarding less than 5 % of the correct matches. $T_{\text{cross,x}}$ and $T_{\text{cross,y}}$ specify the tolerance thresholds. We use $T_{\text{cross,x}} = 0.15 \cdot N_{\text{cols}}$ and $T_{\text{cross,y}} = 0.01 \cdot N_{\text{rows}}$. Figure 2 shows results of the feature matching phase.

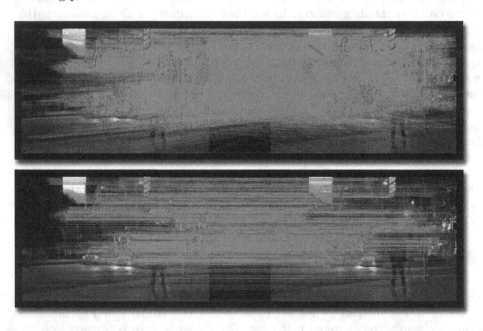

Fig. 2. Matched feature points before and after applying our filter

We use a *random sample consensus* (RANSAC) algorithm to calculate a fundamental matrix $\mathbf{F}$ according to $\mathcal{F}_{\text{filtered}}$. Both images I_b and I_m have been taken with the same camera. Thus, we do not need to create identical twins of cameras (as in the general stereo imaging case). Homography matrices $\mathbf{H}_b$ and $\mathbf{H}_m$ can be computed by using $\mathcal{F}_{\text{filtered}}$ and $\mathbf{F}$ [4]; those matrices transform I_b and I_m into planar perspective views $\hat{I}_b$ and $\hat{I}_m$.

We run an SGM stereo matcher [5] on $\hat{I}_b$ and $\hat{I}_m$, and obtain a disparity map $\hat{d}$ defined on the carrier $\hat{\Omega}$ of $\hat{I}_b$.

Note that without knowing the camera matrix and the relative position of the cameras, the transforms $\mathbf{H}_b$ and $\mathbf{H}_m$ obtained from self-calibration, are not standard rectification transforms. The rectified image $\hat{I}_b$ might be "largely warped",

Fig. 3. *Top*: A rectified image pair $\hat{I}_b$ and $\hat{I}_m$. *Bottom, left to right*: The resulting disparity map $\hat{d}$, the inversely transformed disparity map d, and the joint, bilaterally filtered result.

as shown in Fig. 3, and thus distort the attempted composition. We transform $\hat{d}$ into d according to the inverse transform H_b^{-1}.

A joint bilateral filter [9] is then applied for removing noise from d. See Fig. 3, bottom, for a result after inverse transformation and filtering of the disparity map. Because of lack of texture or limited availability of disparities, disparity information close to the border of the image might be incorrect. This does not affect our application because we only use disparity at highlights.

4   Highlight Registration

As mentioned in Sect. 2.1, star patterns appear only in very high contrast regions, typically at highlights in a night photo. Due to limitations of the dynamic range of the image sensor or of the image file format, luminance and color information in such regions normally gets clipped. We detect these regions in the original image I_b, and estimate the luminance and color information according to depth information and values at adjacent pixels.

4.1   Highlight Detection

To locate valid highlights, we first detect a family $\mathcal{F}_{\text{overexposed}}$ of 4-connected regions S in I_b which are formed by over-exposed pixels, satisfying

$$R_b(p) = G_b(p) = B_b(p) = G_{\max} \tag{4}$$

at all $p \in S$. Some regions in $\mathcal{F}_{\text{overexposed}}$ cannot be considered as a possible source for a star pattern, as occurring in real-world star-effect photos.

For example, overexposed but non-luminous regions such as some metallic patches at buildings, large overexposed regions including the sky (e.g. with a backlight) or a white wall, or very small overexposed regions which are normally just local reflections (e.g. of eyes of a cat) or noisy pixels. To eliminate these items, we extract a subfamily $\mathcal{F}_{\text{highlight}} \subset \mathcal{F}_{\text{overexposed}}$ such that

$$\forall S \left[S \in \mathcal{F}_{\text{highlight}} \leftrightarrow S \in \mathcal{F}_{\text{overexposed}} \wedge \lambda_S < 1.5 \wedge 2 < R_S < 0.03 \cdot N_{\text{cols}} \right] \quad (5)$$

where λ_S is the aspect ratio of the bounding rectangle of S, and R_S is the circumradius of S. The *centroid* of $S \in \mathcal{F}_{\text{highlight}}$, denoted by p_S, is given by

$$p_S = \left(\frac{\mu_{10}(S)}{\mu_{00}(S)}, \frac{\mu_{01}(S)}{\mu_{10}(S)} \right) \quad \text{with} \quad \mu_{ab}(S) = \sum_{(x,y) \in S} x^a \cdot y^b \quad (6)$$

This filter removes a large part of distracting overexposed regions (see Fig. 4), while some tutorials [7, 17] use all the overexposed regions to create star patterns. Experiments show that our strategy performs more naturally (see Sect. 6).

Fig. 4. Highlight detection. From left to right: a map of overexposed pixels for the scene shown in Fig. 3, top, detected overexposed regions, and remaining highlights after applying our filter

4.2 Color Recovery

Highlights are normally the most saturated parts in a night photo, for example, streetlights, traffic signals, or head- or taillights of a car. Though the center of a highlight is by our definition just overexposed without any color information, the adjacent region normally provides strong hints on color due to diffuse reflection or diffraction. Thus we estimate the color information of a highlight based on the color of adjacent pixels.

We first convert I_b into I_{HSV} in the HSV color space following [22]. For $I_b(p) = (R(p), G(p), B(p))$, $V(p) = \max\{R(p), G(p), B(p)\}$, and $\delta(p) = V(p) - \min\{R(p), G(p), B(p)\}$, we have that

$$S(p) = \begin{cases} \delta(p)/V(p) & \text{if} \quad V(p) \neq 0 \\ 0 & \text{otherwise} \end{cases}$$

$$\hat{H}(p) = \begin{cases} 60 \cdot [G(p) - B(p)]/\delta(p) & \text{if} \quad V(p) = R(p) \\ 120 + 60 \cdot [B(p) - R(p)]/\delta(p) & \text{if} \quad V(p) = G(p) \\ 240 + 60 \cdot [R(p) - G(p)]/\delta(p) & \text{if} \quad V(p) = B(p) \end{cases} \tag{7}$$

$$H(p) = \begin{cases} \hat{H}(p) + 360 & \text{if} \quad \hat{H}(p) < 0 \\ \hat{H}(p) & \text{otherwise} \end{cases}$$

For a highlight region S, we select the hue H_S and saturation S_S by detecting the most saturated pixel p in a circular neighborhood Ω_S around S:

$$\forall q\,[q \in \Omega_S \rightarrow S(p) \geq S(q)] \tag{8}$$

Here $S(p)$ is the saturation value of p, and Ω_S is a circular region centered at the centroid p_S having the radius of $1.5 \cdot R_S$, where R_S is the circumradius of S.

4.3 Luminance Estimation

The size of a star pattern in a star-effect photo is related to the luminance value of the corresponding highlight. The real luminance values of highlight regions are lost in a photo due to the limited dynamic range of the image sensor or the image file format. We estimate a possible luminance value V_S for each highlight $S \in \mathcal{F}_{\text{highlight}}$. The goal of such an estimation is to render natural star effects; we do not go so far as understanding the real luminance of the image scene.

We make an assumption that all the light sources with a same color have the same energy. For example, all the streetlights along a street have the same energy, which is stronger than the energy of a traffic light. Thus, we classify the light sources by available color information, and assign a weight parameter $C_{\text{color}}(S)$ to the light source corresponding to S. Empirically, we have that

$$C_{color}(S) = \begin{cases} 0.3, & \text{if} \quad color(S) = \text{Red} \\ 1, & \text{if} \quad color(S) = \text{Yellow} \\ 0.4, & \text{if} \quad color(S) = \text{Green} \\ 0.2, & \text{if} \quad color(S) = \text{Others} \end{cases} \tag{9}$$

with

$$color(S) = \begin{cases} \text{Red} & \text{if} \quad H_S < 30 \vee H_S \geq 330 \\ \text{Yellow} & \text{if} \quad 30 \leq H_S < 75 \\ \text{Green} & \text{if} \quad 75 \leq H_S < 165 \\ \text{Others} & \text{otherwise} \end{cases} \tag{10}$$

This classification covers common light sources in night photos.

We also simply ignore the media between light source and lens, and estimate the luminance V_S of the highlight region according to the distance $D(p)$ between camera and light source, and color information:

$$V_S = \frac{E_S}{4\pi \cdot D(p)^2} \approx C_{\text{intensity}} \cdot C_{\text{color}}(p) \cdot d(p)^2 \tag{11}$$

Here E_S is the energy of the light source corresponding to S – which we do not know. For convenience, we use a global user parameter $C_{\text{intensity}}$ for controlling the "strength" of star effects.

Experiments show that this assumption works well in applications (see Sect. 6).

5   Star Pattern Rendering

The light diffracted by an aperture can be approximately modeled by the *Fraunhofer diffraction equation* [14] because the light sources are normally effectively at infinity. The diffracted light goes into (the system of) optical lenses before it arrives at the image sensor; this sensor introduces further complexity.

Equations (1) and (2) show that the diffraction distribution rule is not related to the strength of the input light. Thus, the pattern keeps the same shape under any luminance condition. A star of a weaker light source looks smaller because the outer-ring of the pattern is "too weak" to be visible. See a real-world example in Fig. 5. Due to the limitation of the dynamic range, the centers of the star patterns (i.e. the "peaks") look all the same. The pattern is stronger inside and weaker outside. Thus, we model the shape of a star pattern by loading an $N \times N$ texture α. The scale N is a user controlled parameter. We define α on a rectangular set Ω_α, having the center of Ω_α as its origin.

Fig. 5. Illustration of the relationship between star pattern and luminance. Photos shot with f/22 and ISO 800. Shutter speeds are, from top-left to bottom-right: 1/4s, 1/2s, 1s, 2s, 4s, and 8s

We render a star pattern for each highlight region S on I_b, and obtain the final result. For each position $p \in \Omega_\alpha$, let

$$I(p + p_S) = I(p + p_S) + \alpha(p)(R_S, G_S, B_S) \tag{12}$$

Here R_S, G_S, and B_S are the RGB color values corresponding to the previously calculated HSV color (H_S, S_S, V_S).

6 Experiments

We implemented our approach on a 3.30 GHz PC with 8.00 GB RAM and no graphics card. The run time is about 3 s for images of $2,400 \times 1,600$ resolution. Figure 6 illustrates star pattern rendering using different strength parameters. Figure 7 illustrates how to control the styles of the star effect using different textures. To control the shape of the star pattern by a camera, photographers need to use different lenses. Comparatively, our method is very convenient in controlling star effects, and thus convenient for artists to try different styles and obtain their favorite feeling.

Fig. 6. Use of different strengths for star-pattern rendering. *Left to right*: Original image, small scale star effect, and large scale star effect

Fig. 7. Application of different star textures on Fig. 6, left

Figure 8 compares our method, a uniform-size star effect, a random-size star effect, and a real-world star-effect photo. The uniform-size star effect is generated manually following a tutorial [17], the random-size star effect is generated using our rendering method but without any use of depth information. The uniform-size star effect also looks appealing, but does not show any space feeling. Such an effect is similar to the style of a common star filter. It can also be noticed that all the overexposed regions are used in the manual process, including those regions that should not make a significant diffraction, as, for example, some sparkles on the water. The random-size star effect looks more flexible. Without understanding the image's content, this effect does not show any space feeling either, and involves false logic. For example, the further-away street light should define a smaller star. In comparison, our depth-aware method performs naturally, and the result is similar to the real-world star-effect photo. Another advantage of our method over manual processing [7,17] is that we can render colorful stars according to the content of the input photo, while the manual process only renders monochromatic stars because the color information of those overexposed regions is lost.

Fig. 8. Comparison between our method (*top-left*), uniform-size star effect (*top-right*), random-size star effect (*bottom-left*), and a real-world star-effect photo, i.e. the "ground truth" (*bottom-right*)

Our method can also simulate the style of a star filter, using a proper star texture (as demonstrated in Fig. 9). The photo on the left is shot at aperture f4, which is a relatively large aperture, and thus does not show any significant star effect. The photo in the middle is shot with a 4-point star filter and with

Fig. 9. Simulation of the style of a star filter. *Left to right*: A photo shot with large aperture (thus does not show any star effect), a photo shot with a star filter, and our result

the same camera parameters as used for the left photo. It can be seen that our result looks similar to the star-filter photo.

Variations in robustness of the applied stereo vision method can affect our star rendering. This is a limitation of our method. Figure 10 shows some failed cases due to failures in depth calculations. The car in the red rectangle of Fig. 10, right, is in an occlusion region (see Fig. 10, middle), thus the depth information is unavailable. As a result, star effect is not applied to the headlight of the car.

Fig. 10. Failed cases due to failures in depth calculations (Color figure online).

7   Conclusion

We present a star-effect simulation method. The key is to obtain depth information from self-calibrated stereo vision, and then estimate the luminance of the highlight regions according to the available depth information. Finally, do a content-aware star-pattern rendering. Experiments show that our results are similar to real-world star-effect photos. Our results are also more natural in their appearance than the results of existing commercial applications. To the best of our knowledge, this is the first research reported on automatically simulating photo-realistic star effects.

Acknowledgements. This project is supported by the China Scholarship Council.

References

1. Blais, F.: Review of 20 years of range sensor development. J. Electron. Imaging **13**, 231–240 (2004)
2. Born, M., Wolf, E.: Principles of Optics. Cambridge University Press, Cambridge (1999)
3. Felzenszwalb, P.F., Huttenlocher, D.P.: Efficient belief propagation for early vision. Int. J. Comput. Vis. **70**, 41–54 (2006)
4. Hartley, R.I.: Theory and practice of projective rectification. Int. J. Comput. Vis. **35**, 115–127 (1999)
5. Hirschmüller, H.: Accurate and efficient stereo processing by semi-global matching and mutual information. In: Proceedings of CVPR, pp. 807–814 (2005)
6. Hermann, S., Klette, R.: Iterative semi-global matching for robust driver assistance systems. In: Lee, K.M., Matsushita, Y., Rehg, J.M., Hu, Z. (eds.) ACCV 2012, Part III. LNCS, vol. 7726, pp. 465–478. Springer, Heidelberg (2013)
7. Hoey, G.: Advanced photoshop starburst filter effect - Week 45 (2009). www.youtube.com/watch?v=lRKp4_EkIvc
8. Khoshelham, K., Elberink, S.O.: Accuracy and resolution of Kinect depth data for indoor mapping applications. Sensors **12**, 1437–1454 (2012)
9. Kopf, J., Cohen, M.F., Lischinski, D., Uyttendaele, M.: Joint bilateral upsampling. ACM Trans. Graph. **26**(3), 96 (2007)
10. Klette, R.: Concise Computer Vision: An Introduction into Theory and Algorithms. Springer, London (2014)
11. Klette, R., Rosenfeld, A.: Digital Geometry: Geometric Methods for Digital Picture Analysis. Morgan Kaufmann, San Francisco (2004)
12. Liu, D., Klette, R.: Fog effect for photography using stereo vision. Vis. Comput. 1–11 (2015). doi:10.1007/s00371-014-1058-7
13. Klette, R., Liu, D., Nicolescu, R.: Bokeh effects based on stereo vision. In: Azzopardi, G., Petkov, N., Yamagiwa, S. (eds.) CAIP 2015. LNCS, vol. 9256, pp. 198–210. Springer, Heidelberg (2015). doi:10.1007/978-3-319-23192-1_17
14. Lipson, A., Lipson, S.G., Lipson, H.: Optical Physics. Cambridge University Press, Cambridge (2010)
15. Lowe, D.G.: Distinctive image features from scale-invariant keypoints Int. J. Comput. Vis. **60**, 91–110 (2004)
16. Lukac, R.: Computational Photography: Methods and Applications. CRC Press, Boca Raton (2010)
17. mahalodotcom: How to create a lens flare effect in Photoshop (2011). www.youtube.com/watch?v=qmL0ct2Ries
18. Ng, R., Levoy, M., Brédif, M., Duval, G., Horowitz, M., Hanrahan, P.: Light field photography with a hand-held plenoptic camera. Stanford University, CSTR 2005–02 (2005)
19. Rublee, E., Rabaud, V., Konolige, K., Bradski, G.: ORB: an efficient alternative to SIFT or SURF. In: Proceedings of ICCV, pp. 2564–2571 (2011)
20. Schechner, Y.Y., Kiryati, N.: Depth from defocus vs. stereo: how different really are they? Int. J. Comput. Vis. **39**, 141–162 (2000)
21. Klette, R., Song, Z.: Robustness of point feature detection. In: Wilson, R., Hancock, E., Bors, A., Smith, W. (eds.) CAIP 2013, Part II. LNCS, vol. 8048, pp. 91–99. Springer, Heidelberg (2013)
22. Smith, A.R.: Color gamut transform pairs. ACM Siggraph Comput. Graph. **12**, 12–19 (1978)
23. Wang, L., Wei, L.Y., Zhou, K., Guo, B., Shum, H.Y.: High dynamic range image hallucination. In: Proceedings of Eurograph, pp. 321–326 (2007)

Computer Vision and Applications

A Robust Stereo Vision with Confidence Measure Based on Tree Agreement

Jeongmok Ha$^{(\boxtimes)}$ and Hong Jeong

Department of Electrical Engineering, Pohang University of Science
and Technology (POSTECH), Cheongam-ro 77, Pohang, South Korea
{jmokha,hjeong}@postech.ac.kr

Abstract. We present an improved non-learning-based confidence measure based on tree agreement for the stereo matching problem. To use confidence information for accurate matching, we propose an improved method to assemble a cost aggregation table with confidence measure. The proposed confidence measure and cost aggregation method were evaluated using the KITTI and HCI datasets. Compared to other non-learning-based confidence measures, the proposed confidence measure showed the best ability to detect wrongly-estimated pixels. By using estimated confidence measure, we showed that the proposed cost aggregation method improved disparity map quality compared to previous methods. The proposed algorithm could estimate disparity relatively accurately even in some very challenging outdoor scenes.

Keywords: Markov random fields · Automotive stereo vision · Confidence measure · Tree agreement · Cost aggregation table

1 Introduction

The stereo vision problem is usually solved by an approximate inference on a *Markov random fields* (MRFs) model [1]. An MRF model may have difficulty matching pixels when the data are corrupted or the smoothness constraints do not satisfy the assumed conditions. Especially, numerous factors can cause mismatches in outdoor scenes, which are important in automotive vision systems; occluded areas [2], textureless areas [3], and repetitive patterns are examples [4]. Although very effective stereo algorithms have been proposed [5,6], these problems are still difficult to solve.

To overcome this limitation, several authors have proposed methods to evaluate the accuracy with which stereo image pairs are matched; i.e., the *confidence* [4]. The confidence measure represents the accuracy with which labels on each pixels are estimated without any ground truth data. Various confidence measures have been proposed [7,8]; they can be categorized into, non-learning-based and learning-based confidence measures.

Non-learning-based confidence measures use the shape of a cost curve, consistency between left and right disparities, and other local information as clues to

© Springer International Publishing Switzerland 2016
T. Bräunl et al. (Eds.): PSIVT 2015, LNCS 9431, pp. 243–256, 2016.
DOI: 10.1007/978-3-319-29451-3_20

find mismatches. Among these methods, *left and right consistency check* (LRC) has been widely used for disparity refinement [9]. Generally, non-learning-based confidence measures are easy to implement, but are not accurate enough to be used. LRC cannot not detect textureless areas, especially in outdoor scenes.

Learning-based confidence measures find the best combination of non-learning-based confidence measures by training them. After various confidence measures have been determined, the best combination of them is obtained. Usually, ensemble learning methods (e.g., random forest [10] and regression forest [11]) are used for the training process. Learning-based methods detect mismatched disparity more accurately than do non-learning-based confidence measures. However, to use learning algorithms for various confidence measures, all confidence measures must be obtained before the training process. This is a troublesome task.

An alternative approach is to use a tree-shaped MRF, and to develop a confidence measurement based on tree agreement [12]. The method is based on the assumption that the full graph is divided into subgraphs, and exploits the property that the convex sum of energy optimized on each subgraph would be the same as the energy optimized on the full graph. The confidence measure is defined as the difference between full graph energy and the convex sum of subgraph energies. This confidence measure works on a *union jack* tree structure with *semi-global matching* (SGM) [13], which is a multidirectional 1D cost-aggregation stereo-matching algorithm.

In this paper, we propose a confidence measure that is based on tree agreement and that uses *cost aggregation table* (CAT) [14–16]. The CAT is a 2D cost aggregation method which is an improved version of SGM; CAT estimates each disparity by aggregating all costs in the image in a short time. Because CAT optimizes the MRF problem by dividing the full graph into four subgraphs, the tree agreement property can be applied easily. To use a confidence measure for stereo matching, we also propose an improved cost aggregation method. The CAT algorithm is used because its pixel selection can be effectively applied to the optimization process.

The contributions of this paper are summarized as follows:

- A tree agreement based confidence measure on four subgraphs is proposed.
- A new cost aggregation method with confidence measure is proposed.
- The proposed confidence measure and cost aggregation method were evaluated with previous methods using the KITTI [17] and HCI [18] datasets.

2   Related Work

Several good survey papers present and evaluate various kinds of confidence measures. One of them presents excellent evaluation of 17 commonly-used confidence measures, and categorizes them well based on the confidence properties [7]. Another paper analyzes various confidence measures on real road scene using the KITTI dataset [8].

Some papers tried to improve disparity results by identifying mismatched or well-matched pixels [19]. A non-parametric scheme was used to learn the probability that errors will match by classifying matches into three cases: correct, nearby foreground, or other wrong depth [20]. To propagate information in the valid pixels into invalid pixels by adaptive filtering, an asymmetric consistency check has been proposed [21]. A credibility map was developed to fuse a high-resolution image with a low-resolution depth map from a *time-of-flight* (ToF) sensor [22]. An algorithm was presented that propagates confidence information by Bayesian approach [23], and the concept of Stixel that extend pixel-level representation into medium-level representation was proposed.

Many approaches have been used to apply machine learning techniques to improve disparity estimation. A combination of learning algorithm and feature selection was proposed to construct a reliable feature set for effective matching process [24]. The perceptron concept that uses prior knowledge in the image has been used for stereo matching [25]. Stability property related to confidence measure have been used to identify subsets unambiguously [26]. A statistical background model for image blocks learned from the image itself has been proposed [27].

Recently, ensemble learning based confidence measures have been proposed. The random forest supervised learning technique has been used to improve depth maps obtained from ToF cameras by improving per-pixel confidence measure with real-world data [28]. A random decision forest framework was used to train confidence measures, and the importance of each confidence measure was ranked by the metric of Gini and permutation [10]. Another learning-based confidence measure [29] differs from previous methods in that it presented how to leverage estimated confidence to increase the accuracy of the disparity estimate by using detected ground control points on an MRF framework. To select an effective confidence measures, the regression forest was used for the training phase [11]; a confidence-based matching cost modulation was also proposed.

Some efforts have been dedicated to modulating cost functions that use confidence measures. An operator was proposed to improve matching reliability by modulating matching cost using confidence measure [30]. A self-aware matching measure [31] was proposed by measuring the correlation coefficient between a cross-matching curve and self-matching curve; this method does not need any additional parameters, and it can be applied without modification to other stereo matching algorithms.

3   Problem Statement

MRFs have been widely used to solve stereo problems. The four-neighbor-connected graph is commonly used because of its simplicity and convenience [1]. A four-neighbor-connected graph $\mathcal{G} = (\mathcal{V}, \mathcal{E})$ consists of a set $\mathcal{V}$ of pixels, and a set $\mathcal{E}$ of edges. Each pixel $\mathbf{p} \in \mathcal{V}$ is a random variable that can have a discrete disparity $d_{\mathbf{p}} \in \mathcal{D}$, where $d_{\mathbf{p}}$ is a disparity of pixel $\mathbf{p}$ and $\mathcal{D}$ is a set of possible disparities. An edge is a pair of two pixels $(\mathbf{p}, \mathbf{q}) \in \mathcal{E}$, where $\mathbf{q} \in \mathcal{V}$; the edge encodes the disparity relationship between the pixels.

The stereo problem is solved by *maximum a posteriori* (MAP) estimation on joint distribution: $p(\mathbf{d}|\mathbf{o}) = p(\mathbf{o}|\mathbf{d})p(\mathbf{d})$, where $p(\cdot)$ represents a probability distribution, $\mathbf{d}$ is a set of all disparities in $\mathcal{V}$, and $\mathbf{o}$ is a set of observation data. The Gibbs distribution [32] can be used to change the a *posteriori* distribution to an energy function. The likelihood and prior terms become data and smoothness terms of the energy function:

$$E(\mathbf{d}) = \sum_{\mathbf{p}\in\mathcal{V}} \phi_{\mathbf{p}}(d_{\mathbf{p}}) + \sum_{(\mathbf{p},\mathbf{q})\in\mathcal{E}} \psi_{(\mathbf{p},\mathbf{q})}(d_{\mathbf{p}}, d_{\mathbf{q}}), \tag{1}$$

where $E(\cdot)$ represents energy function, a unary term $\phi_{\mathbf{p}}(\cdot)$ is a data term on the pixel $\mathbf{p}$, and the pairwise term $\psi_{(\mathbf{p},\mathbf{q})}(\cdot,\cdot)$ represents the smoothness between pixels $\mathbf{p}$ and $\mathbf{q}$. Eq. (1) is the standard energy formulation of MRF models.

By minimizing this energy term, the a set of optimum disparity solution $\mathbf{d}^*$ is estimated:

$$\mathbf{d}^* = \arg\min_{\mathbf{d}\in\mathcal{D}^{|\mathcal{V}|}} E(\mathbf{d}). \tag{2}$$

The goal of the stereo problem is to find disparities that minimize the energy.

4   Confidence Measure with Tree Agreement

In this paper, we use a confidence measure related to *tree agreement* [12] to determine whether or not the disparity of each pixel is well estimated.

The confidence measure related to tree agreement was determined based on *tree-reweighted message passing* (TRW) [33], an representative MAP inference algorithm to find optimum solutions of general labeling problems. TRW optimizes energy function iteratively on each subgraph separately by decomposing a full graph into subgraphs. Then TRW re-parameterizes the estimated results to make the same energy function.

TRW divides a full graph $\mathcal{G}$ into a convex sum of subgraphs $\mathcal{G}^t = (\mathcal{V}^t, \mathcal{E}^t)$, where $t \in \mathcal{T}$ and $\mathcal{T} = \{0, \cdots, T-1\}$ is a set of subgraphs. Each subgraph has its weight ω^t so that $\sum_{t\in\mathcal{T}} \omega^t = 1$. The energy of full graph $E^{\mathcal{G}}(\cdot)$ is weighted convex sum of energy of subgraphs:

$$E^{\mathcal{G}}(\mathbf{d}) = \sum_{t\in\mathcal{T}} \omega^t E^t(\mathbf{d}), \tag{3}$$

where $E^t(\cdot)$ represents the energy of the subgraph t. The optimum result of stereo problem is obtained by finding the minimum energy:

$$\min_{\mathbf{d}\in\mathcal{D}^{|\mathcal{V}|}} E^{\mathcal{G}}(\mathbf{d}) = \min_{\mathbf{d}\in\mathcal{D}^{|\mathcal{V}|}} \sum_{t\in\mathcal{T}} \omega^t E^t(\mathbf{d}). \tag{4}$$

The optimal disparity solution of the stereo problem is found by identifying the disparity set that minimizes the energy function. The minimum energy function has a lower bound because the full graph is divided into subgraphs. On the subgraphs, the estimate on each subgraph is also a solution of the stereo problem.

In the ideal case (in which all disparity estimates are correct), the estimated results on a full graph are the same as the results on the local subgraphs. The full graph consists of a convex sum of subgraphs, so the energy optimized on the full graph must be the same as the sum of energies optimized on each subgraphs. However, in most cases, the energy on the full graph is larger than the sum of energies on subgraphs; the difference can be defined as the confidence of each pixel.

Because the minimum of the sum is always greater or equal to the sum of minima, the minimum energy of the full graph is always greater or equal to the sum of minimum energies of the subgraphs:

$$\min_{\mathbf{d} \in \mathcal{D}^{|\mathcal{V}|}} \sum_{t \in \mathcal{T}} \omega^t E^t(\mathbf{d}) \geq \sum_{t \in \mathcal{T}} \min_{\mathbf{d} \in \mathcal{D}^{|\mathcal{V}|}} \omega^t E^t(\mathbf{d}). \tag{5}$$

The inequality becomes an equality when the optimum disparities of each subgraph are the same as the optimum disparity of the full graph; i.e., in the ideal case in which the disparity of each pixel is well estimated.

In this manner, the difference between left and right hand sides of (5) can be a measurement of the confidence in the estimate; the confidence is defined as the difference between the energy of the full graph and the sum of energies of the subgraphs:

$$\gamma = \min_{\mathbf{d} \in \mathcal{D}^{|\mathcal{V}|}} \sum_{t \in \mathcal{T}} \omega^t E^t(\mathbf{d}) - \sum_{t \in \mathcal{T}} \min_{\mathbf{d} \in \mathcal{D}^{|\mathcal{V}|}} \omega^t E^t(\mathbf{d}), \tag{6}$$

where γ is an uncertainty measure. Because bigger γ increases with the size of the gap between global minimum energy and sum of local minimum energies, γ is actually an uncertainty measure rather than a confidence measure.

5   Proposed Method with Confidence Measure

5.1   Cost Aggregation Table

CAT is an efficient algorithm or structure for the stereo matching problem [14]. CAT divides the full MRF graph into four subgraphs, $\mathcal{T} = (0, 1, 2, 3)$, i.e., north-east, north-west, south-east, and south-west respectively, then initializes the weight of each subgraph as $\omega^t = 1/4$. The subgraphs of CAT are denoted as $\mathcal{G}^0$, $\mathcal{G}^1$, $\mathcal{G}^2$, and $\mathcal{G}^3$. This structure produces approximate MAP inference results in a short time by dividing the full graph into four subgraphs. Because the full graph is divided into four subgraphs, the uncertainty measure based on tree agreement can be used.

We denote a reference pixel as $\mathbf{k} \in \mathcal{V}$; the reference pixel is a pixel whose disparity is to be estimated. The CAT structure is defined differently according to the reference pixel. The subgraphs with the reference node $\mathbf{k}$ is denoted as $\mathcal{G}_{\mathbf{k}}^0$,

$\mathcal{G}_{\mathbf{k}}^1$, $\mathcal{G}_{\mathbf{k}}^2$, and $\mathcal{G}_{\mathbf{k}}^3$, which represent north-east, north-west, south-east, and south-west sides relative to the reference pixel $\mathbf{k}$, respectively.

The joint distribution of the disparity set assumes to consist of the product of distribution of disparities of each pixel and each subgraph:

$$p(\mathbf{d}|\mathbf{o};\mathcal{G}) = \prod_{\mathbf{k}\in\mathcal{V}} p(d_{\mathbf{k}}|\mathbf{o};\mathcal{G}) = \prod_{\mathbf{k}\in\mathcal{V}}\prod_{t\in\mathcal{T}} p(d_{\mathbf{k}}|\mathbf{o};\mathcal{G}_{\mathbf{k}}^t). \tag{7}$$

Although each pixel is estimated independently, estimation of the optimum disparity for each pixel does not require aggregation of all costs in the image every time. With the help of the parents system, all costs can be aggregated in just four scans as follows.

For example, during the first scan, only subgraph $\mathcal{G}^0$ is used to aggregate costs (in the south-east direction). The pixel on the top left corner is set as the seed pixel $\mathbf{s}^0$. The parent pixels $\mathcal{P}_{\mathbf{p}}^t = \{\mathbf{p}_h^t, \mathbf{p}_v^t\}$ of pixel $\mathbf{p}$ are set as their horizontal and vertical adjacent neighbors, e.g., $\mathcal{P}_{\mathbf{p}}^0 = \{(y, x-1), (y-1, x)\}$. Then the costs are aggregated from parent pixels to child pixels. This aggregation step is performed on all four subgraphs independently.

When aggregating costs, a message-passing algorithm based on dynamic programming is used. This algorithm is similar to the cost aggregation method of SGM, but expands the 1D cost aggregation of SGM to 2D. The message is computed considering its smoothness constraint from its parent pixels. The minimum costs of two parent pixels are compared, and the smaller cost is delivered to the child pixel.

The message from parent pixels $\mathcal{P}_{\mathbf{p}}^t$ to pixel $\mathbf{k}$ on subgraph t is defined as:

$$m_{\mathbf{p}}^t(d_{\mathbf{p}}) = \phi_{\mathbf{p}}(d_{\mathbf{p}}) + \min_{\mathbf{q}\in\mathcal{P}_{\mathbf{p}}^t}\left[\min_{d_{\mathbf{q}}}\left[\psi_{(\mathbf{p},\mathbf{q})}(d_{\mathbf{p}}, d_{\mathbf{q}}) + m_{\mathbf{q}}^t(d_{\mathbf{q}})\right]\right], \tag{8}$$

where $m_{\mathbf{p}}^t(\cdot)$ is a message from parent pixels $\mathcal{P}_{\mathbf{p}}^t$ to pixel $\mathbf{p}$. The message is delivered from the parent pixels with smoothness term $\psi_{(\mathbf{p},\mathbf{q})}(\cdot,\cdot)$ to pixel $\mathbf{p}$. This processing is performed iteratively from seed pixel $\mathbf{s}^t$ to the opposite corner pixel. Usually, a census transform [34] is used as the data term, and a two-step penalty function [13] is used as the smoothness term.

After all messages have been computed on every subgraph, belief in the reference pixel $\mathbf{k}$ is defined as the sum of all messages computed on pixel $\mathbf{p}$:

$$b_{\mathbf{p}}(d_{\mathbf{p}}) = \sum_{t\in\mathcal{V}} m_{\mathbf{p}}^t(d_{\mathbf{p}}), \tag{9}$$

where $b_{\mathbf{p}}(\cdot)$ is a belief on pixel $\mathbf{p}$. After beliefs on every pixel are computed, a winner takes all method is used to find the optimum disparity on each pixel:

$$d_{\mathbf{p}}^* = \arg\min_{d_{\mathbf{p}}} b_{\mathbf{p}}(d_{\mathbf{p}}). \tag{10}$$

Algorithms based on subgraph division can use the confidence measure based on tree agreement. With the subgraph division of CAT structure, the proposed

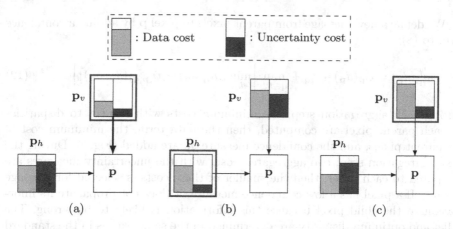

Fig. 1. Diagrams of cost aggregation step with the confidence term for north-east table. (a) Both data and uncertainty costs are lower than the other cost. (b) Uncertainty costs are compared when data costs are same. (c) Both data cost and uncertainty cost of horizontal and vertical pixels are summed and lower cost is propagated to the child pixel.

confidence measure is defined as the difference between the global minimum energy of the full graph and the sum of local minimum energies of the subgraphs. This uncertainty measure can be defined on each pixel $\mathbf{p}$ in the CAT structure:

$$\gamma_\mathbf{p} = \min_{d_\mathbf{p} \in \mathcal{D}} \sum_{t \in \mathcal{T}} \omega^t E^t(d_\mathbf{p}) - \sum_{t \in \mathcal{T}} \min_{d_\mathbf{p} \in \mathcal{D}} \omega^t E^t(d_\mathbf{p}), \qquad (11)$$

where $\gamma_\mathbf{p}$ is a uncertainty measure on pixel $\mathbf{p}$. After all costs in the image are aggregated in the direction of each table $\mathcal{T}$, the confidence of each pixel is computed.

5.2   Cost Aggregation with Confidence Term

The proposed algorithm is based on 2D cost aggregation algorithm on CAT. Because the algorithm is based on message passing, the confidence of the pixel can be propagated with the messages.

The previous CAT algorithm computes messages by finding the minimum cost between horizontal and vertical adjacent pixels. Only the smallest cost in the horizontal and vertical pixels is propagated to the direction of the subgraph. By adding a confidence term to the energy formulation, the costs of pixels for which confidence is high can be chosen while aggregating costs. When one horizontal and one vertical pixel have high confidence, the cost the pixel for which confidence is higher should be aggregated. We propose a new message that identify the pixel for which confidence is highest.

We define a new message from parent pixels to pixel **p** by adding a confidence term to (8):

$$m_{\mathbf{p}}^t(d_{\mathbf{p}}) = \phi_{\mathbf{p}}(d_{\mathbf{p}}) + \gamma_{\mathbf{q}} + \min_{\mathbf{q} \in \mathcal{P}_{\mathbf{p}}^t} \left[\min_{d_{\mathbf{q}}} \left[m_{\mathbf{q}}^t(d_{\mathbf{q}}) + \psi_{(\mathbf{p},\mathbf{q})}(d_{\mathbf{p}}, d_{\mathbf{q}}) \right] \right]. \qquad (12)$$

During each aggregation step, the minimum costs with respect to disparities on each parent pixel are computed, then the data term, the minimum cost of the parent pixels, and the confidence measure $\gamma_{\mathbf{p}}$ are added (Fig. 1). During the next aggregation step, two aggregated costs with the uncertainty measures are compared to each other, then the smaller of these costs is selected for message passing. If a pixel has a low confidence measure, it does not propagate its information to the child pixel because this information is likely to be wrong. The belief and optimum disparity are determined in the same was as in the standard CAT algorithm.

6   Experimental Results

In this section, we present qualitative and quantitative experimental evaluation of confidence measure and stereo accuracy. We used the KITTI dataset [17] for quantitative and qualitative evaluation, and the HCI dataset [18] only for qualitative evaluation because the dataset does not provide ground truth. Empirically determined parameters used; SGM – $P1$: 0.25, $P2$: 5, CAT and proposed algorithm – $P1$: 0.6, $P2$: 12. Our PC simulation environment was Intel i7-3770 processor 3.4 GHz with CPU, 8 GB memory, Microsoft Windows 8.1, Microsoft Visual studio 2013 C++, and OpenCV 3.0.

6.1   Confidence Measure Comparison

We used the KITTI dataset to evaluate the proposed confidence measure and the proposed algorithm. The KITTI dataset is widely used to evaluate disparity estimation algorithms because it provides various stereo image pairs of road scene scenarios; in this trial, the 194 training image pairs with ground truth were used to evaluate the confidence measure and proposed algorithm.

To evaluate the proposed confidence measure, sparsification curve and *area under curve* (AUC) were used [8]. The sparsification curve shows how *pixel error rate* (PER) is affected by removal of pixels that have the lowest confidence measure. Lower AUC decreases when the confidence measure detects mismatched pixels accurately.

Popular non-learning-based confidence measurements for stereo problem were tested [7]; *curvature* (CUR), *naive pear ratio* (PKRN), *maximum margin* (MMN), *naive winner margin* (WMNN), *left right difference* (LRD), and the proposed confidence measure. Cost curves used for the confidence measure were aggregated costs of CAT.

Table 1. The comparison tables of the SGM, CAT, and proposed algorithm on non-occlusion areas and all areas.

		Non-occlusion areas (%)			All areas (%)			
Window	Metrics	SGM	CAT	Proposed	Metrics	SGM	CAT	Proposed
3×3	PER-2px	16.03	13.75	**11.42**	PER-2px	17.87	15.41	**12.94**
	PER-3px	11.35	9.85	**7.93**	PER-3px	13.25	11.52	**9.41**
	PER-4px	8.82	7.69	**6.08**	PER-4px	10.75	9.36	**7.51**
	PER-5px	7.23	6.29	**4.91**	PER-5px	9.17	7.94	**6.30**
	APE (px)	2.07	1.81	**1.56**	APE (px)	2.95	2.45	**2.07**
5×5	PER-2px	11.58	10.06	**8.91**	PER-2px	13.44	11.67	**10.32**
	PER-3px	7.94	7.04	**6.10**	PER-3px	9.82	8.61	**7.42**
	PER-4px	6.05	5.43	**4.67**	PER-4px	7.93	6.97	**5.91**
	PER-5px	4.88	4.42	**3.78**	PER-5px	6.75	5.93	**4.96**
	APE (px)	1.60	1.46	**1.33**	APE (px)	2.43	2.05	**1.78**
7×7	PER-2px	9.99	8.76	**7.96**	PER-2px	11.81	10.28	**9.27**
	PER-3px	6.77	6.03	**5.43**	PER-3px	8.60	7.50	**6.63**
	PER-4px	5.14	4.64	**4.16**	PER-4px	6.94	6.06	**5.27**
	PER-5px	4.14	3.78	**3.39**	PER-5px	5.91	5.16	**4.42**
	APE (px)	1.45	1.34	**1.26**	APE (px)	2.24	1.89	**1.66**
9×9	PER-2px	9.27	8.17	**7.57**	PER-2px	11.05	9.64	**8.22**
	PER-3px	6.25	5.59	**5.14**	PER-3px	8.01	6.98	**6.27**
	PER-4px	4.75	4.31	**3.96**	PER-4px	6.48	5.65	**4.99**
	PER-5px	3.82	3.53	**3.25**	PER-5px	5.52	4.81	**4.20**
	APE (px)	1.39	1.29	**1.24**	APE (px)	2.14	1.81	**1.61**

In most of the sparsification curves of confidence measurements, the proposed confidence measure showed the lowest curve shape among tested confidence measures. AUC curve of all KITTI training images were depicted in the ascending order according to AUC of the proposed confidence measure (Fig. 2). LRD and other confidence measures occasionally achieved lower AUC than the proposed confidence measure, but the proposed confidence measure achieved the lowest AUC in most images.

6.2 Quantitative Evaluation on KITTI Dataset

Three cost aggregation algorithms (SGM, CAT, and the proposed algorithm) were compared to each other using KITTI dataset. Based on KITTI stereo evaluation metrics, PER with threshold 2px, 3px, 4px, and 5px and *average pixel error* (APE) were used for disparity accuracy measurement. All PERs and APEs

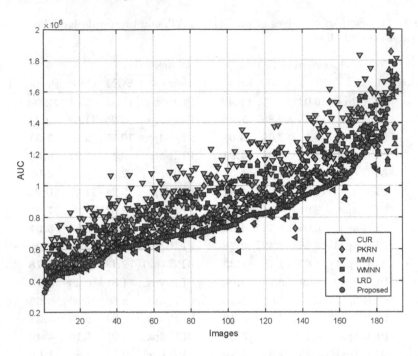

Fig. 2. AUC curve of CUR, PKRN, MMN, WMNN, LRD, and the proposed confidence measure using 194 KITTI training images.

were determined by averaging error results of 194 disparity maps. To determine the effect of window size of census transform, algorithms were operated with 3×3, 5×5, 7×7, and 9×9 window sizes. No disparity refinement technique was used to evaluate the effect of confidence term.

Regardless of window size of census transform, every metric showed that the proposed algorithm was the best among the three algorithms (Table 1). The amount of the error rate reduction on all areas is higher than that on non-occlusion areas; it means that proposed method works effectively in occlusion areas. Disparity maps of CAT and the proposed algorithm showed that some high uncertainty areas on disparity map of CAT were corrected on disparity map of the proposed algorithm (Fig. 3).

6.3 Qualitative Evaluation on HCI Dataset

We used the HCI dataset to show the effect of the confidence term in very challenging stereo scenarios. The HCI dataset provides 11 different kinds of harsh environment scenarios. Because this dataset does not provide ground truth, it was only used to show that proposed algorithm gives stable disparity results

Fig. 3. Three examples of uncertainty maps, and disparity maps of the CAT and CAT with confidence term using KITTI dataset. Top left: left image. Top right: uncertainty map; red: high uncertainty; blue: low uncertainty. Bottom left: disparity maps computed by CAT; red: close to camera; blue: far from camera. Bottom right: disparity maps computed by CAT with confidence term (Color figure online).

even in some harsh environments. Especially, pixel matching in images of night and snow, rain blur, reflecting cars, and sunflare scenarios can be ambiguous and cause false stereo matching results. Disparity maps of CAT and the proposed algorithm were obtained with its confidence measures (Fig. 4). The uncertainty map shows high values in areas in which a harsh environment affects the camera. The proposed algorithm can estimate disparity relatively stable in areas that CAT estimates wrongly.

Fig. 4. Examples of uncertainty map (second column, red: high uncertainty, blue: low uncertainty), disparity map of the CAT (third column, red: close to camera, blue: far from camera), and disparity map of CAT with confidence term (fourth column) using night and snow (first row), rain blur (second row), sunflare (third row), and wet autobahn (fourth row) scenario image pairs of HCI dataset (Color figure online).

7   Conclusions

We proposed a non-learning-based confidence measure that uses the tree agreement property. The proposed confidence measure is based on the fact that convex sum of each subgraph energy must be the same as the energy of full graph if pixel is well matched. To use the new confidence measure, we proposed a new CAT-based cost aggregation method with the confidence term. It could select the cost among horizontal and vertical pixels that has low uncertainty values.

We evaluated the proposed confidence measure and cost aggregation method on the KITTI and HCI datasets. The proposed confidence measure showed lower AUC than all other non-learning-based confidence measures. The proposed cost aggregation with the confidence term achieved more accurate disparity results than did methods that do not use this term. Even on very challenging scenarios provided by the HCI dataset, the proposed combination of confidence measure and cost aggregation method showed reliable disparity results.

Acknowledgments. This work was supported by the Human Resource Training Program for Regional Innovation and Creativity through the Ministry of Education and National Research Foundation of Korea (NRF-2014H1C1A1066380).

References

1. Li, S.Z.: Markov Random Field Modeling in Image Analysis. Springer Science and Business Media, London (2009)
2. Egnal, G., Wildes, R.P.: Detecting binocular half-occlusions: empirical comparisons of five approaches. IEEE Trans. Pattern Anal. Mach. Intell. **24**, 1127–1133 (2002)
3. Manduchi, R., Tomasi, C.: Distinctiveness maps for image matching. In: ICIAP, p. 26. IEEE (1999)
4. Egnal, G., Mintz, M., Wildes, R.P.: A stereo confidence metric using single view imagery with comparison to five alternative approaches. Image Vis. Comput. **22**, 943–957 (2004)
5. Scharstein, D., Szeliski, R.: A taxonomy and evaluation of dense two-frame stereo correspondence algorithms. Int. J. Comput. Vis. **47**, 7–42 (2002)
6. Jeong, H.: Architectures for Computer Vision: From Algorithm to Chip with Verilog. Wiley, USA (2014)
7. Hu, X., Mordohai, P.: A quantitative evaluation of confidence measures for stereo vision. IEEE Trans. Pattern Anal. Mach. Intell. **34**, 2121–2133 (2012)
8. Haeusler, R., Klette, R.: Analysis of KITTI data for stereo analysis with stereo confidence measures. In: Fusiello, A., Murino, V., Cucchiara, R. (eds.) ECCV 2012 Ws/Demos, Part II. LNCS, vol. 7584, pp. 158–167. Springer, Heidelberg (2012)
9. Fua, P.: A parallel stereo algorithm that produces dense depth maps and preserves image features. Mach. Vis. Appl. **6**, 35–49 (1993)
10. Haeusler, R., Nair, R., Kondermann, D.: Ensemble learning for confidence measures in stereo vision. In: IEEE Conference on Computer Vision and Pattern Recognition (CVPR), pp. 305–312. IEEE (2013)
11. Park, M.G., Yoon, K.J.: Leveraging stereo matching with learning-based confidence measures. In: Proceedings of the IEEE Conference on Computer Vision and Pattern Recognition, pp. 101–109 (2015)
12. Drory, A., Haubold, C., Avidan, S., Hamprecht, F.A.: Semi-global matching: a principled derivation in terms of message passing. In: Jiang, X., Hornegger, J., Koch, R. (eds.) GCPR 2014. LNCS, vol. 8753, pp. 43–53. Springer, Heidelberg (2014)
13. Hirschmüller, H.: Stereo processing by semiglobal matching and mutual information. IEEE Trans. Pattern Anal. Mach. Intell. **30**, 328–341 (2008)
14. Ha, J.M., Jeon, J.Y., Bae, G.Y., Jo, S.Y., Jeong, H.: Cost aggregation table: cost aggregation method using summed area table scheme for dense stereo correspondence. In: Bebis, G., et al. (eds.) ISVC 2014, Part I. LNCS, vol. 8887, pp. 815–826. Springer, Heidelberg (2014)
15. Ha, J., Jeon, B., Jun, W., Lee, J., Jeong, H.: An improved 2D cost aggregation method for advanced driver assistance systems. In: 2015 IEEE Intelligent Vehicles Symposium (IV), pp. 89–94. IEEE (2015)
16. Ha, J., Jeon, B., Jeon, J., Jo, S.Y., Jeong, H.: Cost aggregation table: a theoretic derivation on the markov random field and its relation to message passing. In: 22th IEEE International Conference on Image Processing (ICIP). IEEE (2015)

17. Geiger, A., Lenz, P., Urtasun, R.: Are we ready for autonomous driving? the KITTI vision benchmark suite. In: IEEE Conference on Computer Vision and Pattern Recognition (CVPR), pp. 3354–3361. IEEE (2012)
18. Meister, S., Jähne, B., Kondermann, D.: Outdoor stereo camera system for the generation of real-world benchmark data sets. Opt. Eng. **51**, 021107-1 (2012)
19. Kostková, J., Sára, R.: Stratified dense matching for stereopsis in complex scenes. In: BMVC, vol. 5, p. 6. Citeseer (2003)
20. Kong, D., Tao, H.: A method for learning matching errors for stereo computation. In: BMVC, vol. 1, p. 2 (2004)
21. Min, D., Sohn, K.: An asymmetric post-processing for correspondence problem. Sig. Process. Image Commun. **25**, 130–142 (2010)
22. Garcia, F., Mirbach, B., Ottersten, B., Grandidier, F., Cuesta, A.: Pixel weighted average strategy for depth sensor data fusion. In: 17th IEEE International Conference on Image Processing (ICIP), pp. 2805–2808. IEEE (2010)
23. Pfeiffer, D., Gehrig, S., Schneider, N.: Exploiting the power of stereo confidences. In: IEEE Conference on Computer Vision and Pattern Recognition (CVPR), pp. 297–304. IEEE (2013)
24. Lew, M.S., Huang, T.S., Wong, K.: Learning and feature selection in stereo matching. IEEE Trans. Pattern Anal. Mach. Intell. **16**, 869–881 (1994)
25. Cruz, J., Pajares, G., Aranda, J., Vindel, J.: Stereo matching technique based on the perceptron criterion function. Pattern Recogn. Lett. **16**, 933–944 (1995)
26. Šára, R.: Finding the largest unambiguous component of stereo matching. In: Heyden, A., Sparr, G., Nielsen, M., Johansen, P. (eds.) ECCV 2002, Part III. LNCS, vol. 2352, pp. 900–914. Springer, Heidelberg (2002)
27. Sabater, N., Almansa, A., Morel, J.M.: Meaningful matches in stereovision. IEEE Trans. Pattern Anal. Mach. Intell. **34**, 930–942 (2012)
28. Reynolds, M., Dobos, J., Peel, L., Weyrich, T., Brostow, G.J.: Capturing time-of-flight data with confidence. In: IEEE Conference on Computer Vision and Pattern Recognition (CVPR), pp. 945–952. IEEE (2011)
29. Spyropoulos, A., Komodakis, N., Mordohai, P.: Learning to detect ground control points for improving the accuracy of stereo matching. In: IEEE Conference on Computer Vision and Pattern Recognition (CVPR), pp. 1621–1628. IEEE (2014)
30. Gherardi, R.: Confidence-based cost modulation for stereo matching. In: 19th International Conference on Pattern Recognition, ICPR 2008, pp. 1–4. IEEE (2008)
31. Kindermann, R., Snell, J.L., et al.: Markov Random Fields and Their Applications. American Mathematical Society, vol. 1. Providence, RI (1980)
32. Kindermann, R., Snell, J.L., et al.: Markov Random Fields and Their Applications. American Mathematical Society Providence, vol. 1. RI (1980)
33. Kolmogorov, V.: Convergent tree-reweighted message passing for energy minimization. IEEE Trans. Pattern Anal. Mach. Intell. **28**, 1568–1583 (2006)
34. Zabih, R., Woodfill, J.: Non-parametric local transforms for computing visual correspondence. In: Eklundh, J.O. (ed.) Computer Vision ECCV 1994, pp. 151–158. Springer, Heidelberg (1994)

Semantics-Preserving Warping for Stereoscopic Image Retargeting

Chun-Hau Tan[1], Md Baharul Islam[1], Lai-Kuan Wong[1][(✉)], and Kok-Lim Low[2]

[1] Faculty of Computing and Informatics, Multimedia University,
Persiaran Multimedia, 63100 Cyberjaya, Selangor, Malaysia
tanchunhau@hotmail.com, bahar_mag@yahoo.com, lkwong@mmu.edu.my
[2] School of Computing, National University of Singapore, Computing 1,
13 Computing Drive, Singapore 117417, Singapore
lowkl@comp.nus.edu.sg

Abstract. Due to availability and popularity of stereoscopic displays in the recent years, research into stereo image retargeting is receiving considerable attention. In this paper, we extend the tearable image warping method for stereo image retargeting. Our method retargets both the left and right image of the stereo image pair simultaneously to preserve scene consistency, and minimize distortion using a global optimization algorithm. It is also able to preserve stereoscopic properties of the resulting stereo image. Experimental results show that our approach can preserve the global image context better than stereoscopic cropping, preserve structural details better than stereoscopic seam carving, and protect objects better than stereoscopic traditional warping. Besides, compared to scene warping, our approach can guarantee semantic connectedness.

Keywords: Stereo image retargeting · Stereo image warping · Scene consistency · Tearable image warping

1 Introduction

With the recent availability of stereoscopic displays such as 3D monitor, 3D television and stereo camera phone, there is an increasing need for stereo image retargeting techniques. Stereo image retargeting aims to resize a stereo image pair to fit various stereoscopic displays of different aspect ratios and sizes. An ideal stereo image retargeting method should be able to (1) ensure scene consistency, (2) preserve geometric/structural details, and (3) preserve stereoscopic properties between the left and right image. More specifically, scene consistency properties [1,2] include zero object distortion, correct scene occlusion and correct semantic connectedness (consistent physical contacts between objects with their environment in the retargeted image).

Retargeting using simple operators such as scaling and cropping [3] do not guarantee protection of important objects, leading to distortion of objects or loss of important content. Therefore, content-aware stereo retargeting approaches,

© Springer International Publishing Switzerland 2016
T. Bräunl et al. (Eds.): PSIVT 2015, LNCS 9431, pp. 257–268, 2016.
DOI: 10.1007/978-3-319-29451-3_21

which can be categorized into discrete, continuous and hybrid approaches, are gaining more research attention. Discrete approaches [4,5] can produce impressive results for stereo images with simple background but due to its discontinuous nature, object distortion and artifacts are unavoidable for images with complex background. Continuous approaches [6,7] utilize warping to retarget stereoscopic images. Due to their continuous nature, these approaches can preserve semantic connectedness well but distortion to objects and structural details are unavoidable in extreme retargeting cases. Lee et al. [8] propose a hybrid retargeting approach that segments out the objects into object layers, performs warping on the background layer and paste the objects back to the warped background to produce the retargeted image. This approach ensures objects protection and better preserves structural details but does not guarantee semantic connectedness between a segmented object and its background.

To better preserve scene consistency while minimizing artifacts and preserving stereoscopic properties, we propose a novel stereo image retargeting technique based on the tearable image warping technique [2]. Conceptually, in tearable image warping, an object boundary is divided into tearable and non-tearable segments. Tearable segments correspond to where depth discontinuity occurs, and these segments are allowed to break away from its environment, thus allowing the background warping to be distributed more evenly, leading to reduced distortion of structural details. Non-tearable segments correspond to the object boundary that has actual physical contacts with the environment or other objects. These segments help to preserve semantic connectedness by constraining the object to maintain the real contacts in the 3D world. This approach is able to preserve semantic connectedness very well. However, it is designed for single image and thus, unable to preserve the stereoscopic properties of a retargeted stereo image.

The main contribution of this work is to extend the tearable image warping method [2] for stereo image retargeting. The proposed method retargets both the left and right image of the stereo image pair simultaneously to preserve scene consistency, and minimize distortion, through a revised-optimization algorithm. In addition, it successfully maintains consistent stereoscopic properties of the resulting stereo image pair to avoid visual discomfort during viewing. Besides being able to maintain stereoscopic consistency and guarantees semantic connectedness, experimental results show that our approach can preserve structural details better than stereoscopic seam carving, preserve the global image context better than stereo cropping and protect objects better than traditional stereoscopic warping.

2   Related Works

State-of-the-art content-aware, stereo image retargeting can be categorized into discrete, continuous and hybrid approaches. Discrete methods include scene carving [1] and patch-based [5] approaches. As with its 2D counterpart, the geometrically consistent seam carving [4] approach for stereo image retargeting produces good results for non-complex images but fails in complex images and extreme retargeting cases. The shift-map [5] based approach characterizes geometric rearrangement of a stereo image pair. It can preserve the foreground objects well but does not consider the preservation of semantics features like ripples, shadow, symmetry, texture, etc.

Continuous approaches generally utilize warping to retarget a stereo image pair. Niu et al. [7] extend traditional image warping to stereo images with the objective to preserve prominent objects and 3D structure. Chang et al. [6] warping-based approach aims to avoid diplopia (double vision) by optimizing two stereoscopic constraints; vertical alignment for avoiding vertical artifact and horizontal disparity consistency. However, these warping-based approaches cannot avoid object distortion in cases of extreme image retargeting. In addition, the stereoscopic quality of the retargeted images could be reduced because the whole image is warped in a continuous manner, thus disallowing proper occlusions and depth discontinuity to be created.

To address the limitations of the above warping based approaches, Lee et al. [8] proposes scene warping, a hybrid approach that decomposes the input stereo image into several layers according to the depth order and each layer is warped according to its own mesh deformation. The warped layers were then composited together according to depth order to get the retargeted image. This method produces better stereoscopic quality and ensures object protection, but it cannot guarantee the preservation of the semantic connectedness between a foreground object and its background environment, such as shadow and ripples.

3 Our Approach

Our approach extends the tearable warp algorithm [2] for single image retargeting to the stereoscopic domain. The challenge lies in maintaining the stereoscopic properties of the retargeted stereo image pair and ensuring that the object extraction process for both the left and right image is trivial and coherent. Figure 1 illustrates an overview of our approach. Similar to scene warping approach [8], in our tearable warp based approach, an input stereo image pair is first separated into the background and object layers. Then, the background layers are warped and the objects are pasted back onto the background layers to produce the retargeted results. The core difference in our approach is that for each object, an object handle that represents the connection between the object and its background is defined. During the warping process, we constrain the object handles to be kept as rigid as possible and we ensure that the object is pasted onto the warped background to coincide with the object handle. This technique guarantees the preservation of semantic connectedness.

In the following sub-sections, we provide a detail description of our algorithm in three main steps; (1) pre-processing, (2) warping, and (3) image compositing.

3.1 Pre-processing

In the pre-processing phase, given a stereo image pair, we first compute the disparity map using sum of absolute difference (SAD). The disparity values should

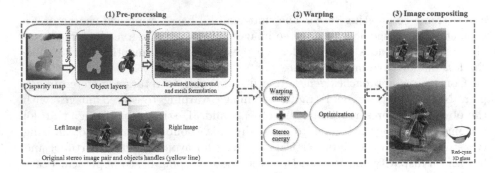

Fig. 1. Overview of our stereo image retargeting approach

be preserved in the retargeted image pair for ensuring comfortable 3D viewing experience. Next, we provide a simple, semi-automatic interface, powered by Grabcut [9] to allow users to select objects on the left image and define their respective handles with just a few clicks. The corresponding object segments and object handles in the right image are then automatically inferred from the left image based on disparity map. Exemplar based inpainting [10] is then used to fill up holes in the background layers. The disparity map for a given stereo image pair, the object segment, and the inpainted background layer for the left image are illustrated in the pre-proessing box of Fig. 1. We can observe that although the inpainting result is imperfect, the artifacts are not shown in the retargeted results illustrated in Fig. 1.

3.2 Warping

Next, we perform triangle-based warping on the inpainted background layer pair to retarget it to the desired target size. Let L denote the left image and R denote the right image. Given the source left and right triangle meshes, M_L and M_R and the respective object handles, the warping process is the problem of mapping M_L and M_R to their target meshes, M'_L and M'_R. During the warping process, we aim to preserve the stereoscopic properties and keep the object handles as rigid as possible. The warping energy attempts to minimize a set of errors that consists of the scale transformation error, the smoothness error and the stereoscopic quality error, subject to a set of constraints. Figure 2 shows the warped background layers where objects handles kept as rigid as possible.

Scale Transformation Error. Let T be the set of all triangles in the input meshes, $M_L \cup M_R$. For each triangle $t \varepsilon T$, we constrain the transformation to non-uniform scaling [2,11], denoted by,

$$G_t = \begin{pmatrix} S_t^x & 0 \\ 0 & S_t^y \end{pmatrix} \tag{1}$$

Fig. 2. Triangular mesh of the (*left*) inpainted background layer and (*right*) the warped background layer (width reduced by 20 %). The shape of the object handle (represented by the yellow lines) in the warped image is preserved rigidly (Color figure online).

where S_t^x and S_t^y are the scale of triangle t in the x and y dimensions respectively. The scale transformation error, E_w is then defined as,

$$E_w = \sum_{t \varepsilon T} A_t \|J_t - G_t\|_F^2 \tag{2}$$

where A_t is the area of triangle t, $\|.\|_F^2$ is the Frobenius norm, and J_t is a 2×2 Jacobian matrix that represents the linear portion of the affine mapping that maps a triangle to its corresponding triangle in $M_L' \cup M_R'$.

Smoothness Error. The smoothness error tries to avoid discontinuity by minimizing the scale difference between neighboring triangles,

$$E_s = \sum_{s,t \varepsilon T} A_{st} \|G_t - G_s\|_F^2 \tag{3}$$

where $A_{st} = (A_s + A_t)/2$ and s, t are adjacent triangles.

Stereoscopic Quality Error. To ensure the stereoscopic properties are preserved, we minimize the change in two stereoscopic properties [8]; (1) disparity between input and output stereo mesh pair, and (2) vertical drift between left and right output meshes. Let (p_i^L, p_i^R) and (q_i^L, q_i^R) denote the sets of corresponding points in the disparity map of the input and output images respectively where p_i^L and p_i^R are the corresponding points of the input meshes, $M_L \cup M_R$ and q_i^L and q_i^R are the corresponding points of the output meshes, $M_L' \cup M_R'$. The stereoscopic quality error is then defined as

$$E_t = \sum_{(q_i^L, q_i^R) \varepsilon M_L' \bigcup M_R'} E_d(q_i^L, q_i^R) + E_v(q_i^L, q_i^R) \tag{4}$$

Fig. 3. Analysis of disparity preservation. (*left*) Original stereo image, (*middle*) retargeted results of single image tearable warping, without consideration for stereoscopic properties preservation, and (*right*) results of our approach that minimizes stereoscopic properties error. Yellow boxes and black dots highlight the comparison of disparity preservation. Green boxes highlight more violation in disparity preservation (Color figure online).

where E_d indicates the disparity consistency, and E_v ensures zero vertical drift.

$$E_d(q_i^L, q_i^R) = \left((q_i^R(x) - q_i^L(x)) - (p_i^R(x) - p_i^L(x)) \right)^2 \tag{5}$$

$$E_v(q_i^L, q_i^R) = (q_i^R(y) - q_i^L(y))^2 \tag{6}$$

where (x) and (y) refers the x and y coordinate of the particular point.

Total Warping Error. The total warping energy function E can be formulated as the weighted sum of the scale transformation error, the smoothness error and the stereoscopic quality error,

$$E = \alpha E_w + \beta E_s + \gamma E_t \tag{7}$$

where α, β, and γ are the corresponding weights.

Constraints. To preserve semantics connectedness, we define the handle shape constraint [2] to rigidly preserve the shape and orientation of the object handles. In addition, the image boundary and object boundary constraints were added to ensure that the original image boundary remains on the boundary and user-defined objects do not move out of the image boundary.

3.3   Image Compositing

At this stage, all objects in both images will be scaled to its respective scale factor S_k and inserted to coincide with its corresponding object handle in the warped background image. The sequence of the insertion of an object to the background image follows the depth order acquired from depth map.

3.4   Optimization Details

We use the CVX Matlab toolbox [12] to find the solution to the convex quadratic function defined in Eq. (7). Weights for the total energy; α, β and γ are set to 1,

Fig. 4. Comparison of our results with stereo cropping [8]. Reducing width by 30 %: (*left*) input left stereo image, (*middle*) stereo cropping [8], and (*right*) our method. Yellow box highlights the important object that is being cropped off (Color figure online).

0.5 and 0.1 respectively. This set of weights is obtained from our experiments. Notably, the γ value is set to a much lower value, 0.1 compared to α and β, in order to avoid smoothness being penalized. Our experiments show that a higher weight for γ will reduce smoothness and cause obvious discontinuity and severe compression in certain part of the retargeted image. The handle shape and image boundary constraints are set as hard constraints while the object boundary is set as inequality constraint. The scale factor, S_k for each object is set to 1.

4   Results and Discussion

The images used to test our approach are collected from Flickr [13], and Yury Golubinskys stereo blog [14]. The results were generated on a desktop with Intel i7 CPU 3.40 GHz and 12 GB memory. The computation time depends on the number of triangles in the triangular meshes used to represent the the stereo image pair. Excluding the time taken for inpainting, which is performed at the pre-processing stage, our algorithm produces retargeted results in about 3.5 to 6 s. For example, it takes 5.5 s to produce the result for a 720 × 480 stereo image that is represented by 1552 triangles.

To illustrate the effectiveness of our approach in preserving the stereoscopic properties, we compare our approach against the naive adoption of single image tearable image warping to the stereoscopic domain. From Fig. 3, it is obvious that the tearable image warping approach designed for single image [2] fails to preserve the disparity consistency. On the contrary, our algorithm successfully minimize the variance of disparity between the original and retargeted stereo images to preserve the stereoscopic properties. Therefore, our results do not cause any visual discomfort to the user during 3D viewing of the retargeted stereo image.

Next, we perform comparison with state-of-the-art stereo retargeting aprroaches. We compare our results with stereo cropping [3], stereo seam carving [4], stereo traditional warping based on non-homogenous scaling [11], and scene

Fig. 5. Extreme Retargeting Results - reducing width by 40 %: (*column 1*) input left stereo image with object handle in yellow, (*column 2*) stereo seam carving [4], (*column 3*) stereo traditional warping [11], and (*column 4*) our approach. Yellow boxes highlight object distortion (Color figure online).

warping [8], where each selected approach corresponds to a category of retargeting approaches; simple operator, discrete, continuous and hybrid approaches respectively. Compared to stereo cropping [3], our approach can better preserve the global image context and reduce loss of important content, as shown in Fig. 4.

Figures 5 and 7 compared our approach with stereo seam carving [4] and stereo traditional warping [11] for cases of extreme retargeting, where width or height is reduced by 40 %. Severe object distortion/compression can be observed for most results of seam carving and traditional warping. On the other hand, our approach achieves zero object distortion as the important objects are not warped during the optimization process. Due to its discrete nature, seam carving

Fig. 6. Our method can better preserve the geometric structure of the arch shape of the pillars. (*left*) Left image of our result and (*right*) left image of result of stereo warping [11].

Fig. 7. Extreme Retargeting Results - reducing height by 40%: (*row 1, column 1,3*) input left stereo image with object handle in yellow, (*row 1, column 2,4*) original stereo image, (*row 2*) stereo seam carving [4], (*row 3*) stereo traditional warping [11], and (*row 4*) our approach. Yellow boxes highlight object distortion (Color figure online).

approach also fails to prevent distortion to geometric structures. Compared to traditional warping [11], as illustrated in Fig. 6, our approach can better preserve geometric structures because in our tearable warping based approach, only object handles needs to be preserved rigidly. Therefore, the compression that occurs during warping can be distributed more evenly to other parts of the image. On the other hand, in the traditional warping approach, the whole area that contains the object needs to be preserved, leaving less space for compression during warping.

Lastly, we compare our results with scene warping [8]. Due to adopting the similar layer-based approach, both scene warping and our approach can avoid object distortion and preserve structural details better than traditional warping and seam carving. In addition, as illustrated in Fig. 8, both of these approaches can allow overlapping based on depth order and thus, can support extreme image retargeting. However, our approach should preserve semantic connectedness better than scene warping. Our optimization algorithm constrains the object handle to be as rigid as possible and thus it can guarantee the preservation of the semantic relationship between an object and its background, as shown in the

Fig. 8. Comparison of results with scene warping - reducing width by 40 %: (*left*) input left stereo image, (*middle*) scene warping [8], and (*right*) our approach.

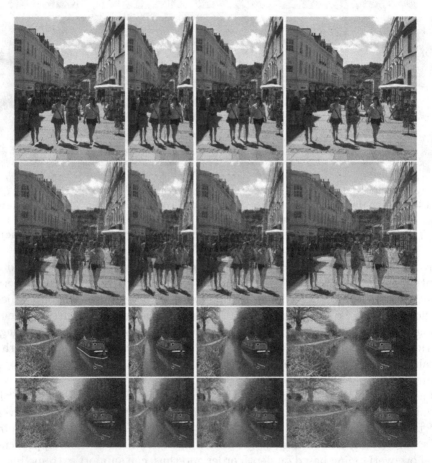

Fig. 9. More results - (*column 1, row 1,3*) Input left stereo image with object handle marked in yellow, (*column 1, row 2, 4*) original stereo image, (*column 2*) reducing width by 40 %, (*column 3*) reducing width by 20 %, and (*column 4*) increasing width by 20 % (Color figure online).

perfect shadow connection in our retargeted results in Fig. 9. We could not show the result of scene warping for comparison on preservation of semantic connectedness due to unavailability of their source code. But, based on theoretical analysis, the shadow may not be well-preserved by scene warping as there is no energy or constraint that guarantees the preservation of semantic connectedness.

Analysis of our results show that our approach is quite robust to background distortion due to the more even distribution of compression throughout the retargeted stereo image. However, in cases of images with very complex geometrical structures, background distortion is still unavoidable. In such cases, additional constraint is needed to preserve the geometrical details. Another potential problem with our approach is the possibility of incorrect propagation of object segments and their respective handles from the left image to the right image of the stereo image pair, due to inaccurate disparity information. To our pleasant surprise, from our experiments, this problem seldom crop up. Finally, our approach requires inpainting, which is still an open problem in computer vision. Although inpainting artifacts are inevitable, in most of our retargeting results, the artifacts are being covered up when objects are pasted onto the warped background during the image compositing stage. For cases where inpainting artificacts are visible, we can allow users to interactively touch up the artifacts.

5   Conclusion

This paper has successfully extended the tearable image warping method [2] to perform stereoscopic image retargeting. This proposed method retargets both the left and right image of the stereo image pair simultaneously using a revised, global optimization algorithm. Experiments show that our approach is able to preserve the stereoscopic properties in the retargeted images and compares favourably with existing methods. Since the warping process does not involve the foreground objects, our method ensures object protection and produces less severe compression compared to stereo seam carving and stereo traditional warping methods, particularly in extreme retargeting cases. The core strength of our method is in its ability to guarantee the preservation of semantic connectedness between an object and its background without distorting the objects, while preserving the stereoscopic properties of the stereo image.

Acknowledgement. This work is supported by FRGS Research Grant No. EP20130326018 and MMU Internal Grant No. IP20131108001.

References

1. Mansfield, A., Gehler, P., Van-Gool, L., Rother, C.: Scene carving: scene consistent image retargeting. In: Daniilidis, K., Maragos, P., Paragios, N. (eds.) ECCV 2010, Part I. LNCS, vol. 6311, pp. 143–156. Springer, Heidelberg (2010)
2. Wong, L.K., Low, K.L.: Tearable image warping for extreme image retargeting. In: Computer Graphics International Conference, pp. 1–8, Bournemouth, UK (2012)

3. Niu, Y., Liu, F., Feng, W.C., Jin, H.: Aesthetics-based stereoscopic photo cropping for heterogeneous displays. IEEE Trans. Multimedia **14**(3), 783–796 (2012)
4. Basha, T., Moses, Y., Avidan, S.: Geometrically consistent stereo seam carving. In: ICCV Conference, pp. 1816–1823, Barcelona, Spain (2011)
5. Qi, S., Ho, J.: Shift-map based stereo image retargeting. In: ACCV Conference, pp. 457–469, Daejeon, Korea (2012)
6. Chang, C.H., Liang, C.K., Chuang, Y.Y.: Content-aware display adaptation and interactive editing for stereoscopic images. IEEE Trans. Multimedia **13**(4), 589–601 (2011)
7. Niu, Y., Feng, W.C., Liu, F.: Enabling warping on stereoscopic images. ACM Trans. Graph. 31(6), Article No. 183 (2012)
8. Lee, K.Y., Chung, C.D., Chuang, Y.Y.: Scene warping: layer-based stereoscopic image resizing. In: CVPR Conference, pp. 49–56, Rhode Island, USA (2012)
9. Rother, C., Kolmogorov, V., Blake, A.: GrabCut - interactive foreground extraction using iterated graph cuts. ACM Trans. Graph. **23**(3), 309–314 (2004)
10. Criminisi, A., Prez, P., Toyama, K.: Region filling and object removal by exemplar-based image inpainting. IEEE Trans. Image Process. **13**(9), 1200–1212 (2004)
11. Jin, Y., Liu, L., Wu, Q.: Nonhomogeneous scaling optimization for real time image resizing. Vis. Comput. **26**(6), 769–778 (2010)
12. CVX: Matlab software for disciplined convex programming. http://cvxr.com/cvx/
13. Flickr. http://www.flickr.com/
14. Yury Golubinsky's blog. http://www.urixblog.com/en/about-en/

Improved Poisson Surface Reconstruction with Various Passive Visual Cues from Multiple Camera Views

Ningqing Qian[✉], Sohaib Kiani, and Bahareh Shakibajahromi

Institut für Nachrichtentechnik, RWTH-Aachen University,
Melatener Straßer 23, 52074 Aachen, Germany
qian@ient.rwth-aachen.de

Abstract. Poisson surface reconstruction with octree is widely used as the last step to retrieve the surface data from the point cloud. When the point cloud is generated by the triangulation of point correspondence in multiple images, the noisy positions of the 3D points and the inaccurate estimation of the normal vectors will impact the quality of the reconstructed surface. In this work, the mesh optimization using multiple visual cues will be applied to improve the output of the Poisson surface reconstruction. Usually, the active cues like shading and focusing require elaborate experimental setup, whereas the passive cues like silhouette and photometric property can be more easily acquired from the raw images. The experimental results show that adaptive integration of the multiple passive visual cues will deliver the surface mesh data with high quality. Besides, the optimization algorithm is easily to parallelize, as each vertex moves independently, which makes it appealing for the real-time 3D reconstruction system.

Keywords: Poisson surface · Multi-view · 3D reconstruction · Silhouette · Photometric consistency

1 Introduction

With the development of new equipments and new methods, the issue of virtually reproduction of the surrounding 3D real world comes back to people's attention. The application areas consist of robotics, entertainment industry, archeology, vehicle industry, etc. A considerable amount of work has been devoted in these areas to achieve 3D reconstruction with high quality regardless of running time. However, in the last decade, the interest in real-time 3D reconstruction systems has increased dramatically. Current real-time reconstruction techniques are bounded either because of the capturing environment or due to the quality of reconstructed surface. This work is aimed to propose a novel efficient algorithm without compromising the quality and robustness of the reconstruction scheme.

Manual modeling is widely used in the film and game industry, where the physical accuracy of the 3D models is less interesting. However, the approach

© Springer International Publishing Switzerland 2016
T. Bräunl et al. (Eds.): PSIVT 2015, LNCS 9431, pp. 269–281, 2016.
DOI: 10.1007/978-3-319-29451-3_22

is quite tedious and time-consuming, which make it inapplicable for large scale scenes modeling. The active 3D laser scanning is an alternative to acquire highly precise 3D models. Multiple scans and even hundreds of scans from many different directions are usually required to obtain complete surface information of the modeled object [2]. However, the limited range and highly controlled illumination condition pose a major challenge for active scanning to further application. The development of time-of-flight (ToF) cameras overcomes the shortcomings of active laser scanning at the cost of low accuracy. With the advent of modern cameras and rapid development in the field of multi-view geometry, image-based modeling becomes the most promising alternative to active scanning. The multi-view 3D reconstruction can be split into two steps:

1. Camera calibration,
2. 3D modeling from calibrated images.

In this work, it is assumed that the images have been already calibrated. The first step towards 3D geometry data acquisition is dense or sparse correspondence matching among neighboring images. After correspondence matching, a 3D point cloud with normal information can be generated as described in [4]. The benefit of using sparse feature point instead of dense disparity map is the quick evaluation of the 3D point cloud, but the accuracy of the output of Poisson surface reconstruction [3] will be dramatically affected. To optimize the Poisson surface mesh, various passive visual cues are explored and applied. The rest of this work is organized as follows: in Sect. 2, we briefly review the related work. In Sect. 3, we introduce the proposed mesh optimization method based on various visual cues. In Sect. 4, we present the experimental results with real objects and evaluate the reconstruction quality with ground-truth data. Conclusions are drawn in Sect. 5.

2   Related Work

The multi-view 3D surface reconstruction can be categorized into variational and non-variational approaches. In variational category, the surface reconstruction problem is formulated as energy minimization problem. Furukawa et al. [1] proposed an accurate modeling which used local photometric consistency and global visibility constraints to extract quasi-dense rectangular patches in 3D space. An iterative deformation algorithm was applied to the generated triangle mesh and the vertices are updated with the following rule [1],

$$\partial(\mathbf{v}) = -w(\mathbf{v})(\nabla f(\mathbf{v}) \cdot \mathbf{N}(v))\mathbf{N}(\mathbf{v}) + (\nabla E_R \cdot \mathbf{N}(\mathbf{v}))\mathbf{N}(\mathbf{v}) + (-\beta_2 \triangle \mathbf{v} + \beta_3 \triangle^2 \mathbf{v}), \quad (1)$$

where the derivative is along the surface normal, $f(\mathbf{v})$ is a scalar photometric discrepancy function and $w(\mathbf{v})$ is an adaptive weight. E_R corresponds to silhouette consistency term and β_2, β_3 are constants to avoid oscillations. This approach requires in average more than 200 iterations to reach the satisfactory surface mesh data [1].

Another variational 3D surface reconstruction is based on the Poisson surface reconstruction. When the oriented point cloud is accurate, Poisson surface reconstruction will deliver very precise surface data. And the octree data structure guarantees the efficiency of execution time and memory consumption without compromising the resolution of the surface. However, this approach does not investigate the visual cues from the objects.

One most recent variational approach is total variation reconstruction [2] that inspires the algorithms proposed in this work, where the energy minimization problem is formulated as a convex form. Consequently, the solution is the globally minimum as compared to other approaches. The passive visual cues are also incorporated in this approach. However, the application of the voxel grids limits the resolution of the surface mesh.

3   Proposed Mesh Optimization Method

As discussed earlier, the focus of the work is on a robust and efficient image-based modeling technique. Mesh optimization with visual cues is applied on the Poisson surface mesh of the sparse or quasi-dense oriented point cloud which is generated by the method proposed in [4]. There is a list of challenges to optimize the Poisson-based mesh:

1. Initial Poisson surface mesh can be very noisy because of the inaccurate and incomplete oriented point cloud.
2. The topology of the triangle meshes should be preserved while the movement of the vertices.
3. Silhouette cue only can not identify the concavities on the surface.
4. Photometric cue is not applicable for homogeneous and textureless objects.
5. The whole process should be efficient regarding to the time cost.

In the following, we will address to these issues in detail.

3.1   One-Ring Neighborhood

Within the mesh topology, every vertex $\mathbf{v}_i$ is connected to multiple vertices, called the one-ring neighborhood $Nei(\mathbf{v}_i) = \{\mathbf{v}_{i1}; \mathbf{v}_{i2}; ...\}$ as illustrated in Fig. 1. The one-ring neighborhood consists of a set of faces surrounding the vertex. The normal vector of the center vertex can be estimated by averaging the enclosing face normal vectors. The movement of the vertex along the normal direction will not change the topology of the triangle meshes. The adjustment of the vertices will result in the surface mesh to extend or to contract.

3.2   Silhouette Consistency

Let M_i be binary mask of image which segments the object from the background and is known as silhouette. Furthermore, let $O \subset \mathbb{R}^3$ be the object of interest.

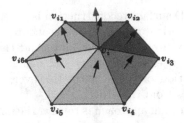

Fig. 1. One-ring neighborhood

The projection of surface $S \subset O$ to the corresponding view P_i that fulfills the silhouette consistency condition should follow the property:

$$P_i \cdot S \in M_i. \tag{2}$$

Although the Eq. 2 is not invertible, the largest possible surface defined as "visual hull" [5] still can be determined. To formalize it as energy minimization problem, the total energy will be expressed as a sum of energy contribution from each individual vertex **v**:

$$E(S) = \sum_{i=1} E_i(\mathbf{v}), \tag{3}$$

$$E_i(\mathbf{v}) = \sum_{p \in \mathbf{N}(\mathbf{v})} \{ \rho(p)_f \left[1 - u(p) \right] + \rho(p)_b u(p) \} . \tag{4}$$

where p is the discrete sample along the normal vector $\mathbf{N}(\mathbf{v})$ of vertex **v** and $\rho(p)_f$ is the silhouette foreground mapping function, which will be '1' inside the foreground and '0' outside the foreground. However, if other segmentation techniques are used, the score will be the value between 0 and 1. Oppositely, $\rho(p)_b$ is '1' inside the background and '0' outside the background as shown in Fig. 2. In Eq. 4, $u(p)$ is the indicator function, which will be '1' inside the object and '0' outside the object. Optimization algorithm used to minimize Eq. 4 is given in Algorithm 1. The basic idea is to first move all vertices lying outside

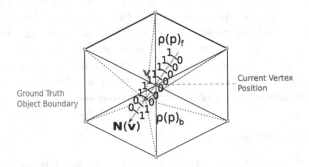

Fig. 2. Silhouette mapping functions along the normal vector $\mathbf{N}(\mathbf{v})$

the surface, not satisfying Eq. 2, inwards until the Eq. 2 stays true for every view. After that, all vertices will be on or inside the surface of the object. So in the second step, all vertices should move outwards as long as Eq. 2 keeps true. The adapted size $\triangle p$ between adjacent sample points along the normal vector is determined by the average edge length around the one-ring neighbor which in turn preserves the topology of the triangle meshes.

Algorithm 1. Silhouette based Optimization

Require: Mesh,calibrated images, silhouettes
Ensure: Silhouette consistent mesh
  1: Load triangular mesh: vertices $\{V\}$, edges $\{E\}$
  2: Load all Images $\{I\}$, all silhouettes/masks $\{M\}$, all projection matrices $\{P\}$
  3: While inward movement of vertices is NOT converged
  4:    For each vertex $\mathbf{v}$
  5:      If $\mathbf{P}_i\mathbf{v} \notin \mathbf{M}_i$ for any view
  6:        Move vertex $\mathbf{v}$ oppositely towards normal direction
  7:    Apply smoothing
  8: While outward movement of vertices is NOT converged
  9:    For each vertex $\mathbf{v}$
 10:      If $\mathbf{P}_i\mathbf{v} \in \mathbf{M}_i$ for all views
 11:        Move vertex $\mathbf{v}$ along normal direction
 12:    Apply smoothing
 13: Save optimized mesh

3.3 Photometric Consistency

Photometric consistency is a good cue to handle concavities on the surface. As before, a photometric consistency map function $\rho(p)$ along the normal vector $\mathbf{N}(\mathbf{v})$, depicted in Fig. 3 is applied to formulate the energy minimization function. The energy contribution of each vertex is given as

$$E(\mathbf{v}_i) = \sum_{p \in \mathbf{N}(\mathbf{v})} \rho(p).\nabla u(p). \tag{5}$$

where $u(p)$ is again object indicator function i.e. '1' inside the object and '0' outside the object.

The photometric consistency works with Lambertian assumption that appearance of a 3D vertex $\mathbf{v}$ is the same in different views. However, by means of realistic capturing setup such a prerequisite is not guaranteed and is also hard to realize. For that reason most image-based reconstruction methods neglect these effects and try to compensate for the color variations using more sophisticated normalized comparison criteria, like NCC[1] scheme. To estimate the photometric

---

[1] Normalized Cross Correlation.

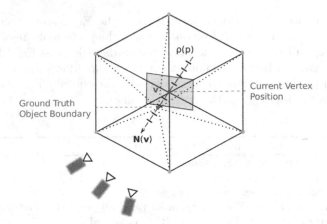

Fig. 3. The mapping function along the normal vector based on photometric consistency

consistency score of the current sample point, a reference camera P_i is determined, of which principal plane tends to perpendicular to the normal vector $\mathbf{N(v)}$. Since the nonlinear distortion in the reference view is relatively small, a square window around the projected sample point in the reference view is selected and split into two triangles T for photometric consistency evaluation. With Barycentric coordinate each discrete pixel within the square window is unprojected to the 3D point inside the square patch. Those unprojected 3D points p_s are again reprojected as p_i into the compared views P_j with sub-pixel accuracy. The NCC between the reference image I_i and a comparison image I_j can now be computed as:

$$\phi NCC^{i,j} = \frac{1}{n} \sum_{s \in T} \frac{(I_i(p_i^s) - \mu_i)(I_j(p_j^s) - \mu_j)}{\sigma_i \sigma_j}. \tag{6}$$

where

$$p_i^{0...n-1} = \mathbf{P}p_s^{0...n-1}, \quad \mu_i = \frac{1}{n} \sum_{s=0}^{n-1} I_i(p_i^s), \quad \sigma_i = \sqrt{\frac{1}{n} \sum_s (I_i(p_i^s) - \mu_i)^2}. \tag{7}$$

The classical photometric consistency estimation generally yields noisy measurement due to homogeneity or repeatability of the texture pattern, which could result in noisy reconstruction. For that reason, more elaborate voting scheme is applied to increase the accuracy of the photometric consistency computation [2]. The idea is to evaluate the contribution of each camera as shown in Eq. 8. The vote is accepted only if the optimum is reached at current sample point. This methodology leads to a considerable increase in the precision of the corresponding photometric consistency map function.

$$VOTE^{i,j} = \begin{cases} 1 & \phi NCC^{i,j} \geq 0.9, \\ 0 & \phi NCC^{i,j} < 0.9. \end{cases}$$

$$Score = \sum_j VOTE^{i,j}.$$ (8)

The photometric consistency map function $\rho(p)$ which is illustrated in Fig. 3 is computed in Eq. 10 at the discrete sample points p_s along the Normal vector $\mathbf{N}(\mathbf{v}_i)$ and Eq. 10 gives one example, where the highlighted positions indicate the adapted vertices on the surface. As can be seen, that the photometric consistency evaluation for the vertex is independent from each other, so the process can be parallelized to run faster.

$$\rho(p_s, \mathbf{v_i}) = 1 - \frac{Score}{Number\ of\ Visible\ Views}$$ (9)

$$\rho = \left.\begin{matrix} 0.9 & 0.4 & 0.5 & 0.6 & \dots \\ 0.9 & 0.4 & 0.3 & 0.4 & \dots \\ 0.6 & 0.4 & 0 & 0.2 & \dots \\ 0.4 & 0.2 & 0.2 & 0.5 & \dots \\ 0.1 & 0.3 & 0.5 & 0.6 & \dots \\ 0.2 & 0.5 & 0.7 & 0.9 & \dots \\ 0.3 & 0.6 & 0.7 & 0.8 & \dots \\ 0.4 & 0.9 & 0.7 & 0.9 & \dots \end{matrix}\right\} Number\ of\ discrete\ sample$$ (10)

$$\underbrace{}_{Number\ of\ vertices}$$

3.4 A Combinatorial Consistency

As shown in Fig. 4, the photometric consistency optimization restores the object in a confined region and the contour of the object can be precisely reconstructed at cost of the lost of details and concavities on the surface. Whereas the silhouette consistency optimization works well to recover the structure details on the surface, but if some part of surface has already lost during Poisson surface reconstruction, it will be never recovered any more.

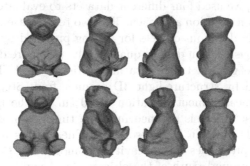

Fig. 4. Visual effects when applying silhouette consistency and photometric consistency separately. The 1st row: Silhouette consistency only. The second row: Photometric consistency only.

Furthermore, the two kinds of optimization can not be applied directly stepwise. Because if the photometric cue is applied first, the silhouette based optimization will fill all the concavities. And the photo-consistency based approach is useless, when operated on the vertices far away from the object surface. To overcome this problem silhouette-based optimization is modified to incorporate multi-view term while optimization.

The goal is to minimize the same energy function Eq. 3 as of silhouettes based optimization. Whereas the mapping functions $\rho(p_s)_f$ and $\rho(p_s)_b$ will be realized differently in this approach. Previously, only silhouette information was considered to determine the mapping functions. Here the state of each discrete sample point p_s in 3D space, whether it is inside or outside the object is determined by measuring photometric consistency score along the visual rays and exploiting the silhouette consistent shape. In detail, after the initial judgement, that the sample point p_s is inside the objects, the modified photometric consistency optimization is followed. As described in Sect. 3.3, NCC score is calculated at discrete sample point p_s^t under a voting scheme. The sample point position p_s^{tmax} which corresponds to the maximum voted NCC scores is considered as the searched point on the surface. If the updated point position p_s^{tmax} is not between the reference camera center and the sample point p_s, the point p_s will be considered outside the surface and the concavity is recovered. Accordingly the mapping functions $\rho(p_s)_f$ and $\rho(p_s)_b$ are updated. For the point p_s which is marked as exterior, it should be moved inwards further along the normal vector. The whole process will run iteratively until the total energy is converged.

The adaptation functions, *smoothing* and *decimation* are also used within the optimization approach, which ensure the topology of the triangle meshes preserves. However, smoothing needs to be stopped when triangular meshes approach the ground truth surface, where the energy function is close to zero. The whole process is summarized again in Algorithm 2.

4 Experiments and Results

In our experiments, we used four different datasets to evaluate the performance of the proposed reconstruction approach. The two test datasets *TempleRing* and *dinoRing* are standard famous objects for testing provided by [6]. Furthermore, to evaluate the reconstruction quality quantitively, two more datasets *totenKopf* and *teddy* with the ground truth data are tested as well. The ground truth data were captured by structure-light 3D scanner from Steinbichler COMET L3D 5M [7] with measurement deviation in $10\,\mu m$ for the measurement field in 100 mm. The test object is scanned multiple times from different angles to provide accurate 3D mesh in high resolution. The objects under observations have all interesting properties like concavities, homogeneity, shadowing, textureless. The captured ground truth of the objects are shown in the second row of Fig. 5(c) and (d). The projection matrices of the datasets *totenKopf* and *teddy* are acquired by camera calibration with known calibration object. A summary of the available datasets is shown in Table 1.

Algorithm 2. A Combinatorial Consistency based Optimization

Require: Mesh,calibrated images
  1: Load Triangular Mesh: vertices $\mathbf{V}$, edges $\mathbf{E}$
  2: Load all Images $\{I\}$, all silhouettes/masks $\{M\}$, all projection matrices $\{P\}$
  3: $\mathbf{D}_i \leftarrow$ Find global visibility correspondence (Depth Maps) for all vertices
  4: While total energy is not minimized
  5:     For each vertex $\mathbf{v}$
  6:         For all discrete sample positions $\mathbf{v}(p_s)$ along $\mathbf{N}(\mathbf{v})$
  7:             If $\mathbf{P}_i\mathbf{v} \in \mathbf{M}_i$ for all $i \in I$
  8:                 Mark position as Interior, i.e. $\rho_f(p_s) = 1$ and $\rho_b(p_s) = 0$
  9:             Otherwise mark position as exterior, i.e. $\rho_f(p_s) = 0$ and $\rho_b(p_s) = 1$
10:     For each vertex $\mathbf{v}$
11:         Find reference and corresponding views
12:         For all discrete sample positions $\mathbf{v}(p_s^t)$ where $\rho_f(p_s) = 1$
13:             While Photo-consistency map along visual ray is not full
14:                 Find barycentric coordinates of square patch around $\mathbf{v}(p_s^t)$
15:                 Find projection and intensities of reference view P_i
16:                 For each corresponding view P_j
17:                     Find projection of square patch onto P_j
18:                     Measure intensities using bilinear Interpolation
19:                     Calculate NCC score, compare it with reference view values
20:                     Use voting scheme to find the maximum photometric consistency score
21:                     If the new point is not located between current position p_s and camera centre
22:                     Then mark point p_s as exterior, i.e. $\rho_f(p_s) = 0$ and $\rho_b(p_s) = 1$
23:     For each vertex $\mathbf{v}$
24:         Move vertex with $v = v + \triangle v$, until $\rho_f(p_s) = 1$
25:         Move vertex with $v = v - \triangle v$, until $\rho_b(p_s) = 1$
26:     Apply Smoothing
27: Save Optimized Mesh

The datasets *templeRing* and *teddy* are rich in texture that makes it easier to find features in images. As expected, the point cloud generated by the framework proposed in [4] covers most of the surface of the object. Simple averaging of the visible visual rays are used to estimate the normal vector of the vertex since sufficient visibility in multiple views. Thus, the Poisson surface mesh is close to the ground truth data. With a combinatorial consistency optimization, the Poisson surface mesh is adapted to the ground truth data.

The datasets *dinoRing* and *totenKopf* are textureless and homogeneous that makes it difficult to extract the features in images. The generated point cloud is almost empty around homogeneous textureless areas. Though with robust normal vector estimation using PCA, the initial Poisson surface mesh is noisy due to sparsity of the point cloud. The silhouette cue helps to recover the missing regions of the Poisson surface and the photometric cue benefits to recover the details on the surface. However, the areas near the teeth of the *totenKopf* was not fully reconstructed due to narrow indentation. To estimate the narrow indentation, the window size of the photometric consistency optimization plays

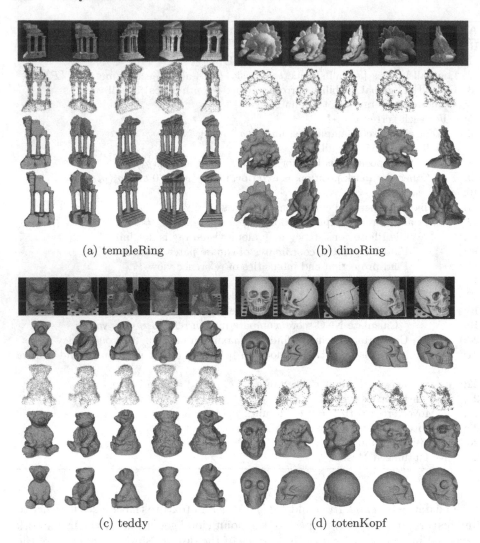

(a) templeRing

(b) dinoRing

(c) teddy

(d) totenKopf

Fig. 5. Experimental datasets. TempleRing/dinoRing: The 1st row - Selected views of the objects. The 2nd row - Oriented point clouds. The 3rd row - Initial Poisson Surface. The 4th row - Optimized Surface. Teddy/totenKopf: The 1st row - Selected views of the objects. The 2nd row - Ground truth data. The 3rd row - Oriented point clouds. The 4th row - Initial Poisson Surface. The 5th row - Optimized Surface.

a vital role. The smaller the window size is employed the better the reconstruction of the narrow concavities. The average number of iterations applied for optimization is about 50 times.

There are no surface meshes reconstructed at the bottom of the objects, as there are no images captured about that region. Therefore in our reconstructed surface, vertices close to bottom of the surface will be far away from

Table 1. Datasets

Datasets	templeRing	dinoRing	teddy	totenKopf
Number of views	47	47	42	60
Ground truth	No	No	Yes	Yes
Resolution (pixel)	640 × 480	640 × 480	2816 × 1880	2816 × 1880

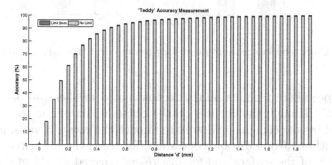

Fig. 6. Accuracy measurement for "teddy" dataset.

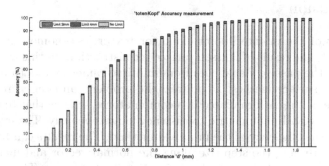

Fig. 7. Accuracy measurement for "totenKopf" dataset.

ground truth. To evaluate the accuracy and completeness of the reconstructed results, the methods introduced in [6] will be applied. The distance of vertices on reconstructed meshes to the nearest vertices on the ground truth meshes is calculated for accuracy measurement, whereas the distance of the vertices on the ground truth meshes to the nearest vertices on the reconstructed meshes for completeness measurement. As depicted in Figs. 6 and 7, the x-axis represents the distance threshold that is tolerant for accuracy measurement and the y-axis represents the portion of the reconstructed vertices within the tolerant threshold. It shows that 90 % of the vertices on the object *teddy* deviate from the ground truth surface meshes within 0.5 mm, whereas 90 % of the vertices on the object *totenKopf* deviate from the ground truth surface meshes within the range 0.95 mm to 1 mm. Intuitively, vertices on ground truth meshes that

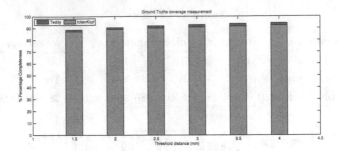

Fig. 8. Completeness measurement for "teddy" and "totenKopf" dataset.

have no proper nearest points on the reconstructed meshes will be regarded as "not covered". Though the vertices on the bottom part of the objects that are not captured by the cameras will greatly impact the completeness, as shown in the Fig. 8, within 1.5 mm distance deviation, for *teddy* the reconstructed meshes covered 88.8 % of the surface and for *totenKopf* covered 87.4 % of the surface.

5   Conclusion

The sparsity of the oriented point cloud for textureless, homogeneous surface severely affects the result of Poisson surface reconstruction. In this work, we have incorporated the passive visual cues from multiple camera views to improve the quality of the surface meshes. To address the problem, an energy minimization of the surface meshes is formulated in a combinatorial scheme that fulfills silhouette consistency and photometric consistency simultaneously. The experimental results prove the efficiency of the proposed method. The results can be improved further by decreasing the step size along the normal vector and increasing the number of iterations at the cost of running time and memory. The independent operation of the vertices provides the opportunity for real-time application.

References

1. Furukawa, Y., Ponce, J.: High-fidelity image-based modeling. In: Technical Report CVR (2006)
2. Kolev, K.: Convexity in image-based 3D surface reconstruction. Computer Vision Group, Department of Computer Science, Technical University Munich, 85748 Garching, Germany (2011)
3. Kazhdan, M., Bolitho, M., Hoppe, H.: Poisson surface reconstruction. In: Proceedings of the Fourth Eurographics Symposium on Geometry Processing, pp. 61–70 (2006)
4. Qian, N., Heisterklaus, I., Bulla, C., Wien, M.: Robust multi-view reconstruction from quasi-dense point cloud and poisson surface mesh. In: Proceedings of 3DTV Conference, pp. 1–4. IEEE, Piscataway (2014)

5. Laurentini, A.: The visual hull concept for visual-based image understanding. In: IEEE Transactions on Pattern Analysis and Machine Intelligence, vol. 16, pp. 150–162. IEEE, Piscataway (1994)
6. Seitz, S.M., Curless, B., Diebel, J., Scharstein, D., Szeliski, R.: A comparison and evaluation of multi-view stereo reconstruction algorithms. In: Proceedings of the Conference on Computer Vision and Pattern Recognition, vol. 1, pp. 519–528. IEEE, Piscataway (2006). http://vision.middlebury.edu/mview/
7. http://www.steinbichler.de

Prediction of Vibrations as a Measure of Terrain Traversability in Outdoor Structured and Natural Environments

Mohammed Abdessamad Bekhti$^{(\boxtimes)}$ and Yuichi Kobayashi

Graduate School of Science and Technology, Shizuoka University, Hamamatsu, Japan
bekhti.m.a@gmail.com, kobayashi.yuichi@shizuoka.ac.jp

Abstract. Terrain recognition is an important task that a mobile robot has to accomplish autonomously to navigate in hazardous territories safely with no additional human monitoring. For this, sensory information should be employed to construct a good model to estimate the degree of traversability of upcoming terrains. In this paper, a regression-based method is proposed to estimate mobile robot vibration from terrain images as a description for terrain traversability. Texture attributes obtained from evaluation of the fractal dimension to describe the terrains were combined with appropriate acceleration features for function approximation using Gaussian Process regression (GP). Results showed effectiveness of the method to predict motion data for different terrain configurations in structured and rough environments.

Keywords: Autonomous mobile robots · Texture features · Acceleration · Gaussian process regression · Terrain traversability

1 Introduction

Autonomous mobile robot navigation in natural environments is a challenging task, due to variety of environment configurations a mobile platform may encounter and lack of a precise prior knowledge of the terrain conditions [1]. Thereby, it is important to design a highly autonomous recognition system that will allow the mobile platform to rely less on human instructions to assess terrain traversability, *i.e.*, terrain representation can evolve through interaction with new terrain scenarios without referring to predefined set of terrain classes such as grass, rocks, mud, etc.

Several sensors to perceive the environment have been used to develop frameworks for traversability. They can be categorized as exteroceptive and proprioceptive sensors [2]. Exteroceptive sensors such as cameras and lasers give a direct representation of the environment. In addition to this, wheel encoders and proprioceptive sensors such as vibration sensors, current sensors, gyroscopes provide complementary information about the environment, and thus the importance of combining both type of sensors to improve terrain recognition and reducing the dependency on human design.

© Springer International Publishing Switzerland 2016
T. Bräunl et al. (Eds.): PSIVT 2015, LNCS 9431, pp. 282–294, 2016.
DOI: 10.1007/978-3-319-29451-3_23

A speed control system was developed based on roughness identification using a 2D laser [3]. Terrain scans return the height of the point on the soil which are compared with measures of flatness obtained by scanning the height of a flat surface in front of vehicle. Based on the comparison of the four parameters used to describe the terrain roughness with predefined thresholds, the speed is controlled to be either reduced, augmented or maintained at the current level.

Shape attributes of the ground were extensively investigated for traversability estimation. The idea is to use 3D environment analysis methods and chart the mobility smoothness in a hierarchical fashion. Based on this, 3D Ladar information was clustered according to scatterness (grass), surfaceness (ground), and linearness (tree trunc) for terrain modeling [4]. 2D lasers are plane scanners and thus unable to describe the geometry of the soil, also obstacle detection (e.g., [5]) may fail if the scanned plane is high. On the other hand, 3D lasers or lidars provide detailed representation of the scenery [6], but still are costly, consume more energy to perform.

Cameras are undoubtedly more preferred since they are much affordable, easier to integrate, and can furnish various information such as color, texture, etc. In this context, several methods have been implemented methods which used both image and geometry data for traversability estimation.

Investigating elevation of height profile allowed detection and categorization of obstacles into negative (ditches, holes) and positive (bump) obstacles [7]. Terrain categorization was done through classification of color information within predefined material-class. Obstacle degree of traversability was inferred by combining range information and classification outcome. In the same context, an algorithm for self-supervise terrain classification combining geometrical and visual features was proposed [8]. With regard to image information, HSV color expressed by a four dimensional vector and wavelet-based texture information were used. Features are then fused using a naive Bayes classifier. Both previously mentioned methods lack use of low level feedback information (proprioceptive data) related to the moving platform that can be used as ground truth.

In the context of proprioceptive data, vibrations generated from interaction of the wheels and the soil was used to perform terrain classification [9]. The acceleration signal is divided into small sections which will serve to evaluate the Power Spectral Density (PSD). To categorize terrain samples Linear Discriminant Analysis (LDA) was employed. Vibration data may provide a good understanding of robot behavior while navigating but it is not enough to anticipate upcoming terrains and scenarios such as obstacles since it is limited to underfoot only.

Latest research projects showed the effectiveness of learning from both exteroceptive and proprioceptive sensory information to estimate the vehicle behavior toward subsequent terrains. Image color information was employed by Krebs et al. to approximate the interaction of the mobile platform and the ground based on a classification framework [10]. The goal of training process was to learn terrain understanding through interaction with several terrain configurations. Rover Terrain Interaction (RTI) attributes were combined with corresponding exteroceptive data to build an inference model. It showed effectiveness for RTI parameters such as slip and vibration.

Regression of terrain traversability based on robot pose was proposed by Ho *et al.* [11]. Vehicle attitude was estimated when running on deformable terrains from an approximation done on rigid grounds and terrain geometry attributes using Gaussian Process regression (GP) [15]. For the final objective of navigation, geometry is just an intermediate representation. It is possible to directly predict motion property from other sensory modalities like cameras which can provide 3D map of the environment.

Image texture information can furnish a detailed representation about terrain natures due to the high dimension of the feature vector compared with color information [10], and thus enables a good prediction for traversability. Nonetheless, classifying terrain using only texture attribute may not be suitable. Another issue in classification framework is the non-consistency of attributed labels, since it relies on the judgment of the designer.

This paper addresses approximation of terrain signature *i.e.*, vibrations from mobile robot motion information based on learned data association of exteroceptive and proprioceptive information using GP regression. With regard to exteroceptive data, texture information based on fractal dimension is used to describe terrain configurations. Also vibration *i.e.*, vertical acceleration generated from interaction between the mobile platform and the soil was considered in this study case. Compared with semi-supervised methods, the proposed framework uses acceleration signals obtained from interaction of the vehicle with the soil as ground truth. The proposed approach is able to estimate the vibration that the mobile platform may encounter when running on a terrain regardless of its nature.

2   Problem Definition

2.1   Objective

A camera and an acceleration sensor are mounted on a four wheel mobile platform as shown in Fig. 1. The camera acquires terrain images and the acceleration sensor registers acceleration signal generated during a sequence of a run. The target is to predict vibration feature as a measure of traversability only from terrain images. This information will be used to understand the vehicle behavior towards subsequent terrains and is expected to enable a safe run.

2.2   Methodology

From terrain images, Region of Interest (ROI) are determined for image feature extraction. In this case study, from every single image two terrain patches (ROIs) will be used. Texture attribute evaluated by measuring the fractal dimension [13] is retained. Registered acceleration signal is divided into small sequences to measure motion features according to extracted terrain patches. For function

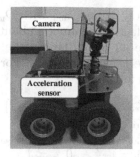

Fig. 1. Pioneer 3AT hardware configuration.

approximation, GP regression is employed to learn data correlation of texture and vibration features. Based on this result, prediction of vibration features is performed using only image information.

3 Regression of Motion Information

3.1 Terrain Patches Identification

From terrain images, patches corresponding to a short range distance will be considered for texture extraction. For this, the camera model is used to define the ROIs (refer to [12] for further details). As shown in Fig. 2, the camera is characterized by the camera frame $\{O_c, x_c, y_c, z_c\}$ whose center is O_c. The following equation translates a point from the world reference frame represented by $P \in \mathbb{R}^4$ to $p \in \mathbb{R}^3$ (both containing one as the last element) onto the image plane:

$$p = \mathbf{K}[\mathbf{R}|t]P, \tag{1}$$

where $[\mathbf{R}|t] \in \mathbb{R}^{4 \times 4}$ is the extrinsic parameter matrix, and $\mathbf{K} \in \mathbb{R}^{4 \times 3}$ is the camera parameter matrix.

The above-mentioned model will be used to determine terrain the vehicle is traversing using robot's wheels base L and width W. As shown in Fig. 3, both camera and world references frame are center of the platform. The world

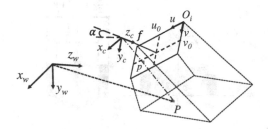

Fig. 2. Camera frame for mapping 3D point mapping onto the image plane.

reference frame is given by $\{O_w, x_w, y_w, z_w\}$ with O_w as origin. The goal of the process is to map points to identify the inner and outer bounds of terrain region crossed by the vehicle. Since all points lay on the same line, only the depth components according to the w_z-axis will vary. For both left and right sides, these points are expressed as follows:

$$\begin{cases} P_{ro} = [\frac{L}{2} + W, \quad 0, \quad z_w] \\ P_{ri} = [\frac{L}{2}, \quad 0, \quad z_w] \\ P_{lo} = [-\frac{L}{2} - W, \quad 0, \quad z_w] \\ P_{li} = [-\frac{L}{2}, \quad 0, \quad z_w] \end{cases}, \tag{2}$$

where P_{ro}, P_{ri} denote the points laying on the right outer and inner bounds respectively and P_{lo}, P_{li} the left outer and inner bounds. Results of this operation are shown in Fig. 4. To increase the number of terrain sample, two terrain patches will be extracted from a single image. Warp perspective transformation is performed to remove the trapezoidal shape introduced when taking a picture.

3.2   Texture Attribute Extraction

Texture attributes are extracted using Segmentation-based Fractal Texture Analysis (SFTA) [13]. The SFTA method consists of two steps. In the first step, the input grayscale image is decomposed into binary images using the Two-Threshold Binary Decomposition (TTBD) [13]. In the second step, each binary image is used to calculate the fractal dimension from its region boundaries. TTBD computes a set of thresholds T, which is acheived by the Multi-level Otsu algorithm [14]. After obtaining the desired threshold number n_t, pairs of contiguous thresholds $T \cup \{n_l\}$ with n_l the highest value in the input gray scale image, associated with pairs of thresholds $\{t, n_t\}$ with $t \in T$, are employed to obtain the binary images as follows

$$I_{x,y}^b = \begin{cases} 1, & \text{if } t_l < I(x,y) \leq t_u \\ 0, & \text{otherwise} \end{cases}, \tag{3}$$

where $I_{x,y}^b$ denotes the binary value of image pixel (x,y), t_l and t_u denote the lower and the upper threshold values respectively. Consequently, $2n_t$ binary

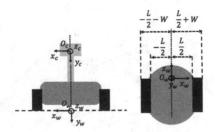

Fig. 3. Mobile robot carrying a camera and layout of both world and camera reference frames.

Fig. 4. Identification of terrain patches for image feature extraction.

images will be obtained. In the application of this paper, SFTA feature vector will include only the fractal dimension of the boundaries. $\Delta(x, y)$ represents the border image of the binary image $I_{x,y}^b$, and is evaluated as

$$\Delta(x, y) = \begin{cases} 1, & \text{if } \exists (x', y') \in N_{x,y} \\ & s.t.\ I_{x',y'}^b = 0 \wedge I_{x,y}^b = 1 \ , \\ 0, & \text{otherwise} \end{cases} \tag{4}$$

where $N_{x,y}$ is the 8-connexity of a pixel (x, y). $\Delta(x, y)$ takes the value one if the pixel at location (x, y) in the related binary image $I_{x,y}^b$ has the value one and having at least one neighbor pixel with zero value. The border image is used to compute the fractal dimension $D \in \mathbb{R}$ by the box counting algorithm as follows

$$D_0(x, y) = \lim_{\varepsilon \to 0} \frac{\log N(\varepsilon)}{\log(\varepsilon^{-1})}, \tag{5}$$

where $N(\varepsilon)$ is the number of hyper-cubes of length ε that fill the object. The resulting SFTA feature vector is denoted by $x \in \mathbb{R}^{2n_t}$.

3.3 Motion Feature Extraction

Let $a_k, k = 1, \cdots, K$ be the vertical acceleration signal translating vibrations during a run on a short range distance with time step k and K is the total time steps. Amplitude distance was retained to describe the motion of the platform, and is given by

$$a_{k_d} = \max_{k=1,\cdots,K} a_k - \min_{k=1,\cdots,K} a_k. \tag{6}$$

3.4 Matching Image and Motion Features

As mentioned above, two short terrain segments are considered for image feature extraction. Accordingly, relevant acceleration segment for motion feature

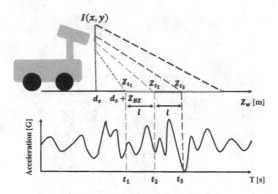

Fig. 5. data acquisition

extraction is matched to image features using coordinate transformation and odometry. As shown in Fig. 5, at time $t = 0$, the robot is located at the origin of the world reference frame. Location to take a new picture is denoted as $Z_{I_i(x,y)}$ and is expressed as

$$Z_{I_i(x,y)} = id_s, \quad i = 1, \cdots, N_{\text{image}}, \tag{7}$$

where d_s denotes sampling distance, and N_{image} is the total number of terrain images acquired during a run. Due to the camera tilt angle α, terrains will be covered from a certain position expressed as

$$Z_{I_i(x,y)} + Z_{\text{BZ}}, \quad i = 1, \cdots, N_{\text{image}}, \tag{8}$$

where Z_{BZ} is area not covered by the image, which is called blind zone. As mentioned above, a short range distance l covered by the images will be retained for image feature extraction. A reason for that is the further a pixel (x, y) is from the camera focus point, the more noise the pixel will be subject to. Thus visual representation of the environment may not be faithful to the real world. Acceleration signal sequence generated by the distance l is used for motion feature extraction, and is bounded according to the ROI as follows

$$A_i = [Z_{I_i(x,y)} + Z_{\text{BZ}}, Z_{I_i(x,y)} + Z_{\text{BZ}} + l], \tag{9}$$

where A_i denotes the ROI.

3.5   Regression Analysis using Gaussian Process (GP)

Gaussian process [15] is used for regression analysis. Let $\mathcal{D} = \{(\boldsymbol{x}_j, y_j), j = 1, \cdots, n\}$ denote a set of training samples with pairs of SFTA feature vector inputs $\boldsymbol{x}_j$ and motion feature outputs $y_j \in \mathbb{R}$, n denotes the total number of training samples. The goal is to evaluate the predictive distribution for the function f_* for test input samples $\boldsymbol{x}_*$. The noise is additive, independent and

(a) Gravel   (b) Stones

(c) Grass   (d) Woodchip

Fig. 6. Natural terrains.

following a normal distribution. The relationship between the function $f(\boldsymbol{x})$ and the observed noisy targets y is given by

$$y_j = f(\boldsymbol{x}_j) + \varepsilon_j, \tag{10}$$

where ε_j is a noise which follows $\mathcal{N}(0, \sigma^2_{\text{noise}})$, where σ^2_{noise} denotes the variance of the noise. The notation $\mathcal{N}(\mathbf{a}, A)$ is retained for the normal distribution with mean $\mathbf{a}$ and covariance A. Gaussian Process regression is a Bayesian algorithm that assumes that *a priori* the function values respond as

$$p(\mathbf{f}|\boldsymbol{x}_1, \boldsymbol{x}_2, \cdots, \boldsymbol{x}_n) = \mathcal{N}(0, K), \tag{11}$$

where $\mathbf{f} = [f_1, f_2, \cdots, f_n]^\top$ contains the latent function values, $f_j = f(\boldsymbol{x}_j)$ and K is a covariance matrix which inputs are provided by the covariance function defined as $K_{ij} = k(\boldsymbol{x}_i, \boldsymbol{x}_j)$. A widely employed covariance function is the squared exponential given by

$$K_{ij} = k(\boldsymbol{x}_i, \boldsymbol{x}_j) = \sigma^2 \exp\left(-\frac{(\boldsymbol{x}_i - \boldsymbol{x}_j)^\top (\boldsymbol{x}_i - \boldsymbol{x}_j)}{2\lambda^2}\right), \tag{12}$$

where σ^2 controls the variance, and λ is the isotropic lengthscale parameter that describes the smoothness of a function.

4   Experiment

4.1   Experiment Settings

To predict motion information based on Gaussian Process regression, the vehicle was engaged extensively in 30 different outdoor environment configurations

(a) Slik asphalt   (b) Granulated asphalt

(c) Tiles   (d) Wood

Fig. 7. Artificial terrains.

to acquire terrain observations (images) and corresponding acceleration signals. The goal of experiment is to assess performance of proposed framework to predict motion features. Samples of terrain configurations are shown in Figs. 6 and 7. Training was done using a set of 1208 terrain patches and corresponding acceleration features. An extra set of 109 image features were used for testing. Experiment parameters were set as follows

- Camera height h: 540 [mm],
- Camera tilt angle α: 31[deg],
- Number of thresholds for SFTA n_t: 8,
- Dimension of SFTA feature vector $x \in \mathbb{R}^{16}$,
- ROI length l: 250 [mm],
- Number of images used for function approximation N_{tr}: 1208,
- Number of images used for prediction N_{pr}: 109,
- Acceleration signal sampling period T_s: 10 [ms],
- Step distance for taking images d_s: 500 [mm].

4.2   Results

Effectiveness of the proposed approach was evaluated based on whether the real motion feature belongs to 1σ trust interval. The results are introduced by Fig. 8. A total of 76 terrain samples of different natures were successfully approximated within the trust interval. Moreover, the fractal dimension offers a discrimination of terrains texture attributes. Principal Component Analysis (PCA) was applied to SFTA feature vector to reduce the dimension from $x \in \mathbb{R}^{16}$ to $z \in \mathbb{R}^2$ to visualize the distribution of the motion information. As shown in Fig. 9, terrain configurations are scattered in different areas.

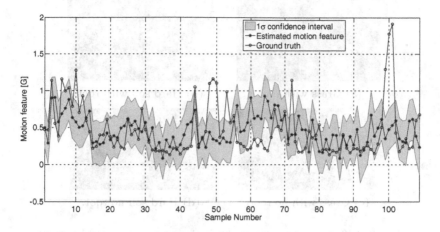

Fig. 8. Approximation of motion features using Gaussian process

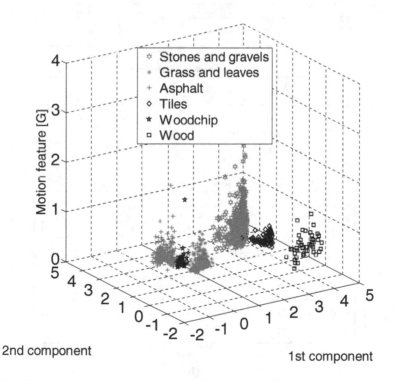

Fig. 9. Distribution of motion information with regard to SFTA for three terrain types: stones and gravels, grass and leaves, granulated and slick asphalt.

(a) Grass with root.   (b) Hard soil with root.

(c) Grass with no root.   (d) Hard soil no root.

Fig. 10. Difference of terrain configurations for same ground nature.

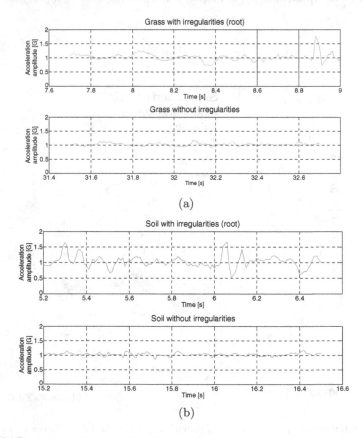

(a)

(b)

Fig. 11. Difference in vibration signal for terrains with and without irregularities: (a) Grass, (b) soil.

4.3 Discussion

The remaining 33 samples were not estimated within the confidence interval. In the case of terrain configurations shown by Fig. 10(a) and (b), where tree roots appear from the ground creating bumps, motion data could not be predicted well. When the mobile platform crosses terrain deformation or irregularity (tree roots, rocks, etc.), acceleration sensor acquires instant high vibration values *i.e.*, motion information is more localized compared with uniform terrains which generates smoother acceleration signal as shown in Fig. 11. On the other hand, image region can include both grass textures and bumps. More localized (with narrower regions) features to take into account irregularities of the soil will improve this problem. Thus, sufficient number of data will be required also for terrain irregularities to achieve a good approximation of motion features.

5   Conclusion and Future Work

In this paper, we introduced a method to assess terrain mobility for mobile robot navigating in outdoor environments based on data association of exteroceptive data (terrain observations) and proprioceptive information (vibrations of the platform). SFTA texture attribute was used to describe the nature of terrains. It can provide a discrimination of terrain texture information and thus the ability to distinguish terrain natures (stones, grass, and asphalt). Using GP regression, a set of training data of different terrain configurations was used for learning by combining both image and motion attributes, and a different set of terrain images was used for validation. Obtained results showed a good motion data prediction with 70 % success rate. SFTA feature vector is a non localized representation of terrain characteristics with regard to the running information which is more local as of its instantaneous nature. A more localized image representation may be suitable for predicting local motion data of the mobile robot when running on a terrain with irregularities. More general problems could influence the image features such as high brightness which may lead to a strong reflectance from the ground. Also, perspective effect of the camera leads to a less appreciation of the details included in the soil.

Acknowledgement. This research was partly supported by JSPS KAKENHI Grant Number 25330305.

References

1. Chilian, A., Hirschmuller, H.: Stereo camera based navigation of mobile robots on rough terrain. In: IEEE/RSJ International Conference on Intelligent Robots and Systems, pp. 4571–4576. IEEE Press (2009)
2. Sancho-Pradel, D., Gao, Y.: A survey on terrain assessment techniques for autonomous operation of planetary robots. J. Br. Interplanetary Soc. **63**, 206–217 (2010)

3. Castelnovi, M., Arkin, R., Collins, T.: Reactive speed control system based on terrain roughness detection. In: IEEE International Conference on Robotics and Automation, pp. 891–896. IEEE Press (2005)
4. Lalonde, J.-F., Vandapel, N., Huber, D.F., Hebert, M.: Natural terrain classification using three-dimensional ladar data for ground robot mobility. J. Field Robot. **23**, 839–861 (2006)
5. Labayrade, R., Gruyer, D., Royere, C., Perrollaz, M., Aubert, D.: Obstacle Detection Based on Fusion Between Stereovision and 2D Laser Scanner. Mobile Robots: Perception and Navigation (2007)
6. Papadakis, P.: Terrain traversability analysis methods for unmanned ground vehicles: a survey. Eng. Appl. Artif. Intel. **26**, 1373–1385 (2013)
7. Bellutta, P., Manduchi, R., Matthies, L., Owens, K., Rankin, A.: Terrain perception for DEMO III. In: IEEE Intelligent Vehicles, pp. 326–331. IEEE Press (2000)
8. Brooks, C.A., Iagnemma, K.D.: Self-supervised classification for planetary rover terrain sensing. In: IEEE Aerospace Conference, pp. 1–9. IEEE Press (2007)
9. Brooks, C., Iagnemma, K., Dubowsky, S.: Vibration-based terrain analysis for mobile robots. In: IEEE International Conference on Robotics and Automation, pp. 3415–3420. IEEE Press (2005)
10. Krebs, A., Pradalier, C., Siegwart, R.: Adaptive rover behavior based on online empirical evaluation: Rover-terrain interaction and near-to-far learning. J. Field Robot. **27**, 158–180 (2010)
11. Ken, H., Peynot, T., Sukkarieh, S.: A near-to-far non-parametric learning approach for estimating traversability in deformable terrain. In: Proceedings of IEEE/RSJ International Conference on Intelligent Robots and Systems, pp. 2827–2833. IEEE Press (2013)
12. Hartley, R., Zisserman, A.: Multiple View Geometry in Computer Vision. Cambridge University Press, Cambridge (2000)
13. Costa, A.F., Humpire-Mamani, G., Traina, A.J.M.: An efficient algorithm for fractal analysis of textures. In: 25th Conference on Graphics, Patterns and Images, pp. 39–46. IEEE Press (2012)
14. Liao, P., Chen, T., Chung, P.: A fast algorithm for multilevel thresholding. J. Inf. Sci. Eng. **17**, 713–727 (2001)
15. Rasmussen, C.E., Williams, C.K.I.: Gaussian Processes for Machine Learning. The MIT Press, Cambridge (2006)

Echo State Network for 3D Motion Pattern Indexing: A Case Study on Tennis Forehands

Boris Bačić[(✉)]

School of Computer and Mathematical Sciences,
Auckland University of Technology, Auckland, New Zealand
`boris.bacic@aut.ac.nz`

Abstract. Open skill sports such as tennis have a large number of swing execution techniques. This study presents a novel approach to event detection and motion pattern indexing of forehand swings captured from fixed location multi-camera represented as a 3D motion data set of multi-time series sampled at 50 Hz. The achieved results utilising Echo State Network (ESN) demonstrate 100 % recognition of tennis forehands from previously unseen test data without ball impact information. In contrast to traditional, heuristic and feature extraction-based algorithmic approaches in exergames and augmented coaching technologies, the proposed ESN paradigm represents a viable and generic approach for future work in temporal and spatial detection and automated analysis of region of interest in human motion data processing.

Keywords: Computational intelligence (CI) · Sport and rehabilitation · Biomechanics · Augmented coaching systems (ACS) · Reservoir computing (RC) · Spiking neural network (SNN)

1 Introduction

Over past decades there has been growing popularity in *exergames*, augmented coaching technology and ubiquitous computing devices with integrated inertial motion sensors. Inertial Measurement Units (IMUs), used for detecting, measuring and quantifying human activity, are becoming ubiquitous for sport equipment, embedded design, or as part of wearable technology (e.g. www.smarttennissensor.sony.net, www. zepp.com or www.xsens.com). Captured motion data related to the human body, sport equipment or projectile/ball trajectory can be obtained as raw time-series or in computed and human interpretable form. Similar to IMUs and Wireless IMUs motion data, computer vision systems such as Microsoft's Kinect for exergames or other general purpose systems (e.g. www.ptgrey.com/stereo-vision-cameras-systems) are able to convert video and depth information as 3D data in near-real-time. While currently available exergames and augmented coaching technology are designed to promoting active life style, the next generation of augmented coaching systems (ACS) are also prototyped to provide autonomous feedback on human motion similar to a coach when helping an athlete to improve stylistic execution of characteristic movement patterns [1–4]. The study addresses the problem area of fast recognition of characteristic movement patterns that is also an integral part of the prototyped ACS architecture

© Springer International Publishing Switzerland 2016
T. Bräunl et al. (Eds.): PSIVT 2015, LNCS 9431, pp. 295–306, 2016.
DOI: 10.1007/978-3-319-29451-3_24

relying on a new computing approach, such as Jaeger's [5, 6] Echo State Network (ESN). The presented ESN-based modelling approach was evaluated for supervised learning and motion pattern recognition such as automated detection and indexing of various tennis forehands from captured 3D motion data.

The following sections briefly describe *reservoir computing*, human motion modelling and tennis-related backgrounds. The mid-section focuses on 3D motion data analysis, experiments and results. The last section provides discussion, critique and concluding remarks.

1.1 Related Work and Prior Studies

The Reservoir Computing (RC) models such as LSM, ESN, Spiking Neural Networks (SNN) and other similar biologically inspired systems are referred in literature as the "third generation" of neural networks that are suited for temporal and spatial problem areas [7, 8]. The third generation of neural networks are also considered as an alternative for fast-processing substitute or complementary technology to traditional neuro-fuzzy, heuristic- and feature extraction-based approaches [9–14]. Preliminary studies on the RC paradigm, idiosyncrasy of human motion [15, 16], and human activity in the equestrian discipline utilising first synthetic and then IMU sensor data [17, 18], suggest that RC paradigm should be further investigated in the contexts of human motion modelling and analysis.

1.2 Tennis and Sport Science Backgrounds

At the end of the wooden racquets era, almost four decades ago, the new racquet materials have enabled the design of larger head sizes and sweet spots. As a result of continuous developments of new synthetic strings, materials and frame production technology, the game of tennis has become increasingly faster so that players have to continuously evolve their competitive game. Furthermore, the new racquet varieties have been designed to suit different tennis player profiles, so it is also common to see a diversity of playing styles, idiosyncrasies of swing techniques and strategies combined with diverse pace and stances [19–21]. Unlike backhands, forehand's winners and defensive shots are common shots at all skill levels. The diversity of forehand idiosyncrasies and execution techniques (from basics to elite competitive levels) is a well investigated area in sport science and biomechanics [21–26].

2 Experimental Setup: Data Collection, Analysis, Pre-processing and ESN Modelling

The motion data set was obtained using nine cameras recording at 50 Hz (ASCII text data exported from SMART-e 900 eMotion/BTS). Exported 3D motion data series, representing a stick figure of a tennis player is obtained by attaching a set of retro-reflective markers ($q = 22$) to a selection of anatomical body landmarks and the racquet. The motion data set includes swings of different velocity, hitting stances and execution techniques. The experiment's motion data set does not include ball information. The motion data set contains a balanced distribution of relatively good and bad swings that are considered *common errors* [27]. The relatively small captured data set was considered sufficient to conduct the preliminary experiments of feasibility of ESN for swing detection without warranting the need for extending the data set with synthetic data (Fig. 2).

A sequence of stick figures (Fig. 1) showing human activity before, during and after a forehand swing was produced from the captured 3D markers' time series.

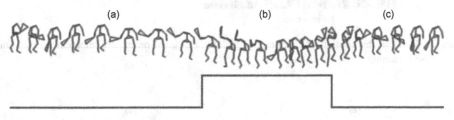

Fig. 1. Temporal and spatial problem area of forehand swing detection. Distinct temporal phases cover: (a) getting into swing position, (b) forehand swing event, and (c) post-swing position recovery. The sequence of 3D stick figures is not shown at equal time distance. The binary signal (green line) indicates expert's arbitrary boundaries of recognised forehand swing (Color figure online).

2.1 Data Analysis and Pre-processing

The captured motion data are summarised as follows:

- Each marker position trajectory is represented with three time series $m_p(n) = (x_p(n), y_p(n), z_p(n))$ in the captured volume, where n is a time-stamp number.
- Each motion datum sample is denoted as frame M within the captured volume. A frame M represents a stick figure, which is an interconnected finite set of three-dimensional markers m_p, where $M = (m_1, m_2, ..., m_q)$, and $p = 1, ..., q$.
- Each swing event S_j (Fig. 1(b)) is a set of k consecutive frames $M(n, ..., n + k)$, $S_j = \{M(n) | n_0 \leq n \leq n_{k-1}\}$ of duration $k/(\text{frame\_rate})$.

As a guideline to ESN modelling, the temporal event of the swing S_j duration is approx. one second (i.e. $mean(k)/(50 \text{ Hz})$). For ESN modelling, in addition to leak rate μ parameter tuning, it is also recommended [12] that spectral radius $\rho(W)$ should be close to 1 for long memory tasks and for mapping signals $x(n)$ into more nonlinear regions of $\tanh(.)$ along with scaling of W^{in} and W.

Before supplying motion data to the ESN model, data pre-processing involved replacing missing values (NaN) and normalisation (1) shown in Fig. 3. For each time-series, normalization within the interval $[-1, 1]$ was implemented as linear scaling:

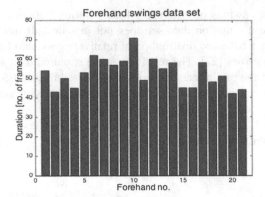

Forehand duration analysis
                                              [no. of frames]

Minimum:	42
Maximum:	71
Mean*:	52.81
Median:	53
Mode:	45
Standard deviation*:	7.61
Range (max — min):	29

*Note: rounded to two decimal places

Fig. 2. Random distribution of relative swing duration, based on expert selection utilised for supervised learning

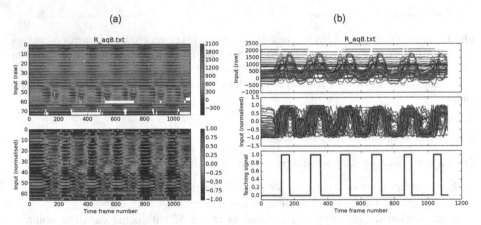

Fig. 3. Preprocessing steps of motion dataset time-series for supervised learning: (a) visualisation of input data pre-processing with (NaN) replacements and normalising to [−1,1], and (b) assigning output labels {0, 1} to forehand events (i.e. 'Teaching signal' for supervised learning).

$$v_{norm} = 2 \cdot \left(\frac{v_{in} - \min(v)}{\max(v) - \min(v)} - 0.5 \right) \qquad (1)$$

Fast linear curve fitting for NaN values processing were implemented as replacements with average neighbouring values where M_j: (NaN $\in M_j$) $\Rightarrow$
$M_j = \text{mean}(M_{j-1}, M_h)$ where NaN $\notin M_h$.

2.2   Echo State Network – Model Description and Parameter Optimisation Results

The chosen ESN classifier for the study is one of the examples of Recurrent Neural Networks (RNNs), where the next state of neural network depends on input signals, connection weights and the previous states of the network (Eqs. (2) and (3)).

The typical ESN operation includes [14, 18, 28] reservoir neuron input signals $u(n)$, activated neuron outputs $x'(n)$ and output of the network $y(n)$ functions:

$$x'(n) = f(W^{in}u(n) + Wx(n-1));$$

$$x(n) = (1 - \mu)x(n-1) + \mu x'(n) \tag{2}$$

The output of the network (3) at the frame number n is a linear transformation of concatenated input and output vectors:

$$y(n) = f^{out}(W^{out}[u(n)|x(n)]) \tag{3}$$

The central component of ESN is a *dynamic reservoir* (Fig. 4), with random recurrent neuron interconnectivity created during the ESN initialisation.

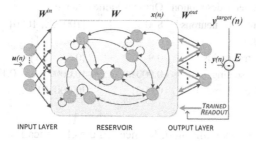

Fig. 4. Reservoir computing: ESN concept and parameters

Where,

n	time frame number	W^{in}	input weights matrix
$u(n)$	input signal e.g. discrete time-series	W	reservoir weights (recurrent synaptic neuron interconnectivity) matrix
$x(n)$	the state vector containing reservoir neurons' activation at time of the frame number n	W^{out}	output weights matrix
$y(n)$	the output function of the network	$\rho(W)$	spectral radius, the largest eigen value of W
$y^{target}(n)$	teaching/target signal utilised for supervised learning of ESN	E	error measure utilised by supervised learning algorithm to obtain $y(n)$ function.

The ESN training or learning task is associated only with the adjustment of the output layer, leaving the input layer and reservoir parameters unchanged. The learning task is optimisation problem aimed to minimise the difference E between the output y (n) and $y^{target}(n)$ signals. One of the commonly used methods here is *ridge regression* (also known as Tikhonov regularization). While the obtained output i.e. readout is expected to be linearly separable into the output classes, the *clipping threshold* parameter is set to map the output signal $y(n)$ to the predicted class. During the ESN initialisation, the sparse random interconnectivity of reservoir neurons is specified by a weight matrix W, scaled by the spectral radius $\rho(W)$. The *input scaling* parameter is associated with reservoir response i.e. linearity or non-linearity of a leaky integrator neuron activation function $f(\cdot)$. Both reservoir neuron activation $f(\cdot)$ and output neuron activation function $f^{out}(\cdot)$, referred in Eqs. (2) and (3), are typically a sigmoidal shape such as element-wise hyperbolic tangent tanh(.) as utilized in the study. In addition, the leak rate μ parameter controls integration with previous i.e. recurrent state of the network.

Preliminary findings on the obtained ESN model and classification of 3D tennis motion data set were produced using the grid search ESN parameter optimisation (as shown in Table 1).

Table 1. Optimized parameters for leaky reservoir ESN model.

Parameter description	Optimal value	Range
Number of neurons	800	[100, ..., 1000]
Leak rate	0.9	[0.3, ..., 1]
Spectral radius	0.9	[0.5, ..., 1]
Input scaling	0.0001	[0.00001, ..., 0.1]
Ridge parameter	0.0001	[0.000001, ..., 0.1]

Note: There were no significant differences in the classification results for the range of 700–1000 neurons (shown in Fig. 6 and Table 2). Leak rate μ parameter between [0.8, 0.9] was found to contribute to *true positive (TP)* vs. *true negative (TN)* class accuracy ratio rather than the overall classification, so it was left to 0.9 to favour classification accuracy of a minority class of forehand swings.

3 Classification Results and Model Visualisation

Classification results (Fig. 5) of the ESN model were obtained utilising four streams of 66 column time-series. Each input frame M would be classified in one of the two output labels were 0 ('No Forehand') and 1 ('Forehand swing').

The obtained leaky ESN classifier is able to detect all forehand swings from the test data. The classifier model was trained with the first 400 frames of each of the four times series data. Compared to the expert's visual forehand detection, the ESN classifier detected 100 % of all forehand events with an occasional difference related to start and stop of the classified swing event.

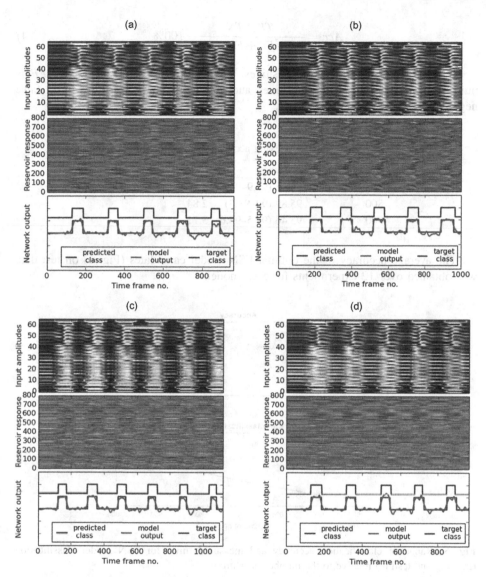

Fig. 5. ESN model – regression output and produced output class on four time-series (a), (b), (c) and (d). Visual representations of excitation patterns of reservoir responses are varying due to the random recurrent connectivity and the diversity of forehand swings.

Visual representation of the classification results (Fig. 5) shows minor errors in individual samples regarding the start and stop of forehands that are executed with different swing speed i.e. time durations (Fig. 2). Given that practical implementation may involve an ESN classifier with lesser neurons to improve processing speed and reduce computational costs, the reported classification accuracy Acc in Eq. (4) is calculated for each time sample within the time series of $(1/50) \cdot (TP + FP + FN + TN)$ duration.

$$Acc = \frac{TP + TN}{TP + FP + FN + TN} \cdot 100\% \tag{4}$$

Where TP is number of true positives, TN is number of true negatives, FP is number of misclassified false positives and FN is number of misclassified false negatives.

Table 2. Individual sample indexing accuracy for optimal model candidates.

No. of neurons	Accuracy	Processing time [s]
700	95.66 (98.9–94)	2.12
800	95.89 (99–93.3)	2.84
900	95.46 (97.5–93.6)	3.71

The average accuracy of the optimal ESN model candidates (Fig. 6) on test data was obtained over 12 experiments for each model.

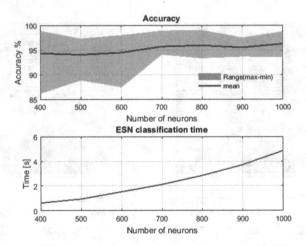

Fig. 6. Range of classification accuracy and measured times for ESN model classification (training and testing) relative to the number of neurons

The processing time was measured on a PC with 3.5 GHz CPU, 16 GB/2.4 GHz RAM, and a solid-state disk, using single CPU processing running on Ubuntu 14.04.

The accuracy achieved was above expectations, given the inclusion of all markers trajectories, fast interpolation and normalisation, and relatively small ESN model training portion (less than 40 %). The occurrence of errors regarding start and stop event samples, is considered as a random combination of classifier performance and possible uncertainties in regards to expert's decision boundaries of forehand event selection (Fig. 5).

4 Discussion, Limitation and Critique

Utilisation of motion data without ball flight, impact vibration or sound information has broad applicability to exergames and augmented sport coaching technology (e.g. pedometers, motion sensors, activity monitors). Since the demonstrated ESN/RC-based approach does not rely on traditional analytical, algorithmic, feature- or heuristic-based approaches, it is contended here that the solution is robust to minor displacement deviation between 3D marker positions and anatomical landmarks commonly used in biomechanics for marker placement representing a human body using a rigid stick figure model. Furthermore, for motion data obtained from video, image and signal processing, presented approach reveals decoupling of the processing of motion data from motion data sources. A strategy for future proofing is supported by enabling system developments with replaceable layers that have minimal dependency on data sources and formats compared to for example, algorithmic approaches that are 'hard-wired' to a specific computer vision system, or other signal sources.

Regarding the selection of development tools, choosing Python for ESN implementation allows portability and flexibility of a range of processing platforms to be utilised for stand-alone or distributed processing (e.g. via web services running on embedded Linux) without licensing and software registration costs. The animated 3D interactive stick figure player was prototyped in Matlab (R13), but due to virtual 3D camera integration requirements for smooth and accurate replay control, it was implemented in Delphi relying on a proprietary developed graphic engine. As a result, the 3D player runs as portable stand-alone executable file in multiple instances, without frame freezing on the single core machines (including Windows XP and Linux Ubuntu via Wine utility). Smooth and accurate replay is considered important for exergames, ACS user experience and for expert validation of human motion. The developed animated 3D interactive stick figure player was accurate enough for the experts (i.e. the author and three other certified tennis coaches) to identify errors and provide assessment and judgment of stylistic execution of the captured forehands.

The decision related to the use of synthetic motion data was influenced by a phenomenon where it is possible to tell whether an animated cartoon character motion was produced synthetically or via motion capture. The experiment decision was to rely only on captured motion data without the ball impact information.

In line with exergames (such as Xbox Kinect sampling at 30 Hz), the relatively small captured data set included variations of sport-specific characteristic motion patterns that were captured in higher precision and sampling rate for prototyping purposes. Motion patterns variations included forehand swings only, without actual ball impact, and with occasional corrupted samples (containing NaN values) due to limitations of utilised computer vision system for motion capture. Unlike with IMU sensors, computer vision systems may not always capture all frame data, which exergame users experience as occasional non-responsive input error. Similarly, in coaching contexts, overlooking a swing by a coach represents a possible human error and it is considered as a False Negative (*FN*) event. For augmented coaching systems, False Positive (*FP*) detection would trigger undesired automated analysis of events that did not occur. The achieved ESN classifier model implies that the RC-based approach represents a viable direction for discovery of fast classifiers that are robust for: utilised imperfect raw 3D data including noise, low sampling rate, fast linear averaging of missing data points, and arbitrary selection of marker placement and topology. Although the chosen grid-search for parameter optimisation is computationally intensive, in all experiments, the ESN model with the obtained parameters performed training and classification in shorter times than actual real-time durations of processed motion sequence. Future work will include combining heterogeneous motion detection and indexing approaches in order to assure additional robustness in processing of the unseen evolved motion patterns. Furthermore, heterogeneous approaches may include domain-specific algorithms (e.g. impact vibration, sound signal analysis) and sliding window-based algorithms (similar to [29]).

5 Conclusions, Recommendations and Future Work

The experimental results and the obtained 100 % of forehand recognition confirm that Reservoir Computing (RC) approaches such as ESN represent a viable generic approach to: 3D motion data pattern detection and indexing, and general Human Motion Modelling and Analysis (HMMA). In spite on computationally expensive parameter optimisation efforts, the resulting ESN model with 800 neurons was considered to be a fast classifier and to work in near-real-time on the 3D motion data set with 66 time-series captured at 50 Hz. Based on generic temporal and spatial event extraction approach, the presented method represents a viable alternative to existing approaches, which are relying on impact information such as sound, vibration or ball rebound that are used by other augmented coaching technologies. The benefits of the presented universal RC-based approach are that there are no requirements for: specific algorithm- or heuristic-based design and development, feature selection or feature extraction based on the available insights. Presented ESN/RC-based approach to extract characteristic motion pattern is applicable to exergames, embedded and ubiquitous augmented coaching technology, kinesiology and other disciplines such as surveillance and monitoring.

Future work will extend to multi-modal motion data collections and investigation of applications of computational intelligence in kinesiology for human motion modelling and analysis towards the advancements of automated augmented coaching systems, intelligent prosthetics and rehabilitation devices.

Acknowledgements. The author wishes to express his appreciation to developers of Oger Toolbox (http://organic.elis.ugent.be/organic/engine) utilised in this study. Tennis data have been obtained in Peharec polyclinic for physical therapy and rehabilitation, Pula (Croatia) during afterhours with support, rigour, watchful critical observations and general biomechanics assistance of Petar Bačić (biomechanics lab specialist and professional tennis coach). The author also wishes to express his gratitude to Dr. Stefan Schliebs, who before moving from academia to commercial research started to work on this project and provided valuable insights into use of Oger Toolbox, Python IDEs and R-Studio.

References

1. Bacic, B.: Bridging the gap between biomechanics and artificial intelligence. In: XXIV International Symposium on Biomechanics in Sports - ISBS 2006, Salzburg, pp. 371–374 (2006)
2. Bacic, B.: Evolving connectionist systems for adaptive sports coaching. In: Ishikawa, M., Doya, K., Miyamoto, H., Yamakawa, T. (eds.) Neural Information Processing, vol. 12, pp. 53–62. Springer, Heidelberg (2008)
3. Bačić, B.: Connectionist methods for data analysis and modelling of human motion in sporting activities. Ph. D. thesis, School of Computer and Mathematical Sciences, AUT University, Auckland (2013)
4. Bačić, B.: Prototyping and user interface design for augmented coaching systems with MATLAB and delphi: implementation of personal tennis coaching system. In: MATLAB Conference 2015, Auckland (2015)
5. Jaeger, H.: The "echo state" approach to analysing and training recurrent neural networks. Technical report, Fraunhofer Institute for Autonomous Intelligent Systems (2001)
6. Jaeger, H.: The "echo state" approach to analysing and training recurrent neural networks - with an erratum note. Technical report, German National Research Center for Information Technology (2010)
7. Schliebs, S.K., Kasabov, N.: Computational modeling with spiking neural networks. In: Kasabov, N. (ed.) Springer Handbook of Bio-/Neuroinformatics, pp. 625–646. Springer, Berlin (2014)
8. Maass, W.: Networks of spiking neurons: the third generation of neural network models. Neural Netw. **10**, 1659–1671 (1997)
9. Paugam-Moisy, H.: Spiking neuron networks a survey. Technical report, IDIAP Research Institute (2006)
10. Jaeger, H., Lukoševičius, M., Popovici, D., Siewert, U.: Optimization and applications of echo state networks with leaky-integrator neurons. Neural Netw. **20**, 335–352 (2007)
11. Verstraeten, D., Schrauwen, B., D'Haene, M., Stroobandt, D.: An experimental unification of reservoir computing methods. Neural Netw. **20**, 391–403 (2007)
12. Lukoševičius, M., Jaeger, H.: Reservoir computing approaches to recurrent neural network training. Comput. Sci. Rev. **3**, 127–149 (2009)
13. Bengio, Y.: Practical recommendations for gradient-based training of deep architectures. In: Montavon, G., Orr, G.B., Müller, K.-R. (eds.) Neural Networks: Tricks of the Trade, 2nd edn. LNCS, vol. 7700, pp. 437–478. Springer, Heidelberg (2012)
14. Tang, F., Tiňo, P., Chen, H.: Learning the deterministically constructed echo state networks. In: 2014 International Joint Conference on Neural Networks (IJCNN), Beijing, pp. 77–83 (2014)
15. Dolinský, J., Takagi, H.: Analysis and modeling of naturalness in handwritten characters. IEEE Trans. Neural Netw. **20**, 1540–1553 (2009)
16. Klette, R., Liu, D.: Inverse skeletal strokes. In: Huang, F., Sugimoto, A. (eds.) PSIVT 2013. LNCS, vol. 8334, pp. 1–11. Springer, Heidelberg (2014)
17. Hunt, D., Schliebs, S.: Continuous classification of spatio-temporal data streams using liquid state machines. In: Huang, T., Zeng, Z., Li, C., Leung, C.S. (eds.) ICONIP 2012, Part IV. LNCS, vol. 7666, pp. 626–633. Springer, Heidelberg (2012)
18. Hunt, D.P., Parry, D., Schliebs, S.: Exploring the applicability of reservoir methods for classifying punctual sports activities using on-body sensors. In: Thirty-Seventh Australasian Computer Science Conference (ACSC 2014), Auckland, pp. 67–73 (2014)

19. The Pusher, Part 2: The Art of Winning, The Pain of Losing https://www.youtube.com/watch?v=q8NOOikjb0c
20. Dunn, M., Goodwill, S., Wheat, J., Haake, S.: Assessing tennis player interactions with tennis courts. In: XXIX International Conference on Biomechanics in Sports, Porto, pp. 859–862 (2011)
21. Bahamonde, R.E., Knudson, D.: Kinetics of the upper extremity in the open and square stance tennis forehand. J. Sci. Med. Sport 6, 88–101 (2003)
22. Rota, S., Hautier, C., Creveaux, T., Champely, S., Guillot, A., Rogowski, I.: Relationship between muscle coordination and forehand drive velocity in tennis. J. Electromyogr. Kinesiol. 22, 294–300 (2012)
23. Reid, M., Elliott, B., Crespo, M.: Mechanics and learning practices associated with the tennis forehand: a review. J. Sports Sci. Med. 12, 225–231 (2013)
24. Landlinger, J., Lindinger, S., Stöggl, T., Wagner, H., Müller, E.: Key factors and timing patterns in the tennis forehand of different skill levels. J. Sports Sci. Med. 9, 643–651 (2010)
25. Knudson, D., Blackwell, J.: Variability of impact kinematics and margin for error in the tennis forehand of advanced players. Sports Eng. 8, 75–80 (2005)
26. Crespo, M., Higueras, J.: Forehands. In: Roetert, J.G. (ed.) World-class Tennis Technique, pp. 147–171. Human Kinetics, Champaign (2001)
27. Knudson, D.V., Morrison, C.S.: Qualitative Analysis of Human Movement. Human Kinetics, Champaign (2002)
28. Ceperic, V., Baric, A.: Reducing complexity of echo state networks with sparse linear regression algorithms. In: UKSim-AMSS 16th International Conference on Computer Modelling and Simulation (UKSim), 2014, pp. 26–31 (2014)
29. Bacic, B.: Towards a neuro fuzzy tennis coach: automated extraction of the region of interest (ROI). In: International Conference on Fuzzy Systems (FUZZ-IEEE) and International Joint Conference on Neural Networks (IJCNN), Budapest, pp. 703–708 (2004)

Image Segmentation and Classification

Multispectral Image Denoising Using Optimized Vector NLM Filter

Ahmed Ben Said[✉] and Sebti Foufou

CSE Department, College of Engineering, Qatar University,
P.O. Box 2713, Doha, Qatar
{abensaid,sfoufou}@qu.edu.qa

Abstract. In this paper, we present a Stein's Unbiased Risk Estimator (SURE) approach for Non-Local Mean filter to denoise multispectral images. We extend this filter to the vector case in order to take advantage from the additional spectral information brought by the multispectral imaging system. Experimental results show that the proposed optimized vector non-local mean filter (OVNLM) presented good denoising performance compared to several other approaches.

Keywords: Multispectral image · Vector non-local mean filter · Stein's Unbiased Risk Estimator

1 Introduction

Nowadays, so many applications rely on images. Computer vision and image processing tasks (classification, segmentation, denoising...) are involved in so many areas such as remote sensing [1,2], motion segmentation [3,4], face recognition [5,6]... Following the growing need for more sophisticated applications and reliable systems, multispectral imaging systems have emerged as a new technology that is able to deal with various problems encountered with broadband systems. Using multispectral images is justified by two main reasons. First, narrow spectral bands exhibit more relevant information compared to conventional broadband color and black and white images. Indeed, we obtain a unique spectral signature of the objects being captured. Such information can be used to enhance the accuracy of image processing applications. Second, by using multispectral images, we are able to separate the illumination information from object reflectance, in contrast to broadband images where it is almost impossible to do this separation. This separated information can now be used to normalize images. For instance, in face recognition applications, near-infrared spectral image can be combined with the visible image [7,8]. This approach has been widely used to construct more effective biometric systems [9–11]. Thermal infrared images have also been widely used. Thermal infrared sensors detect the heat energy radiated from the face which is independent from the illumination as in the case of reflectance [12,13]. Furthermore, thermal infrared is less sensitive to scattering and absorption by smoke or

T. Bräunl et al. (Eds.): PSIVT 2015, LNCS 9431, pp. 309–320, 2016.
DOI: 10.1007/978-3-319-29451-3_25

dust and invariant in case of illumination change [14]. It also allows to reveal anatomical information which is very useful in detecting disguised faces [15].

The quality of a multispectral image has great implications on the efficiency of image processing applications. Environmental corruption such as noise and blur is a common phenomena for any captured images due to many factors. In particular, a multispectral image can be subject to quality degradation due to the imperfectness of sensors [16]. Furthermore, noise is inevitable in all real broadband and multispectral images. Thus, it is essential to have techniques that ensure noise removal to adequate levels in order to increase performance in many image processing applications such as classification and segmentation [17]. Several techniques have been proposed to tackle the problem of multispectral image denoising. The work of Luisier et al. [18] constitutes the state of the art in multispectral image denoising. Authors proposed a denoising algorithm parameterized as a linear expansion of thresholds [19]. Optimization is carried out using Stein's Unbiased Risk Estimator (SURE) [20]. The thresholding function is point wise and wavelet based. A non-redundant orthonormal wavelet transform is applied on the noisy input image. Next, a vector-valued thresholding of individual multichannel wavelet coefficients is performed. Finally, an inverse wavelet transform is applied to obtain the denoised image. The application of an orthonormal wavelet transform is justified by two main properties. First, assuming a white Gaussian noise in the image domain Ω, its wavelet coefficients remain also Gaussian and are independent between subbands. Second, the Mean Square Error (MSE) in Ω is equal to the sum of subbands MSEs.

Authors in [2,21] proposed an optimization framework for the vector bilateral filter using SURE. They proved that within a neighborhood of a given edge pixel, a high Signal to Error (SER) measure is obtained by maximizing the weight attributed to neighbor pixels with similar values and minimizing the weight given to pixels with significant different values. Authors have also demonstrated that the SER of the vector version of the bilateral filter is always greater than the component wise 2D bilateral filter. The optimization scheme is based on the minimization of the MSE. However, the underlying difficulty of this measure is that it involves the original image which is unknown. To overcome this issue, SURE is applied and filter parameters are obtained by minimizing the expression of SURE. The obtained minimization problem is non-linear and is solved numerically using Sequential Quadratic Programming (SQP). Experiments on color and multispectral images have been conducted and comparison using the Peak Signal to Noise Ratio (PSNR) is presented.

Manjon et al. [22] have recently proposed a new algorithm for multispectral image denoising based on the Non-Local Mean (NLM) filter [23]. NLM filter is designed so that it takes advantage of the redundancy exhibited in the image. This redundancy is no longer pixel based but window based. In other words, every small window centered on a pixel is supposed to have many similar windows. These windows can be located anywhere in the image domain Ω and are no longer restricted to the neighborhood. In the multispectral framework, information from various bands are combined and a new weight is proposed. This filter is highly dependent on the choice of three parameters: The radius of the search window, the radius of the neighborhood window and a smoothing parameter that controls the degree of the smoothing. The latter is very important. Indeed, with a small value, little noise will be removed. On the other hand, with a high value, image will be blurred. Authors have set these parameters manually.

In our work, we propose a modified version of the NLM filter we call Optimized Vector NLM (OVNLM) filter, where we take into account the spectral dimension of the data. In addition, we propose an optimization framework to tune the filter parameters.

The remainder of this paper is organized as follows: Sect. 2 gives an overview of the NLM filter. We presents the proposed OVNLM filter in Sect. 3. In Sect. 4, experiments on multispectral images are conducted and comparison with other approaches is presented. We conclude in Sect. 5.

2   Overview of NLM Filter

We consider the following additive noise model:

$$I_{in}(s) = I_{or}(s) + N \tag{1}$$

Where $I_{in}(s)$ and $I_{or}(s)$ are the noisy and original pixels respectively, N is the Gaussian noise and $s \in \Omega$ is the pixel coordinates in the spatial domain. The basic assumption behind the definition of the NLM filter is that we need to take advantage of the high degree of redundancy in the image: the neighborhood of a pixel s is any set of pixels p in the image domain Ω such that a local window surrounding s is similar to the local window surrounding p [23]. The general case of NLM filter is given by:

$$I_{out}(s) = \sum_{p \in \Omega} \omega(s,p) I_{in}(p) \tag{2}$$

$\omega(s,p)$ is the weight calculated for each pixel. It is computed based on a similarity measure between pixels in positions s and p. $\omega(s,p)$ satisfies the following constraints:

$$0 \leq \omega(s,p) \leq 1$$
$$\sum_{p \in \Omega} \omega(s,p) = 1 \tag{3}$$

The similarity between two pixels s and p is measured as a decreasing function of the Gaussian weighted Euclidean distance $\|\cdot\|_{2,a}^2$, where $a > 0$ is the standard deviation of the Gaussian kernel. Let $N(s)$ and $N(p)$ be the pixel vectors of the gray level intensity within a squared neighborhood centered at positions s and p respectively.

$$\omega(s,p) = \frac{1}{C_i} exp \left(-\frac{\|N(s) - N(p)\|_{2,a}^2}{h^2} \right) \tag{4}$$

h^2 acts as a smoothing parameter. C_i is a normalization constant which ensures that $\sum_{p \in \Omega} \omega(s,p) = 1$.

$$C_i = \sum_{p \in \Omega} exp\left(-\frac{\|N(s) - N(p)\|_{2,a}^2}{h^2}\right) \tag{5}$$

The Gaussian weighted Euclidean distance is given by:

$$\|N(s) - N(p)\|_{2,a}^2 = \sum_{k \in K} G_a(k)(N(s-k) - N(p-k))^2 \tag{6}$$

Where K is a local window and $G_\alpha(k)$ is defined as:

$$G_\alpha(k) = \frac{1}{2\pi a^2} exp\left(-\frac{k_1^2 + k_2^2}{2a^2}\right), k = (k_1, k_2) \tag{7}$$

Thus, we can distinguish two main characteristics: the restored pixel is obtained by taking into account the contribution of pixels in the whole image and the weight computation is based on the similarity between local windows. Such characteristics have triggered researchers to design various novel methods [23].

3   Optimized Vector NLM Filter

To take advantage of the additional information brought by the spectral dimension, we extend the NLM filter to the vector case. In the multispectral context, we have the reflectance intensity at a given position in different spectral bands. Thus we are operating on a set of pixel vectors $I = \{(I_s)/s \in \Omega\}$. We define the vector NLM (VNLM) filter as:

$$I_{out}(s) = \sum_{p \in \Omega} \omega(s,p) I_{in}(p) \tag{8}$$

With the new formulation of the weight between two pixels at position s and p defined as:

$$\omega(s,p) = \frac{1}{C_i} exp(\frac{-1}{h^2} \sum_{k \in K} (I_{in}(s-k) - I_{in}(p-k))^T \Phi^{-1} \cdot$$
$$(I_{in}(s-k) - I_{in}(p-k)) \tag{9}$$

If $\Phi = I$, I is the identity matrix-, we have the classical Euclidean distance.

$$C(i) = \sum_{p \in \Omega} exp(-\frac{1}{h^2} \sum_{k \in K} (I_{in}(s-k) - I_{in}(p-k))^T \Phi^{-1} \cdot$$
$$(I_{in}(s-k) - I_{in}(p-k)) \tag{10}$$

The filter depends on two parameters: the smoothing parameter h and the covariance matrix Φ. Thus, we have:

$$I_{out}(s) = f(I_{in}(s), \Theta) \ with \ \Theta = (h, \Phi) \tag{11}$$

Where f is a non linear estimator and Θ is the filter parameter.

Our aim is to optimize the filter parameter Θ so that we can ensure the best parametrization of the filter in order to obtain the best denoising result. The performance of the estimator is generally evaluated using the mean square error (MSE):

$$MSE = \frac{1}{HL} \sum_{s \in \Omega} \|I_{out}(s) - I_{or}(s)\|^2 \tag{12}$$

However, the problem of such estimator is that the ground truth image $I_{or}(s)$ is unknown. MSE can be seen as a random variable of the noise. Its expected value is designated as the Risk R_θ and expressed as:

$$R_\theta = E(MSE) \tag{13}$$

The problem of estimating the risk without the need to dispose of the underlying image $I_{or}(s)$ is approached by Stein's Unbiased Risk Estimator (SURE) [18, 24]. Thus, we have [20]:

$$E\left(\|I_{out}(s) - I_{or}(s)\|^2\right) = E\left(\|I_{out}(s)\|^2\right)$$
$$- 2E\left(I_{out}(s)^T I_{or}(s)\right) + E\left(\|I_{or}(s)\|^2\right) \tag{14}$$

and:

$$E\left(I_{out}(s)^T I_{or}(s)\right) = E\left(f(I_{in}(s), \Theta)^T (I_{in}(s) - n_s)\right)$$
$$= E\left(I_{out}(s)^T I_{in}(s)\right) - E\left(f(I_{in}(s), \Theta)^T n_s\right) \tag{15}$$

If we consider a zero mean multivariate Gaussian noise, we have [18]:

$$E\left(f(I_{in}(s), \Theta)^T n_s\right) = E\left(trace\left\{\Psi^T \nabla_{I_{in}(s)} f(I_{in}(s), \Theta)\right\}\right) \tag{16}$$

With Ψ is the noise covariance matrix. By combining Eqs. 14 and 15, we end up with an expression without $I_{or}(s)$:

$$E\left(\|I_{out}(s) - I_{or}(s)\|^2\right) = E\left(\|I_{out}(s) - I_{in}(s)\|^2\right)$$
$$- trace(\Psi) + 2E\left(Tr\left\{\Psi^T \nabla_{I_{in}(s)} f(I_{in}(s), \Theta)\right\}\right) \tag{17}$$

Thus, the risk $\hat{R}_\theta$ is the unbiased risk estimator of MSE in Eq. 12 and is given by:

$$\hat{R}_\theta = \frac{1}{HL} \sum_{s \in \Omega} E\left(\|I_{out}(s) - I_{in}(s)\|^2\right) - trace(\Psi)$$
$$+ 2\frac{1}{HL} \sum_{s \in \Omega} E\left(trace\left\{\Psi^T \nabla_{I_{in}(s)} f(I_{in}(s))\right\}\right) \tag{18}$$

Where $\nabla_{I_{in}(s)} f(I_{in}(s)) = J_{f(I_{in}(s))}$ is the Jacobian matrix with respect to $I_{in}(s)$. $J_{f(I_{in}(s))}$ is given by [2]:

$$(J_{f(I_{in}(s))})_{i,j} = \frac{\partial f_i(I_{in}(s), \theta)}{\partial I_{in}(s_j)} =$$

$$\frac{\sum_{p \in \Omega} \frac{\partial \chi(p)}{\partial I_{in}(s_j)} I_{in}(s_i) + \delta_{i,j}}{\sum_{p \in \Omega} \chi(p)} - \frac{\left(\sum_{p \in \Omega} \frac{\partial \chi(p)}{\partial I_{in}(s_j)}\right) \left(\sum_{p \in \Omega} \chi(p) I_{in}(s_j)\right)}{\left(\sum_{p \in \Omega} \chi(p)\right)^2} \quad (19)$$

Where $\delta_{i,j}$ is the delta function and $\chi(p)$ is defined as:

$$\chi(p) = exp(-\frac{1}{h^2} \sum_{k \in K} (I_{in}(s-k) - I_{in}(p-k))^T \Phi^{-1}.$$
$$(I_{in}(s-k) - I_{in}(p-k)) \quad (20)$$

With the derivation of $\chi(p)$ (see appendix), we formulate the problem of vector NLM filter as a constrained optimization problem:

$$\begin{cases} (h_{opt}, \Phi_{opt}) = \arg \min_{h,\Phi}(\hat{R}(h, \Phi)) \\ s.t. : h > 0, \Phi \geq 0 \end{cases} \quad (21)$$

Note that in case of using the Euclidean distance, the only parameter to be optimized is h. We solve the constrained non-linear optimization problem using Sequential Quadratic Programming. Given a noisy image and noise covariance matrix which can be estimated with the median absolute deviation method [25], we minimize the risk value based on an optimal choice of parameters $\Theta = (h, \Phi)$ until we reach the maximum number of iteration $iter\_max$ or the risk value decreases below a preset threshold ξ. We implemented this approach in Matlab (R2015a). The minimization is performed using the function $fmincon$. We use a neighborhood window of 7×7.

4   Experimental Results

To assess the performance of our approach, we conduct experiments on multispectral images. We use the database of multispectral face images of IRIS Lab at University of Tennessee [26,27]. The IRIS Lab database was built between August 2005 and March 2006. It consists of 2624 multispectral face images taken along the visible spectrum in addition to thermal images with a resolution of 640×480. RGB images are also generated with a resolution of 2272×1704. These images are taken in different lightening conditions: Halogen light, daylight and fluorescent light. The total size of the database is 8.91 GB. A total of 82 participants were involved from different genders (76 % male, 24 % female), ethnicities as depicted in Table 1, ages, facial expression, genders and hair characteristics (Figs. 1 and 2).

Table 1. Ethnicity percentage in IRIS M^3 database

	Caucasian	Asian	Asian Indian	African descent
%	57 %	23 %	12 %	8 %

We apply the proposed OVLNM algorithm to denoise two mulispectral face images of 25 spectral bands illustrated in Figs. 1 (subject 1) and 2 (subject 2). We compare our approach with the vector SURE-LET [18] approach and MNLM algorithm proposed in [22]. The latter is also inspired from the NLM filter and adapted for multispectral image denoising where parameterization is conducted using ad hoc means. To evaluate the denoising performance, we used the Peak Signal to Noise Ratio (PSNR) metric. Experiments are basically conducted by contaminating original images with an additive Gaussian noise at different levels, then denoising algorithms are applied on the noisy images.

Figure 4 illustrates the PSNR variation with respect to noise standard variation for subject 1. Results demonstrate that OVNLM algorithm exhibits good performance especially in the area with a high level of noise. Indeed, with $\sigma = 100$, the OVNLM has an output PSNR of 23.03 dB compared to 18.62 dB and 18.11 dB obtained with SURE-LET and MNLM respectively. PSNR results for subject 2 are illustrated in Fig. 6. OVNLM exhibits also good performance particularly with heavily corrupted images ($\sigma = 100$). In fact, we obtained for OVNLM a PSNR of 23 dB compared to 18.58 dB and 17 dB with vector SURE-LET and MNLM (Fig. 5).

Fig. 1. Multispectral images for subject 1 in 480 nm, 560 nm and 720 nm

Fig. 2. Multispectral images for subject 2 in 480 nm, 560 nm and 720 nm

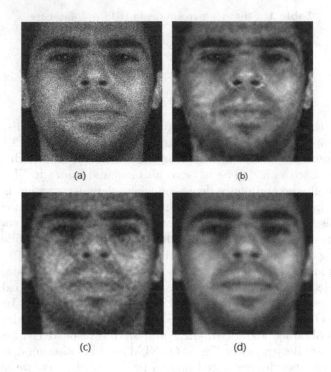

(a)   (b)

(c)   (d)

Fig. 3. Subject 1: (a) Noisy image (b) SURE-LET (c) MNLM (d) Proposed

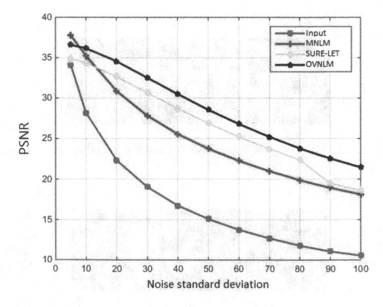

Fig. 4. PSNR curves for subject 1

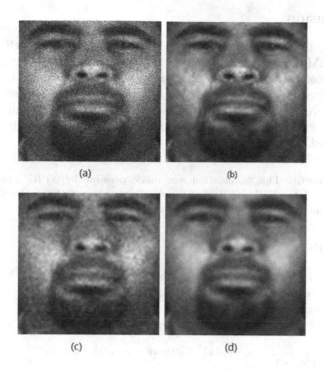

Fig. 5. Subject 2: (a) Noisy image (b) SURE-LET (c) MNLM (d) Proposed

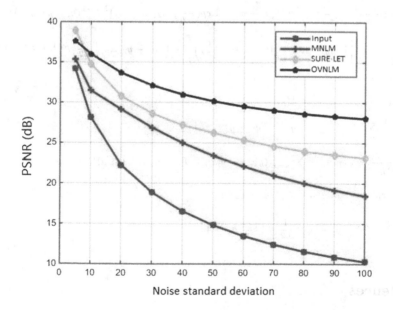

Fig. 6. PSNR curves for subject 2

5   Conclusion

The proposed filter is inspired from the NLM filter. Our approach is based on extending NLM filter to the vector case and applying an optimization approach in order to automatically tune parameters in a way that guarantees better results. Results demonstrate that the proposed approach exhibits promising denoising performance. Nevertheless, the computation burden is still an important issue with NLM in general. Further techniques to speed up the computation should be investigated.

Acknowledgment. This publication was made possible by NPRP grant #4-1165-2-453 from the Qatar National Research Fund (a member of Qatar Foundation). The statements made herein are solely the responsibility of the authors.

A   Appendix

Let: $\chi(p) = exp\left(-\frac{1}{h^2}\sum_{k\in K}(y_{s-k} - y_{p-k})^T \Phi^{-1}(y_{s-k} - y_{p-k})\right).$

- $p - s \in K$:

$$= exp(-\frac{1}{h^2}(y_s - y_p)^T \Phi^{-1}(y_s - y_p)) \cdot exp(-\frac{1}{h^2}(y_{2s-p} - y_s)^T \Phi^{-1}(y_{2s-p} - y_s)).$$

$$exp(-\frac{1}{h^2}\sum_{\substack{k\in K \\ k\notin\{0,p-s\}}}(y_{s-k} - y_{p-k})^T \Phi^{-1}(y_{s-k} - y_{p-k}))$$

$$\implies \frac{\partial\chi(p)}{\partial y_{s_j}} = exp(-\frac{1}{h^2}\sum_{\substack{k\in K \\ k\notin\{0,p-s\}}}(y_{s-k} - y_{p-k})^T \Phi^{-1}(y_{s-k} - y_{p-k})).$$

$$\frac{\partial}{\partial y_{s_j}}(exp(-\frac{1}{h^2}(y_s - y_p)^T \Phi^{-1}(y_s - y_p)) \cdot exp(-\frac{1}{h^2}(y_{2s-p} - y_s)^T \Phi^{-1}(y_{2s-p} - y_s)))$$

$$\frac{\partial\chi(p)}{\partial y_{s_j}} = \chi(p)\left[\left((y_p - y_s)^T \frac{1}{h^2}(\Phi^{-1} + \Phi^{-1T})\right)^T_j + \left((y_s - y_{2s-p})^T \frac{1}{h^2}(\Phi^{-1} + \Phi^{-1T})\right)^T_j\right]$$

- $p - s \notin K$:

$$= exp(-\frac{1}{h^2}(y_s - y_p)^T \Phi^{-1}(y_s - y_p)).$$

$$exp(-\frac{1}{h^2}\sum_{\substack{k\in K \\ k\neq 0}}(y_{s-k} - y_{p-k})^T \Phi^{-1}(y_{s-k} - y_{p-k}))$$

$$\implies \frac{\partial\chi(p)}{\partial y_{s_j}} = exp(-\frac{1}{h^2}\sum_{\substack{k\in K \\ k\neq 0}}(y_{s-k} - y_{p-k})^T \Phi^{-1}(y_{s-k} - y_{p-k})).$$

$$\frac{\partial}{\partial y_{s_j}}(exp(-\frac{1}{h^2}(y_s - y_p)^T \Phi^{-1}(y_s - y_p)))$$

$$\frac{\partial\chi(p)}{\partial y_{s_j}} = \chi(p)\left((y_p - y_s)^T \frac{1}{h^2}(\Phi^{-1} + \Phi^{-1T})\right)^T_j$$

References

1. Landgrebe, D.A.: Signal Theory Methods in Multispectral Remote Sensing. Wiley, Chichester (2003)

2. Peng, H., Rao, R., Dianat, S.: Multispectral image denoising with optimized vector bilateral filter. IEEE Trans. Image Process. **23**(1), 264–273 (2014)
3. Ben Said, A., Hadjidj, R., Foufou, S.: Cluster validity index based on jeffrey divergence. Pattern Anal. Appl. 1–11 (2015)
4. Tron, R., Vidal, R.: A benchmark for the comparison of 3-d motion segmentation algorithms. In: IEEE Conference on Computer Vision and Pattern Recognition, 2007, CVPR 2007, pp. 1–8 (2007)
5. Georghiades, A., Belhumeur, P., Kriegman, D.: From few to many: illumination cone models for face recognition under variable lighting and pose. IEEE Trans. Pattern Anal. Mach. Intell. **23**(6), 643–660 (2001)
6. Lee, K.C., Ho, J., Kriegman, D.: Acquiring linear subspaces for face recognition under variable lighting. IEEE Trans. Pattern Anal. Mach. Intell. **27**(5), 684–698 (2005)
7. Omri, F., Foufou, S.: A novel image texture fusion scheme for improving multispectral face recognition. In: 2014 Tenth International Conference on Signal-Image Technology and Internet-Based Systems (SITIS), pp. 43–48 (2014)
8. Omri, F., Foufou, S., Abidi, M.: NIR and visible image fusion for improving face recognition at long distance. In: Elmoataz, A., Lezoray, O., Nouboud, F., Mammass, D. (eds.) ICISP 2014. LNCS, vol. 8509, pp. 549–557. Springer, Heidelberg (2014)
9. Meraoumia, A., Chitroub, S., Bouridane, A.: Biometric recognition systems using multispectral imaging. In: Hassanien, A.E., Kim, T.H., Kacprzyk, J., Awad, A.I. (eds.) Bio-inspiring Cyber Security and Cloud Services: Trends and Innovations, vol. 70, pp. 321–347. Springer, Heidelberg (2014)
10. Pan, Z., Healey, G., Prasad, M., Tromberg, B.: Face recognition in hyperspectral images. IEEE Trans. Pattern Anal. Mach. Intell. **25**(12), 1552–1560 (2003)
11. Pan, Z., Healey, G.E., Prasad, M., Tromberg, B.J.: Hyperspectral face recognition under variable outdoor illumination. In: Proceedings of SPIE 5425, Algorithms and Technologies for Multispectral, Hyperspectral, and Ultraspectral Imagery X, pp. 520–529 (2004)
12. Kong, S., Heo, J., Boughorbel, F., Zheng, Y., Abidi, B., Koschan, A., Yi, M., Abidi, M.: Multiscale fusion of visible and thermal ir images for illumination-invariant face recognition. Int. J. Comput. Vis. **71**(2), 215–233 (2007)
13. Kong, S.G., Heo, J., Abidi, B.R., Paik, J., Abidi, M.A.: Recent advances in visual and infrared face recognitiona review. Comput. Vis. Image Underst. **97**(1), 103–135 (2005)
14. Socolinsky, D.A., Selinger, A., Neuheisel, J.D.: Face recognition with visible and thermal infrared imagery. Comput. Vis. Image Underst. **91**(12), 72–114 (2003)
15. Pavlidis, I., Symosek, P.: The imaging issue in an automatic face/disguise detection system. In: IEEE Workshop on Computer Vision Beyond the Visible Spectrum: Methods and Applications, 2000. Proceedings, pp. 15–24 (2000)
16. Corner, B.R., Narayanan, R.M., Reichenbach, S.E.: Noise estimation in remote sensing imagery using data masking. Int. J. Remote Sens. **24**(4), 689–702 (2003)
17. Abrams, M.C., Cain, S.C.: Sampling, radiometry, and image reconstruction for polar and geostationary meteorological remote sensing systems (2002)
18. Luisier, F., Blu, T.: Sure-let multichannel image denoising: interscale orthonormal wavelet thresholding. IEEE Trans. Image Process. **17**(4), 482–492 (2008)
19. Blu, T., Luisier, F.: The SURE-LET approach to image denoising. IEEE Trans. Image Process. **16**, 2778–2786 (2007)
20. Stein, C.M.: Estimation of the mean of a multivariate normal distribution. Ann. Stat. **9**(6), 1135–1151 (1981)

21. Peng, H., Rao, R., Dianat, S.: Optimized vector bilateral filter for multispectral image denoising. In: 2012 19th IEEE International Conference on Image Processing (ICIP), pp. 2141–2144 (2012)
22. Manjon, J.V., Robles, M., Thacker, N.A.: Multispectral mri denoising using non-local means. In: Medical Image Understanding and Analysis, pp. 41–46 (2007)
23. Buades, A., Coll, B., Morel, J.: A review of image denoising algorithms, with a new one. Multiscale Model. Simul. 4(2), 490–530 (2005)
24. Chaux, C., Duval, L., Benazza-Benyahia, A., Pesquet, J.: A nonlinear stein-based estimator for multichannel image denoising. IEEE Trans. Signal Process. 56(8), 3855–3870 (2008)
25. Huber, P.: Robust Statistics. Wiley, New York (1981)
26. Bouchech, H., Foufou, S., Koschan, A., Abidi, M.: A kernelized sparsity-based approach for best spectral bands selection for face recognition. Multimedia Tools Appl. 74, 1–24 (2014)
27. Chang, H., Harishwaran, H., Yi, M., Koschan, A., Abidi, B., Abidi, M.: An in door and outdoor, multimodal, multispectral and multi-illuminant database for face recognition. In: Conference on Computer Vision and Pattern Recognition Workshop, 2006. CVPRW 2006, pp. 54–54 (2006)

Scene-Based Non-uniformity Correction with Readout Noise Compensation

Martin Bürker[1]([⊠]) and Hendrik P.A. Lensch[2]

[1] Daimler AG, Wilhelm-Runge-Straße 11, 89081 Ulm, Germany
martin.burker@daimler.com
[2] Department of Computer Science, Computer Graphics,
Tübingen University, Sand 14, 72076 Tübingen, Germany

Abstract. Thermal cameras can not be calibrated as easily as RGB cameras, since their noise characteristics change over time; thus scene-based non-uniformity correction (SBNUC) has been developed. We present a method to boost the convergence of these algorithms by removing the readout noise form the image before it is processed. The readout noise can be estimated by capturing a series of pictures with varying exposure times, fitting a line for each pixel and thereby estimating the bias of the pixel. When this is subtracted from the image a noticeable portion of the noise is compensated. We compare the results of two common SBNUC algorithms with and without this compensation. The mean average error improves by several orders of magnitude, which allows faster convergence with smaller step sizes. The readout noise compensation (RNC) can be used to improve the performance of any SBNUC approach.

1 Introduction

In thermal cameras the noise is both spatially varying and the noise characteristics change over time. Hence, it is necessary to constantly update the noise estimate. Scene-based non-uniformity correction (SBNUC) estimates the noise parameters of the video stream online.

We present a method to estimate the readout noise by capturing a series of images with different exposure times. Adding readout noise compensation (RNC) to existing SBNUC techniques increases the initial image quality drastically.

The variety of SBNUC techniques can be devided in three major groups: Neural net (NN) algorithms assuming neighboring pixels to capture the same brightness, constant statistics/constant range (CR) algorithms assuming a uniform distribution of a pixel's values over time and motion constraint algorithms assuming a scene point can be found at a different location in the following frame. All of these approaches start from an unnecessarily noisy image due to the contained readout noise.

By removing this fixed pattern noise (FPN) the SBNUC algorithm can work on images with less corruption, which leads to faster convergence and better results. We compared NN and CR algorithms with and without RNC to validate the advantage of this method. Since the step size of the adjustment can be reduced it also has beneficial effects on ghosting.

T. Bräunl et al. (Eds.): PSIVT 2015, LNCS 9431, pp. 321–331, 2016.
DOI: 10.1007/978-3-319-29451-3_26

2   Previous Work

The choice of a photometric calibration process for a digital cameras is depending on the wavelength the sensor is sensitive to. For conventional RGB cameras and some infrared cameras the procedure requires the user to take dark frames, where the lens is covered to let no light fall onto the sensor, and flat-fields, where every pixel is illuminated with the same amount of brightness (see Granados et al. [2] for details). For cameras sensitive to mid- and far-infrared it is not possible to take dark frames, since the material to cover the lens would have to be cooled to $0\,K$ or it will emit noticeable radiation.

To overcome this problem special calibration devices called black body radiators have been developed. They have a spatially uniform area of material with the same temperature. The dark frame can be extrapolated by taking measurements at different temperatures.

One of the first methods for SBNUC has been developed by Scribner et al. [9]. They proposed to learn the gain and offset by minimizing the difference to the mean value of the nearest neighbors with steepest descent. This approach is inspired by the way neural nets backpropagate errors to adopt to the desired output. Harris and Chiang [3] assume that the brightness corresponding to a fixed pixel over time follows a Gaussian distribution with zero mean and unit variance. They called it constant-statistics constraint and used it to level out the mean and standard variation of the detector. Geng et al. [1] improved the algorithm by combining the Gaussian kernel with a temporal median. The median filter adds robustness to variation on the sample distribution. Hayat et al. [4] assume a uniform distribution of the signal. The incident radiation is estimated by using the mean and variance of the pixel values in a time window. The minimum and maximum values of the image in that window are used to project the values back to the original domain. This algorithm was refined by Torres, Reeves and Hayat [11] with a recursive method for updating the parameters of the constant range algorithm, which in turn was enhanced by Pezoa et al. [5] by replacing the simple moving average with an exponential moving average. Torres and Hayat [10] also developed a Kalman filter considering gain and offset of the detectors as state variables modeled by a Gauss-Markov process. The Kalman filter approach was then modified by San Martin, Torres and Pezoa [7] assuming that the gain does not change over time and only the offset has to be estimated. A more recent development are interframe registration based methods, like the one proposed by Zuo et al. [14]. They find the translation between two consecutive frames by computing the cross-power spectrum. The phase correlation is limited to pure translations, so this method it best suited for scanning applications where the scene moves parallel to the image plane, or vice versa.

3   Noise Model

There are two different kinds of noise cameras are susceptible to: temporal and spatial. While temporal noise can be easily dealt with by averaging multiple frames, it is often impossible to do so due to motion in the scene or the limited frame rate of the camera. Spatial noise, or non-uniformity is the deviation of the response of each pixel to the same signal.

3.1 Temporal Noise

The variation of a pixels value exposed to the same signal over time is called temporal noise. It is caused by small variations in the conversion of light into electrons and holes (photon shot noise), the temporal variations of electrons and holes generated by the sensors temperature (dark current shot noise) and the noise of the electronic device itself occurring during the charge-to-voltage transfer and analog-to-digital conversion (readout noise).

As stated before, temporal noise can be compensated by averaging multiple consecutive frames. If this not practical the noise is often suppressed by low-pass filtering or more advanced methods in a companion chip in the camera. For calibration purposes, one wants to make sure such noise compensation is turned off since it adds unwanted non-linearity.

3.2 Spatial Noise

The quantum efficiency of the pixels is not uniform throughout the sensor i.e., for the same signal the digital value differs from pixel to pixel. This is called spatial noise and compensated by photometric calibration also known as non-uniformity correction.

Photo-Response Non-uniformity (PRNU). Each pixel consist of a photo-sensitive area in which the light is converted into current. The current is converted into voltage, which is amplified to make the result less susceptible to noise in the readout process. Due to small differences in size and material there are not two identical pixels and hence the resulting value is not the same for the same signal. This is called photo-response non-uniformity and simplified to a per pixel gain factor.

Dark Current Non-uniformity (DCNU). As each pixel responds different to light it also reacts different to temperature. The amount of current generated by temperature is called dark current and the different susceptibility to it is called dark current non-uniformity. It is modeled as an additive offset to the signal.

4 Photometric Calibration

4.1 Camera Model

A camera converts light into digital values. The irradiance $X^{(j)}$ at a pixel position j generates a digital value

$$Y^{(j)} = gt(a^{(j)}X^{(j)} + b^{(j)}) + N_R, \tag{1}$$

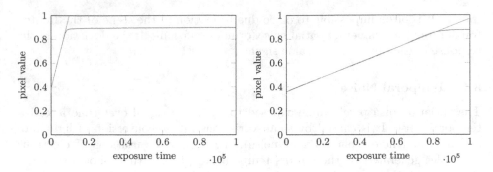

Fig. 1. Two pixels at different positions. On the left a pixel capturing a bright signal; on the right a pixel capturing a dark signal. The blue line represents the pixel value for each exposure time with 100 sampling points. The green line is the estimate of the linear regression (LMS). The values are scaled from 14 bits per pixel to $[0, 1]$, the exposure time is in μs (Color figure online).

where g is a global gain factor, t is the exposure time, $a^{(j)}$ is the per pixel gain induced by PRNU, $b^{(j)}$ is the offset induced by DCNU and N_R is the readout noise. The camera response is assumed to be linear and, unlike in [2], the quantization is omitted (Fig. 1).

4.2   Non-uniformity Correction (NUC)

Most NUC algorithms drop the readout noise N_R and global gain g which simplifies the equation and allows to compute the irradiance $X^{(j)}$ (or some value proportional to it) by estimating the per-pixel gain $a^{(j)}$ and offset $b^{(j)}$, by

$$X^{(j)} \sim \frac{Y^{(j)}/t - b^{(j)}}{a^{(j)}}. \tag{2}$$

As we will show it is not advisable to omit the readout noise. It is neither negligible, nor hard to measure.

5   Readout Noise Compensation

In theory the readout noise is measured by taking a bias frame. That is an image captured with zero integration time which according to the camera model (Eq. 1) would consist only of readout noise. The problem is, no camera can reset and readout the sensor with no delay. This means there is always dark current present in the picture. One way is to set the integration time to the minimum value and cover the lens, as one would taking a dark frame. The captured image should contain only readout noise and very little dark current. We found that the cameras we have access to don't allow a integration time of zero and even very small values were not applied correctly.

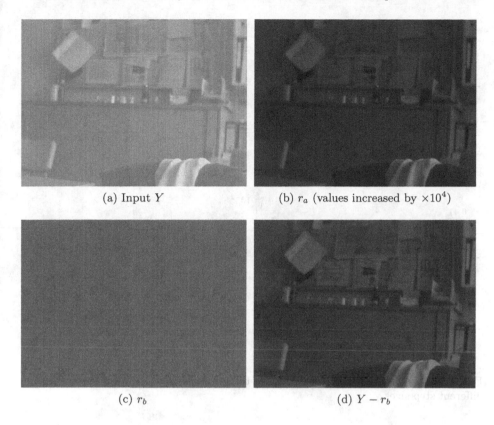

(a) Input Y (b) r_a (values increased by $\times 10^4$)

(c) r_b (d) $Y - r_b$

Fig. 2. The image (a) can be preprocessed by estimating the readout noise (c) and subtracting it from the input.

Another way is to estimate a pixel value with zero integration time by linear regression. This is only possible if the camera response curve is fairly regular i. e., the digital value should change with the same factor as the integration time. For a single pixel j the same scene point is captured with different exposure times $t_1, t_2, ..., t_n$, so the pixel values are

$$
\begin{pmatrix} Y_1^{(j)} \\ Y_2^{(j)} \\ \vdots \\ Y_n^{(j)} \end{pmatrix} = r_a^{(j)} \begin{pmatrix} t_1 \\ t_2 \\ \vdots \\ t_n \end{pmatrix} + r_b^{(j)}, \tag{3}
$$

where r_a and r_b can be estimated by linear regression e.g., least mean square. To get more accurate results, the temporal noise can be reduced by averaging multiple exposures or the number of integration times can be increased. Note that it is not necessary to know the signal $X^{(j)}$ or any of the other variables in

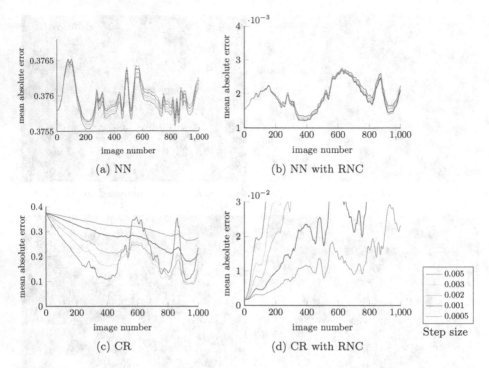

Fig. 3. The mean absolute error (MAE) to the ground truth of the Xenics Bobcat for different step sizes.

Eq. 1, since the parameters

$$r_a^{(j)} = g(a^{(j)} X^{(j)} + b^{(j)}), \text{ and}$$
$$r_b^{(j)} = N_R \tag{4}$$

already comprise them. It is essential that none of the values $Y_i^{(j)}$ is saturated.

We can now simply remove the readout noise by subtracting $r_b^{(j)}$ from the pixel value $Y^{(j)}$ (see Fig. 2).

Readout noise is classified as temporal noise, which means it should not have a different average for different pixels. This means either that there is also a spatial non-uniformity in readout noise, or that the non-uniformity we found is caused by a noise source which our camera model does not contain.

6   Evaluation

Our readout noise compensation (RNC) has been evaluated on two common SBNUC algorithms: neural nets (Scribner et al. [8]) and constant range (Hayat et al. [4]). Both algorithms were implemented on a graphics card with the following improvements:

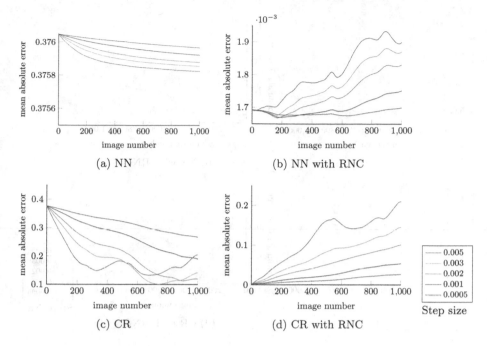

Fig. 4. The mean absolute error to the evaluation data of the Xenics Bobcat for different step sizes.

- The neural net algorithm was implemented with the adaptive learning rate from Torres et al. [12].
- The constant range approach was implemented according to Redlich et al. [6]. The minimum and maximum of the range were set per pixel to the lowest and highest value of the frames processed.

A Xenics Bobcat-640-CL and a Raptor Photonics OWL 640 CameraLink were used for the evaluation. The sequences used were captured with the cameras mounted behind the (uncoated) windshield of a car. Due to the different frame rates, the length of the sequences differ from each other, so we took the first 1000 frames of each sequence. The images were processed in the order they were captured in to simulate an online calibration.

The results are heavily depending on the chosen step size. If it is too small, the algorithm would take longer than needed; if they are too big the algorithm would produce ghosting (overfitting). In general it is advisable to decrease the learning rate over time, which is called annealing (see Zeiler [13]), but for comparison it is sufficient to use a fixed step size.

6.1 Comparison to Ground Truth

The error was measured in mean absolute error (MAE) to a ground truth. The ground truth is the image corrected by flatfielding and dark frame subtraction.

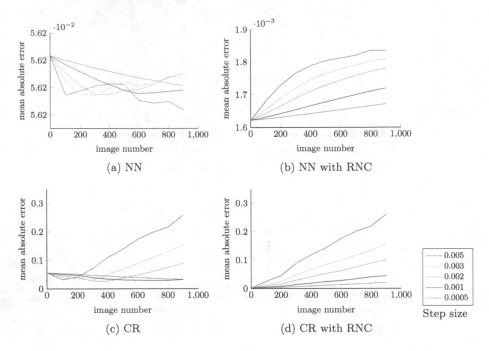

Fig. 5. The mean absolute error to the evaluation data of the Raptor OWL for different step sizes.

For each camera several 50 flatfields and 50 dark frames at operating temperature were acquired. The mean flatfield ff and mean dark frame b are used to calculate the per-pixel gain (similar to [2])

$$a^{(j)} = \frac{ff^{(j)} - b^{(j)}}{1/m \sum_{j=1}^{m} \left(ff^{(j)} - b^{(j)} \right)}. \tag{5}$$

The ground truth is then computed according to Eq. 2. Since it is not used in any of the evaluation algorithms, the global gain is not corrected for. For a valid ground truth it is absolutely necessary to capture dark frames. This is only possible with cameras sensitive to reflected and not thermal light, which is why we used short-wave infrared cameras for the evaluation (Fig. 5).

6.2   Comparison to Evaluation Data Set

The result of each frame is also compared to a random (but fixed) set of 30 images from other sequences. This tests the generality of the current gain and offset. The overfitting to pixels that change only slightly is penalized when choosing uncorrelated images to compute the MAE.

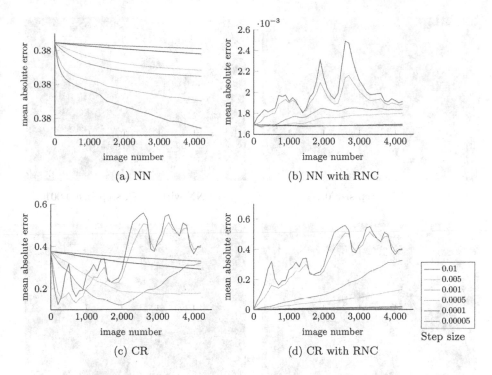

Fig. 6. The mean absolute error to the evaluation data of the Xenics Bobcat for different step sizes.

6.3   Longer Sequence

To make sure we do not stop the evaluation before the algorithms could exploit their full potential, we used a 4235 frame sequence of the Xenics Bobcat (Fig. 6). Also we used a wider range of step sizes with higher values to give the NN the chance to take bigger steps towards a smooth image and smaller values to let the algorithms with RNC slowly decrease the MAE even more.

6.4   Results

As Figs. 3 and 4 show, without RNC the algorithms could not achieve an MAE even close to the error of the pictures with RNC after 1000 frames. The MAE achieved with RNC is around 0.16 %, whereas the lowest MAE achieved without RNC is 9.1 % (CR to ground truth), or 11.7 % (CR to evaluation data). As Fig. 6 shows, even after 4235 frames none of the algorithms could decrease the MAE significantly under the initial error of RNC. The lowest MAE to the evaluation data was achieved by NN with RNC with a step size of 0.002 after 164 frames.

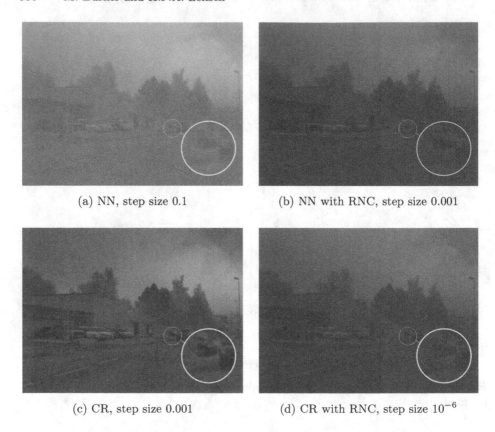

(a) NN, step size 0.1   (b) NN with RNC, step size 0.001

(c) CR, step size 0.001   (d) CR with RNC, step size 10^{-6}

Fig. 7. Frame 1000 of the sequence. The results with RNC (b) and (d) have both an MAE of < 0.002. The NN algorithm (a) shows ghosting and the CR approach (c) still has visible FPN. For displazing purposes, the brightness of (b) and (d) has been increased.

7   Conclusion

We showed that the proposed RNC gives the actual SBNUC algorithm a way better starting point. Figure 7 shows that the remaining non-uniformity after 1000 frames is - with both tested algorithms - hard to see and the MAE is smaller than 0.2 %. Since the RNC is independent from the SBNUC it can be also used with other algorithms than NN and CR. Even without SBNUC the RNC reduces the FPN considerably. Although, for long sequences we recommend to use SBNUC with a low step size, which can smooth out changes in dark current noise that is common in thermal cameras. In theory, once the parameters are known they can be reused unlimited, but this has not been researched and the parameters can be updated every time the camera is not moving.

References

1. Geng, L., Chen, Q., Qian, W., Zhang, Y.: Scene-based nonuniformity correction algorithm based on temporal median filter. J. Opt. Soc. Korea **17**(3), 255–261 (2013)
2. Granados, M., Ajdin, B., Wand, M., Theobalt, C., Seidel, H.P., Lensch, H.P.A.: Optimal HDR reconstruction with linear digital cameras. In: IEEE Computer Society Conference on Computer Vision and Pattern Recognition, vol. 1, pp. 215–222. IEEE, June 2010
3. Harris, J.G., Chiang, Y.M.: Nonuniformity correction using the constant-statistics constraint: analog and digital implementations. In: Proceedings of SPIE, vol. 3061, pp. 895–905 (1997)
4. Hayat, M.M., Torres, S.N., Armstrong, E., Cain, S.C., Yasuda, B.: Statistical algorithm for nonuniformity correction in focal-plane arrays. Appl. Opt. **38**, 772–780 (1999)
5. Pezoa, J.E., Torres, S.N., Córdova, J.P., Reeves, R.A.: An enhancement to the constant range method for nonuniformity correction of infrared image sequences. In: Sanfeliu, A., Martínez Trinidad, J.F., Carrasco Ochoa, J.A. (eds.) CIARP 2004. LNCS, vol. 3287, pp. 525–532. Springer, Heidelberg (2004)
6. Redlich, R., Figueroa, M., Torres, S.N., Pezoa, J.E.: Embedded nonuniformity correction in infrared focal plane arrays using the Constant Range algorithm. Infrared Phys. Technol. **69**, 164–173 (2015)
7. San Martin, C., Torres, S., Pezoa, J.E.: Statistical recursive filtering for offset nonuniformity estimation in infrared focal-plane-array sensors. Infrared Phys. Technol. **51**(6), 564–571 (2008)
8. Scribner, D., Sarkady, K., Kruer, M., Caulfield, J., Hunt, J., Colbert, M., Descour, M.: Adaptive retina-like preprocessing for imaging detector arrays. In: IEEE International Conference on Neural Networks, pp. 1955–1960 (1993)
9. Scribner, D.A., Sarkady, K.A., Caulfield, J.T., Kruer, M.R., Katz, G., Gridley, C.J., Herman, C.: Nonuniformity correction for staring IR focal plane arrays using scene-based techniques. In: Proceedings of SPIE, Aplications of Artificial Neural Networks, vol. 1308, pp. 224–233 (1990)
10. Torres, S.N., Hayat, M.M.: Kalman filtering for adaptive nonuniformity correction in infrared focal-plane arrays. J. Opt. Soc. Am. A Opt. Image Sci. Vis. **20**(3), 470–480 (2003)
11. Torres, S.N., Reeves, R.A.: Scene-based nonuniformity correction method using constant-range: performance and analysis. In: Proceedings of 6th World Multiconference on Systemics, Cybernetics and Informatics, vol. 9, pp. 224–229 (2002)
12. Torres, S.N., Vera, E.M., Reeves, R.A., Sobarzo, S.K.: Adaptive scene-based nonuniformity correction method for infrared-focal plane arrays. In: Holst, G.C. (ed.) Society of Photo-Optical Instrumentation Engineers (SPIE) Conference Series, vol. 5076, pp. 130–139, August 2003
13. Zeiler, M.D.: ADADELTA: An Adaptive Learning Rate Method. arXiv:1212.5701 [cs.LG] (2012)
14. Zuo, C., Chen, Q., Gu, G., Sui, X.: Scene-based nonuniformity correction algorithm based on interframe registration. J. Opt. Soc. Am. A Opt. Image Sci. Vis. **28**(6), 1164–1176 (2011)

A Color Quantization Based on Vector Error Diffusion and Particle Swarm Optimization Considering Human Visibility

Ryosuke Kubota[1(✉)], Hakaru Tamukoh[2], Hideaki Kawano[3], Noriaki Suetake[4],
Byungki Cha[5], and Takashi Aso[5]

[1] Department of Intelligent System Engineering, National Institute of Technology,
Ube College, 2-14-1 Tokiwadai, Ube-shi, Yamaguchi 755-8555, Japan
kubota@ube-k.ac.jp
[2] Graduate School of Life Science and Systems Engineering,
Kyushu Institute of Technology, 2-4 Hibikino, Wakamatsu-ku,
Kitakyushu-shi, Fukuoka 808-0196, Japan
tamukoh@brain.kyutech.ac.jp
[3] Graduate School of Engineering, Kyushu Institute of Technology, 1-1 Sensui-cho,
Tobata-ku, Kitakyushu-shi, Fukuoka 804-8550, Japan
kawano@ecs.kyutech.ac.jp
[4] Graduate School of Science and Engineering, Yamaguchi University, 1677-1
Yoshida, Yamaguchi-shi, Yamaguchi 753-8511, Japan
suetake@sci.yamaguchi-u.ac.jp
[5] Faculty of Management and Information Sciences, Kyushu Institute of Information
Sciences, 6-3-1 Saifu, Dazaifu-shi, Fukuoka 818-0117, Japan
{cha,taso}@kiis.ac.jp

Abstract. In this paper, we propose a new color quantization method
for generation of the color-reduced images. The proposed method
employs a vector error diffusion (VED) method and a particle swarm
optimization (PSO). VED method based on Floyd-Steinberg dithering is
used for display of the color-reduced image. Furthermore, a color palette
used in VED method is optimized by PSO. PSO generates the effective color palette with evaluating a human visibility of the color-reduced
image on the display. The validity and the effectiveness of the proposed
method are confirmed by some experiments.

Keywords: Color quantization · Vector error diffusion · Particle swarm
optimization · Color-reduced image · Restricted color image

1 Introduction

Electronic papers (e-paper) have become increasingly popular for general con-
sumers [1]. The e-paper is a display technology, and has the combination of
viewing characteristics and highly portability as well as those of the ordinary
printed-paper. Recently, some display companies provide not only the monochrome e-papers, but also the color e-papers. In addition, the color e-papers

T. Bräunl et al. (Eds.): PSIVT 2015, LNCS 9431, pp. 332–343, 2016.
DOI: 10.1007/978-3-319-29451-3_27

can display images as well as texts. However, there are no full color e-papers in the present market. Furthermore, the power consumption of the color e-paper becomes large with increasing the number of colors to be displayed. It is thus preferable to display the color-reduced image for long-time using.

In order to generate the color-reduced image, color quantization methods are used generically. The color image quantization is an important issue in the fields of image processing and computer graphics. The popular color quantization methods are popularity algorithm (PA) [2], median cut algorithm (MCA) [2], k-means clustering (KMC) [3] and so on. Those methods generate a color palette containing K colors. After generating the color palette, each pixel value in the full color image is replaced into the quantized value in the color palette. PA chooses the K colors with the highest frequencies, and generates the color palette by using the chosen K colors. PA is very simple, but needs preprocessing, e.g. multilevel dithering, to decrease the number of colors in the original full color image. Further, the essential details in the original full color image cannot be preserved appropriately, because some colors with low frequencies are discarded. On the other hand, MCA and KMC are kinds of partitioning algorithms. MCA divides the color space of the original full color image into K rectangular boxes containing an equal number of pixels in the color space of the original full color image. In other words, MCA splits the color space repeatedly along the median into the rectangular boxes until the desired number of colors is obtained. MCA uses the average color in each rectangular box as one of the colors in the color palette. KMC divides the color space of the original image into K Voronoi spaces (partitions) by using cluster centers. The cluster centers are adjusted so as to minimize the accumulated distance between the cluster center and each pixel value in the Voronoi partition. After adjusting, the K cluster centers are used as the color palette. MCA and KMC can realize certain levels of quantization, when these methods apply to the color quantization in the image. Furthermore, their modified methods, e.g. center cut algorithm [4], RWM-cut algorithm [5,6], fuzzy C-means clustering [7] and so on, have been proposed in order to improve the quantization errors. In recent years, metaheuristic-based color quantization methods have also proposed [8,9].

However, these methods generate pseudo edges, because the similar colors are merged into a certain color coercively. In order to suppress the generation of the pseudo edges, it is required to employ not only the color quantization method, but also the multilevel dithering method as the post-processing. Nevertheless, the color palettes generated by the conventional quantization methods are not suitable for the post-multilevel dithering process, because the conventional color quantization methods focus on only reducing the quantization error. Therefore, a novel color quantization framework is needed to prepare the suitable color palette for effective multilevel dithering.

In this paper, we propose a new color quantization method to improve a quality of the quantized image. In the proposed method, the suitable color palette is found by using a particle swarm optimization (PSO) [10]. PSO is a population-based stochastic optimization method based on swarm intelligence [11] such as a bacteria foraging optimization (BFO) and an artificial bee colony (ABC) algorithms, and it is becoming very popular due to its simplicity of its concept and implementation. The color palette found by PSO is used for the multilevel dithering. As the multilevel dithering method, we employ a vector error diffusion (VED) method [12]. In the search, PSO evaluates a quality of the output image generated by VED with the color palette, which is to be optimized. The evaluation is based on a mean squared error between the original full color image and the output image represented by the full color. In the transformation from the color-reduced output image to the full color output image, the Gaussian filter is employed to consider the visual characteristics of human simply.

The validity and the effectiveness of the proposed method are verified by applying it to some test images.

2   Conventional Color Quantization Methods

2.1   Median Cut Algorithm

In MCA, the full color space divided into K color spaces. In particular, MCA splits a rectangular box in the color space into two rectangular boxes containing equal number of pixels. The cutting plane is decided based on one of the coordinate axes with a largest range of image pixel values, and pass through the median point of the color distribution projected on this axis. The splitting operation is performed repeatedly until that the number of the divided boxes is equal to that of the reduced color, i.e., K colors. At the end of the above-mentioned operation, the average color in each rectangular box is employed as one of the colors in the color palette. In other words, the colors in each rectangular box are merged into the average color.

MCA as well as PA can be performed by a simple procedure. However, the essential details in the full color image cannot be preserved appropriately, because some colors with low frequencies are discarded. Furthermore, the volume in a low-density part of the color space can be very large. Therefore, the quantization error tends to be large.

2.2   K-means Clustering Algorithm

KMC is a very popular method for general clustering. In KMC, input vectors are divided into K groups (clusters). In KMC, a center of each cluster as the centroid of its member input vectors is calculated to find the minimum of a sum-of-squares cost function (quantization error) ϕ represented by:

$$\phi = \sum_{j=1}^{K} \sum_{\ell=1}^{N_{\chi(j)}} \| \boldsymbol{u}_{j,\ell} - \boldsymbol{p}(j) \|, \tag{1}$$

where K is the number of clusters. $\chi(j)$ and $N_{\chi(j)}$ stand for j-th cluster and the number of members in $\chi(j)$, respectively. $\boldsymbol{u}_{j,\ell}$ represents ℓ-th member in $\chi(j)$.

$p(j)$ is the center of mass of the members in $\chi(j)$, and is calculated by:

$$p(j) = \frac{1}{N_{\chi(j)}} \sum_{\ell=1}^{N_{\chi(j)}} u_{j,\ell}. \tag{2}$$

KMC is performed by the following steps:

Step 1: K cluster centers $p(1), p(2), \cdots p(K)$ are initialized by the randomly-selected input vectors.
Step 2: The cluster membership for each input vector is assigned to the nearest cluster center.
Step 3: The cost function represented by Eq. (1) is calculated.
Step 4: The cluster centers are updated by Eq. (2).
Step 5: For each input data and all clusters, Steps from 2 to 4 until all cluster centers converge.

3   Proposed Method

In this paper, we propose a new color quantization method to improve a quality of the reduced-color image. In the proposed method, the appropriate color palette used for a vector error diffusion (VED) process is found by a particle swarm optimization (PSO). In this section, we first describe about VED for multilevel dithering after quantizing the color. Then, a procedure of PSO-based color palette generation method in order to realize the fine VED is described.

3.1   Vector Error Diffusion

VED is one of the multilevel dithering methods. A full color image is transformed into the K-color image by applying VED. The color palette for VED is then represented by $p_{\text{VED}} = \{p(1), p(2), \cdots p(K)\}$. VED is performed by the following processes. First, the closest color $p(k^*)$ is chosen by:

$$k^* = \arg\min_k \|p(k) - I_e(n)\|, \tag{3}$$

where $I_e(n)$ represents a sum of n-th pixel value $I(n)$ in the full color image and the accumulated errors from the neighboring pixels to n-th pixel. In the next step, the n-th pixel $I_o(n)$ in the output image is replaced by $p(k^*)$. Further, an error $e(n)$ of n-th pixel is calculated by:

$$e(n) = I_e(n) - I_o(n). \tag{4}$$

After calculating the error, the weighted error is diffused into the neighboring pixels that have not yet been processed as shown in Fig. 1 based on Floyd-Steinberg method. VED is performed for each pixel along with the horizontal scan line from upper left to lower right.

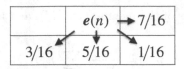

Fig. 1. Diffusion coefficients (weights) with its directions in Floyd-Steinberg method. The cell denoted by $e(n)$ represents the pixel currently being processed.

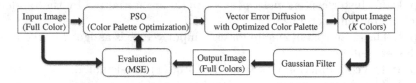

Fig. 2. A conceptual sketch of the proposed method

3.2   Generation of Color Palette by using Particle Swarm Optimization

In the proposed method, the appropriate color palette P_{VED} for employing the above mentioned VED is found by PSO. Figure 2 shows a conceptual sketch of the proposed method. PSO is motivated from the simulation of simplified animal social behaviors such as fish schooling, bird flocking, etc. Further, PSO is becoming very popular due to its simplicity of its concept and implementation.

The ordinary PSO as well as other population-based optimization methods starts with the random initialization of a population of individuals (particles). The particles are updated by exchanging fitness information obtained from the environment with each other. The individuals of the population thus move towards better solutions. Each individual moves with a velocity in the D-dimensional searching space. The velocity is iteratively updated according to its own and the other particles' flying experiences. The position of i-th particle and its fitness value at time step t are represented as $\boldsymbol{x}_i(t) = (x_{i1}(t), x_{i2}(t), \cdots, x_{iD}(t))$ and $f_i(t)$, respectively. The velocity, which corresponds to a rate of the position change, is represented as $\boldsymbol{v}_i(t) = (v_{i1}(t), v_{i2}(t), \cdots, v_{iD}(t))$ for i-th particle at time step t.

In the proposed method, $\boldsymbol{x}_i(t)$, which is the combined color vectors in $\boldsymbol{P}_{\text{VED}}$ (i.e., $D = 3K$), is represented by:

$$\boldsymbol{x}_i(t) = (\boldsymbol{p}(1), \boldsymbol{p}(2), \cdots \boldsymbol{p}(K)). \tag{5}$$

As the initial values of $\boldsymbol{x}_i(0)$, in order to realize the effective search, we employ the noise added color palette obtained by the conventional KMC. In the initialization, the Gaussian noises are added to each element of the particle in order to generate various initial particles similar to the color pallet obtained by the conventional KMC.

In this paper, the purpose of this study is to generate the color-reduced image, which is the effective for visual contact. However, it is inherently difficult to compare the quality of the color-reduced image with that of the full-color input image. Thus, it is required to quantitative evaluation considering the visual contact. In order to evaluate the quality of the color-reduced image with considering the visual characteristics of human, the squared error between the full-color input image and the weighted average of color-reduced image is often used [14]. we thus employ a mean squared error (MSE) as the fitness function defined by:

$$f_i(t) = \frac{1}{N} \sum_{n=1}^{N} \| \boldsymbol{I}(n) - \boldsymbol{I}'_{o,\boldsymbol{x}_i(t)}(n) \|^2, \tag{6}$$

where $\| \cdot \|$ stands for the Euclidean norm. $\boldsymbol{I}(n)$ represents the input image. $\boldsymbol{I}'_{o,\boldsymbol{x}_i(t)}(n)$ stands for the output full color image obtained by VED with the combined color vector $\boldsymbol{x}_i(t)$, and it is calculated by:

$$\boldsymbol{I}'_{o,\boldsymbol{x}_i(t)} = G * \boldsymbol{I}_{o,\boldsymbol{x}_i(t)}, \tag{7}$$

where G and "$*$" stand for a 2-dimensional Gaussian filter and the convolution operator, respectively. N is the number of pixels in the image. The Gaussian filter is employed in order to calculate the weighted average of the color-reduced output image simply.

In the search of the proposed method, PSO finds the solution, which minimizes the fitness function. The PSO in the proposed method evaluates a quality of the output image $\boldsymbol{I}_{o,\boldsymbol{x}_i(t)}(n)$ generated by VED with the color palette $\boldsymbol{x}_i(t)$, i.e., $\boldsymbol{P}_{\text{VED}}$. In the evaluation, a similarity between the input full color image $\boldsymbol{I}(n)$ and the output full color image $\boldsymbol{I}'_{o,\boldsymbol{x}_i(t)}(n)$ are calculated. In the transformation from the color-reduced output image $\boldsymbol{I}_o$ to the full color output image $\boldsymbol{I}'_o(n)$, the Gaussian filter is convoluted to the color-reduced output image. In the searching process, the best position of the i-th particle from step 0 to step t is recorded and represented as $\boldsymbol{b}_i(t) = (b_{i1}(t), b_{i2}(t), \cdots, b_{iD}(t))$. $\boldsymbol{b}_i(t)$ is frequently called personal best position (p-best). Furthermore, the best position in the population from step 0 to step t is represented as $\boldsymbol{g}(t) = (g_1(t), g_2(t), \cdots, g_D(t))$. $\boldsymbol{g}(t)$ is frequently called global best position (g-best). In order to update each particle position, ℓ-th element $v_{i\ell}(t+1)$ in the velocity $\boldsymbol{v}_i(t+1)$ is calculated with its own current, p-best and g-best positions by:

$$v_{i\ell}(t+1) = w(t) \cdot v_{i\ell}(t) + c_1 \cdot r_1 \cdot \{b_{i\ell}(t) - x_{i\ell}(t)\} + c_2 \cdot r_2 \cdot \{g_\ell(t) - x_{i\ell}(t)\}, \tag{8}$$

where $\ell = 1, 2, \cdots, D$. r_1 and r_2 are random values in the range $[0, 1]$. c_1 and c_2 are positive constants. ℓ-th element of the position $\boldsymbol{x}_i(t)$ of the particle is updated with Eq. (8) by:

$$x_{i\ell}(t+1) = x_{i\ell}(t) + v_{i\ell}(t+1). \tag{9}$$

In PSO, each particle in the population shares the information on the global best position with each other. The particle stochastically thus moves by using information on the global and the personal best positions in the searching space. Furthermore, PSO can search the appropriate color palette, which generates the fine color-reduced output image.

4 Experimental Results

In order to verify the performance of the proposed method, it is applied to 8 test images in the standard image database (SIDBA). The size of each image is 256×256.

In this experiment, the quality of the output image generated by the proposed method is compared to those of the output images generated by the conventional MCA and KMC. Furthermore, the performance of the proposed method is tested in cases where $K = 32$ and 64. The conventional MCA has no parameter. In the conventional KMC, the number of iteration is fixed to 100, empirically. In the proposed method, PSO has some parameters. The number of particles is 20. The both parameters c_1 and c_2 are decided to 1.49, which is well-used value in various optimization problems. The weight in the updating and the number of iteration steps are fixed to 0.72 and 50, respectively. Furthermore the Gaussian noise added to each particle in the initialization is generated in the normal distribution $N(0, 5)$. The output images in the conventional methods are generated by VED with the color palettes obtained by MCA and KMC. The window size and variance of the Gaussian filter used for generation of the full color output image are 3×3 pixels and 0.5, respectively.

Table 1 shows the quantization and the mean squared errors after the color quantization by each method in case where $K = 32$. As shown in Table 1, the

Table 1. Quantization error (QE) and mean squared error (MSE) after color quantization in case where $K = 32$. Conv. Methods 1 and 2 are median cut algorithm (MCA) and k-means clustering (KMC), respectively.

Test image	Errors	Conv. Method 1	Conv. Method 2	Prop. Method
Couple	QE	9.11	6.95	7.08
	MSE	99.55	61.72	57.90
Parrots	QE	16.14	13.55	14.92
	MSE	271.25	215.67	199.85
Balloon	QE	10.08	7.10	7.57
	MSE	107.52	66.36	59.12
Girl	QE	14.76	10.36	11.11
	MSE	254.59	116.03	95.46
Milkdrop	QE	11.11	8.60	9.22
	MSE	140.32	94.67	74.65
Sailboat	QE	12.11	10.16	11.79
	MSE	160.07	128.81	106.07
Lenna	QE	10.60	9.36	12.23
	MSE	119.98	119.98	89.26
Mandrill	QE	17.49	15.97	17.16
	MSE	355.76	299.28	241.19

quantization error of the conventional method 2 (KMC) is better than those of the conventional method 1 (MCA) and the proposed method. In other words, KMC can realize the finest color quantization. However, the proposed method can generate the finest output image comparing to the conventional methods from the perspective of the MSE. In addition, the proposed method gives the smaller MSE in case where it is applied to the test images that contain the intricate details and smooth parts. Furthermore, Table 2 shows the quantization and the mean squared errors after the color quantization by each method in case where $K = 64$. The color quantization results in case where $K = 64$ shown in Table 2 denote the same tendency of those in case where $K = 32$.

Figures 3 and 4 show examples of the resulting images in case where $K = 32$. In each figure (a), white boxes show the parts of remarkable improvements by using the proposed method. In Fig. 3, the output image by the proposed method gives natural impression better than that of the conventional method 2, although the MSE of the output image by the proposed method is almost same to that by the conventional method 2. In Fig. 4, there are some dithering artifacts in the output images by the conventional method 1 and 2. On the other hand, the output image by the proposed method has less dithering artifacts than the conventional methods, and can preserve the essential details of the original image. Moreover, it can be observed that the proposed method has high expression ability of intricate detail parts. Figures 5 and 6 show examples of the resulting images in case where

Table 2. Quantization error (QE) and mean squared error (MSE) after color quantization in case where $K = 64$. Conv. Methods 1 and 2 are median cut algorithm (MCA) and k-means clustering (KMC), respectively.

Test image	Errors	Conv. Method 1	Conv. Method 2	Prop. Method
Couple	QE	8.27	5.52	7.01
	MSE	80.66	46.92	46.55
Parrots	QE	12.15	10.05	11.08
	MSE	140.10	122.34	103.72
Balloon	QE	8.09	5.35	5.47
	MSE	70.75	41.09	39.60
Girl	QE	11.44	7.90	8.27
	MSE	157.91	67.25	62.55
Milkdrop	QE	8.20	5.98	6.53
	MSE	88.22	51.11	47.07
Sailboat	QE	10.37	8.12	9.90
	MSE	105.60	76.83	64.32
Lenna	QE	8.30	7.10	8.21
	MSE	84.65	71.46	63.12
Mandrill	QE	14.06	12.58	13.67
	MSE	216.90	206.23	161.39

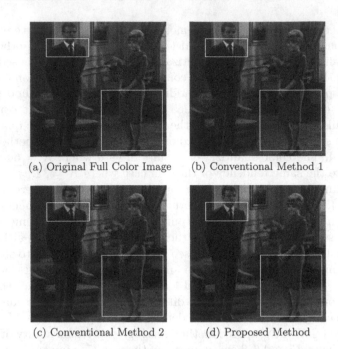

(a) Original Full Color Image   (b) Conventional Method 1

(c) Conventional Method 2   (d) Proposed Method

Fig. 3. Resulting images (Couple) in case where $K=32$

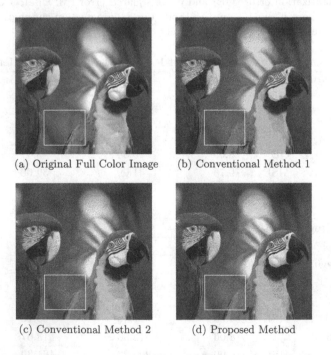

(a) Original Full Color Image   (b) Conventional Method 1

(c) Conventional Method 2   (d) Proposed Method

Fig. 4. Resulting images (Parrots) in case where $K=32$

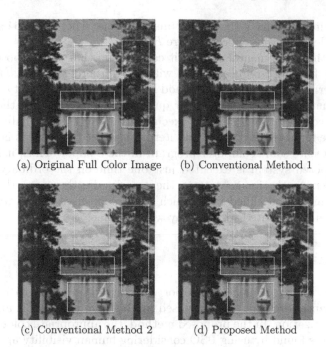

(a) Original Full Color Image   (b) Conventional Method 1

(c) Conventional Method 2   (d) Proposed Method

Fig. 5. Resulting images (Sailboat) in case where $K=64$

(a) Original Full ColorImage   (b) Conventional Method 1

(c) Conventional Method 2   (d) Proposed Method

Fig. 6. Resulting images (Lenna) in case where $K=64$

$K = 64$. The impressions of the output images in case where $K = 64$ also denote the same tendency of those in case where $K = 32$.

Through the experimental results, it can be said that the proposed method generates the fine color-reduced image with low dithering artifacts and pseudo edges. Furthermore, the proposed method has better keeping quality of the original image than the conventional color quantization methods. In the proposed method, the computational cost for executing the PSO is gradually high with increasing the numbers of particle and iteration steps. However, it is inherently difficult to execute some computer program in the e-paper. Thus, it is assumed that the proposed system is executed just one time on the ordinary computer before transferring the image data to the e-paper. Furthermore, the proposed system by using the modified PSO which realizes effective search and GPGPU techniques can be executed without any waiting time.

5   Conclusions

In this paper, we proposed a new color quantization method to improve the quality of quantized image. The proposed method employed VED and PSO for the color quantization. In the proposed method, the appropriate color palette for use of VED was found by using PSO considering human visibility approximated by the Gaussian filter. In the search, PSO evaluates not quantization error, but a quality of the output image. The evaluation is based on the MSE between the original full color image and the output image transformed by the Gaussian filter into the full color.

The validity and the effectiveness of the proposed method were confirmed by applying it to some test images. Future work is to evaluate the quality of the output image based on not only MSE, but also other image quality assessment metrics such as SSIM and FSIM.

Acknowledgments. This work was supported by Japan Society for the Promotion of Science (JSPS) Grant-in-Aid for Challenging Exploratory Research (Grant number 25540111).

References

1. Heikenfeld, J., Drzaic, P., Yeo, J.S., Koch, T.: A critical review of the present and future prospects for electronic paper. J. Soc. Inf. Display **19**, 129–156 (2011)
2. Heckbert, P.: Color image quantization for frame buffer display. ACM Trans. Comput. Graph. (SIGGRAPH) **16**, 297–307 (1982)
3. MacQueen, J.B.,: Some methods for classification and analysis of multivariate observations. In: Proceedings of the Fifth Symposium on Math, Statistics, and Probability, pp. 281–297. University of California Press, Berkeley (1967)
4. Joy, G., Xiang, Z.: Center-cut for color-image quantization. Visual Comput. **10**, 62–66 (1993)

5. Yang, C.Y., Lin, J.C.,: Color quantization by RWM-Cut. In: Proceedings. of the International Conference on Document Analysis and Recognition, pp. 669–672 (1995)
6. Yang, C.Y., Lin, J.C.: RWM-cut for color image quantization. Comput. Graph. **20**, 577–588 (1996)
7. Scheunders, P.: A comparison of clustering algorithms applied to color image quantization. Pattern Recogn. **18**, 1379–1384 (1997)
8. Kaur, R., Girdhar, A., Gupta, A.: Color image quantization based on bacteria foraging optimization. Int. J. Comput. Appl. **25**, 33–42 (2011)
9. Ozturk, C., Hancer, E., Karaboga, D.: Color image quantization: a short review and an application with artificial bee colony algorithm. Informatica **25**, 485–503 (2014)
10. Kennedy, J., Eberhart, R.: Particle swarm optimization. In: Proceedings of 1995 IEEE International Conference Neural Networks, vol. 4, pp. 1942–1948 (1995)
11. Kennedy, J., Eberhart, R., Shi, Y.: Swarm Intelligence. Morgan Kaufmann, San Francisco (2001)
12. Akarun, L., Yardimici, Y., Cetin, A.E.: Adaptive methods for dithering color images. IEEE Trans. Image Proces. **6**, 950–955 (1997)
13. Floyd, R.W., Steinberg, L.: An adaptive algorithm for spatial gray-scale. Proc. Soc. Image Display **17**, 75–77 (1976)
14. Miyahara, M., Kotani, K., Algazi, V.R.: Objective picture quality scale (PQS) for image coding. IEEE Trans. Commun. **46**, 1215–1226 (1998)

Fast Interactive Image Segmentation Using Bipartite Graph Based Random Walk with Restart

Yunfan Du$^{(\boxtimes)}$, Fei Li, and Rujie Liu

Fujitsu Research and Development Center Co., Ltd., Beijing, China
{duyunfan,lifei,rjliu}@cn.fujitsu.com

Abstract. Although random walk with restart(RWR) has been successfully used in interactive image segmentation, the traditional implementation of RWR does not scale for large images. As the images are usually stored on local disk prior to user interaction, we can preprocess the images to save user time. In this paper, we do an offline precomputation that over-segments the input image into superpixels with different scales and then aggregates superpixels and pixels into one bipartite graph which fuses the high level and low level information. Given user scribbles, we do a realtime RWR on the bipartite graph by applying an approximate method which maps the RWR from pixel level to superpixel level. As the number of superpixels is far more less than the number of pixels in the image, our method reduces the amount of user time significantly. The experimental results demonstrate that our method achieves a similar result compared to original RWR along with outperforming in speed.

Keywords: Interactive image segmentation · Random walk with restart · Superpixel · Bipartite graph

1 Introduction

Image segmentation is one of the fundamental but challenging problems in image processing and computer vision. The approaches of unsupervised image segmentation automatically partition an image into coherent regions without any prior knowledge, such as the stochastic clustering [22], mean shift [5], mixture model [19,20], and level sets [11,12]. Unsupervised image segmentation is widely referred as a crucial function of high-level image understanding, which is designed to simulate functionalities of human visual perception such as object recognition [6] and scene parsing [7]. However, the state-of-the-art automatic segmentation methods are still far from the human segmentation performance, which have several problems such as finding the faint object boundaries and separating the highly complicated background in natural images. In order to solve these problems, an interactive method is often preferred when the objects of interest need to be accurately selected and extracted from the background. In this paper, we address this interactive segmentation problem with our fast RWR method.

© Springer International Publishing Switzerland 2016
T. Bräunl et al. (Eds.): PSIVT 2015, LNCS 9431, pp. 344–354, 2016.
DOI: 10.1007/978-3-319-29451-3_28

The task of interactive segmentation is generally to produce a binary segmentation mask of the input image by separating the objects of interest from their background. There is a plenty of literature on the work of interactive image segmentation techniques that have been explored by the investigators during the last decade. The popular graph-based approaches include interactive graph cut [4,18], geodesic distance [3], level sets [16], random walk [9], and RWR [10]. An input image is usually represented by an undirected graph structure where the vertices denote image pixels and edges connect pairs of vertices. Then the problem of interactive segmentation becomes equivalent to partitioning the vertices into disjoint segments. One very successful graph partition technique is RWR, which usually starts random walk from a seed vertex, iteratively moves to its neighborhood vertex, with a probability that is proportional to the weight of the edge between them. There are many RWR related methods including cross modal correlation discovery [17], generative image segmentation [10] and so on. In [10], RWR was incorporated with naive Bayesian theory, which generated an interactive image segmentation method. Pan et al. [17] used RWR to do automatic image captioning.

An important research challenge of RWR is its speed. The solutions of above methods usually need to compute the inverse of matrix. As we all know that the time complexity of matrix inversion approximates $O(N^3)$, which means that the computation cost may become unaffordable in a realtime application, especially for large matrix.

In this paper, we propose a fast interactive segmentation method. Our idea originally inspired by [13]. Li et al. [13] is an unsupervised image segmentation method which can be seen as a fast version of normalized cut. Li et al. [13]'s acceleration work was based on a bipartite graph structure. Li et al. [13] first segmented the input image into superpixels, then aggregated multi-layer superpixels and image pixels into one bipartite graph, and so that highly efficient spectral clustering could be applied on the unbalanced bipartite graph. We introduce the bipartite graph to accelerate interactive image segmentation by modifying the structure of that bipartite graph, we are able to do fast RWR on this graph.

We also notice that some work has been done on bipartite graph based RWR [15,23]. Sun et al. [23] constructed a bipartite graph based on RWR to address two issues: neighborhood formation and anomaly detection while [15] applied bipartite graph based RWR on spatial outlier detection. Sun et al. [23] constructed bipartite graph based on the inner correlation of object set such as conferences vs. authors in a scientific publication network. This construction step limited the application of [23] because only some particular datasets has the inner correlation like conferences vs. authors. Lately, the construction of bipartite graph was generalized to ordinary dataset by [15]. Liu et al. [15] first generated a set of clusters from the ordinary spatial object set, then put the set of clusters and original spatial objects into two disjoint sets of bipartite graph respectively. After the construction of bipartite graph, both [15,23] merged bipartite graph $B_{K \times N}$ and its transpose matrix $B_{K \times N}^T$ into one large adjacency matrix $M_{(K+N) \times (K+N)}$ and then RWR was done on this large adjacency matrix.

Here K is the number of clusters, N is the number of spatial objects. This adjacency matrix is even larger than the adjacency matrix of ordinary RWR, which is usually $M_{N \times N}$. That means that to compute the inverse of large matrix will be more time consuming. Different from their works, we applying an approximate method to map the RWR from pixel level to superpixel level, which significantly reduces the computation cost.

The main contributions of the paper are as follows: 1. We transfer the RWR from pixel level to superpixel level by applying an approximate method. 2. We achieve competitive results compared with original RWR and outperforming in speed.

The rest of the paper is organized as follows: the proposed method is presented in Sect. 2; The experimental results are presented in Sect. 3. Finally, we conclude the paper in Sect. 4.

2   Method

We explain the principle of our fast RWR method and how the bipartite graph accelerates the original RWR in this section. Our method can be divided into two steps: offline and online. In the offline step, we first over-segment the input image into small pixel patches which also known as superpixels, by using some over-segmentation methods such as MeanShift [5], FH [8], Entropy Rate Superpixel [14], Lazy Random Walk [21] and many more. Then we compute the affinity map between each pixel patch and its corresponding superpixels and construct a bipartite graph. In the online step, we do RWR on the constructed bipartite graph.

2.1   Graph Structure

The structure of our bipartite graph is showed in Fig. 1. The bipartite graph can be divided into two sets, one consists of pixels, while the other consists of superpixels with different scales. A pixel will be connected to the superpixels it belongs to. Note that one pixel may be connected to multiple superpixels, because these superpixels are obtained by doing multiple over-segmentation with different scale parameters. The purple arrow in Fig. 1 is one possible random walk path. We can see that the random walk on bipartite graph makes round trip between two sets, so that it is faster than the random walk on ordinary graph which is constructed from pixels.

Given image I with N pixels, to build a bipartite graph, first we need to select some over-segmentation methods to cluster the image pixels into small clusters. The cluster can also be called superpixel in image processing field. After t times of over-segmentation, finally we have $M = \sum_{c=1}^{t} K_c$ superpixels. Here K_c is the number of superpixels we get in the c-th over-segmentation. We vary the value of K_c to get different scales of superpixels. These superpixels can enforce the local coherence and global relationship in the bipartite graph.

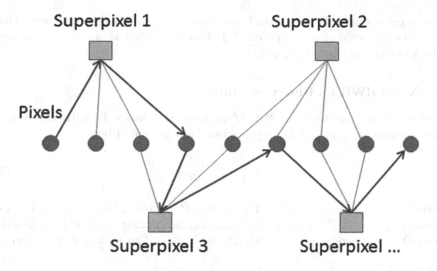

Fig. 1. Structure of our bipartite graph.

After obtaining superpixels, we define a weighted bipartite graph $G = \{V_1 \cup V_2, E\}$. Where $|V_1| = N$ and $|V_2| = M$ are node sets that represent pixels and superpixels respectively and $E \subseteq V_1 \times V_2$. Given two vertices $v_i \in V_1$ and $v_j \in V_2$, the edge that connects the two vertices is defined as $e_{ij} \in E$. The weight of e_{ij} is defined as w_{ij}. Such an edge weight w_{ij} measures the similarity between i-th pixel and the j-th superpixel which the i-th pixel belongs to. Ideally, the superpixels must have some overlapped regions to make sure the RWR can reach every pixel and every superpixel. This is also a limitation for selecting over-segmentation method.

2.2 Edge Weight Measurement

We use the color and spatial information as the feature of image pixels, for example, $p_i = (l_i, a_i, b_i, x_i, y_i)$. Here l_i, a_i, b_i are the color values of p_i, note that the color values are in Lab color space. (x_i, y_i) is the coordinate of p_i in the image. The superpixel can be represented by $q_j = \frac{1}{|C_j|} \sum_{p_i \in C_j} p_i$ and q_j can also be represented by $(l_j, a_j, b_j, x_j, y_j)$. The similarity between the pixels and the superpixels is defined as follow [1]:

$$d_c = \sqrt{(l_i - l_j)^2 + (a_i - a_j)^2 + (b_i - b_j)^2},$$

$$d_s = \sqrt{(x_i - x_j)^2 + (y_i - y_j)^2}, \tag{1}$$

$$w_{ij} = \frac{1}{e^{\sqrt{d_c^2 + \alpha * (\frac{d_s}{T_j})^2}}},$$

where d_c and d_s is the difference between i-th pixel and j-th superpixel in color and spatial space. α is a weight parameter that control the relative importance between color similarity and spatial proximity. T is a normalization factor that represents the scale of j-th superpixel. If j-th superpixel is obtained from c-th over-segmentation, then $T_j = \sqrt{N/K_c}$.

2.3 Naive RWR on Bipartite Graph

Based on G, we construct an $N \times M$ asymmetric matrix B, with $B_{ij} = w_{ij}$. Then the adjacency matrix of graph G can be represented by:

$$W = \begin{pmatrix} 0 & B^T \\ B & 0 \end{pmatrix}. \tag{2}$$

where W is an $(N + M) \times (N + M)$ matrix, B^T is the transpose of B. By row normalizing matrix W, we get the transition probability matrix $P = D^{-1}W$, where D is a diagonal matrix with $D_{ii} = \sum_j W_{ij}$. The matrix P can also be represented by:

$$P = \begin{pmatrix} 0 & \mathcal{B}^T \\ \mathcal{B} & 0 \end{pmatrix}. \tag{3}$$

where $\mathcal{B}$ and $\mathcal{B}^T$ are row normalized matrix B and B^T. The RWR on G will start from initial seed vertices, then converge to a steady state probability distribution u. RWR is usually defined as equation [10]:

$$u = (1 - \gamma) * P * u + \gamma * v, \tag{4}$$

where v is an initial vector that represents seed vertices, γ is the probability that random walk restarts from seed vertices. We can initialize v from user scribbles. u is the steady state probability vector to be solved. The target of RWR is find the converge vector u. Working directly on P will result in a large consumption of time and storage. Next we propose an approximate method to transfer the RWR from P into a far more smaller matrix, in other words, transfer RWR from pixel level to superpixel level.

2.4 Accelerating RWR

First, we process pixels and superpixels separately in Eq. 4:

$$\begin{pmatrix} u_{sp} \\ u_p \end{pmatrix} = (1 - \gamma) \begin{pmatrix} \mathcal{B}^T \cdot u_p \\ \mathcal{B} \cdot u_{sp} \end{pmatrix} + \gamma \begin{pmatrix} v_{sp} \\ v_p \end{pmatrix} \tag{5}$$

where u_p is an $N \times 1$ vector that means the probability that each pixel belongs to certain class, for example c. Similarly, u_{sp} is an $M \times 1$ vector that represents the probability that each superpixel belongs to certain class c. v_p and v_{sp} are the initial probabilities of each pixel and superpixel belongs to c. We can further partition the above equation into two new equations:

$$u_{sp} = (1 - \gamma)\mathcal{B}^T u_p + \gamma v_{sp} \tag{6}$$

$$u_p = (1 - \gamma)\mathcal{B}u_{sp} + \gamma v_p \qquad (7)$$

To accelerate RWR, with the unbalanced bipartite graph B, we approximate u_p and u_{sp} by:

$$\begin{cases} u_p = \mathcal{B}u_{sp}, \\ u_{sp} = \mathcal{B}^T u_p. \end{cases} \qquad (8)$$

Note that matrix $\mathcal{B}$ and $\mathcal{B}^T$ represent the similarity between each pixel and their corresponding superpixels. Briefly speaking, the two equations can be seen as a assumption that the probability of each superpixel belongs to certain class is the sum of the probability of its member pixels belong to the same class. We can easily generalize the assumption to the initial vector:

$$\begin{cases} v_p = \mathcal{B}v_{sp}, \\ v_{sp} = \mathcal{B}^T v_p. \end{cases} \qquad (9)$$

With this simple linear approximation, we can rewrite Eq. 6 by left multiplying Eq. 7 with $\mathcal{B}^T$:

$$\mathcal{B}^T u_p = (1 - \gamma)\mathcal{B}^T \mathcal{B}u_{sp} + \gamma \mathcal{B}^T v_p. \qquad (10)$$

Together with Eqs. 8 and 9, the above equation is equal to:

$$u_{sp} = (1 - \gamma)Q u_{sp} + \gamma v_{sp}, \qquad (11)$$

where $[Q]_{M \times M} = \mathcal{B}^T \mathcal{B}$, then Q_{ij} means the similarity between two superpixels i and j. In other words, the above equation can be seen as doing RWR on the superpixel level. As $K \ll N$, the RWR on matrix Q is far more efficient than on matrix P. The converged vector u_{sp} can be mapped back to the pixel level according to Eq. 8, and the final result is $u_p = \mathcal{B}u_{sp}$.

In conclusion, based on the special structure of bipartite graph and our assumption, we first transfer the RWR from pixel level to superpixel level which can be seen as a downsampling operation. After solving Eq. 11 in superpixel level, we then map the obtained superpixel level class probability information back to the pixel level which can be seen as an upsampling operation. By working on superpixel level, we achieve significant improvement in speed compared to the traditional pixel level RWR. What makes our downsampling and upsampling different is that our operations are based on superpixels with different scales while conventional downsampling is usually on a fixed scale. Benefit from the over-segmentation methods in the offline step, our downsampling and upsampling method has a good property that preserving the region and boundary information of superpixels. Next we will show the performance of our method by some experiments.

3 Results

In this section, experiments are conducted to evaluate the effectiveness of the proposed framework. We have three parts in this section. We first test our approach for interactive image segmentation on the Berkeley Segmentation Datasets

(BSD) of testing images[1], which includes five hundred test images with human annotations as the ground-truth data [2]. The BSD benchmark includes the natural images with abundant colors and different complicated textures, which makes it challenging to segment them even with the user scribbles. Then we compare the error rate of our method with original RWR method [10]. Finally we do a statistic analysis for the computation cost of the two methods.

All the segmentation results are obtained from official released code and the parameters are set to default values. In this section, the scribbles used in our algorithm are presented in the following format: green scribbles are used to indicate the foreground object, blue scribbles are used to indicate the background parts of images. These pixels marked with scirbbles will be used as seed pixels. Then the seed pixels are used to estimate the labels of the unlabeled pixels. We execute all our experiments on an 3.4 Ghz and 24 GB RAM workstation using MATLAB 7.10.

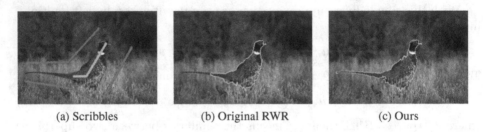

(a) Scribbles   (b) Original RWR   (c) Ours

Fig. 2. Qualitative comparison using images with complex texture. From left to right, (a) scribbles; (b) segmentation result of original RWR; (c) result of our method (Color figure online).

3.1   Qualitative Comparison

Original RWR method [10] has a good performance in complex texture regions. In this part, we choose some images which have complex texture regions from the BSD datasets to show that our method achieves similar performance. Here we select MeanShift [5] and ERS [14] to do over-segmentation in the offline step. We use three different scales of parameters to generate hundreds of superpixels. Generally speaking, the more superpixels, the better segmentation results. But the time cost will increase along with the increment of superpixel number. Figure 2 demonstrates the effect of our method compared with original RWR. As showed in Fig. 2(c), even though there is no scribble at the tail of the bird, our method cuts the tail out precisely. By aggregating different scales of superpixels into one bipartite graph, we can obtain different scales of edge and region information at the same time, so that our method has better boundary coherence in narrow regions with same user scribbles, as showed in Fig. 2.

---

[1] http://www.eecs.berkeley.edu/Research/Projects/CS/vision/grouping/resources. html.

3.2 Quantitative Comparison and Error Estimation

In this part, we will do a quantitative comparison. All images and their ground truth come from BSD datasets. We adopt normalized overlap [10] as accurateness metric:

$$Ac = \frac{S \bigcap G}{S \bigcup G}, \tag{12}$$

where S is the segmented foreground area, G is the ground truth foreground area. In BSD datasets every image usually has 5 grouth truth segmentation results. Here we choose the first one as metric. Ac represents the accuracy of segmentation, is in range$[0, 1]$. The bigger Ac means the higher segmentation accuracy.

Ac = 0.8373   Ac = 0.8573

Ac = 0.8326   Ac = 0.9164

Ac = 0.9451   Ac = 0.9450
(a) Scribbles   (b) original RWR   (c) Ours

Fig. 3. Quantitative comparison using images with complex texture. From left to right, (a) original image with scribbles; (b) results of original RWR; (c) results of ours (Color figure online).

To do a sufficient comparison, we select images with complex texture. As showed in Fig. 3, our method achieve similar result compared to original RWR.

3.3   Time Analysis

As mentioned before, our method can be divided into two steps. Although the offline processing takes a little time, it can be processed automatically prior to user interaction. In the online step, the actual user interaction only needs very little time. As showed in Table 1, our method achieves $20x$ speed up compared to original RWR. The original RWR suffers from computing the inverse of large scale matrix and become infeasible to do a real-time large image segmentation. When the image resolution reaches 1536×1024, original RWR needs about 31 s to make a segmentation, which is definitely unacceptable in an interactive setting.

Table 1. Time cost of RWR and our method in different resolutions.

Resolution	RWR	Ours-offline	Ours-online
289×193	0.85 s	1.2 s	0.04 s
481×321	2.5 s	3.1 s	0.11 s
1536×1024	31 s	45 s	1.2 s

First column is the resolution of input image; second column is the time cost of the offline step of our method; third column is the time cost of the online step of our method

4   Conclusions

In this paper, we have presented a fast interactive image segmentation method. By means of selected over-segmentation methods we first construct an unbalanced bipartite graph which consists of pixels and superpixels with different scales. Then we do random walk on this unbalance bipartite graph and transfer the RWR from pixel level to superpixel level with an approximation equation. In particular, our proposed method has produced competitive and qualitative segmentation results on the BSD datasets. And the experiments demonstrate that our method achieves significant improvement in speed compared to the original RWR.

References

1. Achanta, R., Shaji, A., Smith, K., Lucchi, A., Fua, P., Susstrunk, S.: Slic superpixels compared to state-of-the-art superpixel methods. IEEE Trans. Pattern Anal. Mach. Intell. **34**(11), 2274–2282 (2012)

2. Arbelaez, P., Maire, M., Fowlkes, C., Malik, J.: Contour detection and hierarchical image segmentation. Trans. Pattern Anal. Mach. Intell. **33**(5), 898–916 (2011)
3. Bai, X., Sapiro, G.: A geodesic framework for fast interactive image and video segmentation and matting. In: IEEE 11th International Conference on Computer Vision, pp. 1–8. IEEE (2007)
4. Boykov, Y.Y., Jolly, M.P.: Interactive graph cuts for optimal boundary & region segmentation of objects in nd images. In: 8th IEEE International Conference on Computer Vision, vol. 1, pp. 105–112. IEEE (2001)
5. Comaniciu, D., Meer, P.: Mean shift: a robust approach toward feature space analysis. IEEE Trans. Pattern Anal. Mach. Intell. **24**(5), 603–619 (2002)
6. Divvala, S.K., Hoiem, D., Hays, J.H., Efros, A., Hebert, M., et al.: An empirical study of context in object detection. In: IEEE Conference on Computer Vision and Pattern Recognition, pp. 1271–1278. IEEE (2009)
7. Eigen, D., Fergus, R.: Nonparametric image parsing using adaptive neighbor sets. In: IEEE Conference on Computer vision and pattern recognition, pp. 2799–2806. IEEE (2012)
8. Felzenszwalb, P.F., Huttenlocher, D.P.: Efficient graph-based image segmentation. Int. J. Comput. Vis. **59**(2), 167–181 (2004)
9. Grady, L.: Random walks for image segmentation. IEEE Trans. Pattern Anal. Mach. Intell. **28**(11), 1768–1783 (2006)
10. Kim, T.-H., Lee, S.U., Lee, K.M.: Generative image segmentation using random walks with restart. In: Forsyth, D., Torr, P., Zisserman, A. (eds.) ECCV 2008, Part III. LNCS, vol. 5304, pp. 264–275. Springer, Heidelberg (2008)
11. Li, C., Kao, C.Y., Gore, J.C., Ding, Z.: Minimization of region-scalable fitting energy for image segmentation. IEEE Trans. Image Process. **17**(10), 1940–1949 (2008)
12. Li, C., Xu, C., Gui, C., Fox, M.D.: Distance regularized level set evolution and its application to image segmentation. IEEE Trans. Image Process. **19**(12), 3243–3254 (2010)
13. Li, Z., Wu, X.M., Chang, S.F.: Segmentation using superpixels: a bipartite graph partitioning approach. In: IEEE Conference on Computer Vision and Pattern Recognition, pp. 789–796. IEEE (2012)
14. Liu, M.Y., Tuzel, O., Ramalingam, S., Chellappa, R.: Entropy rate superpixel segmentation. In: IEEE Conference on Computer Vision and Pattern Recognition, pp. 2097–2104. IEEE (2011)
15. Liu, X., Lu, C.T., Chen, F.: Spatial outlier detection: random walk based approaches. In: Proceedings of the 18th SIGSPATIAL International Conference on Advances in Geographic Information Systems, pp. 370–379. ACM (2010)
16. Liu, Y., Yu, Y.: Interactive image segmentation based on level sets of probabilities. IEEE Trans. Visual. Comput. Graph. **18**(2), 202–213 (2012)
17. Pan, J.Y., Yang, H.J., Faloutsos, C., Duygulu, P.: Automatic multimedia cross-modal correlation discovery. In: Proceedings of the 10th ACM SIGKDD International Conference on Knowledge Discovery and Data Mining, pp. 653–658. ACM (2004)
18. Rother, C., Kolmogorov, V., Blake, A.: Grabcut: interactive foreground extraction using iterated graph cuts. ACM Trans. Graph. (TOG) **23**(3), 309–314 (2004)
19. Sanjay-Gopal, S., Hebert, T.J.: Bayesian pixel classification using spatially variant finite mixtures and the generalized em algorithm. IEEE Trans. Image Process. **7**(7), 1014–1028 (1998)

20. Sfikas, G., Nikou, C., Galatsanos, N.: Edge preserving spatially varying mixtures for image segmentation. In: IEEE Conference on Computer Vision and Pattern Recognition, pp. 1–7. IEEE (2008)
21. Shen, J., Du, Y., Wang, W., Li, X.: Lazy random walks for superpixel segmentation. IEEE Trans. Image Process. **23**(4), 1451–1462 (2014)
22. Shental, N., Zomet, A., Hertz, T., Weiss, Y.: Learning and inferring image segmentations using the gbp typical cut algorithm. In: 9th IEEE International Conference on Computer Vision, pp. 1243–1250. IEEE (2003)
23. Sun, J., Qu, H., Chakrabarti, D., Faloutsos, C.: Neighborhood formation and anomaly detection in bipartite graphs. In: 5th IEEE International Conference on Data Mining, pp. 418–425. IEEE (2005)

Adaptive Window Strategy for High-Speed and Robust KLT Feature Tracker

Nirmala Ramakrishnan[1]([✉]), Thambipillai Srikanthan[1], Siew Kei Lam[1], and Gauri Ravindra Tulsulkar[2]

[1] Nanyang Technological University, Singapore, Singapore
rnirms@gmail.com
[2] Manipal Institute of Technology, Manipal, India

Abstract. The Kanade-Lucas-Tomasi tracking (KLT) algorithm is widely used for local tracking of features. As it employs a translation model to find the feature tracks, KLT is not robust in the presence of distortions around the feature resulting in high inaccuracies in the tracks. In this paper we show that the window size in KLT must vary to adapt to the presence of distortions around each feature point in order to increase the number of useful tracks and minimize noisy ones. We propose an adaptive window size strategy for KLT that uses the KLT iterations as an indicator of the quality of the tracks to determine near-optimal window sizes, thereby significantly improving its robustness to distortions. Our evaluations with a well-known tracking dataset show that the proposed adaptive strategy outperforms the conventional fixed-window KLT in terms of robustness. In addition, compared to the well-known affine KLT, our method achieves comparable robustness at an average runtime speedup of 7x.

Keywords: KLT feature tracker · Robust tracker · High-speed tracking

1 Introduction

Feature tracking is an essential step in many computer vision applications, such as global motion estimation, image registration and object tracking, and is used to extract higher level information about camera and/or object motion from the local optical flow vectors of each feature. The Kanade-Lucas-Tomasi (KLT) feature tracking algorithm [1] has been extensively used as it is very effective for small frame-to-frame displacements of features (which is common in video frames), and its low computational complexity enables it to be deployed on resource constrained platforms. In order to handle larger displacements, a multi-resolution approach is presented in [2], which is based on a pyramidal implementation of KLT.

However, KLT assumes that the patch around the feature undergoes only translation motion. Therefore, in the presence of rotation and scaling, KLT is known to suffer from high inaccuracies [3]. This is a severe limitation of KLT

© Springer International Publishing Switzerland 2016
T. Bräunl et al. (Eds.): PSIVT 2015, LNCS 9431, pp. 355–367, 2016.
DOI: 10.1007/978-3-319-29451-3_29

as drastic frame-to-frame rotation is common in many applications, for example videos captured on-board unmanned aerial vehicles that perform bank turns [3].

In this paper, we show that it is necessary for the window size in KLT to adapt to the presence of distortions around the feature points in order to increase the quality of the tracks. We present a novel adaptive window strategy for KLT that does not require explicit error estimate computations. In particular, we show for the first time that the iterations needed to converge within KLT can be used as a crude indicator of the quality of the feature track, thereby providing a simple means to arrive at a suitable window size. The proposed strategy is applied to each level of the pyramid in the pyramidal implementation of KLT to significantly improve the robustness to large displacements and distortions. Our extensive evaluations with simulated as well as annotated tracking datasets show that the proposed strategy significantly outperforms the translation model-based KLT in terms of robustness. In addition, the proposed strategy achieves comparable robustness as the affine model based KLT at 7x run-time speedup.

The paper is organized as follows. Section 2 presents the related work for improving robustness of KLT. Section 3 presents an overview of the KLT algorithm and an analysis of the relationship between the search window size, the motion experienced by the feature and the accuracy of the KLT tracker. Section 4 presents the proposed adaptive window strategy for KLT. In Sect. 5, we show evaluation results with simulated as well as a real annotated tracking dataset [4]. Paper concludes with Sect. 6.

2   Related Work

Feature correspondence algorithms can be classified into two categories: (a) feature matching that uses a rich feature detector-descriptor combination [4], and (b) feature tracking. Feature matching can handle large rotation, scale and view point changes. However frames in video sequences predominantly undergo small translation motion and infrequent rotations/scaling motions between the frames, and therefore feature tracking is more commonly used due to its lower computational complexity.

Several techniques in feature tracking that accommodate the non-translation motions have been proposed and they can be categorized into four groups: (1) fusing the motion data from on-board inertial measurement units (IMUs) [3,5] (2) affine formulation of KLT that replaces the translation model with an affine model [6], (3) computation of error estimates to evaluate the feature tracks [7–9], and (4) employing adaptive window size [10]. The following describes existing work in these groups.

Inertial measurement units (IMUs) can provide the 3D motion of the vehicle and therefore this data can be used to arrive at initial estimates that KLT can then work with and this has been shown to be robust under drastic motions [3,5]. In this paper, we propose a technique that is not dependent on IMUs.

An affine formulation for KLT was proposed in [6] that replaces the translation model for the motion of the feature patch in the search window, with a more complex affine model - this allows the feature patch to undergo rotation, scaling and skew. However, this is highly compute-intensive and real-time performance is achieved only with GPU implementations [11].

Another approach is to evaluate the tracking algorithm in an online manner and discard tracks that are of poorer quality, and a good survey on this area of work is found in [7]. Such evaluations associate an error/uncertainty estimate with every track and this allows the applications that use the feature tracks to detect when KLT is unable to deal with the motion. In [8], the time-reversibility constraint of trackers has been applied to compute a forward-backward error for tracks, and this metric is used to discard potentially erroneous tracks. In [9], theoretical error estimates for KLT tracks is presented, however it is reported that the error estimate computations are so high that they cannot be used in real-world applications in an online manner.

The work in [10], which employs adaptive window size is the most similar to ours. The authors used intensity and disparity variations within the search window to compute uncertainty estimates for the displacement found by the tracking algorithm and find an optimal window size that minimizes this uncertainty estimate. However this iterative window sampling is performed for each core KLT operation to estimate the displacement and this adds a huge computation cost to the tracking algorithm. In contrast, our proposed method does not explicitly compute uncertainty estimates and monitors the KLT performance for a given window size as an indicator of successful tracking. The main contributions of this paper are as follows:

1. We analyze the relationship between the search window size, the motion experienced by the feature and the accuracy of the KLT tracker to show the need for adapting the window size of KLT in order to enhance its robustness to distortions.
2. We propose a novel adaptive window strategy that can be applied to pyramidal KLT implementation. We show that the iterations needed to converge within KLT can be used as a crude indicator of the window size being too small, and this can guide the adaptive strategy to land at a suitable window size.
3. Using simulated as well as a real annotated tracking dataset, we demonstrate that the proposed adaptive strategy outperforms the conventional fixed-window KLT in terms of robustness, and achieves significantly lower runtime without sacrificing robustness when compared to the well-known affine KLT.

3   Overview of KLT Algorithm

The goal of the KLT tracking algorithm is to find the displacement $d = [d_x, d_y]^\top$ for a feature x in two images $I(x)$ and $J(x)$ such that the residual error $\varepsilon(d)$ defined in (1) is minimised:

$$\varepsilon(d) = \sum_W [I(x) - J(x + d)]^2 \tag{1}$$

The residual $\varepsilon(d)$ is the intensity difference computed for a region of support defined by the search window W around the feature x. Given a starting position for d(initialised to $d = 0$), (1) solves the least squares optimization problem by iteratively modifying d as $d \leftarrow d + \Delta d$, through a Newton-Raphson method, such that $\varepsilon(d)$ is minimised. (1) assumes a translation model and is sufficient when the motion between the video frames is uniform. In the presence of fast rotation or scaling motions, this translation model fails. In order to account for the tracking challenge of rotation and scaling with KLT, an affine model was proposed in [6]. The residual error is defined as in (2) with the affine model:

$$\varepsilon(d) = \sum_W [I(x) - J(Ax + d)]^2 \tag{2}$$

Here, A is the affine transformation matrix given by:

$$A = \begin{bmatrix} 1 + d_{xx} & d_{xy} \\ d_{xy} & 1 + d_{yy} \end{bmatrix} \tag{3}$$

The six parameters $(d_x, d_y, d_{xx}, d_{yy}, d_{xy}, d_{yx})$ allow rotation, anisotropic scaling, skew and translation. However, this robustness comes with a computation cost tradeoff. Therefore, we use the translation model as the basis of our proposed method.

3.1   Effect of Search Window Size for Rotation/Scaling

As shown in Fig. 1(a), given a maximum inter-frame displacement d_{max}, it is advisable to setup the search window size $W = 2 * d_{max} + 1$, such that the displacement of the feature is captured within the KLT search window [2]. Figure 1(b) illustrates the translation model assumed by KLT as in (1) in which all the pixels within the search window W have the same displacement given by (d_x, d_y). This assumption is valid only when the feature itself undergoes translation motion. As shown in Fig. 1(c) when there is rotation, the displacement of each of the pixels in W varies and this violates the underlying assumption of a translation motion model by KLT.

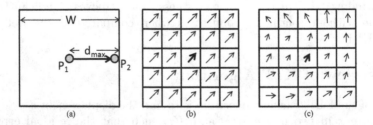

Fig. 1. Search Window Size and Feature Patch Displacement (a) Window size W needs to capture maximum displacement d_{max} (b) Displacements of neighboring pixels for translation motion (c) Displacements of neighboring pixels for rotation motion

Fig. 2. Local feature motions for various global motion (a) translation (b) rotation (c) scaling

When the feature undergoes translation motion alone, having a larger window size is always preferable because any noise in the intensity patterns within the window is averaged out. However, when the frame undergoes rotation or scaling then the pixels within the patch have varying displacement. As we move further away from the center pixel, these variations increase – therefore, relying on the farther away pixels results in higher error in the KLT results. In such cases, typically the center pixel undergoes a small displacement and therefore, this can still be captured with a small window size without including potentially erroneous estimates from far away pixels.

Hence, for images undergoing rotation and scaling, the window size needs to be large enough to capture the displacement of the feature but small enough to not invite potentially erroneous estimates from pixels far from the center of the feature. Similar to the conclusions in [10], there exists an optimum window size that results in the most accurate track for KLT for a given feature patch and inter-frame motion.

When the frame undergoes a rotation or scaling motion, as shown in Fig. 2(b) and (c), then the local displacement and distortion experienced by different features depends on their location in the frame. Therefore, an optimum window size needs to be determined for each individual feature in the presence of global rotation and/or scaling.

3.2 Implications of Fixed Search Window Size with Pyramidal KLT

The KLT tracker employs linear approximation in its core step which works only if the displacement Δd is very small. In order to overcome this limitation, a multi-resolution pyramidal approach was proposed in [2] to deal with larger inter-frame displacements. KLT starts at the highest level of the image pyramids for both frames and the displacement found at this level is up-sampled and used as the initial estimate for the next lower level in the pyramid. This allows the use of a reasonable window size at the highest level to capture a large displacement – for example, with a pyramid of 3 levels, a displacement of 32 pixels is reduced to $32/2^3 = 4$ pixels at the highest level $L3$, and can be captured with a window size of $W = 9$. Once this displacement has been reasonably captured by a higher level and is passed on to the lower level, this lower level needs to only capture any error in this initial estimate.

For example, if the KLT result at $L3$ is 3.75 and the actual displacement is 4 pixels, then we have an error of 0.25 pixels which translates to 0.5 pixels when up-sampled for $L2$. At $L2$, using the same window size of $W = 9$ may be too large for this displacement of 0.5 pixels in the presence of distortions. Therefore, when the displacement itself has to be captured, the window size needs to be large enough. But once it has been captured, and we only need to "refine" this estimate with higher resolution in the lower levels of the pyramid, then a smaller window size is more appropriate to capture the errors in the initial estimates.

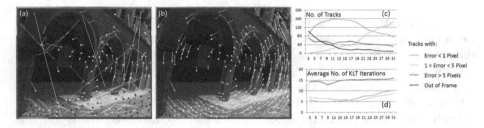

Fig. 3. KLT tracks with in-plane rotation of $10°$ (a) W = (3,3), (b) W = (31,31). For a range of window sizes (x-axis) (c) Total no. of tracks categorised based on tracking error (d) Average no. of iterations taken by KLT to converge for each category of tracks (Color figure online)

In conclusion, KLT is susceptible to errors with a fixed window size in the presence of rotation and scaling. Given a feature with an associated motion, there exists an optimal window size that is large enough to capture the displacement of the feature but small enough to not be affected by the distortion that the neighborhood of the feature undergoes. Based on our analysis in Sects. 3.1 and 3.2, we can conclude:

- In the presence of rotation and scaling, a fixed window size cannot be applied to all features in the frame. It needs to adapt to the motion experienced by each individual feature.
- Within the pyramidal implementation, the displacement that needs to be captured at the highest level is different from the other lower levels, and therefore the window size needs to adapt to the displacement that needs to be captured at each level.

3.3 Tracking Errors and KLT Iterations

Figure 3 shows the KLT tracks for a global in-plane rotation of $10°$. Green dots represent tracks with error less than 1 pixel. Yellow dots represent tracks which have error between 1 and 5 pixels. Red dots represent tracks with error greater than 5 pixels. When the window size is too small to capture the required displacement as in Fig. 3(a), the tracks drift away and result in high tracking error (represented by red tracks) or are pushed out of the frame (represented by blue dots). This is because with a smaller region of support the KLT estimates are easily skewed by noisy pixels within the search window. In contrast when the window size is too large as in Fig. 3(b), the estimates from the noisy pixels get averaged out and the displacement is comfortably captured, resulting in the KLT estimates being close to the final location. However, as there is distortion due to rotation, the far away neighbors tend to skew the KLT estimate and tracking error increases resulting in many yellow tracks. Figure 3(c) shows this trend when window size is varied, which implies that the window size needs to be optimal in order to reduce the chances of a track being red or yellow. Figure 3(d) shows that the average number of iterations is significantly higher for the lost red tracks. However, the yellow tracks converge fast and cannot be distinguished easily from the green tracks at the end of KLT. Therefore, the iterations can be used as an indicator to detect tracking errors caused by a window size that is too small to capture the displacement of the feature.

4 Adaptive Window Size for KLT

We propose an adaptive window strategy for KLT to improve its robustness in the presence of distortions due to rotations and scaling, such that an appropriate window size is chosen for each track resulting in higher number of green tracks and reducing the noisy tracks – both red and yellow. Figure 4 shows the flow of the proposed strategy.

As iterations can indicate tracking error associated with too small a window size, the proposed strategy starts with a small window size and increases the window size only if needed, as indicated by the KLT iterations. Specifically we evaluate the track with the current window size with the following checks:

1. Current track converged within the maximum iterations (*MaxIterations*): The *MaxIterarions* is a user-defined parameter that determines the number of iterations that KLT will run before giving up.
2. Fast convergence for two consecutive window sizes: Not all red tracks hit the maximum iterations. Sometimes, tracks converge fast for a certain window size at a local minimum. However increasing the window size, exposes more of the image and the track is pushed out of the local minimum. In order to prevent such early convergences, we check if the previous window size sampled also had a fast convergence. We set a minimum iterations threshold (=8 iterations) to declare the convergence as fast.
3. Forward-backward error as defined in [8] is within a threshold of 1 pixel: As a final check to reign in lost features (red tracks) that might have converged fast, we employ the forward backward error.

This adaptive window size strategy is applied to each feature at each level of the pyramid in the pyramidal KLT implementation so that an appropriate

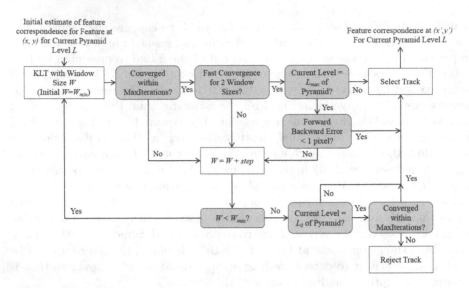

Fig. 4. Adaptive Window Strategy for Each Pyramid Level of the KLT Feature Tracking Algorithm

Fig. 5. Image data used for the simulated motions

window size is used depending on the displacement that needs to be captured at that level of the pyramid. Specifically, this allows the window size to grow as needed at the highest level when the displacement to be captured is unknown. Once the displacement has been captured, at the subsequent lower levels, smaller window sizes result in fast convergences avoiding noisy estimates from far away neighbors in the presence of distortion.

5   Evaluations

In order to evaluate the proposed adaptive window size strategy for KLT, we compare it with these baselines: (a) Conventional translation-model KLT tracking algorithm with a fixed window size W_{fixed}, referred to as *Conv KLT* (b) Affine-model KLT as in [6] with a fixed window size W_{fixed}, referred to as *Affine KLT* henceforth. The proposed method is referred to as *Adaptive KLT*.

We use the KLT implementations in OpenCV v2.4.9 for the conventional (*calcOpticalFlowPyrLK*) and affine KLT (*cvCalcAffineFlowPyrLK*) baselines. We implemented the *Adaptive KLT* by modifying the *calcOpticalFlowPyrLK* function. For the baseline KLT algorithms we used these parameter values:

$W = (31,31)$, *MaxIterations* $= 20$, *minimum Eigen threshold* $= 0.0001$. For the *Adaptive KLT*, $W_{min} = (5,5)$, $W_{max} = (31,31)$, *step* $= 2$, *minIterations* $= 8$. All other parameters are the same as the baseline algorithms.

For our evaluations we selected features using the Shi-Tomasi feature detector [12] and applied each of the variants of the KLT tracker. The correspondence found for each feature is compared with the ground truth and the tracking error is computed. If the error is below 1 pixel, the track is labeled *useful*, else it is labeled as *noisy*. The robustness of the tracker to various motions is determined by the extent to which it can maximize the number of *useful* tracks and minimize the number of *noisy* tracks.

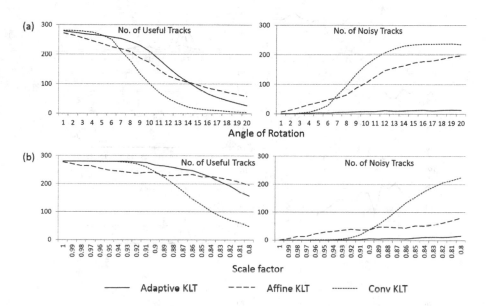

Fig. 6. Number of useful and noisy tracks for varying (a) rotation angles and (b) scale factors

A range of in-plane rotations of angles 0–20° and scale factor of 0-0.8 is applied on the images shown in Fig. 5. The results are shown in Fig. 6 as an average over all the images for a 3-level pyramid implementation. For angles in the range of 1–5°, all the KLT variants perform similarly. In the range of 6–15°, *Conv KLT* sees a drastic drop in the no. of useful features, and a corresponding increase in the no. of noisy features. This indicates an increase in the overall tracking error. The *Affine KLT* is able to salvage many of the noisy tracks and hence shows an improvement in the no. of useful tracks compared to *Conv KLT*. However the *Adaptive KLT* is the most successful in eliminating the noisy tracks and matches the *Affine KLT* in the number of useful tracks reported, thus generating the cleanest feature set among all the KLT variants considered for this range of angles. Beyond 15°, all the 3 variants of KLT are unable to deal with the distortion incurred.

Fig. 7. Sample frames from the tracking dataset used for our evaluations (a) Rotation (b) Perspective Distortion (c) Zoom (d) Shi-Tomasi features (red) selected within the texture area (Color figure online)

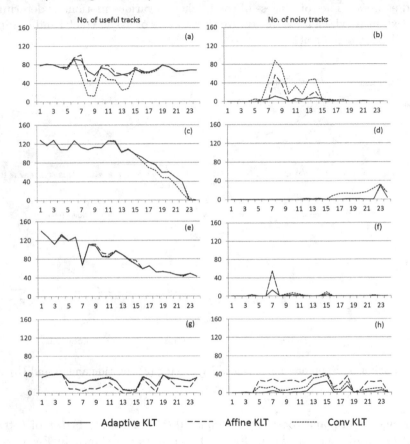

Fig. 8. Robustness Results for Tracking Dataset in [4] (a)-(b) Rotation (c)-(d) Perspective Distortion (e)-(f) Zoom (g)-(h) Panning

We also provide results with a ground truth annotated tracking dataset in [4] shown in Fig. 7, for the videos that incur distortions – rotation, zoom, perspective distortion and panning – for the texture "bu" (building). The Shi-Tomasi features considered are all in the rectangular texture area and features close to the boundary are ignored to eliminate boundary effects as in Fig. 7(d). Features are selected in every frame and tracked in the next frame. As the frame-to-frame motion is very small for this dataset, we skip every other frame and show the

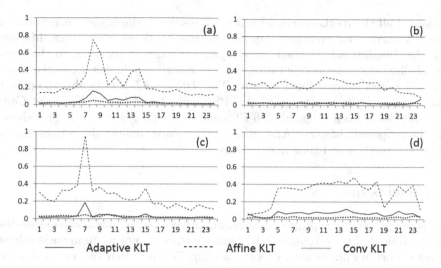

Fig. 9. Computation time (a) Rotation (b) Perspective Distortion (c) Zoom (d) Panning motions

results for this wider baseline video sequence. We use a 2-level pyramid for all the KLT methods.

We show the number of useful and noisy feature tracks for all the KLT variants in Fig. 8. Rotation, as shown in Fig. 8(a), (b), incurs the most interframe distortions among all the 3 motions considered. *Conv KLT* suffers in frames 7–9 and 13–15 and *Affine KLT* improves the number of useful features, however it is unable to keep the noisy tracks to a minimum. *Adaptive KLT* outperforms the *Affine KLT* both in the number of useful and noisy tracks. For perspective distortion, the number of features goes down towards the end of the video sequence as very less area of the texture is seen. *Conv KLT* suffers in terms of robustness, but both *Affine* and *Adaptive KLT* show similar robustness. The zoom video sequence in Fig. 8(e), (f) has a zoom-out motion, and therefore the area covered by the texture goes down as the video progresses. This is reflected in the no. of tracks reported by all KLT variants falling. In frames 6–8 both the *Conv* and *Affine KLT* suffer in terms of number of noisy tracks but *Adaptive KLT* keeps the noisy tracks to a minimum. In the panning video sequence in Fig. 8(g), (h), the displacement is large and the distortion in minimal. *Adaptive KLT* has comparable performance with the *Conv KLT*, but *Affine KLT* is unable to handle the large displacement. Overall, the robustness results show that even though *Affine KLT* is designed to allow distortions in the template patch, it is still outperformed by *Adaptive KLT*. This can be attributed to the large fixed search window size that is used with *Affine KLT* which prevents it from reaching the accuracy, that a more controlled optimal window size reached by the *Adaptive KLT* can offer.

We measured the computation times on a 3.5 GHz Intel (R) Xeon (R) desktop computer. As shown in Fig. 9, *Affine KLT* being the most computationally complex of all the methods considered here, results in the highest computation times – incurring an average computation time 7x times more than *Adaptive KLT*. As *Adaptive KLT* iteratively samples various window sizes, in the presence of distortion, the computation time is marginally higher than the *Conv KLT* which uses a single fixed window. The *Affine KLT* is only able to operate at an average of 5 frames per second (FPS), while the *Adaptive KLT* and *Conv KLT* operates at an average of 39.6 FPS and 41.5 FPS respectively. This shows that the proposed *Adaptive KLT* is not only robust against distortions but it can also be used in real-time applications.

6   Conclusions

In this paper, we have proposed novel adaptive window size strategy for the classical Kanade-Lucas-Tomasi (KLT) feature tracker in order to make it robust against distortions due to rotations and scaling. We show that the search window size determines the accuracy of the KLT feature tracker, and in the presence of distortions around the feature due to rotation and scaling, this window size needs to adapt to the displacement to be captured. The proposed adaptive strategy adopts a controlled selection of window size by sampling various window sizes starting with a small value.

By monitoring the KLT performance in terms of iterations for each window size, our proposed method can determine failure to capture the displacement, and lands at a near-optimal window size when the iterations stabilize. This way, it is able to capture the displacement with a large-enough window size and yet avoids the effects of distortion in the patch. Our evaluations on a tracking dataset show that the proposed strategy significantly outperforms the conventional fixed-window KLT in terms of robustness against rotation and scaling, and achieves the robustness of the more complex affine KLT with 7x faster runtime.

References

1. Lucas, B.D., Kanade, T.: An iterative image registration technique with an application to stereo vision. In: Proceedings of International Joint Conference on Artificial intelligence 1981, pp. 674–679 (1981)
2. Bouguet, J.-Y.: Pyramidal implementation of the Lucas Kanade feature tracker. Intel corporation, Microprocessor research labs (2000)
3. Tanathong, S., Lee, I.: Translation-based KLT tracker under severe camera rotation using GPS/INS data. IEEE Geosci. Remote Sens. Lett. **11**, 64–68 (2014)
4. Gauglitz, S., Höllerer, T., Turk, M.: Evaluation of interest point detectors and feature descriptors for visual tracking. Int. J. Comput. Vis. **94**, 335–360 (2011)
5. Hwangbo, M., Kim, J.-S., Kanade, T.: Inertial-aided KLT feature tracking for a moving camera. In: International Conference on Intelligent Robots and Systems, pp. 1909–1916 (2009)
6. Bouguet, J.-Y.: Pyramidal implementation of the affine Lucas Kanade feature tracker description of the algorithm. Intel Corporation (2001)

7. SanMiguel, J.C., Cavallaro, A., Martínez, J.M.: Adaptive online performance evaluation of video trackers. IEEE Trans. Image Process. **21**, 2812–2823 (2012)
8. Kalal, Z., Mikolajczyk, K., Matas, J.: Forward-backward error: automatic detection of tracking failures. In: 20th International Conference on Pattern Recognition (ICPR), pp. 2756–2759 (2010)
9. Sheorey, S., Keshavamurthy, S., Yu, H., Nguyen, H., Taylor, C.N.: Uncertainty estimation for KLT tracking. In: Jawahar, C.V., Shan, S. (eds.) ACCV 2014 Workshops. LNCS, vol. 9009, pp. 475–487. Springer, Heidelberg (2015)
10. Okutomi, M., Kanade, T.: A locally adaptive window for signal matching. In: 3rd International Conference on Computer Vision, pp. 190–199 (1990)
11. Kim, J.-S., Hwangbo, M., Kanade, T.: Realtime affine-photometric KLT feature tracker on GPU in CUDA framework. In: 12th IEEE International Conference on Computer Vision Workshops, pp. 886–893 (2009)
12. Shi, J., Tomasi, C.: Good features to track. In: IEEE Computer Vision and Pattern Recognition, pp. 593–600 (1994)

Enhanced Phase Correlation for Reliable and Robust Estimation of Multiple Motion Distributions

Matthias Ochs[1]([✉]), Henry Bradler[1], and Rudolf Mester[1,2]

[1] VSI Lab, Goethe University, Frankfurt am Main, Germany
{ochs,bradler,mester}@vsi.cs.uni-frankfurt.de
[2] CVL, ISY, Linköping University, Linköping, Sweden

Abstract. Phase correlation is one of the classic methods for sparse motion or displacement estimation. It is renowned in the literature for high precision and insensitivity against illumination variations. We propose several important enhancements to the phase correlation (PhC) method which render it more robust against those situations where a motion measurement is not possible (low structure, too much noise, too different image content in the corresponding measurement windows). This allows the method to perform self-diagnosis in adverse situations. Furthermore, we extend the PhC method by a robust scheme for detecting and classifying the presence of multiple motions and estimating their uncertainties. Experimental results on the Middlebury Stereo Dataset and on the KITTI Optical Flow Dataset show the potential offered by the enhanced method in contrast to the PhC implementation of OpenCV.

Keywords: Optical flow · Motion estimation · Phase correlation

1 Introduction

Phase Correlation (PhC) is one of the four classical methods for local motion estimation, together with *discrete matching* (a.k.a. block matching), *differential matching* and *spatio-temporal optical flow measurement* (structure tensor). Although the fundamentals of PhC date back to the 1970s [2,4,5], the precise relations between the listed families of approaches have not been analyzed thoroughly in the literature so far. Depending on the characteristics of the data to be processed and to some degree also depending on the scientific community which is regarded (computer vision, geophysical data analysis, time delay estimation, ...), different families of methods are preferred for the task of estimating displacements or 2D motion. For instance, [6,7] are early papers proposing the normalized cross correlation metric. How to optimize the metric is another issue. *Discrete matching* is opposed to *differential approaches* lead by the classic Lucas&Kanade approach [1].

Since Fourier transform is the main element of the PhC method, it shows strong robustness against geometrical and photometric distortions [8–10].

© Springer International Publishing Switzerland 2016
T. Bräunl et al. (Eds.): PSIVT 2015, LNCS 9431, pp. 368–379, 2016.
DOI: 10.1007/978-3-319-29451-3_30

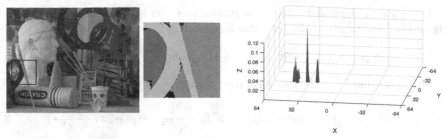

(a) Cell position and disparity map of this cell   (b) Thresholded delta array

Fig. 1. Exemplary result of our enhanced PhC on data from the Middlebury Stereo Dataset. Three different motions (depths) are present in the marked cell (brush, bust and background), causing 3 distinct peaks in the delta array.

Like the classical differential matching schemes, the PhC method, with certain extensions, can achieve subpixel matching accuracy [11]; accuracy of better than 1/100 pixel was claimed by [12,13]. Additional details regarding different variants of PhC algorithms can be found in [10,14–17,21,23]. Some of them describe different ways to achieve subpixel matching accuracy, some others emphasize the advantages of PhC for estimating homogenous displacements for larger images (image registration). Some recent papers considered the use of PhC-based stereo algorithms for remote sensing tasks applied to aerial imagery [18] and for interferometric SAR image co-registration [19]. We refer also to [20] where the PhC stabilizes video sequences against illumination changes and camera shaking. Besides some completely novel approaches, we extend in the present paper several ideas that appear already in [20] and put them on a more systematic basis.

We emphasize that the method presented here does *not* aim at the computation of dense motion fields, but a) makes the classical PhC robust, and b) extends the PhC method towards being able to obtain *distributions* of motion vectors that appear in a given patch. In applications where the patch is assumed to be subjected to a homogeneous translation motion (image registration), this is already the desired result, whereas for complex motion fields these distributions give valuable *prior information* that allows to systematically *initialize* and *guide* a subsequent sparse or (semi-)dense motion estimation procedure.

2   Approach

This section embeds the plain PhC method as it is described in the literature into a framework that checks for potential problematic situations (due to invalid or ambiguous input data) and performs a series of self-checks and filtering steps that are necessary to employ the method in an autonomous mode without user intervention. We provide solid and proven procedures for tuning the different parameters that appear in the enhanced PhC method. The presentation of the PhC method and the proposed extensions are described here for one-dimensional signals; the generalization to more dimensions is straightforward.

Let $y[x_n]$ and $z[x_n]$ be two observations of the same discrete signal $s[x_n]$, where $z[x_n]$ contains a shift by a displacement d:

$$y[x_n] = s[x_n] \quad \text{and} \quad z[x_n] = s[x_n] * \delta[x_n - d] = s[x_n - d]. \tag{1}$$

The orthonormal Fourier transform over a discrete area of size N yields:

$$Y[f_k] = S[f_k] \quad \text{and} \quad Z[f_k] = S[f_k] \cdot \frac{1}{\sqrt{N}} \cdot \exp(-2\pi i \cdot \frac{f_k \cdot d}{N}). \tag{2}$$

For further examination, we isolate the displacement and frequency dependent phase shift between the two signals and introduce the cross-power spectrum $P[f_k]$ and its inverse Fourier transform, the *delta array* $p[x_n]$:

$$P[f_k] \quad \stackrel{\text{def}}{=} \quad \frac{Z[f_k] \cdot Y^*[f_k]}{|Z[f_k]| \cdot |Y[f_k]|} \quad = \quad \exp(-2\pi i \cdot \frac{f_k \cdot d}{N}), \tag{3}$$

$$p[x_n] \quad \stackrel{\text{def}}{=} \quad \mathcal{F}^{-1}(P[f_k]) \quad = \quad \sqrt{N} \cdot \delta[x_n - d]. \tag{4}$$

The delta array $p[x_n]$ consists of an ideal δ-impulse which indicates the relative shift between the two signals $y[x_n]$ and $z[x_n]$. In a realistic setting, with noise[1], multiple motions[2] and without periodicity of the images[3], the delta array is more complex and needs to be analyzed in detail to obtain reliable results.

In the following Sects. 2.1 — 2.4 we introduce several checks and filtering steps which must be performed to let the PhC actually yield reliable and precise results. Steps which need to be applied separately for both patches ($y[x_n]$, $Y[f_k]$ or $z[x_n]$, $Z[f_k]$) are only denoted for the first patch (second patch accordingly).

2.1   Structure Check

First we check if both image patches show sufficient structure to allow the displacement estimation. We compute the gray scale variance of the patches in a weighted manner using the weights $w[x_n]$ of the anti-leakage window:

$$\hat{\sigma}^2 = \left(\sum_{n=1}^{N} w[x_n] \right)^{-1} \sum_{n=1}^{N} w[x_n] \cdot (y[x_n] - \hat{\mu})^2 \quad \text{with} \tag{5}$$

$$\hat{\mu} = \left(\sum_{n=1}^{N} w[x_n] \right)^{-1} \sum_{n=1}^{N} w[x_n] \cdot y[x_n]. \tag{6}$$

Then we compare it against a threshold τ_1 which was experimentally determined:

$$\hat{\sigma}^2 \underset{\text{unstructured}}{\overset{\text{structured}}{\gtrless}} \tau_1. \tag{7}$$

---

[1] $y[x_n] \rightarrow y[x_n] + u[x_n]$, where $u[x_n]$ is assumed to be $\mathcal{N}(0, \sigma_s^2)$ i.i.d.
[2] Due to independent motions within the image or geometric effects (e.g. zoom).
[3] $y[x_n] \rightarrow w[x_n] \cdot y[x_n]$, where $w[x_n]$ is an anti-leakage window (e.g. Tukey).

In our experiments with different datasets[4] we found $\tau_1 \approx 90$ to be a good threshold to distinguish between structured and unstructured patches. Of course this value varies with the noise level of the input images. Due to the normalization of the weights, $w[x_n]$, it is independent of the chosen patch size.

2.2 Spectral Significance Filtering

After the transition to the frequency domain, we need to identify those significant spectral coefficients $Y[f_k]$ and $Z[f_k]$ which represent the main structure of the image patches and thus allow us to determine the displacement d. Therefore we need to suppress the influence of the DC ($f_k = 0$) spectral component of the signal (mean value compensation) as well as the components whose spectral magnitudes are dominated by noise (noise suppression).

Mean Compensation. Since most of the structural information of the image is encoded in the low frequency AC ($f_k \neq 0$) spectral components, it is important to compensate for the gray scale mean *before* the anti-leakage window $w[x_n]$ is applied. Otherwise, these low frequency components would be superimposed by the gray scale mean of the original image patch when the convolution with the Fourier transform of the anti-leakage window $w[x_n]$ is performed[5].

$$Y[f_k] = \mathcal{F}\left(w[x_n] \cdot (y[x_n] - \langle y[x_n]\rangle)\right). \tag{8}$$

Noise Suppression. We also need to suppress those spectral components of $Y[f_k]$ and $Z[f_k]$ whose magnitudes are in the order of magnitude of the noise floor because their phases are only dominated by noise and do not contain any information. To do so, we compute the frequency distributions of $|Y[f_k]|$ and $|Z[f_k]|$ and look for the first interval which is mainly dominated by noise. For a fast approximation, we compute the mean τ_2 of those magnitudes which lie in the smaller half of the frequency distribution. Generally τ_2 might be too large, but this is negligible.

$$|Y[f_k]| \underset{\text{insignificant}}{\overset{\text{significant}}{\gtrless}} \tau_2. \tag{9}$$

2.3 Delta Array Check

After significance filtering has been applied, the cross-power spectrum $P[f_k]$ and the delta array $p[x_n]$ are computed for significant components (see Eqs. 3 and 4). The inverse Fourier transform is an orthonormal transformation, thus:

---

[4] We used a 0.5 Tukey window on Middlebury Stereo and KITTI Optical Flow datasets.

[5] Convolution theorem: $\mathcal{F}(w[x_n] \cdot y[x_n]) = \mathcal{F}(w[x_n]) * \mathcal{F}(y[x_n]) = W[f_k] * Y[f_k]$.

$$\sum_{k=1}^{N} |P[f_k]|^2 = \overbrace{N_{\text{sig}}}^{\text{no. of significant componentens}} = \sum_{n=1}^{N} |p[x_n]|^2 \leq N. \qquad (10)$$

In an ideal case all the energy should concentrate on one δ-impulse which represents the displacement d. Hence we are only interested in those values of $p[x_n]$ which hold a significant amount of the energy known in beforehand (see Eq. 10) and thus represent a dominant motion. The other values which possess a much lower energy are suppressed by computing a threshold τ_3 based on the histogram of the distribution of $|p[x_n]|^2$. We set the histogram range to $[0, N_{\text{sig}}]$ (see Eq. 10), the number of bins to the geometric mean m_{win} of the lengths of the window and the right border of the first bin to be τ_3. In our experiments we verified that energies which represent a relevant motion always lie above this threshold. This check fails if the energies of *all* spectral components are below τ_3.

$$|p[x_n]| \underset{\text{insignificant}}{\overset{\text{significant}}{\underset{<}{\gtrless}}} \tau_3 = \sqrt{\frac{N_{\text{sig}}}{m_{win}}} \qquad (11)$$

2.4   Delta Array Clustering

So far, the tests were described for the one-dimensional case, but for the next check we need the actual two-dimensional representation of the signal. Therefore the delta array is written as $p[\boldsymbol{x}_n]$. In the absence of noise, the inverse Fourier transform of $P[\boldsymbol{f}_k]$ contains a single δ peak, or multiple δ peaks in case of multiple motion. For real data, this / these peak(s) get smeared out and there will be some background noise in the delta array. Hence we only examine the significant (Eq. 11) values of the delta array $p[\boldsymbol{x}_n]$. We define the sets:

$$\mathcal{X} \overset{\text{def}}{=} \{\boldsymbol{x}_n : |p[\boldsymbol{x}_n]| > \tau_3\} \text{ and } \mathcal{P} \overset{\text{def}}{=} \{|p(\boldsymbol{x}_n)| : \boldsymbol{x}_n \in \mathcal{X}\} \ , \ |\mathcal{X}| = |\mathcal{P}| = N_{\text{sig}}. \ (12)$$

These two sets will serve as input for a weighted K-means clustering algorithm.

Initial Phase. The first mean chosen is the point with the largest weight. We iteratively determine $K - 1$ more candidates as the ones with the largest cumulative euclidean distance to the already chosen ones. A set of K covariance matrices $\boldsymbol{\Sigma}_k$ is initialized as two dimensional identity matrices.

Labeling Phase. For each point we calculate the Mahalanobis distance to the current K means $\boldsymbol{m}_k$ and assign the point to the cluster of the mean with minimum distance. Subsequently, we compute means and covariance matrices of the updated clusters using the values of the delta array as weights. This is repeated until either the clusters converge or a predefined maximum number of iterations is reached.

Algorithm 1. weighted k-means using Mahalanobis distance

1: **function** GET_LABELS(k, $\{\boldsymbol{x}_n\}_{n=1,...,N_{\text{sig}}}$, $\{p(\boldsymbol{x}_n)\}_{n=1,...,N_{\text{sig}}}$)
2: $\quad\{\boldsymbol{m}_k\}_{k=1,...,K} \leftarrow$ INITIALIZE_WEIGHTED_MEANS($\{\boldsymbol{x}_n\}, \{p(\boldsymbol{x}_n)\}$)
3: $\quad\{\boldsymbol{\Sigma}_k\}_{k=1,...,K} \leftarrow$ INITIALIZE_COVARIANCE_MATRICES( )
4: $\quad$**repeat**
5: $\qquad$**for** $n \in \{1, ..., N_{\text{sig}}\}$ **do**
6: $\qquad\quad\{d_k\}_{k=1,...,K} \leftarrow$ GET_MAHALANOBIS_DISTANCES($\boldsymbol{x}_n$)
7: $\qquad\quad label_n \leftarrow \arg\min\limits_{k} \{d_k\}_{k=1,...,K}$
8: $\qquad$**end for**
9: $\qquad$UPDATE_WEIGHTED_MEANS( )
10: $\qquad$UPDATE_COVARIANCE_MATRICES( )
11: $\quad$**until** LABELS_CONVERGED( ) **or** MAX_ITER_REACHED( )
12: $\quad$**return** $\{\boldsymbol{m}_k\}_{k=1,...,K}$, $\{\boldsymbol{\Sigma}_k\}_{k=1,...,K}$
13: **end function**

This algorithm returns K means $\boldsymbol{m}_k$ and covariance matrices $\boldsymbol{\Sigma}_k$ which describe the distribution within each cluster. To find the optimal K, the algorithm is run for different values of K and a cost function which sums up the areas of the covariance ellipses and penalizes large values of K (Occam's razor) is minimized:

$$K_{opt} = \arg\min_{K} \sum_{k=1}^{K} \det(\boldsymbol{\Sigma}_k) + a \cdot \exp(b \cdot K). \tag{13}$$

We determined the values of the parameters in our experiments to be

$$a \approx 2.5 \cdot \det(\boldsymbol{\Sigma}_0) \quad \text{and} \quad b \approx 0.5, \tag{14}$$

where $\det(\boldsymbol{\Sigma}_0)$ is the area of the covariance ellipse in the case of only one cluster ($K = 1$).

2.5 Multiresolution

Since the estimation of a relative displacement of the signal in two regarded patches is limited by the patch size[6] and works best when most of the image content is present in both patches, the previously presented steps are performed iteratively on different resolution scales of the image. We employed a Gaussian pyramid with two levels and a scaling of 2 for each image dimension. We used the same patch size on both pyramid levels, performed a first motion estimation on the upper (=lower resolution) pyramid level and transferred the result to the original scale by shifting the patch windows relative to each other according to the (correctly scaled) motion vector determined in the upper pyramid level. This way we ensure that we can deal also with large displacements.

---

[6] Displacements of at most half the patch size are detectable.

3 Experiments

Our enhanced PhC approach allows us to estimate multiple motion distributions. The proposed method is evaluated at the optical flow dataset from the KITTI Vision Benchmark Suite [22] and the Middlebury Stereo Dataset [3]. Due to the fact that the PhC, by construction, aims at determining the *distribution* of motion vectors but not a dense motion field, we could not apply the metrics of these benchmarks which expect a dense motion field. Therefore we can only compare our method against the PhC implementation of OpenCV, which is based on the work of Stone et al. [16], and the ground truth data of the training datasets of the two mentioned benchmarks.

3.1 Middlebury Stereo Dataset

In this experiment, we intend to show that our proposed approach is able to estimate multiple motions within a defined patch. We also want to demonstrate that these estimates are correct and precise. However, PhC is of course only able to detect motions if the moving objects show enough structure. Therefore, we chose the dataset from 2001 as its images exhibit well structured elements.

The 6 image pairs of this stereo dataset are divided into 6 centered patches, each of size 128×128 pixels. These patches are shown as black rectangles in Fig. 2. Since this dataset was originally created for a stereo benchmark, the images are recorded by a left and right camera. Thus we can assume that the captured scene is only translated horizontally, although of course the PhC is not aware of this. The provided disparity maps express exactly this described behavior. Objects which are more far away from the camera exhibit a lower displacement than objects in the near field. The disparity values (represented by the gray level values) describe the 'motion' of an object between two images. For example, two different motions are present in the first patch of the disparity map 2a. The aim of this experiment is to detect exactly these multiple motions within a patch. The total quantity of available displacements of all patches of a specific image pair is listed in the second column of Table 1. Another aspect which has to be considered is that the objects do not necessarily lie in a frontal plane w.r.t. the camera and hence the translation of the object cannot be described with one single disparity value. This means that we observe disparity value *ranges*, not singular values. In our experiment, we computed all such ranges in each patch, which serve as ground truth ranges.

For each patch we executed our enhanced PhC algorithm. The results are shown in Table 1, where they are compared against the OpenCV version of the PhC. Obviously our enhanced PhC is able to estimate a significantly larger amount of motions than the OpenCV PhC. Moreover, the calculated displacements are more precise and more reliable than the OpenCV ones. We estimated every single detected motion correctly, which means that our computed displacements fall within the above stated range of ground truth data. In contrast to that, the OpenCV version does not determine all its detected motions correctly, as it can be seen in the last column of Table 1.

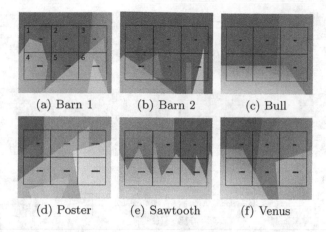

(a) Barn 1   (b) Barn 2   (c) Bull

(d) Poster   (e) Sawtooth   (f) Venus

Fig. 2. All disparity maps from the Middlebury Stereo Dataset 2001 [3] divided into patches. In each patch, the estimated motion is encoded by a colored line. Note: The length of the line (respectively the motion) is scaled by a factor of two for better visualization.

Table 1. We compare the quantity of right estimated motions by our and the OpenCV PhC [16] w.r.t. the occurring motions within each dataset.

Dataset	# gt. motions	est. motions		correct est. motions	
		OpenCV	our PhC	OpenCV	our PhC
Barn 1	15	40 %	67 %	100 %	100 %
Barn 2	13	46 %	77 %	83 %	100 %
Bull	11	54 %	63 %	83 %	100 %
Poster	19	32 %	47 %	100 %	100 %
Sawtooth	13	46 %	54 %	100 %	100 %
Venus	13	46 %	62 %	100 %	100 %
Overall	84	44 %	62 %	94 %	100 %

Using the Middlebury Stereo Dataset, we showed that our enhanced PhC can detect and correctly estimate multiple motions within a patch if the individual objects possess enough structure and cover a reasonable percentage of the patch.

3.2   KITTI Optical Flow Dataset

In the second part of our experiments, we use real world driving scenes and show that our algorithm outperforms the OpenCV PhC in terms of precision and reliability and also simultaneously measures the uncertainties of the estimated motions. Furthermore we show that our four self-diagnostic checks are both useful and work correctly. For the evaluation of our new approach, we took all 194 image pairs from the KITTI Optical Flow Training Dataset [22].

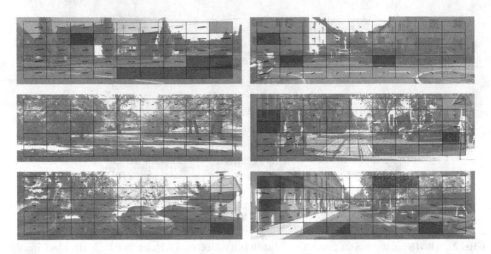

Fig. 3. 6 exemplary results taken from the KITTI Training Dataset which show the performance of our method. The colored lines indicate the length of estimate motions. A red overlay on a patch indicates that one of our checks yielded a negative result and thus no reliable and precise motion estimation is possible.

We did not evaluate our PhC method on the Test Dataset, because ground truth data is not available and the benchmark only accepts sparse or dense motion fields. We cannot provide this because we can only estimate motion distribution within a defined patch. For that reason we analyze the performance of our PhC by dividing each image into 45 non-overlapping patches of 128×64 pixels (cf. Fig. 3) and compare the results of our PhC against the ones from OpenCV and the ground truth from the training dataset. Unfortunately, KITTI does not provide ground truth for the entire image because their *LIDAR* scanner has only a limited field of view. This is why we could only do the evaluation on 6942 of the 8730 possible patches. The KITTI data provides an almost dense motion field within a patch, but we can only compare motion distributions characterized by a mean $\boldsymbol{m}_{n,gt}$ and a covariance matrix $\boldsymbol{\Sigma}_{n,gt}$. Therefore, we determine the parameters of the motion distribution from the ground truth data for the patches $\{c_n\}_{n=1,\ldots,3752}$ where K motions $\boldsymbol{x}_i$ occur in a patch c_n, in the following way:

$$\hat{\boldsymbol{m}}_{n,gt} = \frac{1}{K} \sum_{i=1}^{K} x_i \quad \text{and} \quad \hat{\boldsymbol{\Sigma}}_{n,gt} = \frac{1}{K-1} \sum_{i=1}^{K} (\boldsymbol{x}_i - \hat{\boldsymbol{m}}_{n,gt})(\boldsymbol{x}_i - \hat{\boldsymbol{m}}_{n,gt})^T. \quad (15)$$

With the described self-diagnosis checks, we determined that on 3752 of the 6942 patches, the PhC can provide a reliable motion estimate. On the other patches, one of our proposed checks failed due to low structure, too much noise or too different image patches caused by large displacements. In the Fig. 4a and b, the ordered displacements in horizontal respectively vertical direction are shown for all possible patches. These plots show that our PhC is located much closer to the trend of the ground truth than the OpenCV implementation. Many of the motions computed by OpenCV are either outliers or lie close to the zero line. As opposed to this our PhC produces only a few outliers. Consider to the given integer precision, our results comply well to the ground truth.

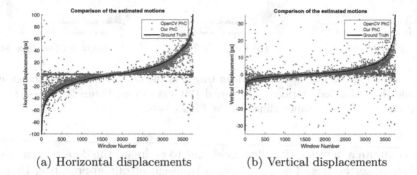

(a) Horizontal displacements   (b) Vertical displacements

Fig. 4. Ordered horizontal and vertical displacements which occur through the 3752 patches where ground truth data and a motion estimate is available.

In the last part of this experiment, we want to show that our motion distribution parameters[7] are well estimated. We chose a relatively pessimistic approach by evaluating $m_{n,eval}$ and $\Sigma_{n,eval}$ for each patch c_n in the following way:

$$m_{n,eval} = \hat{m}_{n,gt} - m_{n,k,PhC} \quad \text{and} \quad \Sigma_{n,eval} = \hat{\Sigma}_{n,gt} + \Sigma_{n,k,PhC}. \tag{16}$$

Figure 5a and b show the histogram of the euclidean lengths of the deviation $\{m\}_{n=1,...,3752,eval}$ between the ground truth and our PhC and the OpenCV PhC respectively. The results show that our PhC provides fewer estimates than the OpenCV PhC, simply because we recognize patches where no reliable motion estimate is possible. Secondly, slightly more displacements are estimated correctly, as it can be seen in histogram bins $[0, 5]$. However, the main advantage of our PhC is that only very few estimates deviate more than 30 pixels to the ground truth. The OpenCV PhC, on the other hand, yields more than 2000 motion estimates which exhibit a deviation of more than 30 pixels w.r.t the ground truth. To evaluate the uncertainty of the estimate, expressed by the 'size' of the covariance matrix, we compute the area A_n of $\Sigma_{n,eval}$ as $A_n = \det(\Sigma_{n,eval})$, which corresponds to the 1σ-area covered by the covariance ellipse. Figure 5c shows the histogram of $\{A\}_{n=1,...,3752}$. Some motions have a relatively high uncertainty (large A_n), but most of the estimated motion distributions are compact (small A_n), which means that their displacements are reliable and precise.

We have evaluated our work on two different datasets. The performance of our enhanced PhC clearly outperforms the OpenCV one. We achieve good estimates of motion distributions if the moving objects possess enough structure and cover a significant part of the patch. As already stated, the purpose of our approach is

---

[7] We do not assume any specific probability distribution.

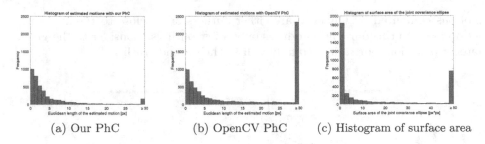

(a) Our PhC   (b) OpenCV PhC   (c) Histogram of surface area

Fig. 5. In the Figs. 5a and b, the euclidean length of the deviation between the ground truth and the estimated motions of two used PhCs is shown. Figure 5c shows the 1σ-area covered by the covariance ellipse of the PhC result.

not to compute a dense optical flow field, but to estimate the dominant motions and their uncertainties. The particular advantage of our approach is that we achieve with very moderate computational effort reliable information about the distribution of the optical flow vectors within a patch - including the case of multiple motions. The runtime of our PhC is roughly 1 ms for a 256×256 pixel patch without any use of multithreading and GPU support on a common PC.

4   Summary and Conclusion

We have shown that the classical PhC method can be made significantly more robust against different sources of malfunction. This has been achieved by a systematic analysis of the effects of noise and the conditioning of the input data (texture, similarity). Obviously, the spatial precision of the method can be extended into the subpixel range by using existing schemes for providing sub-pixel resolution to phase correlation [11–13]. This, however, is independent from the method improvements presented here. We refrained from using any of these schemes in order to present the effects of our modifications in 'clean room conditions', unaffected by other modifications. We emphasize that the standard PhC is a good motion estimator for patches with a homogeneous translational motion field, whereas our extended PhC provides *distributions* for multiple motions in a patch which can be used for local methods that need a good initialization.

References

1. Lucas, B., Kanade, T.: An iterative image registration technique with an application to stereo vision. In: proceedings of the International Joint Conference on Artificial Intelligence, pp. 674–679 (1981)
2. Knapp, C., Carter, G.: The generalized correlation method for estimation of time delay. IEEE Trans. Acoust. Speech Signal Process. **24**(4), 320–327 (1976)
3. Scharstein, D., Szeliski, R.: A taxonomy and evaluation of dense two-frame stereo correspondence algorithms. Intern. J. C.V. **47**(1–3), 7–42 (2002)

4. Pratt, W.K.: Correlation techniques of image registration. IEEE Trans. Aerosp. Electron. Syst. **AES–10**(3), 353–358 (1974)
5. Kuglin, C.D., Hines, D.C.: The Phase Correlation Image Alignment Method. In: Proceedings of the International Conference on Cybernetics and Society, pp. 163–165 (1975)
6. Kumar, B.V.K., Hassebrook, L.: Performance measures for correlation filters. Appl. Opt. **29**(20), 2997–3006 (1990)
7. Greenfeld, J.S.: An operator-based matching system. Photogram. Eng. Remote Sens. **8**(57), 1049–1055 (1991)
8. Tian, Q., Huhns, M.N.: Algorithms for subpixel registration. Comput. Vis. Graph. Image Process. **35**(2), 220–233 (1986)
9. Brown, L.G.: A survey of image registration techniques. ACM Comput. Surv. **24**(4), 325–376 (1992)
10. Zitová, B., Flusser, J.: Image registration methods: a survey. Image Vis. Comput. **21**(11), 977–1000 (2003)
11. Pearson, J.J., Hines, D.C., Golosman, S., Kuglin, C.D.: Video-rate image correlation processor. In: Proceedings of Application of Digital Image Processing, pp. 191–205 (1977)
12. Takita, K., Sasaki, Y., Higuchi, T., Kobayashi, K.: High-accuracy subpixel image registration based on phase-only correlation. IEICE Trans. Fundam. Electron. Commun. **86**(8), 1925–1934 (2003)
13. Takita, K., Muquit, M.A., Aoki, T., Higuchi, T.: A subpixel correspondence search technique for computer vision applications. IEICE Trans. Fundam. Electron. Commun. **E87–A**(8), 1913–1923 (2004)
14. Kirichuk, V.S., Peretjagin, G.I.: Establishing similarity between fragments and a standard. Optoelectron. Instrum. Data Process. **22**(4), 83–87 (1986)
15. Fleet, D.J.: Disparity from local weighted phase-correlation. In: proceedings of the International Conference on Systems, Man and Cybernectis, pp. 48–56 (1994)
16. Stone, H.S., Orchard, M., Chang, E.C., Martucci, S.: A fast direct Fourier-based algorithm for subpixel registration of images. IEEE Trans. Geosci. Remote Sens. **39**(10), 2235–2243 (2001)
17. Guizar-Sicairos, M., Thurman, S.T., Fienup, J.R.: Efficient subpixel image registration algorithms. Opt. Lett. **33**(2), 156–158 (2008)
18. Jung, I.K., Lacroix, S.: High resolution terrain mapping using low altitude aerial stereo imagery. In: proceedings of the International Conference on Computer Vision, pp. 946–951 (2003)
19. Abdelfattah, R., Nicolas, J.M., Tupin, F.: Interferometric SAR image coregistration based on the Fourier Mellin invariant descriptor. IEEE Int. Geosci. Remote Sens. Symp. **3**, 1334–1336 (2002)
20. Eisenbach, J., Mertz, M., Conrad, C., Mester, R.: Reducing camera vibrations and photometric changes in surveillance video. In: proceedings of the International Conference on Advanced Video and Signal Based Surveillance, pp. 69–74 (2013)
21. Foroosh, H., Zerubia, J.B., Berthod, M.: Extension of phase correlation to subpixel registration. IEEE Trans. Image Process. **11**(3), 188–200 (2002)
22. Geiger, A., Lenz, P., Urtasun, R.: Are we ready for autonomous driving? the KITTI vision benchmark suite. In: proceedings of Conference on Computer Vision and Pattern Recognition, pp. 3354–3361 (2012)
23. Morgan, G.L.K., Jian, G.L., Yan, H.: Precise subpixel disparity measurement from very narrow baseline stereo. IEEE Trans. Geosci. Remote Sens. **48**(9), 3424–3433 (2010)

Robust Visual Voice Activity Detection Using Long Short-Term Memory Recurrent Neural Network

Zaw Htet Aung and Panrasee Ritthipravat[(⊠)]

Artificial Intelligence in Medicine Laboratory,
Department of Biomedical Engineering, Mahidol University,
25/25 Puttamonthon 4, Salaya 73170, Nakhon Pathom, Thailand
z.zawhtet.a@ieee.org, panrasee.rit@mahidol.ac.th

Abstract. Many traditional visual voice activity detection systems utilize features extracted from mouth region images which are sensitive to noisy observations of the visual domain. In addition, hyperparameters of the feature extraction process modulating the desired compromise between robustness, efficiency, and accuracy of the algorithm are difficult to be determined. Therefore, a visual voice activity detection algorithm which only utilizes simple lip shape information as features and a Long Short-Term Memory recurrent neural network (LSTM-RNN) as a classifier is proposed. Face detection is performed by structural SVM based on histogram of oriented gradient (HOG) features. Detected face template is used to initialize a kernelized correlation filter tracker. Facial landmark coordinates are then extracted from the tracked face. Centroid distance function is applied to the geometrically normalized landmarks surrounding the outer and inner lip contours. Finally, discriminative (LSTM-RNN) and generative (Hidden Markov Model) methods are used to model the temporal lip shape sequences during speech and non-speech intervals and their classification performances are compared. Experimental results show that the proposed algorithm using LSTM-RNN can achieve a classification rate of 98 % in labeling speech and non-speech periods. It is robust and efficient for realtime applications.

Keywords: Visual voice activity detection · Long short-term memory · Recurrent neural network · Supervised sequence classification

1 Introduction

Voice activity detection plays a significant role in enabling natural and spontaneous Human-Computer and Human-Robot Interaction applications. However, voice activity detection based solely on audio modality faces various challenges in real world environments. The fact that visual information is complimentary to acoustic speech signal has been well founded in the literature. The influence of visual features on the perception of speech has been demonstrated in [1]. It is

© Springer International Publishing Switzerland 2016
T. Bräunl et al. (Eds.): PSIVT 2015, LNCS 9431, pp. 380–391, 2016.
DOI: 10.1007/978-3-319-29451-3_31

well-known in the literature as the McGurk effect. Also, if there is noise corruption in the environment, the availability of lip movement data grants a person an extra 4–6 dB of noise tolerance compared to audio data alone [2].

1.1 Related Works

Many works in the area of visual voice activity detection utilize mouth region image intensity based features. Siatras et al. [3] used variations in the amount and intensity of mouth region pixels as cues for voice activity detection. A case-specific threshold was needed to identify relevant pixels. Ahmad et al. [4] presented a method where changes in the mean intensity values of mouth area during speech and silence periods were modeled by Gaussian Mixture Models. These methods rely solely on image intensities which make them unsuitable for adverse lighting conditions. In [5], Song et al. described a method based on chaos inspired similarity measure to mitigate changes in lighting conditions. However, their classification model depends on a number of predefined thresholds which are not easily generalizable. From the previously described approaches, they do not consider natural lip movements during non-speaking intervals. Aubrey et al. [6] attempted to model both speech and non-speech movements by Hidden Markov Models (HMM), using optical flow vectors computed from consecutive mouth area frames as observations. Additionally, similar approach based on optical flow based mouth image energy feature and bi-level HMM was proposed by Tiawongsombat et al. [7]. Most techniques of the optical flow require appropriate illumination condition and that the displacement of pixels between frames are not abrupt [8]. Moreover, Hidden Markov Models are not suitable for modeling long data sequences because of the independence assumption where each hidden state can depend only on the immediate preceding one.

2 Proposed Method

The technique proposed in this paper only utilizes simple lip shape information extracted from the video sequences containing the speaker's face. First, the speaker's face is detected by histogram of oriented gradients (HOG) based detector [9]. Secondly, the detected face is used as a template to initialize the tracking algorithm [11] and then, in each subsequent frame, the facial landmark coordinates of the tracked face are located using the pretrained shape predictor [9]. Next, the lip shape vectors are geometrically normalized and the centroid distance function is applied to the latter, obtaining the lip shape features. Temporal variations of lip shape during speech and silence periods including non-trivial head motions are modeled using Long Short-Term Memory (LSTM) recurrent neural network. Figure 1 illustrates the overall approach. Details of each step are described as follows.

2.1 Face Detection

Face detection is performed on the initial frames until a face is detected by using the pre-trained sliding window detector provided by [9] which utilizes the

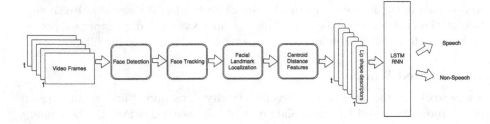

Fig. 1. Proposed approach

structural SVM based classifier trained on histogram of oriented gradient (HOG) features. It has a substantially lower false detections than Viola Jones face detector [10].

2.2 Face Tracking

Kernelized Correlation Filter tracker [11] is then applied. It is an online discriminative tracking algorithm. The object of interest can be continuously tracked while adapting the tracking model to incorporate new information about the former. The KCF tracker exploits the performance and computational efficiency afforded by utilizing cyclically translated samples and by performing corresponding kernel correlations in the Fourier domain. The bounding rectangle returned from the face detector is used to extract the face template to initialize the KCF tracker. Given a base template x of size $(m \times n)$ and the Gaussian-shaped regression targets y of size $(m \times n)$, the dual coefficients $\hat{\alpha}$ to solve the kernelized ridge regression in Fourier Domain is given by

$$\hat{\alpha} = \frac{\hat{y}}{\hat{k}^{xx} + \lambda} \tag{1}$$

where

$\hat{\alpha}$ = DFT (Discrete Fourier Transform) of dual coefficients
$\hat{y}$ = DFT of Gaussian-shaped regression targets
$\hat{k}^{xx}$ = DFT of kernel autocorrelation vector
λ = Regularization term

In the subsequent frames, the kernel crosscorrelation ($\hat{k}^{xz}$) between cyclically shifted versions of base sample x and new candidate patch z can be computed and an $(m \times n)$ map of responses given by the following equation is obtained. $\odot$ represents element-wise multiplication.

$$\hat{f}(z) = \hat{k}^{xz} \odot \hat{\alpha} \tag{2}$$

By calculating the location of the maximum response in the real part of the inverse Discrete Fourier transform of $\hat{f}(z)$ ($Re(\mathcal{F}^{-1}(\hat{f}(z)))$), the location of the tracked face in the current frame can be found. The tracking model is then adapted to the newly found face patch x_n in frame n to reflect the changes.

$$\hat{a}_n = (1 - \eta) * \hat{a}_{n-1} + \eta * (\frac{\hat{y}_{n-1}}{\hat{k}^{x_n x_n} + \lambda}) \tag{3}$$

$$x_n = (1 - \eta) * x_{n-1} + \eta * x_n \tag{4}$$

Here η is the adaptation parameter, $\hat{a}_n$ and x_n are the Fourier transform of dual coefficients and new interpolated base template respectively.

2.3   Landmark Localization and Geometric Normalization

To localize the facial landmarks in the tracked face, an implementation of the method described in [12] is utilized. It has been trained on an IBUG 300-W face landmark dataset to predict the location of 68 facial landmarks in realtime. Here it is defined that the $c_i \in R^2$ be the ith x and y coordinate of lip contour in a face image F. The shape vector $C = (c_1^T, c_2^T, c_3^T, ..., c_{20}^T)$ represents the 20 coordinates of inner and outer lip contours in F. Next, the scale, orientation and translation components of the detected lip landmarks have to be normalized. In this step, it is necessary to find the 2×3 affine transformation matrix $\mathbf{A}$ which maps the vector C onto the coordinate frame with the size of 128×96 as shown in Fig. 2. $\mathbf{A}$ is defined as

$$\mathbf{A} = \begin{bmatrix} \alpha & \beta & [(1 - \alpha) * c_{x\,center} - \beta * c_{y\,center}] \\ -\beta & \alpha & [\beta * c_{x\,center} + (1 - \alpha) * c_{y\,center}] \end{bmatrix} \tag{5}$$

where

$\alpha = $ scale $* \cos \theta$
$\beta = $ scale $* \sin \theta$
$c_{x\,center} = $ x coordinate of mouth center
$c_{y\,center} = $ y coordinate of mouth center
$\theta = $ angle of rotation around c_x and c_y

To get θ and scale, the following equations are computed.

$$\theta = \arctan(\frac{d_y}{d_x}) * \frac{180}{\theta} \tag{6}$$

$$scale = \frac{\gamma * 128}{||c_{lmc} - c_{rmc}||^2} \tag{7}$$

where d_y and d_x are the differences between y and x coordinates of left c_{lmc} and right c_{rmc} mouth corners respectively. γ is the scaling factor.

Finally, the geometrically normalized lip shape vector C_{norm} can be obtained by

$$C_{norm} = \mathbf{A} \begin{bmatrix} C \\ 1 \end{bmatrix}^{\mathbf{T}} \tag{8}$$

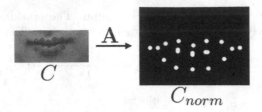

Fig. 2. Lip shape normalization

2.4 Centroid Distance Features

In this step, the centroid distance function [13] (CDF) is applied to the normalized outer and inner lip contour points in C_{norm}. CDF measures the distances between outer and inner lip boundary points and their respective centroids.

$$d^O{}_n = \sqrt{(x^O{}_n - x^O_c)^2 + (y^O{}_n - y^O_c)^2} \tag{9}$$

$$d^I{}_m = \sqrt{(x^I{}_m - x^I_c)^2 + (y^I{}_m - y^I_c)^2} \tag{10}$$

The resulting 20 dimensional feature vector $d_i = [d^O_n \ d^I_m]$ conveys the lip shape information during speech and silence frames.

2.5 LSTM Recurrent Neural Network

Recurrent neural networks (RNNs) belong to a family of supervised learning techniques and they have major advantages over feed forward neural networks and support vector machines in which recurrent neural networks can efficiently capture time dynamics and handle long-range time-dependencies. Moreover, unlike Hidden Markov models (HMM), they do not inherit the flaws of independence assumption where the current state can only depend on a limited number of previous ones. RNNs can model a probability distribution over an arbitrarily long sequence, $P(x_1, x_2, ..., x_T)$, without simplifications necessary to make HMMs mathematically and computationally tractable. At time step t, a recurrent neural network retains a state s_t which encodes the information regarding the entire sequence of previous inputs $(x_1, x_2, ..., x_t)$. Therefore, an RNN can be trained to learn a function f such that

$$s_t = f(s_{t-1}, x_t) \tag{11}$$

For a simple recurrent neural network, the Eq. 11 becomes

$$s_t = \phi(W^{ss} s_{t-1} + W^{sx} x_t) \tag{12}$$

where ϕ is either a logistic sigmoid or hyperbolic tangent nonlinearity. W_{ss} represents the state-to-state connections and W_{sx} represents input-to-hidden state connections. However, simple RNNs cannot effectively learn long-range temporal and non-temporal dependencies since the backpropagated errors may either decay (vanishing gradients) or grow (exploding gradients) across several time steps.

Long Short-Term Memory Recurrent Neural Networks [14,15] are an extension of the original RNNs that address the major short comings of the latter. It achieves this by replacing the traditional hidden recurrent nodes with "LSTM cells" that ensure constant error propagation across time steps. Hence, they are readily suitable to capture the dynamics of lip movements over long temporal scales. An LSTM cell contains a special node (c) with a self-recurrent connection and an input node (I) while the flow of information to and from the cell is controlled by input (i) and output (o) gates. The forget gate (f) determines the persistence of the state of the special memory node. The equations governing the forward propagation mechanisms through an LSTM layer are as follows:

The input node $\boldsymbol{I}$ receives the previous state information of the network $\boldsymbol{s}_{t-1}$ and the current input $\boldsymbol{x}_t$. Then, a squashing function ϕ is applied on the affine transformation of its inputs.

$$\boldsymbol{I}_t = \phi(W^{Ix}\boldsymbol{x}_t + W^{Is}\boldsymbol{s}_{t-1} + \boldsymbol{b}^I) \tag{13}$$

The input and forget gates has the same inputs but the sigmoid nonlinearity σ is used as a gating function to produce a value between 0 and 1. Once learned, the input and forget gates determine how much of new information is allowed into the memory node and how much of previously memorized content should be discarded.

$$i_t = \sigma(W^{ix}\boldsymbol{x}_t + W^{is}\boldsymbol{s}_{t-1} + \boldsymbol{b}^i) \tag{14}$$

$$\boldsymbol{f}_t = \sigma(W^{fx}\boldsymbol{x}_t + W^{fs}\boldsymbol{s}_{t-1} + \boldsymbol{b}^f) \tag{15}$$

Based on the activation values of the input and forget gates, the new internal state $\boldsymbol{c}_t$ of the cell is computed as a weighted sum of the new input information $\boldsymbol{I}_t$ and past internal state $\boldsymbol{c}_{t-1}$. $\odot$ represents element-wise multiplication.

$$\boldsymbol{c}_t = \boldsymbol{I}_t \odot \boldsymbol{i}_t + \boldsymbol{c}_{t-1} \odot \boldsymbol{f}_t \tag{16}$$

The output gate will modulate the extent to which the new state of the LSTM cell will be exposed to the rest of the network. $\boldsymbol{b}^I$, $\boldsymbol{b}^i$, $\boldsymbol{b}^o$, $\boldsymbol{b}^f$ are bias vectors.

$$o_t = \phi(W^{ox}\boldsymbol{x}_t + W^{os}\boldsymbol{s}_{t-1} + \boldsymbol{b}^o) \tag{17}$$

Lastly, the hidden state of the LSTM network is updated according to the following equation.

$$\boldsymbol{s}_t = \boldsymbol{c}_t \odot \boldsymbol{o}_t \tag{18}$$

Single LSTM unit and the overall network architecture can be seen in Figs. 3 and 4 respectively. The HMM-based classification scheme is presented in the next section.

2.6 Hidden Markov Model

In this section, a brief description of the Hidden Markov Model (HMM) which is used to model the time varying lip shape vectors is provided. Hidden Markov Models are probabilistic generative models widely used in a variety of sequence generation and classification tasks. An HMM is parameterized by the initial state distribution π, the state transition matrix A, and the observation model O. Given that there are M hidden states and N dimensional feature vectors, the state variable $X_t \in \{i, j | i, j \in 1, ..., M\}$ and the observation variable $Y_t \in R^N$ at time t can be defined. Then, it follows that

$$\pi(i) = P(X_1 = i) \tag{19}$$

$$A(i, j) = P(X_t = j | X_{t-1} = i) \tag{20}$$

$$O(i) = P(Y_t | X_t = i) \tag{21}$$

From a series of T observations generated by a process c, $Y^c{}_{t=1:T}$, π^c, A^c, and O^c for the model M^c can be estimated using the well-known Baum-Welch [16] algorithm. The classification task using trained HMMs, $M^{c=speech}$ and $M^{c=silence}$, can therefore be formulated using log likelihood of the models.

$$M^{c*} = \underset{c}{\mathrm{argmax}}\, P(Y | M^c) P(M^c) \tag{22}$$

$P(Y^c | M^c)$ is the likelihood defined as the probability of the observed data given the model M^c and $P(M^c)$ is the prior for the model which can be omitted as it is assumed to be uniform.

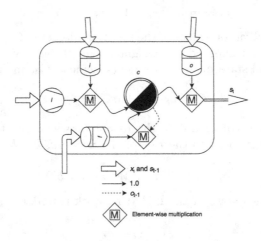

Fig. 3. An LSTM memory cell

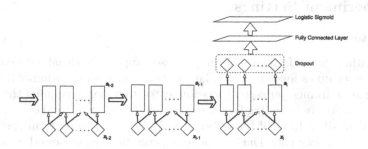

Fig. 4. LSTM network architecture

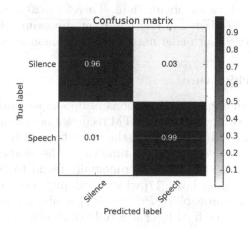

Fig. 5. Confusion matrix for LSTM classification

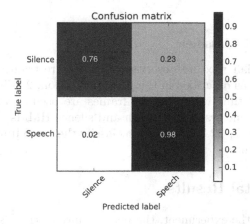

Fig. 6. Confusion matrix for HMM classification

3   Experiment Settings

3.1   Dataset

For evaluating the performance of the proposed approach, visual data collection system was set up as follows. A standard webcam with a resolution of 640 x 480 capturing at 30 frames per second was connected to a laptop running the feature extraction algorithm including face detection and tracking. A total of six subjects were asked to sit in front of the webcam and instructed to perform speech and non-speech lip movements. During the non-speech movement period, in addition to stationary lips, the subjects were instructed to perform typical behaviors such as smiling, laughing, shaking and nodding head, etc. for approximately 5 min. For data collection during speech, each subject was asked to read out loud a collection of Thai words and articles for about 5 min. Therefore, 20 dimensional centroid distance features were collected in realtime from approximately 230000 frames. This process was carried out under uncontrolled common lighting conditions.

3.2   Network Architecture

In this experiment, the temporal evolutions of lip shapes during speaking and non-speaking states are modeled with LSTM recurrent neural network containing one hidden layer of LSTM units. Hence, the input layer of the network receives a 20 dimensional feature vector at each time step. The number of LSTM units in the hidden layer is 100 which is experimentally found to be optimal for the current problem. A dropout layer [17] which randomly sets a certain portion of its inputs to zero with probability P ($P = 0.5$) is also added to reduce over-fitting of the network. The final layer is a fully connected layer with a sigmoid activation function which outputs a value between 0 an 1. Then, the binary cross-entropy between the target and network output values is evaluated. The network is trained using RMSProp [18] algorithm with the initial learning rate set to 0.001.

3.3   HMM-based Classifier

HMMs with Gaussian mixture observation model are trained using the same lip shape sequences as described in the previous section. 20 dimensional feature vectors, spanning a time window of 60 frames are used as training sequences to estimate the parameters of the speech and silence HMMs. The classification scheme described in Eq. 22 is employed to classify the video frame sequences into either speech or silence.

4   Experimental Results

In the first part of the experiment, the performance of the LSTM network and HMM-based classifiers is evaluated on the dataset which contains lip shape features extracted from all subjects. Two HMMs are trained on 75 % of the data

Fig. 7. An example of the program running in realtime

Table 1. Classification rate

	Classification Rate
CDF + LSTM	**98 %**
CDF + HMM	**87 %**

Table 2. Classification accuracies for different subjects using LSTM

Subject	1	2	3	4	5	6
1	-	0.83	0.75	0.95	0.89	0.95
2	0.95	-	0.85	0.96	0.80	0.98
3	0.73	0.78	-	0.98	0.96	0.98
4	0.92	0.79	0.89	-	0.96	0.99
5	0.63	0.71	0.90	0.97	-	0.91
6	0.75	0.80	0.86	0.97	0.90	-

while the remaining 25 % are used for testing. For LSTM-based classifier, the dataset is divided into training, validation and test sets containing 50 To investigate the effectiveness and generalizability of the proposed approach, the two models are trained solely on the centroid distance features extracted from each person and their classification performances are assessed on the datasets of every other subjects. The results of the second experiment are shown in Tables 2 and 3. Even though the LSTM network is trained only on a fraction of the whole dataset, it is still able to classify with high accuracy in most cases whereas the HMM-based classifier shows consistently lower performance. Also, the proposed approach using LSTM network is tested in realtime on a laptop with Intel Core i5 processor and 30 fps webcam with a resolution of 640x480, while performing forward pass on the network every 60 frames. Given that the user's face

Table 3. Classification accuracies for different subjects using HMM

Subject	1	2	3	4	5	6
1	-	0.56	0.47	0.53	0.46	0.55
2	0.52	-	0.54	0.59	0.83	0.69
3	0.52	0.80	-	0.88	0.88	0.86
4	0.53	0.84	0.80	-	0.86	0.90
5	0.56	0.75	0.86	0.96	-	0.97
6	0.63	0.77	0.78	0.94	0.90	-

is detected and tracked correctly, the algorithm can efficiently and accurately classify speech and complex non-speech lip shape sequences (Fig. 7).

5 Conclusion

A novel method for visual voice activity detection with integrated face tracking framework has been proposed. Since the features utilized by this method are simple and purely geometric, the efficiency and robustness of the algorithm is greatly increased. Another contribution of this paper is the use of Long Short-Term Memory neural network to model long range temporal evolutions of lip shapes during periods of speech and non-speech. To the best of the authors' knowledge, this is the first time that a temporal connectionist model is applied to visual voice activity detection. Moreover, the performances of and LSTM recurrent neural network and the classical HMM on visual voice activity detection task, using the proposed features are compared. Experimental results show that the trained network can achieve classification rate of above 98 % and also it is demonstrated that the generalization performance of the proposed approach using LSTM network is better than using HMM.

Acknowledgements. This research was supported by National Science and Technology Development Agency (NSTDA) and National Research Council of Thailand (NRCT).

References

1. McGurk, H., MacDonald, J.: Hearing lips and seeing voices. Nature **264**, 746–748 (1976)
2. Summerfield, Q.: Lipreading and audio-visual speech perception. Philos. Trans. R. Soc. Lond. B Biol. Sci. **335**(1273), 71–78 (1992)
3. Siatras, S., Nikolaidis, N., Krinidis, M., Pitas, I.: Visual lip activity detection and speaker detection using mouth region intensities. IEEE Trans. Circ. Syst. Video Technol. **19**(1), 133–137 (2009)

4. Ahmad, R., Raza, S.P., Malik, H.: Visual speech detection using an unsupervised learning framework. In: 12th International Conference on Machine Learning and Applications (ICMLA), vol. 2, pp. 525–528. 4–7 Dec 2013
5. Song, T., Lee, K., Ko, H.: Visual voice activity detection via chaos based lip motion measure robust under illumination changes. IEEE Trans. Consum. Electron. **60**(2), 251–257 (2014)
6. Aubrey, A.J., Hicks, Y.A., Chambers, J.A.: Visual voice activity detection with optical flow. IET Image Process. **4**(6), 463–472 (2010)
7. Tiawongsombat, P., Jeong, M.-H., Yun, J.-S., You, B.-J., Oh, S.-R.: Robust visual speakingness detection using bi-level HMM. Pattern Recogn. **45**(2), 783–793 (2012). ISSN 0031-3203
8. Roth, S., Lewis, J.P., Sun, D., Black, M.J.: Learning optical flow. In: Forsyth, D., Torr, P., Zisserman, A. (eds.) ECCV 2008, Part III. LNCS, vol. 5304, pp. 83–97. Springer, Heidelberg (2008)
9. King, D.E.: Dlib-ml: a machine learning toolkit. J. Mach. Learn. Res. **10**, 1755–1758 (2009)
10. King, D.E.: Max-Margin Object Detection. CoRR abs/1502.00046 (2015)
11. Henriques, J.F., Caseiro, R., Martins, P., Batista, J.: High-speed tracking with kernelized correlation filters. IEEE Trans. Pattern Anal. Mach. Intell. **37**(3), 583–596 (2015)
12. Kazemi, V., Sullivan, J.: One millisecond face alignment with an ensemble of regression trees. In: Proceedings of the IEEE Conference on Computer Vision and Pattern Recognition (CVPR 2014), pp. 1867–1874. IEEE Computer Society (2014)
13. Mingqiang, Y., Kidiyo, K., Joseph, R.: A Survey of Shape Feature Extraction Techniques. In: Yin, P.Y. (ed.) Pattern Recognition Techniques, Technology and Applications, InTech (2008). doi:10.5772/6237, ISBN: 978-953-7619-24-4
14. Gers, F.A., Schmidhuber, J., Cummins, F.: Learning to forget: continual prediction with LSTM. Neural Comput. **12**(10), 2451–2471 (2000). PubMed PMID: 11032042
15. Hochreiter, S., Schmidhuber, J.: Long short-term memory. Neural Comput. **9**(8), 1735–1780 (1997)
16. Rabiner, L.R.: A tutorial on hidden Markov models and selected applications in speech recognition. Proc. IEEE **77**(2), 257–286 (1989)
17. Srivastava, N., Hinton, G., Krizhevsky, A., Sutskever, I., Salakhutdinov, R.: Dropout: a simple way to prevent neural networks from overfitting. J. Mach. Learn. Res. **15**, 1929–1958 (2014)
18. Dauphin, Y.N., de Vries, H., Chung, J., Bengio, Y.: RMSProp and equilibrated adaptive learning rates for non-convex optimization, CoRR abs/1502.04390 (2015)

Wing-Surface Reconstruction of a Lanner-Falcon in Free Flapping Flight with Multiple Cameras

Martin Heinold[✉] and Christian J. Kähler

Fakultät für Luft- und Raumfahrttechnik, Institut für Strömungsmechanik
und Aerodynamik, Universität der Bundeswehr München,
Werner-Heisenberg-Weg 39, 85577 Neubiberg, Germany
martin.heinold@unibw.de
http://www.unibw.de/lrt7

Abstract. This paper presents a way to reconstruct the upper and lower surface of a curved and textured Lanner-falcon wing in flapping flight. A stereo camera system was used to take images of a free-flying bird in a wind-tunnel. The usage of two cameras allows for the finding of correspondences of sought-after surface points in both cameras. Furthermore, three dimensional coordinates can be triangulated. To get camera points, which belong together, a disparity map is calculated with the help of a Semi-Global Block Matching algorithm. A reduction of the complexity is achieved by rectifying the camera-images on the basis of the epipolar geometry. The analysis shows that the surface structure of a Lanner-falcon and the motion during a specified time-series can be reconstructed with sufficient accuracy.

Keywords: 3D · Stereo · Surface-reconstruction · Lanner-falcon · Flapping flight · Optical flow · Semi-global block matching

1 Introduction

Since the beginning of modern aviation, researchers have tried to learn more about the aerodynamics of free-flying animals because flapping flight is a very good propulsion mechanism at low Reynolds numbers. The possibility to fly at low Reynolds numbers is important in many ways and a huge number of studies have been performed in this area of research. However the aerodynamics of the problem are not yet fully understood. Especially in the future of planetary exploration, small drones that can fly long distances with minimal energy requirements will be of special importance. Birds can be a role model for these probes. For this reason, the shape of bird wings in free flight is of particular importance because most of the aerodynamic properties can be determined by them. Within the "Schwerpunktprogramm 1207" of the German research funding organization (DFG), studies on barn owls in gliding flight were performed [1,4,11]. Stationary cameras and moving camera frames were compared to analyze the advantages and disadvantages of the experimental methods. The data

© Springer International Publishing Switzerland 2016
T. Bräunl et al. (Eds.): PSIVT 2015, LNCS 9431, pp. 392–403, 2016.
DOI: 10.1007/978-3-319-29451-3_32

was evaluated by methods of Optical Flow [4], Stereo Matching [11] and laser light section process [1]. In areas of low texture, Stereo Matching algorithms showed holes as a result of missing image information. The evaluation with correlation windows resulted in a bad resolution and the projection of point patterns on the wing got blurred during a wing beat amplitude. Further investigations on a flapping barn owl by Wolf [12] have shown that a moving camera with a resting coordinate system on the bird can simplify the evaluation of the data. Otherwise a stationary camera allows for the masking of the moving bird from the resting background. In addition, the behavior of a bird during the flight with a moving camera system can change in comparison to its real reactions. In order to measure the wing-surface structures, methods which produce reliable results and do not harm the animal are needed. On this account, methods of Computer Vision (CV) are used to reconstruct objects from two cameras into three dimensional point clouds, without harming or influencing the bird. Our method provides the possibility, after a complete calibration with a 3D two-plane calibration target, to triangulate point clouds (X, Y, Z) in a three dimensional space through unique point correspondences on the camera sensor [6]. On the one hand, the distance between two camera centers (baseline) is fixed and should be as short as possible to reliably determine the displacement field between them. On the other hand, a decrease of the spatial resolution of the point position in the direction of the measurement volume depth for small camera distances is noticed. Therefore a compromise has to be found. An increase of the baseline reduces the measurement uncertainty in the Z-direction, but also leads to occlusions. In this case the search for point correspondences gets ambiguous. In real experimental setups the camera distance can vary between a few centimeters and meters. This paper offers a possibility to obtain unique disparity maps where 3D point clouds of a considered falcon wing are determined.

2   Measurement Setup

The atmospheric wind tunnel of the University of Bundeswehr Munich was used for the measurements of flapping flight of a Lanner-falcon. The wind tunnel has a cross-section of $1.85\,\text{m} \times 1.85\,\text{m}$, a $22\,\text{m}$ long measurement domain and can produce velocities between $2\,\frac{\text{m}}{\text{s}}$ and $45\,\frac{\text{m}}{\text{s}}$. The data was acquired with 4 Phantom v12 high speed cameras from Vision Research. The camera sensor of these cameras generates images with up to $1280 \times 800\,\text{px}$ and can record with $6200\,\frac{\text{frames}}{\text{s}}$ at full resolution. To resolve the motion of a wing up- and downstroke over time precisely, a frame rate for the recordings of $1000\,\frac{\text{frames}}{\text{s}}$ was selected. The measurement object, a Lanner-falcon with a wing span of about $0.9\,\text{m}$, flies through the wind tunnel upstream against an uniform flow. As a result the time of flight in the measurement domain rises and more than one flap can be recorded. At our experiments in the atmospheric wind tunnel at the University of Bundeswehr Munich baselines of $700-900\,\text{mm}$ occurred. The high speed cameras were equipped with Zeiss Distagon $35\,\text{mm}$ lenses with a working distance between camera and measurement object of approximately $1\,\text{m}$. Figure 1 shows the wind

Fig. 1. Two stereo camera systems for upper and lower side view

tunnel with the four mounted cameras and the flow direction in a schematic representation.

3 Calibration

The calibration of the stereoscopic camera system was done in two steps: First, a three dimensional two-plane calibration target was mounted in the measurement domain. Next, the target was moved by rotation and translation within the observation area of both cameras. The arbitrary movement of the calibration pattern requires a calibration with a pinhole camera model. The intrinsic camera parameters A were calculated for every camera, which include the focal length f in mm, the pixel size of the camera sensor s in $\frac{mm}{px}$ and the principal point (u_0, v_0) in px [8]. To get this information, the determined sensor coordinates of the calibration points were assigned to physical positions, whereby a mathematical connection between sensor positions (x, y) and world coordinates (X, Y, Z) was created. Additionally, the extrinsic parameters K for the first camera view of the calibration pattern were fitted. It includes the rotation R with three Euler angles to rotate the coordinate system and a translation t, which moves the coordinate system from the origin in the world coordinate system to the camera sensor. For every other view, the rotation and translation were calculated. The back projection error was finally minimized by a least square algorithm. The relative position of each camera, depending on the calibration target, is defined by the extrinsic parameters. Mathematically, the camera matrix P can be calculated by putting together the intrinsic and extrinsic parameters of every camera (Fig. 2).

$$P = A \cdot K = A \cdot [R|t] \tag{1}$$

$$A = \begin{bmatrix} \frac{f}{s} & 0 & u_0 \\ 0 & \frac{-f}{s} & -v_0 + h \\ 0 & 0 & 1 \end{bmatrix} \tag{2}$$

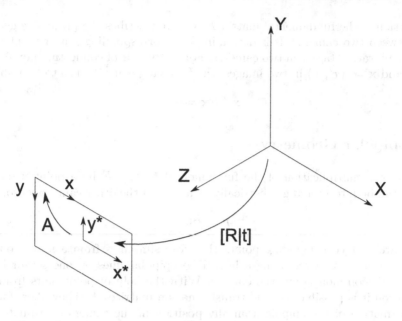

Fig. 2. Transformation between world and camera coordinate system

$$R = R(r_x, r_y, r_z) = R_z \cdot R_y \cdot R_x \tag{3}$$

$$t = \begin{pmatrix} t_x \\ t_y \\ t_z \end{pmatrix} \tag{4}$$

With Eq. (1), it is possible to convert world coordinates into sensor positions.

$$\begin{pmatrix} x \\ y \\ 1 \end{pmatrix} = P \cdot \begin{pmatrix} X \\ Y \\ Z \\ 1 \end{pmatrix} \tag{5}$$

To reduce the complexity of the transformation homogeneous coordinates are used to project a three dimensional frame into a two dimensional frame with just one matrix multiplication. Otherwise a multiplication and a summation need to be performed successively, which increases the computational load. Lens distortions, on the basis of the curvature of the camera lenses, can be eliminated with the radial distortion coefficients (k_1, k_2). Barrel distortion has no further influence on our experimental setup.

$$\begin{pmatrix} x_u \\ y_u \end{pmatrix} = f\left(\begin{pmatrix} x_d \\ y_d \end{pmatrix}, s, k_1, k_2\right) = \begin{pmatrix} x_d \\ y_d \end{pmatrix} \left(1 + \frac{\sqrt{x_d^2 + y_d^2}k_1}{500^2 s} + \frac{(x_d^2 + y_d^2)k_2}{500^3 s^2}\right) \tag{6}$$

In Eq. (6), distorted pixel coordinates (x_d, y_d) are corrected by the radial distortion coefficients to get undistorted pixel positions (x_u, y_u) [8]. Another important connection is the fundamental matrix F, which describes the projective geometry between two cameras. It is determined by corresponding sensor point pairs of the calibration target in two cameras. For every pair of connecting points $\mathbf{x} = (x, y)$ and $\mathbf{x'} = (x', y')$ in two images, the following equation has to be fulfilled:

$$\mathbf{x'}^T F \mathbf{x} = 0 \tag{7}$$

4   Epipolar Geometry

The matrix multiplication of the fundamental Matrix F by a point $\mathbf{x}$ on one sensor can be interpreted geometrically as a line on the other camera sensor (see Fig. 3).

$$l' = F\mathbf{x} \tag{8}$$

The search for corresponding points therefore simplifies from a search on the whole sensor to a search along a line. Two epipolar lines on one sensor intersect in one common point, the epipole. With the help of point pairs from the calibration it is possible to build transformation matrices T. They allow for the transformation of the epipole from any position in the camera coordinate system to a point at infinity, which leads to horizontal epipolar lines. This reduces the correspondence search to a one dimensional problem. If the transformation matrix is applied to every pixel in the image, the picture is rectified [5] (see Fig. 4).

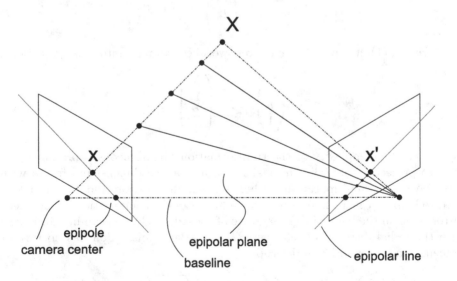

Fig. 3. Epipolar plane between two cameras

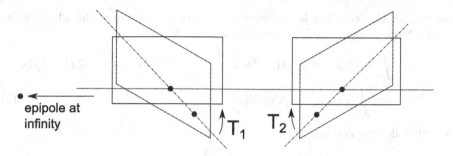

Fig. 4. Transformation of epipole to infinity

5   Calculation of the Displacement Field

The rectified image pairs show, by virtue of a long baseline, disparities in the order of $\gg O(1)$ px. State-of-the-art algorithms do not produce reliable results for those kinds of displacements. The disparity space gets larger with large disparity ranges, which raises the required memory and ambivalent results can occur. Therefore the determination of the complete displacement field V is split into two consecutive steps. In the first step, a coarse displacement field is defined based on manually chosen points. These points are marked at prominent positions in the left camera image. After that, the equivalent points are found in the right image. With the help of n point correspondences $c_i(1 \leq i \leq n)$, a spline is set up with the following equation [2]:

$$f(x,y) = a_1 + a_x x + a_y y + \sum_{i=1}^{n} w_i U(|c_i - (x,y)|) \tag{9}$$

with the help function
$$U(r) = r^2 \log r^2 \tag{10}$$
where r is the geometrical distance between two points

$$r = |(x,y)_1 - (x,y)_2| \tag{11}$$

A displacement field (V_m) is then produced for every point within the image. Based on the rectification all disparities lay along the x-axis in the image. If the left camera image is warped with the disparity map V_m, both camera images are nearly superimposed. The disparities reduce to the order of $O(1)$ and $O(2)$. These can be determined under the use of a Semi-Global Block Matching algorithm [7]. This method creates sparse disparity maps V_f. On positions where a left-right and right-left plausibility check is successful, a disparity is only saved. The computation is done with the OpenCV database on a Nvidia GTX 660 GPU, which leads to a reduction of the calculation time to under 10 s for an image pair with 1280 × 800 px. To fill the holes in V_f, the Optical Flow [3] between the same image pair as before produces estimations for empty areas. The chosen approach for Optical Flow is to minimize an energy function of the whole image in order to get a dense and steady displacement field.

$$E(\mathbf{w}) = \int_\Omega \Psi(|I(\mathbf{x}+\mathbf{w}) - I(\mathbf{x})|^2)\mathrm{d}\mathbf{x} + \gamma \int_\Omega \Psi(|\nabla I(\mathbf{x}+\mathbf{w}) - \nabla I(\mathbf{x})|^2)\mathrm{d}\mathbf{x}$$
$$+ \alpha \int_\Omega \Psi(|\nabla u|^2 + |\nabla v|^2)\mathrm{d}\mathbf{x} \tag{12}$$

with the following comments:

$$\mathbf{w} = \begin{pmatrix} u \\ v \\ 1 \end{pmatrix} \tag{13}$$

$$\Psi(s^2) = \sqrt{s^2 + \epsilon^2} \text{ with } \epsilon = 0.001 \tag{14}$$

The first part of Eq. (12) describes the assumption of constant intensity distribution of a surface, the second term describes the existence of constant gradients along edges and the last one describes the smoothness of the velocity (displacement) field. A sensitivity analysis was performed to choose the parameters α (regularization parameter) and γ (weight parameter) with two synthetic images and a disparity of 50 px between the images.

$$\alpha = 0.0197, \gamma = 100 \tag{15}$$

Furthermore a Gaussian pyramid with a scale factor of 0.8 was used to pursue a coarse-to-fine strategy in the algorithm. Areas of very low texture within the image that do not produce reliable results with the Block Matching algorithm can be closed with values from Optical Flow. The parameters of Semi-Global Block Matching originate from the OpenCV documentation [9].

disparity range:	$[-64, 64]$
left-right-consistency check:	on
windows size:	7 px × 7 px

The complete displacement field is defined as a summation of the single disparity maps.

$$V = V_f + V_m \tag{16}$$

As explained above, Optical Flow and Semi-Global Block Matching carry out spatial smoothing because smooth objects cannot exist with large displacement jumps. To reduce more imperfections, temporal smoothing of the disparity maps is done by transforming displacement fields before and after the considered time step with Optical Flow to the same temporal position. Afterwards, a temporal averaging is implemented.

6   Triangulation and Masking

For every point $\mathbf{x}$ in the left camera image, the summation of this coordinate with the displacement results in the corresponding point $\mathbf{x}'$ in the right camera image. With these point pairs $\mathbf{x}$ and $\mathbf{x}'$ and the camera matrices P_i, which were calculated by the calibration, the world coordinates (X, Y, Z) can be triangulated using the optimal triangulation method [6] (see Fig. 5). Every point inside the camera image, with a corresponding point in the other image, can be reconstructed but in our experiments only the moving falcon is of interest. That's why objects of interest are masked by thresholding the Optical Flows. In this case, only areas with velocities higher than a threshold are integrated into the mask. For the measurement of the Lanner-falcon, the bird is separated from the stationary background of the wind tunnel.

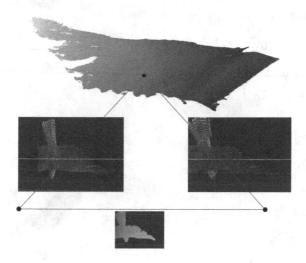

Fig. 5. Schematics of the triangulation with corresponding points

7   Sequence of a Wing Flap

The procedure to generate a 3D point cloud with two cameras at a time step t_0 can be adapted to additional time steps (t_n with $n > 1$) with the same operations. The most time-consuming and not automatic part of the reconstruction, the determination of the manual displacement field V_m, is bypassed with Optical Flow. Correspondences from the first image are transformed with velocity fields to the next time steps, whereby the repeated selection of points is dropped. In Fig. 6, the downstroke of a wing is portrayed. The three reconstructions are taken from images with a time lag of $\Delta t = 20\,\text{ms}$.

8   Upper and Lower Wing Side

At least four cameras are needed to reconstruct the upper and lower side of a flapping bird wing. The calibration with a three dimensional two-plane pattern

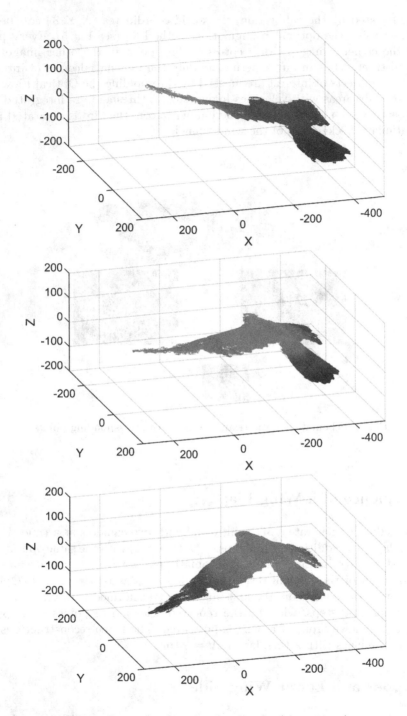

Fig. 6. Sequence of a wing downstroke ($\Delta t = 20$ ms)

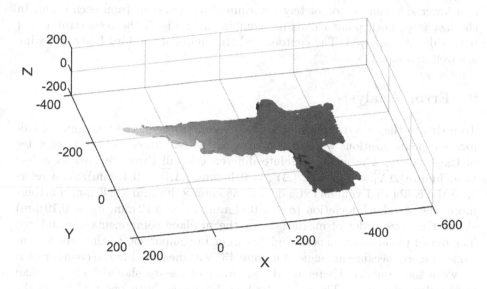

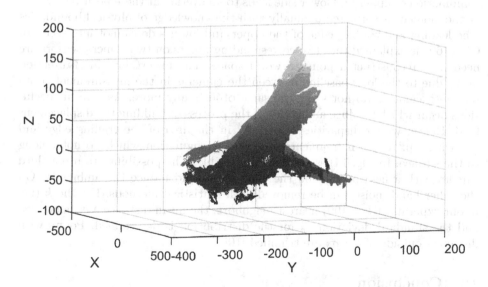

Fig. 7. Upper and lower side of the reconstruction from different view points

allows for the calibration of the cameras which see the front or the backside of the target. Hence, all cameras have the same world coordinate system. The upper and lower side can be completely determined independent from each other. In the last step, both point clouds are combined. In Fig. 7, the reconstruction of both sides is displayed. The contour and the shape of the bird body and wing are well developed.

9   Error Analysis

To estimate the uncertainty of the stereo reconstruction, the triangulated calibration point positions were compared with the real known world coordinates of these points. The mean, absolute difference in all three dimensions is less than 1 mm ($\overline{|\Delta X|} = 0.67\,$mm, $\overline{|\Delta Y|} = 0.46\,$mm, $\overline{|\Delta Z|} = 0.47\,$mm). As a reference the calibrated volume extends over 385 mm × 400 mm × 340 mm. Furthermore, the standard deviation ($\sigma_X = 0.11\,$mm, $\sigma_Y = 0.12\,$mm, $\sigma_Z = 0.19\,$mm) shows the same order of magnitude for the in-plane components σ_X and σ_Y. The out-of-plane component is slightly larger in comparison to the values mentioned before, because an angle of around 43° was measured in the configuration between the cameras. Therefore, the accuracy of the σ_Z should be larger than the in-plane deviation. The mean absolute difference shows one problem of the reconstruction. Thin objects like single feathers at the trailing edge of the wing are highly affected by the reconstruction error because the thickness at this position on the wing is just one order of magnitude higher than the error. So the combination of upper and lower side leads to an overlap at these positions, which at the moment is corrected manually with the knowledge of physical boundaries (the leading and trailing edge of the upper and lower side cannot intersect). In Chap. 6 it is explained that two corresponding points on two camera sensors are needed to reconstruct a point in world space. The uncertainty in Z-direction drops due to the long baseline between the cameras in the measurement setup but both cameras do not show the same objects any more. As a result occlusions occur which produce ambiguity in the process of building the displacement field. Hence, wrong disparities, especially in the area of the trailing edge and the wing tip, result in fragments after the triangulation which do not belong to the surface. In Fig. 6 these outliers are visible. The possibility to use a third camera with a field of view on the wing tip should reduce the ambiguity. On the other hand, noise can be removed with statistical methods. For the k (i.e. in our experiment $k = 100$) nearest neighbors, the mean distance δ is calculated and the standard deviation σ_δ for the distribution is determined. Points with distances outside of $\delta \pm \sigma_\delta$ are trimmed [10].

10   Conclusion

This paper presented a stereoscopic method to reconstruct the surface of a bird wing recorded in free flight in a wind tunnel. The procedure allows for the determination of three dimensional point clouds for a given time sequence with minimal manual influence. It is possible to predict the form of the wing cross-section on different wing span positions from the determined surfaces of the upper and lower wing side in order to calculate aerodynamic properties according to airfoil theory. Also, structures like reverse flow breaks can be visualized with this method. Nevertheless, the approach is applicable to other objects or animals with highly textured surfaces.

References

1. Bachmann, T., Wagner, H.: The three-dimensional shape of serrations at barn owl wings: towards a typical natural serration as a role model for biomimetic applications. J. Anat. **219**, 192–202 (2011)
2. Bookstein, F.L.: Principal warps: thin-plate splines and the decomposition of deformations. IEEE Trans. Pattern Anal. Mach. Intell. **11**, 567–585 (1989)
3. Brox, T., Bruhn, A., Papenberg, N., Weickert, J.: High accuracy optical flow estimation based on a theory for warping. In: Pajdla, T., Matas, J.G. (eds.) ECCV 2004. LNCS, vol. 3024, pp. 25–36. Springer, Heidelberg (2004)
4. Friedl, A., Kähler, C.J.: Measuring and Analyzing the Birds Flight. STAB Fach-Symposium zur Strömungsmechanik, Berlin (2010)
5. Fusiello, A., Trucco, E., Verri, A.: A compact algorithm for rectification of stereo pairs. Mach. Vis. Appl. **12**, 16–22 (2000)
6. Hartley, R., Zisserman, A.: Multiple View Geometry in Computer Vision, 2nd edn. Cambridge University Press, New York (2004). 9. printing
7. Hirschmüller, H.: Accurate and efficient stereo processing by semi-global matching and mutual information. In: IEEE Conference on Computer Vision and Pattern Recognition, vol. 2, pp. 807–814 (2005)
8. LaVision: personal correspondence with employees (2015)
9. OpenCV Documentation. http://docs.opencv.org/modules/calib3d/doc/camera_calibration_and_3d_reconstruction.html#stereosgbm-stereosgbm
10. Rusu, R.B., Marton, Z.C., Blodow, N., Dolha, M., Beetz, M.: Towards 3D point cloud based object maps for household environments. Robot. Auton. Syst. **56**(11), 927–941 (2008)
11. Thomas, W., Robert, K., Thomas, E., Hermann, W.: Shape and deformation measurement of free flying birds in flapping flight. In: Tropea, C., Bleckmann, H. (eds.) Nature-Inspired Fluid Mechanics. NNFM, vol. 119, pp. 135–148. Springer, Heidelberg (2012)
12. Wolf, T., Konrath, R.: Avian wing geometry and kinematics of a free-flying barn owl in flapping flight. Exp. Fluids **56**, 1–23 (2015)

Underwater Active Oneshot Scan with Static Wave Pattern and Bundle Adjustment

Hiroki Morinaga[1]([✉]), Hirohisa Baba[1], Marco Visentini-Scarzanella[1], Hiroshi Kawasaki[1], Ryo Furukawa[2], and Ryusuke Sagawa[3]

[1] Kagoshima University, Kagoshima, Japan
{marco,kawasaki}@ibe.kagoshima-u.ac.jp
[2] Hiroshima City University, Hiroshima, Japan
ryo-f@hiroshima-cu.ac.jp
[3] National Institute of Advanced Industrial Science and Technology,
Tsukuba, Japan
ryusuke.sagawa@aist.go.jp

Abstract. Structured Light Systems (SLS) are widely used for various purposes. Recently, a strong demand to apply SLS to underwater applications has emerged. When SLS is used in an air medium, the stereo correspondence problem can be solved efficiently by epipolar geometry due to the co-planarity of the 3D point and its corresponding 2D points on camera/projector planes. However, in underwater environments, the camera and projector are usually set in special housings and refraction occurs at the interfaces between water/glass and glass/air, resulting in invalid conditions for epipolar geometry which strongly affect the correspondence search process. In this paper, we tackle the problem of underwater 3D shape acquisition with SLS. In this paper, we propose a method to perform 3D reconstruction by calibrating the system as if they are in the air at multiple depth. Since refraction cannot be completely described by a polynomial approximation of distortion model, grid based SLS method solve the problem. Finally, we propose a bundle adjustment method to refine the final result. We tested our method with an underwater SLS prototype, consisting of custom-made diffractive optical element (DOE) laser and underwater housings, showing the validity of the proposed approach.

Keywords: Underwater scan · Camera-projector system · One-shot scan

1 Introduction

Structured Light Systems (SLS) are widely used in various applications such as augmented reality, medical examination, games, movies, etc. A typical SLS consists of a camera and a projector. Usually the projector projects an encoded pattern onto an object's surface, and the images of the object captured by the camera can be easily decoded through knowledge of the projected pattern. Because the technique uses an active pattern projector, the correspondence

© Springer International Publishing Switzerland 2016
T. Bräunl et al. (Eds.): PSIVT 2015, LNCS 9431, pp. 404–418, 2016.
DOI: 10.1007/978-3-319-29451-3_33

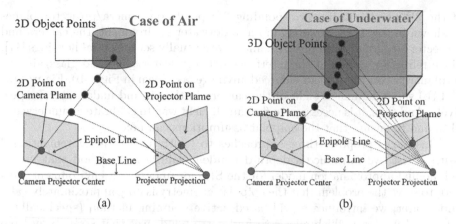

Fig. 1. (a) Epipolar geometry without water. (b) Epipolar geometry with water.

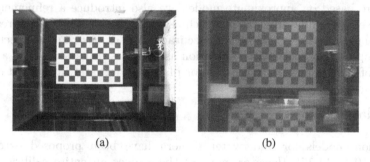

Fig. 2. (a) Capture image without water. (b) Capture image with water.

searching process becomes much easier than passive stereo techniques due to the uniqueness and distinctiveness of the features in the pattern. Therefore, a higher reconstruction accuracy and density can be achieved with active stereo systems, and SLS has become one of the most important non-contact 3D shape measurement methods [5, 18]. In particular, one-shot SLS is one of the main techniques in active scanning of dynamic environments [2, 15].

The most critical factor affecting the accuracy of an SLS is calibration. Before SLS reconstruction of an object by using a fixed pattern, the intrinsic parameters of the camera and projector as well as the extrinsic parameters relating them should be estimated. After calibration, reconstruction is done from epipolar geometry: the epipolar lines corresponding to the feature points detected on the camera images can be drawn on the fixed pattern image which is projected by the projector. Finally the correspondences can be found by searching along these epipolar lines, and 3D reconstruction performed by triangulating the corresponding points [12].

When the SLS operates within an air medium, the correspondence problem can be solved efficiently by the valid epipolar geometry due to the co-planarity of the 3D point and its corresponding 2D points on camera/projector planes as shown in Fig. 1(a). However, in an underwater environment, the camera and projector (regarded as an inverse camera) are usually set in special housings [17]. Since refraction occurs at the interfaces between water/glass and glass/air, the co-planarity condition is not enforced anymore, as shown in Fig. 1(b). Figure 2(a) and (b) show the line of sight of the camera in the air and underwater, respectively. And thus, it is necessary to find an efficient way to calibrate an underwater SLS, and to ensure that the epipolar assumptions can hold.

This paper proposes three approaches to jointly tackle the aforementioned issues. First, we introduce a depth-dependent calibration method that uses a polynomial approximation model for the SLS for underwater environment. Second, to solve the problem that the epipolar geometry is only approximately valid underwater, we introduce a grid-based active scanning method (specifically, a wave grid pattern) which allows to find correspondences that stray away from the epipolar line while still maintaining a good matching performance. Since the results are based on approximate model, we also introduce a refinement algorithm based on bundle adjustment which uses the wave reconstruction results as the initial parameters to achieve high accuracy. We demonstrate the effectiveness of the proposed approach with simulation as well as a real system with a special housing of camera and pattern projector placed underwater in a pool tank.

2 Related Work

Calibration models for underwater camera have been proposed extensively [1,3,6–8,10,13,14,17]. However, none of them gives an entire calibration and reconstruction procedure for an SLS. Because of the correspondence matching problem in SLS, some of the proposed models becomes invalid since the formulated models do not offer a practical strategy for matching and reconstruction. Besides, projector calibration underwater is also a slightly different issue than camera calibration due to the "blindness" of the projector [4].

There are some early works for underwater 3D reconstruction based on approximation model [3,13,14]. Queiroz-Neto et al. proposed an underwater model which simply ignores the effects of the refraction, but earns results with low accuracy due to the non-linear refraction effect [14]. Some approximate methods also have been proposed, such as focal length adjustment [14], lens radial distortion approximation [3] and a combination of the two [13]. Unfortunately, the accuracy of these approximation models are also insufficient to an SLS system for correspondence search using epipolar geometry.

To improve the accuracy of underwater measurement, some physical models for camera calibration and reconstruction have been proposed [1,6–8,10,17]. Agrawal et al. gives a general calibration method for underwater cameras, based on a physical refractive model [1]. They consider that all refractive planes are parallel to each other, and they derive front-projection and back-projection equations for their refractive model. However, it is necessary to solve 4th degree equations even for one refractive plane's case, and 12th degree equations in the

2 plane case in a forward projection situation, and thus, it is difficult to use this method directly for SLS. Sedlazeck *et al.* focus on the underwater light rays which are projected as a curved surface: after learning this surface, perspective projection can be done [17]. According to this method, it is also difficult to tackle the forward projection problem due to the complicated learning phase. Kang *et al.* and Sedlazeck also consider the underwater reconstruction with Structure from Motion (SfM) [6,7]. SfM is a passive way to recover 3D shape of objects, and it is difficult to achieve a dense reconstruction result due to the difficulty of the correspondence searching. Kawahara et al. proposed pixel-wise varifocal camera model, where the focal length of the projection varies pixel-by-pixel, for modeling non-central projection of an underwater camera, and a calibration method for the cameras [8]. They also proposed an active-stereo system composed of a projector and two cameras, where projection of the cameras and the projector is based on their model [9]. Since image-based correspondence search using epipolar lines are not valid for underwater cameras, they applied space carving method, where only photo-consistency is needed.

In terms of SLS for underwater, Campos *et al.* proposed an underwater active stereo system that uses a DOE-based pattern projector [11]. They used a pattern of parallel lines and each line is not coded into local features. Their decoding method (*i.e.*, the method for solving correspondences between the captured image and the projected pattern) relies on the order between the detected lines on the camera image, thus, ambiguity may occur if only a small region of the pattern is detected.

3   Overview

3.1   System Configuration

In this research, we set up a camera-projector system. The camera and projector are set into housings, respectively. The actual configuration is shown in Fig. 3. We made a waterproof housing as shown in Fig. 4(a). Left and right housings are for the cameras, while the center housing is for the laser projector with a diffractive optical element (DOE) of a wave pattern (Fig. 4(b)). Our choice of using two cameras stems from the following reasons:

1. With two cameras and the appropriate baseline it is possible to reconstruct areas occluded in one view, thereby reconstructing a much wider area than with conventional monocular active sensing.
2. By using multiple cameras, our system is equivalent to multi-view stereo, so its accuracy can be further improved with Bundle Adjustment.

3.2   Algorithm

We adopt a coarse to fine approach for reconstruction. First, the approximated model is used to perform the wave grid reconstruction to retrieve coarse shape.

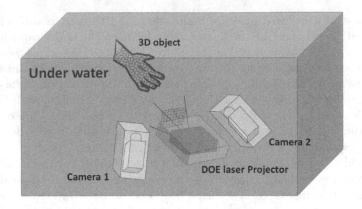

Fig. 3. Set up a camera-projector.

(a)   (b)

Fig. 4. Tool for underwater experiment. (a) Housing. (b) DOE laser projector.

Then, the estimated 3D points are used as initial values for Bundle Adjustment refinement using an accurate non-central projection camera model, which takes into account the refractive environment. The reason why we need the approximation model for the coarse level is that a central projection model does not work in the underwater environment, that means epipolar constraint does not work, however, the epipolar constraint is a key to efficiently find the correspondences with active stereo techniques. Certainly approximation errors inevitably occur at the coarse level, however, those are corrected during the refinement process. Furthermore, there is no practical problem if the deviation of the initial model from the actual model is within the tolerance of the epipolar matching to still produce the correct match.

3.3   Polynomial Approximation of Refraction

Problem Statement. Before introducing our polynomial approximation model for refraction, let us consider the problem when we perform underwater reconstruction with a full physical refraction model. To simplify the model, we only consider the forward-projection considering one refractive layer introduced in [1]. We suppose that a camera and a projector are all set into housings respectively, and assume that the housings' thicknesses can be ignored. Figure 5(a) shows the camera model. Coordinate x shows the refractive plane, and the refractive indices of the media above and below this plane are μ_1 and μ_2 respectively. The blue line shows a ray coming from a 3D point b, and refraction will occur on the intersection with the plane at point $p_1 = (x_1, 0)$. d is the distance between the b and camera plane, x_b is the distance between b and the optical axis z. y_c is the focus of camera. The angle of the incidence is supposed as α and the refracting as β. Based on Snell's law, the following equations are obtained.

$$\frac{\sin \alpha}{\sin \beta} = \frac{\mu_2}{\mu_1} = n, \tag{1}$$

$$\sin \alpha = \frac{x_1}{\sqrt{x_1^2 + y_c^2}}, \sin \beta = \frac{x_b - x_1}{\sqrt{(x_b - x_1)^2 + d^2}}. \tag{2}$$

After some manipulation, the next equation can be obtained,

$$(n^2 - 1)x_1^4 + (-2x_b n + 2x_b)x_1^3$$
$$+(x_b^2 n + y_c^2 n - x_b^2 - d^2)x_1^2 - 2x_b y_c^2 n x_1 + x_b^2 y_c^2 n^2 = 0. \tag{3}$$

By solving this 4th order equation, the corresponding epipolar line on the plane of projector pattern with predefined depth can be calculated for each feature points.

Polynomial Approximation Model. We propose a polynomial approximation of the full physical refraction model. As shown in Fig. 5(b), we consider two kinds of light paths. The blue arrows show the light paths which are outgoing from a 3D point, going through a water-air interface, reflected on the surface of an object, and finally going into a camera. The red ones show the same light paths as if through an air medium. Blue and red light paths are outgoing from b, and incoming to the center of a camera a. p_1 is the intersection point of the blue ray and camera plane, and p_2 is the intersection point of the red ray. The most important factor in the polynomial approximation model is the distance between these p_1 and p_2, which is defined as our approximation error. The relationship between the error and p_1 is defined as the following equation.

$$E(p_1) = \alpha_1 r^2 + \alpha_2 r^4 \tag{4}$$

Although only the x-z plane is drawn in the Fig. 5(b), the same applies to the y-z plane. The r in Eq. (4) represents the 2-dimensional Euclidean distance

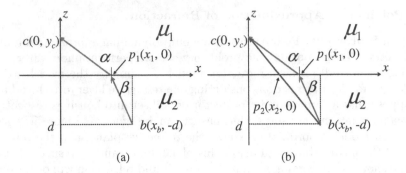

Fig. 5. (a) Physical camera refraction model. (b) Polynomial approximation camera refraction model.

between the center of the camera and p_1 in the 3D coordinate axis xyz. During the calibration phase, not only the extrinsic parameters, but also polynomial approximation parameters α_1 and α_2 are estimated. The pinhole projection can then be represented with the Eq. (4) with the approximation model.

Using the calibration parameters which are calibrated under water, reprojection of 3D points to captured image plane can be done by the following manner. First, 3D points are converted to the camera coordinate system by using the extrinsic parameters, which contains the rotation and translation information, and then, reprojected to the camera plane by using the intrinsic parameter of the camera. Then, the 2D coordinates are further distorted by the Eq. (4). Note that the process is completely same as the ordinary camera reprojection process other than the parameters are estimated under water, and, unlike the air environment, it contains an inevitable error derived from the approximation model, and thus, it should be solved in the further step.

4   Depth Dependent Calibration

4.1   Overview of the Calibration Process

First, the camera and projector are put into their respective housings, and placed into a pool filled with water. After that, the intrinsic parameters of the camera are estimated with a checkerboard [19]. Then, the intrinsic parameters of the projector and the extrinsic parameters between them are estimated by a second calibration using a sphere of known size, described in the next section.

Since the effect of refraction is depth dependent, we conduct the calibration at the multiple depth in the paper. From the multiple calibration results, it is possible to represent the refraction effect with several hyper parameters. However, we take another solution to cope with a depth dependent effect in the paper for simplicity and leave the hyper parameter estimation approach for our future task. In order to retrieve a discrete set of depth-dependent calibration parameters, we put the calibration objects, i.e., checker board planes and sphere, at multiple depth and conduct calibrations independently.

For the selection of the best parameters, the residual errors of epipolar constraints are used. To achieve this, the 3D reconstruction process is conducted for all the parameter sets independently. The sum of residual errors of the correspondences, which are normally errors of epipolar constraints, is calculated and used for the selection of the best result.

4.2   Sphere Based Projector Calibration

For sphere-based calibration, images are captured with the pattern projected onto the sphere as shown in Fig. 6(a). The radius of the spherical surface is known. From the image, points on the spherical contour are sampled. Also, the correspondences between the grid points on the camera image and the grid points on the projected pattern are assigned manually.

For the calibration process, we minimize reprojection errors between the imaged grid points on the sphere and the simulated grid positions, with respect to the extrinsic parameters, the intrinsic parameters of the projector, and the position of the calibration sphere. Figure 6(b) shows how the simulated grid positions are calculated. From a grid point (for example, g_{p1} in Fig. 6(b)) of the projector, the gird projection on the sphere (g_{c1}) is calculated by ray-tracing, and is projected to the camera (g_{i1}). If the ray of the grid point does not intersect with the sphere (for example, g_{p2}), we use intersection of the ray with an auxiliary plane (g_{c2}) that is fronto-parallel and includes the sphere center.

Other than the reprojection errors, points on the spherical contour are also used for the optimization. The line of sight of a contour point ($\tilde{s}$ in Fig. 6(b)) should be tangent to the sphere in the 3D space; thus, the distance between the spherical center ($\mathbf{c}$) and the line should equal to the sphere radius (r). Thus, the difference between the distance from the spherical object and the radius ($\sqrt{\|\mathbf{c}\|^2 - (\tilde{s} \cdot \mathbf{c})} - r$) is also considered to be an error. Thus, the sum of squares of these errors is minimized by using Levenberg-Marquardt method.

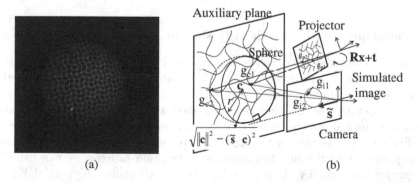

(a)   (b)

Fig. 6. Calibration of intrinsic/extrinsic parameters of the pattern projector by sphere object: (a) pattern projection on a sphere, (b) calibration errors.

5 3D Reconstruction

5.1 Wave Grid Reconstruction

For 3D reconstruction, it is necessary to find matches between points on the image plane and the known projector pattern. In our method, we use a "wave pattern" because of the distinctiveness and uniqueness of its features and its reconstruction density [16]. Figure 7 is an example of the pattern. The correspondences are found through an epipolar search. During the search, the impact of our polynomial approximation on accuracy is limited since the interval between intersections in the wave grid is much larger than the pixel width, and an error of a few pixels does not affect the correspondence search. This feature is important for our underwater scanning method because the polynomial approximation inevitably will create some errors on the epipolar lines, and depth dependent calibration parameters is conducted only with a sparse set of depth values. Since the reconstructed results have some errors because of approximation model and inconsistent shapes because of depth dependent calibration parameters, those errors are effectively solved in the refinement process.

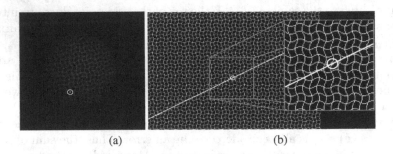

(a)   (b)

Fig. 7. (a) Corresponding point, (b) Epipolar line for (a).

5.2 Refinement with Bundle Adjustment

Refinement of 3D shape as well as camera and projector parameters will be conducted by the following way. We set 3D points and a position of the glass between air and water as parameters to be estimated with bundle adjustment. In terms of the position of the glass, it is described with four parameters consisting of a surface normal and a distance between camera center and surface of the glass. Since we can retrieve a hundred of corresponding points between camera and projector image through the wave reconstruction process, we can calculate the reprojection error by simply solving the fourth order polynomial Eq. (3). Leaven-Marquardt algorithm is used to minimize the error.

The main differences from the ordinary bundle adjustment algorithm, which is used for structure from motion or multiple view stereo method, and ours are two folds. First, we use fourth order polynomial equation to calculate 2D coordinates on the image plane back-projected from 3D points considering a refraction between water and air. Second, we include the rigid transformation parameter of the interface plane between water and air to be estimated in the bundle adjustment process.

Since we can start the optimization from the initial shape calculated by the approximated model, it converges quickly with Leaven-Marquardt algorithm with our implementation. It should be noted that, since the images are undistorted by the parameter of approximation model in underwater environment to retrieve the initial shape, the image is needed again distorted by the approximation parameters and undistorted by ordinary distortion parameters which are estimated by openCV in the air before the bundle adjustment.

6 Experiments

6.1 Depth Dependent Calibration

The experimental environment is shown in Fig. 8. Two Point Grey Research Grasshopper cameras and a DOE laser projector were used. Then, the camera-projector system was placed underwater, and calibrated several times with multiple depth with the proposed technique. Figure 9(a) shows the example of captured image for our sphere calibration. Two depth positions are considered, as the near range, 1 m from the camera 0 and as the far range, 1.5 m. The reason why we made calibration with such few positions is that the assumed depth range was not so wide based on the measurement environment we applied. As wave grid reconstruction applied in our method works using the epipolar constraint, erroneous reconstruction occurs when the projection error turns to be above our matching tolerance. However, such a problem didn't occur under our experimental environment in the paper, because the deviation from the assumed model was still within our tolerance. Note that possibly erroneous connection

Fig. 8. Experimental environment of underwater scan.

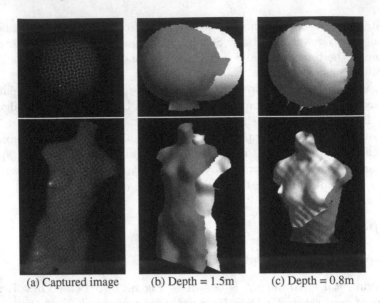

|(a) Captured image | (b) Depth = 1.5m | (c) Depth = 0.8m|

Fig. 9. Reconstruction results of the mannequin at different depth. White shape is reconstructed by left camera and red shape is reconstructed by right camera (Color figure online).

of grids didn't occur because wave grid reconstruction has some effect to correct the errors by using grid pattern connections. After acquiring intrinsic and extrinsic parameters of the system for each depth, the 3D shape of the sphere for calibration is reconstructed to verify the result of the calibration as shown in 1st row of Fig. 9. We can confirm that sphere is correctly reconstructed with the approximation model. It can be observed that two reconstructed shapes from two cameras are apart because they are independently calibrated and reconstructed, and such inconsistency will be efficiently eliminated by our refinement algorithm.

6.2   Wave Oneshot Reconstruction

Then, we captured and reconstructed the 3D shape of a mannequin using wave reconstruction. 2nd row of Fig. 9(a) shows the example of captured image and

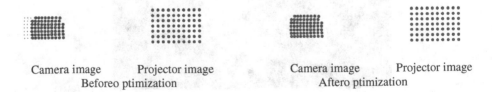

Camera image   Projector image   Camera image   Projector image
    Beforeo ptimization   Aftero ptimization

Fig. 10. Reprojection of camera and projector image. Blue: observed points and Red: reprojected points (Color figure online).

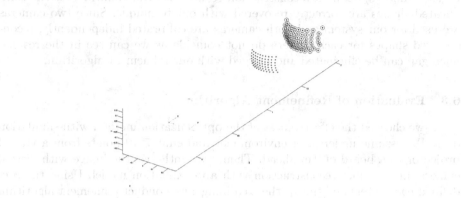

Fig. 11. Reconstructed shape of sphere (Red: Initial position, Blue dot: Ground truth, Blue circle: Refined result) (Color figure online)

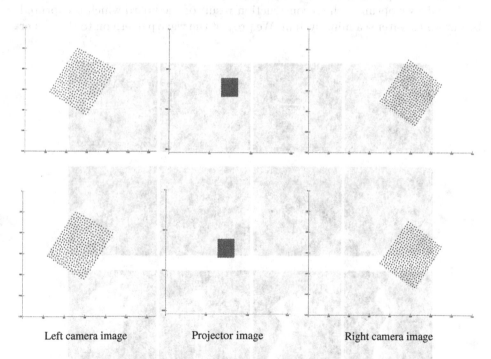

Left camera image   Projector image   Right camera image

Fig. 12. Reprojection of camera and projector image after optimization. 1st row: Before optimization. 2nd row: After optimization. Red points are observed points and green points are reprojected points. Both errors in left and right camera are decreased from initial positions, so that the total error is drastically reduced by LM algorithm (Color figure online).

Fig. 9(b) and (c) shows a reconstruction results. We can confirm that the complicated shapes are correctly recovered with our technique. Since two cameras are used for our system and both cameras are calibrated independently, reconstructed shapes for each camera do not coincide as we can see in the results. Such gap can be eliminated and merged with our refinement algorithm.

6.3 Evaluation of Refinement Algorithm

First, we checked the effectiveness of the optimaization method with simulation data. We assume underwater environment and emit 7*10 points from a virtual projector to a board of 2 m ahead. Then, we synthesize the image with virtual camera and conduct reconstruction with approximation model. Using the predefined parameters and the synthesized image, we conduct refinement algorithm and results are shown in Figs. 10 and 11. From the results, we can confirm that the reprojection error calculated by solving the fourth order polinomial equation considering a refraciton decreases with our bundle adjustment algorithm and correct shapes are reconstructed.

Finally, we optimize the reconstruction result of the board which is captured by our underwater scanning system. We project the wave pattern on to the planer

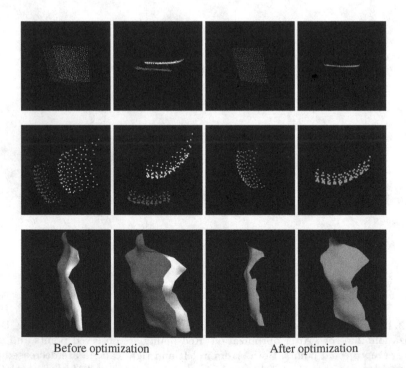

Before optimization   After optimization

Fig. 13. Reconstructed 3D shape (Red: initial position for left camera, white: initial position for right camera and green: final shape after optimization). 1st row: Planer board. 2nd row: Ball. 3rd row: Mannequin (Color figure online).

board, sphere and mannequin and first restored the shape with approximated model, and then, the shape was refined by out bundle adjustment algorithm. As shown in Fig. 12, we can confirm that the reprojection error is drastically decreased and Fig. 13 right two columns (green colored shapes) show that the our refinement algorithm successfully merged two shapes (left two colums, red and white colored shapes) into single consistent shape. For quntitave evaluation, we calculate RMSE for the planer board by fitting the plane to the board and it was drestically decreased from 9.7 mm to 0.7 mm, confirming the effectiveness of our algorithm.

7 Conclusion and Future Work

In this paper, we propose a practical oneshot active 3D scanning method in underwater environment. To realize the system, we propose three solutions. First, we calibarate the camera and projector paremeters with polynomial approximation for multiple depth. Then, shapes are reconstructed by wave reconstruction which allows inevitable errors in epipolar geometry. Finally, 3D shapes are refined by the bundle adjustment algorithm which calculates the actural 2D position on the image plane by solving the fourth order polynomial of phisical model. Experiments are conducted with simulation and real environment showing the effectiveness of our method. Temporal constraint to reconver moving object under water environment is our future work.

References

1. Agrawal, A., Ramalingam, S., Taguchi, Y., Chari, V.: A theory of multi-layer flat refractive geometry. In: CVPR (2012)
2. Aoki, H., Furukawa, R., Aoyama, M., Hiura, S., Asada, N., Sagawa, R., Kawasaki, H., Shiga, T., Suzuki, A.: Noncontact measurement of cardiac beat by using active stereo with waved-grid pattern projection. In: 2013 35th Annual International Conference of the IEEE Engineering in Medicine and Biology Society (EMBC), pp. 1756–1759. IEEE (2013)
3. Ferreira, R., Costeira, J.P., Santos, J.A.: Stereo reconstruction of a submerged scene. In: Marques, J.S., Pérez de la Blanca, N., Pina, P. (eds.) IbPRIA 2005. LNCS, vol. 3522, pp. 102–109. Springer, Heidelberg (2005)
4. Fu, X., Wang, Z., Kawasaki, H., Sagawa, R., Furukawa, R.: Calibration of the projector with fixed pattern and large distortion lens in a structured light system. In: The 13th IAPR Conference on Machine Vision Applications (2013)
5. Hall-Holt, O., Rusinkiewicz, S.: Stripe boundary codes for real-time structured-light range scanning of moving objects. ICCV 2, 359–366 (2001)
6. Jordt-Sedlazeck, A., Jung, D., Koch, R.: Refractive plane sweep for underwater images. In: Weickert, J., Hein, M., Schiele, B. (eds.) GCPR 2013. LNCS, vol. 8142, pp. 333–342. Springer, Heidelberg (2013)
7. Kang, L., Wu, L., Yang, Y.-H.: Two-view underwater structure and motion for cameras under flat refractive interfaces. In: Fitzgibbon, A., Lazebnik, S., Perona, P., Sato, Y., Schmid, C. (eds.) ECCV 2012, Part IV. LNCS, vol. 7575, pp. 303–316. Springer, Heidelberg (2012)

8. Kawahara, R., Nobuhara, S., Matsuyama, T.: A pixel-wise varifocal camera model for efficient forward projection and linear extrinsic calibration of underwater cameras with flat housings. In: 2013 IEEE International Conference on Computer Vision Workshops (ICCVW), pp. 819–824. IEEE (2013)

9. Kawahara, R., Nobuhara, S., Matsuyama, T.: Underwater 3D surface capture using multi-view projectors and cameras with flat housings. IPSJ Trans. Comput. Vis. Appl. **6**, 43–47 (2014)

10. Lavest, J.-M., Rives, G., Lapresté, J.T.: Underwater camera calibration. In: Vernon, D. (ed.) ECCV 2000. LNCS, vol. 1843, pp. 654–668. Springer, Heidelberg (2000)

11. Massot-Campos, M., Oliver-Codina, G.: Underwater laser-based structured light system for one-shot 3D reconstruction. In: 2014 IEEE SENSORS, pp. 1138–1141. IEEE (2014)

12. Mazaheri, M., Momeni, M.: 3D modeling using structured light pattern and photogrammetric epipolar geometry. Int. Arch. Photogrammetry Remote Sens. Spat. Inf. Sci. **37**, 87–90 (2008)

13. Pizarro, O., Eustice, R., Singh, H.: Relative pose estimation for instrumented, calibrated imaging platforms. In: DICTA, pp. 601–612. Citeseer (2003)

14. Queiroz-Neto, J.P., Carceroni, R., Barros, W., Campos, M.: Underwater stereo. In: Proceedings of the 17th Brazilian Symposium on Computer Graphics and Image Processing, pp. 170–177. IEEE (2004)

15. Sagawa, R., Ota, Y., Yagi, Y., Furukawa, R., Asada, N., Kawasaki, H.: Dense 3D reconstruction method using a single pattern for fast moving object. In: ICCV (2009)

16. Sagawa, R., Sakashita, K., Kasuya, N., Kawasaki, H., Furukawa, R., Yagi, Y.: Grid-based active stereo with single-colored wave pattern for dense one-shot 3D scan. In: 3DIMPVT, pp. 363–370 (2012)

17. Sedlazeck, A., Koch, R.: Calibration of housing parameters for underwater stereo-camera rigs. In: BMVC (2011)

18. Young, M., Beeson, E., Davis, J., Rusinkiewicz, S., Ramamoorthi, R.: Viewpoint-coded structured light. In: CVPR, June 2007

19. Zhang, Z.: A flexible new technique for camera calibration. Technical report MSR-TR-98-71, 12 (1998)

Using Image Features and Eye Tracking Device to Predict Human Emotions Towards Abstract Images

Kitsuchart Pasupa[1]([⊠]), Panawee Chatkamjuncharoen[1],
Chotiros Wuttilertdeshar[1], and Masanori Sugimoto[2]

[1] Faculty of Information Technology,
King Mongkut's Institute of Technology Ladkrabang,
Bangkok 10520, Thailand
kitsuchart@it.kmitl.ac.th,
{panawee.c,chotiroswuttilertdeshar}@gmail.com
[2] Department of Computer Science, Hokkaido University,
Sapporo 060-814, Japan
sugi@ist.hokudai.ac.jp

Abstract. Nowadays, emotional semantic image retrieval system enables users to access images that they want in a database according to emotional concept. This leads to affective image classification task which recently attracts researchers' attention. However, different users may experience different emotions depending on where, in the image, they are gazing on. This paper presents an improved prediction method by taking into account the users eye movement as implicit feedback while they are looking at the image. Our experimental results show that using both eye movement information and image feature together to determine users emotion gave more accurate predictions than using image feature alone.

Keywords: Eye movements · Implicit feedback · Emotion · Image retrieval

1 Introduction

Image retrieval is a method for users to search for their desired images in a database. In the past, each image in the database was manually tagged with keywords, then a system retrieved images by keyword matching. However, tagging keywords to a large number of images consumes a lot of resources. Therefore, less-resource-consuming retrieval methods were proposed i.e. automatic tag Image [1] and content-based image retrieval (CBIR). Images are described by lower-level features i.e. texture, color, and shape. CBIR compares features of a given image to every image in a database and then retrieves the images that have similar features to the given image. Recently, CBIR are becoming popular [2]. Examples of CBIR are PicSOM [3] and Google Image Search [4]. In 2006,

© Springer International Publishing Switzerland 2016
T. Bräunl et al. (Eds.): PSIVT 2015, LNCS 9431, pp. 419–430, 2016.
DOI: 10.1007/978-3-319-29451-3_34

Emotion Semantic Image Retrieval (ESIR) [5] was introduced - image search system with emotional concepts. From then on, the number of research studies on ESIR is steadily increasing. Examples of these studies are the following: a study of features of images that classify human emotions using theories of art and psychology [6]; a study of human emotions toward images of abstract art with low-level features [7]; and a study of emotion classification by using Multiple Kernel Learning (MKL) with basic image features – color, shape and texture [8].

In order to enhance the performance of CBIR, a relevance feedback from the user is used to refine the search results such as a mouse click. Clicking is an explicit feedback from a user actualizing his or her intention. A feedback can also be implicit. In 2009, Pasupa and his colleague developed a system that rank images by tracking and using the users unintentional eye movement to identify the ranking on images judged by users; specifically, the system outputs a ranking list of images that are likely to be the desired image [9]. However, the proposed approach is unrealistic and unable to apply to CBIR system because there is no eye movement presented a-priori on all images in database. Hence, Tensor Ranking Support Vector Machine is proposed to solve this problem [10]. In 2010, a CBIR system the so-called "PinView" was successfully developed to use both explicit and implicit feedback [11].

Emotional awareness depends on several factor such as gender, ethnicity, age and educational level. However, in this research, we were interested in using the close connection between human emotion and eye movement to classify the users emotion toward an image. The phrase "Beauty is in the eye of the beholder" leads to the assumption of this study that when several people look at a particular image, their emotions stimulated by the image may be different depending on which area of the image they are gazing on. This paper presents an approach to classify users emotions toward images by using both image feature and eye movement on the assumption that a better classification from using both together can achieve a higher prediction efficiency than using image feature alone.

The paper is organized as follows: Sect. 2 briefly explains theory used in this work. Data collection and feature extraction of this work is explained in Sects. 3 and 4, respectively. Section 5 shows experiment setup followed by its results and discussions in Sect. 6.

2   Theories

2.1   Emotion

Emotion is a feeling affected by stimulation. It can be classified by a dimension approach or a discrete approach.

The dimension approach considers each emotion as a combination of basic emotions that have their own intensities. Following this approach, Plutchik and Kellerman (1986) proposed eight basic emotions, which are joy, sadness, anger, fear, trust, disgust, surprise, and anticipation [12]. These basic emotions can also be combined to create a derived emotion such as love, trust, etc.

On the other hand, the discrete approach considers that each emotion can have different intensities, as mentioned in [13,14]. In this work, we follow Ekman (1972) approach [15]. Six basic emotions were proposed which are anger, disgust, fear, happiness, sadness, and surprise. These six basic emotions are then grouped, in a study by Jack *et al.* (2014), by facial expressions into four categories which are happy, sad, angry, and fear [16]. Jack *et al.* (2014) also reported that fear and surprise have similar facial expressions as disgust and angry.

2.2   Abstract Art

Abstract art is the type of images that convey an artist's emotion or feeling as abstract forms. Wassily Kandinsky, the inventor of abstract art, had mentioned that the main elements of abstract art are colors and forms that are used to express meaning. Abstract art does not directly convey its meaning, thus individual viewers feeling and imagination are needed to interpret a piece of abstract art [17]. Emotions stimulated by a piece of abstract art are caused by each viewers interpretation of it which depends on where in the piece the viewer is gazing on. Therefore, even for the same image, each people can have a different emotion towards it. In this study, an eye tracker was used to record where in pieces of abstract art that viewers were gazing on. These records were then used to find the image features that can be used to classify the viewers emotion towards those pieces of abstract art.

2.3   Relevance Feedback

Relevance feedback is the information that a computer system gets from the user to determine whether the retrieved item is related to the users query or not. This piece of information is then used to optimize the response to the next query. There are two categories of relevance feedback: first, explicit – it is intentional feedback from users that takes time and mental effort such as mouse click, intentional eye movement, voice, and gesture; and second, implicit feedback – it is unintentional feedback that users do automatically. This type of feedback needs to be processed before use, such as heart rate, blood pressure, body temperature, and unintentional eye movement while reading a book or searching for information on a web browser.

2.4   Support Vector Machine

Support Vector Machine (SVM) is a well-known machine learning algorithm that is used to perform classification task. The are evidences that emotions towards images can also be classified by SVM [6–8,18]. SVM classifies data points by using linear hyperplane. Assuming that x_i is a sample vector, x_i pairs with y_i where $y \in \{-1, +1\}$, w is the weight vector, ξ is a non-negative slack variable, and C is a penalty constant. A hyperplane is generated such that the distance between two groups of data is the farthest and the classification error is the lowest, as shown in (1).

$$\min \frac{1}{2}\|\boldsymbol{w}\|^2 + C\sum_{i=1}^{m}\xi_i$$
$$\text{s.t.} \quad y_i(\boldsymbol{w}\cdot\boldsymbol{x}_i - b) \geq 1 - \xi_i, \tag{1}$$
$$\xi \geq 0, i = 1\dots m,$$

where $C > 0$. The decision function is as follow:

$$f(\boldsymbol{x}) = \text{sgn}(\boldsymbol{w}\cdot\boldsymbol{x}_i - b) \tag{2}$$

In real world application, a relationship between two groups of data is usually not linear in most cases, so a kernel trick is used. Examples of kernel functions are Polynomial and Radial Basis Function.

3   Data Collection

In this experiment, 100 sets of data of emotions towards images together with data of eye movements were collected from 20 undergraduate students aged 18–22 (10 males and 10 females) who had regular eyesight and were not wearing glasses. During data collection, our developed software displayed images from a database and collected subjects eye movement data with an eye tracker device at the same time. First, the subject was asked to sit in front of a 13-inch laptop (with a resolution of 1366×768 pixel) and then explained the procedure of the experiment. A subject had to specify his or her emotion towards a displayed image and an experiment operator recorded this information with a keyboard, as shown in Fig. 1. Before the experiment, the subjects were asked to try not to move their head, and the eye tracker was calibrated by having the subjects look at 9 points on the screen (1 point at the center and 8 points at the edges), as shown in Fig. 2a. Also, before skipping to the next image, the subjects were asked to look at an image that consists of a reference point at the center for 3 seconds, as shown in Fig. 2b, in order to make sure that his or her eyes were at the same position for every image.

The Eye Tribe Tracker could connect to a computer or a tablet and tracked eyes with data transfer rate of $30\,\text{Hz}$ and $0.5° - 1°$ accuracy [19]. Abstract art images included in this study were obtained from Machajdik and Hanbury (2010) [6]. These included 228 images classified into 8 emotions – amusement, excitement, contentment, sad, anger, awe, fear, and disgust. However, we did not classify the images into 8 emotions as Wang *et al.* (2006) did, in order to reduce complexity for users to make judgements. Instead, we classified them according to the method of Shaver *et al.* (2001) [20]. Emotions are categorized to be 3 levels: primary, secondary, and tertiary emotion. These 8 emotions were categorized according to these levels of emotion into 4 primary emotions which are happy (amusement, excitement, contentment), sad, anger, and fear (fear, disgust), as in [16]. Images that produce awe emotion were not mentioned in [20], thus they were not considered in this study.

Fig. 1. The setup of eye tracking experiment.

(a)   (b)

Fig. 2. (a) The nine-point calibration, and (b) the reference point screen.

Then, 100 images of 4 emotions (25 images for each emotion) that received the highest users votes – as in Machajdik and Hanbury (2010) [6] – were selected; some are shown in Fig. 3. Experimental results showed that when different people looked at the same image (Fig. 4a), their emotions were different. Users defined their emotion towards the image as fear, anger, and sad, as shown in Fig. 4b, c, and d, respectively.

4   Feature Extraction

For feature extraction in this study, we essentially extracted the color, shape, and texture features from images by using histograms. RGB was used to represent the distribution of color in each pixel of an image. The value of RGB is between 0–255. The shape feature used was as described by Sobel. It shows the magnitude of gradient in an image. The texture feature was extracted with a Gabor function with five scales and eight orientations. In this study, we used only one scale, eight orientations, and a high-pass filter. In order to increase the efficiency of emotional prediction, these features were combined by concatenating the vector of each feature together. These features were extracted from the original image, the original image with eye movement information, and the original image with eye movement information and Gaussian blur as shown in Fig. 5.

Fig. 3. Examples of images used in the study. Happy images are shown in 1st row followed by sad images in 2nd row. Anger and fear images are shown in 3rd, and 4th row, respectively.

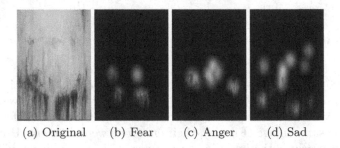

(a) Original   (b) Fear   (c) Anger   (d) Sad

Fig. 4. Different users with different emotions at the same image

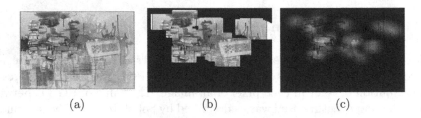

(a)   (b)   (c)

Fig. 5. (a) Original Image, (b) Original image with eye movement information, and (c) Original image with eye movement information and Gaussian blur.

4.1 Original Image

Each original image were represented by the histograms of the distribution of RGB, Sobel and Gabor features at 8, 16, 32, and 64 bin sizes (n_{bin}). The size of color feature vector ($n_{feature}$) is n_{bin}^3 and the size of shape and texture feature vectors is n_{bin}.

4.2 Original Image Processed with Eye Movement Data

Original images were processed with eye movement data using a Gaussian function and the main cause for the change from each original image was which area in the image the subject was gazing on.

Mathematically, the processing can be described as follows. Let $I(x, y)$ be the image where (x, y) is a specified location and $E(x, y)$ is the eye movement information (fixation location). The Gaussian function that processes the image is expressed as

$$g(x_s) = e^{\frac{-x_s^2}{2\sigma}} \qquad (3)$$

where x_s is a size of Gaussian. In this work, x_s is set to 100, 125, and 150 which gives Gaussian at 100×100, 125×125, and 150×150 sizes, respectively. σ is the standard deviation of the Gaussian function, here, we used $\sigma = \frac{x_s}{6}$. We used Gaussian function because it is well-suited for the foveation in human vision [21]. The Gaussian function transforms $E(x, y)$ into heatmap $G(x, y)$. Heatmap quantifies the degree of importance of part of image. Furthermore, $G(x, y)$ is be used to create a binary filter $H(x, y)$,

$$H(x, y) = \begin{cases} 1 \text{ if } G(x, y) > 0 \\ 0 \text{ if } G(x, y) = 0 \end{cases}. \qquad (4)$$

Hence, the processed image is expressed as

$$I_E(x, y) = H(x, y) \times I(x, y) \qquad (5)$$

where $\times$ denote element-wise multiplication.

4.3 Original Image Processed with Eye Movement Data and Gaussian Blur

Instead of using the filter $H(x, y)$ of Sect. 4.2, $G(x, y)$ is applied as the filter to process the original image into this type of processed image,

$$I_G(x, y) = G(x, y) \times I(x, y) \qquad (6)$$

The values of $G(x, y)$ are between 0 and 1. If the value is close to 0, that position of the image is dark, whereas if the value is close to 1, that position is bright.

5 Experiment Setup

In this study, we performed two experiments, one that used each users model and the other one that used a global model, to compare the efficiencies of the 3 features – histograms of RGB colors, Sobel, and Gabor – in the three types of images – original image (I), original image processed with eye movement data (I_E), and original image processed with eye movement data and Gaussian blur (I_G).

In the first experiment, three acquired features were compared by having them predicting each users emotion from his or her user model (20 users). SVM with linear kernel was used. The task is to classify 4 classes of data – happy, sad, anger, and fear, therefore, one-vs-all multi-class classification was considered. We used leave-one-out cross-validation (LOO-CV) technique to obtain the optimal model for each user based on misclassification rate. In this experiment, leave-one-image-out cross validation was applied to find the optimal n_{bin}, size of Gaussian filter, and SVM's C parameter. The adjustable C parameter is between 10^{-6} and 10^4. It should be noted that all data were normalized to zero mean and unit standard deviation.

In the second experiment, a global model constructed from all users data was used with similar setup as in the first experiment to predict the emotions of 10 users but with a leave-one-user-out cross-validation technique instead.

6   Experimental Results and Discussion

6.1   User Model

The effectiveness of emotion classification is reported as percentages of average accuracy of 20 users. The classification results of the three features and a set of four combined features on all three sets of data are compared to a baseline (BL) – that is, when SVM is able to predict only one emotion which is the majority class.

From Table 1, we can see that the average accuracies found from I, I_E, and I_G sets of data are better than that found from BL. Also, I_E and I_G are generally more effective than I but the texture feature of I is more effective than the two. Moreover, using combined features together is more effective than using a single feature alone. In combining them, the size of each feature is taken to be equal, a value in the range of $\{8, 16, 32, 64\}$-bin. We can see that the emotion prediction accuracy obtained from using all three features combined is the best at 48.05 %, while it is 47.60 % for combined color and texture features and 47.20 % for combined color and shape feature. However, using combined shape and texture features gives a worse prediction accuracy than using color feature alone. Therefore, we surmise that including color feature and eye movement in a set of combined features should increase prediction accuracy.

Figure 6 shows a graph of the averages of true positive rates from using every type of features, the most accurate prediction is from using the leftmost feature on the x-axis and the less accurate ones are from left to right (in that strict order for the I_E data set). It can be observed that the trend that a particular feature is more likely to be more or less accurate than the others is the same for the results reported in Table 1 and those reported in Fig. 6.

6.2   Global Model - New User

According to the first experiment, we found that I_E is more accurate than I_G. This might be because some parts of I_G is blurred and leads to information loss problem. Using the best combination of 3 features is more accurate than using any single feature or other combinations of features. Therefore, we chose to use I_E and the best combination of 3 features for predicting the emotions of any new users based on the leave-one-user-out cross-validated data on 10 users which were randomly sampled user.

Table 1. The accuracy of emotion predictions of 20 users (%) - user model.

Feature	BL	I	I_E	I_G
Color	36.35	43.35	**45.85**	45.70
Shape		41.95	**45.80**	44.80
Texture		**43.15**	42.20	42.15
Color+Shape		46.60	**47.20**	46.95
Color+Texture		45.65	**47.60**	45.65
Shape+Texture		41.40	**44.60**	44.45
Color+Shape+Texture		47.10	**48.05**	47.20
Average	36.35	44.17	**45.90**	45.26

From Tables 1 and 2, it can be observed that the average accuracies of the global model are higher than those of user model because the amount of the global models training data (900 images) is more than that of the user models training data (99 images). The results of the global model in Table 3 show that both I and I_E are more accurate than BL and that I_E is generally more accurate than I (55.70 % on average) except for the cases of the 5, 6, 7 subjects, that might be due to the differences in their eye movement behavior and their emotion towards an image to the majority of the subjects. Hence, predictions from the

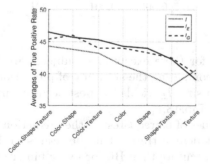

Fig. 6. Average of true positive predictions from using each feature.

Table 2. Average accuracies of the three contenders: I, I_E and BL on global model of 10 users.

User	BL	I	I_E
1	46.00	48.00	**50.00**
2	28.00	51.00	**55.00**
3	35.00	59.00	**65.00**
4	49.00	47.00	**57.00**
5	33.00	**49.00**	48.00
6	46.00	**62.00**	56.00
7	36.00	**55.00**	**55.00**
8	38.00	52.00	**53.00**
9	34.00	55.00	**61.00**
10	52.00	56.00	**57.00**
Average	39.70	53.40	**55.70**

Table 3. Average accuracies and their standard deviations of emotion prediction - global model.

n_{bin}	BL	I	I_E
8	39.70±7.96	51.90±4.23	**52.00±6.13**
16		52.50±5.46	**52.60±5.97**
32		51.30±5.14	**55.00±5.35**
64		50.70±5.14	**53.80±4.76**

Table 4. p-values of paired t-test of the accuracies of emotion prediction of the global model in Table 3.

n_{bin}	I-vs-BL	I_E-vs-BL	I_E-vs-I
8	0.001	0.001	0.955
16	0.002	0.001	0.949
32	0.005	0.001	0.034
64	0.006	0.001	0.001

global model with I_E for these exceptional subjects are less accurate than or equal to I. Moreover, comparing the accuracy of prediction of emotion in global model on the same bin size, I_E yields the best accuracy in all cases followed by I and BL as shown in Table 3.

Table 4 shows p-values of paired t-test of the prediction accuracies of emotion of the global model. It demonstrates that the results in Table 3 that I and I_E are significantly more accurate than BL for every bin size at $p < 0.01$ and that I_E are significantly more accurate than I only for 32, 64 bin size at $p < 0.05$.

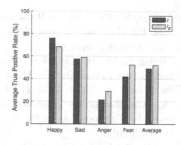

Fig. 7. The average of true positive result for prediction of each emotion in global model.

Figure 7 shows the average of true positive results for each emotion and the average of true positive results for all emotions. It can be seen that I_E is more accurate than I in predicting sad, anger, and fear. Averaged over all emotions, I_E proves to be the best.

7   Conclusion

This paper presents an approach to predict users emotions towards abstract images (happy, sad, anger, and fear) by using (a) eye movement information and (b) low-level image features such as color, shape, and texture. It is found that using both the eye movement information and a set of image features gives more accurate predictions than using image features alone. The best combination of 3 features gives more accurate predictions than any other single feature or combinations. The color feature, either alone or in a combination, has the most positive influence on prediction results. Moreover, increasing the amount of training user data can also improve the prediction accuracy as shown in global model. However, eye movements can degrade the predictions if the users' judgements and eye movement behaviours are different from other users in the training model. Hence, user adaptation should be considered in the future.

Acknowledgments. The research leading to these results has received funding from the ASEAN University Network/Southeast Asia Engineering Education Development Network (AUN/SEED-Net) under the Short-term Research Program in Japan (SRJP 2014). This publication only reflects the authors views.

References

1. Ye, L., Ogunbona, P., Wang, J.: Image content annotation based on visual features. In: 8th IEEE International Symposium on Multimedia, pp. 62–69. IEEE Press, New York (2006)
2. Datta, R., Li, J., Wang, J.Z.: Content-based image retrieval: approaches and trends of the new age. In: 7th ACM SIGMM International Workshop on Multimedia Information Retrieval, pp. 253–262. ACM (2005)

3. Laaksonen, J., Koskela, M., Oja, E.: PicSOM - self-organizing image retrieval with MPEG-7 content descriptors. IEEE Trans. Neural Netw. **13**, 841–853 (2002)
4. Google Image Search. https://images.google.com/
5. Wang, W.-N., Yu, Y.-L., Jiang, S.-M.: Image retrieval by emotional semantics: a study of emotional space and feature extraction. In: IEEE International Conference on Systems, Man and Cybernetics, pp. 3534–3539. IEEE Press, New York (2006)
6. Machajdik, J., Hanbury, A.: Affective image classification using features inspired by psychology and art theory. In: Proceedings of the International Conference on Multimedia, pp. 83–92. ACM (2010)
7. Zhang, H., Augilius, E., Honkela, T., Laaksonen, J., Gamper, H., Alene, H.: Analyzing emotional semantics of abstract art using low-level image features. In: Gama, J., Bradley, E., Hollmén, J. (eds.) IDA 2011. LNCS, vol. 7014, pp. 413–423. Springer, Heidelberg (2011)
8. Zhang, H., Gönen, M., Yang, Z., Oja, E.: Predicting emotional states of images using Bayesian multiple kernel learning. In: Lee, M., Hirose, A., Hou, Z.-G., Kil, R.M. (eds.) ICONIP 2013, Part III. LNCS, vol. 8228, pp. 274–282. Springer, Heidelberg (2013)
9. Pasupa, K., Saunders, C., Szedmak, S., Klami, A., Kaski, S., Gunn, S.: Learning to rank images from eye movements. In: 12th IEEE International Conference on Computer Vision Workshops, pp. 2009–2016. IEEE Press, New York (2009)
10. Hardoon, D.R., Pasupa, K.: Image ranking with implicit feedback from eye movements. In: 2010 Symposium on Eye-Tracking Research & Applications, pp. 291–298. ACM (2010)
11. Auer, P., Hussain, Z., Kaski, S., Klami, A., Kujala, J., Laaksonen, J., Leung, A.P., Pasupa, K., Shawe-Taylor, J.: PinView: implicit feedback in content-based image retrieval. In: Diethe, T., Cristianini, N., Shawe-Taylor, J. (eds.) Proceedings of the Workshop on Applications of Pattern Analysis 2010, vol. 11, pp. 51–57 (2010). Journal of Machine Learning Research
12. Plutchik, R., Kellerman, H.: Emotion: Theory, Research and Experience, vol. 3. Academic Press, New York (1986)
13. Izard, C.E.: Basic emotions, relations among emotions, and emotion-cognition relations. Psychol. Rev. **99**, 561–565 (1992)
14. Vytal, K., Hamann, S.: Neuroimaging support for discrete neural correlates of basic emotions: a voxel-based meta-analysis. J. Cogn. Neurosci. **22**, 2864–2885 (2010)
15. Ekman, P.: Universal and cultural differences in facial expression of emotion. In: Nebraska Symposium on Motivation, vol. 19, pp. 207–284. University of Nebraska Press, Lincoln (1972)
16. Jack, R., Garrod, O., Schyns, P.: Dynamic facial expressions of emotion transmit an evolving hierarchy of signals over time. Curr. Biol. **24**, 187–192 (2014)
17. Galenson, D.W.: Two paths to abstract art: Kandinsky and Malevich. Technical report 12403, National Bureau of Economic Research (2006)
18. Wu, Y., Bauckhage, C., Thurau, C.: The good, the bad, and the ugly: predicting aesthetic image labels. In: 20th International Conference on Pattern Recognition, pp. 1586–1589 (2010)
19. The Eye Tribe. https://theeyetribe.com
20. Shaver, P., Schwartz, J., Kirson, D., O'Connor, C.: Emotional knowledge: further exploration of a prototype approach. In: Parrott, G. (ed.) Emotions in Social Psychology: Essential Readings, pp. 26–56. Psychology Press, Philadelphia (2001)
21. Chang, E.C., Mallat, S., Yap, C.: Wavelet foveation. Appl. Comput. Harmon. Anal. **9**, 312–335 (2000)

Video Surveillance

Personal Authentication Based on 3D Configuration of Micro-feature Points on Facial Surface

Takao Yoshinuma[✉], Hideitsu Hino, and Kazuhiro Fukui

Graduate School of Systems and Information Engineering, University of Tsukuba, Tsukuba, Japan
yoshinuma@cvlab.cs.tsukuba.ac.jp, {hinohide,kfukui}@cs.tsukuba.ac.jp

Abstract. This paper proposes a personal authentication method based on the 3D configuration of micro-feature points such as moles and freckles, plus common feature points such as corners of eyes, edges of mouth and nostrils. The basic idea behind the proposed method is the assumption that such 3D configuration can be uniquely determined by individuals. To compare two configurations of feature points effectively, the concept of 3D shape subspace in a high-dimensional vector space is introduced. With this idea, the task of comparing the sets of feature points is converted to that of measuring the structural similarity between the corresponding shape subspaces. The validity of the proposed method is demonstrated through experiments with feature points from actual face images. In addition, the performance limit of the method is explored using sets of artificially generated feature points.

Keywords: Personal authentication · Facial feature · Shape subspace · Grassmann discriminant analysis

1 Introduction

This paper presents a personal authentication method based on the 3D configuration of micro-feature points, such as moles and freckles, on a facial surface, and facial feature points such as corners of eyes, edges of mouth and nostrils. Common appearance-based face recognition methods [1–7] often fail to distinguish a pair of faces with similar appearance by its nature. In contrast, the most remarkable advantage of the proposed method is that it can distinguish even a pair of twins with the completely same appearance, since the 3D configuration of micro-features includes both inherent and acquired features.

The proposed method is motivated by a 3D object recognition method based on the structure similarity between shape subspaces [8]. In this method, each set of feature points is compactly represented by a linear subspace, which is called shape subspace as shown in Fig. 1. A shape subspace of an image is known to be generated by applying factorization method [9] to the trajectories of a set of feature points, which are extracted and tracked from sequential images. This converts the task of comparing two given sets of feature points to that of measuring

© Springer International Publishing Switzerland 2016
T. Bräunl et al. (Eds.): PSIVT 2015, LNCS 9431, pp. 433–446, 2016.
DOI: 10.1007/978-3-319-29451-3_35

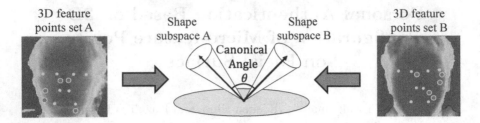

Fig. 1. A conceptual diagram of the proposed framework. Sets of T 3D feature points are extracted from RGB-D images to constitute shape subspaces in T-dimensional vector space, and their similarity is evaluated by the notion of canonical angles.

the structural similarity between two corresponding shape subspaces, by using the canonical angles between them [8]. Suppose there are several different classes (e.g., different persons), and shape subspaces are already enrolled in the system for each class. Then, an input set of feature points is classified into the class with the highest similarity.

The above framework based on the shape subspace can work well under stable lighting condition and no occlusion. However, the framework has the following two issues: (1) stable extraction and tracking of a set of feature points are required, while they are difficult in practical situations, (2) classification ability is insufficient for discriminating persons with very similar 3D structure of feature points.

To address the first issue, we propose an effective method to generate a shape subspace from a single depth image captured by an RGB-D sensor. This method does not require feature points tracking. For the second issue, we enhance the classification ability by introducing a powerful subspace-based classification method called Grassmann discriminant analysis (GDA [10]). An additional issue is that facial feature detection is often error-prone, which may reduce the performance of our method. To deal with this issue, we generate multiple perturbed shape subspaces from an input depth image by repeating the random sampling of reliable feature points, instead of generating one subspace from the depth image.

The validity of the proposed method is demonstrated through simple experiments with feature points from actual face images. In addition, the performance limit of the method is explored using sets of artificially generated feature points, simulating the situation of distinguishing similar faces.

2   Preliminary

The core idea of the proposed method is the use of structural similarity between shape subspaces, which is measured by using the canonical angles between these subspaces. In the following, we firstly explain how to calculate canonical angles from two given sets of facial feature points. Then, we outline the algorithm of Grassmann discriminant analysis for realizing a highly accurate classifier using shape subspaces.

2.1   Definition of Structural Similarity with Canonical Angles

Consider an n_A-dimensional subspace $\mathcal{S}_A$ and an n_B-dimensional subspace $\mathcal{S}_B$, where $n_A \leq n_B$. The principal canonical angle θ_1 is uniquely defined by [11]

$$\cos^2 \theta_1 = \sup_{u \in \mathcal{S}_A, v \in \mathcal{S}_B} \frac{u^\top v}{\|u\|^2 \|v\|^2}, \tag{1}$$

where $\| \cdot \|$ denotes the norm of a vector. Let $\mathbf{Q}_A$ and $\mathbf{Q}_B$ denote the orthogonal projection matrices of the subspaces $\mathcal{S}_A$ and $\mathcal{S}_B$, respectively. Then, $\cos^2 \theta$ for the canonical angle θ between $\mathcal{S}_A$ and $\mathcal{S}_B$ is equal to the eigenvalue of $\mathbf{Q}_A \mathbf{Q}_B$ or $\mathbf{Q}_B \mathbf{Q}_A$ [11]. The largest eigenvalue corresponds to the smallest angle θ_1, whereas the second largest eigenvalue corresponds to the smallest angle θ_2 in a direction perpendicular to that of the largest canonical angle. The values $\cos^2 \theta_l (l = 3, \ldots, n_A)$ are calculated in the same manner.

The simplest classification method using the canonical angles is known as the mutual subspace method (MSM [3]). In this method, the structural similarity φ between $\mathcal{S}_A$ and $\mathcal{S}_B$ is defined by

$$\varphi = \frac{1}{n_A} \sum_{l=1}^{n_A} \cos^2 \theta_l. \tag{2}$$

If two shape subspaces coincide completely with each other, φ is 1, since all canonical angles are zero. The similarity φ gets smaller as the two spaces deviate. The similarity φ is zero when the two subspaces are orthogonal to each other. In the MSM, we calculate the similarities between an input subspace $\mathcal{S}$ and reference subspaces $\mathcal{S}_i$ $(i = 1, 2, \ldots)$. The input subspace is classified into the class with the highest similarity. As explained in detail later, the shape subspaces are 3-dimensional subspaces, hence we can compute three canonical angles. By using them, the similarity between shape subspaces $\mathcal{S}_A$ and $\mathcal{S}_B$ is defined as

$$\mathrm{sim}(\mathcal{S}_A, \mathcal{S}_B) = \frac{1}{3} \sum_{l=1}^{3} \cos^2 \theta_l. \tag{3}$$

2.2   Grassmann Discriminant Analysis

The structural similarity calculated by the MSM is effective for discriminating two sets of facial feature points. However, its classification ability for the structural similarity is insufficient in discriminating persons with very similar feature points configurations.

A linear subspace considered in the MSM is regarded as a point on a Grassmann manifold [12], and the concept underlying the MSM is the computation of distance between points on the Grassmann manifold. To improve the classification ability of the MSM, we introduce the notion of Grassmann discriminant analysis (GDA [10]), which is a generalization of linear discriminant analysis

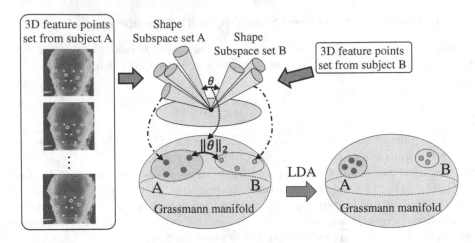

Fig. 2. Conceptual diagram of the use of Grassmann discriminant analysis. Each shape subspace is considered as a point on a Grassmann manifold. Distance between points on the manifold corresponds to the canonical angle between the subspaces.

(LDA [13]) for dealing with a set of data points as a single datum as shown in Fig. 2. Grassmann discriminant analysis can find the classification axis that maximizes the class separability taking the relative similarity between subspaces into account.

Grassmann discriminant analysis is an extension of linear discriminant analysis by replacing vectors for samples with subspaces generated from the set of samples. For this extension, GDA utilizes the kernel trick [14] with the kernel function on the space of subspaces defined as

$$k(\mathcal{S}_i, \mathcal{S}_j) = \mathrm{sim}(\mathcal{S}_i, \mathcal{S}_j), \tag{4}$$

where sim is defined by Eq. (3). We then define the empirical kernel feature map [15] of a shape subspace $\mathcal{S}$ as

$$\boldsymbol{k}(\mathcal{S}) = (k(\mathcal{S}, \mathcal{D}_{1,1}), k(\mathcal{S}, \mathcal{D}_{1,2}), \ldots, k(\mathcal{S}, \mathcal{D}_{2,1}), \ldots, k(\mathcal{S}, \mathcal{D}_{C,N_C}))^{\top}, \tag{5}$$

where $\mathcal{D}_{c,l}(c = 1, \ldots, C, l = 1, \ldots, N_c)$ are subspaces consist of training samples, C is the number of the classes (i.e., each person), and N_c is the number of the samples of class c (i.e., sets of feature points). For the details of GDA, refer to [10].

3   Proposed Framework

In this section, we explain the detail of the proposed framework for person authentication. First, we extract facial feature points by applying the circular separability filter [16] for a gray scale image of a face. Then, we obtain the 3D coordinates of the feature points from a depth image captured with the gray scale image at the same time.

A shape subspace is spanned by the three column vectors of a $T \times 3$ matrix S, which is defined by

$$S = (d_1, d_2, \ldots, d_T)^\top = \begin{pmatrix} x_1 & y_1 & z_1 \\ x_2 & y_2 & z_2 \\ \vdots & \vdots & \vdots \\ x_T & y_T & z_T \end{pmatrix}, \tag{6}$$

where $d_t = (x_t \ y_t \ z_t)^\top$, $(1 \le t \le T)$ denotes the positional vector of the t-th feature point.

In the next subsection, we explain how we extract the feature points on a face. Then, we explain the way we correspond two sets of feature points extracted from two face images.

3.1 Feature Extraction with Separability Filter

The separability filter computes the separability η of two regions of an image as shown in Fig. 3(a). The separability η $(0.0 \le \eta \le 1.0)$ of two regions R_1 and R_2 in an image is calculated as follows.

$$\eta = \frac{\sigma_b^2}{\sigma_T^2}, \tag{7}$$

$$\sigma_b^2 = \frac{q_1}{q}(\bar{P}_1 - \bar{P})^2 + \frac{q_2}{q}(\bar{P}_2 - \bar{P})^2, \tag{8}$$

$$\sigma_T^2 = \frac{1}{q} \sum_{P_i \in (R_1 \cup R_2)} (P_i - \bar{P})^2 = \overline{P^2} - (\bar{P})^2, \tag{9}$$

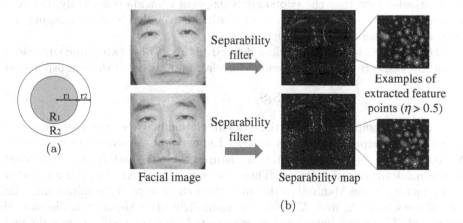

(a)

Separability filter →

Separability filter →

Examples of extracted feature points ($\eta > 0.5$)

Facial image   Separability map

(b)

Fig. 3. Circular separability filter (a) and examples of separability map and extracted feature points ($\eta > 0.5$) (b). In (b), salient features such as eyes, nose, and mouth region are excluded. From another image of the same subject, many feature points are extracted in the almost same position.

where σ_b^2 is the between-class variance, σ_T^2 is the total variance, q_1, q_2 are the numbers of pixels in R_1 and R_2, respectively, and $q = q_1 + q_2$. P_i is the image feature at pixel i, $\bar{P}_1, \bar{P}_2$ are the mean values of the image features in R_1 and R_2. $\bar{P}, \overline{P^2}$ are the mean value and the mean of square of the image features from both regions.

By applying the separability filter on the whole facial image, we can obtain a separability map, where each local maximum point corresponds to the center point of a circular object, such as eyeballs, nostril or moles. The separability map and the example of the extracted feature points are shown in Fig. 3(b). Most of feature points are obtained accurately. The separability can be regarded as a measure of reliability of detection. In addition to them, the separability filter can also extract the corners of eyes and the edges of mouth stably and precisely [18]. See [16–18] for the details of the separability filter.

3.2 Corresponding Feature Points using Autocorrelation Matrix

Although a shape subspace can be easily generated as the column space of the matrix $\mathbf{S}$ as mentioned previously, the generated shape subspace changes if the order of the feature points changes. Therefore, we need to correspond points between two images before calculating the similarity of the shape subspaces.

To deal with this issue, we introduce an effective method for corresponding points from two images based on autocorrelation matrices, which is an extension of the method proposed in [8]. The orthogonal projection matrix was used for corresponding feature points in [8]. In contrast, the autocorrelation matrix is used in this paper. As the autocorrelation remains more information of the feature points, we can conduct the corresponding points more stably. The method is based on the fact that if two shape subspaces are close with respect to canonical angles, the two corresponding autocorrelation matrices can also be close. In the particular case that the two shape subspaces coincide completely, the corresponding autocorrelation matrices also coincide completely after changing the order of the feature points appropriately.

Let $\mathbf{S}_i$ and $\mathbf{S}_j$ be shape matrices defined by Eq. (6) for two shape subspaces $\mathcal{S}_i$ and $\mathcal{S}_j$, respectively. We define autocorrelation matrices of these subspaces as

$$\mathbf{A}_i = \mathbf{S}_i\mathbf{S}_i^\top, \quad \mathbf{A}_j = \mathbf{S}_j\mathbf{S}_j^\top. \tag{10}$$

By iteratively comparing rows of the autocorrelation matrices, we correspond the points in the shape subspaces as follows. Elements of autocorrelation matrices $\mathbf{A}_i$ and $\mathbf{A}_j$ are sorted in column-wise manner, and $\mathbf{A}_i$ and $\mathbf{A}_j$ are re-defined by the resultant sorted matrices. Then, for each row of $\mathbf{A}_i$, find the row index of $\mathbf{A}_j$ such that the Manhattan distance from the row of $\mathbf{A}_i$ is minimum. The pair of rows from $\mathbf{A}_i$ and $\mathbf{A}_j$ found by minimizing the Manhattan distance is associated. This matching procedure is repeated until the residual error defined between the two autocorrelation matrices is lower than a threshold.

3.3   Overall Procedure of the Proposed Framework

We summarize the procedure of the proposed framework, considering the case of classifying an input shape subspace of an unknown person into C person classes. Given a set of N'_c RGB-D images (gray image and depth image for each person).

Learning Phase

1. We detect a set of feature points from each gray scale image. To reduce the influence of the error in detecting feature points as described in Sect. 1, we generate multiple perturbed shape subspaces by randomly selecting feature points from the gray images repeatedly. Consequently, the number of the feature sets of each person class, N'_c, increases to N_c.
2. We set reference shape matrices $\mathbf{S}_{c,l}(c = 1, \ldots, C, l = 1, \ldots, N_c)$ in Eq. (6), and then generate autocorrelation matrices $\mathbf{A}_{c,l}$ in Eq. (10) from them. These autocorrelation matrices are used as the references in the testing phase.

Testing Phase

1. We set input shape matrix $\mathbf{S}_{input}$ from a pair of gray scale image and its corresponding depth image of an unknown person. Then, we generate the autocorrelation matrix $\mathbf{A}_{input}$ to correspond the feature points.
2. We conduct the corresponding process between the input shape matrix $\mathbf{S}_{input}$ and reference shape matrices $\mathbf{S}_{c,l}$. In this process, the input shape matrix $\mathbf{S}_{input}$ is used as the reference. Namely, the row elements of $\mathbf{S}_{c,l}$ are sorted based on the that of input matrix $\mathbf{S}_{input}$.
3. After completing the corresponding process, we calculate the similarity among each reference subspaces using Eq. (3). With the similarities, we calculate a discriminative space (its basis) on the Grassman manifold by applying the GDA to the Gram matrix, which is calculated from the similarities among all the reference subspaces.
4. We project each subspace onto the discriminative space, and calculate the distance between the projected input subspace $\mathcal{S}_{input}$ and reference subspace $\mathcal{S}_{c,l}$. Finally, the input subspace is classified to the class of the nearest reference subspace.

4   Experimental Results and Consideration

We conducted four experiments. (1) To verify the effectiveness of the proposed framework, we evaluated its basic performance for real face data, (2) to show the validity of using the information of 3D configuration, we compared the performances of the methods with 3D configuration and 2D configuration of feature points, (3) to address the issue that the detected facial feature points include errors, we evaluate the effectiveness of using a large number of subspaces obtained by repeated random sampling from the reliable candidates of the feature points, (4) to evaluate the performance limit of the proposed method, we emulate the tough situation of distinguishing between twins.

4.1   Experiment 1

Experimental Condition. We captured a pairs of a depth image and its corresponding gray scale image by using an RGB-D sensor (Microsoft Kinect v2) from 16 subjects. The sensor was about 0.6 m away from the subjects sitting on a chair.

It is desirable to extract 3D coordinates of feature points directly from the pairs. However, it was difficult to extract very unclear and weak feature points, due to the comparatively low resolution of 512×424 pixels. To avoid the problem, we also captured gray scale images with higher resolution of $4,000 \times 6,000$ pixels by using a single-lens reflex camera. The camera was about 1.2 m away from the subjects. We captured 5 high resolution images from subjects in one session. The subjects were asked to stand up and sit down at the beginning of each session to produce natural fluctuations in face direction and position. We repeated the session four times to totally capture 20 images.

We cropped a facial region of 120×120 pixels from the low resolution image and then extracted eight common feature points: the four corners eyes, two nostrils, and two edges of mouth. For the high resolution image, we cropped a facial region of $1,200 \times 1,200$ pixels from the whole image and detected micro-features by applying the separability filter to the region except that of eyes, nostrils, and a mouth as shown in Fig. 3(b). The detected micro-feature is selected by the descending order of the separability. Besides, we manually extracted the eight facial feature points. Figure 4 shows an example of the extracted feature points. Finally, based on the correspondence relation of the positions of the eight facial feature points of the high- and low- resolution images, we obtained 3D coordinates of the feature points.

In many cases, the features on facial surface are affected by factors such as genetic or age of subjects. Therefore, the number of obtainable feature points depends on the subjects. Later in this section, we will see the dependencies of the classification error on the number of extracted feature points.

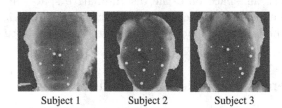

Subject 1   Subject 2   Subject 3

Fig. 4. Examples of the extracted feature points. Small points are edge of eyes, nostril, and corners of the mouth, which are considered as commonly extracted feature points.

The above evaluation procedure is summarized as follows:

1. We obtain the feature points from the images taken from 16 persons. From each person, 20 images are taken, hence the total number of the collected images is 320.

2. We make $N = 16$ persons' shape subspaces by using the obtained feature point sets.
3. Since 20 images were taken from each person, we evaluate the classification accuracy by 20-fold cross validation. That is, we used one image from each of N different persons as test dataset, and the rest $19 \times N$ subspaces from N persons as training datasets for constructing shape subspaces for N classes.

The MSM and GDA were used as classifiers and their accuracies were compared. We considered two simple methods in the classification process:

1-NN: a test sample (a set of feature points) is assigned the class for that of the closest subspace in the registered subspaces. The closeness is measured based on the Euclidean distance in the empirical kernel feature space induced by the kernel function defined in Eq. (4).

Distance to mean: mean points of subspaces for each class is calculated, and a test sample is assigned the class with the closest mean point. For calculating mean points of subspaces, distance is calculated based on the Euclidean distance in the feature space induced by the kernel function defined in Eq. (4).

Results and Discussion. Figure 5(a) and (b) show the error rates (ER) and equal error rates (EER), respectively, obtained by the MSM followed by 1NN method (MSM-1NN), the MSM followed by classification based on the distance to mean vector method (MSM-Mean), GDA followed by 1NN method (GDA-1NN), and GDA followed by the classification based on the distance to mean vector method (GDA-Mean).

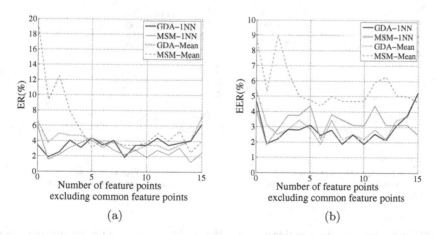

Fig. 5. Error rates (a) and equal error rates (b) of classification. GDA- and MSM-1NN in the legend indicate 1-nearest neighbor method in GDA and MSM, respectively. GDA- and MSM- Mean indicate classification method based on the mean of the distance from all the sample data in each class.

From Fig. 5, MSM-Mean does not show good performance compared to the other three methods. In the sense of ER, the other three methods are comparatively the same. From Fig. 5, we can see that GDA based two methods outperform the other two MSM based methods. The better performance of GDA based methods can be contributed to the fact that GDA can find the most discriminative classification axes in the same manner as LDA, which cannot be obtained by using a simple subspace based method such as the MSM. Finally, it is our surprise that the number of extracted feature points does not have a significant effect on the classification error rates based on GDA. This suggests that, the proposed method is applicable even for person with only few feature points such as moles or freckles on a facial surface.

4.2   Experiment 2

In our proposed framework, the shape subspace is constructed by using the 3D shape matrix defined in Eq. (6). To see the effectiveness of the use of 3D structural information for classification, we performed the following simple experiment. Here, we compared the performances of two methods with the 3D shape matrix in Eq. (6), and with 2D shape matrix which is defined by removing the z axis of the 3D shape matrix. Classification methods are the same as those used in the previous section.

The plots of ER and EER of classification results are shown in Fig. 6(a) and (b), respectively. From these results, we can see that the use of 3D structural information contributes to the improvement of the classification accuracy.

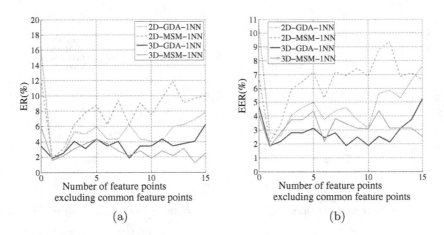

Fig. 6. Error rates (a) and equal error rates (b) of classification. One nearest neighbor based method with GDA and MSM using either 2D or 3D shape matrices are compared.

4.3 Experiment 3

In this experiment, we use the same dataset and settings as Experiment 1 to evaluate the effectiveness of using enhance references with perturbed subspaces, which is described in Sect. 3.3. For this purpose, we compared two types of the methods: "maximum separability" without the enhanced reference references, and "random sampling method" with the enhancement.

In maximum separability, 10 feature points with the 10 highest separabilities were simply selected. Thus, the same as Experiment 1, only 19 shape subspaces were used as the references for each person. In contrast, in "random sampling method", 10 feature points were randomly selected from a set of 15 candidates of feature points with the 15 highest separabilities. By repeating this process 15 times, we obtained 15 sets feature points. In this case, 19 × 15 shape subspaces were used as the reference for each person.

For the random sampling, the average of 5 trials was used as the final result. Table 1 shows the evaluation results of the both methods. In the random sampling, the ER of MSM is 1.19 %, and that of GDA is 1.63 %. In contrast, in the maximum separability, the ER of MSM is 1.88 %, and that of GDA is 3.44 %. From these results, we can see clearly the advantage of the random sampling method. Thus, we conclude that the reference enhancement by the random sampling is valid to solve the problem of the unstable detection of facial feature points.

Table 1. Error rates and equal error rates of Experiment 3. Maximum separability in the table indicates the feature points selection method that chooses 10 feature points from the descending order of the higher separability. Random sampling indicates the method that chooses 10 feature points from 15 candidate feature points which have higher separability 15 times to increase the reference data.

Maximum separability				Random sampling			
ER (%)		EER (%)		ER (%)		EER (%)	
MSM	GDA	MSM	GDA	MSM	GDA	MSM	GDA
1.88	3.44	3.08	1.88	**1.19**	1.63	2.32	**1.75**

4.4 Experiment 4

In this experiment, we consider a more difficult recognition problem of classification between twins. To simulate such tough situation, we generated artificially sets of feature points on a face and explored the performance limit of the proposed method by using them. We should note that the conventional view-based methods in principle cannot distinguish them completely.

Experimental Condition. We took 15 almost frontal face images, which has 160 synthetic micro-feature points (Fig. 7, left), from on a subject. These synthetic feature points were generated by pasting a thin film with dots on the face of a subject. In addition to these micro-feature points, we extracted 8 common feature points, four edges of two eyes, two edges of a mouth, and two nostrils (Fig. 7). We assume that the eight facial feature points are stably extracted, and the artificially generated feature points has the ground truth locations.

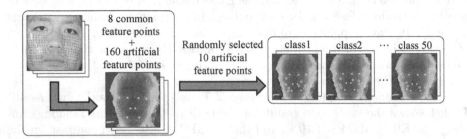

Fig. 7. A schematic diagram of the procedure of Experiment 4. A thin film with markers is pasted on a face to generate synthetic feature points. Then we obtain eight common feature points (the edge of eyes, nostril, and corner of the mouth) and 160 artificial feature points on the film. We select 10 artificial feature points randomly 50 times to generate artificial twins datasets.

Finally, we randomly selected 10 points from the 160 micro-features and obtained shape subspaces from them. The random selection was repeated 50 times to obtain $N(N = 50)$ shape subspaces (Fig. 7, right). These 50 classes correspond to very similar 50 persons with exactly the same eight facial feature points and with different micro-feature points. By conducting the same procedure for each of the 15 face images, each of the 50 person can have 15 sample images.

We performed a classification experiments in the same manner as the Experiment 1. One out of 15 sample feature set was drawn from each class and constituted a test set. The rest 14×50 sets of feature points were used as the training data, and in the same manner as in Experiment 1, the ER and EER of both MSM and GDA based classifiers were evaluated by 15-fold cross validation. The evaluation was repeated 10 times by varying the seed of random number generator for generating the 160 random feature points. The experimental results are summarized in Table 2 and the ROC curve is depicted in Fig. 8. From Table 2, we can see that the proposed method has favorable classification ability. The ER

Table 2. Error rates and equal error rates of simulation for Experiment 4.

ER (%)		EER (%)	
MSM	GDA	MSM	GDA
0.08	**0.00**	0.55	**0.19**

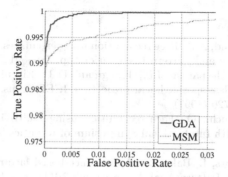

Fig. 8. ROC curve of recognition simulation of the situation of distinguishing between very similar appearance persons.

of the MSM is 0.08 %, while that of GDA is 0.00 %. In addition, from Fig. 8, the results become better when we use GDA as a classifier than in the case when we use the MSM. From the above results, we can conclude that our method with GDA has high classification accuracy even if the objects to discriminate have similar salient feature points such as those observed for twins, when we utilize the micro-feature points and apply GDA using 3D structural shape subspace similarity.

5   Concluding Remarks

In this paper, we proposed a novel framework for personal authentication based on the 3D configuration of micro-feature points, such as moles and freckles, on a facial surface. The proposed framework is instantiated by using the separability filter for feature extraction, feature point association based on the autocorrelation matrix, the notion of shape subspace, and Grassmann discriminant analysis. The usefulness and validity of the proposed framework are examined through a set of simple experiments. From the experimental results, we can confirm that RGB-D images contain features that can be used to form the shape subspace, and GDA offers highly accurate classification results.

The aim of this paper is to introduce a novel framework for person authentication, hence there remains a number of problems to be addressed. Making the feature extraction procedure fully automatic is the most important problem to be addressed. Also, our future works include large scale experiments to evaluate the proposed method, and comparison to state-of-the-art methods in the literature. The reproducibility of feature extraction is not guaranteed, even for the same person. Sensitivity of the proposed method to the feature points extraction should be also examined in more detail, and the way to stably extract feature points from the same person should be also investigated.

Acknowledgement. Part of this work is supported by JSPS KAKENHI Grant Number 25870811.

References

1. Turk, M.A., Pentland, A.P.: Face recognition using eigenfaces. In: IEEE Conference on Computer Vision and Pattern Recognition, pp. 586–591 (1991)
2. Belhumeur, P.N., Hespanha, J.P., Kriegman, D.J.: Eigenfaces vs. Fisherfaces: recognition using class specific linear projection. IEEE Trans. Pattern Anal. Mach. Intell. **19**(7), 711–720 (1997)
3. Fukui, K., Yamaguchi, O.: Face recognition using multi-viewpoint patterns for robot vision. In: 11th International Symposium of Robotics Research, pp. 192–201 (2005)
4. Gross, R., Matthews, I., Baker, S.: Appearance-based face recognition and light-fields. IEEE Trans. Pattern Anal. Mach. Intell. **26**(4), 449–465 (2004)
5. Heseltine, T., Pears, N., Austin, J., Chen, Z.: Face recognition: a comparison of appearance-based approaches. In: VIIth Digital Image Computing: Techniques and Applications, pp. 59–68 (2003)
6. Xianwei, L., Haiyang, Z.: A survey of face recognition methods. In: The 2nd International Conference on Computer Science and Electronics Engineering, pp. 1405–1407 (2013)
7. Li, S.Z., Jain, A.K.: Handbook of Face Recognition. Springer New York, Inc., Secaucus (2005)
8. Igarashi, Y., Fukui, K.: 3D object recognition based on canonical angles between shape subspaces. ACCV 2010. LNCS, vol. 6495, pp. 580–591. Springer, Heidelberg (2010)
9. Tomasi, C., Kanade, T.: Shape and motion from image streams under orthography: a factorization method. Int. J. Comput. Vis. **9**(2), 137–154 (1992)
10. Hamm, J., Lee, D.D.: Grassmann discriminant analysis: a unifying view on subspace-based learning. In: The 25th International Conference on Machine Learning, pp. 376–383 (2008)
11. Chatelin, F.: Eigenvalues of Matrices. Wiley, New York (1993)
12. Mattila, P.: Geometry of Sets and Measures in Euclidean Spaces. Cambridge University Press, New York (1995)
13. Fisher, R.A.: The use of multiple measurements in taxonomic problems. Ann. Eugenics **7**, 179–188 (1936)
14. Shawe-Taylor, J., Cristianini, N.: Kernel Methods for Pattern Analysis. Cambridge University Press, New York (2004)
15. Schölkopf, B., Mika, S., Burges, C.J.C., Knirsch, P., Müller, K.R., Rätsch, G., Smola, A.J.: Input space versus feature space in kernel-based methods. IEEE Trans. Neural Netw. **10**(5), 1000–1017 (1999)
16. Ohkawa, Y., Suryanto, C.H., Fukui, K.: Fast combined separability filter for detecting circular objects. In: 12th IAPR Conference on Machine Vision Applications, pp. 99–103 (2011)
17. Fukui, K., Yamaguchi, O.: Facial feature point extraction method based on combination of shape extraction and pattern matching. Syst. Comput. Jpn. **29**(6), 49–58 (1998)
18. Yuasa, M., Yamaguchi, O.: Real-time face blending by automatic facial feature point detection. In: 8th IEEE International Conference on Automatic Face and Gesture Recognition (FG 2008), pp. 1–6 (2008)

6-DOF Direct Homography Tracking
with Extended Kalman Filter

Hyowon Ha, François Rameau, and In So Kweon[✉]

Robotics and Computer Vision Laboratory, KAIST, Daejeon, South Korea
iskweon@kaist.ac.kr

Abstract. This paper considers a robust direct homography tracking that takes advantage of the known intrinsic parameters of the camera to estimate its pose in real scale, to speed-up the convergence, and to drastically increase the robustness of the tracking. Indeed, our new formulation for direct homography tracking allows us to explicitly solve a 6 Degrees Of Freedom (DOF) rigid transformation between the plane and the camera. Furthermore, it simplifies the integration of the Extended Kalman Filter (EKF) which allows us to increase the computational speed and deal with large motions. For the sake of robustness, our approach also includes a pyramidal optimization using an Enhanced Correlation Coefficient (ECC) based objective function. The experiments show the high efficiency of our approach against state of the art methods and under challenging conditions.

Keywords: ECC · Homography tracking · Pose estimation · EKF

1 Introduction

In the past decade, planar homography tracking has been extensively studied in the field of computer vision since it is an essential tool for a large number of applications, such as visual servoing, robotic navigation, augmented reality and more.

The direct homography tracking pipeline is straightforward; a known image template is tracked along a video sequence by iteratively solving a parametric image alignment problem which minimize the photometric difference between the template and the current image. The estimated parameters from the previous frame are then utilized as an initial guess for the current one. This process is repeated for every new frame in the sequence. This mapping between the coordinates of both images requires an appropriate geometric transformation. For planar tracking using a pinhole camera, the perspective homography is considered to be the most suitable model for general cases [1].

This strategy is very efficient but relies on multiple assumptions, such as a small and smooth inter-frame displacement. This first hypothesis is violated when fast motions are performed, which limits the possible uses for this technique in many practical applications. Hence, many researches have focused on

© Springer International Publishing Switzerland 2016
T. Bräunl et al. (Eds.): PSIVT 2015, LNCS 9431, pp. 447–460, 2016.
DOI: 10.1007/978-3-319-29451-3_36

more efficient objective functions based on different performance criterions like Mutual Information (MI) [2], NCC [3], etc. The goal of the previously mentioned approaches is to increase the robustness against illumination changes and the range of convergence in order to handle larger motions than basic SSD approaches [4]. Nonetheless, a large overlap - of the tracked plane between two consecutive images - is still required to ensure correct tracking. The interested reader can check the results obtained with different direct homography tracking methods under fast motions in [3]. The first attempt specifically designed to deal with fast motion is probably the work of Park *et al.* [8], where the well-known Efficient Second Order Minimization (ESM) tracking [4] is modified to deal with strongly blurred images.

Also, non-direct approaches using sparse features such as edges [5] or points [6] exist but are usually very sensitive to motion blur and strong changes in scale and appearance. Direct approaches tend to be more robust in such challenging conditions. However the feature-based methods are very useful for the re-detection of the target and less prone to drift. In [7], the authors combine the advantages from both approaches in a single hybrid scheme. In this paper, we exclusively focused on the direct tracking approaches.

From the literatures, we acknowledge two facts. First, most of the existing methods focused on uncalibrated camera configurations which consist of the resolution of an 8 degrees of freedom problem in order to solve a homography (up to scale). When the camera pose is needed, the extrinsic parameters are extracted afterwards using the intrinsic parameters of the camera [2]. This homography decomposition does not ensure the orthogonality of the rotation matrix which has to be enforce afterwards. This leads to a slightly biased estimation of the motion. In this work, we propose to include the computation of the extrinsic parameters directly in the tracking process through a reformulation of the problem. If the size of the template is known, the real scale pose estimation can be determined by our method. Moreover, explicitly solving the orientation and position of the camera leads to a more constrained problem less prone to divergence than usual approaches.

Our second observation is that the existing methods are purely deterministic and remains very sensitive to fast motions. In this paper, we propose to include a probabilistic stage in the tracking process. Indeed, our reformulation of the tracking problem allows for the use of the EKF [9,10] to predict the next pose of the camera. Therefore, this prediction can be utilized as an initialization for the next frame. With this approach, we are able to deal with larger inter-frame motions than conventional methods since the predicted initial parameters are closer to the optimal solution. This procedure also strongly increases the convergence speed of the optimization step. To our best knowledge, it is the first attempt to fuse the EKF to direct homography tracking, while the EKF has been intensively adopted to many non-direct tracking methods [5,11].

Another strong assumption for direct homography tracking is the lightness constancy. A large number of works dedicated to this particular problem are available. For instance, in [12], Silveira *et al.* cope with generic illumination changes using an efficient illumination model.

Although it is not the main point of this paper, our approach also takes the local and global illumination changes into consideration, thanks to a robust objective function based on ECC [1]. The range of convergence as well as the speed of the method have also been improved by a pyramidal optimization scheme. However, it is clear that our approach is compatible with any performance criterion. The advantages offered by our method are underlined through multiple experiments where the tracking accuracy, robustness and speed are evaluated.

This paper is organized in the following manner: in the Sect. 2 we describe both the reformulation of the homography under a 6DOF problem and the ECC-based image alignment process. The next section is dedicated to the integration of the Extended Kalman Filter in the tracking scheme. In the Sect. 4, we propose a large number of results demonstrating the accuracy and the speed of our method. Finally this paper ends with a short conclusion.

2   ECC-Based 6-DOF Direct Homography Tracking

In this section, our ECC-based 6-DOF direct homography tracking algorithm is explained in twofold. Firstly, our homography from a 6-DOF pose is explained. Compared to conventional approaches, our homography is modeled using the 6-DOF pose of the camera thanks to its known intrinsic parameters. This new formulation enhances the convergence of the optimization and allows us to apply the EKF. Secondly, our ECC-based tracking algorithm is described in detail. We model the homography-based tracking of a planar object as an ECC-based non-linear least squares problem with 6 unknown parameters which can be solved using a gradient descent approach.

2.1   Homography from a 6-DOF Pose

In computer vision, projective homography is often referred to as a transformation between two images of the same planar object. It is geometrically modeled by the normal direction of the plane, the intrinsic parameters and the poses of the cameras. Practically, it is often utilized to estimate the relative pose of the camera w.r.t. a plane. If we consider two cameras as a and b, the corresponding image points x_a and x_b observed by a and b follow this homographic relationship:

$$x_a \sim K_a \cdot H_{b \to a} \cdot K_b^{-1} \cdot x_b, \tag{1}$$

where $H_{b \to a}$ is a 3×3 homography transformation matrix from b to a and K_a, K_b are the intrinsic camera matrices of a and b.

In this work, we focus on a homography-based tracking scenario where we have a single image for b (*template*) and a series of images for a (*target*). Therefore, we use abbreviated notations *tgt* (*target*) and *tmp* (*template*) in place of a and b respectively (Fig. 1). We design our world coordinate to be centered at the planar object of which the plane equation is $Z = 0$. If an image of

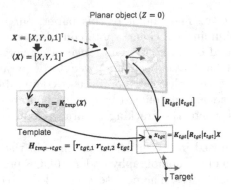

Fig. 1. Our homography relationship between the planar object, template image and the target image.

the planar object is captured by the *target* camera with an intrinsic camera matrix $\mathbf{K}_{tgt}$ and a 6-DOF pose represented as $[\mathbf{R}_{tmp}, \mathbf{t}_{tmp}]$, an arbitrary 3D point $\mathbf{X} = [X, Y, 0, 1]^{\top}$ on the planar object can be projected onto the *target* image as $\mathbf{x}_{tgt} = \mathbf{K}_{tgt}[\mathbf{R}_{tgt}|\mathbf{t}_{tgt}]\mathbf{X}$. By introducing a deprived form $\langle \mathbf{X} \rangle = [X, Y, 1]^{\top}$ to reflect the zero z-value, the projection can be simplified as:

$$\mathbf{x}_{tgt} = \mathbf{K}_{tgt}[\mathbf{r}_{tgt,1}, \mathbf{r}_{tgt,2}, \mathbf{t}_{tgt}]\langle \mathbf{X} \rangle \tag{2}$$

The corresponding point in the *template* image can be calculated by a transformation $\mathbf{K}_{tmp}$ (like an intrinsic camera matrix) so that $\mathbf{x}_{tmp} = \mathbf{K}_{tmp}\langle \mathbf{X} \rangle$ where $\mathbf{K}_{tmp}$ must be predefined w.r.t. the *pixel/mm* scale of the *template* image and the position of the reference coordinate. For instance, if the *template* image consists of $w \times h$ pixels and the actual size of the corresponding rectangle on the planar object is $W \times H$ millimeters, then it can be expressed in the following manner:

$$\mathbf{K}_{tmp} = \begin{bmatrix} \frac{w-1}{W} & 0 & \frac{w-1}{2} \\ 0 & \frac{h-1}{H} & \frac{h-1}{2} \\ 0 & 0 & 1 \end{bmatrix}, \tag{3}$$

thereby enforcing the reference coordinate system to be located at the center of the template image and the pose estimation in metric scale to be achieved.

From Eqs. (1), (2) and (3), the homography from the *template* image to the *target* image, $\mathbf{H}_{tmp \to tgt}$, can be described simply as follows:

$$\mathbf{H}_{tmp \to tgt} = \begin{bmatrix} \mathbf{r}_{tgt,1} & \mathbf{r}_{tgt,2} & \mathbf{t}_{tgt} \end{bmatrix}. \tag{4}$$

2.2 ECC-based Direct Homography Tracking

ECC [1] is one of the image similarity measures which quantify the similarity between two images. Hence, the alignment of the two images can be achieved by maximizing the ECC between them. Given a pair of pixel intensities $I_{tmp}(\boldsymbol{x}_k)$ and $I_{tgt}(\boldsymbol{y}_k)$ for the template image and the target image (respectively at the image coordinates $\boldsymbol{x}_k$ and $\boldsymbol{y}_k$), the alignment problem consists of finding the transformation vector $\boldsymbol{p}$ mapping $\boldsymbol{y}_k = \phi(\boldsymbol{x}_k; \boldsymbol{p})$. In our case, $\boldsymbol{p}$ is a vector of length 6 composed of the rotation vector $\boldsymbol{r}_{tgt}$ and the translation vector $\boldsymbol{t}_{tgt}$ of the *target* camera. In this paper, the vector for pixels' intensities of the template image ($\boldsymbol{i}_{tmp}$) and the target image ($\boldsymbol{i}_{tgt}$) are defined as:

$$\boldsymbol{i}_{tmp} = [I_{tmp}(\boldsymbol{x}_1), I_{tmp}(\boldsymbol{x}_2), \cdots, I_{tmp}(\boldsymbol{x}_K)]^\top, \tag{5}$$

$$\boldsymbol{i}_{tgt}(\boldsymbol{p}) = [I_{tgt}(\boldsymbol{y}_1(\boldsymbol{p})), I_{tgt}(\boldsymbol{y}_2(\boldsymbol{p})), \cdots, I_{tgt}(\boldsymbol{y}_K(\boldsymbol{p}))]^\top. \tag{6}$$

Thus, our ECC-based image alignment problem solving for the optimal vector $\boldsymbol{p}^*$ is defined as follows:

$$\boldsymbol{p}^* = \arg\min_{\boldsymbol{p}} \sum_{k=1}^{K} \left(\frac{I_{tgt}(\boldsymbol{y}_k(\boldsymbol{p})) - \bar{\boldsymbol{i}}_{tgt}}{\left\| \boldsymbol{i}_{tgt} - \bar{\boldsymbol{i}}_{tgt} \right\|} - \frac{I_{tmp}(\boldsymbol{x}_k) - \bar{\boldsymbol{i}}_{tmp}}{\left\| \boldsymbol{i}_{tmp} - \bar{\boldsymbol{i}}_{tmp} \right\|} \right)^2 \tag{7}$$

where $\bar{\boldsymbol{i}}_{tmp}$ and $\bar{\boldsymbol{i}}_{tgt}$ are the mean values of $\boldsymbol{i}_{tmp}$ and $\boldsymbol{i}_{tgt}$, while $\|\cdot\|$ stands for the Euclidean distance.

To solve this non-linear least squares problem, we adopt the Levenberg-Marquardt (LM) [13] algorithm, one of the most famous gradient descent methods. For an efficient use of the LM algorithm, it is essential to compute the Jacobian matrix of the objective function.

Since the image intensity is not a continuous function, we consider its approximation by applying the first-order Taylor expansion for $\boldsymbol{p} = \tilde{\boldsymbol{p}} + \triangle \boldsymbol{p}$ where $\triangle \boldsymbol{p}$ is a vector of perturbations:

$$I_{tgt}(\boldsymbol{y}(\boldsymbol{p})) \approx I_{tgt}(\boldsymbol{y}(\tilde{\boldsymbol{p}})) + \left[\nabla_y I_{tgt}(\boldsymbol{y}(\tilde{\boldsymbol{p}})) \right]^\top \frac{\partial \phi(\boldsymbol{x}; \tilde{\boldsymbol{p}})}{\partial \boldsymbol{p}} \triangle \boldsymbol{p}, \tag{8}$$

where $\nabla_y I_{tgt}(\boldsymbol{y}(\tilde{\boldsymbol{p}}))$ is the vector of the gradient intensities of the image I_{tgt} at $\boldsymbol{y}(\tilde{\boldsymbol{p}})$ and $\frac{\partial \phi(\boldsymbol{x}; \tilde{\boldsymbol{p}})}{\partial \boldsymbol{p}}$ is the Jacobian matrix of the transformation vector mapping ϕ with respect to the parameters. Now, we rewrite Eq. (1) with vector normalization:

$$\hat{\boldsymbol{y}} = \hat{\phi}(\boldsymbol{x}; \boldsymbol{p}) = \mathbf{K}_{tgt} \cdot \mathbf{H}(\boldsymbol{p}) \cdot \mathbf{K}_{tmp}^{-1} \cdot \boldsymbol{x}, \tag{9}$$

$$\boldsymbol{y} = \phi(\boldsymbol{x}; \boldsymbol{p}) = \left[\frac{\hat{y}_1}{\hat{y}_3}, \frac{\hat{y}_2}{\hat{y}_3} \right]^\top, \tag{10}$$

where $\boldsymbol{x}, \boldsymbol{y}$ are the coordinates in the *template* and the *target* images, with $\mathbf{K}_{tmp}$, $\mathbf{K}_{tgt}$ as their intrinsic matrices. Here, $\mathbf{H}(\boldsymbol{p})$ and $\mathbf{K}_{tmp}$ are expressed as defined in Eqs. (3) and (4). To consider the normalization of $\hat{\boldsymbol{y}}$ (Eq. (10)), the vector function $\hat{\phi}$ is divided into three scalar functions $\hat{y}_1 = \hat{\phi}_1(\boldsymbol{x}; \boldsymbol{p})$, $\hat{y}_2 = \hat{\phi}_2(\boldsymbol{x}; \boldsymbol{p})$ and $\hat{y}_3 = \hat{\phi}_3(\boldsymbol{x}; \boldsymbol{p})$. Then, the vector mapping function ϕ is represented by the two components, $\phi_1(\boldsymbol{x}; \boldsymbol{p}) = \hat{\phi}_1(\boldsymbol{x}; \boldsymbol{p})/\hat{\phi}_3(\boldsymbol{x}; \boldsymbol{p})$ and $\phi_2(\boldsymbol{x}; \boldsymbol{p}) = \hat{\phi}_2(\boldsymbol{x}; \boldsymbol{p})/\hat{\phi}_3(\boldsymbol{x}; \boldsymbol{p})$.

The partial derivatives of ϕ with respect to p_i, or the $i\text{-}th$ element of p where $i = 1, \cdots, 6$, can be calculated as follows:

$$\frac{\partial \phi(x)}{\partial p_i} = \left[\frac{\partial \phi_1(x)}{\partial p_i}, \frac{\partial \phi_2(x)}{\partial p_i} \right]^\top, \tag{11}$$

$$\frac{\partial \phi_1(x)}{\partial p_i} = \frac{\partial \hat{\phi}_1(x)}{\partial p_i} \left(\frac{1}{\hat{\phi}_3(x)} \right) - \frac{\partial \hat{\phi}_3(x)}{\partial p_i} \left(\frac{\hat{\phi}_1(x)}{\hat{\phi}_3^2(x)} \right), \tag{12}$$

$$\frac{\partial \phi_2(x)}{\partial p_i} = \frac{\partial \hat{\phi}_2(x)}{\partial p_i} \left(\frac{1}{\hat{\phi}_3(x)} \right) - \frac{\partial \hat{\phi}_3(x)}{\partial p_i} \left(\frac{\hat{\phi}_2(x)}{\hat{\phi}_3^2(x)} \right), \tag{13}$$

where

$$\begin{bmatrix} \frac{\partial \hat{\phi}_1(x)}{\partial p_i} \\ \frac{\partial \hat{\phi}_2(x)}{\partial p_i} \\ \frac{\partial \hat{\phi}_3(x)}{\partial p_i} \end{bmatrix} = \mathbf{K}_{tgt} \cdot \frac{\partial \mathbf{H}}{\partial p_i} \cdot \mathbf{K}_{tmp}^{-1} \cdot x. \tag{14}$$

Since we consider $p = \left[r_{tgt}^\top, t_{tgt}^\top \right]^\top$, the partial derivative of $\mathbf{H}$ depends on the rotation representation. In this paper, we use the Rodrigues' rotation formula. Finally, the Jacobian matrix $\mathbf{J}$ for Eq. (7) is computed as:

$$\mathbf{J} = \begin{bmatrix} J_{1,1} & J_{1,2} & \cdots & J_{1,6} \\ J_{2,1} & J_{2,2} & \cdots & J_{2,6} \\ \vdots & \vdots & \ddots & \vdots \\ J_{K,1} & J_{K,2} & \cdots & J_{K,6} \end{bmatrix}, \tag{15}$$

where

$$J_{k,i} = \left[\nabla_y I_{tgt}(y_k) \right]^\top \begin{bmatrix} \frac{\partial \phi_1(x)}{\partial p_i} \\ \frac{\partial \phi_2(x)}{\partial p_i} \end{bmatrix} / \left\| i_{tgt} - \bar{i}_{tgt} \right\|, \tag{16}$$

by assuming $\bar{i}_{tgt}(p) \approx \bar{i}_{tgt}(\tilde{p})$ and $\left\| i_{tmp}(p) - \bar{i}_{tmp}(p) \right\| \approx \left\| i_{tmp}(\tilde{p}) - \bar{i}_{tmp}(\tilde{p}) \right\|$.

The LM method proceeds through successive iterations from an initial guess $p^{(0)}$ as:

$$p^{(s+1)} = p^{(s)} - \left(\mathbf{J}^\top \mathbf{J} + \lambda \text{diag}(\mathbf{J}^\top \mathbf{J}) \right)^{-1} \mathbf{J}^\top f(p^{(s)}) \tag{17}$$

where f is a function (see Eq. (7)) returning a residual vector of length K, s is the iteration step and λ is the damping factor for the LM method.

3   Integration of Extended Kalman Filter

The Kalman Filter (KF) [14] is a method that uses a series of noisy measurements to produce estimates of the state of a system. However, the basic KF is limited to linear systems while many actual systems (such as the rotational motion model) are inherently non-linear. To overcome this limitation, the Extended Kalman Filter (EKF) [9,10] has been introduced as an extended version of the KF for non-linear systems. To be compatible with non-linearity, the EKF takes advantage of the partial derivatives (Jacobian) of the non-linear system at each time step under the assumption that it is locally linear. Though the EKF is imperfect for estimating an optimal solution due to this hypothesis, it still provides a reliable state prediction with very low computational cost, which is essential for various real-time applications.

We adopt the EKF specifically to provide a well predicted initial pose for our direct homography tracking algorithm instead of using only the previous pose estimation. The EKF consist of three steps; prediction, tracking, and correction. In the prediction step, the EKF produces estimates of the current state variables regarding the camera motion along with their uncertainties. In the tracking step, our ECC-based direct homography tracking algorithm is applied with the predicted pose of the camera, and produces a refined camera pose which we call the measurement. In the correction step, the estimates and the uncertainties are updated based on the new measurement in a weighted averaging manner, where a larger weight is attributed to the estimates with higher certainty.

In this work, we divide the motion model of the camera into two systems: a linear system for the translational motion and a non-linear system for the rotational motion. Even though the two systems can be modelled together in a single EKF scheme, it is more efficient to separate them to reduce the computational cost since they can be regarded as being independent to each other. The details of each model are explained in the following sections. (Please note that the notations in this section are independent of those in Sect. 2.)

3.1 Translational Motion Model

The translational motion can be modeled by the following linear system:

$$t_k = t_{k-1} + v_{k-1}\Delta t + \frac{1}{2}a_{k-1}(\Delta t)^2, \tag{18}$$

$$v_k = v_{k-1} + a_{k-1}\Delta t, \tag{19}$$

$$a_k = a_{k-1}, \tag{20}$$

where the subscript k denotes the time step, Δt is the time interval and $t = [t_x, t_y, t_z]^\top$, $v = [v_x, v_y, v_z]^\top$, $a = [a_x, a_y, a_z]^\top$ are the vectors of the translation, velocity, and acceleration, respectively.

Since it is a linear system, we can apply the basic KF for predicting the current translational motion. The state vector is the concatenation of the translation, velocity and acceleration vectors. Hence, the state transition model can be written as follows:

$$x_k = \begin{bmatrix} t_k \\ v_k \\ a_k \end{bmatrix} = \mathbf{F}_k x_{k-1}, \tag{21}$$

where x_k is the state vector of length 9 and $\mathbf{F}_k$ is the 9 × 9 state transition matrix implying Eqs. (18), (19) and (20). For the sake of clarity, we omit the process noise in the model which is assumed to be a zero mean Gaussian white noise.

At time k, the measurement z_k of the state x_k is modeled as:

$$z_k = \mathbf{H}_k x_k, \tag{22}$$

$$\mathbf{H}_k = \begin{bmatrix} \mathbf{I}_{3\times3} & \mathbf{0}_{3\times3} & \mathbf{0}_{3\times3} \end{bmatrix}, \tag{23}$$

where z_k is the measurement vector of length 3 and $\mathbf{H}_k$ is the 3×9 measurement matrix. Here, z_k is the translation vector estimated by our direct homography tracking which utilizes the predicted translation from Eq. (21) as the initial guess. Again, for simplicity, we do not detail the measurement noise which is also assumed to be zero mean Gaussian white noise.

3.2 Rotational Motion Model

We define the rotational motion model using the quaternions and an angular velocity vector which allow for a closed-form propagation of the rotational motion:

$$q_k = e^{\Omega(w_{k-1})\Delta t} q_{k-1}, \tag{24}$$

$$w_k = w_{k-1}, \tag{25}$$

where k is the time step, q is the quaternion vector of length 4, $w = [w_x, w_y, w_z]^\top$ is the angular velocity vector and $\Omega(w)$ is defined as:

$$\Omega(w) = \frac{1}{2} \begin{bmatrix} 0 & w_z & -w_y & w_x \\ -w_z & 0 & w_x & w_y \\ w_y & -w_x & 0 & w_z \\ -w_x & -w_y & -w_z & 0 \end{bmatrix}. \tag{26}$$

Using the power series expansion, Eq. (24) can be reduced to:

$$q_k = \left[\cos\left(|w_{k-1}|\,\Delta t/2\right) \mathbf{I}_{4\times4} + \frac{2}{|w_{k-1}|} \sin\left(|w_{k-1}|\,\Delta t/2\right) \Omega(w_{k-1}) \right] q_{k-1}. \tag{27}$$

When we define the state vector as the concatenation of the quaternion and the angular velocity vectors, we can apply the EKF on the following non-linear system:

$$x_k = \begin{bmatrix} q_k \\ w_k \end{bmatrix} = f(x_{k-1}), \tag{28}$$

$$z_k = \mathbf{G} x_k, \tag{29}$$

$$\mathbf{G} = \begin{bmatrix} \mathbf{I}_{4\times4} & \mathbf{0}_{4\times3} \end{bmatrix}, \tag{30}$$

with f being the state transition function (which implies Eq. (24), (25), (26) and (27)), z_k the measured quaternion vector of length 4, and $\mathbf{G}$ the measurement matrix.

For implementing the EKF, it is essential to use the Jacobian of f which can be obtained by calculating the partial derivatives with respect to the state variables. For conciseness, the process noise and the measurement noise for the EKF are also omitted in the equations, but were considered in the implementation with their covariance matrices. Please note that x, z are independent to those in Sect. 3.1, where we only intend to follow the conventional notations of the KF. Also, an inclusion of the angular acceleration in the rotation model may improve the performance depending on the tracking scenario.

4   Results

In this section, we propose a large series of experiments with our own data but also against multiple state of the art methods through a template-based tracking benchmark [15].

For our experiments, we used a USB3 *Pointgrey Flea3* camera with a 6 mm lens acquiring images with a spatial resolution of 1328×1048 pixels at 25 frames per second. Our method has been implemented on a computer with a 2 GHz processor and 4 GB of RAM. The initialization of the first frame is done using a simple rectangle detection algorithm.

Our tests focused on multiple aspects: the accuracy of the pose estimation and the speed improvement offered by our approach. Moreover, a comparison against multiple deterministic techniques is also proposed.

4.1   Pose Estimation

One important advantage of our approach is the direct computation of the camera's pose included in the optimization process itself. To highlight the accuracy offered by our method, we developed a practical assessment process which consists of capturing both the target image and a checkerboard - to accurately compute a ground truth pose. Our experimental platform is depicted in Fig. 2. In such a configuration, the coordinate system of the checkerboard and the target image are different, so we propose to compare the displacement of the camera with respect to its first position. The nth camera motion $\mathbf{M}_{o1}^{on} = [\mathbf{R}_{o1}^{on} | \mathbf{t}_{o1}^{on}]$ is nothing but the composition of two transformations. From the checkerboard we compute the ground truth transformation $^{GT}\mathbf{M}_{o1}^{on} = \mathbf{M}_c^{on}(\mathbf{M}_c^{o1})^{-1}$, while the estimated motion from the tracking is computed as follow: $\mathbf{M}_{o1}^{on} = \mathbf{M}_t^{on}(\mathbf{M}_t^{o1})^{-1}$. Thus, the translational discrepancy can be calculated with: $e_t = \sqrt{\sum(\mathbf{t}_{o1}^{on} - {}^{CT}\mathbf{t}_{o1}^{on})}$, and the rotational error is computed as follow: $e_r = acos(\frac{1}{2}(tr((\mathbf{R}_{o1}^{on})^{-1}{}^{GT}\mathbf{R}_{o1}^{on})-1))$. As shown in Fig. 3, we acquired two sequences - *Van Gogh* (1500 images) and *Güell* (1200 images). In both videos a smooth and slow motion of the plane is performed within a distance range between 30 cm and 0.9 m. The pose estimation remains very accurate when the plane is close enough to the camera, as it is the case for the first sequence where the maximum distance is only 45 cm away. Indeed, for the *Van Gogh* sequence the maximum error is under 6 mm. Nonetheless, in the second sequence the distance is larger. In such circumstances the target covers a very small portion of the image which leads to a higher error in the pose estimation. Although the rotation remains accurate, the translational error is increasing up to 30 mm (for a distance of 0.9 m) which represents a percentile error of 3.3 %. This error is low enough for many applications, such as augmented reality.

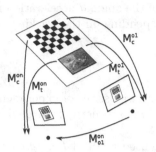

Fig. 2. Illustration of our pose estimation assessment

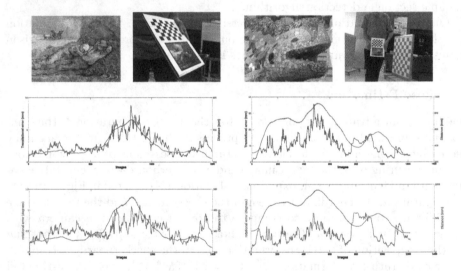

Fig. 3. Pose estimation results, (first row) Template and image sample from both sequences, (left column) Translational and rotational error of the *Van Gogh* sequence, (right column) Translational and rotational error of the *Güell* sequence.

4.2   Speed Evaluation

As claimed previously in this paper, the use of a predictive approach allows us to initialize the non-linear image alignment closer to the optimal minimum. Consequently, the number of needed iterations is reduced, which leads to a significant speed improvement of the algorithm. To emphasize this effect, we acquired a very challenging sequence called *Jung Seop* (which contains 1078 images).

This sequence consists of very fast motions at different distances. Figure 4(b) shows one representative tracking results obtained with our algorithm. On this figure, the green bounding box is the obtained result for the current image and the red bounding box is the previous position of the target which is usually utilized as an initialization in common approaches. Finally, the blue bounding box is the predicted pose from the EKF that we use to initialize our method. It is qualitatively clear that the prediction is closer to the final solution. More results are available in Fig. 5. We tried our algorithm with and without the EKF, and it showed that when the EKF is activated the sequence is fully tracked. Without this prediction step, the tracking failed after only 250 images due to very fast motions. Thus, we compared the required number of iterations in both cases only for the first 250 images of the sequence. For this test, the multi-resolution step is not utilized. We fixed the maximum number of iterations to 100, while the stopping criteria -the absolute difference between two successive updates ϵ - was defined by $\epsilon < 10^{-4}$. The results are available in Fig. 6, it is obvious that our method drastically reduced the number of iterations. For most of the images only 2 iterations are performed with the EKF prediction. In fact, the mean number of iterations with the EKF is 2.8 iterations per image while it is increased to 7.1 iterations without it.

Furthermore, ensuring the initialization to be in the vicinity of convergence leads to a more robust tracking. For instance, in Fig. 5, the warped images are strongly affected by motion blur, but even under these difficult conditions our method can efficiently track the target.

Fig. 4. *Jung Seop* sequence, (a) template image, (b) sample image of the tracking sequence

4.3   Benchmark Experiments

In order to compare our tracking approach against different state of the art methods, in this section we propose a full evaluation using the template-based tracking benchmark by Metaio GmbH [15]. This dataset consists of eight template images (see Fig. 7) with different characteristics: low, repetitive, normal and highly textured. Along with each template image, five video sequences are provided. The first sequence contains large angular motions and the second one includes challenging scale changes. In the third and fourth videos, fast far and fast close motions are performed. Finally, the last sequence is subject to strong illumination changes. The outputs of the tracker are compared with a ground

Fig. 5. Sample from the *Jung Seop* sequence, (first row) tracking results, (second row) corresponding warped images

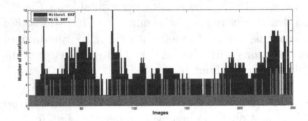

Fig. 6. Number of iterations per image with and without EKF

truth data; if the template position error is larger than 10 pixels, then the target is considered as lost. Consequently, the results are expressed in the percentage of successfully tracked frames.

We compare our method with three other approaches, the first being one of the most common template-based trackers, ESM [4]. The other methods are more recent and employ more efficient and robust objective functions, respectively, based on NCC [3] and MI [2].

For these sequences, our algorithm is configured with 3 multi-scale levels to increase the range of convergence, the EKF is activated and the stopping criterion is fixed at $\epsilon < 10^{-4}$ with a maximum of 20 iterations per scale level. Furthermore, the template image is downscaled to a size of 320×240 pixels to avoid oversampling.

Table 1 contains the results obtained from the algorithms where the highest scores are display in bold. The score difference below 5 % are not taken into account. According to this ranking, it is clear that our method significantly outperforms the compared deterministic approaches for almost every "fast" sequences, which can be directly attributed to the use of a EKF. Moreover, our algorithm also leads to better results under challenging motions such as large distance variations ("Range" sequences).

Fig. 7. Set of templates utilized in the benchmark [15], (from left to right column) low, repetitive, normal, high texturedness

Table 1. Ratio of successfully tracked images from the ESM [4], NCC [3], MI [2], and ours

ESM	Angle	Range	Fast Far	Fast Close	Illumination
Low	100.00%	92.33%	35.00%	21.58%	71.08%
	100.00%	64.17%	10.58%	26.83%	56.25%
Repetitive	61.92%	50.42%	22.50%	50.17%	34.50%
	2.92%	11.33%	6.83%	35.83%	11.33%
Normal	95.42%	77.75%	7.50%	67.08%	76.75%
	99.58%	99.00%	15.67%	86.75%	90.67%
High	0.00%	0.00%	0.00%	0.00%	0.00%
	100.00%	61.42%	22.83%	45.50%	79.67%

NCC	Angle	Range	Fast Far	Fast Close	Illumination
Low	99.7%	76.8%	52.7%	27.6%	100.0%
	100.0%	99.9%	21.6%	66.0%	**100.0%**
Repetitive	100.0%	57.7%	22.2%	68.2%	100.0%
	100.0%	81.3%	12.2%	53.6%	100.0%
Normal	100.0%	96.8%	58.2%	90.5%	100.0%
	99.9%	99.9%	20.1%	80.5%	100.0%
High	93.6%	**52.3%**	9.2%	14.0%	98.9%
	100.0%	51.5%	22.0%	75.0%	100.0%

MI	Angle	Range	Fast Far	Fast Close	Illumination
Low	100.0%	94.1%	75.2%	56.5%	99.5%
	100.0%	98.1%	69.9%	43.7%	93.0%
Repetitive	76.9%	67.9%	22.8%	63.6%	100.0%
	91.3%	67.1%	10.4%	70.5%	96.2%
Normal	99.2%	99.3%	43.9%	86.7%	99.6%
	100.0%	100.0%	14.8%	84.5%	100.0%
High	47.1%	23.2%	7.2%	10.0%	50.6%
	100.0%	69.8%	20.8%	83.8%	100.0%

ECC + EKF	Angle	Range	Fast Far	Fast Close	Illumination
Low	100.00%	**100.00%**	77.08%	**83.33%**	100.00%
	100.00%	100.00%	**100.00%**	**100.00%**	93.00%
Repetitive	100.00%	**100.00%**	41.60%	**85.40%**	100.00%
	100.00%	78.12%	**27.08%**	68.75%	100.00%
Normal	100.00%	100.00%	**93.75%**	89.58%	100.00%
	100.00%	100.00%	**54.16%**	**97.90%**	100.00%
High	**100.00%**	45.83%	**18.75%**	**41.60%**	79.16%
	100.0%	**79.16%**	**56.25%**	85.41%	100.00%

5 Conclusion

In this paper we proposed an efficient direct homography tracking algorithm able to deal with large motions. Our new formulation of the problem leads to two major improvements. Firstly, the pose can be accurately estimated in the tracking process itself, which reduces the number of DOF to 6. Secondly, this reformulation of the problem facilitates the addition of a predictive approach (the EKF) in the tracking process, while most of the state of the art method are purely deterministic. The predicted pose provides better initialization to the iterative image alignment process which allows the algorithm to cope with large motions, it also drastically improves the general robustness of the algorithm.

Many experiments have been proposed in this paper to highlight the advantages offered by our approach. Through these assessments it is clear that our algorithm outperforms state of the art methods for fast motions and provides a very accurate pose of the camera. Furthermore, the proposed method significantly reduces the number of iterations for the non-linear image alignment step.

Acknowledgement. This work was supported by the National Research Foundation of Korea (NRF) grant funded by the Korea government (MSIP) (No. 2010-0028680).

460   H. Ha et al.

References

1. Evangelidis, G.D., Psarakis, E.Z.: Parametric image alignment using enhanced correlation coefficient maximization. IEEE Trans. Pattern Anal. Mach. Intell. **30**(10), 1858–1865 (2008)
2. Dame, A., Marchand, E.: Accurate real-time tracking using mutual information. In: ISMAR (2010)
3. Scandaroli, G.G., Meilland, M., Richa, R.: Improving NCC-based direct visual tracking. In: Fitzgibbon, A., Lazebnik, S., Perona, P., Sato, Y., Schmid, C. (eds.) ECCV 2012, Part VI. LNCS, vol. 7577, pp. 442–455. Springer, Heidelberg (2012)
4. Benhimane, S., Malis, E.: Real-time image-based tracking of planes using efficient second-order minimization. In: IROS (2004)
5. Li, P., Chaumette, F., Tahri, O.: A shape tracking algorithm for visual servoing. In: ICRA (2005)
6. Mondragon, I., Campoy, P., Martinez, C., Olivares-Mendez, M.: 3d pose estimation based on planar object tracking for uavs control. In: ICRA (2010)
7. Kusuma Negara, G.P., Teck, F.W., Yiqun, L.: Hybrid feature and template based tracking for augmented reality application. In: Shan, S., Jawahar, C.V., Jawahar, C.V. (eds.) ACCV 2014 Workshops. LNCS, vol. 9010, pp. 381–395. Springer, Heidelberg (2015)
8. Park, Y., Lepetit, V., Woo, W.: Handling motion-blur in 3d tracking and rendering for augmented reality. IEEE Trans. Vis. Comput. Graphics **18**(9), 1449–1459 (2012)
9. Sorenson, H.W.: Kalman Filtering: Theory and Application. IEEE Press, New York (1985)
10. Broida, T., Chandrashekhar, S., Chellappa, R.: Recursive 3-d motion estimation from a monocular image sequence. IEEE Trans. Aerosp. Electron. Syst. **26**(4), 639–656 (1990)
11. Forster, C., Pizzoli, M., Scaramuzza, D.: Svo: fast semi-direct monocular visual odometry. In: ICRA (2014)
12. Silveira, G., Malis, E.: Real-time visual tracking under arbitrary illumination changes. In: CVPR (2007)
13. Marquardt, D.W.: An algorithm for least-squares estimation of nonlinear parameters. J. Soc. Industr. Appl. Math. **11**(12), 431–441 (1963)
14. Kalman, R.E.: A new approach to linear filtering and prediction problems. J. Fluids Eng. **82**(1), 35–45 (1960)
15. Lieberknecht, S., Benhimane, S., Meier, P., Navab, N.: A dataset and evaluation methodology for template-based tracking algorithms. In: ISMAR (2009)

Tracking a Human Fast and Reliably Against Occlusion and Human-Crossing

Xuan-Phung Huynh, In-Ho Choi, and Yong-Guk Kim[(⊠)]

Department of Computer Engineering, Sejong University, Seoul, Korea
ykim@sejong.ac.kr

Abstract. Tracking a human using the computer vision techniques is essential in the automatic surveillance task. Not only its accuracy and speed but also how it deals with occlusion and human-crossing are the challenges for a reliable tracking framework. Among many, Kernelized Correlation Filter (KCF) has become a state-of-the-art tracker partly because of its high speed, although its performance in dealing diverse situations requires some improvement. We present a new tracking method whereby the reliability is greatly enhanced while maintaining its speed by integrating a Kalman filter with the KCF. The tracker works as follow. After the KCF estimates target's position based on the prediction by the Kalman filter, then the estimated value is given to the updating step of the Kalman filter. During the KCF learning phase, the kernel model is updated using the correct state. Evaluation result using the standard tracking databases suggests that the present tracker outperforms the standard KCF, MOSSE and MIL trackers, respectively. In particular, it is the only tracker that can deal very well with the occlusion and human-crossing tasks, which are the crucial requirements for the high-end surveillance.

Keywords: Surveillance · Human tracking · Occlusion · Human-crossing · Kernelized correlation filters · Kalman filter

1 Introduction

Human tracking has played an important role in the automatic surveillance system [15]. Currently, surveillance [7,13] is contributing vital roles not only in the research but also in the market. Visual tracking is the process of estimating the trajectory of an object in the image plane as it moves around in the scene. According to [15], tracking objects can be complex due to its accuracy and speed as well as how it deals with occlusion and human-crossing cases. Numerous approaches for object tracking have been proposed. Among them, Kernelized Correlation Filter [5,6] has been a state-of-the-art tracker partly because of its high speed and simple implement with only a few lines of code. It is the third performing tracker among many in term of accuracy [10]. And yet, its performance in dealing such occlusion requires some improvement for robust tracking.

© Springer International Publishing Switzerland 2016
T. Bräunl et al. (Eds.): PSIVT 2015, LNCS 9431, pp. 461–472, 2016.
DOI: 10.1007/978-3-319-29451-3_37

In general, a Kalman filter estimates the state of a linear system where state is supposed to be distributed by a Gaussian [2,8,12,15]. It is known that the Kalman filter successfully tracks objects even in the case of occlusion if the assumed type of motion is correctly modeled [2]. This assumption is very strict and it is only suitable for tracking very small objects [15].

Combination of Kalman filter with the kernel method has also been proposed based upon the mean-shift tracking [9,11,17,18]. The mean-shift tracker eliminates the brute force search in the standard template matching and shortens the computation time although it requires that a portion of the objects should be inside a circular region during the initialization stage [15].

In this paper we present a new tracking method whereby the reliability is greatly enhanced while the speed is also maintained by combining a Kalman filter with the KCF. Once KCF estimates a target position based on the prediction by the Kalman filter, the estimated value becomes the observation in updating the object's state. During the KCF learning phase, the correct state of the Kalman filter is utilized to update the kernel model. However, when the tracker meets an occlusion, the Kalman filter omits observation values from KCF and adjusts the state based on the previous state. Experimental results show that the present tracker outperforms the standard KCF, MOSSE (Minimum Output Sum of Squared Error) [1] and MIL (Multiple Instance Learning) trackers [16], respectively. In particular, it is the only tracker that can deal very well with occlusion and human-crossing task, which are critical requirements for the high-end surveillance task.

The rest of the paper is organized as follows. In Sects. 2 and 3, we review the Kernelized Correlation Filter and Kalman Filter, respectively. In Sect. 4, we describe our proposed tracker in detail. In Sect. 5, we present experimental results. Finally, Sect. 6 summarizes this paper.

2   Kernelized Correlation Filters

2.1   Circulant Matrices

KCF trains a linear classifier using both a base sample, i.e. a positive example, and several virtual samples, which serve as the negative examples, obtained by translating it. Here, a cyclic shift operator is utilized in modeling this translation. Because of the cyclic property [4], the signal x becomes identical after n^{th} shifts, and the full set of shifted signals is

$$\{P^u x | u = 0, ..., n - 1\} \tag{1}$$

with P is the permutation matrix [5] and n is the number of translation step.

Element of Eq. (1) is a row of a circulant matrix X

$$X = C(x) = \begin{bmatrix} x_1 & x_2 & x_3 & \dots & x_n \\ x_n & x_1 & x_2 & \dots & x_{n-1} \\ x_{n-1} & x_n & x_1 & \dots & x_{n-2} \\ \cdot & \cdot & \cdot & \cdot & \cdot \\ \cdot & \cdot & \cdot & \cdot & \cdot \\ \cdot & \cdot & \cdot & \cdot & \cdot \\ x_2 & x_3 & x_4 & \dots & x_1 \end{bmatrix} \tag{2}$$

Since all circulant matrices are made diagonal by the discrete Fourier transform (DFT) [4], X can be expressed as

$$X = F\,diag(\hat{x})F^H \tag{3}$$

where F is Discrete Fourier transform (DFT) matrix, and $\hat{x}$ is the DFT of the generating vector.

Equation 3 expresses the eigendecomposition of a general circulant matrix and why KCF is fast when it is implemented.

2.2   Fast Kernel Regression

The kernel matrix $K(n \times n)$ stores the dot-products between all pairs of samples

$$K_{ij} = \kappa(x_i, x_j) = \varphi^T(x_i)\varphi(x_i) \tag{4}$$

with high-dimensional space $\varphi(.)$.

The following kernels satisfy the condition to claim that K is circulant [6]:

- *Radial Basic Function kernels –e.g., Gaussian.*
- *Dot-product kernels –e.g., linear, polynomial.*
- *Additive kernels –e.g., intersection, χ^2 and Hellinger kernels.*
- *Exponentiated additive kernels.*

Therefore, the kernelized version of Ridge Regression is possible to diagonalize

$$\hat{\alpha}^* = \frac{\hat{y}^*}{\hat{k}^{xx} + \lambda} \tag{5}$$

where $K = C(k^{xx})$ is kernel matrix.

Learning phase utilizes Eq. (5) to update the model for next frame.

2.3   Fast Detection

Several candidate patches, **z**, that can be modeled by cyclic shifts are evaluated by the regression function $f(z)$. To compute efficiently, detection phase diagonalizes regression function

$$\hat{f}(z) = \hat{k}^{xz} \odot \hat{\alpha} \tag{6}$$

where k^{xz} is a kernel correlation of **x** and **z**.

During detecting phase, Eq. (6) predicts where is the center of target within the given frame with a learned coefficients α.

2.4   Fast Kernel Correlation

The kernel correlation of two arbitrary vectors, $\mathbf{x}$ and $\mathbf{x}$', is the vector $k^{xx'}$ with elements

$$k_i^{xx'} = \kappa(x', P^{i-1}x) = \varphi^T(x')\varphi(P^{i-1}x) \tag{7}$$

Kernel correlation consists of computing the kernel for all relative shifts of two input vectors. This quadratic complexity can be resolved efficiently by diagonalization with DFT.

Depending on the kernel value being unchanged by unitary transformations, such as the DFT, we can use fast kernel correlation for such kernels: dot-product and radial basic function.

Firstly, with dot-product, we have

$$k_i^{xx'} = g(F^{-1}(\hat{x}^* \odot \hat{x}')) \tag{8}$$

where F^{-1} is inverse of DFT. In particular, for a polynomial kernel

$$k_i^{xx'} = (F^{-1}(\hat{x}^* \odot \hat{x}') + a)^b \tag{9}$$

Secondly, for radial basic function

$$k_i^{xx'} = h(\|x\|^2 + \|x'\|^2 - 2F^{-1}(\hat{x}^* \odot \hat{x}')) \tag{10}$$

As a particularly, useful special case, a Gaussian kernel

$$k_i^{xx'} = exp(-\frac{1}{\sigma^2}(\|x\|^2 + \|x'\|^2 - 2F^{-1}(\hat{x}^* \odot \hat{x}'))) \tag{11}$$

[6] proposed simple Matlab code, with a Gaussian kernel, that can run very fast.

3   Kalman Filter

By assuming the system noise has Gaussian distribution, Kalman filter utilizes the linear dynamical systems to resolve the linear optimal filtering problem. More specifically, x_n is a discrete time system with state at time n. In the next time step $n + 1$, the state is

$$x_{n+1} = F_{n+1,n}x_n + w_{n+1} \tag{12}$$

where $F_{n+1,n}$ is the transition matrix from state x_n to x_{n+1}, and w_{n+1} is white Gaussian noise with zero mean and covariance matrix Q_{n+1}.

While the measurement vector z_{n+1} is given by

$$z_{n+1} = H_{n+1}x_{n+1} + v_{n+1} \tag{13}$$

where H_{n+1} is the measurement matrix and v_{n+1} is white Gaussian noise with zero mean and covariance matrix R_{n+1}, that is independent of noise w_{n+1}. The system gets measurement value for each step then estimates the correct state based on the minimum mean-square error of Eq. (13). The solution is a recursive procedure [2,8] as illustrated in Algorithm 1.

Algorithm 1. Kalman filter

1. Initialization:

$$\hat{x}_0 = E[x_0]$$
$$P_0 = E[(x_0 - E[x_0])(x_0 - E[x_0])^T]$$

2. Prediction:

$$\hat{x}_n^- = F_{n,n-1}\hat{x}_{n-1}$$
$$P_n^- = F_{n,n-1}P_{n-1}F_{n,n-1}^T + Q_n$$
$$G_n = P_n^- H_n^T [H_n P_n^- H_n^T + R_n]^{-1}$$

3. Estimation:

$$\hat{x}_n = \hat{x}_n^- + G_n(z_n - H_n\hat{x}_n^-)$$
$$P_n = (I - G_n H_n)P_n^-$$

Goto the Prediction step for the next prediction.

4   The Proposed Method

We propose a new tracker that improves the KCF tracker by correcting target's position with Kalman filter. It is known that KCF often makes failed prediction for the case of occlusion and human crossing simply because the object is disappear. Moreover, performance of the KCF tracker is often deteriorated for rotation, illumination variation, motion blur and etc. We thought that Kalman filter can improve these limitations. In fact, after the KCF estimates target's position based on the prediction by the Kalman filter, and the estimated value is given to the updating step of the Kalman filter. During the KCF learning phase, our tracker uses the correct state to update the kernel model.

First, the fast detection would acquire the peak value $f_{max}(k)$ at $(x(k), y(k))$ according to formula [6] in the current frame. Then, Kalman filter uses this position to adjust the system state to correct the position by using Algorithm 1. After several frames of progress, when Kalman filter is stable, it can correct the position of the target in the current frame. Then, during the KCF's learning phase, it is able to extract the target's feature successfully for the forthcoming frames.

Secondly, in order to resolve the occlusion as well as human crossing cases, we propose a novel approach. When the peak value is less than threshold T, it is assumed that this is the occlusion case. In other words, KCF would predict the incorrect position in that frame, and we could not use it as a measurement value of Kalman filter. During such case, our tracker will use the target's position based on the prediction step by Algorithm 1, and only this step will run. Figure 1 and Algorithm 2 describe it in detail.

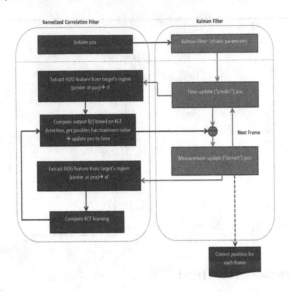

Fig. 1. Flowchart of our tracker, which basically combines KCF and Kalman filter.

Algorithm 2. Kernelized Correlation Filter with Kalman Filter

1. Initialization

   $pos \leftarrow target's\ center\ (first\ frame)$

   $\hat{x}_0 = pos$

   $P_0 = E[(x_0 - E[x_0])(x_0 - E[x_0])^T]$

2. Kalman prediction

   $pos = \hat{x}_n^-$

3. KCF detection

   $zf \leftarrow HOG\ target's\ feature\ (center\ at\ pos)$

   $f_{peak}, pos' \leftarrow max(\hat{k}^{xz} \odot \hat{\alpha})$

   if $f_{peak} < T$ **then**

       Goto step 5

   else

       $z_n = pos'$

       Goto step 4

   end if

4. Kalman estimation

   $pos = \hat{x}_n$

5. KCF learning

   $xf \leftarrow HOG\ target's\ feature\ (cente\ at\ pos)$

   $\hat{\alpha}^* = \frac{\hat{y}^*}{\hat{k}^{xx} + \lambda}$

   Goto step 2 for new frame.

Table 1. Average precision and fps of 5 trackers

	Mean precision (%)	Standard deviation precision (%)	Mean fps	Standard deviation fps
Our tracker	**96.7**	5.7	138	125.3
KCF on HOG	90.7	18.3	148	121.6
KCF on raw pixels	67.9	33.6	152	135.1
MOSSE	55.3	33.4	**254**	207.4
MIL	41.3	33.2	145	41.45

5   Experiments

5.1   Implementation Details

The present tracker is implemented using Matlab library. The pipeline for the tracker is illustrated in Algorithm 2. Some heuristics are used for threshold value T and Kalman filter. For instance, the sampling rate, acceleration magnitude, process noise, and measurement noise are given as 1 frame/s, 0.2, 0.5, and 1.0, respectively. Performance of our tracker is compared against KCF, MIL and MOSSE trackers. All trackers are implemented using Matlab on Windows 7 running on a computer having an i7 CPU with 16 GB RAM.

5.2   Evaluation

Tracking Dataset. To evaluate the performance, we use 38 video sequences, which are taken from the standard tracking benchmark dataset [3,14][1]. These videos consist of different challenges for tracking such as illumination variation, rotation, scale, motion blur, occlusion, and human crossing. Performance of the present tracker is compared with those of KCF, MOSSE, and MIL tracker, respectively, by implementing all trackers within the same computer.

Results. The precision curve and the frame rate (fps) are evaluated for each tracker [6,14]. In this metrics, the ratio of successfully tracked frame is assessed by a set of thresholds within the precision plot. By setting the threshold at 20, we compute the average precision and fps as well as the standard deviation as shown in Table 1. The mean precisions of MIL, MOSSE, KCF, KCF on HOG and our tracker are 41.3, 55.3, 67.9, 90.7 and 96.7 %, respectively. Figure 2 shows the performance curves of five trackers by varying the threshold, suggesting that the present tracker is the best among them. Regarding to the speed, the mean fps of the KCF on HOG case is 148 and the present one runs at 138 fps. Both can run in the real-time applications.

---

[1] Dataset is available at https://goo.gl/2bPKi7.

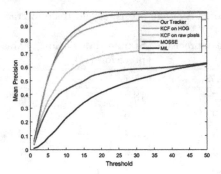

Fig. 2. Comparing the trackers' performance for full datasets.

Table 2. Average precision of 5 trackers with different categories and datasets (%)

Category	Datasets	Our tracker	KCF on HOG	KCF on raw pixels	MOSSE	MIL
Illumination variation	Boy, Car1,Fish, Car2, Crossing, Car24, RedTeam, Car4, CarDark, Crowds, Human8, Man, Mhyang, Singer1, Singer2, Skater, Subway, Sylvester, Trellis, Walking, Suv, Woman	**98.8**	96.4	66.2	56.2	45.6
Rotation	Board, Boy, CarScale, Dancer, Dancer2, David2, David3, Doll, Dudek, Gym, Liquor, Mhyang, MountainBike, RedTeam, Singer2, Skater, Sylvester, Tracjectory10, Tracjectory16, FaceOcc2, Trellis	**95.3**	90.6	72.1	53.7	48.1
Scale variation	Board, Car4, CarDark, CarScale, Dancer, Doll, Dudek, Fish, Jogging, Liquor, Mhyang, RedTeam, Singer1, Singer2, Skater, Sylvester, Tracjectory10, Tracjectory16,Walking, Woman	**94.8**	86.3	65.6	52.1	42.8
Motion blur	Car1, Car24, Woman, CarDark, Dancer, Dancer2, Suv, Doll, Dudek, Fish, Gym, Mhyang, RedTeam, Singer2, Subway, Boy	**98.2**	95.6	67.7	44.5	51.5
Occlusion	Car1, Car24, CarScale, David3, Doll, FaceOcc1, FaceOcc2, Jogging, Liquor, Suv,Tracjectory16, Walking, Woman	**95.1**	81.9	57.8	47.7	36.4
Human-crossing	Crowds, Jogging, Subway, Tracjectory10, Tracjectory16	**97.3**	69.9	60.8	60.2	15.2

To analyze the detail characteristics, the dataset is divided into six categories: illumination variation, rotation, scale, motion blur, occlusion, and human-crossing. The mean precision for each tracker is obtained for each category as shown in Table 2. Figure 3 shows six graphs. As you can see, the present tracker shows great improvement compared with the KCF on HOG tracker, particularly in the categories of the occlusion and human-crossing cases. This result suggests

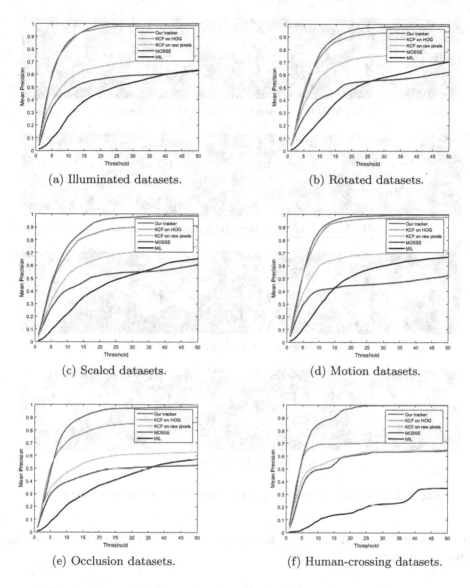

(a) Illuminated datasets.

(b) Rotated datasets.

(c) Scaled datasets.

(d) Motion datasets.

(e) Occlusion datasets.

(f) Human-crossing datasets.

Fig. 3. Comparing the trackers' performance for sequence attribute.

that Kalman filter plays an important role in making a directional decision when the object drifts into occlusion or other object such as human.

Further Analysis for the Human Crossing Case. Since the present tracker shows the best performance for the human-crossing case, it would be necessary to analyze a bit further. Figure 4 demonstrates how 3 trackers, i.e. MIL, MOSSE, and KCF, could not track the walking man correctly except the present one.

(a) MIL tracker starts to fail at these frames.

(b) MOSSE tracker starts to fail at these frames.

(c) KCF tracker starts to fail at these frames.

(d) Our tracker is successful.

Fig. 4. Comparing the trackers' performance for the human-crossing case.

It seems obvious that those trackers could not deal well with occlusion and human-crossing.

6   Conclusions

In this paper, we present a new tracking framework that combines the best features of the Kernelized Correlation filter and Kalman filter. Using the KCF, we acquire an estimation of the target's location, which is corrected by Kalman filter for adapting object's position. It is found that our tracker outperforms the state-of-art trackers such as KCF, MOSSE and MIL. It is particularly excellent in the occlusion and human-crossing cases. Given that KCF is one of the fastest trackers so far, our tracker can be used for the real-time applications such as the high-end surveillance.

Acknowledgments. This research was supported by Basic Science Research Program through the National Research Foundation of Korea (NRF) funded by the Ministry of Education, Science and Technology (NRF-2013R1A1A2006969) and by the MSIP(Ministry of Science, ICT and Future Planning), Korea, under the Global IT Talent support program (IITP-2015-R0134-15-1032) supervised by the IITP(Institute for Information and Communication Technology Promotion).

References

1. Bolme, D.S., Beveridge, J.R., Draper, B., Lui, Y.M., et al.: Visual object tracking using adaptive correlation filters. In: 2010 IEEE Conference on Computer Vision and Pattern Recognition (CVPR), pp. 2544–2550. IEEE (2010)
2. Cuevas, E.V., Zaldivar, D., Rojas, R., et al.: Kalman filter for vision tracking (2005)
3. Ferryman, J., Ellis, A.: Pets 2010: dataset and challenge. In: 2010 Seventh IEEE International Conference on Advanced Video and Signal Based Surveillance (AVSS), pp. 143–150. IEEE (2010)
4. Gray, R.M.: Toeplitz and Circulant Matrices: A Review. Now Publishers Inc, Hanover (2006)
5. Caseiro, R., Martins, P., Batista, J., Henriques, J.F.: Exploiting the circulant structure of tracking-by-detection with kernels. In: Fitzgibbon, A., Lazebnik, S., Perona, P., Sato, Y., Schmid, C. (eds.) ECCV 2012, Part IV. LNCS, vol. 7575, pp. 702–715. Springer, Heidelberg (2012)
6. Henriques, J.F., Caseiro, R., Martins, P., Batista, J.: High-speed tracking with kernelized correlation filters. IEEE Trans. Pattern Anal. Mach. Intell. **37**(3), 583–596 (2015)
7. Huang, T.: Surveillance video: the biggest big data. Computing Now **7**(2) (2014). http://www.computer.org/web/computingnow/archive/february2014. IEEE Computer Society
8. Kalman, R.E.: A new approach to linear filtering and prediction problems. J. Fluids Eng. **82**(1), 35–45 (1960)
9. Karavasilis, V., Nikou, C., Likas, A.: Visual tracking by adaptive kalman filtering and mean shift. In: Konstantopoulos, S., Perantonis, S., Karkaletsis, V., Spyropoulos, C.D., Vouros, G. (eds.) SETN 2010. LNCS, vol. 6040, pp. 153–162. Springer, Heidelberg (2010)
10. Kristan, M., et al.: The visual object tracking VOT2014 challenge results. In: Agapito, Lourdes, Bronstein, Michael M., Rother, Carsten (eds.) ECCV 2014 Workshops. LNCS, vol. 8926, pp. 191–217. Springer, Heidelberg (2015)
11. Lu, H., Zhang, R., Chen, Y.W.: Head detection and tracking by mean-shift and kalman filter. In: 3rd International Conference on Innovative Computing Information and Control, ICICIC 2008, pp. 357–357. IEEE (2008)
12. Mohinder, S.G., Angus, P.A.: Kalman filtering: theory and practice using matlab. John Wileys and Sons, Hoboken (2001)
13. Ojha, S., Sakhare, S.: Image processing techniques for object tracking in video surveillance-a survey. In: 2015 International Conference on Pervasive Computing (ICPC), pp. 1–6. IEEE (2015)
14. Wu, Y., Lim, J., Yang, M.H.: Online object tracking: A benchmark. In: 2013 IEEE Conference on Computer vision and pattern recognition (CVPR), pp. 2411–2418. IEEE (2013)
15. Yilmaz, A., Javed, O., Shah, M.: Object tracking: a survey. ACM Computing Surveys (CSUR) **38**(4), 13 (2006)

16. Zhang, K., Song, H.: Real-time visual tracking via online weighted multiple instance learning. Pattern Recogn. **46**(1), 397–411 (2013)
17. Zhao, J., Qiao, W., Men, G.Z.: An approach based on mean shift and kalman filter for target tracking under occlusion. In: 2009 International Conference on Machine Learning and Cybernetics, vol. 4, pp. 2058–2062. IEEE (2009)
18. Zhu, Z., Ji, Q., Fujimura, K., Lee, K.: Combining kalman filtering and mean shift for real time eye tracking under active IR illumination. In: Proceedings 16th International Conference on Pattern Recognition, vol. 4, pp. 318–321. IEEE (2002)

Biomedical Image Processing
and Analysis

Automatic BI-RADS Classification
of Mammograms

Nabeel Khan[✉], Kaier Wang, Ariane Chan, and Ralph Highnam

Volpara Health Technologies Ltd., Wellington, New Zealand
{nabeel.khan,kyle.wang,ariane.chan,ralph.highnam}@volparasolutions.com

Abstract. Mammograms provide a significant amount of information, which allows the classification of breast tissue into one of four breast density categories. The higher the category score, the greater the amount of dense (fibroglandular) tissue in the breast. These categories were proposed to give an indication of the sensitivity of mammography, but it is also widely acknowledged that breast density is associated with the risk of developing cancer. Thus, accurate and reproducible measures of classifying breast density are important for breast cancer screening and risk assessment.

We present our Volpara^{TM} algorithm to automatically estimate the volumetric breast density (VBD) from mammograms. VBD is the percentage of fibroglandular tissue in the breast and is a physiological measure of the breast composition. Volpara uses a physics model together with image information derived from a mammogram to report the breast density. In this paper, we compare Volpara's VBD with various statistical texture measures across 1179 mammograms. This comparison shows that Volpara has the best performance in categorising breast density with respect to radiologist's readings.

Keywords: Volumetric breast density · Mammogram · Image processing · Texture

1   Introduction

Breast cancer is the most commonly diagnosed cancer in women worldwide and is the second most fatal cancer overall (lung cancer is the first) [1,2]. Breast cancers diagnosed at later stages tend to have poorer outcomes. Therefore, the early detection of breast cancer through mammographic screening is crucial. Mammography is a specific type of imaging that uses a low-dose x-rays to generate digital images of the internal breast structure, referred to as mammograms, for radiologists to review.

The breast is mainly composed of fatty and fibroglandular tissues. The fibroglandular tissue attenuates x-rays to a greater extent than fatty tissue, which makes fibrogalndular tissue appear brighter on mammograms. Since cancers also appear brighter on a mammogram, increased breast density can reduce the sensitivity of mammography. There is a strong correlation between the breast density

© Springer International Publishing Switzerland 2016
T. Bräunl et al. (Eds.): PSIVT 2015, LNCS 9431, pp. 475–487, 2016.
DOI: 10.1007/978-3-319-29451-3_38

and the risk of developing a breast cancer. For instance, women with the densest breasts are at four to six times increased risk of developing breast cancer compared to women with the least dense breasts [3,4]. Therefore, the American College of Radiology has developed a BI-RADS (Breast Imaging-Reporting and Data System) to give an indication of the sensitivity of mammography [5]. The 4th edition of this standard provides four categories:

- **BI-RADS 1:** the breast is almost entirely fatty (<25 % fibroglandular tissue)
- **BI-RADS 2:** there are scattered breast densities (25–50 % fibroglandular tissue)
- **BI-RADS 3:** the breast tissue is heterogeneously dense, which could obscure detection of small masses (51–75 % of fibroglandular tissue)
- **BI-RADS 4:** the breast tissue is extremely dense (>75 % glandular). This may lower the sensitivity of mammography.

An example mammographic image for each BI-RADS category is shown in Fig. 1. If categorised as BI-RADS 3 or 4, the radiologist may recommend the patient for supplementary imaging techniques that are not influenced by dense tissue (e.g. ultrasound or magnetic resonance imaging) to detect a cancer, which may be masked by the dense tissue.

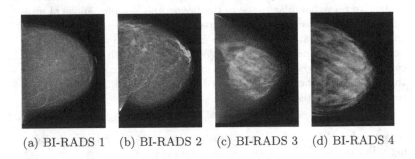

(a) BI-RADS 1   (b) BI-RADS 2   (c) BI-RADS 3   (d) BI-RADS 4

Fig. 1. Sample mammogram for each BI-RADS category.

Various image processing techniques have been recently proposed to classify or quantify the breast density into BI-RADS categories [6–8]. Texture analysis is the most commonly used image processing approach to classify breast density based on a radiologist's BI-RADS scores. Subashini *et al.* [7] segmented the breast image using a histogram-based threshold in which they removed all pixels with gray value less than 40. The statistical texture features (e.g. mean, skewness or uniformity) are then extracted from the processed image and fed to the support vector machine (SVM) to classify the breast density. The authors report an average classification accuracy of 95.44 % over 43 mammograms. Similarly, Sheshadri and Kandaswamy [9] used the image histogram to extract the statistical features (e.g. mean, entropy or standard deviation) and reported an average classification accuracy of 80 % over 320 mammograms. Limitations of the histogram-based approaches include: (1) histogram pattern is variable to noise or contrast (vendors use different algorithms to adjust the image contrast), and (2) thresholding may remove important information, such as valid breast tissue from the breast region during analysis.

Texture-based approaches have shown very good classification accuracy on mammograms in recent research [7,10,11]. However, the main problems associated with these methods are: (1) the number of mammograms used in the studies were small, thus limiting their statistical power, and (2) texture analysis is vulnerable to contrast changes and can give quite different results across mammograms of the same patient. A change in contrast for a mammogram can occur if radiographer applies variable configuration settings during mammographic acquisition, such as x-ray tube voltage or compression force. Therefore, we believe that there is still room for a thorough evaluation of statistical texture measures across a large set of mammograms.

There are also commercial softwares available to estimate the breast density using area-based methods, such as Cumulus [12]. Cumulus is a semi-automated software and widely considered to be the gold standard for breast density work. The area-based methods first segment (automatically or semi-automatically) certain areas of the projected breast and then estimate the breast density from the segmented areas. Area-based methods have shown to correlate well with mammogram sensitivity [3]. However, the area-based methods drive tissue information solely from the image, which highly depends upon on the imaging conditions, such as breast compression and x-ray exposure. However, breast tissue is a three dimensional concept rather than a two dimensional projection. So, it is more reasonable to consider the breast density in term of the volume percentage.

Volpara^{TM} algorithm is a volume-based method and estimates the volume of fibroglandular tissue, and the ratio of that to the breast volume, which gives volumetric breast density. The Volpara algorithm not only provides a very good agreement with the ground truth reading (magnetic resonance imaging data) [13] but is also shown to perform better than Cumulus [14]. The Volpara algorithm uses phase congruency [15] and realistic breast edge models [13,16] to estimate the volumetric breast density and does not use calibration objects as required by some volume-based methods [16,17]. In principle, the calibration object leads to a highly accurate measure of breast density. However, use of a step-wedge is impractical clinically, and needs to be removed by radiographers while imaging large breasts.

In this paper, we examined the correlation between extracted image features (texture and VBD) and one radiologist's BI-RADS readings (score of 1, 2, 3 or 4). We refer to texture analysis and VBD as image measures in the remaining part of the paper. We first separated the extracted image feature data into four groups according to the radiologist's reading. Then, we developed two quality metrics to evaluate how well an image measure can classify images based on the BI-RADS scores. An image measure that gives good data separation between the BI-RADS categories is likely to perform well.

Our paper is structured as follows: Sect. 2 presents the image measures used in this paper, such as statistical texture measures and the Volpara algorithm. Dataset and quality metrics are presented in Sect. 3. Results are discussed in Sect. 4, followed by the conclusion.

2   Image Measures

A typical mammographic image is comprised of the breast region and the background. Some image segments, such as the pectoral muscle and medical labels, do not contribute to the breast density. Therefore, pre-processing is performed on a mammogram to extract a valid breast tissue area, referred as a Region of Interest (ROI), and that region is then used to classify the breast density. In this section, we discuss the image measures used in our work.

2.1   Texture Measures from the Image

We detect a ROI (valid breast tissue region) from a grayscale mammogram and convert it to a one dimensional vector X in which the element x_i ($i = 0, 1, 2, 3, \cdots, m-1$) represents pixel values and m is the total number of pixels. We then compute the texture measures using the following approaches:

– **Standard deviation (STD)** measures a change in the contrast intensity to classify patterns.

$$STD = \sqrt{\frac{1}{m-1} \sum_{i=1}^{m} |x_i - (\frac{1}{m} \sum_{i=1}^{m} x_i)|^2} \tag{1}$$

Heavy textures (random distributions of pixel values) give a high STD value compared to the smooth textures (uniform distributions of pixel values).

– **Entropy (ENT)** measures the randomness of data to characterise the texture of the image.

$$ENT = -\sum_{i=1}^{256} c_i \log 2(c_i) \tag{2}$$

A 256-bin histogram is generated from the vector X and c_i refers to the corresponding histogram counts. We expect a high ENT value for heavy textures and a low ENT value for smooth textures.

– **Skewness (SKW)** measures the inequality of the data distribution about the mean. A negative skewness means that the data is distributed more to the left of the mean (a value smaller than mean) than to its right (a value larger than mean) and vice versa.

$$SKW = \frac{\frac{1}{m} \sum_{i=1}^{m} (x_i - \overline{x})^3}{\left(\sqrt{\sum_{i=1}^{m} (x_i - \overline{x})^2}\right)^3} \tag{3}$$

where $\bar{x}$ is the arithmetic mean. A uniform distribution gives a zero SKW value. Otherwise, SKW value varies depending upon the distribution of pixel values.

2.2   Texture Measures from Gray-Level Co-occurrence Matrix

The texture measures introduced in the previous section do not use spatial information (we converted the image to a 1-D vector). An alternative method for examining image texture is to consider the spatial relationship of pixels of a grayscale mammogram by a gray-level co-occurrence matrix (GLCM) [18, 19]. GLCM estimates the image properties related to second-order statistics by considering the relation between two neighbouring pixels in one offset as the second order texture, where the first pixel is called the reference and the second pixel is called the neighbour. GLCM contains joint probabilities between pairs of pixels, separated by a displacement distance d in a given direction θ.

We have computed GLCM from the ROI and used several displacement values (1, 2, 4, 8 and 16) along with common values of θ (0, 45, 90 or 135) in which we found that the setting $d = 1$ and $\theta = 0$ gave the best results. In this paper, we report the results of this optimal setting.

Let G represent a GLCM matrix (square matrix with L^2 elements) having joint probabilities between pairs in distance d and direction θ. $G_{i,j}$ is the value at i^{th} row and j^{th} column of the matrix G. We computed the following statistical measures from the GLCM:

- **Contrast (CON)** measures the linear dependency of gray levels of neighbouring pixels.

$$\text{CON} = \sum_{i,j} |i - j|^2 G_{i,j} \tag{4}$$

The expected value of CON ranges from 0 to $(L-1)^2$. Heavy textures give a high CON value while smooth textures normally give low CON value.
- **Homogeneity (HOM)** measures the uniformity of non-zero entries in the GLCM.

$$\text{HOM} = \sum_{i,j} \frac{1}{1 - (1 - j)^2} G_{i,j} \tag{5}$$

The value of HOM ranges from 0 to 1. For smooth textures, the homogeneity is high and vice versa. High homogeneity indicates that texture contains multiple repetitive structures.
- **Correlation (COR)** measures gray level linear dependence between the pixels at the specified locations relative to each other.

$$\text{COR} = \sum_{i,j} \frac{(1 - \mu_i)(1 - \mu_j) G_{i,j}}{\sigma_i \sigma_j} \tag{6}$$

where $\mu_{i(j)}$ and $\sigma_{i(j)}$ are means and standard deviations of the G elements at i^{th} (j^{th}) row. Smooth textures gives a high value of COR while heavy textures give a low value of COR. The expected value of COR ranges from 0 to 1.

2.3 Volpara^{TM} Algorithm

Volpara^{TM} algorithm finds pixel values in the breast that correspond to entirely fatty tissue, referred to as P_{fat}, which is used as a reference to compute the thickness of the dense tissue h_d at each pixel location (x, y) based on the following equation [16]:

$$h_d(x, y) = \frac{\ln(P_{x,y}/P_{fat})}{\mu_{fat} - \mu_{dense}} \tag{7}$$

The pixel value P is assumed to be linearly related to the energy imparted to the x-ray detector. The denominator is the effective x-ray attenuation coefficients for fat and dense tissue, receptively. This formula is intrinsically robust to any errors, such as exposure, detector gain or multiplicative variations [20]. Equation (7) generates a density map, where each pixel corresponds to the dense tissue thickness. The volumetric breast density (VBD) is then computed by integrating over the entire breast area in the density map.

Volpara is an FDA-cleared and CE-marked commercial product for breast density assessment. Volpara is currently used in 30 countries with 215 installations at various sites. Volpara is also supplied for research purposes.

3 Dataset and Quality Metrics

Digital mammography imaging generates two types of images for analysis, raw and processed. The visualisation of contrasts is suboptimal in raw images, which makes it hard for radiologists to estimate the breast density. Vendors apply a suitable image processing technique on raw images to generate processed images to allow an improved contrast for radiologist's BI-RADS readings. But processed images tend to vary in contrasts among vendors due to their specific image enhancement algorithm. On the other hand, raw images do not vary and can offer consistent results for density analysis. In this paper, we have therefore used the raw images for analysis.

Each patient normally has one mediolateral oblique (MLO) and one craniocaudal (CC) view for the left and right breasts, respectively. Our data consisted of 1179 mammograms belonging to 296 patients (cases). We used the services of a qualified radiologist to examine the mammograms and assign an average BI-RADS score for each case based on visual assessment.

Each image measure yields a numerical-value for a mammogram in our experiments. We then compute the average value per case, to allow for a direct comparison with the BI-RADS scores, which are assigned on a per case basis. Therefore, all results in this paper are case-based.

The motivation of our study is to analyse the correlation between each image measure and the BI-RADS score. We first separated the numerical-values of each image measure into four groups based on the radiologist's BI-RADS readings. Then, we analysed the separation between values of groups. For example, the values between BI-RADS 1 and BI-RADS 2, and between BI-RADS 1 and BI-RADS

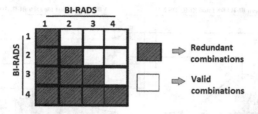

Fig. 2. Valid BI-RADS combinations (upper right triangle elements) used to analyse the image measures.

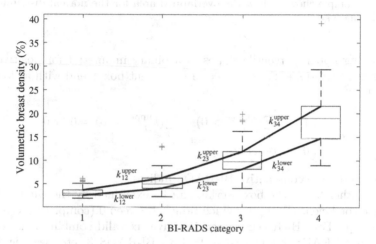

Fig. 3. An example showing box–trend for the boxplot of volumetric breast density (VBD).

3, and so on. As shown in Fig. 2, we had six valid combinations of BI-RADS groups. We selected each valid BI-RADS combination as two distributions and applied a two-tailed t-test to determine if the two distributions were significantly different (as the initial test). We found that the p-values were less than 0.05 for all valid combinations of each image measure. Therefore, t-test could not differentiate between the classification performance of image measures. So, we have developed two new statistical metrics to analyse the classification performance of each image measure.

3.1   Quality-Score (QS)

The performance of an image measure can be evaluated by using a boxplot in terms of the box trends and any overlapping data. As the BI-RADS score is related to the breast density, we expect a consistent (either upwards or downwards) trend for all boxes. To quantitatively examine the box trend, one can simply measure the upper and lower percentile slopes between two consecutive boxes, see Fig. 3 for an example. Each boxplot yields three lower–percentile and

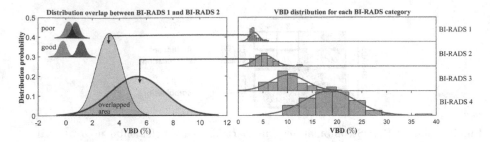

Fig. 4. An example showing how the overlapped area for the normal distributions of VBD is calculated.

corresponding upper–percentile slopes in a binary manner: 1 for positive slope and 0 for negative slope. So we expect a consistent box–trend with a slope sum q of 6 or 0:

$$q = \begin{cases} 1 & \sum_{ij}(k_{ij}^{\text{lower}} > 0) + \sum_{ij}(k_{ij}^{\text{upper}} > 0) = 6 \text{ or } 0 \\ 0 & \text{otherwise} \end{cases} \tag{8}$$

in which i and j are consecutive BI-RADS indices.

On the other hand, the box overlap can be examined by the Bhattacharyya correlation coefficient (BC) [21], which ranges between 0 (complete overlap) and 1 (no overlap). Four BI-RADS categories have six valid combinations (e.g. BI-RADS 1 vs BI-RADS 2 and BI-RADS 1 vs BI-RADS 3, etc. see Fig. 2 for a description). The mean of the BC coefficients for these combinations is combined with the slope sum q to give a quality-score (QS):

$$\text{QS} = q \times \frac{1}{n}\sum_{i=1}^{n}(1 - \text{BC}) \tag{9}$$

where n is the total number of combinations (6 combinations in our case). As a result, an excellent data separation has a QS = 1 whereas a failed separation reads QS = 0.

3.2   Overlap-Area (OA)

To further examine the proposed image measures, we developed another statistical metric that compares the overlapped proportion between data distributions. Again, we first separated the measured image data into four groups based on the radiologist's BI-RADS readings. Then we computed one histogram per BI-RADS category. This gives us four histograms per method. Lastly, we fitted normal distribution curves to histograms as shown in Fig. 4. Few overlaps (overlapped area = 0) between two normal distribution curves indicate an excellent data separation, whereas a complete overlap i.e. where the overlapped area = 1 means that two data sets are statistically the same (failed separation).

Following the above idea, we defined another quality metric as the mean overlap-area (OA) over the six valid combinations of BI-RADS data groups (valid combinations are shown in Fig. 2). Contrary to QS, OA = 0 indicates perfect data separation while OA = 1 indicates a failed separation.

4 Results

Our image measures are applied on a region of interest (ROI) of the raw mammographic image and density map output by Volpara™. The ROI is defined as the inner breast region detected by Volpara algorithm. Note that Volpara's volumetric breast density (VBD) is determined from density map.

The generated boxplots and histograms for each image measure are shown in Figs. 5 and 6 respectively. The computed quality-score (QA) and overlap-area (OA) metrics for each image measure is summarised in Table 1. It is clear that VBD performs the best in classifying the mammograms since it has the largest QS and smallest OA. We also note that correlation (COR) and standard deviation (STD) have comparable performance as VBD. However, Fig. 7 demonstrates that STD is not able to differentiate between fatty (BI-RADS 1) and extremely dense (BI-RADS 4) breasts, which is not acceptable clinically; whereas COR lacks confidence to distinguish breasts of BI-RADS 2 and BI-RADS 3. Moreover, we find that COR is likely to misinterpret a focal density (clustered dense

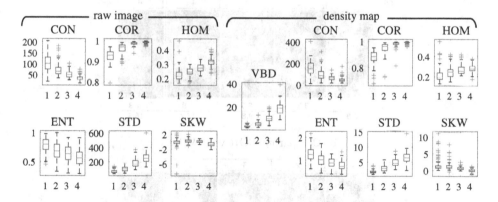

Fig. 5. Boxplots of the proposed image measures for raw images and density maps. In each sub-plot, the x-axis is the BI-RADS score, and the y-axis donates an image measure specified by the title.

Table 1. Results for image measures: (higher QS and lower OA correspond to the best classification performance)

Metric	Raw Images						Density Maps						
	COR	CON	HOM	ENT	STD	SKW	COR	CON	HOM	ENT	STD	SKW	VBD
QS	0.34	0.48	0.28	0.10	0.49	0	0.28	0.46	0.01	0.16	0.48	0	0.58
OA	0.38	0.27	0.44	0.65	0.26	0.53	0.44	0.28	0.67	0.57	0.27	0.42	0.19

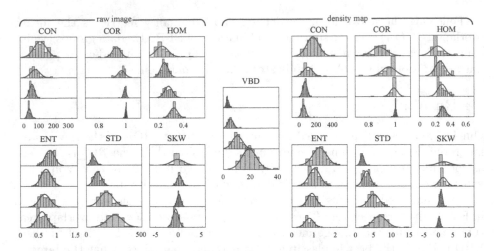

Fig. 6. Histograms and fitted normal distribution curves of the proposed image measures for raw images and density maps. In each subplot, the vertical division from top to bottom represents BI-RADS 1–4. For each sub-plot, the x-axis donates the image measure specified by the title, and the y-axis simply measures the counts for histogram (y-axis labels are removed due to limited space).

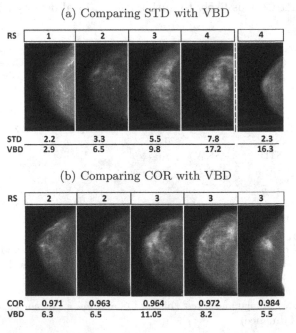

Fig. 7. Sample mammograms with a radiologist's score (RS) at the top of the image and other image measures are at the bottom of the image.

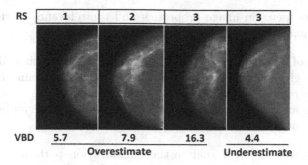

Fig. 8. Sample mammograms with a radiologist's score (RS) at the top of the image and VBD measures are at the bottom of the image.

tissue that can potentially mask tumours) as low BI-RADS category since such tissue structure has repetitive patterns giving large COR values (boxplot suggests that large COR value corresponds to low BI-RADS score). BI-RADS 3 cut-off is very important in countries, such as the United States, where density legislation affects the women. This also limits the applicability of COR in clinics.

Although Volpara showed the best relationship to radiologist's BI-RADS scores, its measure sometimes overestimates or underestimates the VBD compared to radiologist's readings (see Fig. 8 for examples). The issues causing the underestimation or overestimation of breast densities are poor compression, poor breast positioning, or very high x-ray tube voltages. These issues significantly degrade the quality of mammogram and affect the breast density classification. We are working on these issues to improve the precision of the breast density classification.

5   Conclusion

This paper presents a preliminary evaluation of various image measures over a large number of mammograms. For statistical analysis, we have developed two new quality metrics to analyse how well an image measure classifies mammograms based on a radiologist's BI-RADS scores.

Standard deviation (STD) measure is likely to be a good candidate for breast density classification due to its computational efficiency and considerably good image classification. However, STD does not perform well in distinguishing between fatty (BI-RADS 1) and extremely dense (BI-RADS 4) breasts. On the other hand, correlation (COR) measure performs well with fatty and very dense breasts. However, our experiments show that it cannot differentiate properly between breasts of BI-RADS 2 and BI-RADS 3 categories. Our statistical analysis indicates that volumetric breast density (VBD) measure performs relatively better than other image measures in classifying the breast density. It is also worth mentioning that VBD measures a physiological characteristic, and it has significance in terms of the risk of developing breast cancer, whereas other image measures focus on image properties and the relevance to risk is not yet clear. The primary contributions of this paper are two-fold:

1. comparison of six standard statistical texture measures with VBD, to analyse how well a given image measure can classify mammograms based on the radiologist's readings.
2. development of two new statistical methods, quality-score and overlap-area, to evaluate the performance of each image measure.

As further work, we will analyse the classification performance of texture measures on tomosynthesis images. Breast tomosynthesis is a recent break-through in mammography that provides a clearer and more accurate view compared to conventional mammography. Breast tomosynthesis takes multiple slices of the entire breast allowing radiologists to examine through the layers of tissue. However, motion artifacts are likely to occur in sliced images because of the slightly longer exposure time compared to mammograms [22], which can make it difficult to classify the breast density. To our knowledge, there are few studies in evaluating the texture measures on tomosynthesis images till date.

Acknowledgment. We thank Associate Professor Alistair D. A. Steyn-Ross at the University of Waikato for his valuable insights to help us develop the overlap-area metric.

References

1. Sampat, M., Markey, M., Bovik, A.: Computer-Aided Detection and Diagnosis in Mammography. Elsevier Academic Press, Handbook of Image and Video processing. Second edition (2005)
2. Globocan 2012: Estimated cancer incidence, mortality and prevalence wolrdwide in 2012 (2012). http://globocan.iarc.fr/Pages/fact_sheets_population.aspx
3. McCormack, V., dos. Silva, I.: Breast density, parenchymal patterns as markers of breast cancer risk: a meta-analysis. Cancer Epidemiol. Biomark. Prev. **24**(7), 1159–1169 (2006)
4. Subashini, T., Ramalingam, V., Palanivel, S.: Automated assessment of breast tissue density in digital mammograms. Comput. Vis. Image Underst. **114**(1), 33–43 (2010)
5. American College of Radiology. Breast Imaging Reporting and Data System (BI-RADS), 4 (2003)
6. Bosch, A., Munoz, X., Oliver, A., Marti, J.: Modeling and classifying breast tissue density in mammograms. Comput. Vis. Pattern Recog. **2**, 1552–1558 (2006)
7. Subashini, T., Ramalingam, V., Palanivel, S.: Automated assessment of breast tissue density in digital mammograms. Comput. Vis. Image Underst. **114**(1), 33–43 (2009)
8. Kinoshita, S., de Azevedo-Marques, P., Pereira, R., Rodrigues, J., Rangayyan, R.: Content-based retrieval of mammograms using visual features related to breast density patterns. J. Digit. Imaging **20**(2), 172–190 (2007)

9. Sheshadri, H., Kandaswamy, A.: Experimental investigation on breast tissue classification based on statistical feature extraction of mammograms. Comput. Med. Imaging Graph. **31**(1), 46–48 (2006)
10. Kaliyaperumal, V., Selvarajan, S.: Automated characterization of mammographic density for early detection of breast cancer risk. Int. J. Simul. Syst. Sci. Technol. **15**(1), 56–63 (2008)
11. Silva, W., Menotti, D.: Classification of mammograms by the breast composition. In: International Conference on Image Processing, Computer Vision and Pattern Recognition, vol. 6, pp. 1–6 (2012)
12. Byng, J., Boyd, N., Fishell, E., Jong, R., Yaffe, M.: The quantitative analysis of mammographic densities. Physcis Med. Biol. **39**(10), 1629–1638 (1994)
13. Highnam, R., Brady, S.M., Yaffe, M.J., Karssemeijer, N., Harvey, J.: Robust breast composition measurement - volpara^{TM}. In: Martí, J., Oliver, A., Freixenet, J., Martí, R. (eds.) IWDM 2010. LNCS, vol. 6136, pp. 342–349. Springer, Heidelberg (2010)
14. Harvey, J., Highnam, R., Jeffreys, M.: Comparing a new volumetric breast density method (Volpara^{TM}) to cumulus. In: Martí, J., Oliver, A., Freixenet, J., Martí, R. (eds.) IWDM 2010. LNCS, vol. 6136, pp. 408–413. Springer, Heidelberg (2010)
15. Kovesi, P.: Image features from phase congruency. Videre: J. Comput. Vis. Res. **1**(3), 1–26 (1999)
16. van Engeland, S., Snoeren, P., Huisman, H., Boetes, C., Karssemeijer, N.: Volumetric breast density estimation from full-field digital mammograms. IEEE Trans. Med. Imaging **25**(3), 273–282 (2006)
17. Shepherd, J., Herve, L., Landau, J., Fan, B., Kerlikowske, K., Cummings, S.: Novel use of single x-ray absorptiometry for measuring breast density. Technol. Cancer Res. Treat. **4**(2), 173–182 (2005)
18. Kekre, H., Thepade, S., Sarode, T., Suryawanshi, V.: Image retrieval using texture features extracted from glcm, lbg and kpe. Int. J. Comput. Theor. Eng. **2**(5), 1793–8201 (2010)
19. Nikoo, H., Talebi, H., Mirzaei, V.: A supervised method for determining displacement of gray level co-occurrence matrix. In: Machine Vision and Image Processing, pp. 1–5. IEEE (2011)
20. Highnam, R., Brady, M.: Mammographic Image Analysis. Computational Imaging and Vision, vol. 14. Kluwer Academic Publishers, Nijmegen (1999)
21. Bhattacharyya, A.: On a measure of divergence between two statistical populations defined by their probability distribution. Bull. Calcutta Math. Soc. **35**, 99–109 (1943)
22. Helvie, M.: Digital mammography imaging: breast tomosynthesis and advanced applications. Radiol. Clin. North Am. **48**, 917–929 (2010)

Analyzing Muscle Activity and Force with Skin Shape Captured by Non-contact Visual Sensor

Ryusuke Sagawa[1][✉], Yusuke Yoshiyasu[1], Alexander Alspach[2], Ko Ayusawa[1],
Katsu Yamane[2,3], and Adrian Hilton[4]

[1] Intelligent Systems Research Institute, National Institute of Advanced Industrial Science and Technology, Tsukuba, Japan
ryusuke.sagawa@aist.go.jp
[2] Disney Research, Pittsburgh, USA
[3] The Robotics Institute, Carnegie Mellon University, Pittsburgh, USA
[4] Centre for Vision, Speech and Signal Processing, University of Surrey, Guildford, UK

Abstract. Estimating physical information by vision as humans do is useful for the applications with physical interaction in the real world. For example, observing muscle bulging infers how much force a person puts on the muscle to interact with an object or environment. Since the human skin deforms due to muscle activity, it is expected that skin deformation gives information to analyze human motion. This paper demonstrates that biomechanical information can be derived from skin shape by analyzing the relationship between skin deformation, force produced by muscles, and muscle activity. We first obtained the dataset simultaneously acquired by a range sensor, a force sensor, and electromyograph (EMG) sensors. Since recent range sensors based on non-contact visual measurement acquires accurate and dense shape of an object at high frame rate, the deforming skin can be observed. The deformation is calculated by finding the correspondence between a template shape and each range scan. The relationship between skin deformation and other data is learned. In this paper, the following problems are considered: (1) estimating force from skin shape, (2) estimating muscle activity from skin shape, (3) synthesizing skin shape from muscle activity. In the experiments, the database learned from the sensor data can be used for the above problems, and the skin shape gives useful information to explain the muscle activity.

1 Introduction

Geometry of an object is one of the most important information to visually understand a scene. The geometrical analysis by using cameras has been a major topic of computer vision and has been applied to observe and analyze various targets including human motions. Geometrical information by vision is however often not sufficient for effective and safe physical interaction between humans, robots, objects, and the environment. When a robot picks up an object, for example, motion planning and control would be easier if its physical properties

T. Bräunl et al. (Eds.): PSIVT 2015, LNCS 9431, pp. 488–501, 2016.
DOI: 10.1007/978-3-319-29451-3_39

such as weight and compliance are known in advance. It would also be beneficial to know the ground surface properties such as friction coefficient before actually walking on it. For human-robot interaction, knowing a person's muscle tension level is useful for deciding whether the robot should offer physical help. Unfortunately, obtaining such information requires installation of additional force sensors outside the robot, which is not always possible especially in uncontrolled environments.

For humans, it is actually possible to estimate physical quantities only from visual clues in some special cases. For example, we can roughly estimate an object's weight by observing another person holding the object, possibly based on such clues as the person's facial expression, pose, and body shape including muscle bulging, all of which are available through visual sensors. If we can implement a similar inference process, robots would be able to estimate physical quantities without additional sensors.

This paper presents an example of estimating physical quantities from visual information. More specifically, we develop a method for estimating the force applied to the environment by a human subject using muscle geometry data obtained from a projector-camera system. The method is then applied to force estimation of objects dropped onto the subject's hand.

Motion capture (mocap) system is widely used for human motion analysis. The articulated motion of human body is captured by tracking markers attached on the human body. To obtain the physical information, force plates are used to measure the force produced by human body with a mocap system. Since force plates are placed on the floor, the internal forces of a human body cannot be measured directly. To obtain the information of individual muscle, electromyograph (EMG) sensors are often used. The sensors are attached to the skin above the target muscles, and record the electrical activity produced by muscles. Since using these sensors is high cost, it is useful and our future goal if physical information is predicted only by a non-contact visual sensor. In this paper, we use these sensors for training step of the proposed method, and compared to the results in the evaluation.

The idea we adopt in this paper is to observe skin shape based on non-contact visual measurement. If the activity level of a muscle changes, the skin above the muscle deforms according to the muscle shape. It is therefore expected that the skin shape has information to estimate the muscle activity. Since the skin deformation is non-parametric and the difference between individuals is difficult to model, we take an approach to learn the relationship between skin shape, force produced by muscles, and muscle activity with the dataset simultaneously acquired by a range sensor (a.k.a. depth sensor), a force sensor, and EMG sensors.

Range scans are captured frame-by-frame, and it is necessary to calculate the deformation from the acquired data to prepare the dataset. The proposed method consists of four steps: (1) acquire a dataset of various motions with a range sensor, a force sensor, and EMG sensors, (2) extract the feature vector of skin deformation by finding the correspondence between a template shape and range scans, (3) train the database with acquire dataset, and (4) predict force, muscle activity, and skin shape for input variables. The contribution of this paper is summarized as follows.

– It is demonstrated that visual measurement of surface shape can be used to estimate arm muscle activation and force.
– The proposed approach based on learning the relationship succeeds to predict force, muscle activity, and skin shapes each other.

2   Related Work

The analysis of skin deformation is studied in the field of computer graphics. Skin deformation according to body pose is important factor to generate a realistic model of human body. The methods of modeling muscles is classified to three approaches: geometrically-based, physically-based, and data-driven approaches [8]. The first one models the animation effects of muscle contraction and succeeded to model simple muscles. The second approach involves muscle dynamics and tissue properties to model complex scene of muscles. The third approach directly models the skin shape from the data captured by a mocap system or a range sensor. Skin deformation between individuals are modeled in [1]. The deformation of body shape according to poses are modeled in [3]. The muscle deformation is model from the range data obtained by a depth camera in [18]. In [17], the skin deformation is learned with respect to the pose and acceleration of body parts by kernel regression. The acceleration is used as the external force for each body part. In [14], the skin shape of a moving arm with a barbell in the hand is captured, which is used as external force. The relationship between body pose, body shape and external force is learned by kernel ridge regression. The shape is parameterized base on [20]. The relationship learned from the dataset is used for synthesizing skin shape for a new pose and external force. The co-contraction of multiple muscles is not considered in the methods. The problem considered in their paper is an inverse problem of estimating force from skin shape, which is tackled in this paper.

To capture dynamic objects by non-contact visual sensors, various methods have been proposed, which are roughly classified to passive and active methods. From the viewpoint of accuracy and robustness, active methods are easy to apply. In active methods, Time-of-Flight (TOF) cameras and triangulation based methods are widely used. TOF cameras project temporally-modulated light patterns and acquire a depth image at once by capturing the reflections [13]. In triangulation-based methods, two approaches have proposed to capture dynamic object: temporal-encoding [23,27] or spatial-encoding method [12,19,22]. While temporal-encoding methods need to project multiple patterns, a spatial-encoding method is suitable to capture dynamic scenes because a single image of a fixed projector pattern is sufficient for reconstruction.

Since skin deforms nonrigidly, nonrigid surface registration techniques are required to find the correspondence between a template shape and range scans. The surface registration techniques can be divided into three categories in terms of regularizations that they use: smoothness regularization, isometric regularization and conformal regularization. Early approaches [1,2,24,25] are based on smoothness regularization. These techniques are very flexible in that they can

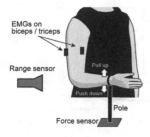

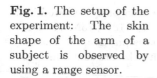

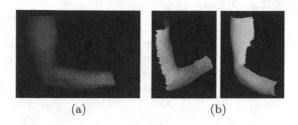

(a)   (b)

Fig. 1. The setup of the experiment: The skin shape of the arm of a subject is observed by using a range sensor.

Fig. 2. (a) An input image of the projector-camera system that casts the static wave-grid pattern on the target. (b) The shape computed from the image (a).

change the shape of the template quite largely; for example, they can deform a sphere into a tooth, if adequate landmarks are given. However, they are poor at preserving template details and mesh structures, which means that they need many landmarks to work properly. In contrast, the isometric (as-rigid-as possible) regularization can preserve original template details and are commonly used in automatic registration techniques [7,9,21]. The drawback of these methods are that they are incapable of handling models with different sizes or those which undergo large local stretching. Recently, the techniques based on conformal (as-similar-as possible) regularization [10,16,26] are proposed to achieve both flexibility in changing shapes and preservation of mesh structure. They are based on angle-preserving deformation.

3 Data Acquisition

In this paper, we analyze the relationship between the skin shape and the muscle activity of a person. However, the shape of skin can be affected by other various conditions. For example, the skin shape depends on the angle of the joint even if the muscle is relaxed, and the muscle mass is different between individuals. Therefore, we simplify the condition considered in this paper, and focus on the relationship between skin shape and muscle activity. Figure 1 shows the setup of the experiment we analyze in this paper. We observe the skin shape of the arm of a subject from the side by using a range sensor. The elbow joint is almost fixed so that the angle is 90 degrees by strapping the wrist to a pole. When the subject pushes down or pulls up the wrist by trying to straighten/bend the elbow, the force transmitted from the pole is measured by the force sensor. In this situation, the force is mainly produced by biceps and triceps muscles. The muscle activity is measured by two EMG sensors placed on the skin above the muscles. Our challenge is to estimate the muscle activity and the produced force from the skin shape, which is the first approach to the best of our knowledge to derive muscle activation from visual observations even in the limited situation.

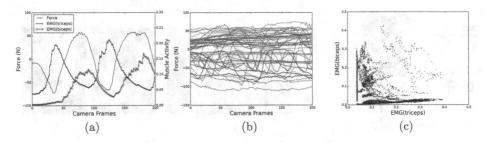

Fig. 3. (a) An example of the force and muscle activity simultaneously acquired in a push-and-pull sequence. (b) The range of force of all sequences is -110~+75N. The force is measured along the vertical axis, and the upward direction is positive. (c) The distribution of the activity of two muscles. It shows that both muscles are simultaneously active a some sequences.

The shape of the skin is deformed according to the muscle activity. We observed the shape of the front and upper arm at 30~50 frames/second by using a projector-camera system proposed in [19]. Since the shape of a front arm is affected by the wrist and hand pose, the wrist angle is fixed to be straight as much as possible and the hand stays open and relaxed during the shape acquisition. The shape of the hand is omitted from the analysis to remove the effect in the experiment. Figure 2 shows one of the frame of the range sensor. (a) is the input image of the projector-camera system that casts the static wave-grid pattern on the target. (b) is the shape computed from the image (a). The image acquisition is synchronized with the force sensor and the EMGs.

We captured three types of the sequences: pull-up, push-down, and push-and-pull motions. In the push-and-pull sequences, the subject changed the force direction during the sequence, while the pole was continuously pulled up or pushed down the pole during the pull-up and push-down sequences. 10 K frames of range scan are obtained in total. An example of the force and muscle activity is shown in Fig. 3(a). The force is measured along the vertical axis, and the upward direction is positive. The range of force of all sequences is -110~+75N as shown in Fig. 3(b). The muscle activity is defined as the integrated EMG signal normalized by the signal of the maximal voluntary contraction (MVC) [11]. If it is close to zero, the muscle is relaxed. Since this sequence is one of the push-and-pull sequences, the co-contraction of the biceps and triceps muscles is observed. Figure 3(c) shows the distribution of the activity of two muscles, and both muscles are simultaneously active in some sequences.

4   Feature Extraction of Skin Deformation

The skin shape deforms according to the muscle activity. We use the deformation of a template shape as the feature vector to explain the state of muscle.The template shape is a range scan with the least muscle activity chosen from all range scans. The deformation of the template shape are calculated for all vertices of each frame. Since the range scans is captured by the range sensor frame-by-frame, the deformation is calculated by finding the correspondence between the template shape and each range scan by the method explained in Sect. 4.2.

4.1 Defining Feature Vector to Explain Skin Deformation

The template shape is represented as a set of 3D vertices. Now, we assume each vertex v of the template shape corresponds to the point $P(v)$ of a range scan. Although we want to extract the skin deformation caused by muscle activity, the difference $P(v) - v$ includes the change of arm pose in addition to the skin deformation. Although the arm is almost fixed in the experiment of this paper, it slightly moves and the elbow angle changes. Additionally, we assume the arm pose does not affect the skin deformation since the arm motion is small. If we know the arm pose, the relationship between $P(v)$ and v is written as

$$P(v) = R(v + d(v)) + t, \tag{1}$$

where R and t are the rotation and translation calculated by the arm pose for the vertex, respectively. $d(v)$ is the vector of skin deformation, which is used as the feature to explain the muscle activity. $d(v)$ is calculated from the correspondence by $d(v) = R^T(P(v) - t) - v$.

Once the skin deformation $d(v)$ is calculated for each vertex of the template shape, the feature vector D_k for k-th range scan is defined by

$$D_k = [d_k(v_1), d_k(v_2), \ldots d_k(v_M)], \tag{2}$$

where M is the number of vertices in the template shape. Since $d_k(v)$ is a three-dimensional vector, the length of feature vector D_k is $3M$.

4.2 Finding Correspondence Between the Template Shape and Each Range Scan

Calculating the skin deformation $d(v)$ is based on finding the correspondence between the template shape and each range scan. The surface of an arm changes according to the arm pose and the muscle activity under the skin. Although the arm pose can be estimated by the registration of articulated model or by using a motion capture system, the residual of the deformation is not explained by an articulated model. Therefore, a method of vertex-wise nonrigid registration between two models is necessary to find the correspondence for each vertex.

Nonrigid registration is achieved using the conformal (angle-preserving) registration technique [26] that can capture spatially-varying scale changes in order to capture muscle bulges. This technique assigns an affine transformation X_i to each vertex of the template shape and optimizes the transformation to attract the template toward a range scan while preserving the angles of triangle meshes as much as possible. We use the as-similar-as possible formulation that constrains

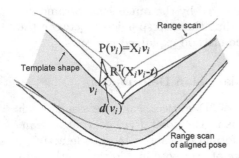

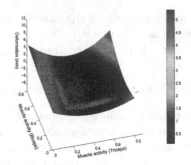

Fig. 4. The template shape and a range scan is represented by black and green curves. The range scan aligned by using the relative pose is represented by the blue curve (Color figure online).

Fig. 5. The curved surface represents the B-spline function fitted to the red points, which are the deformation of captured data (Color figure online).

affine transformations to similarity transformations. Let $X = [X_1 \ldots X_M]^T$ be the affine transformations associated to vertices. We define the cost function

$$E(X) = w_{\text{ASAP}}E_{\text{ASAP}} + w_{\text{reg}}E_{\text{reg}} + w_{\text{Closest}}E_{\text{Closest}}, \tag{3}$$

where E_{ASAP} constrains deformation as similar as possible, E_{reg} acts as a regularization term to avoid extreme local deformation, E_{Closest} penalizes distances between the closest points of template and target surface. The energy is minimized using the alternating optimization technique where the first step optimizes the vertex positions with fixed transformations and the second step optimizes affine transformations with fixed vertex positions.

Once X_i is estimated, the corresponding point is expressed by $P(\boldsymbol{v}_i) = X_i\boldsymbol{v}_i$. To cancel the effect of the pose, The rotation R and translation $\boldsymbol{t}$ are calculated by assuming locally rigid around each vertex. The parameters are estimated by minimizing the following equation:

$$\arg\min_{R,\boldsymbol{t}} \sum_{\boldsymbol{v}' \in N(\boldsymbol{v})} (X_i\boldsymbol{v}' - R\boldsymbol{v}' - \boldsymbol{t})^2, \tag{4}$$

where $N(\boldsymbol{v})$ is the set of neighborhood vertices that satisfies $\| \boldsymbol{v}' - \boldsymbol{v} \| < r$. r is a user-defined threshold of the radius around the vertex.

Figure 4 illustrates the calculation of the skin deformation $d(\boldsymbol{v}_i)$. The template shape and a range scan is represented by black and green curves. The corresponding point $X_i\boldsymbol{v}_i$ for a vertex $\boldsymbol{v}_i$ is found by nonrigid registration. The rotation R and translation $\boldsymbol{t}$ for each vertex of the range scan relative to the template shape is estimated by Eq. (4). The range scan aligned by using R and $\boldsymbol{t}$ is represented by blue curve. $d(\boldsymbol{v}_i)$ is calculated as the difference of the corresponding points between the template shape and the range scan of aligned pose.

5   Learning the Relationship Between Skin Shape, Force, and Muscle Activity

Although the setup of the experiment performed in this paper is simple, multiple muscles affects the skin shape, and the shape of each muscle and the amount of fat under the skin are unknown. It is therefore difficult to model the skin shape based on the muscle model. Instead, we learn the relationship between skin and muscle from the acquired data. We obtained the skin shape, the force produced by an arm, the muscle activity measured by EMG sensors. We consider three problems in this section.

The first problem is estimating the force from the skin shape. If the force is calculated from the skin shape, which is obtained by non-contact sensor, it gives useful information for biomechanical analysis.

The second one is estimating muscle activity from skin shape. The force produced by an arm is the result of multiple active muscles. If the force can be estimated from the skin shape, it should be able to detect the co-contraction of multiple muscles. We clarify if the skin shape reflects the muscle activity.

The third one is the inverse problem of the second one. If the relationship between skin shape and muscle activity is one-to-one correspondence, the skin shape can be synthesized from a given state of muscle activity, which is useful to generate realistic model of human skin.

Since the skin deformation is non-linear, they are problems to determine the non-linear function between the given data and the estimated result. We find the function by learning-based approach. Since the all values of skin deformation, force, and muscle activity are continuous, they are defined as non-linear regression. We chose Random Forests (RF) [4] as the learning method in this paper, which is applied for regression problems [5,6,15].

5.1   Estimating Force from Skin Shape

The first problem is to estimate the force f from a given feature vector D of the skin. The function F_f to be determined is defined as $f = F_f(D)$. In this definition of the problem, the muscle activity is not considered explicitly, and we estimate the force directly from the skin shape. EMG sensors are not necessary for this estimation, we use them to check if the co-contraction is occurred or not as shown in Fig. 3(a).

In the training phase, we have multiple training examples $(D_k, f_k), k = 1, \ldots, L$, which are obtained at L camera frames during data acquisition. The RF algorithm builds multiple decision trees, of which each leaf node stores the values of f. In the predicting phase, a new feature vector of skin deformation D_{new} is given and applied to the decision trees. The predicted value of f for D_{new} is calculated as the average of multiple leaf nodes.

Each training example is constructed from the data of a single camera frame, and the prediction phase is performed frame-by-frame. No temporal information is used in the current implementation. The number of vertices in the template shape is about $8\,K{\sim}15\,K$ points.

5.2   Estimating Muscle Activity from Skin Shape

The second problem is to estimate the muscle activity a from a given feature vector D of the skin. The function F_a to be determined is defined as $a = F_a(D)$. Because we used two EMG sensors in this paper, the activity state a is a two-dimensional vector $a = (a_t, a_b)$, which are activities of triceps and biceps, respectively.

The training and predicting phase is similar to the case of estimating force, but the output of the prediction is a two-dimensional vector a. The prediction phase is also performed frame-by-frame in this estimation.

5.3   Synthesizing Skin Shape from Muscle Activity

The dataset of the third problem is the same with the second one, but the input and output data are swapped. The feature vector D of the skin is estimated from a given muscle activity a. The function F_D to be determined is defined as $D = F_D(a)$, which means we assume the skin shape only depends on the activity of muscles that relates to the skin if the joint angle is known.

The captured shape is actually affected by other reasons such as the activity of another muscle and the error of the measurements. We estimate the function by approximating the measured deformation to determine the deformation vector uniquely with respect to muscle activity a. Since the motion of muscles is smooth, we estimate a B-spline function defined by

$$F_{D,i}(a_t, a_b) = \sum_{t=1,2,3, b=1,2,3} p_{t,b} w_{t,b} \tag{5}$$

$$[w_{t,b}] = A_t^T A_b, \quad A_t = a_t W, \quad A_b = a_b W,$$

for i-th dimension of the feature vector D, where $p_{t,b}(t = 1, 2, 3, b = 1, 2, 3)$ are 9 control parameters of B-spline function, $a_t = [a_t^2, a_t, 1]$, $a_b = [a_b^2, a_b, 1]$, and a 3×3 matrix $W = \frac{1}{2}[1, -2, 1; -2, 2, 0; 1, 1, 0]$. The muscle activities are normalized to the range $0 \sim 1.0$ by using MVC. The total number of parameters are $27M$ for M vertices of the template shape. $p_{t,b}$ for i-th dimension of D is estimated by minimizing the error $\sum_k (F_{D,i}(a_t, a_b) - D_{k,i})^2$, where $D_{k,i}$ is the i-th dimension of D.

Figure 5 shows an example of the approximating function. The curved surface represents the B-spline function fitted to the red points, which are the deformation of captured data. If an activity state a is given, the deformation vector is calculated by $F_D(a)$ for each dimension, and the skin shape for the state is calculated by adding the deformation vector to the template shape. The captured data is expected to cover the space of the input activity a for this approach to work properly.

6   Experiments

In the experiments, we analyze if the skin deformation has sufficient information to explain the force produced by the arm and the muscle activity. First, we

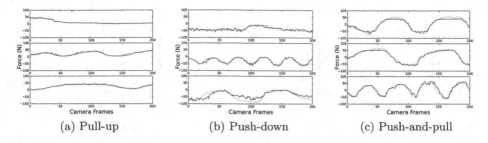

(a) Pull-up	(b) Push-down	(c) Push-and-pull

Fig. 6. The results of predicting force are shown for 9 sequences. The solid curves are the results of prediction and the dotted curves are the values measured by the force sensor: (a) the results of three sequences of pull-up motion. (b) the results of three sequences of push-down motion. (c) the results of three push-and-pull motion.

test the force estimation from the skin shape. We evaluate the accuracy of the predicted force by using the trained database. The accuracy is calculated based on leave-one-out cross-validation by using 48 acquired sequences of 200 frames. Figure 6 shows some of the results of predicting force. The solid curves are the results of prediction and the dotted curves are the values measured by the force sensor. The results of three sequences of pull-up motion is shown in (a). The RMS error of pull-up sequences is 5.31N. Since the maximum force in the sequences is about 75N, the error is less than 10 % of the range. The results of three sequences of push-down motion is shown in (b), and the RMS error is 11.87N, which is larger than that of the pull-up sequences. The reason is considered that the movement of triceps is smaller than that of biceps and the viewing direction of the range sensor was not the best for observing the triceps. The results of push-and-pull motion is shown in (c), and the RMS error is 13.97N. Although the co-contraction occurs in the push-and-pull sequences as shown in Fig. 3(a), the proposed method succeeded to predict the force for each frame.

The next experiment is estimating muscle activity from skin shape. Figure 7 shows the results of predicting muscle activity. The solid curves are the results of prediction and the dotted curves are the values measured by the EMG sensors. The blue curves indicate the values of biceps, and the green curves are those of triceps. The sequences in Fig. 7 are the same ones in Fig. 6. The RMS error of pull-up sequences shown in (a) is 0.0227. The RMS error of push-down motion shown in (b) is 0.0317. The reason that the error is larger than that of the pull-up sequences is considered the same with the force estimation. The results of push-and-pull motion is shown in (c), and the RMS error is 0.0598. Since the error is sufficiently small compared to MVC, the proposed method succeeded to predict the muscle activity from the skin shape. However, the sequences with co-contraction have larger errors than the other sequences. It is considered because the number of training examples with co-contraction were not large enough to construct the database. To increase the training dataset is one of our future work to improve the result.

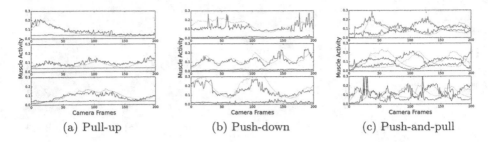

(a) Pull-up   (b) Push-down   (c) Push-and-pull

Fig. 7. The results of predicting muscle activity are shown for the same sequences in Fig. 6. The solid curves are the results of prediction and the dotted curves are the values measured by the EMG sensors. The blue curves indicate the values of biceps, and the green curves are those of triceps. The activity values are normalized by maximal voluntary contraction (MVC) (Color figure online).

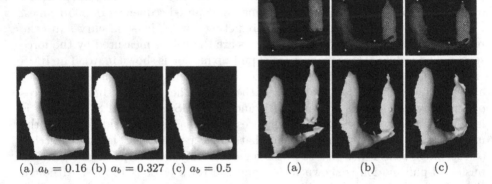

(a) $a_b = 0.16$ (b) $a_b = 0.327$ (c) $a_b = 0.5$ (a)   (b)   (c)

Fig. 8. Three examples of synthesized shapes are shown by changing the biceps activity a_b from 0.16 to 0.5, while the triceps activity a_t is fixed to 0.08. The muscle around the biceps near the inside of the elbow bulges out according to the activation.

Fig. 9. A dynamic scene of catching a dropped bottle is captured. The weights of the bottle are light (0.65 kg) in (b) and heavy (1.80 kg) in (c). The shapes of the arm have difference around the biceps.

The next experiment is synthesizing skin shape from muscle activity. We synthesize the skin shapes based on Eq. (5) for given muscle activity. Figure 8 shows three examples of synthesized shapes by changing the biceps activity a_b from 0.16 to 0.5, while the triceps activity a_t is fixed to 0.08. The muscle around the biceps near the inside of the elbow bulges out according to the activation. 6.5 K frames of the captured data is used as the training set for the approximation. The accuracy of the synthesized deformation vectors is estimated by using 4.9 K frames that are not in the training set. The RMS error of deformation vector is 1.09 mm.

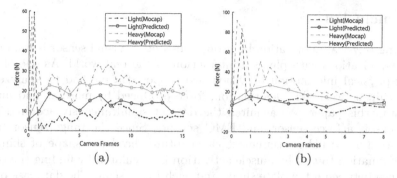

(a)   (b)

Fig. 10. Two examples of predicting force by changing how to catch. The solid lines are the results of the predicted force by observing the arm by the proposed method. The dotted lines are the force calculated from the motion of the bottle obtained by using a motion capture system. The blue lines are the results of a light bottle, while the red lines are those of a heavy bottle. The frame rate of the camera is 30 frames/second, while that of the motion capture system is 120 frames/second (Color figure online).

The last experiment is observing a dynamic scene of catching a dropped bottle shown in Fig. 9(a). We tried to estimate the force during catching by changing the weight of the bottle. Figure 9(b) is the frame at the moment of catching of a light bottle (0.65 kg), and (c) is that of a heavy bottle (1.80 kg). While it is difficult to recognize the difference in the input images, the shapes have difference around the biceps. Figure 10 shows the results of the predicted force by observing the arm by the proposed method (solid lines). The force is compared to the one calculated from the motion of the bottle obtained by using a motion capture system (dotted lines). The blue lines are the results of a light bottle, while the red lines are those of a heavy bottle. The frame rate of the camera is 30 frames/second, while that of the motion capture system is 120 frames/second. Although the frame rate of the camera was not sufficient to observe the impact, the proposed method successfully estimated the force in the following frames. Figure 10(a) and (b) are two examples of predicting the force by changing how to catch. The predicted forces clearly have difference between the light and heavy bottles. Since the motion of the wrist is obtained by nonrigid registration, the weight of the bottle can be estimated from the force and the acceleration of the wrist motion. By using frames that the acceleration is small to reduce the noise in calculating the second order derivative of the motion, the average weights estimated for the light bottle are 0.92 kg and 0.79 kg for these two examples, while those of the heavy bottle are 1.46 kg and 1.57 kg. The error of the estimated weight is 0.1~0.4 kg. The results indicate that the proposed method can recognize which bottle is heavy from the visual information without using contact sensors at the testing phase.

7   Conclusion

Obtaining physical information by using non-contact visual sensor is important for the applications with physical interaction in the real world. As one of estimating physical information by vision, we proposed a method to analyze the relationship between skin deformation, force produced by muscles, and muscle activity in this paper. We acquired the dataset simultaneously acquired by a range sensor, a force sensor, and EMG sensors. Since the range sensor based on non-contact visual measurement can capture the dense shape of skin, the skin deformation caused by muscle activation is calculated by finding the correspondence between a template shape and each range scan. The database of the relationship between skin deformation, force, and muscle activity is constructed by learning based on Random Forests. The proposed method succeeded to three prediction problems: estimating force from skin shape, estimating muscle activity from skin shape, synthesizing skin shape from muscle activity. The results of experiments shows that skin shape obtained by non-contact visual measurement has useful information to estimate the muscle force and muscle activation.

In our future work, we plan to improve the prediction of force and muscle activation. One idea is to construct the database by increasing the parameters of the setup, for example, multiple subject, flexible joint motion, and multiple joints of human body. Additionally, we will observe the motion of the skin at the moment of impact by using a high speed camera to analyze dynamic motion more deeply.

Acknowledgments. This research has been partially supported by JSPS Strategic Young Researchers Overseas Visits Program for Accelerating Brain Circulation, "Joint research for robots beyond human capacity for emergency handling".

References

1. Allen, B., Curless, B., Popović, Z.: The space of human body shapes: reconstruction and parameterization from range scans. ACM Trans. Graph. **22**(3), 587–594 (2003)
2. Amberg, B., Romdhani, S., Vetter, T.: Optimal step nonrigid ICP algorithms for surface registration. In: CVPR (2007)
3. Anguelov, D., Srinivasan, P., Koller, D., Thrun, S., Rodgers, J., Davis, J.: Scape: shape completion and animation of people. ACM Trans. Graph. **24**(3), 408–416 (2005)
4. Breiman, L.: Random forests. Mach. Learn. **45**(1), 5–32 (2001)
5. Criminisi, A., Shotton, J., Konukoglu, E.: Decision forests for classification, regression, density estimation, manifold learning and semi-supervised learning. Technical report, MSR-TR-2011-114, Microsoft Research (2011)
6. Gall, J., Yao, A., Razavi, N., Van Gool, L., Lempitsky, V.: Hough forests for object detection, tracking, and action recognition. IEEE Trans. Pattern Anal. Mach. Intell. **33**(11), 2188–2202 (2011)
7. Huang, Q.X., Adams, B., Wicke, M., Guibas, L.J.: Non-rigid registration under isometric deformations. In: Proceedings of the Symposium on Geometry Processing, pp. 1449–1457 (2008)

8. Lee, D., Glueck, M., Khan, A., Fiume, E., Jackson, K.: Modeling and simulation of skeletal muscle for computer graphics: a survey. Found. Trends Comput. Graph. Vis. **7**(4), 229–276 (2012)

9. Li, H., Sumner, R.W., Pauly, M.: Global correspondence optimization for non-rigid registration of depth scans. In: Proceedings of the Symposium on Geometry Processing, pp. 1421–1430 (2008)

10. Liao, M., Zhang, Q., Wang, H., Yang, R., Gong, M.: Modeling deformable objects from a single depth camera. In: ICCV, pp. 167–174 (2009)

11. Merletti, R.: Standards for reporting EMG data. J. Electromyogr. Kinesiol. **9**(1), III–IV (1999)

12. Microsoft: Xbox 360 Kinect (2010). http://www.xbox.com/en-US/kinect

13. Microsoft: Kinect for Windows (2013). http://www.microsoft.com/en-us/kinectforwindows

14. Neumann, T., Varanasi, K., Hasler, N., Wacker, M., Magnor, M., Theobalt, C.: Capture and statistical modeling of arm-muscle deformations. Comput. Graph. Forum (Proc. of Eurographics) **32**(2pt3), 285–294 (2013)

15. Okada, R.: Discriminative generalized hough transform for object dectection. In: Proceedings of 2009 IEEE 12th International Conference on Computer Vision, pp. 2000–2005 (2009)

16. Papazov, C., Burschka, D.: Deformable 3D shape registration based on local similarity transforms. Comput. Graph. Forum **30**, 1493–1502 (2011)

17. Park, S., Hodgins, J.: Data-driven modeling of skin and muscle deformation. In: ACM TOG (2008)

18. Robertini, N., Neumann, T., Varanasi, K., Theobalt, C.: Capture of arm-muscle deformations using a depth-camera. In: Proceedings of European Conference on Visual Media Production (CVMP), vol. 10 (2013)

19. Sagawa, R., Sakashita, K., Kasuya, N., Kawasaki, H., Furukawa, R., Yagi, Y.: Grid-based active stereo with single-colored wave pattern for dense one-shot 3D scan. In: 3DIMPVT, pp. 363–370 (2012)

20. Sumner, R., Popović, J.: Deformation transfer for triangle meshes. In: SIGGRAPH 2004, ACM SIGGRAPH 2004 Papers, pp. 399–405 (2004)

21. Tevs, A., Bokeloh, M., Wand, M., Schilling, A., Seidel, H.P.: Isometric registration of ambiguous and partial data. In: CVPR, pp. 1185–1192 (2009)

22. Vuylsteke, P., Oosterlinck, A.: Range image acquisition with a single binary-encoded light pattern. J. IEEE Trans. Pattern Anal. Mach. Intell. Arch. **12**(2), 148–164 (1990)

23. Weise, T., Leibe, B., Gool, L.V.: Fast 3D scanning with automatic motion compensation. In: CVPR (2007)

24. Weise, T., Li, H., Van Gool, L., Pauly, M.: Face/off: live facial puppetry. In: Proceedings of the 2009 ACM SIGGRAPH/Eurographics Symposium on Computer Animation, pp. 7–16 (2009)

25. Yeh, I.C., Lin, C.H., Sorkine, O., Lee, T.Y.: Template-based 3D model fitting using dual-domain relaxation. IEEE Trans. Vis. Comput. Graph. **17**(8), 1178–1190 (2010)

26. Yoshiyasu, Y., Ma, W.C., Yoshida, E., Kanehiro, F.: As-conformal-as-possible surface registration. Comput. Graph. Forum **33**(5), 257–267 (2014)

27. Zhang, L., Curless, B., Seitz, S.M.: Spacetime stereo: shape recovery for dynamic scenes. In: IEEE Computer Society Conference on Computer Vision and Pattern Recognition, pp. 367–374 (2003)

Regression as a Tool to Measure Segmentation Quality and Preliminary Indicator of Diseased Lungs

Norliza Mohd. Noor[1]([✉]), Omar Mohd. Rijal[2], Joel Chia Ming Than[1],
Rosminah M. Kassim[3], and Ashari Yunus[4]

[1] UTM Razak School of Engineering and Advanced Technology,
Universiti Teknologi Malaysia, Kuala Lumpur, Malaysia
norliza@utm.my
[2] Institute of Mathematical Sciences, University of Malaya, Kuala Lumpur, Malaysia
[3] Department of Diagnostic Imaging, Kuala Lumpur Hospital,
Kuala Lumpur, Malaysia
[4] Institute of Respiratory Medicine, Kuala Lumpur, Malaysia

Abstract. Segmentation of the lung from HRCT Thorax images was studied. An automatic method of determining segmentation area is proposed. High quality of segmentation is considered achieved when the segmented area from the proposed algorithm is almost identical to the area obtained from the manual tracings by lung expert (ground truth). High correlation between the two types of segmented areas showed that regression may be used as a tool to measure segmentation quality. Supplementary information may also be obtained from the regression plot. Prediction interval may be used as a possible indicator of diseased whilst outliers may show or indicate low segmentation quality or a possible severity of the disease.

Keywords: Lung segmentation · Regression · Segmentation quality · High resolution computed tomography

1 Introduction

Lung segmentation is defined as the separation of the lung regions from background regions to obtain lung region defined by a boundary. Most segmentation techniques can be attributed to the use of thresholding [1–6]. This is because thresholding is particularly effective as the main approach of extracting the region of interest (lungs) from the body region due to the difference in contrast between the two regions. This attribute is due to content of air in the lungs that causes less attenuation of than body regions [6]. Other examples of methods include graph cut [7], texture [8] and active contours [9]. Thus the objective and quantitative evaluation of segmentation is important especially with the array of segmentation methods available today [10].

© Springer International Publishing Switzerland 2016
T. Bräunl et al. (Eds.): PSIVT 2015, LNCS 9431, pp. 502–511, 2016.
DOI: 10.1007/978-3-319-29451-3_40

Limited lung slices or levels can be used to view particular diseases in a particular patient [11]. These levels correspond to different anatomic landmarks and height of the lung as well. There are possible categorisations of levels to three or five level slice viewing. For five levels, the levels can be represented as L1: aortic arch, L2: trachea carina, L3: pulmonary hilar, L4: pulmonary venous confluence and L5: 1–2 cm above right hemi-diaphragm [12].

Segmentation quality can be found using several measures. There are many quality measures used such as volume overlap error, relative volume difference, average symmetric surface difference [13]. For this study, the regression curve which is often overlooked is highlighted to show its capability to exhibit the segmentation quality across levels of the lung. Regression analysis is a powerful tool to show the segmentation quality over a large sample base.

2   Data Collection

High Resolution Computed Tomography (HRCT) scans for 15 normal patients and 81 diseased patients were collected retrospectively from Hospital Kuala Lumpur. The images were obtained using a Siemens SomatomPlus4 CT scanner, and observed by a senior radiologist using SyngoFastView version VX57G27. Each slice was obtained at 10 mm intervals. Patients were at a supine position will full suspended inspiration when scans were taken. Images taken were in the size of 512×512 pixels.

A senior radiologist was tasked to select the five predetermined levels of the lungs to be processed with the segmentation algorithm. The five predetermined levels correspond to anatomical landmarks were selected by senior radiologist as Level 1 (L1) - aortic arch, Level 2 (L2) - trachea carina, Level 3 (L3) - pulmonary hilar, Level 4 (L4) - pulmonary venous confluence, and Level 5 (L5) - 1–2 cm above right hemi-diaphragm.

Since the gold standard or ground truth of segmentation is also done by a human expert, in this study, the manual tracings of the ground truth were done by a trained lung image expert who plotted the borders of the lung using a software interface. The points plotted were saved in a (x,y) coordinate format.

3   Methodology

3.1   Segmentation Algorithm

The segmentation algorithm was developed and tested firstly for the normal patients HRCT scans and was applied to the diseased patients for all five predetermined levels. The segmentation approach used here was able to segment across all levels and in a fast manner. The segmentation algorithm combines known techniques such as thresholding and morphology [12]. The flowchart of the segmentation algorithm is shown in Fig. 1.

The HRCT scan image first undergoes an automatic global thresholding known as Otsu thresholding. This enables the separation the body region from the surrounding region. Secondly objects less than 3000 pixels in area are removed. Next, the body region is applied an empirical threshold of -324HU. This threshold approach separates the lung region from the body region. Morphology operations of dilation and erosion with a square structure element with a size of 3×3 pixels are then executed to smooth lung boundaries. A connected component analysis is done to extract the two lung regions. Besides the body and surrounding there should be two other regions that can be seen to have 8-connectivity. This property is used to detect the presence of both lungs. A check is done to see whether there are two lungs present. If there are not, lung separation operations are executed. Lung regions are then filled and contours are extracted.

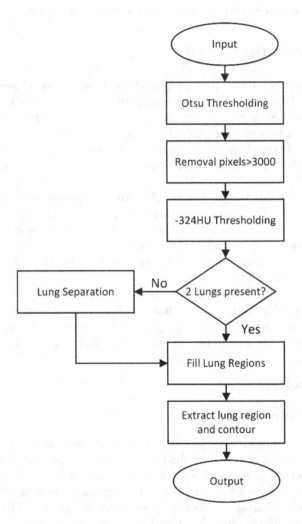

Fig. 1. Flowchart of segmentation algorithm.

3.2 Regression Analysis

Regression analysis, using MINITAB, was done to analyze the relationship between two measurements [14]. The first measurement is the lung area enclosed by the automatically segmented boundary using the segmentation algorithm termed as y. The second measurement is the lung area enclosed by the manually traced lung borders termed as x. The lung area is calculated by summing the area of pixels enclosed and the area of each pixel can calculated as Eq. (1).

$$A = h \times l \tag{1}$$

where A is the area of a pixel in mm^2, h is the pixel height in mm and l the pixel length in mm.

Regression analysis firstly plots the trendline that shows the relationship between x and y. The trendline can be signified by an equation that models the value of y when x changes. The parameters contributing to this model are the slope of the trendline represented by β, and the intersect of the y axis represented by α. The model can be represented as Eq. (2).

$$y = \alpha + \beta x \tag{2}$$

In this study, the prediction intervals (PI) with 95 % probability are also used. A prediction interval can be defined as the range that is likely to contain the response value of a new value of y when there are provided specified settings of the predictors in the model Eq. (3).

$$y = \alpha + \beta x + \epsilon \tag{3}$$

where y is the area of the segmented lung, x is the area of the manually traced lung. α the intersection of y axis β is the slope of the trendline, and ϵ is the random error term.

4 Results

The Fig. 2 shows the sample of good segmentation that the segmentation algorithm was able to produce. The high quality segmentation is signified by the degree of overlap between two contours noticed by the naked eye. There are two contours present; green signifying the automatic segmented borders and red borders signifying the manually traced lung borders. In some instances such as in Fig. 2 the green totally overlaps the red contours. The overlap signifies the high degree of similarity between the automatic segmentation and ground truth.

Next the regression curves for the combined five levels are shown for both dis-eased and normal lungs are presented in Figs. 3 and 4. The X axis represents the ground truth traced lung area and the Y axis represents the automatically segmented lung area. The regression equations are inserted as well in the plots. The dashed lines represent the 95 % prediction intervals. The solid red line represents the fitted linear regression line.

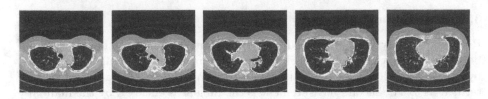

Fig. 2. Samples of high quality segmentation across five levels (Color figure online).

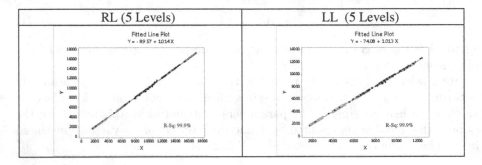

Fig. 3. Regression plots for normal patients right (RL) and left (LL) lungs for five levels combined (Color figure online).

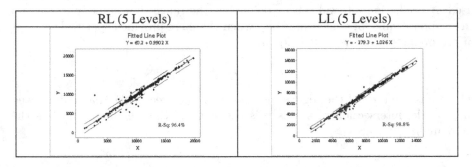

Fig. 4. Regression plots for diseased patients right (RL) and left (LL) lungs for five levels combined (Color figure online).

To further see in detail the segmentation quality, the regression curve of separate five levels of right and left lungs for diseased and normal patients are shown in Figs. 5 and 6. The dashed lines represent the 95 % prediction intervals. The solid red line represents the fitted linear regression line. Again, the X axis represents the ground truth traced lung area and the Y axis represents the automatically segmented lung area.

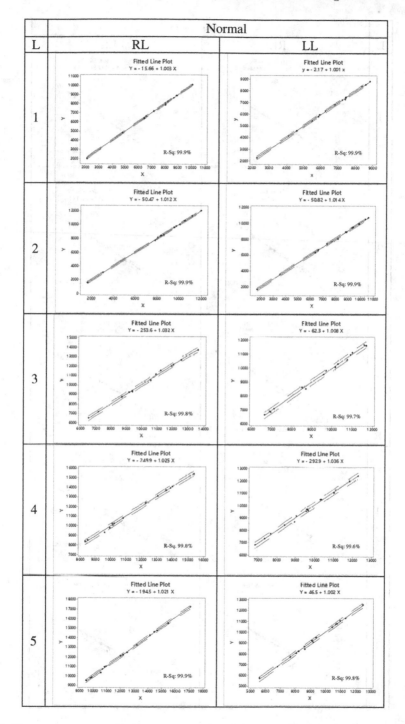

Fig. 5. Regression curves for separate five levels for normal right (RL) and left (LL) lungs for normal lungs (Color figure online).

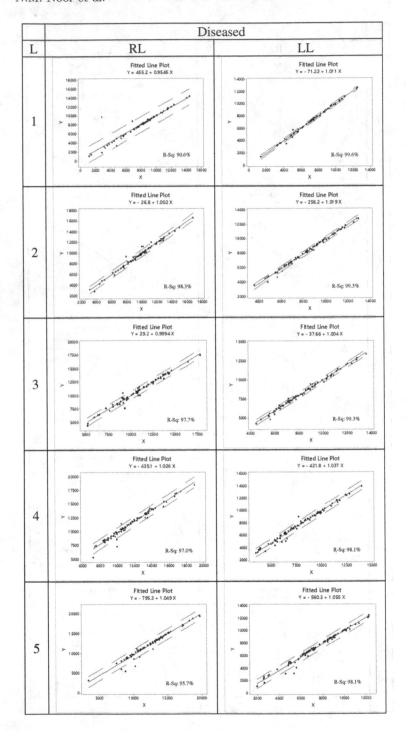

Fig. 6. Regression curves for separate five levels for diseased right (RL) and left (LL) lungs for normal lungs (Color figure online).

5   Discussion

The segmented area from the proposed segmentation algorithm (Y) being highly cor-related to the area obtained by manual tracings (ground truth, X) is the basic definition of segmentation quality. The regression plots in Figs. 3, 4, 5 and 6 showing high correlation strongly suggesting that a high segmentation quality was consistently achieved across all five levels. This is illustrated by the β values of all the regression equations being close to one, this situation being the case for normal lungs and more importantly diseased lungs as well. However, non-zero α values may be considered as deviation of Y from X, but their values are relatively small compared to the magnitude of the segmented area. This result strongly suggest that the proposed segmentation algorithm is promising because it shows the segmentation was able to exhibit segmentation quality similar to ground truth provided by a human expert for most diseased lungs.

As a second indicator of segmentation quality, the regression plots displayed should show points within the prediction interval, this being the general case. It is of interest to note that prediction intervals are wider for disease cases, which could suggest a possible method of differentiating disease cases from normal case.

Absence of outliers in the regression plots may also be used as an indicator of segmentation quality. However, when outliers do exist such observation should be separately studied. For example, in Fig. 7(a)-(b), two samples of such outliers are presented. On further investigation, one observation showed the problem of lung hardening whilst the second observation was a patient with a collapse lung. A senior radiologist has confirmed that the lung hardening case has severe reticular pattern and pulmonary consolidation which are features of Interstitial Lung Disease (ILD). Henceforth outliers whilst suggesting lower segmentation quality may provide other useful information.

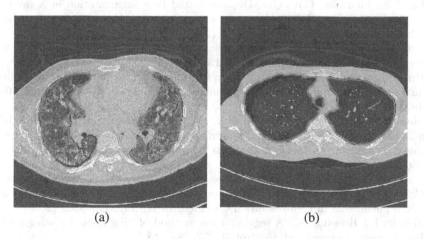

| (a) | (b) |

Fig. 7. Samples of outliers from regression curves (a) due to lung hardening and (b) due to collapse lung.

In summary, the simple regression model may be used as an indicator of segmentation quality while outliers provide useful information of the lung condition.

6   Conclusion

As a conclusion this study showed that the regression plot has managed to show the segmentation quality in detail when comparing five levels of diseased and normal lungs. The width of the prediction interval of the regression plot and outliers may in turn also provide supplementary information of the lung condition.

Acknowledgement. This research is funded by the Universiti Teknologi Malaysia Research University Grant: GUP QK130000.2540.06H35, and Ministry of Higher Education Malaysia and supported by Universiti Malaya.

References

1. Brown, M.S., Goldin, J.G., McNitt-Gray, M.F., Greaser, L.E., Sapra, A., Li, K.-T., Sayre, J.W., Martin, K., Aberle, D.R.: Knowledge-based segmentation of thoracic computed tomography images for assessment of split lung function. Med. Phys. **27**, 592–598 (2000)
2. Brown, M.S., McNitt-Gray, M.F., Mankovich, N.J., Goldin, J.G., Hiller, J., Wilson, L.S., Aberle, D.R.: Method for segmenting chest CT image data using an anatomical model: preliminary results. IEEE Trans. Med. Imaging. **16**, 828–839 (1997)
3. Armato, S.G., Sensakovic, W.F.: Automated lung segmentation for thoracic CT impact on computer-aided diagnosis. Acad. Radiol. **11**, 1011–1021 (2004)
4. Leader, J.K., Zheng, B., Rogers, R.M., Sciurba, F.C., Perez, A., Chapman, B.E., Patel, S., Fuhrman, C.R., Gur, D.: Automated lung segmentation in X-ray computed tomography: development and evaluation of a heuristic threshold-based scheme1. Acad. Radiol. **10**, 1224–1236 (2003)
5. Sun, X., Zhang, H., Duan, H.: 3D computerized segmentation of lung volume with computed tomography. Acad. Radiol. **13**, 670–677 (2006)
6. Hu, S., Hoffman, E.A., Reinhardt, J.M.: Automatic lung segmentation for accurate quantitation of volumetric X-ray CT images. IEEE Trans. Med. Imaging **20**(6), 490–498 (2001)
7. Massoptier, L., Misra, A., Sowmya, A.: Automatic lung segmentation in HRCT images with diffuse parenchymal lung disease using graph-cut. In: 24th International Conference on Image and Vision Computing New Zealand, IVCNZ09, pp. 266–270 (2009)
8. Korfiatis, P., Kalogeropoulou, C., Karahaliou, A., Kazantzi, A., Skiadopoulos, S., Costaridou, L.: Texture classification-based segmentation of lung affected by interstitial pneumonia in high-resolution CT. Med. Phys. **35**, 5290–5302 (2008)
9. Tobata, K., Hospital, K.: A segmentation method of lung areas by using snakes. Int. J. Innov. Comput. Inf. Control. **3**, 277–284 (2007)
10. Zhang, Y.: A review of recent evaluation methods for image segmentation. In: Proceedings of the 6th International Symposium on Signal Processing and its Applications, vol. 1, pp. 148–151 (2001)

11. Kazerooni, E.A., Martinez, F.J., Flint, A., Jamadar, D.A., Gross, B.H., Spizarny, D.L., Cascade, P.N., Whyte, R.I., Lynch, J.P., Toews, G., Lynch 3rd, J.P.: Thin-section CT obtained at 10-mm increments versus limited three-level thin-section CT for idiopathic pulmonary fibrosis: correlation with pathologic scoring. AJR. Am. J. Roentgenol. **169**, 977–983 (1997)

12. Chia, J., Than, M., Noor, N.M., Rijal, O.M., Yunus, A., Kassim, R.M., Chia, J., Noor, N.M., Rijal, O.M., Yunus, A., Kassim, R.M.: Lung segmentation for HRCT thorax images using radon transform and accumulating pixel width. In: 2014 IEEE Region 10 Symposium, pp. 157–161 (2014)

13. Heimann, T., van Ginneken, B., Styner, M.A., Arzhaeva, Y., Aurich, V., Bauer, C., Beck, A., Becker, C., Beichel, R., Bekes, G., Bello, F., Binnig, G., Bischof, H., Bornik, A., Cashman, P.M.M., Chi, Y., Cordova, A., Dawant, B.M., Fidrich, M., Furst, J.D., Furukawa, D., Grenacher, L., Hornegger, J., Kainmller, D., Kitney, R.I., Kobatake, H., Lamecker, H., Lange, T., Lee, J., Lennon, B., Li, R., Li, S., Meinzer, H.-P., Nemeth, G., Raicu, D.S., Rau, A.-M., van Rikxoort, E.M., Rousson, M., Rusko, L., Saddi, K.A., Schmidt, G., Seghers, D., Shimizu, A., Slagmolen, P., Sorantin, E., Soza, G., Susomboon, R., Waite, J.M., Wimmer, A., Wolf, I.: Comparison and evaluation of methods for liver segmentation from CT datasets. IEEE Trans. Med. Imaging **28**(8), 1251–1265 (2009)

14. Montgomery, D.C., Peck, E.A., Vining, G.G.: Introduction to Linear Regression Analysis. John Wiley Sons, New York (2012)

An Image Registration Method with Radial Feature Points Sampling: Application to Follow-Up CT Scans of a Solitary Pulmonary Nodule

Masaki Ishihara[✉], Yuji Matsuda, Masahiko Sugimura, Susumu Endo, Hiroaki Takebe, Takayuki Baba, and Yusuke Uehara

Fujitsu Laboratories Ltd., 1-1, Kamikodanaka 4-chome,
Nakahara-ku, Kawasaki 211-8588, Japan
{ishihara-masaki,matsuda-yuji,suginy,endou.susumu-02,
takebe.hiroaki,baba-t,yuehara}@jp.fujitsu.com

Abstract. In order to support radiologists' follow-up task of two CT scans captured in the past and in the present, we aimed to develop a system that displays both a region of interest (ROI) in one image selected by a radiologist and a corresponding ROI in another image. In this paper, we propose a registration method for the system. A typical registration method identifies several pairs of matched feature points (i.e., matching pairs) between two images within the range of a predefined distance from the ROI's center point (i.e., interest point) to correct a positional shift of an organ caused by heartbeats and breathing. However, low accuracy of registration is often observed because of biased distribution or a small number of matching pairs, depending on the sampling range. We developed a novel registration method that radially and evenly searches for several nearest matching pairs around the interest point and then estimates a translation vector at the interest point as a weighted average of these nearest pairs using a weighting factor based on its distance from the interest point. This method was based on the assumption that the transformation of an interest point work with the transformation of a near point since the lung is a continuum. The results of a comparative evaluation of the existing method and the proposed method on the basis of 15 cases showed that the accuracy of the proposed method was higher than that of the existing method in 13/15 cases. We analyzed the association between the accuracy and the range of sampling and found that the accuracy of the proposed method was similar to the best performance of the existing method with an ideal range of sampling the matching pairs. Finally, we showed evidence that the new method was reasonably consistent in terms of giving the best performance.

Keyword: Image registration

1 Introduction

It is important to monitor temporal changes in the solitary pulmonary nodule (SPN) to enable optimum diagnosis and follow-up treatment. Comparative

© Springer International Publishing Switzerland 2016
T. Bräunl et al. (Eds.): PSIVT 2015, LNCS 9431, pp. 512–525, 2016.
DOI: 10.1007/978-3-319-29451-3_41

reading of medical images by radiologists is indispensable. In this paper, the term 'tumor' is used to describe the SPN, and 'follow-up CT scans' is used to describe the comparative reading task.

It is now possible to visualize each tumor more distinctively through advances in X-ray Computed Tomography (CT) scanning equipment. Accordingly, along with the increase of medical images required for diagnosis, the burden of radiologists has become an issue. For radiologists to expedite diagnosis, computer aided diagnosis (CAD) systems are required. In this paper, we aim to develop a support system for radiologists' follow-up CT scans (such as that in Fig. 1) that satisfies the following requirements:

1. Display of multiple CT images side-by-side.
2. Display of close-up of both of a selected region by a radiologist and the corresponding region in another image.
3. No image deformation except translation and expansion.

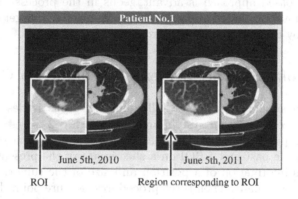

Fig. 1. A proposed support system for follow-up CT scans.

First requirement is needed to compare two CT images captured in the past and present in order to confirm the temporal change in tumor development. At this time, a positional shift of an organ occurs owing to heartbeats, breathing, and body position during CT scanning. For this reason, registration of the same tumor requires an understanding of temporal changes. Second requirement is needed to confirm in detail the change of the tumor and its surroundings. Therefore, the purpose of this paper is not registration of whole CT images, but registration of a region of interest (ROI) selected by the radiologist. Third requirement is needed since incorrect deformation impedes successful diagnosis. Hence, we are not concerned with the deformable image registration or the rigid registration which includes rotation. A simple method of rigid registration which includes translation and expansion in order to align a center of tumor is needed.

Since there are many types of lung cancer, efficient follow-up CT scans is needed. For this reason, we have chosen to target chest CT images. In the lung cancer screening, registration error should be less than 2.5 mm, since tumors larger than 2.5 mm in radius are considered therapeutic objectives [1]. Hence, we set the target of each registration error below 2.5 mm. In consideration of waiting time, processing time is required to be less than two seconds.

The image registration methods can be roughly divided into two approaches, the intensity based approach and the feature based approach [2]. In the intensity based approach [3,4], an image deformation that maximizes the similarity (like normalized cross correlation (NCC)) with iterative operation is computed. Therefore, convergence of iterative operations tends to take a long time. In the feature based approach [5,6], the method detects feature points from two images to be compared and extracts image descriptors in each feature point. Then, the method computes the correspondence of feature points (called a matching pair), which maximizes the similarity of descriptors. Finally, the method obtains a registration result using a matching pair. Xia et al. [5] used phase congruency, and Yang et al. [6] used a salient region as a feature point detector. They commonly used SIFT as a feature descriptor.

The feature based approach is advantageous in the processing speed compared with the intensity based approach. Thus, to meet the target of processing speed, we employ the feature based approach.

2   Outline of a Support System for Follow-Up CT Scans

An outline of a support system for follow-up CT scans is described in this chapter. The procedures of our system are shown in Fig. 2.

First of all, input data of our system are two series of CT images captured in the present and the past and a ROI on a slice image of the present CT images. The ROI means information of a position and size of the tumor, which a user needs to indicate manually. Then three procedures (feature point detection, feature description, and matching) are executed in sequence. As a result, matching pairs of images are obtained for each pair of the slice image of the present and one of several slice images of the past.

The system performs image alignment in two steps by using the obtained matching pairs. First, vertical (superior-inferior) alignment results in finding the slice image of the past corresponding to the slice image of the present. In vertical alignment, a slice image of the past that has the maximum similarity is searched for. Specifically, similarity between slice images is calculated as a number of matching pairs that have higher similarity than a threshold. Next, two-dimensional horizontal (left-right or anterior-posterior) alignment is achieved for two corresponding slice images of the present and the past from their matching pairs. This alignment results in finding a vector of parallel translation between the two images.

Finally, the system outputs the position and size of the region in the past CT images corresponding to the ROI in the present CT images. Our system can provide zooming views of these regions to a user as shown in Fig. 1.

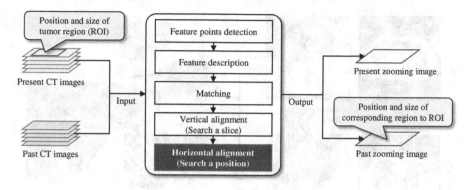

Fig. 2. System architecture of our system.

3   Existing Method of the Feature Based Image Registration and Its Problem

In this chapter, we show an existing method of the feature based image registration and its problem.

3.1   Existing Method of Feature Based Image Registration

In this paper, we define registration as obtaining a matching pair between an organ indicated by an interest point in one image and the same organ in another image. The interest point means a center point of a ROI selected by a radiologist. However, when the interest point is in a tumor, the detection of a matching pair often fails. Since there are temporal changes in the tissues between a pair of images, a matching pair of points is often not found.

Therefore, we assume that the matching pairs in the interest point can be estimated by interpolation of the other matching pairs of the feature points around the interest point [5]. On the basis of this assumption, our method selects several matching pairs of feature points in a sampling region centered at the interest point, and then aggregates these matching pairs as a vector, such as a mean vector (Fig. 3). In order to differentiate an estimated matching pair in the interest point from the other matching pairs around the interest point, we call this estimated relation a translation vector.

3.2   Problems of the Existing Method

In the pilot study, the performance of the existing method was evaluated with several sample cases described below. As a result, it was found that the registration error was 4.4 mm. This result means that the existing method was not acceptable since it did not satisfy the performance requirement (< 2.5 mm). The cause of the problem related to registration errors was analyzed. It was reasonable to suppose that the translation vector was obtained by aggregating several

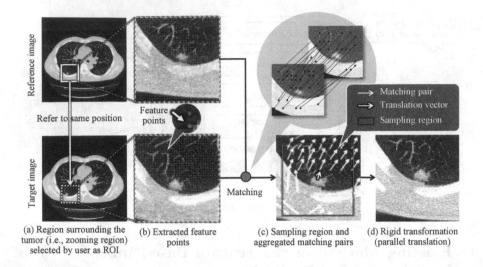

(a) Region surrounding the tumor (i.e., zooming region) selected by user as ROI

(b) Extracted feature points

(c) Sampling region and aggregated matching pairs

(d) Rigid transformation (parallel translation)

Fig. 3. Illustration of image registration based on feature points matching.

matching pairs in the sampling region, such as a rectangle or a circle range of a predefined distance from the interest point. When the obtained translation vector was applied to the registration of a user's selected region, several large errors could be observed depending on the region.

Several reasons for this registration error are described below. One of the reasons was noise errors due to matching pairs not being distributed equally in the lung region. In a similar way, these pairs were also not equally distributed in the sampling region. Therefore, if only a few matching pairs were extracted in the sampling region, the translation vector was susceptible to several incorrect pairs (i.e., noises) included in these pairs (Fig. 4(b)). Another reason was biased errors. If the distribution of the matching pairs in the sampling region was biased, the translation vector was dominantly influenced by several localized pairs (Fig. 4(c)).

These two errors resulted in a wrong translation vector, leading to the registration error. To estimate the correct translation vector, it was found suitable to sample and aggregate the matching pairs using the following two terms:

1. Sampling a sufficient number of matching pairs near the interest point.
2. Sampling evenly distributed matching pairs near the interest point.

4   Proposed Method

In this chapter, we propose a novel sampling method for matching pairs that is robust against bias distribution of the feature points around the interest point. First, regions in the lung that are suitable for feature point matching are explained in Sect. 4.1. Then, our proposed method is described in Sect. 4.2.

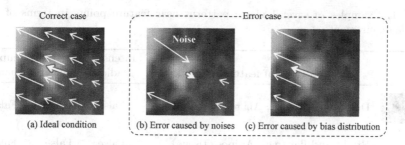

Fig. 4. Illustration of some problems of the basic method.

4.1   Selecting Feature Points

We here explain the method to extract feature points and match these points
between pairs of images. It is necessary to extract feature points as evenly and
minimally as possible, since the calculating cost for matching increases exponen-
tially with the number of these points. Therefore, these points are extracted at
regular intervals (i.e., dense sampling) in the range of a predefined distance from
the interest point. This will enable us to control the number and the distribution
of feature points. Moreover, several points that would obviously yield only low
similarity in the matching process must be eliminated from the candidates of
feature points, since these low similarity points often result in noise errors or
unfound pairs.

According to our early analysis, we can assume that a feature point suitable
for matching satisfies the following requirements:

1. There is a sharp contrast region near the feature point (i.e., characterized
   point by a pattern of luminance change).
2. There are few feature points similar to the feature point in the image (i.e.,
   matching error-resistant point).
3. The feature point does not change much temporally between two images
   captured in the past and present (i.e., the feature point can be extracted
   stably over time).

We show some examples of typical areas in CT scan images and summarize
the relationship between the areas and the above three requirements in Table 1. A
bright line in a dark region is acceptable for all of the requirements and indicates
horizontal vessels or bronchial tubes in a lung region on a slice image. In order
to extract these tissue regions, edge detection is first applied to a slice image. We
apply the Canny edge detector. Next, only points near the edge are extracted
from dense points, and the other points are eliminated. After extraction of feature
points, a luminance change pattern is extracted from each region near these
points as a local feature. We adopted a binary descriptor BRIEF [7] as the local
feature, which is used to calculate similarity in the matching process.

Table 1. Examples of several visual patterns near feature points in terms of each suitable requirement.

#	Visual patterns of feature point	Intensity gradient	Multiple similarity	Temporal change
1	Dark and flat (e.g., Air region in lung)	False	False	False
2	Bright and flat (e.g., Adipose tissue)	False	False	False
3	Local bright point in dark region (e.g., Vertical vessels or bronchial tubes)	**True**	False	False
4	Local dark point in bright region (e.g., Hole in adipose tissue)	**True**	False	False
5	Bright line in dark region (e.g., Horizontal vessels or bronchial tubes)	**True**	**True**	True

4.2   Sampling Matching Pairs

An important part of our proposed method is a sampling method. We supposed that the method of sampling matching pairs satisfied the 1st term as described in Sect. 3.2. Setting a large sampling region is reasonable in order to sample as many matching pairs as possible. However, if a translation vector is estimated from the large sampling region, the assumption that the matching pair of the interest point is identical to the aggregation of the other pairs in the region is not true. In this case, the translation vector averaged all of the pairs in this region, causing a registration error. We should consider that the transformation of the interest point works with the transformation of the near point since the lung is a continuum. Therefore, it is reasonable to assume that the translation vector should be strongly reflected by the pairs near the interest point. For example, we adopted a weighted average according to the distance from the interest point to the nearest feature point.

Next, we suppose that the method of sampling matching pairs satisfies the 2nd term as described previously. If two matching pairs are observed, a matching pair (i.e., a translation vector) of any point on the line through the two points is estimated by a linear interpolation. We can obtain the translation vector in the interest point by sampling at least two nearest matching pairs. One pair is in one direction and the other pair is in an opposite direction as viewed from the interest point. Ideally, if matching pairs in all directions viewed from the interest point are evenly sampled, the translation vector can be estimated precisely by these pairs.

Based on the above concept, we formulated a method for calculating the translation vector v_t:

$$\begin{cases} v_t = \sum_{i=0}^{N-1} v_i \cdot w_i \\ w_i = r_i^{-1} \left(\sum_{j=0}^{N-1} r_j^{-1} \right)^{-1} \end{cases} \qquad (1)$$

In this formulation, v_i indicates the nearest matching pair from the interest point and w_i indicates a weight for v_i. The weight w_i is the inverse of the distance r_i from the interest point to a source point of the nearest matching pair, and they are normalized from 0 to 1 (i.e., $\sum_{i=0}^{N-1} w_i = 1$). This formulation is defined in a polar coordinate system as the interest point is the origin. The upper bound of summation N is a predefined division number of the sampling region.

The sampling method of v_i is described in detail below. First, in a reference image, a radiologist selects a region for zooming and registration. The center point of the ROI is defined as the interest point (Fig. 5(a)). Next, feature points in the range of a predefined distance R_{max} from the interest point are detected and matched. After matching, matching pairs are obtained. The predefined distance is defined as the maximum range of motion of a lung. Next the exact region is radially and evenly divided to N sub-regions around the interest point (Fig. 5(b)). The nearest matching pairs v_i are sampled from each of these sub-regions (Fig. 5(c)). If v_i is not obtained in a sub-region, the v_i is not taken into formulation 1 (i.e., $v_i = 0, r_i^{-1} = 0$).

Based on the above procedure, we formulated a method for calculating the sampled matching pair v_i:

$$\left. \begin{array}{rl} \text{given} & N, R_{max} \\ \text{find} & v_i(r_i, \theta_i) \\ \text{that minimizes} & r_i \\ \text{subject to} & 0 \le r_i < R_{max}, \\ & \dfrac{2\pi}{N} i \le \theta_i < \dfrac{2\pi}{N}(i+1), \\ & i = 0, 1, \cdots, N-1 \end{array} \right\} \qquad (2)$$

The formulation 2 is defined in a two-dimensional polar plane for the purpose of illustration.

5   Experiments

To evaluate the performance, we compared registration errors by two methods. One is a method of estimating the translation vector using a fixed range sampling (called existing method); the other is our proposed method.

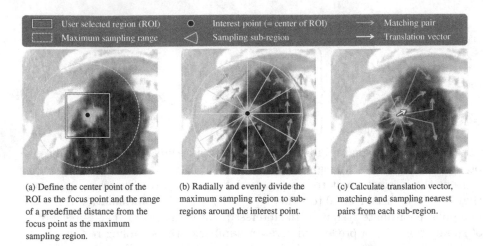

(a) Define the center point of the ROI as the focus point and the range of a predefined distance from the focus point as the maximum sampling region.

(b) Radially and evenly divide the maximum sampling region to sub-regions around the interest point.

(c) Calculate translation vector, matching and sampling nearest pairs from each sub-region.

Fig. 5. Illustration of the sampling algorithm of the proposed method.

5.1 Evaluation Data and Evaluation Method

Chest CT images of five lung cancer patients were used. Fifteen cases in total, consisting of three planes (axial, coronal, and sagittal) for each patient, were used. A case indicates a pair of CT image series, such as previous and current ones, for comparative reading. All cases included tumors in both images for comparison. Capture intervals between images could be several months to several years (about one year on average).

We assumed that a radiologist selects two slice images from two CT image series and selects a region surrounding the tumor as an ROI in a reference image (i.e., previous image). That is, the vertical alignment is done manually due to evaluate only performance of the horizontal alignment. Next, our system provided a zoom view of the regions in both the reference image and the target image (Fig. 1). The accuracy of the registration was evaluated for the local region in the target image corresponding to the ROI in the reference image. We applied feature based registration with the proposed method and the existing method to these CT images. On the assumption of actual usage, the interest point was set to the centroid of the tumor. Table 2 shows details of CT images and the parameters of our proposed method.

First, the original CT images are converted to 16-bit gray scale images. Then each slice image is generated by the maximum intensity projection (MIP) of ±10 slice images. Since MIP image provides the continuous structures such as the blood vessels or the bronchial tubes, the result of edges detection is effectively used for filtering the feature points. Note that before sampling of matching pairs, we applied a method for reducing noise pairs. First, we divided the image into blocks of fixed intervals (e.g., 12 × 12 pixels). We then aggregated these pairs in every block with a 2D histogram, consisting of a distance and an angle made by the matching pairs. The mode of each block was given from the 2D histogram.

We defined the mode as a matching pair. The ground truth for the experiment was obtained manually by registration of the centroid of the tumor on the basis of a radiologist's annotation. The registration error was evaluated using Euclidean distance between an estimated coordinate and a ground truth coordinate.

5.2   Experimental Results

Figure 6 shows registration errors by the existing method and by our proposed method. An average error is shown in the bar chart, and minimum and maximum errors are shown in the bar. In this experiment, the sampling range for the existing method was changed from 10 to 250 pixels at intervals of 10 pixels with the interest point in the center.

Our proposed method achieved lower registration error than the average error by the existing method in 13/15 cases. Moreover, in nine cases, our proposed method achieved a lower registration error than 2.5 mm, which is our target accuracy. The processing time of our proposed method was 0.7 s in total. The processing time of the existing method is similar to the time of our proposed method. The processing time includes 0.5 s for feature extraction and matching and 0.2 s for aggregation of matching pairs and image display. This processing speed satisfies the required performance. For this experiment, a Xeon 3.5 GHz machine with 8 GB RAM was used.

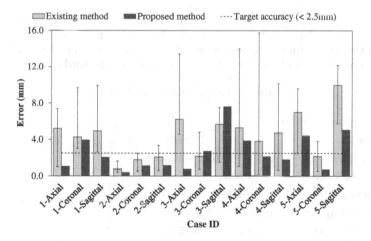

Fig. 6. Registration results of the proposed method and the existing method. The horizontal axis means case ID, and the vertical axis means registration errors. The dashed line means the upper limit of acceptable registration error (2.5 mm). The error bar means the registration error range of trials with gradually changed sampling regions. Therefore, the lower limit of error bar indicates the best performance, and the bar chart of existing method means the average of these trials.

5.3   Discussion

First of all, we discuss the availability of our proposed method. Figure 7 shows the registration errors of case ID 1-Axial, 1-Coronal, and 1-Sagittal by the existing method with varying sampling ranges. If the sampling range was narrow, the registration error tended to increase due to noises and deviations of the distribution of matching pairs. On the other hand, even if the sampling range was

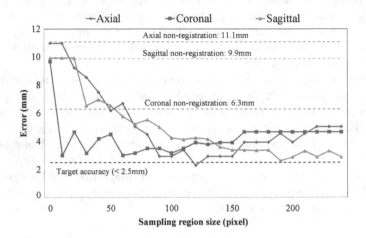

Fig. 7. The registration error of the existing method with varying sampling ranges in case ID 1-Axial, 1-Coronal and 1-Sagittal. The vertical axis shows the registration error and the horizontal one rectangle size of sampling range. The broken line shows the initial error of each plane and our target accuracy (< 2.5 mm).

Table 2. Experimental conditions.

A. Capture conditions	
Image size	512×512 pixels
Pixel spacing	0.781–0.625 mm/pixel
Slice thickness	1 mm
Patient position	Supine position
B. CT image reconstruction conditions	
Gray level range	16-bit (0–65,535)
Reconstruction method	Maximum intensity projection (± 10 slice images)
C. Feature point detection conditions	
Sampling method	Dense sampling (3×3 pixels)
Filtering points	Around edge and inside of ROI
D. Sampling matching pairs conditions	
Sampling range (radius)	40 pixels
Angle interval	30 degrees

wide, the registration error tended to increase due to loss of locality. Figure 7 exactly shows some problems of the existing method described as in Sect. 3.2. Thus, highly accurate registration required an optimal sampling range for the registration.

Table 3. Several sample images of cases 3-Axial and 3-Sagittal, and registration results of the proposed method and the existing method. The far-right images show several matching pairs (green thin arrows) and the translation vector (red bold arrow) obtained by the proposed method.

CaseID	(a)Nodule region image (50×50 pixels)		(b)Diff image between reference and registered target image (50×50 pixels)		(c)Sampling range and vectors
	Reference	Target	Existing	Proposed	
3-Axial					
3-Sagittal					

We compared the difference in the sampling range, which minimizes the registration error in each case. Each plane's histograms that aggregated the optimal sampling range in all cases are shown in Fig. 8. As seen in Fig. 8, there was no significant trend in the sampling range. The optimal sampling range depended on the case. As a result, we confirm that the performance of the proposed method in terms of automatically estimating the optimal sampling range is as good as that of the existing method.

Second, we discuss the advantages and disadvantages of our proposed method with several typical examples. The advantages are explained with case 3-Axial. As seen in Table 3(c) 3-Axial, the proposed method samples a wider range on the side of chest cavity than on the side of chest wall. There are not many vessels or bronchi as landmarks around the interest point in this case. Since the wide range of sampling on the side of chest cavity contributes to search for these landmarks, the registration performance of our proposed method is better than that of the existing method.

Next, the disadvantages are explained with case 3-Sagittal. As seen in Table 3(c) 3-Sagittal, there is mismatching pair that has a very different direction than the other sampled matching pairs. We also analyze other cases that did not achieve the target accuracy. As the result, we found that the mismatching often occurs at the area near the chest wall. Since the edge appears at the boundary of the lung, feature points are extracted in the proposed method. Features extracted from the boundary of the lung are similar to each other and cannot be obtained with unique correspondence. In case 3-Sagittal, we consider that the mismatching pair is strongly reflected in the translation vector since the interest point (i.e. the position of tumor) is near the chest wall.

To solve the problem of mismatching near the lung walls, it is assumed that the registration error is reduced using the corner point detector instead of the feature point near the edge. Thus, we consider integrating a corner point detector such as FAST [8]. In addition, the movable range of the organization within the lung due to heartbeat and breathing depends on the location [9]. Registration errors are expected to be reduced by limiting the range of feature matching using this knowledge.

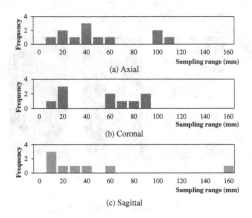

Fig. 8. The frequency of sampling ranges that minimize the registration error in each case. The interval of sampling range is set to 10 mm.

6   Conclusion

In order to support radiologists' follow-up task of two CT scans captured at two different time points, we aimed at developing a system that displays both the ROI in one image selected by a radiologist and the corresponding region for this particular ROI in another image. In this paper, we propose a registration method for the system.

A typical registration method identifies several pairs of matched feature points between two images to correct the positional shift of organs caused by heartbeat and breathing. To determine the vector for transformation of the ROI, the existing method samples several matching pairs in the range of a predefined distance from the interest point. However, low accuracy of registration is often observed due to biased distribution or a low number of matching pairs, depending on the sampling range.

We developed a novel registration method that radially and evenly searches for several nearest matching pairs around the interest point and subsequently estimates a translation vector at the interest point as a weighted average of these nearest pairs using a weighting factor based on its distance from the interest point. The results of comparative evaluation of the existing method and our proposed method using 15 cases showed that the accuracy of our proposed method was better than the accuracy of the existing method in the 13 cases, and the registration error in the nine cases was less than 2.5 mm, which is our target accuracy. We analyzed the association between the accuracy and the range of sampling, and found the accuracy of our proposed method was similar to the best performance of the existing method with an ideal sampling range. Finally, we showed that the proposed method was reasonably consistent in terms of giving a stable performance.

References

1. Guidelines for the management of pulmonary nodules detected by low-dose CT lung cancer screening version 3. The Japanese Society of CT Screening (2013)
2. Sotiras, A., Davatzikos, C., Paragios, N.: Deformable medical image registration: a survey. IEEE Trans. Med. Imaging **32**(7), 1153–1190 (2013)
3. Rueckert, D., Sonoda, L.I., Hayes, C., Hill, D.L.G., Leach, M.O., Hawkes, D.J.: Non-rigid registration using free-form deformations: application to breast MR images. IEEE Trans. Med. Imaging **18**(8), 712–721 (1999)
4. Werner, R., Hermann, S.: High accuracy optical flow for 3D medical image registration using the census cost function. In: Klette, R., Rivera, M., Satoh, S. (eds.) PSIVT 2013. LNCS, vol. 8333, pp. 23–35. Springer, Heidelberg (2014)
5. Xia, R., Zhao, J., Liu, Y.: A robust feature-based registration method of multimodal image using phase congruency and coherent point drift. In: MIPPR 2013: Pattern Recognition and Computer Vision, SPIE 8919, pp. 891903–891903-8 (2013)
6. Yang, J., Blum, R.S., Williams, J.P., Sun, Y., Xu, C.: Non-rigid image registration using geometric features and local salient region features. IEEE Comput. Soc. Conf. Comput. Vis. Pattern Recogn. **1**, 825–832 (2006)
7. Calonder, M., Lepetit, V., Ozuysal, M., Trzcinski, T., Strecha, C., Fua, P.: BRIEF: computing a local binary descriptor very fast. IEEE Trans. Pattern Anal. Mach. Intell. **34**(7), 1281–1298 (2012)
8. Rosten, E., Porter, R., Drummond, T.: FASTER and better: a machine learning approach to corner detection. IEEE Trans. Pattern Anal. Mach. Intell. **32**(1), 105–119 (2010)
9. Seppenwoolde, Y., Shirato, H., Kitamura, K., Shimizu, S., van Herk, M., Lebesque, J.V., Miyasaka, K.: Precise and real-time measurement of 3D tumor motion in lung due to breathing and heartbeat, measured during radiotherapy. Int. J. Radiat. Oncol. Biol. Phys. **53**(4), 822–834 (2002)

Object and Pattern Recognition

Time Consistent Estimation of End-Effectors from RGB-D Data

Xiao Lin[✉], Josep R. Casas, and Montse Pardás

Image Processing Group, Technical University of Catalonia (UPC), Barcelona, Spain
james.linxiao@gmail.com

Abstract. End-effectors are usually related to the location of the free end of a kinematic chain. Each of them contains rich structure information about the entity. Hence, estimating stable end-effectors of different entities enables robust tracking as well as a generic representation. In this paper, we present a system for end-effector estimation from RGB-D stream data. Instead of relying on a specific pose or configuration for initialization, we exploit time coherence without making any assumption with respect to the prior knowledge. This makes the estimation process more robust in a predict-update framework. Qualitative and quantitative experiments are performed against the reference method with promising results.

Keywords: End-effector estimation · Time coherence · Topology representation

1 Introduction

In recent years, Human Motion Analysis (HMA) has made great progress in constrained scenarios. It achieved remarkable results for pose estimation and gesture recognition with isolated human body data. But a large proportion of our visual experience involves analyzing the interactions between humans and objects. We use the term "entities" in this paper to refer to anything that we can model with a star-graph, including humans and objects, as illustrated in Fig. 1. This requires systems to be able to represent different entities in a generic way, which makes it a difficult problem because entities could vary greatly in appearance. Those variations arise not only from changes in illumination and viewpoint, but also due to non-rigid deformations and intra-class variability in shape and other visual properties.

Previous work for generic entity representation mainly focus on two different strategies. First, global representation is usually performed by extracting global features within a bounding box of the entity. This strategy is usually employed when spatial layouts of entity appearances are roughly rigid, such as faces or pedestrians at a distance. It has limited performance in complex scenes, as it highly relies on the extracted features to not only characterize different types of entities, but also cover the intra-class variability. The other way to achieve

© Springer International Publishing Switzerland 2016
T. Bräunl et al. (Eds.): PSIVT 2015, LNCS 9431, pp. 529–543, 2016.
DOI: 10.1007/978-3-319-29451-3_42

a generic representation is to represent the global structure of local descriptors/features of the entity, such as with a Deformable Part based Model (DPM). DPM shows its potential to be generic due to the loose constraints between the part representations. Several DPM based approaches [1,3,7] have proved their ability to represent different kinds of entities by customizing the model with different training data. Similarly, Wang *el al.* [15] take the detection results of a selective search approach [14] as candidates, and represent each candidate with the region-let feature which stands for spatial structure and appearance of some salient small regions. However, these approaches strongly rely on training data to learn the appearance models for the local patches and the spatial models for their global structure. Employing training in the entity representation process makes the model lose its generality to represent other objects except the trained one.

With the motivation of representing generic entities, we seek for the elemental factors among them, which will be of great importance when establishing a simple and more loosely structured generic model in the future. As shown in [10], end-effector is a common factor for both deformable entities and rigid entities (See the human body and chair shown in Fig. 1) while it only changes when the geometric structure of the entity changes, which makes it possible to represent generic entities. Hence, in this paper, we propose a novel way to estimate end-effectors of generic entities based on the topological representation of its 3D point cloud from RGB-D stream data. We exploit time coherence to make the estimation process more robust in a predict-update framework, instead of relying on a specific pose or configuration for initialization. Our contributions can be summarized in the following points:

- We propose a novel way to evaluate the correctness of being an end-effector based on a new approximation of its geodesic distance to the entity centroid.
- Estimating end-effectors without training and initialization provides the proposed system the potential to estimate end-effectors of generic entities in stream data.
- We introduce temporal information to facilitate the task of point cloud end-effector estimation, which makes the proposed system more robust to topology changes caused by occlusion and body part interaction.
- We avoid strongly relying on the previous information and initialization, which provides the system the ability to recover from estimation errors.

In the rest of the paper, we first review the related work in Sect. 2. Then, the input data and preprocessing steps are described in Sect. 3. In Sect. 4, we present a single frame end-effector estimation approach, in which the point cloud is topologically organized into different bands. End-effectors are estimated by analyzing the point cloud topology from its band-based representation. This topology is sometimes not reliable because of the presence of occlusion and parts interaction, which will probably change the topology of the point cloud. Therefore, in Sect. 5, we analyze the end-effector estimation process along time and propose a time coherence guided end-effector estimation approach to address the above mentioned problems. Finally, Sect. 6 shows the quantitative and qualitative experiment results of the proposed method.

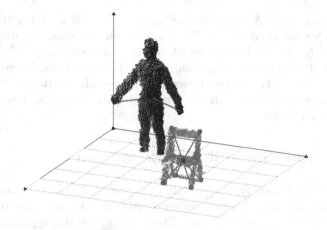

Fig. 1. Different entities represented by end-effectors

2   Related Work

End-effector estimation from RGB-D data is currently an open task as a result of the increasing performance of consumer depth sensors. Baak *el al.* [2] construct a weighted graph for point cloud data by taking each point on the point cloud as a graph node and exploiting the neighborhood structures in the pixel domain to build edges between them. Then, edges are weighted as the Euclidean distances between connected node pairs. End-effectors are searched as the extrema with respect to the centroid of the point cloud using Dijkstra's algorithm. Suau *el al.* [13] employ a level set method in RGB-D data to exploit connectivities over the depth surface in order to extract a topological representation of point clouds. But these two approaches are not effective in solving the problem when deformable entities change the topology of the graph, in which case the detected extrema may not correspond to the position of the end effectors. Schwarz *el al.* [11] propose to use optical flow to handle the topology change problem. Similar to [2], a graph is constructed to represent the topology of the point cloud. Then motion information is employed to disambiguate body parts when occlusion and body part attachment (that is, when end effectors are connected to other body parts) occur. However, they introduce a human body structure in order to segment body parts and rebuild the graph, which makes the model not generic to estimate end-effectors for other entities. Besides, it requires an initialization to start the algorithm by requesting a T-pose at the beginning, which also makes it difficult to recover from the tracking errors.

3   Input Data

A consumer depth sensor provides RGB-D data at video frame rates by analyzing a speckle pattern of infrared light. It captures color and relatively accurate depth data at the same time. A depth image $I_{depth} : Z^2 \to R$ contains the distance $d \in R$ for each pixel position $p \in Z^2$. Thus, given the camera parameters, we can transform the per-pixel distances into a 3D point cloud $C_I \subseteq R^3$. It contains both foreground points and background points. To extract the foreground point cloud $C_{fg} \subseteq R^3$ from the scene, a group of thresholds restricting the activity area in 3D space are involved. In the proposed system, we take the foreground point cloud as input data.

4   Single Frame End-Effector Estimation

An end-effector is defined as the free end of a kinematic chain. Estimating end-effectors for 3D point cloud data requires representing the topology of the point cloud with a well organized structure. Thus, we exploit the approach proposed in [13] to describe the topology of point clouds. Then, a new strategy proposed in [2] for searching the end-effectors from its topology representation is integrated into the proposed system, providing a better performance than the strategy used in [13].

4.1   Point Cloud Topology Description

Geometric Deformable Models (GDMs) [5,8] have proved performance and flexibility on describing topology. They are based on the theory of curve evolution and level set methods [12]. Its basic idea is to evolve the initial contour on the data domain according to predefined internal and external forces. Internal forces lead the actual contour curve to expand itself while keeping its smoothness. External forces are modeled from the data and work against internal forces by countering the curve expansion, which actually makes the contour curve evolve along the topology of the data.

Following the work in [13], the external forces in the proposed system come from the foreground point cloud data $C_{fg} = \{x_i\} \subseteq R^3$ obtained in the previous step. The internal forces are defined as the expansion power. Let $\phi(x, t) : R^3 \to R$ be a level set function which provides an implicit representation of the evolving curve at time t. Let $curve(t)$ be the contour curve as the zero level set of $\phi(x, t)$, and $L_t^0 \subset C_{fg}$ is the subset enclosed by $curve(t)$. The objective is to make $curve(t)$ evolve over C_{fg} while preserving the topological properties of the point cloud data. The way to evolve it from time t to $t+1$ is to expand and include a set of new points regarding the previous level set L_t^0, under the constraints of both proximity and density. Specifically, it is formulated as:

$$L_{t+1} = \{x_i\} \quad if \quad \phi(x_i, t) < \delta_L \quad and \quad \rho(x_i)$$
$$L_{t+1}^0 = L_t^0 \cup L_{t+1} \tag{1}$$

where,

$$\phi(x, t) = \begin{cases} 0 & \forall x \in L_t^0 \\ min(dist_E(x, curve(t))) & \forall x \notin L_t^0 \end{cases} \tag{2}$$

$$\rho(x) = \begin{cases} True & if \quad Num(x, \delta_L) >= \eta_L \\ False & if \quad Num(x, \delta_L) < \eta_L \end{cases} \quad (3)$$

L_{t+1} stands for the set of new points included at time $t+1$ which is called narrow band. The proximity constraint limits the Euclidean distance from points in L_{t+1} shorter than δ_L, and the density constraint is performed by requiring the number of its neighbor points within a ball area of radius δ_L larger than η_L. To complete the formulation, we should define how the contour curve is updated in the sense of point cloud data:

$$curve(t) = \{x_i\} \quad if \begin{cases} x_i \in L_{t+1} \\ \phi(x_i, t) \in [\frac{3}{4}\delta_L, \delta_L] \end{cases} \quad (4)$$

The contour curve at time t is defined as the points which are farther from the previous zero level set. Therefore, the foreground point cloud C_{fg} will be organized into bands at different levels by iterating through Eqs. (1)–(4) from an initial level set L_0^0. Figure 2 shows an example of this process. Narrow bands cover the foreground point cloud, organizing its topology into different bands. However, a band may contain points belonging to different context (e.g. different arms of a human body). To address this, each band L_k is separated into sub-bands with respect to a constraint on the maximal number of points in a sub-band.

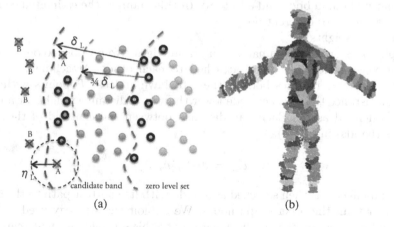

(a)   (b)

Fig. 2. Curve evolution. (a) The green points are the actual zero level set L_t^0, and those with a thick black boundary form $curve(t)$. The blue points are the organized band L_{t+1}, with the $curve(t + 1)$ also marked with thick boundary. Orange points A are rejected to be included in L_{t+1}^0 because of the density constraint. Orange points B are rejected to be included in L_{t+1}^0 because of proximity constraint. (b) An example of a body topology representation, different colors stands for different sub-bands. (Fig. 2(a) is extracted from [13]) (Color figure online)

4.2   Estimating End-Effectors in a Topologically Weighted Graph

The sub-bands obtained in the previous step belong to visible surfaces of the analyzed entity, which also implicitly provides the approximate topology information about its point cloud (See Fig. 2(b)). To utilize these context-wise sub-bands and estimate the end-effectors of a point cloud, we construct a graph based on these sub-bands. The following three points should be considered when constructing the graph:

– Graph nodes
  In this topological graph, the centroid of each sub-band is taken as a graph node.
– Graph root
  As introduced in the second paragraph of Sect. 4.1, an initial zero level set L_0^0 is needed as a starting point in the topology description procedure. Such an origin set is treated as the graph root. The graph root could be a single 3D point or a set of points, depending on the application. In the case of human body, we propose to compute the centroid of the point cloud, and start with the point which has the shortest Euclidean distance to the centroid as a rough initial zero level set and obtain a rough band structure. Then, we use a partition of the point cloud which is composed of the first N level of bands to compute the centroid again. N stands for the size of the massive part of an entity (e.g. N is related to the size of torso in the application of estimating human body end-effectors). In this manner, the estimated centroid is more robust to different poses.
– Edges and weights
  Graph nodes are linked in pairs with graph edges. We propose to only include those edges which link nodes attached to each other. Attachment between node n_i and n_j requires both of them to have at least P points with their closest distance to the other node lower than λ. A distance weight for an edge $w_{i,j}$ is defined as the Euclidean distance between the centroid of these two nodes (bands) in Eq. (5):

$$w_{i,j} = dist_E(n_i, n_j) \tag{5}$$

An end-effector is then searched as a node with its shortest path to the graph root longer than the other graph nodes. We exploit the strategy used in [2] to detect end-effectors on the graph. According to this strategy, we first search the node with the longest shortest path to the target node which is set to be the graph root initially. Then we add edges with zero weight between each node on this path and the target node on the graph and update the target node to the previous detected end-effector. These operations are performed iteratively till the estimated end-effector has the geodesic distance lower than a threshold g. This strategy favours possible end-effectors on the opposite side of the previous detected one while avoiding shortcuts of neighbors.

The geodesic distance of an end-effector is then calculated as the sum of all weights of the included edges on its path to the graph root:

$$dist_G(e_t) = \sum^{edge(i,j) \in path} w_{i,j} \qquad (6)$$

5 Temporal Coherence Guided End-Effector Estimation

For end-effectors extracted by analyzing the topology of a point cloud, one obvious weakness is that the estimation result will be changed with the dynamic changes in the topology due to motion. The main reasons for topology changes are listed below:

- Occlusion
  In this case, part of the surface of the entity is occluded by the occluder (*e.g.* arms of human body), which results in an incomplete point cloud. This is even worse when the auto-occlusions separate naturally connected entity parts.
- Parts interaction
  Articulated entities such as human body deform by moving the rigid parts connected to the articulations. These deformations could lead to interactions between parts like merge and split. For example, the hands are not extremes of a human body when both arms attach tightly to the torso.

End-effectors can only be correctly detected for certain topological configurations of the point cloud. However, once detected, they can be tracked in order to extract the stable configurations that can be used in higher level applications. Therefore, we propose to make use of the temporal information between frames when dealing with the task of end-effector estimation from RGB-D streams data in order not to lose them when the topology changes. We favor the natural detection of end-effectors, but if one was there and has suddenly disappeared (because, for instance, a hand touched the body), we exploit temporal coherence to search back for the end effector and predict its position in the current frame. This introduces the end-effector estimation task into a predict-update framework. The purpose is to guide the single frame based end-effector estimation with temporal information, but only when needed, so that we do not rely much on temporal prediction. This strategy will avoid initialization and make the system flexible enough to escape from tracking errors.

5.1 Predict Phase

The end-effectors detected at a given frame are projected into the next frame, in order to maintain the stability of the detection along time. Let $E_t = \left\{ e_t^1 ... e_t^{M_t} \right\} \subseteq R^3$ be the end-effector set at time t, M_t be the number of end-effectors estimated. Then a dynamic model is defined as $E_{t+1}^{pr} = Dnc(E_t, \theta_t)$, in which E_{t+1}^{pr} stands for the end-effector predictions of E_t, θ_t is the parameter of the dynamic model at time t. We use a motion estimation technique to compute the velocity of each end-effector from time t to $t + 1$ based on color images $\{I^t_{color}, I^{t+1}_{color}\} = \theta_t$. Specifically, forward optical flow is computed using Large Displacement Optical Flow (LDOF) [4]. The obtained optical flow is back-projected from the image plane to the 3D space using depth information and the camera parameters to obtain 3D scene flow in the real world. Consequently, the dynamic model $Dnc(E_t, \theta_t)$ propagates the previous end-effectors estimation to the current frame by using the velocity information in the scene flow.

5.2   Update Phase

We take the end-effectors in E^{pr}_{t+1} obtained in the previous step as a set of end-effector candidates for the current frame. Another set of end-effector candidate E^{est}_{t+1} is estimated locally by analyzing the topology of the current point cloud as explained in Sect. 3. The final end-effectors E_{t+1} will be generated within these two sets of candidates. In order to select the best end-effectors, we propose to establish one-to-one correspondences between elements in E^{pr}_{t+1} and E^{est}_{t+1} so that we can compare each pair of them based on a selection rule and generate the final end-effectors.

End-Effector Correspondence Assignment. To establish the correspondence, we represent the end-effector candidates with features and compute the similarity in the feature space. These features may contain different information such as 3D position, color, local 3D shape etc. In our experiments, we just use the 3D position as the feature for the end-effector candidates and we define the similarity according to the geodesic distance between them with respect to the topologically weighted graph constructed in current frame, which is inversely proportional to the geodesic distance. Note that the position of predicted end-effector candidates are rectified as the closest point on the current point cloud in order to compute the geodesic distance in the current frame. As E^{pr}_{t+1} and E^{est}_{t+1} are two disjoint sets, we construct a weighted bipartite graph by adding all possible edges connecting one vertex in E^{pr}_{t+1} and one in E^{est}_{t+1} and weighting them with similarities. Then, assigning the correspondence between end-effector candidates in E^{pr}_{t+1} and E^{est}_{t+1} is converted to a maximum weighted bipartite graph matching problem. We employ the Hungarian algorithm [6] to solve it.

Evaluate the End-Effector Candidates. Once the correspondence is established, we need to evaluate the proposed candidates in order to generate the final end-effectors. When we obtain an end-effector with a large geodesic distance to the centroid, we are in a pose which strongly hints at the actual presence of an end-effector, and that is where we can rely on, in the end-effector estimation. However, the geodesic distance calculated based on the full shortest path is sensitive to occlusions. Figure 3(a) shows an occluded area on the torso, in which the black line stands for the full shortest path between an end-effector to the graph root and the red line is the approximated path. The occlusion leads to a longer estimated geodesic distance for the end effector candidate placed on the head. Thus, to make it more robust to occlusions, we propose to approximate the shortest path by just taking into account a mid-band in that shortest path when calculating the geodesic distance. Specifically, the approximated geodesic distance for an end-effector candidate estimated at frame t is formulated as the summation of two parts of Euclidean distance:

$$dist_G^{ap}(e_t^i) = dist_E(e_t^i, mid) + dist_E(mid, L_0^0) \tag{7}$$

where mid stands for the mid-band of the shortest path from end-effector candidate e_t^i to the centroid. For the predicted end-effector candidates, since they are not an extrema estimated in the current frame, their distance is assimilated to the approximated geodesic distance in the previous frame. Then, the approximated geodesic distance of an end-effector candidate is calculated for the comparison. The comparison is performed depending on different situations. According to the similarity between a pair of corresponding end-effector candidates, we categorize them into three cases:

- Case A: Related pair. It stands for corresponding candidates with similarity higher than a predefined threshold ε_a.
- Case B: Unrelated pair. It represents corresponding candidates with similarity larger than ε_b but lower than ε_a, which means the corresponding candidates are not the same end-effector although they were matched in the previous step. Threshold ε_b is set to filter out some extreme cases, such as when both of the two matched candidates are valid end-effectors. In this case, as the geodesic distance between two valid end-effectors $dist_G(e_1, e_2)$ is normally larger than the geodesic distance from each of them to the centroid ($dist_G(e_1)$ and $dist_G(e_2)$), we set ε_b with respect to larger one between $dist_G(e_1)$ and $dist_G(e_2)$.
- Case C: Unmatched candidate. As there may be new end-effectors detected in the current frame or tracked end-effectors that do not correspond to any extrema in the current frame, the number of candidates in E_{t+1}^{est} and E_{t+1}^{pr} may not be the same. Thus, there will be candidates which have no correspondence with any other candidates which we call unmatched candidates. Some matched pairs with similarity lower than ε_b are also included as unmatched candidates.

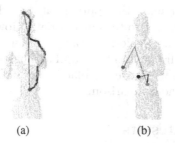

(a)   (b)

Fig. 3. (a) Approximate geodesic path with mid-band. (b) Benefit of geodesic distance updating.

End-Effector Selection and Geodesic Distance Update. Final end-effectors are selected from the end-effector candidates depending on the above mentioned three cases. In cases A and B, we take the end-effector candidate with the longest geodesic distance as a final end-effector. In case C, the candidate will be kept as an end-effector, for a maximum of T frames. If it is not matched (thus becoming case A or B) during these frames, it will be removed. Thus, we can preserve the possibility of tracking correct estimations while avoiding permanent errors.

Finally, we update the geodesic distance of the selected end-effectors by considering both previous and current information according to Eq. (8).

$$dist_G^{ap}(e_{t+1}) = \begin{cases} \alpha \times dist_G^{ap}(e_t) + (1 - \alpha) \times dist_G^{ap}(e_{t+1}^{pr}) \ if \ \ e_t \in E_{t+1}^{pr} \\ dist_G^{ap}(e_{t+1}^{est}) \ \ if \ \ e_t \in E_{t+1}^{est} \end{cases} \quad (8)$$

where the updated geodesic distance of the final end-effector e_{t+1} is defined as the weighted sum of its geodesic distance in frame t and the geodesic distance of its prediction in frame $t + 1$ if this end-effector is from E_{t+1}^{pr}. Otherwise, it is equal to its geodesic distance in frame $t + 1$, as it is newly detected. These end-effectors are treated as the final estimation which will be predicted to the next frame when we process frame $t + 2$. The weight used in Eq. (8) is defined as:

$$\alpha = \sigma^k \quad (9)$$

where k is the number of frames that this end effector has not been related with any end-effector candidate in current estimation (cases B and C). $\sigma \in [0, 1]$ is a penalty factor.

Geodesic distance updating ensures that the proposed method is capable to memorize the occurrence of tracked end-effectors and their geodesic distances at that time while not totally relying on it, which reduces the risk of getting stuck with errors in previous information. Figure 3(b) shows an example of how the proposed system benefits from geodesic distance updating, in which the red point stands for an end-effector candidate estimated from the current data and the black point represents its corresponding candidate in E_{t+1}^{pr}. The black point indicates the correct end-effector position while not being detected from the current frame as both arms attach to the torso. The topology changes caused by body part attachment also make the approximated geodesic distance of the black candidate shorter with respect to the current data. However, as the black candidate is correctly tracked, its geodesic distance, rather than its geodesic distance calculated in the current frame, has been updated based on its information from the motion history, which will leave the black point with the correct end-effector position be favoured in the comparison.

6   Experimental Results

We have evaluated our end-effector estimation approach for a human body end-effector estimation application. Berkely Multimodal Human Action Database

(MHAD) [9] is employed as the benchmark data set, in which eleven different actions are performed in an indoor scenario and captured by two Kinects. These two Kinects are placed diagonally with respect to the subject. In our experiments, we use the RGB-D stream data from the front Kinect. It has been calibrated in advance and the calibration parameters are available in the database. Each frame of the stream for both depth and color image is 640×480 pixels. In the rest of this section, we present the quantitative and qualitative results of the proposed approach while comparing it with the Restricted Narrow Band Level Set (R-NBLS) approach proposed in [13].

6.1   Quantitative Results

We select seven actions in the data base without human object interactions as the quantitative experiment data. Since all the actions are performed five times, we use the first two repetitions in each action sequence, which yields around 70 frames per sequence. We manually marked all the end-effectors for the selected sequences as the ground truth.

We consider that an estimated end-effector is a true positive if it is within a distance threshold with respect to the ground truth. A threshold of 15 cm has been used in the experiments presented in this paper. Three metrics including recall, average distance error and false positive rate are defined as:

$$Recall_t = M_t^{TP}/M_{human} \tag{10}$$

$$\bar{\epsilon}_t = \frac{1}{M_{TP}} \sum_{i=1}^{M_{TP}} dist_E(TP_t^i - GT_t^i) \tag{11}$$

$$FPR_t = M_t^{FP}/M_t \tag{12}$$

We denote the true positive end-effector estimation result at time t as set TP_t and false positive as set FP_t. In Eq. (10), M_t^{TP} represents the number of correctly estimated end-effectors at time t and M_{human} is a constant number which stands for the natural number of end-effectors of human body. In Eq. (11), we calculate the average Euclidean distance error between end-effector TP_t^i in TP_t and its corresponding ground truth GT_t^i. In Eq. (12), M_t^{FP} stands for the number of end-effectors in FP_t and M_t is the number of estimated end-effectors at time t.

By considering the presence of significant occlusions, we divide the test sequences into two groups. The first group contains four actions without significant occlusions: *jumping in place, jumping jack, waving two hands, waving one hand*. The second group consists of three actions with significant occlusions: *bending, punching, clapping*. In Figs. 4, 5 and 6(a), we compare the proposed approach with R-NBLS by evaluating the recall of each frame in the test sequences and average recall of each sequence. The results of the proposed approach and R-NBLS are marked in red and black respectively. Figure 4 shows the results of the first group. In these four sequences, the proposed method keeps tracking the end-effectors detected in the history while comparing them with the current estimations, which yields the continuity in end-effector estimation. This is illustrated in all the sequences as we achieve consistently better results than R-NBLS. Especially in Fig. 4(a), it is clearly showed that the proposed approach memorizes the presence of end-effectors in the history and continuously detects them in the future. Note that the memory for an occurred end-effector could be also dropped when we lose track of it, see $29th$ frame in Fig. 4(b) or $46th$ frame in Fig. 4(c). Figure 5 shows the result of the second group. In these three sequences, there is more noise in the current estimations as significant occlusions caused by the three actions change the topology of the point cloud very often. Besides, end-effectors might not be always visible due to significant occlusions. The results show the robustness of the proposed approach with respect to noisy current estimations. Figure 6(a) presents average recall of each sequence, which results in an overall 91.3 % recall compared to 82.1 % from R-NBLS. We also compute the average distance error for all the sequences as a secondary metrics in Fig. 6(b). It shows that the proposed approach has 7.5 cm average distance error over all the test sequences compared to 7.6 cm of R-NBLS.

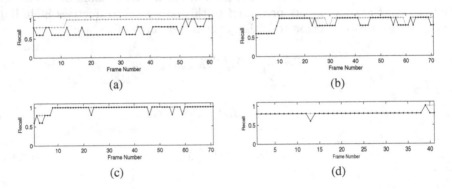

Fig. 4. (a) Jump1 (Jumping in place). (b) Jump2 (Jumping jacks). (c) Wave hand1 (Waving two hands). (d) Wave hand2 (Waving one hand). Black: R-NBLS approach [13]. Red: the proposed approach (Color figure online).

The false positive end-effectors will affect the representation of entities in the future. Thus we also evaluate the False Positive Rate (FPR) in the experiments. As shown in Fig. 6(c), the proposed approach (bars in red) has all the FP rates lower than 4 %.

6.2   Qualitative Result

In Sect. 6.1, we compared quantitatively the performance of the proposed method with R-NBLS. To further analyze them, several example results are discussed in this section.

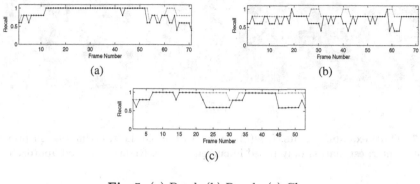

Fig. 5. (a) Bend. (b) Punch. (c) Clap.

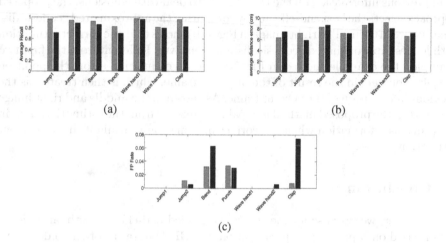

Fig. 6. (a) Average recall for all the test sequences. (b) Average distance error for all the test sequences. (c) False positive rate for all the test sequences (Color figure online).

Figure 7(a) shows three examples of estimation result. In each example, the left image is the estimation result in the previous frame, the image in the middle shows end-effectors estimated just based on the current frame and the right image shows the result of the proposed approach. All the end-effectors are marked in red in this group of figures.

Figure 7(a) presents an estimation result in punching sequence. We can see that the temporal information affects the estimation results by tracking the point in the previous frame and keeping the tracked point when we fail to detect it in the current frame. Figure 7(b) shows the results of a clapping sequence. End-effectors are well estimated in the previous frames while collision occurs in the current frame. Once both hands attach to each other, two end-effectors on both hands are combined into one and a new end-effector on the right shoulder is detected based on the current information. This constitutes an unrelated pair between the newly born end-effector candidate on the shoulder and the end-effector candidate predicted

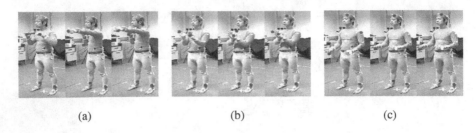

(a)   (b)   (c)

Fig. 7. Three example results: (a)–(c). In each example, Left: estimation in previous frame, Center: estimation only based in current frame, Right: proposed approach.

from previous information on the right hand. To deal with collisions, the proposed approach selects the best end-effector by comparing the approximated geodesic distance between them. The right image in Fig. 7(b) shows that the correct estimation with longest approximated geodesic distance survives. Different from the first two examples, the example showed in Fig. 7(c) has an estimation error (the point on the left shoulder) in the result of the previous frame, which is then treated as the previous information of the current frame. As shown in the middle and right image in Fig. 7(c), the proposed method is capable to recover from the estimation error in the previous information when the correct information is available in the current estimation.

7   Conclusion

In this paper, we propose a time coherence guided end-effector estimation algorithm based on topological representation of RGB-D data. In order to deal with the estimation error caused by topology changes, we employed time coherence by integrating single frame estimation with previous information in a predict-update framework while avoiding strongly relying on it. Therefore, the proposed approach does not require any initialization or prior knowledge about the structure of the entity, which provides the ability to recover from estimation errors and the generality to estimate end-effectors for different entities. In our experiments, we proved that the proposed approach provides robustness for end-effector estimation, with its results outperforming the method in [13] in recall and average false positive rate while achieving similar results in terms of average distance error.

Acknowledgement. This work has been developed in the framework of the project TEC2013-43935-R, financed by the Spanish Ministerio de Economa y Competitividad and the European Regional Development Fund (ERDF).

References

1. Laptev, I., Azizpour, H.: Object detection using strongly-supervised deformable part models. In: Fitzgibbon, A., Lazebnik, S., Perona, P., Sato, Y., Schmid, C. (eds.) ECCV 2012, Part I. LNCS, vol. 7572, pp. 836–849. Springer, Heidelberg (2012)
2. Baak, A., Müller, M., Bharaj, G., Seidel, H., Theobalt, C.: A data-driven approach for real-time full body pose reconstruction from a depth camera. In: Fossati, A., Gall, J., Grabner, H., Ren, X., Konolige, K. (eds.) Consumer Depth Cameras for Computer Vision, pp. 71–98. Springer, London (2013)
3. Bergtholdt, M., Kappes, J., Schmidt, S., Schnörr, C.: A study of parts-based object class detection using complete graphs. Int. J. Comput. Vis. **87**(1–2), 93–117 (2010)
4. Brox, T., Malik, J.: Large displacement optical flow: descriptor matching in variational motion estimation. IEEE Trans. Pattern Anal. Mach. Intell. **33**(3), 500–513 (2011)
5. Caselles, V., Catté, F., Coll, T., Dibos, F.: A geometric model for active contours in image processing. Numer. Math. **66**(1), 1–31 (1993)
6. Kuhn, H.W.: The hungarian method for the assignment problem. Naval Res. Logistics Q. **2**(1–2), 83–97 (1955)
7. Li, J.L., Hao, S., Lim, Y.W., Li, F.F.: Object bank: an object-level image representation for high-level visual recognition. Int. J. Comput. Vis. **107**(1), 20–39 (2014)
8. Malladi, R., Sethian, J.A., Vemuri, B.C.: Shape modeling with front propagation: a level set approach. IEEE Trans. Pattern Anal. Mach. Intell. **17**(2), 158–175 (1995)
9. Ofli, F., Chaudhry, R., Kurillo, G., Vidal, R., Bajcsy, R.: Berkeley mhad: a comprehensive multimodal human action database. In: 2013 IEEE Workshop on Applications of Computer Vision (WACV), pp. 53–60. IEEE (2013)
10. Plagemann, C., Ganapathi, V., Koller, D., Thrun, S.: Real-time identification and localization of body parts from depth images. In: 2010 IEEE International Conference on Robotics and Automation (ICRA), pp. 3108–3113. IEEE (2010)
11. Schwarz, L.A., Mkhitaryan, A., Mateus, D., Navab, N.: Human skeleton tracking from depth data using geodesic distances and optical flow. Image Vis. Comput. **30**(3), 217–226 (2012)
12. Sethian, J.A.: Level set methods and fast marching methods: evolving interfaces in computational geometry, fluid mechanics, computer vision, and materials science, vol. 3. Cambridge University Press (1999)
13. Suau, X., Hidalgo, J.R., Casas, J.R.: Detecting end-effectors on 2.5 d data using geometric deformable models: application to human pose estimation. Comput. Vis. Image Underst. **117**(3), 281–288 (2013)
14. Sande, K., Uijlings, J., Gevers, T., Smeulders, A.: Segmentation as selective search for object recognition. In: 2011 IEEE International Conference on Computer Vision (ICCV), pp. 1879–1886. IEEE (2011)
15. Wang, X.Y., Yang, M., Zhu, S.H., Lin, Y.Q.: Regionlets for generic object detection. In: 2013 IEEE International Conference on Computer Vision (ICCV), pp. 17–24. IEEE (2013)

Volume-Based Semantic Labeling with Signed Distance Functions

Tommaso Cavallari$^{(\boxtimes)}$ and Luigi Di Stefano

Department of Computer Science and Engineering,
University of Bologna, Bologna, Italy
{tommaso.cavallari,luigi.distefano}@unibo.it

Abstract. Research works on the two topics of Semantic Segmentation and SLAM (Simultaneous Localization and Mapping) have been following separate tracks. Here, we link them quite tightly by delineating a category label fusion technique that allows for embedding semantic information into the dense map created by a volume-based SLAM algorithm such as KinectFusion. Accordingly, our approach is the first to provide a semantically labeled dense reconstruction of the environment from a stream of RGB-D images. We validate our proposal using a publicly available semantically annotated RGB-D dataset and (a) employing ground truth labels, (b) corrupting such annotations with synthetic noise, (c) deploying a state of the art semantic segmentation algorithm based on Convolutional Neural Networks.

1 Introduction

In the last years the Computer Vision community renewed its interest in the task of Simultaneous Localization and Mapping by leveraging on RGB-D information. This research trend has been fostered by the development of ever cheaper sensors as well as by the more and more ubiquitous presence of smart mobile platforms, possibly having such sensors on board. Many works tackled issues related to reliable camera tracking, accurate mapping, scalable world representation, efficient sensor relocalization, loop closure detection, map optimization. A major breakthrough in the realm of RGB-D SLAM was achieved by the KinectFusion algorithm [11], which firstly demonstrated real-time and accurate dense surface mapping and camera tracking.

On separate tracks, researchers working on object detection and semantic segmentation proposed many interesting techniques to extract high-level knowledge from images by recognition of object instances or categories and subsequent region labeling. Especially thanks to the recent developments in the field of deep convolutional neural networks, year after year, new benchmark-beating algorithms are proposed that enable to quickly process raw images and extract from them valuable semantic information.

However, just a few works have tried to draw a bridge between the two aforementioned fields, though we believe that both research areas could benefit significantly from tighter integration. Indeed, a SLAM process may be improved

© Springer International Publishing Switzerland 2016
T. Bräunl et al. (Eds.): PSIVT 2015, LNCS 9431, pp. 544–556, 2016.
DOI: 10.1007/978-3-319-29451-3_43

Fig. 1. The left picture shows the standard KinectFusion output. The right picture illustrates the type of output delivered by our technique: a fully labeled dense reconstruction where each surface element is assigned a category tag.

by deploying high-level knowledge on the type of objects encountered while the moving agent explores the environment, whereas object detection and semantic labeling techniques could be ameliorated by deploying multiple views from tracked sensor poses.

In this article we propose a technique capable to obtain incrementally a dense semantic labeling of the environment from a stream of RGB-D images while performing tracking and mapping à la KinectFusion [11]. Therefore, differently from the map concerned only with the 3D shape of the surfaces present in the environment yielded by a typical SLAM algorithm such as KinectFusion, our technique additionally provides a fully labeled map that embodies the information on *what* kind of object (e.g. a wall, chair, bed, pillow, furniture..) each reconstructed surface element belongs to. A view from one of such dense semantic maps is reported in Fig. 1, with each color representing a different category label.

The rest of this article is organized as follows: Sect. 2 discusses briefly some of the most relevant works aimed at connecting semantic perception and SLAM; Sect. 3 describes first the camera tracking and mapping method employed in our work and, subsequently, illustrates our proposal concerning the integration of a semantic labeling algorithm's output within the SLAM framework; finally, Sect. 4 shows how the proposed volume-based semantic labeling technique behaves when feeding it with (*a*) "correct", manually annotated, labels, (*b*) labels corrupted by synthetic noise, (*c*) "real" labels obtained by a state of the art semantic segmentation algorithm.

2 Related Works

As mentioned in the previous section, embedding of semantic informations into SLAM algorithms was addressed by just a few works. A relevant early proposal in this field is the work by Castle et al. [4], where location of planar objects detected by SIFT features are incorporated into a SLAM algorithm based on Extended Kalman Filtering. Later, Civera et al. [5], extended the previous approach to account for non-planar objects. Bao et al. [1] proposed the idea of "Semantic Structure from Motion" to jointly perform the object recognition and SLAM tasks; in their research, tough, they process entire image sequences offline and perform a global optimization on the resulting environmental map. All such approaches, also, do not employ RGB-D informations, relying instead on the processing of several images to estimate the 3D world structure.

On the converse, works exploiting the availability 3D information throughout the entire pipeline are those by Fioraio et al. [7], Salas-Moreno et al. [13] and Xiao et al. [14]. Fioraio proposes a keyframe-based SLAM algorithm where detected objects are inserted as additional constraints in the bundle adjustment process used to estimate camera poses. The work by Salas-Moreno relies instead on a pipeline where only detected objects are used to estimate sensor location by rendering a synthetic view of their placement and aligning the real depth image to such view through the ICP algorithm [12]. Xiao introduces a semantically annotated dataset; while not the main focus of his work, semantic informations on the object location are used during the bundle adjustment process to better constrain the generated reconstruction of the environment. In their work they show a full "semantic loop" where bounding boxes for objects manually labeled in a subset of frames are used to improve the world map; in turn this allows to propagate the labels to previously unlabeled frames in order to reduce the effort needed by the user to annotate the entire sequences.

Therefore, to the best of our knowledge, no previous work has attempted to bridge the gap between semantic segmentation and SLAM in order to achieve a dense semantic reconstruction of the environment from a moving visual sensor.

3   Description of the Method

To obtain a densely labeled map of the environment captured by the sensor, we adopt a volume-based approach. Similarly to KinectFusion [11], the map is represented by a Signed Distance Function [6], but, peculiarly, we also provide each voxel with a label that specifies the type of object appearing in that spatial location together with an indication of the confidence on the assigned label.

To update the information stored into the volume by integrating new measurements, we need to track the RGB-D sensor as it moves within the environment. In KinectFusion [11] camera tracking is performed by ICP-based alignment between the surface associated with the current depth image and that extracted from the TSDF. Later, Bylow et al. [2] and Canelhas et al. [3] proposed to track the camera by direct alignment of the current depth image to the mapped environment encoded into the TSDF as the zero-level isosurface. This newer approach has been proven to be faster and more accurate than the original KinectFusion tracker. In our work, we decided to employ the aforementioned direct camera-tracking method on such considerations of speed and accuracy. More precisely, our code has been obtained by properly modifying a publicly available implementation of the standard KinectFusion algorithm[1] in order to introduce both the direct camera tracking method as well as dense semantic labeling process.

---

[1] https://github.com/Nerei/kinfu_remake.

In the remainder of this section we will describe our proposed approach to achieve integration of semantic labels into the TSDF representation, while we refer the reader to the previously mentioned article by Bylow and colleagues [2] for details on the tracking algorithm's implementation.

3.1   Labeled TSDF

To obtain a densely labeled representation of the environment, we assume the RGB-D sensor output to be fed to a semantic segmentation algorithm. Without lack of generality, the output of such an algorithm can be represented as a "category" map, i.e. a bitmap having the same resolution as the input image wherein each pixel is assigned a discrete label identifying its category or the lack thereof. Moreover, we assume to be provided with a "score" map, where each value represents the confidence of the labeling algorithm in assigning a category to the corresponding pixel of the input image. Different semantic segmentation algorithms may indeed produce their output in heterogeneous formats (e.g. per-pixel categories, labeled superpixels, 2D or 3D bounding boxes, 3D cluster of points, polygons. . .) but it is typically possible to reconcile those into the aforementioned intermediate representation. The reliance on such an algorithm-agnostic format may also allow us to exploit simultenously the output from diverse labeling techniques, either aimed at detection of different categories or in order to combine their predictions by fusing the score maps. As not every semantic segmentation technique can be run in real time for every frame captured by the sensor, our proposed label storage and propagation technique also allows for robust integration of unlabeled frames.

A typical TSDF volume holds for each voxel the (truncated) distance of its center from the closest surface in the environment. A weight (also truncated to a maximum value) is stored alongside the distance to compute a running average of the SDF value while tracking the sensor [11].

To label an element of the volume, several approaches may be envisioned. The most informative is to store, as an histogram, a probability density function representing the probability for a voxel to represent an object of a certain class. Advantage of this approach is the possibility to properly label a multi-category voxel (such as a voxel spatially located between two or more objects), also, analogously to the trilinear interpolation of SDF values, one may interpolate between neighboring voxels to obtain a spatially continuous p.d.f. Unfortunately, practical memory occupancy issues forbid us to rely on such an approach: each voxel already holds an SDF value and a weight, stored as half precision floating point numbers, i.e. 4 bytes of memory storage. With a 512^3 voxel grid this means a memory occupancy of 512 MB, with typical consumer GPU cards rarely providing more than 2-3 GB of total usable memory. An RGB triplet may also be stored for visualization purposes, this requiring 4 more bytes for each voxel[2] and doubling memory occupancy. Hence, by encoding the probability of each

---

[2] Due to memory alignment constraints it is not recommended to store only three bytes per triplet.

class as a half precision float number we could not store probabilities for more than 4-8 categories without filling up all the available GPU memory. Also, since the integration of a new frame into the voxel grid during the "mapping" step of the algorithm requires a visit to each voxel, the more categories one wishes to handle the slower turns out the entire tracking pipeline.

The above considerations lead us to store a single category per voxel, together with a "score" expressing the confidence on the accuracy of the assigned label. Discrete labels are stored as unsigned short numbers while the score is once again an half precision float, which amounts to a total of 8 bytes per voxel including the already existing SDF data. Accordingly, a 512^3 voxel grid requires 1 GB of GPU RAM regardless of the total number of handled categories. Clearly, we lose information using such label encoding as we can no longer represent properly those voxels featuring more than one likely label. Moreover, such a minimal representation mandates special care in implementing the volume update operation to insert new labeled data into the grid, in order to avoid situations where a voxel gets continuously switched between different categories.

3.2   Volume Update Process

Integration of the acquired depth values into the TSDF volume after camera pose estimation is a crucial operation for any volume-based tracking and mapping algorithm. Typically, every voxel is visited in parallel on the GPU (as each is independent from others) and its 3D position is projected onto the depth map to select a pixel. Such depth pixel stores the distance of the camera from the observed surface at the current frame (if available). Analogously, the voxel stores the distance from its center to the closest surface. The stored TSDF value then undergoes an update step consisting in the weighted average between the voxel's distance from the surface (obtained from the depth map) and the current TSDF value. Weight is also increased, up to a maximum value. Infinite weight growth is avoided to allow for temporal smoothing of the estimated surface distance: this approach allows older measurements to be forgotten after a certain number of volume updating steps.

As mentioned, to store semantic information into each voxel, we add a discrete category label together with a floating point score expressing the confidence in the stored label. Hence, a running average approach such as that just described to update the map information cannot be used for the semantic labeling information as different categories cannot be directly confronted. We could store in each voxel the labels as we receive them (by projecting each 3D cell's coordinates onto the label bitmap and sampling the corresponding pixel), but this would be prone to errors as a mislabeled region would possibly overwrite several correct voxel labels acquired in the past. Additionally, not every pixel may be labeled, possibly entire frames when using a slow semantic segmentation technique which cannot be run on every input image.

Therefore, in this work we propose an evidence weighting approach: each time an already labeled voxel is seen and associated to the currently stored category we increment its score. If a labeled voxel in a subsequent frame is assigned to a different category (e.g. due to a labeling error or to being on the seam between two differently labeled regions), we decrement the associated score. Only when the score reaches a negative value we replace the stored category with the new one.

As for the evidence increment/decrement weight applied to the score, we deploy the confidence of the semantic segmentation algorithm, as sampled from the input score map that we assume to be provided together with the labeling output itself. This choice naturally induces an hysteresis-like effect, protecting the consistency of the labels stored into the volume when areas of the input image are assigned to different categories in subsequent frames: typically a mislabeled region has associated a low score, such value then will not bring in enough evidence to change the category associated with a correctly identified area of the space. Conversely, assuming the initial labeling of a region to be wrong (therefore with a low confidence), a correct labeling from subsequent frames will easily be able to replace the initial erroneous tag. A possible pitfall becomes evident if, for any reason, the score associated to a wrong labeling result is very high but, as more frames are integrated into the TSDF volume, stored weights will increase above the maximum score the semantic segmentation algorithm is able to provide; when such a situation is reached, a single incorrect segmentation will not be able to adversely affect the volume contents. An unlabeled area (or entire frame, without lack of generality) has no effect on the volume labeling process: each corresponding voxel will be left unchanged.

Similarly to the geometric integration approach, we clamp the maximum label score for a voxel to allow for an easier change of category if suddenly a region of space is consistently tagged as a different object for several frames (e.g. in non static situations when an object is removed from the scene). Algorithm 1 shows the pseudo-code for the proposed volume-based label updating process.

Algorithm 1. Pseudo-code of the label updating process

---

for all voxels in the volume **do**
    $(i, j) \leftarrow$ projection of the 3D voxel coordinates into the image plane
    $L_{in} \leftarrow$ category associated to the pixel (i, j)
    $W_{in} \leftarrow$ labeling score associated to the pixel (i, j)
    $L_{tsdf} \leftarrow$ category associated to the current voxel
    $W_{tsdf} \leftarrow$ labeling score associated to the current voxel
    if $L_{in} \notin$ (unlabeled, background) **then**
        if $L_{tsdf} =$ unlabeled $\vee W_{tsdf} < 0$ **then**
            $L_{tsdf} \leftarrow L_{in}$
            $W_{tsdf} \leftarrow W_{in}$
        else if $L_{in} = L_{tsdf}$ **then**
            $W_{tsdf} \leftarrow \min(W_{tsdf} + W_{in}, W_{clamp})$
        else
            $W_{tsdf} \leftarrow W_{tsdf} - W_{in}$
        end if
    end if
end for

---

4 Experimental Evaluation

To evaluate the proposed volume labeling approach we performed tests using different types of semantically segmented data. Our tests deploy the video sequences included in the Sun3D dataset [14]. On their website, Xiao et al., provide multiple RGB-D video sequences captured using a Kinect sensor and depicting typical indoor environments such as hotel, conference rooms or lounge areas. Unique to this dataset is the presence of manually acquired accurate object annotations in the form of per-object polygons for multiple sequences. Each object is also given a unique name, which allows us to tell apart several instances of a same category (e.g. in a hotel room sequence we may have "pillow 1" and "pillow 2").

To parse the dataset's own object representation into our intermediate labeling format, described in Subsect. 3.1, we adopted the following approach:

Category Map. Each named object was given an increasing (and unique) integer identifier, afterwards, its bounding polygon was painted as a filled shape into our category bitmap. Being the source data the result of a manual annotation process, partial overlap of the object polygons has not been a concern.

Score Map. Annotated shapes have been manually defined, we therefore consider the *labeling algorithm*'s confidence maximal. Similarly to the category bitmap, we draw each object's bounding polygon onto the score map and fill it with the floating point value 1.0.

Figure 2 shows a frame from the hotel room sequence contained in the aforementioned dataset, we see that each object is correctly labeled and their confidences are maximal due to the manual labeling process.

Fig. 2. Labeled frame from a sequence of the Sun3D dataset. From top left in clockwise order: RGB frame, depth frame, score map and category map. Each map has been drawn in false colors to increase visibility (blue is the minimum value while red is the maximum) (Color figure online).

We will provide two kind of results, first by proving the robustness of the method under presence of synthetic noise in the labeler's output, subsequently, we will show densely labeled volumes for several sequences obtained using either ground truth labeling data or the semantic segmentation produced by a state of the art algorithm and we will evaluate the capability of the proposed fusion technique to reduce the number of erroneously labeled areas in the reconstructed volumes.

4.1 Robustness to Synthetic Label Noise

To investigate on the robustness of the proposed volumetric label integration process with respect to per-pixel semantic segmentation errors, for all the considered sequences, we corrupted the ground-truth category map associated with each frame by employing synthetically generated white noise. Then, we compared the resulting labeled volume to the reference volume obtained by executing the label fusion process based on noiseless ground-truth category maps. In particular, considering only those labels assigned to voxels representing a surface element (i.e. the zero-level isosurface of the TSDF), we compute the volumetric labeling error rate, i.e. the fraction of misclassified surface voxels. Our synthetic noise model is as follows. We sample pixels from the category map with a certain probability so to switch their correct label to wrong ones uniformly selected from the total pool of labels present in the current sequence. We also assign maximum confidence to switched labels.

Figure 3 shows how, though the image labeler output is corrupted (as illustrated in Fig. 4), thanks to the temporal label integration process, the final volume features a consistent labeling where each voxel is likely to have been correctly classified. Even when the probability to corrupt a label is as high as 50 %, the proposed label integration can reduce the final volumetric error rate significantly, i.e. squeezing it down to less than 25 % typically, to much less than 20 % quite often. For more than 50 % of wrong labels per input image the error grows almost linearly with the noise level, the label fusion process still turning out beneficial in terms of noise attenuation: e.g., with as much as 70 % wrong labels per image the amount of misclassified surface voxels is typically less than 50 %.

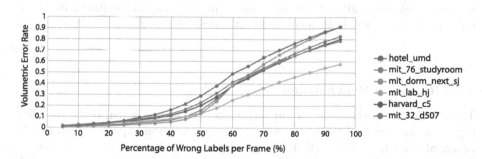

Fig. 3. Volumetric labeling error rate for several sequences of the Sun3D dataset when synthetic noise is added to the ground-truth category labels.

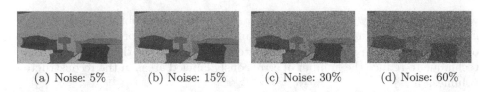

(a) Noise: 5%   (b) Noise: 15%   (c) Noise: 30%   (d) Noise: 60%

Fig. 4. Sample category bitmaps when correct labels are corrupted by increasing amount of noise.

Figure 5 depicts the semantic reconstruction of a portion of the environment explored through the mit_dorm_next_sj sequence. It can be observed that the labeled surface represents accurately both the shape as well as the semantic of the objects present in the environment. The comparison between Fig. 5a and b allows for assessing the effectiveness of the temporal label integration process: though as many as 30 % of the per-pixel labels in each frame are wrong, just a few errors are noticeable with respect to the semantic reconstruction based on perfect noiseless input data. Indeed, such errors are mostly concentrated in the desk area, where the sensor did not linger for multiple frames and thus the evidence weighting process turned out less effective.

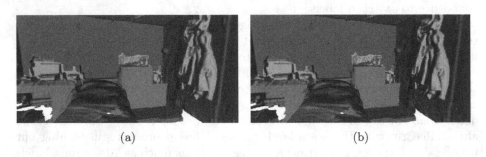

(a)   (b)

Fig. 5. Semantically labeled reconstructions: each surface element is colored according to its category label. Left: reconstruction from noiseless per-pixel category maps. Right: reconstruction when 30 % of the input labels in each map are switched to wrong. Labeling errors are visible by zooming onto the desk area only.

4.2   Results in Real Settings

To evaluate the effectiveness of our technique when using a real semantic labeling algorithm, we used the recent Semantic Segmentation approach proposed by Long, Shelhamer and Darrell [10]. Such algorithm uses a Convolutional Neural Network to produce a per-pixel labeling of an input image. The authors made available several pretrained networks[3] based on the open source Caffe deep learning framework [9]. We chose to employ the "FCN-16s NYUDv2" network due

---

[3] https://github.com/BVLC/caffe/wiki/Model-Zoo#fcn.

to similarities of the category set with the type of objects present in the Sun3D dataset. FCN-16s NYUDv2 processes RGB-D images and produces per-pixel scores for 40 categories defined in [8]. Using the aforementioned algorithm to label each frame of the sequences, we fed our volume labeling pipeline with category maps where each pixel is assigned to the object class having the highest probability, storing then such values into the respective score maps.

Figures 6, 7 and 8 show views from the semantically labeled surfaces obtained by processing some of the sequences of the Sun3D dataset. To allow for better comparative assessment of the performance achievable in real settings, in each Figure we report both the reconstruction obtained by feeding our algorithm with ground truth labels and with the output from the CNN mentioned above. Identifiers from the Sun3D dataset (greater in number than the 40 categories detected by the algorithm in [10]) have been manually mapped onto the associated categories in order to have the same objects in both datasets identified by the same numerical identifier (the Sun3D dataset for example, for the hotel sequence, defines four different pillow objects; we mapped all such identifiers to the single "pillow" category). Based on the comparison to the ground-truth reconstructions, it can be observed that the majority of the labeled regions are consistently and correctly identified by the real algorithm and that, where labeling errors have been made, the associated confidence provided by the proposed label integration technique is likely low (such as in the TV stand in Fig. 7 or on the bed in Fig. 8). In the supplementary material we provide a video depicting fully labeled volumes for the two Sun3D sequences "hotel_umd" and "mit_dorm_next_sj". In the video we show the output of our algorithm when feeding it with manually annotated images and per-pixel categories provided by the CNN.

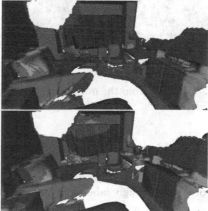

Fig. 6. View from hotel_umd sequence. From the top left, in clockwise order: standard KinectFusion output, semantically labeled view using manually annotated categories, semantically labeled view and related confidence map using the CNN.

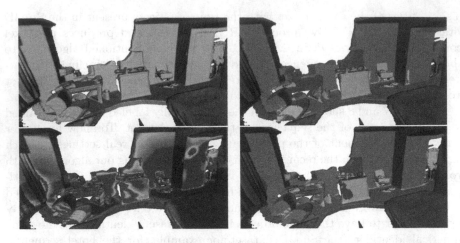

Fig. 7. A second view from the hotel_umd sequence. Images are ordered as in Fig. 6.

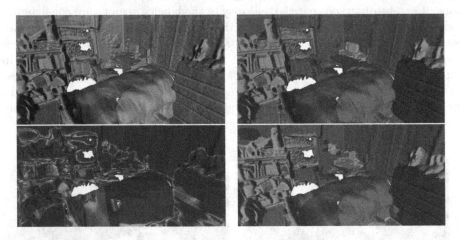

Fig. 8. A view from the mit_dorm_next_sj sequence. Once again, images are ordered as in Fig. 6.

Table 1. Volumetric vs. per-frame labeling. The left side of the table reports the error rates yielded by CNN proposed in [10] on the individual frames of the two Sun3D sequences considered throughout this paper. The rightmost column shows the percentage of voxels wrongly labeled by our volumetric label integration method.

Sequence	Per frame error rate (%)		Volumetric error rate (%)
	Average	Std. Dev	
hotel_umd	34.9	22.6	24.1
mit_dorm_next_sj	26.1	15.7	19.3

Eventually, in Table 1 we assess the benefits brought in by our volumetric label integration technique with respect to per-frame labeling in real settings, i.e. when deploying a real semantic labeling algorithm such as the CNN proposed in [10]. The first part of the table reports per-frame semantic labeling error rates: this metric is computed for each frame using the ground-truth labels provided with the Sun3D dataset so to divide the number of erroneously labeled pixels by the total number of labeled pixels. We show average per-frame error rate and associated standard deviation for the two considered sequences. Then, the rightmost column displays the volumetric error rate, i.e. the percentage of erroneously labeled surface voxels in the final reconstruction of the 3D volume (the same metric as in Fig. 3). Thus, the results in Table 1 vouch how the proposed label integration technique can handle effectively varying and large per-frame labeling errors so to provide a significantly more accurate semantic segmentation of the reconstructed environment. It is also worth pointing out that the volumetric error rates reported in Table 1 turn out higher than those yielded by synthetic label noise (Fig. 3) due to the diverse kinds of labeling errors. Indeed, while in the experiment dealing with synthetic noise each pixel has a uniform and independent probability to be assigned to a wrong category, in real settings it is more likely that large connected image regions get labeled wrongly due to the spatial smoothness constraints enforced by real semantic labeling algorithms, such as e.g. the CNN deployed in our experiments.

5   Final Remarks

We have described the first approach to bridge the gap between semantic segmentation and dense surface mapping and tracking, so as to attain, peculiarly, a semantically labeled dense reconstruction of the environment explored by a moving RGB-D sensor. We have demonstrated its robustness by introduction of significant noise in the labeling fed as input as well as its effectiveness by comparing the labeled surfaces achievable by ground truth semantic data to those obtained by deploying a state of the art semantic segmentation algorithm.

Our goal is to provide a tool usable alongside any kind of semantic perception algorithm in order to incrementally gather high-level knowledge on the environment and store it within the map itself. We also plan to deploy such volumetric semantic data to improve the camera tracking algorithm by exploiting semantic cues together with geometric information to align the current view to the surface embedded into the TSDF volume. Additionally, it will be feasible to raycast in real time a category and confidence bitmap using the data stored into the volume. This will allow the user to obtain a continuous stream of semantically labeled frames, possibly interacting with the system while mapping the space so to either linger on low-confidence regions or even correct or improve the acquired semantic information.

References

1. Bao, S.Y., Savarese, S.: Semantic structure from motion. In: CVPR, 2025–2032 (2011)
2. Bylow, E., Sturm, J., Kerl, C., Kahl, F., Cremers, D.: Real-time camera tracking and 3D reconstruction using signed distance functions. In: Robotics: Science and Systems Conference (2013)
3. Canelhas, D.R., Stoyanov, T., Lilienthal, A.J.: SDF tracker: a parallel algorithm for on-line pose estimation and scene reconstruction from depth images. In: IEEE International Conference on Intelligent Robots and Systems, pp. 3671–3676 (2013)
4. Castle, R.O., Klein, G., Murray, D.W.: Combining monoSLAM with object recognition for scene augmentation using a wearable camera. Image Vis. Comput. **28**(11), 1548–1556 (2010)
5. Civera, J., Galvez-Lopez, D., Riazuelo, L., Tardos, J.D., Montiel, J.M.M.: Towards semantic SLAM using a monocular camera. In: 2011 IEEE/RSJ International Conference on Intelligent Robots and Systems, pp. 1277–1284. IEEE, September 2011
6. Curless, B., Levoy, M.: A volumetric method for building complex models from range images. In: Proceedings of 23rd Annual Conference on Computer Graphics and Interactive Technique - SIGGRAPH 1996, pp. 303–312 (1996)
7. Fioraio, N., Di Stefano, L.: Joint detection, tracking and mapping by semantic bundle adjustment. In: 2013 IEEE Conference on Computer Vision and Pattern Recognition, pp. 1538–1545, June 2013
8. Gupta, S., Arbelaez, P., Malik, J.: Perceptual organization and recognition of indoor scenes from RGB-D images. In: 2013 IEEE Conference on Computer Vision and Pattern Recognition, pp. 564–571. IEEE, June 2013
9. Jia, Y., Shelhamer, E., Donahue, J., Karayev, S., Long, J., Girshick, R., Guadarrama, S., Darrell, T.: Caffe: convolutional architecture for fast feature embedding, June 2014
10. Long, J., Shelhamer, E., Darrell, T.: Fully convolutional networks for semantic segmentation. In: IEEE Conference on Computer Vision and Pattern Recognition (2015)
11. Newcombe, R.A., Davison, A.J., Izadi, S., Kohli, P., Hilliges, O., Shotton, J., Molyneaux, D., Hodges, S., Kim, D., Fitzgibbon, A.: KinectFusion: real-time dense surface mapping and tracking. In: 2011 10th IEEE International Symposium on Mixed and Augmented Reality, pp. 127–136. IEEE, October 2011
12. Rusinkiewicz, S., Levoy, M.: Efficient variants of the ICP algorithm. In: Proceedings of 3-D Digital Imaging and Modeling 2001. In: Third International Conference on IEEE, pp. 145–152 (2001)
13. Salas-Moreno, R.F., Newcombe, R., Strasdat, H., Kelly, P.H., Davison, A.J.: SLAM++: simultaneous localisation and mapping at the level of objects. In: 2013 IEEE Conference on Computer Vision and Pattern Recognition, pp. 1352–1359, June 2013
14. Xiao, J., Owens, A., Torralba, A.: SUN3D: a database of big spaces reconstructed using SfM and object labels. In: Proceedings of IEEE International Conference on Computer Vision, pp. 1625–1632, December 2013

Simultaneous Camera, Light Position and Radiant Intensity Distribution Calibration

Marco Visentini-Scarzanella[(✉)] and Hiroshi Kawasaki

Computer Vision and Graphics Laboratory,
Kagoshima University, Kagoshima, Japan
marco.visentiniscarzanella@gmail.com

Abstract. We propose a practical method for calibrating the position and the Radiant Intensity Distribution (RID) of light sources from images of Lambertian planes. In contrast with existing techniques that rely on the presence of specularities, we prove a novel geometric property relative to the brightness of Lambertian planes that allows to robustly calibrate the illuminant parameters without the detrimental effects of view-dependent reflectance and a large decrease in complexity. We further show closed form solutions for position and RID of common types of light sources. The proposed method can be seamlessly integrated within the camera calibration pipeline, and its validity against the state-of-the-art is shown both on synthetic and real data.

1 Introduction

The problem of devising a usable, accurate calibration routine for the illumination properties of a scene is becoming increasingly relevant. As techniques for 3D reconstruction become more accurate, the focus of the community has shifted towards more complex scenarios where many of the traditional lighting assumptions are no longer valid, e.g., in 3D reconstruction from hand-held devices with on-board lighting [4] or in endoscopic images which are becoming more popular in the community [6]. In these cases, anisotropic lighting combined with unstable or scarce features make traditional feature-based methods prone to errors. On the other hand, especially in medical environments there has been a resurgence of photometric techniques such as Shape-from-Shading (SFS) and Photometric Stereo (PS) [1,2,7,20,22,26], because of their inherent suitability to textureless environments.

However, improvements in algorithmic and mathematical techniques have not been matched by a commensurate improvement in modelling, and in virtually all aforementioned scenarios a realistic modelling of the light sources has been largely ignored. Indeed, in the SFS and PS literature either directional [10,23] or 'omnilight' [20,22,26] light sources are considered. While these models can perform well in controlled conditions, they are not suitable for the challenging environments where these techniques are being applied, with focused lights exhibiting anisotropic Radiant Intensity Distributions (RID) and placed close to the surface. This is also due to a lack of enabling technologies allowing to

© Springer International Publishing Switzerland 2016
T. Bräunl et al. (Eds.): PSIVT 2015, LNCS 9431, pp. 557–571, 2016.
DOI: 10.1007/978-3-319-29451-3_44

easily integrate the estimation of illumination parameters within the standard camera calibration pipeline, with most existing technologies requiring costly and time-intensive hardware solutions [14,16].

Specifically, in this work we address the lack of cheap, practical vision-based techniques for RID calibration by introducing a fully image-based approach to calibration of light position and RID that can be easily integrated in camera calibration routines. Inspired by the first approach to the problem in [11], we extend it with the following contributions:

1. A novel geometric property of shading of Lambertian planes, which relates the light position to global maxima in the intensity.
2. An algebraic method for robustly finding the dominant light axis from global maxima in the intensity only, without the need for complex symmetry search as in [11].
3. Closed-form solutions for position and RID for classes of (an-)isotropic sources.
4. A complete pipeline for joint camera, light position and RID calibration using standard Lambertian calibration boards.

1.1   Related Work

Calibrating the position of a light source is a well-studied problem in computer vision. For distant light sources, all light rays are parallel and is therefore sufficient to estimate a single direction vector, which can be accomplished from the specular highlights produced by illuminating shiny surfaces [3,25]. In the case of point light sources where the assumption of parallel light rays is no longer valid and is therefore necessary to estimate the light position in space, current strategies still employ reflective objects of known geometry such as spheres [13,15,18,27], planes [17], or non-reflective objects with known geometry [24]. Alternative methods requiring specialised hardware such as LEDs and translucent screens [9] or flatbed scanners [19] have also been proposed. Applications have been proposed recently in works on PS using sources with anisotropic RIDs for generic vision [8] as well as medical endoscopy applications [2,21]; however either none or *ad hoc* calibration methods were proposed in the cited works.

While the approaches above only characterise the positional information of the light source, there is a limited number of techniques investigating RID calibration, i.e., determining the angle-dependent attenuation factor relative to the anisotropism of the light source. The only vision-based approach in the literature was proposed by Park *et al.* in [11]. In this method, geometric properties holding under the Lambertian assumption are exploited to calibrate the light source. However, the method is effectively a 2-stage approach where the light position is first estimated using specularities from shiny surfaces, thus contradicting the initial Lambertian assumption. Whenever Lambertian surfaces are considered, the method was shown to have large errors in the position estimation. The contradiction between Lambertian assumption and the use of shiny surfaces can

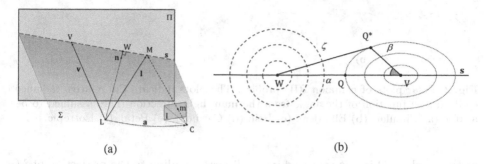

Fig. 1. (a) Geometric setup under consideration. The Lambertian plane Π with surface normal n lit by the point light source L is projected by the camera C on the image plane I. Each 3D point $M \in \Pi$ is projected to a point $m \in I$, and is related to L by the light vector l. Two special points are defined on Π: V, which is the intersection of the dominant light axis v with Π, and W, which is the closest point to L. The triplet (V, W, L) defines the plane Σ, which intersects Π at the line s. (b) Supporting figure for the proof of Lemma 1.

result in a breakdown of the assumptions depending on the light/camera configuration [12]. Finally, from a computational perspective the method leverages the symmetry of the projected light pattern, which on Lambertian surfaces results in a sensitive optimisation process requiring a full 2D search.

Conversely, we improve on the state-of-the-art by proving an additional geometric property of the shading of Lambertian planes. This allows to find the dominant light axis by inspection of the global intensity maxima, without expensive symmetry searches. Moreover, we find a closed-form solution for position and RID for widely used classes of realistic light sources. Finally, we show how we can easily integrate our proposed method within the camera calibration pipeline, using AR markers instead of the traditional checkerboard pattern.

2   Shading of Lambertian Planes Under Near Illumination

In this section, we analyse the reflectance properties of Lambertian textureless planes under near illumination from point light sources. Let Π be a plane in space with known position and orientation (R, l), a unit surface normal $\hat{n} = (n_x, n_y, n_z)$ illuminated by a nearby point light source L. The light source is located at a position $a = (a_x, a_y, a_z)$ from the world origin, which in our formulation coincides with the position of the camera C. The light source is characterised by a dominant unit direction vector $\hat{v}$, and the light vector between a 3D point $M = (x, y, z) \in \Pi$ and L is represented as l. In our notation, 3D points are given in uppercase letters, 2D points as lowercase letters, direction vectors as boldface lowercase letters, matrices as boldface uppercase letters and scalars as Greek letters.

This configuration is shown graphically in Fig. 1a. Under a generic Lambertian reflectance model with an infinitely far away light source, the brightness

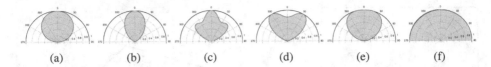

(a)   (b)   (c)   (d)   (e)   (f)

Fig. 2. Polar plots of common RID profiles. The plots indicate the relative radiance emitted as a function of the angle from the main light direction (here assumed to be at 0°). (a) Circular. (b) Elliptical. (c) Bell. (d) Cardioid. (e) Petal. (f) Isotropic.

at the pixel (u, v) in the captured image I corresponding to the projection of M is independent from the viewing direction:

$$I(u, v) = \rho \, \gamma \frac{l \cdot \hat{n}}{\|l\|}, \tag{1}$$

where ρ is the surface albedo and γ is the power of the incident light on the surface. This is the scenario that is traditionally considered in the photometric stereo literature for Lambertian surfaces. However, when a more realistic setup is considered, the factors related to the nearby light source can no longer be ignored. More specifically, while for infinitely far light sources two light rays l_i, l_j would be parallel, in this case they will no longer be parallel and intersect at L. Likewise, the incident light power γ is replaced by the Radiant Intensity Distribution (RID) function $g(\phi)$ of the angle between the normalised light vector $\hat{l}$ and the dominant light direction. Finally, the attenuation term $r^2 = \|l\|^2$ represents the light fall-off which is inversely proportional to the square of the distance between M and L:

$$I(u, v) = \rho \, \frac{g(\phi)}{\|l\|^2} \frac{l \cdot \hat{n}}{\|l\|}. \tag{2}$$

In the equation above, the shape of $g(\phi)$ is determined by the physical characteristics of the light source. Generally, focused lights such as those found on flash cameras, spotlights and endoscopes will exhibit some degree of anisotropism. In Fig. 2 examples of common RIDs are provided. Similarly to the work in [11], our single assumption is that the RID is radially symmetric about L, so that all RIDs can be represented as a 1D function of the angle ϕ.

2.1 Geometric Properties of Illumination Model

Consider the setup shown in Fig. 1a. The plane Σ can be constructed from the triplet of points (V, W, L), where V is the intersection of v and Π, and W is the closest point to L on Π. The intersection of Π and Σ defines the line s. Orientation and position of the calibration plane Π is known to the observer.

In [11] it was shown that for any radially symmmetric RID about the main light axis v, the observed brightness on a Lambertian plane will be bilaterally symmetric. This key result was extended by noticing that the observed brightness is in fact radially symmetric whenever the RID under consideration is isotropic. Thus, it was possible to detect s and Σ through a 2D search for the axis of symmetry, or 1D whenever the light position was already known.

In this section, we prove a further property of this geometric setup: given the shading image of a Lambertian plane, its global maximum will invariably lie on the line s. This allows us to recover the dominant light direction and, for several classes of RID, the light source position directly from the position of the maximal points, without the need for computationally expensive and error-prone symmetry search. More formally, we prove the following:

Lemma 1 (Location of Global Maximum). *Let Π be a Lambertian plane of constant albedo illuminated by a nearby point light source L with dominant view direction v and radially symmetric RID $g(\phi)$, and let s be a line on Π formed by W, the closest point to L on Π, and V, the point of intersection between Π and v. Then, the point where the global maximum of the intensity is reached, Q, will also lie on s.*

Proof by contradiction of Lemma 1. Consider the Lambertian reflectance function in Eq. (2). This can be represented as the product of two functions $f_1(\rho, l, v), f_2(l, n)$:

$$I(u, v) = f_1(\rho, l, v) f_2(l, n),$$
$$f_1(\rho, l, v) = \rho \, g(\hat{l} \cdot \hat{v}),$$
$$f_2(l, n) = \frac{l \cdot n}{\|l\|^3}. \tag{3}$$

By construction, $f_1(\rho, l, v)$ is an elliptical conic section on Π with centre V and symmetrical about s. Also, $f_2(l, n)$ is globally maximised at W: since W is by definition the closest point to L, at W the denominator of $f_2(l, n)$ is minimised. Moreover, as W is the closest point to L it also implies that at W, $l \parallel n$, thereby also maximising the numerator. Since both the distance from L and the angle between l and n will be radially symmetric about W, we conclude that $f_2(l, n)$ is also radially symmetric about W.

The two functions will form isocurves centred at V and W respectively (Fig. 1b). Now consider a globally maximal point Q^* not lying on s. Without loss of generality, let us assume that the distance between V and W is α and let us further assume that this point lies on the β–isocurve of $f_1(\rho, l, v)$, meaning that it lies on a circumference of radius β centred at V. The three points form a triangle $\triangle VWQ^*$, where the length the two known sides is $\overline{VW} = \alpha$ and $\overline{VQ^*} = \beta$ respectively, while the length of the third side $\overline{WQ^*} = \zeta$ can be expressed as:

$$\zeta^2 = \alpha^2 + \beta^2 - 2\alpha\beta \cos \angle WVQ^*. \tag{4}$$

Since both α and β are of fixed length, ζ will have its minimum length when $\angle WVQ^* = 0$, in other words when Q^* lies on s. Let us call this point Q. Since $\overline{WQ} < \overline{WQ^*}$, Q lies on a higher isocurve of $f_2(l, n)$ while lying on the same isocurve of $f_1(\rho, l, v)$ as Q^*. However, this implies that the product of the two functions will yield a higher value for Q than for Q^*, contradicting our initial assumption that the global maximum does not lie on s. $\square$

Corollary 1. When the light source is isotropic, no dominant light direction is present, then $\alpha = 0$ and $Q = W$.

3   Illuminant Properties Estimation

We estimate light position and RID from N purely Lambertian plane images I_i. Perspective distortion-free images $\breve{I}_i$ are first created from the plane position and orientations $(\boldsymbol{R}_i, \boldsymbol{t}_i)$ obtained during AR-marker based camera calibration. Since all images are Lambertian, there are no view-variant effects to compensate for during the perspective correction.

3.1   Dominant Light Axis Estimation

We estimate the dominant light axis $\boldsymbol{v}$ by observing that all planes Σ_i form a pencil around it, each with normal vector $\boldsymbol{v} \times \hat{\boldsymbol{n}}_i$. As the symmetry line $\boldsymbol{s}_i$ is the intersection of Σ_i and Π_i, the segment $L - Q_i$ between the light source and the ith maximal point will also lie on Σ_i and

$$\boldsymbol{v} \times \hat{\boldsymbol{n}}_i \cdot (L - Q_i) = 0. \tag{5}$$

After expansion, and by stacking observations about the maximal points and the plane normals from each of the Π_i planes, we obtain a system $\boldsymbol{Au} = 0$, where $\boldsymbol{A}$ is a rank 5, $N \times 9$ matrix and $\boldsymbol{u}$ a vector of unknowns. Each row $\boldsymbol{A}_i$ of the matrix $\boldsymbol{A}$ and $\boldsymbol{u}$ correspond to:

$$\begin{aligned}
\boldsymbol{A}_i &= [n_z, -n_y, n_x, -n_z, n_y, -n_x, (n_z Q_y - n_y Q_z), (n_x Q_z - n_z Q_x), (n_y Q_x - n_x Q_y)], \\
\boldsymbol{u} &= [v_y L_x, v_z L_x, v_z L_y, v_x L_y, v_x L_z, v_y L_z, v_x, v_y, v_z].
\end{aligned} \tag{6}$$

The elements of $\boldsymbol{v}$ are encoded in the last three rows of the null space of $\boldsymbol{A}$, which is found after a rank 5 approximation of $\boldsymbol{A}$ to minimise the effect of noise followed by SVD. Generally, at this stage any candidate point L_c along $\boldsymbol{v}$ will satisfy Eq. 5, so while the 3 directional components of $\boldsymbol{v}$ can be obtained from the estimate of $\boldsymbol{u}$, the location of L will still be unknown and is estimated with the methods presented in the next sections. Instead, we fix $\boldsymbol{v}$ in space by finding a generic point V_0 on $\boldsymbol{v}$ by stacking the Hessian normal forms of Σ_i: $(\hat{\boldsymbol{n}}_i \times \boldsymbol{v})^{\top} V_0 = (\hat{\boldsymbol{n}}_i \times \boldsymbol{v}) \cdot Q_i$ and solving for V_0.

At least 9 observations are sufficient to obtain a reliable estimate of $\boldsymbol{v}$ from the maximal points only. These are estimated by thresholding the top percentile of the pixel intensities, and calculating the intensity-weighted centroid. Given the smoothness of the reflectance function, this simple procedure is generally sufficient for a reliable estimate.

Corollary 2. When the light position is known, either by design or because of prior specular calibration, the orientation of the dominant light axis can be obtained from only two images and their maximal points. This is particularly important for practical systems.

3.2   Closed-Form Estimation of Light Position and RID

In this section we derive the procedure necessary for estimating light position and RID parameters directly in closed form, with no additional information required apart from the location of the maximal points. This procedure is applicable to both isotropic and regular anisotropic sources, approximating a wide variety of practical scenarios.

(1) Isotropic sources. For isotropic light sources, according to Corollary 1 the maximal points coincide with the closest points on the plane from the light source. Therefore, there is no need to estimate v according to the previous section, and the maximal point Q_i on a plane $(\hat{n}_i, t_i)$ closest to light source L is:

$$Q_i = L + (\hat{n}_i \cdot (t_i - L)) \, \hat{n}_i. \tag{7}$$

Hence, dropping the index i for notation clarity, we can build a linear system given one maximal point:

$$\begin{bmatrix} 1 - n_x^2 & -n_x n_y & -n_x n_z \\ -n_y n_x & 1 - n_y^2 & -n_y n_z \\ -n_z n_x & -n_z n_y & 1 - n_z^2 \end{bmatrix} \begin{bmatrix} L_x \\ L_y \\ L_z \end{bmatrix} = \begin{bmatrix} Q_x - (\hat{n} \cdot t) \, n_x \\ Q_y - (\hat{n} \cdot t) \, n_y \\ Q_z - (\hat{n} \cdot t) \, n_z \end{bmatrix}. \tag{8}$$

Since the matrix above is of rank 2, at least two observations are needed to be stacked together and remove the ambiguity. Therefore, for isotropic sources, given two observations it is possible to calculate the light position. This coincides with the specular case, where at least two views of a specular highlight are necessary to triangulate the light position.

(2) Regular anisotropic sources. For regular anisotropic light sources, we consider RID functions of the form $g(l, v) = \cos(\angle(l, v))^{\mu} = ((l \cdot v) / \|l\|)^{\mu}$, which approximates well the light distributions from spotlights commonly found in halogen or LED light sources, examples of which are shown in Fig. 2a, b. We decide to concentrate on this form as it has been shown to work well in practical scenarios in the photometric stereo literature, e.g., in [8].

To locate L we proceed by first recovering the dominant light axis v according to the procedure outlined earlier. This leaves one degree of freedom for the position of L along the known axis. To simplify our mathematical treatment, we transform the system so that this degree of freedom will translate into a single unknown. To achieve this, we first rotate our complete frame by a matrix R^* so that the resulting vector v^* will be parallel to the vector $u = (0 \; 0 \; 1)^{\mathsf{T}1}$.

The rotated system consists of the new unknown light source position L^* with dominant light vector v^*, the rotated planes Π_i^* with unit normals $\hat{n}_i^*$ and translations t_i^*. After rotating the reference frame, the intersection points V_i^* between the dominant light vector and the planes will be aligned parallel to the z−axis, with (x, y) coordinates equal to (L_x^*, L_y^*), thus leaving a single unknown

---

[1] Full expressions given in the supplementary material.

L_z^* to be calculated. We now parametrise a point P on the intersection line s^* between each plane Π_i^* and Σ_i^*:

$$P(\lambda) = V^* + \lambda \begin{bmatrix} W_x^* - V_x^* \\ W_y^* - V_y^* \\ W_z^* - V_z^* \end{bmatrix}, \tag{9}$$

where we drop the index i for clarity. The intensity function along the intersection line can then be derived as:

$$I(\lambda) = \rho \frac{(P_z^*(\lambda) - L_z^*)^\mu (L^* \cdot \hat{n}^* - P(\lambda) \cdot \hat{n}^*)}{\|L^* - P(\lambda)\|^{(\mu+3)}}. \tag{10}$$

At maximal points W^*, $\frac{\partial I(\lambda)}{\partial \lambda} = 0$. Noting that at these points $\lambda = 1$, we obtain:

$$0 = (W_z^* - L_z^*)^{(\mu+1)} \frac{\mu k_1 k_2 (W_z^* - V_z^*) + (W_z^* - L_z^*)(k_2 (W^* - V^*) \cdot \hat{n}^* + (\mu+3)k_1 k_3)}{\|L^* - W^*\|^{2(\mu+5)}}, \tag{11}$$

where k_1, k_2, k_3 are polynomials in L_z^* of degree 1, 2 and 1 respectively.[1] The zeros of the functions can occur either when one of the $\mu + 1$ repeated roots $(W_z^* - L_z^*)$ is zero or when the numerator is zero. Since the former can never be zero as $L_z^* \neq W_z^*$, the problem of finding the unknowns μ and L_z^* is reduced to finding the zeros of numerator. This is linear in μ and cubic in L_z^*, irrespective of the value of μ. Given that we have at least 9 observations from the estimation of v, the two unknowns can be efficiently estimated using a numerical equation solver. Therefore, from the maximal points only we can retrieve dominant light direction, light location and RID parameters of regular anisotropic light sources.

3.3 Optimisation Procedure for Complex Anisotropic Sources

Light Position Estimation. For lights with complex RIDs, it is more difficult to obtain an analytical expression for the position as a function of maximal points, and we use instead an optimisation procedure. Instead of optimising the full reflectance function which requires RID knowledge, we extend the work in [5], by noting that given N Lambertian planes crossed by a ray l, the intensity of the points $I_i(u_i, v_i)$ on l obeys the following relationship independently of albedo or RID:

$$\sqrt[3]{\frac{I_1(u_1, v_1)}{l \cdot \hat{n}_1}} \|l\|_1 = \cdots = \sqrt[3]{\frac{I_N(u_N, v_N)}{l \cdot \hat{n}_N}} \|l\|_N. \tag{12}$$

We start our search for L by picking the first crossing point L_0 between the planes and v (since we assume that all planes are in front of the light source) and proceeding backwards. For each candidate point L_c, we trace J random rays starting from it, compute their intersections with the planes and obtain the corresponding pixel intensities by projecting using the known calibration parameters. From Eq. (12), we compute the set of observations $r_j = \{r_{1j}, ..., r_{Nj}\}$ relative to each ray. An initial approximation for L is found by minimising the cost based on the variance of the sets r_j:

$$E(L_c) = \frac{1}{JN} \sum_{j \in J} \sum_i^N (r_{ij}(L_c) - \bar{r}_j(L_c))^2. \tag{13}$$

Helped by the RID independency of our formulation, in our experiments we have invariably found $E(j)$ to be convex, as we show in the supplementary material. The single unknown for the light position is found through a Levenberg-Marquadt optimisation of $E(j)$.

RID Parameters Optimisation. Once the position of the light source is known, for complex RIDs it is necessary to estimate the distribution from the observed intensities. In our case, given the view-invariant Lambertian images, the RID is modeled with a 4th order polynomial with five unknown coefficients:

$$g(\boldsymbol{v}, \boldsymbol{l}) = p_4\phi^4 + p_3\phi^3 + p_2\phi^2 + p_1\phi^1 + p_0. \tag{14}$$

Since the RID function has the constraint $g_{\max} = 1$, the albedo is found as the normalising value for the estimated function. We solve the system from Eq. (2) by stacking K observations in the vector $\boldsymbol{b} = I(u, v)\|\boldsymbol{l}\|^3/(\boldsymbol{l} \cdot \hat{\boldsymbol{v}})$ and solving the system $\boldsymbol{Ap} = \boldsymbol{b}$, where $\boldsymbol{A}$ is an $K \times 5$ matrix where each row is the vector of calculated angles $[\phi^4\ \phi^3\ \phi^2\ \phi\ 1]$ between the calculated $\boldsymbol{v}$ and the light vector to the projected 3D position of the plane pixels, while $\boldsymbol{p}$ is the 5×1 vector of unknown coefficients.

4   Results

4.1   Synthetic Data

We generated 20 datasets for each of the 6 RID types in Fig. 2. Each dataset contains a plane observed at 20 positions/orientations. In our experiments, we test the angular error of the estimated dominant view axis, the position error of the source, as well as the MSE between the estimated and ground truth RIDs. The error measures in Fig. 4 are the average of the 20 datasets for each RID type. The proposed method is compared with the state-of-the-art in [11]. For fairness, while it is not a requirement for our proposed method, we ensured that the orientations generated showed enough of the symmetric pattern to avoid failure cases of [11]. Finally, we explore the noise robustness of the technique by injecting increasing percentages of uniformly distributed noise.

As shown in Fig. 4, the proposed method (solid lines) drastically reduces the errors in [11] (dashed) for all RID types. Numerical results are shown in the tables. Different colours of lines represent different RID types. Whenever the

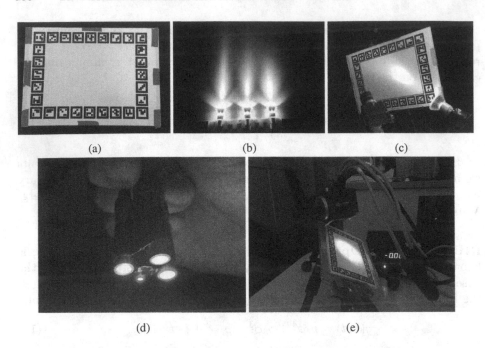

(a)   (b)   (c)

(d)   (e)

Fig. 3. Images from the two experiments with real data. (a) The AR board used for joint camera and light calibration. (b) The lights tested, left to right: narrow, medium and wide cones. (c) Experimental setup. (d) Head of the scope used for the experiment, with the three coloured LEDs around it. (e) Calibration procedure (Color figure online).

closed form solution can be used (i.e. for Circular, Elliptical and Isotropic RIDs), the estimated solution is very robust to noise with error close to zero in both position and RID. The robustness is due to the fact that only intensity maxima need to be found, which can be estimated very reliably. Whenever the optimisation of Sect. 3.3 has to be used, the errors increase, albeit at a slower rate than [11]. Extending the closed form solution to more classes to avoid the optimisation will be the subject of our future work. On the other hand, the method in [11] suffers from inaccuracies in the position estimation, which adversely affect the RID estimation as well. It is important to stress the difference in complexity between the two methods. Mainly due to the 2D symmetry search, our implementation of the method in [11] requires several minutes for each plane, while the proposed method can process the full set in a few seconds. In all cases at a given noise level, our worst performance is better than the best performance of [11].

4.2 Real Data

We test our proposed technique in two separate scenarios. First, with three halogen light bulbs with equal power but different beam widths (Fig. 3b). Second, we

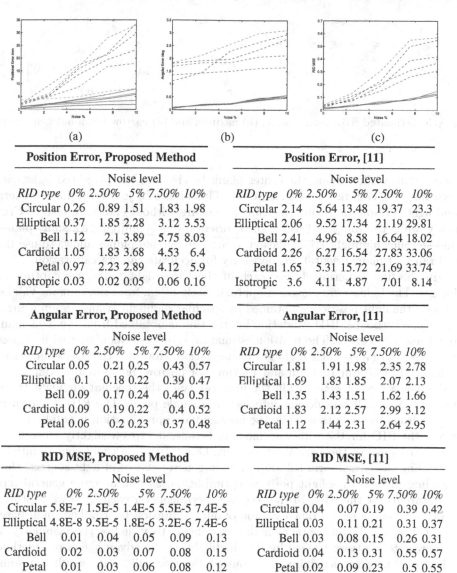

(a)   (b)   (c)

Position Error, Proposed Method

RID type	Noise level				
	0%	2.50%	5%	7.50%	10%
Circular	0.26	0.89	1.51	1.83	1.98
Elliptical	0.37	1.85	2.28	3.12	3.53
Bell	1.12	2.1	3.89	5.75	8.03
Cardioid	1.05	1.83	3.68	4.53	6.4
Petal	0.97	2.23	2.89	4.12	5.9
Isotropic	0.03	0.02	0.05	0.06	0.16

Position Error, [11]

RID type	Noise level				
	0%	2.50%	5%	7.50%	10%
Circular	2.14	5.64	13.48	19.37	23.3
Elliptical	2.06	9.52	17.34	21.19	29.81
Bell	2.41	4.96	8.58	16.64	18.02
Cardioid	2.26	6.27	16.54	27.83	33.06
Petal	1.65	5.31	15.72	21.69	33.74
Isotropic	3.6	4.11	4.87	7.01	8.14

Angular Error, Proposed Method

RID type	Noise level				
	0%	2.50%	5%	7.50%	10%
Circular	0.05	0.21	0.25	0.43	0.57
Elliptical	0.1	0.18	0.22	0.39	0.47
Bell	0.09	0.17	0.24	0.46	0.51
Cardioid	0.09	0.19	0.22	0.4	0.52
Petal	0.06	0.2	0.23	0.37	0.48

Angular Error, [11]

RID type	Noise level				
	0%	2.50%	5%	7.50%	10%
Circular	1.81	1.91	1.98	2.35	2.78
Elliptical	1.69	1.83	1.85	2.07	2.13
Bell	1.35	1.43	1.51	1.62	1.66
Cardioid	1.83	2.12	2.57	2.99	3.12
Petal	1.12	1.44	2.31	2.64	2.95

RID MSE, Proposed Method

RID type	Noise level				
	0%	2.50%	5%	7.50%	10%
Circular	5.8E-7	1.5E-5	1.4E-5	5.5E-5	7.4E-5
Elliptical	4.8E-8	9.5E-5	1.8E-6	3.2E-6	7.4E-6
Bell	0.01	0.04	0.05	0.09	0.13
Cardioid	0.02	0.03	0.07	0.08	0.15
Petal	0.01	0.03	0.06	0.08	0.12

RID MSE, [11]

RID type	Noise level				
	0%	2.50%	5%	7.50%	10%
Circular	0.04	0.07	0.19	0.39	0.42
Elliptical	0.03	0.11	0.21	0.31	0.37
Bell	0.03	0.08	0.15	0.26	0.31
Cardioid	0.04	0.13	0.31	0.55	0.57
Petal	0.02	0.09	0.23	0.5	0.55

Fig. 4. Results from [11] and this work shown as dashed and solid lines respectively. (a), Top tables: light position estimation error in mm. (b), Middle tables: angular estimation error of dominant light vector in degrees. (c), Bottom tables: MSE of estimated RID. All errors measured against different noise levels.

mounted three external (red, blue and green) LEDs with a housing diameter of 7.9 mm on a standard medical endoscope with an onboard camera in a triangular configuration (Fig. 3d). Instead of the traditional checkerboard used for camera calibration, we print on a matte sheet of paper AR markers for camera

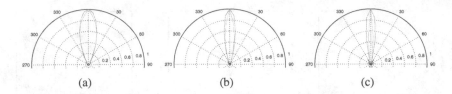

Fig. 5. Estimated RIDs for (a) wide, (b) medium and (c) narrow beam halogen bulbs.

calibration, while leaving the center blank to visualise the projected light pattern for light calibration (Fig. 3a, c, e). This allows to jointly perform camera and light calibration during the same procedure without elaborate setups. Crucially, while the range of feasible plane orientations is limited with shiny planes and specular highlight triangulation, using Lambertian planes allows to use the full range of plane orientations necessary for accurate camera calibration.

In the first experiment, For each of the three light bulbs, we capture 17 images. The lights were placed at approximately 25 cm from the camera. Validation for the light position is obtained by specular highlight triangulation using a shiny checkerboard. RID validation information is obtained from the light manufacturer's datasheet. The position estimation error was calculated with respect to the result of a specular highlight triangulation. However, the positional errors calculated (18.3 mm 12.9 mm and 13.5 mm for narrow, medium and wide beam lights respectively) were within the uncertainty of the specular highlight triangulation, since all rays do not intersect in a single point. The RID is shown in Fig. 5. It can be seen that while the polynomial approximation faithfully reproduces the RID for the wide and medium beams, it gives a slightly loose fit to the sharp spike of the narrow-beam light. Our future work will concentrate on extending the closed form solution to more general classes of light sources, thus avoiding the sensitive light position optimisation, as well as more general representations for the RID. In the second experiment, for each LED we captured 7 images using a scaled down version of our calibration board. The small baseline between light and camera makes it difficult to visualise the symmetry of the projected pattern needed by [11], highlighting the advantage of our method where only brightness maxima are required. Position calibration results are summarised by Fig. 6b, where we show the reconstructed position and orientation of the 3 LEDs reflecting their triangular configuration around the camera (black square in the figure) already shown in Fig. 3d. The correctness of the position was checked by hand and the angle of vergence between the dominant vectors of the 3 LEDs also corresponds to our setup, which was made so that the LED beams would focus at a distance of 7–8 cm. The RID result is shown in Fig. 6a. While we have no ground truth from the manufacturer, we can see that the fitted RID function shows a curve reaching 10 % of its maximal brightness at an angle of ≈25°, corresponding to an approximately elliptical RID, which is expected from a focused light source.

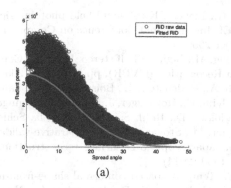
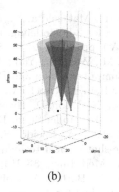

(a)   (b)

Fig. 6. (a) Estimated RID for the endoscope LED. (b) Position calibration results for the coloured LEDs: their position in a triangular configuration around the camera (black square) and slight convergence reflects the real setup.

5 Conclusions

In this paper we propose an approach for calibration of light RID and position that can be integrated within the standard camera calibration pipeline. In particular, we prove a novel property of near lighting on Lambertian planes which allows to calculate the dominant orientation of the light source by observing only the point of maximum intensity on the plane, thus constraining the light position to a single degree of freedom. This, combined with closed-form solutions with particular classes of light sources, allows us to have demonstrably better results for all types of light sources than the state-of-the-art, which instead relies on computationally expensive, sensitive symmetry searches. The method was validated with synthetic data as well as real data with a selection of different light sources and camera types, including an example application with endoscopic data.

Acknowledgments. This work was supported by The Japanese Foundation for the Promotion of Science, Grant-in-Aid for JSPS Fellows no.26.04041.

References

1. Ciuti, G., Visentini-Scarzanella, M., Dore, A., Menciassi, A., Dario, P., Yang, G.Z.: Intra-operative monocular 3D reconstruction for image-guided navigation in active locomotion capsule endoscopy. In: IEEE RAS EMBS International Conference on Biomedical Robotics and Biomechatronics (BioRob), pp. 768–774 (2012)
2. Collins, T., Bartoli, A.: 3D Reconstruction in laparoscopy with close-range photometric stereo. In: Ayache, N., Delingette, H., Golland, P., Mori, K. (eds.) MICCAI 2012, Part II. LNCS, vol. 7511, pp. 634–642. Springer, Heidelberg (2012)
3. Drbohlav, O., Chaniler, M.: Can two specular pixels calibrate photometric stereo? In: IEEE International Conference on Computer Vision (ICCV), vol. 2, pp. 1850–1857, October 2005

4. Higo, T., Matsushita, Y., Joshi, N., Ikeuchi, K.: A hand-held photometric stereo camera for 3-D modeling. In: IEEE International Conference on Computer Vision (ICCV), pp. 1234–1241, September 2009
5. Liao, M., Wang, L., Yang, R., Gong, M.: Light fall-off stereo. In: IEEE Conference on Computer Vision and Pattern Recognition (CVPR), pp. 1–8, June 2007
6. Maier-Hein, L., Groch, A., Bartoli, A., Bodenstedt, S., Boissonnat, G., Chang, P.L., Clancy, N., Elson, D., Haase, S., Heim, E., Hornegger, J., Jannin, P., Kenngott, H., Kilgus, T., Muller-Stich, B., Oladokun, D., Rohl, S., dos Santos, T., Schlemmer, H.P., Seitel, A., Speidel, S., Wagner, M., Stoyanov, D.: Comparative validation of single-shot optical techniques for laparoscopic 3-D surface reconstruction. IEEE Trans. Med. Imag. **33**(10), 1913–1930 (2014)
7. Malti, A., Bartoli, A., Collins, T.: Template-based conformal shape-from-motion-and-shading for laparoscopy. In: Abolmaesumi, P., Joskowicz, L., Navab, N., Jannin, P. (eds.) IPCAI 2012. LNCS, vol. 7330, pp. 1–10. Springer, Heidelberg (2012)
8. Mecca, R., Wetzler, A., Bruckstein, A.M., Kimmel, R.: Near field photometric stereo with point light sources. SIAM J. Imag. Sci. **7**(4), 2732–2770 (2014)
9. Moreno, I., Sun, C.C.: Three-dimensional measurement of light-emitting diode radiation pattern: a rapid estimation. Measur. Sci. Technol. **20**(7), 075306 (2009). http://stacks.iop.org/0957-0233/20/i=7/a=075306
10. Park, J., Sinha, S., Matsushita, Y., Tai, Y.W., Kweon, I.S.: Multiview photometric stereo using planar mesh parameterization. In: IEEE International Conference on Computer Vision (ICCV), pp. 1161–1168, December 2013
11. Park, J., Sinha, S., Matsushita, Y., Tai, Y.W., Kweon, I.S.: Calibrating a non-isotropic near point light source using a plane. In: IEEE Conference on Computer Vision and Pattern Recognition (CVPR), pp. 2267–2274, June 2014
12. Park, J., Sinha, S., Matsushita, Y., Tai, Y.W., Kweon, I.S.: Supplementary material for: 'calibrating a non-isotropic near point light source using a plane', June 2014
13. Powell, M., Sarkar, S., Goldgof, D.: A simple strategy for calibrating the geometry of light sources. IEEE Trans. Pattern Anal. Mach. Intell. **23**(9), 1022–1027 (2001)
14. Rykowski, R., Kostal, H.: Novel approach for led luminous intensity measurement. In: Conference of Society of Photo-Optical Instrumentation Engineers (SPIE), vol. 6910, February 2008
15. Schnieders, D., Wong, K.Y.K.: Camera and light calibration from reflections on a sphere. Comput. Vis. Image Underst. **117**(10), 1536–1547 (2013)
16. Simons, R., Bean, A.: Lighting Engineering: Applied Calculations. Routeledge, London (2012)
17. Stoyanov, D., Elson, D., Yang, G.Z.: Illumination position estimation for 3D soft-tissue reconstruction in robotic minimally invasive surgery. In: IEEE/RSJ International Conference on Intelligent Robots and Systems (IROS), pp. 2628–2633, October 2009
18. Takai, T., Niinuma, K., Maki, A., Matsuyama, T.: Difference sphere: an approach to near light source estimation. In: IEEE Conference on Computer Vision and Pattern Recognition (CVPR), vol. 1, pp. I-98-I-105, June 2004
19. Tan, H.Y., Ng, T.W.: Light-emitting-diode inspection using a flatbed scanner. Opt. Eng. **47**(10), 103602–103602 (2008)
20. Tankus, A., Sochen, N., Yeshurun, Y.: Reconstruction of medical images by perspective shape-from-shading. Int. Conf. Pattern Recogn. (ICPR) **3**, 778–781 (2004)

21. Visentini-Scarzanella, M., Hanayama, T., Masutani, R., Yoshida, S., Kominami, Y., Sanomura, Y., Tanaka, S., Furukawa, R., Kawasaki, H.: Tissue shape acquisition with a hybrid structured light and photometric stereo endoscopic system. In: Luo, X., Reichl, T., Reiter, A., Mariottini, G.L. (eds.) Computer-Assisted and Robotic Endoscopy (CARE). LNCS, pp. 26–37. Springer, Heidelberg (2015)
22. Visentini-Scarzanella, M., Stoyanov, D., Yang, G.Z.: Metric depth recovery from monocular images using shape-from-shading and specularities. In: IEEE International Conference on Image Processing (ICIP), Orlando, USA, pp. 25–28 (2012)
23. Vogiatzis, G.: Self-calibrated, multi-spectral photometric stereo for 3D face capture. Int. J. Comput. Vis. **97**(1), 91–103 (2012)
24. Weber, M., Cipolla, R.: A practical method for estimation of point light-sources. In: British Machine Vision Conference (BMVC), pp. 1–10, September 2001
25. Wong, K.-Y.K., Schnieders, D., Li, S.: Recovering Light Directions and Camera Poses from a Single Sphere. In: Forsyth, D., Torr, P., Zisserman, A. (eds.) ECCV 2008, Part I. LNCS, vol. 5302, pp. 631–642. Springer, Heidelberg (2008)
26. Wu, C., Narasimhan, S.G., Jaramaz, B.: A multi-image shape-from-shading framework for near-lighting perspective endoscopes. Int. J. Comput. Vis. **86**, 211–228 (2010)
27. Zhou, W., Kambhamettu, C.: A unified framework for scene illuminant estimation. Image Vis. Comput. **26**(3), 415–429 (2008)

A General Vocabulary Based Approach for Fine-Grained Object Recognition

Shubhra Aich[✉] and Chil-Woo Lee

Department of Electronics and Computer Engineering,
Chonnam National University, Gwangju, Republic of Korea
s.aich.72@gmail.com, leecw@chonnam.ac.kr, leecw@jnu.ac.kr

Abstract. In this paper, we deal with the classification problem of visually similar objects which is also known as fine-grained recognition. We consider both rigid and non-rigid types of objects. We investigate the classification performance of different combinations of bag-of-visual words models to find out a generalized set of visual words for different types of fine-grained classification. We combine the feature sets using multi-class multiple learning algorithm. We evaluate the models on two datasets; in the non-rigid, deformable object category, Oxford 102 class flower dataset is chosen and 17 class make and model recognition car dataset is selected in the rigid category. Results show that our combination of vocabulary sets provides reasonable accuracies of 81.05 % and 96.76 % in the flower and car datasets, respectively.

1 Introduction

Object recognition is one of the most fundamental problems in computer vision. Most of the researches in this area belong to the classification problem among different categories, like cars, airplanes, animals etc. as we can see from PASCAL [2] and Caltech [3] datasets. Rather than differentiating the objects of different categories, we investigate the recognition problem within single basic category. This is also referred to as fine-grained recognition and in most cases, it requires domain knowledge which very few people have. Recent studies cite show that combination of heterogeneous features covering the aspects of texture, shape and color is successful in fine-grained recognition since the heterogeneity of the feature sets exploit the subtle object properties complementarily. Hence, in this paper, we address this problem in a generalized way by examining different heterogeneous feature combinations to find out a general set of bag-of-features irrespective of the expert level of domain knowledge. For experiment, we consider both rigid and non-rigid types of objects. In the non-rigid category, we choose the problem of flower classification and in the rigid case, we take the problem of make and model recognition of cars into account.

The problem of flower classification appears to be more challenging than multi-category object classification for several reasons. One reason is large inter-species shape and color similarities. Also, mostly the overall shape information

© Springer International Publishing Switzerland 2016
T. Bräunl et al. (Eds.): PSIVT 2015, LNCS 9431, pp. 572–581, 2016.
DOI: 10.1007/978-3-319-29451-3_45

of the flowers is quiet useless because of the high-level of deformation of non-rigid flower petals. Therefore, it is very difficult for the laymen to identify the species of a given flower from a color image with visual inspection. Given only the image, sometimes it becomes even impossible for the botanists or flora-experts to differentiate among visually similar flower categories.

Also, recognition of make and model of cars impose the same kind of problems. Anyone familiar with brand logos can easily identify the brand name only looking at the logo in the cars. However, the logos only provide information about the brand or make of the cars. No information is present about the car models in the logos. Given the image of the frontal side of the cars only, identifying both make and model of that car is impossible for the person not very much familiar with that specific model of that specific brand because of the similar appearances in most cases, especially in case of the models from the same brand.

Sample images from flower and car datasets are shown in Fig. 1 from which high-level of visual similarities within the categories are evident.

Fig. 1. Sample images from Oxford 102 flower dataset [7] and MMR 17 dataset [1]. In case of flowers, first two and last two images have significant visual similarities in shape. In case of cars, overall appearances are similar.

In this paper, we investigate a general combination of color, shape and texture features using multiple kernel learning algorithm of Tang et al. [6]. Our selected bag-of-features model provides substantially high recognition accuracies on both flower and car datasets. The next section gives a review of the most relevant literatures. The methodology is described in Sect. 3. A short description of both datasets and the experimental results on these datasets are illustrated in Sect. 4. Section 5 contains discussion and future work.

2   Related Work

As a major field in computer vision, there are hundreds of papers published on object recognition every year. Here, we cover only the most relevant ones to ours.

Nilsback and Zisserman [7–11] have the first extensive level of work on flower classification. They use a bag-of-words model of combination of HSV, internal and boundary SIFT [4] and HOG [12] with a non-linear multiple kernel support vector machine [5]. Also, later they propose geometric layout features [7] to make all the images of same size and orientation. Our work can be considered a modified extension, improvement and generalization over their work.

Chai et al. [13] proposes two iterative bi-level co-segmentation algorithms (BiCos and BiCos-MT) based on SVM classification using GrabCut [14] and high-dimensional descriptors stacked from the standard sub-descriptors such as, color distribution, SIFT [4], size, location within the image and shape - all extracted from superpixels [15] of single image and multiple images from multiple classes. Finally, they use concatenated bag-of-words histograms of LLC [16] quantized Lab color and three different SIFT descriptors extracted from the forenground region and linear SVM for recognition.

Ito and Kubota [17] use the concept of co-occurrence features for recognition. They propose three heterogeneous co-occurrence features, i.e. color-CoHOG which consists of multiple co-occurrence histograms of oriented gradients including color matching information, CoHED which is the co-occurrence of edge orientation and color difference, CoHD which is the co-occurrence of a pair of color differences and lastly, one homogeneous feature - color histogram [10].

Angelova and Zhu [18] use RGB intensity based pixel affinity for segmentation and max pooling of the LLC [16] encoded HOG features [12] at multiple scales with linear SVM for classification. In the domain of make and model recognition (MMR), there are two types of approaches - one is feature-based and the other is appearance-based. Since our approach belongs to the former category, we only review the relevant approaches in that category.

Petrovic and Cootes [19] first analyze different features including pixel intensities, edge response and orientation, normalized gradients and phase information extracted from the frontal view of the vehicles with k-Nearest Neighbor (kNN) classifier for recognition. Another type of feature-based approach in this domain includes descriptor features like scale-invariant feature transform (SIFT)[4] and speeded up robust features (SURF)[20] as the descriptors. Dlagnekov [21] investigated SIFT based image matching along with two other methods, i.e. Eigencars and shape context matching for recognition. His experiments demonstrated the promising performance of SIFT compared to others. Baran et al. [1] examined the performance of two approaches in the same dataset we use in MMR. The first one is SURF bag-of-features with SVM and the second approach consists of different distance metrics based image matching using the weighted combination of edge histogram descriptors [22], SIFT and SURF.

3   Method

Many object recognition researches leverage segmentation as pre-processing for recognition [1, 7, 13, 18, 23]. Since our focus in this paper is to experiment the combination of bag-of-features using multiple kernel learning, we use simple GrabCut [24] and Haar-like feature detectors [25, 26] to segment the images of flower and car datasets, respectively, prior to applying our recognition framework.

3.1 Features

The low level features extracted from the foreground or object regions to exploit color, shape and texture properties of the objects are HSV color, SIFT, multi-scale dense SIFT and non-overlapping HOG.

HSV Color. HSV colorspace is chosen over RGB, Lab or other spaces because of its less sensitivity to illumination variance [7]. The descriptors are taken as the average of non-overlapping MxM pixel blocks over the entire image. All 3-D descriptors from the training images are then grouped into N clusters by estimating N cluster centroids or visual words using K-means [27]. The values of parameters M and N are chosen experimentally to avoid both high bias and high variance.

SIFT. SIFT descriptors take the local shape and texture properties of the objects in the segmented images into account. However, the original scale estimation procedure of Lowe [4] in the SIFT calculation shows serious drawbacks. Objects naturally appear in images in arbitrarily different scales. In most cases, in natural images, these scales are unknown and so multiple scales should be considered for each feature point. One typical approach is to seek for each feature point a stable, characteristic scale to both reduce the computational complexity of higher level visual systems, as well as improving their performance by focusing on more relevant information. In the original paper of SIFT descriptor [4], Lowe followed this approach. However, this method produces a small set of interest points located near corner structures in the image. Mikolajczyk [28] shows that a scale change of factor 4.4 causes the percent of pixels for which a scale is detected to decrease as little as 38 % for the DoG detector of which in only 10.6 %, the detected scale is correct. To overcome this limitation of scale estimation, instead of using original point localization method of SIFT, we extract SIFT descriptors on a regular grid of spacing M with circular patches of fixed radius R [7,30]. The superiority of this kind of regular point sampling strategies over systems utilizing invariant features generated at stable coordinates and scales is already shown by Nowak et al. [29]. The reason behind this performance boost in [29] is because of having descriptors for many pixels over accurate scales than just having a few with the Lowe's method.

Multi-scale Dense SIFT. SIFT descriptors of fixed size in regular grid points cannot handle larger scale differences. To this end, we incorporate the pyramid histogram of visual words (PHOW) descriptor [30,31], which is a variant of multi-scale dense SIFT. At each point on a regular grid of spacing M, SIFT descriptors are computed over four circular support patches of four fixed radii. Hence, each point is represented by four SIFT descriptors. At last, all the features are vector quantized into N words using K-means algorithm.

Non-overlapping HOG. HOG features [12] are the normalized histograms of oriented gradients with overlaps between the neighboring cells (small blocks of pixels) in a grid. The number of bins B is equal to the number of orientations in the histogram. However, in our calculation, we have used no overlapping between the cells. Also, like SIFT descriptors, we treat B-bin normalized histograms as B-dimensional descriptors and quantize them into N visual words using K-means like the other three features.

3.2   Classifier

We have used multiple kernel learning approach of Tang et al. [6]. This approach uses SVM as its base classifier and a weighted linear combination of kernels, each kernel corresponding to one feature. We use normalized chi-square distance to calculate the similarity matrix and same kernel for each feature. Semi-infinite linear program (SILP) [32] is used in [6] for the purpose of large scale kernel learning. Figure 2 shows the block diagram of our general approach.

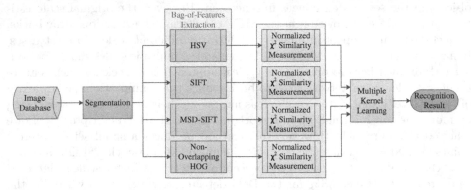

Fig. 2. Block diagram of our approach.

4   Experiment

In this section, we illustrate the experimental results of our proposed feature combination using multiple kernel learning on two fine-grained recognition benchmarks: Oxford 102 flowers [7] and MMR 17 cars [1].

4.1   Datasets

Oxford 102 Flowers. Oxford 102 flowers dataset is introduced by Nilsback and Zisserman [7]. It contains 102 species of flowers and a total of 8189 images. Each category consists of between 40 and 250 images. The species are chosen to be flowers commonly found in United Kingdom. Most of the images in this dataset were collected from the web whereas a few of them were acquired by taking pictures. The dataset is divided into a training set, a validation set and a test set. Training and validation sets each consist of 10 images per class, totaling 1020 images each. Remaining 6149 images belong to the test set.

MMR 17 Cars. This dataset is proposed by Baran et al. [1]. The number of car models in this dataset is 17. It is divided into two separate subsets - one is for training and the other is for testing. The images were collected in various lighting conditions over a period of 12 months. All the images represent front sides of cars taken "en face" or at a little angle (less than 30 degrees). The training set contains a total number of 1360 images with 80 images per class taken outdoor or downloaded from the internet (fifty-fifty). The test set is composed of 2499 images. Each category consists of between 65 and 237 images. The test images, like the training ones, were taken as well from the outdoor as from the internet. In case of test set however, less attention was paid to the quality and size of collected images.

4.2 Results

All the images are first cut according to the smallest bounding box enclosing the foreground segmentation and then they are rescaled to the smallest dimension of 500 pixels before feature extraction in Oxford 102 flower dataset. Table 1 shows the recognition performance for different features and their combinations on this dataset and Table 2 shows the comparison in accuracy with other recent methods. We compare our method with only those which use segmentation prior to recognition to keep the same baseline. On this baseline, our method provides slightly better recognition rate over the recent one of Angelova and Zhu [18].

Table 3 lists the recognition rate for different features and their combinations on MMR 17 dataset. Since any car model may have any arbitrary color,

Table 1. Recognition performance of features on oxford dataset

Features	Recognition rate (%)
HSV	43.36
NO-HOG	37.03
SIFT	57.88
MSD-SIFT	68.27
HSV + NO-HOG	58.79
NO-HOG + SIFT	66.99
SIFT + MSD-SIFT	73.09
HSV + SIFT	70.91
HSV + MSD-SIFT	78.22
NO-HOG + MSD-SIFT	71.56
HSV + NO-HOG + SIFT	75.10
NO-HOG + SIFT + MSD-SIFT	74.32
HSV + NO-HOG + MSD-SIFT	78.63
HSV + NO-HOG + SIFT + MSD-SIFT	81.05

Table 2. Performance comparison on oxford dataset

Method	Recognition rate (%)
Nilsback and Zisserman [7]	72.8
Ito and Cubota [17]	74.8
Nilsback and Zisserman [11]	76.3
Chai et al., BiCos Method [13]	79.4
Chai et al., BiCos-MT Method [13]	80.00
Angelova and Zhu [18]	80.66
This Method	81.05

Table 3. Recognition performance of features on MMR dataset

Features	Recognition rate (%)
NO-HOG	68.39
SIFT	73.99
MSD-SIFT	96.96
NO-HOG + SIFT	66.99
SIFT + MSD-SIFT	96.76
NO-HOG + MSD-SIFT	96.96
NO-HOG + SIFT + MSD-SIFT	96.76

Table 4. Performance comparison on MMR dataset

Method	Recognition rate (%)
Baran et al. [1] SURF-BoW+SVM	91.7
Baran et al. [1] SURF+SIFT+EH	97.2
This work	96.8

it cannot be considered an object property for make and model recognition. Therefore, we exclude HSV color from the feature set for this dataset. From the recognition rates listed in Tables 1 and 3 for different single features, multi-scale dense SIFT (MSD-SIFT) appears to be the best among all. Table 4 shows a comparison of our method with two other approaches recently published by Baran et al. [1]. Our method outperforms the approach using SURF-BoW+SVM in [1] but is slightly behind the other weighted combination of SURF, SIFT and EH. However, in [1], the authors clearly state that this method has significant computational burden of exhaustive high dimensional descriptor matching and so despite achieving higher accuracy, it is infeasible for real-time implementation. Therefore, from the perspective of feasibility in real-time applications, our method shows a performance boost over the recent one (SURF-BoW+SVM).

Parameters. The optimum number of words is 900 for HSV feature in Oxford dataset. For HOG, it is 1500 and for both SIFT and MSD-SIFT, this number is 3000 in both datasets. The block size for averaging in HSV colorspace is 3×3. In case of HOG, 8×8 square cells are used for both datasets with the range of gradient orientation from -180 to +180 degree. Regular grid spacing of 5 pixels is used in the calculation of both SIFT and MSD-SIFT for both datasets. The radius of the descriptors in SIFT is used to be 5 pixels and the magnification factor for MSD-SIFT used is equal to 6. Scales equal to 4, 6, 8 and 10 are used in MSD-SIFT calculation.

5   Discussion and Future Work

In this paper, we experiment on different combination of feature set to find out an effective one across different domain of fine-grained recognition. In this work, we use one non-rigid and one rigid dataset for evaluation. Albeit our feature set provides reasonable accuracies on both datasets compared to the state-of-the-art, it is much less accurate in non-rigid or deformable domain than the rigid one. Hence, one of the main future challenges is to find out an almost equally effective approach in both deformable and rigid domains. Also, future work includes the task of developing similar approaches for large-scale datasets.

Acknowledgment. This research is financially supported by the Ministry of Education, Science and Technology (MEST) and National Research Foundation of Korea (NRF) through the Human Resource Training Project for Regional Innovation.

References

1. Baran, R., Glowacz, A., Matiolanski, A.: The efficient real- and non real-time make and model recognition of cars. Multimedia Tools Appl. **74**, 4269–4288 (2015)
2. Everingham, M., Van Gool, L.J., Williams, C.K.I., Winn, J.M., Zisserman, A.: The pascal visual object classes (VOC) challenge. Int. J. Comput. Vis. **88**(2), 303–338 (2010)
3. Li, F.-F., Fergus, R., Perona, P.: One-shot learning of object categories. IEEE Trans. Pattern Anal. Mach. Intell. **28**(5), 594–611 (2006)
4. Lowe, D.G.: Distinctive image features from scale-invariant keypoints. Int. J. Comput. Vis. **60**(2), 91–110 (2004)
5. Scholkopf, B., Smola, A.: Learning with Kernels. MIT Press, Cambridge (2002)
6. Tang, L., Chen, J., Ye, J.: On multiple kernel learning with multiple labels. In: 21st International Joint Conference on Artificial Intelligence, Pasadena, California, USA, pp. 1255–1260 (2009)
7. Nilsback, M.-E., Zisserman, A.: Automated flower classification over a large number of classes. In: 6th Indian Conference on Computer Vision. Graphics & Image Processing, Bhubaneswar, India, pp. 722–729 (2008)
8. Nilsback, M-E., Zisserman, A.: Delving into the whorl of flower segmentation. In: Proceedings of the British Machine Vision Conference, Warwick, UK, pp. 1–10 (2007)

9. Nilsback, M.-E., Zisserman, A.: Delving deeper into the whorl of flower segmentation. Image Vis. Comput. **28**(6), 1049–1062 (2010)
10. Nilsback, M-E., Zisserman, A.: A visual vocabulary for flower classification. In: IEEE Computer Society Conference on Computer Vision and Pattern Recognition, New York, USA, pp. 1447–1454 (2006)
11. Nilsback, M-E.: An automatic visual flora - segmentation and classification of flowers images. D. Phil. thesis, University of Oxford (2009)
12. Dalal, N., Triggs, B.: Histograms of oriented gradients for human detection. In: 2005 IEEE Computer Society Conference on Computer Vision and Pattern Recognition (CVPR 2005), San Diego, California, USA, pp. 886–893 (2005)
13. Chai, Y., Lempitsky, V.S., Zisserman, A.: BiCoS: a bi-level co-segmentation method for image classification. In: IEEE International Conference on Computer Vision, Barcelona, Spain, pp. 2579–2586 (2011)
14. Rother, C., Kolmogorov, V., Blake, A.: "GrabCut": interactive foreground extraction using iterated graph cuts. ACM Trans. Graph. **23**(3), 309–314 (2004)
15. Felzenszwalb, P.F., Huttenlocher, D.P.: Efficient graph-based image segmentation. Int. J. Comput. Vis. **59**(2), 167–181 (2004)
16. Wang, J., Yang, J., Yu, K., Lv, F., Huang, T.S., Gong, Y.: Locality-constrained linear coding for image classification. In: The Twenty-Third IEEE Conference on Computer Vision and Pattern Recognition, San Francisco, California, USA, pp. 3360–3367 (2010)
17. Ito, S., Kutoba, S. : Object classification using heterogeneous co-occurrence features. In: 11th European Conference on Computer Vision, Heraklion, Crete, Greece, pp. 209–222 (2010)
18. Angelova, A., Zhu, S.: Efficient object detection and segmentation for fine-grained recognition. In: IEEE Conference on Computer Vision and Pattern Recognition, Portland, OR, USA, pp. 811–818 (2013)
19. Petrovic, V.S., Cootes, T.F.: Analysis of features for rigid structure vehicle type recognition. In: British Machine Vision Conference, Kingston, UK, pp. 1–10 (2004)
20. Bay, H., Tuytelaars, T., Van Gool, L.J.: SURF: speeded up robust features. In: 9th European Conference on Computer Vision, Graz, Austria, pp. 404–417 (2006)
21. Dlagnekov, L.: Video-based car surveillance: license plate, make and model recognition. Master's thesis, University of California, San Diego, USA (2005)
22. Park, D.K., Jeon, Y.S., Won, C.S.: Efficient use of local edge histogram descriptor. In: ACM Multimedia 2000 Workshops, Los Angeles, California, USA, pp. 51–54 (2000)
23. Rabinovich, A., Vedaldi, A., Belongie, S.: Does image segmentation improve object categorization? UCSD CSE Technical report, no. CS2007-090, USA (2007)
24. Boykov, Y., Jolly, M-P.: Interactive graph cuts for optimal boundary and region segmentation of objects in N-D images. In: International Conference on Computer Vision, Princeton, NJ, USA, pp. 105–112 (2001)
25. Andrzej, M., Piotr, G.: Automated optimization of object detection classifier using genetic algorithm. In: Dziech, A., Czyżewski, A. (eds.) Multimedia Communications, Services and Security. Communications in Computer and Information Science, vol. 149, pp. 158–164. Springer, Berlin, Heidelberg, Germany (2011)
26. Viola, P.A., Jones, M.J.: Rapid object detection using a boosted cascade of simple features. In: IEEE Computer Society Conference on Computer Vision and Pattern Recognition, Kauai, HI, USA, pp. 511–518 (2001)
27. Csurka, G., Dance, C.R., Fan, L., Willamowski, J., Bray, C.: Visual categorization with bags of keypoints. In: 8th European Conference on Computer Vision, Prague, Czech Republic, pp. 1–22 (2004)

28. Mikolajczyk, K.: Detection of local features invariant to affine transfomations. Ph.D. thesis, Institut National Polytechnique deGrenoble, France (2002)
29. Nowak, E., Jurie, F., Triggs, B. : Sampling strategies for bag-of-features image classification. In: 9th European Conference on Computer Vision, Graz, Austria, pp. 490–503 (2006)
30. Vedaldi, A., Fulkerson, B. : Vlfeat: an open and portable library of computer vision algorithms. In: International Conference on Multimedia, Firenze, Italy, pp. 1469–1472 (2010)
31. Bosch, A., Zisserman, A., Muoz, X., Image Classification using Random Forests and Ferns. In: International Conference on Computer Vision, Rio de Janeiro, Brazil, pp. 1–8 (2007)
32. Sonnenburg, S., Rätsch, G., Schäfer, C., Schölkopf, B.: Large scale multiple kernel learning. J. Mach. Learn. Res. **7**, 1531–1565 (2006)

A Triangle Mesh Reconstruction Method Taking into Account Silhouette Images

Michihiro Mikamo[1](✉), Yoshinori Oki[1], Marco Visentini-Scarzanella[1],
Hiroshi Kawasaki[1], Ryo Furukawa[2], and Ryusuke Sagawa[3]

[1] Graduate School of Science and Engineering, Kagoshima University,
1-21-40, Korimoto, Kagoshima 890-0065, Japan
{mikamo,oki,marco,kawasaki}@ibe.kagoshima-u.ac.jp
http://www.ibe.kagoshima-u.ac.jp/~cgv/index.html
[2] Graduate School of Information Sciences, Hiroshima City University,
3-4-1, Otsukahigashi, Asaminami-ku, Hiroshima 731-3194, Japan
ryo-f@hiroshima-cu.ac.jp
https://www.hiroshima-cu.ac.jp/
[3] National Institute of Advanced Industrial Science and Technology,
1-3-1 Kasumigaseki, Chiyoda-ku, Tokyo 100-8921, Japan
ryusuke.sagawa@aist.go.jp
https://www.aist.go.jp/index_en.html

Abstract. In this paper, we propose a novel approach to reconstruct triangle meshes from point sets by taking the silhouette of the target object into consideration. Recently, many approaches have been proposed for complete 3D reconstruction of moving objects. For example, motion capture techniques are used to acquire 3D data of human motion. However, it needs to attach markers onto the joints, which results in limiting the capturing environments and the number of data that can be acquired. In contrast, to obtain dense data of 3D object, multi-view stereo scanning system is one of the powerful methods. It utilize images taken by several directions and enables to reconstruct 3D dense point sets by using Epipolar geometry. However, it is still challenging problem to reconstruct 3D triangle mesh from the 3D point sets due to the abundant points originated by mismatched points between images. We propose a novel approach to obtain more accurate triangle mesh reconstruction method than the previous one. We take advantage of silhouette images acquired in the process of reconstructing 3D point sets that result in removing noises and compensating holes. Finally, we demonstrate that the proposed method can generate the details of the surface, where the previous method loses from a small number of points.

Keywords: Active measurement system · Projector-camera system · Entire 3D shape · Multi-view image reconstruction

1 Introduction

In this paper, we propose a novel approach to generate triangle meshes based on the silhouette of the target object. Recently, 3D data is becoming one of

© Springer International Publishing Switzerland 2016
T. Bräunl et al. (Eds.): PSIVT 2015, LNCS 9431, pp. 582–593, 2016.
DOI: 10.1007/978-3-319-29451-3_46

the most important information to represent the object motion and shape, such as humans, animals and so on. To acquire such 3D data, several techniques have been invented. One such example is motion capture. To detect the motion of objects, markers are attached onto joints. However, the number of samples acquired is limited to the number of markers. As a result, it is difficult to reconstruct surface information using such devices. On the other hand, to obtain dense 3D point sets, various techniques have been proposed in the literature, including Shape-from-Silhouette [14], Multi-view Stereo (MVS) [8]. Shape from Silhouette is one of the typical methods to acquire the entire shape in dynamic scenes, however surface details usually cannot be recovered correctly. Multi-view stereo can generally yield accurate reconstructions. However, reconstructing accurate point sets and generating 3D triangle mesh from the point sets are still challenging tasks.

Multi-view stereo reconstructs 3D point sets by computing corresponding points by the images captured from several directions. The point sets are refined by silhouette images that are the binary images contouring the object, to remove points originated from calibration error or background textures. After reconstructing the point sets, the points are connected to be a triangle mesh. There are some methods that can generate a 3D mesh, however, they tend to fail to connect the points, especially in the case that the number of the points are small, and lose the details of the surfaces.

The main contribution of this paper is that we propose a novel approach that can generate a triangle mesh with a higher accuracy than the state of the art. This is achieved by integrating the silhouette images of the target object into the mesh generating process. The silhouette images prevent abundant points to be connected to generate a 3D mesh. The proposed method is evaluated using point sets acquired by a multi-view projectors/cameras system. We compare the proposed method with a technique representative of the state of the art, which shows our method can generate surfaces from small number of points. Our method can cover holes that tend to appear in sparse point areas and keep the details on the surfaces.

The paper consists of the following sections. In Sect. 2, we briefly introduce some representative methods whose purpose is reconstructing 3D points or meshes. In Sect. 3, we mention the overview of the multi-view projectors/cameras system that enables to reconstruct the point set from images captured by several directions and how to exploit silhouettes from the images. We explain the details of the proposed method in Sect. 4. Experimental results are mentioned in Sect. 5. Finally we conclude the paper by directing future vision in Sect. 6.

2   Related Work

Lots of techniques have been developed to reconstruct 3D shape by using multi-view stereo technique. We review some of representative methods here.

Several methods use the concept of visual hull such as [5,9,14,16]. Visual hull is computed by taking the intersection of slices of space projected from the target object in the input image. Several techniques utilize visual hull as the initial shape of the 3D model. However, visual hull cannot reconstruct the details of the surfaces. Therefore, improvements are proposed by the articles [5,9].

Volumetric multi-view stereovision techniques decompose the domain into subdivided areas [2,3,6]. These methods tend to be time-consuming or fail to reconstruct 3D shapes because of initial settings of the optimization.

Other approaches for reconstructing 3D shape are well-summarized in Seitz et al. [19]. Labatut et al. also introduces such techniques by categorizing them from several aspects [13].

Surface reconstruction has been actively developed in computer graphics fields such as [1,4,11,12]. Those methods are implicitly assuming that the point sets are dense enough to reconstruct 3D surface. However, point sets acquired by multi-view stereo system are not always sufficient. In addition, density of the points would be different depending on the areas. This is because occlusions occur behind the target object, where the reconstruction would be failed.

The proposed method enables to reconstruct surface from relatively small number of points and space areas. In addition, our method can preserve the shape of the surface without smoothing the details.

3   Overview of the Multi-view Projector Camera System

3.1   System Configuration

For our proposed method, we use the active MVS system proposed by Furukawa et al. [7], where multiple cameras and projectors are used.

In the setup, devices are placed so that they encircle the target object, and the cameras and the projectors are put in alternating order with known position and orientation. The system was setup as shown in Fig. 1. We assume all the

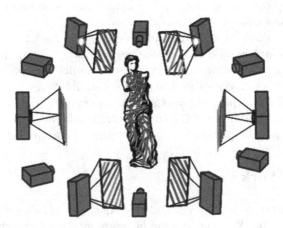

Fig. 1. A setup example to reconstruct the entire shape using six projectors and six cameras.

devices are calibrated (*i.e.* known intrinsic parameters of the devices as well as their relative positions and orientations). The details of the system configuration are explained in the paper [7].

3.2   The Multi-view Projector Camera System

The system obtains triangle meshes by the following steps; capturing images, generating silhouettes, decoding projected patterns, getting point sets of the target object, and finally, reconstructing triangle meshes. The overview of the proposed method is shown in Fig. 2. The process from capturing images to getting point sets are included in the multi-view stereo system. We use the silhouettes of the target object to generate 3D triangle mesh with higher accuracy.

In order to capture the geometry of the object, each of the projectors projects patterns, while the cameras capture the projected patterns as 2D curves on the captured images.

Next, we generate silhouettes to suppress noise from point mismatches resulting in 3D points outside the target object. To this end, we employ a silhouette generating method based on an offline image database composed by the background images taken under all combinations of projectors, in order to be robust to cast shadows [18]. The details of the silhouette extracting method is explained in Sect. 3.3. In the proposed mesh generating process, this silhouette image is also used as a term of a cost function, which brings more accurate reconstruction result than the previous method. Wrong matches inside the object don't affect

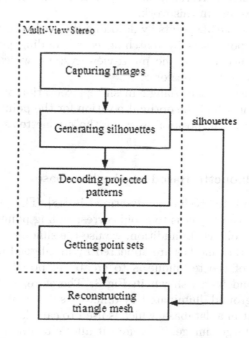

Fig. 2. The overview of the proposed method

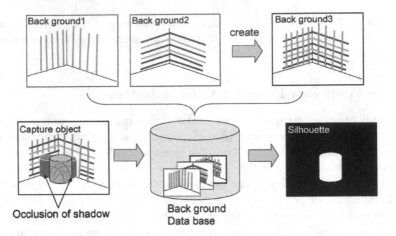

Fig. 3. Workflow for the silhouette extraction.

the cost function because they don't appear on surfaces. The tetrahedra composed of the points are also invisible from outside, therefore, they don't affect the final result.

Decoding the projected patterns is necessary to get the shape information of the target object. However, the color information projected is often lost or corrupted due to the texture of the target object. Several methods are proposed to recover the projected patterns despite the interference of the surface texture, such as [21] which we use in this work.

Next, we compute the 3D points by decoding the projected patterns. Namely, we reconstruct the point sets by matching corresponding points between the captured images. Since we use the multi-view system, we can get six sets of points that come from six projectors.

Finally, we reconstruct the triangle mesh representation of the target object. To do so, first, we must find the optimal position for the point sets. We propose a method to determine this position by using the silhouette as a term of the cost function in Sect. 4.

3.3 Creating Silhouette Based on the Database

In our system, we use the technique described in [18]. The purpose of defining the 3D silhouette of the object is to avoid corresponding points being generated outside of the target object. In addition, we use the silhouette as a term of cost function to prevent that meshes are appeared by misaligned points.

The basic idea of the technique is to create all possible the image areas affected by cast shadows as shown in Fig. 3. Therefore, we capture multiple images of the background illuminated by different subsets of the projectors. All these images are put in a database, which is used to calculate the similarity with each region of the target image. Therefore it allows to find correspondences of background regions even the captured image includes shadows.

During the shape acquisition procedure, similarity is calculated for each patch of the object image against the database using ZNCC (Zero-mean Normalized Cross-Correlation), which allows for linear changes in luminance. However, whenever a candidate patch contains both a subregion with cast shadows as well as one with a clean background, the similarity score is negatively affected. Similarly, at the boundary of the projected lines the perceived color is affected by the demosaicing algorithm, creating instabilities and false matches. In order to alleviate these issues, we consider directly using Bayer pattern images as the input and use an adaptive support-weight [22] when calculating the similarity. Adaptive support-weights work by setting a weight to each pixel of the patch based on color similarity between the center and outer pixels, which we have found experimentally to solve our problem. In all our experiments, we use a 5×5 patch size. The similarity score is used as the data term for a Graph Cut algorithm, which we use for the final segmentation into foreground and background.

4   Triangle Mesh Reconstruction

In this section, we propose a method that enables to generate triangle meshes from point sets. The purpose of the proposed method is to generate accurate polygon meshes by taking advantage of the information obtained from the multi-view stereo system.

Our method stems from the mesh generating technique proposed in the paper [13]. This consists of constructing a triangle mesh by viewing the problem as binary labeling, where labels stand for the points being either inside or outside of the target shape generated by 3D Delaunay triangulation. For optimization, graph cut was used to minimize the following cost function.

$$E(S) = E_{vis}(S) + \lambda_{photo}E_{photo}(S) + \lambda_{area}E_{area}(S) \tag{1}$$

where, S is a set of triangles belonging to the target mesh. $E_{vis}(S)$ is the visibility that indicates whether the triangle set can be seen from the camera or not. The idea is that the triangle set S consists of the surface of the target object is visible from the camera. $E_{vis}(S)$ is represented by the total number of tetrahedra that the ray passes through from each point of a tetrahedron while it reaches the camera. $E_{area}(S)$ is one of the areas of triangles on a tetrahedron.

In our method, we accept the active reconstruction method using multi-view stereo system proposed in the paper [10] to get the point sets of a target object. We used the projection patterns shown in Fig. 4. The advantage of this projection patterns is that we can acquire point sets independent from other projected patterns. The arrangements of the devices are same to Fig. 1.

The process of the proposed triangle-mesh generating method is as follows: First, we merge the point sets to reduce the errors that come from calibration process. Next, we construct 3D Delaunay triangulation by using graph cut. Finally, we solve the optimization problem by Levenberg-Marquadt method to get the resultant triangle mesh.

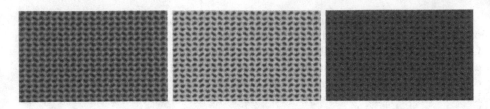

Fig. 4. The wave projection pattern

5 Experiment

5.1 Merging Point Sets

Our system consists of six cameras and six projectors aligned alternately (See Fig. 1). Therefore, we reconstruct three dimensional points using the combinations of cameras and projectors. The minimum component is that a projector is aligned between the two paired of cameras. As a result, each projector has two reconstructed point sets. Then, twelve point sets can be obtained. Point sets obtained by the same projector are supposed to be matched, however, mismatches exist because of the calibration error. We optimize the point sets using SBA (Sparse Bundle Adjustment) [15].

5.2 Computing the Delaunay Triangulation in 3D Space

In the two dimensional space, Delaunay triangulation connects points to be triangles. In the three dimensional space, it connects points with neighboring three points so that they make a tetrahedron. The circumcircles of the triangle do not include the other points, therefore, it is possible to construct mesh structure by the neighboring points. We construct 3D Delaunay map from 3D point sets. To obtain the 3D Delaunay map, we used The Computational Geometry Algorithms Library (CGAL) [20].

5.3 Graph Cut Optimization

The method proposed in the paper [13] generates triangle mesh by regarding the problem as a binary labeling. They assign labels to the tetrahedron so that they stand for inside or outside of the target shape. In the proposed method, we follow this concept, however, we propose a new cost function to prevent noise that would be reconstructed from abundant 3D points.

To add the binary labels, we use graph cut optimization. We optimize the following cost function.

$$E(S) = E_{vis}(S) + \lambda_{sil}E_{sil}(S) + \lambda_{area}E_{area}(S) + \lambda_{length}E_{length}(S) \qquad (2)$$

λ_{sil}, λ_{area}, and λ_{length} are weights for each term. $E_{sil}(S)$ is the total number of white pixels that appear by a tetrahedra being reprojected to be a silhouette image. By using this term, we generate meshes based on the silhouette images, which result in decreasing noises. $E_{area}(S)$ is the energy that decides the surface smoothness. $E_{length}(S)$ is the energy that stands for the sum of the length of the edges by the triangle that consists of tetrahedra.

5.4 Experimental Settings

In our experiment, we used six Point Grey Research Grasshopper cameras (1600 × 1200 pixels), and six LCD video projectors at WXGA resolution. The cameras are synchronized and calibrated prior to the experiment and can capture images at 20 fps. We used a mannequin model as an object.

5.5 Experimental Results

The images captured by the MVS system are shown in the top row of Fig. 5. The wave pattern was projected onto the object. We used the method proposed in the paper [18] to generate silhouette images. The acquired silhouettes images are shown in the bottom row of Fig. 5. The silhouettes are properly obtained without including the texture of background.

Figure 6 illustrates the comparison result. The top row shows the front view and the bottom row shows the back view. We show the merged point set obtained by our system in Fig. 6(a). The number of vertices is 4,654. Despite the low number of vertices, we are able to generate a smooth polygon mesh as shown in Fig. 6(b). Figure 6(c) is the result obtained by the method proposed in [11] and implemented on Meshlab [17]. We tried to find the best parameter settings in the method [11], however we found empirically that the suggested parameters were the best: Octree Depth is 6, Solver Divide is 6, Samples per Node is 1, and Surface offsetting is 1. The computation time is about 0.5 s on the software.

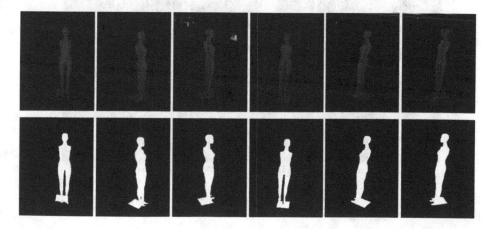

Fig. 5. The captured images (top row) and obtained silhouettes (bottom row)

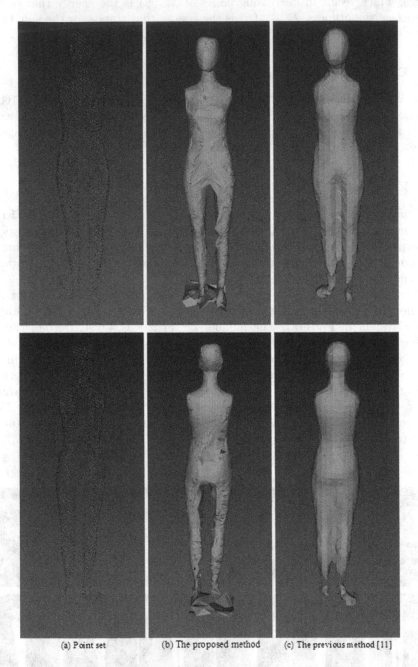

(a) Point set   (b) The proposed method   (c) The previous method [11]

Fig. 6. The comparison between the proposed method (center column(b)) and the previous method [11](right column(c))

In Fig. 6(b), we can see that the proposed method enables to reconstruct areas where detail tends to be lost, such as the area where the points are occluded by the legs, where the points are sparsely distributed. Conversely, these points are connected into contiguous surfaces when using the method in [11] as shown in Fig. 6(c). In addition, noise that existed in the point set was removed by the proposed method in Fig. 6(b), while they can be seen around the object in Fig. 6(c).

Our method still left some bumps. This is caused by the area where the point sets overlapped due to slight calibration errors.

We conducted our experiment under the condition that Intel(R) Core(TM) i7-2600 CPU (3.40 GHz), 16 GB RAM, x64 system. The program was executed on a single core. The total computation time is 756.31 s. The most time-consuming part is the collision judgment between the Delaunay diagram and silhouette images. It takes 379.69 s and accounts for about 50 % of the total computation time. The visibility judgment that the rays count the number of surface across the path takes 362.45 s and accounts for about 48 %.

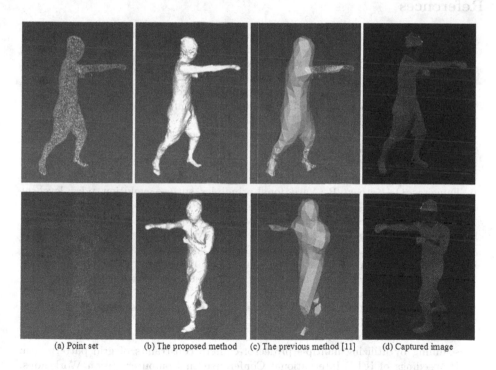

(a) Point set   (b) The proposed method   (c) The previous method [11]   (d) Captured image

Fig. 7. The resultant mesh obtained from complex object

In Fig. 7, we applied our method to data obtained from a posing human subject. The number of vertices is 16,287. Figure 7(d) shows some of the captured images. Again, the results clearly show how our method can better preserve the details in scenes with a low number of vertices.

6   Conclusion

We proposed a novel approach to generate triangle meshes by integrating information from the silhouette images of the target object. By using the silhouette images as a term of the cost function, we are able to successfully remove mismatched points that would result in failure cases during the mesh reconstruction. Consequently, the proposed method can generate triangle meshes from relatively small number of points while preserving the surface details. Especially when compared with the state of the art, our method is able to better preserve the surface details with a small number of vertices.

For our future work, we will explore the parameter space of our proposed method for a better optimization performance. In addition, efficient implementation is another future work. In the proposed algorithm, all the processes can be separated by the minimum projector-camera components. Therefore, the computation time can be reduced by parallel processing such as using GPU.

References

1. Boissonnat, J.-D.: Geometric structures for three-dimensional shape representation. ACM Trans. Graph. **3**(4), 266–286 (1984)
2. Boykov, Y., Lempitsky, V.: From photohulls to photoflux optimization. In: Proceedings of British Machine Vision Conference, vol. 3, pp. 1149–1158 (2006)
3. Broadhurst, A., Drummond, T.W., Cipolla, R.: A probablistic framewrok for space carving. In: Proceedings of IEEE International Conference on Computer Vision, pp. 388–393 (2001)
4. Edelsbrunner, H., Mücke, E.P.: Three-dimensional alpha shapes. ACM Trans. Graph. **13**(1), 43–72 (1994)
5. Esteban, C.H., Schmitt, F.: Silhouette and stereo fusion for 3d object modeling. Comput. Vis. Image Underst. **96**(3), 367–392 (2004)
6. Faugeras, O., Keriven, R.: Variational principles, surface evolution, pdes, level set methods, and the stereo problem. Trans. Image Process. **7**(3), 336–344 (1998)
7. Furukawa, R., Sagawa, R., Delaunoy, A., Kawasaki, H.: Multiview projectors/cameras system for 3d reconstruction of dynamic scenes. In: Proceedings of 4DMOD Workshop on Dynamic Shape Capture and Analysis, pp. 1602–1609 (2011)
8. Furukawa, Y., Ponce, J.: Accurate, dense, and robust multi-view stereopsis. In: Proceedings of IEEE Computer Society Conference on Computer Vision and Pattern Recognition, pp. 1362–1376 (2007)
9. Furukawa, Y., Ponce, J.: Carved visual hulls for image-based modeling. Int. J. Comput. Vis. **81**(1), 53–67 (2009)
10. Kasuya, N., Sagawa, R., Furukawa, R., Kawasaki, H.: One-shot entire shape scanning by utilizing multiple projector-camera constraints of grid patterns. In: Proceedings of IEEE International Conference on Computer Vision Workshops, pp. 299–306 (2013)
11. Kazhdan, M., Bolitho, M., Hoppe, H.: Poisson surface reconstruction. In: Proceedings of the Fourth Eurographics Symposium on Geometry Processing, SGP 2006, pp. 61–70 (2006)
12. Kolluri, R., Shewchuk, J.R., O'Brien, J.F.: Spectral surface reconstruction from noisy point clouds. In: Proceedings of Eurographics/ACM SIGGRAPH Symposium on Geometry Processing, pp. 11–21 (2004)

13. Labatut, P., Pons, J.-P., Keriven, R.: Efficient multi-view reconstruction of large-scale scenes using interest points, delaunay triangulation and graph cuts. In: Proceedings of IEEE 11th International Conference, pp. 1–8 (2007)
14. Laurentini, A.: The visual hull concept for silhouette-based image understanding. IEEE Trans. Pattern Anal. Mach. Intell. **16**(2), 150–162 (1994)
15. Lourakis, M.I.A., Argyros, A.A.: Sba: a software package for generic sparse bundle adjustment. ACM Trans. Math. Softw. **36**(1), 1–2 (2009)
16. Matusik, W., Buehler, C., Raskar, R., Gortler, S.J., McMillan, L.: Image-based visual hulls. ACM Trans. Graph. **6**, 369–374 (2000)
17. Meshlab. http://meshlab.sourceforge.net/
18. Oki, Y., Visentini-Scarzanella, M., Wada, T., Furukawa, R., Kawasaki, H.: Entire shape scan system with multiple pro-cams using texture information and accurate silhouette creating technique. In: Proceedings of the 14th IAPR International Conference Machine Vision Applications, pp. 18–21 (2015)
19. Seitz, S.M., Curless, B., Diebel, J., Scharstein, D., Szeliski, R.: A comparison and evaluation of multi-view stereo reconstruction algorithms. In: Proceedings of IEEE Computer Society Conference on Computer Vision and Pattern Recognition, pp. 519–528 (2006)
20. The Computational Geometry Algorithms Library. http://www.cgal.org/
21. Thibault, Y., Kawasaki, H., Sagawa, R.,. Furukawa, R.: Exemplar based texture recovery technique for active one shot scan. In: Proceedings of the 13th IAPR Conference on Machine Vision Applications, pp. 331–334 (2013)
22. Yoon, K.-J., Kweon, I.S.: Adaptive support-weight approach for correspondence search. IEEE Trans. Pattern Anal. Mach. Intell. **28**(4), 650–656 (2006)

All-Focus Image Fusion and Depth Image Estimation Based on Iterative Splitting Technique for Multi-focus Images

Wen-Nung Lie[1,2(✉)] and Chia-Che Ho[1]

[1] Department of Electrical Engineering,
National Chung Cheng University, Chia-Yi, Taiwan, ROC
[2] AIM-HI, National Chung Cheng University, Chia-Yi, Taiwan, ROC
`ieewnl@ccu.edu.tw`

Abstract. This paper concerns about processing of multi-focus images which are captured by adjusting the positions of the imaging plane step by step so that objects at different depths will have their best focus at different images. Our goal is to synthesize an all-focus image and estimate the corresponding depth image for this multi-focus image set. In contrast to traditional pixel- or block-based techniques, our focus measures are computed based on irregular regions that are iteratively refined/split to adapt to varying image content. At first, an initial all-focus image is obtained and then segmented to get initial region definitions. The regional Focus Evaluation Curve (FEC) along the focal-length axis and a regional label histogram are then analyzed to determine whether a region should be subject to further splitting. After convergence, the final region definitions are used to perform WTA (Winner-take-all) for choosing image pixels of best focus from the image set. Depth image then corresponds to the label image by which image pixels of best focus are chosen. Experiments show that our adaptive region-based algorithm has performances (in synthesis quality, depth map, and speed) superior to other prior works and commercial software that adopt pixel-weighting strategy.

Keywords: All-focus · Multi-focus · Image fusion · Depth image

1 Introduction

3D scanning has been an important research topic for a long time. It can be divided into two types: active and passive. For examples, 3D laser scanner or infrared (IR) illuminator belong to the active type, which actively illuminate light to measure ranges and surface variations based on time-of-flight principle. Passive 3D scanners, however, do not emit any light, but compute the 3D surfaces or even the range values based on the reflection of ambient lights from object surfaces. Generally, the passive type takes an advantage of lower hardware cost, but intensive computing load; the active type however suffers from a higher hardware cost and measurement noise from environment.

The "Depth from Focus" (DFF) [1, 3] and "Depth from Defocus" (DFD) [2] algorithms have been developed for 3D passive measurement/scanning techniques for several years. These two techniques, differing from the traditional stereo-vision type,

© Springer International Publishing Switzerland 2016
T. Bräunl et al. (Eds.): PSIVT 2015, LNCS 9431, pp. 594–604, 2016.
DOI: 10.1007/978-3-319-29451-3_47

use monocular camera, set at different focus lengths or positions of imaging planes for a same view and scene. Since all the pictures are captured at the same viewing angle, there is no occlusion/dis-occlusion problems as in stereo matching problem. This paper will mainly emphasize on the DFF technique to estimate the depth image as well as the all-focus image based on the multiple-focus image set.

In principle, objects at different depths or distances, at a given camera focal length or position of imaging plane, will present different levels of focus on the resulting picture. By varying the focal lengths or positions of imaging planes and analyzing the focusing regions of each image, it is possible for the DFF technique to synthesize an all-focus image by extracting the image pixels of best focus for each image region (e.g., block or patch) from among the set of images. Since each imaging plane position corresponds to a distance where an object has best focus, the depth map can be easily derived from the all-focus image.

The success of DFF technique relies on a reliable focus measure for a given local image patch. Traditional measures include: Gaussian-filtering response [3], Laplacian filtering response [4], variation [5], image quality measure value (IQM) [6], and Modulation Transfer Function (MTF) [7]. Most of them try to estimate the amount of high-frequency components in a local area as a measure of focusing (clarity). Some of them also found applications in camera auto-focusing (AF). However, the most important in DFF is that a good focus measure should be able to discriminate between "focus" and "unfocus" for textureless areas.

Depending on the range of local measure, DFF algorithms can be also categorized into pixel-based [10], block-based, and region-based [8] methods. This categorization depends on the area (pixel, block, or region) where a focus measure is computed and assigned. For pixel-based methods, the resulting focus value map is often noisy and requires post-optimization process. For block or patch-based methods, the regular area shape or improper size often makes it possibly failed around region boundaries. To overcome the above drawbacks, [8] proposes a region-based method, where focus measures are computed for segmented regions of arbitrary shapes. However, their work defined the regions according to the raw and unfocused image set in a one-shot manner without any following refinement, hence cannot adapt to varying image content accurately.

Viewing the all-focus synthesis procedure as an image fusion process, the DFF methods can be classified into pixel-weighting, winner-take-all (WTA) [10], and weight-optimized [9] algorithms. Pixel-weighting methods compute a weight $(0.1 \sim 1.0)$ for each component image when trying to fuse a specific pixel/block/region along the focal length domain. The weight-optimized methods however refine the weights according to similarity/smoothness constraints between adjacent pixels. Though this kind of methods is capable of achieving better result, it is time-consuming and not suitable for time-limited applications. WTA strategy, which assigns one of the weights to be 1.0 and 0.0 for others, is however simpler and popular in many other applications.

Since the results of the pixel- and block-based focus measures are rather noisy and patterned, respectively, we adopt in this paper the region-based strategy (as in [8]) which is capable of adapting shapes of segmented regions to varying image content. Since pixel-weighting and weight-optimized fusions suffer from their high system complexity, the WTA strategy is adopted for fusion in our system. That is to say, we propose a region- and WTA-based algorithm for DFF. At first, we derive an "initial all-focus image" from the original image set by a simple pixel-weighting scheme. Then, a region segmentation algorithm is applied to the initial all-focus image to get the initial region definitions. The focus measures are then computed for each region definition at different focal lengths (or, different positions of imaging plane). By analyzing the time-series (i.e., along the focal length axis) behavior of the focus measures for each region definition, it is decided to split the region definition into multiple sub-regions or not. This process is iterated until no region definitions can be split any more. After convergence, focus measure computations and WTA fusion are applied based on the final region definitions. The depth map can be easily derived from the all-focus image by assigning, for each pixel, the frame position label (corresponding to a specific object distance) which has the highest focus measure. Since all pixels in a converged region have the same frame position label, they will have the same depth.

Though our splitting procedure makes our algorithm more adaptive to different image content, a post processing is still necessary to filter out wrong depth estimates based on a smoothness constraint. A better-quality all-focus image can then be obtained.

2   Iterative Region-Splitting Algorithm

First, we define a multi-focus image set $\mathbf{I} = \{I^1, ..I^k, ..., I^K\}$ (k is the position label and K is the number of images in the set). The iterative region splitting procedure is composed of three parts.

2.1   Initial All-Focus Image Generation

It is known that the amount of high-frequency components around a given pixel can be considered as an index to reflect the level of focusing. For example, the formula in [9] is adopted in this paper:

$$y_{ik} = \theta_{ik}\left[erf\left(\frac{|g_i^k|}{\sigma^k}\right)\right]^K,\tag{1}$$

where i is the pixel index, g_i^k is the high-frequency gradient component, σ^k is the variance of g_i^k for the k-th image, $erf(\cdot)$ stands for the Gaussian error function, θ_{ik} is the frequency of non-zero $|g_i^k|$ around pixel i in image k, and y_{ik} represents the weight at pixel i of the image k. Therefore, each input image k has its own weight map, which can be used to synthesize an initial all-focus image P, as follows:

$$P_i = \sum_{k=1}^{K} w_{ik}I_i^k\tag{2}$$

$$w_{ik} = \frac{y_{ik}}{S_i}, S_i = \sum_{k=1}^{K} y_{ik} \tag{3}$$

where I_i^k represents the value of the pixel i in input image k, and P_i represents the pixel i in the output image P. Clearly, all w_{ik} are summed to be 1.0 for any given pixel i.

2.2   Initial Region Segmentation

The initial region segmentation in this paper is based on the initial all-focus image P (in contrast to [8] which is based on an average image derived from $\mathbf{I}$). The well-known Mean-Shift region segmentation algorithm [11] is applied to achieve the purpose. Note that our initial all-focus image P is basically superior to the average image [8] on quality, hence resulting in a more accurate region segmentation.

2.3   Iterative Region Splitting

The initial region segmentation should be subject to following refinement (splitting). Our strategy is to conduct a time-series analysis. For co-located regions along the focal length axis, a Focusing Evaluation Curve (FEC) is analyzed and derived. If there is no outstanding peak in the FEC such that WTA can be confident, it will be subject to splitting. Here, we use the variation function [5] as our local focus measure:

$$F_s^k = \sum_{(x,y) \in S} [I_{Laplacian}^k(x, y) - \mu_S^k]^2, \tag{4}$$

$$\mu^k = \frac{1}{|S|} \sum_{(x,y) \in S} I_{Laplacian}^k(x, y), \tag{5}$$

where (x, y) are the image coordinates, S represents the indicated region, $|S|$ is the total number of pixels in S, $I_{Laplacian}^k$ means the Laplacian response for the image k, μ_S^k is the average of $I_{Laplacian}^k$ within region S, and F_S^k represents the focus measure for region S in image k. Hence, we get an FEC for each region S: $FEC_S = \{F_S^1, ..., F_S^K\}$. With the analysis of FEC_S, we are capable of making a decision of whether S should be split or not.

Figure 1 shows two examples of FEC_S, where the x axis represents the image number k and the y axis represents the F_S^k value in Eq. (4). The case of single peak in (a) often reveals a single depth in S, hence WTA can be easily applied to extract the frame of best focus (the red line). On the contrary, the case of two peaks in (b) reveal that there might be two objects of different depths in S. Actually, there are other possible behaviors for FEC_S such as flat, multimodal, etc.

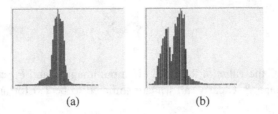

(a)   (b)

Fig. 1. Two examples of FEC curve for a region S: (a) single peak, (b) two peaks.

2.3.1   Classification of a Region S

In this paper, each FEC_S is classified into single-peak (SP), two-peak (TP), and undetermined (x region). For regions of SP type, WTA can be applied to S for fusion; for regions of TP type, S will be split into several sub-regions; for x regions, they should resort to the supporting information from neighboring ones for depth estimation and focusing pixel extraction.

To achieve the above classification, a label histogram (LH) is made for each region S. LH_S is defined as a histogram of the image number of best focus (or, the winner or depth label) for all pixels in S. That is, the focus measure in Eqs. (4) and (5) is modified for pixels as follows:

$$F^k_{(x,y)} = (I^k_{Laplacian}(x, y) - \mu^k_{(x,y)})^2, \tag{6}$$

$$\mu^k_{(x,y)} = \frac{1}{|D|} \sum_{(x,y) \in D} I^k_{Laplacian}(x, y), \tag{7}$$

where D is a fixed window around (x,y). LH_S can be also used to determine whether a single depth of field exists in S. If there is multi-modes in LH_S, a further split into sub-regions is necessary. Since LH_S and FEC_S represent features along the spatial and focal-length domain, respectively, their combination is expected to provide more useful information for region splitting.

This paper proposes three tests to LH_S and FEC_S. The first is to perform a second derivative to FEC_S and count the zero-crossing rate (ZCR). For SP curve, the ZCR is 4 and the peaks and valleys have similar areas. If all the above conditions are satisfied, then an SP is detected for S.

For the second test, local peaks in FEC_S are identified first; then a convexity or concavity indicator γ for the curve from each local peak (LP) to the global peak (GP) is calculated:

$$\gamma_{LP} = \frac{1}{|GP - LP + 1|} \sum_{i=LP}^{GP} U(F^i_S - F^{LP}_S \geq thd), \tag{8}$$

where LP and GP represent the corresponding image numbers, thd is a threshold, and U (.) is a step function ($U(x) = 1$ for $x > 0$ and $U(x) = 0$ for $x \leq 0$). A larger γ_{LP} means more convexity which possibly exists in SP curve. By combining γ_{LP} from all local peaks of FEC_S, we get a global SP indicator SM_1 as follows:

$$SM_1 = \frac{1}{H}\sum_i (\gamma_{LPi} \cdot \beta_{LPi} \cdot F_S^{LPi}), \quad \beta_{LPi} = \|LP_i - GP\|, \quad H = \sum_i (\gamma_{LPi} \cdot \beta_{LPi}) \quad (9)$$

It can be seen that the computation of SM_1 is distance-weighted. If an LP is near to the GP, it might be considered as a noise and given a less weight. A larger SM_1 (approaching 1.0) reveals a higher probability of SP curve. We also perform Eqs. (8) and (9) to LH_S and get another indicator SM_2. Both SM_1 and SM_2 are required to be larger than a threshold so that SP can be identified.

The third is to test the bi-modality (TP) of LH_S. First, the traditional Otsu's algorithm is used to binarize LH_S and get two clusters (with probabilities $P_0, P_1, P_0 + P_1 = 1.0$). If both P_0 and P_1 are between 0.4 ~ 0.6 and the distance (on image index) between two peaks is larger than a threshold, then a TP in the curve LH_S is identified.

For each region S, test 1&2 are performed to FEC_S. When all conditions for SP (in test 1 & 2) are satisfied, SP is identified. Otherwise, test 3 is performed to LH_S. When conditions for TP (in test 3) are satisfied, TP is identified. Otherwise, S is classified as an x-region.

2.3.2 Region Splitting

For any region S that satisfies test 3, it will be split into several parts. Our algorithm takes advantage of the result of Otsu's thresholding in test 3. That is, each pixel in S is classified to be cluster 1 or 2, depending on whether its winning image number is higher (cluster 2) or lower (cluster 1) than the calculated threshold. However, note that the number of connected regions after splitting may be larger than 2. That is, sub-regions for cluster 1 or 2 might be dis-connected. Anyway, each segmented sub-region of S after splitting is conducted for next iteration of tests 1 ~ 3.

2.3.3 Processing of X-Regions

Regions with FEC_S which cannot be classified into SP or TP (such as flat, multi-peak, etc.) are marked as x-regions. Their best focus or depth cannot be derived from WTA based on their own pixel data reliably. Since the number of x-regions is not large, we resort to the help from neighboring regions which have been classified successfully.

Our strategy for processing x-regions is based on the observation of smooth depth change between neighboring regions. First, for each x-region, the depth labels (i.e., the image number of best focus) of its neighboring regions are recorded. The dominant one is hence accepted for the current x-region. Since x-regions themselves might be adjacent to one another, x-regions that have a larger portion of classified neighboring regions should have higher priorities in processing order.

3 Depth Image Post-processing

It is still possible to have some artifacts in either the depth or all-focus image. For example, focus measure F_S^k from defocusing regions might be even larger than that from focused areas, hence resulting in impulse noise in depth image. They should be corrected before further applications.

First, we detect the impulse-noise regions in the depth image. They are defined to be regions that have large depth differences (over a threshold) with respect to the neighboring regions along a total of ρ% (e.g., 70 %) of the outer boundaries. After detection, the depth correction is similar to the processing of x-regions, i.e., using the dominant label/depth from neighboring regions for replacement.

4 Experiment Results

Four test image sets are captured and collected by adjusting positions of the camera imaging plane step by step. They are: "Battery" (65 images), "Screw" (48 images), "PCB" (48 images), and "Tool" (7 images), all are in 640×480 pixels size, as shown in Figs. 2, 3, 4 and 5.

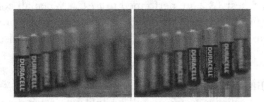

Fig. 2. "Battery" image set

Fig. 3. "Screw" image set

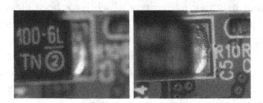

Fig. 4. "PCB" image set

In this paper, we compare the performances in all-focus image synthesis and depth map estimation between four methods: (1) Helicon, (2) Zerene Stacker, (3) [10], and (4) proposed. The first two are actually commercial software. Figures 6, 7, 8 and 9 illustrate the results of all-focus image synthesis and depth map estimation for the 4 methods under comparison. Since the depth maps estimated by Zerene Stacker cannot

Fig. 5. "Tool" image set

be acquired by us, they are not provided in Figs. 6, 7, 8 and 9. On the other hand, the depth maps generated by [10] are different from Helicon's and ours due to its non-linear interpolation/recalculation.

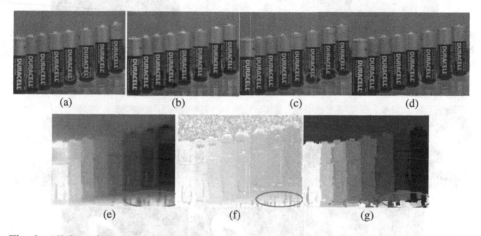

Fig. 6. All-focus image and depth map results for "Battery": (a) (e) Helicon, (b) Zerene Stacker, (c) (f) [10], (d) (g) proposed.

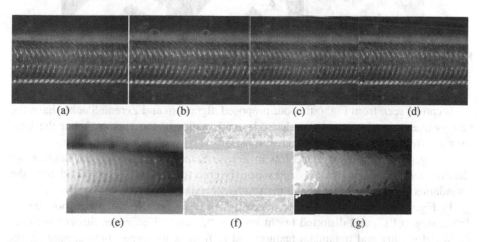

Fig. 7. All-focus image and depth map results for "Screw": (a) (e) Helicon, (b) Zerene Stacker, (c) (f) [10], (d) (g) proposed.

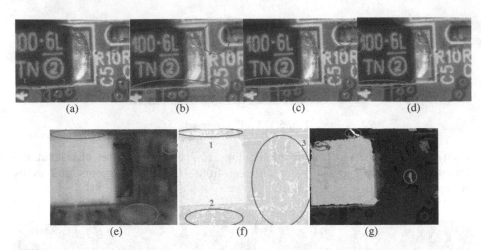

Fig. 8. All-focus image and depth map results for "PCB": (a) (e) Helicon, (b) Zerene Stacker, (c) (f) [10], (d) (g) proposed.

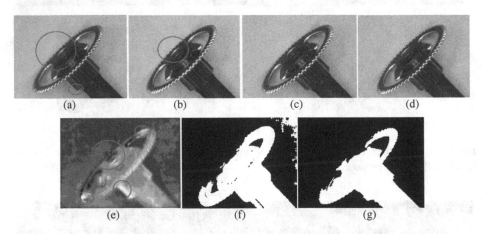

Fig. 9. All-focus image and depth map results for "Tool": (a) (e) Helicon, (b) Zerene Stacker, (c) (f) [10], (d) (g) proposed.

It can be seen from Fig. 6 that our proposed algorithm and Zerene Stacker have the best synthesis result around the electrodes and bodies of the "battery", but the later seems better in the table's reflection surface.

In Fig. 7, there are two dark dots in Zerene Stacker's result. For the depth map, Helicon seems to give wrong depths (too bright) for the background and blur the boundaries between the screw and the top background.

In Fig. 8, Helicon presents geometrical distortion (see the left image boundary), defocusing at "1", and distorted bright spots at "2" and "3"; Zerene Stacker presents slight defocusing and redundant texture; and [10] presents some ripple around object boundaries. For the depth map, our method presents some errors, whereas Helicon blurs the object depth boundaries.

In Fig. 9, our proposed and [10] present better results, while Helicon and Zerene Stacker present slight defocusing. As for the depth map, Helicon presents some errors.

In Figs. 6, 7 and 8, the depth maps generated by [10] are noisy (especially for the background area) and might copy the texture patterns from the color information.

To objectively evaluate the all-focus image fusion performance, the metric proposed in [12] (Q, ranging between 0.0 and 1.0, a higher value means better fusion) are measured for the four methods under comparison. Table 1 gives the result, where "*"'s represent the highest ones. It can be seen that our proposed method outperforms others except for the "Screw" image set. This might be due to the bottom background where some spots are present.

Table 2 shows the comparison in computing time for the 4 methods. The computer platform is Intel Core i7-3770 3.40 GHz with 3.2 GB RAM for Helicom, Zerene Stacker, and our proposed. The method of [10] was however executed on a CPU platform of 2.8 GHz and 16 GB RAM. Obviously, our algorithm (not optimized) is speedy than Helicon and Zerene Stacker in nearly all 4 image sets.

Table 1.   Evaluation of image fusion results.

	Battery	Screw	PCB	Tool
Resolution*images	640x480x65	640x480x48	640x480x48	640x480x7
Helicon	0.32721	0.32846(*)	0.3015	0.4087
Proposed	0.38451(*)	0.27735	0.48273(*)	0.47050(*)
Zerene Stacker	0.27272	0.24245	0.30591	0.4027
[10]	0.35688	0.26358	0.45498	0.47502(*)

Table 2.   Comparison of computing time (sec).

	Battery	Screw	PCB	Tool
Resolution*images	640x480x65	640x480x48	640x480x48	640x480x7
Helicon	12.47	7.86	9.06	3.21
Proposed	12.605	5.949	7.93	2.068
Zerene Stacker	19.89	24.84	15.48	2.89
[10]	10.89	7.43	7.48	1.29

5   Conclusion

This paper proposes a region-based and WTA strategy to synthesize an all-focus image and estimate the depth map for multi-focus images. That is, focus measures are computed based on irregular regions which are able to adapt to varying image content. Our algorithm has a capability of iteratively refining/splitting the segmented regions by analyzing the behaviors of FEC and LH time-series curves.

Software implementation shows that our adaptive region-based algorithm has a performance (in both fusion quality, depth map, and speed) superior to commercial software that adopts pixel-weighting strategy. Future possible improvements include finer classification of a region S so that more suitable arrangement can be made. Other mixed fusion strategy that is more effective than WTA and simpler than pixel-weighting scheme can be also devised.

References

1. Wong, E.: A new method for creating a depth map for camera auto focus using an all in focus picture and 2D scale space matching. In: Proceedings of International Conference Acoustics, Speech and Signal Processing (ICASSP), May 2006
2. Lin, H.-Y., Gu, K.-D.: Depth recovery using defocus blur at infinity. In: Proceedings of International Conference on Pattern Recognition, ICPR (2008)
3. Chen, Y.-C., Wu, Y.-C., Liu, C.-H., Sun, W.-C., Chen, Y.-C.: Depth map generation based on depth from focus. In: Proceedings of IEEE Conference Electronic Devices, Systems and Applications (ICEDSA), pp. 59–63, April 2010
4. Yokota, A., Yoshida, T., Kashiyama, H., Hamamoto, T.: High speed sensing system for depth estimation based on depth from focus by using smart imager. Proc. IEEE ISCAS 1, 564–567 (2005)
5. Wong, E.: A new method for creating a depth map for camera auto focus using an all in focus picture and 2D scale space matching. In: Proceedings of IEEE ICASSP, May 2006
6. Pedraza, J.C., Ohba, K., Rodriguez, J.W., Tanie, K.: All in focus camera vision system for robot navigation and manipulation based on the DFF criteria. Proc. IEEE Conf. Intell. Robots Syst. 2, 758–763 (2001)
7. Wang, T.H., Chiu, C.T.: Low visual difference virtual high dynamic range image synthesizer from a single legacy image. In: Proceedings of IEEE International Conference on Image Processing, pp. 2265– 2268 (2011)
8. Li, Q., Du, J., Song, F., Wang, C., Liu, H., Lu, C.: Region-based multi-focus image fusion using the local spatial frequency. In: Control and Decision Conference (CCDC) (2013)
9. Shen Cheng, R., Jianbo Shi, I., Basu, A.: Generalized random walks for fusion of multi-exposure images. Proc. IEEE Int. Conf. Image Process. 20(12), 3634–3646 (2011)
10. Zeng, Y.-C.: Generation of all-focus images and depth-adjustable images based on pixel blurriness. In: Proceedings of Annual Summit and Conference of Asia-Pacific Signal and Information Processing Association (APSIPA) (2013)
11. Comaniciu, D., Meer, P.: Mean shift: a robust approach toward feature space analysis. IEEE Trans. Pattern Anal. Mach. Intell. 24(5), 603–619 (2002)
12. Xydeas, C.S., Petrovic, V.: Objective image fusion performance measure. Electron. Lett. 36(4), 308–309 (2000)

Stereo Matching Techniques for High Dynamic Range Image Pairs

Huei-Yung Lin$^{(\boxtimes)}$ and Chung-Chieh Kao

Department of Electrical Engineering, National Chung Cheng University,
Chiayi 621, Taiwan
hylin@ccu.edu.tw

Abstract. We investigate the stereo matching techniques for high
dynamic range (HDR) image pairs. It is an emerging topic in computer vision and multimedia applications due to the availability of HDR
image capture devices. The disparity computation will eventually take
the stereo HDR input. In this work, three state-of-the-art stereo matching algorithms are modified and used to test the advantages of HDR
stereo matching. By performing the HDR bit-plane slicing, it is found
that only about 16 bits per channel is required for the HDR image format.
We propose a 16-bit unsigned integer format to store the HDR image,
which allows the available stereo matching algorithms to be adopted
for disparity computation. Experiments and performance evaluation are
carried out using Middlebury stereo datasets.

Keywords: Stereo matching · High dynamic image

1 Introduction

Stereo matching is a core technology of many 3D related applications. In the
multimedia related field, it is commonly used for depth perception, 3D scene
reconstruction, depth-image-based rendering, 3DTV and multi-view stereoscopic
display, etc. While a large number of algorithms have been developed for stereo
correspondence computation in the past few decades [1], it is still difficult to
obtain high quality disparity maps for high dynamic range scenes. The main
reason is that most current CCD and CMOS sensors are only capable of capturing 2 to 4 orders of light intensity whereas the human eyes are sensitive to
around 5 orders of magnitude simultaneously. Consequently, the conventional
stereo matching algorithms cannot be successfully performed on the captured
images due to the presence of over or under exposed regions.

High dynamic range imaging (HDRI or HDR imaging) serves to represent
a real world scene which contains a wide range of luminance change. It adopts
the floating point values to encode the large amount of information, instead of
using integers as in the conventional image formats. While the existing sensor
technology has not caught up to the demands of HDR imaging, a few studios
have managed to develop HDR cameras [2]. Their solutions are fairly expensive

© Springer International Publishing Switzerland 2016
T. Bräunl et al. (Eds.): PSIVT 2015, LNCS 9431, pp. 605–616, 2016.
DOI: 10.1007/978-3-319-29451-3_48

and require a long time to capture the full dynamic range of a scene. Therefore, to generate the HDR content in a budget, methods using conventional cameras to take multiple exposures of the same scene to create a single HDR image are commonly adopted.

In computer vision research areas, stereo matching is considered as one of the most challenging and unsolved problems. Since the publication on the taxonomy of stereo algorithms by Scharstein and Szeliski [3], many researchers have participated in an on-line evaluation to compare the performance and accuracy among different stereo matching techniques. Several image datasets with rectified stereo pairs and ground truth disparity maps are available on the Middlebury stereo website as standard test beds [4]. The addition of new and more complex test image datasets provides different scenes taken under 3 illuminations and each with 3 different exposures [5]. It greatly facilitates the stereo matching research on the high dynamic range domain. By constructing HDR images from the given multi-exposure image pairs, the new datasets are suitable for the development and evaluation of HDR stereo matching algorithms.

Among the stereo matching techniques currently available, a popular method for real-time systems is the Semi-Global Block Matching (SemiGlob) algorithm proposed by Hirschmuller [6]. It achieves relatively good quality results while maintaining low computational complexity. This technique is thus successfully employed in mass production vehicles today. Hosni et al. [7] proposed a framework by applying a cost volume filtering method. They have shown that the spatially smooth labeling where the label transitions are aligned with color edges of the image can be efficiently achieved by smoothing the label costs with a fast edge preserving guided filter [8]. Ham et al. [9] describes a steady state matching probability (SSMP) density function to represent the likelihood where the points among the input stereo images being matched. They also focused on using SSMP density function to achieve a probability-based rendering (PBR) method for reconstructing an intermediate view [10]. To develop and investigate the HDR stereo matching techniques, the above algorithms are selected and integrated in our proposed framework.

Although there exist extensive studies on both stereo matching and HDR related fields, not much work has been done on joining these two subjects. Among the similar topics currently under investigation, the most close one is to produce stereoscopic HDR images or videos for high quality 3D contents [11]. However, it is substantially different from stereo matching on HDR images since the disparity computation is not the critical issue. In general, the stereoscopic HDR applications take rough disparity maps and adopt DIBR (depth-image-based rendering) technique to synthesize the stereoscopic image pairs [12]. Stereo matching on HDR images, instead, focuses on how to derive high quality disparity maps in terms of low bad pixel rates and low computation costs.

In recent years, several stereo matching techniques which take HDR image pairs as input have been proposed. Lin et al. [13] present a method to generate high dynamic range and disparity images by simultaneously capturing the high and low exposure images using a pair of cameras. Selmanović et al. [14] propose a technique to generate 3D stereoscopic HDR content using an HDR and LDR pair by stereo correspondence matching. Sun et al. [15] present an algorithm that generates HDR images from multi-exposed LDR stereo images and use a classic NCC (normalized cross-correlation) stereo matching method to evaluate the results. Akhavan et al. [16] discuss the possibilities for combining state-of-the-art stereo matching algorithms with high dynamic range imaging techniques.

In this paper, we present the stereo matching approach using HDR image pairs. The state-of-the-art stereo matching algorithms originally created to run on the conventional (LDR) stereo images are modified for HDR stereo matching. The performance is evaluated on the HDR stereo pairs generated from the multi-exposure images acquired from the same scene. We also adopt the bit-plane slicing techniques originally developed for the LDR image pairs [17], and investigate the feasibility for HDR stereo matching. Experiments are carried out using Middlebury stereo datasets, and three different HDR stereo matching algorithms are evaluated for performance comparison. The results have demonstrated the feasibility of our approach for stereoscopic HDR applications.

2   HDR Images and Stereo Matching

To obtain the HDR images, Reinhard et al. [18] briefly describes how to generate from multiple exposures. By treating the camera response function linearly, we can generate HDR images from multiple LDR exposures by the following steps:

1. Read the different exposure LDR images;
2. Set thresholds to indicate the over and under-exposed pixel intensities of each image and mark them as invalid;
3. Divide LDR images by the exposure time, bringing intensity values of LDR images into a common domain;
4. Accumulate the pixel values that are properly exposed;
5. Normalize the accumulated array by the number of input LDR images that provide valid pixel data for each position.

In the experiments we find setting thresholds to indicate over and under-exposed pixels of each exposure a critical issue if we want to derive good HDR stereo matching results. It is the key for the HDR input to outperform the original LDR input on the stereo matching results.

Since LDR and HDR images are stored in completely different formats [19], it causes many issues to come up when trying to modify LDR stereo matching algorithms for use on HDR stereo image pairs. Most conventional stereo matching algorithms (e.g., SSD, SAD, and SemiGlob) take grayscale image pairs as input. The process of converting RGB images to grayscale is basically joining information from 3 color channels - eliminating hue and saturation information while retaining the luminance.

For HDR images we use the same equation for the conversion of luminance values to a single two-dimensional array. Although the meaning behind applying the same equation to LDR and HDR images is somewhat different, in the experiments we find this method suitable for stereo matching applications. Some stereo matching algorithms in recent years take color image pairs as inputs and use the obtained color information to calculate their matching costs (such as CostFilter and SSMP). For these algorithms we use the color HDR stereo pairs generated from LDR multi-exposed images as input.

While there are various formats for HDR images, we choose the RGBE floating-point encoding format. The pixel values of HDR images are normalized to a range between 0 and 1. This is critical in our research and discussion towards HDR bit-plane slicing. We can then expand and align the whole fraction into an n-bit consecutive memory space. The variable n is determined according to the pixel with the smallest exponent value in the whole image. For example, suppose there is a pixel with the smallest exponent -5 for an HDR image. To allow all fraction bits in the image to be included, n will be $(-1) \cdot ((-5) - 23)$ with 23 being the number of bits in a fraction of a single precision IEEE 754 format floating point number. This allows all fraction bits to be aligned, and provides straightforward bit-plane slicing with fractions.

After the HDR bit-plane slicing process, we can generate bit-level quantized HDR images. For the first bit-level quantized HDR image, all pixels only contain the 2^{-1} bit position data from their original HDR image. For the second bit-level quantized HDR image, all pixels contain 2^{-1} and 2^{-2} data bits from their original HDR images, etc. As a general representation, the k bit-level quantization generate the image given by

$$I(k) = a_{-1} \cdot 2^{-1} + a_{-2} \cdot 2^{-2} + \cdots + a_{-k} \cdot 2^{-k} \tag{1}$$

3   Algorithm and Evaluation

To generate HDR stereo pairs, we use full resolution images (roughly 1300×1100 resolution) from the new stereo datasets available on the Middlebury Stereo Evaluation website. In the years of 2005 and 2006, the datasets provide a total of 30 different scenes. Each scene consists of multiple rectified views taken under three different illuminations (Illum1, Illum2, Illum3) and each with three different exposures (Exp0, Exp1, Exp2). From observation the 3 exposures of each scene all have a consistent ± 2 exposure value range, which allows us to compare the stereo matching results of different scenes and illuminations having the same baseline setup.

By taking multiple exposures, each image in the sequence will have different pixels properly exposed, and other pixels under or over exposed. However, each pixel will be properly exposed in one or more images in the sequence. Under the assumption that the image capture device is perfectly linear, each exposure may be brought into the same domain by dividing each pixel by the image's exposure time. It is therefore possible and desirable to ignore very dark and very bright pixels in the subsequent computations. We set the pixel intensity threshold to mark as over exposed pixels as 250. Any pixel intensity with a value above this number is considered as over exposed and will not be used in the HDR generation process. The under-exposure threshold is set as 5.

After looking into many state-of-the-art stereo matching algorithms from recent years, it is obvious that many algorithm implementations (designed originally for usage on LDR pairs) take advantage on the output-referred LDR image format using 8 bits per color channel. Almost all implementations coded in C store pixel information in an unsigned 8-bit integer space. This not only saves memory usage but also takes advantage of optimized CPU SIMD (single instruction, multiple data) instructions allowing computation on multiple pixel data simultaneously exploiting data level parallelism, and improving array processing performance significantly. To achieve maximum optimization for data parallelism using SIMD instruction sets, often they are hardcoded into programs, meaning it will be a lot of work for them to run on floating point numbers, i.e., HDR images. Another issue is due to the fact that many widely used image libraries such as OpenCV do not support HDR image formats. If one is to perform any kind of research on HDR images, it would be required to spend numerous hours of coding on basic operations that are available in common LDR image libraries.

In this work, we surveyed top performing stereo matching algorithms and found stereo methods CostFilter, SemiGlob, and SSMP suitable for modification to achieve HDR stereo matching. We then focus on the comparison between HDR and LDR stereo matching results. In the experiments, the original CostFilter, SemiGlob and SSMP algorithms are used to run on the 3 exposures of each scene. Modified versions of these three algorithms are used to run on the HDR stereo pairs created from the 3 different exposure images. The scene 'Midd1' as shown in Fig. 1 is an example of the HDR stereo matching outperforming the conventional methods using LDR exposures as input. This is due to the fact that the over and under-exposed pixel intensity values are properly clipped and eliminated in the HDR generation process. The middle exposure (Exp1), which is the correct exposure indicated by the camera, has the best disparity results among the 3 LDR exposures. The under exposure (Exp0) result is a little worse than Exp1. This is because the under-exposed image (Exp0) have darkened regions leaving not enough data to perform accurate stereo matching. A similar situation happens to the over-exposed image pair. By observing the original LDR images of Exposure 2 (Exp2), we can see that the whole image is way too bright, which causes many details and objects disappeared in the image.

Stereo matching requires pixels to have distinct values between each other in order to find the corresponding location of the same object in left and right stereo pairs. If the pixels are over-exposed leaving no texture or detail for stereo matching methods to compare, the disparity map will have a very poor quality result, no matter how robust the algorithm is capable in the case of correctly exposed stereo input. Although performing stereo matching on under- and over-exposed images alone shows disappointing stereo matching results, combining all exposures into an HDR representation can benefit from the extra image data.

Figure 2 shows the results of another experiment using 'Wood1' dataset. In the image of Exposure 0 (Exp0), we can see many dark regions lacking details of the objects in the scene. In the HDR generation process these under-exposed pixels are not eliminated properly, which causes less accurate HDR stereo matching results. When generating the HDR images from multiple exposures, we use the

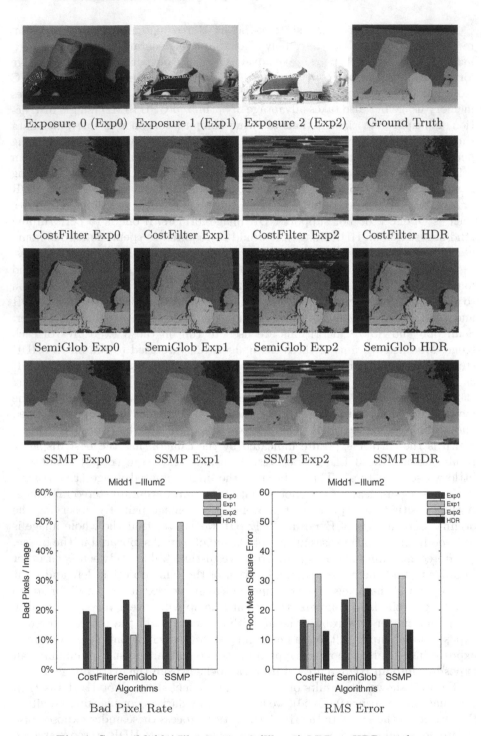

Fig. 1. Scene 'Midd1' Illumination 2 (Illum2) LDR vs HDR results.

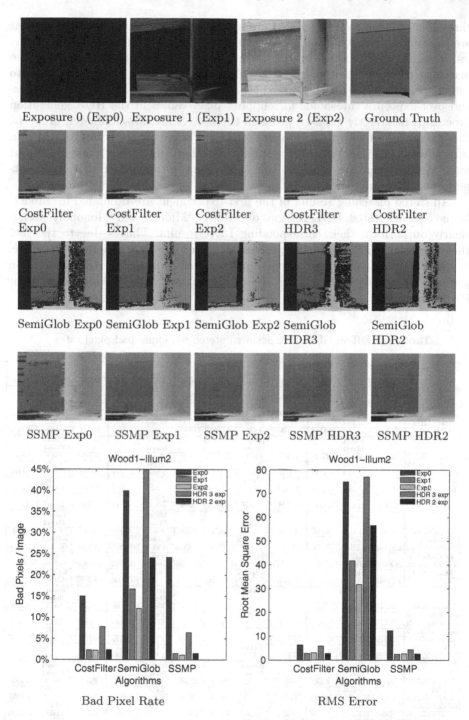

Fig. 2. Scene 'Wood1' Single Illumination (Illum2) LDR vs HDR results. HDR3 indicates created from 3 exposures. HDR2 indicates created from 2 exposures (Exp1, Exp2)

threshold 5 to eliminate pixels that are too dark and 250 to eliminate pixels that are too bright. These parameter settings are clearly not suitable for all scenarios. If we use only Exp1 and Exp2 to generate the HDR images, then the stereo matching results become more acceptable, as illustrated in the figure. Thus, to get the best results from these 3 exposures, we need to find the suitable under- and over-exposure thresholds for clipping pixel values in the HDR generation process. If incorrectly exposed pixels in the images are not eliminated properly, these pixel values will propagate and affect the resulting HDR image, which in turn causes the HDR matching results worse than the correctly exposed LDR ones. We can therefore conclude this experiment with the fact that HDR outperforms LDR only when the intensity clipping thresholds are set properly.

All stereo matching results of the first experiment are tabulated in Table 1. In the 5 scenes tested, HDR versions of 'Midd1', 'Midd2', and 'Monopoly' scenes clearly outperform their corresponding LDR results. This is due to the fact that from the HDR generation process, over-exposed and under-exposed pixel intensity values are properly clipped and eliminated from the HDR generation process. On the other hand, the scenes "Reindeer" and "Wood1" show poor HDR stereo matching results.

Table 1. LDR vs HDR (3 exposures) stereo matching bad pixel rates.

Algorithms	Aloe Illum1			Aloe Illum2			Aloe Illum3			Baby1 Illum1		
	Exp0	Exp1	Exp2	Exp0	Exp1	Exp2	Exp0	Exp1	Exp2	Exp0	Exp1	Exp2
CostFilter-HDR		10.5601			9.485			10.2241			15.8739	
CostFilter-LDR	14.3107	8.6379	7.3832	12.1138	7.6327	6.8886	12.7334	7.6222	6.5761	22.1137	12.61	11.7812
SemiGlob-HDR		25.6981			24.5632			25.7534			31.0712	
SemiGlob-LDR	25.0211	19.5558	18.5555	23.3308	19.2169	18.3614	25.0355	20.468	19.2431	29.8626	19.8844	16.6329
SSMP-HDR		11.0758			10.6646			10.3838			19.9357	
SSMP-LDR	19.8795	10.3882	8.8466	16.289	8.937	7.6195	14.7509	9.0516	7.9415	38.3126	14.0249	12.0671

Algorithms	Baby1 Illum2			Baby1 Illum3			Cloth3 Illum1			Cloth3 Illum2		
	Exp0	Exp1	Exp2	Exp0	Exp1	Exp2	Exp0	Exp1	Exp2	Exp0	Exp1	Exp2
CostFilter-HDR		12.8852			12.2907			3.3194			3.1678	
CostFilter-LDR	18.5774	11.1543	8.7538	16.4616	10.3675	10.2523	4.6538	2.9648	2.8294	3.0355	2.8052	3.1125
SemiGlob-HDR		28.4723			27.9715			11.2368			7.7316	
SemiGlob-LDR	26.6789	17.4644	15.4227	25.9842	16.9775	14.9178	11.4334	7.7863	7.0369	7.5254	6.9861	7.2694
SSMP-HDR		13.6788			12.6247			3.3125			3.4216	
SSMP-LDR	23.3062	11.1051	8.9452	21.1075	10.4442	10.1045	7.1509	3.0636	2.9117	2.8942	2.8062	2.9698

Algorithms	Cloth3 Illum3			Midd1 Illum2			Midd2 Illum2			Monopoly Illum2		
	Exp0	Exp1	Exp2	Exp0	Exp1	Exp2	Exp0	Exp1	Exp2	Exp0	Exp1	Exp2
CostFilter-HDR		2.421232			12.809572			9.509858			6.370229	
CostFilter-LDR	2.318061	2.253166	2.425352	16.562021	15.32695	32.163753	12.233618	11.80046	30.817319	9.712566	18.539122	32.779233
SemiGlob-HDR		23.417206			27.242021			26.40699			31.439887	
SemiGlob-LDR	23.208917	23.550864	24.035603	23.503187	23.968582	50.849491	23.905366	23.052968	49.761127	23.110402	24.31458	50.977137
SSMP-HDR		2.932481			13.248041			10.891008			5.132793	
SSMP-LDR	2.440035	2.442828	2.598794	16.71691	15.179717	31.498245	12.169497	11.711232	28.570909	6.827182	15.108296	32.043236

Algorithms	Reindeer Illum1			Rocks1 Illum1			Rocks1 Illum2			Rocks1 Illum3		
	Exp0	Exp1	Exp2	Exp0	Exp1	Exp2	Exp0	Exp1	Exp2	Exp0	Exp1	Exp2
CostFilter-HDR		11.6935						5.6882			5.7211	
CostFilter-LDR	14.0529	10.3011	11.8272	16.8082	8.094	5.7901	11.349	5.3911	4.3507	8.5694	5.2482	4.6236
SemiGlob-HDR		28.6551			19.0521			17.846			15.4912	
SemiGlob-LDR	27.619	21.7317	21.5128	18.6442	9.8143	7.4289	16.7113	8.9711	7.6411	14.1115	8.9657	7.7281
SSMP-HDR		11.79			4.8183			4.8455			5.1165	
SSMP-LDR	14.5659	9.9756	10.8423	34.9485	7.7635	7.3271	14.6579	4.4092	4.0265	8.066	5.0848	4.6891

Algorithms	Rocks2 Illum1			Rocks2 Illum2			Rocks2 Illum3			Wood1 Illum2		
	Exp0	Exp1	Exp2	Exp0	Exp1	Exp2	Exp0	Exp1	Exp2	Exp0	Exp1	Exp2
CostFilter-HDR		3.0185			3.1024			2.8792			7.7188	
CostFilter-LDR	6.2622	2.7277	2.0433	7.0107	2.8744	2.0678	4.3836	2.4363	2.0873	14.9723	2.2695	2.1733
SemiGlob-HDR		10.9581			12.6551			8.5396			44.875	
SemiGlob-LDR	10.6543	5.5585	4.1695	13.6324	5.4548	3.9418	7.8741	4.7667	3.8864	39.8532	16.6652	12.0399
SSMP-HDR		2.5498			2.5044			2.8934			6.392	
SSMP-LDR	7.5783	2.5392	1.9962	16.4043	2.7289	2.2068	3.9263	2.6156	2.1688	24.1315	1.4503	1.0554

Table 2. The maximum number of bits required to store the pixel radiance values for different scenes.

Scene	Aloe	Baby1	Cloth3	Rocks1	Rocks2	Midd1	Midd2	Monopoly	Reindeer	Wood1
Illum1	14	15	14	17	14	14		13	14	
Illum2	14	14	14	17	14		15			14
Illum3	14	14	14	16	14					

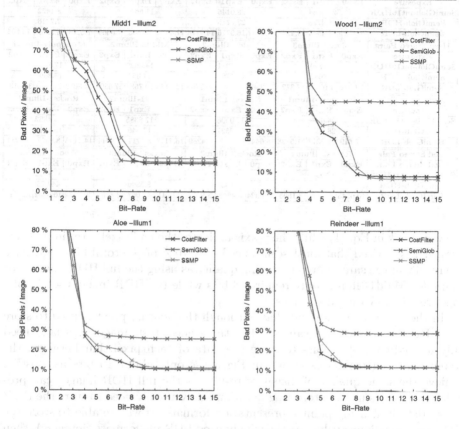

Fig. 3. Some examples of bit-level quantized HDR stereo matching results ('Midd - Illum2', 'Wood1 - Illum2', 'Aloe - Illum1', 'Reindeer - Illum1').

In the second part of experiment and evaluation, we apply the bit-plane slicing technique to generate the bit-level quantized versions of HDR stereo images used in the experiments. Table 2 shows a summary of the maximum required bits to store the radiance information for a pixel in different scene images. The numbers in the table indicate the maximum required value for the variable k given in Eq. (1). In the 'Aloe' scene, for example, all 3 illumination conditions only require 14 bits to store the radiance information. Figure 3 shows some of the bit-level quantization stereo matching results, 'Midd1-Illum2', 'Wood1-Illum2', 'Aloe-Ilum1', and 'Reindeer-Illum1'. The x-axis indicates the value for

Table 3. Comparison of Integer-HDR, HDR and LDR on the bad pixel rate using the algorithm "SemiGlob".

Used Stereo Pairs	Aloe-Illum1			Aloe-Illum2			Aloe-Illum3			Baby1-Illum1		
Exposure	Exp0	Exp1	Exp2	Exp0	Exp1	Exp2	Exp0	Exp1	Exp2	Exp0	Exp1	Exp2
SemiGlob-int16HDR	25.6976			24.576			25.7521			31.0602		
SemiGlob-HDR	25.6981			24.5632			25.7534			31.0712		
SemiGlob-LDR	25.0211	19.5558	18.5555	23.3308	19.2169	18.3614	25.0355	20.468	19.2431	29.8626	19.8844	16.6329

Used Stereo Pairs	Baby1-Illum2			Baby1-Illum3			Cloth3-Illum1			Cloth3-Illum2		
Exposure	Exp0	Exp1	Exp2	Exp0	Exp1	Exp2	Exp0	Exp1	Exp2	Exp0	Exp1	Exp2
SemiGlob-int16HDR	28.4684			28.0146			11.6647			8.1422		
SemiGlob-HDR	28.4723			27.9715			11.2368			7.7316		
SemiGlob-LDR	26.6789	17.4644	15.4227	25.9842	16.9775	14.9178	11.4334	7.7863	7.0369	7.5254	6.9861	7.2694

Used Stereo Pairs	Cloth3-Illum3			Midd1-Illum2			Midd2-Illum2			Monopoly-Illum2		
Exposure	Exp0	Exp1	Exp2	Exp0	Exp1	Exp2	Exp0	Exp1	Exp2	Exp0	Exp1	Exp2
SemiGlob-int16HDR	8.2729			14.7911			14.0629			17.7825		
SemiGlob-HDR	7.8652			14.7794			14.059			17.8097		
SemiGlob-LDR	7.6022	7.0145	7.372	23.3308	11.49	50.2709	12.6123	10.7588	57.6306	14.8002	14.1561	39.4134

Used Stereo Pairs	Reindeer-Illum1			Rocks1-Illum1			Rocks1-Illum2			Rocks1-Illum3		
Exposure	Exp0	Exp1	Exp2	Exp0	Exp1	Exp2	Exp0	Exp1	Exp2	Exp0	Exp1	Exp2
SemiGlob-int16HDR	28.6534			19.0506			17.8385			15.4882		
SemiGlob-HDR	28.6551			19.0521			17.846			15.4912		
SemiGlob-LDR	27.619	21.7317	21.5128	18.6442	9.8143	7.4289	16.7113	8.9711	7.6411	14.1115	8.9657	7.7281

Used Stereo Pairs	Rocks2-Illum1			Rocks2-Illum2			Rocks2-Illum3			Wood1-Illum2		
Used Stereo Pairs	Exp0	Exp1	Exp2	Exp0	Exp1	Exp2	Exp0	Exp1	Exp2	Exp0	Exp1	Exp2
SemiGlob-int16HDR	10.9569			12.6579			8.5416			45.1112		
SemiGlob-HDR	10.9581			12.6551			8.5396			44.875		
SemiGlob-LDR	10.6543	5.5585	4.1695	13.6324	5.4548	3.9418	7.8741	4.7667	3.8864	39.8532	16.6652	12.0399

the variable k in Eq. (1) while the y-axis indicates the bad pixel rate (in percentage). It is surprised that most scenes need only 70 % of the total bits to achieve the results of the same stereo matching quality as using the full HDR image. For example, 'Midd1-Illum2' only requires 8 bits while the HDR image uses 15 bits to store all HDR radiance values.

In the experiments we find that, although the floating point is used to store the HDR's pixel radiance values, all of the scenes (test images) actually need only a maximum of 17 bits to store the data of each pixel. Furthermore, the stereo matching results as shown in Fig. 3 use only about 10 bits at most to achieve the same quality of disparity results as the full HDR images can provide. This brings up an interesting question - do we really need to store the HDR image data in floating point representation formats? If we are able to store the HDR image radiance values as the widely used LDR file formats (integers), then the research towards HDR stereo matching could greatly benefit. Many graphics libraries and state-of-the-art stereo matching methods are already implemented using integers. There is no need to spend numerous efforts on coding or modifying the available stereo matching codes, but focus on enhancing the stereo correspondence methods instead.

To validate the possibility of integer-HDR stereo matching, we convert the HDR images to an 'integer' format, PNG (Portable Network Graphics), for the last part of experiment and evaluation. PNG is a lossless compression format for LDR bitmap images and is the most used lossless image compression format on the internet. In PNG specification there is a 'Truecolor' option capable of storing 16 bits for each channel pixel. Thus, we can store all HDR radiance values in the

PNG file format by shifting the 16 positions of the floating point to the right and store only the resulting integer part of the number while truncating the rest of the bits. It means that the normalized HDR images with the floating point values in the range of 0 – 1 becomes integers with the range of 0 – 65535. We can then read the image data from the stored 'integer-HDR' PNG file and apply the conventional stereo matching algorithms.

Table 3 shows the comparison of bad pixel rates among the disparity maps obtained using PNG-stored 16-bit HDR format (int16-HDR), floating point HDR format and conventional LDR. It shows that the stereo matching quality of 'int16-HDR' is not lost too much, compared to the disparity derived from the original HDR images. This observation is consistent with the HDR encoding research presented by Mantiuk et al. [20]. The HDR pixel values can be represented using as few as 10 – 12 bits for luminance and 8 bits for chrominance without introducing any visible quantization artifacts. Although the proposed technique is mainly used for HDR video encoding, it still proves it still provides a way to represent HDR images with less bits.

4 Conclusion

In this work, the stereo matching techniques for high dynamic range image pairs are investigated. We address the key issues on generating HDR images suitable for achieving high-quality disparity results. Three state-of-the-art stereo matching algorithms are modified and used to test the performance of our HDR stereo technique. From the analysis of HDR bit-plane slicing, it is found that only about 16 bits per channel are required to store HDR images. Moreover, the results show that using 10 bits of image data can achieve the same disparity quality as the full HDR image pair can provide. We propose a 16-bit unsigned integer format to store the HDR image, which allows the available stereo matching algorithms to be adopted for stereo HDR with slight modification. The experiments have demonstrated that the HDR stereo pairs generated with proper thresholds can provide better disparity results compared to the LDR countparts.

References

1. Dhond, U., Aggarwal, J.: Structure from stereo: a review. IEEE Trans. Syst. Man Cybern. 19(6), 1489–1510 (1989)
2. Sbaiz, L., Yang, F., Charbon, E., Susstrunk, S., Vetterli, M.: The gigavision camera. In: Proceedings of the 2009 IEEE International Conference on Acoustics, Speech and Signal Processing, ICASSP 2009. IEEE Computer Society, Washington, DC, pp. 1093–1096 (2009)
3. Scharstein, D., Szeliski, R.: A taxonomy and evaluation of dense two-frame stereo correspondence algorithms. Int. J. Comput. Vis. 47(1–3), 7–42 (2002)
4. Scharstein, D., Szeliski, R.: Middlebury stereo vision page (2002). http://vision.middlebury.edu/stereo

5. Scharstein, D., Pal, C.: Learning conditional random fields for stereo. In: IEEE Conference on Computer Vision and Pattern Recognition, CVPR 2007, pp. 1–8 (2007)
6. Hirschmuller, H.: Stereo processing by semiglobal matching and mutual information. IEEE Trans. Pattern Anal. Mach. Intell. **30**(2), 328–341 (2008)
7. Hosni, A., Rhemann, C., Bleyer, M., Rother, C., Gelautz, M.: Fast cost-volume filtering for visual correspondence and beyond. IEEE Trans. Pattern Anal. Mach. Intell. **35**(2), 504–511 (2013)
8. He, K., Sun, J., Tang, X.: Guided image filtering. In: Daniilidis, Kostas, Maragos, Petros, Paragios, Nikos (eds.) ECCV 2010, Part I. LNCS, vol. 6311, pp. 1–14. Springer, Heidelberg (2010)
9. Ham, B., Min, D., Oh, C., Do, M., Sohn, K.: Probability-based rendering for view synthesis. IEEE Trans. Image Process. **23**(2), 870–884 (2014)
10. Oh, C., Ham, B., Sohn, K.: Probabilistic correspondence matching using random walk with restart. In: Bowden, R., Collomosse, J.P., Mikolajczyk, K., eds.: BMVC, BMVA Press pp. 1–10 (2012)
11. Mann, S., Lo, R., Huang, J., Rampersad, V., Janzen, R.: Hdrchitecture: Real-time stereoscopic hdr imaging for extreme dynamic range. In: ACM SIGGRAPH 2012 Emerging Technologies, SIGGRAPH 2012. ACM, New York, pp. 11:1–11:1 (2012)
12. Zhang, L., Tam, W.: Stereoscopic image generation based on depth images for 3d tv. IEEE Trans. Broadcast. **51**(2), 191–199 (2005)
13. Lin, H.Y., Chang, W.Z.: High dynamic range imaging for stereoscopic scene representation. In: Proceedings of the 16th IEEE International Conference on Image Processing, ICIP 2009. IEEE Press, Piscataway, pp. 4249–4252 (2009)
14. Selmanović, E., Debattista, K., Bashford-Rogers, T., Chalmers, A.: Generating stereoscopic hdr images using hdr-ldr image pairs. ACM Trans. Appl. Percept **10**(1), 3:1–3:18 (2013)
15. Sun, N., Mansour, H., Ward, R.: Hdr image construction from multi-exposed stereo ldr images. In: 2010 17th IEEE International Conference on Image Processing (ICIP), pp. 2973–2976 (2010)
16. Akhavan, T., Yoo, H., Gelautz, M.: A framework for hdr stereo matching using multi-exposed images. In: Proceedings of HDRi2013 - First International Conference and SME Workshop on HDR imaging (2013)
17. Lin, H.Y., Lin, P.Z.: Hierarchical stereo matching with image bit-plane slicing. Mach. Vis. Appl. **24**(5), 883–898 (2013)
18. Reinhard, E., Ward, G., Pattanaik, S., Debevec, P.: High Dynamic Range Imaging: Acquisition, Display, and Image-Based Lighting (The Morgan Kaufmann Series in Computer Graphics). Morgan Kaufmann Publishers Inc., San Francisco, CA, USA (2005)
19. Larson, G.W., Shakespeare, R.: Rendering with Radiance: The Art and Science of Lighting Visualization. Booksurge Llc, New York (2004)
20. Mantiuk, R., Krawczyk, G., Myszkowski, K., Seidel, H.P.: Perception-motivated high dynamic range video encoding. In: ACM SIGGRAPH 2004 Papers, SIGGRAPH 2004. ACM, New York, pp. 733–741 (2004)

Discriminative Properties in Directional Distributions for Image Pattern Recognition

Hayato Itoh[1]([✉]), Atsushi Imiya[2], and Tomoya Sakai[3]

[1] School of Advanced Integration Science, Chiba University, Chiba, Japan
hayato-itoh@graduate.chiba-u.jp
[2] Institute of Management and Information Technologies,
Chiba University, Chiba, Japan
[3] Graduate School of Engineering, Nagasaki University, Nagasaki, Japan

Abstract. We clarify mathematical properties for accurate and robust achievement of the histogram of the oriented gradients method. This method extracts image features from the distribution of gradients by shifting bounding box. We show that this aggregating distribution of local regions extracts low-frequency components of an image. Furthermore, we show that the normalisation of histograms in this method is a nonlinear mapping. Moreover, we show a combination of dominant directional distribution and the Wasserstein distance recognise the image of particular object as accurately as the histogram of oriented gradients method.

1 Introduction

We reformulate the oriented gradients (HoG) method [2] from the viewpoints of gradient-based image pattern recognition and the directional statistics. The gradient-based image recognition is robust against bias change such that illumination changes. The directional statistics compares distribution of the directions of gradients in an image. Gradients are fundamental geometrical features for the segment boundary extraction. The segment boundaries are employed for the detection of a particular object, such as a pedestrian and car, from a scene and a sequence of scenes. In the HoG method, oriented gradients in windowed sequence on the plane yields histogram on the unit circles [6]. To measure differences and similarities among these histogram-based features, we are required to use a well-defined metric for the distributions. For this purpose, we redefined a histogram as a cyclic probability density function by using the directional statistics [4]. The state-of-art methods in the pedestrian detection [1,3,5,9] handle occlusion, non-rigid deformation and scale change of pedestrian images with less detection error than that of the original HoG method. However, almost all the methods still adopt the feature of HoG method. Therefore, clarifying the mathematical properties for accurate and robust achievement of the HoG method derives the new improvements of object detection systems.

By using the Wasserstein distance [8], we introduce the distance among directional statistics. Furthermore, we develop three methods to construct histogram from a distribution of gradients. Combining these three construction methods

© Springer International Publishing Switzerland 2016
T. Bräunl et al. (Eds.): PSIVT 2015, LNCS 9431, pp. 617–630, 2016.
DOI: 10.1007/978-3-319-29451-3_49

and three aggregating method for the local regions of an image, we define directional distribution-based features. Moreover, we explore the mathematical properties of the definition of the HoG method. Finally, we evaluate the performances of the developed directional distribution-based features and HoG feature with L_p-norm and the Wasserstein distance. Our developed features are presented in Sects. 3.1 and 3.2. Comparing these evaluations, we examine what mathematical properties give accurate detection.

2   Mathematical Preliminaries

2.1   Directions and Matching

We assume an image $f(x)$ defined over a finite closed set Ω exists in the intersection of Sobolev space $W^{1,p}$ and bounded variational space. Therefore, $\int_\Omega |\nabla f| dx < \infty$ and $\int_\Omega |\nabla f|^2 dx < \infty$ hold. For gradients of images, we have the following theorem.

Theorem 1. *For functions f and g, iff $\nabla f = \nabla g$, then $f = g + $ constant.*

From Theorem 1, we derive the distance $D(f, g) = \sqrt{\int_{\mathbb{R}^2} |\nabla f - \nabla g|^2 dx}$, which is invariant to a constant bias. Therefore, gradient-based matching is robust against soft illumination change. However, since partial derivative enhances noises, we need blur filtering to remove noises for robust matching based on gradients.

The directional gradient of images $f(x)$ for $x = (x, y)^\top$ in the direction of $\omega = (\cos\theta, \sin\theta)^\top$ is computed as $D(\theta) = \frac{\partial f}{\partial \omega} = \omega^\top \nabla f$. The directional gradient $D(\theta)$ evaluates steepness, smoothness and flatness of f along the direction of vector ω. gradient-based image recognition [2] uses the pair of the direction of gradient $n(x) = \nabla f(x)/\|\nabla f(x)\|_2$ and its magnitude $m(x) = \|\nabla f(x)\|_2$ over the region Ω as $d(f(x)) = (m(x), n(x))$, where $\|\cdot\|_2$ is the L_2-norm. We represent the gradients field of an image as $\Phi(f) = \{d(f(x)) \mid x \in \Omega\}$. Hereafter, to compute the directional angle of each point, we define the operation $\angle(\nabla f(x))$ as $\angle(\nabla f(x)) = \theta$, if $n(x) = \frac{\nabla f}{\|\nabla f\|_2} = (\cos\theta, \sin\theta)^\top$. Figure 1 shows an example of gradient field and its histogram for a local region of an image.

2.2   Aggregating Methods for Local Regions

To measure the difference of two images, the HoG method focuses on the difference of local regions between two images. The HoG method aggregates directional distributions of gradient in local regions of an image. To compute directional distributions of local regions of an image, we define local regions in same manner of Reference [2]. For a fixed point $c \in \mathbb{R}^2$ on an image, positive constant $\alpha \in \mathbb{R}_+$ and positive integer $k \in \mathbb{Z}_+$, using a set of points $x \in \mathbb{R}^2$ and infinity norm$\|\cdot\|_\infty$, we define a local region and bounding box as

$$C(c) = \{c \mid \|x - c\|_\infty < \alpha\}, \quad B(c) = \{x \mid \|x - c\|_\infty < k\alpha\}, \tag{1}$$

which are called cells and blocks, respectively.

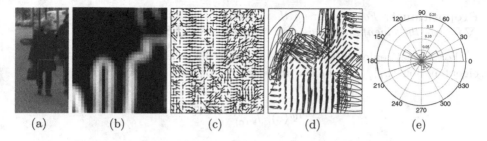

Fig. 1. Example of directional statistics. (a) A grayscale image. (b) Magnitudes of gradients in a local region of the image. (c) Directions of gradients in a local region of the image. (d) A distribution of structure tensors in a local region of the image. (e) A circular histogram constructed with the gradient field.

For practical computation of a cell and block, using a constant α, we select a set of points $\{c_{ij}\}_{i,j=1}^{M,N}$ with the conditions $C(c_{ij}) \cap C(c_{i'j'}) = \emptyset, (i,j) \neq (i',j')$ and $C(c_{11}) \cup C(c_{12}) \cup \ldots, C(c_{MN}) = \Omega$. For $k = 2$, we select a set of blocks $B(c'_l)$ with the condition $c'_l \in \{\mu | \mu = (c_{ij} + c_{ij+1} + c_{i+1j} + c_{i+1j+1})/4\}$, $l = 1, 2, \ldots, (M-1)(N-1)$. The HoG method divides an image by cells, aggregates the cells by blocks and represents an image as a vector by connecting histograms of cells. For vectors, cells, blocks and histograms, we have to select appropriate metrics.

2.3   Histogram of Gradients

We define local and global directional distribution for an image. For local regions $C(c)$ and $B(c)$, using Dirac delta function δ, the operation $\angle(\cdot)$ and magnitude $m(x)$ of gradient at a point x, we construct the normalised histogram in local regions

$$H_w^C(\theta, c) = \frac{\int_{C(c)} m(x)\delta(\theta - \angle(\nabla f))dx}{\int_0^{2\pi} \int_{C(c)} m(x)\delta(\theta - \angle(\nabla f))dx\, d\theta}, \tag{2}$$

$$H_w^B(\theta, c) = \frac{\int_{B(c)} m(x)\delta(\theta - \angle(\nabla f))dx}{\int_0^{2\pi} \int_{B(c)} m(x)\delta(\theta - \angle(\nabla f))dx\, d\theta}, \tag{3}$$

as a probabilistic distribution. We call this histogram directional distribution. Furthermore, for over an image region $\Omega \in \mathbb{R}^2$, we define a normalised global histogram of gradients as

$$H_w^G(\theta) = \frac{\int_{x \in \Omega} m(x)\delta(\theta - \angle(\nabla f))\, dx}{\int_0^{2\pi} \int_{x \in \Omega} m(x)\delta(\theta - \angle(\nabla f))\, dx\, d\theta}. \tag{4}$$

2.4   Histogram of Dominant Directions

For gradients, we have the following property.

Proposition 1. *For f, setting the directional tensor $S = \nabla f \nabla f^\top$, ∇f and $|\nabla f|^2$ are the eigenfunction u_1 and eigenvalue λ_1 of S, respectively.*

For a local region $\Psi(c) \in \{C(c), B(c)\}$ defined around a point $c \in \mathbb{R}^2$, the eigenfunction $\{u_i\}_{i=1}^2$ and eigenvalues $\{\lambda\}_{i=1}^2$ of the structure tensor

$$\bar{S} = \frac{1}{|\Psi(c)|} \int_{\Psi(c)} \nabla f \nabla f^\top dx. \tag{5}$$

are used as the descriptor of f in a local region $\Psi(c)$. Figure 1(d) illustrates a distribution of structure tensors in a local region of an image. Using the pair (λ_1, u_1) of the first eigenvalue and the first eigenvector of $\bar{S}$, the operation $\angle(\cdot)$ and the region Ω of an image, we construct the histogram $h_\mathrm{D}(\theta, \bar{s}(c)) = \int_{c \in \Omega} \lambda_1 \delta(\theta - \angle(u_1)) dc$. This histogram expresses the number of dominant directions for a direction θ in an image. However, if we obtain u_1 as the solution of eigenvalue problem of $\bar{S} u_1 = \lambda u_1$, the range of angle of u_1 is limited in $[0, \frac{\pi}{2}]$, since eigenfunction u_1 lost sign of plus and minus.

For the practical computation, we define the maximum of a histogram in a cell $M^C(c) = \max_\theta H_\mathrm{w}^C(\theta, c)$. Using this maximum, for a constant $\lambda > 0.5$, we define histograms of dominant directions for a cell as

$$h_\mathrm{D}^C(\theta, c) = \begin{cases} H_\mathrm{w}^C(\theta, c), & H_\mathrm{w}^C(\theta, c) \geq \lambda M^C(c) \\ 0, & \text{otherwise.} \end{cases} \tag{6}$$

For the region Ω of an image, we have the global dominant directional distribution as

$$H_\mathrm{D}^G(\theta) = \frac{\int_{c \in \Omega} \int_{x \in B(c)} h_\mathrm{D}^C(\theta, x) dx dc}{\int_0^{2\pi} \int_{c \in \Omega} \int_{x \in B(c)} h_\mathrm{D}^C(\theta, x) dx dc d\theta}. \tag{7}$$

2.5   Gradient-Based Object Detection Method

For a reference image f and a template image g, using a moving window W, the gradient-based feature $F(f)$ of an image f and the metric D for features, gradient-based object detection is achieved by minimising

$$J(f) = D(F(g_W(x)), F(f(x))), \tag{8}$$

where

$$g_W(x) = \chi_W(x) g(x), \quad \chi_W(x) = \begin{cases} 1, & \text{if } x \in W, \\ 0, & \text{otherwise.} \end{cases} \tag{9}$$

To establish high accurate detection, we need to construct discriminative gradient-based feature $F(f)$ and select appropriate metric for this gradient-based feature.

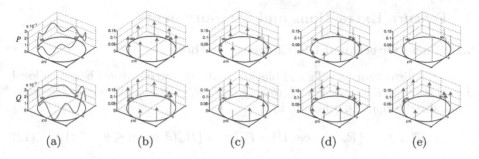

Fig. 2. Examples of the computation of the Wasserstein distances. (a) Two probabilistic distribution on a circle. (b) Sampled data of the two function. (c) and (d)
illustrate the 1-Wasserstein distance and binomial-distribution-based 1-Wasserstein
distance, respectively. The top row in (c) and (d) show the residual values after the
maximum flows moved from each bin of P to bins of Q. The bottom row in (c) and
(d) show the flows that moved from P to Q as maximum flow. These two figures show
that different ground distances give different Wasserstein distances. (e) The state at
the end of the computation. All sampled values of P are moved to bins of Q.

2.6   Wasserstein Distance

The p-Wasserstein distance [8] between a pair of probabilistic distributions $f(x)$
and $g(y)$ for $x \in X$ and $y \in Y$ is

$$W_p(f,g) = \min_{c(x,y)} \left(\int_X \int_Y |f(x) - g(y)|^p c(x,y) dx dy \right)^{1/p}, \tag{10}$$

where $c(x,y)$ is a cost function.

For sampled probabilistic distributions $P = \{p_i\}_{i=1}^n$ and $Q = \{q_j\}_{j=1}^n$ on a
circle, where $p_{i+n} = p_i$ and $q_{j+n} = q_j$, we define ground distance $d_{ij} = |p_i - q_j|$.
The distance between P and Q is computed as

$$D_{\mathrm{W}}(P,Q) = \min_{x_{ij}} \left(\sum_{i=1}^n \sum_{j=1}^n d_{ij}^p x_{ij} \right)^{1/p}, \tag{11}$$

subject to the conditions $\sum_{j=1}^n x_{ij} = p_i$, $\sum_{i=1}^n x_{ij} = q_j$ and $x_{ij} \geq 0$. The
minimisation is achieved by using linear programming to solve the transportation
problem. As a special case of the Wasserstein distance, 1-Wasserstein distance
is known as the Earth Mover's distance [7].

Furthermore, we assume random-walk model for a gap between directional
distributions. We define binomial-distribution-based p-Wasserstein distance as
$d_{ij} = |p_i - q_j| \binom{n}{d_c(i,j)} \frac{1}{2^n}$, where $d_c(i,j) = |i - j|$ for $|i - j| \leq \frac{n}{2}$ and $d_c(i,j) = $
$|i+n-j|$ for $|i-j| > \frac{n}{2}$. This ground distance is weighted by value generated from
the binomial distribution of the difference of indexes i and j. Figure 2 illustrates
these two kinds of Wasserstein distances (Fig. 3).

3 Feature Extractions and Measurements

3.1 Local Directional Distributions Methods

Using the histograms of cells and blocks, we define three features based on local directional distributions. For $H_\mathrm{w}(\theta, c) \in \{H_\mathrm{w}^\mathrm{C}(\theta, c), H_\mathrm{w}^\mathrm{B}(\theta, c)\}$, we define directional distribution (DD) feature as

$$F_\mathrm{DD}(f) = \{P_\mathrm{w}(c) \mid c \in \Omega\}, \quad P_\mathrm{w}(c) = \{H_\mathrm{w}(\theta, c) \mid 0 \leq \theta < 2\pi\}. \quad (12)$$

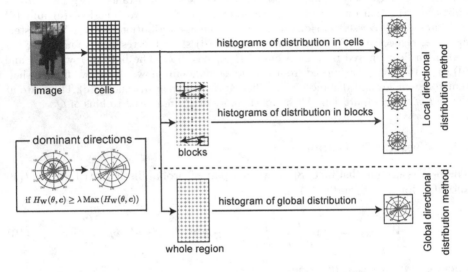

Fig. 3. Flow of feature extractions. There are three flows. The top and middle rows show feature extraction with respect to cells and blocks, respectively. In the top and middle rows, a set of histograms is extracted. The bottom row shows feature extraction from overall region of an image. For these three extractions, we adopt histograms of directional distribution and dominant directional distribution. The left small box summarises the extraction of dominant directional distribution in each cell.

For the extracted features, we construct four methods to measure difference between images. First, for the DD features extracted from cells, we define two discrimination methods. We set $F(f) = \{P(c) \mid c \in \Omega\}$ and $F(g) = \{Q(c) \mid c \in \Omega\}$ are extracted features for images f and g. We define cell-based discrimination method (**C method**) as

$$D_\mathrm{Cell} = \int_{c \in \Omega} D_\mathrm{W}\left(P(c), Q(c)\right) dc, \quad (13)$$

where $D_\mathrm{W}(\cdot, \cdot)$ is the Wasserstein distance. This discrimination method sums the Wasserstein distances of each corresponding cells in two images.

Second, we define block-wise-cell-based discrimination method (**BWC method**) as

$$D_{\text{BWC}} = \int_{c \in \Omega} \int_{x \in B(c)} D_W \left(P(x), Q(x) \right) dx dc. \tag{14}$$

This discrimination method sums the Wasserstein distances of cells in each corresponding blocks in two images. In Eqs. (13) and (14), both $P(c)$ and $Q(c)$ are given by histograms H_w^C defined in Eq. (2) of cells.

Third, for the DD features extracted from blocks, we define block-based discrimination method (**B method**) as

$$D_{\text{Block}} = \int_{c \in \Omega} D_W(P(c), Q(c)) dc, \tag{15}$$

where both $P(c)$ and $Q(c)$ are given by histograms H_w^B defined in Eq. (3) of blocks. This discrimination method sums the Wasserstein distances of each corresponding blocks in two images.

Fourth, for the DD features extracted from cells and blocks, we define L_p-norm. We set $P(c) = \{H_P^C(\theta, c) \mid 0 \le \theta < 2\pi\}$ and $Q(c) = \{H_Q^C(\theta, c) \mid 0 \le \theta < 2\pi\}$ that are given by the histograms H_w^C for two images f and g, respectively. For two images, we define L_p-norm for cells as

$$D_{L_p} = \left(\int_{\Omega} \int_0^{2\pi} |H_P^C(\theta, c) - H_Q^C(\theta, c)|^p d\theta dc \right)^{1/p}. \tag{16}$$

This L_p-norm measures the differences of all the cells dividing images. Furthermore, we define L_p-norm for a collection of block-wise cells as

$$D_{L_p} = \left(\int_{c \in \Omega} \int_{x \in B(c)} \int_0^{2\pi} |H_P^C(\theta, c) - H_Q^C(\theta, c)|^p d\theta dx dc \right)^{1/p}. \tag{17}$$

This L_p-norm measures the differences of all the cells obtained by moving a block.

Moreover, we define L_p-norm for blocks. To define L_p-norm for blocks , we set $P(c) = \{H_P^B(\theta, c) \mid 0 \le \theta < 2\pi\}$ and $Q(c) = \{H_Q^B(\theta, c) \mid 0 \le \theta < 2\pi\}$ that are given by the histograms H_w^B for two images f and g, respectively. Then, we define L_p-norm for a collection of blocks as

$$D_{L_p} = \left(\int_{\Omega} \int_0^{2\pi} |H_P^B(\theta, c) - H_Q^B(\theta, c)|^p d\theta dc \right)^{1/p}. \tag{18}$$

3.2   Global Directional Distribution Method

Let an image f be a blurred image by the Gaussian filtering of the standard deviation σ. For this blurred image f, using a histogram defined in Eq. (4), we construct a global direction distribution (DD) feature

$$F_{\text{DD}}^G(f) = P = \{H_w^G(\theta) | 0 \le \theta < 2\pi\}. \tag{19}$$

This feature represent directional distribution over region of an image by one histogram. Furthermore, using a histogram defined in Eq. (7), we construct dominant directional distribution (DDD) feature as

$$F_{\mathrm{DDD}}^{\mathrm{G}}(f) = P = \{H_{\mathrm{D}}^{\mathrm{G}}(\theta)|0 \leq \theta < 2\pi\}. \tag{20}$$

The both features consist of a histogram of a global directional distribution over an image.

For images f and g, using $F^{\mathrm{G}} \in \{F_{\mathrm{DD}}^{\mathrm{G}}, F_{\mathrm{DDD}}^{\mathrm{G}}\}$, we extract these features $F^{\mathrm{G}}(f) = P$, and $F^{\mathrm{G}}(g) = Q$, respectively. To measure the difference of two features, we define global discrimination method (**G method**) as

$$D_{\mathrm{G}} = D_{\mathrm{W}}(P, Q), \tag{21}$$

where D_{W} is the Wasserstein distance. Furthermore, we define L_p-norm between two features. Setting $P = \{H_P^{\mathrm{G}}(\theta)|0 \leq \theta < 2\pi\}$ and $Q = \{H_Q^{\mathrm{G}}(\theta)|0 \leq \theta < 2\pi\}$, we have

$$D_{L_p} = \left(\int_0^{2\pi} |H_P^{\mathrm{G}}(\theta) - H_Q^{\mathrm{G}}(\theta)|^p d\theta \right)^{1/p}. \tag{22}$$

where both histograms H_P^{G} and H_Q^{G} are given by either of $H_{\mathrm{w}}^{\mathrm{G}}$ or $H_{\mathrm{D}}^{\mathrm{G}}$.

3.3   Histogram of Oriented Gradients Method

We summarises the feature extraction of the HoG method as below.

1. Compute $\Phi(f)$ in the Sect. 2.1.
2. Compute a histogram of gradients defined in Eq. (2) in a local region $C(\mathbf{c})$.
3. By sliding a bounding box, we extract the HoG feature of an image.

We use L_p-normalisation for the histogram in each block with $p = 2$ as

$$H_{\mathrm{H}_p}(\theta, \mathbf{c}) = \frac{H_{\mathrm{w}}^{\mathrm{C}}(\theta, \mathbf{c})}{\left(\int_{\mathbf{x} \in B(\mathbf{c})} \int_0^{2\pi} |H_{\mathrm{w}}^{\mathrm{C}}(\theta, \mathbf{c})|^p d\theta d\mathbf{x} \right)^{1/p}}. \tag{23}$$

Sliding the center $\mathbf{c}$ of the block $B(\mathbf{c})$ over the region Ω of an image f, we extract the HoG feature

$$F_{\mathrm{H}}(f) = \{H_{\mathrm{H}}(\theta, \mathbf{c}) \mid \mathbf{c} \in \Omega, \ 0 \leq \theta < 2\pi\}, \tag{24}$$

where $H_{\mathrm{H}} = H_{\mathrm{H}_2}$.

For two HoG features $F_{\mathrm{H}}(f) = \{H_{\mathrm{H},1}(\theta, \mathbf{c})\}$ and $F_{\mathrm{H}}(g) = \{H_{\mathrm{H},2}(\theta, \mathbf{c})\}$ of images f and g, respectively, we derive the L_p-norm

$$D_{L_p} = \left(\int_\Omega \int_0^{2\pi} |H_{\mathrm{H},1}(\theta, \mathbf{c}) - H_{\mathrm{H},2}(\theta, \mathbf{c})|^p d\theta d\mathbf{c} \right)^{1/p}. \tag{25}$$

Measuring the difference of two HoG features by D_{L_p} is the HoG method in Reference [2]. Furthermore, setting $H_1'(c) = \{\int_{x \in B(c)} H_H^1(\theta, x) dx \,|\, 0 \le \theta < 2\pi\}$ and $H_2'(c) = \{\int_{x \in B(c)} H_H^2(\theta, x) dx \,|\, 0 \le \theta < 2\pi\}$, we define block-based discrimination method

$$D_{\text{Block}} = \int_{c \in \Omega} D_W \left(H_1'(c), H_2'(c) \right) dc. \tag{26}$$

In block-based discrimination method, the difference between the DD and HoG features is how to normalise each histogram of a block. The HoG method defines histogram of a block as connected vectorised histograms of cells and normalised by L_2-norm.

For the L_p-normalisation, we have

Theorem 2. *Assuming $f \in L_1(\Omega) \cap L_2(\Omega)$ for a finite closed set Ω, we have the relation*

$$\|x\|_1 \le \sqrt{\Omega} \|x\|_2 \tag{27}$$

(Proof). For all $f \in L_p$ using the Cauchy-Schwartz inequality, we have

$$\|f\|_1 = \int_\Omega |f(x)| \cdot 1 \, dx \le \left(\int_\Omega |f(x)|^2 dx \right)^{1/2} \left(\int_\Omega 1^2 dx \right)^{1/2} = \sqrt{\Omega} \|x\|_2. \tag{28}$$

(Q.E.D.)

Theorem 3. *If we define mapping $\phi : \frac{f}{\|f\|_1} \mapsto \frac{f}{\|f\|_2}$, then this mapping ϕ is a nonlinear mapping.*

(Proof). If we assume that the transform ϕ is linear, that is, for $\frac{f}{\|f\|_1} = \phi(\frac{f}{\|f\|_2}) = \int_\Omega K(x, y) \frac{f}{\|f\|_2} dy$, K is independent to f. This operator K satisfies the relation $K(x, y) = \frac{\|f\|_2}{\|f\|_1} \delta(x - y)$ for all $f \in H$. Since $\alpha(f) = \frac{\|f\|_2}{\|f\|_1}$ is a function of f, K depends on f. This property of K derives the contradiction to the assumption on ϕ. This contradiction implies that ϕ is non-linear transform.   (Q.E.D.)

For the normalised histograms $H_{H_p}(\theta, c)$ with $p \in \{1, 2\}$, we define the L_1-norm of a block in an image as $D_{L_{1,p}}(c) = \int_0^{2\pi} |H_{H_p}(\theta, c)| d\theta$. Therefore, we rewrite L_1-norm defined Eq. (25) for the HoG feature as $D_{L_{1,p}} = \int_{c \in \Omega} |D_{L_{1,p}}(c)| dc$. with $p \in \{1, 2\}$. From Theorem 2, we have the following inequality

$$D_{L_{1,1}} \le \sqrt{n} D_{L_{1,2}} \tag{29}$$

holds. Here, n is the number of bins of histogram in a block. The connecting of four histograms gives larger upper bound of L_1-norm than that given by only one histogram. Furthermore, from Theorem 3, we can infer that L_2-normalisation makes separation ratio higher than L_1-normalisation in the recognition of HoG features.

4   Numerical Experiments

By comparing the recognition rates of the local and global directional distribution methods, and the HoG method, we examine the mathematical properties that contribute to accurate gradient-based image pattern recognition.

For feature extractions, adopting the same procedure of the original HoG paper in Reference [2], we use 9 and 18 oriented directions $\{\frac{\pi}{9}(i-1)\}_{i=1}^{9}$ and $\{\frac{\pi}{9}(i-1)\}_{i=1}^{18}$. For local and global features, we use nine and 18 directions, respectively. For the HoG feature, we use both nine and 18 directions. The sizes of a cell and block are 8×8 pixels and 2×2 cells, respectively. For the DDD feature, we set $\lambda = 0.9$.

Throughout this section, as metrics, we use L_1- and L_2-norms, and the p-Wasserstein distance with $p = 1$ (**1WD**) and binomial-distribution-based p-Wasserstein distance with $p = 1$ (**B1WD**). For the local directional distribution features, we use C method, B method, BWC method and L_p-norms defined in Eqs. (13), (14), (15), and (16), (18) and (17). For the global directional distribution features, we use G method and L_p-norm defined in Eqs. (21) and (22), respectively. For the HoG feature, we use B method and L_p-norm in Eqs. (25) and (26), respectively.

For the computation of recognition rate, we use INRIA dataset [2] that benefits from high quality annotations of pedestrian in diverse settings (city, beach, mountain, etc.). From the INRIA dataset, we select images that show frontal view of a pedestrian as positive images. These positive images are divided into 38 learning positive images and 115 positive queries. To obtain negative images, we randomly crop 115 background regions of images in the INRIA dataset. We use these negative images as negative queries.

Table 1. Summary of pairs of features and discrimination criteria. For the directional distribution (DD), the histogram of oriented gradients (HoG) and the dominant directional distribution (DDD), this table shows whether each discrimination method is available or not by equation or −, respectively. Features are divided with respect to whether they are based on a local histogram or a global histogram.

region	Local			Global	
feature	DD		HoG	DD	DDD
histogram	H_w^C: eq. (2)	H_w^B: eq. (3)	H_{H_p}: eq. (23)	H_w^G: eq. (4)	H_D^G: eq. (7)
C method: D_{Cell}	eq. (13)	−	−	−	−
B method D_{Block}	−	eq. (15)	eq. (15)	−	−
BWC method D_{BWC}	eq. (14)	−	−	−	−
G method D_G	−	−	−	eq. (21)	eq. (21)
L_p-norm D_{L_p}	eq. (16)	eq. (17)	eq. (18)	eq. (22)	eq. (22)

Algorithm 1: Preliminaries	Algorithm 2: Classification
Input: N_L learning data $\{f_k\}_{k=1}^{N_L}$ **Output**: The median f_M 1. Extract feature F_k of image f_k for all learning data 2. Compute distance $D(F_i, F_j)$ for all pairs of F_i and F_j with $i, j \in \{1, 2, \ldots, N_L\}$ 3. Find the median f_M such that its extracted feature F_M satisfies $F_M = \arg\min_{F_i} \left(\sum_j^{N_L} D(F_i, F_j) \right).$	**Input**: N queries $\{f_i\}_{i=1}^{N}$, an extract feature F_M of the median for a discrimination method $D(\cdot, \cdot)$ and threshold X. **Output**: Labels $\{l_i\}_{i=1}^{N}$, $l_i \in \{1, -1\}$. 1. Extract features $\{F_i\}_{i=1}^{N}$ from all queries $\{f_i\}_{i=1}^{N}$. 2. Compute distance $D(F_M, F_i)$ between the median and query for the all queries. 3. Give a positive label 1 to a query if $D(F_M, F_i) \leq \frac{X}{100} D_{max}$, otherwise, give a negative label -1. Here, D_{max} and X are the largest value in $\{D(F_M, F_i))\}_{i=1}^{N}$ and a criterion for classification.

For all the combinations of feature and discrimination methods shown in Table 1, we compute recognition rates using the Algorithms 1 and 2. In Algorithm 2, threshold X represents that positive queries exist on how large percentage of the whole space that contain all the queries. Therefore, if small threshold gives highest recognition rate, the results mean that a combination of feature and discrimination method achieves discriminative classification.

Figure 4 shows the recognition rates for the local directional distribution method and the HoG method. Figure 5 show the recognition rate for global directional method.

In Fig. 4(a), all the discrimination methods except L_1-norm for blocks give lower recognition rate than 0.5. Figure 4(b) shows that L_1-norms gives highest recognition rate in both nine and 18 directions for the HoG. Figure 5(a)–(d) show that the Gaussian filtering of larger standard deviation gives more discriminative feature. In Fig. 5(e)–(h), 1WD gives highest recognition rate than L_p-norms and B1WD.

Figure 6 shows the relation of the L_1- and L_2-normalisation of histograms of blocks in the HoG feature. Figure 6(a) shows that discrimination given by L_2-normalisation is larger distance among the median and queries than that given by L_1-normalisation. This result is coincident to Theorem 2. Figure 6(b) and (c) show the nonlinear mapping from L_1-normalised HoG feature to L_2-normalised HoG feature increases separation ratio of two categories.

Table 2 summarises the discriminative combinations of a feature and metric. In the context of directional statistics, the combination of WD and DDD feature gives accurate recognition. Using L_1-norm for DDD feature, we can obtain same performance without the extraction of the dominant directions.

Table 2. Summary of discriminative combination of feature and metric.

Extraction method	Local method		Global method	
	DD feature	HoG feature	DD feature	DDD feature
Discriminative metric	L_1	L_1	L_1 and L_2	1WD

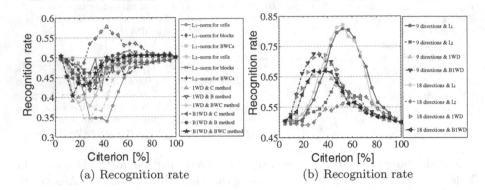

(a) Recognition rate   (b) Recognition rate

Fig. 4. Recognition rate for the local directional distribution method and histogram of oriented gradients method. The vertical and horizontal axes represent recognition rate and criterion, respectively. The L_1-norm gives highest recognition for both methods.

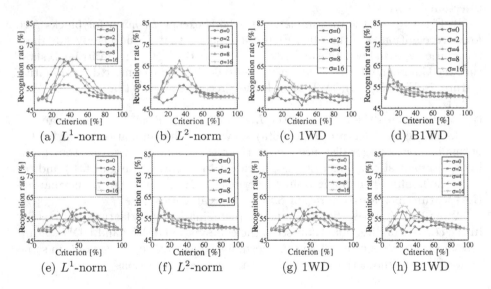

(a) L^1-norm   (b) L^2-norm   (c) 1WD   (d) B1WD

(e) L^1-norm   (f) L^2-norm   (g) 1WD   (h) B1WD

Fig. 5. The recognition rate for the global directional distribution method. Upper and lower rows show the recognition rate for directional distribution feature and dominant directional distribution feature, respectively. The first, second, third and fourth column shows results for L_1-norm, L_2-norm, 1-Wasserstein distance (1WD) and Binomial-distribution-based 1-Wasserstein distance (B1WD), respectively. The vertical and horizontal axes represent the recognition rate and criterion, respectively. The circle, square, six-rayed star, upwards and downwards mark represent results for blurred images with the Gaussian filtering of standard deviations $0, 2, 4, 8, 16$, respectively.

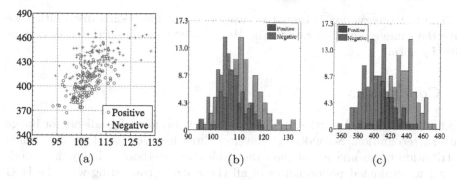

(a)   (b)   (c)

Fig. 6. Distribution of L_1-norms among the median and queries. (a) Relation between L_1-norms for L_1- and L_2-normalised HoG features. The horizontal and vertical axes represent L_1-norms for L_1- and L_2-normalised HoG features, respectively. This relation shows that the mapping ϕ is nonlinear. In (b) and (c), the horizontal and vertical axes represent distances among the median and queries and its probability of occurrence, respectively. L_2-normalisation gives more discriminative distributions to positive and negative queries than L_1-normalisation.

5 Discussion

For the results of experiments in the previous section, we summarise four key observations about feature extraction methods and discrimination methods.

The first observation is that the low-frequency features of an image are important for the image pattern recognition. In generally, an image can be represented as linear combination of orthogonal functions such that low frequency and high frequency sinusoidal functions. The frequency of the features depends on the size of blocks. If the size of divided local region is large, the features with low frequency are extracted. Therefore, the blocks extracted features with low frequency since the size of block is larger than those of cells. In Fig. 4(a), the recognition rates of the block-extracted feature with low frequencies are higher than cell- and block-wise-cell-extracted features. The results of Fig. 5 also imply that the discriminative features of distributions of gradients depend the low frequency components of an image, since the Gaussian filtering extracts the low-frequency components of an image.

The second observation is that L_p-norm for aggregated local regions has a similar role of the bluer filtering of an image, since L_p-norm sums all the differences of local regions. The shapes of graph of recognition rate in Fig. 5(a)–(d) are similar to the shape of the graph of recognition rate for the 1WD and B1WD in Fig. 4(b).

The third observation is that the HoG feature is not the probabilistic distribution of gradients while the HoG feature is a kind of gradient-based feature. Figure 4(a) and (b) show that the HoG gives higher recognition rate than the local directional distribution method. The only difference between the block-wise local feature and HoG feature is the normalisaion procedure.

The last observation is that if we use dominant directional distribution we have the same recognition rate to the HoG features of nine oriented directions with L_2-norm.

6   Conclusions

We firstly introduced metrics for directional distributions of gradients for image pattern recognition. Secondly, we develop three features based on directional distribution of an image and their discrimination methods. Finally, in experiments, we evaluated performances of all the features comparing with the HoG method. The results in our experiments clarify following properties. First, if we use the L_1-norm for the histogram of oriented gradients features, we can establish higher recognition rate than L_2-norm and the Wasserstein distances since the L_2-normalisaion is nonlinear mapping. Second, the global directional distribution is more discriminative feature than the local directional distribution method. Furthermore, results of the global directional distribution method imply that the histogram of oriented gradients method extracts low-frequency features of local regions. Third, the dominant directional distribution is discriminative feature in image pattern recognition. This dominant directional distributions represent edges. Furthermore, using L_1-norm for global directional distribution feature, we can obtain as accurate detection as the combination of the dominant directional distribution and Wasserstein distance without the extraction of dominant directions.

References

1. Benenson, R., Omran, M., Hosang, J., Schiele, B.: Ten years of pedestrian detection, what have we learned? In: Agapito, L., Bronstein, M.M., Rother, C. (eds.) ECCV 2014 Workshops. LNCS, vol. 8926, pp. 613–627. Springer, Heidelberg (2015)
2. Dalal, N., Triggs, B.: Histograms of oriented gradients for human detection. In: CVPR (2005)
3. Dollár, P., Tu, Z., Perona, P. Belongie, S.: Integral channel features. In: BMVC (2009)
4. Mardia, K.V., Jupp, P.E.: Directional Statistics. Wiley, Chichester (2000)
5. Park, D., Zitnick, C.L., Ramanan, D., Dollár, P.: Exploring weak stabilization for motion feature extraction. In: CVPR (2013)
6. Rabin, J., Delon, J., Gousseau, Y.: Transportation distances on the circle. JMIV 41, 147–167 (2011)
7. Rubner, Y., Tomasi, C., Guibas, L.J.: The earth mover's distance as a metric for image retrieval. IJCV 40, 99–121 (2000)
8. Wasserstein, L.N.: Markov processes over denumerable products of spaces describing large systems of automata. Prob. Info. Trans. 5, 47–52 (1969)
9. Yan, J., Zhang, X., Lei, Z., Liao, S., Li, S.Z.: Robust multi-resolution pedestrian detection in traffic scenes. In: CVPR (2013)

Deep Boltzmann Machines for i-Vector Based Audio-Visual Person Identification

Mohammad Rafiqul Alam[1]([✉]), Mohammed Bennamoun[1], Roberto Togneri[2], and Ferdous Sohel[3]

[1] School of Computer Science and Software Engineering,
The University of Western Australia, 35 Stirling Highway,
Crawley, WA 6009, Australia
mohammad.alam@research.uwa.edu.au
[2] School of Electrical, Electronics and Computer Engineering,
The University of Western Australia, 35 Stirling Highway,
Crawley, WA 6009, Australia
[3] School of Engineering and Information Technology, Murdoch University,
90 South Street, Murdoch, WA 6150, Australia

Abstract. We propose an approach using DBM-DNNs for i-vector based audio-visual person identification. The unsupervised training of two Deep Boltzmann Machines DBM_{speech} and DBM_{face} is performed using unlabeled audio and visual data from a set of *background* subjects. The DBMs are then used to initialize two corresponding DNNs for classification, referred to as the $DBM\text{-}DNN_{speech}$ and $DBM\text{-}DNN_{face}$ in this paper. The DBM-DNNs are discriminatively fine-tuned using the back-propagation on a set of training data and evaluated on a set of test data from the *target* subjects. We compared their performance with the cosine distance (cosDist) and the state-of-the-art DBN-DNN classifier. We also tested three different configurations of the DBM-DNNs. We show that DBM-DNNs with two hidden layers and 800 units in each hidden layer achieved best identification performance for 400 dimensional i-vectors as input. Our experiments were carried out on the challenging MOBIO dataset.

1 Introduction

The emergence of smart devices is opening doors to a range of applications such as the e-lodgment of service requests, e-transfer of payments, and e-banking. The viability of such applications would however require a robust and error free biometric system to identify the end users. This is a challenging task due to the significant session variabilities that may be contained in the captured data [1,2]. Recently, audio-visual person recognition on mobile phones has gained a significant attention. For example, two evaluation competitions were organized in 2013 for speaker [3] and face [4] recognition on the MOBIO [5] dataset. In those competitions, the state-of-the-art face and speaker recognition techniques were evaluated. A majority of the speaker recognition systems in [3] used the Total

© Springer International Publishing Switzerland 2016
T. Bräunl et al. (Eds.): PSIVT 2015, LNCS 9431, pp. 631–641, 2016.
DOI: 10.1007/978-3-319-29451-3_50

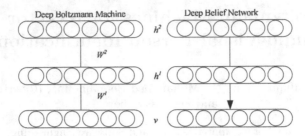

Fig. 1. right: a deep belief network; **left**: a deep Boltzmann machine with undirected edges between the layers.

Variability Modeling (TVM) [6] to learn a total variability matrix (T) which was then used to extract the i-vectors. Recently, in [7,8], TVM was used for both speaker and face verification to achieve one of the top performing results. This motivates the use of i-vectors as features for audio-visual identification.

In addition, learning high level representations using a deep architecture with multiple layers of non-linear information processing has recently gained popularity in the areas of image, audio and speech processing [9,10]. For example, as shown in Fig. 1 right panel, a Deep Belief Network (DBN) is a generative architecture built by stacking multiple layers of restricted Boltzmann machines (RBMs) [11]. A DBN can be converted into a discriminative network, which is referred to as DBN-DNN in [9], by adding a top label layer and using the standard back-propagation algorithm. Although it has been extensively used for speech recognition [9], DBN-DNN was also used for speaker recognition in [12]. In [13] a DBN was used as a pseudo-ivector extractor and then a Probabilistic Linear Discriminant Analysis (PLDA) [14,15] was used for classification. Such greedy layer wise learning of DBNs however limits the network to a single bottom-up pass. It also ignores the top-down influence during the inference process, which may lead to failures in the modeling of variabilities in the case of ambiguous inputs. This motivates the use of Deep Boltzmann Machines (DBMs) as an alternative of DBN.

A DBM is a variant of Boltzmann machine which not only retains the multi-layer architecture but also incorporates the top-down feedback (Fig. 1 left panel). Hence, a DBM has the potential of learning complex internal representations and dealing more robustly the ambiguous inputs (e.g., image or speech) [16]. Similar to the DBN-DNN, a DBM can be converted into a discriminative network, which is referred to as a DBM-DNN [17]. Although they have been used for a variety of classification tasks (e.g., handwritten digit recognition and object recognition [16], query detection [18], phone recognition [17], and multi-modal learning [19]), multi-modal person identification using DBMs has not been well studied. In this paper, we propose to use DBM-DNNs for i-vector based audio-visual person identification on mobile phone data (details in Sect. 4). As opposed to the DBM-DNN in [17] (used for speech recognition), the DBM-DNNs presented in this paper do not use the hidden representations as additional input to the DBM-DNNs. Rather than using DBMs for learning hierarchical representations we use them to learn a set of initial parameters (weights and biases) of the DNNs.

In summary, our contributions in this paper can be listed as follows: **(a)** We use DBM-DNNs for i-vector based audio-visual person identification. To the best of our knowledge, this is the first application of DBM-DNN with i-vectors as inputs. **(b)** We show that a higher accuracy can be achieved with DBM-DNN compared to the cosine distance classifier [6] commonly used in the literature to evaluate i-vector based systems (see Fig. 2) and also the state-of-the-art DBN-DNN **(c)** We study three configurations of DBM-DNN. Our experimental results show that two hidden layers having 800 units each achieved the best accuracy with 400 dimensional i-vectors.

2 Background

In this section, we briefly present the theoretical background of DBMs and the i-vector extraction using TVM.

2.1 Deep Boltzmann Machines

A deep Boltzmann machine is formed by stacking multiple layers of Boltzmann machines as shown in Fig. 1 left panel. In a DBM each layer captures higher-order correlations between the activities of hidden units in the layer below. In [16], some key aspects of DBMs were mentioned: **(i)** potential of learning complex internal representations, **(ii)** high-level representations can be built from a large supply of unlabeled data and very small number of labeled data can be used to slightly fine-tune the model, **(iii)** deal more robustly with ambiguous inputs (e.g., image and speech). Therefore, DBMs are considered a promising tool for solving object and speech/speaker recognition problems [20, 21].

Consider a two-layer DBM with no within-layer connection, Gaussian visible units (e.g., speech, image) $v \in \mathbb{R}^D$ and binary hidden units $h \in \{0, 1\}^P$. Then, the energy for the state v, h^1, h^2 can be defined as:

$$E(v, h^1, h^2 | \theta) = \sum_{i=1}^{D} \frac{(v_i - b_i)^2}{2\sigma_i^2} - \sum_{i=1}^{D} \sum_{j=1}^{P_1} \frac{v_i}{\sigma_i^2} h_j^1 W_{ij}^1 - \sum_{n=1}^{2} \sum_{j=1}^{P_l} c_j^n h_j^n - \sum_{j=1}^{P_1} \sum_{k=1}^{P_2} h_j^1 h_k^2 W_{jk}^2,$$

$$(1)$$

where b and c^n represent the biases of the visible and n-th hidden layer, respectively; σ_i is the standard-deviation of the visible units; W^n represents the synaptic connection weights between the n-th hidden layer and the previous layer; and D and P_n represent the number of units in the visible layer and in the n-th hidden layer, respectively. Here, $\theta = \{b, c, W^1, W^2\}$ represents the set of parameters.

DBMs can be trained with the stochastic maximization of the log-likelihood function. The partial-derivative of the log-likelihood function is:

$$\frac{\partial \mathcal{L}(\theta | v)}{\partial \theta} = \left\langle \frac{\partial E(v_{(t)}, h | \theta)}{\partial \theta} \right\rangle_{data} - \left\langle \frac{\partial E(v, h | \theta)}{\partial \theta} \right\rangle_{model}, \quad (2)$$

where $\langle \cdot \rangle_{data}$ and $\langle \cdot \rangle_{model}$ denote the expectations over the data distribution $P(h | \{v_{(t)}\}, \theta)$ and the model distribution $P(v, h | \theta)$, respectively. The training set

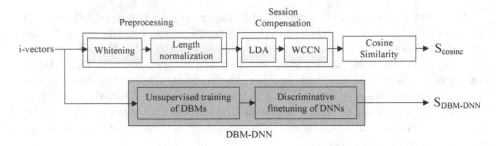

Fig. 2. Steps followed by the cosine distance classifier and the DBM-DNNs to obtain the matching score matrices S_{cosine} and $S_{DBM\text{-}DNN}$, respectively.

$\{v_{(t)}\}_{t=1,\ldots,T}$ contains T samples. Although the update rules are well defined, it is intractable to exactly compute them. Variational approximation is commonly used to compute the expectation over the data distribution and different persistent sampling methods (e.g., [16,22,23]) are used to compute the expectation over the model distribution. A greedy layerwise approach [16] or a two-stage pre-training algorithm [24] can be used to initialize the parameters of DBM.

2.2 Total Variability Modeling (TVM)

Inter-session variability (ISV) [25] and joint factor analysis (JFA) [26] are two session variability modeling techniques widely used for session compensation. Total Variability Modeling (TVM) [6] overcomes the high-dimensionality issue of ISV and JFA. In TVM, each sample in the training set is treated as if it comes from a distinct subject. TVM utilizes the factor analysis as a front-end processing step and extracts low-dimensional i-vector. The TVM training process assumes that the jth sample of subject i is can be represented by the Gaussian Mixture Model (GMM) mean super-vector

$$\mu_{i,j} = m + Tw_{i,j} \tag{3}$$

where m is the speaker- and session-independent mean super-vector obtained from a Universal Background Model (UBM), T is the low-dimensional total variability matrix, and $w_{i,j}$ is the i-vector representation.

The factor analysis process in TVM is used to extract a low-dimensional representation of each sample known as i-vector. An i-vector in its raw form captures the subject-specific information needed for discrimination as well as detrimental session variability. Hence, session compensation (e.g., whitening and i-vector length normalization) and scoring (e.g., PLDA or cosine distance) are performed as separate processes (see Fig. 2).

3   DBM-DNN Classification

In this section, we present the DBM-DNNs for audio-visual person identification. We train two DBMs (e.g., DBM$_{speech}$ and DBM$_{face}$) as shown in Fig. 3, in an

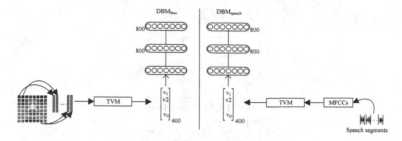

Fig. 3. left: DBM_{face} architecture; **right:** DBM_{speech} architecture. We use 400 dimensional raw i-vectors as inputs to the DBMs.

unsupervised fashion using the raw i-vectors extracted from the unlabeled samples from the *background* subjects. The steps followed in our proposed framework are: **(i)** DBMs pre-training, **(ii)** DBMs fine-tuning, **(iii)** discriminative training of the DBM-DNNs for classification, and **(iv)** fusion.

In the *first* step, we use the two-stage (Stage 1 and 2) pre-training algorithm presented in [24]. In Stage 1, each even-numbered layer of a DBM is trained as an RBM on top of each other. This is a common practice when a DBN is trained. In Stage 2, a model that has the predictive power of the variational parameters given the visible vector is trained. This is done by learning a joint distribution over the visible and hidden vectors using an RBM. In the *second* step, the initial set of parameters are fine-tuned using a layer-by-layer approach. This is similar to the one in [16] except that the visible units at the bottom layer and the hidden units at the top layer are not repeated. This allows the DBMs to adjust the parameters of all the layers (both even and odd) at one go.

In the *third* step, we use the learned DBM parameters to initialize deep neural networks (DNM-DNNs) with a top label layer. The top label layer of a DBM-DNN has as many units as the number of enrolled subjects. The bottom layers have exactly the same architecture as their corresponding DBM. Here, the connection weights between the layer at the top and the one immediately below are randomly initialized. After the initialization, they are discriminatively fine-tuned using a small set of labeled training data and the standard back-propagation algorithm. Finally, at the *fourth* step, we combine the outputs of the DBM-DNNs using the sum fusion, which for an identity j is given by:

$$f_j = \sum_m p_m(v_m, j) \tag{4}$$

where m is the modality assignment (in our case, $m = 1$ represents DBM-DNN$_{speech}$ and $m = 2$ represents DBM-DNN$_{face}$) and $p_m(v_m, j)$ represents the probability of the input v_m belonging to person j (i.e., the value assigned by j-th node of DBM-DNN for v_m). For a given set of observation vectors $o = \{v_1, v_2\}$, a decision is given in favor of the j-th identity if f_j is maximum in the fused score vector $f = [f_1, f_2, \ldots, f_N]$, where N is the number of *target* subjects.

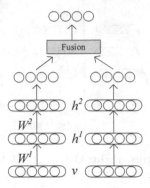

Fig. 4. DBM-DNN$_{speech}$ (left) and DBM-DNN$_{face}$ are initialized with the generative weights of the DBM$_{speech}$ and DBM$_{face}$, respectively, and discriminatingly fine-tuned using the standard back-propagation algorithm. The output scores are fused using the sum rule of fusion.

4   Database and Features

In our experiments, we used the MOBIO dataset which is a collection of videos with speech captured using mobile devices. There are videos from 150 subjects (50 females and 100 males) captured in 12 different sessions over a one-and-a-half-year period. Each session contains 11–21 videos with significant pose and illumination variations (see Fig. 5) as well as different environment noise. We divided the subjects into two sets: (a) *background* (50 subjects: randomly picked 37 males and 13 females to retain the gender representation ratio of the dataset) and (b) *target* (remaining 100 subjects). This was repeated 10 times to ensure the experimental results were not based on a held-out set of data. Therefore, each experimental result presented in this paper represents th e mean of 10 evaluations. In each evaluation, we used the audio and visual data from the *background* subjects for: **(a)** building a UBM to learn the total variability matrix, and **(b)** for the unsupervised training of a DBM. We picked 5 samples each from a set of 6 randomly selected session (out of 12 sessions) from all the *target* subjects as the training data. Similarly, we used 5 samples each from the remaining 6 sessions as the test data.

4.1   Speech Features

We used speech enhancement and voice activity detection algorithms in the VOICEBOX toolbox [27] for preprocessing the speech signals. Then, frames were extracted from each silence removed speech with a window size of 20 ms and sampling rate of 10ms. Then, 12 cepstral coefficients were derived and augmented with the log energy forming a 13 dimensional static feature vector. The delta and acceleration were appended to form the final 13 static + 13 delta + 13 acceleration = 39 dimensional mel frequency cepstral coefficients (MFCCs) feature vector per frame.

Fig. 5. Top row: presence of appearance, background and illumination variations on the video frames in different sessions in MOBIO database; **Bottom row:** detected faces from the video frames.

4.2 Visual Features

Each image is rotated, scaled and cropped to a size of 64×80 pixels. This is done in such a way that the eyes are 16 pixels from the top and separated by 33 pixels. Then, each cropped image is photometrically normalized using the Tan-Triggs algorithm [28]. We extracted 12×12 pixel blocks from a preprocessed image using an exhaustive overlap which led to 3657 blocks per image. Then, the 44 lowest frequency 2D discrete cosine transform (2D-DCT) coefficients [29] excluding the zero frequency coefficient were extracted from each normalized (zero mean and unit variance) image block. The resulting 2D-DCT feature vectors were also normalized to zero mean and unit variance in each dimension with respect to other feature vectors of the image.

5   Results and Analysis

In this section, we present the implementation details, experimental results and analysis. We carried our experiments on the MOBIO dataset and compared the performance of the DBM-DNNs with the DBN-DNN and the cosine distance classifier.

5.1   Implementation

In this section, we evaluate the identification accuracy of the DBM-DNNs and compare with state-of-the-art classifiers, such as the cosine distance classifier [6] and the DBN-DNN. In our experiments, i-vectors were extracted using the MSR Identity Toolbox [30]. We learned 512 mixture gender-independent UBMs for each modality. The rank of the TVM subspace was set to 400 (commonly used in the literature) and 5 iterations of the total variability modeling was carried out. The DBM-DNNs and DBN-DNNs presented in this paper were implemented using the Deepmat toolbox [31] and the same set of learning parameters. The input data was subdivided into mini-batches and the connection weights between the units of two layers were updated after each mini-batch. During the pre-training phase, the parameters of RBM were learned by the contrastive divergence (CD), adaptive learning rate and enhanced gradient techniques as in [32]. The learning rates for Stage 1 and 2 were set to 0.05 and 0.01, respectively.

Table 1. Rank-1 identification rate

Classifier		Speech	Face	Fusion
CosDist		0.775	0.733	0.946
DBN-DNN		0.841	0.802	0.952
DBM-DNN	400-400	0.863	0.830	0.967
	800-800	**0.901**	**0.847**	**0.975**
	1200-1200	0.882	0.836	0.969

Then, persistent contrastive divergence (PCD) and the enhanced gradient were used to fine-tune the DBM parameters with a learning rate of 0.001. In each step, the model was trained for 50 epochs and with a mini-batch size of 100.

We evaluated the performance of the cosine distance classifier, DBN-DNNs (two hidden layers with 400 units each) and three configurations of the DBM-DNNs. Their rank-1 identification rates are reported in Table 1. The overall rank-1 identification rate obtained using the cosine distance classifier is 0.946 which is significantly better than the identification rates of the individual modalities (i.e., 0.775 for speech and 0.733 for face). In Table 1, the results show that deep learning methods significantly improved the identification accuracy. We carried out our experiments using DBM-DNNs and DBN-DNNs with two hidden layers. We used three different configurations for DBM-DNNs: 400-400, 800-800, and 1200-1200, representing the number of units in the hidden layers. Our experimental results in Table 1 show that using DBM-DNNs with 800 units in each hidden layer performed better in terms of individual and overall identification rates compared to the use of 400 or 1200 units in the hidden layers.

In Fig. 6, we also report the Cumulative Match Characteristics (CMC) curves for the individual modalities and their fusion performed using the equally weighted sum rule. The CMC curves for the best DBM-DNN (i.e., 800–800) as shown in Table 1 are reported. It can be seen that the DBM-DNN consistently outperformed the cosine distance classifier and the DBN-DNN. This is because the posteriors obtained using the DBM-DNNs were able to discriminate between the target subjects better than the DBN-DNNs and the cosine distance classifier.

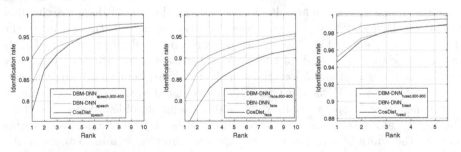

Fig. 6. Cumulative match characteristics (CMC) curves for speech modality (**left**), face modality (**middle**) and fused (**right**).

6   Conclusion

In this paper, we present the first use of DBM-DNNs for i-vector based audio-visual person identification. We compare the performance of DBM-DNNs with the state-of-the-art DBN-DNNs and the cosine distance classifier commonly used in the literature to evaluate i-vector based systems. Our experiments were carried out on the challenging MOBIO dataset. Experimental results show that DBM-DNNs achieved higher accuracies compared to the DBN-DNNs and the cosine distance classifier. We also studied three different configurations of the DBM-DNNs in this paper. Our results show that when a 400 dimensional i-vector is presented to a DBM-DNN with two hidden layers and 800 units each this performed more accurately than the other configurations. The fact that DBMs incorporate top-down feedback in the learning process enables them to learn a good generative model of the underlying data. The performance of the DBM-DNNs and DBN-DNNs under various environmental noise conditions will be an interesting study.

Acknowledgment. This research is supported by Australian Research Council grants DP110103336 and DE120102960.

References

1. Alam, M.R., Bennamoun, M., Togneri, R., Sohel, F.: An efficient reliability estimation technique for audio-visual person identification. In: 2013 8th IEEE Conference on Industrial Electronics and Applications (ICIEA), pp. 1631–1635. IEEE (2013)
2. Alam, M.R., Bennamoun, M., Togneri, R., Sohel, F.: A confidence-based late fusion framework for audio-visual biometric identification. Pattern Recogn. Lett. **52**, 65–71 (2015)
3. Khoury, E., Vesnicer, B., Franco-Pedroso, J., Violato, R., Boulkenafet, Z., Mazaira Fernandez, L.M., Diez, M., Kosmala, J., Khemiri, H., Cipr, T., et al.: The 2013 speaker recognition evaluation in mobile environment. In: Proceedings of the 2013 International Conference on Biometrics (ICB), pp. 1–8. IEEE (2013)
4. Gunther, M., Costa-Pazo, A., Ding, C., Boutellaa, E., Chiachia, G., Zhang, H., de Assis Angeloni, M., Struc, V., Khoury, E., Vazquez-Fernandez, E., et al.: The 2013 face recognition evaluation in mobile environment. In: Proceedings of the 2013 International Conference on Biometrics (ICB), pp. 1–7. IEEE (2013)
5. McCool, C., Marcel, S., Hadid, A., Pietikainen, M., Matejka, P., Cernocky, J., Poh, N., Kittler, J., Larcher, A., Levy, C., et al.: Bi-modal person recognition on a mobile phone: using mobile phone data. In: Proceedings of the 2012 IEEE International Conference on Multimedia and Expo Workshops (ICMEW), pp. 635–640. IEEE (2012)
6. Dehak, N., Kenny, P., Dehak, R., Dumouchel, P., Ouellet, P.: Front-end factor analysis for speaker verification. IEEE Trans. Audio Speech Lang. Process. **19**(4), 788–798 (2011)
7. Wallace, R., McLaren, M.: Total variability modelling for face verification. IET Biometrics **1**(4), 188–199 (2012)

8. Khoury, E., El Shafey, L., McCool, C., Günther, M., Marcel, S.: Bi-modal biometric authentication on mobile phones in challenging conditions. Image Vis. Comput. **32**(12), 1147–1160 (2014)
9. Hinton, G., Deng, L., Yu, D., Dahl, G.E., Mohamed, A.R., Jaitly, N., Senior, A., Vanhoucke, V., Nguyen, P., Sainath, T.N., et al.: Deep neural networks for acoustic modeling in speech recognition: The shared views of four research groups. IEEE Sig. Process. Mag. **29**(6), 82–97 (2012)
10. Yu, D., Deng, L.: Deep learning and its applications to signal and information processing [exploratory dsp]. IEEE Sig. Process. Mag. **28**(1), 145–154 (2011)
11. Hinton, G.E., Salakhutdinov, R.R.: Reducing the dimensionality of data with neural networks. Science **313**(5786), 504–507 (2006)
12. Ghahabi, O., Hernando, J.: Deep belief networks for i-vector based speaker recognition. In: Proceedings of the 2014 IEEE International Conference on Acoustics, Speech and Signal Processing (ICASSP), pp. 1700–1704. IEEE (2014)
13. Vasilakakis, V., Cumani, S., Laface, P.: Speaker recognition by means of deep belief networks. In: Proceedings of the Biometric Technologies in Forensic Science (BTFS) (2013)
14. Brümmer, N., De Villiers, E.: The speaker partitioning problem. In: Odyssey, p. 34 (2010)
15. Kenny, P.: Bayesian speaker verification with heavy-tailed priors. In: Odyssey, p. 14 (2010)
16. Salakhutdinov, R., Hinton, G.E.: Deep boltzmann machines. In: Proceedings of the 2009 International Conference on Artificial Intelligence and Statistics, pp. 448–455 (2009)
17. You, Z., Wang, X., Xu, B.: Investigation of deep boltzmann machines for phone recognition. In: 2013 IEEE International Conference on Acoustics, Speech and Signal Processing (ICASSP), pp. 7600–7603. IEEE (2013)
18. Zhang, Y., Salakhutdinov, R., Chang, H.A., Glass, J.: Resource configurable spoken query detection using deep boltzmann machines. In: 2012 IEEE International Conference on Acoustics, Speech and Signal Processing (ICASSP), pp. 5161–5164. IEEE (2012)
19. Srivastava, N., Salakhutdinov, R.: Multimodal learning with deep boltzmann machines. In: Advances in Neural Information Processing Systems, pp. 2222–2230 (2012)
20. Senoussaoui, M., Dehak, N., Kenny, P., Dehak, R., Dumouchel, P.: First attempt of boltzmann machines for speaker verification. In: Proceedings of the Odyssey 2012-The Speaker and Language Recognition Workshop (2012)
21. Stafylakis, T., Kenny, P., Senoussaoui, M., Dumouchel, P.: Preliminary investigation of boltzmann machine classifiers for speaker recognition. In: Proceedings of the 2012 Odyssey Speaker and Language Recognition Workshop (2012)
22. Salakhutdinov, R.: Learning deep boltzmann machines using adaptive mcmc. In: Proceedings of the 27th International Conference on Machine Learning (ICML), pp. 943–950 (2010)
23. Salakhutdinov, R., Hinton, G.: An efficient learning procedure for deep boltzmann machines. Neural Comput. **24**(8), 1967–2006 (2012)
24. Cho, K.H., Raiko, T., Ilin, A., Karhunen, J.: A two-stage pretraining algorithm for deep boltzmann machines. In: Mladenov, V., Koprinkova-Hristova, P., Palm, G., Villa, A.E.P., Appollini, B., Kasabov, N. (eds.) ICANN 2013. LNCS, vol. 8131, pp. 106–113. Springer, Heidelberg (2013)
25. Vogt, R., Sridharan, S.: Explicit modelling of session variability for speaker verification. Comput. Speech Lang. **22**(1), 17–38 (2008)

26. Kenny, P., Boulianne, G., Ouellet, P., Dumouchel, P.: Joint factor analysis versus eigenchannels in speaker recognition. IEEE Trans. Audio Speech Lang. Process. **15**(4), 1435–1447 (2007)
27. Brookes, M., et al.: Voicebox: Speech processing toolbox for matlab. Software (1997). http://www.ee.ic.ac.uk/hp/staff/dmb/voicebox/voicebox.html. March 2011
28. Tan, X., Triggs, B.: Enhanced local texture feature sets for face recognition under difficult lighting conditions. IEEE Trans. Image Process. **19**(6), 1635–1650 (2010)
29. Sanderson, C., Paliwal, K.K.: Fast features for face authentication under illumination direction changes. Pattern Recog. Lett. **24**(14), 2409–2419 (2003)
30. Sadjadi, S.O., Slaney, M., Heck, L.: MSR identity toolbox v1. 0: A matlab toolbox for speaker recognition research. In: Speech and Language Processing Technical Committee Newsletter (2013)
31. Cho, K.: (2013). https://github.com/kyunghyuncho/deepmat
32. Cho, K., Raiko, T., Ihler, A.T.: Enhanced gradient and adaptive learning rate for training restricted boltzmann machines. In: Proceedings of the 28th International Conference on Machine Learning (ICML), pp. 105–112 (2011)

Improved DSIFT Descriptor Based Copy-Rotate-Move Forgery Detection

Ali Retha Hasoon Khayeat[1,2]([⊠]), Xianfang Sun[1], and Paul L. Rosin[1]

[1] School of Computer Science and Informatices, Cardiff University, Cardiff, UK
{KhayeatAR,SunX2,RosinPL}@Cardiff.ac.uk
[2] Computer Science Department, College of Science, Kerbala University,
Kerbala, Iraq
aliretha@gmail.com

Abstract. In recent years, there has been a dramatic increase in the number of images captured by users. This is due to the wide availability of digital cameras and mobile phones which are able to capture and transmit images. Simultaneously, image-editing applications have become more usable, and a casual user can easily improve the quality of an image or change its content. The most common type of image modification is cloning, or copy-move forgery (CMF), which is easy to implement and difficult to detect. In most cases, it is hard to detect CMF with the naked eye and many possible manipulations (attacks) can be used to make the doctored image more realistic. In CMF, the forger copies part(s) of the image and pastes them back into the same image. One possible transformation is rotation, where an object is copied, rotated and pasted. Rotation-invariant features need to be used to detect Copy-Rotate-Move (CRM) forgery. In this paper we present three contributions. First, a new technique to detect CMF is developed, using Dense Scale-Invariant Feature Transform (DSIFT). Second, a new improved DSIFT descriptor is implemented which is more robust to rotation than Zernike moments. Third, a new method to remove false matching is proposed. Extensive experiments have been conducted to train, evaluate and test the algorithms, the new feature vector and the suggested method to remove false matching. We show that the proposed method can detect forgery in images with blurring, brightness change, colour reduction, JPEG compression, variations in contrast and added noise.

Keywords: Copy-move forgery · Copy-rotate-move · DSIFT descriptor · Zernike moments

1 Introduction

Copy-move is the most common image manipulation (copy and paste), where regions of the image are cloned to hide/cover objects in the scene. If this is done with care, visual detection of cloning will be difficult. Moreover, because the cloned regions can be in any location or can have any shape, searching all possible image portions in different sizes and locations is computationally infeasible.

© Springer International Publishing Switzerland 2016
T. Bräunl et al. (Eds.): PSIVT 2015, LNCS 9431, pp. 642–655, 2016.
DOI: 10.1007/978-3-319-29451-3_51

In Copy-Move Forgery (CMF), part(s) of the image are copied and pasted into the same image but in different places, possibly after a rotation. Moreover, because the copied-pasted region is from the same image, its characteristics (e.g. colour and noise) are compatible with that image. This type of forgery is more challenging to detect than other types, such as splicing and retouching. This is because the usual methods of detecting incompatibilities, using statistical measurements to compare different parts of the image, will be useless for CMF detection [2]. The first method to detect CMF was suggested by Fridrich et al. [7]. They divided the image into overlapping blocks and quantised the discrete cosine transform (DCT) coefficients of each block; they then sorted them lexicographically and checked the similarity between adjacent blocks.

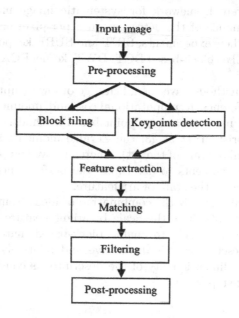

Fig. 1. The general block diagram of CMF detection.

A large number of CMF detection methods have been proposed; most of them follow a common pipeline, as shown in Fig. 1. The general CMF detection system consists of several main steps. The first step is to pre-process the image, for example, by converting the RGB colour image to a greyscale image.

The second step is to extract features from the image. There are two different methods of carrying out this extraction, by dividing the image into blocks (densely) or by detecting interest points in the image (sparsely).

In the first method, the image can be divided into overlapping or non-overlapping blocks, and these blocks can have a square or circular shape. The features are extracted from the blocks. In the second, the numbers and the locations of the interest points vary and depend on the method itself (e.g. SIFT,

MSER, SURF, HOG, etc.). The features are then extracted in the neighbour-hood of the interest points.

The third step is to find the matches (similarity) between extracted features. Many possible methods can be used to locate this similarity. The most common methods either 1/sort the feature vectors lexicographically and compute the Euclidean distance between adjacent stored blocks or 2/build a kd-tree containing all feature vectors and find the 2nd Approximate Nearest Neighbour (2ANN) for each feature. We tested both methods in our work.

In the final step, the false matches should be removed to refine the primary result.

Many methods of detecting CMF have been suggested. Christlein et al. [3] tested the 15 most prominent feature sets by creating a real-world copy-move dataset and a software framework for systematic image manipulation. They analysed the performance of the detection on a per-pixel basis and per-image basis. According to their experiments, SIFT and SURF keypoint-based features work very well, as well as block-based DCT, DWT, kernel PCA, PCA and Zernike moments.

Keypoint-based methods have the advantage of low computational complexity. There is a big difference in computational cost and amount of detected details between block-based methods and keypoint-based methods.

According to Christlein et al. [3] the Zernike moments achieved the most precise detection results (state of the art). Therefore, we compared our improved DSIFT with Zernike moments to determine the performance of our improved DSIFT descriptor versus the state of art feature.

One of our contributions is the combination of ideas from the keypoint and block-based methods. We chose the Scale Invariant Feature Transform (SIFT) method and applied it densely to enable block-based matching. SIFT is the most widely used descriptor; it is distinctive and relatively fast. However, in some cases, the high dimensionality of the descriptor is considered a drawback during the matching step [8].

2   Related Works

Several papers have used SIFT to detect CMF but, as far as we are aware, none have used DSIFT [4] for this purpose. Huang et al. [8] extract SIFT keypoints from the image, and store them in a kd-tree to enable efficient retrieval of the 2nd Nearest Neighbours (2NN). In their work, they used images from the internet. This method can partially detect CMF (one clone only), but there was no consideration of post processing methods and they did not report the accuracy of their method.

Pan and Lyu [12], detected sparse SIFT keypoints, and used the best-bin-first algorithm followed by RANdom Sample Consensus (RANSAC) [6] to estimate the possible geometric transformations. They built a correlation coefficient map between pixels in the same region and applied Gaussian filtering (7×7) to reduce noise and thresholded their results. They used their own forged images and their method failed to detect forgery in some images with translation. Moreover, they falsely detected forgery in some original (untampered) images.

Amerini et al. [1] extracted SIFT features and used 2ANN to find multiple matches between feature vectors. They applied hierarchical clustering to their matched points and used RANSAC to estimate the geometric transform. The authors employed the Columbia photographic image repository [11] and other personal collected images. This method can partially detect multiple cloned regions, but it missed some objects and falsely detected forgery in some cases. Moreover, the authors did not consider forged images with rotation in their work.

Ryu et al. [15] divided the image into overlapping 24×24 blocks and calculated the Zernike moments for each block. They sorted the Zernike feature vectors lexicographically and computed the Euclidean distance between adjacent stored blocks. If the distance is smaller than a specific threshold, they consider these blocks as cloned. They conducted their experiments with 12 TIFF images from their personal collection and other papers. They considered the Copy-Rotate Move (CRM) with rotations in the range of $0°$ to $90°$ in $10°$ steps. In their follow-up paper [14], they computed the 5th order Zernike moments from overlapping blocks to generate their feature vectors. Locality sensitive hashing with Euclidean distances was used to find similar feature vectors. The authors applied RANSAC at the feature level to remove false matches. Then, they tested their work on their forged images, which were rotated between $0°$ to $90°$, in steps of $10°$. They built their forged images by duplicating random square patches, with different sizes, on original images. This makes CMF/CRM detection much easier and produces unrealistic forged images. Moreover, their method generates considerable Pixel False Positives (PFP).

Li et al. [9] followed a different approach. They segmented the image into more than 100 patches, extracted the SIFT features from the whole image and found possible matches using a kd-tree and KNN. They estimated the transformation matrix using RANSAC. Then, they refined their results using an EM-based algorithm. They tested their work on two datasets and were unable to detect forgery in some plain forged images. Moreover, they identified some unforged images as counterfeit.

3   Forgery Detection Algorithms

This section first describes the steps taken to improve the DSIFT descriptor, and then presents our suggested algorithm for CMF detection using our improved DSIFT descriptor. Subsequently, three different methods of removing false matches are discussed, and we propose an algorithm to remove false matches using neighbourhood clustering within a radius.

3.1   Steps to Improve DSIFT

CRM forgery detection requires a rotation-invariant descriptor; thus, we improved the DSIFT descriptor to make it rotation invariant. Based on local image properties, SIFT assigns a dominant orientation for each keypoint. When building the descriptor each patch is rotated according to this orientation so that the subsequent descriptor is robust to rotation [10].

We improved the DSIFT descriptor in two steps; first, we used a different method to compute the dominant orientation, and second, we used circular blocks instead of square ones.

Step one: SIFT uses the following approach to detect dominant orientation for each patch. For each keypoint, compute the gradient orientations in its 16×16 neighbourhood. An orientation histogram is build containing 36 bins covering $360°$. Each value added to the histogram is weighted by its gradient magnitude. The peak in the orientation histogram represents the dominant directions of the keypoint. The standard setting of SIFT uses 36 bins, which causes a quantisation of the estimated dominant orientation, and this error in the orientation will cause problems in the CMF stage. It is possible to increase the number of bins to 360, but this would substantially increase the run time. Obviously, there is a trade-off between quantisation error and robustness. Therefore, we used the following method to detect the dominant orientation in our work.

In our suggested method to improve the detection of dominant orientation, we used the second order and the third order central moments to detect the dominant orientation. This method is more accurate and faster than the SIFT's method for detecting dominant orientation. The second order central moment (moment of inertia) can be used to detect the principle axes of the patch, the region around keypoint. The angle of the principle axis of the least inertia is used to describe the object orientation. This angle has a $180°$ ambiguity; the third central moment (projection skewness) was used to solve this ambiguity. Rotation of an object by $180°$ changes the sign of the projection's skewness on either axis. In other words, the sign of μ_{30} was used to differentiate between the possible orientations [13]. This method works very well and is much faster than the SIFT method (see Sect. 4.3).

Step two: SIFT considers a square region around the keypoint, which increases the border effects on this region. Simply, we considered a circular area instead of square area to reduce the border effects. Each block within a radius of 8 is divided into 4×4 sub-regions. A comparison between circular and square neighbourhoods will be described in Sect. 4.3.

The steps to build our improved DSIFT descriptor are as follows: 1/Transform a colour image into greyscale. 2/At each pixel, consider its 16×16 neighbourhood. 3/Mask each neighbourhood to use only the central disk with a radius equal to 8. 4/Use the moments based method to find the dominant orientation for each circular patch. 5/Rotate each circular patch according to its dominant orientation. 6/Compute the gradient magnitude and orientation for each circular patch. 7/Use the Gaussian function to weight the gradient magnitude. 8/For each 4×4 sub-region in the patch, build an 8 bin histogram. 9/Accumulate each bin according to its gradient magnitude of orientation. 10/Concatenate the 16 histograms to build a 128 element feature vector.

3.2   CMF Detection with Translation/Rotation

Computing DSIFT for a 512×512 image with block size of 16×16 generates 247009 feature vectors. Computing sparse SIFT for the same image size typically generates about 750 to 1350 keypoints/feature vectors. Using SIFT densely increases the running time but provides robust features which are systematically distributed over the whole image.

The full algorithm for CMFD with translation/rotation

```
Input: IRGB % Coloured image
Output: IForgery % Forged image
IG=RGB2Grey(RGB); % Convert coloured image to greyscale image
(M,N)=size(IG);
K=0;
For i=1:M-15
 For j=N-15
  Iij=IG(i:i+15,j:j+15);
  If MAD(Iij)> T1 % Compute Median Absolute Deviation
   K=K+1;
   B(K)=DSIFT(Iij);
  end if
 end for
end for
Tkd=KDtree(B);
For L1=1:K
 V1=B(L1);
 Index=ANN2(V1);
 V2=B(Index);
 If ||V1-V2|| < T2
  List=(V1,V2);
 end if
End for
NCList=Neighbourhood_Clustering (List); % Reduce the false matches
RList=RANSAC(NCList);
IForgery=IRGB.GreenColor(RList);
CC=connected_components_labelling(RList)
For F=1: size(CC)
 If CC(F).area < T3
 IForgery.CC(F).Pixel=IRGB.CC(F).Pixel;%Restore original image colour
 end if
End for
```

Flat regions increase false matches. Such flat regions occur where the pixel intensity values are similar to each other and change smoothly over comparatively large regions (e.g. sky and sea). The similarity between pixel intensity values in a large region produces a large number of similar feature vectors, which are considered as copy-move regions in the matching step. We used the median absolute deviation (MAD) to reduce the effect of flat regions. If the block's MAD value was larger than a threshold, we build the descriptor to those tested block; otherwise, we rejected it. The proposed method reduces the number of the false matches in the flat region(s) and decreases the run time significantly. We considered Neighbourhood Clustering with CRM forgery detection only to decrease the false matches and reduce the number of outliers. Without Neighbourhood Clustering, RANSAC cannot efficiently estimate the transformation because of the large number of outliers. In comparison, the number of outliers is relatively small when only translation is considered.

3.3   False Match Removal

We tested the three following methods to remove potential false matches:

1. Counting shift vectors: This method involved creating a list of coordinates for each potential cloned patch and sorting it. Then, the shift vector (spatial distance) between each related point was computed. If the number of each of the shift vectors was greater than the threshold, the patches were considered to be a forgery. This method is appropriate in the case of translation but not for CRM forgery detection.
2. Neighbourhood Clustering: The copied and pasted blocks each had to comprise at least three neighbouring blocks. This method produced very good result; details of Neighbourhood Clustering are given in Sect. 3.4.
3. RANSAC: This is an iterative method of estimating parameters of a mathematical model from a set of observed data which contains outliers. In the initial stage, RANSAC uses a dataset which is as small as possible; it enlarges this dataset consistently when possible. RANSAC can robustly estimate the geometric transformation between matched points and remove outlier blocks [6]. It can cope with more than 50 % outliers, making it more robust than many other parameter estimation techniques (such as the least median of squares) [17]. Figure 3 is an example of using RANSAC for CMF detection to remove false matching.

3.4   Neighbourhood Clustering

As the second contribution of this paper, we propose a new method to remove false matches by analysing a potential match's neighbourhood. We extensively experimented and optimised all thresholds and parameters (see Fig. 2).

The full algorithm for Neighbourhood Clustering within a radius

```
Input:A={A1,A2,..,An},B={B1,B2,..,Bn};%A & B are lists of coordinates
                           where Bi is a potential match to Ai.
Output:AB={Am1,Bm1,Am2,Bm2,...Amq,Bmq};
% q is the number of matching pairs.
[Tkd,Ind]= KDtree(A);
For i=1:n
 Aa=Tkd(i)=A(Ind(i));
 ai=ANNk(Aa) % Find k Approximate
          Nearest Neighbour{ai1,ai2,..aik} ∈ A
```

```
Count=0;
For j=1: k
 e1=ai(j);
 d1=||Aa-e1|| ;
 if d1 < r % r = specific Radius
 e2= match(B,e1) % Find the matching coordinates of e1 in B.
 Bb=B(Ind(i));
 d2=||Bb-e2||;
  If d2 <= r
   count=count+1;
  End if
 End if
 End for j
 If Count > T
 Add {Aa,Bb} into AB.
 End if
End for i
```

 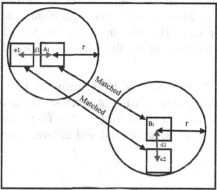

Fig. 2. An example of matching two blocks using the Neighbourhood Clustering method (left), a block diagram of two matched blocks using Neighbourhood Clustering within a radius (right).

4   Experiments and Evaluation Method

4.1   Datasets and Evaluation Method

We tested our method using the image database for Copy-Move Forgery Detection (CoMoFoD) [16]. CoMoFoD consists of 260 forged images categorised into two categories (small 512×512, and large 3000×2000). The small category consists of 200 original images with different types of forgery. We considered only the small images in our work. In the small category, images are divided into 5 different groups according to the applied manipulation, as follows: translation, rotation, scaling, distortion and a combination of all previous manipulations. Moreover, different types of post-processing methods (e.g. blurring, brightness change, colour reduction, JPEG compression, contrast adjustments and added noise), are applied to all forged and original images in each group. The total number of images in the small group is 10400 images with different types of manipulations.

As an example of alternative datasets, CASIA [5] has realistic forgery images which are categorised according to their contents into 9 categories (scene, animal, architecture, character, plant, article, nature indoor and texture). However, it contains limited post-processing methods, specifically JPEG compression and blurring and the majority of the images are small (384 × 256). The MICC-F2000, MICC-F220, MICC-F8multi and MICC-F600 datasets [1] contain 2000, 220, 8 and 600 images, respectively. These datasets have unrealistic forged images and in most cases, the forgery is perceptually very obvious.

We used the F measure at the pixel level to evaluate the accuracy of our results.

4.2 Experiments and Results for CMF/CRM Forgery Detection

A. Experiment to Compute the F Measure with Plain CMF Detection (Translation). We tested 40 different images with plain CMF and could detect forgery in all images, but some false detections were incurred (see Fig. 3). To remove the false matching, we tested three different methods; RANSAC produced the best results with a very short run time, as shown in Table 1.

B. Experiments to Compute the F Measure with CMF Detection (Translation) and Attacks. To create more realistic CMF images and to hide the traces of forgery, the forger could use some post-processing methods. In our work, we considered different types of attack (image blurring, brightness

Fig. 3. From the left: The forged input image, forgery detection with false matches, the result of RANSAC, the generated masks.

Table 1. The results of experiments in translation

Post-processing Method to Remove False Matching	F Measure	Running Time
Without Post-processing	0.8764	155 sec
Shift Vector	0.8792	45 min
Neighbourhood Clustering	0.9123	6.4 min
RANSAC	0.9367	170 sec

Table 2. Comparison between improved DSIFT and Zernike moments for CMF detection with different types of attacks

Attacks	F Measure using improved DSIFT	Detected images with improved DSIFT	F Measure using Zernike moment	Detected images with Zernike moments
Image Blurring, (5 × 5 average filter)	0.7894	38	0.5632	34
Brightness Change Range (0.01, 0.8)	0.8739	40	0.4544	33
Colour Reduction (32 intensity levels)	0.9045	40	0.4999	33
JPEG Compression (quality factor = 40)	0.3819	40	0.6078	33
Contrast Adjustment Range (0.01,0.8)	0.9033	40	0.4868	32

Table 3. Comparison between improved DSIFT and Zernike moments on detection CMF with different levels of noise

The value of White Gaussian Noise (AWGN)	F Measure using improved DSIFT	Detected images with improved DSIFT	F Measure using Zernike moments	Detected images with Zernike moments
0.000001	0.6846	36	0.6362	36
0.000005	0.5424	32	0.5148	31
0.00001	0.4883	32	0.4188	26

change, colour reduction, JPEG compression, contrast adjustments and added noise). We used our suggested method to test 200 images with different types of post-processing. Then, we tested the same images using Zernike moments. In most cases, our improved DSIFT produced better results than Zernike moments, our method detected the forgery in 198 images out of 200 (see Table 2). However, the Zernike moments is more robust to JPEG compression than our method. This is because the DCT operation in JPEG compression has a strong influence on the gradient magnitude, which affected our improved DSIFT.

We used our improved DSIFT to detect CMF with different levels of added noise. We also used Zernike moments to detect CMF with the same noisy images. We achieved satisfactory results and we get better results than Zernike moments, see Table 3 (Fig. 4).

C. Comparison Between Improved DSIFT, Zernike Moments and Original DSIFT. Christlein et al. [3] tested the 15 most prominent features to detect CMF, and Zernike moments achieved the most precise detection results. Therefore, we chose to compare Zernike moments with our method and tested our improved DSIFT descriptor. We conducted experiments on 40 different CoMoFoD images with CMF (translation). In the first experiment, we tested our algorithm on translation, both with and without RANSAC post-processing. In both

Fig. 4. Top row: blurred image (left), detected forgery (centre), generated mask (right). Bottom row: contrast-adjusted image (left), detected forgery (centre), generated mask (right).

cases, our method achieved higher F measure values than Zernike moments (see Table 4). Moreover, the results of using our improved DSIFT and original DSIFT, with translation, were similar.

Table 4. Comparison between improved DSIFT and Zernike moments in CMF

	The average of F Measure using Improved DSIFT	The average of F Measure using Zernike moments
Without post-processing	0.8764	0.8070
With post-processing	0.9367	0.8865

Another experiment was conducted with 40 different images with CRM forgery. These forged images had object(s) rotated by different angles (e.g. $180°, 90°, 10°, 2°, 4°, -4°, 5°, -7°, -3°, 1°$...etc.). In this experiment, we removed false positives in two steps. In the first step, for each potential forgery block, we tested the 8 neighbouring blocks and if we found that at least 3 neighbouring blocks were matched, we forwarded these blocks to the next step. In the second step, we used RANSAC to remove the outliers, which improved the results (see Fig. 5). This experiment illustrated the robustness of our descriptor. We obtained a higher F measure value than we did from Zernike moments and the original DSIFT (see Table 5). Therefore, our suggested improved DSIFT descriptor is more accurate under changes in rotation than Zernike moments and the original DSIFT.

4.3   An Experiment to Test Rotation Invariant of Improved DSIFT

In Sect. 3.1, we described how the level of rotational invariance of the DSIFT descriptor was improved. We also conducted an experiment to test our descriptor.

For 40 different forgery images, we randomly selected 100 blocks from each image and computed our improved DSIFT descriptors for these blocks. Next, we

Fig. 5. Examples of using our proposed method for detection of CRM forgery (True Positive (TP), True Negative (TN), False Positive (FP), False Negative (FN))

Table 5. Comparison between improved DSIFT, Zernike moments and original DSIFT in 40 images with CRM forgery

	The average of F Measure using Improved DSIFT	The average of F Measure using Zernike moments	The average of F Measure using Original DSIFT
Without post-processing	0.4005	0.2899	0.3268
With post-processing	0.7613	0.6398	0.5436

randomly rotated these blocks, considering all possible rotation angles (0°–360°), and computed our improved DSIFT descriptors for these rotated blocks. Then, we computed the Euclidean distance between the descriptors of the original and rotated blocks. The average pairs of Euclidean distance between 4000 improved DSIFT descriptors, built from 4000 different blocks before and after rotation, was 0.0487 (see Fig. 6a).

To compare our improved DSIFT rotation robustness with the original DSIFT, we repeated the previous experiment using the original DSIFT. The average pairs of Euclidean distance between 4000 descriptors (square block), built from 4000 different blocks before and after rotation, was 0.8787 (see Fig. 6b). We then repeated the same experiment using the original DSIFT with circular blocks instead of square ones, and the value of the Euclidean distance was 0.3396 (see Fig. 6c).

4.4 An Experiment to Find the Difference Between Matching Points Algorithms in CMF Detection

From previous works, we found that there are two major methods suggested to find similar blocks in CMF Detection. The first method is sorting the feature vectors lexicographically and computing the dissimilarity value between blocks (the Euclidean distance). The second approach is building the kd-tree and finding the 2ANN. We tested both methods and found them to be similar for translation, but the first method failed with rotation and we could not detect forgery with it.

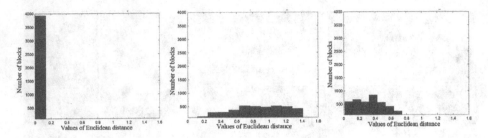

Fig. 6. Histogram of the Euclidean distance between 4000 DSIFT descriptors in: (a) the improved DSIFT (left), (b) the original DSIFT with square blocks (centre), (c) the original DSIFT with circular blocks (right).

To understand the reason for the failure of the first method, we carried out an experiment: We computed the descriptors for two cloned blocks and saved them. Then, we built the descriptors of the whole image, sorted them lexicographically and searched for the two saved descriptors. If the lexicographic sorting worked properly with our method, the two saved descriptors would be adjacent. We found that there were 189 descriptors between the two saved descriptors. The reason for this is that the lexicographical sorting is in a column-wise manner, like a dictionary, so obviously it cannot be used to detect forgery with rotation.

5   Conclusion

In this paper, we considered copy-move forgery incorporating translation and rotation. A new technique was suggested to detect CMF/CRM forgery. We obtained excellent results on translation and very good results on rotation. We improved the accuracy of the rotation robustness of DSIFT; thus, we achieved better results than for Zernike moment in rotation. A new method of removing false matching was developed and extensively tested.

Acknowledgement. This research was supported by the Higher Committee for Education Development (HCED) in Iraq and the School of Computer Science and Informatics, Cardiff University.

References

1. Amerini, I., Ballan, L., Caldelli, R., Del Bimbo, A., Serra, G.: A SIFT-based forensic method for copy-move attack detection, transformation recovery. IEEE Trans. Inf. Forensics Secur. **6**((3 PART 2)), 1099–1110 (2011)
2. Baboo, S.: Automated forensic method for copy-move forgery detection based on Harris interest points and SIFT descriptors. Int. J. Comput. Appl. **27**(3), 9–17 (2011)
3. Christlein, V., Riess, C., Jordan, J., Riess, C., Angelopoulou, E.: An evaluation of popular copy-move forgery detection approaches. IEEE Trans. Inf. Forensics Secur. **7**(6), 1841–1854 (2012)

4. Dalal, N., Triggs, B.: Histograms of oriented gradients for human detection. In: 2005 IEEE Computer Society Conference on Computer Vision and Pattern Recognition (CVPR 2005), vol. 1, pp. 886–893. IEEE (2005)
5. Dong, J., Wang, W., Tan, T.: Casia image tampering detection evaluation database. In: 2013 IEEE China Summit & International Conference on Signal and Information Processing (ChinaSIP), pp. 422–426. IEEE (2013)
6. Fischler, M.A., Bolles, R.C.: Random sample consensus: a paradigm for model fitting with applications to image analysis and automated cartography. Commun. ACM **24**(6), 381–395 (1981)
7. Fridrich, A.J., Soukal, B.D., Lukáš, A.J.: Detection of copy-move forgery in digital images. In: Proceedings of Digital Forensic Research Workshop. Citeseer (2003)
8. Huang, H., Guo, W., Zhang, Y.: Detection of copy-move forgery in digital images using SIFT algorithm. In: 2008 IEEE Pacific-Asia Workshop on Computational Intelligence and Industrial Application, vol. 2, pp. 272–276. IEEE, December 2008
9. Li, J., Li, X., Yang, B., Sun, X.: Segmentation-based image copy-move forgery detection scheme. IEEE Trans. Inf. Forensics Secur. **10**(3), 507–518 (2015)
10. Lowe, D.G.: Distinctive image features from scale-invariant keypoints. Int. J. Comput. Vision **60**(2), 91–110 (2004)
11. Ng, T.-T., Chang, S.-F., Hsu, J., Pepeljugoski, M.: Columbia photographic images and photorealistic computer graphics dataset. ADVENT Tecnical report # 205–2004-5, Columbia University, pp. 1–23 (2005)
12. Pan, X., Lyu, S.: Region duplication detection using image feature matching. IEEE Trans. Inf. Forensics Secur. **5**, 857–867 (2010)
13. Prokop, R.J., Reeves, A.P.: A survey of moment-based techniques for unoccluded object representation and recognition. CVGIP Graph. Models Image Process. **54**, 438–460 (1992)
14. Ryu, S.-J., Kirchner, M., Lee, M.-J., Lee, H.-K.: Rotation invariant localization of duplicated image regions based on Zernike moments. IEEE Trans. Inf. Forensics Secur. **8**(8), 1355–1370 (2013)
15. Lee, H.-K., Lee, M.-J., Ryu, S.-J.: Detection of copy-rotate-move forgery using Zernike moments. In: Böhme, R., Fong, P.W.L., Safavi-Naini, R. (eds.) IH 2010. LNCS, vol. 6387, pp. 51–65. Springer, Heidelberg (2010)
16. Tralic, D., Zupancic, I., Grgic, S., Grgic, M.: CoMoFoD - new database for copy-move forgery detection. In: Proceedings of 55th Internatinal Symposium ELMAR-2013, Number September, pp. 25–27. IEEE (2013)
17. Zuliani, M.: RANSAC for Dummies With examples using the RANSAC toolbox for Matlab^{TM} & Octave and more. I Edizione (2010)

Local Clustering Patterns in Polar Coordinate for Face Recognition

Chih-Wei Lin[1]([✉]) and Kuan-Yin Lu[2]

[1] College of Computer and Information Sciences,
Fujian Agriculture and Forestry University, Fuzhou, China
chihwei1981@ntu.edu.tw
[2] Department of Computer Science and Information Engineering,
National Taiwan University, Taipei, Taiwan, ROC

Abstract. Facial recognition is an important issue and has various practical applications in visual surveillance system. In this paper, we propose a novel local pattern descriptor called the Local Clustering Pattern (LCP) with low computational cost operating in the polar coordinate system for recognizing face. The local derivative variations with multi-direction are considered and that are integrated on the pairwise combinatorial direction. To generate the discriminative local pattern, the features of local derivative variations are transformed into the polar coordinate system by generating the characteristics of distance (r) and angle (θ). LCP is ensemble of several decisions from the clustering algorithm for each pixel in the polar coordinate system (P.C.S.). Differs from the existing local pattern descriptors, such as local binary pattern (LBP) [1,8], local derivation pattern (LDP) [11], and local tetra pattern (LTrP) [7], LCP generates the discriminative local clustering pattern with low-order derivative space and low computational cost which are stable in the process of face recognition. The performance of the proposed method is compared with LBP, LDP, LTrP on the Extended Yale B [4,5] and CAS-PEAL [3] databases.

Keywords: Local pattern descriptors · Local clustering pattern (LCP) · Rectangular coordinate system (R.C.S.) · Polar coordinate system (P.C.S.)

1 Introduction

Due to the intelligence security monitoring is more popular in recent year, the automatical recognizing face is needed for various visual surveillance systems, for example the accessing control system for personal or company to verify the legal/illegal people, policing system for identifying the thief and the robber who presents the illegal behavior in public or private space. To construct an efficient face recognition system, the facial descriptor with discriminated characteristic is required.

Numerous of methodologies are proposed for recognizing face and those can be classified as global and local facial descriptors. The global facial descriptor

© Springer International Publishing Switzerland 2016
T. Bräunl et al. (Eds.): PSIVT 2015, LNCS 9431, pp. 656–666, 2016.
DOI: 10.1007/978-3-319-29451-3_52

describes the facial characteristics with the whole face image, such as Principal Component Analysis (PCA) [6,10], and Linear Discriminant Analysis (LDA) [2,9]. PCA converts the global facial descriptor from high-dimension to low-dimension by using the linear transform methodology to reduce the computational cost. Linear Discriminant Analysis (LDA) also called the Fishers Linear Discriminant is similar to PCA, while it is a supervised methodology. Although the global facial descriptor can extracts the principal component from the facial images, reduces the computational cost, and maintains the variance of the facial image, the performance is sensitive to the change of the environment, such as the change of light.

The flexibilities of the local facial descriptors, such as the local binary pattern (LBP), local derivation pattern (LDP), and local tetra pattern (LTrP), are better than the global facial descriptors, because the spatial structure information is successfully and effectively utilized. The local binary pattern (LBP) generates the local facial descriptor by comparing the gray value between reference pixel and its adjacent pixels for each pixel in the face image. The texture information, such as spots, lines and corners, in the images are extracted. Although LBP considers the spatial information to generate the local facial descriptor, it omits the directional information and is sensitivity when light is slightly changed. The local derivation pattern (LDP) analyzes the turnings between reference pixel and its neighborhoods from the derivative values. The derivative values with four directions are considered to generates the local facial discriptor in the high-order derivative space. However, the turnings between reference pixel and its neighboors is discussed in the same derivative direction. The local tetra pattern (LTrP) utilized the two-dimensional distribution with derivative values in four quadrants to describe the texture informance and that can extracts more discriminative information. Although LTrP considers the derivative variations with two dimensions, there exists two problems: the dimension of facial descriptor and the sensitivity of the features. To comparing with LBP and LDP, the dimension of facial descriptor of LTrP is higher. The features of LTrP in the four quadrants of the rectangular(or Cartesian) coordinate system are altered when illumination is changed.

In this paper, we focus on reducing feature length with low computational cost and improving the accuracy of face recognition. To resolve these issues, we develop a novel pattern descriptor, called local clustering pattern (LCP), to describe the facial texture for recognizing face. Moreover, The proposed local clustering pattern considers the derivative variations with various directions on the pairwise combinatorial directions. To overcome the noise, such as light effect and to generate the stable local pattern discriptor, the facial features with derivative variations are transformed from the rectangular coordinate system with derivative variations into the polar coordinate system by generating the characteristics of distance (r) and angle (θ).

The variations of gradient are the important characteristics in face descriptor for recognizing face. Various methods, such as LDP and LTrP, are attempted to find and utilize the variations of gradient in face images by using derivative variations. The derivative variations change with directions, and that results in the clustering phenomenon. The phenomenon of clustering is more obvious in

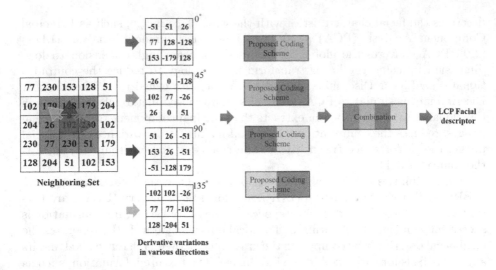

Fig. 1. Overview of generating the proposed local clustering pattern (LCP).

the polar coordinate system than that in the rectangular coordinate system. The ensemble of several decision from the clustering algorithm is applying for encoding local pattern descriptor.

This article is organized as follows: the principles of local clustering pattern (LCP) is presented in Sect. 2. The experimental results are demonstrated in Sect. 3. Finally, conclusions are given in Sect. 4.

2   The Proposed Local Pattern Descriptor

The proposed Local Clustering Pattern (LCP) mainly aims at addressing the problems of reducing feature length with low computational cost and enhancing the accuracy of face recognition. There are three phases to generate the local clustering pattern: (1) To calculate the local derivative variations with various directions. (2) To project the local derivative variations with various directions on the pairwise combinatorial directions from the rectangular coordinate system into the polar coordinate system. (3) Encoding the facial descriptor which is local clustering pattern, as a micropattern for each pixel by applying the clustering algorithm. The details are described in the following subsections, Local Clustering Pattern (LCP) and Coding scheme.

2.1   Local Clustering Pattern (LCP)

The process of generating the proposed local facial descriptor, Local Clustering Pattern (LCP), is shown in Fig. 1. Firstly, we calculate the derivative variations with four directions, 0°, 45°, 90°, and 135°. Then the proposed encoding scheme is carried out including the pairwise combinatorial direction of derivative variations, the coordinate system transformation, and the encoding strategy. Finally, the LCP facial descriptor is generated by integrating four results from the proposed coding scheme.

Given a sub-region image $I(P)$, as shown in Fig. 2(a), in which P_c is the reference pixel and $P_i, i = 1, ..., 8$ are the adjacent pixels around P_c. The first-order derivatives of P_c along $0°$, $45°$, $90°$ and $135°$ directions are denoted as $I'_\alpha(P_c)$, and can be written as

$$I'_\alpha(P_c) = I_\alpha(P_n) - I(P_c) \tag{1}$$

where $\alpha = 0°, 45°, 90°$ and $135°$ are the derivative variation directions.

In this paper, the local clustering pattern is generated based on the derivative variations on the four directions, $0°$, $45°$, $90°$, and $135°$, and those are integrated into four pairwise combinatorial directions of the derivative variations, $0°-45°$, $45°-90°$, $90°-135°$, and $135°-0°$. LCP in pairwise combinatorial direction, α and $\alpha + 45°$, at reference pixel P_c is encoded as

$$LCP_\alpha(P_c) =$$
$$\sum_{n=1}^{N} f_{r,\theta}\left(I'_{\gamma,D}(P_n), I'_{\gamma,D}(P_c)\right) \times 2^{n-1}|_{\gamma \in \{\alpha, \alpha+45°\}, N=8} \tag{2}$$

where $f_{r,\theta}(., .)$ is the proposed coding scheme and that is executed in the polar coordinate system, and $D = 1, 2, 3$ is the distance between reference pixel P_c and its adjacent pixels P_i, as shown in Fig. 2(b). The green, blue, yellow blocks indicate the distances between reference pixel and its adjacent pixels are one, two and three, the formula can be formally define as follow

$$f_{r,\theta}\left(I'_{\gamma,D}(P_n), I'_{\gamma,D}(P_c)\right)\big|_{\gamma \in \{\alpha, \alpha+45°\}} =$$
$$\begin{cases} 0, & if\ I'_{\gamma,D}(P_n)\ and\ I'_{\gamma,D}(P_c) \in C_i \\ 1, & else \end{cases} \tag{3}$$

where C_i is the cluster center.

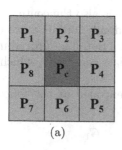

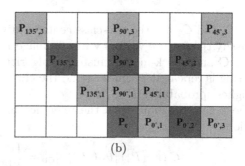

(a)   (b)

Fig. 2. (a) An example of 8-neighbors surrounding reference pixel P_c, (b) the adjacent pixels of P_c with different distances along four directions (Color figure online).

Finally, the LCP at referenced pixel P_c, $LCP(P_c)$, is combinatorial of the four 8-bit binary patterns LCPs, and can be formally as

$$LCP(P_c) = \{LCP_\beta(P_c)|_{\beta=0°,\ 45°,\ 90°,\ 135°}.\qquad(4)$$

2.2 Coding Scheme

The proposed coding scheme is considered as the problem of classification which is executed in the polar coordinate system based on the characteristics of the derivative variations in the pairwise combinatorial directions. In this paper, we utilize four combinations of the derivative variations in the pairwise directions, $0°$–$45°$, $45°$–$90°$, $90°$–$135°$, and $135°$–$0°$, in the rectangular coordinate system (R.C.S.) and those are transformed into the polar coordinate system (P.C.S.) by calculating the distance (r) and angle (θ) for each pair directions of derivative variations. The distance (r) and angle (θ) of P_n are calculated as

$$r_\gamma(P_n) = \sqrt{I'_{\gamma,D}(P_n) + I'_{\gamma+45°,D}(P_n)}|_{\gamma\in\alpha}\qquad(5)$$

$$\theta_\gamma(P_n) = \arctan\frac{I'_{\gamma+45°,D}(P_n)}{I'_{\gamma,D}(P_n)}|_{\gamma\in\alpha}\qquad(6)$$

where $\frac{-\pi}{2} < \theta_\gamma < \frac{\pi}{2}$ is normalized to $0° \sim 360°$.

The feature vectors $\mathbf{v}$ are r_γ and θ_γ coordinates in the polar coordinate system and can be written as

$$\mathbf{v} = [r_\gamma(P_n), \theta_\gamma(P_n)]^T\qquad(7)$$

where $\gamma \in \alpha$ and $n = 1 \sim 9$ are the pixels in the sub-region image $I(P)$ including the reference pixels and its adjacent pixel in the polar coordinate system.

LCP is ensemble of several decisions from the results of clustering. Each clustering result is considered as a problem of a two-class case, whose center vector $\mathbf{C}$ is written as,

$$\mathbf{C} = [C_1, C_2]^T\qquad(8)$$

where C_1 and C_2 are the two-class centers, in which C_1 is also the center of P_c. To classify the feature vectors $\mathbf{v}$ in sub-image I, we randomly initialize two-class centers $\mathbf{C}$ and the k-means clustering algorithm is adopted. The procedure of clustering is repeated T times to find the cluster two-class centers $\mathbf{C}_i$ which has the highest probability $P(\mathbf{C}_i|\mathbf{v})$.

The pixels surround with the reference pixel are encoded as the following equation,

$$C(r_\gamma(P_n), \theta_\gamma(P_n))|_{\gamma\in\alpha} = \begin{cases} 0, & if\ P_n \in C_1 \\ 1, & else \end{cases}\qquad(9)$$

where C_1 is the cluster center which includes P_c.

77	230	153	128	51
102	179	128	179	204
204	26	102	230	102
230	77	230	51	179
128	204	51	102	153

53	240	197	254	73
134	226	108	253	250
207	76	133	250	160
209	72	249	108	254
193	332	145	29	212

$LBP = 11110100$

$LDP_{\alpha=0°} = 10010100$

$LDP_{\alpha=45°} = 11110100$

$LTrP = 20430340$

(a)

$LBP = 10110100$

$LDP_{\alpha=0°} = 10110100$

$LDP_{\alpha=45°} = 10110000$

$LTrP = 21221311$

(b)

Fig. 3. Example of the stability of the existing methods including LBP, LDP, LTrP. (a) The original Image, (b) the image with noise.

Figure 3 shows an example of an original image and the corresponding image after adding Gaussian noise. LBP is encoded by comparing the gray value of the reference pixel with the adjacent pixels, the 7th bit of LBP is changed from 1 to 0. In LDP, we takes two-direction as an example, 0° and 45°. The 6th bit of LDP in 0° direction is changed from 0 to 1, the 3th and 7th bits of LDP in 45° direction are changed from 1 to 0. In LTrP, two directions, 0° and 90°, are considered as an example, the six eighths bits are changed. These methods are susceptible to noise, the encoding results are unstable. Figure 4 demostrates the encoding results of the LCP which takes Fig. 3 with 0° and 45° directions as an example, Fig. 4(a) and (b) are the distributions of the original and that of the noised images, in which C_1 and C_2 are the cluster centers. The characteristics of distance (r) and angle (θ) are more stable than derivative variation and gray values. LCP provides the corresponding pattern even in the situation of that noise and non-monotonic illumination changes.

3 Experimental Results

In this section, we first describe the evaluation of similarity. Then we analyze the accuracy of local clustering pattern (LCP) in the rectangular coordinate system (R.C.S.) and that in polar coordinate system (P.C.S.). After the analysis, we demonstrate the accuracy of LCP by comparing with LBP, LDP, and LTrP. Two publicly available face databases, CAS-PEAL, and Extended Yale B, are used to evaluate the accuracy of these methodologies.

All the original facial images are cropped according to the location of the two eyes and normalized into 64 × 64 pixels. Various derivative modes are compared, $M = [-1, 1]$ means the approximation of the forward derivative and $M = [-1, 0, 1]$ means the approximation of the central derivative.

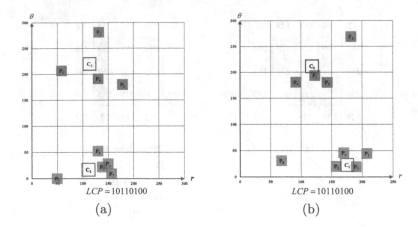

Fig. 4. Example of the stable of LCP takes Fig. 3 as an example (the derivative variations along 0° and 45°). (a) The distribution of the original image of LCP in P.C.S., (b) The distribution of the noise image of LCP in P.C.S.

3.1 Evaluation of Similarity

To measure the similarity, the spatial histogram is adopted for modeling the distribution of each methodology. Three phases are considered: (1) Uniform quantization, (2) Histogram intersection, (3) 1-NN classifier. Firstly, each image is divided into 4×4 sub-regions and the uniform quantization method is applied to reduce the number of histogram bins in each sub-region from 256 to 8. Secondly, the histogram intersection is calculated to evaluate the similarity of two histograms,

$$K\left(H_P, H_G\right) = \sum_{i=1}^{N} \min\left(H_{P_i}, H_{G_i}\right) \tag{10}$$

where $K(.,.)$ is the kernal of histogram intersection to find the minimum value between two histograms, H_{P_i} and H_{G_i}, H_{P_i} is the histogram of the probe image, H_{G_i} is the histogram of the gallery images, and i is the index of the total bins N for each image.

Finally, we utilize 64 run of tests with the 1-NN classifier to evaluate the performance of each methodology.

3.2 Experimental Results of LCP in Various Coordinate System

The concept of clustering in LCP can be applied in both the rectangular coordinate system (R.C.S.) and the polar coordinate system (P.C.S). We first use the Extended Yale B and the CAS-PEAL face databases to evaluate the accuracy of LCP in both R.S.C. and P.S.C.

Figure 5 demonstrates the performance of LCP with various illumination variations in both R.C.S. and P.C.S., in which D is the distance between reference

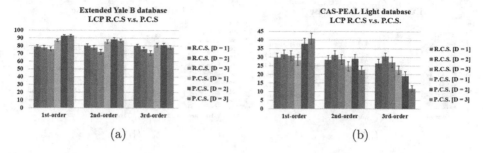

Fig. 5. Experimental results of LCP in both R.C.S. and P.C.S. with various illumination variations. (a) The Extended Yale B database, (b) The CAS-PEAL Light database.

pixel and its adjacent neighbors. From Fig. 5, comparing the performance of LCP in R.C.S. with that in P.C.S., the LCP is the best in the 1st order in P.S.C.

Figure 6 shows the average performance of LCP with CAS-PEAL database in both R.C.S. and P.C.S. From Fig. 6, comparing the performance of LCP in R.C.S with that in P.C.S., the gap of LCP with 1st order derivative in P.S.C. is more obvious than that with other order derivative in both R.C.S. and P.C.S.

From Figs. 5 and 6, with the level of the derivation is increasing, the performance is decreasing either in R.C.S. or in P.C.S. The features of distance (r) and angle (θ) perform better than that of the derivative variations. The best performance of LCP in P.C.S. is obviously better than that in R.C.S. The best performance of LCP in P.C.S. appears with 1st order derivative which has the lowest computation cost. It reveals that the clustering approach applied in P.S.C. is more preferable than that in R.S.C.

3.3   Experimental Results on Extended Yale B Database

The Extended Yale B database contains 2,432 frontal facial images of 38 subjects under 64 different illumination variations. The frontal face images distinctly illuminated from various angles are evaluated.

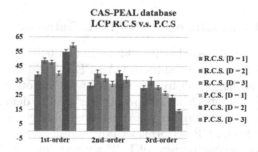

Fig. 6. Experimental results of LCP in both R.C.S. and P.C.S with CAS-PEAL database.

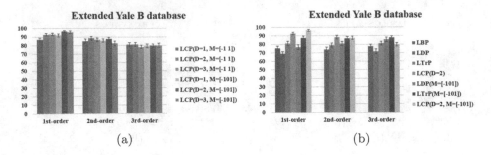

Fig. 7. Exptderimental results on Yale database. (a) LCP with various derivative varia-tions in different distance between neighbor, (b) Comparison results of LCP with other methods.

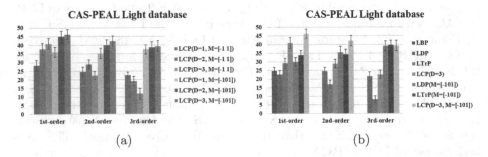

Fig. 8. Exptderimental results on CAS-PEAL Light database. (a) LCP with various derivative variations in different distance between neighbor, (b) Comparsion results of LCP with other methods.

Figure 7(a) shows the performance of the proposed method in various deriva-tive variations with different distance of neighbor. From Fig. 7(a), the best result is presented in 1st order derivation with distance 2 and also has small standard derivation. Figure 7(b) demonstrates the performance of LCP compares with LBP, LDP, LTrP. From Fig. 7(b), LCP performs well in all derivatives with var-ious derivative modes and has the best result in the 1st order derivative.

3.4 Experimental Results on CAS-PEAL Database

The CAS-PEAL light database has 9,060 images of 1,040 subjects, Fig. 8 firstly demonstrates the experimental results in CAS-PEAL light database. The CAS-PEAL light database has 2,450 frontal images with various illumination from different angles and generates from 233 people. Figure 8(a) demonstrates the per-formance of LCP in various derivative variations with different distance between neighbor. From Fig. 8(a), LCP performs well in 1st order derivative with distance 3. Figure 8(b) shows the comparison of LCP with various methodologies, LBP, LDP, and LTrP, in various derivatives. LCP performs well in all derivatives with various derivative modes and has the best result in 1st order derivative.

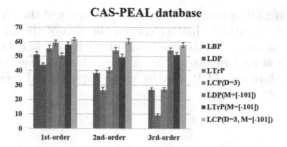

Fig. 9. Comparsion result of LCP with other methods on the CAS-PEAL database.

Figure 9 shows the performance of LCP in CAS-PEAL database. LCP performs well in both derivative modes, the approximation of the forward derivative and the approximation of the central derivative, and has the best result in 1st order derivative with distance 3.

Table 1 shows the feature length of various methodologies. The LBP can be encoded into N-dimensional features depends on the number of neighbors it used. In our study, the 8 dimensional features of LBP is adopted. Although the feature length of LBP is the shortest, the performance of LBP is not ideal in all databases. The feature length of LCP is equal or lesser than LDP and LTrP, while the performance of LCP is the best.

Table 1. Feature length of various methods

Methods	Feature length
LBP	8
LDP	8×4
LTrP	8×13
LCP	8×4

4   Conclusion

In this paper, we design a novel local facial descriptor, Local Clustering Pattern (LCP), for recognizing face. The local derivative variations with various directions on the pairwise combinatorial direction are calculated. To encode the local clustering pattern, LCP, the derivative values with the pairwise combinatorial direction are projected into the polar coordinate system with distance (r) and angle (θ) values. The features, distance (r) and angle (θ), have significantly discriminative for recognizing face. In the polar coordinate system, the clustering phenomenon is obvious, the k-means is applied for clustering the features to generate the ensemble LCP for each pixel.

In the experimental results, we analyze the accuracy of the proposed method (LCP) to compare with LBP, LDP, LTrP on the sets of the Extended Yale B and CAS-PEAL databases. In the condition of the changing light, the proposed method has the best performance, either in the Extended Yale B or CAS-PEAL Light database. Moreover, LCP has the low computational cost and the best performance in both databases.

References

1. Ahonen, T., Hadid, A., Pietikainen, M.: Face description with local binary patterns: application to face recognition. IEEE Trans. Pattern Anal. Mach. Intell. **28**(12), 2037–2041 (2006)
2. Belhumeur, P.N., Hespanha, J.P., Kriegman, D.J.: Eigenfaces vs. fisherfaces: recognition using class specific linear projection. IEEE Trans. Pattern Anal. Mach. Intell. **19**(7), 711–720 (1997)
3. Gao, W., Cao, B., Shan, S., Chen, X., Zhou, D., Zhang, X., Zhao, D.: The caspeal large-scale chinese face database and baseline evaluations. IEEE Trans. Syst. Man Cybern. Part A: Syst. Hum. **38**(1), 149–161 (2008)
4. Georghiades, A.S., Belhumeur, P.N., Kriegman, D.J.: From few to many: Illumination cone models for face recognition under variable lighting and pose. IEEE Trans. Pattern Anal. Mach. Intell. **23**(6), 643–660 (2001)
5. Lee, K.C., Ho, J., Kriegman, D.J.: Acquiring linear subspaces for face recognition under variable lighting. IEEE Trans. Pattern Anal. Mach. Intell. **27**(5), 684–698 (2005)
6. Moghaddam, B., Pentland, A.: Probabilistic visual learning for object representation. IEEE Trans. Pattern Anal. Mach. Intell. **19**(7), 696–710 (1997)
7. Murala, S., Maheshwari, R., Balasubramanian, R.: Local tetra patterns: a new feature descriptor for content-based image retrieval. IEEE Trans. Image Process. **21**(5), 2874–2886 (2012)
8. Ojala, T., Pietikäinen, M., Mäenpää, T.: Multiresolution gray-scale and rotation invariant texture classification with local binary patterns. IEEE Trans. Pattern Anal. Mach. Intell. **24**(7), 971–987 (2002)
9. Swets, D.L., Weng, J.J.: Using discriminant eigenfeatures for image retrieval. IEEE Trans. Pattern Anal. Mach. Intell. **8**, 831–836 (1996)
10. Turk, M., Pentland, A.: Eigenfaces for recognition. J. Cogn. Neurosci. **3**(1), 71–86 (1991)
11. Zhang, B., Gao, Y., Zhao, S., Liu, J.: Local derivative pattern versus local binary pattern: face recognition with high-order local pattern descriptor. IEEE Trans. Image Process. **19**(2), 533–544 (2010)

Computer Vision and Pattern Recognition

Deep Convolutional Neural Network in Deformable Part Models for Face Detection

Dinh-Luan Nguyen[1]([✉]), Vinh-Tiep Nguyen[1], Minh-Triet Tran[1],
and Atsuo Yoshitaka[2]

[1] University of Science, Vietnam National University, HCMC, Vietnam
1212223@student.hcmus.edu.vn,
{nvtiep,tmtriet}@fit.hcmus.edu.vn
[2] School of Information Science,
Japan Advanced Institute of Science and Technology, Nomi, Japan
ayoshi@jaist.ac.jp

Abstract. Deformable Part Models and Convolutional Neural Network are state-of-the-art approaches in object detection. While Deformable Part Models makes use of the general structure between parts and root models, Convolutional Neural Network uses all information of input to create meaningful features. These two types of characteristics are necessary for face detection. Inspired by this observation, first, we propose an extension of DPM by adaptively integrating CNN for face detection called DeepFace DPM and propose a new combined model for face representation. Second, a new way of calculating non-maximum suppression is also introduced to boost up detection accuracy. We use Face Detection Data Set and Benchmark to evaluate the merit of our method. Experimental results show that our method surpasses the highest result of existing methods for face detection on the standard dataset with 87.06 % in true positive rate at 1000 number false positive images. Our method sheds a light in face detection which is commonly regarded as a saturated area.

Keywords: Convolutional neural network · Deformable part models · Face detection · Non-maximum suppression

1 Introduction

Face detection is a classical task in computer vision. Although many methods have been proposed to continuously improve the accuracy, such as using single template approach [1], part-based approach [2,3], and even deep convolutional neural network [4–6], face detection is still an interesting and challenging area because of the different appearances of faces in images.

From different approaches of face detection, we find three things commonly taken into consideration to represent a face: parts of a face, spatial relationship between different parts in a face, and the overall structure of a face. Thus, it is necessary to explore efficient methods to represent parts as well as general face information itself for face detection problem. By choosing appropriate methods

T. Bräunl et al. (Eds.): PSIVT 2015, LNCS 9431, pp. 669–681, 2016.
DOI: 10.1007/978-3-319-29451-3_53

to deputize different aspects of a face, it would be possible to further improve accuracy in face detection.

To deal with representing parts and their spatial relationship, Deformable Part Models (DPM), proposed by Felzenszwalb et al. [7], is one of state-of-the-art methods. DPM uses low level feature HOG combined with latent SVM for classification. Furthermore, it also creates a structure model for representing face model. However, because of using low level feature HOG, DPM is not suitable enough to exploit high level feature of an image to represent the overall structure of a face.

On the other hand, convolutional neural network (CNN) is a new trend in many fields of computer vision, which not only shows its superiority in object detection [8] but also in other tasks such as classification [9], segmentation [6], etc. Using deep neural network for face detection is a favorable method since it wisely gets high level feature of an image through its layered structure. Nevertheless, CNN does not provide explicit relationship between lower level features, such as characteristics of parts in a face. Thus, it may lose potential information about candidate relational structure, which is an important information to improve accuracy especially when dealing with face. Both DPM and CNN have advantages and certain limitations in face detection. DPM provides a more flexible representation of a face with deformable parts while CNN generates a high level feature to represent a face. Therefore, it would be a promising approach to integrate CNN and DPM together to synergize their advantages. In this paper, we inherit DeepPyramid DPM [4], an extension for multiclass object detection, as a baseline and then propose novel method based on DPM for dealing with face detection problem.

Besides, in the post processing step, the method of calculating non-maximum suppression in DPM is so unfair that it treats all bounding boxes as the same value. As a result, a region detected with a low score has the same probability to detect a face to a region with higher score, which is one of the main issues for the vanilla DPM. Some improvements [5,10] also propose other ways for choosing the best bounding box but they are still far from satisfied result. Consequently, a new intuitive way to find bounding box is needed for results returned by DPM.

Main Contribution. There are two key ideas in our system. First, we propose a new representation model for face detection together with constructing a new adaptive way of integrated CNN into DPM. Second, an intuitive calculation for non-maximum suppression is also introduced to boost up detection accuracy. We conduct experiments on the standard dataset Face Detection Data Set and Benchmark (FDDB). The results point out that proposed system is significantly superior to other published works on FDDB. Our method achieves up to 87.06 % in true positive rate, being the state-of-the-art technique.

The rest of our paper is organized as follow. Section 2 reviews some related works on the combination between DPM with CNN and other improvements in face detection using DPM. Our primary contribution for proposing new face model architecture and intuitive non-maximum suppression are carefully discussed in Sect. 3 and Sect. 4 respectively. Section 5 shows experimental results and comparison to other state-of-the-art techniques on FDDB dataset. Finally, conclusion is given in Sect. 6.

2 Related Works

In object detection, there are two main approaches [11]: rigid and part-based methods. In rigid approach, a model captures the whole object and exploits characteristics by using single detection and abstract feature. Based on this idea, some recent works use convolutional neural network for mining high level features and applying to face detection [5,12]. Among them, by achieving competitive result on FDDB dataset, DDFD - an extension of R-CNN [6], proposed by Farfade et al. [13], is one of promising approaches for using CNN in object detection. Besides, Chen et al. [1] proposes a boost cascade technique with shape index feature to align face and conduct detection. Park et al. [14] and Zhang et al. [15] use multi-resolution technique to overcome different scales of face. These approaches, however, have not reached top performance since a rigid based method is not flexible enough to deal with deformable objects, such as a face.

On the other hand, a part-based approach can handle multiple appearances of an object. It captures the patterns of each part and combine them together to get final detection result. Derived from this approach, a tree structured model proposed by Zhu et al. [16] achieves both facial landmarks localization and pose estimation in real time. Pirsiavash and Ramanan [17] create steerable part models to solve different view points of face. Besides, Deformable Part Models (DPM), proposed by Felzenszwalb et al. [7], is one of pioneers in face detection using part-based structure. DPM takes advantage of HOG low level feature as an input for finding root and part models. A root model is used for representing the whole object while a part model which is twice resolution accounts for a changeable objects component. To find the location of a part model, DPM uses a sliding window combined with latent SVM to classify regions. A pyramid image is constructed based on different scales of an image. An extension of Deformable Part Models proposed by Mathias et al. [2] gets the promising result by pre-training carefully. However, applying low level features for learning is so wasteful that it eliminates much useful undiscovered information. Therefore, there is a huge need to replace HOG by another high level feature extracted from input images.

There are just a few works realizing the complementary between DPM and CNN. Work of Ouyang and Wang [12] creates CNN whose inputs are HOG features. This CNN structure also has a deformation layer to deal with occlusion situations. However, this work just focuses on optimizing pedestrian detection. Savalle et al. [8] use deep features extracted from pyramid images instead of using HOG features. This approach gets promising results but the structure for learning features from pyramid images only has five convolutional layers with fine-tuned parameters. Wan et al. [10] use pixel-wise max to form corresponding map from root and nine part filters acquired from three views of an object template. However, this extension of pyramid feature is not adaptive because it fixes the model with nine parts and uses hand-crafted step to split three object templates. Work of Girshick [4] integrates DPM-CNN structure based on features pyramid returned by [8]. To be specific, each pyramid level is convolved with root and part filters to get a convolution map. These maps are processed with a distance transform pooling layer then stacked together to convolve with a spare object geometry filter. Thus, the output of this network is a single channel score map for DPM component. Our method inherits the version 5 of vanilla DPM [7] and DeepPyramid DPM (DP-DPM) [4]. We complement their work by specifying the neural network structure to get it specialized to face detection with raw DPM version.

One of the important parts of a detection model which affects the final result is the post processing step. Non-maximum suppression has been discussed by many works [10,17] and non-maximum suppression is tweaked to fit with the output of each method. In the original DPM and other improvements [2,18,19], non-maximum suppression is usually performed by exploiting the overlapped area of each pair of bounding boxes to select the best one. Thus, this approach does not cover all bounding boxes, especially when dealing with situations in which the boxes are spare and scattered in an image. Besides, Wan et al. [10] create a ranking loss in their network to keep track of promising returned boxes. However, all discussed methods are either too simple [4,7] or complicated [10] and each of them just sticks to a specific model structure. Thus, a general method for adaptively covering all kind of models is necessary to be proposed.

3 Deep Face Deformable Part Models

In this section, we present our new effective face depiction architecture and an integrated convolutional neural network in DPM called DeepFace DPM.

3.1 New Face Representation Model

We review the object model in vanilla DPM [7] and then propose our new model to enhance the original one. DPM uses HOG features to create root and part scores. HOG is calculated by using a pyramid of different scale images and convolution kernel to get gradient value. Different bins of orientation are accumulated by their corresponding size based on gradient orientations.

Part and root filters are constructed from HOG features. The default configuration of DPM having 8 part filters with the fixed size of 6×6 pixels is just a general solution for multiclass detection. In practical use, the accuracy in face detection is affected by the variance of illumination, face's pose direction, occlusion and blur condition. Therefore, from our observation of faces in frontal and side views, we propose a new adaptive model to represent a face which is derived from 4-part model and 5-part model.

To deal with frontal face when the lighting condition is nearly stable, 5 parts are enough for representing 1 forehead, 2 eyes, 1 nose, and 1 mouth. Because of

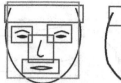

Fig. 1. New integrated model for face representation. 5-part model (left) and 4-part model (right) are used to detect 0° to 45° and 45° to 90° face direction comparing to frontal face respectively.

the vivid forehead, part filter corresponding to it has twice resolution in comparison with the others. Similarly, 4-part model representing 1 forehead, 1 eye, 1 nose, and 1 mouth is introduced to overcome the difficulties of occlusion or changeable illumination face. Figure 1 describes root and part filters in frontal and occluded circumstances. Decision to choose either a 4-part or a 5-part model depends on proposed DeepFace DPM network which is described in details in Fig. 2. The model score for representing face is the output of DeepFace DPM network described in Sect. 3.2. The reason for proposing this new face model is from the observation that when a face is occluded or not in frontal view, we can only see many but not all face components. Thus, using a model with small number of parts which corresponds to occluded situations is sufficient in comparison with the big one.

3.2 DeepFace DPM - A Convolutional Neural Network Integrated in DPM

Extract Coarse Convolutional Feature Pyramid. Given an input image, we scale it up and down into D-scale levels where the original size is at the level $\lfloor D/2 \rfloor$. Since the size of a face is unknown, a feature pyramid is used to deal with different scales in images. We inherit the structure of SuperVision CNN [9] to extract coarse pyramid features. However, we just use 4 layers and eliminate max pooling step at the $4th$ layer to reduce complicated calculations. Thus, the output of this SuperVision CNN process is a coarse pyramid feature as the input for the following 4 or 5-part DPM-CNN architecture.

Integrated 4-5 Part DPM-CNN. Based on the superiority of DPM-CNN architecture [4], we get rid of calculating stack maps process and use the specific 4 part filters per one root filter. Consequently, the component score at each layer is the pyramid distance transform of part convolution. These pyramids are the input for full DPM-CNN with the number of part filters is 5. A max pooling layer is constructed to get the highest correspondent score of model. This score is used as a replacement for the hand-crafted score between root and part filters in the original version of DPM for latent SVM classification afterward.

There are two points in the SuperVision CNN architecture that we solve for face detecting problem. The first thing is that SuperVision network itself is

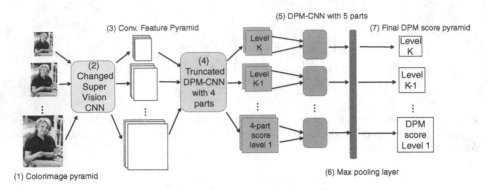

Fig. 2. Proposed model architecture. (1) Color images pyramid is built by resizing an input image with scaling factor 1.5. (2) SuperVision CNN [9] is used to extract feature from an image pyramid. (3) Feature pyramid are constructed from the 4th layer after forward propagation. (4) Convolutional feature pyramid is the input for DPM-CNN [4], which is truncated stack maps process. (5) Each 4-part component feature level goes through full DPM-CNN to get 5-part DMP-CNN feature. (6) Max pooling layer is used for calculating the most promising score result returned by DMP-CNN at each level.

used for classification and detection generic objects. As a consequence, it is not optimized to be used of face detection, which is only focus on round rigid areas. Based on this observation, we scale down 224×224 patches in data augmented process to the size of 112×112. Thus, the input of our network has the size of $112 \times 112 \times 3$. Furthermore, we reduce 1 stride after going through each layer to accumulate more precious high level features. To be specific, the first layer has the stride of 4 pixels while the second, third, and fourth layers use the stride length of 3, 2, and 1 pixels respectively. This way of adjustment means that the more meticulous extracting feature after each layer is, the higher level and important characteristics we get. The second problem with SupperVision CNN is that its output is at $1/16th$ the spatial resolution of the corresponding input. This method for using feature is so deficient that it eliminates any bounding box that has a small size within 16×16 pixels. We completely solve this defect by upscale features at twice resolution in each layer. Combining these solutions together with applying dropout layer not only significantly increases the speed for training but also improves the quality of output features.

4   Intuitive Non-maximum Suppression

In the original version of DPM [7] and other extensions [10,17,18], including DeepPyramidDPM [4] and FaceCascadeCNN [5], Intersection-over-Union exemplar is commonly used to eliminate redundant bounding boxes. To be specific, let B represent a big box and b is a small one. The old traditional method calculates the overlapped region between $S(B) \cap S(b)$ and compares it to the area of

---

Algorithm 1. Intuitive Non-maximum suppression

 Input: $B = \{b_1, b_2, \ldots, b_K\}$
 w, h: width, height of input image
 Output: $B' = \{b'_1, b'_2, \ldots, b'_N\}$
1: **procedure** INTUITIVE NMS
2:    $C = \{c_1, c_2, \ldots, c_N\} \leftarrow MeanShift(B)$
3:    $Tag(b_i) \in L = \{l_1, l_2, \ldots, l_N\}$
4:    $A = 0_{h,w}$
5:    $S_{Bmin,L} = +\infty$
6:    **for** $b_i \in B$ **do**
7:       $A = A + M_{score}(b_i)$
8:       $S_{Bmin,Tag(b_i)} = min(S_{Bmin,Tag(b_i)}, area(b_i))$
9:    **end for**
10:    $C = local\_maximum(A)$
11:    **for** $c_i \in C$ **do**
12:       $b'_i = expand(c_i, S_{Bmin,l_i})$
13:    **end for**
14: **end procedure**

---

the smaller box b. A hard threshold is used to suppress any bounding box that does not satisfy the following constraint:

$$\frac{S(B) \cap S(b)}{S(b)} \geq 50\% \tag{1}$$

Besides, Wan *et al.* [10] proposes an extension to eliminate unnecessary boxes by splitting the condition into two situations depending on whether the bounding boxes are in the same type or not. For different detected object boxes, the criterion is based on

$$\frac{S(B) \cap S(B')}{S(B) \cup S(B')} \geq 75\% \tag{2}$$

where B' is the candidate box of another object. For the same object boxes, the overlap is calculated by

$$\max\left(\frac{S(B) \cap S(b)}{S(B)}, \frac{S(B) \cap S(b)}{S(b)}\right) \geq 50\% \tag{3}$$

These approaches are insufficient since they discard uncommon region between two boxes and treat low score bounding boxes as the same as the big ones. Thus, they may lead to incorrect detect results if candidate boxes are sparse in an image. From these observations, we propose a new intuitive way of calculating bounding boxes described in Algorithm 1 to solve these defects. Given K bounding boxes (B) returned from framework, we classify them into N clusters (C) using MeanShift. Zero matrix A is created with size $h \times w$ to accumulate matrix score area of each bounding box (M_{score}). Besides, minimum size box of each cluster is collected to build the final box (B') from the new cluster center point generated by calculating local maximum over matrix A.

5   Experimental Results

Dataset. We evaluate the merit of our method on Face Detection Data Set and Benchmark (FDDB) [20]. This large scaled dataset contains 2845 images comprising of 5171 faces gathered from news photographs and has wide variety of background, appearance, illumination, and face direction. FDDB uses ellipse coordinator as face annotations. The result of some state-of-the-art techniques are public on FDDB website. Figure 3 shows some FDDB images with their ellipse annotation.

Fig. 3. Some examples and annotation in FDDB dataset. Faces are annotated by using ellipse and cover wide range of size, illumination, looking direction, and occlusion.

To be fair with other methods, we build an upright ellipse for each detected rectangle. In specific, given an output rectangle in size (w, h), we create an ellipse having the same center point of the rectangle and the sizes of the major axis and minor axis of the ellipse are $1.21h$ and $1.11w$ respectively. By adjusting our result for easy evaluation with FDDB dataset, we slightly improve the true positive in overall (from 86.88 % to 87.06 %). The advantage of changing detect region from rectangles to ellipses is described in Table 1.

Evaluation. We use standard evaluation protocol provided with dataset so as to be equitable when comparing with other techniques. There are two kinds of evaluation: continuous and discontinuous one. In the continuous evaluation, it reveals the robust of framework after 10 folds validation by using matching metric of Intersection-over-Union. Meanwhile discontinuous shows the number of false positive and true positive rate. We run our network configuration described in Sect. 3.2 with $D = 15$ scale levels. Table 1 illustrates the results of different DeepFace DPM's configurations. The DeepPyramid DPM with the default configuration using 8 parts is useful for detecting generic object but it does not

Table 1. Comparision between different configurations in FDDB dataset

Configuration	True positive rate at 1000 false positive images
HOG-DPM [7]	65.70 %
HOG-DPM with intuitive NMS	69.86 %
HOG-DPM with 4–5 part model	78.73 %
DeepPyramid DPM [4]	81.29 %
Our method using default DPM object model	82.95 %
Our method w/o using intuitive NMS	84.60 %
Our method with rectangle evaluation	86.88 %
Our best method	**87.06 %**

demonstrate the superiority in face detection. Our integrated DeepFace DPM model points out the advantages with 87.06 % true positive rate at 1000 positive false images while the DeepPyramid DPM only gets 81.29 % in true positive rate. Furthermore, we also compare our system with the HOG-DPM vanilla and others improvements.

From Table 1, using pyramid image scales as raw convolutional features combined with adaptive 4–5 part model for face representation significantly boosts up the accuracy detection. To be specific, HOG-DPM with default configuration

Fig. 4. Selected situations which proposed method shows superiority to DPM and CNN. First row: results detected by DPM. Second row: results detected by CNN (Deep-Pyramid DPM). Third row: results detected by our method.

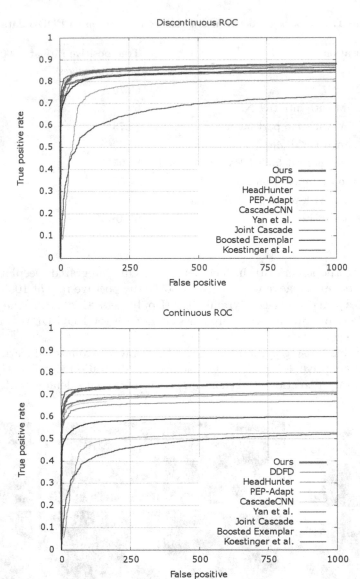

Fig. 5. Comparision with state-of-the-art on FDDB dataset. We compare our result with state-of-the-art methods comprising DDFD [13], HeadHunter [2], PEP-Adapt [3], CasacadeCNN [5], Yan *et al.* [19], Joint Cascade [1], Boosted Exemplar [18], and Koestinger *et al.* [21] (Color figure online).

only get 65.70 % in true positive rate whereas 4–5 part model integrated into HOG-DPM boosts the precision up to 78.73 %. Besides, the method of using high level pyramid features instead of HOG low level features impressively increases 21.36 % (from 65.70 % to 87.06 %) in true positive rate. By using proposed intuitive non-maximum suppression, we avoid a lot of redundant bounding boxes and get the right position for candidate region. HOG-DPM with intuitive non-maximum suppression improves up to 4.16 % (from 65.70 % to 69.86 %) while our system accelerates 2.46 % (from 84.60 % to 87.06 %) in detecting result. Figure 4 shows some difficult situations including different face's pose, direction, illumination, and even stone's face. Our method successfully detects all faces while DPM and CNN miss and have wrong detect in some images.

Compare with State-of-the-Art Techniques. To be equal when comparing our result with other works, we use public results on FDDB website for reference. Our system shows the superiority not only in continuous but also discontinuous score. Figure 5 describes the comparison between our achievement with current state-of-the-art techniques comprising DDFD [13], HeadHunter [2], PEP-Adapt [3], CasacadeCNN [5], Yan *et al.* [19], Joint Cascade [1], Boosted Exemplar [18], and Koestinger *et al.* [21]. Our result gets 87.06 % (discontinuous ROC) and 75.28 % (continuous ROC) in positive rate at 1000 false positive image while the best result of state-of-the-art only achieves 86.13 % and 74.83 % respectively.

Figure 6 shows the comparison between proposed method with traditional NMS. By using our method, the system significantly increases true positive detected bounding boxes. Especially in images having many people, intuitive non-maximum suppression shows the superiority by successful detecting face with different sizes, looking directions, blur condition, and part occlusion. However, a few missing boxes can occur (the red boxes) when comparing with groundtruth because of these faces are nearly occluded and not easily to detect. There are two unsuccessful cases in our framework which are too small blur faces and half occluded ones. Firstly, in the left-most image (small blur faces), face's size so tiny that features for parts and structure between them is not vivid. Hence, it is difficult to exploit features from these faces. However, our framework just misses some situations where faces are too small and nearly occluded by other objects (e.g. racket, image's border). Secondly, in the right-most image, the missed face is occluded by front people. Thus, we nearly just have half information of frontal face. In some circumstances, situation liked this is treated as side-view face. However, in this image, feature may not be enough to be classified either frontal or side-view face.

Fig. 6. Examples of applying intuitive non-maximum suppression method with difficult situations. Green boxes: results detected by traditional NMS, yellow boxes: extra results detected by our method besides green ones, red boxes: missing boxes in comparision with groundtruth (Color figure online).

6   Conclusion

In this paper, two novel techniques are proposed to boost up the capacity of DPM and CNN. Our system reveals the fact that structure learning and deep learning can be integrated together to get the top performance. Besides, new combination of 4–5 part model and intuitive non-maximum suppression significantly increases the accuracy of face detection. The evaluation results show that proposed system is robust and achieves competitive performance in comparison with other state-of-the-arts. Furthermore, it becomes new state-of-the-art on FDDB dataset. This work sheds a light on face detection approach and has potential for practical using in the future.

References

1. Chen, D., Ren, S., Sun, J., Wei, Y., Cao, X.: Joint cascade face detection and alignment. In: Fleet, D., Pajdla, T., Schiele, B., Tuytelaars, T. (eds.) ECCV 2014, Part VI. LNCS, vol. 8694, pp. 109–122. Springer, Heidelberg (2014)
2. Mathias, M., Benenson, R., Pedersoli, M., Van Gool, L.: Face detection without bells and whistles. In: Fleet, D., Pajdla, T., Schiele, B., Tuytelaars, T. (eds.) ECCV 2014, Part IV. LNCS, vol. 8692, pp. 720–735. Springer, Heidelberg (2014)
3. Li, H., Hua, G., Lin, Z., Brandt, J., Yang, J.: Probabilistic elastic part model for unsupervised face detector adaptation. In: 2013 IEEE International Conference on Computer Vision (ICCV), pp. 793–800. IEEE (2013)
4. Girshick, R., Iandola, F., Darrell, T., Malik, J.: Deformable part models are convolutional neural networks. In: Proceedings of the IEEE Conference on Computer Vision and Pattern Recognition (CVPR) (2015)
5. Li, H., Lin, Z., Shen, X., Brandt, J., Hua, G.: A convolutional neural network cascade for face detection. In: Proceedings of the IEEE Conference on Computer Vision and Pattern Recognition, pp. 5325–5334. (2015)
6. Girshick, R., Donahue, J., Darrell, T., Malik, J.: Rich feature hierarchies for accurate object detection and semantic segmentation. In: Proceedings of the IEEE Conference on Computer Vision and Pattern Recognition (CVPR) (2014)
7. Felzenszwalb, P.F., Girshick, R.B., McAllester, D., Ramanan, D.: Object detection with discriminatively trained part-based models. IEEE Trans. Pattern Anal. Mach. Intell. 32, 1627–1645 (2010)
8. Savalle, P.A., Tsogkas, S., Papandreou, G., Kokkinos, I.: Deformable part models with cnn features. In: European Conference on Computer Vision, Parts and Attributes Workshop (2014)
9. Krizhevsky, A., Sutskever, I., Hinton, G.E.: Imagenet classification with deep convolutional neural networks. In: Advances in Neural Information Processing Systems, pp. 1097–1105. (2012)
10. Wan, L., Eigen, D., Fergus, R.: End-to-end integration of a convolutional network, deformable parts model and non-maximum suppression. CoRR abs/1411.5309 (2014)
11. Cho, H., Rybski, P.E., Zhang, W.: Vision-based 3d bicycle tracking using deformable part model and interacting multiple model filter. In: 2011 IEEE International Conference on Robotics and Automation (ICRA), pp. 4391–4398. IEEE (2011)

12. Ouyang, W., Wang, X.: Joint deep learning for pedestrian detection. In: 2013 IEEE International Conference on Computer Vision (ICCV), pp. 2056–2063. IEEE (2013)
13. Farfade, S.S., Saberian, M., Li, L.J.: Multi-view face detection using deep convolutional neural networks. arXiv preprint arXiv:1502.02766 (2015)
14. Park, D., Ramanan, D., Fowlkes, C.: Multiresolution models for object detection. In: Daniilidis, K., Maragos, P., Paragios, N. (eds.) ECCV 2010, Part IV. LNCS, vol. 6314, pp. 241–254. Springer, Heidelberg (2010)
15. Zhang, W., Zelinsky, G., Samara, D.: Real-time accurate object detection using multiple resolutions. In: IEEE 11th International Conference on Computer Vision, 2007, ICCV 2007, pp. 1–8. IEEE (2007)
16. Zhu, X., Ramanan, D.: Face detection, pose estimation, and landmark localization in the wild. In: 2012 IEEE Conference on Computer Vision and Pattern Recognition (CVPR), pp. 2879–2886. IEEE (2012)
17. Pirsiavash, H., Ramanan, D.: Steerable part models. In: 2012 IEEE Conference on Computer Vision and Pattern Recognition (CVPR), pp. 3226–3233. IEEE (2012)
18. Li, H., Lin, Z., Brandt, J., Shen, X., Hua, G.: Efficient boosted exemplar-based face detection. In: 2014 IEEE Conference on Computer Vision and Pattern Recognition (CVPR), pp. 1843–1850. IEEE (2014)
19. Yan, J., Lei, Z., Wen, L., Li, S.Z.: The fastest deformable part model for object detection. In: 2014 IEEE Conference on Computer Vision and Pattern Recognition (CVPR), pp. 2497–2504. IEEE (2014)
20. Jain, V., Learned-Miller, E.G.: Fddb: a benchmark for face detection in unconstrained settings. UMass Amherst Technical report (2010)
21. Kostinger, M., Wohlhart, P., Roth, P.M., Bischof, H. : Robust face detection by simple means. In: DAGM 2012 CVAW Workshop (2012)

Multimodal Gesture Recognition Using Multi-stream Recurrent Neural Network

Noriki Nishida[✉] and Hideki Nakayama

Machine Perception Group, Graduate School of Information Science and Technology,
The University of Tokyo, Tokyo, Japan
`nishida@nlab.ci.i.u-tokyo.ac.jp, nakayama@ci.i.u-tokyo.ac.jp`

Abstract. In this paper, we present a novel method for multimodal gesture recognition based on neural networks. Our multi-stream recurrent neural network (MRNN) is a completely data-driven model that can be trained from end to end without domain-specific hand engineering. The MRNN extends recurrent neural networks with Long Short-Term Memory cells (LSTM-RNNs) that facilitate the handling of variable-length gestures. We propose a recurrent approach for fusing multiple temporal modalities using multiple streams of LSTM-RNNs. In addition, we propose alternative fusion architectures and empirically evaluate the performance and robustness of these fusion strategies. Experimental results demonstrate that the proposed MRNN outperforms other state-of-the-art methods in the Sheffield Kinect Gesture (SKIG) dataset, and has significantly high robustness to noisy inputs.

Keywords: Multimodal gesture recognition · Recurrent neural networks · Long short-term memory · Convolutional neural networks

1 Introduction

Deep neural networks are efficient machine learning models used by many applications in computer vision, speech recognition, and natural language processing. Although various architectures have been proposed in recent years, convolutional neural networks (ConvNets) are currently dominant in a variety of benchmarks in computer vision [1,2]. In many object recognition competitions, such as the ImageNet Large Scale Visual Recognition Challenge (ILSVRC), nearly all top-ranked teams used ConvNets. In recent studies, the error rate of the state-of-the-art models outperforms the human performance [3,4].

On the other hand, in gesture recognition, such a dominant model has not appeared yet. One main reason is that it is difficult for neural networks to simultaneously learn effective image representations and sequential models.

Traditional gesture recognition systems consist of several consecutive stages [5,6]. The first stage involves detecting and segmenting the regions of the objects being focused on (e.g., hands, arms). This stage requires prior knowledge of target gesture domains. In the second stage, features are extracted from the segmented regions. Finally, the last stage classifies input gestures using sequential

© Springer International Publishing Switzerland 2016
T. Bräunl et al. (Eds.): PSIVT 2015, LNCS 9431, pp. 682–694, 2016.
DOI: 10.1007/978-3-319-29451-3_54

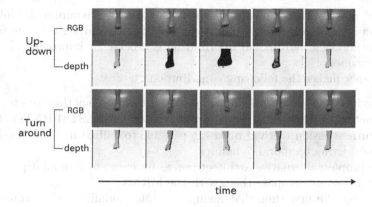

Fig. 1. Two examples in the SKIG dataset [10]. This figure shows that each modality has different importance for different gestures. The upper two rows show a color sequence and a corresponding depth sequence of an example from the "Up-down"category, whereas the lower two rows show an example from the "Turn around" category. It can be seen that depth modality is useful for classifying the upper example. However, in the lower example, the temporal change in the depth modality is very minor, because the key action of the "Turn around" gesture is a hand rotation. Therefore, the color modality should also be considered in classification (Color figure online).

data models such as the Hidden Markov Model (HMM). One of the largest drawbacks of this consecutive approach is that overall performance strongly depends on the quality and the generalization ability of each stage. Moreover, hand-coded heuristics (such as skin color filtering) that are often used during the first stage make the entire system too specific to the target gestures.

Hand-coded heuristics lead to a lack of generality in gesture recognition systems. Representation learning is one of the most efficient methods for addressing this problem [7]. Representation learning focuses on the extraction of effective features from raw data. In particular, multimodal representation learning has attracted increasing attention in machine learning [8,9]. One main reason for this trend is that multimodal information can improve the robustness of classifiers. In general, an object can be described by various modalities, including color image, depth data, sound, and natural language. Each modality is expected to carry different information. Some objects might not be correctly discriminated from others if only a single modality is available. Information from multiple modalities can suppress this type of misclassification. This is also the case for gesture recognition. Some gestures are similar in color modality but are significantly different in depth modality, and vice versa. We show such examples from the SKIG dataset [10] in Fig. 1. The upper two rows are a color sequence and a corresponding depth sequence of an example video from the "Up-down" category. The lower two rows show another example from the "Turn around" category. It is obvious that the depth information is effective for classifying the

"Up-down" gesture. However, the "Turn around" gesture requires color information, because the depth modality changes very slightly throughout the frames. Thus, incorporating multimodal information is crucial for improving classification performance.

This paper makes the following contributions:

- We introduce a novel multimodal-temporal fusion approach that uses recurrent neural networks with Long Short-Term Memory cells (LSTM-RNNs) [11,12]. Our recurrent fusion method makes it possible to embed multiple modalities while considering temporal dynamics.
- We also propose alternative architectures as baselines to fuse multiple temporal modalities and compare them with the MRNN.
- We show for the first time that fusing multiple modalities while considering temporal dynamics is significantly beneficial not only for improving classification performance, but also for increasing robustness to noisy inputs.
- The MRNN outperforms previous approaches and our alternative models in the SKIG dataset, and achieves state-of-the-art performance.

2   Related Work

Our work continues in the path established by Murakami et al. [13]. Both their work and ours propose a data-driven method for gesture recognition that does not require any prior knowledge of target gesture domains. Gesture recognition systems that use a more conventional approach split the entire system into three components: a hand detector, feature extractor, and classifier [5,6]. While there are many works that employ machine learning techniques for gesture recognition, detection and segmentation of key objects (e.g., hands, arms) remain hand-coded. In contrast, in our MRNN, these processes are automatically optimized towards end-to-end classification performance.

Many neural network models have been applied to various tasks in computer vision, including object recognition [3,14], object detection [2], semantic segmentation [15], and image generation [16]. Murakami et al. [13] used Elmen RNN [11] for gesture recognition. They used data collected from data gloves. However, in practice, data gloves are not always available for real-world applications. Ji et al. [17] extended conventional ConvNets to 3D ConvNets for handling videos. Karpathy et al. [18] proposed hierarchically stacked 2D ConvNets for fusing temporal-spatial information. Donahue et al. [19] incorporated a ConvNet with an LSTM-RNN and applied it to action recognition. Molchanov et al. [20] proposed a multimodal gesture recognition model consisting of two streams of 3D ConvNets. They developed a high-resolution 3D ConvNet and a low-resolution 3D ConvNet that are merged in the last layer, and achieved the highest accuracy in the 2015 Vision for Intelligent Vehicles and Applications (VIVA) challenge [9]. Their approach is similar to our early multimodal fusion model; however, we use LSTM-RNNs to extract temporal dynamics. Liu et al. [10] proposed restricted graph-based genetic programming to fuse color and depth modalities. However, their approach requires primitive 3D operations that must be defined before training. The process of choosing these operations limits the model's classification performance. In this paper, we use multiple streams of LSTM-RNNs to fuse multiple temporal modalities. The recurrent nature of our approach allows it to fuse modalities sequentially while considering temporal dependencies. For comparison, we propose alternative architectures that fuse modalities before or after LSTM-RNN streams, and demonstrate that the proposed MRNN is a significantly efficient model in terms of classification performance and robustness to noisy inputs.

3   Multi-stream Recurrent Neural Network

Overview. The purpose of our model is to classify gestures into given categories by utilizing information from multiple modalities. We develop multiple streams of LSTM-RNNs using ConvNets. Each stream receives frame-level inputs at every step from corresponding modalities, and independently represents the temporal dynamics of each modality. To embed the disconnected representation into a common space, we construct an additional LSTM-RNN stream on top of these streams. Figure 2 displays the graphical representation of the MRNN. For comparison, we also propose two alternative architectures: the late multimodal fusion model and the early multimodal fusion model. These models are displayed in Fig. 3(a), (b). In this section, we first explain LSTM-RNNs. We then describe the details of our proposed models.

3.1   RNN with LSTM Cells

A recurrent neural network (RNN) is a straightforward extension of multilayer perceptrons to sequential modeling [11]. Let $\phi(\mathbf{x}_t) \in \mathbb{R}^n$ and $\mathbf{h}_t \in \mathbb{R}^m$ be a nonlinearly transformed input and a hidden state, respectively, at step t. The nonlinear function ϕ is a neural network that extracts the feature vector from the input $\mathbf{x}_t$. For example, ConvNets can be used as ϕ if $\mathbf{x}_t$ is spatial data such as a color image. The neural network ϕ is a portion of the entire architecture, and is optimized simultaneously with the remaining network. Given input sequence $(\phi(\mathbf{x}_1), \dots, \phi(\mathbf{x}_T))$, an RNN computes the hidden sequence $(\mathbf{h}_1, \dots, \mathbf{h}_T)$ using the following equations:

$$\mathbf{h}_t = f(\mathbf{W}_{in}\phi(\mathbf{x}_t) + \mathbf{W}_{hh}\mathbf{h}_{t-1}). \tag{1}$$

Here, we omit the bias term for simplicity. We define $\mathbf{h}_0 = \mathbf{0}$. The activation function f (e.g., sigmoidal function and tanh function) is applied to the input vector in an element-wise manner. In this equation, free parameters are the input-to-hidden weight matrix $\mathbf{W}_{in} \in \mathbb{R}^{m \times n}$, the hidden-to-hidden weight matrix $\mathbf{W}_{hh} \in \mathbb{R}^{m \times m}$, and the parameters of ϕ. This equation represents that the hidden state $\mathbf{h}_t$ is dependent not only on the current input $\mathbf{x}_t$ but also on the previous state $\mathbf{h}_{t-1}$. Therefore, $\mathbf{h}_t$ can represent the sequential dynamics of input sequence $(\mathbf{x}_1, \dots, \mathbf{x}_t)$.

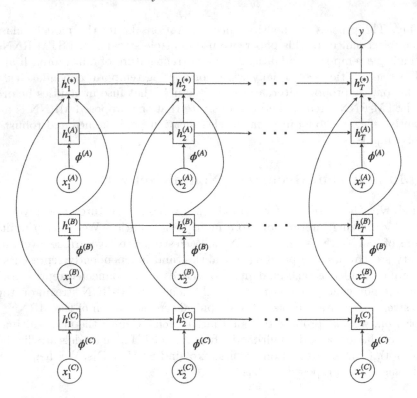

Fig. 2. A graphical representation of the MRNN. The circles represent fully connected layers, the rectangles represent LSTM-RNNs, and the solid lines represent weighted connections. The MRNN has multiple streams of LSTM-RNNs $h_t^{(A)}, h_t^{(B)}, h_t^{(C)}$ that represent the temporal dynamics of input sequences $(x_1^{(A)}, \ldots, x_t^{(A)})$, $(x_1^{(B)}, \ldots, x_t^{(B)})$, $(x_1^{(C)}, \ldots, x_t^{(C)})$ of each modality. We add another LSTM-RNN stream $h_t^{(*)}$ to fuse these modalities while considering temporal dependency $h_{t-1}^{(*)}$. We use appropriate neural network models $\phi^{(A)}, \phi^{(B)}, \phi^{(C)}$ to extract frame-level features from each modality. y denotes a classification result.

The recurrent structure (Eq. (1)) enables the handling of variable-length sequential data. However, it is known that RNNs tend to suffer from vanishing or exploding gradient problems during training [21]. Because of these problems, RNNs cannot remember long-term dependencies in practice. LSTM-RNNs are an elegant method to solve these problems [12]. LSTM-RNNs have been successfully applied to many applications in natural language processing [22,23] and speech recognition [24], outperforming conventional sequential models such as HMMs and an Elman RNN. Figure 4 shows the graphical representation of an LSTM-RNN. An LSTM-RNN is composed of several vectors of same dimension m, a hidden state $\mathbf{h}_t \in \mathbb{R}^m$, a memory cell $\mathbf{c}_t \in \mathbb{R}^m$ and four gates: $\mathbf{g}_t, \mathbf{i}_t, \mathbf{f}_t,$ and $\mathbf{o}_t \in \mathbb{R}^m$. $\mathbf{g}_t, \mathbf{i}_t, \mathbf{f}_t$ and $\mathbf{o}_t$ denote an input modulation gate, an input gate, a

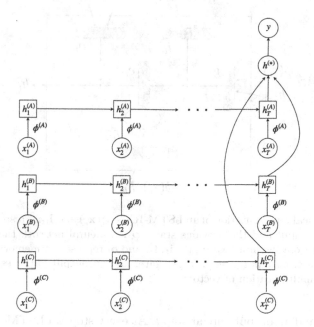

(a) Late multimodal fusion model

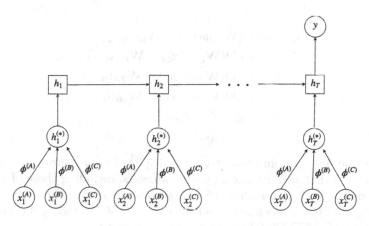

(b) Early multimodal fusion model

Fig. 3. Alternative multimodal fusion models. **(a)** Late multimodal fusion model fuses modalities $(h_T^{(A)}, h_T^{(B)}, h_T^{(C)})$ to $h^{(*)}$ at only the last step. **(b)** Early multimodal fusion model fuses modalities $(\phi^{(A)}(x_t^{(A)}), \phi^{(B)}(x_t^{(B)}), \phi^{(C)}(x_t^{(C)}))$ to $h_t^{(*)}$ at every step before computing the state h_t of the LSTM-RNN. The important difference between these models **(a)**, **(b)** and the MRNN model (Fig. 2) is that the multimodal fusion processes do not depend on temporal dynamics.

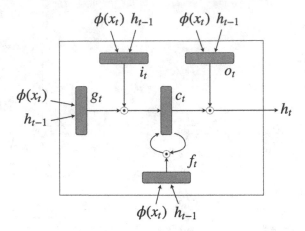

Fig. 4. Graphical representation of an LSTM-RNN. $\phi(\mathbf{x}_t)$ and $\mathbf{h}_{t-1}$ respectively denote a transformed input and the previous state. ϕ is a neural network that extracts the feature vector from the input $\mathbf{x}_t$. $\mathbf{c}_t$, $\mathbf{g}_t$, $\mathbf{i}_t$, $\mathbf{f}_t$, and $\mathbf{o}_t$ represent a memory cell, an input modulation gate, an input gate, a forget gate, and an output gate, respectively. $\odot$ is element-wise multiplication of vectors.

forget gate, and an output gate at step t. At every step, an LSTM-RNN updates its state $\mathbf{h}_t$ using the following equations:

$$\mathbf{g}_t = \tanh(\mathbf{W}_{in}\phi(\mathbf{x}_t) + \mathbf{W}_{hh}\mathbf{h}_{t-1}), \tag{2}$$

$$\mathbf{i}_t = \mathrm{sigmoid}(\mathbf{W}_{ix}\phi(\mathbf{x}_t) + \mathbf{W}_{ih}\mathbf{h}_{t-1}), \tag{3}$$

$$\mathbf{f}_t = \mathrm{sigmoid}(\mathbf{W}_{fx}\phi(\mathbf{x}_t) + \mathbf{W}_{fh}\mathbf{h}_{t-1}), \tag{4}$$

$$\mathbf{o}_t = \mathrm{sigmoid}(\mathbf{W}_{ox}\phi(\mathbf{x}_t) + \mathbf{W}_{oh}\mathbf{h}_{t-1}), \tag{5}$$

$$\mathbf{c}_t = \mathbf{i}_t \odot \mathbf{g}_t + \mathbf{f}_t \odot \mathbf{c}_{t-1}, \tag{6}$$

$$\mathbf{h}_t = \mathbf{o}_t \odot \tanh(\mathbf{c}_t). \tag{7}$$

In these equations, $\odot$ is an element-wise multiplication of vectors.

Please note that we initialize all the parameters, including those of ϕ; moreover, we optimize the parameters of ϕ simultaneously with the other parameters, using mini-batch stochastic gradient descent (SGD) and backpropagation through time (BPTT) [25,26].

3.2   Recurrent Multimodal Fusion

The MRNN is shown in Fig. 2. We develop multiple streams of LSTM-RNNs using ConvNets, the number of which is equal to the number of input modalities. These streams independently update their states according to Eqs. (2)–(7), using input sequences from corresponding modalities. To embed this disconnected information into one common space, we also construct another LSTM-RNN as a fusion stream on top of these streams. At every step, the fusion stream receives the states of the lower streams and fuses them into multimodal-temporal space. Thus, the multimodal fusion process is performed sequentially. Importantly, the fusion structure makes it possible to fuse modalities while considering temporal dependencies. This is the reason we call this fusion strategy "recurrent multimodal fusion". We add a fully connected layer (classification layer) onto the fusion stream. The classification layer receives the last state of the fusion LSTM-RNN. We use the softmax function to compute the probability distribution over categories.

3.3   Late Multimodal Fusion

As an alternative strategy to incorporate multimodal-temporal data, we propose the late multimodal fusion model shown in Fig. 3(a). As with the MRNN, the late multimodal fusion model also employs multiple streams of LSTM-RNNs using ConvNets for each input modality. The difference from the MRNN is that the fusion layer is not an LSTM-RNN but a normal fully connected layer. Thus, the multimodal fusion process is performed independently of temporal dependencies. The fusion layer receives the last states of each stream and embeds them into a common space. The last states of each stream hold information about the temporal dynamics of each input modality. Because the fusion process is performed after the LSTM-RNN streams, we call this method "late multimodal fusion". In this sense, this structure is similar to the model of Molchanov et al. [20], whereas our late multimodal fusion model uses LSTM-RNNs to extract temporal information. As with the MRNN, we add a fully connected layer (classification layer) onto the fusion layer and use the softmax function. The classification layer receives an embedded multimodal feature and predicts the category distribution.

3.4   Early Multimodal Fusion

The early multimodal fusion model we propose is shown in Fig. 3(b). This approach integrates multiple modalities using a fully connected layer (fusion layer) at every step before inputting signals into the LSTM-RNN stream. This is the reason we call this strategy "early multimodal fusion". As with the late multimodal fusion model, this model's multimodal fusion process is performed independently of temporal dependencies. This model has only one LSTM-RNN stream, because the input to the LSTM-RNN is already embedded into a common space by the fusion layer. At every step, the LSTM-RNN receives the embedded feature from the fusion layer and updates its state. As with the other two models, the classification layer predicts the probability distribution over categories using the last state of the LSTM-RNN.

4   Experiments

4.1   Dataset

Using the Sheffiled Kinect Gesture (SKIG) dataset, we compared the MRNN with previous works and our alternative fusion models. The SKIG dataset

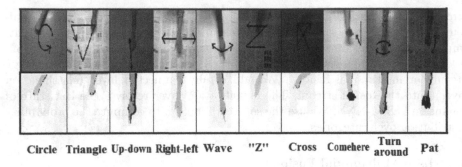

Circle Triangle Up-down Right-left Wave   "Z"   Cross Comehere Turn around Pat

Fig. 5. Examples from the SKIG dataset. This figure is cited from [10].

contains 1080 gesture videos, each belonging to 10 gesture categories. Figure 5 displays some examples from the dataset. Each video consists of two modalities (a color image sequence and a depth data sequence) captured by the Microsoft Kinect sensor. For preprocessing, we downsized all of the frames to 224 × 224, and divided them by 255. All videos are collected from six subjects. We devided all videos into three subsets: subject1+subject2, subject3+subject4, and subject5+subject6. We evaluated our models using 3-fold cross validation, in accordance with the previous works.

It is known that optical flow works effectively for action recognition [27]. We believe that adding temporal information (such as optical flow) to the input of the MRNN improves its classification performance. Given an RGB sequence, we computed dense optical flow based on Gunner Farneback's algorithm [28] using OpenCV. To reduce noise, we apply a bilateral filter to every frame before computing optical flow. As a result, we can obtain a two-channel flow data sequence corresponding to the source RGB sequence.

4.2 Network Architecture

Throughout our experiments, we fixed the dimension size m of the LSTM-RNNs to 512. We also set the dimension size of the fusion layers to 512. The dimension size of the classification layers is 10, which is equal to the number of gesture categories. We used three modalities in our experiments: color image, optical flow, and depth data. Because these modalities are spatial data, we developed the ConvNet architecture based on Network In Network (NIN) [29] as a nonlinear transformer ϕ for each input modality. We show the architecture of the ConvNet that we used in our experiments in Fig. 6. We initialized all parameters (including those of the ConvNets) from a Gaussian distribution, except for hidden-to-hidden weight matrices of the LSTM-RNNs, for which we used an identical matrix according to Le et al. [30].

4.3   Training Settings

We used the cross entropy error as our loss function. We added an L2 regular-izatoin term multiplied by 0.0001 to the loss. We used mini-batch SGD with a learning rate of 0.01. After three epochs, we set the learning rate to 0.001. We set the mini-batch size to 5. We computed all gradients of the parameters using BPTT [25, 26]. We implemented the experimental code with Chainer [31], a Python-based open source library for deep learning, on an NVIDIA TITAN X GPU.

4.4   Experimental Results

We evaluated the test accuracies of the MRNNs (trained on multiple modalities or a single modality) and our alternative fusion models. We report the results in Table 1. The MRNN trained on multiple modalities significantly outperforms the previous works, and provides improved test accuracy. To the best of our knowledge, this accuracy represents the state-of-the-art performance for this dataset. The MRNN trained on multiple modalities also outperforms the other

Table 1. Comparison of test accuracy using the SKIG dataset

Method	Accuracy (%)
Liu et al. [10]	88.7
Choi et al. [32]	91.9
Tung et al. [33]	96.7
Early multimodal fusion	94.1
Late multimodal fusion	94.6
MRNN (color only)	91.6
MRNN (optical flow only)	88.5
MRNN (depth only)	95.9
MRNN	**97.8**

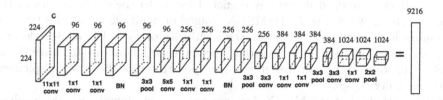

Fig. 6. The architecture of the ConvNet that we used in our experiments. This model has 11 convolution layers (conv), 2 batch normalization layers (BN) [4], and 4 max pooling layers (pool). Each convolution layer is followed by a rectified linear (ReLU) nonlinearity. C is the number of channels of the input frames. We vectorize the last feature maps of size 1024 × 3 × 3 to 9216-dimensional vector.

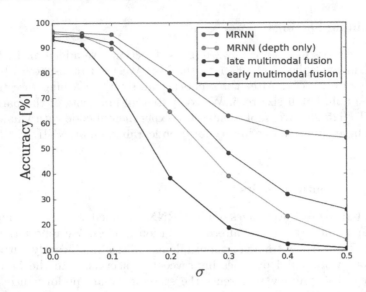

Fig. 7. Test accuracies of the MRNN trained on multiple modalities (red line), the MRNN trained on only depth modality (magenta line), the late multimodal fusion model (green line), and the early multimodal fusion model (blue line). We added Gaussian noise with different standard deviations (denoted by σ) to the depth data of the test inputs. The MRNN trained on multiple modalities successfully utilizes the other modalities to suppress the influence of noise on the depth inputs (Color figure online).

multimodal fusion models. This indicates that a multimodal fusion process that considers temporal dependencies is beneficial for efficient embedding. Compared with the MRNNs trained on a single modality (color only, optical flow only, or depth only), the MRNN trained on multiple modalities also produces better accuracy. Therefore, the MRNN succeeds in utilizing multimodal information effectively.

In our experiments, we also investigated the robustness of the MRNN to noisy inputs. In Fig. 7, we plot the test accuracies when we add Gaussian noise with different standard deviations (denoted by σ) to the depth inputs in the test set. As shown in Fig. 7, the MRNN trained on multiple modalities tends to maintain high accuracy, even when the accuracies of the other models decline. The difference in Fig. 7 indicates that the multimodal fusion structure of ths MRNN provides significant benefits in incorporating modalities to complement each modality.

It is notable that the MRNN does not require any domain-specific localization or segmentation techniques throughout our experiments. The MRNN learns feature extraction, multimodal fusion, and sequential modeling simultaneously in a single architecture in a supervised manner. Therefore, the MRNN is a completely data-driven approach to multimodal gesture recognition, and provides excellent classification performance and high robustness to noisy inputs.

5   Conclusion

In this paper, we proposed a multimodal gesture recognition model that incorporates multiple temporal modalities using multiple streams of LSTM-RNNs. All parameters of the MRNN are optimized towards end-to-end performance in a supervised manner. The MRNN does not require heuristic engineering that is strongly dependent on target gesture domains. We evaluate our recurrent multimodal fusion approach with alternative fusion models. Experimental results indicate that the MRNN (and its multimodal fusion process that considers temporal dependencies) provide significant benefits, and provide excellent classification performance as well as high robustness to noisy inputs. Moreover, the MRNN achieves state-of-the-art performance in the SKIG dataset.

In future, we plan to utilize other modalities such as speech and skeletal data. Moreover, we plan to apply the MRNN to sign language recognition.

Acknowledgments. This work was supported by JST CREST, JSPS KAKENHI Grant Number 26730085. We would like to thank the three anonymous reviewers for their valuable feedback on this work.

References

1. Krizhevsky, A., Sutskever, I., Hinton, G.E.: Imagenet classification with deep convolutional neural networks. In: Proceedings of the NIPS (2012)
2. Girshick, R., Donahue, J., Darrell, T., Malik, J.: Rich feature hierarchies for accurate object detection and semantic segmentation. In: Proceedings of the CVPR (2014)
3. He, K., Zhang, X., Ren, S., Sun, J.: Delving deep into rectifiers: surpassing human-level performance on imagenet classification. In: Proceedings of the ICCV (2015)
4. Ioffe, S., Szegedy, C.: Batch normalization: accelerating deep network training by reducing internal covariate shift. arXiv:1502.03167 (2015)
5. Baraldi, L., Paci, F., Serra, G., Benini, L., Cucchiara, R.: Gesture recognition in ego-centric videos using dense trajectories and hand segmentation. In: Proceedings of the EVW (2014)
6. Darwish, S.M., Madbouly, M.M., Khorsheed, M.B.: Hand gesture recognition for sign language: a new higher order fuzzy HMM approach. Hand **1**, 18565 (2016)
7. Bengio, Y., Courville, A., Vincent, P.: Representation learning: a review and new perspectives. Trans. PAMI **35**(8), 1798–1828 (2013)
8. Wu, J., Cheng, J., Zhao, C., Lu, H.: Fusing multi-modal features for gesture recognition. In: Proceedings of the ICMI (2013)
9. Ohn-Bar, E., Trivedi, M.M.: Hand gesture recognition in real time for automotive interfaces: a multimodal vision-based approach and evaluations. Trans. ITS **15**(6), 2368–2377 (2014)
10. Liu, L., Shao, L.: Learning discriminative representations from RGB-D video data. In: Proceedings of the IJCAI (2013)
11. Elman, J.L.: Finding structure in time. Cogn. Sci. **14**(2), 179–211 (1990)
12. Hochreiter, S., Schmidhuber, J.: Long short-term memory. Neural Comput. **9**(8), 1735–1780 (1997)

13. Murakami, K., Taguchi, H.: Gesture recognition using recurrent neural networks. In: Proceedings of the SIGCHI (1991)
14. Szegedy, C., Liu, W., Jia, Y., Sermanet, P., Reed, S., Anguelov, D., Rabinovich, A.: Going deeper with convolutions. In: Proceedings of the CVPR (2015)
15. Socher, R., Lin, C.C., Manning, C., Ng, A.Y.: Parsing natural scenes and natural language with recursive neural networks. In: Proceedings of the ICML (2011)
16. Gregor, K., Danihelka, I., Graves, A., and Wierstra, D.: DRAW: a recurrent neural network for image generation. arXiv:1502.04623 (2015)
17. Ji, S., Xu, W., Yang, M., Yu, K.: 3D convolutional neural networks for human action recognition. Trans. PAMI **35**(1), 221–231 (2013)
18. Karpathy, A., Toderici, G., Shetty, S., Leung, T., Sukthankar, R., Fei-Fei, L.: Large-scale video classification with convolutional neural networks. In: Proceedings of the CVPR (2014)
19. Donahue, J., Hendricks, L.A., Guadarrama, S., Rohrbach, M., Venugopalan, S., Saenko, K., Darrell, T.: Long-term recurrent convolutional networks for visual recognition and description. In: Proceedings of the CVPR (2014)
20. Molchanov, P., Gupta, S., Kim, K., and Kautz, J.: Hand gesture recognition with 3D convolutional neural networks. In: CVPR Workshop on Hand Gesture Recognition (2015)
21. Bengio, Y., Simard, P., Frasconi, P.: Learning long-term dependencies with gradient descent is difficult. Trans. Neural Netw. **5**(2), 157–166 (1994)
22. Sutskever, I., Vinyals, O., Le, Q.V.: Sequence to sequence learning with neural networks. In: Proceedings of the NIPS (2014)
23. Cho, K., van Merrinboer, B., Bahdanau, D., Bengio, Y.: On the properties of neural machine translation: encoder-decoder approaches. In: SSST-8 (2014)
24. Graves, A., Jaitly, N.: Towards end-to-end speech recognition with recurrent neural networks. In: Proceedings of the ICML (2014)
25. Werbos, P.J.: Backpropagation through time: what it does and how to do it. Proc. IEEE **78**(10), 1550–1560 (1990)
26. Rumelhart, D.E., Hinton, G.E., Williams, R.J.: Learning representations by back-propagating errors. Cogn. Model. **5**, 3 (1988)
27. Simonyan, K., Zisserman, A.: Two-stream convolutional networks for action recognition in videos. In: Proceedings of the NIPS (2014)
28. Farnebäck, G.: Two-Frame Motion Estimation Based on Polynomial Expansion. In: Bigun, J., Gustavsson, T. (eds.) SCIA 2003. LNCS, vol. 2749, pp. 363–370. Springer, Heidelberg (2003)
29. Lin, M., Chen, Q., Yan, S.: Network In network. In: Proceedings of the ICLR (2014)
30. Le, Q.V., Jaitly, N., and Hinton, G.E.: A simple way to initialize recurrent networks of rectified linear units. arXiv:1504.00941 (2015)
31. Chainer. http://chainer.org/
32. Choi, H., Park, H.: A hierarchical structure for gesture recognition using RGB-D sensor. In: Proceedings of the HAI (2014)
33. Tung, P.T., Ngoc, L.Q.: Elliptical density shape model for hand gesture recognition. In: Proceedings of the ICTD (2014)

Image/Video Processing and Analysis

A Spatially Constrained Asymmetric Gaussian Mixture Model for Image Segmentation

Zexuan Ji[⊠], Jinyao Liu, Hengdong Yuan, Yubo Huang, and Quansen Sun

School of Computer Science and Engineering,
Nanjing University of Science and Technology, Nanjing 210094, China
jizexuan@njust.edu.cn

Abstract. Gaussian mixture models with spatial constraint play an important role in image segmentation. Nevertheless, most methods suffer from one or more challenges such as limited robustness to outliers, over-smoothness for segmentations, and lack of flexibility to fit different shapes of observed data. To address above issues, in this paper, we propose a spatially constrained asymmetric Gaussian mixture model for image segmentation. The asymmetric distribution is utilized to fit different shapes of observed data. Then our asymmetric model can be constructed based on the posterior and prior probabilities of within-cluster and between-cluster. Moreover, we introduce two pseudo likelihood quantities which respectively couple neighboring priors of within-cluster and between-cluster based on the Kullback-Leibler divergence. Finally, we derive an expectation maximization algorithm to iteratively maximize the approximation of the lower bound of the data log-likelihood. Experimental results on synthetic and real images demonstrate the superior performance of the proposed algorithm comparing with state-of-the-art segmentation approaches.

Keywords: Image segmentation · Asymmetric Gaussian mixture model · Spatially constraint · Pseudo likelihood quantities

1 Introduction

As one of the most important and difficult tasks in image analysis and computer vision, image segmentation is defined as the partitioning of an image into non-overlapping, consistent regions. Although various image segmentation algorithms have been proposed, automated and accurate segmentation algorithm is still a very challenging research topic due to overlapping intensities, low contrast, noise perturbation, and asymmetric form of the intensity distribution [1].

During the last decades, a number of model-based techniques [2] have been proposed, in which the standard Gaussian mixture models (GMM) [3] is a well-known method that has been widely used due to its simplicity and easiness of implementation. The main advantage of the standard GMM is that the small number of parameters can be efficiently estimated by adopting the expectation maximization (EM) algorithm [4]. However, GMM assumes that each pixel in

© Springer International Publishing Switzerland 2016
T. Bräunl et al. (Eds.): PSIVT 2015, LNCS 9431, pp. 697–708, 2016.
DOI: 10.1007/978-3-319-29451-3_55

an image is independent of its neighbor. Therefore, the performance of GMM is sensitive to outliers. To improve the robustness over noise, mixture models with (hidden) Markov random fields ((H)MRF) have been frequently employed for pixel label [5,6], where the prior distribution varies for every pixel corresponding to each label and depends on the neighboring pixels. Another group of mixture models based on MRF are proposed in [7–10] where a MRF models the joint distribution of the priors of each pixel label. Although the effect of noise on the segmentation result is reduced, most (H)MRF based algorithms lack enough robustness with respect to noise. Moreover, the corresponding computational cost is quite high. On the other hand, only using one distribution for each component in the mixture model is not satisfactory enough for many practical applications. Therefore, the mixture of mixture model and the asymmetric mixture model have been widely studied recently [11–14]. However, without introducing any spatial information, the mixture of mixture model [13] and the asymmetric mixture model [1,11] are still sensitive to the outliers/noise even though these models are more flexible for data distribution.

Motivated by the aforementioned observations, in this paper, we propose a novel spatially constrained asymmetric GMM (SCAGMM) for image segmentation. We firstly modify the asymmetric distribution proposed in [11] to make the model fit different shapes of observed data. Then our asymmetric model can be constructed based on the posterior probabilities and prior probabilities of within-cluster and between-cluster. Similar with the algorithm in [8], to further define the similarity between neighboring priors for within-cluster and between-cluster, we introduce two pseudo-likelihood quantities which respectively couple neighboring priors of within-cluster and between-cluster based on the Kullback-Leibler (KL) divergence. To estimate the involved parameters in the proposed algorithm, we derive an EM algorithm to iteratively maximize the approximation of the lower bound of the data log-likelihood. It is worth mentioning that the proposed prior distributions can be treated as the within-cluster and between-cluster spatial constraint, which are constructed based on the posterior probabilities and prior probabilities of the within-cluster and between-cluster, respectively. They play a role as image filters for smoothing and restoring images corrupted by noise. Therefore, the proposed scheme can simply and efficiently incorporate spatial constraints in an EM framework for image segmentation. The proposed algorithm has been compared to other state-of-the-art segmentation algorithms in both simulated and real images to demonstrate the superior performance of the proposed algorithm.

2   Background

Notations used throughout the paper are denoted as follows. Let $X = \{x_i, i = 1, 2, ..., N\}$ denote the target image, where x_i with dimension D is an observation at the ith pixel of the image. Let the neighborhood of the ith pixel be presented by ∂_i. Labels are denoted by $(\Omega_1, \Omega_2, ..., \Omega_K)$. To segment an image consisting of N pixels into K labels, the finite mixture model assumes that each observation

x_i with dimension D is considered independent of the label $\Omega_k, k = 1, ..., K$. The corresponding density function is given by

$$p(x_i|\Pi, \Theta) = \sum_{k=1}^{K} \pi_{ik} p(x_i|\Omega_k), \tag{1}$$

where $\Pi = \{\pi_{ik}\}, i = \{1, 2, ..., N\}, k = \{1, 2, ..., K\}$ is the set of prior distributions modeling the probability that pixel x_i is in label Ω_k, which satisfies the constraints $0 \leq \pi_{ik} \leq 1$ and $\sum_{k=1}^{K} \pi_{ik} = 1$.

Each distribution $p(x_i|\Omega_k)$ is a component of the mixture model which can be any kind of distribution. In GMM [3], $p(x_i|\Omega_k)$ is the Gaussian distribution $\Phi(x_i|\mu_k, \Sigma_k)$ which can be written in the form

$$\Phi(x_i|\mu_k, \Sigma_k) = \frac{1}{(2\pi)^{D/2}|\Sigma_k|^{1/2}} exp\left\{-\frac{1}{2}(x_i - \mu_k)^T \Sigma_k^{-1}(x_i - \mu_k)\right\}, \tag{2}$$

where μ_k is the mean vector with D dimension, Σ_k is the covariance matrix with $D \times D$ dimension, and $|\Sigma_k|$ is the determinant of Σ_k.

We assume that each pixel i belongs to a single class which is indexed by the hidden random variable z_i. The variable z_i takes values from a discrete set of labels $1, ..., K$. Then, the corresponding generative model for GMM can be shown in Fig. 1(a).

In asymmetric mixture models [1,11], a new asymmetric distribution $p(x_i|\Omega_k)$ is defined to fit different shapes of observed data such as non-Gaussian and non-symmetric:

$$p(x_i|\Omega_k) = \sum_{l=1}^{L} \psi_{kl} p(x_i|\Omega_{kl}), \tag{3}$$

where L is the number of multivariate distribution $p(x_i|\Omega_{kl})$ that is used to model the label Ω_k and ψ_{kl} is called the weighting factor which satisfies the constraints $0 \leq \psi_{kl} \leq 1$ and $\sum_{l=1}^{L} \psi_{kl} = 1$. The motivation to define the distribution in Eq. 3 is based on the fact that non-Gaussian and non-symmetric data can be approximated by multiple multivariate distributions $p(x_i|\Omega_{kl})$. It is worth mentioning that the distribution $p(x_i|\Omega_{kl})$ can be one of the widely used distributions, such as Gaussian distribution, Students t-distribution and generalized Gaussian distribution. The probabilistic graphical model for asymmetric mixture models is shown in Fig. 1(b).

To improve the robustness to the noise for GMMs, MRF distribution is applied to incorporate the spatial correlation amongst prior values

$$p(\Pi) = \frac{1}{Z} exp\left\{-\frac{1}{T} U(\Pi)\right\}, \tag{4}$$

where Z is a normalizing constant, T is a temperature constant, and $U(\Pi)$ is the smoothing prior. The posterior probability density function given by Bayes'rules can be written as

$$p(\Pi, \Theta|X) \propto p(X|\Pi, \Theta)p(\Pi). \tag{5}$$

The involved parameters are usually estimated through maximizing the log-likelihood function of Eq. 5 via the EM algorithm to get the final segmentation labels. These MRF-GMM models can be graphically shown in Fig. 1(c).

Most MRF-based mixture models have been successfully applied to image segmentation by adopting different energy $U(\Pi)$. The main motivation for using this model as opposed to the traditional MRF model on pixel labels is its flexibility with respect to the initial conditions, in which the spatial constraints are directly enforced over the neighboring priors to obtain a smoother energy function and make the algorithm less dependent on the initializations.

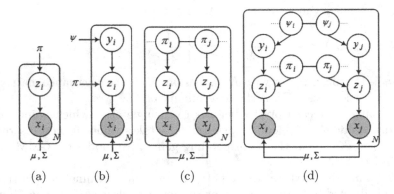

(a)   (b)   (c)   (d)

Fig. 1. The probabilistic graphical models for (a) GMM, (b) asymmetric mixture models, (c) MRF-GMM, and (d) the proposed SCAGMM model.

3   Proposed Algorithm

In this paper, the modified density function $f(x_i|\Pi,\Psi,\Theta)$ for each pixel x_i is defined as

$$f(x_i|\Pi,\Psi,\Theta) = \sum_{k=1}^{K} \pi_{ik} \left(\sum_{l=1}^{L} \psi_{ikl} \Phi(x_i|\mu_{kl}, \Sigma_{kl}) \right) \quad (6)$$

where K is the number of clusters/labels, L is the number of multivariate Gaussian distribution that is used to model the label Ω_k, $\Pi = \{\pi_{ik}\}$ is the set of between-cluster prior distributions modeling the probability that pixel x_i is in label Ω_k, $\Psi = \{\psi_{ikl}\}$ is the set of within-cluster prior distributions modeling the probability that pixel x_i is in the lth component of kth cluster. Θ represents the model parameters. Φ is the Gaussian distribution. Note that the observation x_i is modeled as statistically independent, the joint conditional density of observed data set can be modeled as

$$p(X|\Pi,\Psi,\Theta) = \prod_{i=1}^{N} f(x_i|\Pi,\Psi,\Theta) \quad (7)$$

Based on the Bayes's rules, the posterior probability density function can be written as

$$p(\Pi, \Psi, \Theta | X) \propto p(X | \Pi, \Psi, \Theta) p(\Pi) p(\Psi) \tag{8}$$

Therefore, the probabilistic graphical model for the proposed algorithm can be described as Fig. 1(d).

As in [15], we employ the Besag approximation for modeling the joint density over pixel priors

$$p(\Pi) \approx \prod_{i=1}^{N} p(\pi_i | \pi_{\partial_i}) \quad p(\Psi) \approx \prod_{i=1}^{N} p(\psi_i | \psi_{\partial_i}) \tag{9}$$

where π_{∂_i} and ψ_{∂_i} are respectively defined as mixture distributions over the between-cluster and within-cluster priors of neighboring pixels of pixel i, i.e.,

$$\pi_{\partial_i} = \sum_{j \in \partial_i, j \neq i} \lambda_{ij} \pi_j \quad \psi_{\partial_i} = \sum_{j \in \partial_i, j \neq i} \lambda_{ij} \psi_j \tag{10}$$

where λ_{ij} are positive weights for each pixel $j (j \in \partial_i, j \neq i)$ and satisfies $\sum_j \lambda_{ij} = 1$. It is worth mentioning that the evaluation of these mixtures correspond to convolution operations $\pi_{.k} * \lambda$ and $\psi_{.kl} * \lambda$ for each cluster k and Gaussian component l, where λ is a symmetric linear image filter with zero coefficient in its center and nonnegative coefficients elsewhere that sum to one [8].

For the conditional densities $p(\pi_i | \pi_{\partial_i})$ and $p(\psi_i | \psi_{\partial_i})$, we assume an approximate log-model in the form

$$\begin{aligned} \log p(\pi_i | \pi_{\partial_i}) &= -\alpha [D(\pi_i \| \pi_{\partial_i}) + H(\pi_i)] \\ \log p(\psi_i | \psi_{\partial_i}) &= -\beta [D(\psi_i \| \psi_{\partial_i}) + H(\psi_i)] \end{aligned} \tag{11}$$

where $D(\pi_i \| \pi_{\partial_i})$ is the KL divergence between π_i and π_{∂_i}, and $D(\psi_i \| \psi_{\partial_i})$ is the KL divergence between ψ_i and ψ_{∂_i}, which are always nonnegative and become zero when $\pi_i = \pi_{\partial_i}$ and $\psi_i = \psi_{\partial_i}$. $H(\pi_i)$ and $H(\psi_i)$ are the entropy of the distribution π_i and ψ_i, respectively. To facilitate optimization, we introduce an approximation that makes use of two auxiliaries set of distribution $s_i^{(1)}$ and $s_i^{(2)}$ as follows:

$$\begin{aligned} \log p(\pi_i | \pi_{\partial_i}, s_i^{(1)}) &\approx -\alpha [D(s_i^{(1)} \| \pi_i) + D(s_i^{(1)} \| \pi_{\partial_i}) + H(s_i^{(1)})] \\ \log p(\psi_i | \psi_{\partial_i}, s_i^{(2)}) &\approx -\beta [D(s_i^{(2)} \| \psi_i) + D(s_i^{(2)} \| \psi_{\partial_i}) + H(s_i^{(2)})] \end{aligned} \tag{12}$$

Moreover, we introduce an additional penalty term involving posterior distributions in the form

$$\begin{aligned} &-\frac{1}{4}[D(q_i^{(1)} \| p_i^{(1)}) + D(q_i^{(1)} \| p_{\partial_i}^{(1)}) + H(q_i^{(1)})] \\ &-\frac{1}{4}[D(q_i^{(2)} \| p_i^{(2)}) + D(q_i^{(2)} \| p_{\partial_i}^{(2)}) + H(q_i^{(2)})] \end{aligned} \tag{13}$$

where the coefficient $1/4$ in the penalty term was chosen because it allows a tractable M-step. $q_i^{(1)}$ and $q_i^{(2)}$ are two arbitrary class distributions for pixel i, and two posterior class distributions $p_i^{(1)}$ and $p_i^{(2)}$ can be defined as follows:

$$p_{ik}^{(1)} \equiv \frac{\pi_{ik} \sum_{l=1}^{L} \psi_{ikl} \Phi(x_i|\mu_{kl}, \Sigma_{kl})}{\sum_{m=1}^{K} \left[\pi_{mk} \sum_{l=1}^{L} \psi_{iml} \Phi(x_i|\mu_{ml}, \Sigma_{ml}) \right]} \tag{14}$$

$$p_{ikl}^{(2)} \equiv \frac{\psi_{ikl} \Phi(x_i|\mu_{kl}, \Sigma_{kl})}{\sum_{m=1}^{L} \psi_{ikm} \Phi(x_i|\mu_{km}, \Sigma_{km})} \tag{15}$$

Putting all terms together, the penalized log-likelihood of the observed data yields (ignoring constants)

$$
\begin{aligned}
&L(\Pi, \Psi, \Theta|X) \\
&= \sum_{i=1}^{N} \left\{ log \left(\sum_{k=1}^{K} \pi_{ik} \left(\sum_{l=1}^{L} \psi_{ikl} \Phi(x_i|\mu_{kl}, \Sigma_{kl}) \right) \right) \right. \\
&\quad - \frac{1}{4} [D(q_i^{(1)} \| p_i^{(1)}) + D(q_i^{(1)} \| p_{\partial_i}^{(1)}) + H(q_i^{(1)})] \\
&\quad - \frac{1}{4} [D(q_i^{(2)} \| p_i^{(2)}) + D(q_i^{(2)} \| p_{\partial_i}^{(2)}) + H(q_i^{(2)})] \\
&\quad - \alpha [D(s_i^{(1)} \| \pi_i) + D(s_i^{(1)} \| \pi_{\partial_i}) + H(s_i^{(1)})] \\
&\quad \left. - \beta [D(s_i^{(2)} \| \psi_i) + D(s_i^{(2)} \| \psi_{\partial_i}) + H(s_i^{(2)})] \right\}
\end{aligned}
\tag{16}
$$

Then we utilize EM algorithm to maximize the energy $L(\Pi, \Psi, \Theta|X)$ by coordinate ascent.

E-step: By fixing Π, Ψ and Θ, we can optimize over $s_i^{(1)}$, $s_i^{(2)}$, $q_i^{(1)}$ and $q_i^{(2)}$ for each pixel i and get

$$
\begin{aligned}
s_{ik}^{(1)} &\propto \pi_{ik} \pi_{\partial_i k} & s_{ikl}^{(2)} &\propto \psi_{ikl} \psi_{\partial_i kl} \\
q_{ik}^{(1)} &\propto p_{ik}^{(1)} p_{\partial_i k}^{(1)} & q_{ikl}^{(2)} &\propto p_{ikl}^{(2)} p_{\partial_i kl}^{(2)}
\end{aligned}
\tag{17}
$$

M-step: By fixing $s_i^{(1)}$, $s_i^{(2)}$, $q_i^{(1)}$ and $q_i^{(2)}$, we can maximize $L(\Pi, \Psi, \Theta|X)$ over Π, Ψ and Θ to get the following updating functions for each parameters:

$$\pi_{ik} = \frac{1}{1 + 4\alpha} \left(\frac{1}{4}(q_{ik}^{(1)} + q_{\partial_i k}^{(1)}) + \alpha(s_{ik}^{(1)} + s_{\partial_i k}^{(1)}) \right) \tag{18}$$

$$\psi_{ikl} = \frac{1}{1 + 4\beta} \left(\frac{1}{4}(q_{ikl}^{(2)} + q_{\partial_i kl}^{(2)}) + \beta(s_{ikl}^{(2)} + s_{\partial_i kl}^{(2)}) \right) \tag{19}$$

$$\mu_{kl} = \frac{\sum_{i=1}^{N} (q_{ik}^{(1)} + q_{\partial_i k}^{(1)})(q_{ikl}^{(2)} + q_{\partial_i kl}^{(2)}) x_i}{\sum_{i=1}^{N} (q_{ik}^{(1)} + q_{\partial_i k}^{(1)})(q_{ikl}^{(2)} + q_{\partial_i kl}^{(2)})} \tag{20}$$

$$\Sigma_{kl} = \frac{\sum_{i=1}^{N} (q_{ik}^{(1)} + q_{\partial_i k}^{(1)})(q_{ikl}^{(2)} + q_{\partial_i kl}^{(2)})(x_i - \mu_{kl})(x_i - \mu_{kl})^T}{\sum_{i=1}^{N} (q_{ik}^{(1)} + q_{\partial_i k}^{(1)})(q_{ikl}^{(2)} + q_{\partial_i kl}^{(2)})} \tag{21}$$

4   Experimental Results

In this section, we applied the proposed algorithm SCAGMM to segment the testing images and compared the performances with four state-of-the-art algorithms, including two spatially constrained finite mixture models (a Spatially Constrained Generative Model and an EM algorithm (SCGM) [8], a Fast and Robust Spatially Constrained GMM (FRSCGMM) [10]) and two bounded finite mixture models (Bounded Asymmetric Mixture Model (BAMM) [11], Bounded Generalized Gaussian Mixture Model (BGGMM) [15]). All the algorithms are initialized with k-means algorithm. Unless otherwise specified, the parameters of the proposed algorithm are set as follows. We assume that the number of labels K are given to us for a particular testing image. The number of Gaussian distributions L is assigned a value of three ($L = 3$). The prior parameters α and β are both set as 0.25. All reported results of our algorithm were obtained by using the coefficients of the filter λ shown in Table 1.

Table 1. Coefficients of the filter used in the experiments

0.0256	0.0324	0.0362	0.0324	0.0256
0.0324	0.0362	0.0724	0.0362	0.0324
0.0362	0.0724	0	0.0724	0.0362
0.0324	0.0362	0.0724	0.0362	0.0324
0.0256	0.0324	0.0362	0.0324	0.0256

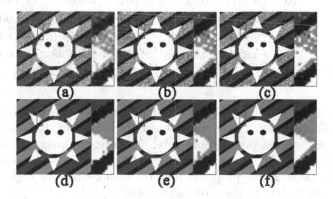

Fig. 2. The experimental results on synthetic image with Gaussian noise. (a) Noisy image, the segmentation results by applying (b) BAMM (MCR=0.0869), (c) BGGMM (MCR=0.0848), (d) SCGM (MCR=0.0058), (e) FRSCGMM (MCR=0.0094), and (f) the proposed SCAGMM algorithm (MCR=0.0040).

In the first experiment, a synthetic image corrupting with Gaussian noise (0 mean, 0.05 variance) as shown in Fig. 2(a) was used to compare the performance of the proposed algorithm with other comparison methods. The image contains four labels with luminance values [0, 1/3, 2/3, 1]. From Fig. 2(b) to (f), we presented the segmentation results obtained by applying BAMM, BGGMM, SCGM, FRSCGMM and SCAGMM, respectively. The marked rectangles show the enlarged partial views of the corresponding regions. From Fig. 2 we can find that the segmentation accuracies of BAMM and BGGMM are quit poor without considering any spatial information. FRSCGMM can get a better result, but the noise suppression ability is still limited. Both the SCGM and the proposed algorithm demonstrate better classification, and segment the image well. Nevertheless, the proposed method can get better segmentation with lower MCR especially for the pixels around the boundaries.

Table 2. MCR values (mean±standard deviation) of segmentations obtained by applying five algorithms on synthetic images with varying noise level.

Type	Level	BAMM	BGGMM	SCGM	FRSCGMM	SCAGMM
Gaussian	0.03	0.2624	0.2717	0.0161	0.0249	**0.0136**
		±0.0781	±0.0824	±0.0104	±0.0267	**±0.0089**
	0.06	0.3776	0.3828	0.1478	0.0579	**0.0337**
		±0.0762	±0.0771	±0.1986	±0.0475	**±0.0229**
Salt&Pepper	0.03	0.0392	0.0203	0.0147	0.0203	**0.0048**
		±0.0072	±0.0017	±0.0029	±0.0017	**±0.0022**
	0.06	0.0496	0.0430	0.0287	0.0430	**0.0105**
		±0.0124	±0.0024	±0.0043	±0.0024	**±0.0044**
Speckle	0.03	0.1524	0.1377	0.0028	0.0036	**0.0036**
		±0.0431	±0.0743	±0.0018	±0.0030	**±0.0035**
	0.06	0.1850	0.1983	0.0396	0.0194	**0.0126**
		±0.0400	±0.0298	±0.0658	±0.0238	**±0.0077**

Then six synthetic images (http://siddhantahuja.wordpress.com/2009/11/21/segmentation-dataset/) were used to test the details of the results obtained by different methods on varying noise level. The original images were corrupted with increasing level of Gaussian noise, salt and pepper noise and speckle noise. As shown in Table 2, the proposed method demonstrates a higher degree of robustness with respect to the given noise level.

In the next experiment, we applied all the algorithms on synthetic T1-weighted 1mm brain MR images selected from BrainWeb [16]. Three example (the 80-th axial, sagittal and coronal slice) brain MR images with 9% noise, together with their segmentation results and ground truths, are shown in Fig. 3. Both the SCGM-EM and FRSCGMM use the similar strategy with the proposed algorithm to construct the spatial information based on the posterior probability and prior probability. However, these two algorithms only use a symmetric smoothing filter over the whole image. The corresponding segmentation results are not satisfied

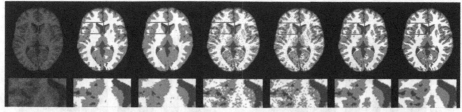

(a) Axial brain MR images (Slice 80th)

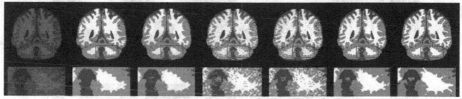

(b) Sagittal brain MR images (Slice 80th)

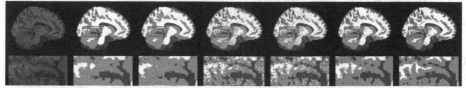

(c) Coronal brain MR images (Slice 80th)

Fig. 3. Illustration of three simulated T1-weighted brain MR images with 9% noise and the corresponding segmentation results obtained by each algorithm. In each subfigure, the images from left to right show the original image, segmentation results obtained by SCGM-EM, FRSCGMM, BAMM, BGGMM and the proposed algorithm, and the ground truth. The enlarged partial view of the corresponding marked region is shown below each figure.

enough for the pixels around boundaries. Moreover, both comparison algorithms may get over-smoothness segmentations and lose the details especially for the CSF tissue. Without considering any spatial information, both BAMM and BGGMM cannot well distinguish the noisy pixels. Comparing with ground truth and segmentations obtained with other algorithms, the proposed algorithm can visually get better results. To statistically show the significant of the proposed algorithm, we tested on 80 brain MR images, in which the level of noise ranges from 3 % to 9 %. The segmentation accuracy for each tissue, i.e. gray matter (GM) and white matter (WM), was measured in terms of average Dice coefficient (DC) [17] values, and the statistical results (means and standard deviations of DC values) are shown in Fig. 4. It should be noted that the value of DC ranges from 0 to 1 with a higher value representing a more accurate segmentation result. This comparison demonstrates that the proposed algorithm produces the most accuracy segmentation (with higher means of DC values) and has the best ability and robustness of denoising (with lower standard deviations of DC values).

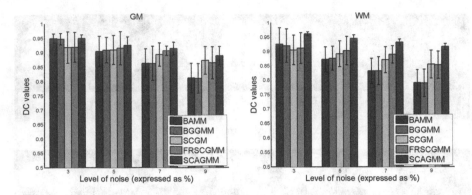

Fig. 4. DC values of GM and WM segmentations obtained by applying five segmentation algorithms to simulated brain MR images with increasing levels of noise.

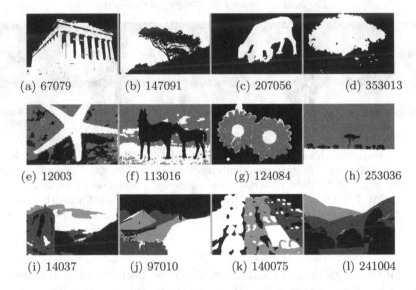

<table>
</table>

(a) 67079   (b) 147091   (c) 207056   (d) 353013

(e) 12003   (f) 113016   (g) 124084   (h) 253036

(i) 14037   (j) 97010   (k) 140075   (l) 241004

Fig. 5. Berkeley image segmentation results by SCAGMM.

Moreover, we showed the segmentation results of real world color images in RGB color space which are selected from Berkeley's image segmentation dataset [18]. A probabilistic evaluation can be achieved by the probabilistic rand (PR) index [19] which takes values between 0 and 1, with a higher value representing a more accurate segmentation result. Fig. 5 shows several segmentation results by applying the proposed SCAGMM algorithm, in which the number of labels is 2, 3, and 4, respectively, from the first column to the third column. It is evident that the proposed algorithm can get satisfactory results for all the testing images. Moreover, a set of color images was used to evaluate the performance of the proposed algorithm against the other four methods. Fig. 6 shows the PR values obtained with all methods for the given set of real world images.

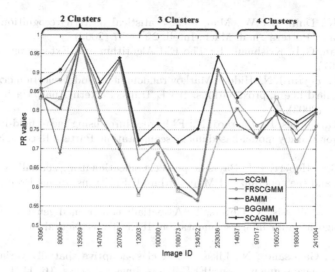

Fig. 6. PR values of segmentation results on 15 Berkeley color images.

As evident from the results, the proposed algorithm outperforms other methods with a higher PR value.

5   Conclusion

To further improve the segmentation accuracy for GMM based algorithm, in this paper, we propose a spatially constrained asymmetric Gaussian mixture model for image segmentation. This algorithm has the flexibility to fit different shapes of observed data, and successfully overcomes the drawbacks of existing EM-type mixture models, including limited robustness to outliers, over-smoothness for segmentations, and limited segmentation accuracy for image details. Our results in synthetic images, brain MR images and real world color images show that the proposed algorithm is capable of producing more accurate segmentation results than several state-of-the-art algorithms. Our future work will focus on how to automatically detect the radius of spatial factor and the number of clusters/labels.

Acknowledgments. This work was supported in part by the National Natural Science Foundation of China under Grant 61401209, in part by the Natural Science Foundation of Jiangsu Province, China under Grant BK20140790, and in part by China Postdoctoral Science Foundation under Grants 2014T70525 and 2013M531364.

References

1. Nguyen, T.M., Jonathan Wu, Q.M.: A nonsymmetric mix-ture model for unsupervised image segmentation. IEEE Trans. Cybern. **43**, 751–765 (2013)
2. Bishop, C.M.: Pattern Recognition and Machine Learning. Springer, New York (2006)

3. Jain, A.K., Duin, R.P.W., Mao, J.C.: Statistical pattern recognition: a review. IEEE Trans. Pattern Anal. Mach. Intell. **22**, 4–37 (2000)

4. McLachlan, G.J., Krishnan, T.: The EM Algorithm and Extensions. Wiley, New York (2007)

5. Forbes, F., Peyrard, N.: Hidden Markov random field model selection criteria based on mean field-like approximations. IEEE Trans. Pattern Anal. Mach. Intell. **25**, 1089–1101 (2003)

6. Celeux, G., Forbes, F., Peyrard, N.: EM procedures using mean field-like approximations for Markov model-based image segmentation. Pattern Recogn. **36**, 131–144 (2003)

7. Sanjay, G.S., Hebert, T.J.: Bayesian pixel classification using spatially variant finite mixtures and the generalized EM algorithm. IEEE Trans. Image Process. **7**, 1014–1028 (1998)

8. Diplaros, A., Vlassis, N., Gevers, T.: A spatially constrained generative model and an EM algorithm for image segmentation. IEEE Trans. Neural Netw. **18**, 798–808 (2007)

9. Nikou, C., Galatsanos, N., Likas, A.: A class-adaptive spatially variant mixture model for image segmentation. IEEE Trans. Image Process. **16**, 1121–1130 (2007)

10. Nguyen, T.M., Jonathan Wu, Q.M.: Fast and robust spatially constrained gaussian mixture model for image segmentation. IEEE Trans. Circ. Syst. Video Technol. **23**, 621–635 (2013)

11. Nguyen, T.M., Jonathan Wu, Q.M., Mukherjee, D., Zhang, H.: A bayesian bounded asymmetric mixture model with segmentation application. IEEE J. Biomed. Health Inform. **18**, 109–119 (2014)

12. Zhang, H., Wu, Q.M.J., Nguyen, T.M.: Image segmentation by a robust modified gaussian mixture model. In: 38th International Conference on Acoustics, Speech, and Signal Processing (ICASSP), pp. 1478–1482. IEEE Press, New York (2013)

13. Browne, R.P., McNicholas, P.D., Sparling, M.D.: Model-based learning using a mixture of mixture of gaussian and uniform distributions. IEEE Trans. Pattern Anal. Mach. Intell. **34**, 814–817 (2014)

14. Nguyen, T.M., Wu, Q.M.J.: Bounded asymmetrical student's-t mixture model. IEEE Trans. Cybern. **44**, 857–869 (2014)

15. Nguyen, T.M., Wu, Q.M.J.: Bounded generalized gaussian mixture model. Pattern Recogn. **47**, 3132–3142 (2014)

16. Rohlfing, T.: Image similarity and tissue overlaps as surrogates for image registration accuracy: widely used but unreliable. IEEE Trans. Med. Imaging **31**, 153–163 (2012)

17. Van Leemput, K., Maes, F., Vandermeulen, D., Suetens, P.: Automated model-based tissue classification of MR images of the brain. IEEE Trans. Med. Imaging **18**, 897–908 (1999)

18. Martin, D., Fowlkes, C., Tal, D., Malik, J.: A database of human segmented natural images and its application to evaluating segmentation algorithms and measuring ecological statistics. In: 8th IEEE International Conference on Computer Vision (ICCV), pp. 416–423. IEEE Press, New York (2001)

19. Unnikrishnan, R., Pantofaru, C., Hebert, M.: A measure for objective evaluation of image segmentation algorithms. In: 8th IEEE Conference on Computer Vision and Pattern Recognition (CVPR), pp. 34–41. IEEE Press, New York (2005)

Object Recognition in Baggage Inspection Using Adaptive Sparse Representations of X-ray Images

Domingo Mery[✉], Erick Svec, and Marco Arias

Departamento de Ciencia de la Computacin, Pontificia Universidad Catlica de Chile,
Av. Vicua Mackenna, 4860(143) Santiago de Chile, Chile
dmery@ing.puc.cl
http://dmery.ing.puc.cl

Abstract. In recent years, X-ray screening systems have been used to safeguard environments in which access control is of paramount importance. Security checkpoints have been placed at the entrances to many public places to detect prohibited items such as handguns and explosives. Human operators complete these tasks because automated recognition in baggage inspection is far from perfect. Research and development on X-ray testing is, however, ongoing into new approaches that can be used to aid human operators. This paper attempts to make a contribution to the field of object recognition by proposing a new approach called Adaptive Sparse Representation (XASR+). It consists of two stages: learning and testing. In the learning stage, for each object of training dataset, several random patches are extracted from its X-ray images in order to construct representative dictionaries. A stop-list is used to remove very common words of the dictionaries. In the testing stage, random test patches of the query image are extracted, and for each test patch a dictionary is built concatenating the 'best' representative dictionary of each object. Using this adapted dictionary, each test patch is classified following the Sparse Representation Classification (SRC) methodology. Finally, the query image is classified by patch voting. Thus, our approach is able to deal with less constrained conditions including some contrast variability, pose, intra-class variability, size of the image and focal distance. We tested the effectiveness of our method for the detection of four different objects. In our experiments, the recognition rate was more than 95 % in each class, and more than 85 % if the object is occluded less than 15 %. Results show that XASR+ deals well with unconstrained conditions, outperforming various representative methods in the literature.

1 Introduction

Baggage inspection using X-ray screening is a priority task that reduces the risk of crime, terrorist attacks and propagation of pests and diseases [1]. Security and safety screening with X-ray scanners has become an important process in public spaces and at border checkpoints [2]. However, inspection is a complex task

© Springer International Publishing Switzerland 2016
T. Bräunl et al. (Eds.): PSIVT 2015, LNCS 9431, pp. 709–720, 2016.
DOI: 10.1007/978-3-319-29451-3_56

because threat items are very difficult to detect when placed in closely packed bags, occluded by other objects, or rotated, thus presenting an unrecognizable view [3]. Manual detection of threat items by human inspectors is extremely demanding [4]. It is tedious because very few bags actually contain threat items, and it is stressful because the work of identifying a wide range of objects, shapes and substances (metals, organic and inorganic substances) takes a great deal of concentration. In addition, human inspectors receive only minimal technological support. Furthermore, during rush hours, they have only a few seconds to decide whether or not a bag contains a threat item [5]. Since each operator must screen many bags, the likelihood of human error becomes considerable over a long period of time even with intensive training. The literature suggests that detection performance is only about 80–90 % [6]. In baggage inspection, automated X-ray testing remains an open question due to: *(i) loss of generality*, which means that approaches developed for one task may not transfer well to another; *(ii) deficient detection accuracy*, which means that there is a fundamental tradeoff between false alarms and missed detections; *(iii) limited robustness* given that requirements for the use of a method are often met for simple structures only; and *(iv) low adaptiveness* in that it may be very difficult to accommodate an automated system to design modifications or different specimens.

There are some contributions in computer vision for X-ray testing such as applications on inspection of castings, welds, food, cargos and baggage screening [7]. For this research proposal, it is very interesting to review the advances in baggage screening that have taken place over the course of this decade. They can be summarized as follows: Some approaches attempt to recognize objects using a single view of mono-energy X-ray images (*e.g.*, the adapted implicit shape model based on visual codebooks [8]) and dual-energy X-ray images (*e.g.*, Gabor texture features [9], bag of words based on SURF features [10] and pseudo-color, texture, edge and shape features [11]). More complex approaches that deal with multiple X-ray images have been developed as well. In the case of mono-energy imaging, see for example the recognition of regular objects using data association in [12] and active vision [13] where a second-best view is estimated. In the case of dual-energy imaging, see the use of visual vocabularies and SVM classifiers in [14]. Progress also has been made in the area of computed tomography. For example, in order to improve the quality of CT images, metal artifact reduction and de-noising [15] techniques were suggested. Many methods based on 3D features for 3D object recognition have been developed (see, for example, RIFT and SIFT descriptors [16], 3D Visual Cortex Modeling 3D Zernike descriptors and histogram of shape index [17]). There are contributions using known recognition techniques (see, for example, bag of words [18] and random forest [19]). As we can see, the progress in automated baggage inspection is modest and still very limited compared to what is needed because X-ray screening systems are still being manipulated by human inspectors. Automated recognition in baggage inspection is far from being perfected given that the appearance of the object of interest can become extremely difficult due to problems of (self-)occlusion, noise, acquisition, clutter, etc.

We believe that algorithms based on sparse representations can be used for this general task because in many computer vision applications, under the assumption that natural images can be represented using sparse decomposition, state-of-the-art results have been significantly improved [20]. Thus, it is possible to cast the problem of recognition into a supervised recognition form with X-ray images images and class levels (*e.g.*, objects to be recognized) using learned features in a unsupervised way. In the sparse representation approach, a dictionary is built from the training X-ray images, and matching is done by reconstructing the query image using a sparse linear combination of the dictionary. Usually, the query image is assigned to the class with the minimal reconstruction error.

Reflecting on the problems confronting recognition of objects, we believe that there are some key ideas that should be present in new proposed solutions. First, it is clear that certain parts of the objects are not providing any information about the class to be recognized (for example occluded parts). For this reason, such parts should be detected and should not be considered by the recognition algorithm. Second, in recognizing any class, there are parts of the object that are more relevant than other parts (for example the sharp parts when recognizing sharp objects like knives). For this reason, relevant parts should be class-dependent, and could be found using unsupervised learning. Third, in the real-world environment, and given that X-ray images are not perfectly aligned and the distance between detector and objects can vary from capture to capture, analysis of fixed parts can lead to misclassification. For this reason, feature extraction should not be in fixed positions, and can be in several random positions. Moreover, it would be possible to use a selection criterion that enables selection of the best regions. Fourth, an object that is present in a query image can be subdivided into 'sub-objects', for different parts (*e.g.*, in case of a handgun there are trigger, muzzle, grip, etc.). For this reason, when searching for images of the same class it would be helpful to search for image parts in all images of the training images instead of similar training images.

Inspired by these key ideas, we propose a method for recognition of objects using X-ray images[1]. Three main contributions of our approach are: (1) A new general algorithm that is able to recognize regular objects: it has been evaluated in the recognition of four different objects. (2) A new representation for the classes to be recognized using random patches: this is based on representative dictionaries learned for each class of the training images, which correspond to a rich collection of representations of selected relevant parts that are particular to a specific class. (3) A new representation for the query X-ray image: this is based on (*i*) a discriminative criterion that selects the 'best' test patches extracted randomly from the query image and (*ii*) and an 'adaptive' sparse representation of the selected patches computed from the 'best' representative dictionary of each class. Using these new representations, the proposed method (XASR+) can achieve high recognition performance under many complex conditions, as shown in our experiments.

---

[1] A similar approach was developed by us for a biometric problem [21].

2   Proposed Method

The proposed XASR+ method consists of two stages: learning and testing (see Fig. 1). In the learning stage, for each object of the training, several random patches are extracted and described from their images in order to built representative dictionaries. In the testing stage, random test patches of the query image are extracted and described, and for each test patch a dictionary is built concatenating the 'best' representative dictionary of each object. Using this adapted dictionary, each test patch is classified in accordance with the Sparse Representation Classification (SRC) methodology [22]. Afterwards, the patches are selected according to a discriminative criterion. Finally, the query image is classified by voting for the selected patches. Both stages will be explained in this section in further detail.

2.1   Model Learning

In the training stage, a set of n object images of k objects is available, where $\mathbf{I}_j^i$ denotes X-ray image j of object i (for $i = 1 \ldots k$ and $j = 1 \ldots n$) as illustrated in Fig. 2. In each image $\mathbf{I}_j^i$, m patches $\mathcal{P}_{jp}^i$ of size $w \times w$ pixels (for $p = 1 \ldots m$) are randomly extracted. They are centered in (x_{jp}^i, y_{jp}^i). In this work, a patch $\mathcal{P}$ is defined as vector:

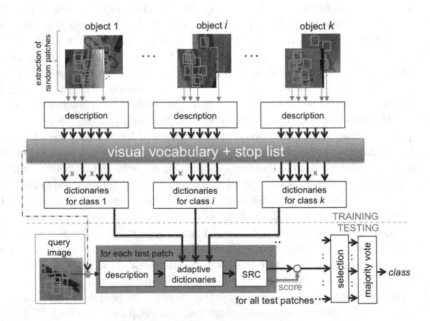

Fig. 1. Overview of the proposed method. The figure illustrates the recognition of three different objects. The shown classes are three: clips, razor blades and springs. There are two stages: Learning and Testing. The stop-list is used to filter out patches that are not discriminating for these classes. The stopped patches are not considered in the dictionaries of each class and in the testing stage.

$$\mathbf{p} = [\,\mathbf{z}\,;\ \alpha r] \in \mathcal{R}^{d+1} \tag{1}$$

where $\mathbf{z} = g(\mathcal{P}) \in \mathcal{R}^d$ is a descriptor of patch $\mathcal{P}$ (*i.e.*, a local descriptor of d elements extracted from the patch); r is the distance of the center of the patch (x^i_{jp}, y^i_{jp}) to the center of the image; and α is a weighting factor between descriptor and location. Description $\mathbf{z}$ must be rotation invariant because the orientation of the object can be anyone. Patch $\mathcal{P}$ is described using a vector that has been normalized to unit length:

$$\mathbf{y} = f(\mathcal{P}) = \frac{\mathbf{p}}{\|\mathbf{p}\|} \in \mathcal{R}^{d+1} \tag{2}$$

In order to eliminate non-discriminative patches, a *stop-list* is computed from a *visual vocabulary*. The visual vocabulary is built using all descriptors $\mathbf{Z} = \{\mathbf{z}^i_{jp}\} \in \mathcal{R}^{d \times knm}$, for $i = 1 \ldots k$, for $j = 1 \ldots n$ and for $p = 1 \ldots m$. Array $\mathbf{Z}$ is clustered using a k-means algorithm in N_v clusters. Thus, a visual vocabulary containing N_v visual words is obtained. In order to construct the stop-list, the *term frequency* 't_f' is computed: $t_f(d, v)$ is defined as the number of occurrences of word v in document d, for $d = 1 \ldots K$, $v = 1 \ldots N_v$. In our case, a document corresponds to an X-ray image, and $K = kn$ is the number of classes in the training dataset. Afterwards, the *document frequency* 'd_f' is computed: $d_f(v) = \sum_d \{t_f(d, v) > 0\}$, *i.e.*, the number of images in the training dataset that contain a word v, for $v = 1 \ldots N_v$. The stop-list is built using words with highest and smallest d_f values: On one hand, visual words with highest d_f values are not discriminative because they occur in almost all images. On the other hand, visual words with smallest d_f are so unusual that they correspond in most of the cases to noise. Usually, the top 5 % and bottom 10 % are stopped [23]. Those patches

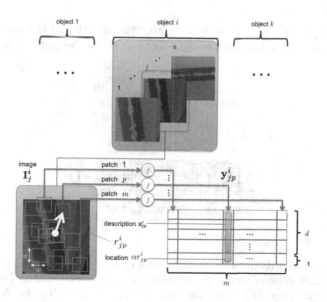

Fig. 2. Extraction and description of m patches of training image j of object i.

of **Z** that belong to the stopped clusters are not considered in the following steps of our algorithm.

Using (2) all extracted patches are described as $\mathbf{y}^i_{jp} = f(\mathcal{P}^i_{jp})$. Thus, for object i an array with the description of all patches is defined as $\mathbf{Y}^i = \{\mathbf{y}^i_{jp}\} \in \mathcal{R}^{(d+1)\times nm}$ (for $j = 1 \ldots n$ and $p = 1 \ldots m$).

The description $\mathbf{Y}^i$ of object i is clustered using k-means algorithm in Q clusters that will be referred to as *parent* clusters:

$$\mathbf{c}^i_q = \text{kmeans}(\mathbf{Y}^i, Q) \tag{3}$$

for $q = 1 \ldots Q$, where $\mathbf{c}^i_q \in \mathcal{R}^{(d+1)}$ is the centroid of parent cluster q of object i. We define $\mathbf{Y}^i_q$ as the array with all samples $\mathbf{y}^i_{jp}$ that belong to the parent cluster with centroid $\mathbf{c}^i_q$. In order to select a reduced number of samples, each parent cluster is clustered again in R *child* clusters:

$$\mathbf{c}^i_{qr} = \text{kmeans}(\mathbf{Y}^i_q, R) \tag{4}$$

for $r = 1 \ldots R$, where $\mathbf{c}^i_{qr} \in \mathcal{R}^{(d+1)}$ is the centroid of child cluster r of parent cluster q of object i. All centroids of child clusters of object i are arranged in an array $\mathbf{D}^i$, and specifically for parent cluster q are arranged in a matrix:

$$\bar{\mathbf{A}}^i_q = [\mathbf{c}^i_{q1} \cdots \mathbf{c}^i_{qr} \cdots \mathbf{c}^i_{qR}]^\mathsf{T} \in \mathcal{R}^{(d+1)\times R} \tag{5}$$

Thus, this arrange contains R representative samples of parent cluster q of object i as illustrated in Fig. 3. The set of all centroids of child clusters of object i ($\mathbf{D}^i$), represents Q representative dictionaries with R descriptions $\{\mathbf{c}^i_{qr}\}$ for $q = 1 \ldots Q, r = 1 \ldots R$.

2.2   Testing

In the testing stage, the task is to determine the identity of the query image $\mathbf{I}^t$ given the model learned in the previous section. From the test image, s selected

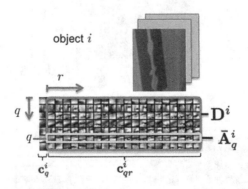

Fig. 3. Representative dictionaries of object i for $Q = 32$ (only for $q = 1 \ldots 7$ is shown) and $R = 20$. Left column shows the centroids $\mathbf{c}^i_q$ of parent clusters. Right columns (orange rectangle called $\mathbf{D}^i$) shows the centroids $\mathbf{c}^i_{qr}$ of child clusters. $\bar{\mathbf{A}}^i_q$ is row q of $\mathbf{D}^i$, *i.e.*, the centroids of child clusters of parent cluster q (Color figure online).

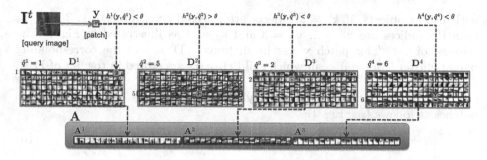

Fig. 4. Adaptive dictionary $\mathbf{A}$ of patch $\mathbf{y}$. In this example there are $k = 4$ objects in the training dataset. For this patch only $k' = 3$ objects are selected. Dictionary $\mathbf{A}$ is built from those objects by selecting all child clusters (of a parent cluster -see blue rectangles-) which has a child cluster with the smallest distance to the patch (see green squares). In this example, object 2 does not have child clusters that are similar enough, i.e., $h^2(\mathbf{y}, \hat{q}^2) > \theta$ (Color figure online).

test patches $\mathcal{P}_p^t$ of size $w \times w$ pixels are extracted and described using (2) as $\mathbf{y}_p^t = f(\mathcal{P}_p^t)$ (for $p = 1 \ldots s$). The selection criterion of a test patch will be explained later in this section.

For each selected test patch with description $\mathbf{y} = \mathbf{y}_p^t$, a distance to each parent cluster q of each object i of the training dataset is measured:

$$h^i(\mathbf{y}, q) = \text{distance}(\mathbf{y}, \bar{\mathbf{A}}_q^i). \tag{6}$$

We tested with several distance metrics. The best performance, however, was obtained by:

$$h^i(\mathbf{y}, q) = \min_r \|\mathbf{y} - \mathbf{c}_{qr}^i\| \text{ for } r = 1 \ldots R, \tag{7}$$

which is the smallest Euclidean distance to centroids of child clusters of parent cluster q as illustrated in Fig. 4. For $\mathbf{y}$ and $\mathbf{c}_{qr}^i$ normalized to unit ℓ_2 norm, the following distance can be used based on (7):

$$h^i(\mathbf{y}, q) = \min_r (1 - <\mathbf{y}, \mathbf{c}_{qr}^i>) \text{ for } r = 1 \ldots R, \tag{8}$$

where the term $< \bullet >$ corresponds to the scalar product that provides a similarity (cosine of angle) between vectors $\mathbf{y}$ and $\mathbf{c}_{qr}^i$. The parent cluster that has the minimal distance is searched:

$$\hat{q}^i = \underset{q}{\text{argmin}} \; h^i(\mathbf{y}, q), \tag{9}$$

which minimal distance is $h^i(\mathbf{y}, \hat{q}^i)$.

For patch $\mathbf{y}$, we select those training objects that have a minimal distance less than a threshold θ in order to ensure a similarity between the test patch and representative object patches. If k' objects fulfill the condition $h^i(\mathbf{y}, \hat{q}^i) < \theta$ for $i = 1 \ldots k$, with $k' \leq k$, we can build a new index $v_{i'}$ that indicates the index of the i'-th selected object for $i' = 1 \ldots k'$. For instance in a training dataset with $k = 4$ objects, if $k' = 3$ objects are selected (*e.g.*, objects 1, 3 and 4), then the indices are $v_1 = 1$, $v_2 = 3$ and $v_3 = 4$ as illustrated in Fig. 4. The selected object i' for patch $\mathbf{y}$ has its dictionary $\mathbf{D}^{v_{i'}}$, and the corresponding parent cluster is $u_{i'} = \hat{q}^{v_{i'}}$, in which child clusters are stored in row $u_{i'}$ of $\mathbf{D}^{v_{i'}}$, *i.e.*, in $\mathbf{A}^{i'} := \bar{\mathbf{A}}^{v_{i'}}_{u_{i'}}$.

Therefore, a dictionary for patch $\mathbf{y}$ is built using the best representative patches as follows (see Fig. 4):

$$\mathbf{A}(\mathbf{y}) = [\, \mathbf{A}^1 \dots \mathbf{A}^{i'} \dots \mathbf{A}^{k'} \,] \in \mathcal{R}^{(d+1) \times Rk'} \tag{10}$$

With this adaptive dictionary $\mathbf{A}$, built for patch $\mathbf{y}$, we can use *Sparse Representation Classification* (SRC) methodology [22]. That is, we look for a sparse representation of $\mathbf{y}$ using the ℓ_1-minimization approach:

$$\hat{\mathbf{x}} = \mathrm{argmin} \|\mathbf{x}\|_1 \quad \text{object to} \quad \mathbf{A}\mathbf{x} = \mathbf{y} \tag{11}$$

The residuals are calculated for the reconstruction for the selected objects $i' = 1 \dots k'$:

$$r_{i'}(\mathbf{y}) = \|\mathbf{y} - \mathbf{A}\delta_{i'}(\hat{\mathbf{x}})\| \tag{12}$$

where $\delta_{i'}(\hat{\mathbf{x}})$ is a vector of the same size of $\hat{\mathbf{x}}$ whose only nonzero entries are the entries in $\hat{\mathbf{x}}$ corresponding to class $v(i') = v_{i'}$. Thus, the class of selected test patch $\mathbf{y}$ will be the class that has the minimal residual, that is it will be

$$\hat{i}(\mathbf{y}) = v(\hat{i}') \tag{13}$$

where $\hat{i}' = \mathrm{argmin}_{i'} r_{i'}(\mathbf{y})$.

Finally, the identity of the query object will be the majority vote of the classes assigned to the s selected test patches $\mathbf{y}^t_p$, for $p = 1 \dots s$:

$$\mathrm{identity}(\mathbf{I}^t) = \mathrm{mode}(\hat{i}(\mathbf{y}^t_1), \dots \hat{i}(\mathbf{y}^t_p), \dots \hat{i}(\mathbf{y}^t_s)) \tag{14}$$

The selection of s patches of query image is as follows:

(*i*) From query image $\mathbf{I}^t$, m patches are randomly extracted and described using (2): $\mathbf{y}^t_j$, for $j = 1 \dots m$, with $m \geq s$.

(*ii*) Each patch $\mathbf{y}^t_j$ is represented by $\hat{\mathbf{x}}^t_j$ using the mentioned adaptive sparse representation according to (11).

(*iii*) The *sparsity concentration index* (SCI) of each patch is computed in order to evaluate how spread are its sparse coefficients [22]. SCI is defined by

$$S_j := \mathrm{SCI}(\mathbf{y}^t_j) = \frac{k \max(\|\delta_{i'}(\hat{\mathbf{x}}^t_j)\|_1)/\|\hat{\mathbf{x}}^t_j\|_1 - 1}{k - 1} \tag{15}$$

If a patch is discriminative enough it is expected that its SCI is large. Note that we use k instead of k' because the concentration of the coefficients related to k classes must be measured.

(*iv*) Array $\{S\}^m_{j=1}$ is sorted in a descended way.

(*v*) The first s patches in this sorted list in which SCI values are greater than a τ threshold are then selected. If only s' patches are selected, with $s' < s$, then the majority vote decision in (14) will be taken with the first s' patches.

3   Experiments

Our method was tested in the recognition of five classes in baggage screening: handguns, *shuriken* (ninja stars), clips, razor blades and background (see some samples in Fig. 5). In our experiments, there are 100 X-ray images per class. All images were resized to 128×128 pixels. We defined the following protocol: from each class, 50 images were randomly chosen for training and one for testing. In order to obtain a better confidence level in the estimation of recognition accuracy[2], the test was repeated 100 times by randomly selecting new 51 images per class each time (50 for training and 1 for testing). The reported accuracy in all of our experiments is the average calculated over the 100 tests[3].

The descriptor used by our method was $LBP_{8,1}^{ri}$, *i.e.*, Local Binary Pattern rotation-invariant with 8 samples and radius 1 [25]. That yields a 36-bin descriptor ($d = 36$). The size of the patch was 24×24 pixels ($w = 24$).

Table 1. Accuracy [%] of each experiment

Occlusion → Method ↓	0 (0%)	15×15 (1.4%)	30×30 (5.5%)	50×50 (15.3%)	70×70 (29.9%)
XASR+	**97.0**	**96.5**	**95.0**	**89.5**	**82.3**
XASR	92.0	92.0	85.5	31.5	20.5
SIFT	91.0	87.6	84.2	78.4	64.6
SRC	94.8	89.4	85.8	81.0	70.6
Vgoogle	87.2	83.6	82.8	70.4	54.6
BoW-KNN	88.6	84.4	82.6	73.8	55.0
BoW-RF	84.4	75.2	73.6	61.0	38.2

In order to evaluate the robustness against occlusion, we corrupted the test images with a square of random gray value of size $a \times a$ pixels located randomly, for $a = 15, 30, 50, 70$ (see example in Table 1). The obtained result is given in first row of Table 1 (see XASR+'s row). We observe that the accuracy was more than 95 % in each class when there is no occlusion, and more than 80 % if the object is occluded less than 30 %.

In order to evaluate the effectiveness of the stop-list, we repeated the same experiment without considering this step. The results are given in the second row of Table 1 (see XASR's row). We observe that the use of a stop-list can increase the accuracy significantly.

---

[2] Ratio of correctly classified samples to the total number of samples.

[3] The code for the MATLAB implementation is available on our webpage http:// dmery.ing.puc.cl/index.php/material/. The X-ray images belong to GDXray database [24].

Fig. 5. Images used in our experiments. The five classes are: handguns, shuriken, razor blades, clips and background.

In addition, we compared our method with four known methods that can be used in object recognition: *(i)* SIFT [26], *(ii)* sparse representation classification (SRC) [22] with SIFT descriptors, *(iii)* efficient visual search based on an information retrieval approach (Vgoogle) [23], and *(iv)* bag of words [27] using KNN (BoW-KNN) and random forest (BoW-RF) [28] with SIFT descriptors. We coded these methods according to the specifications given by the authors in their papers. The parameters were set so as to obtain the best performance. The results are summarized in the corresponding rows of Table 1. Results show that XASR+ deals well with unconstrained conditions in every experiment, achieving a high recognition performance in many conditions and obtaining similar or better performance in comparison with other representative methods in the literature.

The time computing depends on the size of the dictionary that is proportional to the number of classes to be detected. In our experiments with 5 classes the computational time is about 0.2 s per testing image (testing stage) on a Mac Mini Server OS X 10.10.1, processor 2.6 GHz Intel Core i7 with 4 cores and memory of 16GB RAM 1600 MHz DDR3.

4   Conclusions

In this paper, we have presented XASR+, an algorithm that is able to recognize objects automatically in cases with less constrained conditions including some contrast variability, pose, intra-class variability, size of the image and focal distance. We tested the effectiveness of our method for the detection of four different objects: razor blades, *shuriken* (ninja stars) handguns and clips. In our experiments, the recognition rate was more than 95 % in every class. The robustness of our algorithm is due to three reasons: *(i)* the dictionaries learned for each class in the learning stage corresponded to a rich collection of representations of relevant parts which were selected and clustered; *(ii)* the testing stage was based on *adaptive sparse representations* of several random patches using the dictionaries estimated in the previous stage which provided the best match with the patches, and *(iii)* a visual vocabulary and a stop-list used to reject non-discriminative patches in both learning and testing stage.

Acknowledgments. This work was supported by Fondecyt Grant No. 1130934 from CONICYT, Chile.

References

1. Zentai, G.: X-ray imaging for homeland security. In: IEEE International Workshop on Imaging Systems and Techniques (IST 2008), pp. 1–6 (September 2008)
2. Parliament, E.: Aviation security with a special focus on security scanners. European Parliament Resolution (2010/2154(INI)), pp. 1–10 (October 2012)
3. Halbherr, T., Schwaninger, A., Bolfing, A.: How Image Based Factors and Human Factors Contribute to Threat Detection Performance in X-Ray Aviation Security Screening. In: Holzinger, A. (ed.) USAB 2008. LNCS, vol. 5298, pp. 419–438. Springer, Heidelberg (2008)
4. Schwaninger, A., Bolfing, A., Halbherr, T., Helman, S., Belyavin, A., Hay, L.: The impact of image based factors and training on threat detection performance in X-ray screening. In: Proceedings of the 3rd International Conference on Research in Air Transportation, ICRAT 2008, pp. 317–324 (2008)
5. Blalock, G., Kadiyali, V., Simon, D.H.: The Impact of post-9/11 airport security measures on the demand for air travel. J. Law Econ. **50**(4), 731–755 (2007)
6. Michel, S., Koller, S., de Ruiter, J., Moerland, R., Hogervorst, M., Schwaninger, A.: Computer-based training increases efficiency in X-ray image interpretation by aviation security screeners. In: 2007 41st Annual IEEE International Carnahan Conference on Security Technology, pp. 201–206 (October 2007)
7. Mery, D.: Computer Vision for X-Ray Testing. Springer, Heidelberg (2015)
8. Riffo, V., Mery, D.: Automated detection of threat objects using adapted implicit shape model. IEEE Trans. Syst. Man Cybern. Syst. (2015, in press)
9. Uroukov, I., Speller, R.: A preliminary approach to intelligent x-ray imaging for baggage inspection at airports. Sig. Process. Res. **4**, 1–11 (2015)
10. Turcsany, D., Mouton, A., Breckon, T.P.: Improving feature-based object recognition for X-ray baggage security screening using primed visualwords. In: IEEE International Conference on Industrial Technology (ICIT 2013), pp. 1140–1145
11. Zhang, N., Zhu, J.: A study of x-ray machine image local semantic features extraction model based on bag-of-words for airport security. Int. J. Smart Sens. Intell. Syst. **8**(1), 45–64 (2015)
12. Mery, D.: Inspection of complex objects using multiple-x-ray views. IEEE/ASME Trans. Mech. **20**(1), 338–347 (2015)
13. Riffo, V., Mery, D.: Active x-ray testing of complex objects. Insight-Non-Destr. Test. Condition Monit. **54**(1), 28–35 (2012)
14. Schmidt, U., Roth, S., Franzel, T.: Object Detection in Multi-view X-Ray Images. In: Pinz, A., Pock, T., Bischof, H., Leberl, F. (eds.) DAGM and OAGM 2012. LNCS, vol. 7476, pp. 144–154. Springer, Heidelberg (2012)
15. Mouton, A., Flitton, G.T., Bizot, S.: An evaluation of image denoising techniques applied to CT baggage screening imagery. In: IEEE International Conference on Industrial Technology (ICIT 2013), IEEE (2013)
16. Flitton, G., Breckon, T.P., Megherbi, N.: A comparison of 3D interest point descriptors with application to airport baggage object detection in complex CT imagery. Pattern Recogn. **46**(9), 2420–2436 (2013)
17. Megherbi, N., Han, J., Breckon, T.P., Flitton, G.T.: A comparison of classification approaches for threat detection in CT based baggage screening. In: 2012 19th IEEE International Conference on Image Processing (ICIP), pp. 3109–3112. IEEE (2012)
18. Flitton, G., Mouton, A., Breckon, T.P.: Object classification in 3D baggage security computed tomography imagery using visual codebooks. Pattern Recogn. **48**(8), 2489–2499 (2015)

19. Mouton, A., Breckon, T.P.: Materials-based 3D segmentation of unknown objects from dual-energy computed tomography imagery in baggage security screening. Pattern Recogn. **48**(6), 1961–1978 (2015)
20. Tosic, I., Frossard, P.: Dictionary learning. IEEE Sig. Process. Mag. **28**(2), 27–38 (2011)
21. Mery, D., Bowyer, K.: Automatic facial attribute analysis via adaptive sparse representation of random patches. Pattern Recogn. Lett. **68**(Part 2), 260–269 (2015)
22. Wright, J., Yang, A.Y., Ganesh, A., Sastry, S.S., Ma, Y.: Robust face recognition via sparse representation. IEEE Trans. Pattern Anal. Mach. Intell. **31**(2), 210–227 (2009)
23. Sivic, J., Zisserman, A.: Efficient visual search of videos cast as text retrieval. IEEE Trans. Pattern Anal. Mach. Intell. **31**(4), 591–606 (2009)
24. Mery, D., Riffo, V., Zscherpel, U., Mondragón, G., Lillo, I., Zuccar, I., Lobel, H., Carrasco, M.: GDXray: The database of X-ray images for nondestructive testing. J. Nondestr. Eval. **34**(4), 1–12 (2015)
25. Ojala, T., Pietikäinen, M., Mäenpää, T.: Multiresolution gray-scale and rotation invariant texture classification with local binary patterns. IEEE Trans. Pattern Anal. Mach. Intell. **24**(7), 971–987 (2002)
26. Lowe, D.: Distinctive image features from scale-invariant keypoints. Int. J. Comput. Vis. **60**(2), 91–110 (2004)
27. Csurka, G., Dance, C., Fan, L., Willamowski, J., Bray, C.: Visual categorization with bags of keypoints. In: Workshop on Statistical Learning in Computer Vision, ECCV, vol. 1, pp. 1–2, Prague (2004)
28. Moosmann, F., Triggs, B., Jurie, F.: Fast discriminative visual codebooks using randomized clustering forests. In: Twentieth Annual Conference on Neural Information Processing Systems (NIPS 2006), pp. 985–992. MIT Press (2007)

Real-Time Lane Estimation Using Deep Features and Extra Trees Regression

Vijay John[1]($\boxtimes$), Zheng Liu[1], Chunzhao Guo[2], Seiichi Mita[1],
and Kiyosumi Kidono[2]

[1] Toyota Technological Institute, Nagoya, Japan
vijayjohn@toyota-ti.ac.jp
[2] Toyota Central R&D Labs, Nagakute, Japan

Abstract. In this paper, we present a robust real-time lane estimation algorithm by adopting a learning framework using the convolutional
neural network and extra trees. By utilising the learning framework, the
proposed algorithm predicts the ego-lane location in the given image even
under conditions of lane marker occlusion or absence. In the algorithm,
the convolutional neural network is trained to extract robust features
from the road images. While the extra trees regression model is trained
to predict the ego-lane location from the extracted road features. The
extra trees are trained with input-output pairs of road features and ego-
lane image points. The ego-lane image points correspond to Bezier spline
control points used to define the left and right lane markers of the ego-
lane. We validate our proposed algorithm using the publicly available
Caltech dataset and an acquired dataset. A comparative analysis with a
baseline algorithms, shows that our algorithm reports better lane estimation accuracy, besides being robust to the occlusion and absence of lane
markers. We report a computational time of 45 ms per frame. Finally, we
report a detailed parameter analysis of our proposed algorithm.

Keywords: Convolutional neural network · Extra trees · Lane detection · Occlusion

1 Introduction

Urban environment driving often requires to driver to concentrate while driving,
which results in the increase of driver stress and fatigue. To provide assistance to
the drivers, in recent years, there has been significant interest in the development
of advanced driver assistance systems (ADAS) and autonomous vehicles. Within
ADAS, lane detection plays an important role, and is used for applications such
as lane following, lane departure warning, collision warning and vehicle path
planning. The standard lane detection algorithm relies on the robust estimation
of visible lane markers from the camera image, using vision and image processing
algorithms. But the robust estimation of lanes is not trivial. Some of the challenges include degraded or absence of lane markers, lane marker occlusion, lane

© Springer International Publishing Switzerland 2016
T. Bräunl et al. (Eds.): PSIVT 2015, LNCS 9431, pp. 721–733, 2016.
DOI: 10.1007/978-3-319-29451-3_57

marker appearance variations, illumination variations and adverse environmental conditions such as snow and rain. Examples of challenges in the lane detection algorithm are presented in Fig. 1. Researchers often employ constraints such as tracking [1], region-of-interest (ROI) based estimation [2] and prior lanes [3] to overcome these limitations. However, even the use of additional constraints has some limitations and does not completely solve the lane detection problem [4].

In this paper, we propose an alternative scheme to address these issues using a learning framework. The proposed learning framework models the relationship between the entire road image and annotated ego-lane markers for various scenarios. The modeled relationship is then used to predict the ego-lane location within a given test road image. The ego-lane image location is represented using annotated Bezier spline control points, defined for the left and right lane markers. Using training pairs of road images and annotated lane control points, the ego-lane location is estimated in two learning-based steps. In the first step, we utilise the convolutional neural network (CNN) to extract robust and discriminative features from the entire input road image. We train the CNN to perform feature extraction by fine-tuning the pre-trained Places-CNN model [5] using a dataset of road images. In the second step, the extra trees regression algorithm is used to model the relationship between the extracted CNN-based road features and their corresponding annotated ego-lane markers. The trained models are then used to estimate the ego lane location in real-time during the testing phase, by CNN-based feature extraction and extra trees-based ego-lane prediction. Our main contribution to the lane detection literature is the use of a CNN and extra trees-based learning framework to accurately predict the ego-lane location in an image even under conditions of lane occlusion and absence. We validate our proposed algorithm on the publicly available Caltech dataset [6] and an acquired dataset. As shown in our experimental results, the proposed algorithm demonstrates the ability to accurately estimate the ego-lane, besides being robust to occlusion and absence of lane markers. Moreover, we report a real-time computational time of 45 ms per frame. A comparative analysis with the baseline algorithms is shown, along with a detailed parameter analysis. The rest of the paper is structured as follows. In Sect. 2 we report the literature review. The algorithm is presented in Sect. 3, and the experimental results are presented in Sect. 4. Finally, we summarize and conclude the paper in Sect. 5.

Fig. 1. An illustration of the various challenges in the lane detection including the absence of lane markers, degraded lane markers, shadows and occlusions.

2   Literature Review

Lane detection being an important problem in ADAS, has received significant attention in the research community. The summary of lane detection algorithms can be found in the surveys by Hillel et al. [4] and Yenikaya et al. [7]. The literature for the lane detection problem can be categorized into feature extraction techniques [1,2] and model-based techniques [3,8]. In feature extraction techniques, the lane markers are identified from the input image using image processing and fitting algorithms. On the other hand, the model-based techniques are generative models, where candidate lane models are evaluated for optimum fitness with the image-based features. We next present a brief overview of the literature in both the techniques.

In the standard feature extraction technique, the road image is first preprocessed to remove noise. Next, using image thresholding techniques, candidate lane markers are localised in the image. The final lanes are then identified from the candidate set. For example, Andrew et al. [2] localise the lanes in the image by identifying the painted lines on the road, and prune the candidates using orientation and length-based threshold. To enhance the accuracy of feature extraction-based techniques, researchers utilise techniques such as spatial constraints (ROI), tracking and inverse perspective transformations (IPT) into their algorithms. The ROI is used to constrain the lane search to a specific region in the image. While the tracking algorithm is used to incorporate temporal information to enhance the detection accuracy. Arshad et al. [9] utilise an adaptive ROI within their colour-threshold-based lane detection algorithm to identify the lanes. While Choi et al. [1] propose a lane detection algorithm using template matching, RANSAC and Kalman filtering. The template matching framework is used to obtain candidate lanes from the image, which are then pruned using the RANSAC and Kalman filter. In the work by Aly et al. [6], the IPT algorithm is used to generate the top view of the road, which are then filtered using oriented Gaussian filters to obtain candidate lanes. The candidate lanes are pruned using RANSAC and Bezier spline fitting algorithm. In the recent work by Kim et al. [10] a RANSAC and CNN is used to estimate the lanes from the edges in the image. The CNN is trained to generate output binary lane maps from input edge maps containing visible lane markers. The output binary lane maps are then used within the RANSAC algorithm as priors to estimate the lanes. However, the CNN-based output binary lane maps are dependent on the presence of visible lane markers in the input edge maps. Summarising the feature extraction methods, we observe that these methods are simple and easy to implement, but are limited by their dependence on strong lane cues.

In the model-based technique, lane models defined using parameters are used within a model-fitting framework to estimate the lanes. Candidate lane models generated using parameter estimates are evaluated within model-fitting frameworks such as RANSAC, particle filtering, etc. For example, Sehestedt et al. [8] evaluate the candidate lanes using the particle filter in the IPT edge image. In the work by Huang et al. [11], basis curves are used within a probabilistic framework to estimate the lanes. Lane estimates defined by the basis curves, are evaluated with observations from the road in a probabilistic framework. To enhance the accuracy of the lane estimation, the authors integrate the curb detection and road paint detection algorithm in their framework. Similar to the feature extraction techniques, researchers also employ constraints within the model-based framework. For example, Kowasri et al. [3] constrain the particle filters-based model fitting algorithm using lane priors. The lane priors are annotated on the map, and are retrieved by the vehicle during testing. Comparing the two categories of literature, we can observe that the model-based technique are more robust. But the performance of both these methods are affected by degraded lane markers, absence of lane markers, lane occlusion, and adverse weather conditions such as snow and rain. Unlike the aforementioned approaches, in this paper, we propose to address these issues using a learning-based approach by modeling the relationship between road image and annotated lane markers. The modeled relationship is then used to predict ego-lanes for various challenging scenarios.

3   Algorithm

In this paper, we formulate the lane detection problem using two learning algorithms, the CNN and the extra trees. The proposed algorithm consists of a training and testing phase. During the training phase, the CNN is trained to extract D-dim road features $\mathbf{f} \in \mathbb{R}^D$ from the input road image I. Next, the extra trees model is trained to predict the ego-lane in the image using training pairs of input road features $F = \{\mathbf{f}_n\}_{n=1}^N$ and output Bezier splines $\mathbf{B} = \{B_n\}_{n=1}^N$. In the training output, $B_n = [\mathbf{b}_n^l, \mathbf{b}_n^r]$, represents the set of Bezier splines for the n-th image, where $\mathbf{b}_n^l$ and $\mathbf{b}_n^r$ corresponds to the Bezier spline control points for the left and right lane marker. Each Bezier spline is defined using 4 control points or 8 image pixel coordinates. The 8 image pixel coordinates are manually annotated within a predefined ROI in the image, and used for training and testing. In the testing phase, for a given input road image I_t the trained CNN extracts the features $\mathbf{f}_t$. The feature $\mathbf{f}_t$ is then given as an input to the trained extra trees, which subsequently predicts the ego-lane using the output Bezier splines B_t. An overview of our proposed algorithm is shown in Fig. 2. We next present a detailed overview of the training and testing phase.

3.1   Training

Convolutional Neural Network. The convolutional neural network (CNN) is a deep learning framework used for multi-class classification [5]. It has reported state-of-the-art detection and classification result in various image classification, speech recognition applications [5]. The deep learning framework is an end-to-end machine learning framework, where multiple layers of processing are used to simultaneously perform feature extraction and feature classification. To perform the feature extraction and classification, CNN based on the multi-layered perceptron learns the weights and bias in each layer. The lower layers of CNN extract the low level features, while the higher layers learn the high-level features.

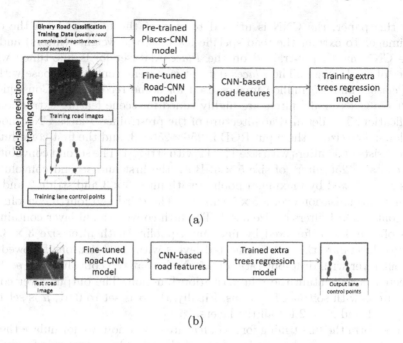

Fig. 2. An overview of the (a) training and (b) testing phase of the proposed algorithm

The extracted features are represented as feature maps in the CNN network. Given the feature maps, CNN performs the feature classification inherently in the final layers. The CNN architecture is represented using convolutional layers, pooling, fully connected layers, drop-out layers and loss layers. The convolutional layers and pooling layers are used in the initial layers to inherently perform feature extraction. The final layers contain the fully connected layers, drop-out layers and loss layers function, which are used to the perform inherent feature classification. To update the weights in the different layers, the stochastic gradient descent is used, where the weights are updated by the following equations.

$$V_{t+1} = \mu V_t - \alpha \nabla L(W_t) \tag{1}$$

$$W_{t+1} = W_t + V_{t+1} \tag{2}$$

where W_t is the previous weight and V_t is the previous weight update at iteration t. V_{t+1} and W_{t+1} are the updated weight update and weights at $t+1$. $\nabla L(W_t)$ is the negative gradient of the previous weight. α is the learning rate for the weight of the negative gradient. μ is the momentum or the weight of the previous update. Additionally, each layer has a learning rate multiplier term for the weights and bias β_w and β_b, respectively. This is used to vary the α during training for each layer to facilitate faster convergence.

In this paper, the CNN is utilised to extract the features from the entire road image. To extract the road specific features, the weights (filters) and bias of the CNN model pre-trained on the *Places* dataset [5] is fine-tuned with a dataset of road images. The *Places* dataset is a scene-centric database with 205 scene classes and 2.5 million images used for scene recognition. Consequently, the Places-CNN model filters are highly tuned for scene feature extraction and classification. The detailed architecture of the pre-trained Places-CNN model is as follows: The size of the input RGB is $256 \times 256 \times 3$, and the first convolutional layer consists of 96 filters with size 11×11 with stride 4. The second convolutional layer contains 256 filters of size 5×5. Both the first and second convolutional layers are followed by maximum pooling with filter 3×3 and stride 2 and local response normalisation over a 5×5 window. The third and fourth convolutional layer contains 384 filters of size 3×3. The fifth convolutional layer contains 256 filters of size 3×3, followed by maximum pooling with filter size 3×3. The next two layers are the fully connected layers with 4096 neurons followed by a drop-out layer with drop-out ratio of 0.5. Note that the convolutional and fully connected layer contain the relu activation function. The output layer contain 205 neurons with softmax functions. Finally, the α is set to 0.01, μ is set to 0.9 and $\beta_w = 1$ and $\beta_b = 2$ for all the layers.

To perform the fine-tuning for road feature extraction, we formulate the multiclass Places-CNN model as a binary road classifier. We adopt this formulation to fine-tune the feature extraction layers of the (C1–C5) through the backpropagation algorithm. To modify the Places-CNN model as a binary classifier, we replace the 205 neurons in the output layer with 2 neurons. Henceforth we refer to this modified binary model, as the road-CNN model. The fine-tuning for the road-CNN model is done using 100000 positive road scene samples and 100000 negative non-road scene samples. Note that the binary classification modification is primarily done to fine-tune the pre-trained feature extraction layers, owing to the CNN's characteristic of network training using backpropagation from the output layers.

During the fine-tuning step, the weights and bias of the road-CNN feature extraction layers, $C1–C5$, are initialised with the corresponding pre-trained weights and biases of the Places-CNN model. On the other hand, the weights and bias for the fully connected layers $FC6–FC8$ or feature classification layers are initialised without the pre-trained weights and bias. To reflect the pre-initialisation, we lower the learning rate α to a lower value 0.001, compared to the Places-CNN model. But, the momentum and learning multipliers (β_w and β_b) for convolutional layers $C1–C5$ are kept the same (0.9,1,2). On the other hand, to enable the feature extraction layers to learn quickly, β_w and β_b for fully connected layers $FC6$ and $FC7$ are set as 2 and 4, while the β_w and β_b for the output layer is set as 10 and 20. The number of training iterations is lowered to 50000. Using the above described parameters, we fine-tune the road-CNN and learn the road-specific weights and bias. The fine-tuned road-CNN is then used to extract the road features, which corresponds to the output feature maps of the fifth pooling layer ($P5$). Consequently, each road feature $\mathbf{f}$ is represented by

256 feature maps of size 7 × 7. Thus generating a 12544 dim feature vector. We refer to this feature vector as the *complete* feature vector. An illustration of the filters and feature maps of the road-CNN model is presented in Fig. 3

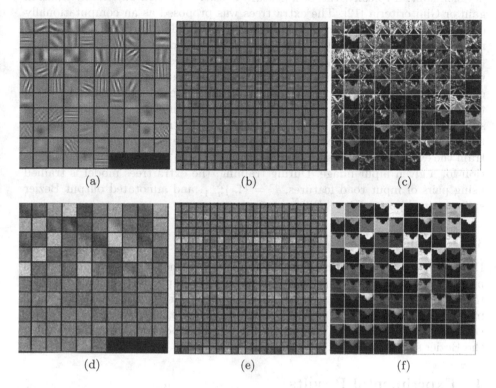

(a)   (b)   (c)

(d)   (e)   (f)

Fig. 3. A visualization of the (a) C1-filters, (b) C2-filters, and (c) C1-feature maps for the fine-tuned road-CNN. The (d) C1-filters, (e) C2-filters and (f) C1-feature maps for the directly-trained road-CNN (Details of this model given in Sect. 4.2)

Extra Trees Regression. The extra trees are an extension of the random forest regression model and proposed by Geurts et al. [12]. The extra trees belong to the class of decision tree-based ensemble learning methods. In decision tree-based ensemble methods, multiple decision trees are used to perform classification and regression tasks [13]. Random forest and extra trees are important algorithms within this class and have reported state-of-the-art performance on many regression tasks with high-dimensional input and outputs [13]. The random forests are trained to perform the regression tasks using the techniques of tree bagging and feature bagging. In tree bagging, each decision tree in the ensemble is trained on a random subset of the training data, generating an ensemble of decision trees. Given, the ensemble of decision trees, the feature bagging technique is used to perform the split at each node in the decision tree. The feature bagging-based split is performed in two steps. In the first step, random subset of features are selected from the previously selected training data subset. In the second step, the best subset feature and its corresponding value are chosen to perform the decision split. Typically, the best feature is selected based on the information gain or Gini criteria [12]. The extra trees was proposed as an computationally efficient and highly randomised extension of the random forest. There are two main differences between the extra trees and the random forest. Firstly, unlike the random forest, the extra trees does not use the tree bagging step to generate the training subset for each tree. The entire training set is used to train all the decision trees in the ensemble. Secondly, in the node-splitting step, the extra trees randomly selects the best feature along with the corresponding value to split the node. These two differences results in the extra trees being less susceptible to overfitting and reporting better performance [12]. In our problem, we train the extra trees regression model with 50 trees to predict the ego-lane location for a given input image. During training, the extra trees model is trained using pairs of input road features, $F = \{\mathbf{f}_n\}_{n=1}^{N}$, and annotated output Bezier spline control points, $\mathbf{B} = \{B_n\}_{n=1}^{N}$.

3.2 Testing

During the real-time testing phase, we use the trained CNN and extra trees model to predict the ego-lane location in an given input test image I_t, resized to $256 \times 256 \times 3$. First, the trained CNN is used to extract the *complete* feature maps or the road features $\mathbf{f}_t$. The road features are then given as an input to the trained extra trees, which outputs the ego-lane location in the image using the Bezier spline control points B_t.

4 Experimental Results

The proposed algorithm was validated with the publically available Caltech dataset [6] and an acquired dataset. We performed a comparative analysis with a baseline algorithm and report a better lane detection accuracy even under occlusion and absence of lane markers. Additionally, a detailed parameter analysis of our algorithm is performed. In the experiments, we validate our proposed method using the Caltech dataset and an acquired dataset. The Caltech dataset has 1224 images with annotated Bezier spline control points, while the acquired dataset contains 2279 frames with manual annotation. The training and testing of our proposed algorithm was done using a 5-fold cross validation scheme on both the datasets. The algorithm is implemented on a Linux machine with Nvidia Geforce GTX960 graphics card using Python and GPU-based Caffe software tool [14]. The scikit machine learning library was used to implement the extra trees.

4.1 Comparative Analysis

In this section, we report the results of a comparative analysis performed with two baseline algorithms. The first baseline algorithm is based on the Hough

Table 1. Det. Accuracy *Caltech*

Algorithm	Lanes	Det. rate
Proposed algo.	2450	98.9 %
ROI-Hough-Ransac.	2450	94.2 %
ROI-Hough.	2450	88.4 %

Table 2. Det. Accuracy *Acquired*

Algorithm	Lanes	Det. rate
Proposed algo.	4560	99.3 %
ROI-Hough-Ransac.	4560	96.8 %
ROI-Hough.	4560	92.6 %

transform-based lane detection framework [9]. In this algorithm, we first identify the lane ROI in the image, and utilise a intensity and colour-based threshold to identify the set of candidate lines. Following morphological operations, the candidate lanes are pruned using the Hough transform. Finally, the two strongest lanes are used to identify the ego-lane markers in the image. In the second baseline, based on the work by Aly et al. [6], we utilise edge information to identify candidate lanes within a lane ROI. The candidate lanes are further pruned by the Hough transform, before estimating the ego-lane using Ransac.

To compare the algorithms, we use their respective lane detection accuracies. An estimated lane marker is considered as a true positive, when the distance between the estimated lane marker points and the ground truth lane marker points is less than 20 pixels. Prior to calculating the Euclidean distance between the lane marker points, a greedy nearest neighbour search is performed to match the estimated spline points with their corresponding ground truth spline points. The lane marker points for the proposed algorithm are derived from the Bezier splines, which are in turn, interpolated from the predicted control points. A similar technique is adopted to extract the ground-truth lane marker points. On the other hand, the lane marker points of the baseline algorithm are directly generated from algorithm's output. Since both our proposed and baseline algorithms only estimates the ego-lane in the final output, every missed lane marker or false negative also corresponds to a false positive. Consequently, we do not report the false positive rate.

The lane detection accuracy between the proposed algorithm and the baseline algorithm is evaluated using the testing subset of each round of the 5-fold cross validation. As shown in Tables 1 and 2, it can be seen that the proposed algorithm reports better lane detection algorithm than the baseline algorithm. Additionally, as shown in Fig. 4, our proposed algorithm estimates the ego-lane for frames, where the lane markers are either occluded or absent. The baseline algorithm fails to detect the lane markers under these conditions. We report a computational time of 45 ms per frame using the GPU, where the CNN-based feature extraction takes an average 44 ms, while the extra trees regression takes 1 ms.

4.2   Parameter Analysis

Here we perform a detailed parameter analysis of our algorithm by reporting the lane detection accuracy. For the parameter analysis, we first evaluate the fine-tuning of the road-CNN model. Second, we evaluate the CNN-based features

Table 3. Det Acc. *Caltech*

Feat-Reg	Ext. trees	Rand forest	Lasso
Complete	98.9 %	95.9 %	95.3 %
HOG	92.9 %	90.3 %	65.1 %
SURF	93.2 %	90.4 %	65.2 %

Table 4. Det Acc. *Acquired*

Feat-Reg	Ext. trees	Rand forest	Lasso
Complete	99.3 %	95.6 %	94.8 %
HOG	91.8 %	90.7 %	76.8 %
SURF	92.6 %	91.4 %	76.7 %

with different feature descriptors. Third, we evaluate the features used as the regression input. Finally, we evaluate the regression models used for the lane prediction.

Fine-Tuned Feature Extraction. In this experiment, we validate the need to fine-tune the pre-trained Places-CNN. To perform the validation, we set-up a directly trained (DT) road-CNN model, where we train all the layers of the road-CNN model without any pre-initialisation using the pre-trained Places-CNN weights and bias. On the other hand, in the fine-tuned road-CNN model we pre-initialise the weights and bias for layers $C1 - C5$. The training for DT road-CNN models is done using thee same binary dataset (100000 positive and 100000 negative samples). Following the training, we evaluate the fine-tuned and directly-trained CNN models on a separate test dataset of 10000 road scenes and 10000 negative scenes and report the classification accuracies. Based on the experimental results, we observe that the fine-tuned road-CNN model achieves a 100 % classification accuracy, while the DT CNN only achieves a 75 % accuracy. This validates the need to adopt a pre-trained network for fine-tuning, instead of directly training the CNN. In Fig. 3, we present the filters and feature maps of the two CNN networks. It can be clearly seen that the fine-tuned filters and feature maps are well-trained, unlike the directly trained filters and features maps.

Different Features. To validate the lane detection accuracy due to the CNN-based road features, we train the regression model with the HOG and SURF-based road features [15] and report the lane detection accuracies. As shown in Tables 3 and 4, the performance of the CNN-based road features is much better than both the HOG and SURF-based features across different regression models.

CNN-Based Feature Descriptor. We perform an experiment by considering different feature descriptors to represent the CNN-based feature (*complete*). For this experiment, we consider three different feature descriptors with reduced dimensions, the *mean*, *phist* and *bhist*. In the *mean* descriptor the 256, 7×7, feature maps in the original feature vector are averaged, resulting in a 49-dim feature vector ($1 \times 7 \times 7$). In the *phist*, a 10-bin histogram is used to represent the distribution of values across the 256 feature maps at each 7×7 map index resulting in a 490-dim feature vector ($10 \times 7 \times 7$). Finally, in the *bhist* the 10-bin histogram is used to represent the feature distribution across 3 disjoint blocks of the 256 feature maps at each 7×7 index. This results in a 1470-dim feature vector ($30 \times 7 \times 7$). Based on our experimental results, we observe that none of

Table 5. Det. Acc *Caltech*

Feat-Reg	Ext. trees	Rand forest	Lasso
Complete	98.9 %	95.9 %	95.3 %
Mean	94.2 %	90.6 %	65 %
PHist	90.5 %	87.0 %	78.3 %
BHist	89.6 %	87.6 %	82 %

Table 6. Det. Acc *Acquired*

Feat-Reg	Ext. trees	Rand forest	Lasso
Complete	99.3 %	95.6 %	94.8 %
Mean	94.0 %	91.1 %	77.7 %
PHist	91.4 %	88.6 %	83.9 %
BHist	95.9 %	94.8 %	93.7 %

the feature descriptors demonstrate an improved lane detection accuracy, inspite of reducing the computational complexity of the regression model. This is shown in Tables 5 and 6.

Different Regression Models. The performance of the extra trees is evaluated in this section. Trained random forest and Lasso regression models are used to predict the lanes for different features and feature descriptors. As observed in all the tables above (Tables 1, 2, 3, 4, 5 and 6), the performance of the extra trees is better than the random forest and the Lasso models, across different features

(a)   (b)   (c)   (d)

(e)   (f)   (g)   (h)

(i)   (j)   (k)   (l)

Fig. 4. Some lane detection examples of our proposed algorithm for challenges scenarios where the ego-lane markers are (a–b) curved, (c) shadowed, (d) shadowed and absent, (e–f) partially occluded, (g) partially occluded, absent with different coloured road surface, (h) occluded and absent, (i–l) absent. The blue splines are the ground truths, while the red splines are the predicted splines. The baseline algorithms fails to detect the ego-lane markers under these conditions.

Fig. 5. Missed lane marker detections by our algorithm, for a hard left turn and suddenly emerging left lanes.

and feature descriptors. Additionally, we can also observe that the performance of the random forest is better than the Lasso model.

Discussion. Based on the experimental results, we observe that the proposed algorithm demonstrates better lane detection accuracy. Additionally, the advantage of the CNN-based road features and extra trees regression model is clearly demonstrated. The algorithm is robust to lane marker occlusions and absent lane markers. The few missed lane detections occur for lane marker scenes which occur rarely, resulting in limited training samples for the extra trees regression. Examples of missed lane detections classes are shown in Fig. 5. Note that this can be addressed by increasing the training samples for the particular class.

5   Conclusion and Future Work

In this paper, a real-time learning-based lane detection is proposed using the convolutional neural network and extra tree regression model. The proposed learning framework models the relationship between the input road image and annotated lane markers, which are then used to perform ego-lane prediction. In the learning framework, the pre-trained Places-convolutional neural network is fine-tuned to extract features from the input road images. These extracted features are used along with annotated ego-lane markers to train the extra trees regression model. The trained extra trees are then used to predict the ego-lanes in real-time, during the testing phase, using the convolutional neural network-based road features. We validate the proposed algorithm on the publicly available Caltech dataset and an acquired dataset, and perform a comparative analysis with baseline lane detection algorithms. Based on our experimental results, we report better lane detection accuracies. More importantly, our proposed approach is not affected by either occlusions or the absence of lane markers. A detailed parameter analysis of the proposed algorithm is also performed. In the future work, we will validate the algorithm on a larger dataset and extend the algorithm to identifying multiple lanes.

References

1. Choi, H., Park, J., Choi, W., Oh, S.: Vision-based fusion of robust lane tracking and forward vehicle detection in a real driving environment. Int. J. Automot. Technol. **13**(4), 653–669 (2012)
2. Andrew, H., Lai, S., Nelson, H., Yung, C.: Lane detection by orientation and length discrimination. IEEE Trans. Syst. Man Cybern. Part B **30**(4), 539–548 (2000)
3. Kowsari, T., Beauchemin, S.S., Bauer, M.A.: Map-based lane and obstacle-free area detection. In: VISAPP (2014)
4. Bar Hillel, A., Lerner, R., Levi, D., Raz, G.: Recent progress in road, lane detection: a survey. Mach. Vis. Appl. **25**(3), 727–745 (2014)
5. Zhou, B., Lapedriza, A., Xiao, J., Torralba, A., Oliva, A.: Learning deep features for scene recognition using places database. In: Advances in Neural Information Processing Systems (2014)
6. Aly, M.: Real time detection of lane markers in urban streets. In: Proceedings of the Intelligent Vehicles Symposium (2008)
7. Yenikaya, S., Yenikaya, G., Düven, E.: Keeping the vehicle on the road: a survey on on-road lane detection systems. ACM Comput. Surv. **46**(1), 2:1–2:43 (2013)
8. Sehestedt, S., Kodagoda, S., Alempijevic, A., Dissanayake, G.: Efficient lane detection and tracking in urban environments. In: Proceedings of the European Conference on Mobile Robots (2007)
9. Arshad, N., Moon, K., Park, S., Kim, J.: Lane detection with moving vehicle using colour information. In: World Congress on Engineering and Computer Science (2011)
10. Kim, J., Lee, M.: Robust lane detection based on convolutional neural network and random sample consensus. In: Yap, K.S., Wong, K.W., Teoh, A., Huang, K., Loo, C.K. (eds.) ICONIP 2014, Part I. LNCS, vol. 8834, pp. 454–461. Springer, Heidelberg (2014)
11. Huang, A.S., Teller, S.: Probabilistic lane estimation for autonomous driving using basis curves. Auton. Robots **31**(2–3), 269–283 (2011)
12. Geurts, P., Ernst, D., Wehenkel, L.: Extremely randomized trees. Mach. Learn. **63**(1), 3–42 (2006)
13. Gall, J., Yao, A., Razavi, N., Van Gool, L., Lempitsky, V.: Hough forests for object detection, tracking, and action recognition. IEEE Trans. Pattern Anal. Mach. Intell. **33**(11), 2188–2202 (2011)
14. Jia, Y., Shelhamer, E., Donahue, J., Karayev, S., Long, J., Girshick, R., Guaddarrame, S., Darrel, T.: Caffe: convolutional architecture for fast feature embedding. arXiv preprint arXiv:1408.5093 (2014)
15. Song, J., Ma, Y., Hu, F., Lao, S., Zhao, Y.: Scalable image retrieval based on feature forest. In: Zha, H., Taniguchi, R., Maybank, S. (eds.) ACCV 2009, Part III. LNCS, vol. 5996, pp. 506–515. Springer, Heidelberg (2010)

Contrast Based Hierarchical Spatial-Temporal Saliency for Video

Trung-Nghia Le[1](✉) and Akihiro Sugimoto[2]

[1] Department of Informatics, SOKENDAI (Graduate University for Advanced
Studies), 2-1-2, Hitotsubashi, Chiyoda-ku, Tokyo 101-8430, Japan
ltnghia@nii.ac.jp
[2] National Institute of Informatics, 2-1-2, Hitotsubashi,
Chiyoda-ku, Tokyo 101-8430, Japan
sugimoto@nii.ac.jp

Abstract. Predicting human attention for video is requires exploiting
temporal knowledge included in the video. We propose a novel hierarchical spatial-temporal saliency model for video based on the center-
surround framework using both static features and temporal features.
Saliency cues are analyzed through a hierarchical segmentation model,
and fused across multiple levels, yielding the spatial-temporal saliency
map. An adaptive temporal window using motion information is also
developed to combine saliency values of consecutive frames in order to
keep temporal consistency across frames. Performance evaluation on several popular benchmark datasets validates that our method outperforms
existing state-of-the-arts.

1 Introduction

Predicting human attention plays a significant part in computer vision, mobile
robotics, and cognitive systems [1]. Saliency detection aims to simulate human
attention by focusing on the most informative and interesting regions in a scene.
Several computational models are developed for human gaze fixation prediction
[2,3], which is important for understanding human attention; while others are
proposed for salient object detection [4,5], which is useful for high-level vision
tasks. In this work, although we focus on the salient object detection aspect, our
proposed saliency model also achieves high performance in predicting human
gaze fixation.

In the real world, visual information is usually composed of dynamic entities
caused by egocentric movements or dynamics of the world. Particularly, in a
dynamic scene, background always changes; different parts corresponding to different elements or objects can move in different directions with different speed
independently. Therefore, predicting human attention for video is challenging
because we have to incorporate a relationship of dynamics between consecutive
frames. Attention models should have ability to fuse current static information and accumulated knowledge on dynamics from the past to deal with the
dynamic nature of scenes including two properties: dynamic background and

T. Bräunl et al. (Eds.): PSIVT 2015, LNCS 9431, pp. 734–748, 2016.
DOI: 10.1007/978-3-319-29451-3_58

entities' independent motion. Several spatial-temporal saliency methods based on motion analysis are proposed for video [4,6]. Some of them can capture scene regions that are important in a spatial-temporal manner [4,7]. However, most of existing methods do not fully exploit the nature of dynamics in a scene. Temporal features expressing motion dynamics of objects in a scene between consecutive frames are not utilized in saliency detection process, either.

In order to effectively use knowledge on dynamics of background and objects in a video, we propose a flexible framework where pixel-based features and region-based features are fused to create a saliency detection method (c.f. Table 1). In this framework, static features and temporal features computed from pixel-based and region-based features are combined together in order to utilize both low-level features of each frame and consistency between consecutive frames. We also present a novel metric for motion information by estimating the number of referenced frames for each single object to keep temporal consistency across frames. Our method overcomes the limitation of the existing method [4] which uses a fixed number of referenced frames and does not concern motion of objects within a scene.

Table 1. Feature classification

	pixel-based feature	region-based feature
static feature	- color - intensity - orientation	- location - objectness
temporal feature	- flow magnitude - flow orientation	- movement

In our method, firstly, we execute a hierarchical segmentation. Saliency map for each segmentation level is then calculated via combination of contrast information and regional characteristics among segmented regions at the same scale level. Our feature maps are combinations of pixel-based features and region-based features. Particularly, pixel-based features consist of low-level image features such as color, intensity, or orientation as well as temporal features such as flow magnitude or flow orientation; while region-based features include spatial features such as location of an object or foreground object as well as movement of an object (c.f. Table 1). An adaptive sliding window in the temporal domain is proposed to relate salient values of frame sequences by exploiting motion information of a segmented region in each frame. Each region in each frame has a different number of referenced frames depending on its motion distribution. Experimental results using two public standard datasets i.e., the Weizmann standard dataset [8] and the SFU dataset [9], show that our proposed method outperforms the state-of-the-arts. Examples of generated saliency maps using our method are shown in Fig. 1.

Fig. 1. Examples of our spatial-temporal saliency model. Top row images are original images. Bottom row images are the corresponding saliency maps using our method.

Our key contributions lie in twofold:

- The first one is that we show the framework, which integrates the contrast information together with regional properties. Although the proposed saliency model is developed based on a contrast based method presented by Zhou et al. [4], it significantly improves performance of the original work.
- The other is that we introduce a novel metric using motion information in order to keep temporal consistency between consecutive frames of each entity in a video. Our method also exploits the dynamic nature of the scene in term of independent motion of entities.

2   Related Work

Many computational models have been recently proposed for saliency detection. The majority of existing visual attention methods are developed using bottom-up computational algorithms, where low-level stimuli in scenes such as color, intensity, or edge are utilized in the center-surround contrast framework. For videos, several spatial-temporal saliency methods based on the center-surround framework are proposed. These methods measure the saliency of a pixel based on its contrast within a local context or the entire image. For instance, the framework proposed by Seo et al. [10] relies on center-surround differences between a local spatial-temporal cube and its neighboring cubes in space-time coordinates. In several center-surround schemes, motion between a pair of frames (e.g. optical flow), which is considered as a low-level feature channel, is used to compute local discrimination of the flow in a spatial neighborhood [4,11].

However, such contrast based saliency models may be ineffective when objects contain small-scale salient patterns; thus saliency could generally be misled by their complexity. Multi-level analysis and hierarchical models are developed to deal with salient small scale structure [4,5]. Some saliency models employ temporal coherence to principles of multi-scale processing to enhance performance [4].

Comparing with the previous work, our saliency method combines various features including primitive pixel-based features (color, intensity, orientation, and flow information) and region-based features (location, objectness and object's movement) through a hierarchical contrast calculation.

Saliency detection for video originates from applying an attention model to each frame of the video separately [12]. However, this kind of process does not achieve high effectiveness because temporal information across frames in the video is disregarded. The problem is even more challenging when dealing with dynamic scenes, where not only objects but also background always changes over time. Dynamics in a video is caused by different dynamic entities of natural scenes or by ego-motion of imaging sensors. Therefore, dynamic textures are integrated into discriminant center-surround saliency detection method to deal with scenes with highly dynamic backgrounds and moving cameras [13]. Accuracy for human egocentric visual attention prediction is also enhanced by adding information of camera's rotation, velocity and direction of movement into the bottom-up saliency model [6]. Differently from existing methods, our spatial-temporal saliency model uses motion information in order to keep temporal consistency across frames.

3   Hierarchical Spatial-Temporal Saliency Model

Figure 2 illustrates the process of our spatial-temporal saliency detection method. First of all, the streaming hierarchical method [14], which runs on arbitrarily long videos with constant, low memory consumption, is executed to hierarchically segment a video into spatial-temporal regions. In order to obtain regions at different scales, we initially construct a 5-level segmentation pyramid. Motion information as well as used features for each frame are extracted in each scale level. From these features, we build feature maps, including contrast information between regions and regional characteristics, in order to calculate saliency entities for regions in each scale level. After that, an Adaptive Temporal Window (ATW) is individually applied to each region to smooth saliency entities between frames by exploiting the motion information, yielding hierarchical saliency maps for each frame. Finally, a spatial-temporal saliency map is generated for each frame by fusing its hierarchical saliency maps.

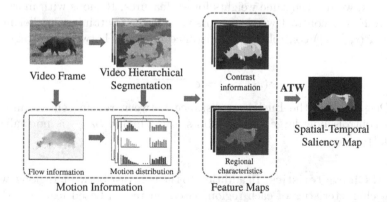

Fig. 2. Pipeline of the proposed spatial-temporal saliency method.

3.1   Saliency Entity Construction

Contrast Information. Human vision reacts to image regions with discriminative features such as unique color, high contrast, different orientation, or complex texture. To estimate attractiveness of regions in a video, contrast metric is usually used to evaluate sensitivity of elements in each frame. The contrast information is based on pixel-based features including static information such as color, intensity, or texture, and dynamic information such as magnitude or orientation of motion. A region with a high level of contrast against surrounding regions can attract human attention and is perceptually more important.

For the i-th region at the l-th scale of the segmentation pyramid at a frame, denoted by $r_{i,l}$, we compute its normalized color histogram in CIE Lab color space, denoted by $\chi_{i,l}^{pf_{col}}$, and distribution of lightness $\chi_{i,l}^{pf_{lig}}$. Gabor filter [15] is used to calculate orientation representation statistics $\chi_{i,l}^{pf_{ori}}$ of the region $r_{i,l}$.

Since human visual system is more sensitive to moving objects than still objects, temporal features are also compared between regions at the same segmentation level. Pixel-wise optical flow [16] is used to analyze motion between consecutive frames. Motion distribution of region $r_{i,l}$ is encoded in two descriptors: $\chi_{i,l}^{pf_{fmag}}$ is a normalized distribution of flow magnitude and $\chi_{i,l}^{pf_{fori}}$ is a normalized histogram of flow orientation.

The contrast of each region is measured as the sum of its feature distances to other regions at the same scale level in the segmentation pyramid with different weight factors:

$$S_{CI_{i,l}} = \sum_{pf} w_{pf} \sum_{j \neq i} |r_{j,l}| \, \omega\left(r_{i,l}, r_{j,l}\right) \left\| \chi_{i,l}^{pf} - \chi_{j,l}^{pf} \right\|, \tag{1}$$

where $|r_{j,l}|$ denotes the number of pixels in region $r_{j,l}$. $\left\| \chi_{i,l}^{pf} - \chi_{j,l}^{pf} \right\|$ is the Chi-Square distance [17] between two histograms, $pf \in \{pf_{col}, pf_{lig}, pf_{ori}, pf_{fmag}, pf_{fori}\}$ denotes one of the five features with corresponding weight w_{pf}. In this work, we use the same weights for all features. Regions with more pixels contribute higher contrast weight factors than those containing smaller number of pixels. $\omega\left(r_{i,l}, r_{j,l}\right)$ controls spatial distance influence between two regions $r_{i,l}$ and $r_{j,l}$:

$$\omega\left(r_{i,l}, r_{j,l}\right) = e^{\frac{-D\left(r_{i,l}, r_{j,l}\right)^2}{\sigma^2}},$$

where $D(r_{i,l}, r_{j,l})$ is the Euclidean distance between region centers and parameter σ controls how large the neighbors are. Finally, $S_{CI_{i,l}}$ is normalized to range $[0, 1]$.

Regional Characteristics. In addition to the contrast between regions, we also compute characteristics of each region based on region-based features. Human vision is biased toward specific spatial information of video such as center of the frame or foreground objects, as well as movements of objects over time. Therefore, our region-based features are based on location, objectness, and movement metrics.

Human eye-tracking studies show that human attention favors the center of natural scenes when watching videos [18]. So, pixels close to the screen center could be salient in many cases. Our location feature is defined as:

$$\chi_{i,l}{}^{rf_{loc}} = \frac{1}{|r_{i,l}|} \sum_{j \in r_{i,l}} e^{\frac{-D(p_j, \bar{p})^2}{\sigma^2}},$$

where $|r_{i,l}|$ denotes the number of pixels in region $r_{i,l}$ and $D(p_j, \bar{p})$ is the Euclidean distance from each pixel p_j in the region to the image center $\bar{p}$.

The second characteristic is objectness of regions, which is based on differences of spatial layout of image regions [19]. Object regions are much less connected to image boundaries than background ones. In contrast, a region corresponding to background tends to be heavily connected to image boundary. In order to compute objectness of each region, each segmented image is first built as an undirected weighted graph by connecting all adjacent regions and assigning their weights as the Euclidean distance between their average colors in the CIE-Lab color space. The objectness feature of region $r_{i,l}$ is written as:

$$\chi_{i,l}{}^{rf_{obj}} = \exp\left(-\frac{BndCon^2(r_{i,l})}{2\sigma^2_{BndCo}}\right),$$

where $BndCon(r_{i,l})$ is the boundary connectivity of region $r_{i,l}$, which is calculated as the ratio of the length along the boundary of region $r_{i,l}$ to the square root of its spanning area. The length along the boundary of region $r_{i,l}$ is the sum of the Geodesic distance [19] from it to regions on the image boundary whereas its spanning area is the sum of the Geodesic distances from it to all regions in the image. σ_{BndCo} is a parameter and we set $\sigma_{BndCo} = 1$ like [19].

Moreover, to encode movement of objects, we capture any sudden speed change in motion of regions. Movement of a region is calculated as displacement of its spatial center over time:

$$\chi_{i,l}^{rf_{mov}} = e^{\lambda \Delta(r_{i,l})},$$

where $\Delta(r_{i,l})$ is the Euclidean distance between the centers of region $r_{i,l}$ in two consecutive frames.

The characteristics of the region $r_{i,l}$ are computed as the sum of its attribute values with different weight factors:

$$S_{RC_{i,l}} = \sum_{rf} w_{rf} \chi_{i,l}^{rf}, \tag{2}$$

where $rf \in \{rf_{loc}, rf_{obj}, rf_{mov}\}$ denotes one of the three features, with corresponding weight factor w_{rf}. In this work, we use the same weights for all features. Finally, $S_{RC_{i,l}}$ is normalized to range $[0, 1]$.

Feature Map Combination. Combining the contrast information and the regional characteristics, we obtain initial saliency entities for all segmentation levels separately:

$$S_{i,l} = S_{CI_{i,l}} S_{RC_{i,l}}.$$

(3)

Finally, the saliency entities are linearly normalized to fixed range $[0, 1]$ in order to guarantee that pixel with value 1 is the maxima of saliency.

3.2   Exploiting Motion Information

Differently from still images, video scenes include both spatial information and temporal information, which is considered as motion information of objects in the scenes. In addition, motion information plays an important role for human perception. Therefore, it is necessary to include motion information into the saliency map for video. To calculate motion information, we first use the pixel-wise optical flow proposed by C. Liu [16] to compute motion magnitude of each pixel in a frame, and then exploit distribution of motion magnitude in each region (c.f. Fig. 3).

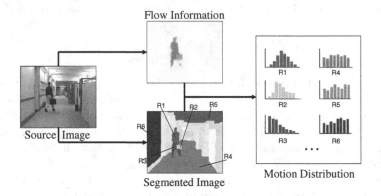

Fig. 3. Motion information calculation.

In a video, it is sometimes hard to distinguish objects from background because every pixel value always changes over time regardless that it belongs to an object or background. Moreover, motion analysis shows that different parts of objects move with various speed and, furthermore, background motion also changes with different speed and direction (c.f. flow information in Fig. 3). This causes fluctuation of object appearances between frames. To reduce this negative effect, saliency entities at each segmentation level at the current frame is combined with neighboring frames, resulting in smoothing saliency values over time. We propose to adaptively use a sliding window in the temporal domain for each region at each frame to capture speed variation by exploiting motion information in the region. After this operation, salient values on contiguous frames become similar, and this generates robust temporal saliency:

$$\tilde{S}_{i,l}^{t} = \frac{1}{\Psi} \sum_{t'=t-\Phi_{i,l}^{t}}^{t} e^{\frac{-D(t,t')^2}{2\Phi_{i,l}^{t}{}^2\sigma^2}} S_{i,l}^{t}, \tag{4}$$

where $S_{i,l}^{t}$ measures saliency entity of region $r_{i,l}$ at frame t, $D(t,t')$ denotes the time difference between two frames, parameter σ controls how large the region at previous frames is. Ψ is the normalization factor of saliency value:

$$\Psi = \sum_{t'=t-\Phi_{i,l}^{t}}^{t} e^{\frac{-D(t,t')^2}{2\Phi_{i,l}^{t}{}^2\sigma^2}},$$

where $\Phi_{i,l}^{t}$ controls the number of participating frames in the operation, expressed as:

$$\Phi_{i,l}^{t} = Me^{-\mu_{i,l}^{t}\frac{\lambda}{\beta_{i,l}^{t}}}, \tag{5}$$

where M and λ are parameters. $\beta_{i,l}^{t} = \frac{\sigma_{i,l}^{t}}{\mu_{i,l}^{t}}$ is the coefficient variation measuring dispersion of motion distribution of each region. $\mu_{i,l}^{t}$ and $\sigma_{i,l}^{t}$ are the mean value and the standard deviation of the motion distribution of region $r_{i,l}$ at frame t.

3.3 Spatial-Temporal Saliency Generation

Normalized hierarchical saliency maps of different scales are combined to create a spatial-temporal saliency map SM by calculating the average over all hierarchical levels:

$$SM_{p}^{t} = \frac{1}{L} \sum_{l=1}^{L} \tilde{S}_{\Omega_{l}(p),l}^{t}, \tag{6}$$

where Ω_l is a function that converts pixel p to the region at scale level l where it belongs. Therefore, all operations are processed pixel-wisely. $\tilde{S}_{\Omega_l(p),l}^{t}$ measures hierarchical saliency value of each pixel generated in the l-th scale of the segmentation pyramid at frame t.

4   Experimental Setup

4.1   Dataset

We used Weizmann human action database [8] and SFU eye-tracking database [9] for all experiments. The Weizmann dataset [8] contains 93 video sequences with static background of nine people performing ten natural actions such as running, walking, jacking, waving, etc. with the ground-truth foreground mask. The SFU dataset [9] contains 12 standard video sequences which have dynamic background and complex scenes with the first and second viewing gaze location data by 15 independent viewers. Fixations of the first viewing in the SFU dataset were used as the ground truth.

4.2   Evaluation Metrics

Precision, Recall, and F-Measure. These metrics are used to evaluate performance of the object location detection at a binarized threshold. Similarly to [20], we used an adaptive threshold for each image, which is determined as twice the mean value of salient values over the entire given image.

The F-measure [20] is the overall performance measure computed by the weighted harmonic of precision and recall: $F_\beta = \frac{(1+\beta^2)Precision \times Recall}{\beta^2 \times Precision + Recall}$. Similarly to [20], we chose $\beta^2 = 0.3$ to weight precision more than recall.

Absolute Correlation Coefficients. The linear Correlation Coefficient (CC) metric [21] focuses on saliency and gaze statistical distributions. To have advantages when comparing average CC from videos, we use Absolute Correlation Coefficient (ACC): $ACC = \left| \frac{\sum_p ((SM(p)-\mu_{SM})(GT(p)-\mu_{GT}))}{\sigma_{SM}\,\sigma_{GT}} \right|$ where SM is the saliency map and GT is the ground truth; $\mu_{SM}, \sigma_{SM}, \mu_{GT}, \sigma_{GT}$ are mean values and standard deviation of SM and GT respectively.

Normalized Scanpath Saliency. The Normalized Scanpath Saliency (NSS) metric [22] focuses on saliency map values at eye gaze positions. This metric quantifies saliency map values at the ground truth locations and normalizes it with saliency variance.

Area Under Curve. In Area Under the Curve (AUC), saliency map is treated as a binary classifier on every pixel where pixels with larger values than a threshold are classified as fixated while the rest of the pixels are classified as non-fixated. To reduce influence of the border cut and the center-bias over AUC, we adopted the shuffled-AUC [23], a standard evaluation method used in many recent works. We used an implementation of the shuffled-AUC metric by Z.Bylinskii [24].

5   Evaluation of the Proposed Method

5.1   Evaluation of Introduction to Regional Characteristics

In a video, each pixel value of each frame always changes over time regardless that it belongs to an object or background. Therefore, contrast information using only pixel-based features cannot effectively highlight objects from dynamic background. However, the combination of regional characteristics, derived from region-based features, and contrast information can overcome this limitation because region-based features reduce fluctuation of pixel values in a region. Therefore, our method effectively predict human attention in videos.

To verify this, we conducted experiments to compare Precision, Recall, F-measure values for salient object detection and ACC, NSS, AUC values for eye fixation obtained from our method (denoted by "with RC") with those without regional characteristics (denoted by "without RC"). Results in Fig. 4 indicates that our method outperforms the others in all metrics.

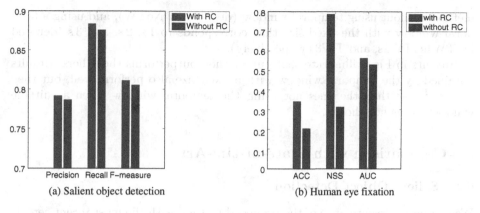

(a) Salient object detection   (b) Human eye fixation

Fig. 4. Regional characteristic evaluation. (a) is experimental results for salient object detection on the Weizmann dataset [8]; (b) is experimental results for human eye fixation on the SFU dataset [9].

5.2 Evaluation of Adaptive Temporal Windows

Although combining saliency values of consecutive frames can have positive effect, the employed window size should depend on motion and background. In contrast to the method using a fixed window size, our method adapts the window size to different motion regions in a video. Therefore, our method efficiently utilizes information from consecutive frames to keep temporal consistency between frames.

To verify this, we performed experiments to compare Precision, Recall, F-measure values for salient object detection and ACC, NSS, AUC values for eye fixation obtained from our method (denoted by ATW) with those from the

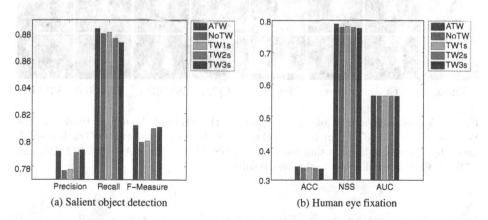

(a) Salient object detection   (b) Human eye fixation

Fig. 5. Adaptive temporal window evaluation. (a) is experimental results for salient object detection on the Weizmann dataset [8]; (b) is experimental results for human eye fixation on the SFU dataset [9].

method without using temporal window (denoted by NoTW), and using a temporal window with the fixed size that corresponds to 1 s, 2 s, and 3 s (denoted by TW1s, TW2s, and TW3s respectively).

Results in Fig. 5 illustrate that our method outperforms the others. Results obtained by the temporal window with a fixed size also perform well, but they can be worse than the ones not using the temporal window when a suitable window size is not chosen.

6   Comparison with State-of-the-Art

6.1   Salient Object Detection

We compared performance of the proposed method with the most recent center-surround contrast based methods using the Weizmann dataset [8]. They are HS [5], LC [25], SAG [26], SO [19], and STS [4]. Among them, LC, SAG, STS are spatial-temporal saliency detection methods, whereas HS and SO are pure spatial methods. We remark that there are some other methods based on the center-surround contrast framework whose results are mostly inferior to the above mentioned methods.

In the first experiment, we used a fixed threshold to binarize saliency maps. In the second experiment, we performed image adaptive binarization of saliency maps. We compared our method with the five methods mentioned above. To evaluate these five methods, we used their publicly available source codes with default configuration set by the authors. Some examples for visual comparison of the methods are shown in Fig. 6, indicating that our method produces the best results on these images.

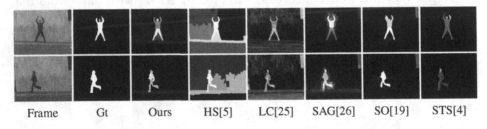

Frame   Gt   Ours   HS[5]   LC[25]   SAG[26]   SO[19]   STS[4]

Fig. 6. Visual comparison of our method to the state-of-the-art methods on the Weizmann dataset [8]. From left to right, original images and ground truth are followed by outputs obtained using our method, HS [5], LC [25], SAG [26], SO [19], and STS [4]. Our method achieves the best results.

Image Binarization by a Fixed Threshold. In this experiment, each saliency map is binarized into a binary mask using a saliency threshold θ (θ is changed from 0 to 1). With each θ, the binalized mask is checked against the

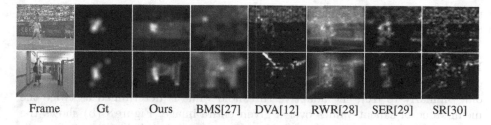

Frame   Gt   Ours   BMS[27]   DVA[12]   RWR[28]   SER[29]   SR[30]

Fig. 7. Visual comparison of our method to the state-of-the-art methods on the SFU dataset [9]. From left to right, original images and ground truth are followed by outputs obtained using our method, BMS [27], DVA [12], RWR [28], SER [10], and SR [29]. Our method achieves the best results.

ground truth to evaluate the accuracy of the salient object detection to compute Precision Recall Curve (PRC) (c.f. Fig. 8 (a)). The PRC is used to evaluate performance of the object location detection because it captures behaviors of both precision and recall under varying thresholds. Therefore, the PRC provides a reliable comparison of how well various saliency maps can highlight salient regions in images.

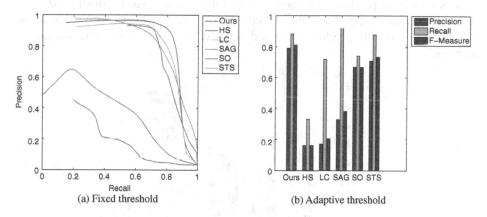

(a) Fixed threshold

(b) Adaptive threshold

Fig. 8. Salient object detection comparison on the Weizmann dataset [8]. (a) is Precision Recall Curves for fixed threshold; (b) is Precision, Recall, and F-Measure for adaptive threshold.

In the PRC, the precision value corresponds to the ratio of salient pixels that are correctly assigned with respect to all the pixels in extracted regions, while the recall value is defined as the percentage of detected salient pixels in relation to the number of salient pixels in the ground truth.gh recall is achieved at the expense of reducing the precision and vice-versa. The results in Fig. 8 (a) show that our method consistently produces saliency maps closer to the ground truth than the others. This is because the precision value of our method is higher than the others at almost each recall value.

Image Adaptive Binarization. In this experiment, an adaptive threshold depending on obtained saliency for each image is used instead of a fixed threshold. Similarly to [20], the adaptive threshold value is determined as twice the mean value of salient values over a given entire image. Figure 8 (b) shows the Precision, Recall, and F-measure values of our method and the other five methods. Our method outperforms the other methods in all three metrics over the Weizmann dataset.

6.2   Eye Fixation Prediction

We compared performance of our proposed method with dynamic saliency detection methods for human fixation such as BMS [27], DVA [12], RWR [28], SER [10], and SR [29] using the SFU dataset. To evaluate these methods, we used their publicly available source codes with default configuration set by the authors. In order to produce eye fixation maps, our saliency maps are blurred by applying Gaussian blur with zero mean and standard deviation σ (we set $\sigma = 7$). Some examples for visual comparison of the methods are shown in Fig. 7, indicating that our method produces the best results on these images. Figure 9 shows the ACC, NSS, and AUC value comparisons of our method with the other methods. As can be seen, our proposed method outperforms the other methods on all metrics.

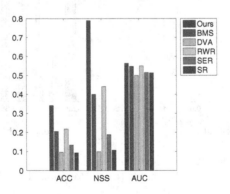

Fig. 9. Eye fixation prediction comparison on the SFU dataset [9], using ACC, NSS, and AUC metrics.

7   Conclusion

In this paper, we present a novel contrast based hierarchical spatial-temporal saliency model for video. Our method effectively integrates pixel-based features and region-based features into a flexible framework so that our method can utilize both static features and temporal features. Saliency values of consecutive frames are combined by an adaptive temporal window to reduce influence of different motion in a scene, thus the proposed method is robust to dynamic scenes. By introducing region-based features and adaptive temporal window, our method effectively incorporate the dynamic nature of scenes into saliency computation. Experimental results show that our method outperforms state-of-the-art methods on two standard benchmark datasets.

A drawback of the proposed method is not using high-level cues, such as semantic features. Our future work will focus on integration of multiple features and semantic knowledge for further improvement.

References

1. Borji, A., Itti, L.: State-of-the-art in visual attention modeling. IEEE Trans. Pattern Anal. Mach. Intell. **35**(1), 185–207 (2013)
2. Judd, T., Ehinger, K., Durand, F., Torralba, A.: Learning to predict where humans look. In: 2009 IEEE 12th International Conference on Computer Vision, pp. 2106–2113. IEEE (2009)
3. Margolin, R., Tal, A., Zelnik-Manor, L.: What makes a patch distinct? In: 2013 IEEE Conference on Computer Vision and Pattern Recognition (CVPR), pp. 1139–1146. IEEE (2013)
4. Zhou, F., Kang, S.B., Cohen, M.: Time-mapping using space-time saliency. In: 2014 IEEE Conference on Computer Vision and Pattern Recognition (CVPR), pp. 3358–3365, June 2014
5. Yan, Q., Xu, L., Shi, J., Jia, J.: Hierarchical saliency detection. In: 2013 IEEE Conference on Computer Vision and Pattern Recognition (CVPR), pp. 1155–1162. IEEE (2013)
6. Yamada, K., Sugano, Y., Okabe, T., Sato, Y., Sugimoto, A., Hiraki, K.: Attention prediction in egocentric video using motion and visual saliency. In: Ho, Y.-S. (ed.) PSIVT 2011, Part I. LNCS, vol. 7087, pp. 277–288. Springer, Heidelberg (2011)
7. Luo, Y., Cheong, L.-F., Cabibihan, J.-J.: Modeling the temporality of saliency. In: Cremers, D., Reid, I., Saito, H., Yang, M.-H. (eds.) ACCV 2014. LNCS, vol. 9005, pp. 205–220. Springer, Heidelberg (2015)
8. Blank, M., Gorelick, L., Shechtman, E., Irani, M., Basri, R.: Actions as space-time shapes. In: Tenth IEEE International Conference on Computer Vision, ICCV 2005, vol. 2, pp. 1395–1402. IEEE (2005)
9. Hadizadeh, H., Enriquez, M.J., Bajic, I.V.: Eye-tracking database for a set of standard video sequences. IEEE Trans. on Image Process. **21**(2), 898–903 (2012)
10. Seo, H.J., Milanfar, P.: Static and space-time visual saliency detection by self-resemblance. J. Vision **9**(12), 15 (2009)
11. Itti, L., Koch, C., Niebur, E.: A model of saliency-based visual attention for rapid scene analysis. IEEE Trans. Pattern Anal. Mach. Intell. **20**(11), 1254–1259 (1998)
12. Hou, X., Zhang, L.: Dynamic visual attention: Searching for coding length increments. In: Advances in Neural Information Processing Systems, pp. 681–688 (2009)
13. Mahadevan, V., Vasconcelos, N.: Spatiotemporal saliency in dynamic scenes. IEEE Trans. Pattern Anal. Mach. Intell. **32**(1), 171–177 (2010)
14. Xiong, C., Xu, C., Corso, J.J.: Streaming hierarchical video segmentation. In: Fitzgibbon, A., Lazebnik, S., Perona, P., Sato, Y., Schmid, C. (eds.) ECCV 2012, Part VI. LNCS, vol. 7577, pp. 626–639. Springer, Heidelberg (2012)

15. Namuduri, K., Mehrotra, R., Ranganathan, N.: Edge detection models based on gabor filters. In: Proceedings of 11th IAPR International Conference on Pattern Recognition, 1992. Vol. III. Conference C: Image, Speech and Signal Analysis, pp. 729–732, August 1992

16. Liu, C.: Beyond Pixels: Exploring New Representations and Applications for Motion Analysis. MIT, Cambridge (2009)

17. Pele, O., Werman, M.: The quadratic-chi histogram distance family. In: Daniilidis, K., Maragos, P., Paragios, N. (eds.) ECCV 2010, Part II. LNCS, vol. 6312, pp. 749–762. Springer, Heidelberg (2010)

18. Tseng, P.H., Carmi, R., Cameron, I.G., Munoz, D.P., Itti, L.: Quantifying center bias of observers in free viewing of dynamic natural scenes. J. Vision 9(7), 4 (2009)

19. Zhu, W., Liang, S., Wei, Y., Sun, J.: Saliency optimization from robust background detection. In: 2014 IEEE Conference on Computer Vision and Pattern Recognition (CVPR), pp. 2814–2821. IEEE (2014)

20. Achanta, R., Hemami, S., Estrada, F., Susstrunk, S.: Frequency-tuned salient region detection. In: IEEE Conference on Computer Vision and Pattern Recognition CVPR 2009, pp. 1597–1604. IEEE (2009)

21. Toet, A.: Computational versus psychophysical bottom-up image saliency: a comparative evaluation study. IEEE Trans. Pattern Anal. Mach. Intell. 33(11), 2131–2146 (2011)

22. Peters, R.J., Iyer, A., Itti, L., Koch, C.: Components of bottom-up gaze allocation in natural images. Vision Res. 45(18), 2397–2416 (2005)

23. Borji, A., Sihite, D.N., Itti, L.: Quantitative analysis of human-model agreement in visual saliency modeling: a comparative study. IEEE Trans. Image Process. 22(1), 55–69 (2013)

24. Bylinskii, Z., Judd, T., Borji, A., Itti, L., Durand, F., Oliva, A., Torralba, A.: Mit saliency benchmark. http://saliency.mit.edu/

25. Zhai, Y., Shah, M.: Visual attention detection in video sequences using spatiotemporal cues. In: Proceedings of the 14th Annual ACM International Conference on Multimedia. pp. 815–824. ACM (2006)

26. Wang, W., Shen, J., Porikli, F.: Saliency-aware geodesic video object segmentation. In: Proceedings of IEEE CVPR (2015)

27. Zhang, J., Sclaroff, S.: Saliency detection: a Boolean map approach. In: 2013 IEEE International Conference on Computer Vision (ICCV), pp. 153–160. IEEE (2013)

28. Kim, H., Kim, Y., Sim, J.Y., Kim, C.S.: Spatiotemporal saliency detection for video sequences based on random walk with restart. IEEE Trans. Image Process. 24(8), 2552–2564 (2015)

29. Hou, X., Zhang, L.: Saliency detection: a spectral residual approach. In: IEEE Conference on Computer Vision and Pattern Recognition CVPR 2007, pp. 1–8. IEEE (2007)

Pattern Recognition

Binary Descriptor Based on Heat Diffusion for Non-rigid Shape Analysis

Xupeng Wang[1,3]([✉]), Ferdous Sohel[2], Mohammed Bennamoun[3], and Hang Lei[1]

[1] School of Information and Software Engineering,
University of Electronic Science and Technology of China, Chengdu, China
201211220104@std.uestc.edu.cn, hlei@uestc.edu.cn
[2] School of Engineering and Information Technology,
Murdoch University, Perth, Australia
F.Sohel@murdoch.edu.au
[3] School of Computer Science and Software Engineering,
The University of Western Australia, Perth, Australia
mohammed.bennamoun@uwa.edu.au

Abstract. This paper presents an efficient feature point descriptor for non-rigid shape analysis. The descriptor is developed based on the properties of the heat diffusion process on a shape. We use, for the first time, the Heat Kernel Signature of a particular time scale to define the scalar field on a manifold. Then, motivated by the successful use of a local reference frame for rigid shape analysis, we construct a repetitive local polar coordinate system, which is invariant under isometric deformations. Finally, a binary descriptor is derived by comparing the intensities of the neighboring points for each feature point. We show that the descriptor is highly discriminative and can be computed simply using 'intensity comparisons' on a shape. Furthermore, its similarity can be evaluated using the Hamming distance, which is very efficient to compute compared with the commonly used L_2 norm. Our experiments demonstrate a superior performance compared to existing techniques on the standard benchmark TOSCA.

Keywords: Non-rigid shape analysis · Local descriptor · Heat diffusion · Binary descriptor

1 Introduction

In 3D shape analysis, the extraction of feature descriptors *aka* local shape descriptors is a fundamental step [18]. Early research on feature based methods mainly focused on rigid shape analysis [10,11]. A large number of descriptors have been developed, such as the local surface patch [9], spin image [14] and rotation projection statistics [12]. The development of non-rigid descriptors is more

This research is supported by China Scholarship Council (CSC No.201406070059) and Australian Research Council grants (DE120102960, DP150100294 and DP150104251).

© Springer International Publishing Switzerland 2016
T. Bräunl et al. (Eds.): PSIVT 2015, LNCS 9431, pp. 751–761, 2016.
DOI: 10.1007/978-3-319-29451-3_59

challenging due to the large degrees of freedom resulting from the local deformations. Several methods have been proposed, such as the geodesic mapping [13] and conformal factors [17]. However, these methods are sensitive to the topological noise and the geometric noise, which are inevitable in these applications. In the recent years, an intrinsic geometric property known as diffusion geometry has become popular and achieves the best performance [2,5,15,18,20,22,23,27]. It is based on the spectral decomposition of the Laplace-Beltrami operator associated with a shape, and uses eigenvalues and eigenvectors to construct the diffusion distance, which provides an intuitive interpretation of the shape properties in terms of spatial frequency [15]. This work falls in the category of diffusion geometric framework.

The Local Binary Descriptor (LBD) has attracted a significant interest in the analysis of 2D images due to its computational simplicity and discriminative power [8,28]. However, little efforts have been made to extend the LBD framework to the field of 3D shape analysis [26]. The key to the development of an LBD for non-rigid shapes is the construction of a repetitive Local Reference Frame (LRF), because the LBD requires an intrinsic order for computation. Several spatial structures have been proposed to facilitate feature descriptors for non-rigid shape analysis. In [29], an LRF is constructed using the surface normal and two vectors which lie on the tangent plane (a common method used for rigid shape descriptors). This LRF is not invariant under non-rigid transformations, because the relative positions of the points will change. In [7], a 'multiple circular geodesic pathways' is defined on the local surface using a fixed number of increasing geodesic distances. Within each circle, points are sampled in a clockwise direction with respect to the surface normal. In [15], the local surface is charted by shooting geodesic outwards from the feature point to form a polar coordinate system, where the 'angle' is defined as tantamount to the geodesic shooting direction, and 'radius' as the geodesic distance. However, neither of the methods solves the problem of orientation ambiguity during the construction of the LRF. In [26], the local surface is modeled as a structure of ordered and concentric rings around the central facet based on the categorization of the facets on its contour. Since it is fully dependent on the structure of the mesh, the LRF is not intrinsic and robust.

In this paper, we develop a local descriptor for non-rigid shape analysis, called Heat Diffusion based Local Binary Descriptor (HD-LBD). There are two main contributions in this paper. **First**, we construct a new repetitive Local Polar Coordinate System (LPCS) which is invariant under isometric transformations. **Second**, we develop a binary descriptor facilitated with the LPCS for non-rigid shape analysis. Experiments were performed to demonstrate the effectiveness of the proposed method.

2   Background

Diffusion geometry is one of the most successful approaches for non-rigid shape analysis. Reuter *et al.* [20] exploited the Laplace-Beltrami spectra as an intrinsic shape descriptor called Shape-DNA. Rustamov *et al.* proposed the Global Point Signature (GPS) [22] by associating each point with an l^2 sequence formed by the eigenfunctions and the eigenvalues of the Laplacian. Sun *et al.* [23] developed the Heat Kernel Signature (HKS) based on the analysis of heat diffusion process. Kokkinos *et al.* [5] introduced the Scale Invariant Heat Kernel Signature (SI-HKS) using Fourier transform. Kokkinos *et al.* [15] developed the Intrinsic Shape Context (ISC) by aggregating HKS of the feature point's local neighborhood to further improve its descriptiveness. In [2], the Wave Kernel Signature (WKS) was proposed based on a different physical model, in which one evaluated the probability of a quantum particle with a certain energy distribution to be located at a point. Litman *et al.* [18] and Windheuser *et al.* [27] used machine learning techniques to learn the spectral descriptor for a specific task (e.g. human recognition). Our work follows on the idea of diffusion geometry. Unlike [5,15,23], we use the HKS of a particular scale to define the scalar field on a manifold.

A large amount of LBDs exist in the field of 2D image analysis. Most of the comparison-based descriptors can be considered to be variants of the local binary pattern proposed in [19], where the intensities of some predefined pairs of neighboring pixels are compared to form a binary string for a feature point. In Binary Robust Independent Elementary Feature (BRIEF) [6], Binary Robust Invariant Scalable Key-point (BRISK) [16], Oriented FAST and Rotated BRIEF (ORB) [21] and Fast Retina Key-point (FREAK) [1], various ways of pixel pairs sampling were proposed. Ordinal Spatial Intensity Distribution (OSID) [24] and the Local Intensity Order Pattern (LIOP) [25] incorporated spatial information to improve the LBD's discriminative ability. The works in [8,30] proposed to use the full ranking of a set of pixels as a local descriptor, which is expected to encode the complete comparative information among pixels. The recent work in [26] proposed a framework to compute the local binary-like-patterns directly on a triangular-mesh. However, their work is specially developed for shapes with photometric and geometric information. To the best of our knowledge, we are the first to develop a local binary descriptor for non-rigid shape analysis.

3 Proposed Method

Suppose we are given a discrete representation of shape as a triangular mesh (V, E, T) with n_V vertices $\{v_1, \ldots, v_{n_V}\}$, n_E edges $\{(v_{i_1}, v_{j_1}), \ldots, (v_{i_{n_E}}, v_{j_{n_E}})\}$ and n_T faces $\{(v_{i_1}, v_{j_1}, v_{k_1}), \ldots, (v_{i_{n_T}}, v_{j_{n_T}}, v_{k_{n_T}})\}$. Our goal is to derive a local shape signature that is invariant under isometric deformations.

An illustrative example of the proposed binary descriptor is given in Fig. 1. Basically our *Heat Diffusion based Local Binary Descriptor* (HD-LBD) is an extension from 2D images to 3D shapes. Therefore, the first step is the definition of scalar functions on manifolds [29] (see Sect. 3.1). Based on the definition of the scalar fields, an intrinsic Local Polar Coordinate System (LPCS) is constructed around the feature point (see Sect. 3.2 for details). Finally, in Sect. 3.3, we aggregate the information of the neighboring surface to form the binary string.

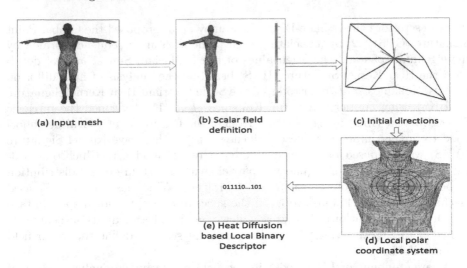

Fig. 1. Block diagram of the Local Heat Diffusion Binary descriptor.

3.1   Scalar Field Definition

We model shapes as Riemannian manifolds M (possibly with boundary) embedded in R^3. Let g be the scalar field defined on M. The real valued function g represents the geometric or photometric information of the shapes. In this paper, we consider the heat diffusion property, explained below.

The heat diffusion process over M is governed by the heat equation,

$$(\triangle_M + \frac{\partial}{\partial t})u(v,t) = 0, \tag{1}$$

where $\triangle_M$ denotes the positive semi-definite Laplace-Beltrami operator of M, a Riemannian equivalent of the Laplacian. The solution $u(v,t)$ describes the amount of heat on the manifold at point v in time t with an initial condition $u(v,0)$. Since M is compact, $u(v,t) = \int_M^\infty h_t(v,v')u(v')dv'$. $h_t(v,v')$ is called heat kernel, and can be thought of as the amount of heat transferred from v to v' in time t given a unit heat source at v. According to the spectral decomposition theorem, the heat kernel can be presented as

$$h_t(v,v') = \sum_{i \geq 1} e^{-\lambda_i t} \Phi_i(v)\Phi_i(v'), \tag{2}$$

where λ_i and Φ_i are the ith eigenvalues and corresponding eigenfunctions of the Laplace-Beltrami operator. Its restriction to the temporal domain results to

$$h_t(v) = \sum_{i \geq 1} e^{-\lambda_i t} \Phi_i^2(v), \tag{3}$$

known as the heat kernel signature. This signature is not only concise and commensurable, but it is still informative and invariant to isometric deformations [23].

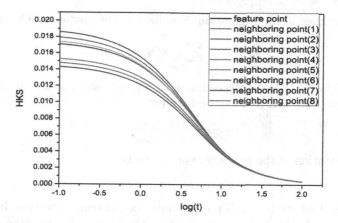

Fig. 2. HKS as a function of t for a feature point and its neighboring points in Fig. 1 (c). A small t separates these points, in which case HKS reflects the local properties of the surface. As t increases, the values of HKS are almost the same, because HKS captures the global structure of a larger neighborhood.

More importantly, the descriptor captures the geometric information of the local surface over a number of scales (multi-scale), which is determined by the time parameter t, as shown in Fig. 2. Particularly, for small values of t, it is related to the manifold curvature according to

$$h_t(v) = \frac{1}{4\pi t} + \frac{K(v)}{12\pi} + \ominus(t), \qquad (4)$$

where $K(v)$ denotes the Gaussian curvature at point v.

Therefore, we adopt HKS over a small t to define the scalar field, which is supposed to reflect the intrinsic property of the local surface around the point v.

3.2 Intrinsic Local Reference Frame

Given a feature point v and a support radius r (defined using the geodesic metric), a local surface M' is cropped from the mesh M. $V_N = \{v_{i1}, \ldots, v_{ik}\}$ are the points lying on M', and $N_1(v)$ is the set of directly connected vertices to v, called *1-ring* neighborhood. The construction of the Local Polar Coordinate System (LPCS) involves two steps: first to find the reference direction and then to chart the surface (see below for details).

Reference Direction. The first and the key step to construct the LPCS is to find its reference direction. Its accuracy directly determines the repeatability of the coordinate system. We adopt the method of intensity centroid [16], which is used to describe the orientation of a key point in the image domain. This method assumes that a corner's intensity is the offset from its centroid, and this vector can be used as an orientation. Specifically, the moments of a patch P are defined as

$$m_{pq} = \sum_{(x_i,y_i) \subseteq P} x_i^p y_i^q I(x_i, y_i), \tag{5}$$

where (x, y) is the cartesian coordinate of a pixel, and I is its intensity. With these moments, the centroid can be found at

$$c = (\frac{m_{10}}{m_{00}}, \frac{m_{01}}{m_{00}}). \tag{6}$$

The orientation of the patch is assumed to be

$$\theta = atan2(m_{01}, m_{10}) \tag{7}$$

In our method, we use $N_1(v)$ to compute the reference direction. In our case, the intensities of the pixels are replaced by the values of $h_t(v)$ (the previously defined scalar function on the shape). The coordinates of $N_1(v)$ are approximated as follows: **first**, we map v's *1-ring* triangles onto the plane partitioning it into several segments with angle ratios remained; **then** a rectangular coordinate system is constructed around the feature point centred at v. Thus, coordinates of all vertexes belonging to $N_1(v)$ are obtained.

Finally, we derive the reference direction of the local polar coordinate system (the face T_i on which the reference direction lies and the deviation angle θ_i from the triangle edge), denoted as R on the *1-ring* triangles and R' on the mapped plane.

Surface Charting. A mesh can be viewed as a piece-wise planar approximation of the underlying smooth surface. Using the standard unfolding procedure in [3], the local surface made up of triangles can be transformed into an image patch that is unevenly sampled. Similar to [15], the construction of the local polar coordinate system consists of 2 steps: directions initialization and propagation. The initial directions are established by first mapping the *1-ring* triangles onto the plane, partitioning the plane into several segments of equal angles with respect to the reference direction, and finally mapping back to the mesh. The order of the directions can be clockwise or counter-clockwise. In order to resolve ambiguities, we adopt a simple yet practical solution similar to [26], that the direction on the mapped plane nearest to the reference frame is chosen as the next. In this way, all the directions (Fig. 1(c)) are ordered in a uniform way. Afterwards, the initial directions are propagated outwards from *1-ring* (using the standard unfolding procedure [3]) until they reach the boundary of the 'image patch' defined by the radius r. Thus, the LPCS (Fig. 1(d)) is constructed, where the 'reference direction' is R and its extension, 'angle' is the angle between the geodesic shooting direction and R, and the 'radius' is the geodesic distance from v.

4   Local Binary Descriptor

With the previously defined scalar function (Sect. 3.1) and the constructed local polar coordinate system (Sect. 3.2), the local surface M' around vertex v can be regarded as an image patch, on which the local binary descriptor is defined. In the case of 2D image analysis, a number of ways are used to extract point pairs for the construction of a local binary descriptor, such as [1,6,16,21]. In our method, we propose the bit vector (defined in Eq. 9) based on all pairwise intensity comparisons, which turned out to be highly discriminative (Sect. 5.3).

To be specific, we define a test τ of a point pair $N_i(p_{i1}, p_{i2})$ on the local surface M' as

$$\tau(h_t; p_{i1}, p_{i2}) = \begin{cases} 1 \text{ if } h_t(p_{i1}) < h_t(p_{i2}) \\ 0 \text{ otherwise} \end{cases} \tag{8}$$

where $h_t(p_i)$ is the value of heat kernel signature with parameter t at $p_i = (\rho_i, \theta_i)$.

The test in Eq. 8 considers only the information at a single point p_i in the neighborhood of v, and is therefore quite noise-sensitive. In order to increase the stability and repeatability of the descriptor, we include all the points falling into each bin of the local polar coordinate system, and use the average of their intensities as a unit for test (the same approach used in [28]).

The choice of the set of location pairs $N_i(p_{i1}, p_{i2})$ uniquely defines a set of binary tests. In our method, we propose a bit string (binary) descriptor with dimension n_d equal to the cardinality of $N_i(p_{i1}, p_{i2})$ as

$$f_{n_d}(p) = \sum_{1<=i<=n_d} 2^{i-1} \tau(h_t; p_{i1}, p_{i2}). \tag{9}$$

5   Experiments

The experiments that we carried out have three main goals. **First**, we examined the repetitiveness of the proposed local reference frame. **Second**, we compared our proposed descriptor with other state-of-the-art techniques to show its effectiveness. **Finally**, we examined the effect of the parameters on the performance of the descriptor.

5.1   Dataset

The performance of our binary descriptor was evaluated on the TOSCA dataset [4]. We followed the experimental protocol in [18] using human shapes (12 female shapes in class 'vitoria', and 2 different male figures containing 7 and 20 poses in class 'david' and 'michael' respectively). In each class, an extrinsically symmetric 'null' shape undergoes near-isometric deformations. Objects within the same class have the same triangulation and an equal number of vertices numbered in a compatible way, which can be used as a per-vertex ground truth correspondence. A typical number of vertices on each shape is about 50000. In order to reduce the computational load and storage complexity, all the shapes were downsampled to 10000 vertices, maintaining compatible triangulations and ground-truth correspondences. We used the finite elements scheme in [20] to obtain the first 400 eigenvalues and eigenvectors of the Laplace-Beltrami operator on each shape. Then, the heat kernel signature was computed in a particular scale according to Fig. 2.

Table 1. The percentage of reference frames lying in the same face computed on 3 different shape classes.

Shape class \\ t	$t=0.1$	$t=1$	$t=10$
David*	0.8423	0.8388	0.8728
Michael*	0.8554	0.8528	0.8803
Victoria*	0.8184	0.8221	0.8446

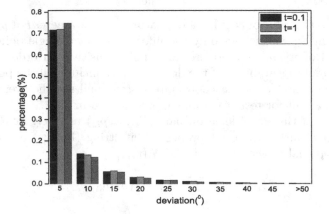

Fig. 3. Deviations of the reference direction for two corresponding points.

5.2 Performance of the Local Polar Coordinate System

To assess the uniqueness of the LPCS, we measured the repetitiveness of its key component - the reference frame (because it determines the initial directions, and the coordinate system is the propagations of initial directions across adjoint triangles in a standard unfolding way). The performance is evaluated in two aspects: the percentage of reference frames lying in the same face, and if so the errors. We randomly sampled 1000 points on the 'null shape', and extracted the corresponding points within each class. The reference directions were computed and compared for each points. According to Sect. 3.1, we choose small t for the computation. The results are summarised in Table 1 and Fig. 3 respectively. When $t = 10$, it achieved the best performance, which we choose to compute the scalar field in the rest of the experiments.

5.3 Performance of the Binary Descriptor

We used a quantitative criteria to evaluate the performance of the descriptor, called Cumulative Match Characteristic (CMC). The CMC curve evaluates the probability of finding the correct match within the first k best matches. The hit rate at k is calculated by sorting all of the distances in ascending order, and calculating the fraction of correct match. We first extracted 500 furthest point

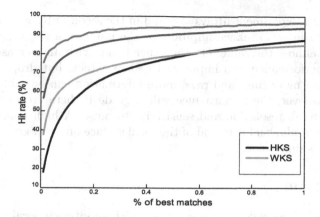

Fig. 4. CMC curves of different descriptors on the TOSCA dataset.

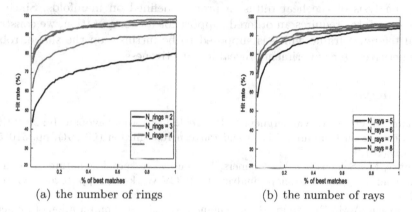

(a) the number of rings   (b) the number of rays

Fig. 5. Influence of parameter selection on the descriptor's performance

samples from the null shapes using the geodesic metric, and then found corresponding points on the deformed shapes. We set rad = 2 ('rad' is the geodesic
distance) between rings, 5 rings and 8 rays respectively, and finally compared
with the method in [18] using the code made available by the authors. From Fig. 4
we can observe that, our proposed descriptor greatly improves the performance
especially at the first few shoots.

5.4   Parameter Selection

Our descriptor has three free parameters: the number of rings/rays and the
geodesic distance between rings (rad), which determine the total area of each
bin in the Local Polar Coordinate System. Here, we set rad = 2. We simulated
various parameters to study the effect of these parameters on the descriptor's
performance. The performance evaluations are shown in Fig. 5 with varying numbers of rings (nRings = 2, 3, 4, 5 and 6) and rays (nRays = 5, 6, 7, 8 and 9),

while in the first experiment nRays = 8 and in the second nRings = 4. It can be observed that the performance improves as the number of rings increases, and then remains almost the same. On the other hand, with an increasing number of rays, the performance also improves to some extent, but drops afterwards. In general, with more rings and rays, more information can be captured by the descriptor. However, the performance will degrade if there are too many rays due to a low mesh resolution and sensitivity to noise. A high number of rings will include redundant information of the local surface and will greatly increases the descriptor's dimension.

6   Conclusion

We introduced a binary descriptor equipped with an intrinsic local polar coordinate system to the field of non-rigid shapes. The descriptor is developed based on the analysis of the heat diffusion process defined on manifolds. Since the binary descriptor requires an ordered support for its computation, we construct a local reference frame which is supposed to be intrinsic on the shape, robust and repetitive. Our experiments reveal its effectiveness.

References

1. Alahi, A., Ortiz, R., Vandergheynst, P.: Freak: fast retina keypoint. In: 2012 IEEE Conference on Computer Vision and Pattern Recognition (CVPR), pp. 510–517. IEEE (2012)
2. Aubry, M., Schlickewei, U., Cremers, D.: The wave kernel signature: a quantum mechanical approach to shape analysis. In: ICCV Workshops, pp. 1626–1633. IEEE (2011)
3. Bronstein, A.M., Bronstein, M.M., Kimmel, R.: Efficient computation of isometry-invariant distances between surfaces. SIAM J. Sci. Comput. **28**(5), 1812–1836 (2006)
4. Bronstein, A.M., Bronstein, M.M., Kimmel, R.: Numerical Geometry of Non-rigid Shapes. Springer Science & Business Media, Berlin (2008)
5. Bronstein, M.M., Kokkinos, I.: Scale-invariant heat kernel signatures for non-rigid shape recognition. In: CVPR, pp. 1704–1711. IEEE (2010)
6. Strecha, C., Fua, P., Lepetit, V., Calonder, M.: BRIEF: binary robust independent elementary features. In: Daniilidis, K., Maragos, P., Paragios, N. (eds.) ECCV 2010, Part IV. LNCS, vol. 6314, pp. 778–792. Springer, Heidelberg (2010)
7. Castellani, U., Cristani, M., Murino, V.: Statistical 3D shape analysis by local generative descriptors. IEEE Trans. Pattern Anal. Mach. Intell. **33**(12), 2555–2560 (2011)
8. Chan, C.H., Yan, F., Kittler, J., Mikolajczyk, K.: Full ranking as local descriptor for visual recognition: a comparison of distance metrics on s_n. Pattern Recogn. **48**(4), 1328–1336 (2015)
9. Chen, H., Bhanu, B.: 3D free-form object recognition in range images using local surface patches. Pattern Recogn. Lett. **28**(10), 1252–1262 (2007)
10. Guo, Y., Bennamoun, M., Sohel, F., Lu, M., Wan, J.: 3D object recognition in cluttered scenes with local surface features: a survey. IEEE Trans. Pattern Anal. Mach. Intell. **36**(11), 2270–2287 (2014)

11. Guo, Y., Bennamoun, M., Sohel, F., Lu, M., Wan, J., Kwok, N.M.: A comprehensive performance evaluation of 3D local feature descriptors. Int. J. Comput. Vis. 1–24 (2015)

12. Guo, Y., Sohel, F., Bennamoun, M., Lu, M., Wan, J.: Rotational projection statistics for 3D local surface description and object recognition. Int. J. Comput. Vis. **105**(1), 63–86 (2013)

13. Hamza, A.B., Krim, H.: Geodesic object representation and recognition. In: Nyström, I., Sanniti di Baja, G., Svensson, S. (eds.) DGCI 2003. LNCS, vol. 2886, pp. 378–387. Springer, Heidelberg (2003)

14. Johnson, A.E., Hebert, M.: Using spin images for efficient object recognition in cluttered 3D scenes. IEEE Trans. Pattern Anal. Mach. Intell. **21**(5), 433–449 (1999)

15. Kokkinos, I., Bronstein, M.M., Litman, R., Bronstein, A.M.: Intrinsic shape context descriptors for deformable shapes. In: CVPR, pp. 159–166. IEEE (2012)

16. Leutenegger, S., Chli, M., Siegwart, R.Y.: Brisk: binary robust invariant scalable keypoints. In: ICCV, pp. 2548–2555. IEEE (2011)

17. Lipman, Y., Funkhouser, T.: Möbius voting for surface correspondence. In: ACM Transactions on Graphics (TOG), vol. 28, p. 72. ACM (2009)

18. Litman, R., Bronstein, A.M.: Learning spectral descriptors for deformable shape correspondence. IEEE Trans. Pattern Anal. Mach. Intell. **36**(1), 171–180 (2014)

19. Ojala, T., Pietikäinen, M., Harwood, D.: A comparative study of texture measures with classification based on featured distributions. Pattern Recogn. **29**(1), 51–59 (1996)

20. Reuter, M., Wolter, F.-E., Shenton, M., Niethammer, M.: Laplace-beltrami eigenvalues and topological features of eigenfunctions for statistical shape analysis. Comput.-Aided Des. **41**(10), 739–755 (2009)

21. Rublee, E., Rabaud, V., Konolige, K., Bradski, G.: Orb: an efficient alternative to sift or surf. In: ICCV, pp. 2564–2571. IEEE (2011)

22. Rustamov, R.M.: Laplace-beltrami eigenfunctions for deformation invariant shape representation. In: Proceedings of the Fifth Eurographics Symposium on Geometry Processing, pp. 225–233. Eurographics Association (2007)

23. Sun, J., Ovsjanikov, M., Guibas, L.: A concise and provably informative multi-scale signature based on heat diffusion. In: Computer Graphics Forum, vol. 28, pp. 1383–1392. Wiley Online Library (2009)

24. Tang, F., Lim, S.H., Chang, N.L., Tao, H.: A novel feature descriptor invariant to complex brightness changes. In: IEEE Conference on Computer Vision and Pattern Recognition, CVPR 2009, pp. 2631–2638. IEEE (2009)

25. Wang, Z., Fan, B., Wu, F.: Local intensity order pattern for feature description. In: 2011 IEEE International Conference on Computer Vision (ICCV), pp. 603–610. IEEE (2011)

26. Werghi, N., Berretti, S., Del Bimbo, A.: The mesh-lbp: a framework for extracting local binary patterns from discrete manifolds (2015)

27. Windheuser, T., Vestner, M., Rodola, E., Triebel, R., Cremers, D.: Optimal intrinsic descriptors for non-rigid shape analysis. In: BMVC (2014)

28. Yang, X., Cheng, K.-T.: Local difference binary for ultrafast and distinctive feature description. IEEE Trans. Pattern Anal. Mach. Intell. **36**(1), 188–194 (2014)

29. Zaharescu, A., Boyer, E., Horaud, R.: Keypoints and local descriptors of scalar functions on 2D manifolds. Int. J. Comput. Vis. **100**(1), 78–98 (2012)

30. Ziegler, A., Christiansen, E., Kriegman, D., Belongie, S.J.: Locally uniform comparison image descriptor. In: Advances in Neural Information Processing Systems, pp. 1–9 (2012)

Table Detection from Slide Images

Xiaoyin Che$^{(\boxtimes)}$, Haojin Yang, and Christoph Meinel

Hasso Plattner Institute, University of Potsdam,
Prof.-Dr.-Helmert-Str. 2-3, 14482 Potsdam, Germany
{xiaoyin.che,haojin.yang,christoph.meinel}@hpi.de

Abstract. In this paper we propose a solution to detect tables from slide images. Presentation slides are one type of document with growing importance. But the layout difference between slides and traditional documents makes many existing table detection methods less effective on slides. The proposed solution works with both high-resolution slide images from digital files and low-resolution slide screenshots from videos. By taking OCR (*Optical Character Recognition*) as initial step, a heuristic analysis on page layout focuses not only on the table structure but also the textual content. The evaluation result shows that the proposed solution achieves an approximate accuracy of 80 %. It is way better than the open-source academic solution Tesseract and also outperforms the commercial software ABBYY FineReader, which is supposed to be one of the best table detection tools.

Keywords: Table detection · Slide image · Table structure

1 Introduction

Table detection is a popular research topic for years. The demand of table detection for numerous of documents, which are stored in libraries, digital archives or on the web, drives the research efforts ahead. But most of these efforts are designed for traditional portrait-oriented, text-dense and book-like documents, which omits one type of frequently used digital document with growing importance in this digitalized new world, the slides.

Presentation slides are widely used in many occasions. The content of slides is vivid, compact and directly focusing on the key points. Therefore "in many organizations, slides also serve a purpose as documentation of information after the presentation has occurred" [1], and special digital library for slides has also been designed [2]. Besides, there are also public slide hosting websites online, such as SlideShare.net, which consists of more than 15 million uploads and is among the top 120 most-visited websites in the world[1]. Furthermore, in the context of education, this never-out-of-date topic, slides play an even more important role. Although whether computer-generated slides are effective in improving the learning outcomes is still under discussion, it is already the basic fact that slides

---

[1] http://www.slideshare.net/about.

© Springer International Publishing Switzerland 2016
T. Bräunl et al. (Eds.): PSIVT 2015, LNCS 9431, pp. 762–774, 2016.
DOI: 10.1007/978-3-319-29451-3_60

have occupied the front of the classroom nowadays [3,4]. With the development of distance learning, especially the wave of MOOC (*Massive Open Online Course*), huge amount of slides are created and uploaded to the internet as supplementary materials to or being included in the lecture videos everyday. Indexing the tables detected within slides could be helpful in both document retrieval and distance learning contexts.

Unfortunately, the slide layout is very diverse and quite different with traditional documents, which makes lots of existing table detection methods less effective. Thus, we propose a solution to detect table from slide images. The input could be either high-resolution slide images transformed directly from digital files, e.g. PPT or PDF, or the screenshots derived from lecture video with comparatively low-resolution. By taking OCR as initial step, the proposed solution will detect rows and columns, locate the potential table areas and then confirm them by exploring both table structure and textual content.

The rest of the paper is organized as follow: Sect. 2 will introduce the related works and why slide is special, Sects. 3–5 will illustrate three main technical procedures of proposed solution respectively and then come the evaluation and conclusion.

2   Related Works

The input of an academic table detection approach could be either born-digital PDF files or scanned document images. With the former a solution can extract metadata from the digital files and then do the layout analysis by them [5–7]. With the latter there are different technical solutions, among which ruling line detection [8–10] and whitespace analysis [11,12] are most popular.

In 2013 a table detection competition was held [13], which enabled all the approaches with either of the above inputs to participate. In addition with 7 academic approaches, the organizer also tested 4 commercial softwares, and the best performer was commercial software ABBYY FineReader 11 with the general accuracy over 98 %. Due to the result analysis, the organizer also reported two factors which caused difficulty for most of the approaches: lack of ruling lines and small tables with fewer than five rows. Unfortunately, they are quite common for slide layout, just as Fig. 1(a, b)[2].

There are more specialties in slide layout which may cause problems for table detection effort, such as dark background with light text, diagrams with lines and annotations, sparse but well-aligned 2-columns layout, etc. By applying the updated version of the best performer, ABBYY FineReader 12, on these example slide images, the table in Fig. 1(b) is missed and false positive detections are found in Fig. 1(c, d). Therefore, we believe a table detection method suitable for slides is highly desirable.

---

[2] The copyright belong to original slide authors or institutions: (a) Mr. William Cockshott, (b) Mr. Avi Pipada, (c) Royal Philips Electronics, (d) Ms. Tamara Bergkamp.

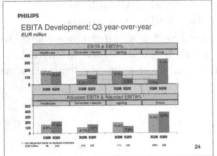
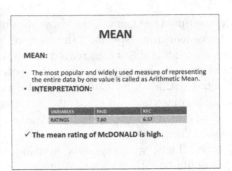
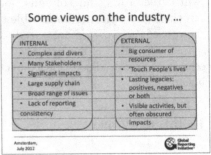

(a) Table without ruling lines

(b) Table with colorful backround and only few cells, missed by FineReader

(c) False positively detected table from a diagram by FineReader

(d) False positively detected table from a 2-columns layout slide by FineReader

Fig. 1. The challenges of detecting table from slides

In recent years, some research works also aim for untraditional document layout. Li et al. [14] proposed an approach for particular business forms by recognizing pre-defined header keywords. Ghanmi and Belaid [15] developed a solution for handwritten chemistry document with conditional random fields. And Seo et al. [16] attempted to detect tables from distorted camera-based document image by locating the junctions, which is still relying on ruling lines.

But none of above is suitable for slides. However, the idea of some earlier approaches based on text bounding box clustering [17,18] could be more inspirational for us. After considering all possibilities, we intend to eliminate all the "shortcuts" and go back to the definition of table: a table is a means of arranging data in rows and columns. To seek row and column structures in slide images will be our initial step.

3   Detection of Rows and Columns

Rows and columns are the indispensable elements of a table. Their existence distinguishes a table from other components in a document, such as a paragraph or a diagram. Therefore, searching and confirming the rows and columns is the premier step of our proposed solution.

After the OCR process, all the textual data within the slide image are stored in text-lines, which include the textual content and the location parameters. Based on them, a virtual bounding box can be created for each text-line recognized, as shown in Fig. 2(a), and then a slide can be simplified as a bunch of such text-lines and a blank background. As a result, the task becomes to judge whether two text-lines, or we say, two bounding boxes locate in a same row or column.

Theoretically it is quite easy to confirm rows. The only requirement is to have two text-lines horizontally locating in a same line. But practically the bounding boxes created for words "Glory" and "name", even with same font, size and actually locating in a same line, may have different heights, and the words "Time" and "map" might even appear interlaced, because of the shapes of letters. In addition with unavoidable and unpredictable OCR errors, a compromised judging mechanism is applied, which requires at least 3/4 of two text-lines vertically overlapp and one cannot be twice the height of the other, or more.

Searching columns is more complicated, with the key issue of alignment. The cells which belong to the same table column must be aligned to the left, to the right or centered. In some special cases, two table cells might coincidently conform to more than one alignment type when they have similar width and same horizontal position. But generally this does not happen to the whole column. Therefore, when we execute the column searching mechanism, one potential column may start with multiple available alignments but end with less as more table cells are involved. The detailed steps are listed below:

1. List all text-lines within current slide as $T_1, T_2,..., T_n$, and then traverse all possible text-line pairs $T_{ij} = \{T_i, T_j\}, 0 < i < j \leq n$.
2. If T_i and T_j are not vertically aligned, ignore 3~6 and go directly to 7.
3. If T_i and T_j are vertically aligned, record all their alignment types in A_{ij}. $A_{ij} \subseteq \{Left, Right, Center\}$ and $A_{ij} \neq \varnothing$.
4. Check whether T_i is already included in any existing column candidate C and whether the intersection of A_C (*the alignment types of* C) and A_{ij} is not empty. ($C \subseteq \{T_1, T_2, ..., T_n\}$, $T_i \in C$ and $A_C \cap A_{ij} \neq \varnothing$).
5. If yes, add T_j into C. And set the intersection of A_C and A_{ij} as new A_C. ($A'_C = A_C \cap A_{ij}$).
6. If no, create a new column candidate $C_{new} = \{T_i, T_j\}$. And set $A_{C_{new}} = A_{ij}$.
7. Continue with next pair.

The above mechanism will create quite a lot of false positive table columns, such as a left-aligned text paragraph, a group of annotation in a diagram, or just several unrelated text-lines coincidently seem to be aligned. We will attempt to eliminate these false positive columns in later procedures, but would not risk missing any possibility to find a potential table column here. It is logical to have two columns horizontally overlapped when they belong to different slide components, but they should be vertically separated to each other. If two horizontally overlapped columns are vertically interlaced, or a text-line is shared by

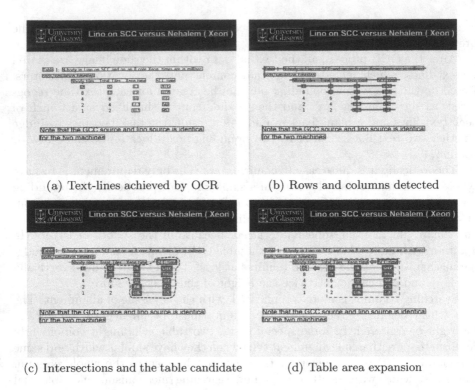

(a) Text-lines achieved by OCR   (b) Rows and columns detected

(c) Intersections and the table candidate   (d) Table area expansion

Fig. 2. An example of table detection process

two columns, it is most likely to be an error leading by OCR inaccuracy and these two columns will be combined together. Figure 2(b) shows all the 7 rows and 5 columns found in the example slide, including false positive ones.

4 Table Area Positioning

4.1 Table Candidate Generation

A table cell is supposed to be the intersection of one row and one column. Rows and columns have already been detected and each of them is a set of several horizontally or vertically aligned text-lines. So the intersected text-lines, each of which belongs to both a row set and a column set, are the most likely table cells. They are the foundation to locate the table area.

Since there might be more than one table in one slide, all the intersected text-lines will be grouped by their rows and columns belonged. Any two text-lines which belong to a same row or column will be grouped together and the effect superimposes. In this way, a text-line is not necessary to share a row or column with all other text-lines in its group but at least share with one of them. Logically the groups should be independent to each other, but when exception happens, which mean one text-line appears in two groups, the two groups will be combined. Any 1-member-group will be directly removed, just like the intersection with text "Table" in left-upper corner of Fig. 2(c).

By now each group represents a potential table candidate. In the following steps they might be modified or eliminated, but never further generated. Any final table confirmed would evolve from one of these potential table candidates. But first of all, they need to be accepted as formal table candidates by the evaluation based on all available information collected from the intersected text-lines involved, including both textual content and location logic.

4.2 Table Candidate Evaluation

There are four measurements with descending importance implemented in the evaluation process of the table candidate. Content mark and standardized column bonus focus on the textual content of the intersected text-lines, while distance deduction and two-column deduction come from the layout. After accumulating the values of all measurements, only the potential table candidates with positive final value will qualify. In this chapter we only introduce the measurements conceptually, detailed parameter configuration can be found online together with the evaluation datasets.

Content Mark evaluates how likely the content of a text-line looks like the content of a table cell. Although there is no standard or regulation illustrating what can be written in a table and what cannot, people prefer to put numbers, percentages, single-words or short phrases into a table, rather than long sentences. So if the content of an intersected text-line belongs to the first 4 catagories, it earns a positive value. And as the length of the content increases, the content mark decreases to 0 or negative. In the end an average content mark will be calculated, which can be either positive or negative.

Standardized Column Bonus can be only positive or 0. In many cases different table rows are used to identify different subjects, while columns are used to list the values of a certain attribute from those subjects, just like Tables 1 and 2. When this happens, most cells of a same column contain same type of content, except for the header row. If the content type of a certain column is digit, which includes number, percentage, fraction, etc., or single word, we believe it is a strong evidence to be a table column and earns a big positive value in the evaluation. We set 75 % as the threshold to determine whether a column contain same type of content, which allows 1 or 2 cells more than the header line to be the exceptions, especially for the digits, because it is not rare for the OCR to misrecognize 'O' and '0', or 'I' and '1'. When a table is reversely designed, with columns to represent subjects and rows for attributes, standardized column bonus does not work, which is why it has no negative value.

Distance Deduction plays a role when two neighboring columns locating too far away horizontally with each other. It is designed for those slides with chart or diagram, whose description texts are sometimes aligned but remotely located. We take the maximum of 1/8 slide width and the correspondent column's width as the reference. If the gap between two neighboring columns is larger than the reference, a deduction will be applied, and the value of this deduction depends on how much larger the gap is. This measurement can be only negative or 0.

Two-Column Deduction is for the special two-column slide layout, like Fig. 1(d), which is a default layout in most of templates of PowerPoint. When applied, the items in these two columns are very likely to be aligned both horizontally and vertically, which is quite similar to a two-column table candidate and fairly probable to be detected as one by previous procedure. In order to decrease such false positive detections, if a vertical axis can be found exactly in the middle of the slide to make the two columns symmetric and these two columns contain more than 80% of all text-lines within the whole slide, a two-column deduction will be applied with a comparatively small negative value, because it is only a weak evidence.

4.3 Table Area Expansion

Generally when we talk about a 3×3 table, it should have 9 cells filled with some content. But it is also possible that there are only 6 cells, with 3 in the first row, 2 in the second and 1 in the third. This kind of "triangle" also belongs to table, but obviously some of its cells cannot be involved in any table candidate by previous procedure, because they are not intersections of the rows and columns. And by simply missing some table cells during the OCR process, just like Fig. 2(a), which happens time to time because of the comparatively small size of the text used inside the table cells, some "triangles" or even more weird shapes could be created unexpectedly, such as the "scribbled" table area in Fig. 2(c). No matter in which way it comes, it goes the same, that the area a table candidate can cover is only a part of the real table. In this step, we aim to fix this problem.

In the beginning we draw a virtual rectangle which covers all the text-lines involved in a table candidate and make this rectangle as the initial table area, as shown in Fig. 2(d). Then we search potential expansion object alongside the rows and the columns which go across the table area. The content of the targeting text-line and its distance to the current table area will be the decisive factors to judge whether this text-line should be added into the relevant table candidate *(detailed configuration can be found online)*. If so, the table area will be updated. After every expansion to the table area, the whole process will restart until there is no further possibility to include new text-line, which means the area does not change after a full searching process.

5 Table Confirmation

A final confirmation will be made on each table area detected. The measurements of the confirmation process focus not only on cells of the table as what we did in Table Candidate Evaluation, but also consider the table area as a whole. Quite a lot of factors need to be included and they generally form 3 aspects: content, structure and appearance. Since a text block might unlikely "survive" as a false positive table area at this late stage, the main task in the final confirmation is to distinguish those table-like charts or diagrams and eliminate them. One prerequisite is applied before the procedure: if a table area has extreme aspect ratio, such as 10:1 or 1:10, it will also be directly denied because no actual table should be like that.

Content Evaluation involves only one factor, the average content mark, M_c. It is similar to what we did in Table Candidate Evaluation, but the text-lines added in the Table Area Expansion process will also count. Theoretically a bigger value of M_c implies a larger probability of detecting an actual table.

Structure Evaluation involves two factors: scale and integrity. Obviously a table area containing lots cells is more likely to be an actual table. So the total number of table cells detected is the best representative of the scale of the table area, which we address as C_T. And the integrity is also very important. For most tables the expected total cell number C_E should be the product of row number r and column number c within the table area. And the table integrity is defined as the ratio of C_T and C_E, with the range of $(0, 1]$. Both these two factors are positively related with the chance of a table area to be confirmed.

Appearance Evaluation includes two positively related factors, the whole table area A_T and the average text height H_t, and a third factor: text density. A table and its content need to be large enough that people can see it clearly, that is why the A_T and H_t are implemented. And text density is defined as the ratio of the sum of areas covered by all text-lines within the table area and A_T. Addressed as D, the text density of an actual table should be neither too large nor too small. Therefore we set 0.2 as the benchmark by the observation of the ground-truth from the training dataset, and the absolute value of the difference between D and the benchmark 0.2 becomes a negatively related factor.

Now we need to take all these factors together into a general considera-tion. Theoretically we know the factors are positively or negatively related with the final result, but on practical level, the distribution of each factor's weight is based on the attempt at the training dataset, without mathematical deduction. The final equation of table confirmation can be illustrated as in (1). When the M_{final} is greater than the threshold (*6.5 for slides*), the table will be confirmed.

$$M_{final} = \frac{e^{M_c}}{3} + \frac{\ln C_T \times C_T}{C_E} + \frac{\ln H_t^2 \times (\ln \ln \sqrt[4]{A_T})^3}{e^{\sqrt[3]{|D-0.2|}}} \tag{1}$$

6   Evaluation

6.1   Datasets and Metrics

There are three datasets in our evaluation process: training set, benchmark set and test set. Both training set and test set consist of slide images, which are collected by ourselves, since we failed to find any public dataset of slides for research purpose. The training set gathers 493 slides from 12 complete presen-tations, which contains 46 tables and is collected from the online learning portal

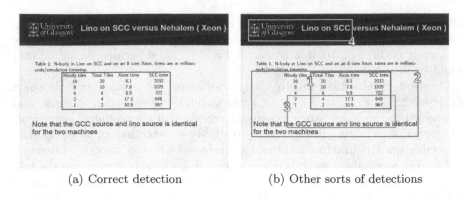

(a) Correct detection   (b) Other sorts of detections

Fig. 3. The catagories of possible detection

Tele-TASK.de[3]. And we select 384 slides from the excerpts of 26 different presentations on Tele-TASK.de and SlideShare.com as the test set. These slides cover various topics such as economy, education, media, information technology, etc., and contain 189 tables in total.

We intend to compare our proposed solution with the open source Tesseract table detection kit [19] and commercial software ABBYY FineReader 12. In order to avoid misusing these tools, we also implemented a benchmark set of traditional documents, which is shared by the competition organizer of [13] and consisting of 238 pages, including 156 tables. All three datasets can be found online[4].

To evaluate the performances we focus on two facts: how the tables in ground-truth get detected and how accurate an actual detection is. For a table in ground-truth there are 5 possibilities in total: correct detection (Fig. 3a), partial detection (Fig. 3b-1), over detection (Fig. 3b-2), partial-and-over detection (Fig. 3b-3) and missed. In actual detections there is an additional false positive category (Fig. 3b-4), and in order to quantify the performances, each detected table is given a precision weight as 1, 0.75, 0.5, 0.25 or 0, based on the proportion of its accurately detected area against the ground-truth. Obviously correct detection values 1, false positive (F.P.) values 0, missed table does not have a value while the others depend.

By accumulating the precision values of all actual detections, a recall rate can be calculated against the ground-truth (G.T.) and a precision rate against the number of total detections (T.D.). Please note, that any over detected table will also value 1 when calculating the recall, because in such cases the whole table is actually detected and the extra redundant area will affect in precision. Finally the F_1-Score of the recall and precision will be taken as the general accuracy.

---

[3] http://www.tele-task.de/.
[4] https://drive.google.com/folderview?id=0B13Cc1a7ebTufmhkdzI5VVhSWnotbkh Lakh5WVVlVlU2NnlMLVZ2QVpuZDJKdUFyOUtPM1E&usp=sharing.

6.2 Experiments on Training and Benchmark Datasets

As we mentioned before, we used the training set to adjust our algorithm. The slide images collected in the training set are directly screenshotted from the desktop stream of lecture videos on Tele-TASK.de. The resolution is 1024×768, but the quality of the images is much worse, which causes a lot of OCR errors. Although we aim to cope with OCR errors in the proposed solution, they would still affect in a negative way. The experiment result can be found in Table 1 in "Proposed-T" row, where "Co." and "Part." are the short terms of "Correct" and "Partial" respectively.

The original materials in the benchmark set are saved in PDF format. We transform these files into high quality images for our context. ABBYY FineReader was the best performer, 98 % accurate, with the same dataset in [13], when taking born-digital PDF files as input. In our experiment FineReader needs to take the images as input and apply its highly reputable commercial OCR tool [20, 21] on the images while detecting table. As a result, FineReader reaches almost 90 % accurate on the benchmark set, which is still very promising. Stats can also be found in Table 1. This result proves the effectiveness of FineReader table detection method on traditional document type. Tesseract works directly with images and its performance on benchmark set can also be referenced.

6.3 Evaluation on Test Dataset

In order to evaluate the proposed solution more comprehensive, we set the slide images in the test set in two different formats: low-resolution screenshot (L) and high-resolution transformed images (H). The resolution of L-images is still 1024×768, for the slide designed in 16:9 ratios there are black edges on the top and the bottom of the slide. But the visual quality of L-images in test set is generally better than those in the training set. We tested all 3 solutions on L-images and the proposed performed the best. H-images are transformed directly from the digital files, either PPT or PDF. They have no unified resolution, but all of them are higher than 1024×768 and visually excellent. All tested solutions perform better on H-images, and the general accuracies of FineReader and proposed solution are almost the same.

From the stats shown in Table 2, we can find out no matter with L-images or H-images, FineReader could achieve more detections than the proposed solution, but also including more false positive detections. The proposed solution tends to make mistakes as over detection, while FineReader is more likely to miss

Table 1. Experiments on training and benchmark datasets

Method-set	G.T.	T.D.	Detection categories						Recall	Precision	F_1-Score
			Co.	Part.	Over	P&O	Miss	F.P.			
Proposed-T	46	39	21	10	5	0	10	3	69.02 %	73.72 %	71.29 %
Tesseract-B	156	111	69	16	7	2	61	17	55.61 %	74.55 %	63.70 %
FineReader-B	156	153	126	21	0	0	10	6	88.62 %	89.87 %	89.24 %

Table 2. Evaluation on test dataset

Method-set	G.T.	T.D.	Detection categories						Recall	Precision	F_1-Score
			Co.	Part.	Over	P&O	Miss	F.P.			
Tesseract-L	189	107	13	34	12	12	118	36	25.93%	41.12%	31.80%
FineReader-L	189	181	109	41	5	2	35	24	73.81%	75.97%	74.87%
Proposed-L	189	169	106	21	26	9	27	7	78.31%	80.18%	**79.23%**
Tessaract-H	189	174	42	42	22	13	74	55	48,81%	47,13%	47,95%
FineReader-H	189	205	142	27	5	0	19	31	84.92%	77.20%	80.87%
Proposed-H	189	194	118	18	32	4	17	22	86.51%	76.03%	**80.93%**

some part of the table. In general, the proposed solution is proven better than FineReader in context of slide images, especially when the input image quality is not so high. On the other hand, Tesseract is no match to either of these two.

By comparing Tables 1 and 2, it is obvious that both Tesseract and FineReader perform less effective on slide images than traditional type of documents, which proves the importance of researching on slide-oriented table detection method. And by analyzing specific instances, we believe our initial aims, such as to avoid recognizing diagram as false positive table, or not to miss the table without ruling line, have been basically fulfilled in the proposed solution. The general accuracy around 80 % is not perfect, but enough for some fundamental applications like indexing table-inclusive slides or generating lecture outline.

7   Conclusion

We proposed a table detection method for slide images and achieved quite positive result. Starting with OCR technology, the proposed solution would first detect the rows and columns, locate the table candidates by searching the row-column intersections, expand the areas of these candidates and finally confirm them. The evaluation result shows that the general accuracy of proposed solution is around 80 %, which slightly outperforms high reputable commercial software ABBYY FineReader and is way better than open source tool Tesseract. In the future, we would like improve our solution by considering more factors and try our definition-based table detection idea on traditional types of documents.

References

1. Nathans-Kelly, T., Nicometo, C.G.: Slide rules: design, build, and archive presentations in the engineering and technical fields. IEEE Trans. Prof. Commun. **58**(2), 232–235 (2015)
2. Canós, J.H., Marante, M.I., Llavador, M.: SliDL: a slide digital library supporting content reuse in presentations. In: Lalmas, M., Jose, J., Rauber, A., Sebastiani, F., Frommholz, I. (eds.) ECDL 2010. LNCS, vol. 6273, pp. 453–456. Springer, Heidelberg (2010)
3. Hill, A., Arford, T., Lubitow, A., Smollin, L.M.: "I'm ambivalent about it" The dilemmas of PowerPoint. Teach. Sociol. **40**(3), 242–256 (2012)

4. Levasseur, D.G., Kanan Sawyer, J.: Pedagogy meets powerpoint: a research review of the effects of computer-generated slides in the classroom. Rev. Commun. **6**(1–2), 101–123 (2006)
5. Fang, J., Gao, L., Bai, K., Qiu, R., Tao, X., Tang, Z.: A table detection method for multipage pdf documents via visual seperators and tabular structures. In: 2011 International Conference on Document Analysis and Recognition (ICDAR), pp. 779–783. IEEE (2011)
6. Liu, Y., Bai, K., Mitra, P., Giles, C.L.: Tableseer: automatic table metadata extraction and searching in digital libraries. In: Proceedings of the 7th ACM/IEEE-CS Joint Conference on Digital Libraries, pp. 91–100. ACM (2007)
7. Yildiz, B., Kaiser, K., Miksch, S.: Pdf2table: a method to extract table information from pdf files. In: IICAI, pp. 1773–1785 (2005)
8. Gatos, B., Perantonis, S.J., Danatsas, D., Pratikakis, I.: Automatic table detection in document images. In: Singh, S., Singh, M., Apte, C., Perner, P. (eds.) ICAPR 2005. LNCS, vol. 3686, pp. 609–618. Springer, Heidelberg (2005)
9. Kasar, T., Barlas, P., Adam, S., Chatelain, C., Paquet, T.: Learning to detect tables in scanned document images using line information. In: 2013 12th International Conference on Document Analysis and Recognition (ICDAR), pp. 1185–1189. IEEE (2013)
10. Tian, Y., Gao, C., Huang, X.: Table frame line detection in low quality document images based on hough transform. In: 2014 2nd International Conference on Systems and Informatics (ICSAI), pp. 818–822. IEEE (2014)
11. Mandal, S., Chowdhury, S., Das, A.K., Chanda, B.: A simple and effective table detection system from document images. Int. J. Doc. Anal. Recogn. **8**(2–3), 172–182 (2006)
12. Wang, Y., Phillips, I.T., Haralick, R.: Automatic table ground truth generation and a background-analysis-based table structure extraction method. In: Proceedings of the Sixth International Conference on Document Analysis and Recognition, pp. 528–532. IEEE (2001)
13. Gobel, M., Hassan, T., Oro, E., Orsi, G.: ICDAR 2013 table competition. In: 2013 12th International Conference on Document Analysis and Recognition (ICDAR), pp. 1449–1453. IEEE (2013)
14. Li, J., Wang, K., Hao, S., Wang, Q.: Location and recognition of free tables in form. In: Zhang, W. (ed.) Software Engineering and Knowledge Engineering: Theory and Practice, pp. 685–692. Springer, Heidelberg (2012)
15. Ghanmi, N., Belaid, A.: Table detection in handwritten chemistry documents using conditional random fields. In: 2014 14th International Conference on Frontiers in Handwriting Recognition (ICFHR), pp. 146–151. IEEE (2014)
16. Seo, W., Koo, H.I., Cho, N.I.: Junction-based table detection in camera-captured document images. Int. J. Doc. Anal. Recogn. **18**(1), 47–57 (2015)
17. Kieninger, T.G.: Table structure recognition based on robust block segmentation. In: International Society for Optics and Photonics Photonics West 1998 Electronic Imaging, pp. 22–32 (1998)
18. Shin, J., Guerette, N.: Table recognition and evaluation. In: Class of 2005 Senior Conference on Natural Language Processing (2005)
19. Shafait, F., Smith, R.: Table detection in heterogeneous documents. In: Proceedings of the 9th IAPR International Workshop on Document Analysis Systems, pp. 65–72. ACM (2010)

20. Blanke, T., Bryant, M., Hedges, M.: Ocropodium: open source ocr for small-scale historical archives. J. Inf. Sci. **38**(1), 76–86 (2012)
21. Chattopadhyay, T., Sinha, P., Biswas, P.: Performance of document image ocr systems for recognizing video texts on embedded platform. In: 2011 International Conference on Computational Intelligence and Communication Networks (CICN), pp. 606–610. IEEE (2011)

Face Search in Encrypted Domain

Wei Qi Yan[1]([✉]) and Mohan S. Kankanhalli[2]

[1] Auckland University of Technology, Auckland, New Zealand
dcsyanwq@email.com
[2] National University of Singapore, Singapore, Singapore

Abstract. Visual information of images and videos usually is encrypted for the purposes of security applications. Straightforward manipulations on the encrypted data without requiring any decryption have the advantage of speed over performing those operations in spatial, temporal, frequency or compressed domain. In this paper, we will investigate encrypted image search. More specifically, given a face image as the target object, we search it amongst encrypted images. We accomplish the search by using a novel method that extracts features and locates the face object region within the given encrypted image. We evaluate the search results by using precision and recall as well as F-measure. Our experiments reveal that there exists a trade-off between the quality of search and the quality of encryption, namely, stronger encryption leads to poorer search results.

Keywords: Image encryption · Object detection · Encrypted domain

1 Introduction

One of straightforward ways of securing digital image transmission is to encrypt the images [11,23,29]. In image encryption, traditional methods like those of asymmetric encryption in public key systems [6] are often adopted, other methods including image scrambling using Hilberts Space-filling Curves (HSC) [17] as well as image sharing based on Chinese Remainder Theorem (CRT) [26] and Visual Cryptography(VC) [20], etc. have also been employed.

Since digital images have relatively huge volume of file size when compared to text, direct manipulations of encrypted images have been highly recommended for the sake of saving space and speeding up the computation [1]. There already has been a slew of inaugural work in this direction. For example, digital image enhancement has been adopted in encrypted domain [14]. Visual features such as histogram and SIFT have been extracted from encrypted domain for a variety of applications [21]. The empirical methods such as clustering and classification on encrypted domain have been developed to group visual objects in categories [30]. Recently, face emotion recognition has been attempted in encrypted domain [22] which is often thought as an important biometric issue, the focus of relevant research work has been shifted from compressed domain to encrypted domain [7,22].

© Springer International Publishing Switzerland 2016
T. Bräunl et al. (Eds.): PSIVT 2015, LNCS 9431, pp. 775–790, 2016.
DOI: 10.1007/978-3-319-29451-3_61

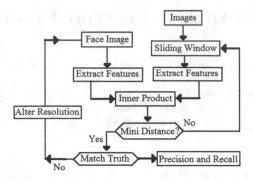

Fig. 1. Flowchart of search in encrypted domain

In this paper, the goal of our research is to accurately find a face within an encrypted image. We perform face object search in scrambled images since scrambling is deemed as a form of encryption. Motivated by face detection and recognition in computer vision [12], search and retrieval in encrypted domain [16, 28], and the mighty value of reuse of encrypted data [18], in this paper we will develop a face object search algorithm based on Hilberts Space-filling Curves (HSC) as shown as Fig. 1.

Given an image, we segment it into identical sized blocks and use DCT (Discrete Cosine Transform) transform to transfer the pixel values to frequency domain. The reason why we select DCT transform is that most of images and videos are stored in JPEG and MPEG formats nowadays which are based on DCT transform. Using DCT transform could greatly reduce our processing time.

We also employ the HSC curves based image scrambling for encrypting the images to make sure that the encrypted image is secure enough. [17] Given an encrypted image having face objects, we search for the encrypted face along scanline order from top-left to bottom-right. The precision and recall as well as F-measure for evaluating the search results are calculated.

Our contributions of this paper are listed below.

(1) *Encrypting digital images using the scrambling algorithm based on Hilberts space-filling curves.* In this paper, we will utilize the HSC based image encryption [2,17] and present our findings along with face object searching. The key for image encryption is a pseudo random number which is used for selecting different HSC curves so as to scramble an image.

(2) *Searching for the given face object hierarchically in the encrypted image and locate it.* We conduct hierarchically search on given encrypted images in multi-resolution. The features are extracted based on mean, variance and histogram which preserve the invariance of the encrypted image. This approach allows the face object to be scaled, rotated or having various lighting conditions in encrypted domain before the search.

(3) *Evaluating performance of face object search in encrypted domain.* In this paper, we take use of the Wild Face Dataset for our experiments. The precision and recall as well as F-measure will be taken into consideration for the search evaluations.

The challenges of this work are to find the given face in encrypted domain hierarchically, there may have many faces within a given image. Our goal in all the cases is to find each face and mark it using a rectangle. The rest of this paper is organized as follows. The related work will be introduced in Sect. 2, our contributions will be presented in Sects. 3 and 4 will provide the experimental results and analysis, conclusion and future work will be stated in Sect. 5.

2   Related Work

With regard to search in encrypted domain, usually lexical features and quantitative features as well as security-specific features are employed for the purposes of confidentiality [15], the domain of these search is usually limited to text encryption. In order to fully utilize the outcomes, homomorphic encryption [8], Yaos Garbled circuits (GC) [19] and reuse of encrypted values [18] have been adapted for data encryption recently [3,11,25].

Homomorphic encryption is a form of encryption that allows computations to be carried out on ciphertexts. A cryptosystem is said to be homomorphic with respect to an operation $\star$, if another operation $\circ$ exists such that, given two plaintexts m_1 and m_2,

$$D(E[m_1] \circ E[m_2]) = m_1 \star m_2 \tag{1}$$

where D and E indicate the decryption and encryption operators respectively. If the function of operation $\star$ is identical to that of the operation $\circ$, the homomorphic encryption satisfies,

$$D(f(E[m])) = D(E(f[m])) = f[m] \tag{2}$$

From functional viewpoint, we have,

$$D(f(E[\cdot])) = D(E(f[\cdot])) = f[\cdot] \tag{3}$$

Namely,

$$D(f(E)) = D(E(f)) = f \tag{4}$$

This indicates the operators f and E are commutative in the encrypted domain.

The homomorphic encryption is possible to be propagated to other media such as image or picture, even audio and video. Based on the prevalent image encryption methods such as Hilberts Space-filling Curves (HSC) based scrambling, the encryptions are able to be iteratively applied to the encrypted images by following the same type of encryption while properties of the homomorphic encryption are still persevered. In this paper, we will take advantage of the HSC based image scrambling as the encryption algorithm and assert the validity of homomorphic encryption in image encrypted domain.

The HSC is with a fractal structure generated by a recursive production rule which has the property of self-similarity and satisfies IFS system, its dimension is a fraction and it is supported by the fixed-point theory. After several rounds of recursions started from the fractal generator, the curve will fill up a given space recursively. If the curve space comprises of raster grids, the curve is utilized for re-ordering each pixel within the discrete space along the pixel order on the curve.

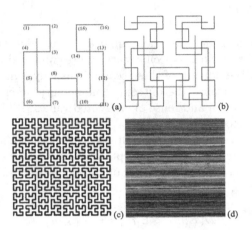

Fig. 2. Generating a HSC curve (a) Fractal generator (b) Generated HSC curve using recursion at resolution 8×8 (c) Generated HSC curve at resolution of 32×32 (d) Scrambled image based on the HSC curve (512×512) in spatial domain.

Generating procedure of a HSC curve is described as Fig. 2(a). In Fig. 2(a), all the pixels on this plane along the HSC curve have been numbered. Figure 2(b) and (c) show the curves at resolutions 8×8 and 32×32 respectively. Figure 2(d) shows a scrambled image of the Lena (512×512) in spatial domain using the 512×512 HSC curve. In a scrambled image, only the pixel locations have been re-ordered, the pixel color information still holds.

Our contribution in this paper is to search for a given face object in encrypted domain. Amongst the existing work, most of them are related to keyword search, this is based on plaintext encryption and ciphertext decryption in the encrypted domain which was derivative from the traditional cryptography.

In face recognition, eigenvalues and eigenvectors are calculated directly from the encrypted images [7] which is based on traditional PCA algorithm. Eigenfaces based recognition algorithm and a combination of known cryptographic techniques, in particular Homomorphic Encryption and Garbled Circuits (GC) have been employed to improve the computational complexity and server client communications [25].

Holomorphic properties of Paillier Cryptosystem specially for Euclidean distance has been used to calculate the distance between two feature vectors. In Paillier Cryptosystem,

$$[|m_1 + m_2|] = [|m_1|][|m_2|] \tag{5}$$

$$[|\alpha \cdot m|] = [|m|]^\alpha \tag{6}$$

Different from those existing work, in this paper our focus is on face object search in encrypted domain. The novelty of this paper lies in that the encryption of digital images is conducted via image scrambling based on the HSC curves; we select mean, variance and histogram as our features and compose them into a feature vector, the distance between feature vectors is calculated by using inner or dot product. We search for the given object in the encrypted domain and evaluate our search results by using precision and recall as well as F-measure.

3   Our Contributions

In image encryption and decryption as well as visual object search, we transform an image from spatial domain to DCT domain first and utilize the DCT coefficients for encryption and decryption. After these operations, we commit inverse DCT / IDCT transforms and transfer the image blocks back to spatial domain for the purpose of displaying. Therefore, in this paper we deal with the DCT transform as our pre-processing, our encryption and decryption are block based scrambling and descrambling. The steps of image search in encryption domain based on HSC curves scrambling are described as below,

Algorithm. Search a given face object in encrypted domain

```
Input: Face image F and image I
Output: Face location in the encrypted image
Step 1. Segment images F and I into the identical size blocks.
Step 2. Use DCT transform on these blocks.
Step 3. Use pseudo random number to select a HSC curve
        for the scrambling
Step 4. Extract the features (mean, variance and histogram)
        from the encrypted image and combine them into a vector
Step 5. Search encrypted image F on encrypted image I by
        calculating the distance between the encrypted F
        and sliding window of I hierarchically
Step 6. Calculate the precision, recall and F-measure for evaluating
        the search results.
```

3.1   Image Encryptions

In this section, we elucidate how digital images are encrypted using HSC curves based image scrambling, we manage the algorithm to serve image encryption and decryption well by adaptively tuning the parameters.

Procedure. As shown in the algorithm, in image encryption we import images in spatial domain and segment them into blocks having identical size, for each block we recursively generate a corresponding HSC curve using the generator presented in Fig. 2(a), the curve starts from very beginning shown in red color, its mouth points in upward.

In the second iteration, for each turning point at start or end, we generate the same shape however the size and orientation will be changed. At the starting point, we rotate the generator for 90 degrees toward the left (anti-clockwise); at the end point, we turn the generator to right for 90 degrees (clockwise), at the other two turning points, the orientations of the generators are the same. We link these generated shapes together and yield the blue curve in Fig. 2(a).

We repeat this step and acquire the black curve shown in Fig. 2(b). If the end resolution is 32 × 32, we take use of the same way to generate Fig. 2(c). The procedure is described as Eq. (7),

$$p_{n+1}(x, y) = HSC(p_n(x, y)), n = 1, 2, \cdots \tag{7}$$

where HSC$(\cdot)$ is the iterative function, $p(x, y)$ is the turning point on the curve, the stop condition for this recursion is the final resolution reached so as to fully fill the given plane, the Hausdorff dimension of this fractal curve is 2.00. [17] The image scrambling procedure is described as,

$$I' = HSC(I) \bmod W \tag{8}$$

where I is the previous image without scrambling, I' is the scrambled image, W is the image width. After generated this HSC curve, we sort the pixel order according to the pixel sequence on the HSC curve shown as Eq. (8). The Eq. (8) first converts points on 2D plane to 1D curve order, then the 1D sequence will be used to fill up the image space line by line from top to bottom, consequently the image is fully scrambled shown as Fig. 2(d) which is exported as the encrypted image.

Figure 3 shows the scrambled images of Lena in different resolutions of the HSC curves. In Fig. 3(a), we scramble each 16 × 16 image blocks in DCT domain using the generated 16 × 16 HSC curve, Fig. 3(b) is based on 32 × 32 blocks meanwhile the Fig. 3(c) is based on 64 × 64 blocks of image scrambling. From our observations, we find that Lena's faces are gradually becoming tougher to be perceived from left to right. From the trade-off perspective, this means that it will be much harder to find a face from Fig. 3(c) than from Fig. 3(a).

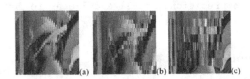

Fig. 3. Image encryption for Lena (512×512) in DCT domain using HSC for the blocks with different size (a) block size: 16 × 16 (b) block size: 32 × 32 (c) block size: 64 × 64

The encryption using HSC based image scrambling in DCT domain changes the pixel sequence spatially, but does not alter color information of image pixels.

Figure 3 shows one of results of image scrambling using the HSC curves based image scrambling in DCT domain with different resolutions.

Security. The security of this encryption is ensured by the key and the scrambling algorithm. This is because the HSC generator has multiple choices, and could be rotated along the clockwise and anti-clockwise directions, the generator has four orientations. Based on different generators, the HSC curves will be completely different. Meanwhile, the image block has multiple choices with various resolutions, the scrambling based on different block sizes will lead to image encryption with different strengths. Larger the bock size, stronger the encryption. Therefore, which HSC curve will be selected at what resolution will be the unique key of the encryption algorithm.

The HSC based image scrambling is different from the traditional encryption algorithms such as RSA, ECC and secret sharing, etc. The reason is that the scrambling completely destroys the order of pixel locations in the image, therefore the pixel neighborhood operations such as edge extraction, SIFT and others, are not possible anymore, especially in the DCT domain. However these geometric information could be detected from those encrypted images using RSA or ECC algorithms sometimes.

3.2   Face Object Search

In this section, we search for a given face object in encrypted domain. Our goal is to find the matched coefficients of the given face object in DCT domain after encryption. Therefore, we seek the face object using a sliding window. We keep the encrypted image at its given size but vary the face object size in a hierarchical multi-resolution search.

The window is initially defined for one face image size. For each window, we traverse the input image completely in scanline order from top to bottom and left to right, calculate the distance between feature vectors of the face image and regions of the encrypted image. When arriving the right-bottom corner of the image, we modify the face image size and search it starting from the left-up corner again, till scanned all sizes of encrypted face image, the procedure is shown as Fig. 4.

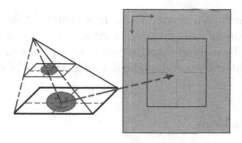

Fig. 4. Sliding windows search for a face object

Feature Selection. Since the images have been encrypted based on DCT domain, the features are used for searching in encryption domain including mean, variance, entropy, etc. The visual features therefore are combined such as Eqs. (9) and (10),

$$V_O = [f_{O1} \quad f_{O2} \quad \cdots \quad f_{Om}] \tag{9}$$

$$V_\Omega = [f_{\Omega 1} \quad f_{\Omega 2} \quad \cdots \quad f_{\Omega m}] \tag{10}$$

where V_O and V_Ω are the relevant features from face object O and sliding window Ω.

Distance Calculation. The feature vectors are employed for the face object search, equation for calculating the distance between feature vectors is shown in Eqs. (11) and (12) which are applied to the cases having invariance in encrypted domain such as rotating, scaling and filliping. After histogram equalization, it is able to be applied to the images having various lighting conditions,

$$\Omega = \arg\min_\Omega \{|V_\Omega(f_1, f_2, \cdots, f_m) - V_O(f_1, f_2, \cdots, f_m)|\} \tag{11}$$

where I_O is the image having face object, V_O is its feature vector; I_Ω is sliding window of the encrypted image for searching, its feature vector is V_Ω. What we like to emphasize in this paper is that the histograms, means and variances are all normalized.

$$\Omega = \arg\max_\Omega \frac{V_O(f_1, f_2, \cdots, f_m) \cdot V_\Omega(f_1, f_2, \cdots, f_m)}{|V_O(f_1, f_2, \cdots, f_m)| \cdot |V_\Omega(f_1, f_2, \cdots, f_m)|} \tag{12}$$

For an example, we search the given object in encrypted domain by using the inner or dot product between two feature vectors first shown as Eq. (12); later we calculate the EMD (Earth Movers Distance) shown as Eq. (13), which is used to refine the image distance for the search in encrypted domain [24].

$$\Omega = \arg\min_\Omega EMD(O, \Omega) = \arg\min_\Omega \frac{\Sigma_i \Sigma_j d_O(i, j) d_\Omega(i, j)}{\min(\Sigma_i w_{pi}, \Sigma_j w_{qj})} \tag{13}$$

where $w_{pi} \geq \Sigma f(i, j)(m \geq i \geq 1)$ and $w_{qj} \geq \Sigma f(i, j)(n \geq j \geq 1)$, $f(i, j) \geq 0$, $d(i, j) \geq 0$.

Multi-resolution Search. While conducting face search in encrypted domain, we have three down-sampling operations: original, half and quarter. The search results '1' or '0' will be merged together using 'or' operations. The finally found region will be generated by merging the detected regions in different resolution together.

3.3   Search Evaluations

In this section, we will detail on how to evaluate search results. Suppose an encrypted face object has been traversed from a large number of encrypted pictures. From the results, we need find true positive *tp*, true negative *tn*; false positive fp and false negative fn. Based on these parameters, we objectively evaluate our search by using precision, recall and F-measure.

In the context of this paper, when a face object is found, we usually refer to search region A and the image region B having intersection, $A \cap B \neq \emptyset$. The corresponding mathematical description is shown as Eq. (14).

$$p = \frac{\Lambda(A \cap B)}{\Lambda(A \cup B)} \cdot 100\% \tag{14}$$

where $\Lambda(\cdot)$ is the area of the specific regions, $p \in [0,1]$. Equation (14) shows how many percent of the face image has been found in the search. If $A \cap B = \emptyset$, that means the search is a failure, we could not get the face object from this image, so $p = 0$.

After we have received the search results, we calculate the recall and precision as well as F-measure utilizing our ground truth. The ground truth tells us whether an image has the designated face or not, it is '0' or '1'. Our results reveal from multi-resolution viewpoint whether we have successfully found the face or not.

If the search results are known, we have,

$$Pr = \frac{Tp}{Tp + Fp} \tag{15}$$

$$Rc = \frac{Tp}{Tp + Fn} \tag{16}$$

where Pr And Rc refer to precision and recall, respectively. Tp, Fp, Fn, and Tn are the true positive, false positive, false negative and true negative in the search. The Tp, Fp, Fn, and Tn show amongst the search results how many search results reflect the ground truth exactly. Furthermore, F-measure is calculated by, Eq. (17),

$$F_m = 2 \cdot \frac{Pr \cdot Rc}{Pr + Rc} \tag{17}$$

4 Results and Analysis

We implement our search algorithm using Matlab platform and encrypted images in DCT domain. Our search results are shown in Figs. 5, 6 and 7 marked with red rectangles.

In Table 1, we encrypt the Lena 512×512 image in blocks using 4 resolutions of HSC curves (resolution 1: 8×8, resolution 2: 16×16, resolution 3: 32×32, resolution 4: 64×64). Table 1 shows that there is a trade-off between the quality of image encryption algorithm and the quality of search. The higher encryption that means the search is more difficult since the visual information has been scrambled using the HSC curves.

Table 2 shows search results that we use the Lena face images (512×512) after 4 Affine transformations (scaling, rotating, horizontal filliping, and vertical

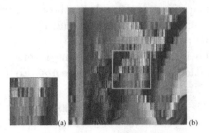

Fig. 5. Searching Lena's face on the scrambled images by using the HSC curve based scrambling (a) Lena's face (164 × 164) in encrypted domain using HSC scrambling after DCT transform; (b) Image Lena (512 × 512) in encrypted domain using HSC scrambling after DCT transform, the red rectangle shows the found region of the visual object (Color figure online).

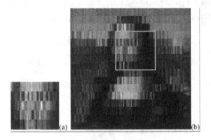

Fig. 6. Searching Mona Lisa's face on the scrambled images by using the HSC curve based scrambling (a) Mona Lisas face (164 × 164) in encrypted domain using HSC scrambling after DCT transform; (b) Image Mona lisa (512 × 512) in encrypted domain using HSC scrambling after DCT transform, the red rectangle shows the found region of the visual object (Color figure online).

Fig. 7. Searching Nicole's face on the scrambled images by using the HSC curve based scrambling (a) Nicoles face (164 × 164) in encrypted domain using HSC scrambling after DCT transform; (b) Nicole (724 × 314) in encrypted domain using HSC scrambling after DCT transform, the red rectangle shows the found region of the visual object (c) Nicoles face on the original color image (Color figure online).

Table 1. Comparisons of HSC encryption in encrypted domain

Resolutions	Block Size	SSIM	DSSIM	NCC	EMD
Resolution 1	8 × 8	0.8227	0.0887	388.1511	0.9811
Resolution 2	16 × 16	0.8340	0.0830	480.3705	2.0861
Resolution 3	32 × 32	0.8618	0.0691	428.1592	3.2792
Resolution 4	64 × 64	0.8631	0.0685	907.2569	5.8470

Table 2. Comparisons of search results after transforms

Transforms	SSIM	DSSIM	NCC	EMD
Scaling	0.8047	0.0977	42.9602	11.7442
Rotating	0.8407	0.0797	291.8372	8.1224
H-flipping	0.8394	0.0803	922.3983	1.9938
V-flipping	0.8805	0.0598	430.1192	2.4320

Table 3. Comparisons of search results of various samples

Pictures	PSNR	SSIM	DSSIM	NCC	EMD
Lena	39.3324	0.8210	0.0895	518.8758	2.3660
Mona Lisa	39.8592	0.8353	0.0823	969.1637	1.4657
Nicola	39.3715	0.8241	0.0879	1578.1183	1.1955

Table 4. Face search in encrypted domain using the Wild dataset

Face Data	Samples	Precision	Recall	F-Measure
Putin	115	0.825	0.3548	0.4962
Agassi	115	0.722	0.2921	0.4629
Clinton	115	0.690	0.2020	0.3125

flipping). It discovers the scaling and flipping transforms did affect the search quality, but the rotating does not affect the result too much, this may be related to the fact that the image size is not changed too much.

Table 3 demonstrates what are the differences between the given human faces and found regions. We calculate the differences using the metrics SSIM(Structural similarity), DSSIM(Structural Dissimilarity), NCC (Normalized Cross Correlation) and EMD (The Earth Mover's Distanc).

Fig. 8. Precision of face search in encrypted domain: 82.5 % (Putin)

Fig. 9. Precision of face search in encrypted domain: 72.22 % (Agassi)

Table 4 shows the corpus of our search related to famous figures. We search the given faces within the encrypted domain, and compare the found face location and the ground truth. From the results, we calculate precision and recall as well as F-measure.

We adopted the LFW Face Database as corpus for searching human faces in encrypted domain, the database of face photographs was designed for studying the problem of unconstrained face recognition. We select 3 figures with a total of 115 images for the algorithm testing (Putin: 40, Agassi: 36, Clinton: 29). The results are shown in Table 4. The precisions of our search are acceptable.

The corresponding images are shown in Figs. 8, 9 and 10.

Fig. 10. Precision of face search in encrypted domain: 69 % (Clinton)

5   Conclusion

In this paper, we search for face objects in encrypted domain. The main purpose is to reuse the encrypted data and save the computation time by directly manipulating on the encrypted data. Our results show the superiority of face object search in encrypted domain. Our contributions are: (1) Image encryption using HSC based image scrambling; (2) Face object search within the given encrypted images; (3) Search evaluation in encrypted domain. In future, we will further investigate the relative issues in encrypted domain, especially for the security and privacy preservation problems in big data associated with social media.

References

1. Bianchi, T., Piva, A., Barni, M.: Composite signal representation for fast and storage-efficient processing of encrypted signals. IEEE Trans. Inf. Forensics Secur. **5**(1), 180–187 (2010)
2. Breinholt, G., Schierz, C.: Algorithm 781: generating hilberts space-filling curve by recursion. ACM Trans. Math. Softw. **24**(2), 184–189 (1998)
3. Cao, N., Wang, C., Li, M., Ren, K., Lou, W.: Privacy-preserving multi-keyword ranked search over encrypted cloud data. IEEE Trans. Parallel Distrib. Syst. **25**(1), 222–233 (2014)

4. Czajkowski, K., Fitzgerald, S., Foster, I., Kesselman, C.: Grid information services for distributed resource sharing. In: 10th IEEE International Symposium on High Performance Distributed Computing, pp. 181–184. IEEE Press, New York (2001)
5. Cheon, J., Lee, H., Seo, J.: A new additive homomorphic encryption based on the co-ACD problem. ACM CCS 2014, pp. 287–298. ACM Press, USA (2014)
6. El-Deen, A., El-Badawy, E., Gobran, S.: Digital image encryption based on RSA algorithm. J. Electron. Commun. Eng. 9(1), 69–73 (2014)
7. Ergun, O.Q.: Privacy preserving face recognition in encrypted domain. In: IEEE Asia Pacific Conference on Circuits and Systems (APCCAS), pp. 643–646 (2014)
8. Gentry, C.: A fully homomorphic encryption scheme. PhD thesis, Stanford University (2009)
9. Hsu, C.Y., Lu, C.S., Pei, S.C.: Image feature extraction in encrypted domain with privacy-preserving SIFT. IEEE Trans. Image Process. 21(11), 4593–4607 (2012)
10. Iftene, S.: General secret sharing based on the Chinese remainder theorem with applications in e-voting. Electron. Notes Theor. Comput. Sci. 186, 67–84 (2007)
11. Kamara, S., Papamanthou, C., Roeder, T.: Dynamic searchable symmetric encryption. In: ACM CCS 2012, USA, pp. 965–976 (2012)
12. Klette, R.: Concise Computer Vision. Springer, London (2014)
13. Lia, L., Abd El-Latif, A., Niu, X.: Elliptic curve ElGamal based homomorphic image encryption scheme for sharing secret images. Sig. Process. 92(4), 1069–1078 (2011)
14. Lathey, A., Atrey, P.K.: Image enhancement in encrypted domain over cloud. ACM Trans. Multimedia Comput. Commun. Appl. 11(3), 38 (2015)
15. Lu, L., Perdisci, R., Lee, W.: SURF: detecting and measuring search poisoning. In: ACM CCS 2011, USA, pp. 467–476 (2011)
16. Lu, W., Swaminathan, A., Varna, A., Wu, M.: Enabling search over encrypted multimedia databases. In: Proceedings of SPIE 7254, Media Forensics and Security (2009)
17. Matias, Y., Shamir, A.: A video scrambling technique based on space filling curves. In: Advances in Cryptology (CRYPTO 1987), pp. 398–416 (1988)
18. Mood, B., Gupta, D., Butler, K., Feigenbaum, J.: Reuse it or lose it: more efficient secure computation through reuse of encrypted values. In: ACM CCS 2014, USA, pp. 282–296 (2014)
19. Naveed, M., Agrawal, S., Prabhakaran1, M. Wang, X., Ayday, E., Hubaux, J., Gunter, C.: Controlled functional encryption. In: ACM CCS 2014, USA, pp. 1280–1291 (2014)
20. Naor, M., Shamir, A.: Visual cryptography. In: De Santis, A. (ed.) EUROCRYPT 1994. LNCS, vol. 950, pp. 1–12. Springer, Heidelberg (1995)
21. Qin, Z., Yan, J., Ren, K., Chen, C.W., Wang, C.: Towards efficient privacy-preserving image feature extraction in cloud computing. In: ACM MM 2014, Orlando, Florida, USA (2014)
22. Rahulamathavan, Y., Phan, R., Jonathon, A., Parish, D.: Facial expression recognition in the encrypted domain based on local fisher discriminant analysis. IEEE Trans. Affect. Comput. 4(1), 83–92 (2013)
23. Rouselakis, Y., Waters, B.: Practical constructions and new proof methods for large universe attribute-based encryption. In: ACM CCS 2013, Germany, pp. 463–474 (2013)
24. Rubner, Y., Tomasi, C., Guibas, L.: The Earth mover's distance as a metric for image retrieval. Int. J. Comput. Vision 40(2), 99–121 (2000)

25. Sadeghi, A., Schneider, T., Wehrenberg, I.: Efficient privacy-preserving face recognition. In: International Conference on Information Security and Cryptology, pp. 229–244 (2009)

26. Shyu, S.J., Chen, Y.R.: Threshold secret image sharing by Chinese remainder theorem. In: IEEE Asia-Pacific Services Computing Conference, pp. 1332–1337 (2008)

27. Suresh, V., Madhavan, C.: Image encryption with space-filling curves. Defence Sci. **62**(1), 46–50 (2012)

28. Song, X., Wagner, D., Perrig, A.: Practical techniques for searches on encrypted data. In: IEEE Symposium on Security and Privacy, pp. 44–55 (2000)

29. Wang, G., Liu, Q., Wu, J.: Hierarchical attribute-based encryption for fine-grained access control in cloud storage services. In: ACM CCS 2010, USA, pp. 735–737 (2010)

30. Wong, W., Cheung, D., Kao, B., Mamoulis, N.: Secure $k - NN$ computation on encrypted databases. In: ACM International Conference on Management of Data, pp. 139–152 (2009)

Author Index

Printed in the United States
By Bookmasters